DISCOVERING STATISTICS USING R

DISCOVERING STATISTICS
USING R

ANDY FIELD | JEREMY MILES | ZOË FIELD

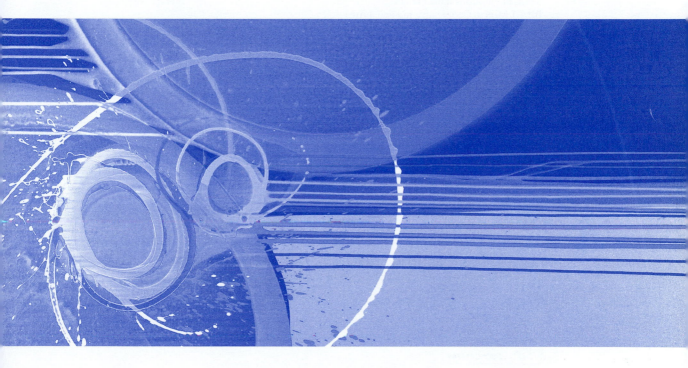

SAGE

Los Angeles | London | New Delhi
Singapore | Washington DC

First published 2012
Reprinted 2013

SAGE Publications Ltd
1 Oliver's Yard
55 City Road
London EC1Y 1SP

SAGE Publications Inc.
2455 Teller Road
Thousand Oaks, California 91320

SAGE Publications India Pvt Ltd
B 1/I 1 Mohan Cooperative Industrial Area
Mathura Road
New Delhi 110 044

SAGE Publications Asia-Pacific Pte Ltd
3 Church Street
#10-04 Samsung Hub
Singapore 049483

Library of Congress Control Number: Available

British Library Cataloguing in Publication data

A catalogue record for this book is available from the British Library

ISBN 978-1-4462-0045-2
ISBN 978-1-4462-0046-9

Typeset by C&M Digitals (P) Ltd, Chennai, India
Printed and bound in Great Britain by Ashford Colour Press Ltd

CONTENTS

3   The R environment   62

8 Logistic regression

12 Factorial ANOVA (GLM 3)

16 Multivariate analysis of variance (MANOVA)   696

PREFACE

Karma Police, arrest this man, he talks in maths, he buzzes like a fridge, he's like a detuned radio.

Radiohead, 'Karma Police', *OK Computer* (1997)

Introduction

Many social science students (and researchers for that matter) despise statistics. For one thing, most of us have a non-mathematical background, which makes understanding complex statistical equations very difficult. Nevertheless, the evil goat-warriors of Satan force our non-mathematical brains to apply themselves to what is, essentially, the very complex task of becoming a statistics expert. The end result, as you might expect, can be quite messy. The one weapon that we have is the computer, which allows us to neatly circumvent the considerable disability that is not understanding mathematics. The advent of computer programs such as SAS, SPSS, R and the like provides a unique opportunity to teach statistics at a conceptual level without getting *too* bogged down in equations. The computer to a goat-warrior of Satan is like catnip to a cat: it makes them rub their heads along the ground and purr and dribble ceaselessly. The only downside of the computer is that it makes it really easy to make a complete idiot of yourself if you don't really understand what you're doing. Using a computer without any statistical knowledge at all can be a dangerous thing. Hence this book. Well, actually, hence a book called *Discovering Statistics Using SPSS*.

I wrote *Discovering Statistics Using SPSS* just as I was finishing off my Ph.D. in Psychology. My main aim was to write a book that attempted to strike a good balance between theory and practice: I wanted to use the computer as a tool for teaching statistical concepts in the hope that you will gain a better understanding of both theory and practice. If you want theory and you like equations then there are certainly better books: Howell (2006), Stevens (2002) and Tabachnick and Fidell (2007) are peerless as far as I am concerned and have taught me (and continue to teach me) more about statistics than you could possibly imagine. (I have an ambition to be cited in one of these books but I don't think that will ever happen.) However, if you want a book that incorporates digital rectal stimulation then you have just spent your money wisely. (I should probably clarify that the stimulation is in the context of an example, you will not find any devices attached to the inside cover for you to stimulate your rectum while you read. Please feel free to get your own device if you think it will help you to learn.)

A second, not in any way ridiculously ambitious, aim was to make this the only statistics textbook that anyone ever needs to buy. As such, it's a book that I hope will become your friend from first year right through to your professorship. I've tried to write a book that can be read at several levels (see the next section for more guidance). There are chapters for first-year undergraduates (1, 2, 3, 4, 5, 6, 9 and 15), chapters for second-year undergraduates (5, 7, 10, 11, 12, 13 and 14) and chapters on more advanced topics that postgraduates might use (8, 16, 17, 18 and 19). All of these chapters should be accessible to everyone, and I hope to achieve this by flagging the level of each section (see the next section).

My third, final and most important aim is make the learning process fun. I have a sticky history with maths because I used to be terrible at it:

| MATHEMATICS ADDL. MATHS. | 43 | 59 | 27= | D | C | His work shows lack of discipline in thought and presentation. I hope it will mature next year. | [initials] |
| CHEMISTRY | | | | | | | |

Above is an extract of my school report at the age of 11. The '27=' in the report is to say that I came equal 27th with another student out of a class of 29. That's almost bottom of the class. The 43 is my exam mark as a percentage. Oh dear. Four years later (at 15) this was my school report:

NAME Andrew Field   FORM 4Q   SUBJECT Mathematics

Andrew's progress in Mathematics has been remarkable. From being a weaker candidate who lacked confidence he has developed into a budding Mathematician. He should achieve a good grade.

	EXAM	
	ATTAINMENT	
	EFFORT	

Date 27/6/88   B.A. Greate   Subject Teacher

What led to this remarkable change? It was having a good teacher: my brother, Paul. In fact I owe my life as an academic to Paul's ability to do what my maths teachers couldn't: teach me stuff in an engaging way. To this day he still pops up in times of need to teach me things (many tutorials in computer programming spring to mind). Anyway, the reason he's a great teacher is because he's able to make things interesting and relevant to me. He got the 'good teaching' genes in the family, but they're wasted because he doesn't teach for a living; they're a little less wasted though because his approach inspires my lectures and books. One thing that I have learnt is that people appreciate the human touch, and so I tried to inject a lot of my own personality and sense of humour (or lack of) into *Discovering Statistics Using …* books. Many of the examples in this book, although inspired by some of the craziness that you find in the real world, are designed to reflect topics that play on the minds of the average student (i.e., sex, drugs, rock and roll, celebrity, people doing crazy stuff). There are also some examples that are there just because they made me laugh. So, the examples are light-hearted (some have said 'smutty' but I prefer 'light-hearted') and by the end, for better or worse, I think you will have some idea of what goes on in my head on a daily basis. I apologize to those who think it's crass, hate it, or think that I'm undermining the seriousness of science, but, come on, what's not funny about a man putting an eel up his anus?

Did I succeed in these aims? Maybe I did, maybe I didn't, but the SPSS book on which this **R** book is based has certainly been popular and I enjoy the rare luxury of having many complete strangers emailing me to tell me how wonderful I am. (Admittedly, occassionally people email to tell me that they think I'm a pile of gibbon excrement but you have to take the rough with the smooth.) It also won the British Psychological Society book award in 2007. I must have done something right. However, *Discovering Statistics Using SPSS* has one very large flaw: not everybody uses SPSS. Some people use **R**. **R** has one fairly big advantage over other statistical packages in that it is free. That's right, it's free. Completely and utterly free. People say that there's no such thing as a free lunch, but they're wrong:

R is a feast of succulent delights topped off with a baked cheesecake and nothing to pay at the end of it.

It occurred to me that it would be great to have a version of the book that used all of the same theory and examples from the SPSS book but written about **R**. Genius. Genius except that I knew very little about **R**. Six months and quite a few late nights later and I know a lot more about **R** than I did when I started this insane venture. Along the way I have been helped by a very nice guy called Jeremy (a man who likes to put eels in his CD player rather than anywhere else), and an even nicer wife. Both of their contributions have been concealed somewhat by our desire to keep the voice of the book mine, but they have both contributed enormously. (Jeremy's contributions are particularly easy to spot: if it reads like a statistics genius struggling manfully to coerce the words of a moron into something approximating factual accuracy, then Jeremy wrote it.)

What are you getting for your money?

This book takes you on a journey (possibly through a very narrow passage lined with barbed wire) not just of statistics but of the weird and wonderful contents of the world and my brain. In short, it's full of stupid examples, bad jokes, smut and filth. Aside from the smut, I have been forced reluctantly to include some academic content. Over many editions of the SPSS book many people have emailed me with suggestions, so, in theory, what you currently have in your hands should answer any question anyone has asked me over the past ten years. It won't, but it should, and I'm sure you can find some new questions to ask. It has some other unusual features:

- **Everything you'll ever need to know**: I want this to be good value for money so the book guides you from complete ignorance (Chapter 1 tells you the basics of doing research) to being an expert on multilevel modelling (Chapter 19). Of course no book that you can actually lift off the floor will contain everything, but I think this one has a fair crack at taking you from novice to postgraduate level expertise. It's pretty good for developing your biceps also.

- **Stupid faces**: You'll notice that the book is riddled with stupid faces, some of them my own. You can find out more about the pedagogic function of these 'characters' in the next section, but even without any useful function they're still nice to look at.

- **Data sets**: There are about 100 data files associated with this book on the companion website. Not unusual in itself for a statistics book, but my data sets contain more sperm (not literally) than other books. I'll let you judge for yourself whether this is a good thing.

- **My life story**: Each chapter is book-ended by a chronological story from my life. Does this help you to learn about statistics? Probably not, but hopefully it provides some light relief between chapters.

- **R tips**: R does weird things sometimes. In each chapter, there are boxes containing tips, hints and pitfalls related to R.

- **Self-test questions**: Given how much students hate tests, I thought the best way to commit commercial suicide was to liberally scatter tests throughout each chapter. These range from simple questions to test what you have just learned to going back to a technique that you read about several chapters before and applying it in a new context. All of these questions have answers to them on the companion website. They are there so that you can check on your progress.

The book also has some more conventional features:

- **Reporting your analysis**: Every single chapter has a guide to writing up your analysis. Obviously, how one writes up an analysis varies a bit from one discipline to another and, because I'm a psychologist, these sections are quite psychology-based. Nevertheless, they should get you heading in the right direction.

- **Glossary**: Writing the glossary was so horribly painful that it made me stick a vacuum cleaner into my ear to suck out my own brain. You can find my brain in the bottom of the vacuum cleaner in my house.

- **Real-world data**: Students like to have 'real data' to play with. The trouble is that real research can be quite boring. However, just for you, I trawled the world for examples of research on really fascinating topics (in my opinion). I then stalked the authors of the research until they gave me their data. Every chapter has a real research example.

Goodbye

The SPSS version of this book has literally consumed the last 13 years or so of my life, and this **R** version has consumed the last 6 months. I am literally typing this as a withered husk. I have no idea whether people use **R**, and whether this version will sell, but I think they should (use **R**, that is, not necessarily buy the book). The more I have learnt about **R** through writing this book, the more I like it.

This book in its various forms has been a huge part of my adult life; it began as and continues to be a labour of love. The book isn't perfect, and I still love to have feedback (good or bad) from the people who matter most: you.

Andy

- Contact details: http://www. discoveringstatistics.com/html/email.html
- Twitter: @ProfAndyField
- Blog: http://www.methodspace.com/profile/ProfessorAndyField

HOW TO USE THIS BOOK

When the publishers asked me to write a section on 'How to use this book' it was obviously tempting to write 'Buy a large bottle of Olay anti-wrinkle cream (which you'll need to fend off the effects of ageing while you read), find a comfy chair, sit down, fold back the front cover, begin reading and stop when you reach the back cover.' However, I think they wanted something more useful. ☺

What background knowledge do I need?

In essence, I assume you know nothing about statistics, but I do assume you have some very basic grasp of computers (I won't be telling you how to switch them on, for example) and maths (although I have included a quick revision of some very basic concepts so I really don't assume anything).

Do the chapters get more difficult as I go through the book?

In a sense they do (Chapter 16 on MANOVA is more difficult than Chapter 1), but in other ways they don't (Chapter 15 on non-parametric statistics is arguably less complex than Chapter 14, and Chapter 9 on the t-test is definitely less complex than Chapter 8 on logistic regression). Why have I done this? Well, I've ordered the chapters to make statistical sense (to me, at least). Many books teach different tests in isolation and never really give you a grip of the similarities between them; this, I think, creates an unnecessary mystery. Most of the tests in this book are the same thing expressed in slightly different ways. So, I wanted the book to tell this story. To do this I have to do certain things such as explain regression fairly early on because it's the foundation on which nearly everything else is built.

However, to help you through I've coded each section with an icon. These icons are designed to give you an idea of the difficulty of the section. It doesn't necessarily mean you can skip the sections (but see Smart Alex in the next section), but it will let you know whether a section is at about your level, or whether it's going to push you. I've based the icons on my own teaching so they may not be entirely accurate for everyone (especially as systems vary in different countries!):

① This means 'level 1' and I equate this to first-year undergraduate in the UK. These are sections that everyone should be able to understand.

② This is the next level and I equate this to second-year undergraduate in the UK. These are topics that I teach my second years and so anyone with a bit of background in statistics should be able to get to grips with them. However, some of these sections will be quite challenging even for second years. These are intermediate sections.

③ This is 'level 3' and represents difficult topics. I'd expect third-year (final-year) UK undergraduates and recent postgraduate students to be able to tackle these sections.

④ This is the highest level and represents very difficult topics. I would expect these sections to be very challenging to undergraduates and recent postgraduates, but postgraduates with a reasonable background in research methods shouldn't find them too much of a problem.

Why do I keep seeing stupid faces everywhere?

Brian Haemorrhage: Brian's job is to pop up to ask questions and look permanently confused. It's no surprise to note, therefore, that he doesn't look entirely different from the author (he has more hair though). As the book progresses he becomes increasingly despondent. Read into that what you will.

Curious Cat: He also pops up and asks questions (because he's curious). Actually the only reason he's here is because I wanted a cat in the book … and preferably one that looks like mine. Of course the educational specialists think he needs a specific role, and so his role is to look cute and make bad cat-related jokes.

Cramming Sam: Samantha hates statistics. In fact, she thinks it's all a boring waste of time and she just wants to pass her exam and forget that she ever had to know anything about normal distributions. So, she appears and gives you a summary of the key points that you need to know. If, like Samantha, you're cramming for an exam, she will tell you the essential information to save you having to trawl through hundreds of pages of my drivel.

Jane Superbrain: Jane is the cleverest person in the whole universe (she makes Smart Alex look like a bit of an imbecile). The reason she is so clever is that she steals the brains of statisticians and eats them. Apparently they taste of sweaty tank tops, but nevertheless she likes them. As it happens she is also able to absorb the contents of brains while she eats them. Having devoured some top statistics brains she knows all the really hard stuff and appears in boxes to tell you really advanced things that are a bit tangential to the main text. (Readers should note that Jane wasn't interested in eating my brain. That tells you all that you need to know about my statistics ability.)

Labcoat Leni: Leni is a budding young scientist and he's fascinated by real research. He says, 'Andy, man, I like an example about using an eel as a cure for constipation as much as the next man, but all of your examples are made up. Real data aren't like that, we need some real examples, dude!' So off Leni went; he walked the globe, a lone data warrior in a thankless quest for real data. He turned up at universities, cornered academics, kidnapped their families and threatened to put them in a bath of crayfish unless he was given real data. The generous ones relented, but others? Well, let's just say their families are sore. So, when you see Leni you know that you will get some real data, from a real research study to analyse. Keep it real.

Oliver Twisted: With apologies to Charles Dickens, Oliver, like the more famous fictional London urchin, is always asking 'Please Sir, can I have some more?' Unlike Master Twist though, our young Master Twisted always wants more statistics information. Of course he does, who wouldn't? Let us not be the ones to disappoint a young, dirty, slightly smelly boy who dines on gruel, so when Oliver appears you can be certain of one thing: there is additional information to be found on the companion website. (Don't be shy; download it and bathe in the warm asp's milk of knowledge.)

R's Souls: People who love statistics are damned to hell for all eternity, people who like **R** even more so. However, **R** and statistics are secretly so much fun that Satan is inundated with new lost souls, converted to the evil of statistical methods. Satan needs a helper to collect up all the souls of those who have been converted to the joy of **R**. While collecting the souls of the statistical undead, they often cry out useful tips to him. He's collected these nuggets of information and spread them through the book like a demonic plague of beetles. When Satan's busy spanking a goat, his helper pops up in a box to tell you some of **R**'s Souls' Tips.

Smart Alex: Alex is a very important character because he appears when things get particularly difficult. He's basically a bit of a smart alec and so whenever you see his face you know that something scary is about to be explained. When the hard stuff is over he reappears to let you know that it's safe to continue. Now, this is not to say that all of the rest of the material in the book is easy, he just lets you know the bits of the book that you can skip if you've got better things to do with your life than read all 1000 pages! So, if you see Smart Alex then you can *skip the section* entirely and still understand what's going on. You'll also find that Alex pops up at the end of each chapter to give you some tasks to do to see whether you're as smart as he is.

What is on the companion website?

In this age of downloading, CD-ROMs are for losers (at least that's what the 'kids' tell me) so I've put my cornucopia of additional funk on that worldwide interweb thing. This has two benefits: 1) the book is *slightly* lighter than it would have been, and 2) rather than being restricted to the size of a CD-ROM, there is no limit to the amount of fascinating extra material that I can give you (although Sage have had to purchase a new server to fit it all on). To enter my world of delights, go to www.sagepub.co.uk/dsur.

How will you know when there are extra goodies on this website? Easy-peasy, Oliver Twisted appears in the book to indicate that there's something you need (or something extra) on the website. The website contains resources for students and lecturers alike:

- **Data files**: You need data files to work through the examples in the book and they are all on the companion website. We did this so that you're forced to go there and once you're there Sage will flash up subliminal messages that make you buy more of their books.

- **R script files**: if you put all of the **R** commands in this book next to each other and printed them out you'd have a piece of paper that stretched from here to the Tarantula Nebula (which actually exists and sounds like a very scary place). If you type all of these commands into **R** you will wear away your fingers to small stumps. I would never forgive myself if you all got stumpy fingers so the website has script files containing every single **R** command in the book (including within chapter questions and activities).

- **Webcasts**: My publisher thinks that watching a film of me explaining what this book is all about will get people flocking to the bookshop. I think it will have people flocking to the medicine cabinet. Either way, if you want to see how truly uncharismatic I am, watch and cringe. There are also a few webcasts of lectures given by me relevant to the content of the book.

- **Self-Assessment Multiple-Choice Questions**: Organized by chapter, these will allow you to test whether wasting your life reading this book has paid off so that you can walk confidently into an examination much to the annoyance of your friends. If you fail said exam, you can employ a good lawyer and sue.

- **Additional material**: Enough trees have died in the name of this book, but still it gets longer and still people want to know more. Therefore, we've written nearly 300 pages, yes, three hundred, of additional material for the book. So for some more technical topics and help with tasks in the book the material has been provided electronically so that (1) the planet suffers a little less, and (2) you won't die when the book falls off of your bookshelf onto your head.

- **Answers**: each chapter ends with a set of tasks for you to test your newly acquired expertise. The chapters are also littered with self-test questions and Labcoat Leni's assignments. How will you know if you get these correct? Well, the companion website contains around 300 pages (that's a different 300 pages to the 300 above) of detailed answers. Will we ever stop writing?

- **Powerpoint slides**: I can't come and personally teach you all. Instead I rely on a crack team of highly skilled and super intelligent pan-dimensional beings called 'lecturers'. I have personally grown each and every one of them in a greenhouse in my garden. To assist in their mission to spread the joy of statistics I have provided them with powerpoint slides for each chapter.

- **Links**: every website has to have links to other useful websites and the companion website is no exception.

- **Cyberworms of knowledge**: I have used nanotechnology to create cyberworms that crawl down your broadband connection, pop out of the USB port of your computer then fly through space into your brain. They re-arrange your neurons so that you understand statistics. You don't believe me? Well, you'll never know for sure unless you visit the companion website …

Happy reading, and don't get sidetracked by Facebook and Twitter.

ACKNOWLEDGEMENTS

This book (in all its SPSS, SAS and R versions) wouldn't have happened if it hadn't been for Dan Wright, who not only had an unwarranted faith in a then-postgraduate to write the first SPSS edition, but also read and commented on draft chapters in all three SPSS editions. Numerous other people have contributed to the SPSS versions of this book, on which this **R** edition is based. I won't list them all here, but particular thanks go to David Hitchin, Laura Murray, Gareth Williams, Lynne Slocombe and Kate Lester, who have given me significant amounts of feedback in various incarnations of this text. Hadley Wickham very kindly gave feedback on my graphing chapter in this **R** version, which led to significant improvements, and Rand Wilcox was incredibly helpful when I couldn't get one of his **R** functions to work. Thanks to them both for generously giving me help.

I have incorporated data sets from real research papers. All of these research papers are studies that I find fascinating and it's an honour for me to have these researchers' data in my book: Hakan Çetinkaya, Tomas Chamorro-Premuzic, Graham Davey, Mike Domjan, Gordon Gallup, Eric Lacourse, Sarah Marzillier, Geoffrey Miller, Peter Muris, Laura Nichols and Achim Schüetzwohl.

Not all contributions are as tangible as those above. With the possible exception of them not understanding why sometimes I don't answer my phone, I could not have asked for more loving and proud parents – a fact that I often take for granted. Also, very early in my career Graham Hole made me realize that teaching research methods didn't have to be dull. My whole approach to teaching has been to steal all of his good ideas and I'm pleased that he has had the good grace not to ask for them back! He is also a rarity in being brilliant, funny *and* nice.

The people at Sage very generously co-funded my wife to help with this book. My editor Mike takes his fair share of crap from me (but what does he expect, he supports Tottenham), he is unfaltering in his efforts to support me and make things happen. Ziyad and Karen at Sage have also been incredibly supportive over many years, and Ian and numerous other people at Sage do magical things. Alex Lee did a fantastic job of turning the characters in my head into characters on the page.

I always write listening to music. For this **R** edition I predominantly enjoyed the following: 1349, Anathema, Behemoth, Blut Aus Nord, Daft Punk, Deathspell Omega, Dio, Enslaved, Genesis, Immortal, I, Iron Maiden, Jethro Tull, Liturgy, Manowar, Marillion, Mastodon, Metallica, Megadeth, Negură Bunget, Opeth, Rush, Sylosis, Týr, W.A.S.P.

Extra big fluffy thanks go to Jeremy Miles for his help with this book. As if this wasn't enough, he also stopped me making a complete and utter fool of myself (in the book – sadly his powers don't extend to everyday life) by pointing out some glaring errors; he's also been a very nice person to know over the past few years (apart from when he's saying that draft sections of my books are, and I quote, 'bollocks'). I particularly enjoyed sharing ranty emails with him about **R**.

All this book-writing nonsense requires many lonely hours (mainly late at night) of typing. Without some wonderful friends to drag me out of my dimly lit room from time to time I'd be even more of a gibbering cabbage than I already am. My eternal gratitude goes to Graham Davey, Ben Dyson, Martin Watts, Sam Cartwright-Hatton, Mark Franklin and their lovely families for reminding me that there is more to life than work. My eternal gratitude to my brothers of metal Doug Martin and Rob Mepham for letting me deafen them with my drumming on a regular basis (www.myspace.com/fracturepattern).

I've saved the best until last: I don't think the words exist to do justice to the thanks deserved by my wife Zoë. Not only has she got a never-ending supply of patience, love and support (even when her husband is being a grumpy, sleep-deprived, withered husk) but she also single-handedly produced the accompanying web materials for this book. I never forget, not even for a nanosecond, how lucky I am.

Dedication

Andy: To my wonderful wife Zoë.

Jeremy: To Susanne, Alex and Daniel.

Zoë: To my grumpy, sleep-deprived, withered but lovable husk.

SYMBOLS USED IN THIS BOOK

Mathematical operators

Σ	This symbol (called sigma) means 'add everything up'. So, if you see something like Σx_i it just means 'add up all of the scores you've collected'.
Π	This symbol means 'multiply everything'. So, if you see something like Πx_i it just means 'multiply all of the scores you've collected'.
$\sqrt{x}$	This means 'take the square root of x'.

Greek symbols

α	The probability of making a Type I error
β	The probability of making a Type II error
β_i	Standardized regression coefficient
χ^2	Chi-square test statistic
χ_F^2	Friedman's ANOVA test statistic
ε	Usually stands for 'error'
η^2	Eta-squared
μ	The mean of a population of scores
ρ	The correlation in the population
σ^2	The variance in a population of data
σ	The standard deviation in a population of data
$\sigma_{\bar{x}}$	The standard error of the mean
τ	Kendall's tau (non-parametric correlation coefficient)
ω^2	Omega squared (an effect size measure). This symbol also means 'expel the contents of your intestine immediately into your trousers'; you will understand why in due course.

English symbols

b_i	The regression coefficient (unstandardized)
df	Degrees of freedom
e_i	The error associated with the ith person
F	F-ratio (test statistic used in ANOVA)
H	Kruskal–Wallis test statistic
k	The number of levels of a variable (i.e. the number of treatment conditions), or the number of predictors in a regression model
$\ln$	Natural logarithm
MS	The mean squared error. The average variability in the data
N, n, n_i	The sample size. N usually denotes the total sample size, whereas n usually denotes the size of a particular group
P	Probability (the probability value, p-value or significance of a test are usually denoted by p)
r	Pearson's correlation coefficient
r_s	Spearman's rank correlation coefficient
r_b, r_{pb}	Biserial correlation coefficient and point–biserial correlation coefficient respectively
R	The multiple correlation coefficient
R^2	The coefficient of determination (i.e. the proportion of data explained by the model)
s^2	The variance of a sample of data
s	The standard deviation of a sample of data
SS	The sum of squares, or sum of squared errors to give it its full title
SS_A	The sum of squares for variable A
SS_M	The model sum of squares (i.e. the variability explained by the model fitted to the data)
SS_R	The residual sum of squares (i.e. the variability that the model can't explain – the error in the model)
SS_T	The total sum of squares (i.e. the total variability within the data)
t	Test statistic for Student's t-test
T	Test statistic for Wilcoxon's matched-pairs signed-rank test
U	Test statistic for the Mann–Whitney test
W_s	Test statistic for the Shapiro–Wilk test and the Wilcoxon's rank-sum test
$\bar{X}$ or $\bar{x}$	The mean of a sample of scores
z	A data point expressed in standard deviation units

SOME MATHS REVISION

1 **Two negatives make a positive**: Although in life two wrongs don't make a right, in mathematics they do! When we multiply a negative number by another negative number, the result is a positive number. For example, $-2 \times -4 = 8$.

2 **A negative number multiplied by a positive one make a negative number**: If you multiply a positive number by a negative number then the result is another negative number. For example, $2 \times -4 = -8$, or $-2 \times 6 = -12$.

3 **BODMAS**: This is an acronym for the order in which mathematical operations are performed. It stands for Brackets, Order, Division, Multiplication, Addition, Subtraction and this is the order in which you should carry out operations within an equation. Mostly these operations are self-explanatory (e.g., always calculate things within brackets first) except for order, which actually refers to power terms such as squares. Four squared, or 4^2, used to be called four raised to the order of 2, hence the reason why these terms are called 'order' in BODMAS (also, if we called it power, we'd end up with BPDMAS, which doesn't roll off the tongue quite so nicely). Let's look at an example of BODMAS: what would be the result of $1 + 3 \times 5^2$? The answer is 76 (not 100 as some of you might have thought). There are no brackets so the first thing is to deal with the order term: 5^2 is 25, so the equation becomes $1 + 3 \times 25$. There is no division, so we can move on to multiplication: 3×25, which gives us 75. BODMAS tells us to deal with addition next: $1 + 75$, which gives us 76 and the equation is solved. If I'd written the original equation as $(1 + 3) \times 5^2$, then the answer would have been 100 because we deal with the brackets first: $(1 + 3) = 4$, so the equation becomes 4×5^2. We then deal with the order term, so the equation becomes $4 \times 25 = 100$!

4 **www.bbc.co.uk/schools/gcsebitesize/maths** is a good site for revising basic maths.

Why is my evil lecturer forcing me to learn statistics?

1

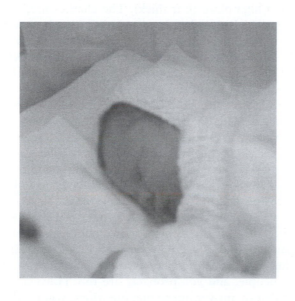

FIGURE 1.1
When I grow up, please don't let me be a statistics lecturer

1.1. What will this chapter tell me? ①

I was born on 21 June 1973. Like most people, I don't remember anything about the first few years of life and like most children I did go through a phase of driving my parents mad by asking 'Why?' every five seconds. 'Dad, why is the sky blue?', 'Dad, why doesn't mummy have a willy?', etc. Children are naturally curious about the world. I remember at the age of 3 being at a party of my friend Obe (this was just before he left England to return to Nigeria, much to my distress). It was a hot day, and there was an electric fan blowing cold air around the room. As I said, children are natural scientists and my little scientific brain was working through what seemed like a particularly pressing question: 'What happens when you stick your finger in a fan?' The answer, as it turned out, was that it hurts – a lot.[1] My point is this: my curiosity to explain the world never went away, and that's why I'm a scientist, and that's also why your evil lecturer is forcing you to learn statistics. It's because you have a curious mind too and you want to answer new and exciting questions. To answer these questions we need statistics. Statistics is a bit like sticking your finger into a revolving fan blade: sometimes it's very painful, but it does give you the power to answer interesting questions. This chapter is going to attempt to explain why statistics are an important part of doing research. We will overview the whole research process, from why we conduct research in the first place, through how theories are generated, to why we need data to test these theories. If that doesn't convince you to read on then maybe the fact that we discover whether Coca-Cola kills sperm will. Or perhaps not.

1.2. What the hell am I doing here? I don't belong here ①

You're probably wondering why you have bought this book. Maybe you liked the pictures, maybe you fancied doing some weight training (it *is* heavy), or perhaps you need to reach something in a high place (it *is* thick). The chances are, though, that given the choice of spending your hard-earned cash on a statistics book or something more entertaining (a nice novel, a trip to the cinema, etc.) you'd choose the latter. So, why have you bought the book (or downloaded an illegal pdf of it from someone who has way too much time on their hands if they can scan a 1000-page textbook)? It's likely that you obtained it because you're doing a course on statistics, or you're doing some research, and you need to know how to analyse data. It's possible that you didn't realize when you started your course or research that you'd have to know this much about statistics but now find yourself inexplicably wading, neck high, through the Victorian sewer that is data analysis. The reason you're in the mess that you find yourself in is because you have a curious mind. You might have asked yourself questions like why people behave the way they do (psychology), why behaviours differ across cultures (anthropology), how businesses maximize their profit (business), how the dinosaurs died (palaeontology), does eating tomatoes protect you against cancer (medicine, biology), is it possible to build a quantum computer (physics, chemistry), is the planet hotter than it used to be and in what regions (geography, environmental studies)? Whatever it is you're studying or researching, the reason you're studying it is probably because you're interested in answering questions. Scientists are curious people, and you probably are too. However, you might not have bargained on the fact that to answer interesting questions, you need two things: data and an explanation of those data.

The answer to 'what the hell are you doing here?' is, therefore, simple: to answer interesting questions you need data. Therefore, one of the reasons why your evil statistics lecturer is forcing you to learn about numbers is because they are a form of data and are vital to the research process. Of course there are forms of data other than numbers that can be used to test and generate theories. When numbers are involved the research involves **quantitative methods**, but you can also generate and test theories by analysing language (such as conversations, magazine articles, media broadcasts and so on).

---

[1] In the 1970s fans didn't have helpful protective cages around them to prevent idiotic 3-year-olds sticking their fingers into the blades.

This involves **qualitative methods** and it is a topic for another book not written by me. People can get quite passionate about which of these methods is *best*, which is a bit silly because they are complementary, not competing, approaches and there are much more important issues in the world to get upset about. Having said that, all qualitative research is rubbish.[2]

How do you go about answering an interesting question? The research process is broadly summarized in Figure 1.2. You begin with an observation that you want to understand, and this observation could be anecdotal (you've noticed that your cat watches birds when they're on TV but not when jellyfish are on)[3] or could be based on some data (you've got several cat owners to keep diaries of their cat's TV habits and have noticed that lots of them watch birds on TV). From your initial observation you generate explanations, or theories, of those observations, from which you can make predictions (hypotheses). Here's where the data come into the process because to test your predictions you need data. First you collect some relevant data (and to do that you need to identify things that can be measured) and then you analyse those data. The analysis of the data may support your theory or give you cause to modify the theory. As such, the processes of data collection and analysis and generating theories are intrinsically linked: theories lead to data collection/analysis and data collection/analysis informs theories! This chapter explains this research process in more detail.

> How do I do research?

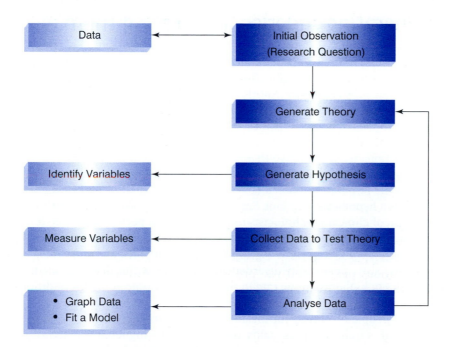

FIGURE 1.2
The research process

---

[2] This is a joke. I thought long and hard about whether to include it because, like many of my jokes, there are people who won't find it remotely funny. Its inclusion is also making me fear being hunted down and forced to eat my own entrails by a hoard of rabid qualitative researchers. However, it made me laugh, a lot, and despite being vegetarian I'm sure my entrails will taste lovely.

[3] My cat does actually climb up and stare at the TV when it's showing birds flying about.

1.3. Initial observation: finding something that needs explaining ①

The first step in Figure 1.2 was to come up with a question that needs an answer. I spend rather more time than I should watching reality TV. Every year I swear that I won't get hooked on *Big Brother*, and yet every year I find myself glued to the TV screen waiting for the next contestant's meltdown (I am a psychologist, so really this is just research – honestly). One question I am constantly perplexed by is why every year there are so many contestants with really unpleasant personalities (my money is on narcissistic personality disorder[4]) on the show. A lot of scientific endeavour starts this way: not by watching *Big Brother*, but by observing something in the world and wondering why it happens.

Having made a casual observation about the world (*Big Brother* contestants on the whole have profound personality defects), I need to collect some data to see whether this observation is true (and not just a biased observation). To do this, I need to define one or more **variables** that I would like to measure. There's one variable in this example: the personality of the contestant. I could measure this variable by giving them one of the many well-established questionnaires that measure personality characteristics. Let's say that I did this and I found that 75% of contestants did have narcissistic personality disorder. These data support my observation: a lot of *Big Brother* contestants have extreme personalities.

1.4. Generating theories and testing them ①

The next logical thing to do is to explain these data (Figure 1.2). One explanation could be that people with narcissistic personality disorder are more likely to audition for *Big Brother* than those without. This is a **theory**. Another possibility is that the producers of *Big Brother* are more likely to select people who have narcissistic personality disorder to be contestants than those with less extreme personalities. This is another theory. We verified our original observation by collecting data, and we can collect more data to test our theories. We can make two predictions from these two theories. The first is that the number of people turning up for an audition that have narcissistic personality disorder will be higher than the general level in the population (which is about 1%). A prediction from a theory, like this one, is known as a **hypothesis** (see Jane Superbrain Box 1.1). We could test this hypothesis by getting a team of clinical psychologists to interview each person at the *Big Brother* audition and diagnose them as having narcissistic personality disorder or not. The prediction from our second theory is that if the *Big Brother* selection panel are more likely to choose people with narcissistic personality disorder then the rate of this disorder in the final contestants will be even higher than the rate in the group of people going for auditions. This is another hypothesis. Imagine we collected these data; they are in Table 1.1.

In total, 7662 people turned up for the audition. Our first hypothesis is that the percentage of people with narcissistic personality disorder will be higher at the audition than the general level in the population. We can see in the table that of the 7662 people at the audition, 854 were diagnosed with the disorder; this is about 11% ($854/7662 \times 100$), which is much higher than the 1% we'd expect. Therefore, hypothesis 1 is supported by the data. The second hypothesis was that the *Big Brother* selection panel have a bias to chose people with narcissistic personality disorder. If we look at the 12 contestants that they selected, 9 of them had the disorder (a massive 75%). If the producers did not have a bias we would

---

[4] This disorder is characterized by (among other things) a grandiose sense of self-importance, arrogance, lack of empathy for others, envy of others and belief that others envy them, excessive fantasies of brilliance or beauty, the need for excessive admiration and exploitation of others.

Table 1.1   A table of the number of people at the Big Brother audition split by whether they had narcissistic personality disorder and whether they were selected as contestants by the producers

	No Disorder	Disorder	Total
Selected	3	9	12
Rejected	6805	845	7650
Total	6808	854	7662

have expected only 11% of the contestants to have the disorder. The data again support our hypothesis. Therefore, my initial observation that contestants have personality disorders was verified by data, then my theory was tested using specific hypotheses that were also verified using data. Data are *very* important!

JANE SUPERBRAIN 1.1

When is a hypothesis not a hypothesis? ①

A good theory should allow us to make statements about the state of the world. Statements about the world are good things: they allow us to make sense of our world, and to make decisions that affect our future. One current example is global warming. Being able to make a definitive statement that global warming is happening, and that it is caused by certain practices in society, allows us to change these practices and, hopefully, avert catastrophe. However, not all statements are ones that can be tested using science. Scientific statements are ones that can be verified with reference to empirical evidence, whereas non-scientific statements are ones that cannot be empirically tested. So, statements such as 'The Led Zeppelin reunion concert in London in 2007 was the best gig ever',[5] 'Lindt chocolate is the best food' and 'This is the worst statistics book in the world' are all non-scientific; they cannot be proved or disproved. Scientific statements can be confirmed or disconfirmed empirically. 'Watching *Curb Your Enthusiasm* makes you happy', 'having sex increases levels of the neurotransmitter dopamine' and 'velociraptors ate meat' are all things that can be tested empirically (provided you can quantify and measure the variables concerned). Non-scientific statements can sometimes be altered to become scientific statements, so 'The Beatles were the most influential band ever' is non-scientific (because it is probably impossible to quantify 'influence' in any meaningful way) but by changing the statement to 'The Beatles were the best-selling band ever' it becomes testable (we can collect data about worldwide record sales and establish whether The Beatles have, in fact, sold more records than any other music artist). Karl Popper, the famous philosopher of science, believed that non-scientific statements were nonsense, and had no place in science. Good theories should, therefore, produce hypotheses that are scientific statements.

I would now be smugly sitting in my office with a contented grin on my face about how my theories and observations were well supported by the data. Perhaps I would quit while I was ahead and retire. It's more likely, though, that having solved one great mystery, my excited mind would turn to another. After another few hours (well, days probably) locked up at home watching *Big Brother* I would emerge triumphant with another profound

---

[5] It was pretty awesome actually.

observation, which is that these personality-disordered contestants, despite their obvious character flaws, enter the house convinced that the public will love them and that they will win.[6] My hypothesis would, therefore, be that if I asked the contestants if they thought that they would win, the people with a personality disorder would say yes.

Let's imagine I tested my hypothesis by measuring their expectations of success in the show, by just asking them, 'Do you think you will win *Big Brother*?'. Let's say that 7 of 9 contestants with personality disorders said that they thought that they will win, which confirms my observation. Next, I would come up with another theory: these contestants think that they will win because they don't realize that they have a personality disorder. My hypothesis would be that if I asked these people about whether their personalities were different from other people they would say 'no'. As before, I would collect some more data and perhaps ask those who thought that they would win whether they thought that their personalities were different from the norm. All 7 contestants said that they thought their personalities were different from the norm. These data seem to contradict my theory. This is known as **falsification,** which is the act of disproving a hypothesis or theory.

It's unlikely that we would be the only people interested in why individuals who go on *Big Brother* have extreme personalities and think that they will win. Imagine these researchers discovered that: (1) people with narcissistic personality disorder think that they are more interesting than others; (2) they also think that they deserve success more than others; and (3) they also think that others like them because they have 'special' personalities.

This additional research is even worse news for my theory: if they didn't realize that they had a personality different from the norm then you wouldn't expect them to think that they were more interesting than others, and you certainly wouldn't expect them to think that others will like their unusual personalities. In general, this means that my theory sucks: it cannot explain all of the data, predictions from the theory are not supported by subsequent data, and it cannot explain other research findings. At this point I would start to feel intellectually inadequate and people would find me curled up on my desk in floods of tears wailing and moaning about my failing career (no change there then).

At this point, a rival scientist, Fester Ingpant-Stain, appears on the scene with a rival theory to mine. In his new theory, he suggests that the problem is not that personality-disordered contestants don't realize that they have a personality disorder (or at least a personality that is unusual), but that they falsely believe that this special personality is perceived positively by other people (put another way, they believe that their personality makes them likeable, not dislikeable). One hypothesis from this model is that if personality-disordered contestants are asked to evaluate what other people think of them, then they will overestimate other people's positive perceptions. To test this hypothesis, Fester Ingpant-Stain collected yet more data. When each contestant came to the diary room[7] they had to fill out a questionnaire evaluating all of the other contestants' personalities, and also answer each question as if they were each of the contestants responding about them. (So, for every contestant there is a measure of what they thought of every other contestant, and also a measure of what they believed every other contestant thought of them.) He found out that the contestants with personality disorders did overestimate their housemates' view of them; in comparison the contestants without personality disorders had relatively accurate impressions of what others thought of them. These data, irritating as it would be for me, support the rival theory that the contestants with personality disorders know they have unusual personalities but believe that these characteristics are ones that others would feel positive about. Fester Ingpant-Stain's theory is quite good: it explains the initial observations and

---

[6] One of the things I like about *Big Brother* in the UK is that year upon year the winner tends to be a nice person, which does give me faith that humanity favours the nice.

[7] The diary room is a private room in the house where contestants can talk to 'big brother' about whatever is on their mind.

brings together a range of research findings. The end result of this whole process (and my career) is that we should be able to make a general statement about the state of the world. In this case we could state: '*Big Brother* contestants who have personality disorders overestimate how much other people like their personality characteristics'.

SELF-TEST
✓ Based on what you have read in this section, what qualities do you think a scientific theory should have?

1.5. Data collection 1: what to measure ①

We have seen already that data collection is vital for testing theories. When we collect data we need to decide on two things: (1) what to measure, (2) how to measure it. This section looks at the first of these issues.

1.5.1. Variables ①

1.5.1.1. Independent and dependent variables ①

To test hypotheses we need to measure variables. Variables are just things that can change (or vary); they might vary between people (e.g., IQ, behaviour) or locations (e.g., unemployment) or even time (e.g., mood, profit, number of cancerous cells). Most hypotheses can be expressed in terms of two variables: a proposed cause and a proposed outcome. For example, if we take the scientific statement 'Coca-Cola is an effective spermicide'[8] then the proposed cause is Coca-Cola and the proposed effect is dead sperm. Both the cause and the outcome are variables: for the cause we could vary the type of drink, and for the outcome these drinks will kill different amounts of sperm. The key to testing such statements is to measure these two variables.

A variable that we think is a cause is known as an **independent variable** (because its value does not depend on any other variables). A variable that we think is an effect is called a **dependent variable** because the value of this variable depends on the cause (independent variable). These terms are very closely tied to experimental methods in which the cause is actually manipulated by the experimenter (as we will see in section 1.6.2). In cross-sectional research we don't manipulate any variables and we cannot make causal statements about the relationships between variables, so it doesn't make sense to talk of dependent and independent variables because all variables are dependent variables in a sense. One possibility is to abandon the terms dependent and independent variable and use the terms **predictor variable** and **outcome variable.** In experimental work the cause, or independent variable, is a predictor, and the effect, or dependent variable, is simply an outcome. This terminology also suits cross-sectional work where, statistically at least, we can use one or more variables to make predictions about the other(s) without needing to imply causality.

[8] Actually, there is a long-standing urban myth that a post-coital douche with the contents of a bottle of Coke is an effective contraceptive. Unbelievably, this hypothesis has been tested and Coke does affect sperm motility, and different types of Coke are more or less effective – Diet Coke is best apparently (Umpierre, Hill, & Anderson, 1985). Nevertheless, a Coke douche is ineffective at preventing pregnancy.

CRAMMING SAM'S TIPS   **Some important terms**

When doing research there are some important generic terms for variables that you will encounter:

- **Independent variable**: A variable thought to be the cause of some effect. This term is usually used in experimental research to denote a variable that the experimenter has manipulated.
- **Dependent variable**: A variable thought to be affected by changes in an independent variable. You can think of this variable as an outcome.
- **Predictor variable**: A variable thought to predict an outcome variable. This is basically another term for independent variable (although some people won't like me saying that; I think life would be easier if we talked only about predictors and outcomes).
- **Outcome variable**: A variable thought to change as a function of changes in a predictor variable. This term could be synonymous with 'dependent variable' for the sake of an easy life.

1.5.1.2. Levels of measurement ①

As we have seen in the examples so far, variables can take on many different forms and levels of sophistication. The relationship between what is being measured and the numbers that represent what is being measured is known as the **level of measurement**. Broadly speaking, variables can be categorical or continuous, and can have different levels of measurement.

A **categorical variable** is made up of categories. A categorical variable that you should be familiar with already is your species (e.g., human, domestic cat, fruit bat, etc.). You are a human or a cat or a fruit bat: you cannot be a bit of a cat and a bit of a bat, and neither a batman nor (despite many fantasies to the contrary) a catwoman (not even one in a nice PVC suit) exist. A categorical variable is one that names distinct entities. In its simplest form it names just two distinct types of things, for example male or female. This is known as a **binary variable**. Other examples of binary variables are being alive or dead, pregnant or not, and responding 'yes' or 'no' to a question. In all cases there are just two categories and an entity can be placed into only one of the two categories.

When two things that are equivalent in some sense are given the same name (or number), but there are more than two possibilities, the variable is said to be a **nominal variable**. It should be obvious that if the variable is made up of names it is pointless to do arithmetic on them (if you multiply a human by a cat, you do not get a hat). However, sometimes numbers are used to denote categories. For example, the numbers worn by players in a rugby team. In rugby, the numbers of shirts denote specific field positions, so the number 10 is always worn by the fly-half (e.g., England's Jonny Wilkinson),[9] and the number 2 is always the hooker (the ugly-looking player at the front of the scrum). These numbers do not tell us anything other than what position the player plays. We could equally have shirts with FH and H instead of 10 and 1. A number 10 player is not necessarily better than a number 1 (most managers would not want their fly-half stuck in the front of the scrum!). It is equally as daft to try to do arithmetic with nominal scales where the categories are denoted by numbers: the number 10 takes penalty kicks, and if the England coach found that Jonny Wilkinson (his number 10) was injured he would not get his number 4 to give number 6 a piggy-back and then take the kick. The only way that nominal data can be used is to consider frequencies. For example, we could look at how frequently number 10s score tries compared to number 4s.

---

[9] Unlike, for example, NFL American football where a quarterback could wear any number from 1 to 19.

JANE SUPERBRAIN 1.2

Self-report data ①

A lot of self-report data are ordinal. Imagine if two judges on *The X Factor* were asked to rate Billie's singing on a 10-point scale. We might be confident that a judge who gives a rating of 10 found Billie more talented than one who gave a rating of 2, but can we be certain that the first judge found her five times more talented than the second? What about if both judges gave a rating of 8: could we be sure they found her equally talented? Probably not: their ratings will depend on their subjective feelings about what constitutes talent (the quality of singing? showmanship? dancing?). For these reasons, in any situation in which we ask people to rate something subjective (e.g., rate their preference for a product, their confidence about an answer, how much they have understood some medical instructions) we should probably regard these data as ordinal although many scientists do not.

So far the categorical variables we have considered have been unordered (e.g., different brands of Coke with which you're trying to kill sperm), but they can be ordered too (e.g., increasing concentrations of Coke with which you're trying to skill sperm). When categories are ordered, the variable is known as an **ordinal variable**. Ordinal data tell us not only that things have occurred, but also the order in which they occurred. However, these data tell us nothing about the differences between values. *The X Factor* is a TV show that is broadcast across the globe in which hopeful singers compete to win a recording contract. It is a hugely popular show, which could (if you take a depressing view) reflect the fact that Western society values 'luck' more than hard work. (This comment in no way reflects my bitterness at spending years learning musical instruments and trying to create orginal music, only to be beaten to musical fame and fortune by a 15-year-old who can sing other people's songs, a bit.) Anyway, imagine the three winners of a particular *X Factor* series were Billie, Freema and Elizabeth. The names of the winners don't provide any information about where they came in the contest; however, labelling them according to their performance does – first, second and third. These categories are ordered. In using ordered categories we now know that the woman who won was better than the women who came second and third. We still know nothing about the differences between categories, though. We don't, for example, know how much better the winner was than the runners-up: Billie might have been an easy victor, getting many more votes than Freema and Elizabeth, or it might have been a very close contest that she won by only a single vote. Ordinal data, therefore, tell us more than nominal data (they tell us the order in which things happened) but they still do not tell us about the differences between points on a scale.

The next level of measurement moves us away from categorical variables and into continuous variables. A **continuous variable** is one that gives us a score for each entity and can take on any value on the measurement scale that we are using. The first type of continuous variable that you might encounter is an **interval variable**. Interval data are considerably more useful than ordinal data and most of the statistical tests in this book rely on having data measured at this level. To say that data are interval, we must be certain that equal intervals on the scale represent equal differences in the property being measured. For example, on www.ratemyprofessors.com students are encouraged to rate their lecturers on several dimensions (some of the lecturers' rebuttals of their negative evaluations are worth a look). Each dimension (i.e., helpfulness, clarity, etc.) is evaluated using a 5-point scale. For this scale to be interval it must be the case that the difference between helpfulness ratings of 1 and 2 is the same as the difference between say 3 and 4, or 4 and 5. Similarly, the difference in helpfulness between ratings of 1 and 3 should be identical to the difference between ratings of 3 and 5. Variables like this that look interval (and are treated as interval) are often ordinal – see Jane Superbrain Box 1.2.

Ratio variables go a step further than interval data by requiring that in addition to the measurement scale meeting the requirements of an interval variable, the ratios of values along the scale should be meaningful. For this to be true, the scale must have a true and meaningful zero point. In our lecturer ratings this would mean that a lecturer rated as 4 would be twice as helpful as a lecturer rated with a 2 (who would also be twice as helpful as a lecturer rated as 1!). The time to respond to something is a good example of a ratio variable. When we measure a reaction time, not only is it true that, say, the difference between 300 and 350 ms (a difference of 50 ms) is the same as the difference between 210 and 260 ms or 422 and 472 ms, but also it is true that distances along the scale are divisible: a reaction time of 200 ms is twice as long as a reaction time of 100 ms and twice as short as a reaction time of 400 ms.

JANE SUPERBRAIN 1.3

Continuous and discrete variables ①

The distinction between discrete and continuous variables can be very blurred. For one thing, continuous variables can be measured in discrete terms; for example, when we measure age we rarely use nanoseconds but use years (or possibly years and months). In doing so we turn a continuous variable into a discrete one (the only acceptable values are years). Also, we often treat discrete variables as if they were continuous. For example, the number of boyfriends/ girlfriends that you have had is a discrete variable (it will be, in all but the very weird cases, a whole number). However, you might read a magazine that says 'the average number of boyfriends that women in their 20s have has increased from 4.6 to 8.9'. This assumes that the variable is continuous, and of course these averages are meaningless: no one in their sample actually had 8.9 boyfriends.

Continuous variables can be, well, continuous (obviously) but also discrete. This is quite a tricky distinction (Jane Superbrain Box 1.3). A truly continuous variable can be measured to any level of precision, whereas a **discrete variable** can take on only certain values (usually whole numbers) on the scale. What does this actually mean? Well, our example in the text of rating lecturers on a 5-point scale is an example of a discrete variable. The range of the scale is 1–5, but you can enter only values of 1, 2, 3, 4 or 5; you cannot enter a value of 4.32 or 2.18. Although a continuum exists underneath the scale (i.e., a rating of 3.24 makes sense), the actual values that the variable takes on are limited. A continuous variable would be something like age, which can be measured at an infinite level of precision (you could be 34 years, 7 months, 21 days, 10 hours, 55 minutes, 10 seconds, 100 milliseconds, 63 microseconds, 1 nanosecond old).

CRAMMING SAM'S TIPS   Levels of measurement

Variables can be split into categorical and continuous, and within these types there are different levels of measurement:

- Categorical (entities are divided into distinct categories):

  ○ Binary variable: There are only two categories (e.g., dead or alive).
  ○ Nominal variable: There are more than two categories (e.g., whether someone is an omnivore, vegetarian, vegan, or fruitarian).

- Ordinal variable: The same as a nominal variable but the categories have a logical order (e.g., whether people got a fail, a pass, a merit or a distinction in their exam).
- Continuous (entities get a distinct score):

  ○ Interval variable: Equal intervals on the variable represent equal differences in the property being measured (e.g., the difference between 6 and 8 is equivalent to the difference between 13 and 15).
  ○ Ratio variable: The same as an interval variable, but the ratios of scores on the scale must also make sense (e.g., a score of 16 on an anxiety scale means that the person is, in reality, twice as anxious as someone scoring 8).

1.5.2.   Measurement error ①

We have seen that to test hypotheses we need to measure variables. Obviously, it's also important that we measure these variables accurately. Ideally we want our measure to be calibrated such that values have the same meaning over time and across situations. Weight is one example: we would expect to weigh the same amount regardless of who weighs us, or where we take the measurement (assuming it's on Earth and not in an anti-gravity chamber). Sometimes variables can be directly measured (profit, weight, height) but in other cases we are forced to use indirect measures such as self-report, questionnaires and computerized tasks (to name but a few).

Let's go back to our Coke as a spermicide example. Imagine we took some Coke and some water and added them to two test tubes of sperm. After several minutes, we measured the motility (movement) of the sperm in the two samples and discovered no difference. A few years passed and another scientist, Dr Jack Q. Late, replicated the study but found that sperm motility was worse in the Coke sample. There are two measurement-related issues that could explain his success and our failure: (1) Dr Late might have used more Coke in the test tubes (sperm might need a critical mass of Coke before they are affected); (2) Dr Late measured the outcome (motility) differently than us.

The former point explains why chemists and physicists have devoted many hours to developing standard units of measurement. If you had reported that you'd used 100 ml of Coke and 5 ml of sperm, then Dr Late could have ensured that he had used the same amount – because millilitres are a standard unit of measurement we would know that Dr Late used exactly the same amount of Coke that we used. Direct measurements such as the millilitre provide an objective standard: 100 ml of a liquid is known to be twice as much as only 50 ml.

The second reason for the difference in results between the studies could have been to do with how sperm motility was measured. Perhaps in our original study we measured motility using absorption spectrophotometry, whereas Dr Late used laser light-scattering techniques.[10] Perhaps his measure is more sensitive than ours.

There will often be a discrepancy between the numbers we use to represent the thing we're measuring and the actual value of the thing we're measuring (i.e., the value we would get if we could measure it directly). This discrepancy is known as **measurement error**. For example, imagine that you know as an absolute truth that you weigh 80 kg. One day you step on the bathroom scales and it says 83 kg. There is a difference of 3 kg between your actual weight and the weight given by your measurement tool (the scales): there is a measurement error of 3 kg. Although properly calibrated bathroom scales should produce only very small measurement errors (despite what we might want to believe when it says we have gained 3 kg), self-report measures do produce measurement error because factors other than the one you're trying to measure will influence how people respond to our measures. Imagine you were completing a questionnaire that asked you whether you had stolen from a shop. If you had, would you admit it, or might you be tempted to conceal this fact?

1.5.3.   Validity and reliability ①

One way to try to ensure that measurement error is kept to a minimum is to determine properties of the measure that give us confidence that it is doing its job properly. The first property is **validity**, which is whether an instrument actually measures what it sets out to measure. The second is **reliability**, which is whether an instrument can be interpreted consistently across different situations.

Validity refers to whether an instrument measures what it was designed to measure; a device for measuring sperm motility that actually measures sperm count is not valid. Things like reaction times and physiological measures are valid in the sense that a reaction time does in fact measure the time taken to react and skin conductance does measure the conductivity of your skin. However, if we're using these things to infer other things (e.g., using skin conductance to measure anxiety) then they will be valid only if there are no other factors other than the one we're interested in that can influence them.

Criterion validity is whether the instrument is measuring what it claims to measure (does your lecturer helpfulness rating scale actually measure lecturers' helpfulness?). In an ideal world, you could assess this by relating scores on your measure to real-world observations. For example, we could take an objective measure of how helpful lecturers were and compare these observations to students' ratings on ratemyprofessor.com. This is often impractical and, of course, with attitudes you might not be interested in the reality so much as the person's perception of reality (you might not care whether they are a psychopath but whether they think they are a psychopath). With self-report measures/questionnaires we can also assess the degree to which individual items represent the construct being measured, and cover the full range of the construct (**content validity**).

Validity is a necessary but not sufficient condition of a measure. A second consideration is reliability, which is the ability of the measure to produce the same results under the same conditions. To be valid the instrument must first be reliable. The easiest way to assess reliability is to test the same group of people twice: a reliable instrument will produce similar scores at both points in time (**test–retest reliability**). Sometimes, however, you will want to measure something that does vary over time (e.g., moods, blood-sugar levels, productivity). Statistical methods can also be used to determine reliability (we will discover these in Chapter 17).

---

[10] In the course of writing this chapter I have discovered more than I think is healthy about the measurement of sperm motility.

1.6. Data collection 2: how to measure ①

1.6.1.　Correlational research methods ①

So far we've learnt that scientists want to answer questions, and that to do this they have to generate data (be they numbers or words), and to generate good data they need to use accurate measures. We move on now to look briefly at how the data are collected. If we simplify things quite a lot then there are two ways to test a hypothesis: either by observing what naturally happens, or by manipulating some aspect of the environment and observing the effect it has on the variable that interests us.

The main distinction between what we could call **correlational** or **cross-sectional research** (where we observe what naturally goes on in the world without directly interfering with it) and **experimental research** (where we manipulate one variable to see its effect on another) is that experimentation involves the direct manipulation of variables. In correlational research we do things like observe natural events or we take a snapshot of many variables at a single point in time. As some examples, we might measure pollution levels in a stream and the numbers of certain types of fish living there; lifestyle variables (smoking, exercise, food intake) and disease (cancer, diabetes); workers' job satisfaction under different managers; or children's school performance across regions with different demographics. Correlational research provides a very natural view of the question we're researching because we are not influencing what happens and the measures of the variables should not be biased by the researcher being there (this is an important aspect of **ecological validity**).

At the risk of sounding like I'm absolutely obsessed with using Coke as a contraceptive (I'm not, but my discovery that people in the 1950s and 1960s actually tried this has, I admit, intrigued me), let's return to that example. If we wanted to answer the question 'Is Coke an effective contraceptive?' we could administer questionnaires about sexual practices (quantity of sexual activity, use of contraceptives, use of fizzy drinks as contraceptives, pregnancy, etc.). By looking at these variables we could see which variables predict pregnancy, and in particular whether those reliant on Coca-Cola as a form of contraceptive were more likely to end up pregnant than those using other contraceptives, and less likely than those using no contraceptives at all. This is the only way to answer a question like this because we cannot manipulate any of these variables particularly easily. Even if we could, it would be totally unethical to insist on some people using Coke as a contraceptive (or indeed to do anything that would make a person likely to produce a child that they didn't intend to produce). However, there is a price to pay, which relates to causality.

1.6.2.　Experimental research methods ①

Most scientific questions imply a causal link between variables; we have seen already that dependent and independent variables are named such that a causal connection is implied (the dependent variable *depends* on the independent variable). Sometimes the causal link is very obvious, as in the research question 'Does low self-esteem cause dating anxiety?'. Sometimes the implication might be subtler – for example, in the question 'Is dating anxiety all in the mind?' the implication is that a person's mental outlook causes them to be anxious when dating. Even when the cause–effect relationship is not explicitly stated, most research questions can be broken down into a proposed cause (in this case mental outlook) and a proposed outcome (dating anxiety). Both the cause and the outcome are variables: for the cause some people will perceive themselves in a negative way (so it is something that varies); and for the outcome, some people will get anxious on dates and others won't (again, this is something that varies). The key to answering the research question is to uncover how the proposed cause and j14the proposed outcome relate to each other; is it the case that the people who have a low opinion of themselves are the same people that get anxious on dates?

What's the difference between experimental and correlational research?

David Hume (see Hume, 1739–40, 1748, for more detail),[11] an influential philosopher, said that to infer cause and effect: (1) cause and effect must occur close together in time (contiguity); (2) the cause must occur before an effect does; and (3) the effect should never occur without the presence of the cause. These conditions imply that causality can be inferred through corroborating evidence: cause is equated to high degrees of correlation between contiguous events. In our dating example, to infer that low self-esteem caused dating anxiety, it would be sufficient to find that whenever someone had low self-esteem they would feel anxious when on a date, that the low self-esteem emerged before the dating anxiety did, and that the person should never have dating anxiety if they haven't been suffering from low self-esteem.

In the previous section on correlational research, we saw that variables are often measured simultaneously. The first problem with doing this is that it provides no information about the contiguity between different variables: we might find from a questionnaire study that people with low self-esteem also have dating anxiety but we wouldn't know whether the low self-esteem or the dating anxiety came first!

Let's imagine that we find that there are people who have low self-esteem but do not get dating anxiety. This finding doesn't violate Hume's rules: he doesn't say anything about the cause happening without the effect. It could be that both low self-esteem and dating anxiety are caused by a third variable (e.g., poor social skills which might make you feel generally worthless but also put pressure on you in dating situations). This illustrates a second problem with correlational evidence: the **tertium quid** ('a third person or thing of indeterminate character'). For example, a correlation has been found between having breast implants and suicide (Koot, Peeters, Granath, Grobbee, & Nyren, 2003). However, it is unlikely that having breast implants causes you to commit suicide – presumably, there is an external factor (or factors) that causes both; for example, low self-esteem might lead you to have breast implants and also attempt suicide. These extraneous factors are sometimes called **confounding variables** or confounds for short.

The shortcomings of Hume's criteria led John Stuart Mill (1865) to add a further criterion: that all other explanations of the cause–effect relationship be ruled out. Put simply, Mill proposed that, to rule out confounding variables, an effect should be present when the cause is present and that when the cause is absent the effect should be absent also. Mill's ideas can be summed up by saying that the only way to infer causality is through comparison of two controlled situations: one in which the cause is present and one in which the cause is absent. This is what *experimental methods* strive to do: to provide a comparison of situations (usually called *treatments* or *conditions*) in which the proposed cause is present or absent.

[11] Both of these can be read online at http://www.utilitarian.net/hume/ or by doing a Google search for David Hume.

As a simple case, we might want to see what effect motivators have on learning about statistics. I might, therefore, randomly split some students into three different groups in which I change my style of teaching in the seminars on the course:

- **Group 1 (positive reinforcement)**: During seminars I congratulate all students in this group on their hard work and success. Even when they get things wrong, I am supportive and say things like 'that was very nearly the right answer, you're coming along really well' and then give them a nice piece of chocolate.

- **Group 2 (punishment)**: This group receives seminars in which I give relentless verbal abuse to all of the students even when they give the correct answer. I demean their contributions and am patronizing and dismissive of everything they say. I tell students that they are stupid, worthless and shouldn't be doing the course at all.

- **Group 3 (no motivator)**: This group receives normal university style seminars (some might argue that this is the same as group 2!). Students are not praised or punished and instead I give them no feedback at all.

The thing that I have manipulated is the teaching method (positive reinforcement, punishment or no motivator). As we have seen earlier in this chapter, this variable is known as the independent variable and in this situation it is said to have three levels, because it has been manipulated in three ways (i.e., motivator has been split into three types: positive reinforcement, punishment and none). Once I have carried out this manipulation I must have some kind of outcome that I am interested in measuring. In this case it is statistical ability, and I could measure this variable using a statistics exam after the last seminar. We have also already discovered that this outcome variable is known as the dependent variable because we assume that these scores will depend upon the type of teaching method used (the independent variable). The critical thing here is the inclusion of the no-motivator group because this is a group in which our proposed cause (motivator) is absent, and we can compare the outcome in this group against the two situations where the proposed cause is present. If the statistics scores are different in each of the motivation groups (cause is present) compared to the group for which no motivator was given (cause is absent) then this difference can be attributed to the type of motivator used. In other words, the motivator used caused a difference in statistics scores (Jane Superbrain Box 1.4).

JANE SUPERBRAIN 1.4

Causality and statistics ①

People sometimes get confused and think that certain statistical procedures allow causal inferences and others don't. This isn't true, it's the fact that in experiments we manipulate the causal variable systematically to see its effect on an outcome (the effect). In correlational research we observe the co-occurrence of variables; we do not manipulate the causal variable first and then measure the effect, therefore we cannot compare the effect when the causal variable is present against when it is absent. In short, we cannot say which variable causes a change in the other; we can merely say that the variables co-occur in a certain way. The reason why some people think that certain statistical tests allow causal inferences is because historically certain tests (e.g., ANOVA, *t*-tests) have been used to analyse experimental research, whereas others (e.g., regression, correlation) have been used to analyse correlational research (Cronbach, 1957). As you'll discover, these statistical procedures are, in fact, mathematically identical.

1.6.2.1. Two methods of data collection ①

When we collect data in an experiment, we can choose between two methods of data collection. The first is to manipulate the independent variable using different participants. This method is the one described above, in which different groups of people take part in each experimental condition (a **between-groups**, **between-subjects**, or **independent design**). The second method is to manipulate the independent variable using the same participants. Simplistically, this method means that we give a group of students positive reinforcement for a few weeks and test their statistical abilities and then begin to give this same group punishment for a few weeks before testing them again, and then finally giving them no motivator and testing them for a third time (a **within-subject** or **repeated-measures design**). As you will discover, the way in which the data are collected determines the type of test that is used to analyse the data.

1.6.2.2. Two types of variation ①

Imagine we were trying to see whether you could train chimpanzees to run the economy. In one training phase they are sat in front of a chimp-friendly computer and press buttons which change various parameters of the economy; once these parameters have been changed a figure appears on the screen indicating the economic growth resulting from those parameters. Now, chimps can't read (I don't think) so this feedback is meaningless. A second training phase is the same except that if the economic growth is good, they get a banana (if growth is bad they do not) – this feedback is valuable to the average chimp. This is a repeated-measures design with two conditions: the same chimps participate in condition 1 *and* in condition 2.

Let's take a step back and think what would happen if we did *not* introduce an experimental manipulation (i.e., there were no bananas in the second training phase so condition 1 and condition 2 were identical). If there is no experimental manipulation then we expect a chimp's behaviour to be similar in both conditions. We expect this because external factors such as age, gender, IQ, motivation and arousal will be the same for both conditions (a chimp's gender etc. will not change from when they are tested in condition 1 to when they are tested in condition 2). If the performance measure is reliable (i.e., our test of how well they run the economy), and the variable or characteristic that we are measuring (in this case ability to run an economy) remains stable over time, then a participant's performance in condition 1 should be very highly related to their performance in condition 2. So, chimps who score highly in condition 1 will also score highly in condition 2, and those who have low scores for condition 1 will have low scores in condition 2. However, performance won't be *identical*, there will be small differences in performance created by unknown factors. This variation in performance is known as **unsystematic variation**.

If we introduce an experimental manipulation (i.e., provide bananas as feedback in one of the training sessions), then we do something different to participants in condition 1 than what we do to them in condition 2. So, the *only* difference between conditions 1 and 2 is the manipulation that the experimenter has made (in this case that the chimps get bananas as a positive reward in one condition but not in the other). Therefore, any differences between the means of the two conditions is probably due to the experimental manipulation. So, if the chimps perform better in one training phase than the other then this *has* to be due to the fact that bananas were used to provide feedback in one training phase but not the other. Differences in performance created by a specific experimental manipulation are known as **systematic variation.**

Now let's think about what happens when we use different participants – an independent design. In this design we still have two conditions, but this time different participants participate in each condition. Going back to our example, one group of chimps receives training without feedback, whereas a second group of different chimps does receive feedback on their performance via bananas.[12] Imagine again that we didn't have an experimental manipulation. If we did nothing to the groups, then we would still find some variation in behaviour between the groups because they contain different chimps who will vary in their ability, motivation, IQ and other factors. In short, the type of factors that were held constant in the repeated-measures design are free to vary in the independent-measures design. So, the unsystematic variation will be bigger than for a repeated-measures design. As before, if we introduce a manipulation (i.e., bananas) then we will see additional variation created by this manipulation. As such, in both the repeated-measures design and the independent-measures design there are always two sources of variation:

- **Systematic variation**: This variation is due to the experimenter doing something to all of the participants in one condition but not in the other condition.

- **Unsystematic variation**: This variation results from random factors that exist between the experimental conditions (natural differences in ability, the time of day, etc.).

The role of statistics is to discover how much variation there is in performance, and then to work out how much of this is systematic and how much is unsystematic.

In a repeated-measures design, differences between two conditions can be caused by only two things: (1) the manipulation that was carried out on the participants, or (2) any other factor that might affect the way in which a participant performs from one time to the next. The latter factor is likely to be fairly minor compared to the influence of the experimental manipulation. In an independent design, differences between the two conditions can also be caused by one of two things: (1) the manipulation that was carried out on the participants, or (2) differences between the characteristics of the participants allocated to each of the groups. The latter factor in this instance is likely to create considerable random variation both within each condition and between them. Therefore, the effect of our experimental manipulation is likely to be more apparent in a repeated-measures design than in a between-group design because in the former unsystematic variation can be caused only by differences in the way in which someone behaves at different times. In independent designs we have differences in innate ability contributing to the unsystematic variation. Therefore, this error variation will almost always be much larger than if the same participants had been used. When we look at the effect of our experimental manipulation, it is always against a background of 'noise' caused by random, uncontrollable differences between our conditions. In a repeated-measures design this 'noise' is kept to a minimum and so the effect of the experiment is more likely to show up. This means that, other things being equal, repeated-measures designs have more power to detect effects than independent designs.

1.6.3. Randomization ①

In both repeated-measures and independent-measures designs it is important to try to keep the unsystematic variation to a minimum. By keeping the unsystematic variation as small as possible we get a more sensitive measure of the experimental manipulation. Generally, scientists use the **randomization** of participants to treatment conditions to achieve this goal.

[12] When I say 'via' I don't mean that the bananas developed little banana mouths that opened up and said 'well done old chap, the economy grew that time' in chimp language. I mean that when they got something right they received a banana as a reward for their correct response.

Many statistical tests work by identifying the systematic and unsystematic sources of variation and then comparing them. This comparison allows us to see whether the experiment has generated considerably more variation than we would have got had we just tested participants without the experimental manipulation. Randomization is important because it eliminates most other sources of systematic variation, which allows us to be sure that any systematic variation between experimental conditions is due to the manipulation of the independent variable. We can use randomization in two different ways depending on whether we have an independent- or repeated-measures design.

Let's look at a repeated-measures design first. When the same people participate in more than one experimental condition they are naive during the first experimental condition but they come to the second experimental condition with prior experience of what is expected of them. At the very least they will be familiar with the dependent measure (e.g., the task they're performing). The two most important sources of systematic variation in this type of design are:

- **Practice effects**: Participants may perform differently in the second condition because of familiarity with the experimental situation and/or the measures being used.

- **Boredom effects**: Participants may perform differently in the second condition because they are tired or bored from having completed the first condition.

Although these effects are impossible to eliminate completely, we can ensure that they produce no systematic variation between our conditions by **counterbalancing** the order in which a person participates in a condition.

We can use randomization to determine in which order the conditions are completed. That is, we randomly determine whether a participant completes condition 1 before condition 2, or condition 2 before condition 1. Let's look at the teaching method example and imagine that there were just two conditions: no motivator and punishment. If the same participants were used in all conditions, then we might find that statistical ability was higher after the punishment condition. However, if every student experienced the punishment after the no-motivator seminars then they would enter the punishment condition already having a better knowledge of statistics than when they began the no-motivator condition. So, the apparent improvement after punishment would not be due to the experimental manipulation (i.e., it's not because punishment works), but because participants had attended more statistics seminars by the end of the punishment condition compared to the no-motivator one. We can use randomization to ensure that the number of statistics seminars does not introduce a systematic bias by randomly assigning students to have the punishment seminars first or the no-motivator seminars first.

If we turn our attention to independent designs, a similar argument can be applied. We know that different participants participate in different experimental conditions and that these participants will differ in many respects (their IQ, attention span, etc.). Although we know that these confounding variables contribute to the variation between conditions, we need to make sure that these variables contribute to the unsystematic variation and *not* the systematic variation. The way to ensure that confounding variables are unlikely to contribute systematically to the variation between experimental conditions is to randomly allocate participants to a particular experimental condition. This should ensure that these confounding variables are evenly distributed across conditions.

A good example is the effects of alcohol on personality. You might give one group of people 5 pints of beer, and keep a second group sober, and then count how many fights each person gets into. The effect that alcohol has on people can be very variable because of different tolerance levels: teetotal people can become very drunk on a small amount, while alcoholics need to consume vast quantities before the alcohol affects them. Now, if you allocated a bunch of teetotal participants to the condition that consumed alcohol, then you might find no difference between them and the sober group (because the teetotal participants are all unconscious after the first glass and so can't become involved in any fights). As such, the person's prior experiences with alcohol will create systematic variation that cannot be dissociated from the effect of the experimental manipulation. The best way to reduce this eventuality is to randomly allocate participants to conditions.

SELF-TEST

✓ Why is randomization important?

1.7. Analysing data ①

The final stage of the research process is to analyse the data you have collected. When the data are quantitative this involves both looking at your data graphically to see what the general trends in the data are, and also fitting statistical models to the data.

1.7.1. Frequency distributions ①

Once you've collected some data a very useful thing to do is to plot a graph of how many times each score occurs. This is known as a **frequency distribution**, or **histogram**, which is a graph plotting values of observations on the horizontal axis, with a bar showing how many times each value occurred in the data set. Frequency distributions can be very useful for assessing properties of the distribution of scores. We will find out how to create these types of charts in Chapter 4.

Frequency distributions come in many different shapes and sizes. It is quite important, therefore, to have some general descriptions for common types of distributions. In an ideal world our data would be distributed symmetrically around the centre of all scores. As such, if we drew a vertical line through the centre of the distribution then it should look the same on both sides. This is known as a **normal distribution** and is characterized by the bell-shaped curve with which you might already be familiar. This shape basically implies that the majority of scores lie around the centre of the distribution (so the largest bars on the histogram are all around the central value). Also, as we get further away from the centre the bars get smaller, implying that as scores start to deviate from the centre their frequency is decreasing. As we move still further away from the centre our scores become very infrequent (the bars are very short). Many naturally occurring things have this shape of distribution. For example, most men in the UK are about 175 cm tall,[13] some are a bit taller or shorter but most cluster around this value. There will be very few men who are really tall (i.e., above 205 cm) or really short (i.e., under 145 cm). An example of a normal distribution is shown in Figure 1.3.

What is a frequency distribution and when is it normal?

---

[13] I am exactly 180 cm tall. In my home country this makes me smugly above average. However, I'm writing this in the Netherlands where the average male height is 185 cm (a massive 10 cm higher than the UK), and where I feel like a bit of a dwarf.

FIGURE 1.3
A 'normal'
distribution (the
curve shows the
idealized shape)

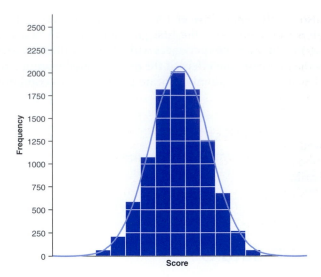

There are two main ways in which a distribution can deviate from normal: (1) lack of symmetry (called **skew**) and (2) pointyness (called **kurtosis**). Skewed distributions are not symmetrical and instead the most frequent scores (the tall bars on the graph) are clustered at one end of the scale. So, the typical pattern is a cluster of frequent scores at one end of the scale and the frequency of scores tailing off towards the other end of the scale. A skewed distribution can be either **positively skewed** (the frequent scores are clustered at the lower end and the tail points towards the higher or more positive scores) or **negatively skewed** (the frequent scores are clustered at the higher end and the tail points towards the lower or more negative scores). Figure 1.4 shows examples of these distributions.

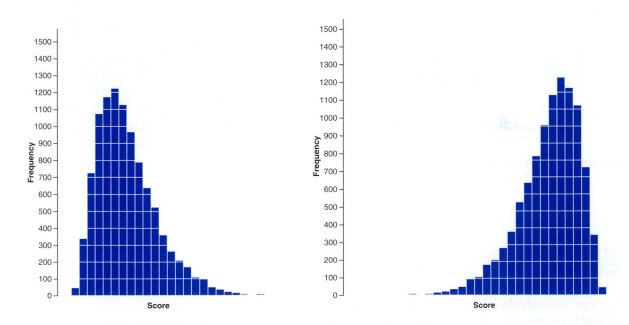

FIGURE 1.4   A positively (left-hand figure) and negatively (right-hand figure) skewed distribution

Distributions also vary in their *kurtosis*. Kurtosis, despite sounding like some kind of exotic disease, refers to the degree to which scores cluster at the ends of the distribution (known as the *tails*) and how pointy a distribution is (but there are other factors that can affect how pointy the distribution looks – see Jane Superbrain Box 2.3). A distribution with *positive kurtosis* has many scores in the tails (a so-called heavy-tailed distribution) and is pointy. This is known as a **leptokurtic** distribution. In contrast, a distribution with *negative kurtosis*is is relatively thin in the tails (has light tails) and tends to be flatter than normal. This distribution is called **platykurtic**. Ideally, we want our data to be normally distributed (i.e., not too skewed, and not too many or too few scores at the extremes!). For everything there is to know about kurtosis read DeCarlo (1997).

In a normal distribution the values of skew and kurtosis are 0 (i.e., the tails of the distribution are as they should be). If a distribution has values of skew or kurtosis above or below 0 then this indicates a deviation from normal: Figure 1.5 shows distributions with kurtosis values of +4 (left panel) and −1 (right panel).

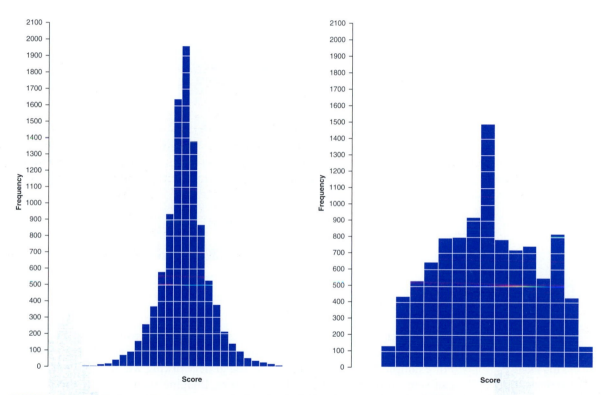

FIGURE 1.5   Distributions with positive kurtosis (leptokurtic, left) and negative kurtosis (platykurtic, right)

1.7.2. The centre of a distribution ①

We can also calculate where the centre of a frequency distribution lies (known as the **central tendency**). There are three measures commonly used: the mean, the mode and the median.

1.7.2.1. The mode ①

The **mode** is simply the score that occurs most frequently in the data set. This is easy to spot in a frequency distribution because it will be the tallest bar! To calculate the mode, simply place the data in ascending order (to make life easier), count how many times each score occurs, and the score that occurs the most is the mode! One problem with the mode is that it can often take on several values. For example, Figure 1.6 shows an example of a distribution with two modes (there are two bars that are the highest), which is said to be **bimodal**. It's also possible to find data sets with more than two modes (**multimodal**). Also, if the frequencies of certain scores are very similar, then the mode can be influenced by only a small number of cases.

FIGURE 1.6
A bimodal
distribution

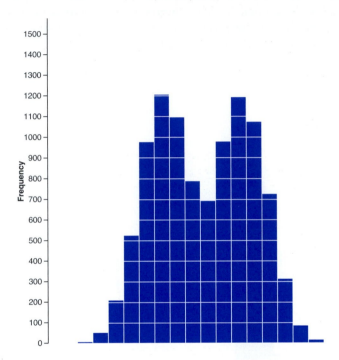

1.7.2.2. The median

What are the mode, median and mean?

Another way to quantify the centre of a distribution is to look for the middle score when scores are ranked in order of magnitude. This is called the **median**. For example, Facebook is a popular social networking website, in which users can sign up to be 'friends' of other users. Imagine we looked at the number of friends that a selection (actually, some of my friends) of 11 Facebook users had. Number of friends: 108, 103, 252, 121, 93, 57, 40, 53, 22, 116, 98.

To calculate the median, we first arrange these scores into ascending order: 22, 40, 53, 57, 93, 98, 103, 108, 116, 121, 252.

Next, we find the position of the middle score by counting the number of scores we have collected (n), adding 1 to this value, and then dividing by 2. With 11 scores, this gives us $(n + 1)/2 = (11 + 1)/2 = 12/2 = 6$. Then, we find the score that is positioned at the location we have just calculated. So, in this example we find the sixth score:

22, 40, 53, 57, 93, (98,) 103, 108, 116, 121, 252

Median

This works very nicely when we have an odd number of scores (as in this example) but when we have an even number of scores there won't be a middle value. Let's imagine that we decided that because the highest score was so big (more than twice as large as the next biggest number), we would ignore it. (For one thing, this person is far too popular and we hate them.) We have only 10 scores now. As before, we should rank-order these scores: 22, 40, 53, 57, 93, 98, 103, 108, 116, 121. We then calculate the position of the middle score, but this time it is $(n + 1)/2 = 11/2 = 5.5$. This means that the median is halfway between the fifth and sixth scores. To get the median we add these two scores and divide by 2. In this example, the fifth score in the ordered list was 93 and the sixth score was 98. We add these together ($93 + 98 = 191$) and then divide this value by 2 ($191/2 = 95.5$). The median number of friends was, therefore, 95.5.

The median is relatively unaffected by extreme scores at either end of the distribution: the median changed only from 98 to 95.5 when we removed the extreme score of 252. The median is also relatively unaffected by skewed distributions and can be used with ordinal, interval and ratio data (it cannot, however, be used with nominal data because these data have no numerical order).

1.7.2.3. The mean ①

The **mean** is the measure of central tendency that you are most likely to have heard of because it is simply the average score and the media are full of average scores.[14] To calculate the mean we simply add up all of the scores and then divide by the total number of scores we have. We can write this in equation form as:

$$\overline{X} = \frac{\sum_{i=1}^{n} x_i}{n} \tag{1.1}$$

This may look complicated, but the top half of the equation simply means 'add up all of the scores' (the x_i just means 'the score of a particular person'; we could replace the letter i with each person's name instead), and the bottom bit means divide this total by the number of scores you have got (n). Let's calculate the mean for the Facebook data. First, we add up all of the scores:

$$\sum_{i=1}^{n} x_i = 22 + 40 + 53 + 57 + 93 + 98 + 103 + 108 + 116 + 121 + 253$$
$$= 1063$$

We then divide by the number of scores (in this case 11):

$$\overline{X} = \frac{\sum_{i=1}^{n} x_i}{n} = \frac{1063}{11} = 96.64$$

The mean is 96.64 friends, which is not a value we observed in our actual data (it would be ridiculous to talk of having 0.64 of a friend). In this sense the mean is a statistical model – more on this in the next chapter.

---

[14] I'm writing this on 15 February 2008, and to prove my point the BBC website is running a headline about how PayPal estimates that Britons will spend an average of £71.25 each on Valentine's Day gifts, but uSwitch.com said that the average spend would be £22.69!

If you calculate the mean without our extremely popular person (i.e., excluding the value 252), the mean drops to 81.1 friends. One disadvantage of the mean is that it can be influenced by extreme scores. In this case, the person with 252 friends on Facebook increased the mean by about 15 friends! Compare this difference with that of the median. Remember that the median hardly changed if we included or excluded 252, which illustrates how the median is less affected by extreme scores than the mean. While we're being negative about the mean, it is also affected by skewed distributions and can be used only with interval or ratio data.

If the mean is so lousy then why do we use it all of the time? One very important reason is that it uses every score (the mode and median ignore most of the scores in a data set). Also, the mean tends to be stable in different samples.

1.7.3.   The dispersion in a distribution ①

It can also be interesting to try to quantify the spread, or dispersion, of scores in the data. The easiest way to look at dispersion is to take the largest score and subtract from it the smallest score. This is known as the **range** of scores. For our Facebook friends data, if we order these scores we get 22, 40, 53, 57, 93, 98, 103, 108, 116, 121, 252. The highest score is 252 and the lowest is 22; therefore, the range is $252 - 22 = 230$. One problem with the range is that because it uses only the highest and lowest score it is affected dramatically by extreme scores.

If you have done the self-test task you'll see that without the extreme score the range drops dramatically from 230 to 99 – less than half the size!

One way around this problem is to calculate the range when we exclude values at the extremes of the distribution. One convention is to cut off the top and bottom 25% of scores and calculate the range of the middle 50% of scores – known as the **interquartile range**. Let's do this with the Facebook data. First we need to calculate what are called **quartiles**. Quartiles are the three values that split the sorted data into four equal parts. First we calculate the median, which is also called the **second quartile**, which splits our data into two equal parts. We already know that the median for these data is 98. The **lower quartile** is the median of the lower half of the data and the **upper quartile** is the median of the upper half of the data. One rule of thumb is that the median is not included in the two halves when they are split (this is convenient if you have an odd number of values), but you can include it (although which half you put it in is another question). Figure 1.7 shows how we would calculate these values for the Facebook data. Like the median, the upper and lower quartile need not be values that actually appear in the data (like the median, if each half of the data had an even number of values in it then the upper and lower quartiles would be the average of two values in the data set). Once we have worked out the values of the quartiles, we can calculate the interquartile range, which is the difference between the upper and lower quartile. For the Facebook data this value would be $116 - 53 = 63$. The advantage of the interquartile range is that it isn't affected by extreme scores at either end of the distribution. However, the problem with it is that you lose a lot of data (half of it in fact !).

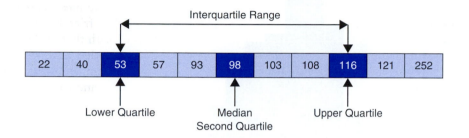

FIGURE 1.7
Calculating quartiles and the interquartile range

SELF-TEST

✓ Twenty-one heavy smokers were put on a treadmill at the fastest setting. The time in seconds was measured until they fell off from exhaustion: 18, 16, 18, 24, 23, 22, 22, 23, 26, 29, 32, 34, 34, 36, 36, 43, 42, 49, 46, 46, 57

Compute the mode, median, mean, upper and lower quartiles, range and interquartile range

1.7.4. Using a frequency distribution to go beyond the data ①

Another way to think about frequency distributions is not in terms of how often scores actually occurred, but how likely it is that a score would occur (i.e., probability). The word 'probability' induces suicidal ideation in most people (myself included) so it seems fitting that we use an example about throwing ourselves off a cliff. Beachy Head is a large, windy cliff on the Sussex coast (not far from where I live) that has something of a reputation for attracting suicidal people, who seem to like throwing themselves off it (and after several months of rewriting this book I find my thoughts drawn towards that peaceful chalky cliff top more and more often). Figure 1.8 shows a frequency distribution of some completely made-up data of the number of suicides at Beachy Head in a year by people of different ages (although I made these data up, they are roughly based on general suicide statistics such as those in Williams, 2001). There were 172 suicides in total and you can see that the suicides were most frequently aged between about 30 and 35 (the highest bar). The graph also tells us that, for example, very few people aged above 70 committed suicide at Beachy Head.

I said earlier that we could think of frequency distributions in terms of probability. To explain this, imagine that someone asked you 'How likely is it that a person who committed suicide at Beachy Head is 70 years old?' What would your answer be? The chances are that if you looked at the frequency distribution you might respond 'not very likely' because you can see that only 3 people out of the 172 suicides were aged around 70. What about

FIGURE 1.8
Frequency
distribution
showing the
number of
suicides at
Beachy Head in a
year by age

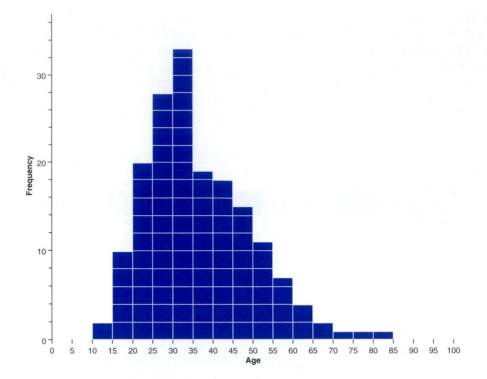

FIGURE 1.8
Frequency
distribution
showing the
number of
suicides at
Beachy Head in a
year by age

if someone asked you 'how likely is it that a 30-year-old committed suicide?' Again, by looking at the graph, you might say 'it's actually quite likely' because 33 out of the 172 suicides were by people aged around 30 (that's more than 1 in every 5 people who committed suicide). So based on the frequencies of different scores it should start to become clear that we could use this information to estimate the probability that a particular score will occur. We could ask, based on our data, 'what's the probability of a suicide victim being aged 16–20?' A probability value can range from 0 (there's no chance whatsoever of the event happening) to 1 (the event will definitely happen). So, for example, when I talk to my publishers I tell them there's a probability of 1 that I will have completed the revisions to this book by April 2011. However, when I talk to anyone else, I might, more realistically, tell them that there's a .10 probability of me finishing the revisions on time (or put another way, a 10% chance, or 1 in 10 chance that I'll complete the book in time). In reality, the probability of my meeting the deadline is 0 (not a chance in hell) because I never manage to meet publisher's deadlines! If probabilities don't make sense to you then just ignore the decimal point and think of them as percentages instead (i.e., .10 probability that something will happen = 10% chance that something will happen).

I've talked in vague terms about how frequency distributions can be used to get a rough idea of the probability of a score occurring. However, we can be precise. For any distribution of scores we could, in theory, calculate the probability of obtaining a score of a certain size – it would be incredibly tedious and complex to do it, but we could. To spare our sanity, statisticians have identified several common distributions. For each one they have worked out mathematical formulae that specify idealized versions of these distributions (they are specified in terms of a curved line). These idealized distributions are known as **probability distributions** and from these distributions it is possible to calculate the probability of getting particular scores based on the frequencies with which a particular score occurs in a distribution with these common shapes. One of these 'common' distributions is the normal distribution, which I've already mentioned in section 1.7.1. Statisticians have calculated the probability of certain scores occurring in a normal distribution with a mean of 0 and a standard deviation of 1. Therefore, if we have any data that are shaped like a normal distribution, then if the mean and standard deviation are 0 and 1 respectively we can use the tables of probabilities for the normal distribution to see how likely it is that a particular score will occur in the data (I've produced such a table in the Appendix to this book).

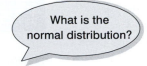

The obvious problem is that not all of the data we collect will have a mean of 0 and standard deviation of 1. For example, we might have a data set that has a mean of 567 and a standard deviation of 52.98. Luckily any data set can be converted into a data set that has a mean of 0 and a standard deviation of 1. First, to centre the data around zero, we take each score (X) and subtract from it the mean of all scores ($\bar{X}$). Then, we divide the resulting score by the standard deviation (s) to ensure the data have a standard deviation of 1. The resulting scores are known as **z-scores** and, in equation form, the conversion that I've just described is:

$$z = \frac{X - \bar{X}}{s} \qquad\qquad (1.2)$$

The table of probability values that have been calculated for the standard normal distribution is shown in the Appendix. Why is this table important? Well, if we look at our suicide data, we can answer the question 'What's the probability that someone who threw themselves off Beachy Head was 70 or older?' First we convert 70 into a z-score. Suppose the mean of the suicide scores was 36, and the standard deviation 13; then 70 will become $(70 - 36)/13 = 2.62$. We then look up this value in the column labelled 'Smaller Portion' (i.e., the area above the value 2.62). You should find that the probability is .0044, or, put another way, only a 0.44% chance that a suicide victim would be 70 years old or more. By looking at the column labelled 'Bigger Portion' we can also see the probability that a suicide victim was aged 70 or less. This probability is .9956, or, put another way, there's a 99.56% chance that a suicide victim was less than 70 years old.

Hopefully you can see from these examples that the normal distribution and z-scores allow us to go a first step beyond our data in that from a set of scores we can calculate the probability that a particular score will occur. So, we can see whether scores of a certain size are likely or unlikely to occur in a distribution of a particular kind. You'll see just how useful this is in due course, but it is worth mentioning at this stage that certain z-scores are particularly important. This is because their value cuts off certain important percentages of the distribution. The first important value of z is 1.96 because this cuts off the top 2.5% of the distribution, and its counterpart at the opposite end (−1.96) cuts off the bottom 2.5% of the distribution. As such, taken together, this value cuts off 5% of scores, or, put another way, 95% of z-scores lie between −1.96 and 1.96. The other two important benchmarks are ±2.58 and ±3.29, which cut off 1% and 0.1% of scores respectively. Put another way, 99% of z-scores lie between −2.58 and 2.58, and 99.9% of them lie between −3.29 and 3.29. Remember these values because they'll crop up time and time again.

SELF-TEST

✓ Assuming the same mean and standard deviation for the Beachy Head example above, what's the probability that someone who threw themselves off Beachy Head was 30 or younger?

1.7.5. Fitting statistical models to the data ①

Having looked at your data (and there is a lot more information on different ways to do this in Chapter 4), the next step is to fit a statistical model to the data. I should really just write 'insert the rest of the book here', because most of the remaining chapters discuss the various models that you can fit to the data. However, I do want to talk here briefly about two very important types of hypotheses that are used when analysing the data. Scientific statements, as we have seen, can be split into testable hypotheses. The hypothesis or prediction that comes from your theory is usually saying that an effect will be present. This hypothesis is called the **alternative hypothesis** and is denoted by H_1. (It is sometimes also called the **experimental hypothesis** but because this term relates to a specific type of methodology it's probably best to use 'alternative hypothesis'.) There is another type of hypothesis, though, and this is called the **null hypothesis** and is denoted by H_0. This hypothesis is the opposite of the alternative hypothesis and so would usually state that an effect is absent. Taking our *Big Brother* example from earlier in the chapter we might generate the following hypotheses:

- Alternative hypothesis: *Big Brother* contestants will score higher on personality disorder questionnaires than members of the public.

- Null hypothesis: *Big Brother* contestants and members of the public will not differ in their scores on personality disorder questionnaires.

The reason that we need the null hypothesis is because we cannot prove the experimental hypothesis using statistics, but we can reject the null hypothesis. If our data give us confidence to reject the null hypothesis then this provides support for our experimental hypothesis. However, be aware that even if we can reject the null hypothesis, this doesn't prove the experimental hypothesis – it merely supports it. So, rather than talking about accepting or rejecting a hypothesis (which some textbooks tell you to do) we should be talking about 'the chances of obtaining the data we've collected assuming that the null hypothesis is true'.

Using our *Big Brother* example, when we collected data from the auditions about the contestant's personalities we found that 75% of them had a disorder. When we analyse our data, we are really asking, 'Assuming that contestants are no more likely to have personality disorders than members of the public, is it likely that 75% or more of the contestants would have personality disorders?' Intuitively the answer is that the chances are very low: if the null hypothesis is true, then most contestants would not have personality disorders because they are relatively rare. Therefore, we are very unlikely to have got the data that we did if the null hypothesis were true.

What if we found that only 1 contestant reported having a personality disorder (about 8%)? If the null hypothesis is true, and contestants are no different in personality than the general population, then only a small number of contestants would be expected to have a personality disorder. The chances of getting these data if the null hypothesis is true are, therefore, higher than before.

When we collect data to test theories we have to work in these terms: we cannot talk about the null hypothesis being true or the experimental hypothesis being true, we can only talk in terms of the probability of obtaining a particular set of data if, hypothetically speaking, the null hypothesis was true. We will elaborate on this idea in the next chapter.

Finally, hypotheses can also be directional or non-directional. A directional hypothesis states that an effect will occur, but it also states the direction of the effect. For example, 'readers will know more about research methods after reading this chapter' is a one-tailed hypothesis because it states the direction of the effect (readers will know more). A non-directional hypothesis states that an effect will occur, but it doesn't state the direction of the effect. For example, 'readers' knowledge of research methods will change after they have read this chapter' does not tell us whether their knowledge will improve or get worse.

What have I discovered about statistics? ①

Actually, not a lot because we haven't really got to the statistics bit yet. However, we have discovered some stuff about the process of doing research. We began by looking at how research questions are formulated through observing phenomena or collecting data about a 'hunch'. Once the observation has been confirmed, theories can be generated about why something happens. From these theories we formulate hypotheses that we can test. To test hypotheses we need to measure things and this leads us to think about the variables that we need to measure and how to measure them. Then we can collect some data. The final stage is to analyse these data. In this chapter we saw that we can begin by just looking at the shape of the data but that ultimately we should end up fitting some kind of statistical model to the data (more on that in the rest of the book). In short, the reason that your evil statistics lecturer is forcing you to learn statistics is because it is an intrinsic part of the research process and it gives you enormous power to answer questions that are interesting; or it could be that they are a sadist who spends their spare time spanking politicians while wearing knee-high PVC boots, a diamond-encrusted leather thong and a gimp mask (that'll be a nice mental image to keep with you throughout your course). We also discovered that I was a curious child (you can interpret that either way). As I got older I became more curious, but you will have to read on to discover what I was curious about.

Key terms that I've discovered

Alternative hypothesis	Experimental hypothesis
Between-group design	Experimental research
Between-subject design	Falsification
Bimodal	Frequency distribution
Binary variable	Histogram
Boredom effect	Hypothesis
Categorical variable	Independent design
Central tendency	Independent variable
Confounding variable	Interquartile range
Content validity	Interval variable
Continuous variable	Kurtosis
Correlational research	Leptokurtic
Counterbalancing	Level of measurement
Criterion validity	Lower quartile
Cross-sectional research	Mean
Dependent variable	Measurement error
Discrete variable	Median
Ecological validity	Mode

Multimodal	Range
Negative skew	Ratio variable
Nominal variable	Reliability
Normal distribution	Repeated-measures design
Null hypothesis	Second quartile
Ordinal variable	Skew
Outcome variable	Systematic variation
Platykurtic	*Tertium quid*
Positive skew	Test–retest reliability
Practice effect	Theory
Predictor variable	Unsystematic variation
Probability distribution	Upper quartile
Qualitative methods	Validity
Quantitative methods	Variables
Quartile	Within-subject design
Randomization	z-scores

Smart Alex's tasks

Smart Alex knows everything there is to know about statistics and **R**. He also likes nothing more than to ask people stats questions just so that he can be smug about how much he knows. So, why not really annoy him and get all of the answers right!

- **Task 1**: What are (broadly speaking) the five stages of the research process? ①

- **Task 2**: What is the fundamental difference between experimental and correlational research? ①

- **Task 3**: What is the level of measurement of the following variables? ①

  a. The number of downloads of different bands' songs on iTunes.
  b. The names of the bands that were downloaded.
  c. The position in the iTunes download chart.
  d. The money earned by the bands from the downloads.
  e. The weight of drugs bought by the bands with their royalties.
  f. The type of drugs bought by the bands with their royalties.
  g. The phone numbers that the bands obtained because of their fame.
  h. The gender of the people giving the bands their phone numbers.
  i. The instruments played by the band members.
  j. The time they had spent learning to play their instruments.

- **Task 4**: Say I own 857 CDs. My friend has written a computer program that uses a webcam to scan the shelves in my house where I keep my CDs and measure how many I have. His program says that I have 863 CDs. Define measurement error. What is the measurement error in my friend's CD-counting device? ①

- **Task 5**: Sketch the shape of a normal distribution, a positively skewed distribution and a negatively skewed distribution. ①

Answers can be found on the companion website.

Further reading

Field, A. P., & Hole, G. J. (2003). *How to design and report experiments*. London: Sage. (I am rather biased, but I think this is a good overview of basic statistical theory and research methods.)

Miles, J. N. V., & Banyard, P. (2007). *Understanding and using statistics in psychology: a practical introduction*. London: Sage. (A fantastic and amusing introduction to statistical theory.)

Wright, D. B., & London, K. (2009). *First steps in statistics* (2nd ed.). London: Sage. (This book is a very gentle introduction to statistical theory.)

Interesting real research

Umpierre, S. A., Hill, J. A., & Anderson, D. J. (1985). Effect of Coke on sperm motility. *New England Journal of Medicine*, *313*(21), 1351.

2

Everything you ever wanted to know about statistics (well, sort of)

2.1. What will this chapter tell me? ①

As a child grows, it becomes important for them to fit models to the world: to be able to reliably predict what will happen in certain situations. This need to build models that accurately reflect reality is an essential part of survival. According to my parents (conveniently I have no memory of this at all), while at nursery school one model of the world that I was particularly enthusiastic to try out was 'If I get my penis out, it will be really funny'. No doubt to my considerable disappointment, this model turned out to be a poor predictor of positive outcomes. Thankfully for all concerned, I soon learnt that the model 'If I get my penis out at nursery school the teachers and mummy and daddy are going to be quite annoyed' was a better 'fit' of the observed data. Fitting models that accurately reflect the observed data is important to establish whether a theory is true. You'll be delighted to know that this chapter is all about fitting statistical models (and not about my penis). We edge sneakily away from the frying pan of research methods and trip accidentally into the fires of statistics hell. We begin by discovering what a statistical model is by using the mean as a straightforward example. We then see how we can use the properties of data to go beyond the data we have collected and to draw inferences about the world at large. In a nutshell, then, this chapter lays the foundation for the whole of the rest of the book, so it's quite important that you read it or nothing that comes later will make any sense. Actually, a lot of what comes later probably won't make much sense anyway because *I've* written it, but there you go.

2.2. Building statistical models ①

We saw in the previous chapter that scientists are interested in discovering something about a phenomenon that we assume actually exists (a 'real-world' phenomenon). These real-world phenomena can be anything from the behaviour of interest rates in the economic market to the behaviour of undergraduates at the end-of-exam party. Whatever the phenomenon we desire to explain, we collect data from the real world to test our hypotheses about the phenomenon. Testing these hypotheses involves building statistical models of the phenomenon of interest.

The reason for building statistical models of real-world data is best explained by an analogy. Imagine an engineer wishes to build a bridge across a river. That engineer would be pretty daft if she just built any old bridge, because the chances are that it would fall down. Instead, an engineer collects data from the real world: she looks at bridges in the real world and sees what materials they are made from, what structures they use and so on (she might even collect data about whether these bridges are damaged!). She then uses this information to construct a model. She builds a scaled-down version of the real-world bridge because it is impractical, not to mention expensive, to build the actual bridge itself. The model may differ from reality in several ways – it will be smaller for a start – but the engineer will try to build a model that best fits the situation of interest based on the data available. Once the model has been built, it can be used to predict things about the real world: for example, the engineer might test whether the bridge can withstand strong winds by placing the model in a wind tunnel. It seems obvious that it is important that the model is an accurate representation of the real world. Social scientists do much the same thing as engineers: they build models of real-world processes in an attempt to predict how these processes operate under certain conditions (see Jane Superbrain Box 2.1 below). We don't have direct access to the processes, so we collect data that represent the processes and then use these data to build statistical models (we reduce the process to a statistical model). We then use this statistical model to make predictions about the real-world phenomenon. Just like the engineer, we want our models to be as accurate as possible so that we can be confident that the predictions we make are also accurate. However, unlike engineers we don't have access to the real-world situation and so we can only ever infer things about psychological, societal, biological or economic processes based upon the models we build. If we want our inferences to be accurate then the statistical model we build must represent the data collected (the observed data) as closely as

Why do we build statistical models?

possible. The degree to which a statistical model represents the data collected is known as the **fit** of the model.

Figure 2.2 illustrates the kinds of models that an engineer might build to represent the real-world bridge that she wants to create. The first model (a) is an excellent representation of the real-world situation and is said to be a good fit (i.e., there are a few small differences but the model is basically a very good replica of reality). If this model is used to make predictions about the real world, then the engineer can be confident that these predictions will be very accurate, because the model so closely resembles reality. So, if the model collapses in a strong wind, then there is a good chance that the real bridge would collapse also. The second model (b) has some similarities to the real world: the model includes some of the basic structural features, but there are some big differences from the real-world bridge (namely the absence of one of the supporting towers). This is what we might term a moderate fit (i.e., there are some differences between the model and the data but there are also some great similarities). If the engineer uses this model to make predictions about the real world then these predictions may be inaccurate and possibly catastrophic (e.g.the model predicts that the bridge will collapse in a strong wind, causing the real bridge to be closed down, creating 100-mile tailbacks with everyone stranded in the snow; all of which was unnecessary because the real bridge was perfectly safe – the model was a bad representation of reality). We can have some confidence, but not complete confidence, in predictions from this model. The final model (c) is completely different from the real-world situation; it bears no structural similarities to the real bridge and is a poor fit (in fact, it might more accurately be described as an abysmal fit!). As such, any predictions based on this model are likely to be completely inaccurate. Extending this analogy to science, we can say that it is important when we fit a statistical model to a set of data that this model fits the data well. If our model is a poor fit of the observed data then the predictions we make from it will be equally poor.

FIGURE 2.2
Fitting models
to real-world
data (see text for
details)

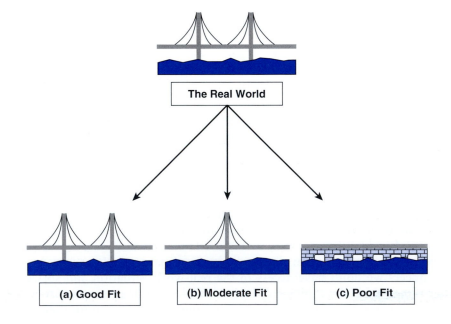

JANE SUPERBRAIN 2.1
Types of statistical models ①

As behavioural and social scientists, most of the models that we use to describe data tend to be **linear models**. For example, analysis of variance (ANOVA) and regression are identical systems based on linear models (Cohen, 1968), yet they have different names and, in psychology at least, are used largely in different contexts due to historical divisions in methodology (Cronbach, 1957).

A linear model is simply a model that is based upon a straight line; this means that we are usually trying to summarize our observed data in terms of a straight line. Suppose we measured how many chapters of this book a person had read, and then measured their spiritual enrichment. We could represent these hypothetical data in the form of a scatterplot in which each dot represents an individual's score on both variables (see section 4.5). Figure 2.3 shows two versions of such a graph summarizing the pattern of these data with either a straight (left) or curved (right) line. These graphs illustrate how we can fit different types of models to the same data. In this case we can use a straight line to represent our data and it shows that the more chapters a person reads, the less their spiritual enrichment. However, we can also use a curved line to summarize the data and this shows that when most, or all, of the chapters have been read, spiritual enrichment seems to increase slightly (presumably because once the book is read everything suddenly makes sense – yeah, as if!). Neither of the two types of model is necessarily correct, but it will be the case that one model fits the data better than another and this is why when we use statistical models it is important for us to assess how well a given model fits the data.

It's possible that many scientific disciplines are progressing in a biased way because most of the models that we tend to fit are linear (mainly because books like this tend to ignore more complex curvilinear models). This could create a bias because most published scientific studies are ones with statistically significant results and there may be cases where a linear model has been a poor fit to the data (and hence the paper was not published), yet a non-linear model would have fitted the data well. This is why it is useful to plot your data first: plots tell you a great deal about what models should be applied to data. If your plot seems to suggest a non-linear model then investigate this possibility (which is easy for me to say when I don't include such techniques in this book!).

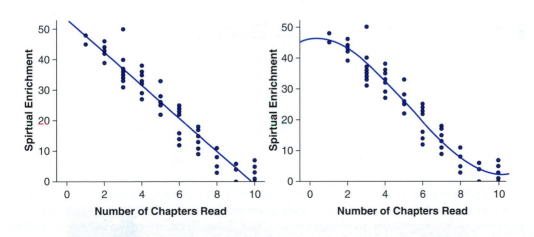

FIGURE 2.3
A scatterplot of the same data with a linear model fitted (left), and with a non-linear model fitted (right)

2.3. Populations and samples ①

As researchers, we are interested in finding results that apply to an entire **population** of people or things. For example, psychologists want to discover processes that occur in all humans, biologists might be interested in processes that occur in all cells, economists want to build models that apply to all salaries, and so on. A population can be very general (all human beings) or very narrow (all male ginger cats called Bob). Usually, scientists strive to infer things about general populations rather than narrow ones. For example, it's not very interesting to conclude that psychology students with brown hair who own a pet hamster named George recover more quickly from sports injuries if the injury is massaged (unless, like René Koning,[1] you happen to be a psychology student with brown hair who has a pet hamster named George). However, if we can conclude that *everyone's* sports injuries are aided by massage this finding has a much wider impact.

Scientists rarely, if ever, have access to every member of a population. Psychologists cannot collect data from every human being and ecologists cannot observe every male ginger cat called Bob. Therefore, we collect data from a small subset of the population (known as a **sample**) and use these data to infer things about the population as a whole. The bridge-building engineer cannot make a full-size model of the bridge she wants to build and so she builds a small-scale model and tests this model under various conditions. From the results obtained from the small-scale model the engineer infers things about how the full-sized bridge will respond. The small-scale model may respond differently than a full-sized version of the bridge, but the larger the model, the more likely it is to behave in the same way as the full-size bridge. This metaphor can be extended to scientists. We never have access to the entire population (the real-size bridge) and so we collect smaller samples (the scaled-down bridge) and use the behaviour within the sample to infer things about the behaviour in the population. The bigger the sample, the more likely it is to reflect the whole population. If we take several random samples from the population, each of these samples will give us slightly different results. However, on average, large samples should be fairly similar.

2.4. Simple statistical models ①

2.4.1. The mean: a very simple statistical model ①

One of the simplest models used in statistics is the mean, which we encountered in section 1.7.2.3. In Chapter 1 we briefly mentioned that the mean was a statistical model of the data because it is a hypothetical value that doesn't have to be a value that is actually observed in the data. For example, if we took five statistics lecturers and measured the number of friends that they had, we might find the following data: 1, 2, 3, 3 and 4. If we take the mean number of friends, this can be calculated by adding the values we obtained, and dividing by the number of values measured: (1 + 2 + 3 + 3 + 4)/5 = 2.6. Now, we know that it is impossible to have 2.6 friends (unless you chop someone up with a chainsaw and befriend their arm, which frankly is probably not beyond your average statistics lecturer) so the mean value is a *hypothetical* value. As such, the mean is a model created to summarize our data.

---

[1] A brown-haired psychology student with a hamster called Sjors (Dutch for George, apparently) who, after reading one of my web resources, emailed me to weaken my foolish belief that this is an obscure combination of possibilities.

2.4.2.   Assessing the fit of the mean: sums of squares, variance and standard deviations ①

With any statistical model we have to assess the fit (to return to our bridge analogy we need to know how closely our model bridge resembles the real bridge that we want to build). With most statistical models we can determine whether the model is accurate by looking at how different our real data are from the model that we have created. The easiest way to do this is to look at the difference between the data we observed and the model fitted. Figure 2.4 shows the number of friends that each statistics lecturer had, and also the mean number that we calculated earlier on. The line representing the mean can be thought of as our model, and the circles are the observed data. The diagram also has a series of vertical lines that connect each observed value to the mean value. These lines represent the **deviance** between the observed data and our model and can be thought of as the error in the model. We can calculate the magnitude of these deviances by simply subtracting the mean value ($\bar{x}$) from each of the observed values (x_i).[2] For example, lecturer 1 had only 1 friend (a glove puppet of an ostrich called Kevin) and so the difference is $x_1 - \bar{x} = 1 - 2.6 = -1.6$. You might notice that the deviance is a negative number, and this represents the fact that our model *overestimates* this lecturer's popularity: it predicts that he will have 2.6 friends yet in reality he has only 1 friend (bless him!). Now, how can we use these deviances to estimate the accuracy of the model? One possibility is to add up the deviances (this would give us an estimate of the total error). If we were to do this we would find that (don't be scared of the equations, we will work through them step by step – if you need reminding of what the symbols mean there is a guide at the beginning of the book):

total error = sum of deviances

$$= \sum (x_i - \bar{x}) = (-1.6) + (-0.6) + (0.4) + (0.4) + (1.4) = 0$$

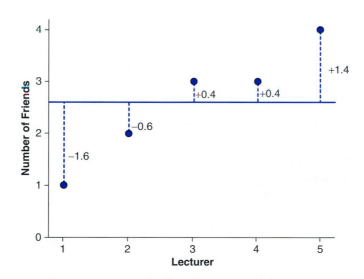

FIGURE 2.4
Graph showing the difference between the observed number of friends that each statistics lecturer had, and the mean number of friends

So, in effect the result tells us that there is no total error between our model and the observed data, so the mean is a perfect representation of the data. Now, this clearly isn't true: there were errors but some of them were positive, some were negative and they have

---

[2] The x_i simply refers to the observed score for the *i*th person (so the *i* can be replaced with a number that represents a particular individual). For these data: for lecturer 1, $x_i = x_1 = 1$; for lecturer 3, $x_i = x_3 = 3$; for lecturer 5, $x_i = x_5 = 4$.

simply cancelled each other out. It is clear that we need to avoid the problem of which direction the error is in and one mathematical way to do this is to square each error,[3] that is multiply each error by itself. So, rather than calculating the sum of errors, we calculate the sum of squared errors. In this example:

$$
\begin{aligned}
\text{sum of squared errors (SS)} &= \sum(x_i - \bar{x})(x_i - \bar{x}) \\
&= (-1.6)^2 + (-0.6)^2 + (0.4)^2 + (0.4)^2 + (1.4)^2 \\
&= 2.56 + 0.36 + 0.16 + 0.16 + 1.96 \\
&= 5.20
\end{aligned}
$$

The **sum of squared errors** (SS) is a good measure of the accuracy of our model. However, it is fairly obvious that the sum of squared errors is dependent upon the amount of data that has been collected – the more data points, the higher the SS. To overcome this problem we calculate the average error by dividing the SS by the number of observations (N). If we are interested only in the average error for the sample, then we can divide by N alone. However, we are generally interested in using the error in the sample to estimate the error in the population and so we divide the SS by the number of observations minus 1 (the reason why is explained in Jane Superbrain Box 2.2). This measure is known as the **variance** and is a measure that we will come across a great deal:

$$
\text{variance } (s^2) = \frac{\text{SS}}{N-1} = \frac{\sum (x_i - \bar{x})^2}{N-1} = \frac{5.20}{4} = 1.3 \tag{2.1}
$$

JANE SUPERBRAIN 2.2

Degrees of freedom ②

Degrees of freedom (*df*) are a very difficult concept to explain. I'll begin with an analogy. Imagine you're the manager of a rugby team and you have a team sheet with 15 empty slots relating to the positions on the playing field. There is a standard formation in rugby and so each team has 15 specific positions that must be held constant for the game to be played. When the first player arrives, you have the choice of 15 positions in which to place him. You place his name in one of the slots and allocate him to a position (e.g., scrum-half) and, therefore, one position on the pitch is now occupied. When the next player arrives, you have the choice of 14 positions but you still have the freedom to choose which position this player is allocated. However, as more players arrive, you will reach the point at which 14 positions have been filled and the final player arrives. With this player you have no freedom to choose

where he plays – there is only one position left. Therefore there are 14 degrees of freedom; that is, for 14 players you have some degree of choice over where they play, but for 1 player you have no choice. The degrees of freedom are one less than the number of players.

In statistical terms the degrees of freedom relate to the number of observations that are free to vary. If we take a sample of four observations from a population, then these four scores are free to vary in any way (they can be any value). However, if we then use this sample of four observations to calculate the standard deviation of the population, we have to use the mean of the sample as an estimate of the population's mean. Thus we hold one parameter constant. Say that the mean of the sample was 10; then we assume that the population mean is 10 also and we keep this value constant. With this parameter fixed, can all four scores from our sample vary? The answer is no, because to keep the mean constant only three values are free to vary. For example, if the values in the sample were 8, 9, 11, 12 (mean = 10) and we changed three of these values to 7, 15 and 8, then the final value *must* be 10 to keep the mean constant. Therefore, if we hold one parameter constant then the degrees of freedom must be one less than the sample size. This fact explains why when we use a sample to estimate the standard deviation of a population, we have to divide the sums of squares by $N - 1$ rather than N alone.

---

[3] When you multiply a negative number by itself it becomes positive.

The variance is, therefore, the average error between the mean and the observations made (and so is a measure of how well the model fits the actual data). There is one problem with the variance as a measure: it gives us a measure in units squared (because we squared each error in the calculation). In our example we would have to say that the average error in our data (the variance) was 1.3 friends squared. It makes little enough sense to talk about 1.3 friends, but it makes even less to talk about friends squared! For this reason, we often take the square root of the variance (which ensures that the measure of average error is in the same units as the original measure). This measure is known as the **standard deviation** and is simply the square root of the variance. In this example the standard deviation is:

$$
s = \sqrt{\frac{\sum(x_i - \bar{x})^2}{N-1}}
$$
$$
= \sqrt{1.3}
$$
$$
= 1.14
$$

(2.2)

The sum of squares, variance and standard deviation are all, therefore, measures of the 'fit' (i.e., how well the mean represents the data). Small standard deviations (relative to the value of the mean itself) indicate that data points are close to the mean. A large standard deviation (relative to the mean) indicates that the data points are distant from the mean (i.e., the mean is not an accurate representation of the data). A standard deviation of 0 would mean that all of the scores were the same. Figure 2.5 shows the overall ratings (on a 5-point scale) of two lecturers after each of five different lectures. Both lecturers had an average rating of 2.6 out of 5 across the lectures. However, the first lecturer had a standard deviation of 0.55 (relatively small compared to the mean). It should be clear from the graph that ratings for this lecturer were consistently close to the mean rating. There was a small fluctuation, but generally his lectures did not vary in popularity. As such, the mean is an accurate representation of his ratings. The mean is a good fit to the data. The second lecturer, however, had a standard deviation of 1.82 (relatively high compared to the mean). The ratings for this lecturer are clearly more spread from the mean; that is, for some lectures he received very high ratings, and for others his ratings were appalling. Therefore, the mean is not such an accurate representation of his performance because there was a lot of variability in the popularity of his lectures. The mean is a poor fit to the data. This illustration should hopefully make clear why the standard deviation is a measure of how well the mean represents the data.

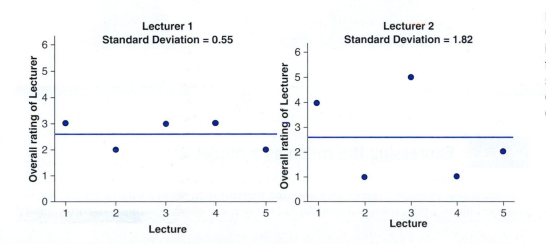

FIGURE 2.5
Graphs illustrating data that have the same mean but different standard deviations

JANE SUPERBRAIN 2.3

The standard deviation and the shape of the distribution ①

As well as telling us about the accuracy of the mean as a model of our data set, the variance and standard deviation also tell us about the shape of the distribution of scores. As such, they are measures of dispersion like those we encountered in section 1.7.3. If the mean represents the data well then most of the scores will cluster close to the mean and the resulting standard deviation is small relative to the mean. When the mean is a worse representation of the data, the scores cluster more widely around the mean (think back to Figure 2.5) and the standard deviation is larger. Figure 2.6 shows two distributions that have the same mean (50) but different standard deviations. One has a large standard deviation relative to the mean ($SD = 25$) and this results in a flatter distribution that is more spread out, whereas the other has a small standard deviation relative to the mean ($SD = 15$) resulting in a more pointy distribution in which scores close to the mean are very frequent but scores further from the mean become increasingly infrequent. The main message is that as the standard deviation gets larger, the distribution gets fatter. This can make distributions look platykurtic or leptokurtic when, in fact, they are not.

FIGURE 2.6
Two distributions with the same mean, but large and small standard deviations

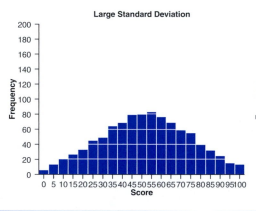
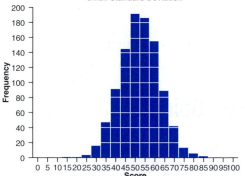

2.4.3. Expressing the mean as a model ②

The discussion of means, sums of squares and variance may seem a sidetrack from the initial point about fitting statistical models, but it's not: the mean is a simple statistical model that can be fitted to data. What do I mean by this? Well, everything in statistics essentially boils down to one equation:

$$\text{outcome}_i = (\text{model}) + \text{error}_i \tag{2.3}$$

This just means that the data we observe can be predicted from the model we choose to fit to the data plus some amount of error. When I say that the mean is a simple statistical model, then all I mean is that we can replace the word 'model' with the word 'mean' in that equation. If we return to our example involving the number of friends that statistics lecturers have and look at lecturer 1, for example, we observed that they had one friend and the mean of all lecturers was 2.6. So, the equation becomes:

$$\text{outcome}_{\text{lecturer1}} = \bar{X} + \varepsilon_{\text{lecturer1}}$$
$$1 = 2.6 + \varepsilon_{\text{lecturer1}}$$

From this we can work out that the error is 1 − 2.6, or −1.6. If we replace this value in the equation we get 1 = 2.6 − 1.6 or 1 = 1. Although it probably seems like I'm stating the obvious, it is worth bearing this general equation in mind throughout this book because if you do you'll discover that most things ultimately boil down to this one simple idea!

Likewise, the variance and standard deviation illustrate another fundamental concept: how the goodness of fit of a model can be measured. If we're looking at how well a model fits the data (in this case our model is the mean) then we generally look at deviation from the model, we look at the sum of squared error, and in general terms we can write this as:

$$\text{deviation} = \sum (\text{observed} - \text{model})^2 \tag{2.4}$$

Put another way, we assess models by comparing the data we observe to the model we've fitted to the data, and then square these differences. Again, you'll come across this fundamental idea time and time again throughout this book.

2.5. Going beyond the data ①

Using the example of the mean, we have looked at how we can fit a statistical model to a set of observations to summarize those data. It's one thing to summarize the data that you have actually collected, but usually we want to go beyond our data and say something general about the world (remember in Chapter 1 that I talked about how good theories should say something about the world). It's one thing to be able to say that people in our sample responded well to medication, or that a sample of high-street stores in Brighton had increased profits leading up to Christmas, but it's more useful to be able to say, based on our sample, that all people will respond to medication, or that all high-street stores in the UK will show increased profits. To begin to understand how we can make these general inferences from a sample of data we can first look not at whether our model is a good fit to the sample from which it came, but whether it is a good fit to the *population* from which the sample came.

2.5.1.   The standard error ①

We've seen that the standard deviation tells us something about how well the mean represents the sample data, but I mentioned earlier on that usually we collect data from samples because we don't have access to the entire population. If you take several samples from a population, then these samples will differ slightly; therefore, it's also important to know how well a particular sample represents the population. This is where we use the **standard error**. Many students get confused about the difference between the standard deviation and the standard error (usually because the difference is never explained clearly). However, the standard error is an important concept to grasp, so I'll do my best to explain it to you.

We have already learnt that social scientists use samples as a way of estimating the behaviour in a population. Imagine that we were interested in the ratings of all lecturers (so lecturers in general were the population). We could take a sample from this population. When someone takes a sample from a population, they are taking one of many possible samples. If we were to take several samples from the same population, then each sample has its own mean, and some of these sample means will be different.

Figure 2.7 illustrates the process of taking samples from a population. Imagine that we could get ratings of all lecturers on the planet and that, on average, the rating is 3 (this is the *population mean, μ*). Of course, we can't collect ratings of all lecturers, so we use a sample. For each of these samples we can calculate the average, or *sample mean*. Let's imagine we took nine different samples (as in the diagram); you can see that some of the samples have the same mean as the population but some have different means: the first sample of lecturers were rated, on average, as 3, but the second sample were, on average, rated as only 2. This illustrates **sampling variation**: that is, samples will vary because they contain different members of the population; a sample that by chance includes some very good lecturers will have a higher average than a sample that, by chance, includes some awful lecturers! We can actually plot the sample means as a frequency distribution, or histogram,[4] just like I have done in the diagram. This distribution shows that there were three samples that had a mean of 3, means of 2 and 4 occurred in two samples each, and means of 1 and 5 occurred in only one sample each. The end result is a nice symmetrical distribution known as a **sampling distribution**. A sampling distribution is simply the frequency distribution of sample means[5] from the same population. In theory you need to imagine that we're taking hundreds or thousands of samples to construct a sampling distribution, but I'm just using nine to keep the diagram simple.[6] The sampling distribution tells us about the behaviour of samples from the population, and you'll notice that it is centred at the same value as the mean of the population (i.e., 3). This means that if we took the average of all sample means we'd get the value of the population mean. Now, if the average of the sample means is the same value as the population mean, then if we knew the accuracy of that average we'd know something about how likely it is that a given sample is representative of the population. So how do we determine the accuracy of the population mean?

Think back to the discussion of the standard deviation. We used the standard deviation as a measure of how representative the mean was of the observed data. Small standard deviations represented a scenario in which most data points were close to the mean, a large standard deviation represented a situation in which data points were widely spread from the mean. If you were to calculate the standard deviation between *sample means* then this too would give you a measure of how much variability there was between the means of

---

[4] This is just a graph of each sample mean plotted against the number of samples that has that mean – see section 1.7.1 for more details.

[5] It doesn't have to be means, it can be any statistic that you're trying to estimate, but I'm using the mean to keep things simple.

[6] It's worth pointing out that I'm talking hypothetically. We don't need to *actually* collect these samples because clever statisticians have worked out what these sampling distributions would look like and how they behave.

different samples. The standard deviation of sample means is known as the **standard error of the mean (SE)**. Therefore, the standard error could be calculated by taking the difference between each sample mean and the overall mean, squaring these differences, adding them up, and then dividing by the number of samples. Finally, the square root of this value would need to be taken to get the standard deviation of sample means, the standard error.

Of course, in reality we cannot collect hundreds of samples and so we rely on approximations of the standard error. Luckily for us some exceptionally clever statisticians have demonstrated that as samples get large (usually defined as greater than 30), the sampling distribution has a normal distribution with a mean equal to the population mean, and a standard deviation of:

$$\sigma_{\bar{X}} = \frac{s}{\sqrt{N}} \tag{2.5}$$

This is known as the **central limit theorem** and it is useful in this context because it means that if our sample is large we can use the above equation to approximate the standard error (because, remember, it is the standard deviation of the sampling distribution).[7] When the sample is relatively small (fewer than 30) the sampling distribution has a different shape, known as a t-distribution, which we'll come back to later.

CRAMMING SAM'S TIPS   The standard error

The standard error is the standard deviation of sample means. As such, it is a measure of how representative a sample is likely to be of the population. A large standard error (relative to the sample mean) means that there is a lot of variability between the means of different samples and so the sample we have might not be representative of the population. A small standard error indicates that most sample means are similar to the population mean and so our sample is likely to be an accurate reflection of the population.

2.5.2.   Confidence intervals ②

2.5.2.1. Calculating confidence intervals ②

Remember that usually we're interested in using the sample mean as an estimate of the value in the population. We've just seen that different samples will give rise to different values of the mean, and we can use the standard error to get some idea of the extent to which sample means differ. A different approach to assessing the accuracy of the sample mean as an estimate of the mean in the population is to calculate boundaries within which we believe the true value of the mean will fall. Such boundaries are called **confidence intervals**. The basic idea behind confidence intervals is to construct a range of values within which we think the population value falls.

Let's imagine an example: Domjan, Blesbois, and Williams (1998) examined the learnt release of sperm in Japanese quail. The basic idea is that if a quail is allowed to copulate with a female quail in a certain context (an experimental chamber) then this context will serve as a cue to copulation and this in turn will affect semen release (although during the

---

[7] In fact it should be the *population* standard deviation (σ) that is divided by the square root of the sample size; however, for large samples this is a reasonable approximation.

FIGURE 2.7
Illustration of
the standard
error (see text
for details)

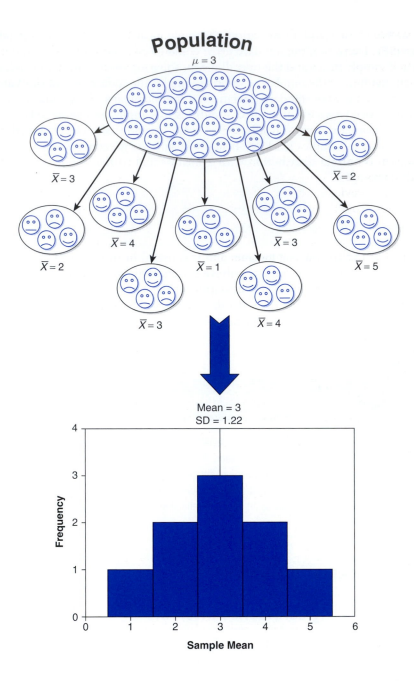

test phase the poor quail were tricked into copulating with a terry cloth with an embalmed female quail head stuck on top).[8] Anyway, if we look at the mean amount of sperm released in the experimental chamber, there is a true mean (the mean in the population); let's imagine it's 15 million sperm. Now, in our actual sample, we might find the mean amount of sperm released was 17 million. Because we don't know the true mean, we don't really know whether our sample value of 17 million is a good or bad estimate of this value. What we can do instead is use an interval estimate: we use our sample value as the mid-point, but set a lower and upper limit as well. So, we might say, we think the true value of the mean sperm release is somewhere between 12 million and 22 million spermatozoa (note that 17 million falls exactly between these values). Of course, in this case the true value (15 million)

[8] This may seem a bit sick, but the male quails didn't appear to mind too much, which probably tells us all we need to know about male mating behaviour.

does falls within these limits. However, what if we'd set smaller limits, what if we'd said we think the true value falls between 16 and 18 million (again, note that 17 million is in the middle)? In this case the interval does not contain the true value of the mean. Let's now imagine that you were particularly fixated with Japanese quail sperm, and you repeated the experiment 50 times using different samples. Each time you did the experiment again you constructed an interval around the sample mean as I've just described. Figure 2.8 shows this scenario: the circles represent the mean for each sample with the lines sticking out of them representing the intervals for these means. The true value of the mean (the mean in the population) is 15 million and is shown by a vertical line. The first thing to note is that the sample means are different from the true mean (this is because of sampling variation as described in the previous section). Second, although most of the intervals do contain the true mean (they cross the vertical line, meaning that the value of 15 million spermatozoa falls somewhere between the lower and upper boundaries), a few do not.

Up until now I've avoided the issue of how we might calculate the intervals. The crucial thing with confidence intervals is to construct them in such a way that they tell us something useful. Therefore, we calculate them so that they have certain properties: in particular, they tell us the likelihood that they contain the true value of the thing we're trying to estimate (in this case, the mean).

Typically we look at 95% confidence intervals, and sometimes 99% confidence intervals, but they all have a similar interpretation: they are limits constructed such that for a certain percentage of the time (be that 95% or 99%) the true value of the population mean will fall within these limits. So, when you see a 95% confidence interval for a mean, think of it like this: if we'd collected 100 samples, calculated the mean and then calculated a confidence interval for that mean (a bit like in Figure 2.8) then for 95 of these samples, the confidence intervals we constructed would contain the true value of the mean in the population.

To calculate the confidence interval, we need to know the limits within which 95% of means will fall. How do we calculate these limits? Remember back in section 1.7.4 that I said that 1.96 was an important value of z (a score from a normal distribution with a mean of 0 and standard deviation of 1) because 95% of z-scores fall between −1.96 and 1.96. This means that if our sample means were normally distributed with a mean of 0 and a standard error of 1, then the limits of our confidence interval would be −1.96 and +1.96. Luckily we know from the central limit theorem that in large samples (above about 30) the sampling distribution will be normally distributed (see section 2.5.1). It's a pity then that our mean and standard deviation are unlikely to be 0 and 1; except not really because, as you might remember, we can convert scores so that they do have a mean of 0 and standard deviation of 1 (z-scores) using equation (1.2):

$$z = \frac{X - \bar{X}}{s}$$

If we know that our limits are −1.96 and 1.96 in z-scores, then to find out the corresponding scores in our raw data we can replace z in the equation (because there are two values, we get two equations):

$$1.96 = \frac{X - \bar{X}}{s} \qquad\qquad -1.96 = \frac{X - \bar{X}}{s}$$

We rearrange these equations to discover the value of X:

$$1.96 \times s = X - \bar{X} \qquad\qquad -1.96 \times s = X - \bar{X}$$
$$(1.96 \times s) + \bar{X} = X \qquad\qquad (-1.96 \times s) + \bar{X} = X$$

FIGURE 2.8

The confidence intervals of the sperm counts of Japanese quail (horizontal axis) for 50 different samples (vertical axis)

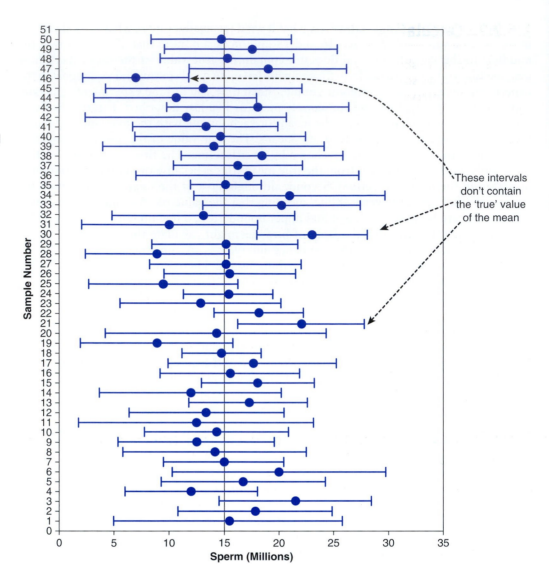

Therefore, the confidence interval can easily be calculated once the standard deviation (s in the equation above) and mean ($\bar{X}$ in the equation) are known. However, in fact we use the standard error and not the standard deviation because we're interested in the variability of sample means, not the variability in observations within the sample. The lower boundary of the confidence interval is, therefore, the mean minus 1.96 times the standard error, and the upper boundary is the mean plus 1.96 standard errors:

$$\text{lower boundary of confidence interval} = \bar{X} - (1.96 \times SE)$$
$$\text{upper boundary of confidence interval} = \bar{X} + (1.96 \times SE)$$

As such, the mean is always in the centre of the confidence interval. If the mean represents the true mean well, then the confidence interval of that mean should be small. We know that 95% of confidence intervals contain the true mean, so we can assume this confidence interval contains the true mean; therefore, if the interval is small, the sample mean must be very close to the true mean. Conversely, if the confidence interval is very wide then the sample mean could be very different from the true mean, indicating that it is a bad representation of the population. You'll find that confidence intervals will come up time and time again throughout this book.

2.5.2.2. Calculating other confidence intervals ②

The example above shows how to compute a 95% confidence interval (the most common type). However, we sometimes want to calculate other types of confidence interval such as a 99% or 90% interval. The −1.96 and 1.96 in the equations above are the limits within which 95% of z-scores occur. Therefore, if we wanted a 99% confidence interval we could use the values within which 99% of z-scores occur (−2.58 and 2.58). In general, then, we could say that confidence intervals are calculated as:

$$\text{lower boundary of confidence interval} = \bar{X} - \left(z_{\frac{1-p}{2}} \times SE \right)$$

$$\text{upper boundary of confidence interval} = \bar{X} + \left(z_{\frac{1-p}{2}} \times SE \right)$$

in which p is the probability value for the confidence interval. So, if you want a 95% confidence interval, then you want the value of z for (1–0.95)/2 = 0.025. Look this up in the 'smaller portion' column of the table of the standard normal distribution (see the Appendix) and you'll find that z is 1.96. For a 99% confidence interval we want z for (1–0.99)/2 = 0.005, which from the table is 2.58. For a 90% confidence interval we want z for (1–0.90)/2 = 0.05, which from the table is 1.64. These values of z are multiplied by the standard error (as above) to calculate the confidence interval. Using these general principles, we could work out a confidence interval for any level of probability that takes our fancy.

2.5.2.3. Calculating confidence intervals in small samples ②

The procedure that I have just described is fine when samples are large, but for small samples, as I have mentioned before, the sampling distribution is not normal, it has a t-distribution. The t-distribution is a family of probability distributions that change shape as the sample size gets bigger (when the sample is very big, it has the shape of a normal distribution). To construct a confidence interval in a small sample we use the same principle as before but instead of using the value for z we use the value for t:

$$\text{lower boundary of confidence interval} = \bar{X} - (t_{n-1} \times SE)$$

$$\text{upper boundary of confidence interval} = \bar{X} + (t_{n-1} \times SE)$$

The n − 1 in the equations is the degrees of freedom (see Jane Superbrain Box 2.2) and tells us which of the t-distributions to use. For a 95% confidence interval we find the value of t for a two-tailed test with probability of .05, for the appropriate degrees of freedom.

SELF-TEST

✓ In section 1.7.2.2 we came across some data about the number of friends that 11 people had on Facebook. We calculated the mean for these data as 96.64 and standard deviation as 61.27. Calculate a 95% confidence interval for this mean.
✓ Recalculate the confidence interval assuming that the sample size was 56.

2.5.2.4. Showing confidence intervals visually ②

What's an error bar?

Confidence intervals provide us with very important information about the mean, and, therefore, you often see them displayed on graphs. (We will discover more about how to create these graphs in Chapter 4.) The confidence interval is usually displayed using something called an error bar, which just looks like the letter 'I'. An error bar can represent the standard deviation, or the standard error, but more often than not it shows the 95% confidence interval of the mean. So, often when you see a graph showing the mean, perhaps displayed as a bar or a symbol (section 4.9), it is often accompanied by this funny I-shaped bar. Why is it useful to see the confidence interval visually?

We have seen that the 95% confidence interval is an interval constructed such that in 95% of samples the true value of the population mean will fall within its limits. We know that it is possible that any two samples could have slightly different means (and the standard error tells us a little about how different we can expect sample means to be). Now, the confidence interval tells us the limits within which the population mean is likely to fall (the size of the confidence interval will depend on the size of the standard error). By comparing the confidence intervals of different means we can start to get some idea about whether the means came from the same population or different populations.

Taking our previous example of quail sperm, imagine we had a sample of quail and the mean sperm release had been 9 million sperm with a confidence interval of 2 to 16. Therefore, we know that the population mean is probably between 2 and 16 million sperm. What if we now took a second sample of quail and found the confidence interval ranged from 4 to 15? This interval overlaps a lot with our first sample:

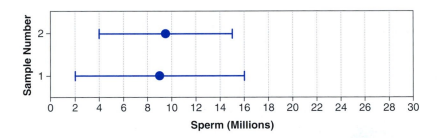

The fact that the confidence intervals overlap in this way tells us that these means could plausibly come from the same population: in both cases the intervals are likely to contain the true value of the mean (because they are constructed such that in 95% of studies they will), and both intervals overlap considerably, so they contain many similar values. What if the confidence interval for our second sample ranges from 18 to 28? If we compared this to our first sample we'd get:

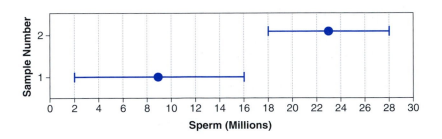

Now, these confidence intervals don't overlap at all. So, one confidence interval, which is likely to contain the population mean, tells us that the population mean is somewhere between 2 and 16 million, whereas the other confidence interval, which is also likely to contain the population mean, tells us that the population mean is somewhere between 18 and 28. This suggests that either our confidence intervals both do contain the population mean, but they come from different populations (and, therefore, so do our samples), or both samples come from the same population but one of the confidence intervals doesn't contain the population mean. If we've used 95% confidence intervals then we know that the second possibility is unlikely (this happens only 5 times in 100 or 5% of the time), so the first explanation is more plausible.

OK, I can hear you all thinking 'so what if the samples come from a different population?' Well, it has a very important implication in experimental research. When we do an experiment, we introduce some form of manipulation between two or more conditions (see section 1.6.2). If we have taken two random samples of people, and we have tested them on some measure (e.g., fear of statistics textbooks), then we expect these people to belong to the same population. If their sample means are so different as to suggest that, in fact, they come from different populations, why might this be? The answer is that our experimental manipulation has induced a difference between the samples.

To reiterate, when an experimental manipulation is successful, we expect to find that our samples have come from different populations. If the manipulation is unsuccessful, then we expect to find that the samples came from the same population (e.g., the sample means should be fairly similar). Now, the 95% confidence interval tells us something about the likely value of the population mean. If we take samples from two populations, then we expect the confidence intervals to be different (in fact, to be sure that the samples were from different populations we would not expect the two confidence intervals to overlap). If we take two samples from the same population, then we expect, if our measure is reliable, the confidence intervals to be very similar (i.e., they should overlap completely with each other).

This is why error bars showing 95% confidence intervals are so useful on graphs, because if the bars of any two means do not overlap then we can infer that these means are from different populations – they are significantly different.

CRAMMING SAM'S TIPS   Confidence intervals

A confidence interval for the mean is a range of scores constructed such that the population mean will fall within this range in 95% of samples.

The confidence interval is not an interval within which we are 95% confident that the population mean will fall.

2.6. Using statistical models to test research questions ①

In Chapter 1 we saw that research was a five-stage process:

1 Generate a research question through an initial observation (hopefully backed up by some data).

2 Generate a theory to explain your initial observation.

3   Generate hypotheses: break your theory down into a set of testable predictions.

4   Collect data to test the theory: decide on what variables you need to measure to test your predictions and how best to measure or manipulate those variables.

5   Analyse the data: fit a statistical model to the data – this model will test your original predictions. Assess this model to see whether or not it supports your initial predictions.

This chapter has shown that we can use a sample of data to estimate what's happening in a larger population to which we don't have access. We have also seen (using the mean as an example) that we can fit a statistical model to a sample of data and assess how well it fits. However, we have yet to see how fitting models like these can help us to test our research predictions. How do statistical models help us to test complex hypotheses such as 'is there a relationship between the amount of gibberish that people speak and the amount of vodka jelly they've eaten?' or 'is the mean amount of chocolate I eat higher when I'm writing statistics books than when I'm not?'. We've seen in section 1.7.5 that hypotheses can be broken down into a null hypothesis and an alternative hypothesis.

SELF-TEST

✓ What are the null and alternative hypotheses for the following questions:

1. 'Is there a relationship between the amount of gibberish that people speak and the amount of vodka jelly they've eaten?'

2. 'Is the mean amount of chocolate eaten higher when writing statistics books than when not?'

Most of this book deals with *inferential statistics*, which tell us whether the alternative hypothesis is likely to be true – they help us to confirm or reject our predictions. Crudely put, we fit a statistical model to our data that represents the alternative hypothesis and see how well it fits (in terms of the variance it explains). If it fits the data well (i.e., explains a lot of the variation in scores) then we assume our initial prediction is true: we gain confidence in the alternative hypothesis. Of course, we can never be completely sure that either hypothesis is correct, and so we calculate the probability that our model would fit if there were no effect in the population (i.e., the null hypothesis is true). As this probability decreases, we gain greater confidence that the alternative hypothesis is actually correct and that the null hypothesis can be rejected. This works provided we make our predictions before we collect the data (see Jane Superbrain Box 2.4).

To illustrate this idea of whether a hypothesis is likely, Fisher (1925/1991) (Figure 2.9) describes an experiment designed to test a claim by a woman that she could determine, by tasting a cup of tea, whether the milk or the tea was added first to the cup. Fisher thought that he should give the woman some cups of tea, some of which had the milk added first and some of which had the milk added last, and see whether she could correctly identify them. The woman would know that there are an equal number of cups in which milk was added first or last but wouldn't know in which order the cups were placed. If we take the simplest situation in which there are only two cups then the woman has a 50% chance of guessing correctly. If she did guess correctly we wouldn't be that confident in concluding that she can tell the difference between cups in which the milk was added first from those in which it was added last, because even by guessing she would be correct half of the time.

JANE SUPERBRAIN 2.4

Cheating in research ①

The process I describe in this chapter works only if you generate your hypotheses and decide on your criteria for whether an effect is significant before collecting the data. Imagine I wanted to place a bet on who would win the Rugby World Cup. Being an Englishman, I might want to bet on England to win the tournament. To do this I'd: (1) place my bet, choosing my team (England) and odds available at the betting shop (e.g., 6/4); (2) see which team wins the tournament; (3) collect my winnings (if England do the decent thing and actually win).

To keep everyone happy, this process needs to be equitable: the betting shops set their odds such that they're not paying out too much money (which keeps them happy), but so that they do pay out sometimes (to keep the customers happy). The betting shop can offer any odds before the tournament has ended, but it can't change them once the tournament is over (or the last game has started). Similarly, I can choose any team

before the tournament, but I can't then change my mind half way through, or after the final game!

The situation in research is similar: we can choose any hypothesis (rugby team) we like before the data are collected, but we can't change our minds halfway through data collection (or after data collection). Likewise we have to decide on our probability level (or betting odds) before we collect data. *If* we do this, the process works. However, researchers sometimes cheat. They don't write down their hypotheses before they conduct their experiments, sometimes they change them when the data are collected (like me changing my team after the World Cup is over), or, worse still, decide on them after the data are collected! With the exception of some complicated procedures called *post hoc* tests, this is cheating. Similarly, researchers can be guilty of choosing which significance level to use after the data are collected and analysed, like a betting shop changing the odds after the tournament.

Every time that you change your hypothesis or the details of your analysis you appear to increase the chance of finding a significant result, but in fact you are making it more and more likely that you will publish results that other researchers can't reproduce (which is very embarrassing!). If, however, you follow the rules carefully and do your significance testing at the 5% level you at least know that in the long run at most only 1 result out of every 20 will risk this public humiliation.

(With thanks to David Hitchin for this box, and with apologies to him for turning it into a rugby example!)

However, what about if we complicated things by having six cups? There are 20 orders in which these cups can be arranged and the woman would guess the correct order only 1 time in 20 (or 5% of the time). If she got the correct order we would be much more confident that she could genuinely tell the difference (and bow down in awe of her finely tuned palate). If you'd like to know more about Fisher and his tea-tasting antics see David Salsburg's excellent book *The Lady Tasting Tea* (Salsburg, 2002). For our purposes the take-home point is that only when there was a very small probability that the woman could complete the tea-task by luck alone would we conclude that she had genuine skill in detecting whether milk was poured into a cup before or after the tea.

It's no coincidence that I chose the example of six cups above (where the tea-taster had a 5% chance of getting the task right by guessing), because Fisher suggested that 95% is a useful threshold for confidence: only when we are 95% certain that a result is genuine (i.e., not a chance finding) should we accept it as being true.[9] The opposite way to look at this is to say that if there is only a 5% chance (a probability of .05) of something occurring by chance then we can accept that it is a genuine effect: we say it is a *statistically significant* finding (see Jane Superbrain Box 2.5 to find out how the criterion of .05 became popular!).

---

[9] Of course, in reality, it might not be true – we're just prepared to believe that it is!

FIGURE 2.9
Sir Ronald A.
Fisher, probably
the cleverest
person ever
($p < .0001$)

JANE SUPERBRAIN 2.5

Why do we use .05? ①

This criterion of 95% confidence, or a .05 probability, forms the basis of modern statistics, and yet there is very little justification for it. How it arose is a complicated mystery to unravel. The significance testing that we use today is a blend of Fisher's idea of using the probability value p as an index of the weight of evidence against a null hypothesis, and Jerzy Neyman and Egron Pearson's idea of testing a null hypothesis *against* an alternative hypothesis. Fisher objected to Neyman's use of an alternative hypothesis (among other things), and Neyman objected to Fisher's exact probability approach (Berger, 2003; Lehmann, 1993). The confusion arising from both parties' hostility to each other's ideas led scientists to create a sort of bastard child of both approaches.

This doesn't answer the question of why we use .05. Well, it probably comes down to the fact that back in the days before computers, scientists had to compare their test statistics against published tables of 'critical values' (they did not have **R** to calculate exact probabilities for them). These critical values had to be calculated by exceptionally clever people like Fisher. In his incredibly influential textbook *Statistical Methods for Research Workers*

(Fisher, 1925)[10] Fisher produced tables of these critical values, but to save space produced tables for particular probability values (.05, .02 and .01). The impact of this book should not be underestimated (to get some idea of its influence 25 years after publication see Mather, 1951; Yates, 1951) and these tables were very frequently used – even Neyman and Pearson admitted the influence that these tables had on them (Lehmann, 1993). This disastrous combination of researchers confused about the Fisher and Neyman–Pearson approaches and the availability of critical values for only certain levels of probability led to a trend to report test statistics as being significant at the now infamous $p < .05$ and $p < .01$ (because critical values were readily available at these probabilities).

However, Fisher acknowledged that the dogmatic use of a fixed level of significance was silly: 'no scientific worker has a fixed level of significance at which from year to year, and in all circumstances, he rejects hypotheses; he rather gives his mind to each particular case in the light of his evidence and his ideas'(Fisher, 1956).

The use of effect sizes (section 2.6.4) strikes a balance between using arbitrary cut-off points such as $p < .05$ and assessing whether an effect is meaningful within the research context. The fact that we still worship at the shrine of $p < .05$ and that research papers are more likely to be published if they contain significant results does make me wonder about a parallel universe where Fisher had woken up in a $p < .10$ kind of mood. My filing cabinet full of research with p just bigger than .05 gets published and I am Vice-Chancellor of my university (although, if this were true, the parallel universe version of my university would be in utter chaos, but it would have a campus full of cats).

---

[10] You can read this online at http://psychclassics.yorku.ca/Fisher/Methods/

2.6.1. Test statistics ①

We have seen that we can fit statistical models to data that represent the hypotheses that we want to test. Also, we have discovered that we can use probability to see whether scores are likely to have happened by chance (section 1.7.4). If we combine these two ideas then we can test whether our statistical models (and therefore our hypotheses) are significant fits of the data we collected. To do this we need to return to the concepts of systematic and unsystematic variation that we encountered in section 1.6.2.2. Systematic variation is variation that can be explained by the model that we've fitted to the data (and, therefore, due to the hypothesis that we're testing). Unsystematic variation is variation that cannot be explained by the model that we've fitted. In other words, it is error, or variation not attributable to the effect we're investigating. The simplest way, therefore, to test whether the model fits the data, or whether our hypothesis is a good explanation of the data we have observed, is to compare the systematic variation against the unsystematic variation. In doing so we compare how good the model/hypothesis is at explaining the data against how bad it is (the error):

$$\text{test statistic} = \frac{\text{variance explained by the model}}{\text{variance not explained by the model}} = \frac{\text{effect}}{\text{error}}$$

This ratio of systematic to unsystematic variance or effect to error is a **test statistic**, and you'll discover later in the book there are lots of them: t, F and χ^2 to name only three. The exact form of this equation changes depending on which test statistic you're calculating, but the important thing to remember is that they all, crudely speaking, represent the same thing: the amount of variance explained by the model we've fitted to the data compared to the variance that can't be explained by the model (see Chapters 7 and 9 in particular for a more detailed explanation). The reason why this ratio is so useful is intuitive really: if our model is good then we'd expect it to be able to explain more variance than it can't explain. In this case, the test statistic will be greater than 1 (but not necessarily significant).

A test statistic is a statistic that has known properties; specifically, we know how frequently different values of this statistic occur. By knowing this, we can calculate the probability of obtaining a particular value (just as we could estimate the probability of getting a score of a certain size from a frequency distribution in section 1.7.4). This allows us to establish how likely it would be that we would get a test statistic of a certain size if there were no effect (i.e., the null hypothesis were true). Field and Hole (2003) use the analogy of the age at which people die. Past data have told us the distribution of the age of death. For example, we know that on average men die at about 75 years old, and that this distribution is top heavy; that is, most people die above the age of about 50 and it's fairly unusual to die in your twenties. So, the frequencies of the age of demise at older ages are very high but are lower at younger ages. From these data, it would be possible to calculate the probability of someone dying at a certain age. If we randomly picked someone and asked them their age, and it was 53, we could tell them how likely it is that they will die before their next birthday (at which point they'd probably punch us!). Also, if we met a man of 110, we could calculate how probable it was that he would have lived that long (it would be a very small probability because most people die before they reach that age). The way we use test statistics is rather similar: we know their distributions and this allows us, once we've calculated the test statistic, to discover the probability of having found a value as big as we have. So, if we calculated a test statistic and its value was 110 (rather like our old man) we can then calculate the probability of obtaining a value that large. The more variation our model explains (compared to the variance it can't explain), the bigger the test statistic will be, and the more unlikely it is to occur by chance (like our 110-year-old man). So, as test statistics get bigger, the probability of them occurring becomes smaller. When this probability falls below .05 (Fisher's criterion), we accept this as giving us enough confidence to assume that the test statistic is as large as it is because our model explains a sufficient amount of variation to reflect what's genuinely happening in the real world (the population). The test statistic is said

JANE SUPERBRAIN 2.6

What we can and can't conclude from a significant test statistic ②

The importance of an effect: We've seen already that the basic idea behind hypothesis testing involves us generating an experimental hypothesis and a null hypothesis, fitting a statistical model to the data, and assessing that model with a test statistic. If the probability of obtaining the value of our test statistic by chance is less than .05 then we generally accept the experimental hypothesis as true: there is an effect in the population. Normally we say 'there is a *significant* effect of …'. However, don't be fooled by that word 'significant', because even if the probability of our effect being a chance result is small (less than .05) it doesn't necessarily follow that the effect is important. Very small and unimportant effects can turn out to be statistically significant just because huge numbers of people have been used in the experiment (see Field & Hole, 2003: 74).

Non-significant results: Once you've calculated your test statistic, you calculate the probability of that test statistic occurring by chance; if this probability is greater than .05 you reject your alternative hypothesis. However, this does *not* mean that the null hypothesis is true. Remember that the null hypothesis is that there is no effect in the population. All that a non-significant result tells us is that the effect is not big enough to be anything other than a chance finding – it doesn't tell us that the effect is zero. As Cohen (1990) points out, a non-significant result should never be interpreted as (despite the fact that it often is) 'no difference between means' or 'no relationship between variables'. Cohen also points out that the null hypothesis is *never* true because we know from sampling distributions (see section 2.5.1) that two random samples will have slightly different means, and even though these differences can be very small (e.g., one mean might be 10 and another might be 10.00001) they are nevertheless different. In fact, even such a small difference would be deemed as statistically significant if a big enough sample were used. So, significance testing can never tell us that the null hypothesis is true, because it never is!

Significant results: OK, we may not be able to accept the null hypothesis as being true, but we can at least conclude that it is false when our results are significant, right? Wrong! A significant test statistic is based on probabilistic reasoning, which severely limits what we can conclude. Again, Cohen (1994), who was an incredibly lucid writer on statistics, points out that formal reasoning relies on an initial statement of fact followed by a statement about the current state of affairs, and an inferred conclusion. This syllogism illustrates what I mean:

- If a man has no arms then he can't play guitar:
  o This man plays guitar.
  o Therefore, this man has arms.

The syllogism starts with a statement of fact that allows the end conclusion to be reached because you can deny the man has no arms (the antecedent) by denying that he can't play guitar (the consequent).[11] A comparable version of the null hypothesis is:

- If the null hypothesis is correct, then this test statistic cannot occur:
  o This test statistic has occurred.
  o Therefore, the null hypothesis is false.

This is all very nice except that the null hypothesis is not represented in this way because it is based on probabilities. Instead it should be stated as follows:

- If the null hypothesis is correct, then this test statistic is highly unlikely:
  o This test statistic has occurred.
  o Therefore, the null hypothesis is highly unlikely.

If we go back to the guitar example we could get a similar statement:

- If a man plays guitar then he probably doesn't play for Fugazi (this is true because there are thousands of people who play guitar but only two who play guitar in the band Fugazi!):
  o Guy Picciotto plays for Fugazi.
  o Therefore, Guy Picciotto probably doesn't play guitar.

This should hopefully seem completely ridiculous – the conclusion is wrong because Guy Picciotto does play guitar. This illustrates a common fallacy in hypothesis testing. In fact significance testing allows us to say very little about the null hypothesis.

[11] Thanks to Philipp Sury for unearthing footage that disproves my point (http://www.parcival.org/2007/05/22/when-syllogisms-fail/).

to be *significant* (see Jane Superbrain Box 2.6 for a discussion of what statistically significant actually means). Given that the statistical model that we fit to the data reflects the hypothesis that we set out to test, then a significant test statistic tells us that the model would be unlikely to fit this well if the there was no effect in the population (i.e., the null hypothesis was true). Therefore, we can reject our null hypothesis and gain confidence that the alternative hypothesis is true (but, remember, we don't accept it – see section 1.7.5).

2.6.2.   One- and two-tailed tests ①

We saw in section 1.7.5 that hypotheses can be directional (e.g., 'the more someone reads this book, the more they want to kill its author') or non-directional (i.e., 'reading more of this book could increase or decrease the reader's desire to kill its author'). A statistical model that tests a directional hypothesis is called a **one-tailed test**, whereas one testing a non-directional hypothesis is known as a **two-tailed test**.

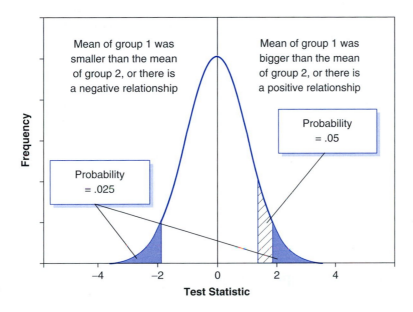

FIGURE 2.10
Diagram to show the difference between one- and two-tailed tests

Imagine we wanted to discover whether reading this book increased or decreased the desire to kill me. We could do this either (experimentally) by taking two groups, one who had read this book and one who hadn't, or (correlationally) by measuring the amount of this book that had been read and the corresponding desire to kill me. If we have no directional hypothesis then there are three possibilities. (1) People who read this book want to kill me more than those who don't so the difference (the mean for those reading the book minus the mean for non-readers) is positive. Correlationally, the more of the book you read, the more you want to kill me – a positive relationship. (2) People who read this book want to kill me less than those who don't so the difference (the mean for those reading the book minus the mean for non-readers) is negative. Correlationally, the more of the book you read, the less you want to kill me – a negative relationship. (3) There is no difference between readers and non-readers in their desire to kill me – the mean for readers minus the mean for non-readers is exactly zero. Correlationally, there is no relationship between reading this book and wanting to kill me. This final option is the null hypothesis. The direction of the test statistic (i.e., whether it is positive or negative) depends on whether

Why do you need two tails?

the difference is positive or negative. Assuming there is a positive difference or relationship (reading this book makes you want to kill me), then to detect this difference we have to take account of the fact that the mean for readers is bigger than for non-readers (and so derive a positive test statistic). However, if we've predicted incorrectly and actually reading this book makes readers want to kill me less then the test statistic will actually be negative.

What are the consequences of this? Well, if at the .05 level we needed to get a test statistic bigger than say 10 and the one we get is actually −12, then we would reject the hypothesis even though a difference does exist. To avoid this we can look at both ends (or tails) of the distribution of possible test statistics. This means we will catch both positive and negative test statistics. However, doing this has a price because to keep our criterion probability of .05 we have to split this probability across the two tails: so we have .025 at the positive end of the distribution and .025 at the negative end. Figure 2.10 shows this situation – the tinted areas are the areas above the test statistic needed at a .025 level of significance. Combine the probabilities (i.e., add the two tinted areas together) at both ends and we get .05, our criterion value. Now if we have made a prediction, then we put all our eggs in one basket and look only at one end of the distribution (either the positive or the negative end, depending on the direction of the prediction we make). So, in Figure 2.10, rather than having two small tinted areas at either end of the distribution that show the significant values, we have a bigger area (the lined area) at only one end of the distribution that shows significant values. Consequently, we can just look for the value of the test statistic that would occur by chance with a probability of .05. In Figure 2.10, the lined area is the area above the positive test statistic needed at a .05 level of significance. Note on the graph that the value that begins the area for the .05 level of significance (the lined area) is smaller than the value that begins the area for the .025 level of significance (the tinted area). This means that if we make a specific prediction then we need a smaller test statistic to find a significant result (because we are looking in only one tail of the distribution), but if our prediction happens to be in the wrong direction then we'll miss out on detecting the effect that does exist. In this context it's important to remember what I said in Jane Superbrain Box 2.4: you can't place a bet or change your bet when the tournament is over. If you didn't make a prediction of direction before you collected the data, you are too late to predict the direction and claim the advantages of a one-tailed test.

2.6.3. Type I and Type II errors ①

We have seen that we use test statistics to tell us about the true state of the world (to a certain degree of confidence). Specifically, we're trying to see whether there is an effect in our population. There are two possibilities in the real world: there is, in reality, an effect in the population, or there is, in reality, no effect in the population. We have no way of knowing which of these possibilities is true; however, we can look at test statistics and their associated probability to tell us which of the two is more likely. Obviously, it is important that we're as accurate as possible, which is why Fisher originally said that we should be very conservative and only believe that a result is genuine when we are 95% confident that it is – or when there is only a 5% chance that the results could occur if there was not an effect (the null hypothesis is true). However, even if we're 95% confident there is still a small chance that we get it wrong. In fact there are two mistakes we can make: a Type I and a Type II error. A **Type I error** occurs when we believe that there is a genuine effect in our population, when in fact there isn't. If we use Fisher's criterion then the probability of this error is .05 (or 5%) when there is no effect in the population – this value is known as the **α-level**. Assuming there is no effect in our population, if we replicated our data collection 100 times we could expect that on five occasions we would obtain a test statistic large enough to make us think that there was a genuine effect in the population even though there isn't. The opposite is a **Type II error**, which occurs when we believe that there is no effect in the population when, in reality, there is. This would occur when we obtain a small test statistic (perhaps because there is a lot of natural variation between our samples). In an ideal world, we want the probability of this error to be very small (if there is an effect in the population then it's important that we can detect it). Cohen (1992) suggests that the maximum acceptable probability of a Type II error would be .2 (or 20%) – this is called the β-**level**. That would mean that if we took 100 samples of data from a population in which an effect exists, we would fail to detect that effect in 20 of those samples (so we'd miss 1 in 5 genuine effects).

There is obviously a trade-off between these two errors: if we lower the probability of accepting an effect as genuine (i.e., make α smaller) then we increase the probability that we'll reject an effect that does genuinely exist (because we've been so strict about the level at which we'll accept that an effect is genuine). The exact relationship between the Type I and Type II error is not straightforward because they are based on different assumptions: to make a Type I error there has to be no effect in the population, whereas to make a Type II error the opposite is true (there has to be an effect that we've missed). So, although we know that as the probability of making a Type I error decreases, the probability of making a Type II error increases, the exact nature of the relationship is usually left for the researcher to make an educated guess (Howell, 2006, gives a great explanation of the trade-off between errors).

2.6.4.   Effect sizes ②

The framework for testing whether effects are genuine that I've just presented has a few problems, most of which have been briefly explained in Jane Superbrain Box 2.6. The first problem we encountered was knowing how important an effect is: just because a test statistic is significant doesn't mean that the effect it measures is meaningful or important. The solution to this criticism is to measure the size of the effect that we're testing in a standardized way. When we measure the size of an effect (be that an experimental manipulation or the strength of a relationship between variables) it is known as an **effect size**. An effect size is simply an objective and (usually) standardized measure of the magnitude of observed effect. The fact that the measure is standardized just means that we can compare effect sizes across different studies that have measured different variables, or have used different scales of measurement (so an effect size based on speed in milliseconds could be compared to an effect size based on heart rates). Such is the utility of effect size estimates that the American Psychological Association is now recommending that all psychologists report these effect sizes in the results of any published work. So, it's a habit well worth getting into.

Can we measure how important an effect is?

Many measures of effect size have been proposed, the most common of which are Cohen's *d*, Pearson's correlation coefficient *r* (Chapter 6) and the odds ratio (Chapter 18). Many of you will be familiar with the correlation coefficient as a measure of the strength of relationship between two variables (see Chapter 6 if you're not); however, it is also a very versatile measure of the strength of an experimental effect. It's a bit difficult to reconcile how the humble correlation coefficient can also be used in this way; however, this is only because students are typically taught about it within the context of non-experimental research. I don't want to get into it now, but as you read through Chapters 6, 9 and 10 it will (I hope!) become clear what I mean. Personally, I prefer Pearson's correlation coefficient, *r*, as an effect size measure because it is constrained to lie between 0 (no effect) and 1 (a perfect effect).[12] However, there are situations in which d may be favoured; for example, when group sizes are very discrepant r can be quite biased compared to d (McGrath & Meyer, 2006).

Effect sizes are useful because they provide an objective measure of the importance of an effect. So, it doesn't matter what effect you're looking for, what variables have been measured, or how those variables have been measured – we know that a correlation coefficient of 0 means there is no effect, and a value of 1 means that there is a perfect effect. Cohen (1988, 1992) has also made some widely used suggestions about what constitutes a large or small effect:

- $r = .10$ (**small effect**): In this case the effect explains 1% of the total variance.

- $r = .30$ (**medium effect**): The effect accounts for 9% of the total variance.

- $r = .50$ (**large effect**): The effect accounts for 25% of the variance.

It's worth bearing in mind that r is not measured on a linear scale, so an effect with $r = .6$ isn't twice as big as one with $r = .3$. Although these guidelines can be a useful rule of thumb to assess the importance of an effect (regardless of the significance of the test statistic), it is worth remembering that these 'canned' effect sizes are no substitute for evaluating an effect size within the context of the research domain where it is being used (Baguley, 2004; Lenth, 2001).

A final thing to mention is that when we calculate effect sizes we calculate them for a given sample. When we looked at means in a sample we saw that we used them to draw inferences about the mean of the entire population (which is the value in which we're actually interested). The same is true of effect sizes: the size of the effect in the population is the value in which we're interested, but because we don't have access to this value, we use the effect size in the sample to estimate the likely size of the effect in the population. We can also combine effect sizes from different studies researching the same question to get better estimates of the population effect sizes. This is called **meta-analysis** – see Field (2001, 2005b).

2.6.5. Statistical power ②

Effect sizes are an invaluable way to express the importance of a research finding. The effect size in a population is intrinsically linked to three other statistical properties: (1) the sample size on which the sample effect size is based; (2) the probability level at which we will accept an effect as being statistically significant (the α-level); and (3) the ability of a test to detect an effect of that size (known as the statistical **power**, not to be confused with statistical powder, which is an illegal substance that makes you understand statistics better). As such, once we know three of these properties, then we can always calculate the remaining one. It will also depend on whether the test is a one- or two-tailed test (see section 2.6.2). Typically, in psychology we use an α-level of .05 (see earlier) so we know this value already. The power of a test is the probability that a given test will find an effect assuming that one exists in the population. If you think back you might recall that we've already come across the probability of failing to detect an effect when one genuinely exists (β, the probability of a Type II error). It follows that the probability of detecting an effect if one exists must be the opposite of the probability of not detecting that effect (i.e., $1 - \beta$). I've also mentioned that Cohen (1988, 1992) suggests that we would hope to have a .2 probability of failing to detect a genuine effect, and so the corresponding level of power that he recommended was $1 - .2$, or .8. We should aim to achieve a power of .8, or an 80% chance of detecting an effect if one genuinely exists. The effect size in the population can be estimated from the effect size in the sample, and the sample size is

[12] The correlation coefficient can also be negative (but not below −1), which is useful when we're measuring a relationship between two variables because the sign of r tells us about the direction of the relationship, but in experimental research the sign of r merely reflects the way in which the experimenter coded their groups (see Chapter 6).

determined by the experimenter anyway so that value is easy to calculate. Now, there are two useful things we can do knowing that these four variables are related:

1 **Calculate the power of a test**: Given that we've conducted our experiment, we will have already selected a value of α, we can estimate the effect size based on our sample, and we will know how many participants we used. Therefore, we can use these values to calculate β, the power of our test. If this value turns out to be .8 or more we can be confident that we achieved sufficient power to detect any effects that might have existed, but if the resulting value is less, then we might want to replicate the experiment using more participants to increase the power.

2 **Calculate the sample size necessary to achieve a given level of power**: Given that we know the value of α and β, we can use past research to estimate the size of effect that we would hope to detect in an experiment. Even if no one had previously done the exact experiment that we intend to do, we can still estimate the likely effect size based on similar experiments. We can use this estimated effect size to calculate how many participants we would need to detect that effect (based on the values of α and β that we've chosen).

The latter use is the more common: to determine how many participants should be used to achieve the desired level of power. The actual computations are very cumbersome, but fortunately there are now computer programs available that will do them for you (one example is G*Power, which is free and can be downloaded from a link on the companion website; another is nQuery Adviser, but this has to be bought!). Also, Cohen (1988) provides extensive tables for calculating the number of participants for a given level of power (and vice versa). Based on Cohen (1992), we can use the following guidelines: if we take the standard α-level of .05 and require the recommended power of .8, then we need 783 participants to detect a small effect size ($r = .1$), 85 participants to detect a medium effect size ($r = .3$) and 28 participants to detect a large effect size ($r = .5$).

What have I discovered about statistics? ①

OK, that has been your crash course in statistical theory! Hopefully your brain is still relatively intact. The key point I want you to understand is that when you carry out research you're trying to see whether some effect genuinely exists in your population (the effect you're interested in will depend on your research interests and your specific predictions). You won't be able to collect data from the entire population (unless you want to spend your entire life, and probably several after-lives, collecting data) so you use a sample instead. Using the data from this sample, you fit a statistical model to test your predictions, or, put another way, detect the effect you're looking for. Statistics boil down to one simple idea: observed data can be predicted from some kind of model and an error associated with that model. You use that model (and usually the error associated with it) to calculate a test statistic. If that model can explain a lot of the variation in the data collected (the probability of obtaining that test statistic is less than .05) then you infer that the effect you're looking for genuinely exists in the population. If the probability of obtaining that test statistic is more than .05, then you conclude that the effect was too small to be detected. Rather than rely on significance, you can also quantify the effect in your sample in a standard way as an *effect size* and this can be helpful in gauging the importance of that effect. We also discovered that I managed to get myself into trouble at nursery school. It was soon time to move on to primary school and to new and scary challenges. It was a bit like using **R** for the first time!

Key terms that I've discovered

α-level
β-level
Central limit theorem
Confidence interval
Degrees of freedom
Deviance
Effect size
Fit
Linear model
Meta-analysis
One-tailed test
Population
Power

Sample
Sampling distribution
Sampling variation
Standard deviation
Standard error
Standard error of the mean (SE)
Sum of squared errors (SS)
Test statistic
Two-tailed test
Type I error
Type II error
Variance

Smart Alex's tasks

- Task 1: Why do we use samples? ①

- Task 2: What is the mean and how do we tell if it's representative of our data? ①

- Task 3: What's the difference between the standard deviation and the standard error? ①

- Task 4: In Chapter 1 we used an example of the time taken for 21 heavy smokers to fall off a treadmill at the fastest setting (18, 16, 18, 24, 23, 22, 22, 23, 26, 29, 32, 34, 34, 36, 36, 43, 42, 49, 46, 46, 57). Calculate the sums of squares, variance, standard deviation, standard error and 95% confidence interval of these data. ①

- Task 5: What do the sum of squares, variance and standard deviation represent? How do they differ? ①

- Task 6: What is a test statistic and what does it tell us? ①

- Task 7: What are Type I and Type II errors? ①

- Task 8: What is an effect size and how is it measured? ②

- Task 9: What is statistical power? ②

Answers can be found on the companion website.

Further reading

Cohen, J. (1990). Things I have learned (so far). *American Psychologist*, *45*(12), 1304–1312.
Cohen, J. (1994). The earth is round (*p* < .05). *American Psychologist*, *49*(12), 997–1003. (A couple of beautiful articles by the best modern writer of statistics that we've had.)

Field, A. P., & Hole, G. J. (2003). *How to design and report experiments*. London: Sage. (I am rather biased, but I think this is a good overview of basic statistical theory.)

Miles, J. N. V., & Banyard, P. (2007). *Understanding and using statistics in psychology: a practical introduction*. London: Sage. (A fantastic and amusing introduction to statistical theory.)

Wright, D. B., & London, K. (2009). *First steps in statistics* (2nd ed.). London: Sage. (This book has very clear introductions to sampling, confidence intervals and other important statistical ideas.)

Interesting real research

Domjan, M., Blesbois, E., & Williams, J. (1998). The adaptive significance of sexual conditioning: Pavlovian control of sperm release. *Psychological Science*, 9(5), 411–415.

3

The R environment

FIGURE 3.1
All I want for
Christmas is …
some tasteful
wallpaper

3.1. What will this chapter tell me? ①

At about 5 years old I moved from nursery (note that I moved, I was not 'kicked out' for showing my …) to primary school. Even though my older brother was already there, I remember being really scared about going. None of my nursery school friends were going to the same school and I was terrified about meeting lots of new children. I arrived in my classroom, and as I'd feared, it was full of scary children. In a fairly transparent ploy to make me think that I'd be spending the next 6 years building sand castles, the teacher told me to play in the sand pit. While I was nervously trying to discover whether I could build a pile of sand high enough to bury my head in, a boy came and joined me. He was Jonathan Land, and he was really nice. Within an hour he was my new best friend (5-year-olds are fickle …) and I loved school. Sometimes new environments seem scarier than they really are. This chapter introduces you to a scary new environment: **R**. The **R** environment is a generally more unpleasant environment in which to spend time than your normal environment; nevertheless, we have to spend time there if we are to analyse our data. The purpose of this chapter is, therefore, to put you in a sand pit with a 5-year-old called Jonathan. I will orient you in your new home and reassure you that everything will be fine. We will explore how **R** works and the key windows in **R** (the *console, editor and graphics/quartz windows*). We will also look at how to create variables, data sets, and import and manipulate data.

3.2. Before you start ①

R is a free software environment for statistical computing and graphics. It is what's known as 'open source', which means that unlike commercial software companies that protectively hide away the code on which their software is based, the people who developed **R** allow everyone to access their code. This open source philosophy allows anyone, anywhere to contribute to the software. Consequently, the capabilities of **R** dynamically expand as people from all over the world add to it. **R** very much embodies all that is good about the World Wide Web.

3.2.1.   The R-chitecture ①

In essence, **R** exists as a base package with a reasonable amount of functionality. Once you have downloaded **R** and installed it on your own computer, you can start doing some data analysis and graphs. However, the beauty of **R** is that it can be expanded by downloading **packages** that add specific functionality to the program. Anyone with a big enough brain and a bit of time and dedication can write a package for other people to use. These packages, as well as the software itself, are stored in a central location known as the **CRAN** (Comprehensive R Archive Network). Once a package is stored in the CRAN, anyone with an Internet connection can download it from the CRAN and install it to use within their own copy of **R**. **R** is basically a big global family of fluffy altruistic people contributing to the goal of producing a versatile data analysis tool that is free for everyone to use. It's a statistical embodiment of The Beatles' utopian vision of peace, love and humanity: a sort of 'give *p*s a chance'.

  The CRAN is central to using **R**: it is the place from where you download the software and any packages that you want to install. It would be a shame, therefore, if the CRAN were one day to explode or be eaten by cyber-lizards. The statistical world might collapse. Even assuming the cyber-lizards don't rise up and overthrow the Internet, it is still a busy place. Therefore, rather than have a single CRAN location that everyone accesses, the CRAN is 'mirrored' at different places across the globe. 'Mirrored' simply means that there are identical versions of the CRAN scattered across the world. As a resident of the UK, I might access a CRAN location in the UK, whereas if you are in a different country you would likely access the copy of the CRAN in your own country (or one nearby). Bigger countries, such as the US, have multiple CRANs to serve them: the basic philosophy is to choose a CRAN that is geographically close to you.

FIGURE 3.2
Users download R and install packages (uploaded by statisticians around the world) to their own computer via their nearest CRAN

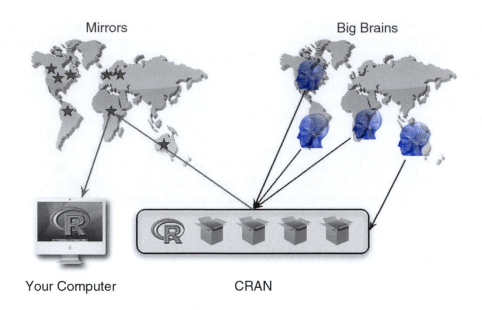

Figure 3.2 shows schematically what we have just learnt. At the centre of the diagram is the CRAN: a repository of the base **R** software and hundreds of packages. People with big brains from all over the world write new packages and upload them into the CRAN for others to use. The CRAN itself is mirrored at different places across the globe (which just means there are multiple copies of it). As a user of **R** you download the software, and install any packages that you want to use via your nearest CRAN.

The idea of needing to install 'packages' into a piece of software to get it to do something for you might seem odd. However, whether you realize it or not many programs work in this way (just less obviously so). For example, the statistical package SPSS has a base version, but also has many modules (for example, the bootstrapping module, advanced statistics, exact tests and so on). If you have not paid for these modules then certain options will be unavailable to you. Many students do not realize that SPSS has this modular format because they use it at a university and the university has paid for all of the modules that they need. Similarly, in Microsoft Excel you need to load the data analysis add-in before you can use certain facilities. **R** is not unusual in having a modular system, and in being modular it has enormous flexibility: as new statistical techniques are developed, contributors can react quickly to produce a package for R; a commercial organization would likely take much longer to include this new technique.

3.2.2. Pros and cons of R ①

The main advantages of using **R** are that it is free, and it is a versatile and dynamic environment. Its open source format and the ability of statisticians to contribute packages to the CRAN mean that there are many things that you can do that cannot be done in commercially available packages. In addition, it is a rapidly expanding tool and can respond quickly to new developments in data analysis. These advantages make **R** an extremely powerful tool.

The downside to **R** is mainly ease of use. The ethos of **R** is to work with a command line rather than a graphical user interface (GUI). In layman's terms this means typing instructions rather than pointing, clicking, and dragging things with a mouse. This might seem weird at first and a rather 'retro' way of working but I believe that once you have mastered a few fairly simple things, **R**'s written commands are a much more efficient way to work.

3.2.3. Downloading and installing R ①

To install **R** onto your computer you need to visit the project website (http://www.R-project.org/). Figure 3.3 shows the process of obtaining the installation files. On the main project page, on the left-hand side, click on the link labelled 'CRAN'. Remember from the previous section that there are various copies (mirrors) of the CRAN across the globe; therefore, the link to the CRAN will navigate you to a page of links to the various 'mirror' sites. Scroll down this list to find a mirror near to you (for example, in the diagram

FIGURE 3.3
Downloading R

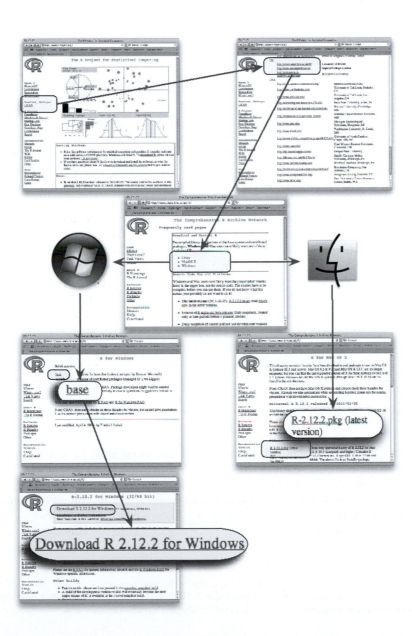

I have highlighted the mirror closest to me, http://www.stats.bris.ac.uk/R/) and click the link. Once you have been redirected to the CRAN mirror that you selected, you will see a web page that asks you which platform you use (Linux, MacOS or Windows). Click the link that applies to you. We're assuming that most readers use either Windows or MacOS.

If you click on the 'Windows' link, then you'll be taken to another page with some more links; click on 'base', which will redirect you to the webpage with the link to the setup file, once there click on the link that says 'Download R 2.12.2 for Windows',[1] which will initiate the download of the **R** setup file. Once this file has been downloaded, double-click on it and you will enter a (hopefully) familiar install procedure.

If you click on the 'MacOS' link you will be taken directly to a page from where you can download the install package by clicking on the link labelled 'R-2.12.2.pkg' (please read the footnote about version numbers). Clicking this link will download the install file; once downloaded, double-click on it and you will enter the normal MacOS install procedure.

3.2.4.   Versions of R ①

At the time of writing, the current version of **R** is 2.12.2; however, the software updates fairly regularly so we are confident that by the time anyone is actually reading this, there will be a newer release (possibly several). Notice that the format of the version number is *major.minor.patch*, which means that we are currently on major version 2, minor version 12 and patch 2. Changes in the patch number happen fairly frequently and usually reflect fixes of minor bugs (so, for example, version 2.12.3 will come along pretty quickly but won't really be a substantial change to the software, just some housekeeping). Minor versions come less regularly (about every 6 months) and still reflect a collection of bug fixes and minor housekeeping that keeps the software running optimally. Major releases are quite rare (the switch from version 1 to version 2 happened in 2006). As such, apart from minor fixes, don't worry if you are using a more recent version of **R** than the one we're using: it won't make any difference, or shouldn't do. The best advice is to update every so often but other than that don't worry too much about which version you're using; there are more important things in life to worry about.

Which version of R do I need to use this book?

3.3. Getting started ①

Once you have installed **R** you can activate it in the usual way. In windows go to the start menu (the big windows icon in the bottom left of the screen) select 'All Programs', then scroll down to the folder labelled 'R', click on it, and then click on the **R** icon (Figure 3.4). In MacOS, go to your 'Applications' folder, scroll down to the **R** icon and click on it (Figure 3.4).

---

[1] At the time of writing the current version of **R** is 2.12.2, but by the time you read this book there will have been an update (or possibly several), so don't be surprised if the '2.12.2' in the link has changed to a different number. This difference is not cause for panic, the link will simply reflect the version number of **R**.

3.3.1. The main windows in R ①

There are three windows that you will use in **R**. The main window is called the **console** (Figure 3.4) and it is where you can both type commands and see the results of executing these commands (in other words, see the output of your analysis). Rather than writing commands directly into the console you can also write them in a separate window (known as the **editor** window). Working with this window has the advantage that you can save collections of commands as a file that you can reuse at another point in time (perhaps to rerun the analysis, or to run a similar analysis on a different set of data). I generally tend to work in this way rather than typing commands into the console because it makes sense to me to save my work in case I need to replicate it, and as you do more analyses you begin to have a repository of **R** commands that you can quickly adapt when running a new analysis. Ultimately you have to do what works for you. Finally, if you produce any graphics or graphs they will appear in the **graphics** window (this window is labelled **quartz** in MacOS).

FIGURE 3.4
Getting **R** started

3.3.2. Menus in R ①

Once **R** is up and running you'll notice a menu bar similar to the ones you might have seen in other programs. Figure 3.4 shows the console window and the menu bar associated with this window. There are some subtle differences between Windows and MacOS versions of **R** and we will look at each version in the following two sections. At this stage, simply note that there are several menus at the top of the screen (e.g., File Edit View) that can be activated by using the computer mouse to move the on-screen arrow onto the desired menu and then pressing the left mouse button once (I'll call pressing this button *clicking*). When you have clicked on a menu, a menu box will appear that displays a list of options that can be activated by moving the on-screen arrow so that it is pointing at the desired option and then clicking with the mouse. Often, selecting an option from a menu makes a window appear; these windows are referred to as *dialog boxes*. When referring to selecting options in a menu I will use arrows to notate the menu paths; for example, if I were to say that you should select the *Save <u>A</u>s ...* option in the *<u>F</u>ile* menu, you will see **File⇒Save As ...**

Before we look at Windows and MacOS versions of **R**, it's worth saying that there are no *substantive* differences: all of the commands in the book work equally as well on Windows or MacOS. Other than pointing out a few differences in the next two sections, we won't talk about Windows and MacOS again because it won't make a difference to how you follow the book. If you happen to use Windows and see a screenshot from MacOS (or vice versa), this is not cause for a nervous breakdown – I promise.

3.3.2.1. R in Windows ①

In **R** for Windows, the menus available depend upon which window is active; Table 3.1 provides an overview of the main menus and their contents. The specific content of a particular menu also changes according to the window that's active. For example, when you are in the *graphics* and *editor* windows the *File* menu pretty much only gives you the option to save, copy or print the graphic or text displayed in the window, but in the *console* window you have many more options. Most options in the menus can also be accessed with keyboard shortcuts (see R's Souls' Tip 3.1).

R's Souls' Tip 3.1 Keyboard shortcuts ①

Within the menus of software packages on Windows some letters are underlined: these underlined letters represent the *keyboard shortcut* for accessing that function. It is possible to select many functions without using the mouse, and the experienced keyboard user may find these shortcuts faster than manoeuvring the mouse arrow to the appropriate place on the screen. The letters underlined in the menus indicate that the option can be obtained by simultaneously pressing *Alt* on the keyboard and the underlined letter. So, to access the *Save <u>A</u>s...* option, using only the keyboard, you should press *Alt* and F on the keyboard simultaneously (which activates the *<u>F</u>ile* menu), then, keeping your finger on the *Alt* key, press A (which is the underlined letter). If these underlined letters are not visible, they can be displayed by pressing the *Alt* key.

As well as the menus there is also a set of *icons* at the top of the data editor window (see Figure 3.4) that are shortcuts to specific facilities. All of these facilities can be accessed via the menu system but using the icons will save you time. Table 3.2 gives a brief overview of these icons and their functions.

Table 3.1 Overview of the menus in R for Windows

Menu	Console	Editor	Graphics
File: This menu allows you to do general things such as saving the workspace (i.e., analysis output – see section 3.4), scripts or graphs. Likewise, you can open previously saved files and print graphs, data or output. In essence, it contains all of the options that are customarily found in *File* menus.	✓	✓	✓
Edit: This menu contains edit functions such as *cut* and *paste*. From here you can also clear the console (i.e., remove all of the text from it), activate a rudimentary data editor, and change how the GUI looks (for example, by default the console shows black text on white background, you can change the colour of both the background and text).	✓	✓	
View: This menu lets you select whether or not to see the toolbar (the buttons at the top of the window) and whether to show a status bar at the bottom of the window (which isn't particularly interesting).	✓		
Misc: This menu contains options to stop ongoing computations (although the ESC key does a quicker job), to list any objects in your working environment (these would be objects that you have created in the current session – see section 3.4), and also to select whether **R** autocompletes words and filenames for you (by default it does).	✓		
Packages: This menu is very important because it is where you load, install and update packages. You can also set your default CRAN mirror so that you always head to that location.	✓	✓	
Window: If you have multiple windows, this menu allows you to change how the windows in **R** are arranged.	✓	✓	✓
Help: This is an invaluable menu because it offers you online help (links to frequently asked questions, the **R** webpage etc.), offline help (pdf manuals, and system help files).	✓	✓	
Resize: This menu is for resizing the image in the graphics window so that it is a fixed size, it is scaled to fit the window but retains its aspect ratio (fit to window), or it expands to fit the window but does not maintain its aspect ratio (R mode).			✓

3.3.2.2. R in MacOS ①

As with any software package for MacOS, the **R** menus appear at the top of the screen. Table 3.3 provides an overview of the main menus and their contents. We will refer back to these menus at various points so by all means feel free to explore them, but don't worry

Table 3.2 Overview of the icons in R for Windows

Icon	Description	Console	Editor	Graphics
	This icon gives you the option to open a previously saved file.	✓	✓	
	Clicking this button opens a dialog box that enables you to load a workspace file (see section 3.4).	✓		
	This icon enables you to save files. It will save the file you are currently working on (be it the console screen or a script file). If the file hasn't already been saved the *Save Data As* dialog box will appear.	✓	✓	
	Clicking this button copies anything selected in the console window to the clipboard.	✓		
	Clicking this button pastes the contents of the Windows clipboard to the console window.	✓		
	Clicking this button copies anything selected in the console window to the clipboard and automatically pastes it into the command line (useful for rerunning earlier commands).	✓		
	Clicking this button stops the **R** processor from whatever it is doing (if you have started **R** on a task, gone and made the dinner and returned to find it still chugging away trying to finish, then you might need to click this button and have a rethink).	✓		
	This icon activates a dialog box for printing whatever you are currently working on (what is printed depends on which window is active).	✓	✓	✓
	In the editor window clicking this button will run a line of code or a block of selected code. It's quicker to use the keyboard though (see section 3.4).		✓	
	Clicking this button returns the focus to the console widow.		✓	✓
	Clicking this button copies the contents of the graphics window to the clipboard as a Windows metafile.			✓

too much at this stage about what specific menu options do. As well as the menus there is a set of *icons* at the top of both the editor and console windows, which provide shortcuts to specific facilities. All of these facilities can be accessed via the menu system or by typing commands, but using the icons can save you time. Table 3.4 overviews of these icons and their functions.

Table 3.3 Overview of the menus in R for MacOS

Menu
File: This menu allows you to do general things such as saving scripts or graphs. Likewise, you can open previously saved files and print graphs, data or output. In essence, it contains all of the options that are customarily found in *File* menus.
Edit: This menu contains edit functions such as *cut* and *paste*. From here you can also clear the console (i.e., remove all of the text from it), execute commands, find a particular bit of text and so on.
Format: This menu lets you change the text styles used (colour, font, etc.).
Workspace: This menu enables you to save the workspace (i.e., analysis output – see section 3.4), load an old workspace or browse your recent workspace files.
Packages & Data: This menu is very important because it is where you load, install and update packages.
Misc: This menu enables you to set or change the working directory. The working directory is the default location where **R** will search for and save files (see section 3.4.4).
Window: If you have multiple windows, this menu allows you to change how the windows in **R** are arranged.
Help: This is an invaluable menu because it offers you a searchable repository of help and frequently asked questions.

3.4. Using R ①

3.4.1. Commands, objects and functions ①

I have already said that **R** uses 'commands' that are typed into the console window. As such, unlike other data analysis packages with which you might be familiar (e.g., SPSS, SAS), there are no friendly dialog boxes that you can activate to run analyses. Instead, everything you want to do has to be typed into the console (or executed from a script file). This might sound like about as much fun as having one of the living dead slowly chewing on your brain, but there are advantages to working in this way: although there is a steep initial learning curve, after time it becomes very quick to run analyses.

Commands in **R** are generally made up of two parts: **objects** and **functions**. These are separated by '<-', which you can think of as meaning 'is created from'. As such, the general form of a command is:

```
Object<-function
```

Which means 'object is created from function'. An object is anything created in **R**. It could be a variable, a collection of variables, a statistical model, etc. Objects can be single values (such as the mean of a set of scores) or collections of information; for example, when you run an analysis, you create an object that contains the output of that analysis, which means that this object contains many different values and variables. Functions are the things that you do in **R** to create your objects. In the console, to execute a command you simply type it into the console and press the return key. (You can put more than one command on a single line if you prefer – see R's Souls' Tip 3.2)

Table 3.4   Overview of the icons in R for MacOS

Icon	Description	Console	Editor
	Clicking this button stops the **R** processor from whatever it is doing.	✓	
	Clicking this button opens a dialog box that enables you to select a previously saved script or data file.	✓	
	Clicking this button opens a new graphics (quartz) window.	✓	
	Clicking this button opens the X11 window; X11 is a device that some **R** packages use.	✓	
	Clicking this button opens a dialog box into which you can enter your system password. This will enable **R** to run system commands. Frankly, I have never touched this button and I suspect it is to be used only by people who actually know what they're doing.	✓	
	Clicking this button activates a sidebar on the console window that lists all of your recently executed commands.	✓	
	Clicking this button opens the *Preferences* dialog box, from which you can change the console colours (amongst other things).	✓	
	Clicking this button opens a dialog box from which you can select and open a previously saved script file. This file will open in the editor window.	✓	
	Clicking this button opens a new editor window in which you can create a new script file.	✓	
	This icon activates a dialog box for printing whatever you are currently working on (what is printed depends on which window is active).	✓	✓
	Clicking this button saves the script file that you're working on. If you have not already saved the file, clicking this button activates a *Save As …* dialog box.		✓
	Clicking this button quits **R**.	✓	

Figure 3.5 shows a very simple example in which we have created an object called 'metallica', which is made up of the four band members' (pre 2001) names. The function used is the *concatenate function* or **c()**, which groups things together. As such, we have written each band member's name (in speech marks and separated by commas), and by enclosing them in *c()* we bind them into a single entity or object, which we have called 'metallica'. If we type this command into the console then when we hit the return key on the keyboard the object that we have called 'metallica' is created. This object is stored in memory so we can refer back to it in future commands. Throughout this book, we denote commands entered into the command line in this way:

R's Souls' Tip 3.2 Running multiple commands at once①

The command line format of **R** tends to make you think that you have to run commands one at a time. Even if you use the **R** editor it is tempting to put different commands on a new line. There's nothing wrong with doing this, and it can make it easier to decipher your commands if you go back to a long script months after you wrote it. However, it can be useful to run several commands in a single line. Separating them with a semicolon does this. For example, the two commands:

```
metallica<-metallica[metallica != "Jason"]

metallica<-c(metallica, "Rob")
```

can be run in a single line by using a semicolon to separate them:

```
metallica<-metallica[metallica != "Jason"]; metallica<-c(metallica, "Rob")
```

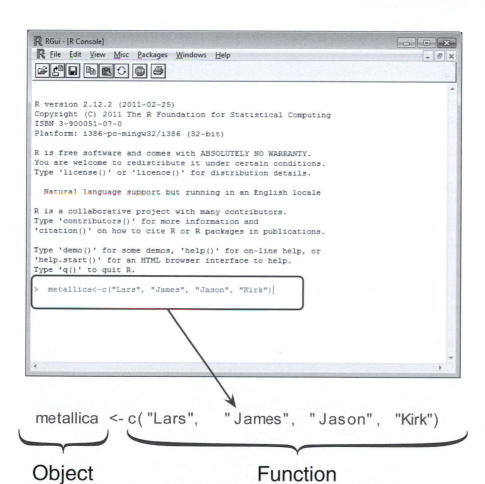

FIGURE 3.5
Using the command line in **R**

```
metallica<-c("Lars","James","Jason","Kirk")
```

Now we have created an object called 'metallica' we can do things with it. First, we can have a look at its contents by typing 'metallica' (or 'print(metallica)' works too) into the command line and hitting the return key:

```
metallica
```

The contents of the object 'metallica' will be displayed in the console window. Throughout the book we display output as follows:

```
[1] "Lars" "James" "Jason" "Kirk"
```

Note that **R** has printed into the console the contents of the object 'metallica', and the contents are simply the four band members' names. You need to be very careful when you type commands and create objects in **R**, because it is case sensitive (see R's Souls' Tip 3.3).

R's Souls' Tip 3.3   R is case sensitive ①

R is case sensitive, which means that if the same things are written in upper or lower case, **R** thinks that they are completely different things. For example, we created a variable called **metallica**; if we asked to see the contents of **Metallica** (note the capital M), **R** would tell us that this object didn't exist. If we wanted to completely confuse ourselves we could actually create a variable called **Metallica** (with a capital M) and put different data into it than in the variable **metallica** (with a small m), and **R** would have no problem with us doing so. As far as **R** is concerned, **metallica** and **Metallica** are as different to each other as variables called **earwax** and **doseOfBellendium**.

This case sensitivity can create problems if you don't pay attention. Functions are generally lower case so you just need to avoid accidentally using capitals, but every so often you find a function that has a capital letter (such as *as.Date()* used in this chapter) and you need to make sure you have typed it correctly. For example, if you want to use the function *data.frame()* but type *data.Frame()* or *Data.Frame()* you will get an error. If you get an error, check that you have typed any functions or variable names exactly as they should be.

We can do other things with our newly created object too. The Metallica fans amongst you will probably be furious at me for listing the pre 2001 line up of the band. In 2001 bassist Jason Newstead left the band and was replaced by Rob Trujillo. Even as I type, there are hoards of Metallica fans with precognition about the contents of this book queuing outside my house and they have dubbed me unforgiven. Personally I'm a big fan of Rob Trujillo, he's given the band a solid kick up the backside, and so let's put him in his rightful place in the band. We currently have a 'metallica' object that contains Jason. First we can change our object to eject Jason (harsh, I know). To get rid of Jason in **R** we can use this command:

```
metallica<-metallica[metallica != "Jason"]
```

This just means that we're re-creating the object 'metallica', the '<-' means that 'we're creating it from' and our function is *metallica[metallica != "Jason"]* which means 'use the object metallica, but get rid of (!=) Jason'. A simple line of text and Jason is gone, which was probably a lot less hassle than his actual ousting from the band. If only Lars and James had come to me for advice. If we have a look at our 'metallica' object now we'll see that it contains only three names. We can do this by simply typing 'metallica' and hitting the return key. Below shows the command and the output:

```
metallica
```

```
[1] "Lars" "James" "Kirk"
```

Now let's add Rob Trujillo to the band. To do this we can again create an object called 'metallica' (which will overwrite our previous object), and we can use the concatenate command to take the old 'metallica' object and add "Rob" to it. The command looks like this:

```
metallica<-c(metallica, "Rob")
```

If we execute this command (by pressing return) and again look at the contents of 'metallica' we will see that Rob has been added to the band:

```
metallica
```

```
[1] "Lars" "James" "Kirk" "Rob"
```

SELF-TEST

✓ Create an object that represents your favourite band (unless it's Metallica, in which case use your second favourite band) and that contains the names of each band member. If you don't have a favourite band, then create an object called *friends* that contains the names of your five best friends.

3.4.2. Using scripts ①

Although you can execute commands from the console, I think it is better to write commands in the **R** editor and execute them from there. A document of commands written in the **R** editor is known as a **script**. There are several advantages to this way of working. First, at the end of your session you can save the script file, which can be reloaded in the future if you need to re-create your analysis. Rerunning analyses, therefore, becomes a matter of loading a file and hitting a few buttons – it will take less than 10 seconds. Often in life you need to run analyses that are quite similar to ones that you have run before; if you have a repository of scripts then it becomes fairly quick to create new ones by editing an existing one or cutting and pasting commands from existing scripts and then editing the variable names. Personally I find that using old scripts to create new ones speeds things up a lot, but this could be because I'm pretty hopeless at remembering how to do things in **R**. Finally, I often mess things up and run commands that throw error messages back in my face; if these commands are written directly into the console then you have to rewrite the whole command (or cut and paste the wrong command and edit it), whereas if you ran the command from the editor window then you can edit the command directly without having to cut and paste it (or rewrite it), and execute it. Again, it's a small saving in time, but these savings add up until eventually the savings outweigh the actual time you're spending doing the task and then time starts to run backwards. I was 56 when I started writing this book, but thanks to using the editor window in **R** I am now 37.

FIGURE 3.6
Executing commands from the **R** editor window

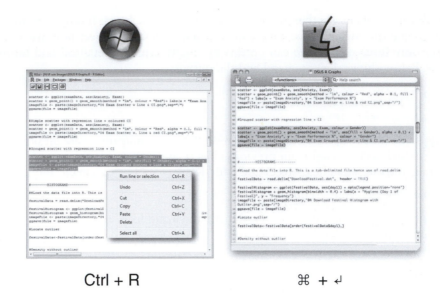

Ctrl + R   ⌘ + ↵

Figure 3.6 shows how to execute commands from the editor window. Assuming you have written some commands, all you need to do is to place the cursor in the line containing the command that you want to execute, or if you want to execute many commands in one go then highlight a block of commands by dragging over them while holding down the left mouse button. Once your commands are highlighted, you can execute them in one of several ways.

In Windows, you have a plethora of choices: you can (1) click on ▣; (2) click the right mouse button while in the editor window to activate a menu, then click with the left mouse button on the top option which is to run the command (see Figure 3.6); (3) go through the main menus by selecting **Edit⇒Run line or selection**; or (4) press and hold down the *Ctrl* key, and while holding it down press and release the letter *R* on the keyboard (this is by far the quickest option). In the book we notate pressing a key while another is held down as 'hold + press', for example *Ctrl + R* means press the *R* key while holding down the *Ctrl* key.

In MacOS you can run the highlighted commands, or the current line, through the menus by selecting **Edit⇒Execute**, but as with Windows the keyboard shortcut is much quicker: press and hold down the *cmd* key (⌘), and while holding it down press and release the return key (↵). In case you skipped the previous paragraph, we will notate pressing a key while another is held down as 'hold + press', for example ⌘ + ↵ means press the ↵ key while holding down the ⌘.

You'll notice that the commands appear in the console window as they are executed, along with any consequences of those commands (for example, if one of your commands asks to view an object the contents will be printed in the console just the same as if you had typed the command directly into the console).

3.4.3. The R workspace ①

As you work on a given data set or analysis, you will create many objects, all of which are stored in memory. The collection of objects and things you have created in a session is known as your **workspace**. When you quit **R** it will ask you if you want to save your current workspace. If you choose to save the workspace then you are saving the contents of the console window and any objects that have been created. The file is known as an **R** image and is saved in a file with .RData at the end. You can save the workspace at any time using the **File⇒Save Workspace ...** menu in **Windows** or in MacOS make sure you are in the console window and select **File⇒Save As ....**

3.4.4. Setting a working directory ②

By default, when you try to do anything (e.g., open a file) from **R** it will go to the directory in which the program is stored on your computer. This is fine if you happen to store all of your data and output in that folder, but it is highly unlikely that you do. If you don't then every time you want to load or save a file you will find yourself wasting time using the menus to navigate around your computer to try to find files, and you will probably lose track of things you save because they have been dumped in **R**'s home folder. You will also end up having to specify the exact file path for every file you save/access. For example, assuming that you're using Windows, your user name is 'Andy F' (because you've stolen my identity), you have a folder in your main documents folder called 'Data' and within that you have another folder called 'R Book Examples', then if you want to access this folder (to save or load a file) you'd have to use this file path:

C:/Users/Andy F/Documents/Data/R Book Examples

So, to load a file called **data.dat** from this location you would need to execute the following command:

```
myData = read.delim("C:/Users/Andy F/Documents/Data/R Book Examples/data.dat")
```

Don't worry about what this command means (we'll get to that in due course), I just want you to notice that it is going to get pretty tedious to keep typing 'C:/Users/Andy F/Documents/Data/R Book Examples' every time you want to load or save something.

If you use **R** as much as I do then all this time typing locations has two consequences: (1) all those seconds have added up and I have probably spent weeks typing file paths when I could have been doing something useful like playing my drum kit; (2) I have increased my chances of getting RSI in my wrists, and if I'm going to get RSI in my wrists I can think of more enjoyable ways to achieve it than typing file paths (drumming again, obviously).

The best piece of advice I can give you is to establish a **working directory** at the beginning of your **R** session. This is a directory in which you want to store your data files, any scripts associated with the analysis or your workspace. Basically, anything to do with a session. To begin with, create this folder (in the usual way in Windows or MacOS) and place the data files you'll be using in that folder. Then, when you start your session in **R** change the working directory to be the folder that you have just created. Let's assume again that you're me (Andy F), that you have a folder in 'My Documents' called 'Data' and within that you have created a folder called 'R Book Examples' in which you have placed some data files that you want to analyse. To set the working directory to be this folder, we use the **setwd()** command to specify this newly created folder as the working directory:

setwd("C:/Users/Andy F/Documents/Data/R Book Examples")

By executing this command, we can now access files in that folder directly without having to reference the full file path. For example, if we wanted to load our **data.dat** file again, we can now execute this command:

myData = read.delim("data.dat")

Compare this command with the one we wrote earlier; it is much shorter because we can now specify only the file name safe in the knowledge that **R** will automatically try to find the file in 'C:/Users/Andy F/Documents/Data/R Book Examples'. If you want to check what the working directory is then execute this command:

```
getwd()
```

Executing this command will display the current working directory in the console window.[2]

In MacOS you can do much the same thing except that you won't have a C drive. Assuming you are likely to work in your main user directory, the easiest thing to do is to use the ' ~ ' symbol, which is a shorthand for your user directory. So, if we use the same file path as we did for Windows, we can specify this as:

```
setwd("~/Documents/Data/R Book Examples")
```

The ~ specifies the MacOS equivalent of 'C:/Users/Andy F'. Alternatively, you can navigate to the directory that you want to use using the **Misc⇒Change Working Directory** menu path (or ⌘ + D).

Throughout the book I am going to assume that for each chapter you have stored the data files somewhere that makes sense to you and that you have set this folder to be your working directory. If you do not do this then you'll find that commands that load and save files will not work.

3.4.5.   Installing packages ①

Earlier on I mentioned that **R** comes with some base functions ready for you to use. However, to get the most out of it we need to install packages that enable us to do particular things. For example, in the next chapter we look at graphs, and to create the graphs in that chapter we use a package called *ggplot2*. This package does not come pre-installed in **R** so to work through the next chapter we would have to install *ggplot2* so that **R** can access its functions.

You can install packages in two ways: through the menus or using a command. If you know the package that you want to install then the simplest way is to execute this command:

```
install.packages("package.name")
```

in which 'package.name' is replaced by the name of the package that you'd like installed. For example, we have (hopefully) written a package containing some functions that are used in the book. This package is called DSUR, therefore, to install it we would execute:

```
install.packages("DSUR")
```

Note that the name of the package must be enclosed in speech marks.

Once a package is installed you need to reference it for **R** to know that you're using it. *You need to install the package only once[3] but you need to reference it each time you start a new session of R*. To reference a package, we simply execute this general command:

```
library(package.name)
```

---

[2] In Windows, the filepaths can also be specified using '\\' to indicate directories, so that "C:/Users/Andy F/Documents/Data/R Book Examples" is exactly the same as "C: \\Users\\Andy F\\Documents\\Data\\R Book Examples". **R** tends to return filepaths in the '\\' form, but will accept it if you specify them using '/'. Try not to be confused by these two different formats. MacOS users don't have these tribulations.

[3] This isn't strictly true: if you upgrade to a new version of **R** you will have to reinstall all of your packages again.

in which 'package.name' is replaced by the name of the package that you'd like to use. Again, if we want to use the *DSUR* package we would execute:

`library(DSUR)`

Note that in this command the name of the package *is not* enclosed in speech marks.

Alternatively you can manage packages through the menu system. Figure 3.7 overviews the menus for managing packages. In Windows if you select **Packages⇒Install package(s)…** a window will open that first asks you to select a CRAN. Having selected the CRAN nearest to you from the list and clicked on ⌷ OK ⌷, a new dialog box will open that lists all of the available packages. Click on the one or ones that you want (you can select several by holding down the *Ctrl* key as you click) and then click on ⌷ OK ⌷. This will have the same effect as using the *install.packages()* command. You can load packages by selecting **Packages⇒Load package…**, which opens a dialog box with all of the available packages that you could load. Select the one(s) you want to load and then click on ⌷ OK ⌷. This has the same effect as the *library()* command.

In MacOS if you select **Packages & Data⇒Package Installer** a window will open. Click on ⌷ Get List ⌷ and a list of all the available packages appears. Click on the one or ones that you want (you can select several by holding down the ⌘ key as you click) and then click on

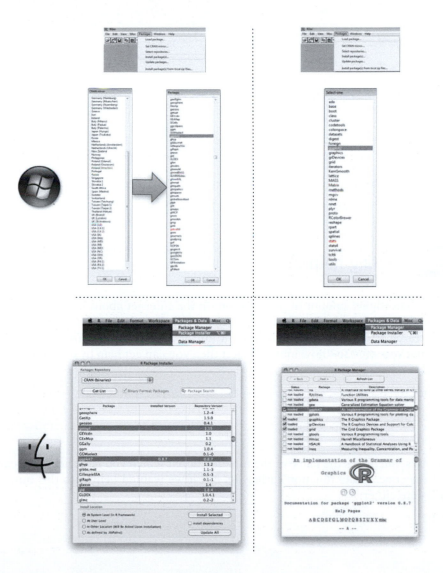

FIGURE 3.7
Installing and loading packages through the menus in **R**

(Install Selected). This will have the same effect as using the *install.packages()* command. You can load packages by selecting **Packages & Data⇒Package Manager**, which opens a dialog box with all of the available packages that you could load. Click on the tick boxes next to the one(s) you want to load. This has the same effect as the *library()* command.

One entertaining (by which I mean annoying) consequence of any Tom, Dick or Harriet being able to contribute packages to **R** is that you sometimes encounter useful functions that have the same name as different functions in different packages. For example, there is a *recode()* function that exists in both the *Hmisc* and *car* packages. Therefore, if you have both of these packages loaded you will need to tell **R** which particular recode function you want to use (see R's Souls' Tip 3.4).

R's Souls' Tip 3.4   Disambiguating functions ①

Occasionally you might stumble across two functions in two different packages that have the same name. For example, there is a *recode()* function in both the *Hmisc* and *car* packages. If you have both packages loaded and you try to use *recode()*, **R** won't know which one to use or will have a guess (perhaps incorrectly). This situation is easy to rectify: you can specify the package when you use the function as follows:

```
package::function()
```

For example, if we want to use the *recode()* function in the *car* package we would write:

```
car::recode()
```

but to use the one in *Hmisc* we would write:

```
Hmisc::recode()
```

Here is an example where we recode a variable using *recode()* from the *car* package:

```
variableName <-car::recode(variableName, "2=0;0=2")
```

3.4.6.   Getting help ①

There is an enormous amount of information on the Internet about using **R**, and I generally find that if I get stuck I can find help with a quick Google (or whatever search engine you use) search. However, there is help built into **R** as well. If you are using a particular function and you want to know more about it then you can get help by executing the **help()** command:

```
help(function)
```

or by executing:

```
?function
```

In both cases *function* is the name of the function about which you need help. For example, we used the concatenate function earlier on, *c()*, if we wanted help with this function we could execute either:

```
help(c)
```

or

```
?c
```

These commands open a new window with the help documentation for that function. Be aware that the help files are active only if you have loaded the package to which the function belongs. Therefore, if you try to use help but the help files are not found, check that you have loaded the relevant package with the *library()* command.

3.5. Getting data into R ①

3.5.1. Creating variables ①

You can enter data directly into R. As we saw earlier on, you can use the *c()* function to create objects that contain data. The example we used was a collection of names, but you can do much the same with numbers. Earlier we created an object containing the names of the four members of metallica. Let's do this again, but this time call the object *metallicaNames*. We can create this object by executing the following command:

```
metallicaNames<-c("Lars","James","Kirk","Rob")
```

We now have an object called *metallicaNames* containing the band members' names. When we create objects it is important to name them in a meaningful way and you should put some thought into the names that you choose (see R's Souls' Tip 3.7).

Let's say we wanted another object containing the ages of each band member. At the time of writing, their ages are 47, 47, 48 and 46, respectively. We can create a new object called *metallicaAges* in the same way as before, by executing:

```
metallicaAges<-c(47, 47, 48, 46)
```

Notice that when we specified names we placed the names in quotes, but when we entered their ages we did not. The quotes tell **R** that the data are not numeric. Variables that consist of data that are text are known as **string variables**. Variables that contain data that are numbers are known as **numeric variables**. **R** and its associated packages tend to be able to treat data fairly intelligently. In other words, we don't need to tell **R** that a variable is numeric or not, it sort of works it out for itself – most of the time at least. However, string values should always be placed in quotes, and numeric values are never placed in quotes (unless you want them to be treated as text rather than numbers).

3.5.2. Creating dataframes ①

We currently have two separate objects: *metallicaNames* and *metallicaAges*. Wouldn't it be nice to combine them into a single object? We can do this by creating a **dataframe**. You can think of a dataframe as a spreadsheet (so, like the contents of the data editor in SPSS, or a worksheet in Excel). It is an object containing variables. There are other ways to combine variables in **R** but dataframes are the way we will most commonly use because of their versatility (R's Souls' Tip 3.5). If we want to combine *metallicaNames* and *metallicaAges* into a dataframe we can use the **data.frame()** function:

```
metallica<-data.frame(Name = metallicaNames, Age = metallicaAges)
```

In this command we create a new object (called *metallica*) and we create it from the function *data.frame()*. The text within the *data.frame()* command tells **R** how to build the dataframe. First it tells **R** to create an object called 'Name', which is equal to the existing object *metallicaNames*. Then it tells **R** to create an object called 'Age', which is equal to the existing object *metallicaAges*. We can look at the contents of the dataframe by executing:

```
metallica
```

You will see the following displayed in the console:

```
Name Age

1 Lars    47
2 James   47
3 Kirk    48
4 Rob     46
```

As such, our dataframe consists of two variables (**Name** and **Age**), the first is the band member's name, and the second is their age. Now that the dataframe has been created we can refer to these variables at any point using the general form:

```
dataframe$variableName
```

For example, if we wanted to use the ages of metallica, we could refer to this variable as:

```
metallica$Age
```

similarly, if we want the **Name** variable we could use:

```
metallica$Name
```

Let's add a new variable that contains the age of each member's eldest child; we will call this variable **childAge**. According to an Internet search, James's (Cali) and Lars's (Myles) eldest children were both born in 1998, Kirk's (Angel) was born in 2006 and Rob's (Tye-Orion) in 2004. At the time of writing, this makes them 12, 12, 4 and 6, respectively. We can add this variable using the *c()* function as follows:

```
metallica$childAge<-c(12, 12, 4, 6)
```

This command is fairly straightforward: *metallica$childAge* simply creates the variable **childAge** in the pre-existing dataframe *metallica*. As always the '<-' means 'create from', then the *c()* function allows us to collect together the numbers representing each member's eldest child's age (in the appropriate order).

We can look at the contents of the dataframe by executing:

```
metallica
```

You will see the following displayed in the console:

```
  Name Age childAge

1 Lars    47       12
2 James   47       12
3 Kirk    48        4
4 Rob     46        6
```

Notice that the new variable has been added.

Sometimes, especially with large dataframes, it can be useful to list the variables in the dataframe. This can be done using the **names()** function. You simply specify the name of the dataframe within the brackets; so, if we want to list the variables in the *metallica* dataframe, we would execute:

```
names(metallica)
```

The output will be a list of the variable names in the dataframe:

```
[1] "Name"      "Age"        "childAge"
```

In this case, **R** lists the names of the three variables in the dataframe.

R's Souls' Tip 3.5   The list() and cbind() functions ①

Dataframes are not the only way to combine variables in **R**: throughout the book you will find us using the *list()* and *cbind()* functions to combine variables. The *list()* function creates a list of separate objects; you can imagine it as though it is your handbag (or manbag) but nicely organized. Your handbag contains lots of different objects: lipstick, phone, iPod, pen, etc. Those objects can be different, but that doesn't stop them being collected into the same bag. The *list()* function creates a sort of bag into which you can place objects that you have created in **R**. However, it's a well-organized bag and so objects that you place in it are given a number to indicate whether they are the first, second etc. object in the bag. For example, if we executed these commands:

```
metallica<-list(metallicaNames, metallicaAges)
```

instead of the *data.frame()* function from the chapter, we would create a **R**-like handbag called *metallica* that looks like this:

```
[[1]]
[1] "Lars"  "James" "Kirk"  "Rob"
[[2]]
[1] 47 47 48 46
```

Object [1] in the bag is the list of names, and object [2] in the bag is the list of ages.

The function *cbind()* is used simply for pasting columns of data together (you can also use *rbind()* to combine rows of data together). For example, if we execute:

```
metallica<-cbind(metallicaNames, metallicaAges)
```

instead of the *data.frame()* function from the chapter, we would create a matrix called *metallica* that looks like this:

```
     metallicaNames metallicaAges
[1,] "Lars"         "47"
[2,] "James"        "47"
[3,] "Kirk"         "48"
[4,] "Rob"          "46"
```

Notice that the end result is that the two variables have been pasted together as different columns in the same object. However, notice that the numbers are in quotes; this is because the variable containing names is text, so it causes the ages to be text as well. For this reason, *cbind()* is most useful for combining variables of the same type.

In general, dataframes are a versatile way to store variables: unlike *cbind()*, *data.frame()* stores variables of different types together (trivia note: *cbind()* works by using the *data.frame()* function so they're basically the same). Therefore, we tend to work with dataframes; however, we will use *list()* sometimes because some functions like to work with lists of variables, and we will sometimes use *cbind()* as a quick method for combining numeric variables.

3.5.3.   Calculating new variables from exisiting ones ①

Although we're not going to get into it too much here (but see Chapter 5), we can also use arithmetic and logical operators to create new variables from existing ones. Table 3.5 overviews some of the basic operators that are used in **R**. As you can see, there are many operations with which you will be familiar (but see R's Souls' Tip 3.6) that you can use on variables: you can add them (using +), subtract them (using −), divide them (using /), and multiply them (using *). We will encounter these and the others in the table as we progress through the book. For now, though, we will look at a simple example to give you a sense that dataframes are versatile frameworks for storing and manipulating data.

Table 3.5   Some of main operators that can be used in R

Operator	What it does
+	Adds things together
−	Subtracts things
*	Multiplies things
/	Divides things
^ or **	Exponentiation (i.e., to the power of, so, x^2 or x**2 is x^2, x^3 is x^3 and so on)
<	Less than
<=	Less than or equal to
>	Greater than
>=	Greater than or equal to
==	Exactly equals to (this might confuse you because you'll be used to using '=' as the symbol for 'equals', but in **R** you usually use '==')
!=	Not equal to
!x	Not x
x | y	x OR y (e.g., name == "Lars"|"James" means 'the variable name is equal to either Lars or James')
x & y	x AND y (e.g., age == 47 & name == "James" means 'the variable age is equal to 47 and the variable name is equal to James')
isTRUE(x)	Test if x is TRUE

R's Souls' Tip 3.6 Equals signs ①

A common cause of errors in **R** is that you will have spent your whole life using the symbol '=' when you want to say 'equals'. For example, you'll all be familiar with the idea that age = 37 is interpreted as 'age equals 37'. However, in a transparent attempt to wilfully confuse us, **R** uses the symbol '==' instead. At first, you might find that if you get error messages it is because you have used '=' when you should have used '=='. It's worth checking your command to see whether you have inadvertently let everything you have ever learnt about equals signs get the better of you.

If we wanted to find out how old (roughly) each band member was when he had their first child, then we can subtract his eldest child's age from his current age. We can store this information in a new variable (**fatherhoodAge**). We would create this new variable as follows:

```
metallica$fatherhoodAge<- metallica$Age – metallica$childAge
```

This command is again straightforward: *metallica$fatherhoodAge* simply creates the variable called **fatherhoodAge** in the existing dataframe (*metallica*). The '<-' means 'create from', then follows the instructions about how to create it; we ask that the new variable is the child's age (which is the variable **childAge** in the *metallica* data set, referred to as *metallica$childAge*) subtracted from (−) the member's age (*metallica$Age*). Again, if we look at the dataframe by executing

```
metallica
```

we see that a new variable has been created containing the age of each band member when they had their first child. We can see from this that James and Lars were both 35 years old, Kirk was 44 and Rob was 40.

```
  Name Age childAge fatherhoodAge
1 Lars   47       12            35
2 James  47       12            35
3 Kirk   48        4            44
4 Rob    46        6            40
```

R's Souls' Tip 3.7   Naming variables ①

There are conventions about naming variables and objects in **R**. Unfortunately these conventions sometimes contradict each other. For example, the Google style guide for **R** recommends that 'Variable names should have all lower case letters and words separated with dots (.)'. So, for example, if you had a variable representing children's anxiety levels you might name it **child.anxiety** but should not name it **child_anxiety** and definitely not **Child_Anxiety**. However, Hadley (see the second URL at the end of this tip) recommends 'Variable names … should be lowercase. Use _ to separate words within a name. … Strive for concise but meaningful names'. In which case, **child_anxiety** would be fine.

I tend to use an old programming convention of capitalizing all but the first word. So, I would name the variable **childAnxiety**, which waves its buttocks at the aforementioned conventions. I also sometimes use underscores … that's just the kind of rebellious guy I am.

The one thing that we can all agree on is that variable names should be meaningful and concise. This skill can take some time and effort to perfect, and I can imagine that you might think that it is a waste of your time. However, as you go through your course accumulating script files, you will be grateful that you did. Imagine you had a variable called 'number of times I wanted to shoot myself during Andy Field's statistics lecture'; then you might have called the variable 'shoot'. All of your analysis and output will simply refer to 'shoot'. That's all well and good, but what happens in three weeks' time when you look at your analysis again? The chances are that you'll probably think 'What did shoot stand for? Number of shots at goal? Number of shots I drank?' Imagine the chaos you could get into if you had used an acronym for the variable 'workers attending news kiosk'. Get into a good habit and spend a bit of time naming objects in **R** in a meaningful way. The aforementioned style guides might also help you to become more consistent than I am in your approach to naming:

- http://google-styleguide.googlecode.com/svn/trunk/google-r-style.html
- https://github.com/hadley/devtools/wiki/Style

3.5.4.   Organizing your data ①

When inputting a new set of data, you must do so in a logical way. The most logical way (and consistent with other packages like SPSS and SAS) that we usually use is known as the **wide format**. In the wide format *each row represents data from one entity while each column represents a variable*. There is no discrimination between independent and dependent variables: both types should be placed in a separate column. The key point is that each row represents one entity's data (be that entity a human, mouse, tulip, business, or water sample). Therefore, any information about that case should be entered across the data editor. For example, imagine you were interested in sex differences in perceptions of pain created by hot and cold stimuli. You could place some people's hands in a bucket of very cold water for a minute and ask them to rate how painful they thought the experience was on a scale of 1 to 10. You could then ask them to hold a hot potato and again measure their perception of pain. Imagine I was a participant. You would have a single row representing my data, so there would be a different column for my name, my gender, my pain perception for cold water and my pain perception for a hot potato: Andy, male, 7, 10.

The column with the information about my gender is a grouping variable (also known as a **factor**): I can belong to either the group of males or the group of females, but not both. As such, this variable is a between-group variable (different entities belong to different groups). Rather than representing groups with words, **R** uses numbers and words. This involves assigning each group a number, and a label that descibes the group. Therefore, between-group variables are represented by a single column in which the group to which the person belonged is defined using a number and label (see section 3.5.4.3). For example, we might decide that if a person is male then we give them the number 0, and if they're female we give them the number 1. We then have to tell **R** that every time it sees a 1 in a particular column the person is a female, and every time it sees a 0 the person is a male. Variables that specify to which of several groups a person belongs can be used to split up data files (so in the pain example you could run an analysis on the male and female participants separately – see section 5.5.3).

Finally, the two measures of pain are a repeated measure (all participants were subjected to hot and cold stimuli). Therefore, levels of this variable (see R's Souls' Tip 3.8) can be entered in separate columns (one for pain perception for a hot stimulus and one for pain perception for a cold stimulus).

R's Souls' Tip 3.8 Entering data ①

There is a simple rule for how variables are typically arranged in an **R** dataframe: data from different things go in different rows of the dataframe, whereas data from the same things go in different columns of the dataframe. As such, each person (or mollusc, goat, organization, or whatever you have measured) is represented in a different row. Data within each person (or mollusc, etc.) go in different columns. So, if you've prodded your mollusc, or human, several times with a pencil and measured how much it twitches as an outcome, then each prod will be represented by a column.

In experimental research this means that any variable measured with the same participants (a repeated measure) should be represented by several columns (each column representing one level of the repeated-measures variable). However, any variable that defines different groups of things (such as when a between-group design is used and different participants are assigned to different levels of the independent variable) is defined using a single column. This idea will become clearer as you learn about how to carry out specific procedures. (This golden rule is not as golden as it seems at first glance – often data need to be arranged in a different format – but it's a good place to start and it's reasonable easy to rearrange a dataframe – see section 3.9.)

Imagine we were interested in looking at the differences between lecturers and students. We took a random sample of five psychology lecturers from the University of Sussex and five psychology students and then measured how many friends they had, their weekly

Table 3.6 Some data with which to play

Name	Birth Date	Job	No. of Friends	Alcohol (units)	Income (p.a.)	Neuroticism
Ben	03-Jul-1977	Lecturer	5	10	20,000	10
Martin	24-May-1969	Lecturer	2	15	40,000	17
Andy	21-Jun-1973	Lecturer	0	20	35,000	14
Paul	16-Jul-1970	Lecturer	4	5	22,000	13
Graham	10-Oct-1949	Lecturer	1	30	50,000	21
Carina	05-Nov-1983	Student	10	25	5,000	7
Karina	08-Oct-1987	Student	12	20	100	13
Doug	16-Sep-1989	Student	15	16	3,000	9
Mark	20-May-1973	Student	12	17	10,000	14
Zoë	12-Nov-1984	Student	17	18	10	13

alcohol consumption (in units), their yearly income and how neurotic they were (higher score is more neurotic). These data are in Table 3.6.

3.5.4.1. Creating a string variable ①

The first variable in our data set is the name of the lecturer/student. This variable consists of names; therefore, it is a *string variable*. We have seen how to create string variables already: we use the *c()* function and list all values in quotations so that **R** knows that it is string data. As such, we can create a variable called **name** as follows:

```
name<-c("Ben", "Martin", "Andy", "Paul", "Graham", "Carina", "Karina", "Doug", "Mark", "Zoe")
```

We do not need to specify the level at which this variable was measured (see section 1.5.1.2) because **R** will automatically treat it as *nominal* because it is a string variable, and therefore represents only names of cases and provides no information about the order of cases, or the magnitude of one case compared to another.

3.5.4.2. Creating a date variable ①

Notice that the second column in our table contains dates (birth dates, to be exact). To enter **date variables** into **R** we use much the same procedure as with a string variable, except that we need to use a particular format, and we need to tell **R** that the data are dates if we want to do any date-related computations. We can convert dates written as text into date objects using the **as.Date()** function. This function takes strings of text, and converts them into dates; this is important if you want to do things like subtract dates from one another. For example, if you want to work out how old someone was when you tested him or her, you could take the date on which they were tested and subtract from it the date they were born. If you have not converted these objects from strings to date objects this subtraction won't work (see R's Souls' Tip 3.9).

R's Souls' Tip 3.9 Dates ①

If you want to do calculations involving dates then you need to tell **R** to treat a variable as a date object. Let's look at what happens if we don't. Imagine two variables (**husband** and **wife**) that contain the birthdates of four men and their respective wives. We might create these variables and enter these birthdates as follows:

```
husband<-c("1973-06-21", "1970-07-16", "1949-10-08", "1969-05-24")
```

```
wife<-c("1984-11-12", "1973-08-02", "1948-11-11", "1983-07-23")
```

If we want to now calculate the age gap between these partners, then we could create a new variable, **agegap**, which is the difference between the two variables (husband − wife):

```
agegap <- husband-wife
```

We'd find this rather disappointing message in the console:

```
Error in husband - wife : non-numeric argument to binary operator
```

This message is **R**'s way of saying 'What the hell are trying to get me to do? These are words; I can't subtract letters from each other.'

However, if we use the *as.Date()* function when we create the variables then **R** knows that the strings of text are dates:

```
husband<-as.Date(c("1973-06-21", "1970-07-16", "1949-10-08", "1969-05-24"))
```

```
wife<-as.Date(c("1984-11-12", "1973-08-02", "1948-11-11", "1983-07-23"))
```

If we try again to calculate the difference between the two variables:

```
agegap <- husband-wife
```

```
agegap
```

we get a more sensible output:

```
Time differences in days
```

```
[1] -4162 -1113   331 -5173
```

This output tells us that in the first couple the wife is 4162 days younger than her husband (about 11 years), for the third couple the wife is 331 days older (just under a year).

The *as.Date()* function is placed around the function that we would normally use to enter a series of strings. Normally if we enter strings we use the form:

```
variable<-c("string 1", "string 2", "string 3", etc.)
```

For dates, these strings need to be in the form yyyy-mm-dd. In other words, if we want to enter the date 21 June 1973, then we would enter it as "1973-06-21". As such, we could create a variable called **birth_date** containing the dates of birth by executing the following command:

```
birth_date<-as.Date(c("1977-07-03", "1969-05-24", "1973-06-21", "1970-07-16",
"1949-10-10", "1983-11-05", "1987-10-08", "1989-09-16", "1973-05-20",
"1984-11-12"))
```

Note that we have entered each date as a text string (in quotations) in the appropriate format (yyyy-mm-dd). By enclosing these data in the *as.Date()* function, these strings are converted to date objects.

3.5.4.3. Creating coding variables/factors ①

A coding variable (also known as a grouping variable or factor) is a variable that uses numbers to represent different groups of data. As such, it is a *numeric variable*, but these numbers represent names (i.e., it is a nominal variable). These groups of data could be levels of a treatment variable in an experiment, different groups of people (men or women, an experimental group or a control group, ethnic groups, etc.), different geographic locations, different organizations, etc.

In experiments, coding variables represent independent variables that have been measured between groups (i.e., different participants were assigned to different groups). If you were to run an experiment with one group of participants in an experimental condition and a different group of participants in a control group, you might assign the experimental group a code of 1 and the control group a code of 0. When you come to put the data into **R** you would create a variable (which you might call **group**) and type in the value 1 for any participants in the experimental group, and 0 for any participant in the control group. These codes tell **R** that all of the cases that have been assigned the value 1 should be treated as belonging to the same group, and likewise for the cases assigned the value 0. In situations other than experiments, you might simply use codes to distinguish naturally occurring groups of people (e.g., you might give students a code of 1 and lecturers a code of 0). These codes are completely arbitrary; for the sake of convention people typically use 0, 1, 2, 3, etc., but in practice you could have a code of 495 if you were feeling particularly arbitrary.

We have a coding variable in our data: the one describing whether a person was a lecturer or student. To create this coding variable, we follow the steps for creating a normal variable, but we also have to tell **R** that the variable is a coding variable/factor and which numeric codes have been assigned to which groups.

First, we can enter the data and then worry about turning these data into a coding variable. In our data we have five lecturers (who we will code with 1) and five students (who we will code with 2). As such, we need to enter a series of 1s and 2s into our new variable, which we'll call **job**. The way the data are laid out in Table 3.6 we have the five lecturers followed by the five students, so we can enter the data as:

```
job<-c(1,1,1,1,1,2,2,2,2,2)
```

In situations like this, in which all cases in the same group are grouped together in the data file, we could do the same thing more quickly using the **rep()** function. This function takes the general form of *rep(number to repeat, how many repetitions)*. As such, *rep(1, 5)* will repeat the number 1 five times. Therefore, we could generate our **job** variable as follows:

```
job<-c(rep(1, 5),rep(2, 5))
```

Whichever method you use the end results is the same:

```
job
```

```
[1] 1 1 1 1 1 2 2 2 2 2
```

To turn this variable into a factor, we use the **factor()** function. This function takes the general form:

```
factor(variable, levels = c(x,y, … z), labels = c("label1", "label2", …
"label3"))
```

This looks a bit scary, but it's not too bad really. Let's break it down: *factor(variableName)* is all you really need to create the factor – in our case *factor(job)* would do the trick. However, we need to tell **R** which values we have used to denote different groups and we do this with *levels = c(1,2,3,4, …)*; as usual we use the *c()* function to list the values we have used. If we have used a regular series such as 1, 2, 3, 4 we can abbreviate this as *c(1:4)*, where the colon simply means 'all the values between'; so, *c(1:4)* is the same as *c(1,2,3,4)* and *c(0:6)* is the same as *c(0,1,2,3,4,5,6)*. In our case, we used 1 and 2 to denote the two groups, so we could specify this as *c(1:2)* or *c(1,2)*. The final step is to assign labels to these levels using *labels = c("label", …)*. Again, we use *c()* to list the labels that we wish to assign. You must list these labels in the same order as your numeric levels, and you need to make sure you have provided a label for each level. In our case, 1 corresponds to lecturers and 2 to students, so we would want to specify labels of "Lecturer" and "Student". As such, we could write *levels = c("Lecturers", "Students")*. If we put all of this together we get this command, which we can execute to transform **job** into a coding variable:

```
job<-factor(job, levels = c(1:2), labels = c("Lecturer", "Student"))
```

Having converted **job** to a factor, **R** will treat it as a nominal variable. A final way to generate factors is to use the *gl()* function – the 'gl' stands for general (factor) levels. This function takes the general form:

```
newFactor<-gl(number of levels, cases in each level, total cases, labels = c("label1", "label2"…))
```

which creates a factor variable called *newFactor*; you specify the number of levels or groups of the factor, how many cases are in each level/group, optionally the total number of cases (the default is to multiply the number of groups by the number of cases per group), and you can also use the *labels* option to list names for each level/group. We could generate the variable job as follows:

```
job<-gl(2, 5, labels = c("Lecturer", "Student"))
```

The end result is a fully-fledged coding variable (or factor):

```
[1] Lecturer Lecturer Lecturer Lecturer Lecturer Student Student Student
Student Student
```

   With any factor variable you can see the factor levels and their order by using the **levels()** function, in which you enter the name of the factor. So, to see the levels of our variable **job** we could execute:

```
levels(job)
```

which will produce this output:

```
[1] "Lecturer" "Student"
```

In other words, we know that the variable job has two levels and they are (in this order) *Lecturer* and *Student*. We can also use this function to set the levels of a variable. For example, imagine we wanted these levels to be called *Medical Lecturer* and *Medical Student*, we could execute:

```
levels(job)<-c("Medical Lecturer", "Medical Student")
```

This command will rename the levels associated with the variable job (note, the new names are entered as text with speech marks, and are wrapped up in the *c()* function). You can also use this function to reorder the levels of a factor – see R's Souls' Tip 3.13.

   This example should clarify why in experimental research grouping variables are used for variables that have been measured between participants: because by using a coding variable it is impossible for a participant to belong to more than one group. This situation should occur in a between-group design (i.e., a participant should not be tested in both the experimental and the control group). However, in repeated-measures designs (within subjects) each participant is tested in every condition and so we would not use this sort of coding variable (because each participant does take part in every experimental condition)

3.5.4.4.   Creating a numeric variable ①

Numeric variables are the easiest ones to create and we have already created several of these already in this chapter. Our next four variables are **friends, alcohol, income** and **neurotic**. These are all numeric variables and you can use what you have learnt so far to create them (I hope!).

SELF-TEST

✓ Use what you have learnt about creating variables in **R** to create variables called **friends**, **alcohol**, **income** and **neurotic** containing the data in Table 3.6.

Hopefully you have tried out the exercise, and if so you should have executed the following commands:

```
friends<-c(5,2,0,4,1,10,12,15,12,17)

alcohol<-c(10,15,20,5,30,25,20,16,17,18)

income<-c(20000,40000,35000,22000,50000,5000,100,3000,10000,10)

neurotic<-c(10,17,14,13,21,7,13,9,14,13)
```

SELF-TEST

✓ Having created the variables in Table 3.6, construct a dataframe containing them all called *lecturerData*.

Having created the individual variables we can bind these together in a dataframe. We do this by executing this command:

```
lecturerData<-data.frame(name,birth_date,job,friends,alcohol,income,
neurotic)
```

If we look at the contents of this dataframe you should hopefully see the same as Table 3.6:

```
> lecturerData
```

	name	birth_date	job	friends	alcohol	income	neurotic
1	Ben	1977-07-03	Lecturer	5	10	20000	10
2	Martin	1969-05-24	Lecturer	2	15	40000	17
3	Andy	1973-06-21	Lecturer	0	20	35000	14
4	Paul	1970-07-16	Lecturer	4	5	22000	13
5	Graham	1949-10-10	Lecturer	1	30	50000	21
6	Carina	1983-11-05	Student	10	25	5000	7
7	Karina	1987-10-08	Student	12	20	100	13
8	Doug	1989-09-16	Student	15	16	3000	9
9	Mark	1973-05-20	Student	12	17	10000	14
10	Zoe	1984-11-12	Student	17	18	10	13

3.5.5. Missing values ①

Although as researchers we strive to collect complete sets of data, it is often the case that we have missing data. Missing data can occur for a variety of reasons: in long questionnaires participants accidentally (or, depending on how paranoid you're feeling, deliberately just to annoy you) miss out questions; in experimental procedures mechanical faults can lead to a datum not being recorded; and in research on delicate topics (e.g., sexual behaviour) participants may exert their right not to answer a question. However, just because we have missed out on some data for a participant doesn't mean that we have to ignore the data we do have (although it sometimes creates statistical difficulties). Nevertheless, we do need to tell **R** that a value is missing for a particular case. The principle behind missing values is quite similar to that of coding variables in that we use a code to represent the missing data point. In **R**, the code we use is NA (in capital letters), which stands for 'not available'. As such, imagine that participants 3 and 10 had not completed their neuroticism questionnaire, then we could have recorded their missing data as follows when we created the variable:

```
neurotic<-c(10,17,NA,13,21,7,13,9,14,NA)
```

Note that if you have missing values then you sometimes need to tell functions in **R** to ignore them (see R's Souls' Tip 3.10).

R's Souls' Tip 3.10 Missing values and functions ①

Many functions include a command that tells **R** how to deal with missing values. For example, many functions include the command *na.rm = TRUE*, which means remove the NA values before doing the computation. For example, the function *mean()* returns the mean of a variable, so that

```
mean(metallica$childAge)
```

will give us the mean age of Metallica's eldest children. However, if we have missing data we can include the command *na.rm = TRUE* to tell **R** to ignore missing values before computing the mean:

```
mean(metallica$childAge, na.rm = TRUE)
```

This function is covered in more detail in Chapter 5. For now, just appreciate that individual functions often have commands for dealing with missing values and that we will try to flag these as we go along.

3.6. Entering data with R Commander ①

It is also possible to do some basic data editing (and analysis) using a package called *Rcmdr* (short for R Commander). This package loads a windows style interface for basic data manipulation and analysis. This tool is very useful for novices or people who are freaked out by typing commands. It is particularly useful for making minor changes to dataframes. To install and load *Rcmdr*, use the menus (see section 3.4.5) or execute these commands:

```
install.packages("Rcmdr", dependencies = TRUE)
```

```
library(Rcmdr)
```

It is important that you remember the capital 'R' in 'Rcmdr' (R's Souls' Tip 3.3). Note that when we install it we specify *dependencies = TRUE*. When a package uses other packages, these are known as dependencies (because the package depends upon them to work). *Rcmdr* is a windows interface for using lots of different functions, therefore, it relies on a lot of other packages. If we don't install all of these packages as well, then much of the functionality of *Rcmdr* will be lost. By setting *dependencies = TRUE* we install not just *Rcmdr* but also all of the other packages upon which it relies (because it uses a lot, installing it can take a few minutes).[4]

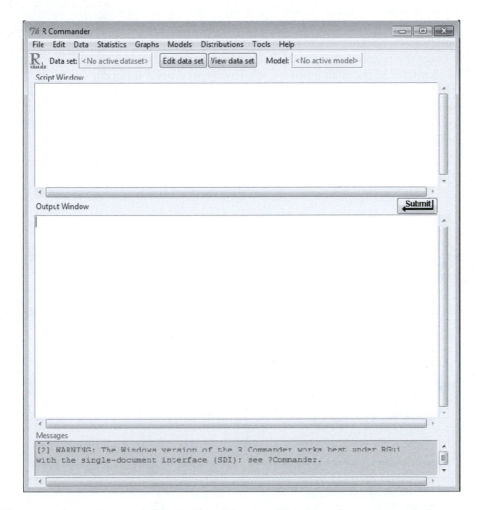

FIGURE 3.8
The main window of R Commander

When you have executed *library(Rcmdr)* you will notice that a new window appears (Figure 3.8). This window has a lot of new menus that you can access to do various things (such as edit data or run basic analyses). These menus offer a windows-based interface for running functions within different packages. We think that as you gain experience with **R** you will prefer to use commands, but for some commonly used analyses we will show you how to use R Commander to get you started. The menu structure is basically identical on Windows and MacOS.

---

[4] If you have installed other packages then it's possible that *Rcmdr* has been installed by one of them; nevertheless, it is worth installing it yourself and including the setting *dependencies = TRUE* to ensure that all of the packages upon which *Rcmdr* depends are installed also.

3.6.1.   Creating variables and entering data with R Commander ①

One particularly useful feature of R Commander is that it offers a basic spreadsheet style interface for entering data (i.e., like Excel). As such, we can enter data in a way that is probably already familiar to us. To create a new dataframe select **Data⇒New data set…**, which opens a dialog box that enables you to name the dataframe (Figure 3.9). For the lecturer data let's stick with the name *lecturerData*; enter this name into the box labelled *Enter name for data set* and then click on ⬚ OK ⬚. A spreadsheet style window will open. You can create variables by clicking at the top of a column, which opens a dialog box into which you can enter the name of the variable, and whether the variable is numeric or text/string (labelled *character* in the dialog box). Each row represents a different entity and, having named the variables, you can enter the relevant information for each entry – as shown for the current data in Figure 3.9. To save the data simply close this window. (You cannot create a new data set in this way in MacOS; however, you can edit an existing dataframe by selecting **Data⇒Load data set….**)

FIGURE 3.9
Entering data using R Commander

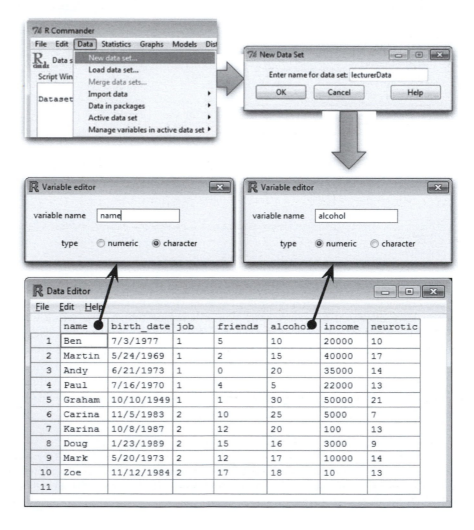

3.6.2. Creating coding variables with R Commander ①

The variable **job** represents different groups of people so we need to convert this variable to a factor or coding variable. We saw how to do this in section 3.5.4.3 using the *factor()* function. We can do the same in R Commander by selecting the **Data⇒Manage variables in active data set⇒Convert numeric variables to factors…** menu. This activates a dialog box with a list of the variables in your data set on the left (Figure 3.10). Select the variable that you want to convert (in this case **job**). If you want to create the coding variable as a new variable in your dataframe then type a name for this new variable in the space labelled *New variable name or prefix for multiple variables:* otherwise leave this space blank (as I have in the figure) and it will overwrite the existing variable. If you want to type some labels for the levels of your coding variable (generally I would recommend that you do) then select Supply level names ⊙ and click on OK. A new dialog box will open with spaces in which you can type the labels associated with each level of your coding variables. As you can see, in Figure 3.10 I have typed in 'Lecturer' and 'Student' next to the numbers that represent them in the variable **job**. When you have added these levels click on OK and **job** will be converted to a factor.

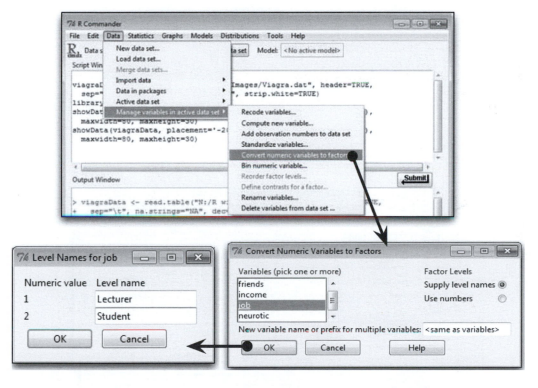

FIGURE 3.10
Creating a coding variable using R Commander

3.7. Using other software to enter and edit data ①

Although you can enter data directly into **R**, if you have a large complicated data set then the chances are that you'll want to use a different piece of software that has a spreadsheet style window into which you can enter data. We will assume in this section that you are going to use Microsoft Excel, because it is widely available and, therefore, it's more likely that you have it on your computer than specialist packages such as SPSS and SAS. If you want to know how to enter data into SPSS and SAS then please consult my other books (Field, 2009; Field & Miles, 2010). If you do not have Excel then OpenOffice is an excellent free alternative for both MacOS and Windows (http://www.openoffice.org/).

OLIVER TWISTED

Please, Sir, can I have some more … SPSS?

'Secret Party for Statistics Slaves?' froths Oliver as he drowns in a puddle of his own saliva. No, Oliver, it's a statistics package. 'Bleagehammm' splutters Oliver as his excitement grows into a rabid frenzy. If you would like to know how to set up data files in SPSS then there is an excerpt from my other book on the companion website.

To enter data you will typically use the wide format so you should apply the same rule as we have already mentioned in this chapter: *each row represents data from one entity while each column represents a variable or levels of a variable*. In Figure 3.11 I have entered the

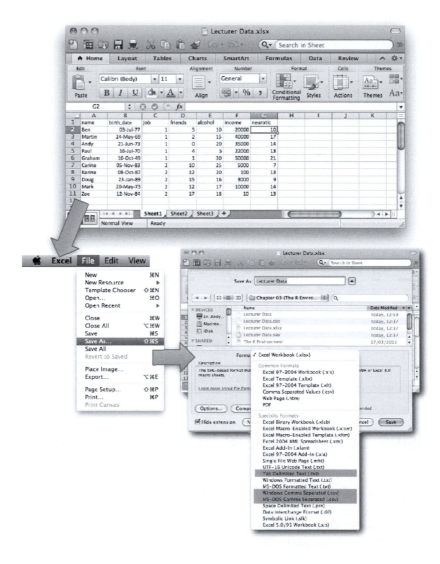

FIGURE 3.11
Laying out wide format data in Excel and exporting to an **R**-friendly format

lecturer data in Excel in this format. Notice that each person is represented by a row in the spreadsheet, whereas each variable is represented as a column. Notice also that I have entered the values for **job** as numbers rather than text. In Excel we could have entered 'Lecturer' and 'Student' rather than the values of 1 and 2. **R** will have imported this variable as a string variable in this case, rather than as a numeric variable. Often **R** will treat these sorts of string variables intelligently (i.e., in this case it would realize that this variable is a factor or coding variable and treat it accordingly), but it can be useful not to assume that **R** will do what you think it will and explicitly define variables as factors once the data have been imported.

3.7.1. Importing data ①

Once your data are entered into Excel, OpenOffice, SPSS or whatever, we need a way to get the data file into a dataframe in **R**. The usual way to do this is to export the file from Excel/SPSS etc. in a format that **R** can import; however, the **foreign** package can be used to import directly data files from SPSS (*.sav*), STATA (*.dta*), *Systat* (*.sys*, *.syd*), Minitab (*.mtp*), and SAS (*XPORT* files). It is probably the safest (in terms of knowing that what you're actually importing is what you think you're importing), to export from your software of choice into an **R**-friendly format.

The two most commonly used **R**-friendly formats are tab-delimited text (*.txt* in Excel and *.dat* in SPSS) and comma-separated values (*.csv*). Both are essentially plain text files (see R's Souls' Tip 3.11). It is very easy to export these types of files from Excel and other software packages. Figure 3.11 shows the process. Once the data are entered in the desired format, simply use the ▣ S̲ave As... menus to open the *Save A̲s...* dialog box. Select the location in which you'd like the file to be saved (a sensible choice is the working directory that you have set in **R**). By default, Excel will try to save the file as an Excel file (*.xlsx* or *.xls*); however, we can change the format by clicking on the drop-down list labelled *Save as t̲ype* (*Format* on MacOS). The drop-down list contains a variety of file types, but the two that are best for **R** are *Text (Tab delimited)* and *CSV (Comma delimited)*. Select one of these file types, type a name for your file and click on ▢ S̲ave... ▢. The end result will be either a *.txt* file or a *.csv* file. The process for exporting data from SPSS (and other packages) is much the same.

If we have saved the data as a CSV file, then we can import these data to a dataframe using the *read.csv* function. The general form of this function is:

```
dataframe.name<-read.csv("filename.extension", header = TRUE)
```

Let's imagine we had stored our lecturer data in a CSV file called **Lecturer Data.csv** (you can find this file on the companion website). To load these data into a dataframe we could execute the following command:

```
lecturerData = read.csv("C:/Users/Andy F/Documents/Data/R Book Examples/Lecturer
Data.csv", header = TRUE)
```

This command will create a dataframe called *lecturerData* based on the file called 'Lecturer Data.csv' which is stored in the location 'C:/Users/Andy F/Documents/Data/R Book Examples/'.[5] I urged you in section 3.4.4 to set up a working directory that relates to the location of your files for the current session. If we executed this command:[6]

---

[5] For MacOS users the equivalent command would be
```
lecturerData = read.csv("~/Documents/Data/R Book Examples/Lecturer Data.csv",
header = TRUE)
```

[6] On a Mac the equivalent command would be
```
setwd("~/Documents/Data/R Book Examples")
```

R's Souls' Tip 3.11 CSV and tab-delimited file formats ①

Comma-separated values (CSV) and tab-delimited file formats are really common ways to save data. Most software that deals with numbers will recognize these formats, and when exporting and importing data it is wise to chose one of them. The beauty of these formats is that they store the data as plain text, without any additional nonsense that might confuse a particular piece of software. The formats differ only in which character is used to separate different values (CSV uses a comma, tab-delimited uses a tab space). If we think back to our Metallica data, this would be stored in a tab-delimited file as:

```
Name Age childAge fatherhoodAge
Lars   47  12   35
James  47  12   35
Kirk   48  4    44
Rob    46  6    40
```

Notice that each piece of data is separated by a tab space. In a CSV file, the data would look like this:

```
Name,Age,childAge,fatherhoodAge
Lars,47,12,35
James,47,12,35
Kirk,48,4,44
Rob,46,6,40
```

The information is exactly the same as the tab-delimited file, except that a comma instead of a tab separates each value. When a piece of software (R, Excel, SPSS, etc.) reads the file like this into a spreadsheet, it knows (although sometimes you have to tell it) that when it 'sees' a comma or a tab it simply places the next value in a different column than the previous one.

```
Setwd("C:/Users/Andy F/Documents/Data/R Book Examples")
```

then we could access the file by executing this less cumbersome command:

```
lecturerData<-read.csv("Lecturer Data.csv", header = TRUE)
```

The *header = TRUE* in the command tells **R** that the data file has variable names in the first row of the file (if you have saved the file without variable names then you should use *header = FALSE*). If you're really struggling with the concept of file paths, which would be perfectly understandable, then see R's Souls' Tip 3.12.

Let's look at the data:

```
> lecturerData
      name birth_date  job friends alcohol income  neurotic
1  Ben     03-Jul-77    1     5      10    20000    10
2  Martin  24-May-69    1     2      15    40000    17
3  Andy    21-Jun-73    1     0      20    35000    14
4  Paul    16-Jul-70    1     4       5    22000    13
5  Graham  10-Oct-49    1     1      30    50000    21
6  Carina  05-Nov-83    2    10      25     5000     7
7  Karina  08-Oct-87    2    12      20      100    13
8  Doug    23-Jan-89    2    15      16     3000     9
9  Mark    20-May-73    2    12      17    10000    14
10 Zoe     12-Nov-84    2    17      18       10    13
```

Note that the dates have been imported as strings, and the **job** variable contains numbers. So that **R** knows that this variable is a factor we would have to convert it using the *factor()* function.

SELF-TEST

✓ Using what you have learnt about how to use the *factor()* function, see if you can work out how to convert the **job** variable to a factor.

Similarly, if you had saved the file as a tab-delimited text file from Excel (**Lecturer Data.txt**) or SPSS (**Lecturer Data.dat**), you could use the *read.delim()* function to import these files. This function takes the same form as the *read.csv()* function, except that you specify a tab-delimited file. Assuming you had set your working directory correctly, we would execute:

```
lecturerData<-read.delim("Lecturer Data.dat", header = TRUE)
lecturerData<-read.delim("Lecturer Data.txt", header = TRUE)
```

Typically we provide data files for chapters as *.dat* files, so you will use the *read.delim()* function a lot.

R's Souls' Tip 3.12 The file.choose() function ①

Some people really struggle with the idea of specifying file locations in **R**. This confusion isn't a reason to be ashamed; most of us have spent our lives selecting files through dialog boxes rather than typing horribly long strings of text. Although if you set your working directory and manage your files I think the process of locating files becomes manageable, if you really can't get to grips with that way of working the alternative is to use the *choose. file()* function. Executing this function opens a standard dialog box allowing you to navigate to the file you want.

You can incorporate this function into *read.csv()* and *read.delim()* as follows:

```
lecturerData<-read.csv(file.choose(), header = TRUE)
lecturerData<-read.delim(file.choose(), header = TRUE)
```

The effect that this has is that when you execute the command, a dialog box will appear and you can select the file that you want to import.

3.7.2. Importing SPSS data files directly ①

You can also import directly from SPSS data files (and other popular packages). To give you some practice, we have provided the data as a *.sav* file (**Lecturer Data.sav**). First we need to install and load the package called *foreign* either using the menus (see section 3.4.5) or by executing these commands:

```
install.packages("foreign")
```
```
library(foreign)
```

The command to read in SPSS data files is *read.spss()* and it works in a similar way to the other import functions that we have already seen; however, there are a couple of extra things that we need to think about. First, let's just execute the command to import our SPSS data file:

```
lecturerData<-read.spss("Lecturer Data.sav",use.value.labels=TRUE, to.data.
frame=TRUE)
```

The basic format is the same as before: we have created a dataframe called *lecturerData*, and we have done this from the file named **Lecturer Data.sav**. There are two additional instructions that we have used, the first is *use.value.labels = TRUE*. This command tells **R** that if a variable is set up as a factor or coding variable in SPSS then it should be imported as a factor. If you set this value to FALSE, then it is imported as a numeric variable (in this case you would get a variable containing 1s and 2s). The second command is *to.data.frame=TRUE*, which self-evidently tells **R** to import the file as a dataframe. Without this command (or if it is set to FALSE), you get lots of horrible junk imported and nobody likes junk. Let's have a look at the dataframe:

```
> lecturerData
      name      birth_date      job    friends alcohol income neurotic
1   Ben       12456115200 Lecturer       5      10    20000      10
2   Martin    12200198400 Lecturer       2      15    40000      17
3   Andy      12328848000 Lecturer       0      20    35000      14
4   Paul      12236313600 Lecturer       4       5    22000      13
5   Graham    11581056000 Lecturer       1      30    50000      21
6   Carina    12656217600  Student      10      25     5000       7
7   Karina    12780028800  Student      12      20      100      13
8   Doug      12820896000  Student      15      16     3000       9
9   Mark      12326083200  Student      12      17    10000      14
10  Zoe       12688444800  Student      17      18       10      13
```

Two things to note: first, unlike when we imported the CSV file, **job** has been imported as a factor rather than a numeric variable (this is because we used the *use.value.labels = TRUE* command). Importing this variable as a factor saves us having to convert it in a separate command as we did for the CSV command. Second, the dates look weird. In fact, they look very weird. They barely even resemble dates. Unfortunately, the explanation for this is a little complicated and involves the way in which **R** stores dates (dates are stored as days relative to 1 January 1970 – don't ask me why). What has happened is that **R** has actually been clever in noticing that **birth_date** was set up in SPSS as a date variable. Therefore, it has converted it into its own time format. To convert it back to a form that we can actually understand we need to execute this command:

```
lecturerData$birth_date<-as.Date(as.POSIXct(lecturerData$birth_date,
origin="1582-10-14"))
```

This takes the variable **birth_date** from the *lecturerData* dataframe (*lecturerData$birth_date*) and re-creates it as a date variable. Hours poking around the Internet to work out the underlying workings of this command have led me to the conclusion that I should just accept that it works and not question the magic. Anyway, if we execute this command and have another look at the dataframe we find that the dates now appear as sensible dates:

```
> lecturerData
      name    birth_date     job    friends alcohol income neurotic
1   Ben      1977-07-03 Lecturer       5      10   20000      10
2   Martin   1969-05-24 Lecturer       2      15   40000      17
3   Andy     1973-06-21 Lecturer       0      20   35000      14
4   Paul     1970-07-16 Lecturer       4       5   22000      13
5   Graham   1949-10-10 Lecturer       1      30   50000      21
6   Carina   1983-11-05  Student      10      25    5000       7
7   Karina   1987-10-08  Student      12      20     100      13
8   Doug     1989-01-23  Student      15      16    3000       9
9   Mark     1973-05-20  Student      12      17   10000      14
10  Zoe      1984-11-12  Student      17      18      10      13
```

3.7.3. Importing data with R Commander ①

You can access the *read.delim()*, *read.csv()* and *read.spss()* commands through the R Commander interface too. Select **Data⇒Import data** to activate a submenu that enables you open a text file, SPSS, Minitab, STATA or Excel file (Figure 3.12). If you select a text file then a dialog box is opened into which you can place a name for the dataframe (in the box labelled *Enter name for data set:*), select whether variable names are included in the file, and what characters you have used to indicate missing values. By default, it assumes you want to open a file on your computer, and that a white space separates data values. For CSV and tab-delimited files you need to change this default to *Commas* or *Tabs* respectively (you can also specify a non-standard text character). Finally, by default it is assumed that a full stop denotes a decimal point, but in some locations a comma is used: if you live in one of these locations you should again choose the default. Having set these options, click on ⬚ OK ⬚ to open a standard 'open file' dialog box, choose the file you want to open and then click on ⬚ Open ⬚.

Opening an SPSS file is much the same except that there are fewer options (Figure 3.12). The dialog box for importing an SPSS file again asks for a name for the dataframe, but then asks only whether variables that you have set up as coding variables should be converted to factors (see section 3.5.4.3). The default is to say yes (which is the same as specifying *use.value.labels = TRUE*, see section 3.7.2). Again, once you have set these options, click

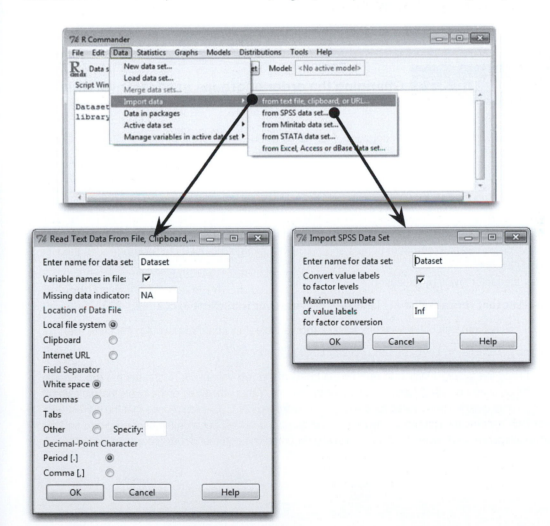

FIGURE 3.12
Importing data with R Commander

on [OK] to open a standard dialog box that enables you to navigate to the file you want to open, select it, and then click on [Open].

3.7.4. Things that can go wrong ①

You can come across problems when importing data into **R**. One common problem is if you have used spaces in your variable names. Programs like SPSS don't allow you to do this, but in Excel there are no such restrictions. One way to save yourself a lot of potential misery is just never to use variable names with spaces. Notice, for example, that for the variable **birth_date** I used an underscore (or 'hard space') to denote the space between the words; other people prefer to use a period (i.e., birth.date). Whatever you choose, avoiding spaces can prevent many import problems.

Another common problem is if you forget to replace missing values with 'NA' in the data file (see section 3.5.5). If you get an error when trying to import, double-check that you have put 'NA' and not left missing values as blank.

Finally, **R** imports variables with text in them intelligently: if different rows have the same text strings in them, **R** assumes that the variable is a factor and creates a factor variable with levels corresponding to the text strings. It orders these levels alphabetically. However, you might want the factor levels in a different order, in which case you need to reorder them – see R's Souls' Tip 3.13.

R's Souls' Tip 3.13 Changing the order of groups in a factor variable ①

Imagine we imported a variable, **job**, that contained information about which of three jobs a person had in a hospital: "Porter", "Nurse", "Surgeon". **R** will order the levels alphabetically, so the resulting factor levels will be:

1. Nurse
2. Porter
3. Surgeon

However, you might want them to be ordered differently. For example, perhaps you consider a porter to be a baseline against which you want to compare nurses and surgeons. It might be useful to have porter as the first level rather than the second.

We can reorder the factor levels by executing:

```
variableName<-factor(variableName, levels = levels(variableName)[c(2, 1, 3)])
```

in which variableName is the name of the variable. For our **job** variable, this command would, therefore, be:

```
job<-factor(job, levels = levels(job)[c(2, 1, 3)])
```

This command uses the *factor()* function to reorder the levels of the **job** variable. It re-creates the **job** variable based on itself, but then uses the *levels()* function to reorder the groups. We put the order of the levels that we'd like in the *c()* function, so in this case we have asked for the levels to be ordered 2, 1, 3, which means that the current second group (*porter*) will become the first group, the current first group (*nurse*) will become the second group and the current third group (*surgeon*) stays as the third group. Having executed this command, our groups will be ordered:

1. Porter
2. Nurse
3. Surgeon

3.8. Saving data ①

Having spent hours typing in data, you might want to save it. As with importing data, you can export data from **R** in a variety of formats. Again, for the sake of flexibility we recommend exporting to tab-delimited text or CSV (see R's Souls' Tip 3.11) because these formats can be imported easily into a variety of different software packages (Excel, SPSS, SAS, STATA, etc.). To save data as a tab-delimited file, we use the *write.table()* command and for a CSV we can use *write.csv()*.

The *write.table()* command takes the general form:

```
write.table(dataframe, "Filename.txt", sep="\t", row.names = FALSE)
```

We replace *dataframe* with the name of the dataframe that we would like to save and "Filename.txt" with the name of the file.[7] The command *sep=""* sets the character to be used to separate data values: whatever you place between the "" will be used to separate data values. As such, if we want to create a CSV file we could write *sep = ","* (which tells **R** to separate values with a comma), but to create a tab-delimited text file we would write *sep = "\t"* (where we have written \t between quotes, which represents the tab key), and we could also create a space-delimited text file by using *sep = " "* (note that there is a space between the quotes). Finally, *row.names = FALSE* just prevents **R** from exporting a column of row numbers (the reason for preventing this is because **R** does not name this column so it throws the variable names out of sync). Earlier on we created a dataframe called *metallica*. To export this dataframe to a tab-delimited text file called **Metallica Data.txt**, we would execute this command:

```
write.table(metallica, "Metallica Data.txt", sep="\t", row.names = FALSE)
```

The *write.csv()* command takes the general form:

```
write.csv(dataframe, "Filename.csv")
```

As you can see, it is much the same as the *write.table()* function. In fact, it is the *write.table()* function but with *sep = ","* as the default.[8] So, to save the metallica dataframe as a CSV file we can execute:

```
write.csv(metallica, "Metallica Data.csv")
```

3.9. Manipulating data ③

3.9.1. Selecting parts of a dataframe ②

Sometimes (especially with large dataframes) you might want to select only a small portion of your data. This could mean choosing particular variables, or selecting particular cases. One way to achieve this goal is to create a new dataframe that contains only the variables or cases that you want. To select cases, we can execute the general command:

```
newDataframe <- oldDataframe[rows, columns]
```

---

[7] Remember that if you have not set a working directory during your session then this filename will need to include the full location information. For example, "C:/Users/Andy F/Documents/Data/R Book Examples/Filename. txt" or "~/Documents/Data/R Book Examples/Filename.txt" in MacOS. Hopefully, it is becoming ever clearer why setting the working directory is a good thing to do.

[8] If you live in certain parts of western Europe, you might want to use *write.csv2()* instead which outputs the file in the format conventional for that part of the world: it uses ';' to separate values, and ',' instead of '.' to represent the decimal point.

This command creates a new dataframe (called *newDataframe*) that contains the specified *rows* and *columns* from the old dataframe (called *oldDataframe*). Let's return to our lecturer data (in the dataframe that we created earlier called *lecturerData*); imagine that we wanted to look only at the variables that reflect some aspect of their personality (for example, alcohol intake, number of friends, and neuroticism). We can create a new dataframe (*lecturerPersonality*) that contains only these three variables by executing this command:

```
lecturerPersonality <- lecturerData[, c("friends", "alcohol", "neurotic")]
```

Note first that we have not specified *rows* (there is nothing before the comma); this means that all rows will be selected. Note also that we have specified *columns* as a list of variables with each variable placed in quotes (be careful to spell them exactly as they are in the original dataframe); because we want several variables, we put them in a list using the *c()* function. If you look at the contents of the new dataframe you'll see that it now contains only the three variables that we specified:

```
> lecturerPersonality
    friends alcohol   neurotic
1         5      10         10
2         2      15         17
3         0      20         14
4         4       5         13
5         1      30         21
6        10      25          7
7        12      20         13
8        15      16          9
9        12      17         14
10       17      18         13
```

Similarly, we can select specific cases of data by specifying an instruction for *rows* in the general function. This is done using a logical argument based on one of the operators listed in Table 3.5. For example, let's imagine that we wanted to keep all of the variables, but look only at the lecturers' data. We could do this by creating a new dataframe (*lecturer Only*) by executing this command:

```
lecturerOnly <- lecturerData[job=="Lecturer",]
```

Note that we have not specified *columns* (there is nothing after the comma); this means that all variables will be selected. However, we have specified *rows* using the condition *job == "Lecturer"*. Remember that the '==' means 'equal to', so we have basically asked **R** to select any rows for which the variable **job** is exactly equal to the word 'Lecturer' (spelt exactly as we have). The new dataframe contains only the lecturers' data:

```
> lecturerOnly
     Name          DoB         job    friends alcohol income   neurotic
1 Ben      1977-07-03 Lecturer         5      10   20000         10
2 Martin   1969-05-24 Lecturer         2      15   40000         17
3 Andy     1973-06-21 Lecturer         0      20   35000         14
4 Paul     1970-07-16 Lecturer         4       5   22000         13
5 Graham   1949-10-10 Lecturer         1      30   50000         21
```

We can be really cunning and specify both rows and columns. Imagine that we wanted to select the personality variables but only for people who drink more than 10 units of alcohol. We could do this by executing:

```
alcoholPersonality <- lecturerData[alcohol > 10, c("friends", "alcohol", "neurotic")]
```

Note that we have specified *rows* using the condition *alcohol > 10*, which means 'select any cases for which the value of the variable **alcohol** is greater than 10. Also, we have specified *columns* as in our original example, *c("friends", "alcohol", "neurotic")*, which means we will select only the three listed variables. You'll see that the new dataframe contains the same data as the *lecturerPersonality* dataframe except that cases 1 and 4 have been dropped because their scores on alcohol were not greater than 10:

```
> alcoholPersonality

    friends alcohol    neurotic
2         2      15          17
3         0      20          14
5         1      30          21
6        10      25           7
7        12      20          13
8        15      16           9
9        12      17          14
10       17      18          13
```

3.9.2.   Selecting data with the subset() function ②

Another way to select parts of your dataframe is to use the **subset()** function. This function takes the general form:

```
newDataframe<-subset(oldDataframe, cases to retain, select = c(list of
variables))
```

Therefore, you create a new dataframe (*newDataframe*) from an exisiting dataframe (*oldDataframe*). As in the previous section, you have to specify a condition that determines which cases are retained. This is usually some kind of logical argument based on one or more of the operators listed in Table 3.5; for example in our *lecturerData* if we wanted to retain cases who drank a lot we could set a condition of *alcohol > 10*, if we wanted neurotic alcoholics we could set a condition of *alcohol > 10 & neurotic > 15*. The *select* command is optional, but can be used to select specific variables from the original dataframe.

Let's re-create a couple of the examples from the previous section but using the *subset()* command. By comparing these commands to the ones in the previous section you can get an idea of the similarity between the methods. First, if we want to select only the lecturers' data we could do this by executing:

```
lecturerOnly <- subset(lecturerData, job=="Lecturer")
```

Second, if we want to select the personality variables but only for people who drink more than 10 units of alcohol we could execute this command:

```
alcoholPersonality <- subset(lecturerData, alcohol > 10, select = c("friends",
"alcohol", "neurotic"))
```

Note that we have specified *rows* using the condition *alcohol > 10*, which means 'select any cases for which the value of the variable **alcohol** is greater than 10'. Also, we have specified *that* we want only the variables **friends**, **alcohol**, and **neurotic** by listing them as part of the *select* command. The resulting *lecturerPersonality* dataframe will be the same as the one in the previous section.

As a final point, it is worth noting that some functions have a *subset()* command within them that allows you to select particular cases of data in much the same way as we have done here (i.e., using logical arguments).

3.9.3.   Dataframes and matrices ②

So far in this chapter we have looked at storing data within dataframes. Dataframes are a useful way to store data because they can contain data of different types (i.e., both numeric and string variables). Sometimes, however, functions in **R** do not work on dataframes – they are designed instead to work on a **matrix**. Frankly, this is a nuisance. Luckily for us we can convert a dataframe to a matrix using the **as.matrix()** function. This function takes the general form:

```
newMatrix <- as.matrix(dataframe)
```

in which *newMatrix* is the matrix that you create, and *dataframe* is the dataframe from which you create it.

   Despite what Hollywood would have you believe, a matrix does not enable you to jump acrobatically through the air, Ninja style, as time seemingly slows so that you can gracefully contort to avoid high-velocity objects. I have worked with matrices many times, and I have never (to my knowledge) stopped time, and would certainly end up in a pool of my own innards if I ever tried to dodge a bullet. The sad reality is that a matrix is just a grid of numbers. In fact, it's a lot like a dataframe. The main difference between a dataframe and a matrix is that a matrix can contain only numeric variables (it cannot contain string variables or dates). As such, we can convert only the numeric bits of a dataframe to a matrix. If you try to convert any string variables or dates, your ears will become turnips. Probably.

   If we want to create a matrix we have to first select only numeric variables. We did this in the previous section when we created the *alcoholPersonality* dataframe. Sticking with this dataframe then, we could convert it to a matrix (which I've called *alcoholPersonalityMatrix*) by executing this command:

```
alcoholPersonalityMatrix <- as.matrix(alcoholPersonality)
```

This command creates a matrix called *alcoholPersonalityMatrix* from the *alcoholPersonality* dataframe. Remember from the previous section that *alcoholPersonality* was originally made up of parts of the *lecturerData* dataframe; it would be equally valid to create the matrix directly from this dataframe but selecting the bits that we want in the matrix just as we did when creating *alcoholPersonality*:

```
alcoholPersonalityMatrix <- as.matrix(lecturerData[alcohol > 10,
c("friends", "alcohol", "neurotic")])
```

Notice that the commands in the brackets are identical to those we used to create *alcoholPersonality* in the previous section.

3.9.4. Reshaping data ③

Once you have typed your data into **R**, Sod's law says you'll discover that it's in the wrong format. Throughout this chapter we have taught you to use the wide format of data entry; however, there is another format known as the **long** or **molten format**. Figure 3.13 shows the difference between wide and long/molten format data. As we have seen, in wide format each person's data is contained in a single row of the data. *Scores on different variables are placed in different columns.* In Figure 3.13, the first participant has a score of 32 on the first

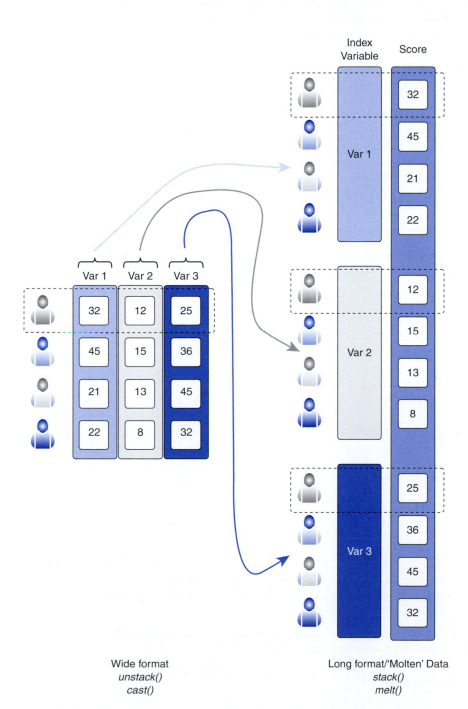

FIGURE 3.13
'Wide' format data places each person's scores on several variables in different columns, whereas 'long format' or 'molten' data places scores for all variables in a single column

variable, a score of 12 in the second variable and a score of 25 on the third. *In long/molten format, scores on different variables are placed in a single column.* It's as though the columns representing the different variables have been 'stacked' on top of each other to make a single column. Notice in the figure that the same scores are present but they are now in a single column. So that we know to what variable a score belongs a new variable has been added (called an *index variable*) that indicates whether the score was from the first, second or third variable. If we look at our first participant again, we can see that his three scores of 32, 12 and 25 are still present, but they are in the same column now; the index variable tells us to which variable the score relates. These formats are quite different, but fortunately there are functions that convert between the two. This final section looks at these functions.

Let's look at an example of people who had their life satisfaction measured at four points in time (if you want to know more about this example, see section 19.7.2). The data are in the file **Honeymoon Period.dat**. Let's first create a dataframe called *satisfactionData* based on this file by executing the following command:

```
satisfactionData = read.delim("Honeymoon Period.dat", header = TRUE)
```

Figure 3.14 shows the contents of this dataframe. The data have been inputted in wide format: each row represents a person. Notice also that four different columns represent the repeated-measures variable of time. However, there might be a situation (such as in Chapter 19), where we need the variable **Time** to be represented by a single column (i.e., in long format). This format is shown in Figure 3.15. To put the hypothetical example in Figure 3.13 into a real context, let's again compare the two data structures.

FIGURE 3.14
The life satisfaction data in 'wide' format'

Person	Satisfaction_Base	Satisfaction_6_Months	Satisfaction_12_Months	Satisfaction_18_Months	Gender
1	6	6	5	2	0
2	7	7	8	4	1
3	4	6	2	2	1
4	6	9	4	1	0
5	6	7	6	6	0
6	5	10	4	2	1
7	6	6	4	2	0
8	2	5	4	NA	0
9	10	9	5	6	0
10	10	10	10	9	0
11	8	8	10	9	0
12	6	10	9	9	0
13	7	8	9	6	1
14	6	7	9	5	0
15	9	10	8	6	1
16	10	10	8	6	1
17	1	2	1	NA	1
18	5	6	7	3	0
19	6	10	10	6	1
20	5	6	NA	NA	0
21	3	7	5	6	0
22	3	4	4	2	1
23	7	6	4	2	0
24	3	4	2	NA	0
25	9	10	8	NA	1

In the wide format (Figure 3.14), each person is represented by a single row of data. Their life satisfaction is represented at four points in time by four columns. In contrast, the long format (Figure 3.15) replaces the four columns representing different time points with two new variables:

R Data Editor

row.names	Person	Gender	variable	value
1	1	0	Satisfaction_Base	6
116	1	0	Satisfaction_6_Months	6
231	1	0	Satisfaction_12_Months	5
346	1	0	Satisfaction_18_Months	2
2	2	1	Satisfaction_Base	7
117	2	1	Satisfaction_6_Months	7
232	2	1	Satisfaction_12_Months	8
347	2	1	Satisfaction_18_Months	4
3	3	1	Satisfaction_Base	4
118	3	1	Satisfaction_6_Months	6
233	3	1	Satisfaction_12_Months	2
348	3	1	Satisfaction_18_Months	2
4	4	0	Satisfaction_Base	6
119	4	0	Satisfaction_6_Months	9
234	4	0	Satisfaction_12_Months	4
349	4	0	Satisfaction_18_Months	1
5	5	0	Satisfaction_Base	6
120	5	0	Satisfaction_6_Months	7
235	5	0	Satisfaction_12_Months	6
350	5	0	Satisfaction_18_Months	6
6	6	1	Satisfaction_Base	5
121	6	1	Satisfaction_6_Months	10
236	6	1	Satisfaction_12_Months	4
351	6	1	Satisfaction_18_Months	2
7	7	0	Satisfaction_Base	6
122	7	0	Satisfaction_6_Months	6
237	7	0	Satisfaction_12_Months	4
352	7	0	Satisfaction_18_Months	2
8	8	0	Satisfaction_Base	2
123	8	0	Satisfaction_6_Months	5
238	8	0	Satisfaction_12_Months	4

FIGURE 3.15 The life satisfaction data in the 'long' or 'molten' form[9]

- **An outcome variable**: This variable contains the scores for each person at each time point. In this case it contains all of the values for life satisfaction that were previously contained in four columns. It is the column labelled 'value' in Figure 3.15.
- **An index variable**: A variable that tells you from which column the data originate. It is the column labelled 'variable' in Figure 3.15. Note that it takes on four values that represent baseline, 6 months, 12 months and 18 months. As such, this variable contains information about the time point to which each life satisfaction score belongs.

Each person's data, therefore, is now represented by four rows (one for each time point) instead of one. Variables such as **Gender** that are invariant over the time points have the same value within each person at each time point; however, our outcome variable (life satisfaction) does vary over the four time points (the four rows for each person).

[9] If you look at your own data then you will probably see something a bit different because your data will be ordered by **variable**. I wanted to show how each person had 4 rows of data so I created a new dataframe *(restructuredData.sorted)* that sorted the data by **Person** rather than **Time**; I did this using: restructuredData.sorted<-restructuredData[order(Person),].

FIGURE 3.16
The satisfaction
data after
running
the stack()
command.

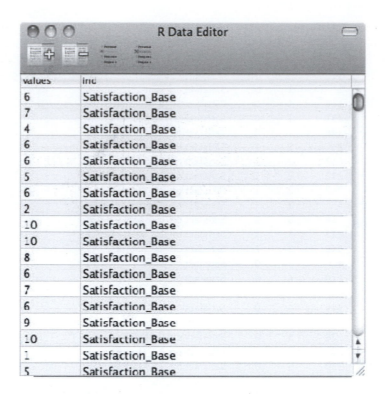

FIGURE 3.16
The satisfaction
data after
running
the stack()
command.

To change between wide and long data formats we can use the **melt()** and **cast()** commands from the *reshape* package, or for simple data sets we can use *stack()* and *unstack()*. Let's look at **stack()** and **unstack()** first. These functions pretty much do what they say on the tin: one of them stacks columns and the other unstacks them. We can use the stack function in the following general form:

```
newDataFrame<-stack(oldDataFrame, select = c(variable list))
```

In short, we create a new dataframe based on an existing one. The *select = c()* is optional, but is a way to select a subset of variables that you want to stack. So, for the current data, we want to stack only the life satisfaction scores (we do not want to stack **Gender** as well). Therefore, we could execute:

```
satisfactionStacked<-stack(satisfactionData,   select   =   c("Satisfaction_
Base",  "Satisfaction_6_Months",  "Satisfaction_12_Months",  "Satisfaction_
18_Months"))
```

This command will create a dataframe called *satisfactionStacked*, which is the variables **Satisfaction_Base, Satisfaction_6_Months, Satisfaction_12_Months,** and **Satisfaction_18_ Months** from the dataframe *satisfactionData* stacked up on top of each other. You can see the result in Figure 3.16 or by executing:

```
satisfactionStacked
```

Notice in Figure 3.16 that the scores for life satisfaction are now stored in a single column (called **values**), and an index variable (called **ind**) has been created that tells us from which column the data originate. If we want to undo our handywork, we can use the *unstack()* function in much the same way:

```
satisfactionUnstacked<-unstack(satisfactionStacked)
```

Executing this command creates a new dataframe called *satisfactionUnstacked* that is based on unstacking the *satisfactionStacked* dataframe. In this case, **R** could make an intelligent guess at how to unstack the data because we'd just used the *stack()* function to create it; however, sometimes you will need to tell **R** how to do the unstacking. In this case, the command takes the following general form:

```
newDataFrame<-unstack(oldDataFrame, scores ~ columns)
```

in which *scores* is the name of the variable containing your scores (for our current dataframe this is **values**) and *columns* is the name of the variable that indicates the variable to which the score belongs (**ind** in the current dataframe). Therefore, to make sure it's going to unstack in the way we want it to, we could fully specify the function as:

R has restructured my brain …

```
satisfactionUnstacked<-unstack(satisfactionStacked, values
~ ind)
```

Note that *values~ind* tells **R** that within the *satisfactionStacked* dataframe, **values** contains the scores to be unstacked, and **ind** indicates the columns into which these scores are unstacked.

The *stack()* and *unstack()* functions are fine for simple operations, but to gain more control over the data restructuring we should use the *reshape* package. To install this package execute:

```
install.packages("reshape")
library(reshape)
```

This package contains two functions: *melt()* for 'melting' wide data into the long format, and *cast()* for 'casting' so-called molten data (i.e., long format) into a new form (in our current context we'll cast it into a wide format, but you can do other things too).

To restructure the *satisfactionData* dataframe we create a new dataframe (which I have unimaginatively called *restructuredData*). This dataframe is based on the existing data (*satisfactionData*), but we use *melt()* to turn it into 'molten' data. This function takes the general form:

```
newDataFrame<-melt(oldDataFrame, id = c(constant variables), measured =
c(variables that change across columns))
```

We will have a look at each option in turn:

- **id**: This option specifies any variables in the dataframe that do not vary over time. For these data we have two variables that don't vary over time, the first is the person's identifier (**Person**), and the second is their gender (**Gender**). We can specify these variables as *id = c("Person", "Gender")*.

- **measured**: This option specifies the variables that do vary over time or are repeated measures (i.e., scores within the same entity). In other words, it specifies the names of variables currently in different columns that you would like to be restructured so that they are in different rows. We have four columns that we want to restructure (**Satisfaction_Base, Satisfaction_6_Months, Satisfaction_12_Months, Satisfaction_18_Months**). These can be specified as: *measured= c ("Satisfaction_Base", "Satisfaction_6_Months", "Satisfaction_12_Months", "Satisfaction_18_Months")*.

If we piece all of these options together, we get the following command:

```
restructuredData<-melt(satisfactionData, id = c("Person", "Gender"), mea-
sured = c("Satisfaction_Base", "Satisfaction_6_Months", "Satisfaction_12_
Months", "Satisfaction_18_Months"))
```

If you execute this command, you should find that your data has been restructured to look like Figure 3.15.

To get data from a molten state into the wide format we use the *cast()* function, which takes the general form:

```
newData<-cast(moltenData, variables coded within a single column ~
variables coded across many columns, value = "outcome variable")
```

This can be quite confusing. Essentially you write a formula that specifies on the left any variables that do not vary within an entity. These are the variables that we specified in the *id* option when we made the data molten. In other words, they are things that do not change (such as name, gender) and that you would enter as a coding variable in the wide format. On the right-hand side of the formula you specify any variable that represents something that changes within the entities in your data set. These are the variables that we specified in the *measured* option when we made the data molten. So these could be measures of the same variable taken at different time points (such as in a repeated-measures or longitudinal design). In other words, this is the variable that you would like to be split across multiple columns in the wide format. The final option, *value*, enables you to specify a variable in the molten data that contains the actual scores. In our current example we have only one outcome variable so we don't need to include this option (**R** will work out which column contains the scores), but it is useful to know about if you have more complicated data sets that you want to restructure.

If we look at the data that we have just melted (*restructuredData*), we have four variables (Figure 3.15):

- **Person**: This variable tells us to which person the data belong. Therefore, this variable does not change within an entity (it identifies them).

- **Gender**: This variable tells us the gender of a person. This variable does not change within an entity (for a given person its value does not change).

- **variable**: This variable identifies different time points at which life satisfaction was measured. As such it does vary within each person (note that each person has four different time points within the column labelled 'variable').

- **value**: This variable contains the life satisfaction scores.

Given that we put variables that don't vary on the left of the formula and those that do on the right, we need to put **Gender** and **Person** on the left, and **variable** on the right; our formula will, therefore, be 'Person + Gender ~ variable'. The variable called **value** contains the scores that we want to restructure, so we can specify this by including the option value = "value" (although note that because we have only one outcome variable we actually don't need this option, I'm including it just so you understand what it does). Our final command will be:

```
wideData<-cast(restructuredData, Person + Gender ~ variable, value = "value")
```

Executing this command creates a new dataframe (*wideData*) that should, hopefully, look a bit like Figure 3.14.

OLIVER TWISTED

Please, Sir, can I have some more … data restructuring?

'Why don't you teach us about *reshape()*?' taunts Oliver. 'Is it because your brain is the size of a grape?' No, Oliver, it's because I think *cast()* and *melt()* are simpler. 'Grape brain, grape brain, grape brain…' sings Oliver as I reach for my earplugs. It is true that there is a *reshape()* function that can be used to restructure data; there is a tutorial on the companion website.

What have I discovered about statistics? ①

This chapter has provided a basic introduction to the **R** environment. We've seen that **R** is free software that you can download from the Internet. People with big brains contribute packages that enable you to carry out different tasks in **R**. They upload these packages to a mystical entity known as the CRAN, and you download them from there into your computer. Once you have installed and loaded a package you can use the functions within it.

We also saw that **R** operates through written commands. When conducting tasks in **R**, you write commands and then execute them (either in the console window, or using a script file). It was noteworthy that we learned that we cannot simply write "**R**, can you analyse my data for me please" but actually have to use specific functions and commands. Along the way, we discovered that **R** will do its best to place obstacles in our way: it will pedantically fail to recognize functions and variables if they are not written exactly as they should be, it will spew out vitriolic error messages if we miss punctuation marks, and it will act aloof and uninterested if we specify incorrectly even the smallest detail. It believes this behaviour to be character building.

You also created your first data set by specifying some variables and inputting some data. In doing so you discovered that we can code groups of people using numbers (coding variables) and discovered that rows in the data represent different entities (or cases of data) and columns represent different variables. Unless of course you use the long format, in which case a completely different set of rules apply. That's OK, though, because we learnt how to transform data from wide to long format. The joy that brought to us can barely be estimated.

We also discovered that I was scared of my new school. However, with the help of Jonathan Land my confidence grew. With this new confidence I began to feel comfortable not just at school but in the world at large. It was time to explore.

R packages used in this chapter

foreign | Rcmdr

R functions used in this chapter

as.Date()	names()
as.matrix()	print()
c()	read.csv()
cast()	read.delim()
choose.file()	read.spss()
data.frame()	recode()
factor()	rep()
getwd()	reshape()
gl()	setwd()
help()	stack()
install.packages()	subset()
levels()	unstack()
library()	write.csv()
mean()	write.table()
melt()	

Key terms that I've discovered

Console window	Numeric variable
CRAN	Package
Dataframe	Object
Date variable	Quartz window
Editor window	script
Factor	String variable
Function	Wide format data
Graphics window	Working directory
Long format data	Workspace
Matrix	

Smart Alex's tasks

- **Task 1**: Smart Alex's first task for this chapter is to save the data that you've entered in this chapter. Save it somewhere on the hard drive of your computer (or a USB stick if you're not working on your own computer). Give it a sensible title and save it somewhere easy to find (perhaps create a folder called 'My Data Files' where you can save all of your files when working through this book).

- **Task 2**: Your second task is to enter the data below. These data show the score (out of 20) for 20 different students, some of whom are male and some female, and some of whom were taught using positive reinforcement (being nice) and others who were taught using punishment (electric shock). Just to make it hard, the data should not be entered in the same way that they are laid out below:

Male		Female	
Electric Shock	**Being Nice**	**Electric Shock**	**Being Nice**
15	10	6	12
14	9	7	10
20	8	5	7
13	8	4	8
13	7	8	13

- **Task 3**: Research has looked at emotional reactions to infidelity and found that men get homicidal and suicidal and women feel undesirable and insecure (Shackelford, LeBlanc, & Drass, 2000). Let's imagine we did some similar research: we took some men and women and got their partners to tell them they had slept with someone else. We then took each person to two shooting galleries and each time gave them a gun and 100 bullets. In one gallery was a human-shaped target with a picture of their own face on it, and in the other was a target with their partner's face on it. They were left alone with each target for 5 minutes and the number of bullets used was measured. The data are below; enter them into **R** and save them as **Infidelity.csv** (clue: they are not entered in the format in the table!).

Male		Female	
Partner's Face	Own Face	Partner's Face	Own Face
69	33	70	97
76	26	74	80
70	10	64	88
76	51	43	100
72	34	51	100
65	28	93	58
82	27	48	95
71	9	51	83
71	33	74	97
75	11	73	89
52	14	41	69
34	46	84	82

Answers can be found on the companion website.

Further reading

There are many good introductory **R** books on the market that go through similar material to this chapter. Here a few:

Crawley, M. (2007). *The R book*. Chichester: Wiley. (A really good and thorough book. You could also try his *Statistics: An Introduction Using R*, published by Wiley in 2005.)

Venables, W. N., & Smith, D. M., and the R Development Core Team (2002). *An introduction to R*. Bristol: Network Theory.

Zuur, A. F., Ieno, E. N., & Meesters, E. H. W. G. (2009) *A beginner's guide to R*. Dordrecht: Springer-Verlag.

There are also many good web resources:

- The main project website: http://www.r-project.org/
- Quick-R, a particular favourite of mine, is an excellent introductory website: http://www.statmethods.net/index.htm
- John Fox's R Commander website: http://socserv.mcmaster.ca/jfox/Misc/Rcmdr/

4 Exploring data with graphs

4.1. What will this chapter tell me? ①

As I got a bit older I used to love exploring. At school they would teach you about maps and how important it was to know where you were going and what you were doing. I used to have a more relaxed view of exploration and there is a little bit of a theme of me wandering off to whatever looked most exciting at the time. I got lost at a holiday camp once when I was about 3 or 4. I remember nothing about this but apparently my parents were frantically running around trying to find me while I was happily entertaining myself (probably by throwing myself head first out of a tree or something). My older brother, who was supposed to be watching me, got a bit of flak for that but he was probably working out equations to bend time and space at the time. He did that a lot when he was 7. The careless explorer in me hasn't really gone away: in new cities I tend to just wander off and hope for the best, and usually get lost and fortunately usually don't die (although I tested my luck once by wandering through part of New Orleans where apparently tourists get mugged a lot – it seemed fine to me). When exploring data you can't afford not to have a map; to explore data in the way that the 6-year-old me used to explore the world is to spin around 8000 times while drunk and then run along the edge of a cliff. Wright (2003) quotes Rosenthal who said that researchers should 'make friends with their data'. This wasn't meant to imply that people who use statistics may as well befriend their data because the data are the only friend they'll have; instead Rosenthal meant that researchers often rush their analysis. Wright makes the analogy of a fine wine: you should savour the bouquet and delicate flavours to truly enjoy the experience. That's perhaps overstating the joys of data analysis, but rushing your analysis is, I suppose, a bit like gulping down a bottle of wine: the outcome is messy and incoherent! To negotiate your way around your data you need a map. Maps of data are called graphs, and it is into this tranquil and tropical ocean that we now dive (with a compass and ample supply of oxygen, obviously).

4.2. The art of presenting data ①

4.2.1. Why do we need graphs ①

Graphs are a really useful way to look at your data before you get to the nitty-gritty of actually analysing them. You might wonder why you should bother drawing graphs – after all, you are probably drooling like a rabid dog to get into the statistics and to discover the answer to your really interesting research question. Graphs are just a waste of your precious time, right? Data analysis is a bit like Internet dating (actually it's not, but bear with me): you can scan through the vital statistics and find a perfect match (good IQ, tall, physically fit, likes arty French films, etc.) and you'll think you have found the perfect answer to your question. However, if you haven't looked at a picture, then you don't really know how to interpret this information – your perfect match might turn out to be Rimibald the Poisonous, King of the Colorado River Toads, who has genetically combined himself with a human to further his plan to start up a lucrative rodent farm (they like to eat small rodents).[1] Data analysis is much the same: inspect your data with a picture, see how it looks and only then think about interpreting the more vital statistics.

Why should I bother with graphs?

4.2.2. What makes a good graph? ①

Before we get down to the nitty-gritty of how to draw graphs in **R**, I want to begin by talking about some general issues when presenting data. **R** (and other packages) make it very easy to produce very snazzy-looking graphs, and you may find yourself losing

---

[1] On the plus side, he would have a long sticky tongue and if you smoke his venom (which, incidentally, can kill a dog) you'll hallucinate (if you're lucky, you'd hallucinate that he wasn't a Colorado river toad–human hybrid).

consciousness at the excitement of colouring your graph bright pink (really, it's amazing how excited my undergraduate psychology students get at the prospect of bright pink graphs – personally I'm not a fan of pink). Much as pink graphs might send a twinge of delight down your spine, I want to urge you to remember why you're doing the graph – it's not to make yourself (or others) purr with delight at the pinkness of your graph, it's to present information (dull, perhaps, but true).

Tufte (2001) wrote an excellent book about how data should be presented. He points out that graphs should, among other things:

- Show the data.
- Induce the reader to think about the data being presented (rather than some other aspect of the graph, like how pink it is).
- Avoid distorting the data.
- Present many numbers with minimum ink.
- Make large data sets (assuming you have one) coherent.
- Encourage the reader to compare different pieces of data.
- Reveal data.

However, graphs often don't do these things (see Wainer, 1984, for some examples).

Let's look at an example of a bad graph. When searching around for the worst example of a graph that I have ever seen, it turned out that I didn't need to look any further than myself – it's in the first edition of the SPSS version of this book (Field, 2000). Overexcited by SPSS's ability to put all sorts of useless crap on graphs (like 3-D effects, fill effects and so on – Tufte calls these **chartjunk**), I literally went into some weird orgasmic state and produced an absolute abomination (I'm surprised Tufte didn't kill himself just so he could turn in his grave at the sight of it). The only consolation was that because the book was published in black and white, it's not pink! The graph is reproduced in Figure 4.2 (you

FIGURE 4.2

A cringingly bad example of a graph from the first edition of the SPSS version of this book

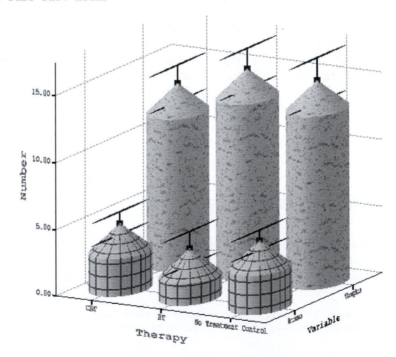

should compare this to the more sober version in this edition, Figure 16.4). What's wrong with this graph?

× The bars have a 3-D effect: Never use 3-D plots for a graph plotting two variables: it obscures the data.[2] In particular it makes it hard to see the values of the bars because of the 3-D effect. This graph is a great example because the 3-D effect makes the error bars almost impossible to read.

× Patterns: The bars also have patterns, which, although very pretty, merely distract the eye from what matters (namely the data). These are completely unnecessary.

× Cylindrical bars: What's that all about, eh? Again, they muddy the data and distract the eye from what is important.

× Badly labelled y-axis: 'number' of what? Delusions? Fish? Cabbage-eating sea lizards from the eighth dimension? Idiots who don't know how to draw graphs?

Now take a look at the alternative version of this graph (Figure 4.3). Can you see what improvements have been made?

✓ A 2-D plot: The completely unnecessary third dimension is gone, making it much easier to compare the values across therapies and thoughts/behaviours.

✓ The y-axis has a more informative label: We now know that it was the number of obsessive thoughts or actions per day that was being measured.

✓ Distractions: There are fewer distractions like patterns, cylindrical bars and the like!

✓ Minimum ink: I've got rid of superfluous ink by getting rid of the axis lines and by using lines on the bars rather than grid lines to indicate values on the y-axis. Tufte would be pleased.[3]

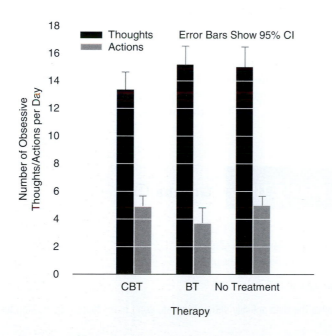

FIGURE 4.3
Figure 4.2 drawn properly

---

[2] If you do 3-D plots when you're plotting only two variables then a bearded statistician will come to your house, lock you in a room and make you write I μυστ νοτ δο 3–Δ γραπησ 75,172 times on the blackboard. Really, they will.

[3] Although he probably over-prescribes this advice: grid lines are more often than not very useful for interpreting the data.

4.2.3. Lies, damned lies, and ... erm ... graphs ①

Governments lie with statistics, but scientists shouldn't. How you present your data makes a huge difference to the message conveyed to the audience. As a big fan of cheese, I'm often curious about whether the urban myth that it gives you nightmares is true. Shee (1964) reported the case of a man who had nightmares about his workmates: 'He dreamt of one, terribly mutilated, hanging from a meat-hook.[4] Another he dreamt of falling into a bottomless abyss. When cheese was withdrawn from his diet the nightmares ceased.' This would not be good news if you were the minister for cheese in your country.

FIGURE 4.4
Two graphs about cheese

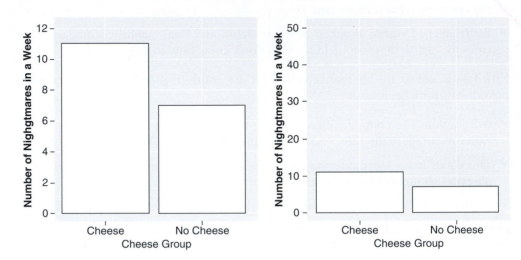

Figure 4.4 shows two graphs that, believe it or not, display exactly the same data: the number of nightmares had after eating cheese. The left-hand panel shows how the graph should probably be scaled. The y-axis reflects the maximum of the scale, and this creates the correct impression: that people have more nightmares about colleagues hanging from meat-hooks if they eat cheese before bed. However, as minister for cheese, you want people to think the opposite; all you have to do is rescale the graph (by extending the y-axis way beyond the average number of nightmares) and there suddenly seems to be little difference. Tempting as it is, don't do this (unless, of course, you plan to be a politician at some point in your life).

CRAMMING SAM'S TIPS   Graphs ①

✓ The vertical axis of a graph is known as the y-axis of the graph.
✓ The horizontal axis of a graph is known as the x-axis of the graph.

If you want to draw a good graph follow the cult of Tufte:

✓ Don't create false impressions of what the data actually show (likewise, don't hide effects!) by scaling the y-axis in some weird way.
✓ Abolish chartjunk: Don't use patterns, 3-D effects, shadows, pictures of spleens, photos of your Uncle Fred or anything else.
✓ Avoid excess ink: don't include features unless they are necessary to interpret or understand the data.

---

[4] I have similar dreams, but that has more to do with some of my workmates than cheese!

4.3. Packages used in this chapter ①

The basic version of **R** comes with a *plot()* function, which can create a wide variety of graphs (type *?plot* in the command line for details) and the *lattice()* package is also helpful. However, throughout this chapter I use Hadley Wickham's **ggplot2** package (Wickham, 2009). I have chosen to focus on this package because I like it. I wouldn't take it out for a romantic meal, but I do get genuinely quite excited by some of the stuff it can do. Just to be very clear about this, it's a very different kind of excitement than that evoked by a romantic meal with my wife.

The *ggplot2* package excites me because it is a wonderfully versatile tool. It takes a bit of time to master it (I still haven't really got to grips with the finer points of it), but once you have, it gives you an extremely flexible framework for displaying and annotating data. The second great thing about *ggplot2* is it is based on Tufte's recommendations about displaying data and Wilkinson's grammar of graphics (Wilkinson, 2005). Therefore, with basically no editing we can create Tufte-pleasing graphs. You can install *ggplot2* by executing the following command:

```
install.packages("ggplot2")
```

You then need to activate it by executing the command:

```
library(ggplot2)
```

4.4. Introducing ggplot2 ①

There are two ways to plot graphs with *ggplot2*: (1) do a quick plot using the *qplot()* function; and (2) build a plot layer by layer using the *ggplot()* function. Undoubtedly the **qplot()** function will get you started quicker; however, the **ggplot()** function offers greater versatility so that is the function that I will use throughout the chapter. I like a challenge.

There are several concepts to grasp that help you to understand how *ggplot2* builds graphs. Personally, I find some of the terminology a bit confusing so I apologize if occasionally I use different terms than those you might find in the *ggplot2* documentation.

4.4.1. The anatomy of a plot ①

A graph is made up of a series of layers. You can think of a layer as a plastic transparency with something printed on it. That 'something' could be text, data points, lines, bars, pictures of chickens, or pretty much whatever you like. To make a final image, these transparencies are placed on top of each other. Figure 4.5 illustrates this process: imagine you begin with a transparent sheet that has the axes of the graph drawn on it. On a second transparent sheet you have bars representing different mean scores. On a third transparency you have drawn error bars associated with each of the means. To make the final graph, you put these three layers together: you start with the axes, lay the bars on top of that, and finally lay the error bars on top of that. The end result is an error bar graph. You can extend the idea of layers beyond the figure: you could imagine having a layer that contains labels for the axes, or a title, and again, you simply lay these on top of the existing image to add more features to the graph.

As can be seen in Figure 4.5, each layer contains visual objects such as bars, data points, text and so on. Visual elements are known as *geoms* (short for 'geometric objects') in *ggplot2*. Therefore, when we define a layer, we have to tell **R** what geom we want displayed on that layer (do we want a bar, line dot, etc.?). These geoms also have aesthetic properties that determine what they look like and where they are plotted (do we want red bars or green ones? do we want our data point to be a triangle or a square? etc.). These aesthetics (*aes()* for short) control the appearance of graph elements (for example, their colour, size, style and location). Aesthetics can be defined in general for the whole plot, or individually for a specific layer. We'll come back to this point in due course.

FIGURE 4.5

In *ggplot2* a plot is made up of layers

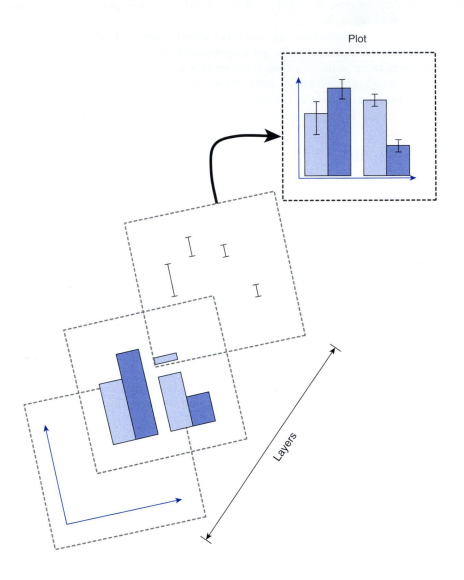

To recap, the finished plot is made up of layers, each layer contains some geometric element (such as bars, points, lines, text) known as a geom, and the appearance and location of these geoms (e.g., size, colour, shape used) is controlled by the aesthetic properties (*aes()*). These aesthetics can be set for all layers of the plot (i.e., defined in the plot as a whole) or can be set individually for each geom in a plot (Figure 4.6). We will learn more about geoms and aesthetics in the following sections.

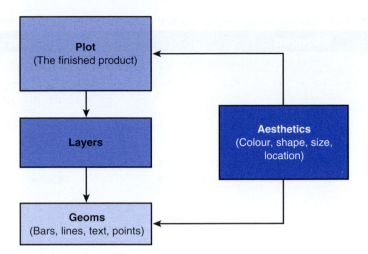

FIGURE 4.6
The anatomy of a
graph

4.3.2. Geometric objects (geoms) ①

There are a variety of geom functions that determine what kind of geometric object is printed on a layer. Here is a list of a few of the more common ones that you might use (for a full list see the *ggplot2* website http://had.co.nz/ggplot2/):

- *geom_bar()*: creates a layer with bars representing different statistical properties.
- *geom_point()*: creates a layer showing the data points (as you would see on a scatterplot).
- *geom_line()*: creates a layer that connects data points with a straight line.
- *geom_smooth()*: creates a layer that contains a 'smoother' (i.e., a line that summarizes the data as a whole rather than connecting individual data points).
- *geom_histogram()*: creates a layer with a histogram on it.
- *geom_boxplot()*: creates a layer with a box–whisker diagram.
- *geom_text()*: creates a layer with text on it.
- *geom_density()*: creates a layer with a density plot on it.
- *geom_errorbar()*: creates a layer with error bars displayed on it.
- *geom_hline()* and *geom_vline()*: create a layer with a user-defined horizontal or vertical line, respectively.

Notice that each geom is followed by '()', which means that it can accept aesthetics that specify how the layer looks. Some of these aesthetics are required and others are optional. For example, if you want to use the text geom then you have to specify the text that you want to print and the position at which you want to print it (using *x* and *y* coordinates), but you do not have to specify its colour.

In terms of required aesthetics, the bare minimum is that each geom needs you to specify the variable or variables that the geom represents. It should be self-evident that *ggplot2* can't create the geom without knowing what it is you want to plot! Optional aesthetics take on default values but you can override these defaults by specifying a value. These are attributes of the geom such as the colour of the geom, the colour to fill the geom, the type

Table 4.1 Aesthetic properties associated with some commonly used geoms

	Required	Optional
geom_bar()	x: the variable to plot on the *x*-axis	colour size fill linetype weight alpha
geom_point()	x: the variable to plot on the *x*-axis y: the variable to plot on the *y*-axis	shape colour size fill alpha
geom_line()	x: the variable to plot on the *x*-axis y: the variable to plot on the *y*-axis	colour size linetype alpha
geom_smooth()	x: the variable to plot on the *x*-axis y: the variable to plot on the *y*-axis	colour size fill linetype weight alpha
geom_histogram()	x: the variable to plot on the *x*-axis	colour size fill linetype weight alpha
geom_boxplot()	x: the variable to plot ymin: lower limit of 'whisker' ymax: upper limit of 'whisker' lower: lower limit of the 'box' upper: upper limit of the 'box' middle: the median	colour size fill weight alpha
geom_text()	x: the horizontal coordinate of where the text should be placed y: the vertical coordinate of where the text should be placed label: the text to be printed all of these can be single values or variables containing coordinates and labels for multiple items	colour size angle hjust (horizontal adjustment) vjust (vertical adjustment) alpha
geom_density()	x: the variable to plot on the *x*-axis y: the variable to plot on the *y*-axis	colour size fill linetype weight alpha

Table 4.1 *(Continued)*

	Required	Optional
geom_errorbar()	x: the variable to plot ymin, ymax: lower and upper value of error bar	colour size linetype width alpha
geom_hline(), *geom_vline()*	yintercept = value xintercept = value (where value is the position on the x- or y-axis where you want the vertical/horizontal line)	colour size linetype alpha

of line to use (solid, dashed, etc.), the shape of the data point (triangle, square, etc.), the size of the geom, and the transparency of the geom (known as alpha). Table 4.1 lists some common geoms and their required and optional aesthetic properties. Note that many of these aesthetics are common across geoms: for example, alpha, colour, linetype and fill can be specified for most of geoms listed in the table.

4.4.3. Aesthetics ①

We have already seen that aesthetics control the appearance of elements within a geom or layer. As already mentioned, you can specify aesthetics for the plot as a whole (such as the variables to be plotted, the colour, shape, etc.) and these instructions will filter down to any geoms in the plot. However, you can also specify aesthetics for individual geoms/layers and these instructions will override those of the plot as a whole. It is efficient, therefore, to specify things like the data to be plotted when you create the plot (because most of the time you won't want to plot different data for different geoms) but to specify idiosyncratic features of the geom's appearance within the geom itself. Hopefully, this process will become clear in the next section.

For now, we will simply look at *how* to specify aesthetics in a general sense. Figure 4.7 shows the ways in which aesthetics are specified. First, aesthetics can be set to a specific value (e.g., a colour such as red) or can be set to vary as a function of a variable (e.g., displaying data for different experimental groups in different colours). If you want to set an aesthetic to a specific value then you don't specify it within the *aes()* function, but if you want an aesthetic

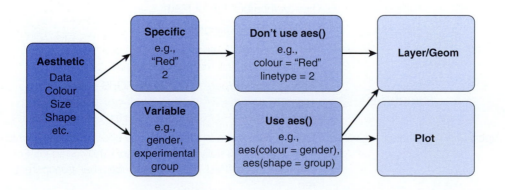

FIGURE 4.7
Specifying aesthetics in *ggplot2*

to vary then you need to place the instruction within *aes()*. Finally, you can set both specific and variable aesthetics at the layer or geom level of the plot, but you cannot set specific values at the plot level. In other words, if we want to set a specific value of an aesthetic we must do it within the *geom()* that we're using to create the particular layer of the plot.

Table 4.2 lists the main aesthetics and how to specify each one. There are, of course, others, and I can't cover the entire array of different aesthetics, but I hope to give you an idea of how to change some of the more common attributes that people typically want to change. For a comprehensive guide read Hadley Wickham's book (Wickham, 2009). It should be clear from Table 4.2 that most aesthetics are specified simply by writing the name of the aesthetic, followed by an equals sign, and then something that sets the value: this can be a variable (e.g., *colour = gender*, which would produce different coloured aesthetics for males and females) or a specific value (e.g., *colour = "Red"*).

Table 4.2 Specifying optional aesthetics

Aesthetic	Option	Outcome
Linetype	linetype = 1	Solid line (default)
	linetype = 2	Hashed
	linetype = 3	Dotted
	linetype = 4	Dot and hash
	linetype = 5	Long hash
	linetype = 6	Dot and long hash
Size	size = value	Replace 'value' with a value in mm (default size = 0.5). Larger values than 0.5 give you fatter lines/larger text/bigger points than the default whereas smaller values will produce thinner lines/smaller text and points than the default.
	e.g., size = 0.25	Produces lines/points/text of 0.25mm
Shape	shape = integer, shape = "x"	The integer is a value between 0 and 25, each of which specifies a particular shape. Some common examples are below. Alternatively, specify a single character in quotes to use that character (shape = "A" will plot each point as the letter A).
	shape = 0	Hollow square (15 is a filled square)
	shape = 1	Hollow circle (16 is a filled circle)
	shape = 2	Hollow triangle (17 is a filled triangle)
	shape = 3	'+'
	shape = 5	Hollow rhombus (18 for filled)
	shape = 6	Hollow inverted triangle
Colour	colour = "Name"	Simply type the name of a standard colour. For example, colour = "Red" will make the geom red.
	colour = "#RRGGBB"	Specify exact colours using the RRGGBB system. For example, colour = "#3366FF" produces a shade of blue, whereas colour = "#336633" produces a dark green.
Alpha	alpha(colour, value)	Colours can be made transparent by specifying alpha, which can range from 0 (fully transparent) to 1 (fully opaque). For example, alpha("Red", 0.5) will produce a half transparent red.

4.4.4. The anatomy of the ggplot() function ①

The command structure in *ggplot2* follows the anatomy of the plot described above in a very literal way. You begin by creating an object that specifies the plot. You can, at this stage set any aesthetic properties that you want to apply to all layers (and geoms) within the plot. Therefore, it is customary to define the variables that you want to plot at this top level. A general version of the command might look like this:

```
myGraph <- ggplot(myData, aes(variable for x axis, variable for y axis))
```

In this example, we have created a new graph object called *myGraph*, we have told *ggplot* to use the dataframe called *myData*, and we put the names of the variables to be plotted on the *x* (horizontal) and *y* (vertical) axis within the *aes()* function. Not to labour the point, but we could also set other aesthetic values at this top level. As a simple example, if we wanted our layers/geoms to display data from males and females in different colours then we could specify (assuming the variable **gender** defines whether a datum came from a man or a woman):

```
myGraph <- ggplot(myData, aes(variable for x axis, variable for y axis,
colour = gender))
```

In doing so any subsequent geom that we define will take on the aesthetic of producing different colours for males and females, assuming that this is a valid aesthetic for the particular geom (if not, the colour specification is ignored) and that we don't override it by defining a different colour aesthetic within the geom itself.

At this level you can also define options using the *opts()* function. The most common option to set at this level is a title:

```
+ opts(title = "Title")
```

Whatever text you put in the quotations will appear as your title exactly as you have typed it, so punctuate and capitalize appropriately.

So far we have created only the graph object: there are no graphical elements, and if you try to display *myGraph* you'll get an error. We need to add layers to the graph containing geoms or other elements such as labels. To add a layer we literally use the 'add' symbol (+). So, let's assume we want to add bars to the plot, we can execute this command:

```
myGraph + geom_bar()
```

This command takes the object *myGraph* that we have already created, and adds a layer containing bars to it. Now that there are graphical elements, *ggplot2* will print the graph to a window on your screen. If we want to also add points representing the data to this graph then we add '+ geom_point()' to the command and rerun it:

```
myGraph + geom_bar() + geom_point()
```

As you can see, every time you use a '+' you add a layer to the graph, so the above example now has two layers: bars and points. You can add any or all of the geoms that we have already described to build up your graph layer by layer. Whenever we specify a geom we can define an aesthetic for it that overrides any aesthetic setting for the plot as a whole. So, let's say we have defined a new graph as:

```
myGraph <- ggplot(myData, aes(variable for x axis, variable for y axis,
colour = gender))
```

but we want to add points that are blue (and do not vary by gender), then we can do this as:

```
myGraph + geom_point(colour = "Blue")
```

Note that because we've set a specific value we have not used the *aes()* function to set the colour. If we wanted our points to be blue triangles then we could simply add the shape command into the geom specification too:

```
myGraph + geom_point(shape = 17, colour =" "Blue")
```

We can also add a layer containing things other than geoms. For example, axis labels can be added by using the *labels()* function:

```
myGraph + geom_bar() + geom_point() + labels(x = "Text", y = "Text")
```

in which you replace the word "Text" (again keep the quotations) with the label that you want. You can also apply themes, faceting and options in a similar manner (see sections 4.4.6 and 4.10).

4.4.5.   Stats and geoms ③

We have already encountered various geoms that map onto common plots used in research: *geom_histogram*, *geom_boxplot*, *geom_smooth*, *geom_bar* etc. (see Table 4.1). At face value it seems as though these geoms require you to generate the data necessary to plot them. For example, the boxplot geom requires that you tell it the minimum and maximum values of the box and the whiskers as well as the median. Similarly, the errorbar geom requires you to feed in the minimum and maximum values of the bars. Entering the values that the geom needs is certainly an option, but more often than not you'll want to just create plots directly from the raw data without having to faff about computing summary statistics. Luckily, *ggplot2* has some built-in functions called 'stats' that can be either used by a geom to get the necessary values to plot, or used directly to create visual elements on a layer of a plot.

Table 4.3 shows a selection of stats that geoms use to generate plots. I have focused only on the stats that will actually be used in this book, but there are others (for a full list see http://had.co.nz/ggplot2/). Mostly, these stats work behind the scenes: a geom uses them without you knowing about it. However, it's worth knowing about them because they enable you to adjust the properties of a plot. For example, imagine we want to plot a histogram, we can set up our plot object (*myHistogram*) as:

```
myHistogram <- ggplot(myData, aes(variable))
```

which has been defined as plotting the variable called **variable** from the dataframe *myData*. As we saw in the previous section, if we want a histogram, then we simply add a layer to the plot using the histogram geom:

```
myHistogram + geom_histogram()
```

That's it: a histogram will magically appear. However, behind the scenes the histogram geom is using the *bin* stat to generate the necessary data (i.e., to bin the data). We could get exactly the same histogram by writing:

```
myHistogram + geom_histogram(aes(y = ..count..))
```

The *aes(y = ..count..)* is simply telling *geom_histogram* to set the *y*-axis to be the *count* output variable from the *bin* stat, which *geom_histogram* will do by default. As we can see from Table 4.3, there are other variables we could use though. Let's say we wanted our histogram to show the density rather than the count. Then we can't rely on the defaults and we would have to specify that *geom_histogram* plots the *density* output variable from the *bin* stat on the *y*-axis:

```
myHistogram + geom_histogram(aes(y = ..density..))
```

Table 4.3 Some of the built-in 'stats' in *ggplot2*

Stat	Function	Output Variables	Useful Parameters	Associated Geom
bin	Bins data	**count**: number of points in bin **density**: density of points in bin, scaled to integrate to 1 **ncount**: count, scaled to maximum of 1 **ndensity**: density, scaled to maximum of 1	**binwidth**: bin width **breaks**: override bin width with specific breaks to use **width**: width of bars	histogram
boxplot	Computes the data necessary to plot a boxplot	**width**: width of boxplot **ymin**: lower whisker **lower**: lower hinge, 25% quantile **middle**: median **upper**: upper hinge, 75% quantile **ymax**: upper whisker		boxplot
density	Density estimation	**density**: density estimate **count**: density × number of points **scaled**: density estimate, scaled to maximum of 1		density
qq	Compute data for Q-Q plots	**sample**: sample quantiles **theoretical**: theoretical quantiles	quantiles	point
smooth	Create a smoother plot	**y**: predicted value **ymin**: lower pointwise CI around the mean **ymax**: upper pointwise CI around the mean **se**: standard error	**method**: e.g., lm, glm, gam, loess **formula**: formula for smoothing **se**: display CI (true by default) **level**: level of CI to use (0.95 by default)	smooth
summary	Summarize data		**fun.y**: determines the function to plot on the y-axis (e.g., fun.y = mean)	bar, errorbar, pointrange, linerange

Similarly, by default, *geom_histogram* uses a bin width of the range of scores divided by 30. We can use the parameters of the *bin* stat to override this default:

```
myHistogram + geom_histogram(aes(y = ..count..), binwidth = 0.4)
```

As such, it is helpful to have in mind the relationship between geoms and stats when plotting graphs. As we go through the chapter you will see how stats can be used to control what is produced by a geom, but also how stats can be used directly to make a layer of a plot.

4.4.6.   Avoiding overplotting ②

Plots can become cluttered or unclear because (1) there is too much data to present in a single plot, and (2) data on a plot overlap. There are several positioning tools in *ggplot2* that help us to overcome these problems. The first is a position adjustment, defined very simply as:

```
position = "x"
```

in which *x* is one of five words:

- *dodge*: positions objects so that there is no overlap at the side.

- *stack* and *fill*: positions objects so that they are stacked. The *stack* instruction stacks objects in front of each other such that the largest object is at the back and smallest at the front. The *fill* instruction stacks objects on top of one other (to make up stacks of equal height that are partitioned by the stacking variable).

- *identity*: no position adjustment.

- *jitter*: adds a random offset to objects so that they don't overlap.

Another useful tool for avoiding overplotting is faceting, which basically means splitting a plot into subgroups. There are two ways to do this. The first is to produce a grid that splits the data displayed by the plot by combinations of other variables. This is achieved using *facet_grid()*. The second way is to split the data displayed by the plot by a single variable either as a long ribbon of individual graphs, or to wrap the ribbon onto the next line after a certain number of plots such that a grid is formed. This is achieved using *facet_wrap()*.

Figure 4.8 shows the differences between *facet_grid()* and *facet_wrap()* using a concrete example. Social networking sites such as Facebook offer an unusual opportunity to carefully manage your self-presentation to others (i.e., do you want to appear to be cool when in fact you write statistics books, appear attractive when you have huge pustules all over your face, fashionable when you wear 1980s heavy metal band t-shirts and so on).

FIGURE 4.8
The difference between *facet_grid()* and *facet_wrap()*

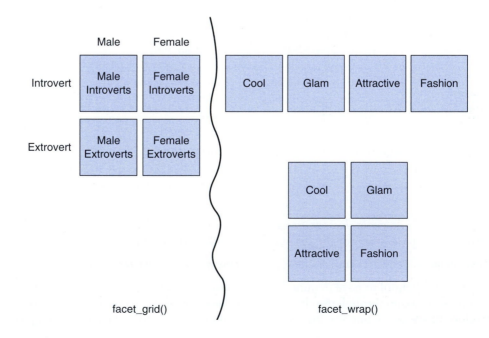

A study was done that examined the relationship between narcissism and other people's ratings of your profile picture on Facebook (Ong et al., 2011). The pictures were rated on each of four dimensions: coolness, glamour, fashionableness and attractiveness. In addition, each person was measuresd on introversion/extroversion and also their gender recorded. Let's say we wanted to plot the relationship between narcissism and the profile picture ratings. We would have a lot of data because we have different types of rating, males and females and introverts and extroverts. We could use *facet_grid()* to produce plots of narcissism vs. photo rating for each combination of gender and extroversion. We'd end up with a grid of four plots (Figure 4.8). Alternatively, we could use *facet_wrap()* to split the plots by the type of rating (cool, glamorous, fashionable, attractive). Depending on how we set up the command, this would give us a ribbon of four plots (one for each type of rating) or we could wrap the plots to create a grid formation (Figure 4.8).

To use faceting in a plot, we add one of the following commands:

```
+ facet_wrap( ~ y, nrow = integer, ncol = integer)
```

```
+ facet_grid(x ~ y)
```

In these commands, *x* and *y* are the variables by which you want to facet, and for facet_ wrap *nrow* and *ncol* are optional instructions to control how the graphs are wrapped: they enable you to specify (as an integer) the number of rows or columns that you would like. For example, if we wanted to facet by the variables **gender** and **extroversion**, we would add this command:

```
facet_grid(gender ~ extroversion)
```

If we wanted to draw different graphs for the four kinds of rating (**Rating_Type**), we could add:

```
+ facet_wrap( ~ Rating_Type)
```

This would give us an arrangement of graphs of one row and four columns (Figure 4.8); if we wanted to arrange these in a 2 by 2 grid (Figure 4.8) then we simply specify that we want two columns:

```
+ facet_wrap( ~ Rating_Type, ncol = 2)
```

or, indeed, two rows:

```
+ facet_wrap( ~ Rating_Type, nrow = 2)
```

4.4.7. Saving graphs ①

Having created the graph of your dreams, you'll probably want to save it somewhere. There are lots of options here. The simplest (but least useful in my view) is to use the *File* menu to save the plot as a pdf file. Figure 4.9 shows the stages in creating and saving a graph. Like anything in **R**, you first write a set of instructions to generate the graph. You select and execute these instructions. Having done this your graph appears in a new window. Click inside this window to make it active, then go to the **File⇒Save As** menu to open a standard dialog box to save the file in a location of your choice.

Personally, I prefer to use the *ggsave()* function, which is a versatile exporting function that can export as PostScript (.eps/.ps), tex (pictex), pdf, jpeg, tiff, png, bmp, svg and wmf (in Windows only). In its basic form, the structure of the function is very simple:

```
ggsave(filename)
```

FIGURE 4.9
Saving a graph
manually

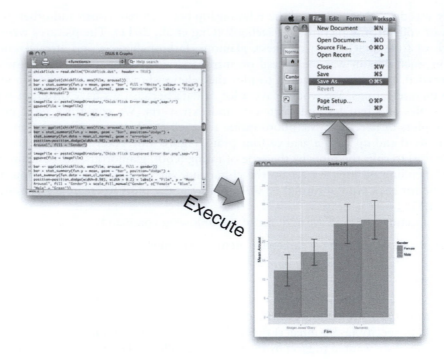

FIGURE 4.9
Saving a graph manually

Here *filename* should be a text string that defines where you want to save the plot and the filename you want to use. The function automatically determines the format to which you want to export from the file extension that you put in the filename, so:

```
ggsave("Outlier Amazon.png")
```

will export as a png file, whereas

```
ggsave("Outlier Amazon.tiff")
```

will export as a tiff file. In the above examples I have specified only a filename, and these files will, therefore be saved in the current working directory (see section 3.4.4). You can, however, use a text string that defines an exact location, or create an object containing the file location that is then passed into the *ggsave()* function (see R's Souls' Tip 4.1). There are several other options you can specify, but mostly the defaults are fine. However, sometimes you might want to export to a specific size, and this can be done by defining the width and height of the image in inches: thus

```
ggsave("Outlier Amazon.tiff", width = 2, height = 2)
```

should save a tiff file that is 2 inches wide by 2 inches high.

4.4.8. Putting it all together: a quick tutorial ②

We have covered an enormous amount of ground in a short time, and have still only scratched the surface of what can be done with *ggplot2*. Also, we haven't actually plotted anything yet! In this section we will do a quick tutorial in which we put into practice various things that we have discussed in this chapter to give you some concrete experience of using *ggplot2* and to illustrate how some of the basic functionality the package works.

R's Souls' Tip 4.1   Saving graphs ③

By default *ggsave()* saves plots in your working directory (which hopefully you have set as something sensible). I find it useful sometimes to set up a specific location for saving images and to feed this into the *ggsave()* function. For example, executing:

```
imageDirectory<-file.path(Sys.getenv("HOME"),   "Documents",   "Academic",   "Books",
"Discovering Statistics", "DSUR I Images")
```

uses the *file.path()* and *Sys.getenv()* functions to create an object *imageDirectory* which is a text string defining a folder called 'DSUR I Images', which is in a folder called 'Discovering Statistics' in a folder called 'Books' in a folder called 'Academic' which is in my main 'Documents' folder. On my computer (an iMac) this command sets *imageDirectory* to be:

```
"/Users/andyfield/Documents/Academic/Books/Discovering Statistics/DSUR I Images"
```

Sys.getenv("HOME") is a quick way to get the filepath of your home directory (in my case */Users/andy-field/*), and we use the *file.path()* function to paste the specified folder names together in an intelligent way based on the operating system that you use. Because I use a Mac it has connected the folders using an '/', but if I used Windows it would have used '\\' instead (because this is the symbol Windows uses to denote folders).

Having defined this location, we can use it to create a file path for a new image:

```
imageFile <- file.path(imageDirectory,"Graph.png")
ggsave(imageFile)
```

This produces a text string called *imageFile*, which is the filepath we have just defined (*imageDirectory*) with the filename that we want (*Graph.png*) added to it. We can reuse this code for a new graph by just changing the filename specified in *imageFile*:

```
imageFile <- file.path(imageDirectory,"Outlier Amazon.png")
ggsave(imageFile)
```

Earlier in the chapter we mentioned a study that looked at ratings of Facebook profile pictures (rated on coolness, fashion, attractiveness and glamour) and predicting them from how highly the person posting the picture scores on narcissism (Ong et al., 2011). The data are in the file **FacebookNarcissism.dat**.

First set your working directory to be the location of the data file (see section 3.4.4). Then create a dataframe called *facebookData* by executing the following command:

```
facebookData <- read.delim("FacebookNarcissism.dat", header = TRUE)
```

Figure 4.10 shows the contents of the dataframe. There are four variables:

1 **id**: a number indicating from which participant the profile photo came.

2 **NPQC_R_Total**: the total score on the narcissism questionnaire.

3 **Rating_Type**: whether the rating was for coolness, glamour, fashion or attractiveness (stored as strings of text).

4 **Rating**: the rating given (on a scale from 1 to 5).

FIGURE 4.10
The
facebookData
dataframe

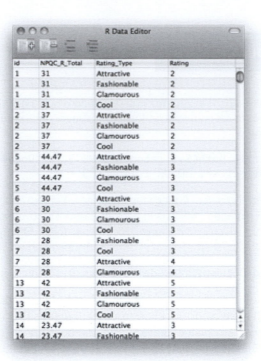

First we need to create the plot object, which I have called, for want of a more original idea, *graph*. Remember that we initiate this object using the *ggplot()* function, which takes the following form:

```
graph <- ggplot(myData, aes(variable for x axis, variable for y axis))
```

To begin with, let's plot the relationship between narcissism (**NPQC_R_Total**) and the profile ratings generally (**Rating**). As such, we want **NPQC_R_Total** plotted on the *x*-axis and **Rating** on the *y*-axis. The dataframe containing these variables is called *facebookData* so we type and execute this command:

```
graph <- ggplot(facebookData, aes(NPQC_R_Total, Rating))
```

This command simply creates an object based on the *facebookData* dataframe and specifies the aesthetic mapping of variables to the *x*- and *y*-axes. Note that these mappings are contained within the *aes()* function. When you execute this command nothing will happen: we have created the object, but there is nothing to print.

If we want to see something then we need to take our object (*graph*) and add some visual elements. Let's start with something simple and add dots for each data point. This is done using the *geom_point()* function. If you execute the following command you'll see the graph in the top left panel of Figure 4.11 appear in a window on your screen:

```
graph + geom_point()
```

If we don't like the circles then we can change the shape of the points by specifying this for the geom. For example, executing:

```
graph + geom_point(shape = 17)
```

will change the dots to triangles (top right panel of Figure 4.11). By changing the number assigned to *shape* to other values you will see different shaped points (see section 4.4.3). If we want to change the size of the dots rather than the shape, this is easily done too by specifying a value (in mm) that you want to use for the 'size' aesthetic. Executing:

```
graph + geom_point(size = 6)
```

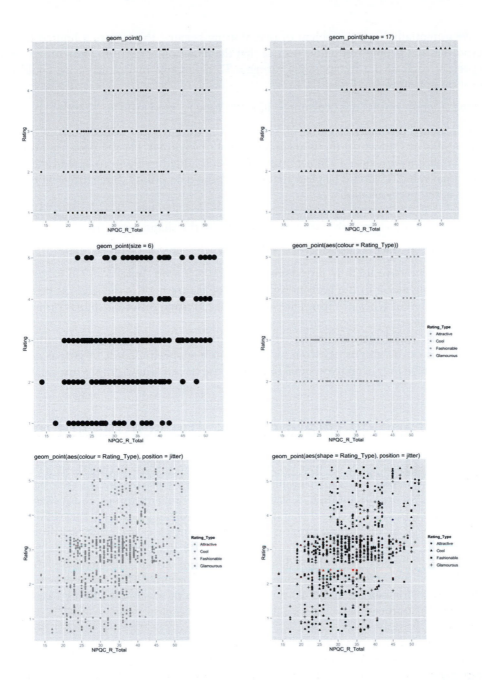

FIGURE 4.11
Different aesthetics for the point geom

creates the graph in the middle left panel of Figure 4.11. Note that the default shape has been used (because we haven't specified otherwise), but the size is larger than by default. At this stage we don't know whether a rating represented coolness, attractiveness or whatever. It would be nice if we could differentiate different ratings, perhaps by plotting them in different colours. We can do this by setting the colour aesthetic to be the variable **Rating_Type**. Executing this command:

```
graph + geom_point(aes(colour = Rating_Type))
```

creates the graph in the middle right panel of Figure 4.11, in which, onscreen, different types of ratings are now presented in different colours.[5]

[5] Note that here we set the colour aesthetic by enclosing it in aes() whereas in the previous examples we did not. This is because we're setting the value of colour based on a variable, rather than a single value.

We potentially have a problem of overplotting because there were a limited number of responses that people could give (notice that the data points fall along horizontal lines that represent each of the five possible ratings). To avoid this overplotting we could use the position option to add jitter:

```
graph + geom_point(aes(colour = Rating_Type), position = "jitter")
```

Notice that the command is the same as before; we have just added *position = "jitter"*. The results are shown in the bottom left panel of Figure 4.11; the dots are no longer in horizontal lines because a random value has been added to them to spread them around the actual value. It should be clear that many of the data points were sitting on top of each other in the previous plot.

Finally, if we wanted to differentiate rating types by their shape rather than using a colour, we could change the colour aesthetic to be the shape aesthetic:

```
graph + geom_point(aes(shape = Rating_Type), position = "jitter")
```

Note how we have literally just changed *colour = Rating_Type* to *shape = Rating_Type*. The resulting graph in the bottom right panel of Figure 4.11 is the same as before except that the different types of ratings are now displayed using different shapes rather than different colours.

This very rapid tutorial has hopefully demonstrated how geoms and aesthetics work together to create graphs. As we now turn to look at specific kinds of graphs, you should hopefully have everything you need to make sense of how these graphs are created.

4.5. Graphing relationships: the scatterplot ①

How do I draw a graph of the relationship between two variables?

Sometimes we need to look at the relationships between variables. A **scatterplot** is a graph that plots each person's score on one variable against their score on another. A scatterplot tells us several things about the data, such as whether there seems to be a relationship between the variables, what kind of relationship it is and whether any cases are markedly different from the others. We saw earlier that a case that differs substantially from the general trend of the data is known as an *outlier* and such cases can severely bias statistical procedures (see Jane Superbrain Box 4.1 and section 7.7.1.1 for more detail). We can use a scatterplot to show us if any cases look like outliers.

4.5.1. Simple scatterplot ①

This type of scatterplot is for looking at just two variables. For example, a psychologist was interested in the effects of exam stress on exam performance. So, she devised and validated a questionnaire to assess state anxiety relating to exams (called the Exam Anxiety Questionnaire, or EAQ). This scale produced a measure of anxiety scored out of 100. Anxiety was measured before an exam, and the percentage mark of each student on the exam was used to assess the exam performance. The first thing that the psychologist should do is draw a scatterplot of the two variables. Her data are in the file **ExamAnxiety.dat** and you should load this file into a dataframe called *examData* by executing:

```
examData <- read.delim("Exam Anxiety.dat", header = TRUE)
```

Figure 4.12 shows the contents of the dataframe. There are five variables:

1 **Code**: a number indicating from which participant the scores came.
2 **Revise**: the total hours spent revising.
3 **Exam**: mark on the exam as a percentage.
4 **Anxiety**: the score on the EAQ.
5 **Gender**: whether the participant was male or female (stored as strings of text).

R Data Editor

Code	Revise	Exam	Anxiety	Gender
1	4	40	86.298	Male
2	11	65	88.716	Female
3	27	80	70.178	Male
4	53	80	61.312	Male
5	4	40	89.522	Male
6	22	70	60.506	Female
7	16	20	81.462	Female
8	21	55	75.82	Female
9	25	50	69.372	Female
10	18	40	82.268	Female
11	18	45	79.044	Male
12	16	85	80.656	Male
13	13	70	70.178	Male
14	18	50	75.014	Female
15	98	95	34.714	Male
16	1	70	95.164	Male
17	14	95	75.82	Male
18	29	95	79.044	Female
19	4	50	91.134	Female
20	23	60	64.536	Male
21	14	80	80.656	Male

FIGURE 4.12 The *examData* dataframe

First we need to create the plot object, which I have called *scatter*. Remember that we initiate this object using the *ggplot()* function. The contents of this function specify the dataframe to be used (*examData*) and any aesthetics that apply to the whole plot. I've said before that one aesthetic that is usually defined at this level is the variables that we want to plot. To begin with, let's plot the relationship between exam anxiety (**Anxiety**) and exam performance (**Exam**). We want **Anxiety** plotted on the *x*-axis and **Exam** on the *y*-axis. Therefore, to specify these variables as an aesthetic we type *aes(Anxiety, Exam)*. Therefore, the final command that we execute is:

```
scatter <- ggplot(examData, aes(Anxiety, Exam))
```

This command creates an object based on the *examData* dataframe and specifies the aesthetic mapping of variables to the *x*- and *y*-axes. When you execute this command nothing will happen: we have created the object, but there is nothing to print.

If we want to see something then we need to take our object (*scatter*) and add a layer containing visual elements. For a scatterplot we essentially want to add dots, which is done using the *geom_point()* function.

```
scatter + geom_point()
```

If we want to add some nice labels to our axes then we can also add a layer with these on using *labs()*:

```
scatter + geom_point() + labs(x = "Exam Anxiety", y = "Exam
Performance %")
```

FIGURE 4.13
Scatterplot of
exam anxiety
and exam
performance

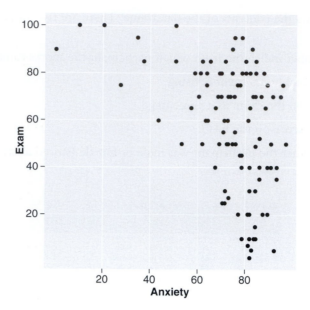

If you execute this command you'll see the graph in Figure 4.13. The scatterplot tells us that the majority of students suffered from high levels of anxiety (there are very few cases that had anxiety levels below 60). Also, there are no obvious outliers in that most points seem to fall within the vicinity of other points. There also seems to be some general trend in the data, such that low levels of anxiety are almost always associated with high examination marks (and high anxiety is associated with a lot of variability in exam marks). Another noticeable trend in these data is that there were no cases having low anxiety and low exam performance – in fact, most of the data are clustered in the upper region of the anxiety scale.

4.5.2. Adding a funky line ①

You often see scatterplots that have a line superimposed over the top that summarizes the relationship between variables (this is called a **regression line** and we will discover more about it in Chapter 7). The scatterplot you have just produced won't have a funky line on it yet, but don't get too depressed because I'm going to show you how to add this line now.

How do I fit a regression line to a scatterplot?

In *ggplot2* terminology a regression line is known as a 'smoother' because it smooths out the lumps and bumps of the raw data into a line that summarizes the relationship. *The geom_smooth() function provides the functionality to add lines (curved or straight) to summarize the pattern within your data.*

To add a smoother to our existing scatterplot, we would simply add the *geom_smooth()* function and execute it:

```
scatter + geom_point() + geom_smooth() + labs(x = "Exam Anxiety",
y = "Exam Performance %")
```

Note that the command is exactly the same as before except that we have added a smoother in a new layer by typing + *geom_smooth()*. The resulting graph is shown in Figure 4.14. Note that the scatterplot now has a curved line (a 'smoother') summarizing the relationship between exam anxiety and exam performance. The shaded area around the line is the 95% confidence interval around the line. We'll see in due course how to remove this shaded error or to recolour it.

The smoothed line in Figure 4.14 is very pretty, but often we want to fit a straight line (or linear model) instead of a curved one. To do this, we need to change the 'method'

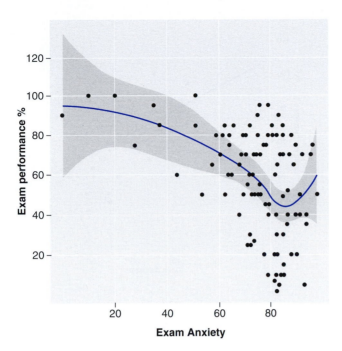

FIGURE 4.14
Scatterplot of
exam anxiety
against exam
performance
with a smoother
added

associated with the smooth geom. In Table 4.3 we saw several methods that could be used for the smooth geom: *lm* fits a linear model (i.e., a straight line) and you could use *rlm* for a robust linear model (i.e., less affected by outliers).[6] So, to add a straight line (rather than curved) we change *geom_smooth()* to include this instruction:

```
+ geom_smooth(method = "lm")
```

We can also change the appearance of the line: by default it is blue, but if we wanted a red line then we can simply define this aesthetic within the geom:

```
+ geom_smooth(method = "lm", colour = "Red")
```

Putting this together with the code for the simple scatterplot, we would execute:

```
scatter <- ggplot(examData, aes(Anxiety, Exam))
scatter + geom_point() + geom_smooth(method = "lm", colour = "Red")+ labs(x
= "Exam Anxiety", y = "Exam Performance %")
```

The resulting scatterplot is shown in Figure 4.15. Note that it looks the same as Figure 4.13 and Figure 4.14 except that a red (because we specified the colour as red) regression line has been added.[7] As with our curved line, the regression line is surrounded by the 95% confidence interval (the grey area). We can switch this off by simply adding *se = F* (which is short for 'standard error = False') to the *geom_smooth()* function:

```
+ geom_smooth(method = "lm", se = F)
```

We can also change the colour and transparency of the confidence interval using the *fill* and *alpha* aesthetics, respectively. For example, if we want the confidence interval to be blue like the line itself, and we want it fairly transparent we could specify:

```
geom_smooth(method = "lm", alpha = 0.1, fill = "Blue")
```

---

[6] You must have the *MASS* package loaded to use this method.

[7] You'll notice that the figure doesn't have a red line but what you see on your screen does, that's because this book isn't printed in colour which makes it tricky for us to show you the colourful delights of **R**. In general, use the figures in the book as a guide only and read the text with reference to what you actually see on your screen.

FIGURE 4.15
A simple
scatterplot with
a regression line
added

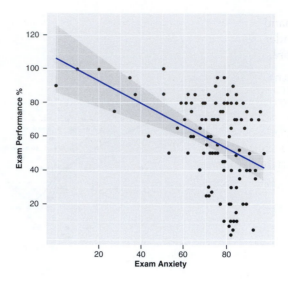

FIGURE 4.16
Manipulating
the appearance
of the
confidence
interval around
the regression
line

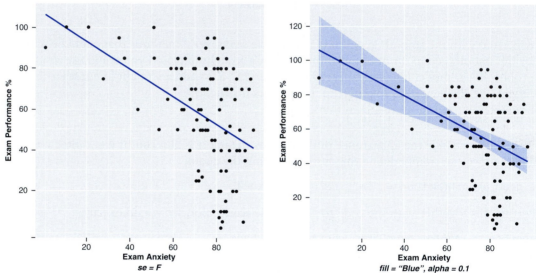

Note that transparency can take a value from 0 (fully transparent) to 1 (fully opaque) and so we have set a fairly transparent colour by using 0.1 (after all we want to see the data points underneath). The impact of these changes can be seen in Figure 4.16.

4.5.3. Grouped scatterplot ①

What if we want to see whether male and female students had different reactions to exam anxiety? To do this, we need to set **Gender** as an aesthetic. This is fairly straightforward. First, we define gender as a colour aesthetic when we initiate the plot object:

```
scatter <- ggplot(examData, aes(Anxiety, Exam, colour = Gender))
```

Note that this command is exactly the same as the previous example, except that we have added 'colour = Gender' so that any geoms we define will be coloured differently for men and women. Therefore, if we then execute:

```
scatter + geom_point + geom_smooth(method = "lm")
```

we would have a scatterplot with different coloured dots and regression lines for men and women. It's as simple as that. However, our lines would have confidence intervals and both intervals would be shaded grey, so we could be a little more sophisticated and add some instructions into *geom_smooth()* that tells it to also colour the confidence intervals according to the **Gender** variable:

```
scatter + geom_point() + geom_smooth(method = "lm", aes(fill = Gender), alpha
= 0.1)
```

Note that we have used *fill* to specify that the confidence intervals are coloured according to **Gender** (note that because we are specifying a variable rather than a single colour we have to place this option within *aes()*). As before, we have also manually set the transparency of the confidence intervals to be 0.1.

As ever, let's add some labels to the graph:

```
+ labs(x = "Exam Anxiety", y = "Exam Performance %", colour = "Gender")
```

Note that by specifying a label for 'colour' I am setting the label that will be used on the legend of the graph. The finished command to be executed will be:

```
scatter + geom_point() + geom_smooth(method = "lm", aes(fill = Gender), alpha
= 0.1) + labs(x = "Exam Anxiety", y = "Exam Performance %", colour = "Gender")
```

Figure 4.17 shows the resulting scatterplot. The regression lines tell us that the relationship between exam anxiety and exam performance was slightly stronger in males (the line is steeper) indicating that men's exam performance was more adversely affected by anxiety than women's exam anxiety. (Whether this difference is significant is another issue – see section 6.7.1.)

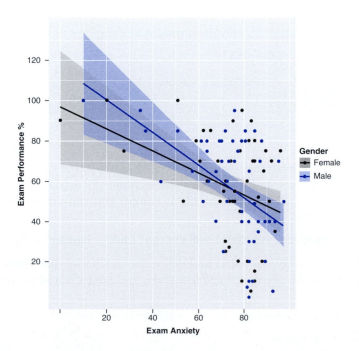

FIGURE 4.17
Scatterplot of exam anxiety and exam performance split by gender

SELF-TEST

✓ Go back to the Facebook narcissism data from the earlier tutorial. Plot a graph that shows the pattern in the data using only a line.
✓ Plot different coloured lines for the different types of rating (cool, fashionable, attractive, glamorous).
✓ Add a layer displaying the raw data as points.
✓ Add labels to the axes.

4.6. Histograms: a good way to spot obvious problems ①

In this section we'll look at how we can use frequency distributions to screen our data.[8] We'll use an example to illustrate what to do. A biologist was worried about the potential health effects of music festivals. So, one year she went to the Download Music Festival[9] (for those of you outside the UK, you can pretend it is Roskilde Festival, Ozzfest, Lollopalooza, Wacken or something) and measured the hygiene of 810 concert-goers over the three days of the festival. In theory each person was measured on each day but because it was difficult to track people down, there were some missing data on days 2 and 3. Hygiene was measured using a standardized technique (don't worry, it *wasn't* licking the person's armpit) that results in a score ranging between 0 (you smell like a corpse that's been left to rot up a skunk's arse) and 4 (you smell of sweet roses on a fresh spring day). Now I know from bitter experience that sanitation is not always great at these places (the Reading Festival seems particularly bad) and so this researcher predicted that personal hygiene would go down dramatically over the three days of the festival. The data file, **DownloadFestival.dat**, can be found on the companion website. We encountered histograms (frequency distributions) in Chapter 1; we will now learn how to create one in **R** using these data.

SELF-TEST

✓ What does a histogram show?

Load the data into a dataframe (which I've called *festivalData*); if you need to refresh your memory on data files and dataframes see section 3.5. Assuming you have set the working directory to be where the data file is stored, you can create the dataframe by executing this command:

```
festivalData <- read.delim("DownloadFestival.dat", header = TRUE)
```

Now we need to create the plot object and define any aesthetics that apply to the plot as a whole. I have called the object *festivalHistogram*, and have created it using the *ggplot()*

---

[8] An alternative way to graph the distribution is a density plot, which we'll discuss later.

[9] http://www.downloadfestival.co.uk

function. The contents of this function specify the dataframe to be used (*festivalData*) and any aesthetics that apply to the whole plot. I've said before that one aesthetic that is usually defined at this level is the variables that we want to plot. To begin with let's plot the hygiene scores for day 1, which are in the variable **day1**. Therefore, to specify this variable as an aesthetic we type *aes(day1)*. I have also decided to turn the legend off so I have added *opts(legend.position = "none")* to do this (see R's Souls' Tip 4.2):

```
festivalHistogram <- ggplot(festivalData, aes(day1)) + opts(legend.position
= "none")
```

Remember that having executed the above command we have an object but no graphical layers, so we will see nothing. To add the graphical layer we need to add the histogram geom to our existing plot:

```
festivalHistogram + geom_histogram()
```

Executing this command will create a graph in a new window. If you are happy using the default options then this is all there is to it; sit back and admire your efforts. However, we can tidy the graph up a bit. First, we could change the bin width. I would normally play around with different bin widths to get a feel for the distribution. To save time, let's just change it to 0.4. We can do this by inserting a command within the histogram geom:

```
+ geom_histogram(binwidth = 0.4)
```

We should also provide more informative labels for our axes using the *labs()* function:

```
+ labs(x = "Hygiene (Day 1 of Festival)", y = "Frequency")
```

As you can see, I have simply typed in the labels I want (within quotation marks) for the horizontal (*x*) and vertical (*y*) axes. Making these two changes leaves us with this command, which we must execute to see the graph:

```
festivalHistogram + geom_histogram(binwidth = 0.4) + labs(x = "Hygiene (Day
1 of Festival)", y = "Frequency")
```

The resulting histogram is shown in Figure 4.18. The first thing that should leap out at you is that there appears to be one case that is very different than the others. All of the

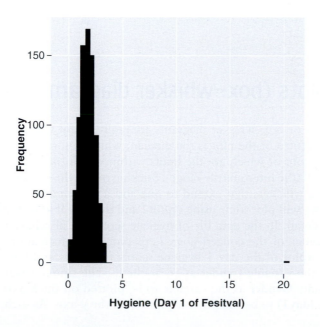

FIGURE 4.18
Histogram of the day 1 Download Festival hygiene scores

scores appear to be squashed up at one end of the distribution because they are all less than 5 (yielding a very pointy distribution) except for one, which has a value of 20. This is an **outlier**: a score very different than the rest (Jane Superbrain Box 4.1). Outliers bias the mean and inflate the standard deviation (you should have discovered this from the self-test tasks in Chapters 1 and 2) and screening data is an important way to detect them. You can look for outliers in two ways: (1) graph the data with a histogram (as we have done here) or a boxplot (as we will do in the next section); or (2) look at z-scores (this is quite complicated, but if you want to know see Jane Superbrain Box 4.2).

The outlier shown on the histogram is particularly odd because it has a score of 20, which is above the top of our scale (remember our hygiene scale ranged only from 0 to 4) and so it must be a mistake (or the person had obsessive compulsive disorder and had washed themselves into a state of extreme cleanliness).

R's Souls' Tip 4.2   Removing legends ③

By default *ggplot2* produces a legend on the right-hand side of the plot. Mostly this legend is a useful thing to have. However, there are occasions when you might like it to go away. This is achieved using the *opts()* function either when you set up the plot object, or when you add layers to the plot. To remove the legend just add:

```
+ opts(legend.position="none")
```

For example, either

```
myGraph <- ggplot(myData, aes(variable for x axis, variable for y axis)) + opts(legend.position="none")
```

or

```
myGraph <- ggplot(myData, aes(variable for x axis, variable for y axis))
myGraph + geom_point() + opts(legend.position="none")
```

will produce a graph without a figure legend.

4.7. Boxplots (box–whisker diagrams) ①

Did someone say a box of whiskas?

Boxplots or box–whisker diagrams are really useful ways to display your data. At the centre of the plot is the median, which is surrounded by a box the top and bottom of which are the limits within which the middle 50% of observations fall (the interquartile range). Sticking out of the top and bottom of the box are two whiskers that extend to one and a half times the interquartile range. First, we will plot some using *ggplot2* and then we'll look at what they tell us in more detail. In the data file of hygiene scores we also have information about the gender of the concert-goer. Let's plot this information as well. To make our boxplot of the day 1 hygiene scores for males and females, we will need to set the variable **Gender** as an aesthetic. The simplest way to do this is just to specify **Gender** as the variable to be plotted on the x-axis, and the hygiene scores (**day1**) to be the variable plotted on the y-axis. As such, when we initiate

JANE SUPERBRAIN 4.1

What is an outlier? ①

An outlier is a score very different from the rest of the data. When we analyse data we have to be aware of such values because they bias the model we fit to the data. A good example of this bias can be seen by looking at the mean. When I published my first book (the first edition of the SPSS version of this book), I was quite young, I was very excited and I wanted everyone in the world to love my new creation and me. Consequently, I obsessively checked the book's ratings on Amazon.co.uk. These ratings can range from 1 to 5 stars. Back in 2002, my first book had seven ratings (in the order given) of 2, 5, 4, 5, 5, 5, and 5. All but one of these ratings are fairly similar (mainly 5 and 4) but the first rating was quite different from the rest – it was a rating of 2 (a mean and horrible rating). The graph plots seven reviewers on the horizontal axis and their ratings on the vertical axis and there is also a horizontal line that represents the mean rating (4.43 as it happens). It should be clear that all of the scores except one lie close to this line. The score of 2 is very different and lies some way below the mean. This score is an example of an outlier – a weird and unusual

person (sorry, I mean score) that deviates from the rest of humanity (I mean, data set). The dashed horizontal line represents the mean of the scores when the outlier is not included (4.83). This line is higher than the original mean, indicating that by ignoring this score the mean increases (it increases by 0.4). This example shows how a single score, from some mean-spirited badger turd, can bias the mean; in this case the first rating (of 2) drags the average down. In practical terms this had a bigger implication because Amazon rounded off to half numbers, so that single score made a difference between the average rating reported by Amazon as a generally glowing 5 stars and the less impressive 4.5 stars. (Nowadays Amazon sensibly produces histograms of the ratings and has a better rounding system.) Although I am consumed with bitterness about this whole affair, it has at least given me a great example of an outlier! (Data for this example were taken from http://www.amazon.co.uk/ in about 2002.)

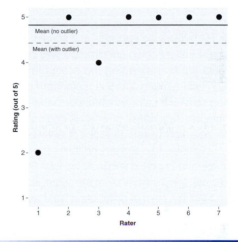

our plot object rather than set a single variable as an aesthetic as we did for the histogram (*aes(day1)*), we set **Gender** and **day1** as variables (*aes(Gender, day1)*). Having initiated the plot object (I've called it *festivalBoxplot*), we can simply add the boxplot geom as a layer (*+ geom_boxplot()*) and add some axis labels with the *labs()* function as we did when we created a histogram. To see the graph we therefore simply execute these two lines of code:

```
festivalBoxplot <- ggplot(festivalData, aes(gender, day1))
festivalBoxplot + geom_boxplot() + labs(x = "Gender", y = "Hygiene (Day 1 of Festival)")
```

The resulting boxplot is shown in Figure 4.19. It shows a separate boxplot for the men and women in the data. Note that the outlier that we detected in the histogram is shown up as a point on the boxplot (we can also tell that this case was a female). An outlier is an extreme score, so the easiest way to find it is to sort the data:

```
festivalData<-festivalData[order(festivalData$day1),]
```

SELF-TEST

✔ Remove the outlier and replot the histogram.

JANE SUPERBRAIN 4.2

Using z-scores to find outliers ③

To check for outliers we can look at *z*-scores. We saw in section 1.7.4 that *z*-scores are simply a way of standardizing a data set by expressing the scores in terms of a distribution with a mean of 0 and a standard deviation of 1. In doing so we can use benchmarks that we can apply to any data set (regardless of what its original mean and standard deviation were). To look for outliers we could convert our variable to *z*-scores and then count how many fall within certain important limits. If we take the absolute value (i.e., we ignore whether the *z*-score is positive or negative) then in a normal distribution we'd expect about 5% to have absolute values greater than 1.96 (we often use 2 for convenience), and 1% to have absolute values greater than 2.58, and none to be greater than about 3.29.

I have written a function that gets **R** to count them for you called *outlierSummary()*. To use the function you

need to load the package associated with this book (see section 3.4.5), you then simply insert the name of the variable that you would like summarized into the function and execute it. For example, to count the number of *z*-scores with absolute values above our three cut-off values in the **day2** variable, we can execute:

```
outlierSummary(festivalData$day2)
```

```
Absolute z-score greater than 1.96 =  6.82 %
Absolute z-score greater than 2.58 =  2.27 %
Absolute z-score greater than 3.29 =  0.76 %
```

The output produced by this function is shown above. We would expect to see 5% (or less) with an absolute value greater than 1.96, 1% (or less) with an absolute value greater than 2.58, and we'd expect no cases above 3.29 (these cases are significant outliers). For hygiene scores on day 2 of the festival, 6.82% of *z*-scores had absolute values greater than 1.96. This is slightly more than the 5% we would expect in a normal distribution. Looking at values above 2.58, we would expect to find only 1%, but again here we have a higher value of 2.27%. Finally, we find that 0.76% of cases were above 3.29 (so 0.76% are significant outliers). This suggests that there may be slightly too many outliers in this variable and we might want to do something about them.

OLIVER TWISTED

Please, Sir, can I have some more … complicated stuff?

'Graphs are for laughs, and functions are full of fun' thinks Oliver as he pops a huge key up his nose and starts to wind the clockwork mechanism of his brain. We don't look at functions for another couple of chapters, which is why I've skipped over the details of how the *outlierSummary()* function works. If, like Oliver, you like to wind up your brain, the additional material for this chapter, on the companion website, explains how I wrote the function. If that doesn't quench your thirst for knowledge then you're a grain of salt.

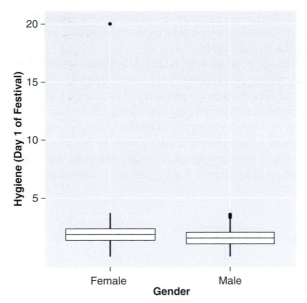

FIGURE 4.19
Boxplot of
hygiene scores
on day 1 of
the Download
Festival split by
gender

This command takes *festivalData* and sorts it by the variable **day1**. All we have to do now is to look at the last case (i.e., the largest value of **day1**) and change it. The offending case turns out to be a score of 20.02, which is probably a mistyping of 2.02. We'd have to go back to the raw data and check. We'll assume we've checked the raw data and it should be 2.02, and that we've used R Commander's data editor (see section 3.6 or the online materials for this chapter) to replace the value 20.02 with the value 2.02 before we continue this example.

SELF-TEST

✓ Now we have removed the outlier in the data, try
  replotting the boxplot. The resulting graph should look
  like Figure 4.20.

Figure 4.20 shows the boxplots for the hygiene scores on day 1 after the outlier has been corrected. Let's look now in more detail about what the boxplot represents. First, it shows us the lowest score (the lowest point of the bottom whisker, or a dot below it) and the highest (the highest point of the top whisker of each plot, or a dot above it). Comparing the males and females we can see they both had similar low scores (0, or very smelly) but the women had a slightly higher top score (i.e., the most fragrant female was more hygienic than the cleanest male).

The lowest edge of the white box is the lower quartile (see section 1.7.3); therefore, the distance between the bottom of the vertical line and the lowest edge of the white box is the range between which the lowest 25% of scores fall. This range is slightly larger for women than for men, which means that if we take the most unhygienic 25% females then there is more variability in their hygiene scores than the lowest 25% of males. The box (the white area) shows the interquartile range (see section 1.7.3): that is, 50% of the scores are bigger than the lowest part of the white area but smaller than the top part of the white area. These boxes are of similar size in the males and females.

The top edge of the white box shows the value of the upper quartile (see section 1.7.3); therefore, the distance between the top edge of the white box and the top of the vertical line shows the range between which the top 25% of scores fall. In the middle of the white box is a line that represents the value of the median (see section 1.7.2). The median for females is higher than for males, which tells us that the middle female scored higher, or was more hygienic, than the middle male.

Boxplots show us the range of scores, the range between which the middle 50% of scores fall, and the median, the upper quartile and lower quartile score. Like histograms, they also tell us whether the distribution is symmetrical or skewed. If the whiskers are the same length then the distribution is symmetrical (the range of the top and bottom 25% of scores is the same); however, if the top or bottom whisker is much longer than the opposite whisker then the distribution is asymmetrical (the range of the top and bottom 25% of scores is different). Finally, you'll notice some dots above the male boxplot. These are cases that are deemed to be outliers. In Chapter 5 we'll see what can be done about these outliers.

FIGURE 4.20

Boxplot of hygiene scores on day 1 of the Download Festival split by gender, after the outlier has been corrected

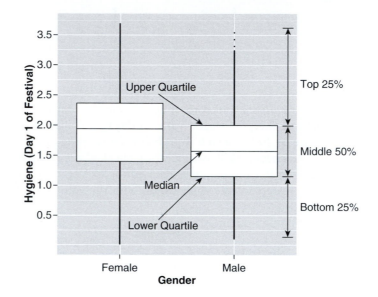

SELF-TEST

✓ Produce boxplots for the day 2 and day 3 hygiene scores and interpret them.

4.8. Density plots ①

Density plots are rather similar to histograms except that they smooth the distribution into a line (rather than bars). We can produce a density plot in exactly the same way as a histogram, except using the density geom: *geom_density()*. Assuming you have removed the outlier for the festival data set,[10] initiate the plot (which I have called *density*) in the same way as for the histogram:

```
density <- ggplot(festivalData, aes(day1))
```

---

[10] If you haven't there is a data file with it removed and you can load this into a dataframe called *festivalData* by executing:

```
festivalData <- read.delim("DownloadFestival(No Outlier).dat", header = TRUE)
```

Then, to get the plot simply add the *density_geom()* function:

`density + geom_density()`

We can also add some labels by including:

`+ labs(x = "Hygiene (Day 1 of Festival)", y = "Density Estimate")`

in the command. The resulting plot is shown in Figure 4.21.

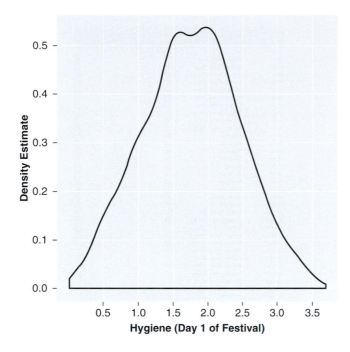

FIGURE 4.21
A density plot of
the Download
Festival data

4.9. Graphing means ③

4.9.1. Bar charts and error bars ②

Bar charts are a common way for people to display means. The *ggplot2* package does not
differentiate between research designs, so you plot bar charts in the same way regardless of
whether you have an independent, repeated-measures or mixed design. Imagine that a film
company director was interested in whether there was really such a thing as a 'chick flick'
(a film that typically appeals to women more than men). He took 20 men and 20 women
and showed half of each sample a film that was supposed to be a 'chick flick' (*Bridget
Jones's Diary*), and the other half of each sample a film that didn't fall into the category
of 'chick flick' (*Memento*, a brilliant film by the way). In all cases he measured their physiological arousal as an indicator of how much they enjoyed the film. The data are in a file
called **ChickFlick.dat** on the companion website. Load this file into a dataframe called
chickFlick by executing this command (I'm assuming you have set the working directory to
be where the data file is stored):

`chickFlick <- read.delim("ChickFlick.dat",  header = TRUE)`

Figure 4.22 shows the data. Note there are three variables:

- **gender**: specifies the gender of the participant as text.
- **film**: specifies the film watched as text.
- **arousal**: is their arousal score.

Each row in the data file represents a different person.

FIGURE 4.22
The **ChickFlick.
dat** data

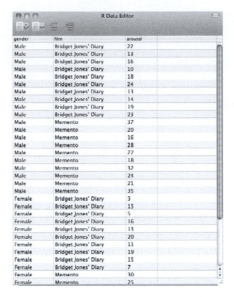

4.9.1.1 Bar charts for one independent variable ②

To begin with, let's just plot the mean arousal score (*y*-axis) for each film (*x*-axis). We can set this up by first creating the plot object and defining any aesthetics that apply to the plot as a whole. I have called the object *bar*, and have created it using the *ggplot()* function. The function specifies the dataframe to be used (*chickFlick*) and has set **film** to be plotted on the *x*-axis, and **arousal** to be plotted on the *y*-axis:

```
bar <- ggplot(chickFlick, aes(film, arousal))
```

This is where things get a little bit tricky; because we want to plot a summary of the data (the mean) rather than the raw scores themselves, we have to use a stat (section 4.4.5) to do this for us. Actually, we already used a stat when we plotted the boxplot in an earlier section, but we didn't notice because the boxplot geom sneaks off when we're not looking and uses the *bin* stat without us having to really do anything. However, if we want means then we have no choice but to dive head first into the pit of razors that is a *stat*. Specifically we are going to use *stat_summary()*.

The *stat_summary()* function takes the following general form:

```
stat_summary(function = x, geom = y)
```

Functions can be specified either for individual points (*fun.y*) or for the data as a whole (*fun.data*) and are set to be common statistical functions such as 'mean', 'median' and so on. As you might expect, the *geom* option is a way of telling the stat which geom to use to represent the function, and this can take on values such as 'errorbar', 'bar' and 'pointrange' (see Table 4.3). The *stat_summary()* function takes advantage of several built-in functions

Table 4.4 Using *stat_summary()* to create graphs

Option	Plots	Common geom
fun.y = mean	The mean	geom = "bar"
fun.y = median	The median	geom = "bar"
fun.data = mean_cl_normal()	95% confidence intervals assuming normality	geom = "errorbar" geom = "pointrange"
fun.data = mean_cl_boot()	95% confidence intervals based on a bootstrap (i.e., not assuming normality)	geom = "errorbar" geom = "pointrange"
mean_sdl()	Sample mean and standard deviation	geom = "errorbar" geom = "pointrange"
fun.data = median_hilow()	Median and upper and lower quantiles	geom = "pointrange"

from the *Hmisc* package, which should automatically be installed. Table 4.4 summarizes these functions and how they are specified within the *stat_summary()* function.

If we want to add the mean, displayed as bars, we can simply add this as a layer to 'bar' using the *stat_summary()* function:

```
bar + stat_summary(fun.y = mean, geom = "bar", fill = "White", colour
= "Black"
```

How do I plot an error bar graph?

As shown in Table 4.4, *fun.y = mean* computes the mean for us, *geom = "bar"* displays these values as bars, *fill = "White"* makes the bars white (the default is dark grey and you can replace with a different colour if you like), and *colour = "Black"* makes the outline of the bars black.

If we want to add error bars to create an **error bar chart**, we can again add these as a layer using *stat_summary()*:

```
+ stat_summary(fun.data = mean_cl_normal, geom = "pointrange")
```

This command adds a standard 95% confidence interval in the form of the pointrange geom. Again, if you like you could change the colour of the pointrange geom by setting its colour as described in Table 4.2.

Finally, let's add some nice labels to the graph using *lab()*:

```
+ labs(x = "Film", y = "Mean Arousal")
```

To sum up, if we put all of these commands together we can create the graph by executing the following command:

```
bar + stat_summary(fun.y = mean, geom = "bar", fill = "White", colour =
"Black") + stat_summary(fun.data = mean_cl_normal, geom = "pointrange") +
labs(x = "Film", y = "Mean Arousal")
```

Figure 4.23 shows the resulting bar chart. This graph displays the means (and the 95% confidence interval of those means) and shows us that on average, people were more aroused by *Memento* than they were by *Bridget Jones's Diary*. However, we originally wanted to look for gender effects, so we need to add this variable into the mix.

SELF-TEST

✓ Change the geom for the error bar to 'errorbar' and change its colour to red. Replot the graph.
✓ Plot the graph again but with bootstrapped confidence intervals.

FIGURE 4.23
Bar chart of the
mean arousal for
each of the two
films

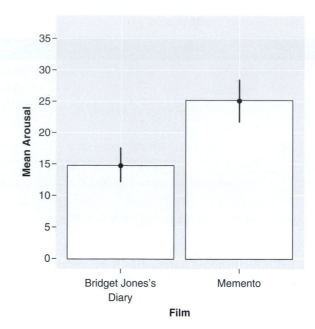

4.9.1.2. Bar charts for several independent variables ②

If we want to factor in gender we could do this in several ways. First we could set an aesthetic (such as colour) to represent the different genders, but we could also use faceting to create separate plots for men and women. We could also do both. Let's first look at separating men and women on the same graph. This takes a bit of work, but if we build up the code bit by bit the process should become clear.

First, as always we set up our plot object (again I've called it *bar*). This command is the same as before, except that we have set the *fill* aesthetic to be the variable **gender**. This means that any geom specified subsequently will be filled with different colours for men and women.

```
bar <- ggplot(chickFlick, aes(film, arousal, fill = gender))
```

If we want to add the mean, displayed as bars, we can simply add this as a layer to *bar* using the *stat_summary()* function as we did before, but with one important difference: we have to specify *position = "dodge"* (see section 4.4.6) so that the male and female bars are forced to stand side-by-side, rather than behind each other.

```
bar + stat_summary(fun.y = mean, geom = "bar", position="dodge")
```

As before, *fun.y = mean* computes the mean for us, *geom = "bar"* displays these values as bars.

If we want to add error bars we can again add these as a layer using *stat_summary()*:

```
+ stat_summary(fun.data = mean_cl_normal, geom = "errorbar", position = posi-
tion_dodge(width=0.90), width = 0.2)
```

This command is a bit more complicated than before. Note we have changed the geom to *errorbar*; by default these bars will be as wide as the bars displaying the mean, which looks a bit nasty, so I have reduced their width with *width = 0.2*, which should make them 20% of the width of the bar (which looks nice in my opinion). The other part of the command is that we have again had to use the *dodge* position to make sure that the error bars stand side-by-side. In this case *position = position_dodge(width=0.90)* does the trick, but you might have to play around with the values of *width* to get what you want.

Finally, let's add some nice labels to the graph using *lab()*:

```
+ labs(x = "Film", y = "Mean Arousal", fill = "Gender")
```

Notice that as well as specifying titles for each axis, I have specified a title for *fill*. This will give a title to the legend on the graph (if we omit this option the legend will be given the variable name as a title, which might be OK for you if you are less anally retentive than I am).

To sum up, if we put all of these commands together we can create the graph by executing the following command:

```
bar + stat_summary(fun.y = mean, geom = "bar", position="dodge") + stat_
summary(fun.data = mean_cl_normal, geom = "errorbar", position = position_
dodge(width = 0.90), width = 0.2) + labs(x = "Film", y = "Mean Arousal", fill
= "Gender")
```

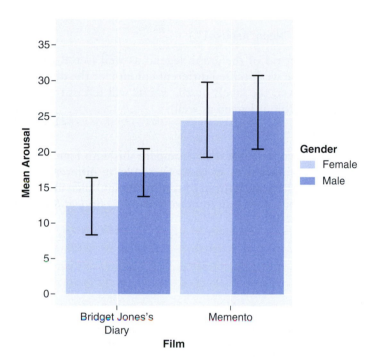

FIGURE 4.24

Bar chart of the mean arousal for each of the two films

Figure 4.24 shows the resulting bar chart. It looks pretty good, I think. It is possible to customise the colours that are used to fill the bars also (see R's Souls' Tip 4.3). Like the simple bar chart, this graph tells us that arousal was overall higher for *Memento* than for *Bridget Jones's Diary*, but it also splits this information by gender. The mean arousal for *Bridget Jones's Diary* shows that males were actually more aroused during this film than females. This indicates they enjoyed the film more than the women did. Contrast this with *Memento*, for which arousal levels are comparable in males and females. On the face of it, this contradicts the idea of a 'chick flick': it actually seems that men enjoy chick flicks more than the so-called 'chicks' do (probably because it's the only help we get to understand the complex workings of the female mind☺).

The second way to express gender would be to use this variable as a facet so that we display different plots for males and females:

```
bar <- ggplot(chickFlick, aes(film, arousal, fill = film))
```

Executing the above command sets up the graph in the same way as before. Note, however, that we do not need to use 'fill = gender' because we do not want to vary the colour by gender. (You can omit the fill command altogether, but I have set it so that the bars representing the different films are filled with different colours.) We set up the bar in the same way as before, except that we do not need to set the position to dodge because we are no longer plotting different bars for men and women on the same graph:

```
bar + stat_summary(fun.y = mean, geom = "bar")
```

We set up the error bar in the same way as before, except again we don't need to include a dodge:

```
+ stat_summary(fun.data = mean_cl_normal, geom = "errorbar", width = 0.2)
```

To get different plots for men and women we use the facet option and specify **gender** as the variable by which to facet:

```
+ facet_wrap( ~ gender)
```

We add labels as we did before:

```
+ labs(x = "Film", y = "Mean Arousal")
```

I've added an option to get rid of the graph legend as well (see R's Souls' Tip 4.2). I've included this option because we specified different colours for the different films so *ggplot* will create a legend; however, the labels on the *x*-axis will tell us to which film each bar relates so we don't need a colour legend as well):

```
+ opts(legend.position = "none")
```

The resulting graph is shown in Figure 4.25; compare this with Figure 4.24 and note how by using **gender** as a facet rather than an aesthetic results in different panels for men and women. The graphs show the same pattern of results though: men and women differ little in responses to *Memento*, but men showed more arousal to *Bridget Jones's Diary*.

FIGURE 4.25

The mean arousal (and 95% confidence interval) for two different films displayed as different graphs for men and women using *facet_wrap()*

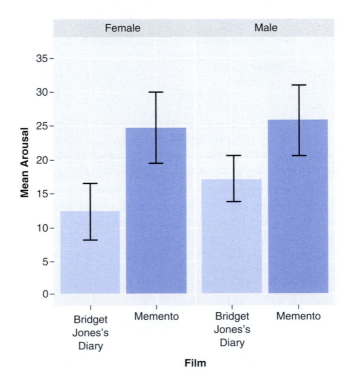

R's Souls' Tip 4.3 Custom colours ②

If you want to override the default fill colours, you can do this using the *scale_fill_manual()* function. For our chick flick data, for example, if we wanted blue bars for females and green for males then we can add the following command:

```
+ scale_fill_manual("Gender", c("Female" = "Blue", "Male" = "Green"))
```

Alternatively, you can use very specific colours by specifying colours using the RRGGBB system. For example, the following produces very specifically coloured blue and green bars:

```
+ scale_fill_manual("Gender", c("Female" = "#3366FF", "Male" = "#336633"))
```

Try adding these commands to the end of the command we used to generate Figure 4.24 and see the effect it has on the bar colours. Then experiment with other colours.

4.9.2. Line graphs ②

4.9.2.1. Line graphs of a single independent variable ②

Hiccups can be a serious problem: Charles Osborne apparently got a case of hiccups while slaughtering a hog (well, who wouldn't?) that lasted 67 years. People have many methods for stopping hiccups (a surprise, holding your breath), but actually medical science has put its collective mind to the task too. The official treatment methods include tongue-pulling manoeuvres, massage of the carotid artery, and, believe it or not, digital rectal massage (Fesmire, 1988). I don't know the details of what the digital rectal massage involved, but I can probably imagine. Let's say we wanted to put digital rectal massage to the test (as a cure for hiccups, I mean). We took 15 hiccup sufferers, and during a bout of hiccups administered each of the three procedures (in random order and at intervals of 5 minutes) after taking a baseline of how many hiccups they had per minute. We counted the number of hiccups in the minute after each procedure. Load the file **Hiccups.dat** from the companion website into a dataframe called *hiccupsData* by executing (again assuming you have set your working directory to be where the file is located):

```
hiccupsData <- read.delim("Hiccups.dat",  header = TRUE)
```

Figure 4.26 shows the data. Note there are four variables:

- **Baseline**: specifies the number of hiccups at baseline.

- **Tongue**: specifies the number of hiccups after tongue pulling.

- **Carotid**: specifies the number of hiccups after carotid artery massage.

- **Rectum**: specifies the number of hiccups after digital rectal massage.

FIGURE 4.26
The Hiccups.dat
data

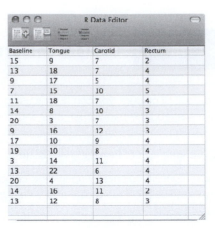

Baseline	Tongue	Carotid	Rectum
15	9	7	2
13	18	7	4
9	17	5	4
7	15	10	5
11	18	7	4
14	8	10	3
20	3	7	3
9	16	12	3
17	10	9	4
19	10	8	4
3	14	11	4
13	22	6	4
20	4	13	4
14	16	11	2
13	12	8	3

Each row in the data file represents a different person, so these data are laid out as a repeated-measures design, with each column representing a different treatment condition and every person undergoing each treatment.

These data are in the wrong format for *ggplot2* to use. We need all of the scores stacked up in a single column and then another variable that specifies the type of intervention.

SELF-TEST

✓ Thinking back to Chapter 3, use the *stack()* function to restructure the data into long format.

We can rearrange the data as follows (see section 3.9.4):

```
hiccups<-stack(hiccupsData)
names(hiccups)<-c("Hiccups","Intervention")
```

Executing these commands creates a new dataframe called *hiccups*, which has the number of hiccups in one column alongside a new variable containing the original variable name associated with each score (i.e., the column headings) in the other column (Figure 4.27). The *names()* function just assigns names to these new variables in the order that they appear in the dataframe. To plot a categorical variable in *ggplot()* it needs to be recognized as a factor, so we also need to create new variable in the *hiccups* dataframe called **Intervention_Factor**, which is just the **Intervention** variable converted into a factor:

```
hiccups$Intervention_Factor <- factor(hiccups$Intervention, levels =
hiccups$Intervention)
```

We are now ready to plot the graph. As always we first create the plot object and define the variables that we want to plot as aesthetics:

```
line <- ggplot(hiccups, aes(Intervention_Factor, Hiccups))
```

I have called the object *line*, and have created it using the *ggplot()* function. The function specifies the dataframe to be used (*hiccups*) and has set **Intervention_Factor** to be plotted on the *x*-axis, and **Hiccups** to be plotted on the *y*-axis.

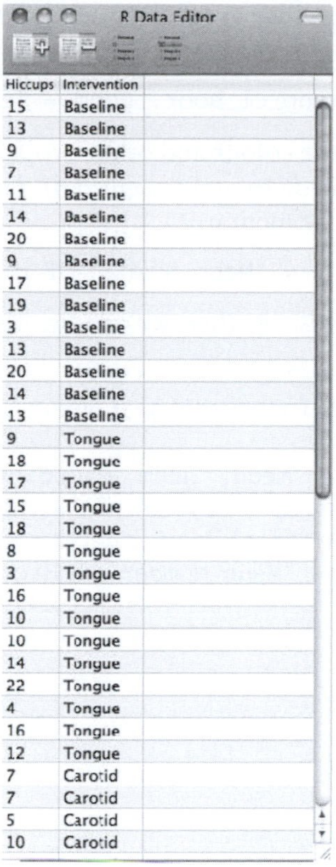

Hiccups	Intervention
15	Baseline
13	Baseline
9	Baseline
7	Baseline
11	Baseline
14	Baseline
20	Baseline
9	Baseline
17	Baseline
19	Baseline
3	Baseline
13	Baseline
20	Baseline
14	Baseline
13	Baseline
9	Tongue
18	Tongue
17	Tongue
15	Tongue
18	Tongue
8	Tongue
3	Tongue
16	Tongue
10	Tongue
10	Tongue
14	Tongue
22	Tongue
4	Tongue
16	Tongue
12	Tongue
7	Carotid
7	Carotid
5	Carotid
10	Carotid

FIGURE 4.27 The hiccups data in long format

Just as we did for our bar charts, we are going to use *stat_summary()* to create the mean values within each treatment condition. Therefore, as with the bar chart, we create a layer using *stat_summary()* and add this to the plot:

```
line + stat_summary(fun.y = mean, geom = "point")
```

Note that this command is exactly the same as for a bar chart, except that we have chosen the point geom rather than a bar. At the moment we have a plot with a symbol representing each group mean. If we want to connect these symbols with a line then we use *stat_summary()* again, we again specify *fun.y* to be the mean, but this time choose the *line* geom. To make the line display we also need to set an aesthetic of *group = 1*; this is because we are joining summary points (i.e., points that summarize a group) rather than individual data points. Therefore, we specify the line as:

```
+ stat_summary(fun.y = mean, geom = "line", aes(group = 1))
```

The above command will add a solid black line connecting the group means. Let's imagine we want this line to be blue, rather than black, and dashed rather than solid, we can simply add these aesthetics into the above command as follows:

```
+ stat_summary(fun.y = mean, geom = "line", aes(group = 1), colour = "Blue",
linetype = “dashed”)
```

Now let's add an error bar to each group mean. We can do this by adding another layer using *stat_summary()*. When we plotted an error bar on the bar chart we used a normal error bar, so this time let's add an error bar based on bootstrapping. We set the function for the data to be *mean_cl_boot* (*fun.data = mean_cl_boot*) – see Table 4.4 – and set the geom to be *errorbar* (you could use *pointrange* as we did for the bar chart if you prefer):

```
+ stat_summary(fun.data = mean_cl_boot, geom = "errorbar")
```

The default error bars are quite wide, so I recommend setting the width parameter to 0.2 to make them look nicer:

```
+ stat_summary(fun.data = mean_cl_boot, geom = "errorbar", width = 0.2)
```

You can, of course, also change the colour and other properties of the error bar in the usual way (e.g., by adding *colour = "Red"* to make them red). Finally, we will add some labels to the *x*- and *y*-axes using the *labs()* function:

```
+ labs(x = "Intervention", y = "Mean Number of Hiccups")
```

If we put all of these commands together, we can create the graph by executing the following command:

```
line <- ggplot(hiccups, aes(Intervention_Factor, Hiccups))

line + stat_summary(fun.y = mean, geom = "point") + stat_summary(fun.y =
mean, geom = "line", aes(group = 1),colour = "Blue", linetype = "dashed")
+ stat_summary(fun.data = mean_cl_boot, geom = "errorbar", width = 0.2) +
labs(x = "Intervention", y = "Mean Number of Hiccups")
```

FIGURE 4.28
Line chart with error bars of the mean number of hiccups at baseline and after various interventions

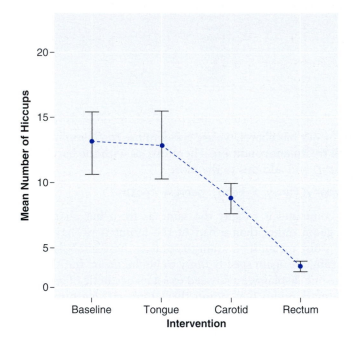

The resulting graph in Figure 4.28 displays the mean number of hiccups at baseline and after the three interventions (and the confidence intervals of those means based on bootstrapping). As we will see in Chapter 9, the error bars on graphs of repeated-measures designs aren't corrected for the fact that the data points are dependent; I don't want to get into the reasons why here because I want to keep things simple, but if you're doing a graph of your own data then I would read section 9.2 before you do.

We can conclude that the amount of hiccups after tongue pulling was about the same as at baseline; however, carotid artery massage reduced hiccups, but not by as much as a good old fashioned digital rectal massage. The moral here is: if you have hiccups, find something digital and go amuse yourself for a few minutes.

4.9.2 2.   Line graphs for several independent variables ②

We all like to text-message (especially students in my lectures who feel the need to text-message the person next to them to say 'Bloody hell, this guy is so boring I need to poke out my own eyes'). What will happen to the children, though? Not only will they develop super-sized thumbs, they might not learn correct written English. Imagine we conducted an experiment in which a group of 25 children was encouraged to send text messages on their mobile phones over a six-month period. A second group of 25 children was forbidden from sending text messages for the same period. To ensure that kids in this latter group didn't use their phones, this group was given armbands that administered painful shocks in the presence of radio waves (like those emitted from phones).[11] The outcome was a score on a grammatical test (as a percentage) that was measured both before and after the intervention. The first independent variable was, therefore, text message use (text messagers versus controls) and the second independent variable was the time at which grammatical ability was assessed (baseline or after 6 months). The data are in the file **Text Messages.dat**.

   Load this file into a dataframe called *textData* by executing this command (I'm assuming you have set the working directory to be where the data file is stored):

```
textData <- read.delim("TextMessages.dat", header = TRUE)
```

Figure 4.29 shows the data. Note there are three variables:

- **Group**: specifies whether they were in the text message group or the control group.
- **Baseline**: grammar scores at baseline.
- **Six_months**: grammar scores after 6 months.

   Each row in the data file represents a different person. These data are again in the wrong format for *ggplot2*. Instead of the current wide format, we need the data in long (i.e., molten) format (see section 3.9.4). This format will have the following variables:

- **Group**: specifies whether they were in the text message group or the control group.
- **Time**: specifies whether the score relates to baseline or 6 months.
- **Grammar_Score**: the grammar scores.

SELF-TEST

✓ Restructure the data to a new dataframe called *textMessages* that is in long format. Use the *factor()* function (see section 3.5.4.3) to convert the 'Time' variable to a factor with levels called 'Baseline' and '6 Months'.

   Assuming that you have done the self-test, you should now have a dataframe called *textMessages* that is formatted correctly for *ggplot2*. As ever, we set up our plot object (I've called it *line*). This command is the same as before, except that we have set the 'fill' aesthetic to be the variable **Group**. This means that any geom specified subsequently will

---

[11] Although this punished them for any attempts to use a mobile phone, because other people's phones also emit microwaves, an unfortunate side effect was that these children acquired a pathological fear of anyone talking on a mobile phone.

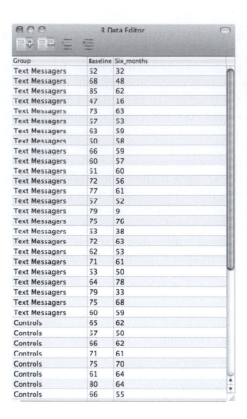

be filled with different colours for text messagers and the control group. Note that we have specified the data to be the *textMessages* dataframe, and for **Time** to be plotted on the *x*-axis and **Grammar_Score** on the *y*-axis.

```
line <- ggplot(textMessages, aes(Time, Grammar_Score, colour = Group))
```

If we want to add the means, displayed as symbols, we can add this as a layer to *line* using the *stat_summary()* function just as we did in the previous section:

```
line + stat_summary(fun.y = mean, geom = "point")
```

To add lines connecting the means we can add these as a layer using *stat_summary()* in exactly the same way as we did in the previous section. The main difference is that because in this example we have more than one group, rather than setting *aes(group = 1)* as we did before, we now set this aesthetic to be the variable (**Group**) that differentiates the different sets of means (*aes(group = Group)*):

```
+ stat_summary(fun.y = mean, geom = "line", aes(group = Group))
```

We can also add a layer containing error bars and a layer containing labels using the same commands as the previous example:

```
+ stat_summary(fun.data = mean_cl_boot, geom = "errorbar", width = 0.2) +
labs(x = "Time", y = "Mean Grammar Score", colour = "Group")
```

If we put all of these commands together we can create the graph by executing the following command:

```
line + stat_summary(fun.y = mean, geom = "point") + stat_summary(fun.y =
mean, geom = "line", aes(group = Group)) + stat_summary(fun.data = mean_cl_
boot, geom = "errorbar", width = 0.2) + labs(x = "Time", y = "Mean Grammar
Score", colour = "Group")
```

SELF-TEST

✓ Use what you have learnt to repeat the text message data plot but to also have different symbols for text messagers and controls and different types of lines.

Figure 4.30 shows the resulting chart. It shows that at baseline (before the intervention) the grammar scores were comparable in our two groups; however, after the intervention, the grammar scores were lower in the text messagers than in the controls. Also, if you look at the dark blue line you can see that text messagers' grammar scores have fallen over the 6 months; compare this to the controls (the red line on your screen, or black in the figure) whose grammar scores are fairly similar over time. We could, therefore, conclude that text messaging has a detrimental effect on children's understanding of English grammar and civilization will crumble, with Abaddon rising cackling from his bottomless pit to claim our wretched souls. Maybe.

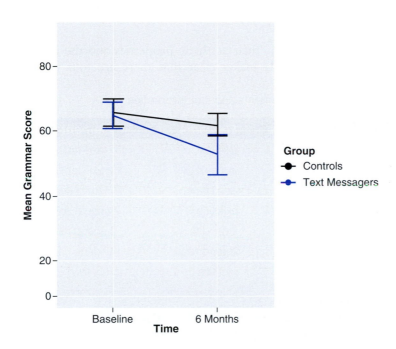

FIGURE 4.30
Error bar graph of the mean grammar score over 6 months in children who were allowed to text-message versus those who were forbidden

4.10. Themes and options ①

I mentioned earlier that *ggplot2* produces Tufte-friendly graphs. In fact, it has two built-in themes. The default is called *theme_grey()*, which follows Tufte's advice in that it uses grid lines to ease interpretation but makes them have low visual impact so that they do not distract the eye from the data. The second theme is a more traditional black and white theme called *theme_bw()*. The two themes are shown in Figure 4.31.

As well as these global themes, the *opts()* function allows you to control the look of specific parts of the plot. For example, you can define a title, set the properties of that title

FIGURE 4.31
Default graph
styles in *ggplot2*:
the left panel
shows *theme_
grey()*, the right
panel shows
theme_bw()

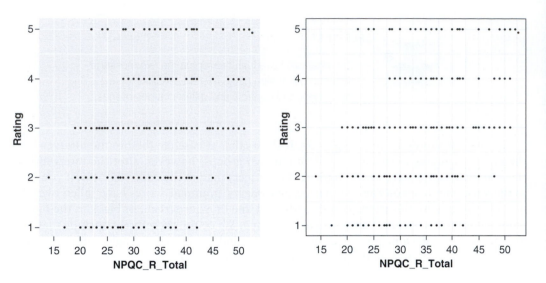

(size, font, colour, etc.). You can also change the look of axes, grid lines, background panels and text. You apply theme and formatting instructions by adding a layer to the plot:

```
myGraph + geom_point() + opts()
```

Table 4.5 shows these themes, their aesthetic properties and the elements of the plot associated with them. The table makes clear that there are four types of theme that

Table 4.5   Summary of theme elements and their properties

Theme	Properties	Elements	Element Description
theme_text()	family face colour size hjust vjust angle lineheight	axis.text.x axis.text.y axis.title.x axis.title.y legend.text legend.title plot.title strip.text.x strip.text.y	x-axis label y-axis label Horizontal tick labels Vertical tick labels Legend labels Legend name Plot title Horizontal facet label text Vertical facet label text
theme_line()	colour size linetype	panel.grid.major panel.grid.minor	Major grid lines Minor grid lines
theme_segment()	colour size linetype	axis.line axis.ticks	Line along an axis Axis tick marks
theme_rect()	colour size linetype fill	legend.background legend.key panel.background panel.background plot.background strip.background	Background of legend Background under legend key Background of panel Border of panel Background of the entire plot Background of facet labels

determine the appearance of text (*theme_text*), lines (*theme_line*), axes (*theme_segment*) and rectangles (*theme_rect*). Each of these themes has properties that can be adjusted; so for all of them you can adjust size and colour, for text you can also adjust things like the font family and angle, for rectangles you can change the fill colour and so on. Different elements of a plot can be changed by adjusting the particular theme attached to that element. So, for example, if we wanted to change the colour of the major grid lines to blue, we would have to do this by setting the colour aesthetic of the *panel.grid.major* element using *theme_line()*. Aesthetic properties are set in the same way as described in section 4.4.3. Therefore, we would do this as follows:

```
+ opts(panel.grid.major = theme_line(colour = "Blue"))
```

Similarly, we could make the axes have blue lines with:

```
+ opts(axis.line = theme_segment(colour = "Blue"))
```

or dashed lines by using:

```
+ opts(axis.line = theme_segment(linetype = 2))
```

The possibilities are endless, and I can't explain them all without killing several more rainforests, but I hope that you get the general idea.

What have I discovered about statistics? ①

This chapter has looked at how to inspect your data using graphs. We've covered a lot of different graphs. We began by covering some general advice on how to draw graphs and we can sum that up as minimal is best: no pink, no 3-D effects, no pictures of Errol your pet ferret superimposed on the graph – oh, and did I mention no pink? We have looked at graphs that tell you about the distribution of your data (histograms, boxplots and density plots), that show summary statistics about your data (bar charts, error bar charts, line charts, drop-line charts) and that show relationships between variables (scatterplots). Throughout the chapter we looked at how we can edit graphs to make them look minimal (and of course to colour them pink, but we know better than to do that, don't we?).

We also discovered that I liked to explore as a child. I was constantly dragging my dad (or was it the other way around?) over piles of rocks along any beach we happened to be on. However, at this time I also started to explore great literature, although unlike my cleverer older brother who was reading Albert Einstein's papers (well, Isaac Asimov) as an embryo, my literary preferences were more in keeping with my intellect, as we will see.

R packages used in this chapter

ggplot2

R functions used in this chapter

file.path()	ggplot()
geom_boxplot()	ggsave()
geom_density()	labs()
geom_histogram()	opts()
geom_line()	qplot()
geom_point()	stat_summary()
geom_smooth()	Sys.getenv()

Key terms that I've discovered

Bar chart	Line chart
Boxplot (box–whisker plot)	Outlier
Chartjunk	Regression line
Density plot	Scatterplot
Error bar chart	

Smart Alex's tasks

- **Task 1**: Using the data from Chapter 3 (which you should have saved, but if you didn't, re-enter it from Table 3.6), plot and interpret the following graphs: ①

  o An error bar chart showing the mean number of friends for students and lecturers.
  o An error bar chart showing the mean alcohol consumption for students and lecturers.
  o An error line chart showing the mean income for students and lecturers.
  o An error line chart showing the mean neuroticism for students and lecturers.
  o A scatterplot with regression lines of alcohol consumption and neuroticism grouped by lecturer/student.

- **Task 2**: Using the **Infidelity** data from Chapter 3 (see Smart Alex's Task 3), plot a clustered error bar chart of the mean number of bullets used against self and partner for males and females. ①

Answers can be found on the companion website.

Further reading

Tufte, E. R. (2001). *The visual display of quantitative information* (2nd ed.). Cheshire, CT: Graphics Press.

Wainer, H. (1984). How to display data badly. *American Statistician*, *38*(2), 137–147.

Wickham, H. (2009). *ggplot2: Elegant graphics for data analysis*. New York: Springer.

Wilkinson, L. (2005). *The grammar of graphics*. New York: Springer-Verlag.

Wright, D. B., & Williams, S. (2003). Producing bad results sections. *The Psychologist*, *16*, 646–648. (This is a very accessible article on how to present data. Dan usually has this article on his website so Google Dan Wright to find where his web pages are located.)

Web resources:

http://junkcharts.typepad.com/ is an amusing look at bad graphs.
http://had.co.nz/ggplot2/ is the official *ggplot2* website (and very useful it is, too).

Interesting real research

Fesmire, F. M. (1988). Termination of intractable hiccups with digital rectal massage. *Annals of Emergency Medicine*, *17*(8), 872.

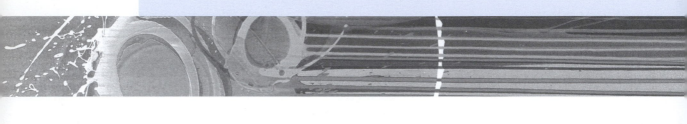

Exploring assumptions

5

FIGURE 5.1
I came first in
the competition
for who has the
smallest brain

5.1. What will this chapter tell me? ①

When we were learning to read at primary school, we used to read versions of stories by the famous storyteller Hans Christian Andersen. One of my favourites was the story of the ugly duckling. This duckling was a big ugly grey bird, so ugly that even a dog would not bite him. The poor duckling was ridiculed, ostracized and pecked by the other ducks. Eventually, it became too much for him and he flew to the swans, the royal birds, hoping that they would end his misery by killing him because he was so ugly. As he stared into the water, though, he saw not an ugly grey bird but a beautiful swan. Data are much the same. Sometimes they're just big, grey and ugly and don't do any of the things that they're supposed to do. When we get data like these, we swear at them, curse them, peck them and hope that they'll fly away and be killed by the swans. Alternatively, we can try to force our data into becoming beautiful swans. That's what this chapter is all about: assessing how much of an ugly duckling of a data set you have, and discovering how to turn it into a swan. Remember, though, a swan can break your arm.[1]

5.2. What are assumptions? ①

Some academics tend to regard assumptions as rather tedious things about which no one really need worry. When I mention statistical assumptions to my fellow psychologists they tend to give me that raised eyebrow, 'good grief, get a life' look and then ignore me. However, there are good reasons for taking assumptions seriously. Imagine that I go over to a friend's house, the lights are on and it's obvious that someone is at home. I ring the doorbell and no one answers. From that experience, I conclude that my friend hates me and that I am a terrible, unlovable person. How tenable is this conclusion? Well, there is a reality that I am trying to tap (i.e., whether my friend likes or hates me), and I have collected data about that reality (I've gone to his house, seen that he's at home, rung the doorbell and got no response). Imagine that in reality my friend likes me (he's a lousy judge of character); in this scenario, my conclusion is false. Why have my data led me to the wrong conclusion? The answer is simple: I had assumed that my friend's doorbell was working and under this assumption the conclusion that I made from my data was accurate (my friend heard the bell but chose to ignore it because he hates me). However, this assumption was not true – his doorbell was not working, which is why he didn't answer the door – and as a consequence the conclusion I drew about reality was completely false. It pays to check assumptions and your doorbell batteries.

Why bother with assumptions?

Enough about doorbells, friends and my social life: the point to remember is that when assumptions are broken we stop being able to draw accurate conclusions about reality. Different statistical models assume different things, and if these models are going to reflect reality accurately then these assumptions need to be true. This chapter is going to deal with some particularly ubiquitous assumptions so that you know how to slay these particular beasts as we battle our way through the rest of the book. However, be warned: some tests have their own unique two-headed, fire-breathing, green-scaled assumptions and these will jump out from behind a mound of blood-soaked moss and try to eat us alive when we least expect them to. Onward into battle …

5.3. Assumptions of parametric data ①

What are the assumptions of parametric data?

Many of the statistical procedures described in this book are **parametric tests** based on the normal distribution (which is described in section 1.7.4). A parametric test is one that requires data from one of the large catalogue of distributions that statisticians have described, and for data to be parametric certain assumptions must be true. If you use a parametric test when your data are not parametric then the results are likely to be inaccurate. Therefore, it is very important that you check the assumptions before deciding which statistical test is appropriate. Throughout

---

[1] Although it is theoretically possible, apparently you'd have to be weak boned, and swans are nice and wouldn't do that sort of thing.

this book you will become aware of my obsession with assumptions and checking them. Most parametric tests based on the normal distribution have four basic assumptions that must be met for the test to be accurate. Many students find checking assumptions a pretty tedious affair, and often get confused about how to tell whether or not an assumption has been met. Therefore, this chapter is designed to take you on a step-by-step tour of the world of parametric assumptions. Now, you may think that assumptions are not very exciting, but they can have great benefits: for one thing, you can impress your supervisor/lecturer by spotting all of the test assumptions that they have violated throughout their careers. You can then rubbish, on statistical grounds, the theories they have spent their lifetime developing – and they can't argue with you,[2] but they can poke your eyes out. The assumptions of parametric tests are:

1   **Normally distributed data**: This is a tricky and misunderstood assumption because it means different things in different contexts. For this reason I will spend most of the chapter discussing this assumption. In short, the rationale behind hypothesis testing relies on having something that is normally distributed (in some cases it's the sampling distribution, in others the errors in the model), and so if this assumption is not met then the logic behind hypothesis testing is flawed (we came across these principles in Chapters 1 and 2).

2   **Homogeneity of variance**: This assumption means that the variances should be the same throughout the data. In designs in which you test several groups of participants this assumption means that each of these samples comes from populations with the same variance. In correlational designs, this assumption means that the variance of one variable should be stable at all levels of the other variable (see section 5.7).

3   **Interval data**: Data should be measured at least at the interval level. This assumption is tested by common sense and so won't be discussed further (but do read section 1.5.1.2 again to remind yourself of what we mean by interval data).

4   **Independence**: This assumption, like that of normality, is different depending on the test you're using. In some cases it means that data from different participants are independent, which means that the behaviour of one participant does not influence the behaviour of another. In repeated-measures designs (in which participants are measured in more than one experimental condition), we expect scores in the experimental conditions to be non-independent for a given participant, but behaviour between different participants should be independent. As an example, imagine two people, Paul and Julie, were participants in an experiment where they had to indicate whether they remembered having seen particular photos earlier on in the experiment. If Paul and Julie were to confer about whether they'd seen certain pictures then their answers would *not* be independent: Julie's response to a given question would depend on Paul's answer, and this would violate the assumption of independence. If Paul and Julie were unable to confer (if they were locked in different rooms) then their responses should be independent (unless they're telepathic): Julie's should not influence Paul's responses. In regression, however, this assumption also relates to the errors in the regression model being uncorrelated, but we'll discuss that more in Chapter 7.

We will, therefore, focus in this chapter on the assumptions of normality and homogeneity of variance.

---

[2] When I was doing my Ph.D., we were set a task by our statistics lecturer in which we had to find some published papers and criticize the statistical methods in them. I chose one of my supervisor's papers and proceeded to slag off every aspect of the data analysis (and I was being *very* pedantic about it all). Imagine my horror when my supervisor came bounding down the corridor with a big grin on his face and declared that, unbeknownst to me, he was the second marker of my essay. Luckily, he had a sense of humour and I got a good mark.☺

5.4. Packages used in this chapter ①

Some useful packages for exploring data are *car*, *ggplot2* (for graphs), *pastecs* (for descriptive statistics) and *psych*. Of course, if you plan to use R Commander then you need the *Rcmdr* package installed too (see section 3.6). If you do not have these packages installed, you can install them by executing the following commands:

```
install.packages("car"); install.packages("ggplot2");
install.packages("pastecs"); install.packages("psych")
```

You then need to load these packages by executing the commands:

```
library(car);    library(ggplot2);    library(pastecs);    library(psych);
library(Rcmdr)
```

5.5. The assumption of normality ①

We encountered the normal distribution back in Chapter 1, we know what it looks like and we (hopefully) understand it. You'd think then that this assumption would be easy to understand – it just means that our data are normally distributed, right? Actually, no. In many statistical tests (e.g., the *t*-test) we assume that the sampling distribution is normally distributed. This is a problem because we don't have access to this distribution – we can't simply look at its shape and see whether it is normally distributed. However, we know from the central limit theorem (section 2.5.1) that if the sample data are approximately normal then the sampling distribution will be also. Therefore, people tend to look at their sample data to see if they are normally distributed. If so, then they have a little party to celebrate and assume that the sampling distribution (which is what actually matters) is also. We also know from the central limit theorem that in big samples the sampling distribution tends to be normal anyway – regardless of the shape of the data we actually collected (and remember that the sampling distribution will tend to be normal regardless of the population distribution in samples of 30 or more). As our sample gets bigger, then, we can be more confident that the sampling distribution is normally distributed (but see Jane Superbrain Box 5.1).

The assumption of normality is also important in research using regression (or general linear models). General linear models, as we will see in Chapter 7, assume that errors in the model (basically, the deviations we encountered in section 2.4.2) are normally distributed.

In both cases it might be useful to test for normality, and that's what this section is dedicated to explaining. Essentially, we can look for normality visually, look at values that quantify aspects of a distribution (i.e., skew and kurtosis) and compare the distribution we have to a normal distribution to see if it is different.

5.5.1. Oh no, it's that pesky frequency distribution again: checking normality visually ①

We discovered in section 1.7.1 that frequency distributions are a useful way to look at the shape of a distribution. In addition, we discovered how to plot these graphs in section 4.4.8. Therefore, we are already equipped to look for normality in our sample using a graph. Let's return to the Download Festival data from Chapter 4. Remember that a biologist had visited the Download Festival (a rock and heavy metal festival in the UK) and assessed people's hygiene over the three days of the festival using a standardized technique that results in a score ranging between 0 (you smell like a rotting corpse that's hiding up a skunk's anus) and 4 (you smell of sweet roses on a fresh spring day). The data file can be downloaded from the companion website (**DownloadFestival.dat**) – remember to use the version of the data for which the outlier has been corrected (if you haven't a clue what I mean, then read section 4.4.8 or your graphs will look very different from mine!).

SELF-TEST

✓ Using what you learnt in Chapter 4, plot histograms for the hygiene scores for the three days of the Download Festival. (For reasons that will become apparent, use *geom_histogram(aes(y = ..density..)* rather than *geom_histogram()*.)

When you drew the histograms, this gave you the distributions. It might be nice to also have a plot of what a normal distribution looks like, for comparison purposes. Even better would be if that we could put a normal distribution onto the same plot. Well, we can using the power of *ggplot2*. First, load in the data:

```
dlf <- read.delim("DownloadFestival.dat", header=TRUE)
```

To draw the histogram, you should have used code something like:

```
hist.day1 <- ggplot(dlf, aes(day1)) + opts(legend.position = "none") +
geom_histogram(aes(y = ..density..), colour = "black", fill = "white") +
labs(x = "Hygiene score on day 1", y = "Density")
```

```
hist.day1
```

To see what this function is doing we can break down the command:

- *ggplot(dlf, aes(day1))*: This tells **R** to plot the **day1** variable from the *dlf* dataframe.

- *opts(legend.position = "none")*: This command gets rid of the legend of the graph.

- *geom_histogram(aes(y=..density..), colour = "black", fill="white")*: This command plots the histogram, sets the line colour to be black and the fill colour to be white. Notice that we have asked for a density plot rather than frequency because we want to plot the normal curve.

- *labs(x = "Hygiene score on day 1", y = "Density")*: this command sets the labels for the x- and y-axes.

We can add another layer to the chart, which is a normal curve. We need to tell *ggplot2* what mean and standard deviation we'd like on that curve though. And what we'd like is the same mean and standard deviation that we have in our data. To add the normal curve, we take the existing histogram object (*hist.day1*) and add a new layer that uses *stat_function()* to produce a normal curve and lay it on top of the histogram:

```
hist.day1 + stat_function(fun = dnorm, args = list(mean = mean(dlf$day1,
na.rm = TRUE), sd = sd(dlf$day1, na.rm = TRUE)), colour = "black", size = 1)
```

The **stat_function()** command draws the normal curve using the function **dnorm()**. This function basically returns the probability (i.e., the density) for a given value from a normal distribution of known mean and standard deviation. The rest of the command specifies the mean as being the mean of the **day1** variable after removing any missing values (*mean = mean (dlf$day1, na.rm = TRUE)*), and the standard deviation as being that of **day1** (), *sd = sd(dlf$day1, na.rm = TRUE)*). We also set the line colour as black and the line width as 1.[3]

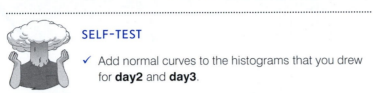

SELF-TEST

✓ Add normal curves to the histograms that you drew for **day2** and **day3**.

There is another useful graph that we can inspect to see if a distribution is normal called a **Q-Q plot** (quantile–quantile plot; a **quantile** is the proportion of cases we find below a certain value). This graph plots the cumulative values we have in our data against the cumulative probability of a particular distribution (in this case we would specify a normal distribution). What this means is that the data are ranked and sorted. Each value is compared to the expected value that the score should have in a normal distribution and they are plotted against one another. If the data are normally distributed then the actual scores will have the same distribution as the score we expect from a normal distribution, and you'll get a lovely straight diagonal line. If values fall on the diagonal of the plot then the variable is normally distributed, but deviations from the diagonal show deviations from normality.

To draw a Q-Q plot using the *ggplot2* package, we can use the **qplot()** function in conjunction with the *qq* statistic. Execute the following code:

```
qqplot.day1 <- qplot(sample = dlf$day1, stat="qq")
```

```
qqplot.day1
```

(Note that by default *ggplot2* assumes you want to compare your distribution with a normal distribution – you can change that if you want to, but it's so rare that we're not going to worry about it here.)

SELF-TEST

✓ Create Q-Q plots for the variables **day2** and **day3**.

Figure 5.2 shows the histograms (from the self-test task) and the corresponding Q-Q plots. The first thing to note is that the data from day 1 look a lot more healthy since we've removed the data point that was mistyped back in section 4.7. In fact the distribution is amazingly normal looking: it is nicely symmetrical and doesn't seem too pointy or flat – these are good things! This is echoed by the Q-Q plot: note that the data points all fall very close to the 'ideal' diagonal line.

---

[3] I have built up the histogram and normal plot in two stages because I think it makes it easier to understand what you're doing, but you could build the plot in a single command:

```
hist.day1 <- ggplot(dlf, aes(day1)) + opts(legend.position = "none") + geom_
histogram(aes(y = ..density..), colour = "black", fill = "white") + labs(x =
"Hygiene score on day 1", y = "Density") + stat_function(fun = dnorm, args =
list(mean = mean(dlf$day1, na.rm = TRUE), sd = sd(dlf$day1, na.rm = TRUE)), colour
= "black", size = 1)
```

```
hist.day1
```

FIGURE 5.2
Histograms (left)
and Q-Q plots
(right) of the
hygiene scores
over the three
days of the
Download Festival

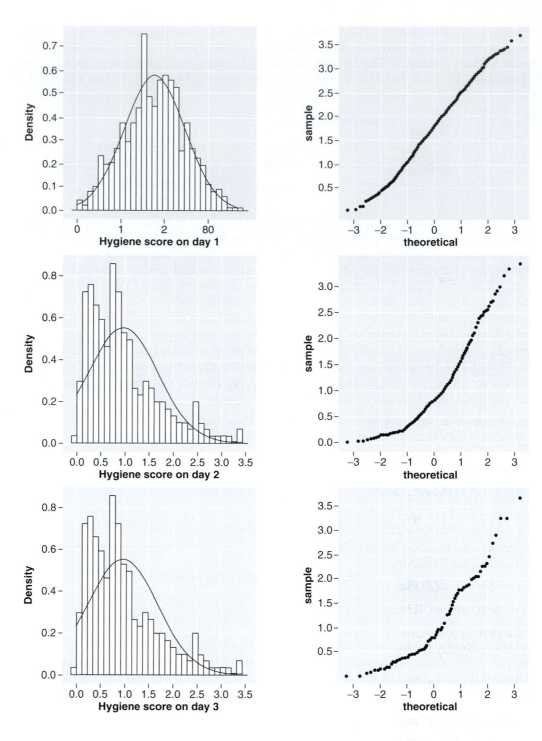

However, the distributions for days 2 and 3 are not nearly as symmetrical. In fact, they both look positively skewed. Again, this can be seen in the Q-Q plots by the data values deviating away from the diagonal. In general, what this seems to suggest is that by days 2 and 3, hygiene scores were much more clustered around the low end of the scale. Remember that the lower the score, the less hygienic the person is, so this suggests that generally people became smellier as the festival progressed. The skew occurs because a substantial minority insisted on upholding their levels of hygiene (against all odds!) over the course of the festival (I find baby wet-wipes are indispensable). However, these skewed distributions might cause us a problem if we want to use parametric tests. In the next section we'll look at ways to try to quantify the skew and kurtosis of these distributions.

5.5.2. Quantifying normality with numbers ①

It is all very well to look at histograms, but they are subjective and open to abuse (I can imagine researchers sitting looking at a completely distorted distribution and saying 'yep, well Bob, that looks normal to me', and Bob replying 'yep, sure does'). Therefore, having inspected the distribution of hygiene scores visually, we can move on to look at ways to quantify the shape of the distributions and to look for outliers. To further explore the distribution of the variables, we can use the **describe()** function, in the *psych* package.

```
describe(dlf$day1)
```

We can also use the **stat.desc()** function of the *pastecs* package,[4] which takes the general form:

```
stat.desc(variable name, basic = TRUE, norm = FALSE)
```

In this function, we simply name our variable and by default (i.e., if we simply name a variable and don't include the other commands) we'll get a whole host of statistics including some basic ones such as the number of cases (because *basic = TRUE* by default) but not including statistics relating to the normal distribution (because *norm = FALSE* by default). To my mind the basic statistics are not very useful so I usually specify *basic = FALSE* (to get rid of these), but in the current context it is useful to override the default and specify *norm = TRUE* so that we get statistics relating to the distribution of scores. Therefore, we could execute:

```
stat.desc(dlf$day1, basic = FALSE, norm = TRUE)
```

Note that we have specified the variable **day1** in the *dlf* dataframe, asked *not* to see the basic statistics (*basic = FALSE*) but asked to see the normality statistics (*norm = TRUE*).

We can also use *describe()* and *stat.desc()* with more than one variable at the same time, using the *cbind()* function to combine two or more variables (see R's Souls' Tip 3.5).

```
describe(cbind(dlf$day1, dlf$day2, dlf$day3))
```

```
stat.desc(cbind(dlf$day1, dlf$day2, dlf$day3), basic = FALSE, norm = TRUE)
```

Note that in each case we have simply replaced a single variable with *cbind(dlf$day1, dlf$day2, dlf$day3)* which combines the three variables **day1**, **day2**, and **day3** into a single object.

A second way to describe more than one variable is to select the variable names directly from the data set (see section 3.9.1):

```
describe(dlf[,c("day1", "day2", "day3")])
```

```
stat.desc(dlf[, c("day1", "day2", "day3")], basic = FALSE, norm = TRUE)
```

---

[4] There's always a second way to do something with **R**. And often a third, fourth and fifth way. While writing this book Jeremy and I would often look at each other's bits (and sometimes what we'd written too) and then send an email saying 'oh, I didn't know you could do that, I always use a different function in a different package'. People can become quite attached to their 'favourite' way of doing things in **R**, but obviously we're way too cool to have favourite ways of doing stats, which is why I didn't at all insist on adding reams of stuff on *stat.desc()* because I prefer it to Jeremy's crappy old *describe()* function.

Remember that we can select rows and columns using *[rows, columns]*, therefore, *dlf[, c("day1", "day2", "day3")]* means from the *dlf* dataframe select all of the rows (because nothing is specified before the comma) and select the columns labelled *day1*, *day2*, and *day3* (because we have specified *c("day1", "day2", "day3")*).

R's Souls' Tip 5.1   Funny numbers ①

You might notice that **R** sometimes reports numbers with the letter 'e' placed in the mix just to confuse you. For example, you might see a value such as 9.612 e−02 and many students find this notation confusing. Well, this notation means 9.612×10^{-2} (which might be a more familiar notation, or could be even more confusing). OK, some of you are still confused. Well think of e−02 as meaning 'move the decimal place 2 places to the left', so 9.612 e−02 becomes 0.09612. If the notation read 9.612 e−01, then that would be 0.9612, and if it read 9.612 e−03, that would be 0.009612. Likewise, think of e+02 (notice the minus sign has changed) as meaning 'move the decimal place 2 places to the right'. So 9.612 e+02 becomes 961.2.

The results of these commands are shown in Output 5.1 (*describe*) and Output 5.2 (*stat.desc*). These outputs basically contain the same values[5] although they are presented in a different notation in Output 5.2 (see R's Souls' Tip 5.1). We can see that, on average, hygiene scores were 1.77 (out of 4) on day 1 of the festival, but went down to 0.96 and 0.98 on days 2 and 3, respectively. The other important measures for our purposes are the skew and the kurtosis (see section 1.7.1). The values of skew and kurtosis should be zero in a normal distribution. Positive values of skew indicate a pile-up of scores on the left of the distribution, whereas negative values indicate a pile-up on the right. Positive values of kurtosis indicate a pointy and heavy-tailed distribution, whereas negative values indicate a flat and light-tailed distribution. The further the value is from zero, the more likely it is that the data are not normally distributed. For day 1 the skew value is very close to zero (which is good) and kurtosis is a little negative. For days 2 and 3, though, there is a skew of around 1 (positive skew).

Although the values of skew and kurtosis are informative, we can convert these values to *z*-scores. We saw in section 1.7.4 that a *z*-score is simply a score from a distribution that has a mean of 0 and a standard deviation of 1. We also saw that this distribution has known properties that we can use. Converting scores to a *z*-score can be useful (if treated with suitable caution) because (1) we can compare skew and kurtosis values in different samples that used different measures, and (2) we can see how likely our values of skew and kurtosis are to occur. To transform any score to a *z*-score you simply subtract the mean of the distribution (in this case zero) and then divide by the standard deviation of the distribution (in this case we use the standard error). Skew and kurtosis are converted to *z*-scores in exactly this way.

$$z_{skewness} = \frac{S - 0}{SE_{skewness}} \qquad z_{kurtosis} = \frac{K - 0}{SE_{kurtosis}}$$

---

[5] The observant will notice that the values of kurtosis differ, this is because *describe()* produces an unbiased estimate (DeCarlo, 1997) whereas *stat.desc()* produces a biased one.

In the above equations, the values of S (skew) and K (kurtosis) and their respective standard errors are produced by **R**. These z-scores can be compared against values that you would expect to get by chance alone (i.e., known values for the normal distribution shown in the Appendix). So, an absolute value greater than 1.96 is significant at $p < .05$, above 2.58 is significant at $p < .01$, and above 3.29 is significant at $p < .001$. Large samples will give rise to small standard errors and so when sample sizes are big, significant values arise from even small deviations from normality. In smallish samples it's OK to look for values above 1.96; however, in large samples this criterion should be increased to the 2.58 one and in very large samples, because of the problem of small standard errors that I've described, no criterion should be applied. If you have a large sample (200 or more) it is more important to look at the shape of the distribution visually and to look at the value of the skew and kurtosis statistics rather than calculate their significance.

```
var n   mean   sd median trimmed mad  min  max range skew kurtosis se
 1 809 1.77 0.69   1.79    1.77 0.70 0.02 3.69 3.67 0.00   -0.41 0.02
 2 264 0.96 0.72   0.79    0.87 0.61 0.00 3.44 3.44 1.08    0.82 0.04
 3 123 0.98 0.71   0.76    0.90 0.61 0.02 3.41 3.39 1.01    0.73 0.06
```

Output 5.1

```
                     day1          day2          day3
median        1.790000000  7.900000e-01  7.600000e-01
mean          1.770828183  9.609091e-01  9.765041e-01
SE.mean       0.024396670  4.436095e-02  6.404352e-02
CI.mean.0.95  0.047888328  8.734781e-02  1.267805e-01
var           0.481514784  5.195239e-01  5.044934e-01
std.dev       0.693912663  7.207801e-01  7.102770e-01
coef.var      0.391857702  7.501022e-01  7.273672e-01
skewness     -0.003155393  1.082811e+00  1.007813e+00
skew.2SE     -0.018353763  3.611574e+00  2.309035e+00
kurtosis     -0.423991408  7.554615e-01  5.945454e-01
kurt.2SE     -1.234611514  1.264508e+00  6.862946e-01
normtest.W    0.995907247  9.083185e-01  9.077513e-01
normtest.p    0.031846386  1.281495e-11  3.804334e-07
```

Output 5.2

The *stat.desc()* function produces *skew.2SE* and *kurt.2SE*, which are the skew and kurtosis value divided by 2 standard errors. Remember that z is significant if it is greater than 2 (well, 1.96), therefore this statistic is simply the equations above in a slightly different format. We have said that if the skew divided by its standard error is greater than 2 then it is significant (at $p < .05$), which is the same as saying that if the skew divided by 2 times the standard error is greater than 1 then it is significant (at $p < .05$). In other words, if *skew.2SE* or *kurt.2SE* are greater than 1 (ignoring the plus or minus sign) then you have significant skew/kurtosis (at $p < .05$); values greater than 1.29 indicate significance at $p < .01$, and above 1.65 indicate significance at $p < .001$. However, as I have just said, you would only use this criterion in fairly small samples so you need to interpret these values of *skew.2SE* or *kurt.2SE* cautiously.

For the hygiene scores, the values of *skew.2SE* are −0.018, 3.612, and 2.309 for days 1, 2 and 3 respectively, indicating significant skew on days 2 and 3; the values of *kurt.2SE* are −1.235, 1.265, and 0.686, indicating significant kurtosis on days 1 and 2, but not day 3. However, bear in mind what I just said about large samples because our sample size is pretty big so the histograms are better indicators of the shape of the distribution.

The output of *stat.desc()* also gives us the Shapiro–Wilk test of normality, which we look at in some detail in section 5.6. For the time being, just note that the test and its probability value can be found in Output 5.2 labelled as *normtest.W* and *normtest.p*.

R's Souls' Tip 5.2 Changing how many decimal places are displayed in your output ①

Output 5.2 looks pretty horrible because of all of the decimal places and the scientific notation (i.e., 7.900000e–01). Most of this precision is unnecessary for everyday purposes. However, we can easily convert our output using the **round()** function. This function takes the general form:

```
round(object that we want to round, digits = x)
```

Therefore, we can stick an object into this function and then set *digits* to be the number of decimal places that we want. For example, if we wanted Output 5.2 to be displayed to 3 decimal places we could execute:

```
round(stat.desc(dlf[, c("day1", "day2", "day3")]), basic = FALSE, norm = TRUE), digits = 3)
```

Note that we have simply placed the original command (*stat.desc(dlf[, c("day1", "day2", "day3")], basic = FALSE, norm = TRUE*)) within the *round()* function, and then set digits to be 3. The result is a more palatable output:

```
               day1    day2    day3
median        1.790   0.790   0.760
mean          1.771   0.961   0.977
SE.mean       0.024   0.044   0.064
CI.mean.0.95  0.048   0.087   0.127
var           0.482   0.520   0.504
std.dev       0.694   0.721   0.710
coef.var      0.392   0.750   0.727
skewness     -0.003   1.083   1.008
skew.2SE     -0.018   3.612   2.309
kurtosis     -0.424   0.755   0.595
kurt.2SE     -1.235   1.265   0.686
normtest.W    0.996   0.908   0.908
normtest.p    0.032   0.000   0.000
```

CRAMMING SAM'S TIPS   Skew and kurtosis

- To check that the distribution of scores is approximately normal, we need to look at the values of skew and kurtosis in the output.
- Positive values of skew indicate too many low scores in the distribution, whereas negative values indicate a build-up of high scores.
- Positive values of kurtosis indicate a pointy and heavy-tailed distribution, whereas negative values indicate a flat and light-tailed distribution.
- The further the value is from zero, the more likely it is that the data are not normally distributed.
- You can test the significance of these values of skew and kurtosis, but these tests should not be used in large samples (because they are likely to be significant even when skew and kurtosis are not too different from normal).

5.5.3. Exploring groups of data ①

Sometimes we have data in which there are different groups of entities (cats and dogs, different universities, people with depression and people without, for example). There are several ways to produce basic descriptive statistics for separate groups of people (and we will come across some of these methods in section 5.6.1). However, I intend to use this opportunity to introduce you to the **by()** function and reintroduce the *subset()* function from Chapter 3. These functions allow you to specify a grouping variable which splits the data, or to select a subset of cases.

You're probably getting sick of the hygiene data from the Download Festival so let's use the data in the file **RExam.dat.** This file contains data regarding students' performance on an **R** exam. Four variables were measured: **exam** (first-year **R** exam scores as a percentage), **computer** (measure of computer literacy as a percentage), **lecture** (percentage of **R** lectures attended) and **numeracy** (a measure of numerical ability out of 15). There is a variable called **uni** indicating whether the student attended Sussex University (where I work) or Duncetown University. Let's begin by looking at the data as a whole.

5.5.3.1. Running the analysis for all data ①

To begin with, open the file **RExam.dat** by executing:

```
rexam <- read.delim("rexam.dat", header=TRUE)
```

The variable **uni** will have loaded in as numbers rather than as text, because that was how it was specified in the data file; therefore, we need to set the variable **uni** to be a factor by executing (see section 3.5.4.3):

```
rexam$uni<-factor(rexam$uni, levels = c(0:1), labels = c("Duncetown University", "Sussex University"))
```

Remember that this command takes the variable **uni** from the *rexam* dataframe (*rexam$uni*), specifies the numbers used to code the two universities, 0 and 1 (*levels = c(0:1)*), and then assigns labels to them so that 0 represents Duncetown University, and 1 represents Sussex University (*labels = c("Duncetown University", "Sussex University")*).

SELF-TEST

✓ Using what you have learnt so far, obtain descriptive statistics and draw histograms of first-year exam scores, computer literacy, numeracy and lectures attended.

Assuming you completed the self-test, you should see something similar to what's in Output 5.3 (I used *stat.desc()*) and Figure 5.3. From Output 5.3, we can see that, on average, students attended nearly 60% of lectures, obtained 58% in their **R** exam, scored only 51% on the computer literacy test, and only 4.85 out of 15 on the numeracy test. In addition, the standard deviation for computer literacy was relatively small

FIGURE 5.3
Histograms
of the **R** exam
data

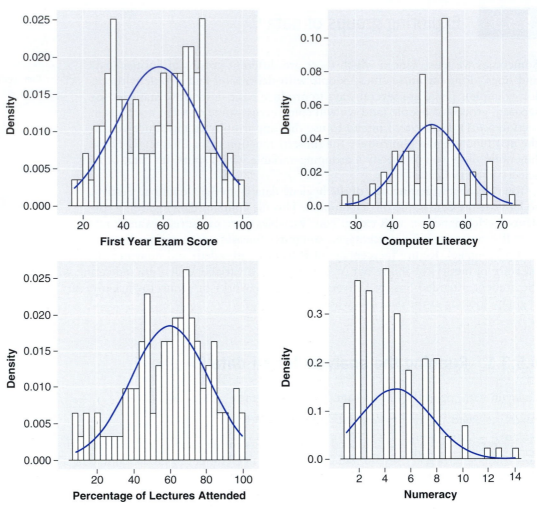

compared to that of the percentage of lectures attended and exam scores. The other important measures are the skew and the kurtosis, and their associated tests of significance. We came across these measures earlier on and found that we can interpret absolute values of *kurt.2SE* and *skew.2SE* greater than 1, 1.29, and 1.65 as significant $p < .05$, $p < .01$, and $p < .001$, respectively. We can see that for skew, numeracy scores are significantly positively skewed ($p < .001$) indicating a pile-up of scores on the left of the distribution (so most students got low scores). For kurtosis, prior exam scores are significant ($p < .05$).

The histograms show us several things. The exam scores are very interesting because this distribution is quite clearly not normal; in fact, it looks suspiciously bimodal (there are two peaks, indicative of two modes). This observation corresponds with the earlier information from the table of descriptive statistics. It looks as though computer literacy is fairly normally distributed (a few people are very good with computers and a few are very bad, but the majority of people have a similar degree of knowledge), as is the lecture attendance. Finally, the numeracy test has produced very positively skewed data (i.e., the majority of people did very badly on this test and only a few did well). This corresponds to what the skew statistic indicated.

	exam	computer	lectures	numeracy
median	60.000	51.500	62.000	4.000
mean	58.100	50.710	59.765	4.850
SE.mean	2.132	0.826	2.168	0.271
CI.mean.0.95	4.229	1.639	4.303	0.537
var	454.354	68.228	470.230	7.321
std.dev	21.316	8.260	21.685	2.706
coef.var	0.367	0.163	0.363	0.558
skewness	-0.104	-0.169	-0.410	0.933
skew.2SE	-0.215	-0.350	-0.849	1.932
kurtosis	-1.148	0.221	-0.285	0.763
kurt.2SE	-1.200	0.231	-0.298	0.798
normtest.W	0.961	0.987	0.977	0.924
normtest.p	0.005	0.441	0.077	0.000

Output 5.3

Descriptive statistics and histograms are a good way of getting an instant picture of the distribution of your data. This snapshot can be very useful: for example, the bimodal distribution of **R** exam scores instantly indicates a trend that students are typically either very good at statistics or struggle with it (there are relatively few who fall in between these extremes). Intuitively, this finding fits with the nature of the subject: statistics is very easy once everything falls into place, but before that enlightenment occurs it all seems hopelessly difficult.

5.5.3.2. Running the analysis for different groups ①

If we want to obtain separate descriptive statistics for each of the universities, we can use the *by()* function.[6] The *by()* function takes the general form:

```
by(data = dataFrame, INDICES = grouping variable, FUN = a function that you
want to apply to the data)
```

In other words, we simply enter the name of our dataframe or variables that we'd like to analyse, we specify a variable by which we want to split the output (in this case, it's **uni**, because we want separate statistics for each university), and we tell it which function we want to apply to the data (in this case we could use *describe* or *stat.desc*). Therefore, to get descriptive statistics for the variable **exam** for each university separately using describe, we could execute:

```
by(data = rexam$exam, INDICES = rexam$uni, FUN = describe)
```

To do the same, but using *stat.desc()* instead of *describe()* we could execute:

```
by(data = rexam$exam, INDICES = rexam$uni, FUN = stat.desc)
```

In both cases, we can get away with not explicitly using *data*, *INDICES* and *FUN* as long as we order the variables in the order in the functions above; so, these commands have the same effect as those above:

```
by(rexam$exam, rexam$uni, describe)
by(rexam$exam, rexam$uni, stat.desc)
```

Finally, you can include any options for the function you're using by adding them in at the end; for example, if you're using *stat.desc()* you can specify not to have basic statistics and to have normality statistics by including those options:

```
by(rexam$exam, rexam$uni, stat.desc, basic = FALSE, norm = TRUE)
```

---

[6] *by()* is what is known as a 'wrapper' function – that is, it takes a more complicated function and simplifies it for people like me. *by()* is a wrapper for a very powerful and clever function, called *tapply()*, which can do all sorts of things, but is harder to use, so we use *by()* instead, which just takes our commands and turns them into commands for *tapply()*.

If we want descriptive statistics for multiple variables, then we can use *cbind()* (see R's Souls' Tip 3.5) to include them within the *by()* function. For example, to look at the descriptive statistics of both the previous **R** exam and the numeracy test, we could execute:

```
by(cbind(data=rexam$exam,data=rexam$numeracy), rexam$uni, describe)
```

or

```
by(rexam[, c("exam", "numeracy")], rexam$uni, stat.desc, basic = FALSE,
norm = TRUE)
```

Note that the resulting Output 5.4 (which was created using *describe* rather than *stat.desc*) is split into two sections: first the results for students at Duncetown University, then the results for those attending Sussex University. From these tables it is clear that Sussex students scored higher on both their **R** exam (called V1 here) and the numeracy test than their Duncetown counterparts. In fact, looking at the means reveals that, on average, Sussex students scored an amazing 36% more on the **R** exam than Duncetown students, and had higher numeracy scores too (what can I say, my students are the best).

```
INDICES: Duncetown University
   var  n  mean    sd median trimmed  mad min max range skew kurtosis   se
V1   1 50 40.18 12.59     38   39.85 12.60  15  66    51 0.29    -0.57 1.78
V2   2 50  4.12  2.07      4    4.00  2.22   1   9     8 0.48    -0.48 0.29
-------------------------------------------------------------------
INDICES: Sussex University
   var  n  mean    sd median trimmed  mad min max range skew kurtosis   se
V1   1 50 76.02 10.21     75   75.70 8.90  56  99    43 0.26    -0.26 1.44
V2   2 50  5.58  3.07      5    5.28 2.97   1  14    13 0.75     0.26 0.43
```

Output 5.4

Next, we'll look at the histograms. It might be possible to use *by()* with *ggplot2()* to draw histograms, but if it is the command will be so complicated that no one will understand it. A simple way, therefore, to create plots for different groups is to use the *subset()* function, which we came across in Chapter 3 (section 3.9.2) to create an object containing only the data in which we're interested. For example, if we wanted to create separate histograms for the Duncetown and Sussex Universities then we could create new dataframes that contain data from only one of the two universities. For example, execute:

```
dunceData<-subset(rexam, rexam$uni=="Duncetown University")
sussexData<-subset(rexam, rexam$uni=="Sussex University")
```

These commands each create a new dataframe that is based on a subset of the *rexam* dataframe; the subset is determined by the condition in the function. The first command contains the condition *rexam$uni==“Duncetown University”*, which means that if the value of the variable **uni** is exactly equal to the phrase "Duncetown University" then the case is selected. In other words, it will retain all cases for which **uni** is Duncetown University. Therefore, I've called the resulting dataframe *dunceData*. The second command does the same thing but this time specifies that **uni** must be exactly equal to the phrase 'Sussex University'. The resulting dataframe, *sussexData*, contains only the Sussex University scores. This is a quick and easy way to split groups; however, you need to be careful that the term you specify to select cases (e.g., 'Duncetown University') exactly matches (including capital letters and spaces) the labelling in the data set otherwise you'll end up with an empty data set.

Having created our separate dataframes, we can generate histograms using the same commands as before, but specifying the dataframe for the subset of data. For example, to create a histogram of the numeracy scores for Duncetown University, we could execute:

```
hist.numeracy.duncetown <- ggplot(dunceData, aes(numeracy)) + opts(legend.
position = "none") + geom_histogram(aes(y = ..density..), fill = "white",
colour = "black", binwidth = 1) + labs(x = "Numeracy Score", y = "Density")
+   stat_function(fun=dnorm,   args=list(mean   =   mean(dunceData$numeracy,
na.rm = TRUE), sd = sd(dunceData$numeracy, na.rm = TRUE)), colour = "blue",
size=1)
hist.numeracy.duncetown
```

Compare this code with that in section 5.5.1; note that it is exactly the same, but we have used the *dunceData* dataframe instead of using the whole data set.[7] We could create the same plot for the Sussex University students by simply using *sussexData* in place of *dunceData* in the command.

We could repeat these commands for the exam scores by replacing 'numeracy' with 'exam' throughout the commands above (this will have the effect of plotting exam scores rather than numeracy scores). Figure 5.4 shows the histograms of exam scores and numeracy split according to the university attended. The first interesting thing to note is that for

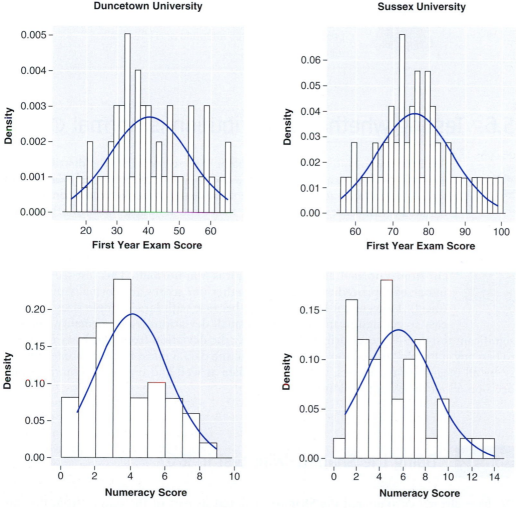

FIGURE 5.4
Distributions of exam and numeracy scores for Duncetown University and Sussex University students

[7] Note that I have included 'binwidth = 1' (see Chapter 4) for the numeracy scores because it makes the resulting plot look better; for the other variables this option can be excluded because the default bin width produces nice-looking plots.

exam marks the distributions are both fairly normal. This seems odd because the overall distribution was bimodal. However, it starts to make sense when you consider that for Duncetown the distribution is centred on a mark of about 40%, but for Sussex the distribution is centred on a mark of about 76%. This illustrates how important it is to look at distributions within groups. If we were interested in comparing Duncetown to Sussex it wouldn't matter that overall the distribution of scores was bimodal; all that's important is that each group comes from a normal distribution, and in this case it appears to be true. When the two samples are combined, these two normal distributions create a bimodal one (one of the modes being around the centre of the Duncetown distribution, and the other being around the centre of the Sussex data). For numeracy scores, the distribution is slightly positively skewed (there is a larger concentration at the lower end of scores) in both the Duncetown and Sussex groups. Therefore, the overall positive skew observed before is due to the mixture of universities.

SELF-TEST

✓ Repeat these analyses for the computer literacy and percentage of lectures attended and interpret the results.

5.6. Testing whether a distribution is normal ①

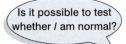

Is it possible to test whether *I* am normal?

Another way of looking at the problem is to see whether the distribution as a whole deviates from a comparable normal distribution. The **Shapiro–Wilk** test does just this: it compares the scores in the sample to a normally distributed set of scores with the same mean and standard deviation. If the test is non-significant ($p > .05$) it tells us that the distribution of the sample is not significantly different from a normal distribution. If, however, the test is significant ($p < .05$) then the distribution in question is significantly different from a normal distribution (i.e., it is non-normal). This test seems great: in one easy procedure it tells us whether our scores are normally distributed (nice!). However, it has limitations because with large sample sizes it is very easy to get significant results from small deviations from normality, and so a significant test doesn't necessarily tell us whether the deviation from normality is enough to bias any statistical procedures that we apply to the data. I guess the take-home message is: by all means use these tests, but plot your data as well and try to make an informed decision about the extent of non-normality.

5.6.1.   Doing the Shapiro–Wilk test in R ①

We have already encountered the Shapiro–Wilk test as part of the output from the *stat. desc()* function (see Output 5.2 and, for these data, Output 5.3). However, we can also use the **shapiro.test()** function. This function takes the general form:

```
shapiro.test(variable)
```

in which *variable* is the name of the variable that you'd like to test for normality. Therefore, to test the **exam** and **numeracy** variables for normality we would execute:

```
shapiro.test(rexam$exam)
shapiro.test(rexam$numeracy)
```

The output is shown in Output 5.5. Note that the value of *W* corresponds to the value of *normtest.W*, and the *p*-value corresponds to *normtest.p* from the *stat.desc()* function (Output 5.3). For each test we see the test statistic, labelled *W*, and the *p*-value. Remember that a significant value (*p*-value less than .05) indicates a deviation from normality. For both numeracy ($p = .005$) and **R** exam scores ($p < .001$), the Shapiro–Wilk test is highly significant, indicating that both distributions are not normal. This result is likely to reflect the bimodal distribution found for exam scores, and the positively skewed distribution observed in the numeracy scores. However, these tests confirm that these deviations were *significant* (but bear in mind that the sample is fairly big).

```
        Shapiro-Wilk normality test

data:   rexam$exam
W = 0.9613, p-value = 0.004991


        Shapiro-Wilk normality test

data:   rexam$numeracy
W = 0.9244, p-value = 2.424e-05
```

Output 5.5

As a final point, bear in mind that when we looked at the exam scores for separate groups, the distributions seemed quite normal; now if we'd asked for separate Shapiro–Wilk tests for the two universities we might have found non-significant results. In fact, let's try this out, using the *by()* function we came across earlier. We use *shapiro.test* as the FUN instead of describe or *stat.desc*, which we have used before (although *stat.desc* would also give you the Shapiro–Wilk test as part of the output so you could use this function also):

```
by(rexam$exam, rexam$uni, shapiro.test)
by(rexam$numeracy, rexam$uni, shapiro.test)
```

You should get Output 5.6 for the exam scores, which shows that the percentages on the **R** exam are indeed normal within the two groups (the *p*-values are greater than .05). This is important because *if our analysis involves comparing groups, then what's important is not the overall distribution but the distribution in each group.*

```
rexam$uni: Duncetown University

        Shapiro-Wilk normality test

data:  dd[x, ]
W = 0.9722, p-value = 0.2829

-----------------------------------------------------------------
rexam$uni: Sussex University

        Shapiro-Wilk normality test

data:  dd[x, ]
W = 0.9837, p-value = 0.7151
```

Output 5.6

For numeracy scores (Output 5.7) the tests are still significant indicating non-normal distributions both for Duncetown University ($p = .015$), and Sussex University ($p = .007$).

```
rexam$uni: Duncetown University

        Shapiro-Wilk normality test

data:  dd[x, ]
W = 0.9408, p-value = 0.01451


------------------------------------------------------------------


rexam$uni: Sussex University

        Shapiro-Wilk normality test

data:  dd[x, ]
W = 0.9323, p-value = 0.006787
```

Output 5.7

We can also draw Q-Q plots for the variables, to help us to interpret the results of the Shapiro–Wilk test (see Figure 5.5).

```
qplot(sample = rexam$exam, stat="qq")
qplot(sample = rexam$numeracy, stat="qq")
```

The normal Q-Q chart plots the values you would expect to get if the distribution were normal (theoretical values) against the values actually seen in the data set (sample values). If the data are normally distributed, then the observed values (the dots on the chart) should fall exactly along a straight line (meaning that the observed values are the same as you would expect to get from a normally distributed data set). Any deviation of the dots from the line represents a deviation from normality. So, if the Q-Q plot looks like a wiggly snake then you have some deviation from normality. Specifically, when the line sags consistently below the diagonal, or consistently rises above it, then this shows that the kurtosis differs from a normal distribution, and when the curve is S-shaped, the problem is skewness.

In both of the variables analysed we already know that the data are not normal, and these plots (see Figure 5.5) confirm this observation because the dots deviate substantially from the line. It is noteworthy that the deviation is greater for the numeracy scores, and this is consistent with the higher significance value of this variable on the Shapiro–Wilk test.

FIGURE 5.5
Normal Q-Q plots of numeracy and **R** exam scores

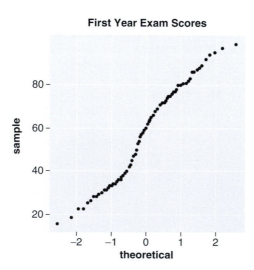

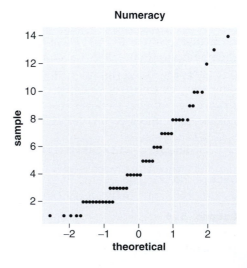

| 5.6.2. | Reporting the Shapiro–Wilk test ① |

The test statistic for the Shapiro–Wilk test is denoted by W; we can report the results in Output 5.5 in the following way:

✓ The percentage on the **R** exam, $W = 0.96$, $p = .005$, and the numeracy scores, $W = 0.92$, $p < .001$, were both significantly non-normal.

CRAMMING SAM'S TIPS **Normality tests**

- The Shapiro–Wilk test can be used to see if a distribution of scores significantly differs from a normal distribution.
- If the Shapiro–Wilk test is significant (p-value less than .05) then the scores are significantly different from a normal distribution.
- Otherwise, scores are approximately normally distributed.
- **Warning**: In large samples this test can be significant even when the scores are only slightly different from a normal distribution. Therefore, they should always be interpreted in conjunction with histograms, or Q-Q plots, and the values of skew and kurtosis.

5.7. Testing for homogeneity of variance ①

So far I've concentrated on the assumption of normally distributed data; however, at the beginning of this chapter I mentioned another assumption: homogeneity of variance. This assumption means that as you go through levels of one variable, the variance of the other should not change. If you've collected groups of data then this means that the variance of your outcome variable or variables should be the same in each of these groups. If you've collected continuous data (such as in correlational designs), this assumption means that the variance of one variable should be stable at all levels of the other variable. Let's illustrate this with an example. An audiologist was interested in the effects of loud concerts on people's hearing. So, she decided to send 10 people on tour with the loudest band she could find, Motörhead. These people went to concerts in Brixton (London), Brighton, Bristol, Edinburgh, Newcastle, Cardiff and Dublin and after each concert the audiologist measured the number of hours after the concert that these people had ringing in their ears.

Figure 5.6 shows the number of hours that each person had ringing in his or her ears after each concert (each person is represented by a circle). The horizontal lines represent the average number of hours that there was ringing in the ears after each concert and these means are connected by a line so that we can see the general trend of the data. Remember that for each concert, the circles are the scores from which the mean is calculated. Now, we can see in both graphs that the means increase as the people go to more concerts. So, after the first concert their ears ring for about 12 hours, but after the second they ring for about 15–20 hours, and by the final night of the tour, they ring for about 45–50 hours (2 days). So, there is a cumulative effect of the concerts on ringing in the ears. This pattern is found in both graphs; the difference between the graphs is not in terms of the means (which are roughly the same), but in terms of the spread of scores around the mean. If you look at the left-hand graph, the spread of scores around the mean stays the same after each concert (the scores are fairly tightly packed around the mean). Put it another way, if you measured the vertical distance between the lowest score and the highest score after the Brixton concert, and then did the same after the other concerts, all of these distances would be fairly similar. Although the means increase, the spread of scores for hearing loss is the same at each level of the concert variable (the spread of scores is the same after Brixton, Brighton, Bristol, Edinburgh, Newcastle, Cardiff and Dublin). This is what we mean by *homogeneity of variance*. The right-hand graph shows a different picture: if you look at the spread of scores after the Brixton concert, they are quite tightly packed around the mean (the vertical distance from the lowest score to the highest score is small), but after the Dublin show (for example) the scores are very spread out around the mean (the vertical distance from the lowest score to the highest score is large). This is an example of *heterogeneity of variance*: that is, at some levels of the concert variable the variance of scores is different than other levels (graphically, the vertical distance from the lowest to highest score is different after different concerts).

FIGURE 5.6
Graphs illustrating data with homogeneous (left) and heterogeneous (right) variances

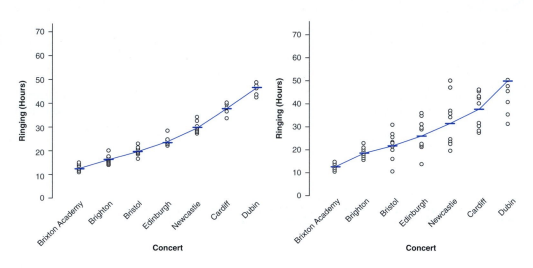

5.7.1.   Levene's test ①

Hopefully you've got a grip of what homogeneity of variance actually means. Now, how do we test for it? Well, we could just look at the values of the variances and see whether they are similar. However, this approach would be very subjective and probably prone to academics thinking 'Ooh look, the variance in one group is only 3000 times larger than the variance in the other: that's roughly equal'. Instead, in correlational analysis such as regression we tend to use graphs (see section 7.9.5) and for groups of data we tend to use a test called **Levene's test** (Levene, 1960). Levene's test tests the null hypothesis that the variances in different groups are equal (i.e., the difference between the variances is zero). It's a very simple and elegant test that works by doing a one-way ANOVA (see Chapter 10) conducted on the deviation scores; that is, the absolute difference between each score and the mean of the group from which it came (see Glass, 1966, for a very readable explanation).[8] For now, all we need to know is that if Levene's test is significant at $p \leq .05$ then we can conclude that the null hypothesis is incorrect and that the variances are significantly different – therefore, the assumption of homogeneity of variances has been violated. If, however, Levene's test

[8] We haven't covered ANOVA yet, so this explanation won't make much sense to you now, but in Chapter 10 we will look in more detail at how Levene's test works.

is non-significant (i.e., $p > .05$) then the variances are roughly equal and the assumption is tenable.

5.7.1.1. Levene's test with R Commander ①

First we'll load the data into R Commander. Choose **Data ⇒ Import data ⇒ from text file, clipboard, or URL…** and then select the file **RExam.dat** (see section 3.7.3). Before we can conduct Levene's test we need to convert **uni** to a factor because at the moment it is simply 0s and 1s so **R** doesn't know that it's a factor – see section 3.6.2 to remind yourself how to do that. Once you have done this you should be able to select **Statistics⇒Variances⇒Levene's test** (you won't be able to select it unless **R** can 'see' a factor in the dataframe). Choosing this option in the menu opens the dialog box shown in Figure 5.7. You need to select a grouping variable. R Commander has realized that you only have one variable that could be the grouping variable – because it is the only factor – and that's **uni**. Therefore, it has already selected this variable.

Choose the variable on the right that you want to test for equality of variances across the groups defined by **uni**. You can choose median or mean for the centring – the median tends to be more accurate and is the default; I use this default throughout the book. Run the analysis for both **exam** and **numeracy**. Output 5.8 shows the results.

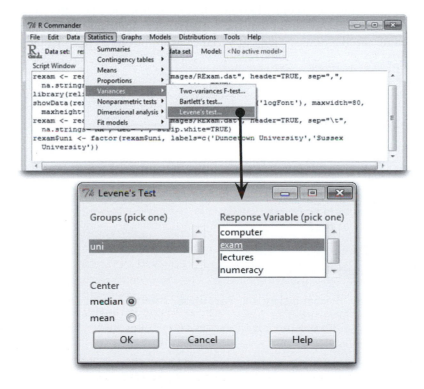

FIGURE 5.7
Levene's test in R Commander

5.7.1.2. Levene's test with R ①

To use Levene's test, we use the **leveneTest()** function from the *car* package. This function takes the general form:

```
leveneTest(outcome variable, group, center = median/mean)
```

Therefore, we enter two variables into the function: first the outcome variable of which we want to test the variances; and second, the grouping variable, which must be a factor. We can just enter these variables and Levene's test will centre the variables using the median (which is slightly preferable), but if we want to override this default and centre using the mean then we can add the option *center = "mean"*. Therefore, for the exam scores we could execute:

```
leveneTest(rexam$exam, rexam$uni)
leveneTest(rexam$exam, rexam$uni, center = mean)
```

For the numeracy scores we would execute (note that all we have changed is the outcome variable):

```
leveneTest(rexam$numeracy, rexam$uni)
```

5.7.1.3. Levene's test output ①

Output 5.8 shows the output for Levene's test for exam scores (using the median), exam scores (centring using the mean) and numeracy scores. The result is non-significant for the **R** exam scores (the value in the *Pr (>F)* column is more than .05) regardless of whether we centre with the median or mean. This indicates that the variances are not significantly different (i.e., they are similar and the homogeneity of variance assumption is tenable). However, for the numeracy scores, Levene's test is significant (the value in the *Pr (>F)* column is less than .05) indicating that the variances are significantly different (i.e., they are not the same and the homogeneity of variance assumption has been violated).

```
> leveneTest(rexam$exam, rexam$uni)

Levene's Test for Homogeneity of Variance (center = median)
      Df F value Pr(>F)
group  1  2.0886 0.1516
      98


> leveneTest(rexam$exam, rexam$uni, center = mean)

Levene's Test for Homogeneity of Variance (center = mean)
      Df F value Pr(>F)
group  1  2.5841 0.1112
      98


> leveneTest(rexam$numeracy, rexam$uni)

Levene's Test for Homogeneity of Variance (center = median)
      Df F value  Pr(>F)
group  1   5.366 0.02262 *
      98

Output 5.8
```

5.7.2. Reporting Levene's test ①

Levene's test can be denoted with the letter F and there are two different degrees of freedom. As such you can report it, in general form, as $F(df1, df2) =$ value, $Pr (>F)$. So, for the results in Output 5.8 we could say:

✓ For the percentage on the **R** exam, the variances were similar for Duncetown and Sussex University students, $F(1, 98) = 2.09$, *ns*, but for numeracy scores the variances were significantly different in the two groups, $F(1, 98) = 5.37$, $p = .023$.

<table>
<tr><td>5.7.3.</td><td>Hartley's F_{max}: the variance ratio ①</td></tr>
</table>

As with the Shapiro–Wilk test (and other tests of normality), when the sample size is large, small differences in group variances can produce a Levene's test that is significant (because, as we saw in Chapter 1, the power of the test is improved). A useful double check, therefore, is to look at **Hartley's F_{max}** – also known as the **variance ratio** (Pearson & Hartley, 1954). This is the ratio of the variances between the group with the biggest variance and the group with the smallest variance. This ratio was compared to critical values in a table published by Hartley. Some of the critical values (for a .05 level of significance) are shown in Figure 5.8 (see Oliver Twisted); as you can see, the critical values depend on the number of cases per group (well, $n - 1$ actually), and the number of variances being compared. From this graph you can see that with sample sizes (*n*) of 10 per group, an F_{max} of less than 10 is more or less always going to be non-significant, with 15–20 per group the ratio needs to be less than about 5, and with samples of 30–60 the ratio should be below about 2 or 3.

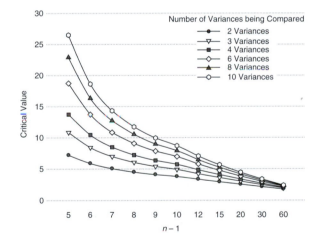

FIGURE 5.8
Selected critical values for Hartley's F_{max} test

OLIVER TWISTED

Please Sir, can I have some more … Hartley's F_{max}?

Oliver thinks that my graph of critical values is stupid. 'Look at that graph,' he laughed, 'it's the most stupid thing I've ever seen since I was at Sussex Uni and I saw my statistics lecturer, Andy Fie…'. Well, go choke on your gruel you Dickensian bubo, because the full table of critical values is in the additional material for this chapter on the companion website.

CRAMMING SAM'S TIPS   **Homogeneity of variance**

- Homogeneity of variance is the assumption that the spread of scores is roughly equal in different groups of cases, or more generally that the spread of scores is roughly equal at different points on the predictor variable.
- When comparing groups, this assumption can be tested with Levene's test.
- If Levene's test is significant ($Pr (>F)$ in the **R** output is less than .05) then the variances are significantly different in different groups.
- Otherwise, homogeneity of variance can be assumed.
- The variance ratio is the largest group variance divided by the smallest. This value needs to be smaller than the critical values in Figure 5.8.
- **Warning**: In large samples Levene's test can be significant even when group variances are not very different. Therefore, it should be interpreted in conjunction with the variance ratio.

5.8. Correcting problems in the data ②

The previous section showed us various ways to explore our data; we saw how to look for problems with our distribution of scores and how to detect heterogeneity of variance. In Chapter 4 we also discovered how to spot outliers in the data. The next question is what to do about these problems.

5.8.1. Dealing with outliers ②

If you detect outliers in the data there are several options for reducing the impact of these values. However, before you do any of these things, it's worth checking that the data have been entered correctly for the problem cases. If the data are correct then the three main options you have are:

1   *Remove the case*: This entails deleting the data from the person who contributed the outlier. However, this should be done only if you have good reason to believe that this case is not from the population that you intended to sample. For example, if you were investigating factors that affected how much cats purr and one cat didn't purr at all, this would likely be an outlier (all cats purr). Upon inspection, if you discovered that this cat was actually a dog wearing a cat costume (hence why it didn't purr), then you'd have grounds to exclude this case because it comes from a different population (dogs who like to dress as cats) than your target population (cats).

2   *Transform the data*: Outliers tend to skew the distribution and, as we will see in the next section, this skew (and, therefore, the impact of the outliers) can sometimes be reduced by applying **transformations** to the data.

3   *Change the score*: If transformation fails, then you can consider replacing the score. This on the face of it may seem like cheating (you're changing the data from what was actually corrected); however, if the score you're changing is very unrepresentative and biases your statistical model anyway then changing the score is the lesser of two evils! There are several options for how to change the score:

a *The next highest score plus one*: Change the score to be one unit above the next highest score in the data set.

b *Convert back from a z-score*: A *z*-score of 3.29 constitutes an outlier (see Jane Superbrain Box 4.1), so we can calculate what score would give rise to a *z*-score of 3.29 (or perhaps 3) by rearranging the *z*-score equation in section 1.7.4, which gives us $X = (z \times s) + \overline{X}$. All this means is that we calculate the mean ($\overline{X}$) and standard deviation (*s*) of the data; we know that *z* is 3 (or 3.29 if you want to be exact) so we just add three times the standard deviation to the mean, and replace our outliers with that score.

c *The mean plus two standard deviations*: A variation on the above method is to use the mean plus two times the standard deviation (rather than three times the standard deviation).

5.8.2. Dealing with non-normality and unequal variances ②

5.8.2.1. Transforming data ②

This section is quite hair raising so don't worry if it doesn't make much sense – many undergraduate courses won't cover transforming data so feel free to ignore this section if you want to.

We saw in the previous section that you can deal with outliers by transforming the data and that these transformations are also useful for correcting problems with normality and the assumption of homogeneity of variance. The idea behind transformations is that you do something to every score to correct for distributional problems, outliers or unequal variances. Although some students often (understandably) think that transforming data sounds dodgy (the phrase 'fudging your results' springs to some people's minds!), in fact it isn't because you do the same thing to all of your scores.[9] As such, transforming the data won't change the relationships between variables (the relative differences between people for a given variable stay the same), but it does change the differences between different variables (because it changes the units of measurement). Therefore, if you are looking at relationships between variables (e.g., regression) it is alright just to transform the problematic variable, but if you are looking at differences within variables (e.g., change in a variable over time) then you need to transform all levels of those variables.

What do I do if my data are not normal?

Let's return to our Download Festival data (**DownloadFestival.dat**) from earlier in the chapter. These data were not normal on days 2 and 3 of the festival (section 5.4). Now, we might want to look at how hygiene levels changed across the three days (i.e., compare the mean on day 1 to the means on days 2 and 3 to see if people got smellier). The data for days 2 and 3 were skewed and need to be transformed, but because we might later compare the data to scores on day 1, we would also have to transform the day 1 data (even though scores were not skewed). If we don't change the day 1 data as well, then any differences in hygiene scores we find from day 1 to day 2 or 3 will be due to us transforming one variable and not the others.

---

[9] Although there aren't statistical consequences of transforming data, there may be empirical or scientific implications that outweigh the statistical benefits (see Jane Superbrain Box 5.1).

Table 5.1 Data transformations and their uses

Data Transformation	Can Correct For
Log transformation (log(X_i)): Taking the logarithm of a set of numbers squashes the right tail of the distribution. As such it's a good way to reduce positive skew. However, you can't take the log of zero or negative numbers, so if your data tend to zero or produce negative numbers you need to add a constant to all of the data before you do the transformation. For example, if you have zeros in the data then do log(X_i + 1), or if you have negative numbers add whatever value makes the smallest number in the data set positive.	Positive skew, unequal variances
Square root transformation ($\sqrt{X_i}$): Taking the square root of large values has more of an effect than taking the square root of small values. Consequently, taking the square root of each of your scores will bring any large scores closer to the centre – rather like the log transformation. As such, this can be a useful way to reduce positive skew; however, you still have the same problem with negative numbers (negative numbers don't have a square root).	Positive skew, unequal variances
Reciprocal transformation (1/X_i): Dividing 1 by each score also reduces the impact of large scores. The transformed variable will have a lower limit of 0 (very large numbers will become close to 0). One thing to bear in mind with this transformation is that it reverses the scores: scores that were originally large in the data set become small (close to zero) after the transformation, but scores that were originally small become big after the transformation. For example, imagine two scores of 1 and 10; after the transformation they become 1/1 = 1 and 1/10 = 0.1: the small score becomes bigger than the large score after the transformation. However, you can avoid this by reversing the scores before the transformation, by finding the highest score and changing each score to the highest score minus the score you're looking at. So, you do a transformation 1/($X_{Highest} - X_i$).	Positive skew, unequal variances
Reverse score transformations: Any one of the above transformations can be used to correct negatively skewed data, but first you have to reverse the scores. To do this, subtract each score from the highest score obtained, or the highest score + 1 (depending on whether you want your lowest score to be 0 or 1). If you do this, don't forget to reverse the scores back afterwards, or to remember that the interpretation of the variable is reversed: big scores have become small and small scores have become big!	Negative skew

There are various transformations that you can do to the data that are helpful in correcting various problems.[10] However, whether these transformations are necessary or useful is quite a complex issue (see Jane Superbrain Box 5.1). Nevertheless, because they *are* used by researchers Table 5.1 shows some common transformations and their uses.

5.8.2.2. Choosing a transformation ②

Given that there are many transformations that you can do, how can you decide which one is best? The simple answer is trial and error: try one out and see if it helps and if it doesn't

[10] You'll notice in this section that I keep writing X_i. We saw in Chapter 1 that this refers to the observed score for the *i*th person (so, the *i* could be replaced with the name of a particular person, thus for Graham, $X_i = X_{Graham}$ = Graham's score, and for Carol, $X_i = X_{Carol}$ = Carol's score).

then try a different one. If you are looking at differences between variables you *must apply the same transformation to all variables* (you cannot, for example, apply a log transformation to one variable and a square root transformation to another). This can be quite time consuming.

JANE SUPERBRAIN 5.1

To transform or not to transform, that is the question ③

Not everyone agrees that transforming data is a good idea; for example, Glass, Peckham and Sanders (1972), in a very extensive review, commented that 'the payoff of normalizing transformations in terms of more valid probability statements is low, and they are seldom considered to be worth the effort' (p. 241). In which case, should we bother?

The issue is quite complicated (especially for this early in the book), but essentially we need to know whether the statistical models we apply perform better on transformed data than they do when applied to data that violate the assumption that the transformation corrects. If a statistical model is still accurate even when its assumptions are broken it is said to be a **robust test** (section 5.8.4). I'm not going to discuss whether particular tests are robust here, but I will discuss the issue for particular tests in their respective chapters. The question of whether to transform is linked to this issue of robustness (which in turn is linked to what test you are performing on your data).

A good case in point is the *F*-test in ANOVA (see Chapter 10), which is often claimed to be robust (Glass et al., 1972). Early findings suggested that *F* performed as it should in skewed distributions and that transforming the data helped as often as it hindered the accuracy of *F* (Games & Lucas, 1966). However, in a lively but informative exchange, Levine and Dunlap (1982) showed that transformations of skew did improve the performance of *F*; however, in a response, Games (1983) argued

that their conclusion was incorrect, which Levine and Dunlap (1983) contested in a response to the response. Finally, in a response to the response to the response, Games (1984) pointed out several important questions to consider:

1. The central limit theorem (section 2.5.1) tells us that in big samples the sampling distribution will be normal regardless, and this is what's actually important, so the debate is academic in anything other than small samples. Lots of early research did indeed show that with samples of 40 the normality of the sampling distribution was, as predicted, normal. However, this research focused on distributions with light tails and subsequent work has shown that with heavy-tailed distributions larger samples would be necessary to invoke the central limit theorem (Wilcox, 2005). This research suggests that transformations might be useful for such distributions.

2. By transforming the data you change the hypothesis being tested (when using a log transformation and comparing means you change from comparing arithmetic means to comparing geometric means). Transformation also means that you're now addressing a different construct than the one originally measured, and this has obvious implications for interpreting that data (Gelman & Hill, 2007; Grayson, 2004).

3. In small samples it is tricky to determine normality one way or another (tests such as Shapiro–Wilk will have low power to detect deviations from normality and graphs will be hard to interpret with so few data points).

4. The consequences for the statistical model of applying the 'wrong' transformation could be worse than the consequences of analysing the untransformed scores.

As we will see later in the book, there is an extensive library of robust tests that can be used and which have considerable benefits over transforming data. The definitive guide to these is Wilcox's (2005) outstanding book.

5.8.3. Transforming the data using R ②

5.8.3.1. Computing new variables ②

Transformations are very easy using **R**. We use one of two general commands:

```
newVariable <- function(oldVariable)
```

in which *function* is the function we will use to transform the variable. Or possibly:

```
newVariable <- arithmetic with oldVariable(s)
```

Let's first look at some of the simple arithmetic functions:

+	**Addition**: We can add two variables together, or add a constant to our variables. For example, with our hygiene data, 'day1 + day2' creates a column in which each row contains the hygiene score from the column labelled *day1* added to the score from the column labelled *day2* (e.g., for participant 1: 2.65 + 1.35 = 4). In **R** we would execute: `dlf$day1PlusDay2 <- dlf$day1 + dlf$day2` which creates a new variable **day1PlusDay2** in the *dlt* dataframe based on adding the variables **day1** and **day2**.
−	**Subtraction**: We can subtract one variable from another. For example, we could subtract the day 1 hygiene score from the day 2 hygiene score. This creates a new variable in our dataframe in which each row contains the score from the column labelled *day1* subtracted from the score from the column labelled *day2* (e.g., for participant 1: 1.35 − 2.65 = −1.30). Therefore, this person's hygiene went down by 1.30 (on our 5-point scale) from day 1 to day 2 of the festival. In **R** we would execute: `dlf$day2MinusDay1 <- dlf$day2 - dlf$day1` which creates a new variable **day2MinusDay1** in the *dlf* dataframe based on subtracting the variable **day1** from **day2**.
*	**Multiply**: We can multiply two variables together, or we can multiply a variable by any number. In **R**, we would execute: `dlf$day2Times5 <- dlf$day1 * 5` which creates a new variable **day2Times5** in the *dlf* dataframe based on multiplying **day1** by 5.
** OR ^	**Exponentiation**: Exponentiation is used to raise the preceding term by the power of the succeeding term. So 'day1**2' or 'day1 ^ 2' (it doesn't matter which you use) creates a column that contains the scores in the *day1* column raised to the power of 2 (i.e., the square of each number in the *day1* column: for participant 1, $2.65^2 = 7.02$). Likewise, 'day1**3' creates a column with values of *day1* cubed. In **R**, we would execute either: `dlf$day2Squared <- dlf$day2 ** 2` or `dlf$day2Squared <- dlf$day2 ^ 2` both of which create a new variable **day2Squared** in the *dlf* dataframe based on squaring values of **day2**.

<	**Less than**: This is a logical operator – that means it gives the answer TRUE (or 1) or FALSE (or 0). If you typed 'day1 < 1', **R** would give the answer TRUE to those participants whose hygiene score on day 1 of the festival was less than 1 (i.e., if *day1* was 0.9999 or less). So, we might use this if we wanted to look only at the people who were already smelly on the first day of the festival. In **R** we would execute: ```dlf$day1LessThanOne <- dlf$day1 < 1``` to create a new variable **day1LessThanOne** in the *dlf* dataframe for which the values are TRUE (or 1) if the value of **day1** is less than 1, but FALSE (or 0) if the value of **day1** is greater than 1.
<=	**Less than or equal to**: This is the same as above but returns a response of TRUE (or 1) if the value of the original variable is equal to or less than the value specified. In **R** we would execute: ```dlf$day1LessThanOrEqualOne <- dlf$day1 <= 1``` to create a new variable **day1LessThanOrEqualOne** in the *dlf* dataframe for which the values are TRUE (or 1) if the value of **day1** is less than or equal to 1, but FALSE (or 0) if the value of **day1** is greater than 1.
>	**Greater than**: This is the opposite of the less than operator above. It returns a response of TRUE (or 1) if the value of the original variable is greater than the value specified. In **R** we would execute: ```dlf$day1GreaterThanOne <- dlf$day1 > 1``` to create a new variable **day1GreaterThanOne** in the *dlf* dataframe for which the values are TRUE (or 1) if the value of **day1** is greater than 1, but FALSE (or 0) if the value of **day1** is less than 1.
>=	**Greater than or equal to**: This is the same as above but returns a response of TRUE (or 1) if the value of the original variable is equal to or greater than the value specified. In **R** we would execute: ```dlf$day1GreaterThanOrEqualOne <- dlf$day1 >= 1``` to create a new variable **day1GreaterThanOrEqualOne** in the *dlf* dataframe for which the values are TRUE (or 1) if the value of **day1** is greater than or equal to 1, but FALSE (or 0) if the value of **day1** is less than 1.
==	**Double equals** means 'is equal to?' It's a question, rather than an assignment, like a single equals (=). Therefore, if we write something like *dlf$gender == "Male"* we are asking 'is the value of the variable **gender** in the *dlf* dataframe equal to the word 'Male'? In **R**, if we executed: ```dlf$male <- dlf$gender == "Male"``` we would create a variable **male** in the *dlf* dataframe that contains the value TRUE if the variable **gender** was the word 'Male' (spelt as it is specified, including capital letters) and FALSE in all other cases.
!=	**Not equal to.** The opposite of ==. In **R**, if we executed: ```dlf$notMale <- dlf$gender != "Male"``` we would create a variable **notMale** in the *dlf* dataframe that contains the value TRUE if the variable **gender** was *not* the word 'Male' (spelt as it is specified including capital letters) and FALSE otherwise.

Some of the most useful functions are listed in Table 5.2, which shows the standard form of the function, the name of the function, an example of how the function can be used and what **R** would output if that example were used. There are several basic functions for calculating means, standard deviations and sums of columns. There are also functions such as the square root and logarithm that are useful for transforming data that are skewed, and we will use these functions now.

Table 5.2 Some useful functions

Function	Name	Input example	Output
rowMeans()	Mean for a row	rowMeans(cbind (dlf$day1, dlf$day2, dlf$day3), na.rm = TRUE)	For each row, **R** calculates the mean hygiene score across the three days of the festival. *na.rm* tells **R** whether to exclude missing values from the calculation (see R's Souls' Tip 5.3).
rowSums()	Sums for a row	rowSums(cbind (dlf$day1, dlf$day2, dlf$day3), na.rm = TRUE)	For each row, **R** calculates the sum of the hygiene scores across the three days of the festival. *na.rm* tells **R** whether to exclude missing values from the calculation (see R's Souls' Tip 5.4).
sqrt()	Square root	sqrt(dlf$day2)	Produces a column containing the square root of each value in the column labelled *day2*
abs()	Absolute value	abs(dlf$day1)	Produces a variable that contains the absolute value of the values in the column labelled *day1* (absolute values are ones where the signs are ignored: so −5 becomes +5 and +5 stays as +5)
log10()	Base 10 logarithm	log10(dlf$day1)	Produces a variable that contains the logarithm (to base 10) values of the variable *day1*.
log()	Natural logarithm	log10(dlf$day1)	Produces a variable that contains the natural logarithm values of the variable *day1*.
is.na()	Is missing?	is.na(dlf$day1)	This is used to determine if a variable is missing or not. If the variable is missing, the case will be assigned TRUE (or 1); if the case is not missing, the case will be assigned FALSE (or 0).

R's Souls' Tip 5.3 The is.na() function and missing data ③

If we want to count missing data, we can use *is.na()*. For example, if we want to know whether a person is missing for their day 2 hygiene score, we use:

```
dlf$missingDay2 <- is.na(dlf$day2)
```

But we can then use that variable in some clever ways. How many people were missing on day 2? Well, we know that the variable we just created is TRUE (or 1) if they are missing, so we can just add them up:

```
sum(dlf$missingDay2)
```

If we want to be lazy, we can embed those functions in each other, and not bother to create a variable:

```
(sum(is.na(dlf$day2))
```

which tells us that 546 scores are missing. What proportion of scores is that? Well, we have a 1 if they are missing, and a zero if not. So the mean of that variable will be the proportion which are missing:

```
mean(is.na(dlf$day2))
```

This tells us that the mean is 0.674, so 67.4% of people are missing a hygiene score on day 2.

5.8.3.2. The log transformation in R ②

Now we've found out some basic information about the how to compute variables, let's use it to transform our data. To transform the variable **day1**, and create a new variable **logday1**, we execute this command:

```
dlf$logday1 <- log(dlf$day1)
```

This command creates a variable called **logday1** in the *dlf* dataframe, which contains values that are the natural log of the values in the variable **day1**.

For the day 2 hygiene scores there is a value of 0 in the original data, and there is no logarithm of the value 0. To overcome this we should add a constant to our original scores before we take the log of those scores. Any constant will do, provided that it makes all of the scores greater than 0. In this case our lowest score is 0 in the data set so we can simply add 1 to all of the scores and that will ensure that all scores are greater than zero.

The advantage of adding 1 is that the logarithm of 1 is equal to 0, so people who scored a zero before the transformation score a zero after the transformation. To do this transformation we would execute:

```
dlf$logday1 <- log(dlf$day1 + 1)
```

This command creates a variable called **logday1** in the *dlf* dataframe, which contains values that are the natural log of the values in the variable **day1** after 1 has been added to them.

SELF-TEST

✓ Have a go at creating similar variables **logday2** and **logday3** for the **day2** and **day3** variables. Plot histograms of the transformed scores for all three days.

5.8.3.3. The square root transformation in R ②

To do a square root transformation, we run through the same process, by using a name such as *sqrtday1*. Therefore, to create a variable called **sqrtday1** that contains the square root of the values in the variable **day1**, we would execute:

```
dlf$sqrtday1 <- sqrt(day1)
```

SELF-TEST

✓ Repeat this process for **day2** and **day3** to create variables called **sqrtday2** and **sqrtday3**. Plot histograms of the transformed scores for all three days.

5.8.3.4. The reciprocal transformation in R ②

To do a reciprocal transformation on the data from day 1, we don't use a function, we use an arithmetic expression: 1/variable. However, the day 2 data contain a zero value and if we try to divide 1 by 0 then we'll get an error message (you can't divide by 0). As such we need to add a constant to our variable just as we did for the log transformation. Any constant will do, but 1 is a convenient number for these data. We could use a name such as *recday1*, and to create this variable we would execute:

```
dlf$recday1 <- 1/(dlf$day1 + 1)
```

SELF-TEST

✓ Repeat this process for **day2** and **day3**. Plot histograms of the transformed scores for all three days.

5.8.3.5. The ifelse() function in R ②

The *ifelse()* function is used to create a new variable, or change an old variable, depending on some other values. This function takes the general form:

```
ifelse(a conditional argument, what happens if the argument is TRUE, what happens if the argument if FALSE)
```

This function needs three arguments: a conditional argument to test, what to do if the test is true, and what to do if the test is false. Let's use the original data where there was an outlier in the **day1** hygiene score. We can detect this outlier because we know that the highest score possible on the scale was 4. Therefore, we could set our conditional argument to be *dlf$day1 > 4*, which means we're saying 'if the value of **day1** is greater than 4 then …'. The rest of the function tells it what to do, for example, we might want to set it to missing (NA) if the score is over 4, but keep it as the old score if the score is not over 4. In which case we could execute this command:

```
dlf$day1NoOutlier <- ifelse(dlf$day1 > 4, NA, dlf$day1)
```

This command creates a new variable called **day1NoOutlier** which takes the value NA if **day1** is greater than 4, but is the value of **day1** if **day1** is less than 4:

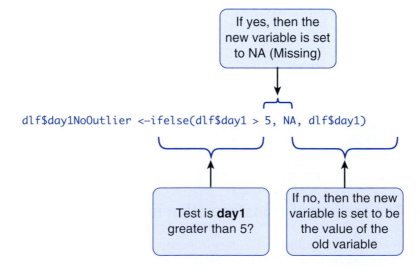

R's Souls' Tip 5.4 Careful with missing data ③

If you have any missing data in your variables, you need to be careful when using functions such as *rowMeans()*, to get the answer that you want. The problem is what you do when you have some missing values. Here's a problem: I have 2 oranges and 3 apples. How many fruits do I have? Obviously, I have a total of 5 fruits.

You have 2 oranges, and we don't know how many apples – this value is missing. How many fruits do you have? We could say that you have 2. Or we could say that we don't know: the answer is missing. If you add apples and oranges in **R**, most functions will tell you that the answer is NA (unknown).

```
apples <- 2
oranges <- NA
apples + oranges
```

```
[1] NA
```

The *rowSums* and *rowMeans* functions will allow you to choose what to do with missing data, by using the *na.rm* option, which asks 'should missing values (*na*) be removed (*rm*)?'

To obtain the mean hygiene score across three days, removing anyone with any missing values, we would use:

```
dlf$meanHygiene <- rowMeans(cbind(dlf$day1, dlf$day2, dlf$day3))
```

But a lot of people would be missing. If we wanted to use everyone who had at least one score for the three days, we would add *na.rm = TRUE*:

```
dlf$meanHygiene <- rowMeans(cbind(dlf$day1, dlf$day2, dlf$day3), na.rm = TRUE)
```

But what would we do if we had 100 days of hygiene scores? And if we didn't mind if people were missing one or two scores, but we didn't want to calculate a mean for people who only had one score? Well, we'd use the *is.na()* function first, to count the number of missing variables.

```
dlf$daysMissing <- rowSums (cbind (is.na(dlf$day1),
                                   is.na(dlf$day2),
                                   is.na(dlf$day3)))
```

(It's OK to break a command across rows like that, and sometimes it makes it easier to see that you didn't make a mistake.) Then we can use the *ifelse()* function to calculate values only for those people who have a score on at least two days:

```
dlf$meanHygiene <- ifelse(dlf$daysMissing < 2, NA,
                          rowMeans(cbind( dlf$day1,
                                          dlf$day2,
                                          dlf$day3),
                          na.rm=TRUE))
```

Notice how I've used spacing so it's clear which arguments go with which function? That makes it (slightly) easier to avoid making mistakes.[11]

5.8.3.6. The effect of transformations ②

Figure 5.9 shows the distributions for days 1 and 2 of the festival after the three different transformations. Compare these to the untransformed distributions in Figure 5.2. Now, you can see that all three transformations have cleaned up the hygiene scores for day 2:

---

[11] It still took me three tries to get this right.

the positive skew is reduced (the square root transformation in particular has been useful). However, because our hygiene scores on day 1 were more or less symmetrical to begin with, they have now become slightly negatively skewed for the log and square root transformation, and positively skewed for the reciprocal transformation![12] If we're using scores

FIGURE 5.9
Distributions of the hygiene data on day 1 and day 2 after various transformations

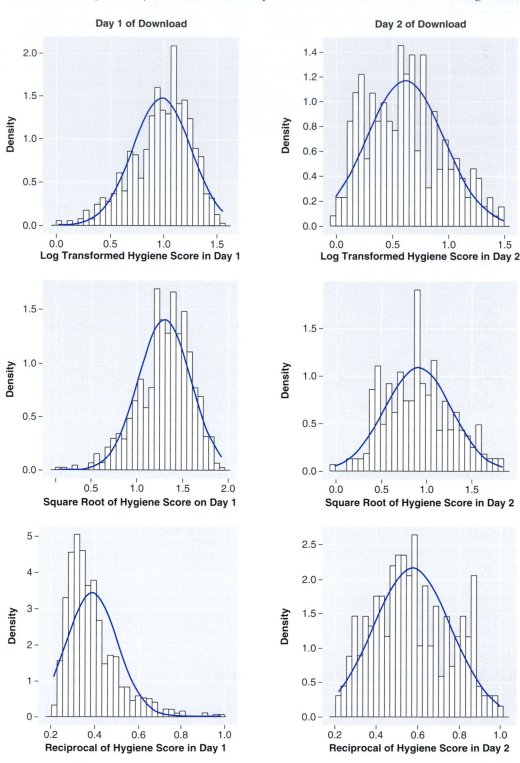

[12] The reversal of the skew for the reciprocal transformation is because, as I mentioned earlier, the reciprocal has the effect of reversing the scores.

from day 2 alone then we could use the transformed scores; however, if we wanted to look at the change in scores then we'd have to weigh up whether the benefits of the transformation for the day 2 scores outweigh the problems it creates in the day 1 scores – data analysis can be frustrating sometimes!

5.8.4.   When it all goes horribly wrong ③

It's very easy to think that transformations are the answers to all of your broken assumption prayers. However, as we have seen, there are reasons to think that transformations are not necessarily a good idea (see Jane Superbrain Box 5.1), and even if you think that they are they do not always solve the problem, and even when they do solve the problem they often create different problems in the process. This happens more frequently than you might imagine (messy data are the norm).

What do I do if my transformation doesn't work?

If you find yourself in the unenviable position of having irksome data then there are some other options available to you (other than sticking a big samurai sword through your head). The first is to use a test that does not rely on the assumption of normally distributed data, and as you go through the various chapters of this book I'll point out these tests – there is also a whole chapter dedicated to them later on.[13] One thing that you will quickly discover about non-parametric tests is that they have been developed for only a fairly limited range of situations. So, happy days if you want to compare two means, but sad and lonely days listening to Joy Division if you have a complex experimental design.

A much more promising approach is to use robust methods (which I mentioned in Jane Superbrain Box 5.1). These tests have developed as computers have got more sophisticated (doing these tests without computers would be only marginally less painful than ripping off your skin and diving into a bath of salt). How these tests work is beyond the scope of this book (and my brain), but two simple concepts will give you the general idea. Some of these procedures use a **trimmed mean**. A trimmed mean is simply a mean based on the distribution of scores after some percentage of scores has been removed from each extreme of the distribution. So, a 10% trimmed mean will remove 10% of scores from the top and bottom before the mean is calculated. With trimmed means you have to specify the amount of trimming that you want; for example, you must decide to trim 5%, 10% or perhaps even 20% of scores. A similar robust measure of location is an **M-estimator**, which differs from a trimmed mean in that the amount of trimming is determined empirically. In other words, rather than the researcher deciding before the analysis how much of the data to trim, an M-estimator determines the optimal amount of trimming necessary to give a robust estimate of, say, the mean. This has the obvious advantage that you never over- or under-trim your data; however, the disadvantage is that it is not always possible to reach a solution. In other words, robust tests based on M-estimators don't always give you an answer.

We saw in Chapter 2 that the accuracy of the mean depends on a symmetrical distribution, but a trimmed mean (or M-estimator) produces accurate results even when the distribution is not symmetrical, because by trimming the ends of the distribution we remove outliers and skew that bias the mean. Some robust methods work by taking advantage of the properties of the trimmed mean and M-estimator.

---

[13] For convenience a lot of textbooks refer to these tests as *non-parametric tests* or *assumption-free* tests and stick them in a separate chapter. Actually neither of these terms are particularly accurate (none of these tests is assumption-free) but in keeping with tradition I've put them in a chapter on their own (Chapter 15), ostracized from their 'parametric' counterparts and feeling lonely.

The second general procedure is the **bootstrap** (Efron & Tibshirani, 1993). The idea of the bootstrap is really very simple and elegant. The problem that we have is that we don't know the shape of the sampling distribution, but normality in our data allows us to infer that the sampling distribution is normal (and hence we can know the probability of a particular test statistic occurring). Lack of normality prevents us from knowing the shape of the sampling distribution unless we have big samples (but see Jane Superbrain Box 5.1). Bootstrapping gets around this problem by estimating the properties of the sampling distribution from the sample data. In effect, the sample data are treated as a population from which smaller samples (called bootstrap samples) are taken (putting the data back before a new case is drawn). The statistic of interest (e.g., the mean) is calculated in each sample, and by taking many samples the sampling distribution can be estimated (rather like in Figure 2.7). The standard error of the statistic is estimated from the standard deviation of this sampling distribution created from the bootstrap samples. From this standard error, confidence intervals and significance tests can be computed. This is a very neat way of getting around the problem of not knowing the shape of the sampling distribution. The bootstrap can be used in conjunction with trimmed means and M-estimators. For a fairly gentle introduction to the concept of bootstrapping see Wright, London, and Field (2011).

There are numerous robust tests based on trimmed means, bootstrapping and M-estimators described by Rand Wilcox (Figure 5.10) in his definitive text (Wilcox, 2005). He has also written functions in **R** to do these tests (which, when you consider the number of tests in his book, is a feat worthy of anyone's respect and admiration). We cover quite a few of these tests in this book.

There are two ways to access these functions: from a package, and direct from Wilcox's website. The package version of the tests is called *WRS* (although it is what's known as a beta version, which means it is not complete).[14] To access this package in **R** we need to execute:

```
install.packages("WRS", repos="http://R-Forge.R-project.org")
library(WRS)
```

This is a standard install procedure, but note that we have to include *repos=http://R-Forge.R-project.org* because it is not a full package and this instruction tells **R** where to find the package. This package is not always implemented in the most recent versions of **R** (because it is only a beta) and it is not kept as up to date as Wilcox's webpage, so although we tend to refer to the package, to be consistent with the general ethos of downloading packages, you should also consider sourcing the functions from Wilcox's website. One advantage of the website is that he keeps the functions very up to date. To source the functions from his website, execute:

```
source("http://www-rcf.usc.edu/~rwilcox/Rallfun-v14")
```

This command uses the **source()** function to access the webpage where Wilcox stores the functions (as a text file). *Rallfun-v14* is the name of the file (short for 'R all functions – version 14'). Without wishing to state the obvious, you need to be connected to the Internet for this command to work. Depending on this book's shelf-life, it is possible that the name of the file might change (most likely to *Rallfun-v15* or *Rallfun-v16*), so if you get an error try replacing the *v14* at the end with *v15* and so on. It's also possible that Rand might move his webpage (http://www-rcf.usc.edu/~rwilcox/) in which case Google him, locate the latest Rallfun file and replace the URL in the source function above with the new one. Having either loaded the package or sources the file from the web, you now have access to all of the functions in Wilcox's book.

[14] Actually, all of the functions are there, but there is very little documentation about what they do, which is why it is only at the 'beta' stage rather than being a full release.

FIGURE 5.10
The absolute
legend that is Rand
Wilcox, who is the
man you almost
certainly ought to
thank if you want
to do a robust test
in **R**

What have I discovered about statistics? ①

'You promised us swans,' I hear you cry, 'and all we got was normality this, homosome-thingorother that, transform this, it's all a waste of time that. Where were the bloody swans?!' Well, the Queen owns them all so I wasn't allowed to have them. Nevertheless, this chapter did negotiate Dante's eighth circle of hell (Malebolge), where data of deliberate and knowing evil dwell. That is, data that don't conform to all of those pesky assumptions that make statistical tests work properly. We began by seeing what assumptions need to be met for parametric tests to work, but we mainly focused on the assumptions of normality and homogeneity of variance. To look for normality we rediscovered the joys of frequency distributions, but also encountered some other graphs that tell us about deviations from normality (Q-Q plots). We saw how we can use skew and kurtosis values to assess normality and that there are statistical tests that we can use (the Shapiro–Wilk test). While negotiating these evildoers, we discovered what homogeneity of variance is, and how to test it with Levene's test and Hartley's F_{max}. Finally, we discovered redemption for our data. We saw we can cure their sins, make them good, with transformations (and on the way we discovered some of the uses of the $by()$ function and the transformation functions). Sadly, we also saw that some data are destined always to be evil.

We also discovered that I had started to read. However, reading was not my true passion; it was music. One of my earliest memories is of listening to my dad's rock and soul records (back in the days of vinyl) while waiting for my older brother to come home from school, so I must have been about 3 at the time. The first record I asked my parents to buy me was 'Take on the World' by Judas Priest, which I'd heard on *Top of the Pops* (a now defunct UK TV show) and liked. This record came out in 1978 when I was 5. Some people think that this sort of music corrupts young minds. Let's see if it did …

R packages used in this chapter

car	psych
ggplot2	Rcmdr
pastecs	

R functions used in this chapter

abs()	qplot()
by()	rowMeans()
cbind()	rowSums()
describe()	round()
dnorm()	shapiro.test()
ifelse()	source()
is.na()	sqrt()
leveneTest()	stat.desc()
log()	stat_function()
log10()	tapply()

Key terms that I've discovered

Bootstrap	Normally distributed data
Hartley's F_{max}	Parametric test
Heterogeneity of variance	Q-Q plot
Homogeneity of variance	Quantile
Independence	Robust test
Interval data	Shapiro–Wilk test
Levene's test	Transformation
Log	Trimmed mean
M-estimator	Variance ratio

Smart Alex's tasks

- **Task 1**: Using the **ChickFlick.dat** data from Chapter 4, check the assumptions of normality and homogeneity of variance for the two films (ignore gender): are the assumptions met? ①
- **Task 2**: Remember that the numeracy scores were positively skewed in the **RExam. dat** data (see Figure 5.5)? Transform these data using one of the transformations described in this chapter: do the data become normal? ②

Answers can be found on the companion website.

Further reading

Tabachnick, B. G., & Fidell, L. S. (2007). *Using multivariate statistics* (5th ed.). Boston: Allyn & Bacon. (Chapter 4 is the definitive guide to screening data!)

Wilcox, R. R. (2005). *Introduction to robust estimation and hypothesis testing* (2nd ed.). Burlington, MA: Elsevier. (Quite technical, but this is the definitive book on robust methods.)

Wright, D. B., London, K., & Field, A. P. (2011). Using bootstrap estimation and the plug-in principle for clinical psychology data. *Journal of Experimental Psychopathology*, 2(2), 252–270. (A fairly gentle introduction to bootstrapping in **R**.)

Correlation

6

FIGURE 6.1
I don't have a photo from Christmas 1981, but this was taken about that time at my grandparents' house. I'm trying to play an 'E' by the looks of it, no doubt because it's in 'Take on the World'.

6.1. What will this chapter tell me? ①

When I was 8 years old, my parents bought me a guitar for Christmas. Even then, I'd desperately wanted to play the guitar for years. I could not contain my excitement at getting this gift (had it been an *electric* guitar I think I would have actually exploded with excitement). The guitar came with a 'learn to play' book and, after a little while of trying to play what was on page 1 of this book, I readied myself to unleash a riff of universe-crushing power onto the world (well, 'Skip to my Lou' actually). But, I couldn't do it. I burst into tears and ran upstairs to hide.[1] My dad sat with me and said 'Don't worry, Andy, everything is hard to begin with, but the more you practise the easier it gets.' In his comforting words, my dad was inadvertently teaching me about the relationship, or correlation, between two variables. These two variables could be related in three ways: (1) *positively related*, meaning that the more I practised my guitar, the better a guitar player I would become (i.e., my dad was telling me the truth); (2) *not related* at all, meaning that as I practised the guitar my playing ability would remain completely constant (i.e., my dad has fathered a cretin); or (3) *negatively related*, which would mean that the more I practised my guitar the worse a guitar player I would become (i.e., my dad has fathered an indescribably strange child). This chapter looks first at how we can express the relationships between variables statistically by looking at two measures: *covariance* and the *correlation coefficient*. We then discover how to carry out and interpret correlations in **R**. The chapter ends by looking at more complex measures of relationships; in doing so it acts as a precursor to multiple regression, which we discuss in Chapter 7.

6.2. Looking at relationships ①

In Chapter 4 I stressed the importance of looking at your data graphically before running any other analysis on them. I just want to begin by reminding you that our first starting point with a correlation analysis should be to look at some scatterplots of the variables we have measured. I am not going to repeat how to get **R** to produce these graphs, but I am going to urge you (if you haven't done so already) to read section 4.5 before embarking on the rest of this chapter.

6.3. How do we measure relationships? ①

6.3.1. A detour into the murky world of covariance ①

The simplest way to look at whether two variables are associated is to look at whether they *covary*. To understand what **covariance** is, we first need to think back to the concept of variance that we met in Chapter 2. Remember that the variance of a single variable represents the average amount that the data vary from the mean. Numerically, it is described by:

$$\text{Variance}(s^2) = \frac{\sum (x_i - \bar{x})^2}{N-1} = \frac{\sum (x_i - \bar{x})(x_i - \bar{x})}{N-1} \tag{6.1}$$

The mean of the sample is represented by $\bar{x}$, x_i is the data point in question and N is the number of observations (see section 2.4.1). If we are interested in whether two variables are related, then we are interested in whether changes in one variable are met with similar changes in the other variable. Therefore, when one variable deviates from its mean we would expect the other variable to deviate from its mean in a similar way. To illustrate what I mean, imagine we took five people and subjected them to a certain number of advertisements promoting toffee sweets, and then measured how many packets of those sweets each

---

[1] This is not a dissimilar reaction to the one I have when publishers ask me for new editions of statistics textbooks.

Table 6.1 Adverts watched and toffee purchases

Participant:	1	2	3	4	5	Mean	s
Adverts watched	5	4	4	6	8	5.4	1.67
Packets bought	8	9	10	13	15	11.0	2.92

person bought during the next week. The data are in Table 6.1 as well as the mean and standard deviation (s) of each variable.

If there were a relationship between these two variables, then as one variable deviates from its mean, the other variable should deviate from its mean in the same or the directly opposite way. Figure 6.2 shows the data for each participant (light blue circles represent the number of packets bought and dark blue circles represent the number of adverts watched); the grey line is the average number of packets bought and the blue line is the average number of adverts watched. The vertical lines represent the differences (remember that these differences are called *deviations*) between the observed values and the mean of the relevant variable. The first thing to notice about Figure 6.2 is that there is a very similar pattern of deviations for both variables. For the first three participants the observed values are below the mean for both variables, for the last two people the observed values are above the mean for both variables. This pattern is indicative of a potential relationship between the two variables (because it seems that if a person's score is below the mean for one variable then their score for the other will also be below the mean).

So, how do we calculate the exact similarity between the patterns of differences of the two variables displayed in Figure 6.2? One possibility is to calculate the total amount of deviation but we would have the same problem as in the single variable case: the positive and negative deviations would cancel out (see section 2.4.1). Also, by simply adding the deviations, we would gain little insight into the relationship between the variables. Now, in the single variable case, we squared the deviations to eliminate the problem of positive and negative deviations cancelling out each other. When there are two variables, rather than squaring each deviation, we can multiply the deviation for one variable by the corresponding deviation for the second variable. If both deviations are positive or negative then this will give us a positive value (indicative of the deviations being in the same direction), but

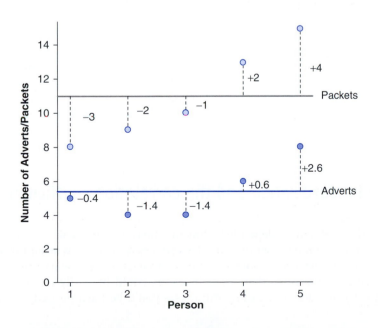

FIGURE 6.2

Graphical display of the differences between the observed data and the means of two variables

if one deviation is positive and one negative then the resulting product will be negative (indicative of the deviations being opposite in direction). When we multiply the deviations of one variable by the corresponding deviations of a second variable, we get what is known as the **cross-product deviations**. As with the variance, if we want an average value of the combined deviations for the two variables, we must divide by the number of observations (we actually divide by $N - 1$ for reasons explained in Jane Superbrain Box 2.2). This averaged sum of combined deviations is known as the **covariance**. We can write the covariance in equation form as in equation (6.2) – you will notice that the equation is the same as the equation for variance, except that instead of squaring the differences, we multiply them by the corresponding difference of the second variable:

$$\text{cov}(x, y) = \frac{\sum (x_i - \bar{x})(y_i - \bar{y})}{N - 1} \tag{6.2}$$

For the data in Table 6.1 and Figure 6.2 we reach the following value:

$$
\begin{aligned}
\text{cov}(x, y) &= \frac{\sum (x_i - \bar{x})(y_i - \bar{y})}{N - 1} \\
&= \frac{(-0.4)(-3) + (-1.4)(-2) + (-1.4)(-1) + (0.6)(2) + (2.6)(4)}{4} \\
&= \frac{1.2 + 2.8 + 1.4 + 1.2 + 10.4}{4} \\
&= \frac{17}{4} \\
&= 4.25
\end{aligned}
$$

Calculating the covariance is a good way to assess whether two variables are related to each other. A positive covariance indicates that as one variable deviates from the mean, the other variable deviates in the same direction. On the other hand, a negative covariance indicates that as one variable deviates from the mean (e.g., increases), the other deviates from the mean in the opposite direction (e.g., decreases).

There is, however, one problem with covariance as a measure of the relationship between variables and that is that it depends upon the scales of measurement used. So, covariance is not a standardized measure. For example, if we use the data above and assume that they represented two variables measured in miles then the covariance is 4.25 (as calculated above). If we then convert these data into kilometres (by multiplying all values by 1.609) and calculate the covariance again then we should find that it increases to 11. This dependence on the scale of measurement is a problem because it means that we cannot compare covariances in an objective way – so, we cannot say whether a covariance is particularly large or small relative to another data set unless both data sets were measured in the same units.

6.3.2. Standardization and the correlation coefficient ①

To overcome the problem of dependence on the measurement scale, we need to convert the covariance into a standard set of units. This process is known as **standardization**. A very basic form of standardization would be to insist that all experiments use the same units of measurement, say metres – that way, all results could be easily compared. However, what happens if you want to measure attitudes – you'd be hard pushed to measure them in metres. Therefore, we need a unit of measurement into which any scale of measurement can be converted. The unit of measurement we use is the *standard deviation*. We came across this measure in section 2.4.1 and saw that, like the variance, it is a measure of the average deviation from the mean. If we divide any distance from the mean by the standard deviation, it gives us that distance in standard deviation units. For example, for the data in Table 6.1, the standard deviation for the number of packets bought is approximately 3.0 (the exact value is 2.92). In Figure 6.2 we can see that the observed value for participant 1 was 3 packets less than the mean (so there was an error of −3 packets of sweets). If we divide this deviation, −3, by the standard deviation, which is approximately 3, then we get a value of −1. This tells us that the difference between participant 1's score and the mean was −1 standard deviation. So, we can express the deviation from the mean for a participant in standard units by dividing the observed deviation by the standard deviation.

It follows from this logic that if we want to express the covariance in a standard unit of measurement we can simply divide by the standard deviation. However, there are two variables and, hence, two standard deviations. Now, when we calculate the covariance we actually calculate two deviations (one for each variable) and then multiply them. Therefore, we do the same for the standard deviations: we multiply them and divide by the product of this multiplication. The standardized covariance is known as a **correlation coefficient** and is defined by equation (6.3), in which s_x is the standard deviation of the first variable and s_y is the standard deviation of the second variable (all other letters are the same as in the equation defining covariance):

$$r = \frac{\text{cov}_{xy}}{s_x s_y} = \frac{\sum(x_i - \bar{x})(y_i - \bar{y})}{(N-1)s_x s_y} \tag{6.3}$$

The coefficient in equation (6.3) is known as the **Pearson product-moment correlation coefficient** or **Pearson correlation coefficient** (for a really nice explanation of why it was originally called the 'product-moment' correlation, see Miles & Banyard, 2007) and was invented by Karl Pearson (see Jane Superbrain Box 6.1).[2] If we look back at Table 6.1 we see that the standard deviation for the number of adverts watched (s_x) was 1.67, and for the number of packets of crisps bought (s_y) was 2.92. If we multiply these together we get $1.67 \times 2.92 = 4.88$. Now, all we need to do is take the covariance, which we calculated a few pages ago as being 4.25, and divide by these multiplied standard deviations. This gives us $r = 4.25/4.88 = .87$.

By standardizing the covariance we end up with a value that has to lie between −1 and +1 (if you find a correlation coefficient less than −1 or more than +1 you can be sure that something has gone hideously wrong!). A coefficient of +1 indicates that the two variables are perfectly positively correlated, so as one variable increases, the other increases by a proportionate amount. Conversely, a coefficient of −1 indicates a perfect negative relationship: if one variable increases, the other decreases by a proportionate amount. A coefficient of zero indicates no linear relationship at all and so if one variable changes, the other stays the same. We also saw in section 2.6.4 that because the correlation coefficient is a standardized measure of an observed effect, it is a commonly used measure of the size of an effect and that values of ±.1 represent a small effect, ±.3 is a medium effect and ±.5 is a large effect (although I re-emphasize my caveat that these canned effect sizes are no substitute for interpreting the effect size within the context of the research literature).

---

[2] You will find Pearson's product-moment correlation coefficient denoted by both r and R. Typically, the upper-case form is used in the context of regression because it represents the multiple correlation coefficient; however, for some reason, when we square r (as in section 6.5.4.3) an upper case R is used. Don't ask me why − it's just to confuse me, I suspect.

JANE SUPERBRAIN 6.1

Who said statistics was dull? ①

Students often think that statistics is dull, but back in the early 1900s it was anything but dull, with various prominent figures entering into feuds on a soap opera scale. One of the most famous was between Karl Pearson and Ronald Fisher (whom we met in Chapter 2). It began when Pearson published a paper of Fisher's in his journal but made comments in his editorial that, to the casual reader, belittled Fisher's work. Two years later Pearson's group published work following on from Fisher's paper without consulting him. The antagonism persisted with Fisher turning down a job to work in Pearson's group and publishing 'improvements' on Pearson's ideas. Pearson for his part wrote in his own journal about apparent errors made by Fisher.

Another prominent statistician, Jerzy Neyman, criticized some of Fisher's most important work in a paper delivered to the Royal Statistical Society on 28 March 1935 at which Fisher was present. Fisher's discussion of the paper at that meeting directly attacked Neyman. Fisher more or less said that Neyman didn't know what he was talking about and didn't understand the background material on which his work was based. Relations soured so much that while they both worked at University College London, Neyman openly attacked many of Fisher's ideas in lectures to his students. The two feuding groups even took afternoon tea (a common practice in the British academic community of the time) in the same room but at different times! The truth behind who fuelled these feuds is, perhaps, lost in the mists of time, but Zabell (1992) makes a sterling effort to unearth it.

Basically, then, the founders of modern statistical methods were a bunch of squabbling children. Nevertheless, these three men were astonishingly gifted individuals. Fisher, in particular, was a world leader in genetics, biology and medicine as well as possibly the most original mathematical thinker ever (Barnard, 1963; Field, 2005c; Savage, 1976).

6.3.3. The significance of the correlation coefficient ③

Although we can directly interpret the size of a correlation coefficient, we have seen in Chapter 2 that scientists like to test hypotheses using probabilities. In the case of a correlation coefficient we can test the hypothesis that the correlation is different from zero (i.e., different from 'no relationship'). If we find that our observed coefficient was very unlikely to happen if there was no effect in the population, then we can gain confidence that the relationship that we have observed is statistically meaningful.

There are two ways that we can go about testing this hypothesis. The first is to use our trusty z-scores that keep cropping up in this book. As we have seen, z-scores are useful because we know the probability of a given value of z occurring, if the distribution from which it comes is normal. There is one problem with Pearson's r, which is that it is known to have a sampling distribution that is not normally distributed. This is a bit of a nuisance, but luckily, thanks to our friend Fisher, we can adjust r so that its sampling distribution *is* normal as follows (Fisher, 1921):

$$z_r = \frac{1}{2}\log_e\left(\frac{1+r}{1-r}\right) \qquad (6.4)$$

The resulting z_r has a standard error of:

$$SE_{z_r} = \frac{1}{\sqrt{N-3}} \qquad (6.5)$$

For our advert example, our $r = .87$ becomes 1.33 with a standard error of .71.

We can then transform this adjusted r into a z-score just as we have done for raw scores, and for skewness and kurtosis values in previous chapters. If we want a z-score that represents the size of the correlation relative to a particular value, then we simply compute a z-score using the value that we want to test against and the standard error. Normally we want to see whether the correlation is different from 0, in which case we can subtract 0 from the observed value of r and divide by the standard error (in other words, we just divide z_r by its standard error):

$$z = \frac{z_r}{SE_{z_r}} \tag{6.6}$$

For our advert data this gives us $1.33/.71 = 1.87$. We can look up this value of z (1.87) in the table for the normal distribution in the Appendix and get the one-tailed probability from the column labelled 'Smaller Portion'. In this case the value is .0307. To get the two-tailed probability we simply multiply the one-tailed probability value by 2, which gives us .0614. As such the correlation is significant, $p < .05$, one-tailed, but not two-tailed.

In fact, the hypothesis that the correlation coefficient is different from 0 is usually (**R**, for example, does this) tested not using a z-score, but using a t-statistic with $N - 2$ degrees of freedom, which can be directly obtained from r:

$$t_r = \frac{r\sqrt{N-2}}{\sqrt{1-r^2}} \tag{6.7}$$

You might wonder then why I told you about z-scores, then. Partly it was to keep the discussion framed in concepts with which you are already familiar (we don't encounter the t-test properly for a few chapters), but also it is useful background information for the next section.

6.3.4. Confidence intervals for r ③

Confidence intervals tell us something about the likely value (in this case of the correlation) in the population. To understand how confidence intervals are computed for r, we need to take advantage of what we learnt in the previous section about converting r to z_r (to make the sampling distribution normal), and using the associated standard errors. We can then construct a confidence interval in the usual way. For a 95% confidence interval we have (see section 2.5.2.1):

lower boundary of confidence interval $= \bar{X} - (1.96 \times SE)$

upper boundary of confidence interval $= \bar{X} + (1.96 \times SE)$

In the case of our transformed correlation coefficients these equations become:

lower boundary of confidence interval $= z_r - (1.96 \times SE_{z_r})$

upper boundary of confidence interval $= z_r + (1.96 \times SE_{z_r})$

For our advert data this gives us $1.33 - (1.96 \times .71) = -0.062$, and $1.33 + (1.96 \times .71) = 2.72$. Remember that these values are in the z_r metric and so we have to convert back to correlation coefficients using:

$$r = \frac{e^{(2z_r)} - 1}{e^{(2z_r)} + 1}$$ (6.8)

This gives us an upper bound of $r = .991$ and a lower bound of -0.062 (because this value is so close to zero the transformation to z has no impact).

CRAMMING SAM'S TIPS   Correlation

- A crude measure of the relationship between variables is the *covariance*.
- If we standardize this value we get *Pearson's correlation coefficient, r*.
- The correlation coefficient has to lie between −1 and +1.
- A coefficient of +1 indicates a perfect positive relationship, a coefficient of −1 indicates a perfect negative relationship, and a coefficient of 0 indicates no linear relationship at all.
- The correlation coefficient is a commonly used measure of the size of an effect: values of ±.1 represent a small effect, ±.3 is a medium effect and ±.5 is a large effect. However, if you can, try to interpret the size of correlation within the context of the research you've done rather than blindly following these benchmarks.

6.3.5.   A word of warning about interpretation: causality ①

Considerable caution must be taken when interpreting correlation coefficients because they give no indication of the direction of *causality*. So, in our example, although we can conclude that as the number of adverts watched increases, the number of packets of toffees bought increases also, we cannot say that watching adverts *causes* you to buy packets of toffees. This caution is for two reasons:

- **The third-variable problem**: We came across this problem in section 1.6.2. To recap, in any correlation, causality between two variables cannot be assumed because there may be other measured or unmeasured variables affecting the results. This is known as the *third-variable* problem or the *tertium quid* (see section 1.6.2 and Jane Superbrain Box 1.1).

- **Direction of causality**: Correlation coefficients say nothing about which variable causes the other to change. Even if we could ignore the third-variable problem described above, and we could assume that the two correlated variables were the only important ones, the correlation coefficient doesn't indicate in which direction causality operates. So, although it is intuitively appealing to conclude that watching adverts causes us to buy packets of toffees, there is no *statistical* reason why buying packets of toffees cannot cause us to watch more adverts. Although the latter conclusion makes less intuitive sense, the correlation coefficient does not tell us that it isn't true.

6.4. Data entry for correlation analysis ①

Data entry for correlation, regression and multiple regression is straightforward because each variable is entered in a separate column. If you are preparing your data in software other than **R** then this means that, for each variable you have measured, you create a variable in the spreadsheet with an appropriate name, and enter a participant's scores across one row of the spreadsheet. There may be occasions on which you have one or more categorical variables (such as gender) and these variables can also be entered in a column – see section 3.7 for more detail.

As an example, if we wanted to calculate the correlation between the two variables in Table 6.1 we would enter these data as in Figure 6.3. You can see that each variable is entered in a separate column, and each row represents a single individual's data (so the first consumer saw 5 adverts and bought 8 packets).

If you have a small data set you might want to enter the variables directly into **R** and then create a dataframe from them. For the advert data this can be done by executing the following commands (see section 3.5):

```
adverts<-c(5,4,4,6,8)
packets<-c(8,9,10,13,15)
advertData<-data.frame(adverts, packets)
```

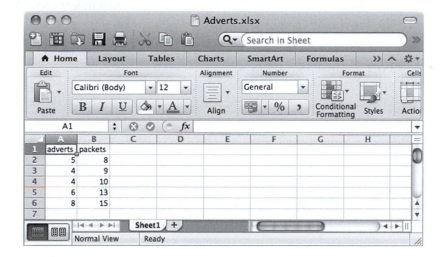

FIGURE 6.3
Data entry for correlation using Excel

SELF-TEST

✓ Enter the advert data and use *ggplot2* to produce a scatterplot (number of packets bought on the *y*-axis, and adverts watched on the *x*-axis) of the data.

6.5. Bivariate correlation ①

There are two types of correlation: *bivariate* and *partial*. A **bivariate correlation** is a correlation between two variables (as described at the beginning of this chapter) whereas a **partial correlation** (see section 6.6) looks at the relationship between two variables while 'controlling' the effect of one or more additional variables. Pearson's product-moment correlation coefficient (described earlier), Spearman's rho (see section 6.5.5) and Kendall's tau (see section 6.5.6) are examples of bivariate correlation coefficients.

Let's return to the example from Chapter 4 about exam scores. Remember that a psychologist was interested in the effects of exam stress and revision on exam performance. She had devised and validated a questionnaire to assess state anxiety relating to exams (called the Exam Anxiety Questionnaire, or EAQ). This scale produced a measure of anxiety scored out of 100. Anxiety was measured before an exam, and the percentage mark of each student on the exam was used to assess the exam performance. She also measured the number of hours spent revising. These data are in **Exam Anxiety.dat** on the companion website. We already created scatterplots for these data (section 4.5) so we don't need to do that again.

6.5.1. Packages for correlation analysis in R ①

There are several packages that we will use in this chapter. Some of them can be accessed through R Commander (see the next section) but others can't. For the examples in this chapter you will need the packages *Hmisc*, *polycor*, *boot*, *ggplot2* and *ggm*. If you do not have these packages installed (some should be installed from previous chapters), you can install them by executing the following commands (*boot* is part of the base package and doesn't need to be installed):

```
install.packages("Hmisc"); install.packages("ggm");
install.packages("ggplot2"); install.packages("polycor")
```

You then need to load these packages by executing the commands:

```
library(boot); library(ggm); library(ggplot2); library(Hmisc);
library(polycor)
```

6.5.2. General procedure for correlations using R Commander ①

To conduct a bivariate correlation using R Commander, first initiate the package by executing (and install it if you haven't – see section 3.6):

```
library(Rcmdr)
```

You then need to load the data file into R Commander by using the **Data⇒Import data⇒from text file, clipboard, or URL…** menu (see section 3.7.3). Once the data are loaded in a dataframe (I have called the dataframe *examData*), you can use either the **Statistics⇒Summaries⇒Correlation matrix…** or the **Statistics⇒Summaries⇒Correlation test…** menu to get the correlation coefficients. These menus and their dialog boxes are shown in Figure 6.4.

The *correlation matrix* menu should be selected if you want to get correlation coefficients for more than two variables (in other words, produce a grid of correlation coefficients); the *correlation test* menu should be used when you want only a single correlation coefficient. Both menus enable you to compute Pearson's product-moment correlation and Spearman's correlation, and both can be used to produce *p*-values associated with these correlations. However, there are some important differences too: the correlation test menu enables you to compute Kendall's correlation, produces a confidence interval and allows you to select both two-tailed and one-tailed tests, but can be used to compute only one correlation coefficient at a time; in contrast, the correlation matrix cannot produce Kendall's correlation but can compute partial correlations, and can also compute multiple correlations from a single command.

Let's look at the *Correlation Matrix* dialog box first. Having accessed the main dialog box, you should find that the variables in the dataframe are listed on the left-hand side of the dialog box (Figure 6.4). You can select the variables that you want from the list by clicking with the mouse while holding down the *Ctrl* key. **R** will create a grid of correlation coefficients for all of the combinations of variables that you have selected. This table is called a correlation matrix. For our current example, select the variables **Exam**, **Anxiety** and **Revise**. Having selected the variables of interest you can choose between three correlation coefficients: Pearson's product-moment correlation coefficient (Pearson product-moment ⊙), Spearman's rho (Spearman rank-order   ⊙) and a partial correlation (Partial ⊙). Any of these can be selected by clicking on the appropriate tick-box with a mouse. Finally, if you would like *p*-values for the correlation coefficients then select[3] Pairwise p-values for Pearson or Spearman correlations ☑ .

For the *correlation test* dialog box you will again find that the variables in the dataframe are listed on the left-hand side of the dialog box (Figure 6.4). You can select only two by clicking with the mouse while holding down the *Ctrl* key. Having selected the two variables of interest, choose between three correlation coefficients: Pearson's product-moment correlation coefficient (Pearson product-moment ⊙), Spearman's rho (Spearman rank-order   ⊙) and Kendall's tau (Kendall's tau ⊙). In addition, it is possible to specify whether or not the test is one- or two-tailed (see section 2.6.2). To recap, a two-tailed test (the default) should be used when you cannot predict the nature of the relationship (i.e., 'I'm not sure whether exam anxiety will improve or reduce exam marks'). If you have a non-directional hypothesis like this, click

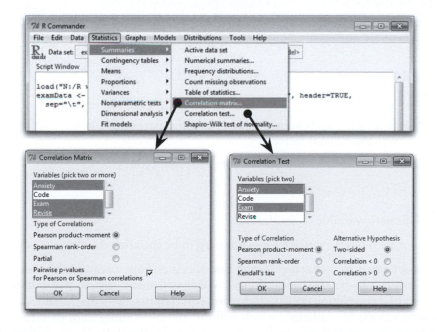

FIGURE 6.4
Conducting a bivariate correlation using R Commander

---

[3] Selecting this option changes the function that R Commander uses to generate the output. If this option is not selected then the function *cor()* is used, but if it is selected *rcorr()* is used (which is part of the *Hmisc* package). The main implication is that *rcorr()* reports the results to only 2 decimal places (see the next section for a full description of these functions).

on Two-sided ⊙. A one-tailed test should be selected when you have a directional hypothesis. With correlations, the direction of the relationship can be positive (e.g., 'the more anxious someone is about an exam, the better their mark will be') or negative (e.g., 'the more anxious someone is about an exam, the worse their mark will be'). A positive relationship means that the correlation coefficient will be greater than 0; therefore, if you predict a positive correlation coefficient then select Correlation < 0 ⊙. However, if you predict a negative relationship then the correlation coefficient will be less than 0, so select Correlation < 0 ⊙. For both the *correlation matrix* and *correlation test* dialog boxes click on OK to generate the output.

6.5.3. General procedure for correlations using R ①

To compute basic correlation coefficients there are three main functions that can be used: **cor(), cor.test()** and **rcorr()**. Table 6.2 shows the main differences between the three functions. The functions *cor()* and *cor.test()* are part of the base system in **R**, but *rcorr()* is part of the *Hmisc* package, so make sure you have it loaded.

Table 6.2 should help you to decide which function is best in a particular situation: if you want a confidence interval then you will have to use *cor.test()*, and if you want correlation coefficients for multiple pairs of variables then you cannot use *cor.test()*; similarly, if you want *p*-values then *cor()* won't help you. You get the gist.

Table 6.2 Attributes of different functions for obtaining correlations

Function	Pearson	Spearman	Kendall	p-values	CI	Multiple Correlations?	Comments
cor()	✓	✓	✓			✓	
cor.test()	✓	✓	✓	✓	✓		
rcorr()	✓	✓			✓	✓	2 d.p. only

We will look at each function in turn and see what parameters it uses. Let's start with *cor()*, which takes the general form:

```
cor(x,y, use = "string", method = "correlation type")
```

in which:

- *x* is a numeric variable or dataframe.

- *y* is another numeric variable (does not need to be specified if *x* above is a dataframe).

- *use* is set equal to a character string that specifies how missing values are handled. The strings can be: (1) "everything", which will mean that **R** will output an NA instead of a correlation coefficient for any correlations involving variables containing missing values; (2) "all.obs", which will use all observations and, therefore, returns an error message if there are any missing values in the data; (3) "complete.obs", in which correlations are computed from only cases that are complete for all variables – sometimes known as *excluding cases listwise* (see R's Souls' Tip 6.1); or (4) "pairwise. complete.obs", in which correlations between pairs of variables are computed for cases that are complete for those two variables – sometimes known as *excluding cases pairwise* (see R's Souls' Tip 6.1).

- *method* enables you to specify whether you want "pearson", "spearman" or "kendall" correlations (note that all are written in lower case). If you want more than one type you can specify a list using the *c()* function; for example, *c("pearson", "spearman")* would produce both types of correlation coefficients.

If we stick with our exam anxiety data, then we could get Pearson correlations between all variables by specifying the dataframe (*examData*):

```
cor(examData, use = "complete.obs", method = "pearson")
```

If we want a single correlation between a pair of variables (e.g., **Exam** and **Anxiety**) then we'd specify both variables instead of the dataframe:

```
cor(examData$Exam, examData$Anxiety, use = "complete.obs", method = "pearson")
```

We can get a different type of correlation (e.g., Kendall's tau) by changing the *method* command:

```
cor(examData$Exam, examData$Anxiety, use = "complete.obs", method = "kendall")
```

We can also change how we deal with missing values, for example, by asking for pairwise exclusion:

```
cor(examData$Exam,    examData$Anxiety,    use    =    "pairwise.complete.obs",
method = "kendall")
```

R's Souls' Tip 6.1 Exclude cases pairwise or listwise? ①

As we discover various functions in this book, many of them have options that determine how missing data are handled. Sometimes we can decide to exclude cases 'pairwise' or 'listwise'. Listwise means that if a case has a missing value for any variable, then they are excluded from the whole analysis. So, for example, in our exam anxiety data if one of our students had reported their anxiety and we knew their exam performance but we didn't have data about their revision time, then their data would not be used to calculate any of the correlations: *they would be completely excluded from the analysis*. Another option is to exclude cases on a pairwise basis, which means that if a participant has a score missing for a particular variable or analysis, then their data are excluded only from calculations involving the variable for which they have no score. For our student about whom we don't have any revision data, this means that their data would be excluded when calculating the correlation between exam scores and revision time, and when calculating the correlation between exam anxiety and revision time; however, the student's scores would be *included* when calculating the correlation between exam anxiety and exam performance because for this pair of variables we have both of their scores.

The function *rcorr()* is fairly similar to *cor()*. It takes the general form:

```
rcorr(x,y, type = "correlation type")
```

in which:

- *x* is a numeric variable or matrix.

- *y* is another numeric variable (does not need to be specified if *x* above is a matrix).

- *type* enables you to specify whether you want "pearson" or "spearman" correlations. If you want both you can specify a list as *c("pearson", "spearman")*.

A couple of things to note: first, this function does not work on dataframes, so you have to convert your dataframe to a matrix first (see section 3.9.2); second, this function excludes cases pairwise (see R's Souls' Tip 6.1) and there is no way to change this setting. Therefore, if you have two numeric variables (that are not part of a dataframe) called **Exam** and **Anxiety** then you could compute the Pearson correlation coefficient and its *p*-value by executing:

```
rcorr(Exam, Anxiety, type = "pearson")
```

Similarly, you could compute Pearson correlations (and their *p*-values) between all variables in a matrix called *examData* by executing:

```
rcorr(examData, type = "pearson")
```

The function *cor.test()* can be used only on pairs of variables (not a whole dataframe) and takes the general form:

```
cor.test(x, y, alternative = "string", method = "correlation type", conf.
level = 0.95)
```

in which:

- *x* is a numeric variable.
- *y* is another numeric variable.
- *alternative* specifies whether you want to do a two-tailed test (*alternative = "two. sided"*), which is the default, or whether you predict that the correlation will be less than zero (i.e., negative) or more than zero (i.e., positive), in which case you can use *alternative = "less"* and *alternative = "greater"*, respectively.
- *method* is the same as for *cor()* described above.
- *conf.level* allows you to specify the width of the confidence interval computed for the correlation. The default is *0.95* (*conf.level = 0.95*) and if this is what you want then you don't need to use this command, but if you wanted a 90% or 99% confidence interval you could use *conf.level = 0.9* and *conf.level = 0.99*, respectively. Confidence intervals are produced only for Pearson's correlation coefficient.

Using our exam anxiety data, if we want a single correlation coefficient, its two-tailed *p*-value and 95% confidence interval between a pair of variables (for example, **Exam** and **Anxiety**) then we'd specify it much like we did for *cor()*:

```
cor.test(examData$Exam, examData$Anxiety, method = "pearson")
```

If we predicted a negative correlation then we could add in the *alternative* command:

```
cor.test(examData$Exam, examData$Anxiety, alternative = "less"), method =
"pearson")
```

We could also specify a different confidence interval than 95%:

```
cor.test(examData$Exam, examData$Anxiety, alternative = "less"), method =
"pearson", conf.level = 0.99)
```

Hopefully you get the general idea. We will now move on to look at some examples of specific types of correlation coefficients.

OLIVER TWISTED

Please Sir, can I have some more … variance and covariance?

Oliver is so excited to get onto analysing his data that he doesn't want me to spend pages waffling on about variance and covariance. 'Stop writing, you waffling fool,' he says. 'I want to analyse my data.' Well, he's got a point. If you want to find out more about two functions for calculating variances and covariances that are part of the *cor()* family, then the additional material for this chapter on the companion website will tell you.

6.5.4. Pearson's correlation coefficient ①

6.5.4.1. Assumptions of Pearson's *r* ①

Pearson's (Figure 6.5) correlation coefficient was described in full at the beginning of this chapter. Pearson's correlation requires only that data are interval (see section 1.5.1.2) for it to be an accurate measure of the linear relationship between two variables. However, if you want to establish whether the correlation coefficient is significant, then more assumptions are required: for the test statistic to be valid the sampling distribution has to be normally distributed and as we saw in Chapter 5 we assume that it is if our sample data are normally distributed (or if we have a large sample). Although typically, to assume that the sampling distribution is normal, we would want both variables to be normally distributed, there is one exception to this rule: one of the variables can be a categorical variable provided there are only two categories (in fact, if you look at section 6.5.7 you'll see that this is the same as doing a *t*-test, but I'm jumping the gun a bit). In any case, if your data are non-normal (see Chapter 5) or are not measured at the interval level then you should use a different kind of correlation coefficient or use bootstrapping.

FIGURE 6.5
Karl Pearson

6.5.4.2. Computing Pearson's *r* using R ①

That's a confusing title. We have already gone through the nuts and bolts of using R Commander and the command line to calculate Pearson's *r*. We're going to use the exam anxiety data to get some hands-on practice.

SELF-TEST

✓ Load the **Exam Anxiety.dat** file into a dataframe called *examData*.

Let's look at a sample of this dataframe:

```
   Code Revise Exam Anxiety Gender
1     1      4   40  86.298    Male
2     2     11   65  88.716  Female
3     3     27   80  70.178    Male
4     4     53   80  61.312    Male
5     5      4   40  89.522    Male
6     6     22   70  60.506  Female
7     7     16   20  81.462  Female
8     8     21   55  75.820  Female
9     9     25   50  69.372  Female
10   10     18   40  82.268  Female
```

The first issue we have is that some of the variables are not numeric (**Gender**) and others are not meaningful numerically (**code**). We have two choices here. The first is to make a new dataframe by selecting only the variables of interest) – we discovered how to do this in section 3.9.1. The second is to specify this subset within the *cor()* command itself. If we choose the first method then we should execute:

```
examData2 <- examData[, c("Exam", "Anxiety", "Revise")]
cor(examData2)
```

The first line creates a dataframe (*examData2*) that contains all of the cases, but only the variables **Exam**, **Anxiety** and **Revise**. The second command creates a table of Pearson correlations between these three variables (note that Pearson is the default so we don't need to specify it and because there are no missing cases we do not need the *use* command).

Alternatively, we could specify the subset of variables in the *examData* dataframe as part of the *cor()* function:

```
cor(examData[, c("Exam", "Anxiety", "Revise")])
```

The end result is the same, so it's purely down to preference. With the first method it is a little easier to see what's going on, but as you gain confidence and experience you might find that you prefer to save time and use the second method.

```
              Exam     Anxiety      Revise
Exam     1.0000000  -0.4409934   0.3967207
Anxiety -0.4409934   1.0000000  -0.7092493
Revise   0.3967207  -0.7092493   1.0000000
```

Output 6.1: Output for a Pearson's correlation

Output 6.1 provides a matrix of the correlation coefficients for the three variables. Each variable is perfectly correlated with itself (obviously) and so $r = 1$ along the diagonal of the table. Exam performance is negatively related to exam anxiety with a Pearson correlation coefficient of $r = -.441$. This is a reasonably big effect. Exam performance is positively related to the amount of time spent revising, with a coefficient of $r = .397$, which is also a reasonably big effect. Finally, exam anxiety appears to be negatively related to the time spent revising, $r = -.709$, which is a substantial effect size. In psychological terms, this all means that as anxiety about an exam increases, the percentage mark obtained in that exam decreases. Conversely, as the amount of time revising increases, the percentage obtained in the exam increases. Finally, as revision time increases, the student's anxiety about the exam decreases. So there is a complex interrelationship between the three variables.

Correlation coefficients are effect sizes, so we can interpret these values without really needing to worry about *p*-values (and as I have tried to drum into you, because *p*-values are related to sample size, there is a lot to be said for not obsessing about them). However, if you are the type of person who obsesses about *p*-values, then you can use the *rcorr()*

function instead and *p* yourself with excitement at the output it produces. First, make sure you have loaded the *Hmisc* package by executing:

```
library(Hmisc)
```

Next, we need to convert our dataframe into a matrix using the *as.matrix()* command. We can include only numeric variables so, just as we did above, we need to select only the numeric variables within the *examData* dataframe. To do this, execute:

```
examMatrix<-as.matrix(examData[, c("Exam", "Anxiety", "Revise")])
```

Which creates a matrix called *examMatrix* that contains only the variables **Exam**, **Anxiety**, and **Revise** from the *examData* dataframe. To get the correlation matrix we simply input this matrix into the *rcorr()* function:[4]

```
rcorr(examMatrix)
```

As before, I think that the method above makes it clear what we're doing, but more experienced users could combine the previous two commands into a single one:

```
rcorr(as.matrix(examData[, c("Exam", "Anxiety", "Revise")]))
```

Output 6.2 shows the same correlation matrix as Output 6.1, except rounded to 2 decimal places. In addition, we are given the sample size on which these correlations are based, and also a matrix of *p*-values that corresponds to the matrix of correlation coefficients above. Exam performance is negatively related to exam anxiety with a Pearson correlation coefficient of $r = -.44$ and the significance value is less than .001 (it is approximately zero). This significance value tells us that the probability of getting a correlation coefficient this big in a sample of 103 people if the null hypothesis were true (there was no relationship between these variables) is very low (close to zero in fact). Hence, we can gain confidence that there is a genuine relationship between exam performance and anxiety. Our criterion for significance is usually .05 (see section 2.6.1) so we can say that all of the correlation coefficients are significant.

```
         Exam Anxiety Revise
Exam     1.00   -0.44   0.40
Anxiety -0.44    1.00  -0.71
Revise   0.40   -0.71   1.00

n= 103


P
         Exam Anxiety Revise
Exam            0       0
Anxiety  0              0
Revise   0      0
```

Output 6.2

It can also be very useful to look at confidence intervals for correlation coefficients. Sadly, we have to do this one at a time (we can't do it for a whole dataframe or matrix). Let's look at the correlation between exam performance (**Exam**) and exam anxiety (**Anxiety**). We can compute the confidence interval *using cor.test()* by executing:

```
cor.test(examData$Anxiety, examData$Exam)
```

---

[4] The *ggm* package also has a function called *rcorr()*, so if you have this package installed, **R** might use that function instead, which will produce something very unpleasant on your screen. If so, you need to put *Hmisc::* in front of the commands to make sure **R** uses *rcorr()* from the *Hmisc* package (R's Souls' Tip 3.4):

```
Hmisc::rcorr(examMatrix)
Hmisc::rcorr(as.matrix(examData[, c("Exam", "Anxiety", "Revise")]))
```

Note that we have specified only the variables because by default this function produces Pearson's *r* and a 95% confidence interval. Output 6.3 shows the resulting output; it reiterates that the Pearson correlation between exam performance and anxiety was −.441, but tells us that this was highly significantly different from zero, $t(101) = -4.94$, $p < .001$. Most important, the 95% confidence ranged from −.585 to − .271, which does not cross zero. This tells us that in all likelihood, the population or actual value of the correlation is negative, so we can be pretty content that exam anxiety and exam performance are, in reality, negatively related.

```
        Pearson's product-moment correlation

data:  examData$Anxiety and examData$Exam
t = -4.938, df = 101, p-value = 3.128e-06
alternative hypothesis: true correlation is not equal to 0
95 percent confidence interval:
 -0.5846244 -0.2705591
sample estimates:
      cor
-0.4409934
```

Output 6.3

SELF-TEST

✓ Compute the confidence intervals for the relationships between the time spent revising (**Revise**) and both exam performance (**Exam**) and exam anxiety (**Anxiety**).

6.5.4.3. Using R^2 for interpretation ①

Although we cannot make direct conclusions about causality from a correlation, we can take the correlation coefficient a step further by squaring it. The correlation coefficient squared (known as the **coefficient of determination**, R^2) is a measure of the amount of variability in one variable that is shared by the other. For example, we may look at the relationship between exam anxiety and exam performance. Exam performances vary from person to person because of any number of factors (different ability, different levels of preparation and so on). If we add up all of this variability (rather like when we calculated the sum of squares in section 2.4.1) then we would have an estimate of how much variability exists in exam performances. We can then use R^2 to tell us how much of this variability is shared by exam anxiety. These two variables had a correlation of -0.4410 and so the value of R^2 will be $(-0.4410)^2 = 0.194$. This value tells us how much of the variability in exam performance is shared by exam anxiety.

If we convert this value into a percentage (multiply by 100) we can say that exam anxiety shares 19.4% of the variability in exam performance. So, although exam anxiety was highly correlated with exam performance, it can account for only 19.4% of variation in exam scores. To put this value into perspective, this leaves 80.6% of the variability still to be accounted for by other variables.

You'll often see people write things about R^2 that imply causality: they might write 'the variance in *y accounted for* by *x*', or 'the variation in one variable *explained* by the other'. However, although R^2 is an extremely useful measure of the substantive importance of an effect, it cannot be used to infer causal relationships. Exam anxiety might well share 19.4% of the variation in exam scores, but it does not necessarily cause this variation.

We can get **R** to compute the coefficient of determination by remembering that "^2" means 'squared' in **R**-speak. Therefore, for our *examData2* dataframe (see earlier) if we execute:

```
cor(examData2)^2
```

instead of:

```
cor(examData2)
```

then you will see be a matrix containing r^2 instead of r (Output 6.4).

```
          Exam    Anxiety    Revise
Exam    1.0000000 0.1944752 0.1573873
Anxiety 0.1944752 1.0000000 0.5030345
Revise  0.1573873 0.5030345 1.0000000
```

Output 6.4

Note that for exam performance and anxiety the value is 0.194, which is what we calculated above. If you want these values expressed as a percentage then simply multiply by 100, so the command would become:

```
cor(examData2)^2 * 100
```

6.5.5. Spearman's correlation coefficient ①

Spearman's correlation coefficient (Spearman, 1910), r_s, is a non-parametric statistic and so can be used when the data have violated parametric assumptions such as non-normally distributed data (see Chapter 5). You'll sometimes hear the test referred to as Spearman's rho (pronounced 'row', as in 'row your boat gently down the stream'). Spearman's test works by first ranking the data (see section 15.4.1), and then applying Pearson's equation (equation (6.3)) to those ranks.

I was born in England, which has some bizarre traditions. One such oddity is the World's Biggest Liar competition held annually at the Santon Bridge Inn in Wasdale (in the Lake District). The contest honours a local publican, 'Auld Will Ritson', who in the nineteenth century was famous in the area for his far-fetched stories (one such tale being that Wasdale turnips were big enough to be hollowed out and used as garden sheds). Each year locals are encouraged to attempt to tell the biggest lie in the world (lawyers and politicians are apparently banned from the competition). Over the years there have been tales of mermaid farms, giant moles, and farting sheep blowing holes in the ozone layer. (I am thinking of entering next year and reading out some sections of this book.)

Imagine I wanted to test a theory that more creative people will be able to create taller tales. I gathered together 68 past contestants from this competition and asked them where they were placed in the competition (first, second, third, etc.) and also gave them a creativity questionnaire (maximum score 60). The position in the competition is an ordinal variable (see section 1.5.1.2) because the places are categories but have a meaningful order (first place is better than second place and so on). Therefore, Spearman's correlation coefficient should be used (Pearson's r requires interval or ratio data). The data for this study are in the file **The Biggest Liar.dat**. The data are in two columns: one labelled **Creativity** and one labelled **Position** (there's actually a third variable in there but we will ignore it for the time being). For the **Position** variable, each of the categories described above has been coded with a numerical value. First place has been coded with the value 1, with positions being labelled 2, 3 and so on.

The procedure for doing a Spearman correlation is the same as for a Pearson correlation except that we need to specify that we want a Spearman correlation instead of Pearson, which is done using *method = "spearman"* for *cor()* and *cor.test()*, and *type = "spearman"* for *rcorr()*. Let's load the data into a dataframe and then create a dataframe by executing:

```
liarData = read.delim("The Biggest Liar.dat",  header = TRUE)
```

or if you haven't set your working directory, execute this command and use the dialog box to select the file:

```
liarData = read.delim(file.choose(),  header = TRUE)
```

SELF-TEST

✓ See whether you can use what you have learned so far to compute a Spearman's correlation between **Position** and **Creativity**.

To obtain the correlation coefficient for a pair of variables we can execute:

```
cor(liarData$Position, liarData$Creativity, method = "spearman")
```

Note that we have simply specified the two variables of interest, and then set the method to be a Spearman correlation. The output of this command will be:

```
[1] -0.3732184
```

If we want a significance value for this correlation we could either use *rcorr()* by executing (remembering that we have to first convert the dataframe to a matrix):

```
liarMatrix<-as.matrix(liarData[, c("Position", "Creativity")])
rcorr(liarMatrix)
```

or simply use *cor.test()*, which has the advantage that we can set a directional hypothesis. I predicted that more creative people would tell better lies. Doing well in the competition (i.e., telling better lies) actually equates to a lower number for the variable **Position** (first place = 1, second place = 2 etc.), so we're predicting a negative relationship. High scores on **Creativity** should equate to a lower value of **Position** (because a low value means you did well!). Therefore, we predict that the correlation will be less than zero, and we can reflect this prediction by using *alternative = "less"* in the command:

```
cor.test(liarData$Position,  liarData$Creativity,  alternative  =  "less",
method = "spearman")
```

FIGURE 6.6
Charles
Spearman,
ranking furiously

```
        Spearman's rank correlation rho
data:  liarData$Position and liarData$Creativity
S = 71948.4, p-value = 0.0008602
alternative hypothesis: true rho is less than 0
sample estimates:
       rho
-0.3732184
```

Output 6.5

Output 6.5 shows the output for a Spearman correlation on the variables **Creativity** and **Position**. The output is very similar to that of the Pearson correlation (except that confidence intervals are not produced – if you want one see the section on bootstrapping): the correlation coefficient between the two variables is fairly large ($-.373$), and the significance value of this coefficient is very small ($p < .001$). The significance value for this correlation coefficient is less than .05; therefore, it can be concluded that there is a significant relationship between creativity scores and how well someone did in the World's Biggest Liar competition. Note that the relationship is negative: as creativity increased, position decreased. Remember that a low number means that you did well in the competition (a low number such as 1 means you came first, and a high number like 4 means you came fourth). Therefore, our hypothesis is supported: as creativity increased, so did success in the competition.

SELF-TEST

✓ Did creativity cause success in the World's Biggest Liar competition?

6.5.6. Kendall's tau (non-parametric) ①

Kendall's tau, τ, is another non-parametric correlation and it should be used rather than Spearman's coefficient when you have a small data set with a large number of tied ranks. This means that if you rank all of the scores and many scores have the same rank, then Kendall's tau should be used. Although Spearman's statistic is the more popular of the two coefficients, there is much to suggest that Kendall's statistic is actually a better estimate of the correlation in the population (see Howell, 1997: 293). As such, we can draw more accurate generalizations from Kendall's statistic than from Spearman's. To carry out Kendall's correlation on the World's Biggest Liar data simply follow the same steps as for Pearson and Spearman correlations but use *method = "kendall"*:

```
cor(liarData$Position, liarData$Creativity, method = "kendall")
```

```
cor.test(liarData$Position,  liarData$Creativity,  alternative  =  "less",
method = "kendall")
```

The output is much the same as for Spearman's correlation.

```
        Kendall's rank correlation tau
data:  liarData$Position and liarData$Creativity
z = -3.2252, p-value = 0.0006294
alternative hypothesis: true tau is less than 0
sample estimates:
       tau
-0.3002413
```

Output 6.6

You'll notice from Output 6.6 that the actual value of the correlation coefficient is closer to zero than the Spearman correlation (it has increased from −.373 to −.300). Despite the difference in the correlation coefficients we can still interpret this result as being a highly significant relationship (because the significance value of .001 is less than .05). However, Kendall's value is a more accurate gauge of what the correlation in the population would be. As with the Pearson correlation, we cannot assume that creativity caused success in the World's Best Liar competition.

SELF-TEST

✓ Conduct a Pearson correlation analysis of the advert data from the beginning of the chapter.

6.5.7.   Bootstrapping correlations ③

Another way to deal with data that do not meet the assumptions of Pearson's *r* is to use bootstrapping. The *boot()* function takes the general form:

```
object<-boot(data, function, replications)
```

in which *data* specifies the dataframe to be used, *function* is a function that you write to tell *boot()* what you want to bootstrap, and *replications* is a number specifying how many bootstrap samples you want to take (I usually set this value to 2000). Executing this command creates an *object* that has various properties. We can view an estimate of bias, and an empirically derived standard error by viewing *object*, and we can display confidence intervals based on the bootstrap by executing *boot.ci(object)*.

When using the *boot()* function with correlations (and anything else for that matter) the tricky bit is writing the function (R's Souls' Tip 6.2). If we stick with our biggest liar data and want to bootstrap Kendall tau, then our function will be:

```
bootTau<-function(liarData,i)cor(liarData$Position[i],liarData$Creativity[i],
use = "complete.obs", method = "kendall")
```

Executing this command creates an object called *bootTau*. The first bit of the function tells **R** what input to expect in the function: in this case we need to feed a dataframe (*liarData*) into the function and a variable that has been called *i* (which refers to a particular bootstrap sample). The second part of the function specifies the *cor()* function, which is the thing we want to bootstrap. Notice that *cor()* is specified in exactly the same way as when we did the original Kendall correlation except that for each variable we have added *[i]*, which again just refers to a particular bootstrap sample. If you want to bootstrap a Pearson or Spearman correlation you do it in exactly the same way except that you specify *method = "pearson"* or *method = "spearman"* when you define the function.

To create the bootstrap object, we execute:

```
library(boot)
boot_kendall<-boot(liarData, bootTau, 2000)
boot_kendall
```

The first command loads the *boot* package (in case you haven't already initiated it). The second command creates an object (*boot_kendall*) based on bootstrapping the *liarData* dataframe using the *bootTau* function that we previously defined and executed. The second line displays a summary of the *boot_kendall* object. To get the 95% confidence interval for the *boot_kendall* object we execute:[5]

```
boot.ci(boot_kendall)
```

Output 6.7 shows the contents of both *boot_kendall* and also the output of the *boot.ci()* function. First, we get the original value of Kendall's tau (–.300), which we computed in the previous section. We also get an estimate of the bias in that value (which in this case is very small) and the standard error (0.098) based on the bootstrap samples. The output from *boot.ci()* gives us four different confidence intervals (the basic bootstrapped CI, percentile and BCa). The good news is that none of these confidence intervals cross zero, which gives us good reason to think that the population value of this relationship between creativity and success at being a liar is in the same direction as the sample value. In other words, our original conclusions stand.

```
ORDINARY NONPARAMETRIC BOOTSTRAP


Call:
boot(data = liarData, statistic = bootTau, R = 2000)

Bootstrap Statistics :
      original        bias    std. error
t1* -0.3002413 0.001058191    0.097663



> boot.ci(boot_kendall)

BOOTSTRAP CONFIDENCE INTERVAL CALCULATIONS
Based on 2000 bootstrap replicates

CALL :
boot.ci(boot.out = boot_kendall)

Intervals :
Level       Normal              Basic
95%    (-0.4927, -0.1099 )   (-0.4956, -0.1126 )

Level     Percentile            BCa
95%    (-0.4879, -0.1049 )   (-0.4777, -0.0941 )
Calculations and Intervals on Original Scale
Warning message:
In boot.ci(boot_kendall) :
  bootstrap variances needed for studentized intervals
```

Output 6.7

SELF-TEST

✓ Conduct bootstrap analysis of the Pearson and Spearman correlations for the *examData2* dataframe.

---

[5] If we want something other than a 95% confidence interval we can add *conf = x*, in which *x* is the value of the confidence interval as a proportion. For example, we can get a 99% confidence interval by executing:

```
boot.ci(boot_kendall, conf = 0.99)
```

R's Souls' Tip 6.2   Writing functions ③

What happens if there is not a function available in **R** to do what you want to do? Simple, write your own function. The ability to write your own functions is a very powerful feature of **R**. With a sufficient grasp of the **R** environment (and the maths behind whatever you're trying to do) you can write a function to do virtually anything for you (apart from making coffee). To write a function you need to execute a string of commands that define the function. They take this general format:

```
nameofFunction<-function(inputObject1, inputObject2, etc.)
{
        a set of commands that do things to the input object(s)
        a set of commands that specify the output of the function
}
```

Basically, you name the function (any name you like, but obviously one that tells you what the function does is helpful). The *function()* tells **R** that you're writing a function, and you need to place within the brackets anything you want as input to the function: this can be any object in **R** (a model, a dataframe, a numeric value, text, etc.). A function might just accept one object, or there might be many. The names you list in the brackets can be whatever you like, but again it makes sense to label them based on what they are (e.g., if you need to input a dataframe then it makes sense to give the input a label of *dataframe* so that you remember what it is that the function needs). You then use {} to contain a set of instructions that tell **R** what to do with the objects that have been input into the function. These are usually some kind of calculations followed by some kind of instruction about what to return from the function (the output).

Imagine that **R** doesn't have a function for computing the mean and we wanted to write one (this will keep things familiar). We could write this as:

```
meanOfVariable<-function(variable)
{
        mean<-sum(variable)/length(variable)
        cat("Mean = ", mean)
}
```

Executing this command creates a function called *meanOfVariable* that expects a variable to be entered into it. The bits in {} tell **R** what to do with the variable that is entered into the function. The first line computes the mean using the function *sum()* to add the values in the variable that was entered into the function, and the function *length()* counts how many scores are in the variable. Therefore, *mean<-sum(variable)/length(variable)* translates as mean = sum of scores/number of scores (which, of course, is the definition of the mean). The final line uses the *cat()* function to print the text "Mean =" and the value of *mean* that we have just computed.

Remember the data about the number of friends that statistics lecturers had that we used to explore the mean in Chapter 2 (section 2.4.1). We could enter these data by executing:

```
lecturerFriends = c(1,2,3,3,4)
```

Having executed our function, we can use it to find the mean. We simply execute:

```
meanOfVariable(lecturerFriends)
```

This tells **R** that we want to use the function *meanOfVariable()*, which we have just created, and that the variable we want to apply this function to is **lecturerFriends**. Executing this command gives us:

```
Mean =  2.6
```

In other words, **R** has printed the text 'Mean =' and the value of the mean computed by the function (just as we asked it to). This value is the same as the one we calculated in section 2.4.1, so the function has worked. The beauty of functions is that having executed the commands that define it, we can use this function over and over again within our session (which saves time).

As a final point, just to be clear, when we define our function we can name things anything we like. For example, although I named the input to the function 'variable' to remind myself what the function needs, I could have named it 'HarryTheHungryHippo' if I had wanted to. Provided that I carry this name through to the commands within the function, it will work:

```
meanOfVariable<-function(HarryTheHungryHippo)
{
    mean<-sum(HarryTheHungryHippo)/length(HarryTheHungryHippo)
    cat("Mean = ", mean)
}
```

Note that within the function I now apply the *sum()* and *length()* functions to *HarryTheHungryHippo* because this is the name that I gave to the input of the function. It will work, but people will be probably confused about what *HarryTheHungryHippo* is when they read your code.

6.5.8. Biserial and point-biserial correlations ③

The biserial and point-biserial correlation coefficients are distinguished by only a conceptual difference, yet their statistical calculation is quite different. These correlation coefficients are used when one of the two variables is **dichotomous** (i.e., it is categorical with only two categories). An example of a dichotomous variable is being pregnant, because a woman can be either pregnant or not (she cannot be 'a bit pregnant'). Often it is necessary to investigate relationships between two variables when one of the variables is dichotomous. The difference between the use of biserial and point-biserial correlations depends on whether the dichotomous variable is discrete or continuous. This difference is very subtle. A discrete, or true, dichotomy is one for which there is no underlying continuum between the categories. An example of this is whether someone is dead or alive: a person can be only dead or alive, they can't be 'a bit dead'. Although you might describe a person as being 'half-dead' – especially after a heavy drinking session – they are clearly still alive if they are still breathing! Therefore, there is no continuum between the two categories. However, it is possible to have a dichotomy for which a continuum does exist. An example is passing or failing a statistics test: some people will only just fail while others will fail by a large margin; likewise some people will scrape a pass while others will excel. So although participants fall into only two categories there is an underlying continuum along which people lie. Hopefully, it is clear that in this case there is some kind of continuum underlying the dichotomy, because some people passed or failed more dramatically than others. The **point-biserial correlation** coefficient (r_{pb}) is used when one variable is a discrete dichotomy (e.g., pregnancy), whereas the **biserial correlation** coefficient (r_b) is used when one variable is a continuous dichotomy (e.g., passing or failing an exam).

Imagine that I was interested in the relationship between the gender of a cat and how much time it spent away from home (what can I say? I love cats so these things interest me). I had heard that male cats disappeared for substantial amounts of time on long-distance roams around the neighbourhood (something about hormones driving them to find mates) whereas female cats tended to be more homebound. So, I used this as a purr-fect (sorry!) excuse to go and visit lots of my friends and their cats. I took a note of the gender of the cat and then asked the owners to note down the number of hours that their cat was absent from home over a week. Clearly the time spent away from home is measured at an interval level – and let's assume it meets the other assumptions of parametric data – while the gender of the cat is discrete dichotomy. A point-biserial correlation has to be calculated and this is simply a Pearson correlation when the dichotomous variable is coded with 0 for one category and 1 for the other.

Let's load the data in the file **pbcorr.csv** and have a look at it. These data are in the CSV format, so we can load them as (assuming you have set the working directory correctly):

```
catData = read.csv("pbcorr.csv", header = TRUE)
```

Note that we have used the *read.csv()* function because the file is a .csv file. To look at the data execute:

```
catData
```

A sample of the data is as follows:

```
   time gender recode
1    41      1      0
2    40      0      1
3    40      1      0
4    38      1      0
5    34      1      0
6    46      0      1
7    42      1      0
8    42      1      0
9    47      1      0
10   42      0      1
11   45      1      0
12   46      1      0
13   44      1      0
14   54      0      1
```

There are three variables:

- **time**, which is the number of hours that the cat spent away from home (in a week).

- **gender**, is the gender of the cat, coded as 1 for male and 0 for female.

- **recode**, is the gender of the cat but coded the opposite way around (i.e., 0 for male and 1 for female). We will come to this variable later, but for now ignore it.

SELF-TEST

✓ Carry out a Pearson correlation on **time** and **gender**.

Congratulations: if you did the self-test task then you have just conducted your first point-biserial correlation. See, despite the horrible name, it's really quite easy to do. If you didn't do the self-test then execute:

```
cor.test(catData$time, catData$gender)
```

You should find that you can see Output 6.8. The point-biserial correlation coefficient is $r_{pb} = .378$, which has a significance value of .003. The significance test for this correlation is actually the same as performing an independent-samples *t*-test on the data (see Chapter 9). The sign of the correlation (i.e., whether the relationship was positive or negative) will depend entirely on which way round the coding of the dichotomous variable was made. To prove that this is the case, the data file **pbcorr.dat** has an extra variable called **recode** which is the same as the variable **gender** except that the coding is reversed (1 = female, 0 = male). If you repeat the Pearson correlation using **recode** instead of **gender** you will find that the correlation coefficient becomes −.378. The sign of the coefficient is completely dependent on which category you assign to which code and so we must ignore all information about the direction of the relationship. However, we can still interpret R^2 as before. So in this example, $R^2 = .378^2 = .143$. Hence, we can conclude that gender accounts for 14.3% of the variability in time spent away from home.

SELF-TEST

✓ Carry out a Pearson correlation on **time** and **recode**.

```
        Pearson's product-moment correlation

data:   catData$time and catData$gender
t = 3.1138, df = 58, p-value = 0.002868
alternative hypothesis: true correlation is not equal to 0
95 percent confidence interval:
 0.137769 0.576936
sample estimates:
       cor
0.3784542
```

Output 6.8

Imagine now that we wanted to convert the point-biserial correlation into the biserial correlation coefficient (r_b) (because some of the male cats were neutered and so there might be a continuum of maleness that underlies the gender variable). We must use equation (6.9) in which p is the proportion of cases that fell into the largest category and q is the proportion of cases that fell into the smallest category. Therefore, p and q are simply the number of male and female cats. In this equation y is the ordinate of the normal distribution at the point where there is $p\%$ of the area on one side and $q\%$ on the other (this will become clearer as we do an example):

$$r_b = \frac{r_{pb}\sqrt{pq}}{y}$$

(6.9)

To calculate p and q, we first need to use the **table()** function to compute the frequencies of males and female cats. We will store these frequencies in a new object called *catFrequencies*. We then use this object to compute the proportion of male and female cats using the **prop.table()** function. We execute these two commands as follows:

```
catFrequencies<-table(catData$gender)
prop.table(catFrequencies)
```

The resulting output tells us that the proportion of male cats (1) was .467 (this is q because it is the smallest portion) and the proportion of females (0) was .533 (this is p because it is the largest portion):

```
        0          1
0.5333333  0.4666667
```

To calculate y, we use these values and the values of the normal distribution displayed in the Appendix. Figure 6.7 shows how to find the ordinate (the value in the column labelled y)

when the normal curve is split with .467 as the smaller portion and .533 as the larger portion. The figure shows which columns represent p and q and we look for our values in these columns (the exact values of 0.533 and 0.467 are not in the table so instead we use the nearest values that we can find, which are .5319 and .4681, respectively). The ordinate value is in the column y and is .3977.

FIGURE 6.7
Getting the 'ordinate' of the normal distribution

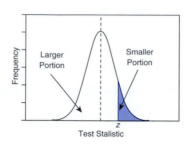

z	Larger Portion	Smaller Portion	y		z	Larger Portion	Smaller Portion	y
.00	.50000	.50000	.3989		.12	.54776	.45224	.3961
.01	.50399	.49601	.3989		.13	.55172	.44828	.3956
.02	.50		39		.14	.55567	.44433	.3951
.03	.51					.5962	.44038	.3945
		.48405	.3			.5356	.43644	.3939
		.48006	.3			.5749	.43251	.3932
		.47508	.3982		.18	.57142	.42858	.3925
.07	.52790	.47210	.3980		.19	.57535	.42465	.3918
.08	.53188	.46812	.3977		.20	.57926	.42074	.3910
.09	.53586	.46414	.3973		.21	.58317	.41683	.3902
.10	.53983	.46017	.3970		.22	.58706	.41294	.3894
.11	.54380	.45620	.3965		.23	.59095	.40905	.3885

If we replace these values in equation (6.9) we get .475 (see below), which is quite a lot higher than the value of the point-biserial correlation (0.378). This finding just shows you that whether you assume an underlying continuum or not can make a big difference to the size of effect that you get:

$$r_b = \frac{r_{pb}\sqrt{pq}}{y} = \frac{.378\sqrt{.533 \times .467}}{.3977} = .475$$

If this process freaks you out, then luckily you can get **R** to do it for you by installing the *polycor* package and using the *polyserial()* function. You can simply specify the two variables of interest within this function just as you have been doing for every other correlation in this chapter. Execute this command:

```
polyserial(catData$time, catData$gender)
```

and the resulting output:

```
[1]  0.4749256
```

confirms out earlier calculation.

You might wonder, given that you can get **R** to calculate the biserial correlation in one line of code, why I got you to calculate it by hand. It's entirely plausible that I'm just a nasty person who enjoys other people's pain. An alternative explanation is that the values of p and q are about to come in handy so it was helpful to show you how to calculate them. I'll leave you to decide which explanation is most likely.

To get the significance of the biserial correlation we need to first work out its standard error. If we assume the null hypothesis (that the biserial correlation in the population is zero) then the standard error is given by (Terrell, 1982):

$$SE_{r_b} = \frac{\sqrt{pq}}{y\sqrt{N}} \tag{6.10}$$

This equation is fairly straightforward because it uses the values of p, q and y that we already used to calculate the biserial r. The only additional value is the sample size (N), which in this example was 60. So our standard error is:

$$SE_{r_b} = \frac{\sqrt{.533 \times .467}}{.3977 \times \sqrt{60}} = .162$$

The standard error helps us because we can create a z-score (see section 1.7.4). To get a z-score we take the biserial correlation, subtract the mean in the population and divide by the standard error. We have assumed that the mean in the population is 0 (the null hypothesis), so we can simply divide the biserial correlation by its standard error:

$$z_{r_b} = \frac{r_b - \bar{r}_b}{SE_{r_b}} = \frac{r_b - 0}{SE_{r_b}} = \frac{r_b}{SE_{r_b}} = \frac{.475}{.162} = 2.93$$

We can look up this value of z (2.93) in the table for the normal distribution in the Appendix and get the one-tailed probability from the column labelled 'Smaller Portion'. In this case the value is .00169. To get the two-tailed probability we simply multiply the one-tailed probability value by 2, which gives us .00338. As such the correlation is significant, $p < .01$.

CRAMMING SAM'S TIPS Correlaion coefficients

- We can measure the relationship between two variables using *correlation coefficients*.
- These coefficients lie between −1 and +1.
- *Pearson's correlation coefficient*, r, is a parametric statistic and requires interval data for both variables. To test its significance we assume normality too.
- *Spearman's correlation coefficient*, r_s, is a non-parametric statistic and requires only ordinal data for both variables.
- *Kendall's correlation coefficient*, τ, is like Spearman's r_s but probably better for small samples.
- The *point-biserial correlation coefficient*, r_{pb}, quantifies the relationship between a continuous variable and a variable that is a discrete dichotomy (e.g., there is no continuum underlying the two categories, such as dead or alive).
- The *biserial correlation coefficient*, r_b, quantifies the relationship between a continuous variable and a variable that is a continuous dichotomy (e.g., there is a continuum underlying the two categories, such as passing or failing an exam).

6.6. Partial correlation ②

6.6.1. The theory behind part and partial correlation ②

I mentioned earlier that there is a type of correlation that can be done that allows you to look at the relationship between two variables when the effects of a third variable are held constant. For example, analyses of the exam anxiety data (in the file **Exam Anxiety. dat**) showed that exam performance was negatively related to exam anxiety, but positively related to revision time, and revision time itself was negatively related to exam anxiety. This scenario is complex, but given that we know that revision time is related to both exam anxiety and exam performance, then if we want a pure measure of the relationship between exam anxiety and exam performance we need to take account of the influence of revision time. Using the values of R^2 for these relationships (refer back to Output 6.4), we know that exam anxiety accounts for 19.4% of the variance in exam performance, that revision time accounts for 15.7% of the variance in exam performance, and that revision time accounts for 50.2% of the variance in exam anxiety. If revision time accounts for half of the variance in exam anxiety, then it seems feasible that at least some of the 19.4% of variance in exam performance that is accounted for by anxiety is the same variance that is accounted for by revision time. As such, some of the variance in exam performance explained by exam anxiety is not *unique* and can be accounted for by revision time. A correlation between two variables in which the effects of other variables are held constant is known as a **partial correlation.**

Let's return to our example of exam scores, revision time and exam anxiety to illustrate the principle behind partial correlation (Figure 6.8). In part 1 of the diagram there is a box for exam performance that represents the total variation in exam scores (this value would be the variance of exam performance). There is also a box that represents the variation in exam anxiety (again, this is the variance of that variable). We know already that exam anxiety and exam performance share 19.4% of their variation (this value is the correlation coefficient squared). Therefore, the variations of these two variables overlap (because they share variance) creating a third box (the blue cross hatched box). The overlap of the boxes representing exam performance and exam anxiety is the common variance. Likewise, in part 2 of the diagram the shared variation between exam performance and revision time is illustrated. Revision time shares 15.7% of the variation in exam scores. This shared variation is represented by the area of overlap (the dotted-blue lines box). We know that revision time and exam anxiety also share 50% of their variation; therefore, it is very probable that some of the variation in exam performance shared by exam anxiety is the same as the variance shared by revision time.

Part 3 of the diagram shows the complete picture. The first thing to note is that the boxes representing exam anxiety and revision time have a large overlap (this is because they share 50% of their variation). More important, when we look at how revision time and anxiety contribute to exam performance we see that there is a portion of exam performance that is shared by both anxiety and revision time (the white area). However, there are still small chunks of the variance in exam performance that are unique to the other two variables. So, although in part 1 exam anxiety shared a large chunk of variation in exam performance, some of this overlap is also shared by revision time. If we remove the portion of variation that is also shared by revision time, we get a measure of the unique relationship between exam performance and exam anxiety. We use partial correlations to find out the size of the unique portion of variance. Therefore, we could conduct a partial correlation between exam anxiety and exam performance while 'controlling' for the effect of revision time. Likewise, we could carry out a partial correlation between revision time and exam performance while 'controlling' for the effects of exam anxiety.

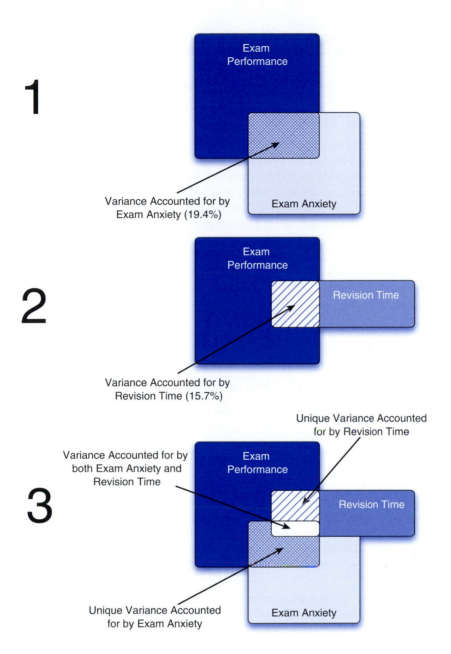

FIGURE 6.8
Diagram showing the principle of partial correlation

6.6.2. Partial correlation using R ②

We will use the *examData2* dataframe again, so if you haven't got this loaded then execute these commands:

```
examData = read.delim("Exam Anxiety.dat", header = TRUE)
examData2 <- examData[, c("Exam", "Anxiety", "Revise")]
```

This will import the **Exam Anxiety.dat** file and create a dataframe containing only the three variables of interest. We will conduct a partial correlation between exam anxiety and exam performance while 'controlling' for the effect of revision time. To compute a partial

correlation and its significance we will use the **pcor()** and **pcor.test()** functions respectively. These are part of the *ggm* package, so first load this:

```
library(ggm)
```

The general form of *pcor()* is:

```
pcor(c("var1", "var2", "control1", "control2" etc.), var(dataframe))
```

Basically, you enter a list of variables as strings (note the variable names have to be in quotes) using the *c()* function. The first two variables should be those for which you want the partial correlation; any others listed should be variables for which you'd like to 'control'. You can 'control' for the effects of a single variable, in which case the resulting coefficient is known as a *first-order partial correlation*; it is also possible to control for the effects of two (a *second-order partial correlation*), three (a *third-order partial correlation*), or more variables at the same time. The second part of the function simply asks for the name of the dataframe (in this case *examData2*). For the current example, we want the correlation between exam anxiety and exam performance (so we list these variables first) controlling for exam revision (so we list this variable afterwards). As such, we can execute the following command:

```
pcor(c("Exam", "Anxiety", "Revise"), var(examData2))
```

Executing this command will print the partial correlation to the console. However, I find it useful to create an object containing the partial correlation value so that we can use it in other commands. As such, I suggest that you execute this command to create an object called *pc*:

```
pc<-pcor(c("Exam", "Anxiety", "Revise"), var(examData2))
```

We can then see the partial correlation and the value of R^2 in the console by executing:

```
pc
pc^2
```

The general form of *pcor.test()* is:

```
pcor(pcor object, number of control variables, sample size)
```

Basically, you enter an object that you have created with *pcor()* (or you can put the *pcor()* command directly into the function). We created a partial correlation object called *pc*, had only one control variable (**Revise**) and there was a sample size of 103; therefore we can execute:

```
pcor.test(pc, 1, 103)
```

to see the significance of the partial correlation.

```
> pc

[1] -0.2466658

> pc^2

[1] 0.06084403

> pcor.test(pc, 1, 103)
$tval

[1] -2.545307


$df

[1] 100


$pvalue

[1] 0.01244581
```

Output 6.9

Output 6.9 shows the output for the partial correlation of exam anxiety and exam performance controlling for revision time; it also shows the squared value that we calculated ($pc\char94 2$), and the significance value obtained from *pcor.test()*. The output of *pcor()* is the partial correlation for the variables **Anxiety** and **Exam** but controlling for the effect of **Revision**. First, notice that the partial correlation between exam performance and exam anxiety is −.247, which is considerably less than the correlation when the effect of revision time is not controlled for ($r = -.441$). In fact, the correlation coefficient is nearly half what it was before. Although this correlation is still statistically significant (its *p*-value is .012, which is still below .05), the relationship is diminished. In terms of variance, the value of R^2 for the partial correlation is .06, which means that exam anxiety can now account for only 6% of the variance in exam performance. When the effects of revision time were not controlled for, exam anxiety shared 19.4% of the variation in exam scores and so the inclusion of revision time has severely diminished the amount of variation in exam scores shared by anxiety. As such, a truer measure of the role of exam anxiety has been obtained. Running this analysis has shown us that exam anxiety alone does explain some of the variation in exam scores, but there is a complex relationship between anxiety, revision and exam performance that might otherwise have been ignored. Although causality is still not certain, because relevant variables are being included, the third variable problem is, at least, being addressed in some form.

These partial correlations can be done when variables are dichotomous (including the 'third' variable). So, for example, we could look at the relationship between bladder relaxation (did the person wet themselves or not?) and the number of large tarantulas crawling up your leg, controlling for fear of spiders (the first variable is dichotomous, but the second variable and 'controlled for' variables are continuous). Also, to use an earlier example, we could examine the relationship between creativity and success in the World's Biggest Liar competition, controlling for whether someone had previous experience in the competition (and therefore had some idea of the type of tale that would win) or not. In this latter case the 'controlled for' variable is dichotomous.[6]

6.6.3. Semi-partial (or part) correlations ②

In the next chapter, we will come across another form of correlation known as a **semi-partial correlation** (also referred to as a **part correlation**). While I'm babbling on about partial correlations it is worth my explaining the difference between this type of correlation and semi-partial correlation. When we do a partial correlation between two variables, we control for the effects of a third variable. Specifically, the effect that the third variable has on *both* variables in the correlation is controlled. In a semi-partial correlation we control for the effect that the third variable has on only one of the variables in the correlation. Figure 6.9 illustrates this principle for the exam performance data. The partial correlation that we

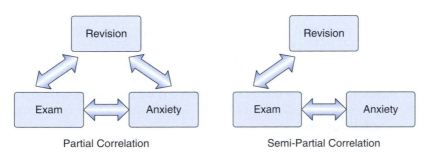

Partial Correlation   Semi-Partial Correlation

FIGURE 6.9
The difference between a partial and a semi-partial correlation

---

[6] Both these examples are, in fact, simple cases of hierarchical regression (see the next chapter) and the first example is also an example of analysis of covariance. This may be confusing now, but as we progress through the book I hope it'll become clearer that virtually all of the statistics that you use are actually the same things dressed up in different names.

calculated took account not only of the effect of revision on exam performance, but also of the effect of revision on anxiety. If we were to calculate the semi-partial correlation for the same data, then this would control for only the effect of revision on exam performance (the effect of revision on exam anxiety is ignored). Partial correlations are most useful for looking at the unique relationship between two variables when other variables are ruled out. Semi-partial correlations are, therefore, useful when trying to explain the variance in one particular variable (an outcome) from a set of predictor variables. (Bear this in mind when you read Chapter 7.)

CRAMMING SAM'S TIPS   **Partial and semi-partial correlation**

- A *partial correlation* quantifies the relationship between two variables while controlling for the effects of a third variable on *both* variables in the original correlation.
- A *semi-partial correlation* quantifies the relationship between two variables while controlling for the effects of a third variable on only *one* of the variables in the original correlation.

6.7. Comparing correlations ③

6.7.1. Comparing independent *r*s ③

Sometimes we want to know whether one correlation coefficient is bigger than another. For example, when we looked at the effect of exam anxiety on exam performance, we might have been interested to know whether this correlation was different in men and women. We could compute the correlation in these two samples, but then how would we assess whether the difference was meaningful?

SELF-TEST

✓ Use the *subset()* function to compute the correlation coefficient between exam anxiety and exam performance in men and women.

If we did this, we would find that the correlations were $r_{\text{Male}} = -.506$ and $r_{\text{Female}} = -.381$. These two samples are independent; that is, they contain different entities. To compare these correlations we can again use what we discovered in section 6.3.3 to convert these coefficients to z_r (just to remind you, we do this because it makes the sampling distribution normal and, therefore, we know the standard error). If we do the conversion, then we get z_r (males) $= -.557$ and z_r (females) $= -.401$. We can calculate a z-score of the differences between these correlations as:

$$z_{\text{Difference}} = \frac{z_{r_1} - z_{r_2}}{\sqrt{\dfrac{1}{N_1 - 3} + \dfrac{1}{\sqrt{N_2 - 3}}}}$$

(6.11)

We had 52 men and 51 women so we would get:

$$z_{\text{Difference}} = \frac{-.557 - (-.401)}{\sqrt{\frac{1}{49} + \frac{1}{48}}} = \frac{-.156}{0.203} = -0.768$$

We can look up this value of z (0.768; we can ignore the minus sign) in the table for the normal distribution in the Appendix and get the one-tailed probability from the column labelled 'Smaller Portion'. In this case the value is .221. To get the two-tailed probability we simply multiply the one-tailed probability value by 2, which gives us .442. As such the correlation between exam anxiety and exam performance is not significantly different in men and women (see Oliver Twisted for how to do this using **R**).

OLIVER TWISTED

Please Sir, can I have some more … functions?

'These equations are rubbish,' says Oliver, 'they're too confusing and I hate them. Can't we get **R** to do it for us while we check Facebook?' Well, no, you can't. Except you sort of can by writing your own function. 'Write my own function!!' screams Oliver whilst trying to ram his computer keyboard into his mouth. 'You've got to be joking, you steaming dog colon, I can barely write my own name.' Luckily for you Oliver, I've done it for you. To find out more, read the additional material for this chapter on the companion website. Or check Facebook, the choice is yours.

6.7.2. Comparing dependent *r*s ③

If you want to compare correlation coefficients that come from the same entities then things are a little more complicated. You can use a *t*-statistic to test whether a difference between two dependent correlations from the same sample is significant. For example, in our exam anxiety data we might want to see whether the relationship between exam anxiety (*x*) and exam performance (*y*) is stronger than the relationship between revision (*z*) and exam performance. To calculate this, all we need are the three *r*s that quantify the relationships between these variables: r_{xy}, the relationship between exam anxiety and exam performance (−.441); r_{zy}, the relationship between revision and exam performance (.397); and r_{xz}, the relationship between exam anxiety and revision (−.709). The *t*-statistic is computed as (Chen & Popovich, 2002):

$$t_{\text{Difference}} = (r_{xy} - r_{zy}) \sqrt{\frac{(n-3)(1+r_{xz})}{2(1 - r_{xy}^2 - r_{xz}^2 - r_{zy}^2 + 2r_{xy}r_{xz}r_{zy})}} \tag{6.12}$$

Admittedly that equation looks hideous, but really it's not too bad: it just uses the three correlation coefficients and the sample size *N*.

Put in the numbers from the exam anxiety example (*N* was 103) and you should end up with:

$$t_{\text{Difference}} = (-.838) \sqrt{\frac{29.1}{2(1 - .194 - .503 - .158 + 0.248)}} = -5.09$$

This value can be checked against the appropriate critical value in the Appendix with $N-3$ degrees of freedom (in this case 100). The critical values in the table are 1.98 ($p < .05$) and 2.63 ($p < .01$), two-tailed. As such we can say that the correlation between exam anxiety and exam performance was significantly higher than the correlation between revision time and exam performance (this isn't a massive surprise, given that these relationships went in the opposite directions to each other).

OLIVER TWISTED

Please Sir, can I have some more … comparing of correlations?

'Are you having a bloody laugh with that equation?' yelps Oliver. 'I'd rather smother myself with cheese sauce and lock myself in a room of hungry mice.' Yes, yes, Oliver, enough of your sexual habits. To spare the poor mice I have written another **R** function to run the comparison mentioned in this section. For a guide on how to use them read the additional material for this chapter on the companion website. Go on, be kind to the mice!

6.8. Calculating the effect size ①

Calculating effect sizes for correlation coefficients couldn't be easier because, as we saw earlier in the book, correlation coefficients *are* effect sizes! So, no calculations (other than those you have already done) necessary! However, I do want to point out one caveat when using non-parametric correlation coefficients as effect sizes. Although the Spearman and Kendall correlations are comparable in many respects (their power, for example, is similar under parametric conditions), there are two important differences (Strahan, 1982).

First, we saw for Pearson's r that we can square this value to get the proportion of shared variance, R^2. For Spearman's r_s we can do this too because it uses the same equation as Pearson's r. However, the resulting R_s^2 needs to be interpreted slightly differently: it is the proportion of variance in the *ranks* that two variables share.

Can I use r^2 for non-parametric correlations?

Having said this, R_s^2 is usually a good approximation for R^2 (especially in conditions of near-normal distributions). Kendall's τ, however, is not numerically similar to either r or r_s and so τ^2 does not tell us about the proportion of variance shared by two variables (or the ranks of those two variables).

Second, Kendall's τ is 66–75% smaller than both Spearman's r_s and Pearson's r, but r and r_s are generally similar sizes (Strahan, 1982). As such, if τ is used as an effect size it should be borne in mind that it is not comparable to r and r_s and should not be squared. A related issue is that the point-biserial and biserial correlations differ in size too (as we saw in this chapter, the biserial correlation was bigger than the point-biserial). In this instance you should be careful to decide whether your dichotomous variable has an underlying continuum, or whether it is a truly discrete variable. More generally, when using correlations as effect sizes you should remember (both when reporting your own analysis and when interpreting others) that the choice of correlation coefficient can make a substantial difference to the apparent size of the effect.

6.9. How to report correlation coefficents ①

Reporting correlation coefficients is pretty easy: you just have to say how big they are and what their significance value was (although the significance value isn't *that* important because the correlation coefficient is an effect size in its own right!). Five things to note are that: (1) if you follow the conventions of the American Psychological Association, there should be no zero before the decimal point for the correlation coefficient or the probability value (because neither can exceed 1); (2) coefficients are reported to 2 decimal places; (3) if you are quoting a one-tailed probability, you should say so; (4) each correlation coefficient is represented by a different letter (and some of them are Greek); and (5) there are standard criteria of probabilities that we use (.05, .01 and .001). Let's take a few examples from this chapter:

- ✓ There was a significant relationship between the number of adverts watched and the number of packets of sweets purchased, $r = .87$, p (one-tailed) $< .05$.

- ✓ Exam performance was significantly correlated with exam anxiety, $r = -.44$, and time spent revising, $r = .40$; the time spent revising was also correlated with exam anxiety, $r = -.71$ (all $ps < .001$).

- ✓ Creativity was significantly related to how well people did in the World's Biggest Liar competition, $r_s = -.37$, $p < .001$.

- ✓ Creativity was significantly related to how well people did in the World's Biggest Liar competition, $\tau = -.30$, $p < .001$. (Note that I've quoted Kendall's τ here.)

- ✓ The gender of the cat was significantly related to the time the cat spent away from home, $r_{pb} = .38$, $p < .01$.

- ✓ The gender of the cat was significantly related to the time the cat spent away from home, $r_b = .48$, $p < .01$.

Scientists, rightly or wrongly, tend to use several *standard* levels of statistical significance. Primarily, the most important criterion is that the significance value is less than .05; however, if the exact significance value is much lower then we can be much more confident about the strength of the effect. In these circumstances we like to make a big song and dance about the fact that our result isn't just significant at .05, but is significant at a much lower level as well (hooray!). The values we use are .05, .01, .001 and .0001. You are rarely going to be in the fortunate position of being able to report an effect that is significant at a level less than .0001!

When we have lots of correlations we sometimes put them into a table. For example, our exam anxiety correlations could be reported as in Table 6.3. Note that above the diagonal I have reported the correlation coefficients and used symbols to represent different levels of significance. Under the table there is a legend to tell readers what symbols represent. (Actually, none of the correlations were non-significant or had p bigger than .001, so most of these are here simply to give you a reference point – you would normally include symbols that you had actually used in the table in your legend.) Finally, in the lower part of the table I have reported the sample sizes. These are all the same (103), but sometimes when you have missing data it is useful to report the sample sizes in this way because different values of the correlation will be based on different sample sizes. For some more ideas on how to report correlations have a look at Labcoat Leni's Real Research 6.1.

Table 6.3 An example of reporting a table of correlations

	Exam Performance	Exam Anxiety	Revision Time
Exam Performance	1	−.44***	.40***
Exam Anxiety	103	1	−.71***
Revision Time	103	103	1

ns = not significant ($p > .05$), * $p < .05$, ** $p < .01$, *** $p < .001$

Labcoat Leni's Real Research 6.1   Why do you like your lecturers? ①

Chamorro-Premuzic, T., et al. (2008). *Personality and Individual Differences*, *44*, 965–976.

As students you probably have to rate your lecturers at the end of the course. There will be some lecturers you like and others that you hate. As a lecturer I find this process horribly depressing (although this has a lot to do with the fact that I tend focus on negative feedback and ignore the good stuff). There is some evidence that students tend to pick courses of lecturers whom they perceive to be enthusastic and good communicators. In a fascinating study, Tomas Chamorro-Premuzic and his colleagues (Chamorro-Premuzic, Furnham, Christopher, Garwood, & Martin, 2008) tested a slightly different hypothesis, which was that students tend to like lecturers who are like themselves. (This hypothesis will have the students on my course who like my lectures screaming in horror.)

First of all, the authors measured students' own personalities using a very well-established measure (the NEO-FFI) which gives rise to scores on five fundamental personality traits: Neuroticism, Extroversion, Openness to experience, Agreeableness and Conscientiousness. They also gave students a questionnaire that asked them to rate how much they wanted their lecturer to have each of a list of characteristics. For example, they would be given the description 'warm: friendly, warm, sociable, cheerful, affectionate, outgoing' and asked to rate how much they wanted to see this in a lecturer from −5 (they don't want this characteristic at all) through 0 (the characteristic is not important) to +5 (I really want this characteristic in my lecturer). The characteristics on the questionnaire all related to personality characteristics measured by the NEO-FFI. As such, the authors had a measure of how much a student had each of the five core personality characteristics, but also a measure of how much they wanted to see those same characteristics in their lecturer.

In doing so, Tomas and his colleagues could test whether, for instance, extroverted students want extrovert lecturers. The data from this study (well, for the variables that I've mentioned) are in the file **Chamorro-Premuzic. dat**. Run some Pearson correlations on these variables to see if students with certain personality characteristics want to see those characteristics in their lecturers. What conclusions can you draw?

Answers are in the additional material on the companion website (or look at Table 3 in the original article, which will also show you how to report a large number of correlations).

What have I discovered about statistics? ①

This chapter has looked at ways to study relationships between variables. We began by looking at how we might measure relationships statistically by developing what we already know about variance (from Chapter 1) to look at variance shared between variables. This shared variance is known as *covariance*. We then discovered that when data are parametric we can measure the strength of a relationship using Pearson's correlation coefficient, *r*. When data violate the assumptions of parametric tests we can use Spearman's r_s, or for small data sets Kendall's τ may be more accurate. We also saw that correlations can be calculated between two variables when one of those variables is a dichotomy (i.e., composed of two categories); when the categories have no underlying continuum then we use the point-biserial correlation, r_{pb}, but when the categories do have an underlying continuum we use the biserial correlation, r_b. Finally, we looked at the difference between *partial correlations*, in which the relationship between two variables is measured controlling for the effect that one or more variables has on both of those variables, and *semi-partial correlations*, in which the relationship between two variables is measured controlling for the effect that one or more variables has on only one of those variables. We also discovered that I had a guitar and, like my favourite record of the time, I was ready to 'Take on the World'. Well, Wales at any rate …

R packages used in this chapter

boot	Polycor
ggm	Rcmdr
ggplot2	
Hmisc	

R functions used in this chapter

boot()	polyserial()
boot.ci()	prop.table()
cor()	rcorr()
cor.test()	read.csv()
pcor()	read.delim()
pcor.test()	table()

Key terms that I've discovered

Biserial correlation	Kendall's tau
Bivariate correlation	Partial correlation
Coefficient of determination	Pearson correlation coefficient
Correlation coefficient	Point-biserial correlation
Covariance	Semi-partial correlation
Cross-product deviations	Spearman's correlation coefficient
Dichotomous	Standardization

Smart Alex's tasks ①

- **Task 1:** A student was interested in whether there was a positive relationship between the time spent doing an essay and the mark received. He got 45 of his friends and timed how long they spent writing an essay (**hours**) and the percentage they got in the essay (**essay**). He also translated these grades into their degree classifications (**grade**): in the UK, a student can get a first-class mark (the best), an upper-second-class mark, a lower second, a third, a pass or a fail (the worst). Using the data in the file **EssayMarks.dat** find out what the relationship was between the time spent doing an essay and the eventual mark in terms of percentage and degree class (draw a scatterplot too!). ①

- **Task 2:** Using the **ChickFlick.dat** data from Chapter 3, is there a relationship between gender and arousal? Using the same data, is there a relationship between the film watched and arousal? ①

- **Task 3:** As a statistics lecturer I am always interested in the factors that determine whether a student will do well on a statistics course. One potentially important factor is their previous expertise with mathematics. Imagine I took 25 students and looked at their degree grades for my statistics course at the end of their first year at university: first, upper second, lower second or third class. I also asked these students what grade they got in their GCSE maths exams. In the UK, GCSEs are school exams taken at age 16 that are graded A, B, C, D, E or F (an A grade is better than all of the lower grades). The data for this study are in the file **grades.csv**. Carry out the appropriate analysis to see if GCSE maths grades correlate with first-year statistics grades. ①

Answers can be found on the companion website.

Further reading

Chen, P. Y., & Popovich, P. M. (2002). *Correlation: Parametric and nonparametric measures.* Thousand Oaks, CA: Sage.

Howell, D. C. (2006). *Statistical methods for psychology* (6th ed.). Belmont, CA: Duxbury. (Or you might prefer his *Fundamental Statistics for the Behavioral Sciences,* also in its 6th edition, 2007. Both are excellent texts that are a bit more technical than this book, so they are a useful next step.)

Miles, J. N. V., & Banyard, P. (2007). *Understanding and using statistics in psychology: A practical introduction.* London: Sage. (A fantastic and amusing introduction to statistical theory.)

Wright, D. B., & London, K. (2009). *First steps in statistics* (2nd ed.). London: Sage. (This book is a very gentle introduction to statistical theory.)

Interesting real research

Chamorro-Premuzic, T., Furnham, A., Christopher, A. N., Garwood, J., & Martin, N. (2008). Birds of a feather: Students' preferences for lecturers' personalities as predicted by their own personality and learning approaches. *Personality and Individual Differences, 44,* 965–976.

Regression

7

7.1. What will this chapter tell me? ①

Although none of us can know the future, predicting it is so important that organisms are hard-wired to learn about predictable events in their environment. We saw in the previous chapter that I received a guitar for Christmas when I was 8. My first foray into public performance was a weekly talent show at a holiday camp called 'Holimarine' in Wales (it doesn't exist any more because I am old and this was 1981). I sang a Chuck Berry song called 'My Ding-a-ling'[1] and to my absolute amazement I won the

---

[1] It appears that even then I had a passion for lowering the tone of things that should be taken seriously.

competition.[2] Suddenly other 8-year-olds across the land (well, a ballroom in Wales) worshipped me (I made lots of friends after the competition). I had tasted success, it tasted like praline chocolate, and so I wanted to enter the competition in the second week of our holiday. To ensure success, I needed to know why I had won in the first week. One way to do this would have been to collect data and to use these data to predict people's evaluations of children's performances in the contest from certain variables: the age of the performer, what type of performance they gave (singing, telling a joke, magic tricks), and maybe how cute they looked. A regression analysis on these data would enable us to predict future evaluations (success in next week's competition) based on values of the predictor variables. If, for example, singing was an important factor in getting a good audience evaluation, then I could sing again the following week; however, if jokers tended to do better then I could switch to a comedy routine. When I was 8 I wasn't the sad geek that I am today, so I didn't know about regression analysis (nor did I wish to know); however, my dad thought that success was due to the winning combination of a cherub-looking 8-year-old singing songs that can be interpreted in a filthy way. He wrote me a song to sing in the competition about the keyboard player in the Holimarine Band 'messing about with his organ', and first place was mine again. There's no accounting for taste.

7.2. An introduction to regression ①

How do I fit a straight line to my data?

In the previous chapter we looked at how to measure relationships between two variables. These correlations can be very useful, but we can take this process a step further and predict one variable from another. A simple example might be to try to predict levels of stress from the amount of time until you have to give a talk. You'd expect this to be a negative relationship (the smaller the amount of time until the talk, the larger the anxiety). We could then extend this basic relationship to answer a question such as 'if there's 10 minutes to go until someone has to give a talk, how anxious will they be?' This is the essence of regression analysis: we fit a model to our data and use it to predict values of the dependent variable (DV) from one or more independent variables (IVs).

Regression analysis is a way of predicting an outcome variable from one predictor variable (**simple regression**) or several predictor variables (**multiple regression**). This tool is incredibly useful because it allows us to go a step beyond the data that we collected.

In section 2.4.3 I introduced you to the idea that we can predict any data using the following general equation:

$$\text{outcome}_i = (\text{model}) + \text{error}_i \tag{7.1}$$

This just means that the outcome we're trying to predict for a particular person can be predicted by whatever model we fit to the data plus some kind of error. In regression, the model we fit is linear, which means that we summarize a data set with a straight line (think back to Jane Superbrain Box 2.1). As such, the word 'model' in the equation above simply gets replaced by 'things' that define the line that we fit to the data (see the next section).

With any data set there are several lines that could be used to summarize the general trend, and so we need a way to decide which of many possible lines to choose. For the sake

---

[2] I have a very grainy video of this performance recorded by my dad's friend on a video camera the size of a medium-sized dog that had to be accompanied at all times by a battery pack the size and weight of a tank. Maybe I'll put it up on the companion website …

of making accurate predictions we want to fit a model that *best* describes the data. The simplest way to do this would be to use your eye to gauge a line that looks as though it summarizes the data well. You don't need to be a genius to realize that the 'eyeball' method is very subjective and so offers no assurance that the model is the best one that could have been chosen. Instead, we use a mathematical technique called the *method of least squares* to establish the line that best describes the data collected.

7.2.1.   Some important information about straight lines ①

I mentioned above that in our general equation the word 'model' gets replaced by 'things that define the line that we fit to the data'. In fact, any straight line can be defined by two things: (1) the slope (or gradient) of the line (usually denoted by b_1); and (2) the point at which the line crosses the vertical axis of the graph (known as the *intercept* of the line, b_0). In fact, our general model becomes equation (7.2) below in which Y_i is the outcome that we want to predict and X_i is the *i*th participant's score on the predictor variable.[3] Here b_1 is the gradient of the straight line fitted to the data and b_0 is the intercept of that line. These parameters b_1 and b_0 are known as the **regression coefficients** and will crop up time and time again in this book, where you may see them referred to generally as b (without any subscript) or b_i (meaning the b associated with variable i). There is a residual term, ε_i, which represents the difference between the score predicted by the line for participant i and the score that participant i actually obtained. The equation is often conceptualized without this residual term (so ignore it if it's upsetting you); however, it is worth knowing that this term represents the fact that our model will not fit the data collected perfectly:

$$Y_i = (b_0 + b_1 X_i) + \varepsilon_i \tag{7.2}$$

A particular line has a specific intercept and gradient. Figure 7.2 shows a set of lines that have the same intercept but different gradients, and a set of lines that have the same gradient but different intercepts. Figure 7.2 also illustrates another useful point: the gradient of the line tells us something about the nature of the relationship being described. In Chapter 6 we saw how relationships can be either positive or negative (and I don't mean the difference between getting on well with your girlfriend and arguing all the time!). A line that has a gradient with a positive value describes a positive relationship, whereas a line with a negative gradient describes a negative relationship. So, if you look at the graph in Figure 7.2 in which the gradients differ but the intercepts are the same, then the red line describes a positive relationship whereas the green line describes a negative relationship. Basically then, the gradient (b_1) tells us what the model looks like (its shape) and the intercept (b_0) tells us where the model is (its location in geometric space).

If it is possible to describe a line knowing only the gradient and the intercept of that line, then we can use these values to describe our model (because in linear regression the model we use is a straight line). So, the model that we fit to our data in linear regression can be conceptualized as a straight line that can be described mathematically by equation (7.2). With regression we strive to find the line that best describes the data collected, then estimate the gradient and intercept of that line. Having defined these values, we can insert

---

[3] You'll sometimes see this equation written as:

$Y_i = (\beta_0 + \beta_1 X_i) + \varepsilon_i$

The only difference is that this equation has got βs in it instead of bs and in fact both versions are the same thing, they just use different letters to represent the coefficients.

FIGURE 7.2
Lines with the same gradients but different intercepts, and lines that share the same intercept but have different gradients

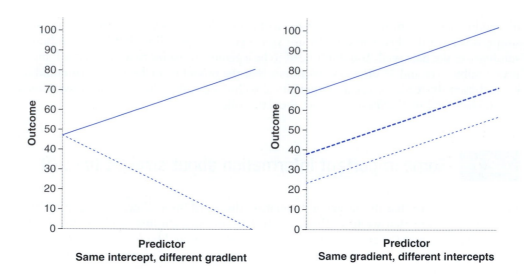

Same intercept, different gradient   Same gradient, different intercepts

different values of our predictor variable into the model to estimate the value of the outcome variable.

7.2.2.   The method of least squares ①

I have already mentioned that the method of least squares is a way of finding the line that best fits the data (i.e., finding a line that goes through, or as close to, as many of the data points as possible). This 'line of best fit' is found by ascertaining which line, of all of the possible lines that could be drawn, results in the least amount of difference between the observed data points and the line. Figure 7.3 shows that when any line is fitted to a set of data, there will be small differences between the values predicted by the line and the data that were actually observed.

Back in Chapter 2 we saw that we could assess the fit of a model (the example we used was the mean) by looking at the deviations between the model and the actual data collected. These deviations were the vertical distances between what the model predicted and each data point that was actually observed. We can do exactly the same to assess the fit of a regression line (which, like the mean, is a statistical model). So, again we are interested in the vertical differences between the line and the actual data because the line is our model: we use it to predict values of *Y* from values of the *X* variable. In regression these differences are usually called **residuals** rather than deviations, but they are the same thing. As with the mean, data points fall both above (the model underestimates their value) and below (the model overestimates their value) the line, yielding both positive and negative differences. In the discussion of variance in section 2.4.2 I explained that if we sum positive and negative differences then they tend to cancel each other out and that to circumvent this problem we square the differences before adding them up. We do the same thing here. The resulting squared differences provide a gauge of how well a particular line fits the data: if the squared differences are large, the line is not representative of the data; if the squared differences are small, the line is representative.

You could, if you were particularly bored, calculate the sum of squared differences (or SS for short) for every possible line that is fitted to your data and then compare these 'goodness-of-fit' measures. The one with the lowest SS is the line of best fit. Fortunately we don't have to do this because the method of least squares does it for us: it selects the

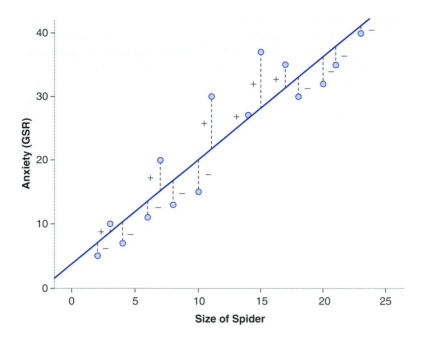

FIGURE 7.3
This graph shows a scatterplot of some data with a line representing the general trend. The vertical lines (dotted) represent the differences (or residuals) between the line and the actual data

line that has the lowest sum of squared differences (i.e., the line that best represents the observed data). How exactly it does this is by using a mathematical technique for finding maxima and minima and this technique is used to find the line that minimizes the sum of squared differences. I don't really know much more about it than that to be honest, so I tend to think of the process as a little bearded wizard called Nephwick the Line Finder who just magically finds lines of best fit. Yes, he lives inside your computer. The end result is that Nephwick estimates the value of the slope and intercept of the 'line of best fit' for you. We tend to call this line of best fit a regression line (or more generally a **regression model**).

7.2.3. Assessing the goodness of fit: sums of squares, R and R^2 ①

Once Nephwick the Line Finder has found the line of best fit it is important that we assess how well this line fits the actual data (we assess the goodness of fit of the model). We do this because even though this line is the best one available, it can still be a lousy fit to the data. In section 2.4.2 we saw that one measure of the adequacy of a model is the sum of squared differences (or more generally we assess models using equation (7.3) below). If we want to assess the line of best fit, we need to compare it against something, and the thing we choose is the most basic model we can find. So we use equation (7.3) to calculate the fit of the most basic model, and then the fit of the best model (the line of best fit), and basically if the best model is any good then it should fit the data significantly better than our basic model:

$$\text{deviation} = \sum(\text{observed} - \text{model})^2 \tag{7.3}$$

This is all quite abstract so let's look at an example. Imagine that I was interested in predicting physical and downloaded album sales (Y) from the amount of money spent advertising that album (X). One day my boss came in to my office and said 'Andy, I know you wanted to be a rock star and you've ended up working as my stats-monkey, but how

How do I tell if my model is good?

many albums will we sell if we spend £100,000 on advertising?' If I didn't have an accurate model of the relationship between album sales and advertising, what would my best guess be? Well, probably the best answer I could give would be the mean number of album sales (say, 200,000) because on average that's how many albums we expect to sell. This response might well satisfy a brainless record company executive (who didn't offer my band a recording contract). However, what if he had asked 'How many albums will we sell if we spend £1 on advertising?' Again, in the absence of any accurate information, my best guess would be to give the average number of sales (200,000). There is a problem: whatever amount of money is spent on advertising I always predict the same levels of sales. As such, the mean is a model of 'no relationship' at all between the variables. It should be pretty clear then that the mean is fairly useless as a model of a relationship between two variables – but it is the simplest model available.

So, as a basic strategy for predicting the outcome, we might choose to use the mean, because on average it will be a fairly good guess of an outcome. Using the mean as a model, we can calculate the difference between the observed values, and the values predicted by the mean (equation (7.3)). We saw in section 2.4.1 that we square all of these differences to give us the sum of squared differences. This sum of squared differences is known as the **total sum of squares** (denoted SS_T) because it is the total amount of differences present when the most basic model is applied to the data. This value represents how good the mean is as a model of the observed data. Now, if we fit the more sophisticated model to the data, such as a line of best fit, we can again work out the differences between this new model and the observed data (again using equation (7.3)). In the previous section we saw that the method of least squares finds the best possible line to describe a set of data by minimizing the difference between the model fitted to the data and the data themselves. However, even with this optimal model there is still some inaccuracy, which is represented by the differences between each observed data point and the value predicted by the regression line. As before, these differences are squared before they are added up so that the directions of the differences do not cancel out. The result is known as the *sum of squared residuals* or **residual sum of squares** (SS_R). This value represents the degree of inaccuracy when the best model is fitted to the data. We can use these two values to calculate how much better the regression line (the line of best fit) is than just using the mean as a model (i.e., how much better is the best possible model than the worst model?). The improvement in prediction resulting from using the regression model rather than the mean is obtained by calculating the difference between SS_T and SS_R. This difference shows us the reduction in the inaccuracy of the model resulting from fitting the regression model to the data. This improvement is the **model sum of squares** (SS_M). Figure 7.4 shows each sum of squares graphically.

If the value of SS_M is large then the regression model is very different from using the mean to predict the outcome variable. This implies that the regression model has made a big improvement to how well the outcome variable can be predicted. However, if SS_M is small then using the regression model is little better than using the mean (i.e., the regression model is no better than taking our 'best guess'). A useful measure arising from these sums of squares is the proportion of improvement due to the model. This is easily calculated by dividing the sum of squares for the model by the total sum of squares. The resulting value is called R^2 and to express this value as a percentage you should multiply it by 100. R^2 represents the amount of variance in the outcome explained by the model (SS_M) relative to how much variation there was to explain in the first place (SS_T). Therefore, as a percentage, it represents the percentage of the variation in the outcome that can be explained by the model:

$$R^2 = \frac{SS_M}{SS_T} \tag{7.4}$$

This R^2 is the same as the one we met in Chapter 6 (section 6.5.4.3) and you might have noticed that it is interpreted in the same way. Therefore, in simple regression we can take

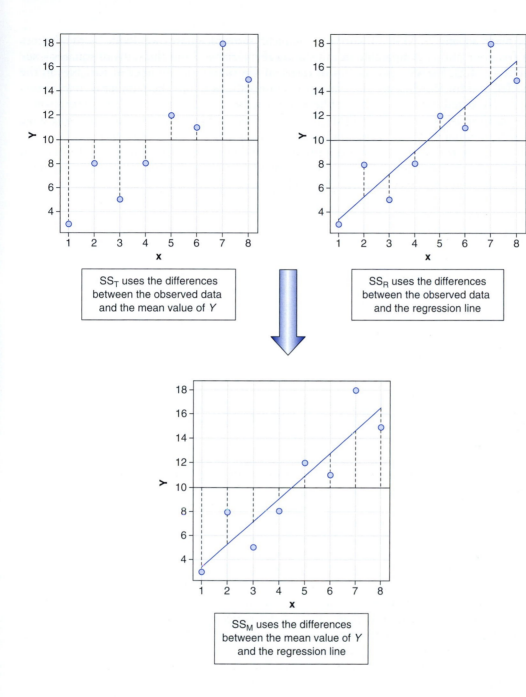

FIGURE 7.4
Diagram showing
from where the
regression sums
of squares derive

SS$_T$ uses the differences between the observed data and the mean value of Y

SS$_R$ uses the differences between the observed data and the regression line

SS$_M$ uses the differences between the mean value of Y and the regression line

the square root of this value to obtain Pearson's correlation coefficient. As such, the correlation coefficient provides us with a good estimate of the overall fit of the regression model, and R^2 provides us with a good gauge of the substantive size of the relationship.

A second use of the sums of squares in assessing the model is through the F-test. I mentioned way back in Chapter 2 that test statistics (like F) are usually the amount of systematic variance divided by the amount of unsystematic variance, or, put another way, the model compared against the error in the model. This is true here: F is based upon the ratio of the improvement due to the model (SS$_M$) and the difference between the model and the observed data (SS$_R$). Actually, because the sums of squares depend on the number of differences that we have added up, we use the average sums of squares (referred to as the **mean squares** or MS). To work out the mean sums of squares we divide by the degrees of freedom (this is comparable to calculating the variance from the sums of squares – see section 2.4.2). For SS_M the degrees of freedom are simply the number of variables in the model, and for SS_R they are the number of observations minus the number of parameters being estimated (i.e., the number of beta coefficients including the constant). The result is the mean squares for the model (MS_M) and the residual mean squares (MS_R). At this stage it isn't essential that you understand how the mean squares are derived (it is explained in Chapter 10). However, it is important that you understand that the **F-ratio** (equation (7.5)) is a measure of how much the model has improved the prediction of the outcome compared to the level of inaccuracy of the model.

$$F = \frac{MS_M}{MS_R} \qquad \qquad \qquad (7.5)$$

If a model is good, then we expect the improvement in prediction due to the model to be large (so MS_M will be large) and the difference between the model and the observed data to be small (so MS_R will be small). In short, a good model should have a large F-ratio (greater than 1 at least) because the top of equation (7.5) will be bigger than the bottom. The exact magnitude of this F-ratio can be assessed using critical values for the corresponding degrees of freedom (as in the Appendix).

7.2.4.   Assessing individual predictors ①

We've seen that the predictor in a regression model has a coefficient (b_1), which in simple regression represents the gradient of the regression line. The value of b represents the change in the outcome resulting from a unit change in the predictor. If the model was useless at predicting the outcome, then if the value of the predictor changes, what might we expect the change in the outcome to be? Well, if the model is very bad then we would expect the change in the outcome to be zero. Think back to Figure 7.4 (see the panel representing SS_T) in which we saw that using the mean was a very bad way of predicting the outcome. In fact, the line representing the mean is flat, which means that as the predictor variable changes, the value of the outcome does *not* change (because for each level of the predictor variable, we predict that the outcome will equal the mean value). The important point here is that a bad model (such as the mean) will have regression coefficients of 0 for the predictors. A regression coefficient of 0 means: (1) a unit change in the predictor variable results in no change in the predicted value of the outcome (the predicted value of the outcome does not change at all); and (2) the gradient of the regression line is 0, meaning that the regression line is flat. Hopefully, you'll see that it logically follows that if a variable significantly predicts an outcome, then it should have a b-value significantly different from zero. This hypothesis is tested using a t-test (see Chapter 9). The **t-statistic** tests the null hypothesis that the value of b is 0: therefore, if it is significant we gain confidence in the hypothesis that the b-value is significantly different from 0 and that the predictor variable contributes significantly to our ability to estimate values of the outcome.

Like F, the t-statistic is also based on the ratio of explained variance against unexplained variance or error. Well, actually, what we're interested in here is not so much variance but whether the b we have is big compared to the amount of error in that estimate. To estimate how much error we could expect to find in b we use the standard error. The standard error tells us something about how different b-values would be across different samples. We could take lots and lots of samples of data regarding album sales and advertising budgets and calculate the b-values for each sample. We could plot a frequency distribution of these samples to discover whether the b-values from all samples would be relatively similar, or whether they would be very different (think back to section 2.5.1). We can use the standard deviation of this distribution (known as the *standard error*) as a measure of the similarity of b-values across samples. If the standard error is very small, then it means that most samples are likely to have a b-value similar to the one in our sample (because there is little variation across samples). The t-test tells us whether the b-value is different from 0 relative to the variation in b-values across samples. When the standard error is small even a small deviation from zero can reflect a meaningful difference because b is representative of the majority of possible samples.

Equation (7.6) shows how the t-test is calculated and you'll find a general version of this equation in Chapter 9 (equation (9.1)). The $b_{expected}$ term is simply the value of b that we would expect to obtain if the null hypothesis were true. I mentioned earlier that the null hypothesis is that b is 0 and so this value can be replaced by 0. The equation simplifies to become the observed value of b divided by the standard error with which it is associated:

$$t = \frac{b_{observed} - b_{expected}}{SE_b}$$

$$= \frac{b_{observed}}{SE_b} \qquad (7.6)$$

The values of t have a special distribution that differs according to the degrees of freedom for the test. In regression, the degrees of freedom are $N - p - 1$, where N is the total sample size and p is the number of predictors. In simple regression when we have only one predictor, so this gives $N - 2$. Having established which t-distribution needs to be used, the observed value of t can then be compared to the values that we would expect to find if there was no effect (i.e., $b = 0$): if t is very large then it is unlikely to have occurred when there is no effect (these values can be found in the Appendix). **R** provides the exact probability that the observed value (or a larger one) of t would occur if the value of b was, in fact, 0. As a general rule, if this observed significance is less than .05, then scientists assume that b is significantly different from 0; put another way, the predictor makes a significant contribution to predicting the outcome.

7.3. Packages used in this chapter ①

There are several packages we will use in this chapter. Some, but not all, can be accessed through R Commander. You will need the packages *boot* (for bootstrapping), *car* (for regression diagnostics) and *QuantPsyc* (to get standardized regression coefficients). If you don't have these packages installed you'll need to install them (*boot* comes pre-installed) by executing:

```
install.packages("car"); install.packages("QuantPsyc")
```

Then you need to load the packages by executing these commands (although *boot* is installed with the base stats package, you still need to load it):

```
library(boot); library(car); library(QuantPsyc)
```

7.4. General procedure for regression in R ①

7.4.1. Doing simple regression using R Commander ①

So far, we have seen a little of the theory behind regression, albeit restricted to the situation in which there is only one predictor. To help clarify what we have learnt so far, we will go through an example of a simple regression using **R**. Earlier on I asked you to imagine that I worked for a record company and that my boss was interested in predicting album sales from advertising. There are some data for this example in the file **Album Sales 1.dat**.

To conduct a regression analysis using R Commander, first initiate the package by executing the command:

```
library(Rcmdr)
```

Once you have initiated the package, you need to load the data file into **R**. You can read **Album Sales 1.dat** into R Commander by using **Data ⇒ Import data ⇒ from text file, clipboard, or URL...** (see section 3.7.3). We can click on View data set to look at the data and check they were read into **R** properly. Figure 7.5 shows the data: there are 200 rows,

FIGURE 7.5
Extract from the album sales data

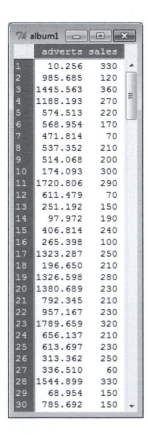

each one representing a different album. There are also two columns, one representing the sales of each album (in thousands) in the week after release and the other representing the amount (in thousands of pounds) spent promoting the album before release. This is the format for entering regression data: the outcome variable and any predictors should be entered in different columns, and each row should represent independent values of those variables.

The pattern of the data is shown in Figure 7.6, and it should be clear that a positive relationship exists: so, the more money spent advertising the album, the more it is likely to sell. Of course there are some albums that sell well regardless of advertising (top left of scatterplot), but there are none that sell badly when advertising levels are high (bottom right of scatterplot). The scatterplot also shows the line of best fit for these data: bearing in mind that the mean would be represented by a flat line at around the 200,000 sales mark, the regression line is noticeably different.

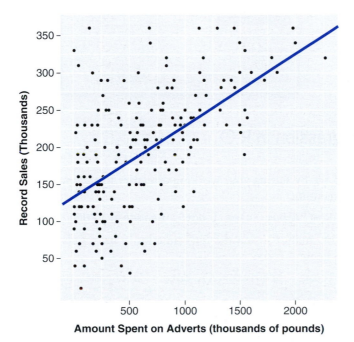

FIGURE 7.6
Scatterplot showing the relationship between album sales and the amount spent promoting the album

To find out the parameters that describe the regression line, and to see whether this line is a useful model, we need to run a regression analysis. In R Commander, choose **Statistics⇒Fit models⇒Linear regression** to activate the linear regression dialog box (Figure 7.7). On the left we choose a response variable – this is the outcome, or dependent variable. On the right we choose an explanatory (predictor, or independent) variable. In this case our outcome is **sales** so we have highlighted this variable in the list labelled *Response variable (pick one)*, and the predictor variable is **adverts**, so we have selected this variable in the list labelled *Explanatory variables (pick one or more)*. At the top of the dialog box, there is a box labelled *Enter name for model:* by default R Commander has named the model *albumSales.1*. By replacing the text in this box we can change that name of the model, for example, to *albumSalesModel* or whatever makes sense to you. When you have selected your variables and named the model, click on ⌷ OK ⌷. The resulting output is described in section 7.5.

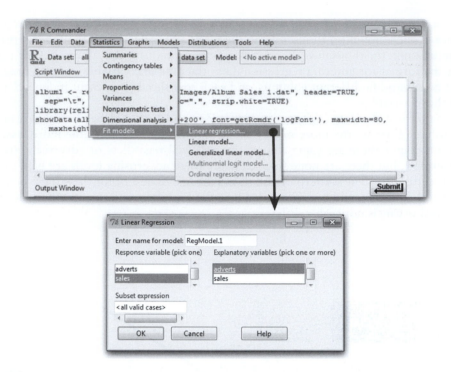

7.4.2. Regression in R ①

First load the data file by setting your working directory to the location of the file (see section 3.4.4) and executing:

```
album1<-read.delim("Album Sales 1.dat", header = TRUE)
```

We run a regression analysis using the *lm()* function – lm stands for 'linear model'. This function takes the general form:

```
newModel<-lm(outcome ~ predictor(s), data = dataFrame, na.action = an action))
```

in which:

- *newModel* is an object created that contains information about the model. We can get summary statistics for this model by executing *summary(newModel)* and *summary. lm(newModel)* for specific parameters of the model.

- *outcome* is the variable that you're trying to predict, also known as the dependent variable. In this example it will be the variable **sales**.

- *predictor(s)* lists the variable or variables from which you're trying to predict the outcome variable. In this example it will be the variable **adverts**. In more complex designs we can specify several predictors but we'll come to that in due course.

- *dataFrame* is the name of the dataframe from which your outcome and predictor variables come.

- *na.action* is an optional command. If you have complete data (as we have here) you can ignore it, but if you have missing values (i.e., NAs in the dataframe) then it can be useful – see R's Souls' Tip 19.2).

The important part to note (especially important because many analyses in the rest of the book uses some variant of *lm()*) is that within the function we write a formula that specifies the model that we want to estimate. This model takes the form:

```
outcome variable ~ predictor variable
```

in which ~ (tilde) means 'predicted from'. (We can't write '=' because that would confuse **R**, plus we're not saying the outcome is *equal* to the predictor, just that the outcome has something to do with the predictor.)

As with functions we have come across before, we can reference variables in two ways: we can either put the whole variable name, including the dataframe:

```
albumSales.1 <- lm(album1$sales ~ album1$adverts)
```

or we can tell **R** what dataframe to use (using *data = nameOfDataFrame*), and then specify the variables without the *dataFrameName$* before them:

```
albumSales.1 <- lm(sales ~ adverts, data = album1)
```

I prefer this second method, but both of these commands create an object called *albumSales1* that contains information about the model. (Note that the command we have just written is the same as the command that R Commander generates for us using the menus.)

R's Souls' Tip 7.1   Missing data ①

Often data sets have missing data, which might be denoted with a placeholder such as 'NA', 'Missing', or a number that denotes missing such as 9999. As we have seen before, when missing data are imported into **R** you typically get an NA in your dataframe to denote the missing value.

If you try to estimate a model with dataframes that have missing values you will get an error because *lm()* does not know what to do with the NAs that it finds in the data. Therefore, you can add *na.action = action* to the function to let it know what to do. There are two main options:

1. *na.action = na.fail*: This is the default and it simply means that if there are any missing values the model will fail to compute.
2. *na.action = na.omit or na.exclude*: This estimates the model but excludes any case that has any missing data on any variable in the model (this is sometimes known as casewise deletion). There are subtle differences between the two but they are so subtle I haven't worked out what they are.

Therefore, if we had missing values in the data we should specify our album sales model as:

```
albumSales.1 <- lm(sales ~ adverts, data = album1, na.action = na.exclude)
```

7.5. Interpreting a simple regression ①

We have created an object called *albumSales.1* that contains the results of our analysis. We can show the object by executing:

```
summary(albumSales.1)
```

which displays the information in Output 7.1.

```
Call:
lm(formula = sales ~ adverts, data = album1)

Residuals:
     Min       1Q    Median       3Q      Max
-152.949   -43.796   -0.393   37.040   211.866
```

```
Coefficients:
            Estimate Std. Error t value Pr(>|t|)
(Intercept) 1.341e+02  7.537e+00  17.799   <2e-16 ***
adverts     9.612e-02  9.632e-03   9.979   <2e-16 ***
---
Signif. codes:  0 '***' 0.001 '**' 0.01 '*' 0.05 '.' 0.1 ' ' 1

Residual standard error: 65.99 on 198 degrees of freedom
Multiple R-squared: 0.3346,      Adjusted R-squared: 0.3313
F-statistic: 99.59 on 1 and 198 DF,  p-value: < 2.2e-16
```

Output 7.1

7.5.1. Overall fit of the object model ①

Let's start at the bottom of Output 7.1:

```
Multiple R-squared: 0.3346,      Adjusted R-squared: 0.3313
```

This part of the output provides the value of R^2 and adjusted R^2 for the model that has been derived. For these data, R^2 has a value of .335. Because there is only one predictor, this value represents the square of the simple correlation between advertising and album sales – we can find the square root of R^2 by running:

```
sqrt(0.3346)
```

Which **R** tells us is:

```
[1] 0.5784462
```

The Pearson correlation coefficient is, therefore, 0.58. (You can confirm this by running a correlation using what you were taught in Chapter 6.) The value of R^2 of .335 also tells us that advertising expenditure can account for 33.5% of the variation in album sales. In other words, if we are trying to explain why some albums sell more than others, we can look at the variation in sales of different albums. There might be many factors that can explain this variation, but our model, which includes only advertising expenditure, can explain approximately 33% of it. This means that 67% of the variation in album sales cannot be explained by advertising alone. Therefore, there must be other variables that have an influence also.

The next part of Output 7.1 reports the results of an analysis of variance (ANOVA – see Chapter 10):

```
F-statistic: 99.59 on 1 and 198 DF,  p-value: < 2.2e-16
```

It doesn't give us all of the sums of squares, it just gives the important part: the *F*-ratio, which is calculated using equation (7.5), and the associated significance value of that *F*-ratio. For these data, *F* is 99.59, which is significant at $p < .001$[4] (because the value

---

[4] Remember that when R wants to show small or large numbers it uses exponential notation. So 2.2e–16 means "2.2 with the decimal place moved 16 places to the left, and add zeros as necessary", which means: 0.00000000000000022. That's a very small number indeed.

labelled p-value is less than .001). This result tells us that there is less than a 0.1% chance that an F-ratio this large would happen if the null hypothesis were true. Therefore, we can conclude that our regression model results in significantly better prediction of album sales than if we used the mean value of album sales. In short, the regression model overall predicts album sales significantly well.

7.5.2. Model parameters ①

The ANOVA tells us whether the model, overall, results in a significantly good degree of prediction of the outcome variable. However, the ANOVA doesn't tell us about the individual contribution of variables in the model (although in this simple case there is only one variable in the model and so we can infer that this variable is a good predictor).

How do I interpret b-values?

The final part of Output 7.1 that we will look at (for now) is the part labelled *Coefficients*. This part contains the model parameters (the beta values) and the significance of these values. We saw in equation (7.2) that b_0 was the Y intercept and this value is the value in the *Estimate* column for the (intercept). (Notice that **R** puts intercept in brackets, because it's in a list of variables, but it's not a real variable). So, from the table shown in Output 7.1, we can say that b_0 is 134.1, and this can be interpreted as meaning that when no money is spent on advertising (when $X = 0$), the model predicts that 134,100 albums will be sold (remember that our unit of measurement was thousands of albums). We can also read off the value of b_1 from the row labelled *adverts* and this value represents the gradient of the regression line. It is 0.096. Although this value is the slope of the regression line, it is more useful to think of this value as representing *the change in the outcome associated with a unit change in the predictor*. Therefore, if our predictor variable is increased by one unit (if the advertising budget is increased by 1), then our model predicts that 0.096 units of extra albums will be sold. Our units of measurement were thousands of pounds and thousands of albums sold, so we can say that for an increase in advertising of £1000 the model predicts 96 (0.096 × 1000 = 96) extra album sales. As you might imagine, this investment is pretty bad for the record company: it invests £1000 and gets only 96 extra sales.

We saw earlier that, in general, values of the regression coefficient b represent the change in the outcome resulting from a unit change in the predictor and that if a predictor is having a significant impact on our ability to predict the outcome then this b should be different from 0 (and big relative to its standard error). We also saw that the t-test tells us whether the b-value is different from 0. **R** provides the exact probability that the observed value of t would occur if the value of b in the population were 0. If this observed significance is less than .05, then scientists agree that the result reflects a genuine effect (see Chapter 2). For these two values, the probabilities are <2e−16 (which means 15 zeros, followed by a 2) and so we can say that the probability of these t-values (or larger) occurring if the values of b in the population were 0 is less than .001. Therefore, the bs are different from 0 and we can conclude that the advertising budget makes a significant contribution ($p < .001$) to predicting album sales.

SELF-TEST

✓ How is the t in Output 7.1 calculated? Use the values in the output to see if you can get the same value as **R**.

7.5.3. Using the model ①

So far, we have discovered that we have a useful model, one that significantly improves our ability to predict album sales. However, the next stage is often to use that model to make some predictions. The first stage is to define the model by replacing the *b*-values in equation (7.2) with the values from the output. In addition, we can replace the *X* and *Y* with the variable names so that the model becomes:

$$\text{album sales}_i = b_0 + b_1 \text{ advertising budget}_i$$
$$= 134.14 + (0.096 \times \text{advertising budget}_i) \tag{7.7}$$

It is now possible to make a prediction about album sales, by replacing the advertising budget with a value of interest. For example, imagine a recording company executive wanted to spend £100,000 on advertising a new album. Remembering that our units are already in thousands of pounds, we can simply replace the advertising budget with 100. He would discover that album sales should be around 144,000 for the first week of sales:

$$\text{album sales}_i = 134.14 + (0.096 \times \text{advertising budget}_i)$$
$$= 134.14 + (0.096 \times 100)$$
$$= 143.74 \tag{7.8}$$

SELF-TEST

✓ How many units would be sold if we spent £666,000 on advertising the latest album by black metal band Abgott?

CRAMMING SAM'S TIPS   **Simple regression**

- Simple regression is a way of predicting values of one variable from another.
- We do this by fitting a statistical model to the data in the form of a straight line.
- This line is the line that best summarizes the pattern of the data.
- We have to assess how well the line fits the data using:

  ○ R^2, which tells us how much variance is explained by the model compared to how much variance there is to explain in the first place. It is the proportion of variance in the outcome variable that is shared by the predictor variable.
  ○ *F*, which tells us how much variability the model can explain relative to how much it can't explain (i.e., it's the ratio of how good the model is compared to how bad it is).

- The *b*-value tells us the gradient of the regression line and the strength of the relationship between a predictor and the outcome variable. If it is significant ($Pr(>|t|) < .05$ in the **R** output) then the predictor variable significantly predicts the outcome variable.

7.6. Multiple regression: the basics ②

To summarize what we have learnt so far, in simple linear regression the outcome variable Y is predicted using the equation of a straight line (equation (7.2)).
Given that we have collected several values of Y and X, the unknown parameters
in the equation can be calculated. They are calculated by fitting a model to the
data (in this case a straight line) for which the sum of the squared differences
between the line and the actual data points is minimized. This method is called
the method of least squares. Multiple regression is a logical extension of these
principles to situations in which there are several predictors. Again, we still use
our basic equation:

> What is the difference
> between simple and
> multiple regression?

$$\text{outcome}_i = (\text{model}) + \text{error}_i$$

but this time the model is slightly more complex. It is basically the same as for simple
regression except that for every extra predictor you include, you have to add a coefficient;
so, each predictor variable has its own coefficient, and the outcome variable is predicted
from a combination of all the variables multiplied by their respective coefficients plus a
residual term (see equation (7.9) – the brackets aren't necessary, they're just to make the
connection to the general equation above):

$$Y_i = (b_0 + b_1 X_{1i} + b_2 X_{2i} + \ldots + b_n X_{ni}) + \varepsilon_i \tag{7.9}$$

Y is the outcome variable, b_1 is the coefficient of the first predictor (X_1), b_2 is the coefficient
of the second predictor (X_2), b_n is the coefficient of the nth predictor (X_{ni}), and ε_i is the difference between the predicted and the observed value of Y for the ith participant. In this
case, the model fitted is more complicated, but the basic principle is the same as simple
regression. That is, we seek to find the linear combination of predictors that correlate
maximally with the outcome variable. Therefore, when we refer to the regression model in
multiple regression, we are talking about a model in the form of equation (7.9).

7.6.1. An example of a multiple regression model ②

Imagine that our recording company executive was interested in extending his model of
album sales to incorporate another variable. We know already that advertising accounts for
33% of variation in album sales, but a much larger 67% remains unexplained. The record
executive could measure a new predictor in an attempt to explain some of the unexplained
variation in album sales. He decides to measure the number of times the album is played
on Radio 1 (the UK's biggest national radio station) during the week prior to release. The
existing model that we derived using **R** (see equation (7.7)) can now be extended to include
this new variable (**airplay**):

$$\text{Album Sales}_i = (b_0 + b_1 \text{ advertising budget}_i + b_2 \text{ airplay}_i) + \varepsilon_i \tag{7.10}$$

The new model is based on equation (7.9) and includes a b-value for both predictors (and,
of course, the constant). If we calculate the b-values, we could make predictions about
album sales based not only on the amount spent on advertising but also in terms of radio
play. There are only two predictors in this model and so we could display this model
graphically in three dimensions (Figure 7.8).

FIGURE 7.8
Scatterplot of
the relationship
between album
sales, advertising
budget and radio
play

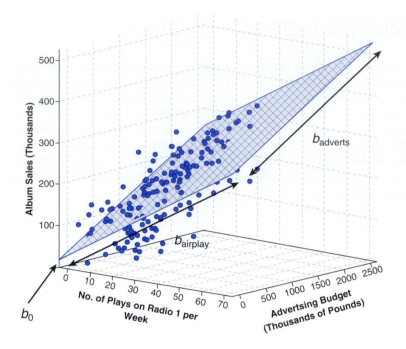

Equation (7.9) describes the tinted trapezium in the diagram (this is known as the regression *plane*) and the dots represent the observed data points. Like simple regression, the plane fitted to the data aims to best predict the observed data. However, there are invariably some differences between the model and the real-life data (this fact is evident because some of the dots do not lie exactly on the tinted area of the graph). The *b*-value for advertising describes the slope of the left and right sides of the regression plane, whereas the *b*-value for airplay describes the slope of the top and bottom of the regression plane. Just like simple regression, knowledge of these two slopes tells us about the shape of the model (what it looks like) and the intercept locates the regression plane in space.

It is fairly easy to visualize a regression model with two predictors, because it is possible to plot the regression plane using a 3-D scatterplot. However, multiple regression can be used with three, four or even ten or more predictors. Although you can't immediately visualize what such complex models look like, or visualize what the *b*-values represent, you should be able to apply the principles of these basic models to more complex scenarios.

7.6.2.   Sums of squares, *R* and R^2 ②

When we have several predictors, the partitioning of sums of squares is the same as in the single variable case except that the model we refer to takes the form of equation (7.9) rather than simply being a 2-D straight line. Therefore, SS_T can be calculated that represents the difference between the observed values and the mean value of the outcome variable. SS_R still represents the difference between the values of *Y* predicted by the model and the observed values. Finally, SS_M can still be calculated and represents the difference between the values of *Y* predicted by the model and the mean value. Although the computation of these values is much more complex than in simple regression, conceptually these values are the same.

When there are several predictors we can't look at the simple R^2, and instead **R** produces a multiple R^2. Multiple R^2 is the square of the correlation between the observed values of *Y* and the values of *Y* predicted by the multiple regression model. Therefore, large values of multiple R^2 represent a large correlation between the predicted and observed values of the outcome. A multiple R^2 of 1 represents a situation in which the model perfectly predicts the observed data. As such, multiple R^2 is a gauge of how well the model predicts the observed data. It follows that the resulting R^2 can be interpreted in the same way as in simple regression: it is the amount of variation in the outcome variable that is accounted for by the model.

7.6.3. Parsimony-adjusted measures of fit ②

The big problem with R^2 is that when you add more variables to the model, it will always go up. If you are deciding which of two models fits the data better, the model with more predictor variables in will always fit better. The **Akaike information criterion (AIC)**[5] is a measure of fit which penalizes the model for having more variables – a little like adjusted R^2. The AIC is defined as:

$$AIC = n\ln\left(\frac{\text{SSE}}{n}\right) + 2k$$

in which n is the number of cases in the model, ln is the natural log, SSE is the sum of square errors for the model, and k is the number of predictor variables. We are not going to worry too much about this equation, other than to notice that the final part – the $2k$ – is the part that does all the work.

Imagine we add a variable to the model; usually this would increase R^2, and hence SSE would be reduced. But imagine that this variable does not change the fit of the model *at all*. What will happen to the AIC? Well, the first part will be the same: n and SSE are unchanged. What will change is k: it will be higher, by one (because we have added a variable). Hence, when we add this variable to the model, the AIC will be higher by 2. A larger value of the AIC indicates worse fit, corrected for the number of variables.

There are a couple of strange things about the AIC. One of them is there are no guidelines for how much larger is 'a lot' and how much larger is 'not very much': If the AIC is bigger, the fit is worse; if the AIC is smaller, fit is better.

The second thing about the AIC is that it makes sense to compare the AIC only between models of the same data. The AIC doesn't mean anything on its own: you cannot say that a value of the AIC of 10 is small, or that a value for the AIC of 1000 is large. The only thing you do with the AIC is compare it to other models with the same outcome variable.

R also provides the option of a second measure of parsimony adjusted model fit, called the *Bayesian information criterion (BIC)*, but that is rather beyond the level of this book.

7.6.4. Methods of regression ②

If we are interested in constructing a complex model with several predictors, how do we decide which predictors to use? A great deal of care should be taken in selecting predictors for a model because the values of the regression coefficients depend upon the variables in

[5] Hirotsugu Akaike (pronounced A-Ka-Ee-Kay) was a Japanese statistician who gave his name to the AIC, which is used in a huge range of different places. You get some idea of this range when you find out that the paper in which the AIC was proposed was published in a journal called *IEEE Transactions on Automatic Control*.

the model. Therefore, the predictors included and the way in which they are entered into the model can have a great impact. In an ideal world, predictors should be selected based on past research.[6] If new predictors are being added to existing models then select these new variables based on the substantive *theoretical* importance of these variables. One thing *not* to do is select hundreds of random predictors, bung them all into a regression analysis and hope for the best. In addition to the problem of selecting predictors, there are several ways in which variables can be entered into a model. When predictors are all completely uncorrelated, the order of variable entry has very little effect on the parameters calculated; however, we rarely have uncorrelated predictors and so the method of predictor selection is crucial.

7.6.4.1. Hierarchical ②

In **hierarchical regression** predictors are selected based on past work and the experimenter decides in which order to enter the predictors into the model. As a general rule, known predictors (from other research) should be entered into the model first in order of their importance in predicting the outcome. After known predictors have been entered, the experimenter can add any new predictors into the model. New predictors can be entered either all in one go, in a stepwise manner, or hierarchically (such that the new predictor suspected to be the most important is entered first).

7.6.4.2. Forced entry ②

Forced entry is a method in which all predictors are forced into the model simultaneously. Like hierarchical, this method relies on good theoretical reasons for including the chosen predictors, but unlike hierarchical the experimenter makes no decision about the order in which variables are entered. Some researchers believe that this method is the only appropriate method for theory testing (Studenmund & Cassidy, 1987) because stepwise techniques are influenced by random variation in the data and so seldom give replicable results if the model is retested.

7.6.4.3. Stepwise methods ②

Stepwise regressions are generally frowned upon by statisticians, and **R** is not as good at running automated stepwise regressions as some other statistics programs we could mention. However, I'm still going to tell you how to do them, but be aware that if you can't do a stepwise regression in the same way in **R** that you can in another program, that's because the other program was written 40 years ago when people didn't know better. In **stepwise regression** decisions about the order in which predictors are entered into the model are based on a purely mathematical criterion.

  When you carry out a stepwise regression in **R**, you need to specify a direction. In the *forward* direction, an initial model is defined that contains only the constant (b_0). The computer then searches for the predictor (out of the ones available) that best predicts the outcome variable – it does this by selecting the predictor that has the highest simple correlation with the outcome. If this predictor improves the ability of the model to predict the outcome, then this predictor is retained in the model and the computer searches for

---

[6] I might cynically qualify this suggestion by proposing that predictors be chosen based on past research that has utilized good methodology. If basing such decisions on regression analyses, select predictors based only on past research that has used regression appropriately and yielded reliable, generalizable models.

a second predictor. The criterion used for selecting this second predictor is that it is the variable that has the largest semi-partial correlation with the outcome. Let me explain this in plain English. Imagine that the first predictor can explain 40% of the variation in the outcome variable; then there is still 60% left unexplained. The computer searches for the predictor that can explain the biggest part of the remaining 60% (so it is not interested in the 40% that is already explained). As such, this semi-partial correlation gives a measure of how much 'new variance' in the outcome can be explained by each remaining predictor (see section 6.6). The predictor that accounts for the most new variance is added to the model and, if it makes a contribution to the predictive power of the model, it is retained and another predictor is considered.

R has to decide when to stop adding predictors to the model, and it does this based on the Akaike information criterion which was described above: a lower AIC indicates a better model. A variable is kept in the model only if it improves (i.e., lowers) the AIC, and if no variable can lower the AIC further, the model is stopped.

The *backward* method is the opposite of the forward method in that the computer begins by placing all predictors in the model and then by looking to see if the AIC goes down when each variable is removed. If a variable is removed, the contribution of the remaining predictors is then reassessed and the process continues until removing any variable causes AIC to increase.

The final direction is called 'both' by **R** (and stepwise by some other programs). This method, as the name implies, goes in both directions. It starts the in same way as the forward method, except that each time a predictor is added to the equation, a removal test is made of the least useful predictor. As such the regression equation is constantly being reassessed to see whether any redundant predictors can be removed.

If you do decide to use a stepwise method then the backward direction is preferable to the forward method. This is because of **suppressor effects**, which occur when a predictor has an effect but only when another variable is held constant. Forward selection is more likely than backward elimination to exclude predictors involved in suppressor effects. As such, the forward method runs a higher risk of making a Type II error (i.e., missing a predictor that does in fact predict the outcome).

7.6.4.4. All-subsets methods ②

The problem with stepwise methods is that they assess the fit of a variable based on the other variables that were in the model. Some people use the analogy of getting dressed to describe this problem. If a stepwise regression method was selecting your clothes, it would decide what clothes you should wear, based on the clothes it has already selected. If, for example, it is a cold day, a stepwise selection method might choose a pair of trousers to put on first. But if you are wearing trousers already, it is difficult to get your underwear on: stepwise methods will decide that underwear does not fit, and you will therefore go without. A better method is all-subsets regression. As the name implies, all-subsets regression tries every combination of variables, to see which one gives the best fit (fit is determined by a statistic called Mallows' C_p, which we are not going to worry about). The problem with all-subsets regression is that as the number of predictor variables increases, the number of possible subsets increases exponentially. If you have two predictor variables, A and B, then you have 4 possible subsets: none of them, A alone, B alone, or A and B. If you have three variables (A, B, C), the possible subsets are none, A, B, C, AB, AC, BC, ABC, making 8 subsets. If you have 10 variables, there are 1024 possible subsets. In the days when computers were slower and running a regression analysis might take a couple of minutes, running 1024 regressions might take a day or so. Thankfully, computers aren't slow any more, and so this method is feasible – it's just that other programs have not yet caught up with **R**, so you tend to come across this method less.

7.6.4.5. Choosing a method ②

R allows you to opt for any one of these methods and it is important to select an appropriate one. The three directions of stepwise selection (forward, backward and both) and all-subsets regression all come under the general heading of *stepwise methods* because they all rely on the computer selecting variables based upon mathematical criteria. Many writers argue that this takes many important methodological decisions out of the hands of the researcher. What's more, the models derived by computer often take advantage of random sampling variation and so decisions about which variables should be included will be based upon slight differences in their semi-partial correlation. However, these slight statistical differences may contrast dramatically with the theoretical importance of a predictor to the model. There is also the danger of over-fitting (having too many variables in the model that essentially make little contribution to predicting the outcome) and underfitting (leaving out important predictors) the model. For this reason stepwise methods are best avoided except for exploratory model building. If you must do a stepwise regression then it is advisable to **cross-validate** your model by splitting the data (see section 7.7.2.2).

When there is a sound theoretical literature available, then base your model upon what past research tells you. Include any meaningful variables in the model in their order of importance. After this initial analysis, repeat the regression but exclude any variables that were statistically redundant the first time around. There are important considerations in deciding which predictors should be included. First, it is important not to include too many predictors. As a general rule, the fewer predictors the better, and certainly include only predictors for which you have a good theoretical grounding (it is meaningless to measure hundreds of variables and then put them all into a regression model). So, be selective and remember you should have a decent sample size – see section 7.7.2.3.

7.7. How accurate is my regression model? ②

When we have produced a model based on a sample of data there are two important questions to ask. First, does the model fit the observed data well, or is it influenced by a small number of cases? Second, can my model generalize to other samples? These questions are vital to ask because they affect how we use the model that has been constructed. These questions are also, in some sense, hierarchical because we wouldn't want to generalize a bad model. However, it is a mistake to think that because a model fits the observed data well we can draw conclusions beyond our sample. **Generalization** is a critical additional step, and if we find that our model is not generalizable, then we must restrict any conclusions based on the model to the sample used. First, we will look at how we establish whether a model is an accurate representation of the actual data, and in section 7.7.2 we move on to look at how we assess whether a model can be used to make inferences beyond the sample of data that has been collected.

7.7.1.   Assessing the regression model I: diagnostics ②

To answer the question of whether the model fits the observed data well, or if it is influenced by a small number of cases, we can look for outliers and influential cases (the difference is explained in Jane Superbrain Box 7.1). We will look at these in turn.

JANE SUPERBRAIN 7.1

The difference between residuals and influence statistics ③

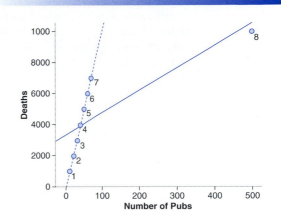

In this section I describe two ways to look for cases that might bias the model: residual and influence statistics. To illustrate how these measures differ, imagine that the Mayor of London at the turn of the last century was interested in how drinking affected mortality. London is divided up into different regions called boroughs, and so he might measure the number of pubs and the number of deaths over a period of time in eight of his boroughs. The data are in a file called **pubs.dat**.

The scatterplot of these data reveals that without the last case there is a perfect linear relationship (the dashed straight line). However, the presence of the last case (case 8) changes the line of best fit dramatically (although this line is still a significant fit to the data – do the regression analysis and see for yourself).

What's interesting about these data is when we look at the residuals and influence statistics. The residual for case 8 is the second *smallest*: this outlier produces a very small residual (most of the non-outliers have larger residuals) because it sits very close to the line that has been fitted to the data. How can this be? Look at the influence statistics below and you'll see that they're massive for case 8: it exerts a huge influence over the model.

	Residual	Cook's Distance	Leverage (Hat Value)	DFBeta (Intercept)	DFBeta (Pubs)
1	−2495.34	0.21	0.17	−509.62	1.39
2	−1638.73	0.09	0.16	−321.10	0.80
3	−782.12	0.02	0.15	−147.08	0.33
4	74.49	0.00	0.14	13.47	−0.03
5	931.10	0.02	0.14	161.47	−0.27
6	1787.71	0.08	0.13	297.70	−0.41
7	2644.32	0.17	0.13	422.68	−0.44
8	−521.42	227.14	0.99	3351.53	−85.65

As always when you see a statistical oddity, you should ask what was happening in the real world. The last data point represents the City of London, a tiny area of only 1 square mile in the centre of London where very few people lived but where thousands of commuters (even then) came to work and had lunch in the pubs. Hence the pubs didn't rely on the resident population for their business and the residents didn't consume all of their beer! Therefore, there was a massive number of pubs.

This illustrates that a case exerting a massive influence can produce a small residual – so look at both. (I'm very grateful to David Hitchin for this example, and he in turn got it from Dr Richard Roberts.)

7.7.1.1. Outliers and residuals ②

An outlier is a case that differs substantially from the main trend of the data (see Jane Superbrain Box 4.1). Figure 7.9 shows an example of such a case in regression. Outliers can cause your model to be biased because they affect the values of the estimated regression coefficients. For example, Figure 7.9 uses the same data as Figure 7.3 except that the score of one participant has been changed to be an outlier (in this case a person who was very calm in the presence of a very big spider). The change in this one point has had a dramatic effect on the regression model chosen to fit the data. With the outlier present, the regression model changes: its gradient is reduced (the line becomes flatter) and the intercept increases (the new line will cross the Y-axis at a higher point). It should be clear from this diagram that it is important to try to detect outliers to see whether the model is biased in this way.

FIGURE 7.9
Graph demonstrating the effect of an outlier. The dashed line represents the original regression line for these data (see Figure 7.3), whereas the solid line represents the regression line when an outlier is present

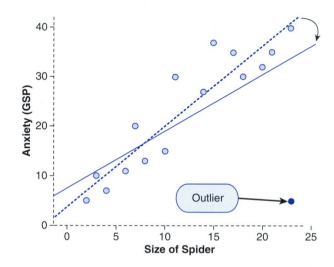

How do you think that you might detect an outlier? Well, we know that an outlier, by its nature, is very different from all of the other scores. This being true, do you think that the model will predict that person's score very accurately? The answer is *no*: looking at Figure 7.9, it is evident that even though the outlier has biased the model, the model still predicts that one value very badly (the regression line is long way from the outlier). Therefore, if we were to work out the differences between the data values that were collected, and the values predicted by the model, we could detect an outlier by looking for large differences. This process is the same as looking for cases that the model predicts inaccurately. The differences between the values of the outcome predicted by the model and the values of the outcome observed in the sample are known as *residuals*. These residuals represent the error present in the model. If a model fits the sample data well then all residuals will be small (if the model was a perfect fit to the sample data – all data points fall on the regression line – then all residuals would be zero). If a model is a poor fit to the sample data then the residuals will be large. Also, if any cases stand out as having a large residual, then they could be outliers.

The *normal* or **unstandardized residuals** described above are measured in the same units as the outcome variable and so are difficult to interpret across different models. What we can do is to look for residuals that stand out as being particularly large. However, we cannot define a universal cut-off point for what constitutes a large residual. To overcome this problem, we use **standardized residuals**, which are the residuals divided by an estimate of their standard deviation. We came across standardization in section 6.3.2 as a means of converting variables into a standard unit of measurement (the standard deviation); we also came across z-scores (see section 1.7.4) in which variables are converted into standard deviation units (i.e., they're converted into scores that are distributed around a mean of 0 with a standard deviation of 1). By converting residuals into z-scores (standardized residuals) we can compare residuals from different models and use what we know about the properties of z-scores to devise universal guidelines for what constitutes an acceptable (or unacceptable) value. For example, we know from Chapter 1 that in a normally distributed sample, 95% of z-scores should lie between -1.96 and $+1.96$, 99% should lie between -2.58 and $+2.58$, and 99.9% (i.e., nearly all of them) should lie between -3.29 and $+3.29$. Some general rules for standardized residuals are derived from these facts: (1) standardized residuals with an absolute value greater than 3.29 (we can use 3 as an approximation) are cause for concern because in an average sample a value this high is unlikely to happen by chance; (2) if more than 1% of our sample cases have standardized residuals with an absolute value greater than 2.58 (we usually just say 2.5) there is evidence that the level of error within our model is unacceptable (the model is a fairly poor fit of the sample data); and (3) if more than 5% of cases have standardized residuals with an absolute value greater than 1.96 (we can use 2 for convenience) then there is also evidence that the model is a poor representation of the actual data.

7.7.1.2. Influential cases ③

As well as testing for outliers by looking at the error in the model, it is also possible to look at whether certain cases exert undue influence over the parameters of the model. So, if we were to delete a certain case, would we obtain different regression coefficients? This type of analysis can help to determine whether the regression model is stable across the sample, or whether it is biased by a few influential cases. Again, this process will unveil outliers.

There are several residual statistics that can be used to assess the influence of a particular case. One statistic is the **adjusted predicted value** for a case when that case is excluded from the analysis. In effect, the computer calculates a new model without a particular case and then uses this new model to predict the value of the outcome variable for the case that was excluded. If a case does not exert a large influence over the model then we would expect the adjusted predicted value to be very similar to the predicted value when the case is included. Put simply, if the model is stable then the predicted value of a case should be the same regardless of whether or not that case was used to calculate the model. The difference between the adjusted predicted value and the original predicted value is known as DFFit (see below). We can also look at the residual based on the adjusted predicted value: that is, the difference between the adjusted predicted value and the original observed value. When this residual is divided by the standard error it gives a standardized value known as the **studentized residual**. This residual can be compared across different regression analyses because it is measured in standard units, and is called a studentized residual because it follows a Student's t-distribution.

The studentized residuals are very useful to assess the influence of a case on the ability of the model to predict that case. However, they do not provide any information about how a case influences the model as a whole (i.e., the impact that a case has on the model's ability to predict *all* cases). One statistic that does consider the effect of a single case on the model as a whole is **Cook's distance**. Cook's distance is a measure of the overall influence of a case on the model, and Cook and Weisberg (1982) have suggested that values greater than 1 may be cause for concern.

A second measure of influence is **hat values** (sometimes called **leverage**), which gauge the influence of the observed value of the outcome variable over the predicted values. The average leverage value is defined as $(k+1)/n$, in which k is the number of predictors in the model and n is the number of participants.[7] Leverage values can lie between 0 (indicating that the case has no influence whatsoever) and 1 (indicating that the case has complete

---

[7] You may come across the average leverage denoted as p/n, in which p is the number of parameters being estimated. In multiple regression, we estimate parameters for each predictor and also for a constant and so p is equivalent to the number of predictors plus one $(k + 1)$.

influence over prediction). If no cases exert undue influence over the model then we would expect all of the leverage values to be close to the average value $((k + 1)/n)$. Hoaglin and Welsch (1978) recommend investigating cases with values greater than twice the average $(2(k + 1)/n)$ and Stevens (2002) recommends using three times the average $(3(k + 1)/n)$ as a cut-off point for identifying cases having undue influence. We will see how to use these cut-off points later. However, cases with large leverage values will not necessarily have a large influence on the regression coefficients because they are measured on the outcome variables rather than the predictors.

It is possible to run the regression analysis with a case included and then rerun the analysis with that same case excluded. If we did this, undoubtedly there would be some difference between the b coefficients in the two regression equations. This difference would tell us how much influence a particular case has on the parameters of the regression model. To take a hypothetical example, imagine two variables that had a perfect negative relationship except for a single case (case 30). If a regression analysis was done on the 29 cases that were perfectly linearly related then we would get a model in which the predictor variable X perfectly predicts the outcome variable Y, and there are no errors. If we then ran the analysis but this time include the case that didn't conform (case 30), then the resulting model would have different parameters. Some data are stored in the file **dfbeta.dat** that illustrate such a situation. Try running a simple regression first with all the cases included and then with case 30 deleted. The results are summarized in Table 7.1, which shows: (1) the parameters for the regression model when the extreme case is included or excluded; (2) the resulting regression equations; and (3) the value of Y predicted from participant 30's score on the X variable (which is obtained by replacing the X in the regression equation with participant 30's score for X, which was 1).

Table 7.1   The difference in the parameters of the regression model when one case is excluded

Parameter (b)	Case 30 Included	Case 30 Excluded	Difference
Constant (intercept)	29.00	31.00	−2.00
Predictor (gradient)	−0.90	−1.00	0.10
Model (regression line):	$Y = (-0.9)X + 29$	$Y = (-1)X + 31$	
Predicted Y	28.10	30.00	−1.90

When case 30 is excluded, these data have a perfect negative relationship; hence the coefficient for the predictor (b_1) is −1 (remember that in simple regression this term is the same as Pearson's correlation coefficient), and the coefficient for the constant (the intercept, b_0) is 31. However, when case 30 is included, both parameters are reduced[8] and the difference between the parameters is also displayed. The difference between a parameter estimated using all cases and estimated when one case is excluded is known as the **DFBeta** in **R**. DFBeta is calculated for every case and for each of the parameters in the model. So, in our hypothetical example, the DFBeta for the constant is −2, and the DFBeta for the predictor variable is 0.1. By looking at the values of DFBeta, it is possible to identify cases that have a large influence on the parameters of the regression model.

A related statistic is the **DFFit**, which is the difference between the predicted value for a case when the model is calculated including that case and when the model is calculated excluding that case: in this example the value is −1.90 (see Table 7.1). If a case is not

---

[8] The value of b_1 is reduced in absolute size because the data no longer have a perfect linear relationship and so there is now variance that the model cannot explain.

influential then its DFFit should be zero – hence, we expect non-influential cases to have small DFFit values.

7.7.1.3. A final comment on diagnostic statistics ②

There are a lot of diagnostic statistics that should be examined after a regression analysis, and it is difficult to summarize this wealth of material into a concise conclusion. However, one thing I would like to stress is a point made by Belsey, Kuh, and Welsch (1980) who noted the dangers inherent in these procedures. The point is that diagnostics are tools that enable you to see how good or bad your model is in terms of fitting the sampled data. They are a way of assessing your model. They are *not*, however, a way of justifying the removal of data points to effect some desirable change in the regression parameters (e.g., deleting a case that changes a non-significant *b*-value into a significant one). Stevens (2002, p. 135), as ever, offers excellent advice:

> If a point is a significant outlier on Y, but its Cook's distance is < 1, there is no real need to delete that point since it does not have a large effect on the regression analysis. However, one should still be interested in studying such points further to understand why they did not fit the model.

7.7.2. Assessing the regression model II: generalization ②

When a regression analysis is done, an equation can be produced that is correct for the sample of observed values. However, in the social sciences we are usually interested in generalizing our findings outside the sample. So, although it can be useful to draw conclusions about a particular sample of people, it is usually more interesting if we can then assume that our conclusions are true for a wider population. For a regression model to generalize we must be sure that underlying assumptions have been met, and to test whether the model does generalize we can look at cross-validating it.

7.7.2.1. Checking assumptions ②

To draw conclusions about a population based on a regression analysis done on a sample, several assumptions must be true (see Berry, 1993):

- **Variable types**: All predictor variables must be quantitative or categorical (with two categories), and the outcome variable must be quantitative, continuous and unbounded. By 'quantitative' I mean that they should be measured at the interval level and by 'unbounded' I mean that there should be no constraints on the variability of the outcome. If the outcome is a measure ranging from 1 to 10 yet the data collected vary between 3 and 7, then these data are constrained.

- **Non-zero variance**: The predictors should have some variation in value (i.e., they do not have variances of 0).

- **No perfect multicollinearity**: There should be no perfect linear relationship between two or more of the predictors. So, the predictor variables should not correlate too highly (see section 7.7.2.4).

- **Predictors are uncorrelated with 'external variables'**: *External variables* are variables that haven't been included in the regression model which influence the outcome variable.[9] These variables can be thought of as similar to the 'third variable' that was discussed with reference to correlation. This assumption means that there should be no external variables that correlate with any of the variables included in the regression model. Obviously, if external variables do correlate with the predictors, then the conclusions we draw from the model become unreliable (because other variables exist that can predict the outcome just as well).

- **Homoscedasticity**: At each level of the predictor variable(s), the variance of the residual terms should be constant. This just means that the residuals at each level of the predictor(s) should have the same variance (**homoscedasticity**); when the variances are very unequal there is said to be **heteroscedasticity** (see section 5.7 as well).

- **Independent errors**: For any two observations the residual terms should be uncorrelated (or independent). This eventuality is sometimes described as a lack of **autocorrelation**. This assumption can be tested with the **Durbin–Watson test**, which tests for serial correlations between errors. Specifically, it tests whether adjacent residuals are correlated. The test statistic can vary between 0 and 4, with a value of 2 meaning that the residuals are uncorrelated. A value greater than 2 indicates a negative correlation between adjacent residuals, whereas a value less than 2 indicates a positive correlation. The size of the Durbin–Watson statistic depends upon the number of predictors in the model and the number of observations. As a very conservative rule of thumb, values less than 1 or greater than 3 are definitely cause for concern; however, values closer to 2 may still be problematic depending on your sample and model. **R** also provides a *p*-value of the autocorrelation. Be very careful with the Durbin–Watson test, though, as it depends on the order of the data: if you reorder your data, you'll get a different value.

- **Normally distributed errors**: It is assumed that the residuals in the model are random, normally distributed variables with a mean of 0. This assumption simply means that the differences between the model and the observed data are most frequently zero or very close to zero, and that differences much greater than zero happen only occasionally. Some people confuse this assumption with the idea that predictors have to be normally distributed. Predictors do not need to be normally distributed (see section 7.12).

- **Independence**: It is assumed that all of the values of the outcome variable are independent (in other words, each value of the outcome variable comes from a separate entity).

- **Linearity**: The mean values of the outcome variable for each increment of the predictor(s) lie along a straight line. In plain English this means that it is assumed that the relationship we are modelling is a linear one. If we model a non-linear relationship using a linear model then this obviously limits the generalizability of the findings.

This list of assumptions probably seems pretty daunting but, as we saw in Chapter 5, assumptions are important. When the assumptions of regression are met, the model that we get for a sample can be accurately applied to the population of interest (the coefficients and parameters of the regression equation are said to be *unbiased*). Some people assume that this means that when the assumptions are met the regression model from a sample is always identical to the model that would have been obtained had we been able to test the

---

[9] Some authors choose to refer to these external variables as part of an error term that includes any random factor in the way in which the outcome varies. However, to avoid confusion with the residual terms in the regression equations I have chosen the label 'external variables'. Although this term implicitly washes over any random factors, I acknowledge their presence here.

entire population. Unfortunately, this belief isn't true. What an unbiased model does tell us is that *on average* the regression model from the sample is the same as the population model. However, you should be clear that even when the assumptions are met, it is possible that a model obtained from a sample may not be the same as the population model – but the likelihood of them being the same is increased.

7.7.2.2. Cross-validation of the model ③

Even if we can't be confident that the model derived from our sample accurately represents the entire population, there are ways in which we can assess how well our model can predict the outcome in a different sample. Assessing the accuracy of a model across different samples is known as cross-validation. If a model can be generalized, then it must be capable of accurately predicting the same outcome variable from the same set of predictors in a different group of people. If the model is applied to a different sample and there is a severe drop in its predictive power, then the model clearly does *not* generalize. As a first rule of thumb, we should aim to collect enough data to obtain a reliable regression model (see the next section). Once we have a regression model there are two main methods of cross-validation:

- **Adjusted R^2**: In **R**, not only is the value of R^2 calculated, but also an **adjusted R^2**. This adjusted value indicates the loss of predictive power or **shrinkage**. Whereas R^2 tells us how much of the variance in Y is accounted for by the regression model from our sample, the adjusted value tells us how much variance in Y would be accounted for if the model had been derived from the population from which the sample was taken. **R** derives the adjusted R^2 using Wherry's equation. However, this equation has been criticized because it tells us nothing about how well the regression model would predict an entirely different set of data (how well can the model predict scores of a different sample of data from the same population?). One version of R^2 that does tell us how well the model cross-validates uses Stein's formula (see Stevens, 2002):

$$adjusted\ R^2 = 1 - \left[\left(\frac{n-1}{n-k-1}\right)\left(\frac{n-2}{n-k-2}\right)\left(\frac{n+1}{n}\right)\right](1-R^2)$$

(7.11)

  In Stein's equation, R^2 is the unadjusted value, n is the number of participants and k is the number of predictors in the model. For the more mathematically minded of you, it is worth using this equation to cross-validate a regression model.

- **Data splitting**: This approach involves randomly splitting your data set, computing a regression equation on both halves of the data and then comparing the resulting models. When using stepwise methods, cross-validation is a good idea; you should run the stepwise regression on a random selection of about 80% of your cases. Then force this model on the remaining 20% of the data. By comparing values of the R^2 and b-values in the two samples you can tell how well the original model generalizes (see Tabachnick & Fidell, 2007, for more detail).

7.7.2.3. Sample size in regression ③

In the previous section I said that it's important to collect enough data to obtain a reliable regression model. Well, how much is enough? You'll find a lot of rules of thumb floating about, the two most common being that you should have 10 cases of data for each

How much data should I collect?

predictor in the model, or 15 cases of data per predictor. So, with five predictors, you'd need 50 or 75 cases respectively (depending on the rule you use). These rules are very pervasive (even I used the 15 cases per predictor rule in the first edition of this book) but they oversimplify the issue considerably. In fact, the sample size required will depend on the size of effect that we're trying to detect (i.e., how strong the relationship is that we're trying to measure) and how much power we want to detect these effects. The simplest rule of thumb is that the bigger the sample size, the better! The reason is that the estimate of R that we get from regression is dependent on the number of predictors, k, and the sample size, N. In fact the expected R for random data is $k/(N-1)$, and so with small sample sizes random data can appear to show a strong effect: for example, with six predictors and 21 cases of data, $R = 6/(21-1) = .3$ (a medium effect size by Cohen's criteria described in section 6.3.2). Obviously for random data we'd want the expected R to be 0 (no effect) and for this to be true we need large samples (to take the previous example, if we had 100 cases, not 21, then the expected R would be a more acceptable .06).

It's all very well knowing that larger is better, but researchers usually need some more concrete guidelines (much as we'd all love to collect 1000 cases of data, it isn't always practical). Green (1991) makes two rules of thumb for the *minimum* acceptable sample size, the first based on whether you want to test the overall fit of your regression model (i.e., test the R^2), and the second based on whether you want to test the individual predictors within the model (i.e., test the b-values of the model). If you want to test the model overall, then he recommends a minimum sample size of $50 + 8k$, where k is the number of predictors. So, with five predictors, you'd need a sample size of $50 + 40 = 90$. If you want to test the individual predictors then he suggests a minimum sample size of $104 + k$, so again taking the example of five predictors you'd need a sample size of $104 + 5 = 109$. Of course, in most cases we're interested both in the overall fit and in the contribution of individual predictors, and in this situation Green recommends you calculate both of the minimum sample sizes I've just described, and use the one that has the largest value (so in the five-predictor example, we'd use 109 because it is bigger than 90).

Now, these guidelines are all right as a rough and ready guide, but they still oversimplify the problem. As I've mentioned, the sample size required actually depends on the size of the effect (i.e., how well our predictors predict the outcome) and how much statistical power we want to detect these effects. Miles and Shevlin (2001) produce some extremely useful graphs that illustrate the sample sizes needed to achieve different levels of power, for different effect sizes, as the number of predictors vary. For precise estimates of the sample size you should be using, I recommend using these graphs. I've summarized some of the general findings in Figure 7.10. This diagram shows the sample size required to achieve a high level of power (I've taken Cohen's, 1988, benchmark of .8) depending on the number of predictors and the size of expected effect. To summarize the graph very broadly: (1) if you expect to find a large effect then a sample size of 80 will always suffice (with up to 20 predictors) and if there are fewer predictors then you can afford to have a smaller sample; (2) if you're expecting a medium effect, then a sample size of 200 will always suffice (up to 20 predictors), you should always have a sample size above 60, and with six or fewer predictors you'll be fine with a sample of 100; and (3) if you're expecting a small effect size then just don't bother unless you have the time and resources to collect at least 600 cases of data (and many more if you have six or more predictors).

7.7.2.4. Multicollinearity ②

Multicollinearity exists when there is a strong correlation between two or more predictors in a regression model. Multicollinearity poses a problem only for multiple regression because (without wishing to state the obvious) simple regression requires only one

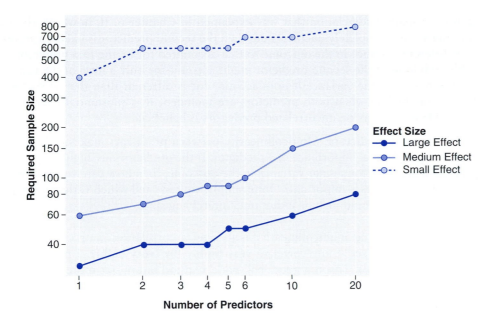

FIGURE 7.10
Graph to show
the sample
size required
in regression
depending on
the number
of predictors
and the size of
expected effect

predictor. **Perfect collinearity** exists when at least one predictor is a perfect linear combination of the others (the simplest example being two predictors that are perfectly correlated – they have a correlation coefficient of 1). If there is perfect collinearity between predictors it becomes impossible to obtain unique estimates of the regression coefficients because there are an infinite number of combinations of coefficients that would work equally well. Put simply, if we have two predictors that are perfectly correlated, then the values of b for each variable are interchangeable. The good news is that perfect collinearity is rare in real-life data. The bad news is that less than perfect collinearity is virtually unavoidable. Low levels of collinearity pose little threat to the models generated by **R**, but as collinearity increases there are three problems that arise:

- **Untrustworthy bs**: As collinearity increases so do the standard errors of the b coefficients. If you think back to what the standard error represents, then big standard errors for b coefficients means that these bs are more variable across samples. Therefore, it means that the b coefficient in our sample is less likely to represent the population. Crudely put, multicollinearity means that the b-values are less trustworthy. Don't lend them money and don't let them go for dinner with your boy- or girlfriend. Of course if the bs are variable from sample to sample then the resulting predictor equations will be unstable across samples too.

- **It limits the size of R**: Remember that R is a measure of the multiple correlation between the predictors and the outcome and that R^2 indicates the variance in the outcome for which the predictors account. Imagine a situation in which a single variable predicts the outcome variable fairly successfully (e.g., $R = .80$) and a second predictor variable is then added to the model. This second variable might account for a lot of the variance in the outcome (which is why it is included in the model), but the variance it accounts for is the same variance accounted for by the first variable. In other words, once the variance accounted for by the first predictor has been removed, the second predictor accounts for very little of the remaining variance (the second variable accounts for very little *unique variance*). Hence, the overall variance in the outcome accounted for by the two predictors is little more than when only one predictor is used (so R might increase from .80 to .82). This idea is connected to the notion of partial correlation that was explained in Chapter 6. If, however, the two predictors are completely uncorrelated, then the second predictor is likely to account for different variance in the outcome to that accounted for by the first predictor. So, although in itself the second predictor might account for only a little of the variance in the outcome, the variance it does account for is different than that of the other predictor (and so when both predictors are included, R is substantially larger, say .95). Therefore, having uncorrelated predictors is beneficial.

- **Importance of predictors**: Multicollinearity between predictors makes it difficult to assess the individual importance of a predictor. If the predictors are highly correlated, and each accounts for similar variance in the outcome, then how can we know which of the two variables is important? Quite simply, we can't tell which variable is important – the model could include either one, interchangeably.

One way of identifying multicollinearity is to scan a correlation matrix of all of the predictor variables and see if any correlate very highly (by 'very highly' I mean correlations of above .80 or .90). This is a good 'ball park' method but misses more subtle forms of multicollinearity. Luckily, **R** can produce various collinearity diagnostics, one of which is the *variance inflation factor* (VIF). The VIF indicates whether a predictor has a strong linear relationship with the other predictor(s). Although there are no hard and fast rules about what value of the VIF should cause concern, Myers (1990) suggests that a value of 10 is a good value at which to worry. What's more, if the average VIF is greater than 1, then multicollinearity may be biasing the regression model (Bowerman & O'Connell, 1990). Related to the VIF is the **tolerance** statistic, which is its reciprocal (1/VIF). As such, values below 0.1 indicate serious problems, although Menard (1995) suggests that values below 0.2 are worthy of concern.

If none of this has made any sense then have a look at Hutcheson and Sofroniou (1999, pp. 78–85) who give a really clear explanation of multicollinearity.

7.8. How to do multiple regression using R Commander and R ②

7.8.1. Some things to think about before the analysis ②

A good strategy to adopt with regression is to measure predictor variables for which there are sound theoretical reasons for expecting them to predict the outcome. Run a regression analysis in which all predictors are entered into the model and examine the output to see which predictors contribute substantially to the model's ability to predict the outcome. Once you have established which variables are important, rerun the analysis including only the important predictors and use the resulting parameter estimates to define your regression model. If the initial analysis reveals that there are two or more significant predictors, then you could consider running a forward stepwise analysis (rather than forced entry) to find out the individual contribution of each predictor.

I have spent a lot of time explaining the theory behind regression and some of the diagnostic tools necessary to gauge the accuracy of a regression model. It is important to remember that **R** may appear to be very clever, but in fact it is not. Admittedly, it can do lots of complex calculations in a matter of seconds, but what it can't do is control the quality of the model that is generated – to do this requires a human brain (and preferably a trained one). **R** will happily generate output based on any garbage you decide to feed into it and will not judge the results or give any indication of whether the model can be generalized or if it is valid. However, **R** provides the statistics necessary to judge these things, and at this point our brains must take over the job – which is slightly worrying (especially if your brain is as small as mine).

7.8.2. Multiple regression: running the basic model ②

7.8.2.1. Multiple regression using R Commander: the basic model ②

Imagine that the record company executive was now interested in extending the model of album sales to incorporate other variables. He decides to measure two new variables: (1) the number of times songs from the album are played on Radio 1 during the week prior to release (**airplay**); and (2) the attractiveness of the band (**attract**). Before an album is released, the executive notes the amount spent on advertising, the number of times songs from the album are played on radio the week before release, and the attractiveness of the band. He does this for 200 different albums (each made by a different band). Attractiveness was measured by asking a random sample of the target audience to rate the attractiveness of each band on a scale from 0 (hideous potato-heads) to 10 (gorgeous sex objects). The mode attractiveness given by the sample was used in the regression (because he was interested in what the majority of people thought, rather than the average of people's opinions). The data are in a file called **Album Sales 2.dat**.

	adverts	sales	airplay	attract
1	10.256	330	43	10
2	985.685	120	28	7
3	1445.563	360	35	7
4	1188.193	270	33	7
5	574.513	220	44	5
6	568.954	170	19	5
7	471.814	70	20	1
8	537.352	210	22	9
9	514.068	200	21	7
10	174.093	300	40	7
11	1720.806	290	32	7
12	611.479	70	20	2
13	251.192	150	24	8
14	97.972	190	38	6
15	406.814	240	24	7
16	265.398	100	25	5
17	1323.287	250	35	5
18	196.650	210	36	8
19	1326.598	280	27	8
20	1380.689	230	33	8
21	792.345	210	33	7
22	957.167	230	28	6
23	1789.659	320	30	9
24	656.137	210	34	7
25	613.697	230	49	7
26	313.362	250	40	8
27	336.510	60	20	4
28	1544.899	330	42	7
29	68.954	150	35	8
30	785.692	150	8	6

FIGURE 7.11
The **Album Sales 2.dat** data

To conduct a multiple regression using R Commander, first initiate the package by executing (and install it if you haven't – see section 3.6):

`library(Rcmdr)`

You can read the data file **Album Sales 2.dat** into **R** using the **Data** ⇒ **Import data** ⇒ **from text file, clipboard, or URL...** menu (see section 3.7.3). Then you can look at the data, by clicking on [View data set]. You should note that each variable has its own column (the same layout as for correlation) and each row represents a different album. So, the first album had £10,256 spent advertising it, sold 330,000 copies, received 43 plays on Radio 1 the week before release, and was made by a band that the majority of people rated as gorgeous sex objects (Figure 7.11).

The executive has past research indicating that advertising budget is a significant predictor of album sales, and so he should include this variable in the model first. His new variables (**airplay** and **attract**) should, therefore, be entered into the model *after* advertising budget. This method is hierarchical (the researcher decides in which order to enter variables into the model based on past research). The record executive needs to run two models. In his first model, the predictor will be **adverts**. In the second model, the predictors will be **adverts**, **airplay** and **attract**.

FIGURE 7.12
Dialog boxes for conducting multiple regression using R Commander

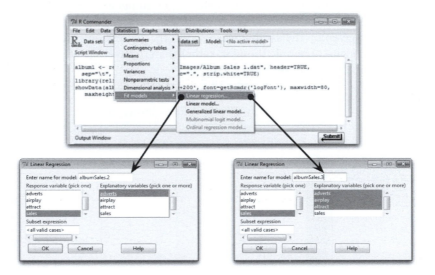

We can use R Commander to run the model by selecting **Statistics** ⇒ **Fit models** ⇒ **Linear regression...** (Figure 7.12). For the first model (left dialog box in Figure 7.12) we select **sales** as the response variable, and **adverts** as the explanatory variable. We have named this model *albumSales.2*. When you have selected your variables and named the model, click on [OK]. The resulting output is described in section 7.8.3.1.

For the second model we choose three explanatory variables, **adverts**, **attract** and **sales**. To select multiple variables you can either 'swipe' over all the variables you are interested in with the mouse (if they are next to each other), or hold down the *Ctrl* key (*cmd* on a Mac) while you click on each one (if they are not next to each other). When you have selected your variables and named the model, click on [OK]. The resulting output is also described in section 7.8.3.1.

7.8.2.2. Multiple regression using R: the basic model ②

First load the data file by setting your working directory to the location of the file (see section 3.4.4) and executing:

```
album2<-read.delim("Album Sales 2.dat", header = TRUE)
```

We can again run the regression analysis using the *lm()* function. We need to create two models: the first, *albumSales.2*, will have **adverts** as a predictor. The second, *albumSales.3*, will have **adverts**, **airplay** and **attract** as predictors.

The first model is the same as the one we created in section 7.4.2 and we can create it by executing the following command:

```
albumSales.2 <- lm(sales ~ adverts, data = album2)
```

To remind you, this creates a model called *albumSales.2*, in which the variable **sales** is predicted from the variable **adverts** (*sales ~ adverts*). The *data* = simply tells **R** which dataframe contains the variables we're using in the model.

To create the second model, we need to specify additional predictors, and we can do this in the same way that we added predictors to the regression equation itself: we simply use '+' to add them into the model. Therefore, if we want to predict **sales** from the variables **adverts**, **airplay** and **attract**, then our model is specified as *sales ~ adverts + airplay + attract*. It basically looks the same as the regression equation but without the *b*s. Therefore, to create this model we would execute:

```
albumSales.3 <- lm(sales ~ adverts + airplay + attract, data = album2)
```

This command creates a model *albumSales.3*, in which the variable **sales** is predicted from the variables **adverts**, **airplay** and **attract**. We could also have used the **update()** function to do this because this model is simply adding new predictors to the previous model (R's Souls' Tip 19.3).

R's Souls' Tip 7.2 The update() function②

Writing out the models in full can be helpful to understand how the *lm()* function works: I think it's useful to see how the code relates to the equation that describes the model. However, the *update()* function is a quicker way to add new things to old models. In our example our model *albumSales.3* is the same as the previous model, *albumSales.2*, except that we added two variables (**attract** and **airplay**). Look at the two model specifications:

```
albumSales.2 <- lm(sales ~ adverts, data = album2)
albumSales.3 <- lm(sales ~ adverts + airplay + attract, data = album2)
```

Note that they are identical except that the second model has two new variables added as predictors. Using the *update()* function we can create the second model in less text:

```
albumSales.3<-update(albumSales.2, .~. + airplay + attract)
```

This function, like the longhand one, creates a new model called *albumSales.3*, and it does this by updating an existing model. The first part of the parenthesis tells **R** *which* model to update (in this case we want to update the model called *albumSales.2*). The *.~.* means 'keep the outcome and predictors the same as the baseline model': the dots mean 'keep the same' so the fact that we put dots on both sides of the ~ means that we want to keep both the outcome and predictors the same as in the baseline model. The *+ airplay + attract* means 'add **airplay** and **attract** as predictors'. Therefore, '*.~. + airplay + attract*' can be interpreted as 'keep the same outcomes and predictors as the baseline model but add **airplay** and **attract** as predictors.

7.8.3. Interpreting the basic multiple regression ②

7.8.3.1. The model summary ②

To see the output of these models we need to use the *summary()* function (in which we simply place the name of the model). To see the output of our models, execute:

```
summary(albumSales.2)
summary(albumSales.3)
```

The summary of the *albumSales.2* model is shown in Output 7.2, whereas the summary of *albumSales.3* is in Output 7.3.

```
Call: lm(formula = sales ~ adverts, data = album2)

Residuals:
    Min       1Q   Median       3Q      Max
-152.949  -43.796   -0.393   37.040  211.866

Coefficients:
            Estimate Std. Error t value Pr(>|t|)
(Intercept) 1.341e+02  7.537e+00  17.799   <2e-16 ***
adverts     9.612e-02  9.632e-03   9.979   <2e-16 ***
---
Signif. codes:  0 '***' 0.001 '**' 0.01 '*' 0.05 '.' 0.1 ' ' 1

Residual standard error: 65.99 on 198 degrees of freedom
Multiple R-squared: 0.3346,       Adjusted R-squared: 0.3313
F-statistic: 99.59 on 1 and 198 DF,  p-value: < 2.2e-16
```

Output 7.2

```
Call: lm(formula = sales ~ adverts + airplay + attract, data = album2)

Residuals:
    Min       1Q   Median       3Q      Max
-121.324  -28.336   -0.451   28.967  144.132

Coefficients:
             Estimate Std. Error t value Pr(>|t|)
(Intercept) -26.612958  17.350001  -1.534    0.127
adverts       0.084885   0.006923  12.261  < 2e-16 ***
airplay       3.367425   0.277771  12.123  < 2e-16 ***
attract      11.086335   2.437849   4.548 9.49e-06 ***
---
Signif. codes:  0 '***' 0.001 '**' 0.01 '*' 0.05 '.' 0.1 ' ' 1

Residual standard error: 47.09 on 196 degrees of freedom
Multiple R-squared: 0.6647,       Adjusted R-squared: 0.6595
F-statistic: 129.5 on 3 and 196 DF,  p-value: < 2.2e-16
```

Output 7.3

Let's look first at the R^2 statistics at the bottom of each summary. This value describes the overall model (so it tells us whether the model is successful in predicting album sales). Remember that we ran two models: *albumSales.2* refers to the first stage in the hierarchy when only advertising budget is used as a predictor, *albumSales.3* refers to when all three predictors are used. At the beginning of each output, **R** reminds us of the command that we ran to get each model.

When only advertising budget is used as a predictor, the R^2 statistic is the square of simple correlation between advertising and album sales (0.578^2). In fact all of the statistics for *albumSales.2* are the same as the simple regression model earlier (see *albumSales.1* in section 7.5). The value of R^2, we already know, is a measure of how much of the variability in the outcome is accounted for by the predictors. For the first model its value is .335, which means that advertising budget accounts for 33.5% of the variation in album sales. However, when the other two predictors are included as well (*albumSales.3* in Output 7.3), this value increases to .665, or 66.5% of the variance in album sales. Therefore, if advertising accounts for 33.5%, we can tell that attractiveness and radio play account for an additional 33.0%.[10] So the inclusion of the two new predictors has explained quite a large amount of the variation in album sales.

The adjusted R^2 gives us some idea of how well our model generalizes, and ideally we would like its value to be the same, or very close to, the value of R^2. In this example the difference for the final model (Output 7.3) is small (in fact the difference between the values is $.665 - .660 = .005$ (about 0.5%)). This shrinkage means that if the model were derived from the population rather than a sample it would account for approximately 0.5% less variance in the outcome. Advanced students might like to apply Stein's formula to the R^2 to get some idea of its likely value in different samples. Stein's formula was given in equation (7.11) and can be applied by replacing n with the sample size (200) and k with the number of predictors (3):

$$\text{adjusted } R^2 = 1 - \left(\frac{200-1}{200-3-1} \times \frac{200-2}{200-3-2} \times \frac{200+1}{200} \right)(1-0.665)$$
$$= 1 - (1.015 \times 1.015 \times 1.005) \times 0.335$$
$$= 1 - 0.347$$
$$= 0.653$$

This value is very similar to the observed value of R^2 (.665), indicating that the cross-validity of this model is very good.

CRAMMING SAM'S TIPS **Model fit**

The fit of the regression model can be assessed with the model fit. Look for the R^2 to tell you the proportion of variance explained by the model. Multiply this value by 100 to give the percentage of variance explained by the model.

7.8.3.2. Model parameters ②

So far we have looked at the overall fit of the model. The next part of the output to consider is the parameters of the model. Now, the first step in our hierarchy was to include advertising budget (as we did for the simple regression earlier in this chapter) and so the parameters for the first model are identical to the parameters obtained in Output 7.1. Therefore, we

[10] That is, $33\% = 66.5\% - 33.5\%$ (this value is known as the R^2 *change*).

will be concerned only with the parameters for the final model (in which all predictors were included). Output 7.3 shows the estimate, standard error, *t*-value and *p*-value.

Remember that in multiple regression the model takes the form of equation (7.9) and in that equation there are several unknown quantities (the *b*-values). The first column gives us estimates for these *b*-values, and these values indicate the individual contribution of each predictor to the model (notice that in the first model, **R** is using the slightly annoying 1.341e+02 notation, which means 'move the decimal point two places to the right', so this value is equal to 134.1). If we replace the *b*-values in equation (7.9) we find that we can define the model as follows:

$$\text{sales}_i = b_0 + b_1\text{advertising}_i + b_2\text{airplay}_i + b_3\text{attractiveness}_i$$
$$= -26.61 + (0.08 \text{ advertising}_i) + (3.37 \text{ airplay}_i) + (11.09 \text{ attractiveness}_i)$$

The *b*-values tell us about the relationship between album sales and each predictor. If the value is positive we can tell that there is a positive relationship between the predictor and the outcome, whereas a negative coefficient represents a negative relationship. For these data all three predictors have positive *b*-values indicating positive relationships. So, as advertising budget increases, album sales increase; as plays on the radio increase, so do album sales; and finally more attractive bands will sell more albums. The *b*-values tell us more than this, though. They tell us to what degree each predictor affects the outcome *if the effects of all other predictors are held constant*:

- **Advertising budget** (*b* = 0.085): This value indicates that as advertising budget increases by one unit, album sales increase by 0.085 units. Both variables were measured in thousands; therefore, for every £1000 more spent on advertising, an extra 0.085 thousand albums (85 albums) are sold. This interpretation is true only if the effects of attractiveness of the band and airplay are held constant.

- **Airplay** (*b* = 3.367): This value indicates that as the number of plays on radio in the week before release increases by one, album sales increase by 3.367 units. Therefore, every additional play of a song on radio (in the week before release) is associated with an extra 3.367 thousand albums (3367 albums) being sold. This interpretation is true only if the effects of attractiveness of the band and advertising are held constant.

- **Attractiveness** (*b* = 11.086): This value indicates that a band rated one unit higher on the attractiveness scale can expect additional album sales of 11.086 units. Therefore, every unit increase in the attractiveness of the band is associated with an extra 11.086 thousand albums (11,086 albums) being sold. This interpretation is true only if the effects of radio airplay and advertising are held constant.

Each of these beta values has an associated standard error indicating to what extent these values would vary across different samples, and these standard errors are used to determine whether or not the *b*-value differs significantly from zero. As we saw in section 7.5.2, a *t*-statistic can be derived that tests whether a *b*-value is significantly different from 0. In simple regression, a significant value of *t* indicates that the slope of the regression line is significantly different from horizontal, but in multiple regression, it is not so easy to visualize what the value tells us. Well, it is easiest to conceptualize the *t*-tests as measures of whether the predictor is making a significant contribution to the model. Therefore, if the *t*-test associated with a *b*-value is significant (if the value in the column labelled $Pr(>|t|)$ is less than .05) then the predictor is making a significant contribution to the model. The smaller the value of $Pr(>|t|)$ (and the larger the value of *t*), the greater the contribution of that predictor. For this model, the advertising budget, $t(196) = 12.26$, $p < .001$, the amount of radio play prior to release, $t(196) = 12.12$, $p < .001$, and attractiveness of the band,

$t(196) = 4.55$, $p < .001$, are all significant predictors of album sales.[11] From the magnitude of the t-statistics we can see that the advertising budget and radio play had a similar impact, whereas the attractiveness of the band had less impact.

The b-values and their significance are important statistics to look at; however, the standardized versions of the b-values are in many ways easier to interpret (because they are not dependent on the units of measurement of the variables). To obtain the standardized beta estimates (usually denoted by β_i) we need to use a function called **lm.beta()**. This is found in the *QuantPsyc* package, and so you need to install and load this package (see section 7.3). All we need to do is to specify our model within this function and then execute it. Therefore, to get standardized betas for the *albumSales.3* model, we execute:

```
lm.beta(albumSales.3)
```

The resulting output is:

```
  adverts    airplay    attract
0.5108462  0.5119881  0.1916834
```

These estimates tell us the number of standard deviations by which the outcome will change as a result of one standard deviation change in the predictor. The standardized beta values are all measured in standard deviation units and so are directly comparable: therefore, they provide a better insight into the 'importance' of a predictor in the model. The standardized beta values for airplay and advertising budget are virtually identical (0.512 and 0.511, respectively) indicating that both variables have a comparable degree of importance in the model (this concurs with what the magnitude of the t-statistics told us).

- **Advertising budget** (*standardized* $\beta = .511$): This value indicates that as advertising budget increases by one standard deviation (£485,655), album sales increase by 0.511 standard deviations. The standard deviation for album sales is 80,699 and so this constitutes a change of 41,240 sales ($0.511 \times 80,699$). Therefore, for every £485,655 more spent on advertising, an extra 41,240 albums are sold. This interpretation is true only if the effects of attractiveness of the band and airplay are held constant.

- **Airplay** (*standardized* $\beta = .512$): This value indicates that as the number of plays on radio in the week before release increases by 1 standard deviation (12.27), album sales increase by 0.512 standard deviations. The standard deviation for album sales is 80,699 and so this constitutes a change of 41,320 sales ($0.512 \times 80,699$). Therefore, if Radio 1 plays the song an extra 12.27 times in the week before release, 41,320 extra album sales can be expected. This interpretation is true only if the effects of attractiveness of the band and advertising are held constant.

- **Attractiveness** (*standardized* $\beta = .192$): This value indicates that a band rated one standard deviation (1.40 units) higher on the attractiveness scale can expect additional album sales of 0.192 standard deviations units. This constitutes a change of 15,490 sales ($0.192 \times 80,699$). Therefore, a band with an attractiveness rating 1.40 higher than another band can expect 15,490 additional sales. This interpretation is true only if the effects of radio airplay and advertising are held constant.

Next we need to think about the confidence intervals. We know the estimate, the standard error of the estimate, and the degrees of freedom, and so it would be relatively straightforward to calculate the confidence intervals for each estimate. It would be even more

---

[11] For all of these predictors I wrote $t(196)$. The number in parentheses is the degrees of freedom. We saw in section 7.2.4 that in regression the degrees of freedom are $N - p - 1$, where N is the total sample size (in this case 200) and p is the number of predictors (in this case 3). For these data we get $200 - 3 - 1 = 196$.

straightforward to make **R** do that, using the **confint()** function. Again, we simply put the name of the regression model into the function and execute it; therefore, to get confidence intervals for the parameters in the model *albumSales.3*, we execute:

<code>confint(albumSales.3)</code>

The results are shown in Output 7.4. Imagine that we collected 100 samples of data measuring the same variables as our current model. For each sample we could create a regression model to represent the data. If the model is reliable then we hope to find very similar parameters in all samples. Therefore, each sample should produce approximately the same *b*-values. The confidence intervals of the unstandardized beta values are boundaries constructed such that in 95% of these samples these boundaries will contain the true value of *b* (see section 2.5.2). Therefore, if we'd collected 100 samples, and calculated the confidence intervals for *b*, we are saying that 95% of these confidence intervals would contain the true value of *b*. Therefore, we can be fairly confident that the confidence interval we have constructed for this sample will contain the true value of *b* in the population. This being so, a good model will have a small confidence interval, indicating that the value of *b* in this sample is close to the true value of *b* in the population. The sign (positive or negative) of the *b*-values tells us about the direction of the relationship between the predictor and the outcome. Therefore, we would expect a very bad model to have confidence intervals that cross zero, indicating that in some samples the predictor has a negative relationship to the outcome whereas in others it has a positive relationship. In this model, the two best predictors (advertising and airplay) have very tight confidence intervals, indicating that the estimates for the current model are likely to be representative of the true population values. The interval for attractiveness is wider (but still does not cross zero), indicating that the parameter for this variable is less representative, but nevertheless significant.

```
                    2.5 %        97.5 %
(Intercept) -60.82960967    7.60369295
adverts       0.07123166    0.09853799
airplay       2.81962186    3.91522848
attract       6.27855218   15.89411823
```

Output 7.4

CRAMMING SAM'S TIPS   Model parameters

The individual contribution of variables to the regression model can be found in the **Coefficients** part of the output from the *summary()* of the model. If you have done a hierarchical regression then look at the values for the final model. For each predictor variable, you can see if it has made a significant contribution to predicting the outcome by looking at the column labelled *Pr(>|t|)*: values less than .05 are significant. You should also look at the standardized beta values because these tell you the importance of each predictor (bigger absolute value = more important).

7.8.4.   Comparing models ②

We did a hierarchical regression, which means we need to compare the fit of the two models, and see if the R^2 is significantly higher in the second model than in the first. The significance of R^2 can be tested using an F-ratio, and this F is calculated from the following equation (in which N is the number of cases or participants, and k is the number of predictors in the model):

$$F = \frac{(N-k-1)R^2}{k(1-R^2)}$$

The first model (*albumSales.2*) causes R^2 to change from 0 to .335, and this change in the amount of variance explained gives rise to an F-ratio of 99.59, which is significant with a probability less than .001. Bearing in mind for this first model that we have only one predictor (so $k = 1$) and 200 cases ($N = 200$), this F comes from the equation above:

$$F_{\text{Model1}} = \frac{(200-1-1)0.334648}{1(1-0.334648)} = 99.587$$

The addition of the new predictors (*albumSales.3*) causes R^2 to increase by a further .330 (see above). We can calculate the F-ratio for this change using the same equation, but because we're looking at the change in models we use the change in R^2, R^2_{Change}, and the R^2 in the new model (model 2 in this case, so I've called it R^2_2) and we also use the change in the number of predictors, k_{Change} (model 1 had one predictor and model 2 had three predictors, so the change in the number of predictors is $3 - 1 = 2$), and the number of predictors in the new model, k_2 (in this case because we're looking at model 2):

$$\begin{aligned} F_{\text{Change}} &= \frac{(N-k_2-1)R^2_{\text{Change}}}{k_{\text{Change}}(1-R^2_2)} \\ &= \frac{(200-3-1)\times 0.330}{2(1-0.664668)} \\ &= 96.44 \end{aligned}$$

The degrees of freedom for this change are k_{Change} (in this case 2) and $N-k_2-1$ (in this case 196). As such, the change in the amount of variance that can be explained is significant, $F(2, 196) = 96.44$, $p < .001$. The change statistics therefore tell us about the difference made by adding new predictors to the model.

7.8.4.1. Comparing models with R Commander ②

To compare two hierarchical models using R Commander we choose **Models ⇒ Hypothesis tests ⇒ Compare two models...** (Figure 7.13). Note that there are two lists of models that we have previously created in the current session of R Commander. Both lists contain the same models, which are the *albumSales.1*, *albumSales.2*, and *albumSales.3* models. We want to compare *albumSales.2* with *albumSales.3* so we need to click on *albumSales.2* in the list labelled *First model (pick one)* and then click on *albumSales.3* in the list labelled *Second model (pick one)*. Once the two models are selected, click on OK to make the comparison. The resulting output is described in the following section.

FIGURE 7.13
Comparing regression models using **R** commander

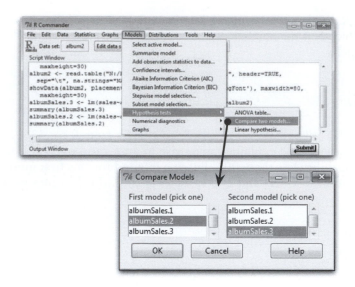

7.8.4.2. Comparing models using R ②

To compare models using **R** we use the **anova()** function, which takes the general form:

```
anova(model.1, model.2, … , model.n)
```

which simply means that we list the models that we want to compare in the order in which we want to compare them. It's worth noting that we can only compare hierarchical models; that is to say, the second model must contain everything that was in the first model plus something new, and the third model must contain everything in the second model plus something new, and so on. Using this principle, we can compare *albumSales.2* with *albumSales.3* by executing:

```
anova(albumSales.2, albumSales.3)
```

Output 7.5 shows the results of this comparison. Note that the value of *F* is 96.44, which is the same as the value that we calculated by hand at the beginning of this section. The value in column labelled *Pr(>F)* is 2.2e−16 (i.e., 2.2 with the decimal place moved 16 places to the left, or a very small value indeed); we can say that *albumSales.3* significantly improved the fit of the model to the data compared to *albumSales.2*, $F(2, 196) = 96.44$, $p < .001$.

```
Analysis of Variance Table

Model 1: album2$sales ~ album2$adverts
Model 2: album2$sales ~ album2$adverts + album2$airplay + album2$attract
  Res.Df    RSS Df  Sum of Sq    F      Pr(>F)
1    198 862264
2    196 434575  2     427690 96.447 < 2.2e-16 ***
---
Signif. codes:  0 '***' 0.001 '**' 0.01 '*' 0.05 '.' 0.1 ' ' 1
```

Output 7.5

CRAMMING SAM'S TIPS   **Assessing model improvement in hierarchical regression**

If you have done a hierarchical regression then you can assess the improvement of the model at each stage of the analysis by looking at the change in R^2 and testing whether this change is significant using the *anova()* function.

7.9. Testing the accuracy of your regression model ②

7.9.1. Diagnostic tests using R Commander ②

R Commander will allow you to run a range of diagnostic tests and other modifications to your model – these are found in the Models menu, shown in Figure 7.14. The menus are listed below with a brief description of what functions they enable you to access. We will not look at any particular function in detail because, in general, we think it is quicker to use commands, and we outline a general strategy for testing the accuracy of your regression model in the next two sections.

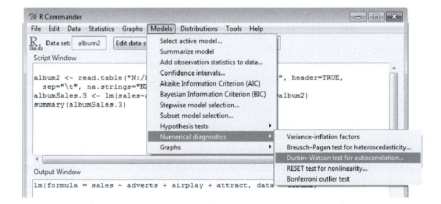

FIGURE 7.14
Regression diagnostics using R Commander

- **Select active model…**: This menu allows you to choose a regression model that you would like to get more information on.

- **Summarize model**: This command produces a summary of the model, by running the *summary()* function.

- **Add observation statistics to data…**: If you run this command, it will create the outlier detection statistics for each case, and then it will merge these into your original dataframe, creating new variables in the dataframe called **hatvalue**, **covratio**, etc.

- **Confidence intervals…**: Produces the confidence intervals for the model.

- **Akaike Information Criterion (AIC)**: This command will display the AIC for the model, which is used to select between models (see section 7.6.3).

- **Bayesian Information Criterion (BIC)**: We have not discussed the BIC in detail, but it is a similar measure to the AIC.

- **Stepwise model selection…**: Used for stepwise model selection to add and remove variables from the model to try to obtain the best fit possible, with the fewest variables. Usually not advised.

- **Subset model selection…**: Slightly (but only slightly) better than stepwise model selection, this tries combinations of variables to try to obtain the best fit, with various penalties for having too many variables.

- **Hypothesis tests**: This menu has three options. The first (**ANOVA table…**) produces sums of squares and *F*-statistics for each predictor variable in the model. You usually want type III sums of squares (see Jane Superbrain Box 11.1).[12] The second option (**Compare two models…**) allows you to do hierarchical regression by comparing the fit of two models. Finally the third option (**Linear hypothesis…**) is involved in analyses that go beyond the material in this chapter.

- **Numerical diagnostics**: This gives a number of other diagnostic tests, of which we have covered the **Variance inflation factors** (VIF) and **Durbin–Watson test**.

- **Graphs**: Several diagnostic graphs are available. It might surprise you, given its length and how long it has taken you to read, that there is anything not covered in this chapter, but we do not cover these graphs.

7.9.2.   Outliers and influential cases ②

The diagnostics that we have examined so far all relate to either the overall model, or to a specific variable. The other type of diagnostic we can look at relates to cases: each case (making up a row in the data set) has a value, hence these are called casewise diagnostics. These diagnostics were described in section 7.7.1. There are various functions that we can use to obtain different casewise diagnostics and in general they take the form of:

```
function(regressionModel)
```

In other words, all we need to do is place the name of our regression model (in this case *albumSales.3*) into the function and execute it. As we did earlier, we can distinguish these measures by whether they help us to identify outliers or influential cases:

- *Outliers*: Residuals can be obtained with the **resid()** function, standardized residuals with the **rstandard()** function and studentized residuals with the **rstudent()** function.

- *Influential cases*: Cook's distances can be obtained with the **cooks.distance()** function, DFBeta with the **dfbeta()** function, DFFit with the **dffits()** function, hat values (leverage) with the **hatvalues()** function, and the covariance ratio with the **covratio()** function.

If we merely execute these functions, **R** will print a long list of values to the console for us, which isn't very useful. Instead, we can store the values in the dataframe, which will enable us to look at them more easily. We can store them in the dataframe by simply creating a new variable within the dataframe and setting the value of this variable to be one of the functions we've just discussed. Remember from section 3.5.2, that to add a variable to a dataframe we execute a command with this general format:

```
dataFrameName$newVariableName<-newVariableData
```

In other words, we create the variable by specifying a name for it and appending this to the name of the dataframe to which we want to add it, then on the right-hand side of the command we specify what the variable contains (with some arithmetic or a function, etc.). Therefore, to create a variable in our *album2* dataframe that contains the residuals for each case, we would execute:

```
album2$residuals<-resid(albumSales.3)
```

[12] Statisticians can get quite hot under the collar about the different types of sums of squares. However, if you ask for type III sums of squares, you'll get the same *p*-values that you get in the model summary. That's why we like them here.

This creates a variable called **residuals** in the dataframe called *album2* (*album2$residuals*) that contains the residuals from the *albumSales.3* model (*resid(albumSales.3)*). Similarly, we can add all of the other residuals and casewise statistics by executing:

```
album2$standardized.residuals<- rstandard(albumSales.3)
album2$studentized.residuals<-rstudent(albumSales.3)
album2$cooks.distance<-cooks.distance(albumSales.3)
album2$dfbeta<-dfbeta(albumSales.3)
album2$dffit<-dffits(albumSales.3)
album2$leverage<-hatvalues(albumSales.3)
album2$covariance.ratios<-covratio(albumSales.3)
```

If you look at the data, you'll see that as well as the original variables, the dataframe now contains variables containing the casewise statistics. For example, if you execute:

```
album2
```

You will see the contents of the dataframe (I've edited the column names, suppressed some of the columns, and included only the first six rows of data):[13]

```
adverts  sales airplay attract resid    stz.r   stu.r cooks dfbeta
10.256   330    43       10    100.080  2.177   2.199 0.059 -5.422
985.685  120    28       7    -108.949 -2.323  -2.350 0.011  0.216
1445.563 360    35       7     68.442  1.469   1.473 0.011 -0.659
1188.193 270    33       7      7.024  0.150   0.150 0.000 -0.045
574.513  220    44       5     -5.753 -0.124  -0.123 0.000 -0.149
568.954  170    19       5     28.905  0.618   0.617 0.001  1.143
...       ...   ...      ...    ...     ...     ...   ...    ...
```

Having created these new variables it might be a good idea to save the data (see section 3.8), which we can do by executing:

```
write.table(album2, "Album Sales With Diagnostics.dat", sep = "\t", row.names
= FALSE)
```

First, let's look at the standardized residuals. I mentioned in section 7.7.1.1 that in an ordinary sample we would expect 95% of cases to have standardized residuals within about ±2. We have a sample of 200, therefore it is reasonable to expect about 10 cases (5%) to have standardized residuals outside these limits. One of the nice things about **R** is that it automatically considers those standardized residuals to be data, so we can examine them just like we examine data. For example, if you execute the command:

```
album2$standardized.residuals > 2 | album2$standardized.residuals < -2
```

then **R** will tell you for every case if the residual is less than −2 or greater than 2 (remember that the '|' symbol in the command means 'or', so the command asks 'is the standardized residual greater than 2 or smaller than −2?'). The command produces the following output:

```
TRUE   TRUE FALSE FALSE FALSE FALSE FALSE FALSE FALSE   TRUE FALSE FALSE
FALSE FALSE FALSE FALSE FALSE FALSE FALSE FALSE FALSE FALSE FALSE FALSE
FALSE FALSE FALSE FALSE FALSE FALSE FALSE FALSE FALSE FALSE FALSE FALSE
FALSE FALSE FALSE FALSE FALSE FALSE FALSE FALSE FALSE FALSE  TRUE FALSE
FALSE FALSE FALSE  TRUE FALSE FALSE TRUE FALSE FALSE FALSE FALSE FALSE
TRUE FALSE FALSE FALSE FALSE FALSE FALSE TRUE FALSE FALSE FALSE FALSE
FALSE FALSE FALSE FALSE FALSE FALSE FALSE FALSE FALSE FALSE FALSE FALSE
FALSE FALSE FALSE FALSE FALSE FALSE FALSE FALSE FALSE FALSE etc.
```

---

[13] To save space, I wanted the values rounded to 3 decimal places so I executed:

```
round(album2, digits = 3)
```

For each case, it tells us whether it is TRUE that they have a residual more than 2 or less than −2 (i.e., a large residual), or FALSE, that they do not (i.e., the residual falls between ± 2). As before, we can store this information as a new variable in our dataframe by executing:

```
album2$large.residual<-album2$standardized.residuals>2|album2$standardized.residuals < -2
```

Now we have a variable that we can use. To use it, it is useful to remember that **R** stores 'TRUE' as 1, and 'FALSE' as 0. Because of that, we can use the *sum()* function to get the sum of the variable **large.residual**, and this will be the number of cases with a large residual. To use the *sum()* function we simply enter into it the variable that we want to sum; therefore, to find out how many large residuals there are we can execute:

```
sum(album2$large.residual)
```

```
[1] 12
```

In other words, **R** will tell you that only 12 cases had a large residual (which we defined as one bigger than 2 or smaller than −2). It might be better to know not just how many cases there are, but also which cases they are. We can do this by selecting only those cases for which the variable **large.residual** is TRUE. Remember from section 3.9.1 that we can select parts of the data set by using *dataFrame[rows, columns]* in which we can specify conditions for *rows* and *columns* that tell **R** what we want to see. If we set rows to be *album2$large.residual*, then we will see only those rows for which **large.residual** is TRUE. If we don't want to see all of the columns, we could also list the columns that we do want to see by providing a list of variable names. For example, if we execute:

```
album2[album2$large.residual,c("sales", "airplay", "attract", "adverts", "standardized.residuals")]
```

we will see the variables (or columns) labelled **sales**, **airplay**, **attract**, **adverts** and **standardized.residuals** but only for cases for which large.residual is TRUE. Output 7.6 shows these values. From this output we can see that we have 12 cases (6%) that are outside of the limits: therefore, our sample is within 1% of what we would expect. In addition, 99% of cases should lie within ±2.5 and so we would expect only 1% of cases to lie outside of these limits. From the cases listed here, it is clear that two cases (1%) lie outside of the limits (cases 164 and 169). Therefore, our sample appears to conform to what we would expect for a fairly accurate model. These diagnostics give us no real cause for concern except that case 169 has a standardized residual greater than 3, which is probably large enough for us to investigate this case further.

We have saved a range of other casewise diagnostics from our model. One useful strategy is to use the casewise diagnostics to identify cases that you want to investigate further. Let's continue to look at the diagnostics for the cases of interest. Let's look now at the leverage (hat value), Cook's distance and covariance ratio for these 12 cases that have large residuals. We can do this by using the same command as before, but listing different variables (columns) in the data set:

```
album2[album2$large.residual , c("cooks.distance", "leverage", "covariance.ratios")]
```

Executing this command prints the variables (or columns) labelled **cooks.distance**, **leverage**, and **covariance.ratios** but only for cases for which large.residual is TRUE. Output 7.7 shows these values; none of them has a Cook's distance greater than 1 (even case 169 is well below this criterion), so none of the cases is having an undue influence on the model. The average leverage can be calculated as 0.02 ($k + 1/n = 4/200$) and so we are looking for values either twice as large as this (0.04) or three times as large (0.06) depending on which statistician you trust most (see section 7.7.1.2). All cases are within the boundary of three times the average and only case 1 is close to two times the average.

	sales	airplay	attract	adverts	standardized.residuals
1	330	43	10	10.256	2.177404
2	120	28	7	985.685	-2.323083
10	300	40	7	174.093	2.130289
47	40	25	8	102.568	-2.460996
52	190	12	4	405.913	2.099446
55	190	33	8	1542.329	-2.455913
61	300	30	7	579.321	2.104079
68	70	37	7	56.895	-2.363549
100	250	5	7	1000.000	2.095399
164	120	53	8	9.104	-2.628814
169	360	42	8	145.585	3.093333
200	110	20	9	785.694	-2.088044

Output 7.6

	cooks.distance	leverage	covariance.ratios
1	0.058703882	0.047190526	0.9712750
2	0.010889432	0.008006536	0.9201832
10	0.017756472	0.015409738	0.9439200
47	0.024115188	0.015677123	0.9145800
52	0.033159177	0.029213132	0.9599533
55	0.040415897	0.026103520	0.9248580
61	0.005948358	0.005345708	0.9365377
68	0.022288983	0.015708852	0.9236983
100	0.031364021	0.027779409	0.9588774
164	0.070765882	0.039348661	0.9203731
169	0.050867000	0.020821154	0.8532470
200	0.025134553	0.022539842	0.9543502

Output 7.7

There is also a column for the covariance ratio. We saw in section 7.7.1.2 that we need to use the following criteria:

- $CVR_i > 1 + [3(k + 1)/n] = 1 + [3(3 + 1)/200] = 1.06$;

- $CVR_i < 1 - [3(k + 1)/n] = 1 - [3(3 + 1)/200] = 0.94$.

Therefore, we are looking for any cases that deviate substantially from these boundaries. Most of our 12 potential outliers have CVR values within or just outside these boundaries. The only case that causes concern is case 169 (again) whose CVR is some way below the bottom limit. However, given the Cook's distance for this case, there is probably little cause for alarm.

You could have requested other diagnostic statistics and from what you know from the earlier discussion of them you would be well advised to glance over them in case of any unusual cases in the data. However, from this minimal set of diagnostics we appear to have a fairly reliable model that has not been unduly influenced by any subset of cases.

CRAMMING SAM'S TIPS **Influential cases**

You need to look for cases that might be influencing the regression model:

- Look at standardized residuals and check that no more than 5% of cases have absolute values above 2, and that no more than about 1% have absolute values above 2.5. Any case with a value above about 3 could be an outlier.
- Look at the values of Cook's distance: any value above 1 indicates a case that might be influencing the model.
- Calculate the average leverage (the number of predictors plus 1, divided by the sample size) and then look for values greater than twice or three times this average value.
- Calculate the upper and lower limit of acceptable values for the covariance ratio, CVR. The upper limit is 1 plus three times the average leverage, whereas the lower limit is 1 minus three times the average leverage. Cases that have a CVR falling outside these limits may be problematic.

7.9.3. Assessing the assumption of independence ②

In section 7.7.2.1 we discovered that we can test the assumption of independent errors using the Durbin–Watson test. We can obtain this statistic along with a measure of autocorrelation and a *p*-value in **R** using the **durbinWatsonTest()** (careful, that's a lower case *d* at the start, and upper case *W* and *T*) or, equivalently, **dwt()** function. All you need to do is to name your regression model within the function and execute it. So, for example, to see the Durbin–Watson test for our *albumSales.3* model, we would execute:

```
durbinWatsonTest(albumSales.3)
```

or

```
dwt(albumSales.3)
```

both of which do the same thing. As a conservative rule I suggested that values less than 1 or greater than 3 should definitely raise alarm bells. The closer to 2 that the value is, the better, and for these data (Output 7.8) the value is 1.950, which is so close to 2 that the assumption has almost certainly been met. The *p*-value of .7 confirms this conclusion (it is very much bigger than .05 and, therefore, not remotely significant). (The *p*-value is a little strange, because it is bootstrapped, and so, for complex reasons that we don't want to go into here, it is not always the same every time you run the command.)

```
lag Autocorrelation D-W Statistic p-value
  1      0.0026951     1.949819      0.7
 Alternative hypothesis: rho != 0
```

Output 7.8

7.9.4. Assessing the assumption of no multicollinearity ②

The VIF and tolerance statistics (with tolerance being 1 divided by the VIF) are useful statistics to assess collinearity. We can obtain the VIF using the **vif()** function. All we need to do is to specify the model name within the function; so, for example, to get the VIF statistics for the *albumSales.3* model, we execute:

```
vif(albumSales.3)
```

The tolerance doesn't have its own function, but we can calculate it very easily, if we remember that tolerance = 1/VIF. Therefore, we can get the values by executing:

```
1/vif(albumSales.3)
```

It can be useful to look at the average VIF too. To calculate the average VIF we can add the VIF values for each predictor and divide by the number of predictors (*k*):

$$\text{VIF} = \frac{\sum_{i=1}^{k} \overline{\text{VIF}}}{k} = \frac{1.015 + 1.043 + 1.038}{3} = 1.032$$

Alternatively, we can ask **R** to do it for us by placing the *vif* command above into the *mean()* function and executing:

```
mean(vif(albumSales.3))

vif(albumSales.3)

 adverts  airplay  attract
1.014593 1.042504 1.038455

1/vif(albumSales.3)

  adverts   airplay   attract
0.9856172 0.9592287 0.9629695

mean(vif(albumSales.3))

[1] 1.03185
```

Output 7.9

These statistics are shown in Output 7.9 (the VIF first, then the tolerance, then the mean VIF). There are a few guidelines from section 7.7.2.4 that can be applied here:

- If the largest VIF is greater than 10 then there is cause for concern (Bowerman & O'Connell, 1990; Myers, 1990).
- If the average VIF is substantially greater than 1 then the regression may be biased (Bowerman & O'Connell, 1990).
- Tolerance below 0.1 indicates a serious problem.
- Tolerance below 0.2 indicates a potential problem (Menard, 1995).

For our current model the VIF values are all well below 10 and the tolerance statistics all well above 0.2. Also, the average VIF is very close to 1. Based on these measures we can safely conclude that there is no collinearity within our data.

CRAMMING SAM'S TIPS   **Checking for multicollinearity**

To check for multicollinearity, use the VIF values. If these values are less than 10 then that indicates there probably isn't cause for concern. If you take the average of VIF values, and this average is not substantially greater than 1, then that also indicates that there's no cause for concern.

7.9.5.   Checking assumptions about the residuals ②

As a final stage in the analysis, you should visually check the assumptions that relate to the residuals (or errors). For a basic analysis it is worth plotting the standardized residual (y-axis) against the predicted value (x-axis), because this plot is useful to determine whether the assumptions of random errors and homoscedasticity have been met. If we wanted to produce high-quality graphs for publication we would use *ggplot2()* – see R's Souls' Tip 7.3. However, if we're just looking at these graphs to check our assumptions, we'll use the simpler (but not as nice) **plot()** and **hist()** functions.

The first useful graph is a plot of fitted values against residuals. This should look like a random array of dots evenly dispersed around zero. If this graph funnels out, then the chances are that there is heteroscedasticity in the data. If there is any sort of curve in this graph then the chances are that the data have violated the assumption of linearity. Figure 7.15 shows several examples of plots of standardized predicted values against standardized residuals. The top left panel shows a situation in which the assumptions of linearity and homoscedasticity have been met. The top right panel shows a similar plot for a data set that violates the assumption of homoscedasticity. Note that the points form the shape of a funnel so they become more spread out across the graph. This funnel shape is typical of heteroscedasticity and indicates increasing variance across the residuals. The bottom left panel shows a plot of some data in which there is a non-linear relationship between the outcome and the predictor. This pattern is shown up by the residuals. There is a clear curvilinear trend in the residuals. Finally, the bottom right panel illustrates a situation in which the data not only represent a non-linear relationship, but also show heteroscedasticity. Note first the curved trend in the data, and then also note that at one end of the plot the points are very close together whereas at the other end they are widely dispersed. When these assumptions have been violated you will not see these exact patterns, but hopefully these plots will help you to understand the types of anomalies you should look out for.

It is easy to get this plot in **R**: we can simply enter the name of the regression model into the *plot()* function. One of the clever things about **R** is that when you ask it to perform an action on something, it looks at what that something is before it decides what to do. For example, when we ask **R** to summarize something, using *summary(x)*, if x is a continuous variable it will give the mean, but if x is a factor (categorical) variable, it will give counts. And if x is a regression model, it gives the parameters, R^2, and a couple of other things. The same happens when we use *plot()*. When you specify a regression model in the *plot()* function, **R** decides that you probably want to see four plots – the first of which is the residuals plotted against the fitted values.

This plot is shown in Figure 7.16; compare this plot to the examples shown in Figure 7.15. Hopefully, it's clear to you that the graph for the residuals in our album sales model shows a fairly random pattern, which is indicative of a situation in which the assumptions of linearity, randomness and homoscedasticity have been met.

The second plot that is produced by the *plot()* function is a Q-Q plot, which shows up deviations from normality (see Chapter 5). The straight line in this plot represents a normal distribution, and the points represent the observed residuals. Therefore, in a perfectly normally distributed data set, all points will lie on the line. This is pretty much what we see for the record sales data (Figure 7.17, left-hand side). However, next to the normal probability plot of the record sales data is an example of a plot for residuals that deviate from normality. In this plot, the dots are very distant from the line (at the extremes), which indicates a deviation from normality (in this particular case skew).

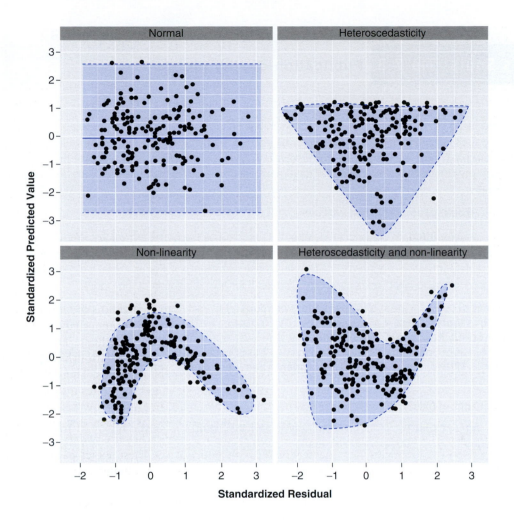

FIGURE 7.15
Plots of predicted (fitted) values against standardized residuals

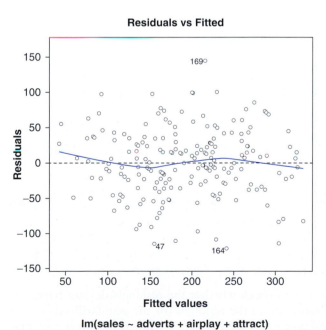

FIGURE 7.16
Plot of residuals against predicted (fitted) values for the album sales model

R's Souls' Tip 7.3 **Publication-quality plots②**

The model that is produced by *lm()* is a type of data set, which has variables in it. One of those variables is the predicted (or fitted) values for each case. It's called *fitted.values*, and we can refer to it just like we refer to any other variable, by using a $ sign: so, *albumSales.3$fitted.values* gives us the predicted values of the model *albumSales.3*. We can save these values in our original dataframe just as we did for the other casewise diagnostic variables by executing:

```
album2$fitted <- albumSales.3$fitted.values
```

We now have a new variable, **fitted**, in our original dataframe that contains the predicted values. We also have the studentized residuals stored in the variable **studentized.residuals**. Using what we learnt in Chapters 4 and 5, we can therefore create publication-standard plots by using these two variables. For example, we could plot a histogram of the studentized residuals by executing (see Chapter 5 for an explanation of this code):

```
histogram<-ggplot(album2, aes(studentized.residuals)) + opts(legend.position = "none") + geom_histogram(aes(y = ..density..), colour = "black", fill = "white") + labs(x = "Studentized Residual", y = "Density")
histogram + stat_function(fun = dnorm, args = list(mean = mean(album2$studentized.residuals, na.rm = TRUE), sd = sd(album2$studentized.residuals, na.rm = TRUE)), colour = "red", size = 1)
```

We could create a Q-Q plot of these values by executing:

```
qqplot.resid <- qplot(sample = album2$studentized.residuals, stat="qq") + labs(x = "Theoretical Values", y = "Observed Values")
```

Finally, we could plot a scatterplot of studentized residuals against predicted values by executing:

```
scatter <- ggplot(album2, aes(fitted, studentized.residuals))
scatter + geom_point() + geom_smooth(method = "lm", colour = "Blue")+ labs(x = "Fitted Values", y = "Studentized Residual")
```

The resulting graphs look like this:

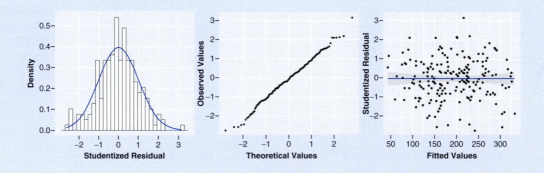

Another useful way to check whether the residuals deviate from a normal distribution is to inspect the histogram of the residuals (or the standardized or studentized residuals). We can obtain this plot easily using the *hist()* function. We simply place a variable name

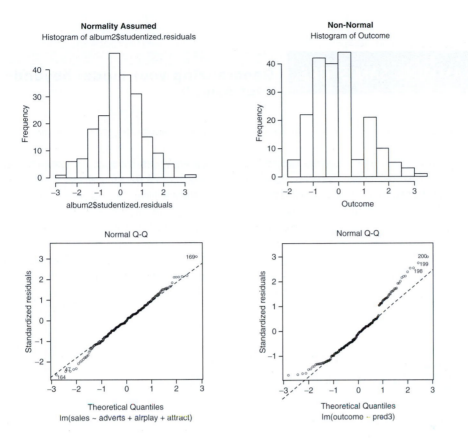

FIGURE 7.17

Histograms and Q-Q plots of normally distributed residuals (left-hand side) and non-normally distributed residuals (right-hand side)

into this function and it will plot us a histogram. We saved the studentized residuals in our dataframe earlier so we could enter this variable into the function and execute it:

```
hist(album2$studentized.residuals)
```

If you haven't saved the studentized residuals into your dataframe you can generate the same plot by entering the *rstudent()* function that we used earlier directly into *hist()*:

```
hist(rstudent(albumSales.3))
```

Figure 7.17 shows the histogram of the data for the current example (left-hand side). The histogram should look like a normal distribution (a bell-shaped curve). For the record company data, the distribution is roughly normal. Compare this histogram to the non-normal histogram next to it and it should be clear that the non-normal distribution is skewed (asymmetrical). So, you should look for a distribution that has the same shape as the one for the album sales data: any deviation from this shape is a sign of non-normality – the greater the deviation, the more non-normally distributed the residuals. For both the histogram and normal Q-Q plots, the non-normal examples are extreme cases and you should be aware that the deviations from normality are likely to be subtler.

We could summarize by saying that the model appears, in most senses, to be both accurate for the sample and generalizable to the population. Therefore, we could conclude that in our sample advertising budget and airplay are fairly equally important in predicting album sales. Attractiveness of the band is a significant predictor of album sales but is less important than the other two predictors (and probably needs verification because of possible heteroscedasticity). The assumptions seem to have been met and so we can probably assume that this model would generalize to any album being released.

CRAMMING SAM'S TIPS **Generalizing your model beyond your sample**

You need to check some of the assumptions of regression to make sure your model generalizes beyond your sample:

- Look at the graph of the standardized residuals plotted against the fitted (predicted) values. If it looks like a random array of dots then this is good. If the dots seem to get more or less spread out over the graph (look like a funnel) then this is probably a violation of the assumption of homogeneity of variance. If the dots have a pattern to them (i.e., a curved shape) then this is probably a violation of the assumption of linearity. If the dots seem to have a pattern and are more spread out at some points on the plot than others then this probably reflects violations of both homogeneity of variance *and* linearity. Any of these scenarios puts the validity of your model into question. Repeat the above for all partial plots too.
- Look at a histogram of the residuals too. If the histogram looks like a normal distribution (and the Q-Q plot looks like a diagonal line), then all is well. If the histogram looks non-normal, then things are less good. Be warned, though: distributions can look very non-normal in small samples even when they are normal!

7.9.6. What if I violate an assumption? ②

It's worth remembering that you can have a perfectly good model for your data (no out-liers, influential cases, etc.) and you can use that model to draw conclusions about your sample, even if your assumptions are violated. However, it's much more interesting to generalize your regression model and this is where assumptions become important. If they have been violated then you cannot generalize your findings beyond your sample. The options for correcting for violated assumptions are a bit limited. If residuals show problems with heteroscedasticity or non-normality you could try transforming the raw data – but this won't necessarily affect the residuals. If you have a violation of the linearity assumption then you could see whether you can do logistic regression instead (described in the next chapter). Finally, you could do a robust regression, and this topic is next on our agenda.

7.10. Robust regression: bootstrapping ③

We saw in Section 6.5.7 that we could bootstrap our estimate of a correlation to obtain the statistical significance and confidence intervals, and that this meant we could relax the distributional assumptions. We can do the same thing with regression estimates. When I showed you how to bootstrap correlations, we used the *boot* package, and we're going to use the same procedure again.[14]

We first encountered bootstrapping and the *boot()* function in Chapter 6, but it won't hurt to recap. When we use the *boot()* function, it takes the general form of:

```
object<-boot(data, function, replications)
```

---

[14] There is a package called *simpleboot*, which has a function called *lm.boot()*. However, at the time of writing, although *simpleboot* is very easy to use to bootstrap, obtaining things like the confidence intervals after you have bootstrapped is much harder.

in which *data* specifies the dataframe you want to use, *function* is the function you want to bootstrap, and *replications* is the number of bootstrap samples you want to use. (More is always better, but takes longer – I find 2000 to be a nice compromise.)

As we did for correlations, we need to write a function (R's Souls' Tip 6.2) we want to bootstrap. We'll write one called *bootReg()* – this function is a little more complex than the function we wrote for the correlation, because we are interested in more than one statistic (we have an intercept and three slope parameters to bootstrap). The function we need to execute is:

```
bootReg <- function (formula, data, indices)
{
d <- data [i,]
fit <- lm(formula, data = d)
return(coef(fit))
}
```

Executing this command creates an object called *bootReg*. The first bit of the function tells **R** what input to expect in the function: in this case we need to feed into the function a regression formula (just like what we'd put into the *lm()* function, so something like *y* ~ *a* + *b*), a dataframe, and a variable that has been called *i* (which refers to a particular bootstrap sample, just as it did in the correlation example). Let's look at what the bits of the function do:

- *d <- data [i,]*: This creates a dataframe called *d*, which is a subset of the dataframe entered into the function. The *i* again refers to a particular bootstrap sample.

- *fit <- lm(formula, data = d)*: This creates a regression model called *fit* using the *lm()* function (notice that the formula that we enter into the *bootReg* function is used within *lm()* to generate the model).

- *return(coef(fit))*: The *return()* function, as the name suggests, just determines what our function *bootReg* returns to us. The function *coef()* is one that extracts the coefficients from a regression object; therefore, *return(coef(fit))* means that the output of *bootReg* will be the intercept and any slope coefficients for predictors in the model.

Having created this function (remember to execute the code), we can use the function to obtain the bootstrap samples:

```
bootResults<-boot(statistic = bootReg, formula = sales ~ adverts + airplay +
attract, data = album2, R = 2000)
```

Executing this command creates an object called *bootResults* that contains the bootstrap samples. We use the *boot()* function to get these. Within this function we tell it to use the function *bootReg()* that we just created (*statistic = bootReg*); because that function requires a formula and dataframe, we specify the model as we did for the original model (*formula = sales ~ adverts + airplay + attract*), and name the dataframe (*data = album2*). As such, everything in the *boot()* function is something that we specified as being necessary input for the *bootReg()* function when we defined it. The only new thing is *R*, which sets the number of bootstrap samples (in this case we have set it to 2000, which means we will throw these instructions into the *bootReg()* function 2000 different times and save the results in *bootResults* each time.

Instead of one statistic, we need to obtain bootstrap confidence intervals for the intercept, and the three slopes for **advert**, **airplay** and **attract**. We can do this with the *boot.ci()* function that we encountered in Chapter 6. However, **R** doesn't know the names of the statistics in *bootResults*, so we instead have to use their location in the *bootResults* object (because **R** does know this information). The intercept is the first thing in *bootResults*, so to obtain the bootstrapped confidence interval for the intercept we use index = 1:

```
boot.ci(bootResults, type = "bca", index = 1)
```

Note that we enter the object from which the confidence intervals will come (*bootResults*), and *index* to tell **R** where in bootResults to look (*index = 1*), and specify the type of confidence interval that we want (in this case bias corrected and accelerated, *type = "bca"*). The locations of the coefficients for **adverts**, **airplay** and **attract** are given by *index* values of 2, 3 and 4, respectively, so we can get the bootstrap confidence intervals for those predictors by executing:

```
boot.ci(bootResults, type = "bca", index = 2)
boot.ci(bootResults, type = "bca", index = 3)
boot.ci(bootResults, type = "bca", index = 4)
```

```
BOOTSTRAP CONFIDENCE INTERVAL CALCULATIONS
Based on 2000 bootstrap replicates

CALL :
boot.ci(boot.out = bootResults, type = "bca", index = 1)

Intervals :
Level       BCa
95%   (-58.49,    5.17 )
Calculations and Intervals on Original Scale

> boot.ci(bootResults , type="bca", index=2)

BOOTSTRAP CONFIDENCE INTERVAL CALCULATIONS
Based on 2000 bootstrap replicates

CALL :
boot.ci(boot.out = bootResults, type = "bca", index = 2)

Intervals :
Level       BCa
95%   ( 0.0715,  0.0992 )
Calculations and Intervals on Original Scale

> boot.ci(bootResults , type="bca", index=3)

BOOTSTRAP CONFIDENCE INTERVAL CALCULATIONS
Based on 2000 bootstrap replicates

CALL :
boot.ci(boot.out = bootResults, type = "bca", index = 3)

Intervals :
Level       BCa
95%   ( 2.736,  3.980 )
Calculations and Intervals on Original Scale

> boot.ci(bootResults , type="bca", index=4)

BOOTSTRAP CONFIDENCE INTERVAL CALCULATIONS
Based on 2000 bootstrap replicates
CALL :
boot.ci(boot.out = bootResults, type = "bca", index = 4)
```

```
Intervals :
Level       BCa
95%   ( 6.52, 15.32 )
Calculations and Intervals on Original Scale
```

Output 7.10

This gives us Output 7.10, which shows the confidence interval for the intercept is from −58.49 to 5.17 (remember that because of how bootstrapping works, you won't get exactly the same result as me, but it should be very close). Compare that with the confidence interval we found using the plug-in approach, shown in Output 7.4, which was from −60.83 to 7.60; the bootstrap results are pretty close.

The first predictor (but second variable) was **adverts**. The plug-in approach gave us a confidence interval from 0.071 to 0.099; the bootstrap confidence interval is from 0.072 to 0.099. Next came **airplay**, which had a plug-in confidence interval from 2.82 to 3.92 and a bootstrap confidence interval from 2.74 to 3.98. Finally, **attract** had a plug-in confidence interval from 6.28 to 15.89 and a bootstrap confidence interval from 6.52 to 15.32. All of the bootstrap confidence intervals are very close to the plug-in confidence intervals, suggesting that we did not have a problem of non-normal distribution in the model.

7.11. How to report multiple regression ②

If you follow the American Psychological Association guidelines for reporting multiple regression then the implication seems to be that tabulated results are the way forward. The APA also seem in favour of reporting, as a bare minimum, the standardized betas, their significance value and some general statistics about the model (such as the R^2). If you do decide to do a table then the beta values and their standard errors are also very useful. Personally I'd like to see the constant as well because then readers of your work can construct the full regression model if they need to. Also, if you've done a hierarchical regression you should report these values at each stage of the hierarchy. So, basically, you want to reproduce the table labelled *Estimates* from the output and omit some of the non-essential information. For the example in this chapter we might produce a table like that in Table 7.2.

Look back through the output in this chapter and see if you can work out from where the values came. Things to note are: (1) I've rounded off to 2 decimal places throughout; (2) in line with APA convention, I've omitted 0 from the probability values, as these cannot exceed 1. All other values can, so the 0 is included.

Table 7.2 How to report multiple regression

	ΔR^2	B	SE B	β	P
Step 1	0.34				<.001
Constant		134.14	7.54		<.001
Advertising budget		0.10	0.01	0.58*	<.001
Step 2	0.33				<.001
Constant		−26.61	17.35		.127
Advertising budget		0.09	0.01	0.51*	<.001
Plays on BBC Radio 1		3.37	0.28	0.51*	<.001
Attractiveness		11.09	2.44	0.19*	<.001

Labcoat Leni's Real Research 7.1   Why do you like your lecturers? ①

Chamorro-Premuzic, T., et al. (2008). *Personality and Individual Differences, 44*, 965–976.

In the previous chapter we encountered a study by Chamorro-Premuzic et al. in which they measured students' personality characteristics and asked them to rate how much they wanted these same characteristics in their lecturers (see Labcoat Leni's Real Research 6.1 for a full description). In that chapter we correlated these scores; however, we could go a step further and see whether students' personality characteristics predict the characteristics that they would like to see in their lecturers.

The data from this study are in the file **Chamorro-Premuzic.dat**. Labcoat Leni wants you to carry out five multiple regression analyses: the outcome variable in each of the five analyses is how much students want to see

neuroticism, extroversion, openness to experience, agreeableness and conscientiousness. For each of these outcomes, force Age and Gender into the analysis in the first step of the hierarchy, then in the second block force in the five student personality traits (Neuroticism, Extroversion, Openness to experience, Agreeableness and Conscientiousness). For each analysis create a table of the results.

Answers are in the additional material on the companion website (or look at Table 4 in the original article).

7.12. Categorical predictors and multiple regression ③

Often in regression analysis you'll collect data about groups of people (e.g., ethnic group, gender, socio-economic status, diagnostic category). You might want to include these groups as predictors in the regression model; however, we saw from our assumptions that variables need to be continuous or categorical with only two categories. We saw in section 6.5.7 that a point-biserial correlation is Pearson's *r* between two variables when one is continuous and the other has two categories coded as 0 and 1. We've also learnt that simple regression is based on Pearson's *r*, so it shouldn't take a great deal of imagination to see that, like the point-biserial correlation, we could construct a regression model with a predictor that has two categories (e.g., gender). Likewise, it shouldn't be too inconceivable that we could then extend this model to incorporate several predictors that had two categories. All that is important is that we code the two categories with the values of 0 and 1. Why is it important that there are only two categories and that they're coded 0 and 1? Actually, I don't want to get into this here because this chapter is already too long, the publishers are going to break my legs if it gets any longer, and I explain it anyway later in the book (sections 9.4.2 and 10.2.3), so, for the time being, just trust me!

7.12.1. Dummy coding ③

The obvious problem with wanting to use categorical variables as predictors is that often you'll have more than two categories. For example, if you'd measured religious affiliation you might have categories of Muslim, Jewish, Hindu, Catholic, Buddhist, Protestant, Jedi (for those of you not in the UK, we had a census here in 2001 in which a significant portion of people put down Jedi as their religion). Clearly these groups cannot be distinguished using a single variable coded with zeros and ones. In these cases we can use what we call **dummy variables.** Dummy coding is a way of representing groups of people using only zeros and ones. To do it, we have to create several variables; in fact, the number of variables we need is one less than the number of groups we're recoding. There are eight basic steps:

1 Count the number of groups you want to recode and subtract 1.

2 Create as many new variables as the value you calculated in step 1. These are your dummy variables.

3 Choose one of your groups as a baseline (i.e., a group against which all other groups should be compared). This should usually be a control group, or, if you don't have a specific hypothesis, it should be the group that represents the majority of people (because it might be interesting to compare other groups against the majority).

4 Having chosen a baseline group, assign that group values of 0 for all of your dummy variables.

5 For your first dummy variable, assign the value 1 to the first group that you want to compare against the baseline group. Assign all other groups 0 for this variable.

6 For the second dummy variable assign the value 1 to the second group that you want to compare against the baseline group. Assign all other groups 0 for this variable.

7 Repeat this until you run out of dummy variables.

8 Place all of your dummy variables into the regression analysis!

Let's try this out using an example. In Chapter 4 we came across an example in which a biologist was worried about the potential health effects of music festivals. She collected some data at the Download Festival, which is a music festival specializing in heavy metal. The biologist was worried that the findings that she had were a function of the fact that she had tested only one type of person: metal fans. Perhaps it's not the festival that makes people smelly, maybe it's only metal fans at festivals that get smellier (as a metal fan, I would at this point sacrifice the biologist to Satan for being so prejudiced). Anyway, to answer this question she went to another festival that had a more eclectic clientele. The Glastonbury Music Festival attracts all sorts of people because many styles of music are performed there. Again, she measured the hygiene of concert-goers over the three days of the festival using a technique that results in a score ranging between 0 (you smell like you've bathed in sewage) and 4 (you smell of freshly baked bread). Now, in Chapters 4 and 5, we just looked at the distribution of scores for the three days of the festival, but now the biologist wanted to look at whether the type of music you like (your cultural group) predicts whether hygiene decreases over the festival. The data are in the file called **GlastonburyFestivalRegression. dat**. This file contains the hygiene scores for each of three days of the festival, but it also contains a variable called **change**, which is the change in hygiene over the three days of the festival (so it's the change from day 1 to day 3).[15] Finally, the biologist categorized people according to their musical affiliation: if they mainly liked alternative music she called them 'indie kid', if they mainly liked heavy metal she called them a 'metaller', and if they mainly liked hippy/folky/ambient type music then she labelled them a 'crusty'. Anyone not falling into these categories was labelled 'no musical affiliation'.

The first thing we should do is calculate the number of dummy variables. We have four groups, so there will be three dummy variables (one less than the number of groups). Next we need to choose a baseline group. We're interested in comparing those who have different musical affiliations against those who don't, so our baseline category will be 'no musical affiliation'. We give this group a code of 0 for all of our dummy variables. For our first

---

[15] Not everyone could be measured on day 3, so there is a change score only for a subset of the original sample.

dummy variable, we could look at the 'crusty' group, and to do this we give anyone that was a crusty a code of 1, and everyone else a code of 0. For our second dummy variable, we could look at the 'metaller' group, and to do this we give anyone that was a metaller a code of 1, and everyone else a code of 0. We have one dummy variable left and this will have to look at our final category: 'indie kid'; we give anyone who was an indie kid a code of 1, and everyone else a code of 0. The resulting coding scheme is shown in Table 7.3. The thing to note is that each group has a code of 1 on only one of the dummy variables (except the base category that is always coded as 0).

Table 7.3 Dummy coding for the Glastonbury Festival data

	Dummy Variable 1	Dummy Variable 2	Dummy Variable 3
Crusty	1	0	0
Indie Kid	0	1	0
Metaller	0	0	1
No Affiliation	0	0	0

This being **R**, there are several ways to code dummy variables. We're going to have a look at the **contrasts()** function, because we will use it time and time again later in the book. First let's load the data by executing:

```
gfr<-read.delim(file="GlastonburyFestivalRegression.dat", header = TRUE)
```

This creates a dataframe called *gfr* (because we didn't want to have to keep typing *glastonburyFestivalRegression*). These data look like this (the first 10 cases only):

```
   ticknumb                 music day1 day2 day3 change
1      2111               Metaller 2.65 1.35 1.61  -1.04
2      2229                 Crusty 0.97 1.41 0.29  -0.68
3      2338 No Musical Affiliation 0.84   NA   NA     NA
4      2384                 Crusty 3.03   NA   NA     NA
5      2401 No Musical Affiliation 0.88 0.08   NA     NA
6      2405                 Crusty 0.85   NA   NA     NA
7      2467              Indie Kid 1.56   NA   NA     NA
8      2478              Indie Kid 3.02   NA   NA     NA
9      2490                 Crusty 2.29   NA   NA     NA
10     2504 No Musical Affiliation 1.11 0.44 0.55  -0.56
```

Note that the variable **music** contains text; therefore, **R** has intelligently decided to create this variable as a factor, and treat the levels in alphabetical order (level 1 = crusty, level 2 = indie kid, 3 = metaller, and 4 = no musical affiliation). We can use the *contrast()* function on this variable to set contrasts because it is a factor. There are several built-in contrasts that we can set (these are described in Chapter 10, Table 10.6, when we get into this topic in more detail). For now, all I'll say is that in a situation in which we want to compare all groups to a baseline we can execute this command:

```
contrasts(gfr$music)<-contr.treatment(4, base = 4)
```

The *contrasts(gfr$music)* simply sets the contrast for the variable **music** in the *gfr* dataframe. The **contr.treatment()** function sets a contrast based on comparing all groups to a baseline (a.k.a. treatment) condition. This function takes the general form:

```
contr.treatment(number of groups, base = number representing the baseline group)
```

Therefore, in our command we have told **R** that there are four groups, and to use the last group as the baseline condition. We can see what this command has done by looking at the **music** variable by executing:

```
gfr$music
```

Note that it now has a *contrasts* attribute:

```
attr(,"contrasts")
                      1 2 3
Crusty                1 0 0
Indie Kid             0 1 0
Metaller              0 0 1
No Musical Affiliation 0 0 0
Levels: Crusty Indie Kid Metaller No Musical Affiliation
```

You can see three contrasts that related to those that we discussed in Table 7.3. This method is the quickest way, but personally I prefer to set the contrasts manually. This preference is not masochism, but because you can then give your contrasts informative names (there is nothing worse than seeing an output with 'contrast1' in it and having no idea what contrast 1 is). To do this, we create variables that reflect each of the dummy variables in Table 7.3:

```
crusty_v_NMA<-c(1, 0, 0, 0)
indie_v_NMA<-c(0, 1, 0, 0)
metal_v_NMA<-c(0, 0, 1, 0)
```

We have created three variables, the first (*crusty_v_NMA*) contains the codes for the first dummy variable. Note that we have listed the codes in the order of the factor levels for **music** (so, the first group, crusty, gets a code of 1, the others a code of 0) and given it a name that reflects what it compares (crusty vs. no musical affiliation); therefore, when we see it in the output we will know what it represents. Similarly, the second variable (*indie_v_NMA*) contains the codes for the second dummy variable. Again we list the codes in the order of the factor levels for **music** (so, the second group, indie kid, gets a code of 1, the others a code of 0). You get the idea.

Having created the dummy variables, we can bind them together using *cbind()* – see R's Souls' Tip 3.5 – and set them as the contrasts in a similar way to before, by executing:

```
contrasts(gfr$music)<-cbind(crusty_v_NMA, indie_v_NMA, metal_v_NMA)
```

When we inspect the **music** variable now, it again has the same contrasts, but they have more helpful names than before:

```
attr(,"contrasts")
                       crusty_v_NMA indie_v_NMA metal_v_NMA
Crusty                            1           0           0
Indie Kid                         0           1           0
Metaller                          0           0           1
No Musical Affiliation            0           0           0
Levels: Crusty Indie Kid Metaller No Musical Affiliation
```

7.12.2. Regression with dummy variables ③

Now you've created the dummy variables, you can run the regression in the same way as for any other kind of regression, by executing:

```
glastonburyModel<-lm(change ~ music, data = gfr)
```

```
summary(glastonburyModel)
```

The fact that we have set contrasts for the variable **music** means that the three dummy variables will be entered into the model in a single step. This is one reason why setting contrasts is a useful way to handle categorical predictors (but see R's Souls' Tip 7.4).

R's Souls' Tip 7.4 A small confession ②

Before we move on, I have a small confession to make. **R** will actually dummy-code your data for you. When you put a variable as a predictor into a regression, **R** looks to see what kind of variable it is. Most variables in **R** are considered 'numeric'. But some variables are considered to be 'factors' – a factor is a variable that **R** knows to be categorical. I mentioned that when we loaded the data **R** would intelligently create the variable **music** as a factor. If you enter a string variable or a factor into a regression equation, **R** knows that it is categorical, and so will dummy-code it for you. So, you can skip all the dummy coding nonsense and simply execute:

```
lm(change ~ music, data = gfr)
```

So why didn't I tell you that to start with? There are three reasons. First, to interpret the results you need to understand what **R** is doing. Second, we often want to decide what category is going to be the reference category when we create the dummy variables, based on the meaning of the data. **R** doesn't know what the data mean (it's not *that* clever), so it chooses the first group to be the reference (in this case it would have chosen *crusty*, which was not what we want). Finally, and I know I keep going on about this, if we set our contrasts manually we can give them helpful names.

```
Call:
lm(formula = change ~ music, data = gfr)

Residuals:
     Min       1Q   Median       3Q      Max
-1.82569 -0.50489  0.05593  0.42430  1.59431

Coefficients:
                   Estimate Std. Error t value Pr(>|t|)
(Intercept)        -0.55431    0.09036  -6.134 1.15e-08 ***
musiccrusty_v_NMA  -0.41152    0.16703  -2.464   0.0152 *
musicindie_v_NMA   -0.40998    0.20492  -2.001   0.0477 *
musicmetal_v_NMA    0.02838    0.16033   0.177   0.8598
---
Signif. codes:  0 '***' 0.001 '**' 0.01 '*' 0.05 '.' 0.1 ' ' 1

Residual standard error: 0.6882 on 119 degrees of freedom
  (687 observations deleted due to missingness)
Multiple R-squared: 0.07617,    Adjusted R-squared: 0.05288
F-statistic:  3.27 on 3 and 119 DF,  p-value: 0.02369
```

Output 7.11

Output 7.11 shows the summary of the regression model (it also shows the command that you run to get the model). This shows that by entering the three dummy variables we can explain 7.6% of the variance in the change in hygiene scores (R^2 expressed as a percentage). In other words, 7.6% of the variance in the change in hygiene can be explained by the musical affiliation of the person. The F-statistic (which shows the same thing as the R^2 change statistic because there is only one step in this regression) tells us that the model is significantly better at predicting the change in hygiene scores than having no model (or, put another way, the 7.6% of variance that can be explained is a significant amount). Most of this should be clear from what you've read in this chapter already; what's more interesting is how we interpret the individual dummy variables.

Let's look at the coefficients for the dummy variables. The first thing to notice is that each dummy variable appears in the table with its name (because we named them, otherwise they'd be called something unhelpful like *contrast1*). The first dummy variable (**crusty_v_NMA**) shows the difference between the change in hygiene scores for the no-affiliation group and the crusty group. Remember that the beta value tells us the change in the outcome due to a unit change in the predictor. In this case, a unit change in the predictor is the change from 0 to 1. As such it shows the shift in the change in hygiene scores that results from the dummy variable changing from 0 to 1. By including all three dummy variables at the same time, our baseline category is always zero, so this actually represents the difference in the change in hygiene scores if a person has no musical affiliation, compared to someone who is a crusty. This difference is the difference between the two group means.

To illustrate this fact, I've produced a table (Output 7.12) of the group means for each of the four groups by executing this command:

```
round(tapply(gfr$change, gfr$music, mean, na.rm=TRUE), 3)
```

These means represent the average change in hygiene scores for the three groups (i.e., the mean of each group on our outcome variable). If we calculate the difference in these means for the no-affiliation group and the crusty group, we get crusty − no affiliation = $(-0.966) - (-0.554) = -0.412$. In other words, the change in hygiene scores is greater for the crusty group than it is for the no-affiliation group (crusties' hygiene decreases more over the festival than those with no musical affiliation). This value is the same as the regression estimate value in Output 7.11. So, the beta values tell us the relative difference between each group and the group that we chose as a baseline category. This beta value is converted to a t-statistic and the significance of this t reported. This t-statistic is testing, as we've seen before, whether the beta value is 0, and when we have two categories coded with 0 and 1, that means it's testing whether the difference between group means is 0. If it is significant then it means that the group coded with 1 is significantly different from the baseline category − so, it's testing the difference between two means, which is the context in which students are most familiar with the t-statistic (see Chapter 9). For our first dummy variable, the t-test is significant, and the beta value has a negative value so we could say that the change in hygiene scores goes down as a person changes from having no affiliation to being a crusty. Bear in mind that a decrease in hygiene scores represents more change (you're becoming smellier) so what this actually means is that hygiene decreased significantly more in crusties compared to those with no musical affiliation.

Crusty	Indie Kid	Metaller	No Musical Affiliation
-0.966	-0.964	-0.526	-0.554

Output 7.12

For the second dummy variable (**indie_v_NMA**), we're comparing indie kids to those that have no musical affiliation. The beta value again represents the shift in the change in hygiene scores if a person has no musical affiliation, compared to someone who is an indie kid. If we calculate the difference in the group means for the no-affiliation group and the indie kid group, we get indie kid − no affiliation = $(-0.964) - (-0.554) = -0.410$. It should be no surprise to you by now that this is the unstandardized beta value in Output 7.11. The t-test is significant, and the beta value has a negative value so, as with the first dummy variable, we could say that the change in hygiene scores goes down as a person changes from having no affiliation to being an indie kid. Bear in mind that a decrease in hygiene scores represents more change (you're becoming smellier) so what this actually means is that hygiene decreased significantly more in indie kids compared to those with no musical affiliation.

Moving on to our final dummy variable (**metal_v_NMA**), this compares metallers to those that have no musical affiliation. The beta value again represents the shift in the change in hygiene scores if a person has no musical affiliation, compared to someone who is a metaller. If we calculate the difference in the group means for the no affiliation group and the metaller group, we get metaller − no affiliation = $(-0.526) - (-0.554) = 0.028$. This value is again the same as the unstandardized beta value in Output 7.11. For this last dummy variable, the t-test is not significant, so we could say that the change in hygiene scores is the same if a person changes from having no affiliation to being a metaller. In other words, the change in hygiene scores is not predicted by whether someone is a metaller compared to if they have no musical affiliation.

So, overall this analysis has shown that, compared to having no musical affiliation, crusties and indie kids get significantly smellier across the three days of the festival, but metallers don't.

This section has introduced some really complex ideas that I expand upon in Chapters 9 and 10. It might all be a bit much to take in, and so if you're confused or want to know more about why dummy coding works in this way, I suggest reading sections 9.4.2 and 10.2.3 and then coming back here. Alternatively, read Hardy's (1993) excellent monograph!

What have I discovered about statistics? ①

This chapter is possibly the longest book chapter ever written, and if you feel like you aged several years while reading it then, well, you probably have (look around, there are cobwebs in the room, you have a long beard, and when you go outside you'll discover a second ice age has been and gone, leaving only you and a few woolly mammoths to populate the planet). However, on the plus side, you now know more or less everything you ever need to know about statistics. Really, it's true; you'll discover in the coming chapters that everything else we discuss is basically a variation on the theme of regression. So, although you may be near death having spent your life reading this chapter (and I'm certainly near death having written it) you are a stats genius – it's official!

We started the chapter by discovering that at 8 years old I could have really done with regression analysis to tell me which variables are important in predicting talent competition success. Unfortunately I didn't have regression, but fortunately I had my dad instead (and he's better than regression). We then looked at how we could use statistical models to make similar predictions by looking at the case of when you have one predictor and one outcome. This allowed us to look at some basic principles such as the equation of a straight line, the method of least squares, and how to assess how well our model fits the data using some important quantities that you'll come across in future chapters: the model sum of squares, SS_M, the residual sum of squares, SS_R, and the total sum of squares, SS_T. We used these values to calculate several important statistics such as R^2 and the F-ratio. We also learnt how to do a regression using **R**, and how we can plug the resulting beta values into the equation of a straight line to make predictions about our outcome.

Next, we saw that the question of a straight line can be extended to include several predictors and looked at different methods of placing these predictors in the model (hierarchical, forced entry, stepwise). Then we looked at factors that can affect the accuracy of a model (outliers and influential cases) and ways to identify these factors. We then moved on to look at the assumptions necessary to generalize our model beyond the sample of data we've collected before discovering how to do the analysis using **R**, and how to interpret the output, create our multiple regression model and test its reliability and generalizability. I finished the chapter by looking at how we can use categorical predictors in regression. In general, multiple regression is a long process and should be done with care and attention to detail. There are a lot of important things to consider and you should approach the analysis in a systematic fashion. I hope this chapter helps you to do that!

So, I was starting to get a taste for the rock-idol lifestyle: I had friends, a fortune (well, two gold-plated winner's medals), fast cars (a bike) and dodgy-looking 8-year-olds were giving me suitcases full of lemon sherbet to lick off mirrors. However, my parents and teachers were about to impress reality upon my young mind …

R packages used in this chapter

boot	QuantPsyc
car	

R functions used in this chapter

anova()	lm()
confint()	lm.beta()
contrasts()	mean()
contr.treatment()	plot()
cooks.distance()	resid()
covratio()	return()
coef()	rstandard()
dfbeta()	rstudent()
dffits()	sqrt()
durbinWatsonTest()	sum()
dwt()	summary()
hatvalues()	update()
hist()	vif()

Key terms that I've discovered

Adjusted predicted value	b_i
Adjusted R^2	β_i
Akaike information criterion (AIC)	Cook's distance
Autocorrelation	Covariance ratio

Cross-validation	Perfect collinearity
Deleted residual	Regression coefficient
DFBeta	Regression model
DFFit	Residual
Dummy variables	Residual sum of squares
Durbin–Watson test	Shrinkage
F-ratio	Simple regression
Generalization	Standardized DFBeta
Goodness of fit	Standardized DFFit
Hat values	Standardized residuals
Heteroscedasticity	Stepwise regression
Hierarchical regression	Studentized deleted residuals
Homoscedasticity	Studentized residuals
Independent errors	Suppressor effects
Leverage	t-statistic
Mean squares	Tolerance
Model sum of squares	Total sum of squares
Multicollinearity	Unstandardized residuals
Multiple R^2	Variance inflation factor
Multiple regression	

Smart Alex's tasks

- **Task 1**: Run a simple regression for the **pubs.dat** data in Jane Superbrain Box 7.1, predicting **mortality** from number of **pubs**. Try repeating the analysis but bootstrapping the regression parameters. ②

- **Task 2**: A fashion student was interested in factors that predicted the salaries of catwalk models. She collected data from 231 models. For each model she asked them their salary per day on days when they were working (**salary**), their age (**age**), how many years they had worked as a model (**years**), and then got a panel of experts from modelling agencies to rate the attractiveness of each model as a percentage, with 100% being perfectly attractive (**beauty**). The data are in the file **Supermodel. dat**. Unfortunately, this fashion student bought some substandard statistics text and so doesn't know how to analyse her data.☺ Can you help her out by conducting a multiple regression to see which variables predict a model's salary? How valid is the regression model? ②

- **Task 3**: Using the Glastonbury data from this chapter, which you should've already analysed, comment on whether you think the model is reliable and generalizable. ③

- **Task 4**: A study was carried out to explore the relationship between **Aggression** and several potential predicting factors in 666 children who had an older sibling. Variables measured were **Parenting_Style** (high score = bad parenting practices), **Computer_Games** (high score = more time spent playing computer games), **Television** (high score = more time spent watching television), **Diet** (high score = the child has a good diet low in additives), and **Sibling_Aggression** (high score = more aggression seen in their older sibling). Past research indicated that parenting style and sibling aggression were good predictors of the level of aggression in the younger child. All other variables were treated in an exploratory fashion. The data are in the file **ChildAggression.dat**. Analyse them with multiple regression. ②

Answers can be found on the companion website.

Further reading

Bowerman, B. L., & O'Connell, R. T. (1990). *Linear statistical models: An applied approach* (2nd ed.). Belmont, CA: Duxbury. (This text is only for the mathematically minded or postgraduate students but provides an extremely thorough exposition of regression analysis.)

Hardy, M. A. (1993). *Regression with dummy variables*. Sage University Paper Series on Quantitative Applications in the Social Sciences, 07-093. Newbury Park, CA: Sage.

Howell, D. C. (2006). *Statistical methods for psychology* (6th ed.). Belmont, CA: Duxbury. (Or you might prefer his *Fundamental Statistics for the Behavioral Sciences,* also in its 6th edition, 2007. Both are excellent introductions to the mathematics behind regression analysis.)

Miles, J. N. V. & Shevlin, M. (2001). *Applying regression and correlation: A guide for students and researchers*. London: Sage. (This is an extremely readable text that covers regression in loads of detail but with minimum pain – highly recommended.)

Stevens, J. (2002). *Applied multivariate statistics for the social sciences* (4th ed.). Hillsdale, NJ: Erlbaum. Chapter 3.

Interesting real research

Chamorro-Premuzic, T., Furnham, A., Christopher, A. N., Garwood, J., & Martin, N. (2008). Birds of a feather: Students' preferences for lecturers' personalities as predicted by their own personality and learning approaches. *Personality and Individual Differences*, 44, 965–976.

8 Logistic regression

FIGURE 8.1
Practising for my
career as a rock
star by slaying
the baying throng
of Grove Primary
School at the age
of 10. (Note the
girl with her hands
covering her ears.)

8.1. What will this chapter tell me? ①

We saw in the previous chapter that I had successfully conquered the holiday camps of
Wales with my singing and guitar playing (and the Welsh know a thing or two about good
singing). I had jumped on a snowboard called oblivion and thrown myself down the black
run known as world domination. About 10 metres after starting this slippery descent I
hit the lumpy patch of ice called 'adults'. I was 9, life was fun, and yet every adult that I
seemed to encounter was obsessed with my future. 'What do you want to be when you
grow up?' they would ask. I was 9 and 'grown-up' was a lifetime away; all I knew was that I
was going to marry Clair Sparks (more about her in the next chapter) and that I was a rock

legend who didn't need to worry about such adult matters as having a job. It was a difficult question, but adults require answers and I wasn't going to let them know that I didn't care about 'grown-up' matters. We saw in the previous chapter that we can use regression to predict future outcomes based on past data, when the outcome is a continuous variable, but this question had a categorical outcome (e.g., would I be a fireman, a doctor, an evil dictator?). Luckily, though, we can use an extension of regression called logistic regression to deal with these situations. What a result; bring on the rabid wolves of categorical data. To make a prediction about a categorical outcome, then, as with regression, I needed to draw on past data: I hadn't tried conducting brain surgery, neither had I experience of sentencing psychopaths to prison sentences for eating their husbands, nor had I taught anyone. I had, however, had a go at singing and playing guitar; 'I'm going to be a rock star' was my prediction. A prediction can be accurate (which would mean that I *am* a rock star) or it can be inaccurate (which would mean that I'm writing a statistics textbook). This chapter looks at the theory and application of **logistic regression**, an extension of regression that allows us to predict categorical outcomes based on predictor variables.

8.2. Background to logistic regression ①

In a nutshell, logistic regression is multiple regression but with an outcome variable that is a categorical variable and predictor variables that are continuous or categorical. In its simplest form, this means that we can predict which of two categories a person is likely to belong to given certain other information. A trivial example is to look at which variables predict whether a person is male or female. We might measure laziness, pig-headedness, alcohol consumption and number of burps that a person does in a day. Using logistic regression, we might find that all of these variables predict the gender of the person, but the technique will also allow us to predict whether a person, not in our original data set, is likely to be male or female. So, if we picked a random person and discovered they scored highly on laziness, pig-headedness, alcohol consumption and the number of burps, then the regression model might tell us that, based on this information, this person is likely to be male. Admittedly, it is unlikely that a researcher would ever be interested in the relationship between flatulence and gender (it is probably too well established by experience to warrant research), but logistic regression can have life-saving applications. In medical research logistic regression is used to generate models from which predictions can be made about the likelihood that a tumour is cancerous or benign (for example). A database of patients can be used to establish which variables are influential in predicting the malignancy of a tumour. These variables can then be measured for a new patient and their values placed in a logistic regression model, from which a probability of malignancy could be estimated. If the probability value of the tumour being malignant is suitably low then the doctor may decide not to carry out expensive and painful surgery that in all likelihood is unnecessary. We might not face such life-threatening decisions but logistic regression can nevertheless be a very useful tool. When we are trying to predict membership of only two categorical outcomes the analysis is known as **binary logistic regression**, but when we want to predict membership of more than two categories we use **multinomial (or polychotomous) logistic regression**.

8.3. What are the principles behind logistic regression? ③

I don't wish to dwell on the underlying principles of logistic regression because they aren't necessary to understand the test (I am living proof of this fact). However, I do wish to draw a few parallels to normal regression so that you can get the gist of what's going on using a framework that will be familiar to you already (what do you mean you haven't read the regression chapter yet!). To keep things simple I'm going to explain binary logistic regression, but most of the principles extend easily to when there are more than two outcome categories. Now would be a good time for those with equation-phobia to look away. In simple linear regression, we saw that the outcome variable Y is predicted from the equation of a straight line:

$$Y_i = b_0 + b_1 X_{1i} + \varepsilon_i \qquad (8.1)$$

in which b_0 is the Y intercept, b_1 is the gradient of the straight line, X_1 is the value of the predictor variable and ε is a residual term. Given the values of Y and X_1, the unknown parameters in the equation can be estimated by finding a solution for which the squared distance between the observed and predicted values of the dependent variable is minimized (the method of least squares).

This stuff should all be pretty familiar by now. In multiple regression, in which there are several predictors, a similar equation is derived in which each predictor has its own coefficient. As such, Y is predicted from a combination of each predictor variable multiplied by its respective regression coefficient:

$$Y_i = b_0 + b_1 X_{1i} + b_2 X_{2i} + \dots + b_n X_{ni} + \varepsilon_i \qquad (8.2)$$

in which b_n is the regression coefficient of the corresponding variable X_n. In logistic regression, instead of predicting the value of a variable Y from a predictor variable X_1 or several predictor variables (Xs), we predict the *probability* of Y occurring given known values of X_1 (or Xs). The logistic regression equation bears many similarities to the regression equations just described. In its simplest form, when there is only one predictor variable X_1, the logistic regression equation from which the probability of Y is predicted is given by:

$$P(Y) = \frac{1}{1 + e^{-(b_0 + b_1 X_{1i})}} \qquad (8.3)$$

in which $P(Y)$ is the probability of Y occurring, e is the base of natural logarithms, and the other coefficients form a linear combination much the same as in simple regression. In fact, you might notice that the bracketed portion of the equation is identical to the linear regression equation in that there is a constant (b_0), a predictor variable (X_1) and a coefficient (or weight) attached to that predictor (b_1). Just like linear regression, it is possible to extend this equation so as to include several predictors. When there are several predictors the equation becomes:

$$P(Y) = \frac{1}{1 + e^{-(b_0 + b_1 X_{1i} + b_2 X_{2i} + \dots b_n X_{ni})}} \qquad (8.4)$$

Equation (8.4) is the same as the equation used when there is only one predictor except that the linear combination has been extended to include any number of predictors. So, whereas the one-predictor version of the logistic regression equation contained the simple linear regression equation within it, the multiple-predictor version contains the multiple regression equation.

Despite the similarities between linear regression and logistic regression, there is a good reason why we cannot apply linear regression directly to a situation in which the outcome variable is categorical. The reason is that one of the assumptions of linear regression is that the relationship between variables is linear. We saw in section 7.7.2.1 how important it is that the assumptions of a model are met for it to be accurate. Therefore, for linear regression to be a valid model, the observed data should contain a linear relationship. When the outcome variable is categorical, this assumption is violated (Berry, 1993). One way around this problem is to transform the data using the logarithmic transformation (see Berry & Feldman, 1985, and Chapter 5). This transformation is a way of expressing a non-linear relationship in a linear way. The logistic regression equation described above is based on this principle: it expresses the multiple linear regression equation in logarithmic terms (called the *logit*) and thus overcomes the problem of violating the assumption of linearity.

The exact form of the equation can be arranged in several ways but the version I have chosen expresses the equation in terms of the probability of Y occurring (i.e., the probability that a case belongs in a certain category). The resulting value from the equation, therefore, varies between 0 and 1. A value close to 0 means that Y is very unlikely to have occurred, and a value close to 1 means that Y is very likely to have occurred. Also, just like linear regression, each predictor variable in the logistic regression equation has its own coefficient. When we run the analysis we need to estimate the value of these coefficients so that we can solve the equation. These parameters are estimated by fitting models, based on the available predictors, to the observed data. The chosen model will be the one that, when values of the predictor variables are placed in it, results in values of Y closest to the observed values. Specifically, the values of the parameters are estimated using **maximum-likelihood estimation**, which selects coefficients that make the observed values most likely to have occurred. So, as with multiple regression, we try to fit a model to our data that allows us to estimate values of the outcome variable from known values of the predictor variable or variables.

8.3.1.   Assessing the model: the log-likelihood statistic ③

We've seen that the logistic regression model predicts the probability of an event occurring for a given person (we would denote this as $P(Y_i)$, the probability that Y occurs for the *i*th person), based on observations of whether or not the event did occur for that person (we could denote this as Y_i, the actual outcome for the *i*th person). So, for a given person, Y will be either 0 (the outcome didn't occur) or 1 (the outcome did occur), and the predicted value, $P(Y)$, will be a value between 0 (there is no chance that the outcome will occur) and 1 (the outcome will certainly occur). We saw in multiple regression that if we want to assess whether a model fits the data we can compare the observed and predicted values of the outcome (if you remember, we use R^2, which is the Pearson correlation between observed values of the outcome and the values predicted by the regression model). Likewise, in logistic regression, we can use the observed and predicted values to assess the fit of the model. The measure we use is the **log-likelihood**:

$$\text{log-likelihood} = \sum_{i=1}^{N} \left[Y_i ln\left(P(Y_i) \right) + (1 - Y_i) ln\left(1 - P(Y_i) \right) \right]$$

(8.5)

The log-likelihood is based on summing the probabilities associated with the predicted and actual outcomes (Tabachnick & Fidell, 2007). The log-likelihood statistic is analogous to the residual sum of squares in multiple regression in the sense that it is an indicator of how much unexplained information there is after the model has been fitted. It, therefore, follows that large values of the log-likelihood statistic indicate poorly fitting statistical models, because the larger the value of the log-likelihood, the more unexplained observations there are.

8.3.2. Assessing the model: the deviance statistic ③

The **deviance** is very closely related to the log-likelihood: it's given by

$$\text{deviance} = -2 \times \text{log-likelihood}$$

The deviance is often referred to as **−2LL** because of the way it is calculated. It's actually rather convenient to (almost) always use the deviance rather than the log-likelihood because it has a chi-square distribution (see Chapter 18 and the Appendix), which makes it easy to calculate the significance of the value.

Now, it's possible to calculate a log-likelihood or deviance for different models and to compare these models by looking at the difference between their deviances. One use of this is to compare the state of a logistic regression model against some kind of baseline state. The baseline state that's usually used is the model when only the constant is included. In multiple regression, the baseline model we use is the mean of all scores (this is our best guess of the outcome when we have no other information). In logistic regression, if we want to predict the outcome, what would our best guess be? Well, we can't use the mean score because our outcome is made of zeros and ones and so the mean is meaningless. However, if we know the frequency of zeros and ones, then the best guess will be the category with the largest number of cases. So, if the outcome occurs 107 times, and doesn't occur only 72 times, then our best guess of the outcome will be that it occurs (because it occurs more often than it doesn't). As such, like multiple regression, our baseline model is the model that gives us the best prediction when we know nothing other than the values of the outcome: in logistic regression this will be to predict the outcome that occurs most often – that is, the logistic regression model when only the constant is included. If we then add one or more predictors to the model, we can compute the improvement of the model as follows:

$$\chi^2 = \left(-2LL(\text{baseline})\right) - \left(-2LL(\text{new})\right)$$
$$= 2LL(\text{new}) - 2LL(\text{baseline})$$
$$df = k_{\text{new}} - k_{\text{baseline}}$$

(8.6)

So, we merely take the new model deviance and subtract from it the deviance for the baseline model (the model when only the constant is included). This difference is known as a likelihood ratio,[1] and has a chi-square distribution with degrees of freedom equal to the number of parameters, k, in the new model minus the number of parameters in the baseline model. The number of parameters in the baseline model will always be 1 (the constant is the only parameter to be estimated); any subsequent model will have degrees of freedom equal to the number of predictors plus 1 (i.e., the number of predictors plus one parameter representing the constant).

8.3.3. Assessing the model: R and R^2 ③

When we talked about linear regression, we saw that the multiple correlation coefficient R and the corresponding R^2 were useful measures of how well the model fits the data. We've

[1] You might wonder why it is called a 'ratio' when a 'ratio' usually means something is divided by something else, and we're not dividing anything here: we're subtracting. The reason is that if you subtract logs of numbers, it's the same as dividing the numbers. For example, $10/5 = 2$ and (try it on your calculator) $\log(10) - \log(5) = \log(2)$

also just seen that the likelihood ratio is similar in that it is based on the level of correspondence between predicted and actual values of the outcome. However, you can calculate a more literal version of the multiple correlation in logistic regression known as the R-statistic. This R-statistic is the partial correlation between the outcome variable and each of the predictor variables, and it can vary between −1 and 1. A positive value indicates that as the predictor variable increases, so does the likelihood of the event occurring. A negative value implies that as the predictor variable increases, the likelihood of the outcome occurring decreases. If a variable has a small value of R then it contributes only a small amount to the model.

The equation for R is:

$$R = \sqrt{\frac{z^2 - 2df}{-2LL(\text{baseline})}}$$ (8.7)

The $-2LL$ term is the deviance for the baseline model, z^2 is the *Wald statistic* calculated as described in section 8.3.5, and the degrees of freedom can be read from the summary table for the variables in the equation. However, because this value of R is dependent upon the **Wald statistic** it is by no means an accurate measure (we'll see in section 8.3.5 that the Wald statistic can be inaccurate under certain circumstances). For this reason the value of R should be treated with some caution, and it is invalid to square this value and interpret it as you would in linear regression.

There is some controversy over what would make a good analogue to the R^2 in linear regression, but one measure described by Hosmer and Lemeshow (1989) can be easily calculated. Hosmer and Lemeshow's (R_L^2) measure is calculated as:

$$R_L^2 = \frac{-2LL(\text{model})}{-2LL(\text{baseline})}$$ (8.8)

As such, R_L^2 is calculated by dividing the model chi-square, which represents the change from the baseline (based on the log-likelihood) by the baseline $-2LL$ (the deviance of the model before any predictors were entered). Given what the model chi-square represents, another way to express this is:

$$R_L^2 = \frac{\left(-2LL(\text{baseline})\right) - \left(-2LL(\text{new})\right)}{-2LL(\text{baseline})}$$

R_L^2 is the proportional reduction in the absolute value of the log-likelihood measure and as such it is a measure of how much the badness of fit improves as a result of the inclusion of the predictor variables. It can vary between 0 (indicating that the predictors are useless at predicting the outcome variable) and 1 (indicating that the model predicts the outcome variable perfectly).

Cox and Snell's R_{CS}^2 (1989) is based on the deviance of the model ($-2LL$(new)) and the deviance of the baseline model ($-2LL$(baseline)), and the sample size, n:

$$R_{CS}^2 = 1 - \exp\left(\frac{\left(-2LL(\text{new})\right) - \left(-2LL(\text{baseline})\right)}{n}\right)$$ (8.9)

However, this statistic never reaches its theoretical maximum of 1. Therefore, Nagelkerke (1991) suggested the following amendment (**Nagelkerke's R_N^2**):

$$R_N^2 = \frac{R_{CS}^2}{1 - \exp\left(-\dfrac{-2LL(\text{baseline})}{n}\right)} \tag{8.10}$$

Although all of these measures differ in their computation (and the answers you get), conceptually they are somewhat similar. So, in terms of interpretation they can be seen as similar to the R^2 in linear regression in that they provide a gauge of the substantive significance of the model.

8.3.4. Assessing the model: information criteria ③

As we saw with linear regression, in section 7.6.3, we can use the Akaike information criterion (AIC) and the Bayes information criterion (BIC) to judge model fit. These two criteria exist to solve a problem with R^2: that every time we add a variable to the model, R^2 increases. We want a measure of fit that we can to compare two models which penalizes a model that contains more predictor variables. You can think of this as the price you pay for something: you get a better value of R^2, but you pay a higher price, and was that higher price worth it? These information criteria help you to decide.

The AIC is the simpler of the two; it is given by:

$$AIC = -2LL + 2k$$

in which $-2LL$ is the deviance (described above) and k is the number of predictors in the model. The BIC is the same as the AIC but adjusts the penalty included in the AIC (i.e., $2k$) by the number of cases:

$$BIC = -2LL + 2k \times \log(n)$$

in which n is the number of cases in the model.

8.3.5. Assessing the contribution of predictors: the z-statistic ②

As in linear regression, we want to know not only how well the model overall fits the data, but also the individual contribution of predictors. In linear regression, we used the estimated regression coefficients (b) and their standard errors to compute a t-statistic. In logistic regression there is an analogous statistic – the **z-statistic** – which follows the **normal distribution**. Like the t-test in linear regression, the z-statistic tells us whether the b coefficient for that predictor is significantly different from zero. If the coefficient is significantly different from zero then we can assume that the predictor is making a significant contribution to the prediction of the outcome (Y):

$$z = \frac{b}{SE_b} \tag{8.11}$$

Equation (8.11) shows how the z-statistic is calculated and you can see it's basically identical to the t-statistic in linear regression (see equation (7.6)): it is the value of the regression coefficient divided by its associated standard error. The z-statistic is usually used to ascertain whether a variable is a significant predictor of the outcome; however, it is probably more accurate to examine the likelihood ratio statistics. The reason why the z-statistic should be used a little cautiously is because, when the regression coefficient (b) is large, the standard error tends to become inflated, resulting in the z-statistic being underestimated (see Menard, 1995). The inflation of the standard error increases the probability of rejecting a predictor as being significant when in reality it is making a significant contribution to the model (i.e., you are more likely to make a Type II error). The z-statistic was developed by Abraham Wald (Figure 8.2), and is thus sometimes known as the Wald statistic.

8.3.6. The odds ratio ③

More crucial to the *interpretation* of logistic regression is the value of the **odds ratio**, which is the exponential of B (i.e., e^B or exp(B)) and is an indicator of the change in odds resulting from a unit change in the predictor. As such, it is similar to the b coefficient in logistic regression but easier to understand (because it doesn't require a logarithmic transformation). When the predictor variable is categorical the odds ratio is easier to explain, so imagine we had a simple example in which we were trying to predict whether or not someone got pregnant from whether or not they used a condom last time they made love. The **odds** of an event occurring are defined as the probability of an event occurring divided by the probability of that event not occurring (see equation (8.12)) and should not be confused with the more colloquial usage of the word to refer to probability. So, for example, the odds of becoming pregnant are the probability of becoming pregnant divided by the probability of not becoming pregnant:

$$\text{odds} = \frac{P(\text{event})}{P(\text{no event})}$$

$$P(\text{event } Y) = \frac{1}{1 + e^{-(b_0 + b_1 X_{1i})}}$$

(8.12)

$$P(\text{no event } Y) = 1 - P(\text{event } Y)$$

To calculate the change in odds that results from a unit change in the predictor, we must first calculate the odds of becoming pregnant given that a condom *wasn't* used. We then calculate the odds of becoming pregnant given that a condom *was* used. Finally, we calculate the proportionate change in these two odds.

To calculate the first set of odds, we need to use equation (8.3) to calculate the probability of becoming pregnant given that a condom wasn't used. If we had more than one predictor we would use equation (8.4). There are three unknown quantities in this equation: the coefficient of the constant (b_0), the coefficient for the predictor (b_1) and the value of the predictor itself (X). We'll know the value of X from how we coded the condom use variable (chances are we would've used 0 = condom wasn't used and 1 = condom was used). The values of b_1 and b_0 will be estimated for us. We can calculate the odds as in equation (8.12).

Next, we calculate the same thing after the predictor variable has changed by one unit. In this case, because the predictor variable is dichotomous, we need to calculate the odds of getting pregnant, given that a condom *was* used. So, the value of X is now 1 (rather than 0).

We now know the odds before and after a unit change in the predictor variable. It is a simple matter to calculate the proportionate change in odds by dividing the odds after a unit change in the predictor by the odds before that change:

$$\Delta\text{odds} = \frac{\text{odds after a unit change in the predictor}}{\text{original odds}}$$

(8.13)

This proportionate change in odds is the odds ratio, and we can interpret it in terms of the change in odds: if the value is greater than 1 then it indicates that as the predictor increases, the odds of the outcome occurring increase. Conversely, a value less than 1 indicates that as the predictor increases, the odds of the outcome occurring decrease. We'll see how this works with a real example shortly.

8.3.7.   Methods of logistic regression ②

As with multiple regression (section 7.6.4), there are several different methods that can be used in logistic regression.

8.3.7.1. The forced entry method ②

The default method of conducting the regression is simply to place predictors into the regression model in one block, and estimate parameters for each predictor.

8.3.7.2. Stepwise methods ②

If you are undeterred by the criticisms of stepwise methods in the previous chapter, then you can select either a forward or a backward stepwise method, or a combination of them.

When the forward method is employed the computer begins with a model that includes only a constant and then adds single predictors to the model based on the criterion that adding the variable must improve the AIC or BIC (whichever you chose). The computer proceeds until none of the remaining predictors have decreased the criterion.

The opposite of the forward method is the backward method. This method uses the same criteria, but instead of starting the model with only a constant, it begins the model with all predictors included. The computer then tests whether any of these predictors can be removed from the model without increasing the information criterion. If it can, it is removed from the model, and the variables are all tested again.

Better than these two simple methods are the backward/forward and the forward/backward methods. These are hybrids of the two methods – the forward/backward approach starts off doing a forward method, but each time a variable is added, it tests whether it's worth removing any variables.

8.3.7.3. How do I select a method? ②

As with ordinary regression (previous chapter), the method of regression chosen will depend on several things. The main consideration is whether you are testing a theory or merely carrying out exploratory work. As noted earlier, some people believe that stepwise methods have no value for theory testing. However, stepwise methods are defensible when used in situations where causality is not of interest and you merely wish to find a model to fit your data (Agresti & Finlay, 1986; Menard, 1995). Also, as I mentioned for ordinary regression, if you do decide to use a stepwise method then the backward method is preferable to the forward method. This is because of **suppressor effects**, which occur when a predictor has a significant effect but only when another variable is held constant. Forward selection is more likely than backward elimination to exclude predictors involved in suppressor effects. As such, the forward method runs a higher risk of making a Type II error.

Which method should I use?

8.4. Assumptions and things that can go wrong ④

8.4.1. Assumptions ②

Logistic regression shares some of the assumptions of normal regression:

1 **Linearity**: In ordinary regression we assumed that the outcome had linear relationships with the predictors. In logistic regression the outcome is categorical and so this assumption is violated. As I explained before, this is why we use the log (or logit) of the data. The linearity assumption in logistic regression, therefore, is that there is a linear relationship between any continuous predictors and the logit of the outcome variable. This assumption can be tested by looking at whether the interaction term between the predictor and its log transformation is significant (Hosmer & Lemeshow, 1989). We will go through an example in section 8.8.1.

2 **Independence of errors**: This assumption is the same as for ordinary regression (see section 7.7.2.1). Basically it means that cases of data should not be related; for example, you cannot measure the same people at different points in time (well, you can actually, but then you have to use a multilevel model – see Chapter 19).

3 **Multicollinearity**: Although not really an assumption as such, multicollinearity is a problem as it was for ordinary regression (see section 7.7.2.1). In essence, predictors should not be too highly correlated. As with ordinary regression, this assumption can be checked with tolerance and VIF statistics, the eigenvalues of the scaled, uncentred cross-products matrix, the condition indices and the variance proportions. We go through an example in section 8.8.1.

Logistic regression also has some unique problems of its own (not assumptions, but things that can go wrong). **R** solves logistic regression problems by an iterative procedure (R's Souls' Tip 8.1). Sometimes, instead of pouncing on the correct solution quickly, you'll notice nothing happening: **R** begins to move infinitely slowly, or appears to have got fed up with you asking it to do stuff and gone on strike. If it can't find a correct solution, then sometimes it actually does give up, quietly offering you (without any apology) a result that is completely incorrect. Usually this is revealed by implausibly large standard errors. Two situations can provoke this situation, both of which are related to the ratio of cases to variables: incomplete information and complete separation.

R's Souls' Tip 8.1 Error messages about 'failure to converge' ③

Many statistical procedures use an *iterative process*, which means that **R** attempts to estimate the parameters of the model by finding successive approximations of those parameters. Essentially, it starts by estimating the parameters with a 'best guess'. It then attempts to approximate them more accurately (known as an *iteration*). It then tries again, and then again, and so on through many iterations. It stops either when the approximations of parameters converge (i.e., at each new attempt the 'approximations' of parameters are the same or very similar to the previous attempt), or it reaches the maximum number of attempts (iterations).

Sometimes you will get an error message in the output that says something like

```
Warning messages:
1: glm.fit: algorithm did not converge
```

What this means is that **R** has attempted to estimate the parameters the maximum number of times (as specified in the options) but they are not converging (i.e., at each iteration **R** is getting quite different estimates). This certainly means that you should ignore any output that **R** has produced, and it might mean that your data are beyond help.

8.4.2. Incomplete information from the predictors ④

Imagine you're trying to predict lung cancer from smoking and whether or not you eat tomatoes (which are believed to reduce the risk of cancer). You collect data from people who do and don't smoke, and from people who do and don't eat tomatoes; however, this isn't sufficient unless you collect data from all combinations of smoking and tomato eating. Imagine you ended up with the following data:

Do you smoke?	Do you eat tomatoes?	Do you have cancer?
Yes	No	Yes
Yes	Yes	Yes
No	No	Yes
No	Yes	??????

Observing only the first three possibilities does not prepare you for the outcome of the fourth. You have no way of knowing whether this last person will have cancer or not based on the other data you've collected. Therefore, **R** will have problems unless you've collected data from all combinations of your variables. This should be checked before you run the analysis using a crosstabulation table, and I describe how to do this in Chapter 18. While you're checking these tables, you should also look at the expected frequencies in each cell of the table to make sure that they are greater than 1 and no more than 20% are less than 5 (see section 18.5). This is because the goodness-of-fit tests in logistic regression make this assumption.

This point applies not only to categorical variables, but also to continuous ones. Suppose that you wanted to investigate factors related to human happiness. These might include age, gender, sexual orientation, religious beliefs, levels of anxiety and even whether a person is right-handed. You interview 1000 people, record their characteristics, and whether they are happy ('yes' or 'no'). Although a sample of 1000 seems quite large, is it likely to include an 80-year-old, highly anxious, Buddhist, left-handed lesbian? If you found one such person and she was happy, should you conclude that everyone else in the same category is happy? It would, obviously, be better to have several more people in this category to confirm that this combination of characteristics predicts happiness. One solution is to collect more data.

As a general point, whenever samples are broken down into categories and one or more combinations are empty it creates problems. These will probably be signalled by coefficients that have unreasonably large standard errors. Conscientious researchers produce and check multiway crosstabulations of all categorical independent variables. Lazy but cautious ones don't bother with crosstabulations, but look carefully at the standard errors. Those who don't bother with either should expect trouble.

8.4.3. Complete separation ④

A second situation in which logistic regression collapses might surprise you: it's when the outcome variable can be perfectly predicted by one variable or a combination of variables! This is known as **complete separation.**

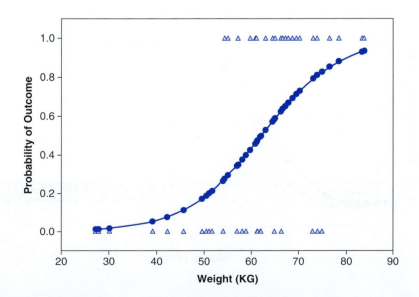

Figure 8.3
An example of the relationship between weight (*x*-axis) and a dichotomous outcome variable (*y*-axis, 1 = Burglar, 0 = Teenager) – note that the weights in the two groups overlap

Let's look at an example: imagine you placed a pressure pad under your doormat and connected it to your security system so that you could detect burglars when they creep in at night. However, because your teenage children (which you would have if you're old enough and rich enough to have security systems and pressure pads) and their friends are often coming home in the middle of the night, when they tread on the pad you want it to work out the probability that the person is a burglar and not one of your teenagers. Therefore, you could measure the weight of some burglars and some teenagers and use logistic regression to predict the outcome (teenager or burglar) from the weight. The graph (Figure 8.3) would show a line of triangles at zero (the data points for all of the teenagers you weighed) and a line of triangles at 1 (the data points for burglars you weighed). Note that these lines of triangles overlap (some teenagers are as heavy as burglars). We've seen that in logistic regression, **R** tries to predict the probability of the outcome given a value of the predictor. In this case, at low weights the fitted probability follows the bottom line of the plot, and at high weights it follows the top line. At intermediate values it tries to follow the probability as it changes.

Imagine that we had the same pressure pad, but our teenage children had left home to go to university. We're now interested in distinguishing burglars from our pet cat based on weight. Again, we can weigh some cats and weigh some burglars. This time the graph (Figure 8.4) still has a row of triangles at zero (the cats we weighed) and a row at 1 (the burglars) but this time the rows of triangles do not overlap: there is no burglar who weighs the same as a cat – obviously there were no cat burglars in the sample (groan now at that sorry excuse for a joke). This is known as perfect separation: the outcome (cats and burglars) can be perfectly predicted from weight (anything less than 15 kg is a cat, anything more than 40 kg is a burglar). If we try to calculate the probabilities of the outcome given a certain weight then we run into trouble. When the weight is low, the probability is 0, and when the weight is high, the probability is 1, but what happens in between? We have no data between 15 and 40 kg on which to base these probabilities. The figure shows two possible probability curves that we could fit to these data: one much steeper than the other. Either one of these curves is valid, based on the data we have available. The lack of data means that **R** will be uncertain about how steep it should make the intermediate slope and it will try to bring the centre as close to vertical as possible, but its estimates veer unsteadily towards infinity (hence large standard errors).

FIGURE 8.4

An example of complete separation – note that the weights (x-axis) of the two categories in the dichotomous outcome variable (y-axis, 1 = Burglar, 0 = Cat) do not overlap

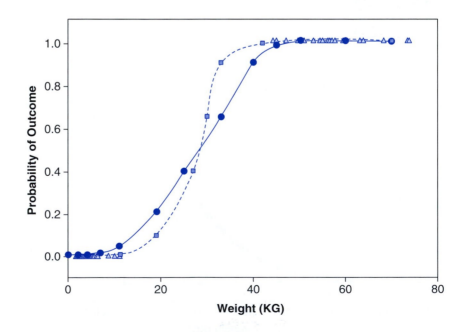

This problem often arises when too many variables are fitted to too few cases. Often the only satisfactory solution is to collect more data, but sometimes a neat answer is found by using a simpler model.

CRAMMING SAM'S TIPS   **Issues in logistic regression**

- In logistic regression, like ordinary regression, we assume linearity, no multicollinearity and independence of errors.
- The linearity assumption is that each predictor has a linear relationship with the log of the outcome variable.
- If we created a table that combined all possible values of all variables then we should ideally have some data in every cell of this table. If we don't then we should watch out for big standard errors.
- If the outcome variable can be predicted perfectly from one predictor variable (or a combination of predictor variables) then we have *complete separation*. This problem creates large standard errors too.

8.5. Packages used in this chapter ①

There are several packages we will use in this chapter. Some, but not all, can be accessed through R Commander. You will need the packages *car* (to recode variables and test multicollinearity) and *mlogit* (for multinomial logistic regression). If you don't have these packages installed you'll need to install them and load them.

```
install.packages("car"); install.packages("mlogit")
```

Then you need to load the packages by executing these commands:

```
library(car); library(mlogit)
```

8.6. Binary logistic regression: an example that will make you feel eel ②

It's amazing what you find in academic journals sometimes. It's a bit of a hobby of mine trying to unearth bizarre academic papers (really, if you find any, email them to me). I believe that science should be fun, and so I like finding research that makes me laugh. A research paper by Lo and colleagues is the one that (so far) has made me laugh the most (Lo, Wong, Leung, Law, & Yip, 2004). Lo et al. report the case of a 50-year-old man who presented himself at the Accident and Emergency Department (ED for the Americans) with abdominal pain. A physical examination revealed peritonitis so they took an X-ray of the man's abdomen. Although it somehow slipped the patient's mind to mention this to the receptionist upon arrival at the hospital, the X-ray revealed the shadow of an eel. The authors don't directly quote the man's response to this news, but I like to imagine it was something to the effect of 'Oh, that! Erm, yes, well I didn't think it was terribly relevant to my abdominal pain so I didn't mention it, but I did insert an eel into my anus this morning. Do you think that's the problem?' Whatever he *did* say, the authors report that he admitted to inserting an eel into his anus to 'relieve constipation'.

I can have a lively imagination at times, and when I read this article I couldn't help thinking about the poor eel. There it was, minding its own business swimming about in a river (or fish tank possibly), thinking to itself 'Well, today seems like a nice day, there are no

Can an eel cure constipation?

eel-eating sharks about, the sun is out, the water is nice, what could possibly go wrong?' The next thing it knows, it's being shoved up the anus of a man from Hong Kong. 'Well, I didn't see that coming', thinks the eel. Putting myself in the mindset of an eel for a moment, he has found himself in a tight dark tunnel, there's no light, there's a distinct lack of water compared to his usual habitat, and he probably fears for his life. His day has gone *very* wrong. How can he escape this horrible fate? Well, doing what any self-respecting eel would do, he notices that his prison cell is fairly soft and decides 'bugger this,[2] I'll *eat* my way out of here'. Unfortunately he didn't make it, but he went out with a fight (there's a fairly unpleasant photograph in the article of the eel biting the splenic flexure).

The authors conclude that 'Insertion of a live animal into the rectum causing rectal perforation has never been reported. This may be related to a bizarre healthcare belief, inadvertent sexual behavior , or criminal assault. However, the true reason may never be known.' Quite.

OK, so this is a really grim tale.[3] It's not really very funny for the man or the eel, but it did make me laugh. Of course my instant reaction was that sticking an eel up your anus to 'relieve constipation' is the poorest excuse for bizarre sexual behaviour I have ever heard. But upon reflection I wondered if I was being harsh on the man – maybe an eel up the anus really can cure constipation. If we wanted to test this, we could collect some data. Our outcome might be 'constipated' vs. 'not constipated', which is a dichotomous variable that we're trying to predict. One predictor variable would be intervention (eel up the anus) vs. waiting list (no treatment). We might also want to factor how many days the patient had been constipated before treatment. This scenario is perfect for logistic regression (but not for eels). The data are in **Eel.dat**.

I'm quite aware that many statistics lecturers do not share my unbridled joy at discussing eel-created rectal perforations with students, so I have named the variables in the file more generally:

- outcome (dependent variable): **Cured** (cured or not cured);
- predictor (independent variable): **Intervention** (intervention or no treatment);
- predictor (independent variable): **Duration** (the number of days before treatment that the patient had the problem).

In doing so, your tutor can adapt the example to something more palatable if they wish to, but you will secretly know that the example is all about putting eels up your bum.

8.6.1. Preparing the data ①

To carry out logistic regression, the data must be entered as for normal regression: they are arranged in whatever data editor you use in three columns (one representing each variable). First load the data file by setting your working directory to the location of the file (see section 3.4.4) and executing:

```
eelData<-read.delim("eel.dat", header = TRUE)
```

[2] Literally.

[3] As it happens, it isn't an isolated grim tale. Through this article I found myself hurtling down a road of morbid curiosity that was best left untravelled. Although the eel was my favourite example, I could have chosen from a very large stone (Sachdev, 1967), a test tube (Hughes, Marice, & Gathright, 1976), a baseball (McDonald & Rosenthal, 1977), an aerosol deodorant can, hose pipe, iron bar, broomstick, penknife, marijuana, bank notes, blue plastic tumbler, vibrator and primus stove (Clarke, Buccimazza, Anderson, & Thomson, 2005), or (a close second place to the eel) a toy pirate ship, with or without pirates I'm not sure (Bemelman & Hammacher, 2005). So, although I encourage you to send me bizarre research, if it involves objects in the rectum then probably don't, unless someone has managed to put Buckingham Palace up there.

This creates a dataframe called *eelData*. We can look at the data using the **head()** function, which shows the first six rows of the dataframe entered into the function:

```
head(eelData)
```

```
  Cured   Intervention     Duration
1 Not Cured No Treatment        7
2 Not Cured No Treatment        7
3 Not Cured No Treatment        6
4     Cured No Treatment        8
5     Cured Intervention       7
6     Cured No Treatment        6
```

Note that we have three variables in different columns. The categorical data have been entered as text. For example, the variable **Cured** is made up of the phrases *Cured* and *Not Cured*. When we read in data that are text strings like this, **R** helpfully converts them to factors. It doesn't tell us that it has done this, it just does it.

When we do logistic regression, we want to do it with numbers, not words. In creating the factors **R** also helpfully assigned some numbers to the variables. There is no end to how helpful **R** will try to be. The trouble is that the numbers that **R** has assigned might not be the numbers that we want. In fact, **R** creates levels of the factor by taking the text strings in alphabetical order and assigning them ascending numerical values. In other words, for **Cured** we have two categories and **R** will have ordered these categories alphabetically (i.e., 'Cured' and 'Not Cured'). So, *Cured* will be the baseline category because it is first. Likewise, for **Intervention** the categories were *Intervention* and *No Treatment*, so given the alphabetic order *Intervention* will be the baseline category.

However, it makes more sense to code both of these variables the opposite way around. For **Cured** it would be good if *Not Cured* was the baseline, or first category, because then we would know that the model coefficients reflect the probability of being cured (which is what we want to know) rather than the probability of not being cured. Similarly, for **Intervention** it would be useful if *No Treatment* were the first category (i.e., the baseline). Fortunately, the function **relevel()** lets us specify the baseline category for a factor. It takes the general form:

```
newFactor<-relevel(oldFactor, "baseline category")
```

In other words, we can create a factor by specifying an existing factor, and simply writing the name of the baseline category in quotes. For **Cured** and **Intervention**, it makes most sense not to create new factors, but just to overwrite the existing ones, therefore, we specify these variables as both the new and old factors; this will simply respecify the baseline category of the existing variables. Execute these commands:

```
eelData$Cured<-relevel(eelData$Cured, "Not Cured")
eelData$Intervention<-relevel(eelData$Intervention, "No Treatment")
```

The variable **Cured** now has *Not Cured* as the first level (i.e., the baseline category), and **Intervention** now has *No Treatment* as the baseline category. Having set our baseline categories, we can get on with the analysis.

8.6.2. The main logistic regression analysis ②

8.6.2.1. Basic logistic regression analysis using R Commander ②

First, import the data, using the **Data⇒Import data⇒from text file, clipboard, or URL…** menu to set the import options and choose the file **eel.dat** (see section 3.7.3). As discussed in the previous section, **R** will import the variables **Cured** and **Intervention** as factors

FIGURE 8.5
Reordering
a factor in R
Commander

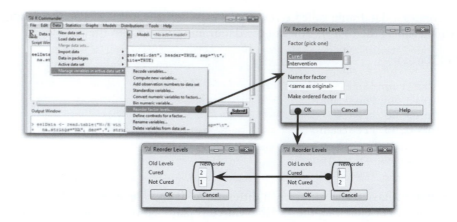

(because they contain text) but we might not like the baseline category that it sets by default. Therefore, the first thing that we need to do is to set the baseline category to one that we want. We can do this by selecting **Data⇒Manage variables in active data set⇒Reorder factor levels…** as shown in Figure 8.5. In the first dialog box there is a list of factors (labelled *Factor (pick one)*); select the factor that you want to reorder (I have selected **Cured**). By default the function will simply overwrite the existing factor, which is why the *Name for factor* box contains *<same as original>*; however, if you want to create a new variable then replace the text in this box with a new name. Having selected a factor and named it, click on ⬚OK⬚. The next dialog box displays the categories contained within the selected factor and their order. Note that we have two categories – *Cured* and *Not Cured* – and the 1 and 2 reflects their order (*Cured* is first, and *Not Cured* second). We want to reverse this order, so we need to change the numbers so that *Cured* is 2 and *Not Cured* is 1 (which will make it the baseline category). Once you have edited the numbers to reflect the order you want click on ⬚OK⬚ to make the change. You can repeat the process for the **Intervention** variable.

We will carry out a hierarchical regression: in model 1, we'll include only **Intervention** as a predictor, and then in model 2 we'll add **Duration**. Let's create the first model. To run binary logistic regression, choose **Statistics⇒Fit models⇒Generalized linear model…** to access the dialog box in Figure 8.6. In the box labelled *Enter name for model:* we enter a

FIGURE 8.6
Dialog box for
generalized linear
models in R
Commander

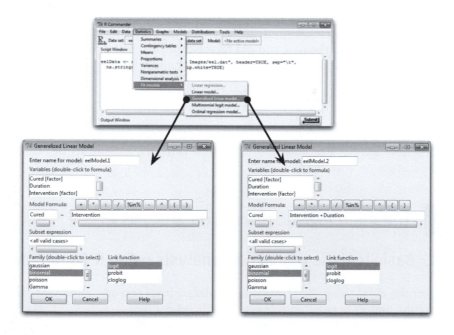

name for the model we are going to estimate; I've called it *eelModel.1*. Next, we need to create the formula that described the model. The formula consists of an outcome variable, which should be a dichotomous factor variable for logistic regression. In our case, the variable is **Cured**. (Notice that R Commander has labelled the variable as a factor in the list of variables.) First double-click on **Cured**, which will move it to box under the label *Model Formula:* (which is where the cursor would be). Having specified the outcome variable, the cursor will hop into the box to the right, which is where we want to put any predictors. There are several buttons above this box that make it easy for us to add useful things like '+' (to add predictors), or '*' (for interaction terms) or even brackets. We can build the predictors up by double-clicking on them in the list of variables and adding appropriate symbols. In model 1 we want only **Intervention** as a predictor, so double-click on this variable in the list (the completed box should look like the left-hand box in Figure 8.6).

When we use a generalized linear model we need to specify a family and link function. The family relates to the type of distribution that we assume; for example, if we choose Gaussian, that means we are assuming a normal distribution. We would choose this for linear regression. For logistic regression we choose binomial. We also need to choose a link function – for logistic regression, we choose the logit. R Commander helpfully selects these by default.

We generate the second model in much the same way. In the box labelled *Enter name for model:* enter a name for the model; I've called it *eelModel.2*. Next, double-click on **Cured**, to move it to the left-hand box under the label *Model Formula:* (which is where the cursor would be). Then to specify the predictors, double-click on **Intervention** to move it to the right-hand box under the label *Model Formula:*, then type '+' or click on ⊞, then double-click on **Duration** in the list to move it to the formula box. The finished dialog box should look like the right-hand dialog box in box in Figure 8.6.

8.6.3. Basic logistic regression analysis using R ②

To do logistic regression, we use the **glm()** function. The *glm()* function is very similar to the *lm()* function that we saw in Chapter 7. While *lm* stands for 'linear model', *glm* stands for 'generalized linear model' – that is, the basic linear model that has been generalized to other sorts of situations. The general form of this function is:

```
newModel<-glm(outcome ~ predictor(s), data = dataFrame, family = name of a
distribution, na.action = an action)
```

in which:

- *newModel* is an object created that contains information about the model. We can get summary statistics for this model by executing *summary(newModel)*.

- *outcome* is the variable that you're trying to predict, also known as the dependent variable. In this example it will be the variable **Cured**.

- *predictor(s)* lists the variable or variables from which you're trying to predict the outcome variable. In this example it will be the variables **Cured** and **Duration**.

- *dataFrame* is the name of the dataframe from which your outcome and predictor variables come.

- *family* is the name of a distribution (e.g., Gaussian, binomial, poisson, gamma).

- *na.action* is an optional command. If you have complete data (as we have here) you can ignore it, but if you have missing values (i.e., NAs in the dataframe) then it can be useful – see R's Souls' Tip 7.1).

The format, as you can see, is extremely similar to *lm()* in that we specify a formula that describes our model, we specify the dataframe that contains the variables in the formula, and we can use *na.action* to determine how to deal with missing cases. The only difference is a new option called *family*. This enables us to tell **R** the detail of the kind of regression that we want to do: by specifying the distribution on which our model is based. If we were doing an ordinary regression (as in Chapter 7) we could set this option to Gaussian (which is another name for a normal distribution) because ordinary regression is based on a normal distribution. Logistic regression is based on a binomial distribution, so we need to set this option to *family = binomial()*.[4]

We will carry out a hierarchical regression: in model 1, we'll include only **Intervention** as a predictor, and then in model 2 we'll add **Duration**. To create the first model we can execute:

```
eelModel.1 <- glm(Cured ~ Intervention, data = eelData, family = binomial())
```

This command creates a model called *eelModel.1* in which **Cured** is predicted from only **Intervention** (*Cured ~ Intervention*) based on a logit function. Similarly, we can create the second model by executing:

```
eelModel.2 <- glm(Cured ~ Intervention + Duration, data = eelData, family =
binomial())
```

This command creates a model called *eelModel.2* in which **Cured** is predicted from both **Intervention** and **Duration** (*Cured ~ Intervention + Duration*).

8.6.4.   Interpreting a basic logistic regression ②

To see the models that we have just generated we need to execute the *summary()* function (remembering to put the model name into the function):

```
summary(eelModel.1)
summary(eelModel.2)
```

The results are shown in Outputs 8.1 and 8.3 and are discussed in the next two sections.

8.6.5.   Model 1: Intervention only ②

Output 8.1 shows the model summary for model 1, which used **Intervention** to predict **Cured**. First, we should look at the summary statistics about the model. The overall fit of the model is assessed using the deviance statistic (to recap: this is -2 times the log-likelihood). Remember that larger values of the deviance statistic indicate poorer-fitting statistical models. **R** provides two deviance statistics: the null deviance and the residual deviance. The null deviance is the deviance of the model that contains no predictors other

---

[4] **R** has a number of useful defaults. If you don't specify a family, **R** assumes that you want to use a Gaussian family of distributions, which is the same as using *lm()*. In addition, you can specify a link function for the binomial family. The logit and probit are two commonly used link functions, which are specified as *Binomial(link = "logit")* and *Binomial(link = "probit")*. If you don't specify a link function, **R** chooses the logit link function for you, which is what is needed for logistic regression so we don't need to explicitly use a link function in our model.

than the constant – in other words, $-2LL$(baseline).[5] The residual deviance is the deviance for the model – in other words, $-2LL$(new).

```
Call:
glm(formula = Cured ~ Intervention, family = binomial(), data = eelData)

Deviance Residuals:
    Min       1Q   Median       3Q      Max
-1.5940  -1.0579   0.8118   0.8118   1.3018

Coefficients:
                        Estimate Std. Error z value Pr(>|z|)
(Intercept)              -0.2877     0.2700  -1.065  0.28671
InterventionIntervention  1.2287     0.3998   3.074  0.00212 **
---
Signif. codes:  0 '***' 0.001 '**' 0.01 '*' 0.05 '.' 0.1 ' ' 1

(Dispersion parameter for binomial family taken to be 1)

    Null deviance: 154.08  on 112  degrees of freedom
Residual deviance: 144.16  on 111  degrees of freedom
AIC: 148.16

Number of Fisher Scoring iterations: 4
```

Output 8.1

At this stage of the analysis the value of the deviance for the model should be less than the value for the null model (when only the constant was included in the model) because lower values of $-2LL$ indicate that the model is predicting the outcome variable more accurately. For the null model, $-2LL = 154.08$, but when **Intervention** has been included this value has been reduced to 144.16. This reduction tells us that the model is better at predicting whether someone was cured than it was before **Intervention** was added.

The question of how much better the model predicts the outcome variable can be assessed using the *model chi-square statistic*, which measures the difference between the model as it currently stands and the model when only the constant was included. We saw in section 8.3.1 that we could assess the significance of the change in a model by taking the log-likelihood of the new model and subtracting the log-likelihood of the baseline model from it. The value of the model chi-square statistic works on this principle and is, therefore, equal to $-2LL$ with **Intervention** included minus the value of $-2LL$ when only the constant was in the model ($154.08 - 144.16 = 9.92$). This value has a chi-square distribution and so its statistical significance can be calculated easily. In this example, the value is significant at a .05 level and so we can say that overall the model is predicting whether a patient is cured or not significantly better than it was with only the constant included. The model chi-square is an analogue of the *F*-test for the linear regression (see Chapter 7). In an ideal world we would like to see a non-significant overall $-2LL$ (indicating that the amount of unexplained data is minimal) and a highly significant model chi-square statistic (indicating that the model including the predictors is significantly better than without those predictors). However, in reality it is possible for both statistics to be highly significant.

We can use **R** to automatically calculate the model chi-square and its significance. We can do this by treating the output model as data. The object *eelModel.1* has a number of

---

[5] You can try this by running a model with only an intercept. Use:

```
eelModel.0 <- glm(Cured ~ 1, data = eelData, family = binomial())
summary(eelModel.0)
```

variables associated with it. Two of these are the *deviance* and *null.deviance*. By subtracting the deviance from the null deviance we can find the improvement, which gives us a chi-square statistic. We can reference these variables the same as any other: by appending the variable name to the model using dollar sign. To calculate this value execute:

```
modelChi <- eelModel.1$null.deviance - eelModel.1$deviance
```

This creates a value called *modelChi* that is the deviance for the model *eelModel.1* subtracted from the null deviance from the same model. We can see the value by executing:

```
modelChi
```

```
[1] 9.926201
```

As you can see, this value corresponds to the one we calculated by hand (allowing for differences in rounding). Similarly, the degrees of freedom for the model are stored in the variable *df.residual* and for the null model are stored as *df.null*. These are the values of 111 and 112 in Output 8.1. We can compute the degrees of freedom associated with the chi-square statistic that we just computed by subtracting the degrees of freedom exactly as we did for the deviance values. Execute:

```
chidf <- eelModel.1$df.null - eelModel.1$df.residual
```

This creates a value called *chidf* that is the degrees of freedom for the model *eelModel.1* subtracted from the degrees of freedom for the null model. We can see the value by executing:

```
chidf
```

```
[1] 1
```

As you can see, the change in degrees of freedom is 1, which reflects the fact that we have only one variable in the model.

To calculate the probability associated with this chi-square statistic we can use the **pchisq()** function. This function needs two things: the value of chi-square (which we have just computed as *modelChi*) and the degrees of freedom (which we have just computed as *chidf*). The probability we want is 1 minus the value of the *pchisq()* function, which we can obtain by executing:

```
chisq.prob <- 1 - pchisq(modelChi, chidf)
```

This command creates an object called *chisq.prob*, which is 1 minus the result of the *pchisq()* function (note that we have placed the variables containing of the chi-square statistic and its degrees of freedom directly into this function). To see the value we execute:

```
chisq.prob
```

```
[1] 0.001629425
```

In other words, the *p*-value is .002 (rounded to three decimal places); because this probability is less than .05, we can reject the null hypothesis that the model is not better than chance at predicting the outcome. This value is the likelihood ratio *p*-value of the model because we only had one predictor in the model. We can report that including **Intervention** produced a significant improvement in the fit of the model, $\chi^2(1) = 9.93$, $p = .002$.

Next, we consider the coefficients. This part is crucial because it tells us the estimates for the coefficients for the predictors included in the model. This section of the output gives us the coefficients and statistics for the variables that have been included in the model at this point (namely **Intervention** and the constant). The *b*-value is the same as the *b*-value in linear regression: they are the values that we need to replace in equation (8.4) to establish the probability that a case falls into a certain category. We saw in linear regression that the value of *b* represents the change in the outcome resulting from a unit change in the predictor variable. The interpretation of this coefficient in logistic regression is very similar in that it represents the change in the *logit* of the outcome variable associated with a one-unit change in the predictor variable. The logit of the outcome is simply the natural logarithm of the odds of *Y* occurring.

The crucial statistic is the z-statistic which has a normal distribution and tells us whether the b coefficient for that predictor is significantly different from zero.[6] If the coefficient is significantly different from zero then we can assume that the predictor is making a significant contribution to the prediction of the outcome (Y). We came across the z-statistic in section 8.3.4 and saw that it should be used cautiously because when the regression coefficient (b) is large, the standard error tends to become inflated, resulting in the z-statistic being underestimated (see Menard, 1995). However, for these data it seems to indicate that having the intervention (or not) is a significant predictor of whether the patient is cured (note that the significance of the z-statistic is less than .05). We could say that **Intervention** was a significant predictor of being cured, $b = 1.23$, $z = 3.07$, $p < .002$.

In section 8.3.3 we saw that we could calculate an analogue of R using equation (8.7). For these data, the z-statistic and its df can be read from the **R** output (3.074 and 1, respectively), and the null model deviance was 154.08. Therefore, R can be calculated as:

$$R = \sqrt{\frac{3.074^2 - 2 \times 1}{154.08}} = 0.22 \tag{8.14}$$

In the same section we saw that Hosmer and Lemeshow's measure (R_L^2) is calculated by dividing the model chi-square by the original $-2LL$. In this example the model chi-square after **Intervention** has been entered into the model is 9.93 (calculated as *modelChi* above), and the original $-2LL$ (before any variables were entered) was 154.08 (the *deviance.null*). So, $R_L^2 = 9.93/154.08 = .06$, which is different from the value we would get by squaring the value of R given above ($R^2 = .22^2 = 0.05$).

We can get **R** to do this calculation for us by executing:

```
R2.hl<-modelChi/eelModel.1$null.deviance
R2.hl
```

```
[1] 0.06442071
```

The first command simply takes the value of the model chi-square (which we have already calculated as *modelChi*, and divides it by the $-2LL$ for the original model (*eelModel.1$null.deviance*)). This is a direct analogue of the equation given earlier in the chapter. The second command displays the value, which is .064.

We also saw two other measures of R^2 that were described in section 8.3.3, Cox and Snell's and Nagelkerke's. There are functions available in **R** to calculate these, but they're a bit of a pain to find and use. It's easy enough, however, to write commands in **R** to calculate them. We can write the equation for the Cox and Snell statistic as:

```
R.cs <- 1 - exp ((eelModel.1$deviance - eelModel.1$null.deviance) /113)
R.cs
```

```
[1] 0.08409487
```

The first command uses the $-2LL$ for the model (*eelModel.1$deviance*) and the null model (*eelModel.1$null.deviance*) and divides the difference by the sample size (in this case 113, but you will need to change this value for other data sets). The second command will display the result: a value of .084. We can use this value to calculate Nagelkerke's estimate also. Again, we just write out the equation in **R**-speak:

```
R.n <- R.cs /(1-(exp(-(eelModel.1$null.deviance/113))))
R.n
```

```
[1] 0.112992
```

The first command uses the value we just calculated, *R.cs*, and adjusts it using the $-2LL$ for the null model (*eelModel.1$null.deviance*) and the sample size (which, again you'll need to

[6] You might also come across a Wald statistic – this is the square of the z-statistic and is distributed as chi-square.

change for other data sets, but is 113 in the current one). The second command will display the result: a value of .113.

Alternatively you could write a function to calculate all three R^2-values from a model, which has the advantage that you can reuse the function for other models (R's Souls' Tip 8.2). As you can see, all of the values of R^2 differ, but they can be used as effect size measures for the model.

R's Souls' Tip 8.2   Writing a function to compute R^2 ③

We saw in (R's Souls' Tip 6.2) that it's possible to write functions to do things for us in **R**. If we were running several logistic regression models it would get fairly tedious to keep typing out the commands to calculate the various values of R^2. Therefore, we could wrap them up in a function. We'll call this function *logisticPseudoR2s* so that we know what it does, and we'll enter a logistic regression model (we've named this *LogModel*) into it as the input. To create the function execute:

```
logisticPseudoR2s <- function(LogModel) {
     dev <- LogModel$deviance
     nullDev <- LogModel$null.deviance
     modelN <- length(LogModel$fitted.values)
     R.l <-  1 -  dev / nullDev
     R.cs <- 1- exp ( -(nullDev - dev) / modelN)
     R.n <- R.cs / ( 1 - ( exp (-(nullDev / modelN))))
     cat("Pseudo R^2 for logistic regression\n")
     cat("Hosmer and Lemeshow R^2  ", round(R.l, 3), "\n")
     cat("Cox and Snell R^2        ", round(R.cs, 3), "\n")
     cat("Nagelkerke R^2           ", round(R.n, 3),   "\n")
   }
```

Taking each line in turn:

- *dev<-LogModel$deviance* extracts the model deviance ($-2LL$(new)) of the model entered into the function and calls it *dev*.
- *nullDev<-LogModel$null.deviance* extracts the baseline deviance ($-2LL$(baseline)) of the model entered into the function and calls is *nullDev*.
- *modelN<-length(LogModel$fitted.values)* uses the *length()* function on the fitted value to compute the sample size, which it calls *modelN*.
- *R.l <- 1 - dev/nullDev* computes Hosmer and Lemeshow's measure (R_L^2) using the values extracted from the model and calls it *R.l*.
- *R.cs<- 1- exp (-(nullDev - dev)/modelN)*: computes Cox and Snell's measure (R_{CS}^2) using the values extracted from the model and calls it *R.cs*.
- *R.n <- R.cs / (1 - (exp (-(nullDev / modelN))))* computes Nagelkerke's measure (R_N^2) using the values extracted from the model and calls it *R.n*.
- *cat()*: The last four lines use the *cat()* function to print the text in quotes, plus the various versions of R^2 rounded to three decimal places.

To use the function on our model, we simply place the name of the logistic regression model (in this case *eelModel.1*) into the function and execute:

```
logisticPseudoR2s(eelModel.1)
```

The output will be:

```
Pseudo R^2 for logistic regression
Hosmer and Lemeshow R^2    0.064
Cox and Snell R^2          0.084
Nagelkerke R^2             0.113
```

The final thing we need to think about is the odds ratios, which were described in section 8.3.6. To calculate the change in odds that results from a unit change in the predictor for this example, we must first calculate the odds of a patient being cured given that they *didn't* have the intervention. We then calculate the odds of a patient being cured given that they *did* have the intervention. Finally, we calculate the proportionate change in these two odds.

To calculate the first set of odds, we need to use equation (8.12) to calculate the probability of a patient being cured given that they *didn't* have the intervention. The parameter coding at the beginning of the output told us that patients who did not have the intervention were coded with a 0, so we can use this value in place of X. The value of b_1 has been estimated for us as 1.229 (see *Coefficients:* in Output 8.1), and the coefficient for the constant can be taken from the same table and is −0.288. We can calculate the odds as:

$$P(\text{Cured}) = \frac{1}{1+e^{-(b_0+b_1X_1)}} = \frac{1}{1+e^{-[-0.288+(1.229\times 0)]}} = .428$$

$$P(\text{Not Cured}) = 1 - P(\text{Cured}) = 1 - .428 = .527$$

$$\text{odds} = \frac{.428}{.572} = 0.748 \tag{8.15}$$

Now we calculate the same thing after the predictor variable has changed by one unit. In this case, because the predictor variable is dichotomous, we need to calculate the odds of a patient being cured, given that they have had the intervention. So, the value of the intervention variable, X, is now 1 (rather than 0). The resulting calculations are as follows:

$$P(\text{Cured}) = \frac{1}{1+e^{-(b_0+b_1X_1)}} = \frac{1}{1+e^{-[-0.288+(1.229\times 1)]}} = .719$$

$$P(\text{Not Cured}) = 1 - P(\text{Cured}) = 1 - .719 = .281$$

$$\text{odds} = \frac{.719}{.281} = 2.559 \tag{8.16}$$

We now know the odds before and after a unit change in the predictor variable. It is now a simple matter to calculate the proportionate change in odds by dividing the odds after a unit change in the predictor by the odds before that change:

$$\Delta\text{odds} = \frac{\text{odds after a unit change in the predictor}}{\text{original odds}}$$

$$= \frac{2.56}{0.75} \tag{8.17}$$

$$= 3.41$$

We can also calculate the odds ratio as the exponential of the b coefficient for the predictor variables. These coefficients are stored in a variable called *coefficients*, which is part of the model we created. Therefore, we can access this variable as:

```
eelModel.1$coefficients
```

This just means 'the variable called *coefficients* within the model called *eelModel.1*'. It's a simple matter to apply the **exp()** function to this variable to find out the odds ratio:

```
exp(eelModel.1$coefficients)
```

Executing this command will display the odds ratio for the predictors in the model:

```
            (Intercept)  InterventionIntervention
            0.750000                   3.416667
```

The odds ratio for **Intervention** (3.417) is the same as we calculated above (allowing for differences in rounding). We can interpret the odds ratio in terms of the change in odds. If the value is greater than 1 then it indicates that as the predictor increases, the odds of the outcome occurring increase. Conversely, a value less than 1 indicates that as the predictor increases, the odds of the outcome occurring decrease. In this example, we can say that the odds of a patient who is treated being cured are 3.42 times higher than those of a patient who is not treated.

We can also calculate confidence intervals for the odds ratios. To obtain confidence intervals of the parameters, we use the *confint()* function – just as we did for ordinary regression. We can also exponentiate these with the *exp()* function. To get the confidence intervals execute:

```
exp(confint(eelModel.1))
```

This function computes the confidence intervals for the coefficients in the model (*confint(eelModel.1)*) and then uses *exp()* to exponentiate them. The resulting output is in Output 8.2. The way to interpret this confidence interval is the same as any other confidence interval (section 2.5.2): if we calculated confidence intervals for the value of the odds ratio in 100 different samples, then these intervals would encompass the actual value of the odds ratio in the population (rather than the sample) in 95 of those samples. In this case, we can be fairly confident that the population value of the odds ratio lies between 1.58 and 7.63.[7] However, our sample could be one of the 5% that produces a confidence interval that 'misses' the population value.

```
                          2.5 %    97.5 %
(Intercept)             0.4374531 1.268674
InterventionIntervention 1.5820127 7.625545
```

Output 8.2

The important thing about this confidence interval is that it doesn't cross 1 (the values at each end of the interval are greater than 1). This is important because values greater than 1 mean that as the predictor variable increases, so do the odds of (in this case) being cured. Values less than 1 mean the opposite: as the predictor variable increases, the odds of being cured decrease. The fact that both the lower and upper limits of our confidence interval are above 1 gives us confidence that the direction of the relationship that we have observed is true in the population (i.e., it's likely that having an intervention compared to not increases the odds of being cured). If the lower limit had been below 1 then it would tell us that there is a chance that in the population the direction of the relationship is the opposite to what we have observed. This would mean that we could not trust that our intervention increases the odds of being cured.

8.6.6. Model 2: Intervention and Duration as predictors ②

Now let's return to model 2 (*eelModel.2*), which we ran a long time ago. Recall that in model 2 we added the variable **Duration** to our model. Output 8.3 shows the output for the summary of this model. You can see that the *b* estimate for **Duration** is −0.008, a pretty small number. In addition, the probability value associated with that variable is not significant: the value of 0.964 is larger than .05.

---

[7] If you ever run analysis with **R** and another package and compare the results, you might find different confidence intervals. That's because some packages use Wald test based confidence intervals, whereas **R** uses likelihood ratio based confidence intervals and thus avoids the problems of the Wald test that we identified earlier.

Comparing model 1 with model 2, we can see that the deviance for the two models is the same (144.16), suggesting that model 2 is not an improvement over model 1. In addition, we can see that the AIC is higher in model 2 (150.16) than model 1 (148.16), indicating that model 1 is the better model.

```
Call:
glm(formula = Cured ~ Intervention + Duration, family = binomial(),
    data = eelData)

Deviance Residuals:
    Min       1Q    Median       3Q      Max
-1.6025  -1.0572    0.8107   0.8161   1.3095

Coefficients:
                        Estimate Std. Error z value Pr(>|z|)
(Intercept)            -0.234660   1.220563  -0.192  0.84754
InterventionIntervention 1.233532   0.414565   2.975  0.00293 **
Duration               -0.007835   0.175913  -0.045  0.96447
---
Signif. codes:  0 '***' 0.001 '**' 0.01 '*' 0.05 '.' 0.1 ' ' 1

(Dispersion parameter for binomial family taken to be 1)

    Null deviance: 154.08  on 112  degrees of freedom
Residual deviance: 144.16  on 110  degrees of freedom
AIC: 150.16

Number of Fisher Scoring iterations: 4
```

Output 8.3

We can again compare the models by finding the difference in the deviance statistics. This difference is chi-square distributed. We can find this difference in two ways. First, we can subtract one deviance from the other as we did before. An easier method though, is to use the *anova()* function (see section 7.8.4). The *anova()* function has the advantage that it also calculates the degrees of freedom for us; but the disadvantage is that it doesn't calculate the significance. If we do the calculations manually we can use the same commands as before, except that rather than using the *null.deviance* and *df.null* variables, we use the *deviance* and *df.residual* variables for the two models we're comparing: in each case we subtract model 2 from model 1:

```
modelChi <- eelModel.1$deviance - eelModel.2$deviance
chidf <- eelModel.1$df.residual - eelModel.2$df.residual
chisq.prob <- 1 - pchisq(modelChi, chidf)
modelChi; chidf; chisq.prob

[1] 0.001983528
[1] 1
[1] 0.9644765
```

You should find that the difference between the models (*modelChi*) is 0.00198, with one degree of freedom (*chidf*), and a *p*-value (*chisq.prob*) of 0.964. As this value is greater than .05, we can conclude that model 2 (with **Intervention** and **Duration** as predictors) is not a significant improvement over model 1 (which included only **Intervention** as a predictor).

With the *anova()* function, remember that we simply list the models in the order in which we want to compare them. Therefore, to compare our two models we would execute:

```
anova(eelModel.1, eelModel.2)
```

This produces Output 8.4, which confirms (but was easier to do) that the difference between the models is 0.00198.

```
Analysis of Deviance Table

Model 1: Cured ~ Intervention
Model 2: Cured ~ Intervention + Duration
  Resid. Df Resid. Dev Df  Deviance
1       111     144.16
2       110     144.16  1 0.0019835
```

Output 8.4

CRAMMING SAM'S TIPS   Deviance

- The overall fit of the final model is shown by the *deviance* statistic and its associated chi-square statistic. If the significance of the chi-square statistic is less than .05, then the model is a significant fit to the data.
- Check the table labelled *Coefficients:* to see which variables significantly predict the outcome.
- For each variable in the model, look at the *z*-statistic and its significance (which again should be below .05).
- More important, though, use the odds ratio for interpretation. You can obtain this using *exp(model$coefficients)*, where *model* is the name of your model. If the value is greater than 1 then as the predictor increases, the odds of the outcome occurring increase. Conversely, a value less than 1 indicates that as the predictor increases, the odds of the outcome occurring decrease. For the aforementioned interpretation to be reliable the confidence interval of the odds ratio should not cross 1.

8.6.7.   Casewise diagnostics in logistic regression ②

8.6.7.1. Obtaining residuals ②

As with linear regression, it is possible to calculate residuals (see section 7.7.1.1). These residual variables can then be examined to see how well the model fits the observed data. The commands to obtain residuals are the same as those we encountered for linear regression in section 7.9. To obtain residuals, we can use the *resid()* function and include the model name within it.

Fitted values for logistic regression are a little different from linear regression. The fitted values are the predicted probabilities of Y occurring given the values of each predictor for a given participant. As such, they are derived from equation (8.4) for a given case. We can also calculate a predicted group membership, based on the most likely outcome for each person based on the model. The group memberships are based on the predicted probabilities, and I will explain these values in more detail when we consider how to interpret the residuals. Predicted probabilities are obtained with the *fitted()* function (again, we simply supply the model name to the function).

As with ordinary regression, then, we can add these casewise diagnostic variables to our dataframe by creating new variables to contain them and then using the various functions we encountered in section 7.9 to populate these variables with the appropriate values. For example, as a basic set of diagnostic statistics we might execute:[8]

---

[8] You might want to save the file after creating these variables by executing:
`write.table(eelData, "Eel With Diagnostics.dat", sep = "\t", row.names = FALSE)`

```
eelData$predicted.probabilities<-fitted(eelModel.1)
eelData$standardized.residuals<-rstandard(eelModel.1)
eelData$studentized.residuals<-rstudent(eelModel.1)
eelData$dfbeta<-dfbeta(eelModel.1)
eelData$dffit<-dffits(eelModel.1)
eelData $leverage<-hatvalues(eelModel.1)
```

To reiterate a point from the previous chapter, running a regression without checking how well the model fits the data is like buying a new pair of trousers without trying them on – they might look fine on the hanger but get them home and you find you're Johnny-tight-pants. The trousers do their job (they cover your legs and keep you warm) but they have no real-life value (because they cut off the blood circulation to your legs, which then have to be amputated). Likewise, regression does its job regardless of the data – it will create a model – but the real-life value of the model may be limited (see section 7.7).

8.6.7.2. Predicted probabilities ②

Let's take a look at the predicted probabilities. We can use the *head()* function again just to look at the first few cases. Execute:

```
head(eelData[,  c("Cured",  "Intervention",  "Duration",  "predicted.
probabilities")])
```

This command uses *head()* to display the first six cases, and we have selected a subset of variables from the *eelData* dataframe (see section 3.9.1).

```
      Cured Intervention Duration predicted.probabilities
1 Not Cured No Treatment        7               0.4285714
2 Not Cured No Treatment        7               0.4285714
3 Not Cured No Treatment        6               0.4285714
4     Cured No Treatment        8               0.4285714
5     Cured Intervention       7               0.7192982
6     Cured No Treatment        6               0.4285714
```

Output 8.5

Output 8.5 shows the values of the predicted probabilities as well as the initial data. We found from the model that the only significant predictor of being cured was having the intervention. This could have a value of either 1 (have the intervention) or 0 (no intervention). If these two values are placed into equation (8.4) with the respective regression coefficients, then the two probability values are derived. In fact, we calculated these values as part of equations (8.15) and (8.16), and you should note that the calculated probabilities – *P*(Cured) in these equations – correspond to the values of the predicted probabilities. These values tells us that when a patient is not treated (**Intervention** = 0, No Treatment), there is a probability of .429 that they will be cured – basically, about 43% of people get better without any treatment. However, if the patient does have the intervention (**Intervention** = 1, yes), there is a probability of .719 that they will get better – about 72% of people treated get better. When you consider that a probability of 0 indicates no chance of getting better, and a probability of 1 indicates that the patient will definitely get better, the values obtained provide strong evidence that having the intervention increases your chances of getting better (although the probability of recovery without the intervention is still not bad).

Assuming we are content that the model is accurate and that the intervention has some substantive significance, then we could conclude that our intervention (which, to remind you, was putting an eel up the anus) is the single best predictor of getting better (not being constipated). Furthermore, the duration of the constipation pre-intervention and its interaction with the intervention did not significantly predict whether a person got better.

8.6.7.3. Interpreting residuals ②

Our conclusions so far are fine in themselves, but to be sure that the model is a good one, it is important to examine the residuals.

We saw in the previous chapter that the main purpose of examining residuals in any regression is to (1) isolate points for which the model fits poorly, and (2) isolate points that exert an undue influence on the model. To assess the former we examine the residuals, especially the studentized residuals, standardized residuals and deviance statistics. To assess the latter we use influence statistics such as Cook's distance, DFBeta and leverage statistics. These statistics were explained in detail in section 7.7 and their interpretation in logistic regression is the same; for more detail consult the previous chapter. To remind you of the main ones, Table 8.1 summarizes them.

If you have saved your residuals in the dataframe then you could look at them by executing something like:

```
eelData[, c("leverage", "studentized.residuals", "dfbeta")]
```

This command will print the leverage, studentized residuals and dfbeta values for model.

OLIVER TWISTED

Please Sir, can I have some more … diagnostics?

'What about the trees?' protests eco-warrior Oliver. 'These outputs take up so much room, why don't you put them on the website instead?' It's a valid point so I have produced a table of the diagnostic statistics for this example, but it's in the additional material for this chapter on the companion website.

The basic residual statistics for this example (leverage, studentized residuals and DFBeta values) are pretty good: note that all cases have DFBetas less than 1, and leverage statistics are very close to the calculated expected value of 0.018. All in all, this means that there are no influential cases having an effect on the model. The studentized residuals all have values of less than ±2 and so there seems to be very little here to concern us.

You should note that these residuals are slightly unusual because they are based on a single predictor that is categorical. This is why there isn't a lot of variability in the values of

Table 8.1   Summary of residual statistics

Name	Comment
Leverage	Lies between 0 (no influence) and 1 (complete influence). The expected leverage is $(k +1)/N$, where k is the number of predictors and N is the sample size. In this case it would be $2/113 = .018$
Studentized residual Standardized residual	Only 5% should lie outside ±1.96, and about 1% should lie outside ±2.58. Cases above 3 are cause for concern and cases close to 3 warrant inspection
DFBeta for the constant DFBeta for the first predictor (**Intervention**)	Should be less than 1

the residuals. Also, if substantial outliers or influential cases had been isolated, you are not justified in eliminating these cases to make the model fit better. Instead these cases should be inspected closely to try to isolate a good reason why they were unusual. It might simply be an error in inputting data, or it could be that the case was one which had a special reason for being unusual: for example, there were other medical complications that might contribute to the constipation that were noted during the patient's assessment. In such a case, you may have good reason to exclude the case and duly note the reasons why.

CRAMMING SAM'S TIPS   **Diagnostic statistics**

You need to look for cases that might be influencing the logistic regression model:

- Look at standardized residuals and check that no more than 5% of cases have absolute values above 2, and that no more than about 1% have absolute values above 2.5. Any case with a value above about 3 could be an outlier.
- Calculate the average leverage (the number of predictors plus 1, divided by the sample size) and then look for values greater than twice or three times this average value.
- Look for absolute values of DFBeta greater than 1.

8.6.8. Calculating the effect size ②

We've already seen that we can use the odds ratio (see section 8.3.6) as an effect size measure.

8.7. How to report logistic regression ②

My personal view is that you should report logistic regression much the same as linear regression (see section 7.11). I'd be inclined to tabulate the results, unless it's a very simple model. As a bare minimum, report the beta values and their standard errors and significance value and some general statistics about the model (such as the R^2 and goodness-of-fit statistics). I'd also highly recommend reporting the odds ratio and its confidence interval. If you include the constant, readers of your work can construct the full regression model if they need to. You might also consider reporting the variables that were not significant predictors because this can be as valuable as knowing about which predictors were significant.

For the example in this chapter we might produce a table like that in Table 8.2. Hopefully you can work out from where the values came by looking back through the chapter so far. As with multiple regression, I've rounded off to 2 decimal places throughout; for the R^2 and p-values, in line with APA convention, there is no zero before the decimal point (because these values cannot exceed 1) but for all other values less than 1 the zero is present; the significance of the variable is denoted by an asterisk with a footnote to indicate the significance level being used.

Table 8.2   How to report logistic regression

	B (SE)	95% CI for odds ratio		
		Lower	Odds ratio	Upper
Included				
Constant	−0.29 (0.27)			
Intervention	1.23* (0.40)	1.56	3.42	7.48

Note. R^2 = .06 (Hosmer–Lemeshow), .08 (Cox–Snell), .11 (Nagelkerke). Model $\chi^2(1) = 9.93$, $p < .01$. * $p < .01$.

8.8. Testing assumptions: another example ②

This example was originally inspired by events in the soccer World Cup of 1998 (a long time ago now, but such crushing disappointments are not easily forgotten). Unfortunately for me (being an Englishman), I was subjected to watching England get knocked out of the competition by losing a penalty shootout. Reassuringly, six years later I watched England get knocked out of the European Championship in another penalty shootout. Even more reassuring, a few years after that I saw them fail to even qualify for the European Championship (not a penalty shootout this time, just playing like cretins).

Why do the England football team always miss penalties?

Now, if I were the England coach, I'd probably shoot the spoilt overpaid prima donnas, or I might be interested in finding out what factors predict whether or not a player will score a penalty. Those of you who hate soccer can read this example as being factors that predict success in a free throw in basketball or netball, a penalty in hockey or a penalty kick in rugby or field goal in American football. Now, this research question is perfect for logistic regression because our outcome variable is a dichotomy: a penalty can be either scored or missed. Imagine that past research (Eriksson, Beckham, & Vassell, 2004; Hoddle, Batty, & Ince, 1998) had shown that there are two factors that reliably predict whether a penalty kick will be missed or scored. The first factor is whether the player taking the kick is a worrier (this factor can be measured using a measure such as the Penn State Worry Questionnaire, PSWQ). The second factor is the player's past success rate at scoring (so whether the player has a good track record of scoring penalty kicks). It is fairly well accepted that anxiety has detrimental effects on the performance of a variety of tasks and so it was also predicted that state anxiety might be able to account for some of the unexplained variance in penalty success.

This example is a classic case of building on a well-established model, because two predictors are already known and we want to test the effect of a new one. So, 75 soccer players were selected at random and before taking a penalty kick in a competition they were given a state anxiety questionnaire to complete (to assess anxiety before the kick was taken). These players were also asked to complete the PSWQ to give a measure of how much they worried about things generally, and their past success rate was obtained from a database. Finally, a note was made of whether the penalty was scored or missed. The data can be found in the file **penalty.dat**, which contains four variables – each in a separate column:

- **Scored**: This variable is our outcome and it is coded such that 0 = penalty missed and 1 = penalty scored.
- **PSWQ**: This variable is the first predictor variable and it gives us a measure of the degree to which a player worries.

- **Previous**: This variable is the percentage of penalties scored by a particular player in their career. As such, it represents previous success at scoring penalties.

- **Anxious**: This variable is our third predictor and it is a variable that has not previously been used to predict penalty success. It is a measure of state anxiety before taking the penalty.

SELF-TEST

✓ We learnt how to do hierarchical regression in the previous chapter with linear regression and in this chapter with logistic regression. Try to conduct a hierarchical logistic regression analysis on these data. Enter **Previous** and **PSWQ** in the first block and **Anxious** in the second. There is a full guide on how to do the analysis and its interpretation in the additional material on the companion website.

8.8.1. Testing for multicollinearity ③

First, if you haven't already, read the data into a new dataframe, which we'll call *penaltyData*, by setting your working directory to the location of the file (see section 3.4.4) and executing:

```
penaltyData<-read.delim("penalty.dat", header = TRUE)
```

In section 7.7.2.4 we saw how multicollinearity can affect the standard error parameters of a regression model. Logistic regression is just as prone to the biasing effect of collinearity and it is essential to test for collinearity following a logistic regression analysis. We look for collinearity in logistic regression in exactly the same way we look for it in linear regression. First, let's re-create the model with all three predictors from the self-help task (in case you haven't done it). We can create the model by executing:

```
penaltyModel.2 <- glm(Scored ~ Previous + PSWQ + Anxious, data = penaltyData,
family = binomial())
```

This command creates a model (*penaltyModel.2*) in which the variable **Scored** is predicted from **PSWQ**, **Anxious**, and **Previous** (*Scored ~ Previous + PSWQ + Anxious*). Having created this model, we can get the VIF and tolerance as we did in Chapter 7 by entering the model name into the *vif()* function from the *car* package. Execute:

```
vif(penaltyModel.2)
1/vif(penaltyModel.2)
```

The first line gives you the VIF values and the second the tolerance (which is simply the reciprocal of the VIF).

```
Previous      PSWQ     Anxious
35.227113   1.089767  35.581976

   Previous        PSWQ      Anxious
0.02838723  0.91762767  0.02810412
```

Output 8.6

The results are shown in Output 8.6. These values indicate that there is a problem of collinearity: a VIF over 10 is usually considered problematic (see section 7.7.2.4 for more details). The result of this analysis is pretty clear-cut: there is collinearity between state anxiety and previous experience of taking penalties, and this dependency results in the model becoming biased.

SELF-TEST

✓ Using what you learned in Chapter 6, carry out a Pearson correlation between all of the variables in this analysis. Can you work out why we have a problem with collinearity?

If you have identified collinearity then, unfortunately, there's not much that you can do about it. One obvious solution is to omit one of the variables (so for example, we might stick with the model from block 1 that ignored state anxiety). The problem with this should be obvious: there is no way of knowing which variable to omit. The resulting theoretical conclusions are meaningless because, statistically speaking, any of the collinear variables could be omitted. There are no statistical grounds for omitting one variable over another. Even if a predictor is removed, Bowerman and O'Connell (1990) recommend that another equally important predictor that does not have such strong multicollinearity replace it. They also suggest collecting more data to see whether the multicollinearity can be lessened. Another possibility when there are several predictors involved in the multicollinearity is to run a factor analysis on these predictors and to use the resulting factor scores as a predictor (see Chapter 17). The safest (although unsatisfactory) remedy is to acknowledge the unreliability of the model. So, if we were to report the analysis of which factors predict penalty success, we might acknowledge that previous experience significantly predicted penalty success in the first model, but propose that this experience might affect penalty taking by increasing state anxiety. This statement would be highly speculative because the correlation between **Anxious** and **Previous** tells us nothing of the direction of causality, but it would acknowledge the inexplicable link between the two predictors. I'm sure that many of you may find the lack of remedy for collinearity grossly unsatisfying – unfortunately statistics is frustrating sometimes!

8.8.2.   Testing for linearity of the logit ③

In this example we have three continuous variables, therefore we have to check that each one is linearly related to the log of the outcome variable (**Scored**). I mentioned earlier in this chapter that to test this assumption we need to run the logistic regression but include predictors that are the interaction between each predictor and the log of itself (Hosmer & Lemeshow, 1989). We need to create the interaction terms of each of the variables with its log, using the *log()* function (section 5.8.3.2). First, let's do the PSWQ variable; well call the interaction of PSWQ with its log *logPSWQInt*, and we create this variable by executing:

```
penaltyData$logPSWQInt <- log(penaltyData$PSWQ)*penaltyData$PSWQ
```

This command creates a new variable called *logPSWQInt* in the *penaltyData* dataframe that is the variable **PSWQ** (*penaltyData$PSWQ*) multiplied by the log of that variable (*log(penaltyData$PSWQ)*).

SELF-TEST

✓ Try creating two new variables that are the natural logs of **Anxious** and **Previous**. (Remember that 0 has no log, so if any of the variables have a zero, you'll need to add a constant – see section 5.8.3.2.)

The dataframe will now look like this:

```
PSWQ Anxious Previous      Scored    logPSWQInt logAnxInt logPrevInt
18       21       56 Scored Penalty    52.02669  63.93497  226.41087
17       32       35 Scored Penalty    48.16463 110.90355  125.42316
16       34       35 Scored Penalty    44.36142 119.89626  125.42316
14       40       15 Scored Penalty    36.94680 147.55518   41.58883
 5       24       47 Scored Penalty     8.04719  76.27329  181.94645
 1       15       67 Scored Penalty     0.00000  40.62075  282.70702
etc.
```

Note that there are three new variables that reflect the interaction between each predictor and the log of that predictor.

To test the assumption we need to redo the analysis exactly the same as before, except that we should put all variables in a single block (i.e., we don't need to do it hierarchically), and we also need to put in the three new interaction terms of each predictor and its log. We create the model by executing:

```
penaltyTest.1 <- glm(Scored ~ PSWQ + Anxious + Previous + logPSWQInt +
logAnxInt + logPrevInt, data=penaltyData, family=binomial())
summary(penaltyTest.1)
```

This command creates a model (*penaltyTest.1*) in which the variable **Scored** is predicted from PSWQ, Anxious, Previous and the variables we created to be the interaction of these variables with their logs (**logPSWQInt**, **logAnxInt**, and **logPrevInt**). We then use the *summary()* function to display the model.

```
Coefficients:
              Estimate Std. Error z value Pr(>|z|)
(Intercept)   -3.57212   15.00782  -0.238    0.812
PSWQ          -0.42218    1.10255  -0.383    0.702
Anxious       -2.64804    2.79283  -0.948    0.343
Previous       1.66905    1.48005   1.128    0.259
logPSWQInt     0.04388    0.29672   0.148    0.882
logAnxInt      0.68151    0.65177   1.046    0.296
logPrevInt    -0.31918    0.31687  -1.007    0.314
```

Output 8.7

Output 8.7 shows the part of the output that tests the assumption. We're interested only in whether the interaction terms are significant. Any interaction that is significant indicates that the main effect has violated the assumption of linearity of the logit. All three interactions have significance values (the values in the column $Pr(>|z|)$) greater than .05, indicating that the assumption of linearity of the logit has been met for **PSWQ**, **Anxious** and **Previous**.

Labcoat Leni's Real Research 8.1   Mandatory suicide? ②

Lacourse, E., et al. (2001). *Journal of Youth and Adolescence*, *30*, 321–332.

Although I have fairly eclectic tastes in music, my favourite kind of music is heavy metal. One thing that is mildly irritating about liking heavy metal is that everyone assumes that you're a miserable or aggressive bastard. When not listening (and often while listening) to heavy metal, I spend most of my time researching clinical psychology: I research how anxiety develops in children. Therefore, I was literally beside myself with excitement when a few years back I stumbled on a paper that combined these two interests: Lacourse, Claes, and Villeneuve (2001) carried out a study to see whether a love of heavy metal could predict suicide risk. Fabulous stuff!

Eric Lacourse and his colleagues used questionnaires to measure several variables: suicide risk (yes or no), marital status of parents (together or divorced/separated), the extent to which the person's mother and father were neglectful, self-estrangement/powerlessness (adolescents who have negative self-perceptions, are bored with life, etc.), social isolation (feelings of a lack of support), normlessness (beliefs that socially disapproved behaviours can be used to achieve certain goals), meaninglessness (doubting that school is relevant to gaining employment) and drug use. In addition, the authors measured liking of heavy metal; they included the sub-genres of classic (Black Sabbath, Iron Maiden), thrash metal (Slayer, Metallica), death/black metal (Obituary, Burzum) and gothic (Marilyn Manson). As well as liking, they measured behavioural manifestations of worshipping these bands (e.g., hanging posters, hanging out with other metal fans) and vicarious music listening (whether music was used when angry or to bring out aggressive moods). They used logistic regression to predict suicide risk from these predictors for males and females separately.

The data for the female sample are in the file **Lacourse et al. (2001) Females.dat**. Labcoat Leni wants you to carry out a logistic regression predicting **Suicide_Risk** from all of the predictors (forced entry). (To make your results easier to compare to the published results, enter the predictors in the same order as in Table 3 in

the paper: **Age**, **Marital_Status**, **Mother_Negligence**, **Father_Negligence**, **Self_Estrangement**, **Isolation**, **Normlessness**, **Meaninglessness**, **Drug_Use**, **Metal**, **Worshipping**, **Vicarious**). Create a table of the results. Does listening to heavy metal predict girls' suicide? If not, what does?

Answers are in the additional material on the companion website (or look at Table 3 in the original article).

8.9. Predicting several categories: multinomial logistic regression ③

What do I do when I have more than two outcome categories?

I mentioned earlier that it is possible to use logistic regression to predict membership of more than two categories and that this is called multinomial logistic regression. Essentially, this form of logistic regression works in the same way as binary logistic regression, so there's no need for any additional equations to explain what is going on (hooray!). The analysis breaks the outcome variable down into a series of comparisons between two categories (which helps explain why no extra equations are really necessary). For example, if you have three outcome categories (*A*, *B* and *C*), then the analysis will consist of two comparisons. The form that these comparisons take depends on how you specify the analysis: you can compare everything against your first category (e.g., *A* vs. *B* and *A* vs. *C*), or your last category (e.g., *A* vs. *C* and *B* vs. *C*), or a custom category, for example category *B* (e.g., *B* vs. *A* and *B* vs. *C*). In practice, this means that you have to select a baseline category. The important parts of the analysis and output are much the same as we have just seen for binary logistic regression.

Let's look at an example. There has been some work looking at how men and women evaluate chat-up lines (Bale, Morrison, & Caryl, 2006; Cooper, O'Donnell, Caryl, Morrison, & Bale, 2007). This research has looked at how the content (e.g., whether the chat-up line is funny, has sexual content, or reveals desirable personality characteristics) affects how favourably the chat-up line is viewed. To sum up this research, it has found that men and women like different things in chat-up lines: men prefer chat-up lines with a high sexual content, and women prefer chat-up lines that are funny and show good moral fibre.

Imagine that we wanted to assess how *successful* these chat-up lines were. We did a study in which we recorded the chat-up lines used by 348 men and 672 women in a nightclub. Our outcome was whether the chat-up line resulted in one of the following three events: the person got no response or the recipient walked away, the person obtained the recipient's phone number, or the person left the nightclub with the recipient. Afterwards, the chat-up lines used in each case were rated by a panel of judges for how funny they were (0 = not funny at all, 10 = the funniest thing that I have ever heard), sexuality (0 = no sexual content at all, 10 = very sexually direct) and whether the chat-up line reflected good moral values (0 = the chat-up line does not reflect good characteristics, 10 = the chat-up line is very indicative of good characteristics). For example, 'I may not be Fred Flintstone, but I bet I could make your bed rock' would score high on sexual content, low on good characteristics and medium on humour; 'I've been looking all over for *you*, the woman of my dreams' would score high on good characteristics, low on sexual content and low on humour (as well as high on cheese, had it been measured). We predict based on past research that the success of different types of chat-up line will interact with gender.

This situation is perfect for multinomial regression. The data are in the file **Chat-Up Lines.dat**. There is one outcome variable (**Success**) with three categories (no response, phone number, go home with recipient) and four predictors: funniness of the chat-up line (**Funny**), sexual content of the chat-up line (**Sex**), degree to which the chat-up line reflects good characteristics (**Good_Mate**) and the gender of the person being chatted up (**Female** – scored as 1 = female, 0 = male). Read this data file into a dataframe called *chatData* by setting your working directory to the location of the file (see section 3.4.4) and executing:

```
chatData<-read.delim("Chat-Up Lines.dat", header = TRUE)
```

8.9.1. Running multinomial logistic regression in R ③

It's possible to use R Commander to do multinomial logistic regression, but it uses a command that I think is a little less friendly than the one I prefer. Hence, in this section, you will need to use commands. It's not so bad though. Honest. We are going to use a function called **mlogit()** from the package of the same name (so make sure it is installed and loaded).

```
          Success Funny Sex Good_Mate Gender
1     Get Phone Number    3   7         6   Male
2 Go Home with Person    5   7         2   Male
3     Get Phone Number    4   6         6   Male
4 Go Home with Person    3   7         5   Male
5     Get Phone Number    5   1         6   Male
6     Get Phone Number    4   7         5   Male
etc.
```

Output 8.8

The data currently look like Output 8.8: data for each person are stored as a row (i.e., the data are wide format – see section 3.9). The outcome (**Success**) and **Gender** are stored as text, therfore **R** should have imported these variables as factors. We can check this by entering each variable into the **is.factor()** function:

```
is.factor(chatData$Success)
is.factor(chatData$Gender)
```

You should find that you get the response TRUE for both, which means that **R** has imported these variables as factors, which is what we want. (If these variables were not factors I could convert them, by placing them into the **as.factor()** function and executing.)

One consideration at this point is that **Gender** will have been imported as a factor with 'female' as the baseline category (because female is before male alphabetically – see the first example in the chapter). All of our predictions are based on females behaving differently than males, so it would be better (in terms of framing out interpretation) to have 'male' as the baseline category. We saw earlier in the chapter that we can achieve this change by executing:

```
chatData$Gender<-relevel(chatData$Gender, ref = 2)
```

This command resets the levels of the variable **Gender** such that the reference or baseline category is the category currently set as 2 (i.e., males become the reference category).[9]

Before we can run a multinomial logistic regression, we need to get the data into a particular format. Instead of having one row per person, we need to have one row per person per category of the outcome variable. Each row will contain TRUE if the person was assigned to that category, and FALSE if they weren't. If that doesn't make sense, you shouldn't worry: first, because it will make sense in a minute; and second, because we can use the **mlogit.data()** function to convert our data into the correct format. This function takes the general form:

```
newDataframe<-mlogit.data(oldDataFrame, choice = "outcome variable", shape
= "wide"/"long")
```

It actually has a quite a few more options than this, but we really need to use only the basic options. This function creates a new dataframe from an old dataframe (specified in the function). We need to tell the function the name of the categorical outcome variable, because this is the variable it uses to restructure the data. In this example the outcome variable is **Success**. Finally, we tell the function the shape of our original dataframe (wide or long) – in this case our data are wide format. Therefore, to restructure the current data we could execute:

```
mlChat <- mlogit.data(chatData, choice = "Success", shape = "wide")
```

This command will create a new dataframe called *mlChat* (which takes a lot less typing than 'multinomial logit chat-up lines') from the existing dataframe (*chatData*). We tell the function that the outcome variable is **Success** (*choice = "Success"*) and the format of the original dataframe is wide (*shape = "wide"*). The new dataframe looks like Output 8.9.

```
                        Success Funny Sex Good_Mate Gender chid
1.Get Phone Number         TRUE    3   7         6   Male    1
1.Go Home with Person     FALSE    3   7         6   Male    1
1.No response/Walk Off    FALSE    3   7         6   Male    1
2.Get Phone Number        FALSE    5   7         2   Male    2
2.Go Home with Person      TRUE    5   7         2   Male    2
2.No response/Walk Off    FALSE    5   7         2   Male    2
etc.
```

Output 8.9

---

[9] Making this change will affect the parameter estimates for the main effects, but not for the interaction terms, which are the effects in which we're actually interested.

Now let's compare Output 8.9 with the first six rows of the original dataframe (*chatData*) in Output 8.8. The first person in the *chatData* dataframe was assigned to the category of 'get phone number'. In the new dataframe, that person has been split into three rows, each labelled 1 on the far left (to indicate that this is person 1). Next to each 1 is one of the three possible outcomes: get phone number, go home, and no response/walk off. The third column tells us which of those events occurred. The first person, remember, was assigned to the 'get phone number' category, so in the new dataframe they have been given a response of TRUE next to 'get phone number' but in the next two rows (which represent the same person's responses but to the other two possible outcomes) they have been assigned FALSE (because these outcomes didn't happen). The next variable in *mlChat* is **Funny**. The first row in the original data set (Output 8.8) has a score a 3 on this variable; because this person's data are now spread over three rows, the first three rows (which represent one person) score a 3 on this variable in *mlChat* (Output 8.9). Hopefully you can see how the data have been restructured.

Now we are ready to run the multinomial logistic regression, using the *mlogit()* function. The *mlogit*() function looks very similar to the *glm*() function that we met earlier in the chapter for logistic regression. It takes the general form:

```
newModel<-mlogit(outcome ~ predictor(s), data = dataFrame, na.action = an
action, reflevel = a number representing the baseline category for the
outcome)
```

in which:

- *newModel* is an object created that contains information about the model. We can get summary statistics for this model by executing *summary(newModel)*.

- *outcome* is the variable that you're trying to predict. In this example it will be the variable **Success**.

- *predictor(s)* lists the variable or variables from which you're trying to predict the outcome variable.

- *dataFrame* is the name of the dataframe from which your outcome and predictor variables come.

- *na.action* is an optional command. If you have complete data (as here) you can ignore it, but if you have missing values (i.e., NAs in the dataframe) then it can be useful – see R's Souls' Tip 7.1).

- *relevel* is a number representing the outcome category that you want to use as a baseline.

As you can see, the basic idea is the same as the *lm()* and *glm()* commands with which you should be familiar. However, one important difference is that we need to specify the reference or baseline category.

SELF-TEST

✓ Think about the three categories that we have as an outcome variable. Which of these categories do you think makes most sense to use as a baseline category?

The best option is probably "No response / Walk off". This is referenced with number 3 in the data (it is the third category listed in Output 8.9). We can specify this by using *reflevel = 3* in the function.

The next issue is what to include within the model. In this example, the main effects are not particularly interesting: based on past research, we don't necessarily expect funny chat-up lines to be successful, but we do expect them to be more successful when used on women than on men. What this prediction implies is that the *interaction* of **Gender** and **Funny** will be significant. Similarly, chat-up lines with a high sexual content might not be successful overall, but we expect them to be relatively successful when used on men. Again, this means that we might not expect the **Sex** main effect to be significant, but we do expect the **Sex**×**Gender** interaction to be significant. As such, we need to enter these interaction terms (**Sex**×**Gender** and **Funny**×**Gender**) into the model. To evaluate these interactions we must also include the main effects. However, we are not particularly interested in higher-order interactions such as **Sex**×**Funny**×**Gender** because we don't (theoretically) predict the success of chat-up lines should vary across genders with the combination of being sexy and funny. We can, therefore, create the model by executing:

```
chatModel <- mlogit(Success ~ 1 | Good_Mate + Funny + Gender + Sex +
Gender:Sex +  Funny:Gender, data = mlChat, reflevel = 3)
```

This command looks (as I said) very like the *glm()* model. However, notice that instead of the outcome variable just being **Success** we write '*Success~1 |*'. We won't worry about why, that's just how you do it. Then you put the formula, as with the *glm()* or the *lm()* functions. Notice that the model contains all main effects but just two interactions: **Sex**×**Gender** and **Funny**×**Gender**.

8.9.2. Interpreting the multinomial logistic regression output ③

The summary of the model can be obtained by executing:

```
summary(chatModel)
```

SELF-TEST

✓ What does the log-likelihood measure?

```
Call:
mlogit(formula = Success ~ 1 | Good_Mate + Funny + Gender + Sex +
    Gender:Sex + Funny:Gender, data = mlChat, reflevel = 3, method = "nr",
    print.level = 0)

Frequencies of alternatives:
No response/Walk Off     Get Phone Number   Go Home with Person
            0.39216               0.47549               0.13235
```

```
nr method
6 iterations, 0h:0m:0s
g'(-H)^-1g = 0.00121
successive fonction values within tolerance limits


Coefficients :
                                        Estimate Std. Error t-value  Pr(>|t|)
altGet Phone Number                     -1.783070  0.669772 -2.6622 0.0077631 **
altGo Home with Person                  -4.286354  0.941398 -4.5532 5.284e-06 ***
altGet Phone Number:Good_Mate            0.131840  0.053726  2.4539 0.0141306 *
altGo Home with Person:Good_Mate         0.130019  0.083521  1.5567 0.1195351
altGet Phone Number:Funny                0.139389  0.110126  1.2657 0.2056135
altGo Home with Person:Funny             0.318456  0.125302  2.5415 0.0110376 *
altGet Phone Number:GenderFemale        -1.646223  0.796247 -2.0675 0.0386891 *
altGo Home with Person:GenderFemale     -5.626369  1.328589 -4.2348 2.287e-05 ***
altGet Phone Number:Sex                  0.276206  0.089197  3.0966 0.0019577 **
altGo Home with Person:Sex               0.417283  0.122083  3.4180 0.0006307 ***
altGet Phone Number:GenderFemale:Sex    -0.348326  0.105875 -3.2900 0.0010020 **
altGo Home with Person:GenderFemale:Sex -0.476639  0.163434 -2.9164 0.0035409 **
altGet Phone Number:Funny:GenderFemale   0.492441  0.139992  3.5176 0.0004354 ***
altGo Home with Person:Funny:GenderFemale 1.172404  0.199240  5.8844 3.996e-09 ***
---
Signif. codes:  0 '***' 0.001 '**' 0.01 '*' 0.05 '.' 0.1 ' ' 1


Log-Likelihood: -868.74
McFadden R^2:  0.13816
Likelihood ratio test : chisq = 278.52 (p.value=< 2.22e-16)
```

Output 8.10

Output 8.10 shows the model parameters. There's a lot of information scattered about in there to look at. We get a log-likelihood ratio of the overall model. Remember that the log-likelihood is a measure of how much unexplained variability there is in the data; therefore, the difference or change in log-likelihood indicates how much new variance has been explained by the model. The chi-square test tests the decrease in unexplained variance from the baseline model (if you ran that model you would find the log-likelihood was -1008.00)[10] to the final model (-868.74), which is a difference of 139.26. We need to multiply this by 2 to get the chi-square test (because we want to compare the $-2LL$ so we multiply by 2), which gives 278.52. This change is significant, which means that our final model explains a significant amount of the original variability (in other words, it's a better fit than the original model). Just above the likelihood ratio test we are also given a McFadden R^2, a measure of effect size.

To help with the interpretation we can exponentiate the coefficients, using the *exp()* function, as we did with the logistic coefficients. These coefficients are stored in a variable called *coefficients* attached to the model, so we can access them using *chatModel$coefficients*. To see the exponentiated versions of them, we could execute:

```
exp(chatModel$coefficients)
```

---

[10] If you like, try this out by executing (note that all of the main effects and predictors are removed from the formula, so this represents a model including only the intercept):

```
chatBase<-mlogit(Success ~ 1, data = mlChat, reflevel = 3)
summary(chatBase)
```

The resulting output is a bit horrible, and we can make it nicer by asking **R** to print the variable as a dataframe by enclosing the above command in the *data.frame()* function:

```
data.frame(exp(chatModel$coefficients))
```

The resulting odds ratios are shown in Output 8.11.

	exp.chatModel.coefficients.
altGet Phone Number	0.16812128
altGo Home with Person	0.01375498
altGet Phone Number:Good_Mate	1.14092570
altGo Home with Person:Good_Mate	1.13885057
altGet Phone Number:Funny	1.14957104
altGo Home with Person:Funny	1.37500360
altGet Phone Number:GenderFemale	0.19277659
altGo Home with Person:GenderFemale	0.00360163
altGet Phone Number:Sex	1.31811957
altGo Home with Person:Sex	1.51783194
altGet Phone Number:GenderFemale:Sex	0.70586855
altGo Home with Person:GenderFemale:Sex	0.62086652
altGet Phone Number:Funny:GenderFemale	1.63630634
altGo Home with Person:Funny:GenderFemale	3.22974620

Output 8.11

Now let's look at the individual parameter estimates from Outputs 8.10 and 8.11. Note that each predictor has two parameters associated with it. This is because these parameters compare pairs of outcome categories. We specified *No response/walk off* as our reference category; therefore, the parts of the table outputs labelled *Get Phone Number* are comparing this category against the *No response/walk off* category. Similarly, the parts labelled *Go home with person* are comparing this category against the *No response/walk off* category.

We can get confidence intervals for these coefficients using the *confint()* function (and again we exponentiate to make these confidence intervals for the odds ratios). Execute:

```
exp(confint(chatModel))
```

The resulting confidence intervals are shown in Output 8.12.

	2.5 %	97.5 %
altGet Phone Number	0.0452388315	0.62478988
altGo Home with Person	0.0021734046	0.08705211
altGet Phone Number:Good_Mate	1.0268939646	1.26762012
altGo Home with Person:Good_Mate	0.9668821194	1.34140512
altGet Phone Number:Funny	0.9263950895	1.42651186
altGo Home with Person:Funny	1.0755891423	1.75776681
altGet Phone Number:GenderFemale	0.0404843865	0.91795423
altGo Home with Person:GenderFemale	0.0002664414	0.04868514
altGet Phone Number:Sex	1.1066999501	1.56992797
altGo Home with Person:Sex	1.1948318258	1.92814902
altGet Phone Number:GenderFemale:Sex	0.5735912484	0.86865066
altGo Home with Person:GenderFemale:Sex	0.4506952417	0.85529022
altGet Phone Number:Funny:GenderFemale	1.2436632929	2.15291265
altGo Home with Person:Funny:GenderFemale	2.1856202907	4.77267737

Output 8.12

Let's look at the effects one by one; because we are just comparing two categories the interpretation is the same as for binary logistic regression (so if you don't understand my conclusions reread the start of this chapter). First let's look at the parts of the outputs for the *Get phone number* category compared to the *No response/walk off* category

- **Good_Mate:** Whether the chat-up line showed signs of good moral fibre significantly predicted whether you got a phone number or no response, $b = 0.13$, $p < .05$. The odds ratio (1.141) tells us that as this variable increases, so as chat-up lines show one more unit of moral fibre, the change in the odds of getting a phone number (rather than no response) is 1.14. In short, you're more likely to get a phone number than not if you use a chat-up line that demonstrates good moral fibre.

- **Funny:** Whether the chat-up line was funny did not significantly predict whether you got a phone number or no response, $b = 0.14$, $p > .05$. Note that although this predictor is not significant, the odds ratio (1.15) is approximately the same as for the previous predictor (which was significant). So, the effect size is comparable, but the non-significance stems from a relatively higher standard error. (Note that this effect is superseded by the interaction with gender below.)

- **Gender:** The gender of the person being chatted up significantly predicted whether they gave out their phone number or gave no response, $b = -1.65$, $p < .05$. This is the effect of females compared to males. The odds ratio tells us that as gender changes from male (0) to female (1) the change in the odds of giving out a phone number compared to not responding is 0.19. In other words, the odds of a man giving out his phone number compared to not responding are $1/0.19 = 5.26$ times the odds for a woman. Men are cheap.

- **Sex:** The sexual content of the chat-up line significantly predicted whether you got a phone number or no response, $b = 0.28$, $p < .01$. The odds ratio tells us that as the sexual content increased by a unit, the change in the odds of getting a phone number (rather than no response) is 1.32. In short, you're more likely to get a phone number than not if you use a chat-up line with high sexual content. (But this effect is superseded by the interaction with gender.)

- **Funny×Gender:** The success of funny chat-up lines depended on whether they were delivered to a man or a woman because in interaction these variables predicted whether or not you got a phone number, $b = 0.49$, $p < .001$. Bearing in mind how we interpreted the effect of gender above, the odds ratio tells us that as gender changes from male (0) to female (1) in combination with funniness increasing, the change in the odds of giving out a phone number compared to not responding was 1.64. In other words, as funniness increases, women become more likely to hand out their phone number than men. Funny chat-up lines are more successful when used on women than men.

- **Sex×Gender:** The success of chat-up lines with sexual content depended on whether they were delivered to a man or a woman because in interaction these variables predicted whether or not you got a phone number, $b = -0.35$, $p < .01$. Bearing in mind how we interpreted the interaction above (note that b is negative here but positive above), the odds ratio tells us that as gender changes from male (0) to female (1) in combination with the sexual content increasing, the change in the odds of giving out a phone number compared to not responding is 0.71. In other words, as sexual content increases, women become *less* likely than men to hand out their phone number. Chat-up lines with a high sexual content are more successful when used on men than women.

Now let's look at the individual parameter estimates for the *Go home with person* category compared to the *No response/walk off* category. We can interpret these effects as follows:

- **Good_Mate**: Whether the chat-up line showed signs of good moral fibre did not significantly predict whether you went home with the date or got no response, $b = 0.13$, $p > .05$. In short, you're not significantly more likely to go home with the person if you use a chat-up line that demonstrates good moral fibre.

- **Funny**: Whether the chat-up line was funny significantly predicted whether you went home with the date or no response, $b = 0.32$, $p < .05$. The odds ratio tells us that as chat-up lines are one unit funnier, the change in the odds of going home with the person (rather than no response) is 1.38. In short, you're more likely to go home with the person than get no response if you use a chat-up line that is funny. (This effect, though, is superseded by the interaction with gender below.)

- **Female**: The gender of the person being chatted up significantly predicted whether they went home with the person or gave no response, $b = -5.63$, $p < .001$. The odds ratio tells us that as gender changes from male (0) to female (1) the change in the odds of going home with the person compared to not responding is 0.004. In other words, the odds of a man going home with someone compared to not responding are $1/0.004 = 250$ times more likely than for a woman. Men are *really* cheap.

- **Sex**: The sexual content of the chat-up line significantly predicted whether you went home with the date or got no response, $b = 0.42$, $p < .01$. The odds ratio tells us that as the sexual content increased by a unit, the change in the odds of going home with the person (rather than no response) is 1.52: you're more likely to go home with the person than not if you use a chat-up line with high sexual content. (Note that this effect is superseded by the interaction with gender below.)

- **Funny×Gender**: The success of funny chat-up lines depended on whether they were delivered to a man or a woman because in interaction these variables predicted whether or not you went home with the date, $b = 1.17$, $p < .001$. The odds ratio tells us that as gender changes from female (0) to male (1) in combination with funniness increasing, the change in the odds of going home with the person compared to getting no response is 3.23. As funniness increases, women become more likely to go home with the person than men. Funny chat-up lines are more successful when used on women compared to men.

- **Sex×Gender**: The success of chat-up lines with sexual content depended on whether they were delivered to a man or a woman because in interaction these variables predicted whether or not you went home with the date, $b = -0.48$, $p < .01$. The odds ratio tells us that as gender changes from male (0) to female (1) in combination with the sexual content increasing, the change in the odds of going home with the date compared to not responding is 0.62. As sexual content increases, women become less likely than men to go home with the person. Chat-up lines with sexual content are more successful when used on men than women.

SELF-TEST

✓ Use what you learnt earlier in this chapter to check the assumptions of multicollinearity and linearity of the logit.

8.9.3. Reporting the results

We can report the results as with binary logistic regression using a table (see Table 8.3). Note that I have split the table by the outcome categories being compared, but otherwise it is the same as before. These effects are interpreted as in the previous section.

Table 8.3 How to report multinomial logistic regression

	B (SE)	95% CI for odds ratio		
		Lower	Odds Ratio	Upper
Phone number vs. no response				
Intercept	−1.78 (0.67)**			
Good Mate	0.13 (0.05)*	1.03	1.14	1.27
Funny	0.14 (0.11)	0.93	1.15	1.43
Female	−1.65 (0.80)*	0.04	0.19	0.92
Sexual Content	0.28 (0.09)**	1.11	1.32	1.57
Female × Funny	0.49 (0.14)***	1.24	1.64	2.15
Female × Sex	−0.35 (0.11)*	0.57	0.71	0.87
Going home vs. no response				
Intercept	−4.29 (0.94)***			
Good Mate	0.13 (0.08)	0.97	1.14	1.34
Funny	0.32 (0.13)*	1.08	1.38	1.76
Female	−5.63 (1.33)***	0.00	0.00	0.05
Sexual Content	0.42 (0.12)**	1.20	1.52	1.93
Female × Funny	1.17 (0.20)***	2.19	3.23	4.77
Female × Sex	−0.48 (0.16)**	0.45	0.62	0.86

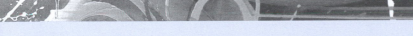

What have I discovered about statistics? ①

At the age of 10 I thought I was going to be a rock star. Such was my conviction about this that even today (many years on) I'm still not entirely sure how I ended up *not* being a rock star (lack of talent, not being a very cool person, inability to write songs that don't make people want to throw rotting vegetables at you, are all possible explanations). Instead of the glitzy and fun life that I anticipated I am instead reduced to writing chapters about things that I don't even remotely understand.

We began the chapter by looking at why we can't use linear regression when we have a categorical outcome, but instead have to use binary logistic regression (two outcome categories) or multinomial logistic regression (several outcome categories). We then looked into some of the theory of logistic regression by looking at the regression equation and what it means. Then we moved onto assessing the model and talked about the log-likelihood statistic and the associated chi-square test. I talked about different methods of obtaining equivalents to R^2 in regression (Hosmer– Lemeshow, Cox–Snell and Nagelkerke). We also discovered the z-statistic and odds ratio. The rest of the chapter looked at three examples using **R** to carry out various logistic regressions. So, hopefully, you should have a pretty good idea of how to conduct and interpret a logistic regression by now.

Having decided that I was going to be a rock star I put on my little denim jacket with Iron Maiden patches sewn onto it and headed off down the rocky road of stardom. The first stop was … my school.

R packages used in this chapter

car | mlogit

R functions used in this chapter

anova() | hatvalues()
as.factor() | head()
binomial() | is.factor()
confint() | log()
dfbeta() | mlogit()
dffits() | mlogit.data()
exp() | pchisq()
factor() | relevel()
fitted() | rstandard()
function() | rstudent()
glm() | summary()
 | vif()

Key terms that I've discovered

−2LL | Main effect
Binary logistic regression | Maximum-likelihood estimation
Chi-square distribution | Multinomial logistic regression
Complete separation | Nagelkerke's R_N^2
Cox and Snell's R_{CS}^2 | Normal distribution
Deviance | Odds
Hosmer and Lemeshow's R_L^2 | Odds ratio
Interaction effect | Polychotomous logistic regression
Likelihood | Suppressor effects
Logistic regression | Wald statistic
Log-likelihood | z-statistic

Smart Alex's tasks

- **Task 1**: A psychologist was interested in whether children's understanding of display rules can be predicted from their age, and whether the child possesses a theory of mind. A display rule is a convention of displaying an appropriate emotion in a given situation. For example, if you receive a Christmas present that you don't like, the appropriate emotional display is to smile politely and say 'Thank you, Auntie Kate, I've always wanted a rotting cabbage'. The inappropriate emotional display is to start crying and scream 'Why did you buy me a rotting cabbage, you selfish old bag?' Using appropriate display rules has been linked to having a theory of mind (the ability to understand what another person might be thinking). To test this theory, children were given a false belief task (a task used to measure whether someone has a theory of mind), a display rule task (which they could either pass or fail) and their age in months was measured. The data are in **Display.dat**. Run a logistic regression to see whether possession of display rule understanding (did the child pass the test? – yes/no) can be predicted from possession of a theory of mind (did the child pass the false belief task? – yes/no), age in months and their interaction. ③

- **Task 2**: Recent research has shown that lecturers are among the most stressed workers. A researcher wanted to know exactly what it was about being a lecturer that created this stress and subsequent burnout. She took 467 lecturers and administered several questionnaires to them that measured: **Burnout** (burnt out or not), **Perceived Control** (high score = low perceived control), **Coping Style** (high score = high ability to cope with stress), **Stress from Teaching** (high score = teaching creates a lot of stress for the person), **Stress from Research** (high score = research creates a lot of stress for the person) and **Stress from Providing Pastoral Care** (high score = providing pastoral care creates a lot of stress for the person). The outcome of interest was burnout, and Cooper, Sloan, and Williams's (1988) model of stress indicates that perceived control and coping style are important predictors of this variable. The remaining predictors were measured to see the unique contribution of different aspects of a lecturer's work to their burnout. Can you help her out by conducting a logistic regression to see which factors predict burnout? The data are in **Burnout.dat**. ③

- **Task 3**: A health psychologist interested in research into HIV wanted to know the factors that influenced condom use with a new partner (relationship less than 1 month old). The outcome measure was whether a condom was used (**use**: condom used = 1, not used = 0). The predictor variables were mainly scales from the Condom Attitude Scale (CAS) by Sacco, Levine, Reed, and Thompson (1991): **gender** (gender of the person); **safety** (relationship safety, measured out of 5, indicates the degree to which the person views this relationship as 'safe' from sexually transmitted disease); **sexexp** (sexual experience, measured out of 10, indicates the degree to which previous experience influences attitudes towards condom use); **previous** (a measure not from the CAS, this variable measures whether or not the couple used a condom in their previous encounter: 1 = condom used, 0 = not used, 2 = no previous encounter with this partner); **selfcon** (self-control, measured out of 9, indicates the degree of self-control that a person has when it comes to condom use, i.e., whether they get carried away with the heat of the moment, or exert control); **perceive** (perceived risk, measured out of 6, indicates the degree to which the person feels at risk from unprotected sex). Previous research (Sacco, Rickman, Thompson, Levine, & Reed, 1993) has shown that gender, relationship safety and perceived risk predict condom use. Carry out an appropriate analysis to verify these previous findings, and to test whether self-control, previous usage and sexual experience can predict any of the remaining variance in condom use. (1) Interpret all important parts of the **R** output. (2) How reliable is the final model? (3) What are the probabilities that participants 12, 53 and 75 will use a condom? (4) A female who used a condom in her previous encounter with her new partner scores 2 on all variables except perceived risk (for which she scores 6). Use the model to estimate the probability that she will use a condom in her next encounter. Data are in the file **condom.dat**. ③

Answers can be found on the companion website.

Further reading

Hutcheson, G., & Sofroniou, N. (1999). *The multivariate social scientist*. London: Sage. Chapter 4.

Menard, S. (1995). *Applied logistic regression analysis*. Sage University Paper Series on Quantitative Applications in the Social Sciences, 07-106. Thousand Oaks, CA: Sage. (This is a fairly advanced text, but great nevertheless. Unfortunately, few basic-level texts include logistic regression so you'll have to rely on what I've written!)

Miles, J. & Shevlin, M. (2001). *Applying regression and correlation: A guide for students and researchers*. London: Sage. (Chapter 6 is a nice introduction to logistic regression.)

Interesting real research

Bale, C., Morrison, R., & Caryl, P. G. (2006). Chat-up lines as male sexual displays. *Personality and Individual Differences*, *40*(4), 655–664.

Bemelman, M., & Hammacher, E. R. (2005). Rectal impalement by pirate ship: A case report. *Injury Extra*, *36*, 508–510.

Cooper, M., O'Donnell, D., Caryl, P. G., Morrison, R., & Bale, C. (2007). Chat-up lines as male displays: Effects of content, sex, and personality. *Personality and Individual Differences*, *43*(5), 1075–1085.

Lacourse, E., Claes, M., & Villeneuve, M. (2001). Heavy metal music and adolescent suicidal risk. *Journal of Youth and Adolescence*, *30*(3), 321–332.

Lo, S. F., Wong, S. H., Leung, L. S., Law, I. C., & Yip, A. W. C. (2004). Traumatic rectal perforation by an eel. *Surgery*, *135*(1), 110–111.

Comparing two means

9

FIGURE 9.1
My (probably)
eighth birthday.
From left to right:
my brother Paul
(who still hides
behind cakes
rather than have
his photo taken),
Paul Spreckley,
Alan Palsey, Clair
Sparks and me

9.1. What will this chapter tell me? ①

Having successfully slayed audiences at holiday camps around the country, my next step towards global domination was my primary school. I had learnt another Chuck Berry song ('Johnny B. Goode'), but also broadened my repertoire to include songs by other artists (I have a feeling 'Over the Edge' by Status Quo was one of them).[1] Needless to say, when the opportunity came to play at a school assembly I jumped at it. The headmaster tried to have

[1] This would have been about 1982, so just before they became the most laughably bad band on the planet. Some would argue that they were *always* the most laughably bad band on the planet, but they were the first band that I called my favourite band.

me banned,[2] but the show went on. It was a huge success (I want to reiterate my earlier point that 10-year-olds are very easily impressed). My classmates carried me around the playground on their shoulders. I was a hero. Around this time I had a childhood sweetheart called Clair Sparks. Actually, we had been sweethearts since before my new-found rock legend status. I don't think the guitar playing and singing impressed her much, but she rode a motorbike (really, a little child's one) which impressed *me* quite a lot; I was utterly convinced that we would one day get married and live happily ever after. I was utterly convinced, that is, until she ran off with Simon Hudson. Being 10, she probably literally did run off with him – across the playground. To make this important decision of which boyfriend to have, Clair had needed to compare two men (Andy and Simon) to see which one was better; sometimes in science we want to do the same thing, to compare one man against another to see if there is evidence that one is different from the other. Sorry, did I write 'man'? I forgot the 'e': this chapter is about the process of comparing two means, not men.

9.2. Packages used in this chapter ①

There are several packages we will use in this chapter. You will need the packages *pastecs* (for descriptive statistics), *ggplot2* (for graphs), *WRS* (for robust methods) and of course *Rcmdr* (R Commander) if you're going to use that rather than commands (see section 3.6). If you don't have these packages installed you'll need to install them by executing:

```
install.packages("ggplot2"); install.packages("pastecs"); install.packages
("WRS")
```

Then you need to load the packages by executing these commands:

```
library(ggplot2); library(pastecs); library(WRS)
```

9.3. Looking at differences ①

Rather than looking at relationships between variables, researchers are sometimes interested in looking at differences between groups of people. In particular, in experimental research we often want to manipulate what happens to people so that we can make causal inferences. For example, if we take two groups of people and randomly assign one group a programme of dieting pills and the other group a programme of sugar pills (which they think will help them lose weight) then if the people who take the dieting pills lose more weight than those on the sugar pills we can infer that the diet pills caused the weight loss. This is a powerful research tool because it goes one step beyond merely observing variables and looking for relationships (as in correlation and regression).[3] This chapter is the first of many that look at this kind of research scenario, and we start with the simplest scenario: when we have two groups, or, to be more specific, when we want to compare two means. As we have seen (Chapter 1), there are two different ways of collecting data:

---

[2] Seriously! Can you imagine a headmaster banning a 10-year-old from assembly? By this time I had an electric guitar and he used to play hymns on an acoustic guitar; I can assume only that he somehow lost all perspective on the situation and decided that a 10-year-old blasting out some Quo in a squeaky little voice was subversive or something.

[3] People sometimes get confused and think that certain statistical procedures allow causal inferences and others don't. This isn't true (see Jane Superbrain Box 1.4).

we can either expose different people to different experimental manipulations (*between-group* or *independent* design), or take a single group of people and expose them to different experimental manipulations at different points in time (*repeated-measures design*). Sometimes people are tempted to compare artificially created groups by, for example, dividing people into groups based on a median score; however, this is generally a bad idea (see Jane Superbrain Box 9.1).

JANE SUPERBRAIN 9.1

Are median splits the devil's work? ②

Often in research papers you see that people have analysed their data using a 'median split'. In our spider phobia example, this means that you measure scores on a spider phobia questionnaire and calculate the median. You then classify anyone with a score above the median as a 'phobic', and those below the median as 'non-phobic'. In doing this you 'dichotomize' a continuous variable. This practice is quite common, but is it sensible?

MacCallum, Zhang, Preacher, and Rucker (2002) wrote a splendid paper pointing out various problems on turning a perfectly decent continuous variable into a categorical variable:

1. Imagine there are four people: Peter, Birgit, Jip and Kiki. We measure how scared of spiders they are as a percentage and get Jip (100%), Kiki (60%), Peter (40%) and Birgit (0%). If we split these four people at the median (50%) then we're saying that Jip and Kiki are the same (they get a score of 1 = phobic) and Peter and Birgit are the same (they both get a score of 0 = not phobic). In reality, Kiki and Peter are the most similar of the four people, but they have been put in different groups. So, median splits change the original information quite dramatically (Peter and Kiki are originally very similar but become very different after the split, Jip and Kiki are relatively dissimilar originally but become identical after the split).

2. Effect sizes get smaller: if you correlate two continuous variables then the effect size will be larger than if you correlate the same variables after one of them has been dichotomized. Effect sizes also get smaller in ANOVA and regression.

3. There is an increased chance of finding spurious effects.

So, if your supervisor has just told you to do a median split, have a good think about whether it is the right thing to do (and read MacCallum et al.'s paper). One of the rare situations in which dichotomizing a continuous variable is justified, according to MacCallum et al., is when there is a clear theoretical rationale for distinct categories of people based on a meaningful break point (i.e., not the median); for example, phobic versus not phobic based on diagnosis by a trained clinician would be a legitimate dichotomization of anxiety.

9.3.1. A problem with error bar graphs of repeated-measures designs ①

We saw in Chapter 4 that it is important to visualize group differences using error bars. We're now going to look at a problem that occurs when we graph repeated-measures error bars. To do this, we're going to look at an example that I use throughout this chapter (not because I am too lazy to think up different data sets, but because it allows me to illustrate various things). The example relates to whether arachnophobia (fear of spiders) is specific to real spiders or whether pictures of spiders can evoke similar levels of anxiety.

Table 9.1   Data from **spiderLong.dat**

Participant	Group	Anxiety
1	Picture	30
2	Picture	35
3	Picture	45
4	Picture	40
5	Picture	50
6	Picture	35
7	Picture	55
8	Picture	25
9	Picture	30
10	Picture	45
11	Picture	40
12	Picture	50
13	Real Spider	40
14	Real Spider	35
15	Real Spider	50
16	Real Spider	55
17	Real Spider	65
18	Real Spider	55
19	Real Spider	50
20	Real Spider	35
21	Real Spider	30
22	Real Spider	50
23	Real Spider	60
24	Real Spider	39

Twenty-four arachnophobes were used in all. Twelve were asked to play with a big hairy tarantula spider with big fangs and an evil look in its eight eyes. Their subsequent anxiety was measured. The remaining 12 were shown only pictures of the same big hairy tarantula and again their anxiety was measured. The data are in Table 9.1 (and **spiderLong.dat** if you're having difficulty entering them into **R** yourself). Remember that each row in the data represents a different participant's data. Therefore, you need a column representing the group to which they belonged and a second column representing their anxiety.

SELF-TEST

✓ Enter these data into a dataframe called *spiderLong*. Using what you learnt in Chapter 4, plot an error bar graph of the spider data.

Table 9.2 Data from **spiderWide.dat**

Participant	Picture (anxiety score)	Real (anxiety score)
1	30	40
2	35	35
3	45	50
4	40	55
5	50	65
6	35	55
7	55	50
8	25	35
9	30	30
10	45	50
11	40	60
12	50	39

OK, now let's imagine that we'd collected these data using the *same* participants; that is, all participants had their anxiety rated after seeing the real spider, but also after seeing the picture (in counterbalanced order obviously). The data would now be arranged differently in **R**. Instead of having a coding variable, and a single column with anxiety scores in, we would arrange the data in two columns (one representing the **picture** condition and one representing the **real** condition). The data are displayed in Table 9.2 (and **spiderWide.dat** if you're having difficulty entering them into **R** yourself). Note that the anxiety scores are identical to the between-group data (Table 9.1) – it's just that we're pretending that they came from the same people rather than different people.

SELF-TEST

✓ Enter these data into a dataframe called *spiderWide*.

Figure 9.2 shows the error bar graphs from the two different designs. Remember that the data are exactly the same, all that has changed is whether the design used the same participants (repeated measures) or different (independent). Now, we discovered in Chapter 1 that repeated-measures designs eliminate some extraneous variables (such as age, IQ and so on) and so can give us more sensitivity in the data. Therefore, we would expect our graphs to be different: the repeated-measures graph should reflect the increased sensitivity in the design. Looking at the two error bar graphs, can you spot this difference between the graphs?

I can't either; and this is the problem. The graphs should not be the same. The moral is: Don't use error bar graphs when you have repeated measures groups. Or if you do, adjust the data before you plot the graph (Loftus & Masson, 1994).

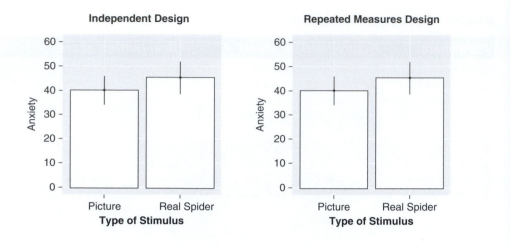

FIGURE 9.2
Two error bar graphs of anxiety data in the presence of a real spider or a photograph. The data on the left are treated as though they are different participants, whereas those on the right are treated as though they are from the same participants

9.3.2. Step 1: calculate the mean for each participant ②

To correct the repeated-measures error bars requires several steps, but none of them are particularly difficult. To begin with, we need to calculate the average anxiety for each participant. We're using the *spiderWide* dataframe so participants' scores are stored in two columns, therefore we need to simply add these columns and divide by 2 by executing:

```
spiderWide$pMean<-(spiderWide$picture + spiderWide$real)/2
```

This command creates a variable called **pMean** in the dataframe *spiderWide*, by adding the scores for **picture** and **real** (from the same dataframe) and dividing by 2.

9.3.3. Step 2: calculate the grand mean ②

The *grand mean* is the mean of all scores (regardless of from which condition the score comes) and so for the current data this value will be the mean of all 24 scores. A fairly simple way to calculate this value is to use the *c()* function, with which we're familiar, to combine the picture and real variables into a single variable, and then apply the *mean()* function to this new variable. We can do this is a single command:

```
grandMean<-mean(c(spiderWide$picture, spiderWide$real))
```

Executing this command creates a variable called **grandMean**, which is the mean of **picture** and **real** combined into a single variable (*c(spiderWide$picture, spiderWide$real)*); in other words, it's the mean of all scores.

9.3.4. Step 3: calculate the adjustment factor ②

If you look at the variable labelled **pMean**, you should notice that the values for each participant are different, which tells us that some people had greater anxiety than others did across the conditions. The fact that participants' mean anxiety scores differ represents individual differences between different people (so it represents the fact that some of the participants are generally more scared of spiders than others). These differences in natural anxiety contaminate the error bar graphs, which is why if we don't adjust the values that we plot, we will get the same graph as if an independent design had been used. Loftus and Masson (1994) argue that to eliminate this contamination we should equalize the means between participants (i.e., adjust the scores in each condition such that when we take the mean score across conditions, it is the same for all participants). To do this, we need to calculate an adjustment factor by subtracting each participant's mean score (**pMean**) from the grand mean (**grandMean**):

```
spiderWide$adj<-grandMean-spiderWide$pMean
```

Executing this command creates a variable **adj** (short for adjustment) in the *spiderWide* dataframe by taking the variable **grandMean** (which we just computed) and subtracting from it the mean anxiety for each participant (which is stored in the variable **pMean**, which we computed earlier on). The dataframe now looks like this:

```
  picture real pMean   adj
1      30   40  35.0   8.5
2      35   35  35.0   8.5
3      45   50  47.5  -4.0
4      40   55  47.5  -4.0
5      50   65  57.5 -14.0
6      35   55  45.0  -1.5
etc.
```

There is a new variable in the data editor called **adj**. The scores in this column represent the difference between each participant's mean anxiety and the mean anxiety level across all participants. You'll notice that some of the values are positive, and these participants are ones who were less anxious than average. Other participants were more anxious than average, and they have negative adjustment scores. We can now use these adjustment values to eliminate the between-subject differences in anxiety.

9.3.5. Step 4: create adjusted values for each variable ②

So far, we have calculated the difference between each participant's mean score and the mean score of all participants (the grand mean). This difference can be used to adjust the existing scores for each participant. First we need to adjust the scores in the **picture** condition. All we do is take the original score (**picture**) and add to it the value of the adjustment (**adj**):

```
spiderWide$picture_adj<-spiderWide$picture + spiderWide$adj
```

Executing this command creates a variable **picture_adj** in the *spiderWide* dataframe by adding the adjustment (*spiderWide$adj*) to the original anxiety scores after seeing the picture (*spiderWide$picture*). We can do exactly the same to create adjusted values of **real**:

```
spiderWide$real_adj<-spiderWide$real + spiderWide$adj
```

Executing this command creates a variable **real_adj** in the *spiderWide* dataframe by adding the adjustment (*spiderWide$adj*) to the original anxiety scores after seeing the real spider (*spiderWide$real*). The dataframe now looks like this:

```
  picture real pMean   adj picture_adj real_adj
1      30   40  35.0   8.5        38.5     48.5
2      35   35  35.0   8.5        43.5     43.5
3      45   50  47.5  -4.0        41.0     46.0
4      40   55  47.5  -4.0        36.0     51.0
5      50   65  57.5 -14.0        36.0     51.0
6      35   55  45.0  -1.5        33.5     53.5
etc.
```

Now, the variables **real_adj** and **picture_adj** represent the anxiety experienced in each condition, adjusted so as to eliminate any between-subject differences. If you don't believe me, then use the *mean()* function to create a variable **pMean2** that is the average of **real_adj** and **picture_adj** (just like we did in section 9.3.2). You should find that the value in this column is the same for every participant, thus proving that the between-subject variability in means is gone: the value will be 43.50 – the grand mean. We can also wrap all of these steps together in a function for use with other dataframes (R's Souls' Tip 9.1).

SELF-TEST

✓ Create an error bar chart of the mean of the adjusted values that you have just made (**real_adj** and **picture_adj**).

FIGURE 9.3
Error bar graph of the adjusted values of the *spiderWide* dataframe

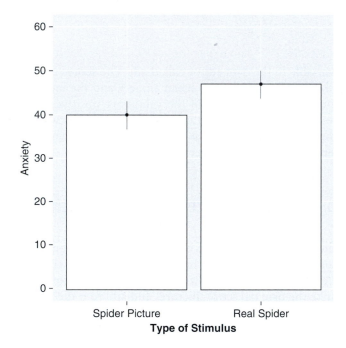

The resulting error bar graph is shown in Figure 9.3. Compare this graph to the graphs in Figure 9.2 – what differences do you see? The first thing to notice is that the means in the two conditions have not changed. However, the error bars have changed: they have got smaller. Also, whereas in Figure 9.2 the error bars overlap, in this new graph they do not. In Chapter 2 we discovered that when error bars do not overlap we can be fairly confident that our samples have not come from the same population (and so our experimental manipulation has been successful). Therefore, when we plot the proper error bars for the repeated-measures data it shows the extra sensitivity that this design has: the differences between conditions appear to be significant, whereas when different participants are used, there does not appear to be a significant difference. (Remember that the means in both situations are identical, but the sampling error is smaller in the repeated-measures design.) I expand upon this point in section 9.7.

R's Souls' Tip 9.1 How to impress your friends ③

The process we went through to adjust the scores for the fact they were from a repeated-measures design could be wrapped up in a function (see R's Souls' Tip 6.2). This would enable us to apply the function to a dataframe, which would be useful if we wanted to adjust lots of pairs of variables. The function would look like this:

```
rmMeanAdjust<-function(dataframe)
{
        varNames<-names(dataframe)
        pMean<-(dataframe[,1] + dataframe[,2])/2
        grandmean<-mean(c(dataframe[,1], dataframe[,2]))
        adj<-grandmean-pMean
        varA_adj<-dataframe[,1] + adj
        varB_adj<-dataframe[,2] + adj
        output<-data.frame(varA_adj, varB_adj)
        names(output)<-c(paste(varNames[1], "Adj", sep = "_"), paste(varNames[2],
"_Adj", sep = "_"))
        return(output)
}
```

Executing these commands creates a function called *rmMeanAdjust* which takes a dataframe as input, and outputs a dataframe containing the adjusted scores. Let's look at the contents of the function:

- *varNames<-names(dataframe)* gets the names of the variables in the dataframe entered into the function and stores them in *varNames*.
- *pMean<-(dataframe[,1] + dataframe[,2])/2* computes **pMean** by adding the first and second columns of the dataframe and diving by 2.
- *grandmean<-mean(c(dataframe[,1], dataframe[,2]))* computes the grand mean by merging the first two columns of the dataframe and computing the mean.
- *adj<-grandmean-pMean* calculates the adjustment for each row of the dataframe by subtracting **pMean** from **grandmean**.
- *varA_adj<-dataframe[,1] + adj* creates a new variable (**varA_adj**) that is the first column of the dataframe plus the adjustment factor.
- *varB_adj<-dataframe[,2] + adj* creates a new variable (**varB_adj**) that is the second column of the dataframe plus the adjustment factor.
- *output<-data.frame(varA_adj, varB_adj)* binds **varA_adj** and **varB_adj** together in a dataframe named *output*.
- *names(output)<-c(paste(varNames[1], "adj", sep = "_"), paste(varNames[2], "_adj", sep = "_"))* renames the columns of the dataframe as the name of the original variable in the original dataframe plus "_adj". So, a variable called **picture** becomes **picture_adj**.
- *return(output)* returns the dataframe of adjusted values.

We can now use this function on a dataframe (remember that it will adjust the first two columns of the dataframe so we're assuming that we're entering a column dataframe with the scores for the two repeated-measures conditions in each column). We apply the function to the original dataframe *spiderWide* (the one that contained only **picture** and **real**) by executing:

```
rmMeanAdjust(spiderWide)
```

The result is:

	picture_adj	real__adj
1	38.5	48.5
2	43.5	43.5
3	41.0	46.0
4	36.0	51.0
5	36.0	51.0
6	33.5	53.5
7	46.0	41.0
8	38.5	48.5
9	43.5	43.5
10	41.0	46.0
11	33.5	53.5
12	49.0	38.0

Pretty cool, I think you'll agree. By 'cool', I mean sad, obviously.

9.4. The *t*-test ①

What's the difference between the independent and dependent *t*-test?

We have seen in previous chapters that the *t*-test is very versatile: it can be used to test whether a correlation coefficient is different from 0; it can also be used to test whether a regression coefficient, *b*, is different from 0. However, it can also be used to test whether two group means are different. It is to this use that we now turn.

The simplest form of experiment that can be done is one with only one independent variable that is manipulated in only two ways and only one outcome is measured. More often than not the manipulation of the independent variable involves having an experimental condition and a control group (see Field & Hole, 2003). Some examples of this kind of design are:

- Is the movie *Scream 2* scarier than the original *Scream*? We could measure heart rates (which indicate anxiety) during both films and compare them.

- Does listening to music while you work improve your work? You could get some people to write an essay (or book!) while listening to their favourite music, and then write a different essay while working in silence (this is a control group). You could then compare the essay marks.

- Does listening to Andy's favourite music improve your work? You could repeat the above but rather than letting people work with their favourite music, you could play them some of my favourite music (as listed in the acknowledgements) and watch the quality of their work plummet.

The *t*-test can analyse these sorts of scenarios. Of course, there are more complex experimental designs and we will look at these in subsequent chapters. There are, in fact, two different *t*-tests and the one you use depends on whether the independent variable was manipulated using the same participants or different:

- **Independent-means *t*-test**: This test is used when there are two experimental conditions and different participants were assigned to each condition (this is sometimes called the *independent-measures* or *independent-samples t*-test).

- **Dependent-means *t*-test:** This test is used when there are two experimental conditions and the same participants took part in both conditions of the experiment (this test is sometimes referred to as the *matched-pairs* or *paired-samples t*-test).

9.4.1.   Rationale for the *t*-test ①

Both *t*-tests have a similar rationale, which is based on what we learnt in Chapter 2 about hypothesis testing:

- Two samples of data are collected and the sample means calculated. These means might differ by either a little or a lot.

- If the samples come from the same population, then we expect their means to be roughly equal (see section 2.5.1). Although it is possible for their means to differ by chance alone, we would expect large differences between sample means to occur very infrequently. Under the null hypothesis we assume that the experimental manipulation has no effect on the participants: therefore, we expect the sample means to be very similar.

- We compare the difference between the sample means that we collected to the difference between the sample means that we would expect to obtain if there were no effect (i.e., if the null hypothesis were true). We use the standard error (see section 2.5.1) as a gauge of the variability between sample means. If the standard error is small, then we expect most samples to have very similar means. When the standard error is large, large differences in sample means are more likely. If the difference between the samples we have collected is larger than we would expect based on the standard error then we can assume one of two things:
  - o There is no effect and sample means in our population fluctuate a lot and we have, by chance, collected two samples that are atypical of the population from which they came.
  - o The two samples come from different populations but are typical of their respective parent population. In this scenario, the difference between samples represents a genuine difference between the samples (and so the null hypothesis is incorrect).

- As the observed difference between the sample means gets larger, the more confident we become that the second explanation is correct (i.e., that the null hypothesis should be rejected). If the null hypothesis is incorrect, then we gain confidence that the two sample means differ because of the different experimental manipulation imposed on each sample.

I mentioned in section 2.6.1 that most test statistics can be thought of as the 'variance explained by the model' divided by the 'variance that the model can't explain'. In other words, effect/error. When comparing two means the 'model' that we fit to the data (the effect) is the difference between the two group means. We saw also in Chapter 2 that means vary from sample to sample (sampling variation) and that we can use the standard error as a measure of how much means fluctuate (in other words, the error in the estimate of the mean). Therefore, we can also use the standard error of the differences between the two means as an estimate of the error in our model (or the error in the difference between means). Therefore, we calculate the *t*-test using the following equation:

$$t = \frac{\text{observed difference between sample means} - \text{expected difference between population means (if null hypothesis is true)}}{\text{estimate of the standard error of the difference between two sample means}} \qquad (9.1)$$

The top half of the equation is the 'model' – our model being that the difference between means (which we expect to be non-zero) is bigger than the expected difference (which in most cases will be zero). The bottom half is the 'error'. So, just as I said in Chapter 2, we're basically getting the test statistic by dividing the model (or effect) by the error in the model. The exact form that this equation takes depends on whether the same or different participants were used in each experimental condition.

9.4.2. The *t*-test as a general linear model ②

A lot of you might think it's odd that a *t*-test can be used to test whether a correlation coefficient (or *b* in regression) is different from 0 and yet now I'm telling you that it can be used to test differences between two means. You might well be thinking 'but correlations and *b*s show relationships, not differences between means – what is this fool going on about?'. You may be starting not to trust me, or stuffing the book in a box to post it back for a refund.

I used to think this too until I read a fantastic paper by Cohen (1968), which made me realize what I'd been missing; the complex, thorny, weed-infested and Andy-eating-tarantula-inhabited world of statistics suddenly turned into a beautiful meadow filled with tulips and little bleating lambs all jumping for joy at the wonder of life. Actually, I'm still a bumbling fool trying desperately to avoid having the blood sucked from my flaccid corpse by the tarantulas of statistics, but it was a good paper. Recall from section 2.4.3 that all statistical procedures are basically the same, they're just more or less elaborate versions of this simple model:

$$\text{outcome}_i = (\text{model}) + \text{error}_i$$

In Chapter 7 we saw that the *t*-test was used to test whether the regression coefficient of a predictor was equal to zero. The experimental design for which the independent *t*-test is used can be conceptualized as a regression equation (after all, there is one independent variable (predictor) and one dependent variable (outcome)). If we want to predict our outcome, then we can use the general equation that I've repeated above.

If we want to use a linear model, then we saw that this general equation becomes equation (7.2) in which the model is defined by the slope and intercept of a straight line. Equation (9.2) shows a very similar equation in which A_i is the dependent variable (outcome), b_0 is the intercept, b_1 is the weighting of the predictor and G_i is the independent variable (predictor). Now, I've also included the same equation but with some of the letters replaced with what they represent in the spider experiment (so A = **anxiety**, G = **group**). When we run an experiment with two conditions, the independent variable has only two values (group 1 or group 2). There are several ways in which these groups can be coded (in the spider example we coded group 1 with the value 0 and group 2 with the value 1). This coding variable is known as a *dummy variable* and values of this variable represent groups of entities. We have come across this coding in section 7.12:

$$A_i = (b_0 + b_1 G_i) + \varepsilon_i$$
$$\text{anxiety}_i = (b_0 + b_1 \text{group}_i) + \varepsilon_i$$

$$(9.2)$$

Using the spider example, we know that the mean **anxiety** of the picture group was 40, and that the **group** variable is equal to 0 for this condition. Look at what happens when the

group variable is equal to 0 (the picture condition): equation (9.2) becomes (if we ignore the residual term)

$$\overline{X}_{\text{picture}} = b_0 + (b_1 \times 0)$$
$$b_0 = \overline{X}_{\text{picture}}$$
$$b_0 = 40$$

Therefore, b_0 (the intercept) is equal to the mean of the picture group (i.e., it is the mean of the group coded as 0). Now let's look at what happens when the **group** variable is equal to 1. This condition is the one in which a real spider was used, and the mean **anxiety** ($\overline{X}_{\text{real}}$) of this condition was 47. Remembering that we have just found out that b_0 is equal to the mean of the picture group ($\overline{X}_{\text{picture}}$), equation (9.2) becomes

$$\overline{X}_{\text{real}} = b_0 + (b_1 \times 1)$$
$$\overline{X}_{\text{real}} = \overline{X}_{\text{picture}} + b_1$$
$$b_1 = \overline{X}_{\text{real}} - \overline{X}_{\text{picture}}$$
$$b_1 = 47 - 40$$
$$= 7$$

b_1, therefore, represents the difference between the group means. As such, we can represent a two-group experiment as a regression equation in which the coefficient of the independent variable (b_1) is equal to the difference between group means, and the intercept (b_0) is equal to the mean of the group coded as 0. In regression, the t-test is used to ascertain whether the regression coefficient (b_1) is equal to 0, and when we carry out a t-test on grouped data we, therefore, test whether the difference between group means is equal to 0.

SELF-TEST

✔ Let me prove that I'm not making it up as I go along. Using the *lm()* function, run a regression on the data in **spiderLong.dat** with **Group** as the predictor and **Anxiety** as the outcome.

The resulting **R** output should contain the regression summary table shown in Output 9.1. The first thing to notice is the value of the constant (b_0): its value is 40, the same as the mean of the base category (the picture group). The second thing to notice is that the value of the regression coefficient b_1 is 7, which is the difference between the two group means ($47 - 40 = 7$). Finally, the t-statistic, which tests whether b_1 is significantly different from zero, is not significant, indicating that b_1 (i.e., the difference between group means) is not significantly different from zero.

```
Call:
lm(formula = Anxiety ~ Group, data = spiderLong)

Residuals:
   Min     1Q Median     3Q    Max
 -17.0   -8.5    1.5    8.0   18.0
```

```
Coefficients:
                  Estimate Std. Error t value Pr(>|t|)
(Intercept)         40.000      2.944  13.587 3.53e-12 ***
GroupReal Spider     7.000      4.163   1.681    0.107
---
Signif. codes:  0 '***' 0.001 '**' 0.01 '*' 0.05 '.' 0.1 ' ' 1

Residual standard error: 10.2 on 22 degrees of freedom
Multiple R-squared: 0.1139,      Adjusted R-squared: 0.07359
F-statistic: 2.827 on 1 and 22 DF,  p-value: 0.1068
```

Output 9.1

Although we have looked at the situation in which the different groups are independent (i.e., different entities are tested in different conditions) repeated-measures designs can be conceptualized in much the same way; however, because in this situation data points will not be independent it's more complicated to explain how it works (and also unnecessary). However, we will get into this subject more in Chapters 13, 14 and 19. For now, I hope to have demonstrated that differences between means can be represented in terms of linear models. If you have understood this section, then you are well on your way to understanding the next six chapters of this book.

9.4.3. Assumptions of the *t*-test ①

Given that the *t*-test is basically regression, it has much the same assumptions. Both the independent *t*-test and the dependent *t*-test are *parametric tests* based on the normal distribution (see Chapter 5). Therefore, they assume:

- The sampling distribution is normally distributed. In the dependent *t*-test this means that the sampling distribution of the *differences* between scores should be normal, not the scores themselves (see section 9.6.3.4).
- Data are measured at least at the interval level.

The independent *t*-test, because it is used to test different groups of people, also assumes:

- Scores in different treatment conditions are independent (because they come from different people).
- Homogeneity of variance – well, at least in theory we assume equal variances, but in reality we don't (Jane Superbrain Box 9.2).

These assumptions were explained in detail in Chapter 5 and, in that chapter, I emphasized the need to check these assumptions before you reach the point of carrying out your statistical test. Let's now look at each of the two *t*-tests in more detail.

9.5. The independent *t*-test ①

9.5.1. The independent *t*-test equation explained ①

We'll stick with the situation in which different entities have been tested in the different conditions of your experiment. This is a situation in which the independent *t*-test is used.

JANE SUPERBRAIN 9.2

What about the assumption of homogeneity of variance? ②

You might have read about homogeneity of variance as being an assumption that is made by the independent *t*-test. It is the same assumption that we came across in regression, as the homoscedasticity assumption, and statisticians used to recommend testing for it (using Levene's test) and if the assumption was violated, use an adjustment to correct for it. However, more recently statisticians have stopped using this approach, for two reasons. First, violating this assumption only matters if you have unequal group sizes; if you don't have unequal group sizes, the assumption is pretty much irrelevant and can be ignored. Second, the tests of homogeneity of variance tend to work very well when you have equal group sizes and large samples (when it doesn't matter as much if you have violated the assumption) and don't work as well with unequal group sizes and smaller samples – which is exactly when it matters.

Plus, there is an adjustment (called Welch's *t*-test) which is able to correct for violation of this assumption – it's quite hard to do if you have to do it by hand, but very easy to do if you have a computer. If you have violated the assumption, a correction is made – and if you haven't violated the assumption, a correction is not made, so you might as well always do Welch's *t*-test and forget about the assumption. If you're really interested in this, I like the article by Zimmerman (2004).

If you choose not to think about the *t*-test and calculating the *t*-statistic as a form of regression, then you can think of it in terms of two equations that differ depending on whether the samples contain an equal number of people. We can calculate the *t*-statistic by using a numerical version of equation (9.1); in other words, we are comparing the model or effect against the error. When different participants participate in different conditions, pairs of scores will differ not just because of the experimental manipulation, but also because of other sources of variance (such as individual differences between participants' motivation, IQ, etc.). Therefore, we make comparisons on a *per condition* basis (by looking at the overall effect in a condition):

$$t = \frac{(\overline{X}_1 - \overline{X}_2) - (\mu_1 - \mu_2)}{\text{estimate of the standard error}}$$

(9.3)

Instead of looking at differences between pairs of scores, we now look at differences between the overall means of the two samples and compare them to the differences we would expect to get between the means of the two populations from which the samples come. If the null hypothesis is true then the samples have been drawn from the same population. Therefore, under the null hypothesis $\mu_1 = \mu_2$ and therefore, $\mu_1 - \mu_2 = 0$. Therefore, under the null hypothesis the equation becomes

$$t = \frac{(\overline{X}_1 - \overline{X}_2)}{\text{estimate of the standard error}}$$

(9.4)

For the independent *t*-test we are looking at differences between groups and so we divide by the standard deviation of differences between groups. We can apply the logic of sampling distributions to this situation. Now, imagine we took several pairs of samples – each pair containing one sample from the two different populations – and compared the means of these samples. From what we have learnt about sampling distributions, we know that the majority of samples from a population will have fairly similar means. Therefore, if we took several pairs of samples (from different populations), the differences between the sample means will be similar across pairs. However, often the difference between a pair of sample means will deviate by a small amount and very occasionally it will deviate by a large amount. If we could plot a sampling distribution of the differences between every pair of sample means that could be taken from two populations, then we would find that it had a normal distribution with a mean equal to the difference between population means ($\mu_1 - \mu_2$). The sampling distribution would tell us by how much we can expect the means of two (or more) samples to differ. As before, the standard deviation of the sampling distribution (the standard error) tells us how variable the differences between sample means are by chance alone. If the standard deviation is high then large differences between sample means can occur by chance; if it is small then only small differences between sample means are expected. It, therefore, makes sense that we use the standard error of the sampling distribution to assess whether the difference between two sample means is statistically meaningful or simply a chance result. Specifically, we divide the difference between sample means by the standard deviation of the sampling distribution.

So, how do we obtain the standard deviation of the sampling distribution of differences between sample means? Well, we use the **variance sum law**, which states that the variance of a difference between two independent variables is equal to the sum of their variances (see, for example, Howell, 2006). This statement means that the variance of the sampling distribution is equal to the sum of the variances of the two populations from which the samples were taken. We saw earlier that the standard error is the standard deviation of the sampling distribution of a population. We can use the sample standard deviations to calculate the standard error of each population's sampling distribution:

$$\text{SE of sampling distribution of population 1} = \frac{s_1}{\sqrt{N_1}}$$

$$\text{SE of sampling distribution of population 2} = \frac{s_2}{\sqrt{N_2}}$$

Therefore, remembering that the variance is simply the standard deviation squared, we can calculate the variance of each sampling distribution:

$$\text{variance of sampling distribution of population 1} = \left(\frac{s_1}{\sqrt{N_1}}\right)^2 = \frac{s_1^2}{N_1}$$

$$\text{variance of sampling distribution of population 2} = \left(\frac{s_2}{\sqrt{N_2}}\right)^2 = \frac{s_2^2}{N_2}$$

The variance sum law means that to find the variance of the sampling distribution of differences we merely add together the variances of the sampling distributions of the two populations:

$$\text{variance of sampling distribution of differences} = \frac{s_1^2}{N_1} + \frac{s_2^2}{N_2}$$

To find out the standard error of the sampling distribution of differences we merely take the square root of the variance (because variance is the standard deviation squared):

$$\text{SE of sampling distribution of differences} = \sqrt{\frac{s_1^2}{N_1} + \frac{s_2^2}{N_2}}$$

Therefore, equation (9.4) becomes:

$$t = \frac{\overline{X}_1 - \overline{X}_2}{\sqrt{\dfrac{s_1^2}{N_1} + \dfrac{s_2^2}{N_2}}} \tag{9.5}$$

Equation (9.5) is true only when the sample sizes are equal. Often in science it is not possible to collect samples of equal size (because, for example, people may not complete an experiment). When we want to compare two groups that contain different numbers of participants then equation (9.5) is not appropriate. Instead the pooled variance estimate *t*-test is used, which takes account of the difference in sample size by *weighting* the variance of each sample. We saw in Chapter 1 that large samples are better than small ones because they more closely approximate the population; therefore, we weight the variance by the size of sample on which it's based (we actually weight by the number of degrees of freedom, which is the sample size minus 1). Therefore, the pooled variance estimate is:

$$s_p^2 = \frac{(n_1 - 1)s_1^2 + (n_2 - 1)s_2^2}{n_1 + n_2 - 2}$$

This is simply a weighted average in which each variance is multiplied (weighted) by its degrees of freedom, and then we divide by the sum of weights (or sum of the two degrees of freedom). The resulting weighted average variance is then just replaced in the *t*-test equation:

$$t = \frac{\overline{X}_1 - \overline{X}_2}{\sqrt{\dfrac{s_p^2}{n_1} + \dfrac{s_p^2}{n_2}}}$$

We can compare the obtained value of *t* against the maximum value we would expect to get by chance alone in a *t*-distribution with the same degrees of freedom (these values can be found in the Appendix); if the value we obtain exceeds this critical value we can be confident that this reflects an effect of our independent variable. One thing that should be apparent from the equation for *t* is that to compute it you don't actually need any raw data. All you need are the means, standard deviations and sample sizes (see R's Souls' Tip 9.2).

The derivation of the *t*-statistic is merely to provide a conceptual grasp of what we are doing when we carry out a *t*-test using **R**. Therefore, if you don't know what on earth I'm babbling on about then don't worry about it (just spare a thought for my cat: he has to listen to this rubbish all the time) because **R** knows how to do it and that's all that matters.

9.5.2. Doing the independent *t*-test ①

I have probably bored most of you to the point of wanting to eat your own legs by now. Equations are boring and that is why **R** was invented to help us minimize our contact with them. Using our spider data again (**spiderLong.dat**), we have 12 arachnophobes who were exposed to a picture of a spider and 12 different spider-phobes who were exposed to a real-life tarantula (the groups are coded using the variable **Group**). Their anxiety was measured in each condition (**Anxiety**). I have already described how the data are arranged (see section 9.2), so we can move straight onto doing the test itself.

R's Souls' Tip 9.2 Computing *t* from means, *SD*s and *N*s ③

You can compute a *t*-test in **R** from only the two group means, the two group standard deviations and the two group sizes. First we'll calculate: **x1** (mean of group 1), **x2** (mean of group 2), **sd1** (standard deviation of group 1), **sd2** (standard deviation of group 2), **n1** (sample size of group 1) and **n2** (sample size of group 2).

```
x1 <- mean(spiderLong[spiderLong$Group=="Real Spider",]$Anxiety)
x2 <- mean(spiderLong[spiderLong$Group=="Picture",]$Anxiety)
sd1 <- sd(spiderLong[spiderLong$Group=="Real Spider",]$Anxiety)
sd2 <- sd(spiderLong[spiderLong$Group=="Picture",]$Anxiety)
n1 <- length(spiderLong[spiderLong$Group=="Real Spider",]$Anxiety)
n2 <- length(spiderLong[spiderLong$Group=="Picture",]$Anxiety)
```

Now we can calculate the *t*-test by writing and executing a function (see R's Souls' Tip 6.2):

```
ttestfromMeans<-function(x1, x2, sd1, sd2, n1, n2)
{
        df<-n1 + n2 - 2
        poolvar<-(((n1-1)*sd1^2)+((n2-1)*sd2^2))/df
        t<-(x1-x2)/sqrt(poolvar*((1/n1)+(1/n2)))
        sig<-2*(1-(pt(abs(t),df)))
        paste("t(df = ", df, ") = ", t, ", p = ", sig, sep = "")
}
```

Executing these commands creates a function called *ttestfromMeans* which takes the means, standard deviations and sample sizes of the two groups, and outputs the resulting *t*-test to compare those two means. Let's look at the contents of the function:

- *df<-n1 + n2 - 2* computes the degrees of freedom.
- *poolvar<-(((n1-1)*sd1 ^ 2)+((n2-1)*sd2 ^ 2))/df* computes the pooled variance estimate, s_p^2
- *t <-(x1-x2)/sqrt(poolvar*((1/n1)+(1/n2)))* computes the *t*-statistic.
- *sig<-2*(1-(pt(abs(t),df)))* calculates the *p*-value.
- *paste("t(df = ", df, ") = ", t, ", p = ", sig, sep = " ")* pastes together some text and the values of *t*, *df* and the *p*-value to print to the console.

We can now use this function on the means, standard deviations and sample sizes that we computed earlier by executing:

```
ttestfromMeans(x1, x2, sd1, sd2, n1, n2)
```

The result is the same as if we'd computed it from the raw data (see Output 9.3):

```
[1] "t(df = 22) = 1.68134561495341, p = 0.106839192382597"
```

9.5.2.1. General procedure for the independent *t*-test ①

To conduct an independent *t*-test you should follow this general procedure:

1 *Enter data.*

2 *Explore your data*: as with any analysis, it's a good idea to begin by graphing your data and computing some descriptive statistics. You should also check distributional assumptions (see Chapter 5).

3 *Compute the test*: you can then run the *t*-test. Depending on what you found in the previous step, you might need to run a robust version of the test.

4 *Calculate an effect size*: it is useful to quantify your effect with an effect size.

We will work through these steps in turn.

9.5.2.2. Entering data ①

One of the strange things about the *t*-test using **R** is that if you use the **t.test()** function, it actually doesn't matter how you enter your data: you can enter it in both wide or long format: it does not matter at all because the function contains an option *paired = TRUE/ FALSE*, which tells it whether to treat data as dependent or independent. However, R Commander does care, so we'll stick to convention and enter the data in a long format, which R Commander expects. You should have already entered the data if you completed the self-help test earlier in the chapter; if not, you can enter the data as:

```
Group<-gl(2, 12, labels = c( "Picture", "Real Spider"))
Anxiety<-c(30, 35, 45, 40, 50, 35, 55, 25, 30, 45, 40, 50, 40, 35, 50, 55, 65, 55, 50, 35, 30, 50, 60, 39)
```

The data are entered in two columns (one called **Group** which specifies whether a real spider or picture was used and one called **Anxiety** which indicates the person's anxiety when faced with the picture/real spider). These commands create a variable called **Anxiety** with the 24 anxiety scores contained within it, and a variable called **Group**, which uses the *gl()* function to create a factor variable with two groups each containing 12 participants. Finally, we can merge these variables into a dataframe called *spiderLong* by executing:

```
spiderLong<-data.frame(Group, Anxiety)
```

9.5.2.3. The independent *t*-test using R Commander ①

As always, first import the data, using **Data⇒Import data⇒from text file, clipboard, or URL...** (see section 3.7.3), click OK and choose the file **spiderLong.dat**.

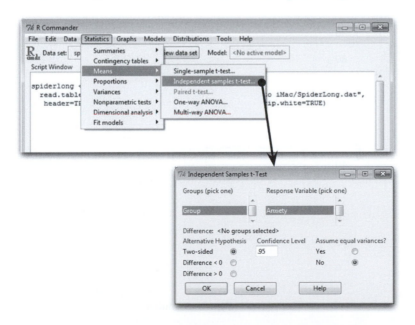

FIGURE 9.4
The independent *t*-test using R Commander

To run an independent *t*-test, choose **Statistics⇒Means⇒Independent samples t-test**. Figure 9.4 shows the dialog box that appears. On the left-hand side, in the list labelled *Groups (pick one)*, choose a variable that distinguishes your two experimental groups. R Commander expects this variable to be a factor – there is only one in our data set, so this variable has been highlighted already (**Group**). On the right-hand side, in the list labelled *Response Variable (pick one)*, choose the outcome variable. R Commander expects this variable to be numeric, and has highlighted the only variable in our data set, **Anxiety**.

Our hypothesis is two-sided (or two-tailed), so that option can be left as it is, and we'd like 95% confidence intervals – although if we'd like a different confidence level, we can change .95 to a different value (.99, to get 99% confidence intervals, for example). Finally, we don't want to make the assumption of equal variances: if we make the assumption, and we're wrong, then our *p*-value will be wrong; however, if we don't make the assumption when it would have been OK to make the assumption, it doesn't matter, because the *p*-value won't change (Jane Superbrain Box 9.2). To run the analysis click on OK. The output is described in section 9.5.2.6.

9.5.2.4. Exploring data and testing assumptions ①

In Chapter 4 we saw that it is always a good idea to look at a graph of your data. In this case we will produce a line graph with error bars.

SELF-TEST

✓ Use *ggplot2* to produce a boxplot and bar chart with error bars showing confidence intervals for the spider data.

The bar chart should look like Figure 9.2 and the boxplot is shown in Figure 9.5. The bar chart shows that the error bars overlap, indicating that, on face value, there are no

FIGURE 9.5
Boxplot of the anxiety data

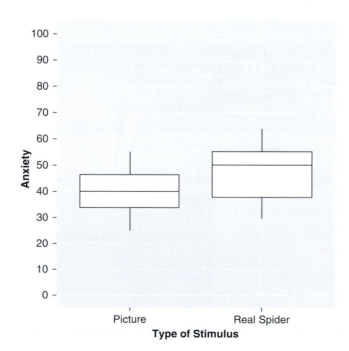

between-group differences (although this measure is only approximate). The boxplot shows that the spread of scores was reasonably similar in the two groups, although the real spider condition exhibits a spread of scores below the median that is wider than that above the median.

To get some descriptive statistics for each group we can use the *by()* function that we encountered in Chapter 5. Remember that this function takes the general form:

```
by(variable, group, output)
```

in which *variable* is the thing that you want to summarize (in this case **Anxiety**), *group* is the variable that defines the groups by which you want to organize the output (in this case **Group**), and *output* is a function that tells **R** what output you would like to see (i.e., the mean). If we use the function **stat.desc()** from the package *pastecs* then **R** will output a host of useful descriptive statistics). Therefore, by combining *by()* and *stat.desc()*, we can get a table of descriptives for each group in a single line of code:

```
by(spiderLong$Anxiety, spiderLong$Group, stat.desc, basic = FALSE, norm =
TRUE)
```

Output 9.2 shows the resulting descriptive statistics (I have edited the output slightly to fit the page so you will see more decimal places). From this output, we can see that the group who saw the picture of the spider had a mean anxiety of 40, with a standard deviation of 9.29. What's more, the standard error of that group (the standard deviation of the sampling distribution) is 2.68 ($SE = 9.293/\sqrt{12} = 9.293/3.464 = 2.68$). In addition, the table tells us that the average anxiety level in participants who were shown a real spider was 47, with a standard deviation of 11.03 and a standard error of 3.18 ($SE = 11.029/\sqrt{12} = 11.029/3.464 = 3.18$). Also, both normality tests are non-significant ($p = .852$ for the picture group and $p = .621$ for the real group) implying that we can probably assume normality of errors in the model.

```
spiderLong$Group: Picture
median    mean  SE.mean CI.mean.0.95  var   std.dev coef.var
40.000   40.000  2.683    5.905       86.364  9.293   0.232

skewness  skew.2SE  kurtosis  kurt.2SE  normtest.W  normtest.p
0.000      0.000    -1.394    -0.566     0.965       0.852
------------------------------------------------------------
:
spiderLong$Group: Real Spider
median    mean  SE.mean CI.mean.0.95  var   std.dev coef.var
50.000   47.000  3.1834   7.007       121.636 11.029  0.235

skewness  skew.2SE  kurtosis  kurt.2SE  normtest.W  normtest.p
-0.006    -0.004    -1.460    -0.592     0.949       0.621
```

Output 9.2

9.5.2.5. The independent *t*-test using R ①

To do a *t*-test we use the function *t.test()*. There are two different ways that you can use this function and it depends on whether your group data are in a single column (as they are in **spiderLong.dat**) or if they are in two different columns (as they are in **spiderWide.dat**). If you have the data for different groups stored in a single column, then the *t.test()* function is used like the *lm()* function (in other words, like a regression):

```
newModel<-t.test(outcome ~ predictor, data = dataFrame, paired = FALSE/TRUE)
```

in which:

- *newModel* is an object created that contains information about the model. We can get summary statistics for this model by executing the name of the model.

- *outcome* is a variable that contains the scores for the outcome measure (in this case **Anxiety**).

- *predictor* is a variable that tells us to which group a score belongs (in this case **Group**).

- *dataFrame* is the name of the dataframe containing the aforementioned variables.

- *paired* determines whether or not you want to do a paired/dependent *t*-test (in which case include *paired = TRUE*) or an independent *t*-test (in which case exclude the option because this is the default, or include *paired = FALSE*).

However, if you have the data for different groups stored in two columns, then the *t.test()* function takes this form:

```
newModel<-t.test(scores group 1, scores group 2, paired = FALSE/TRUE)
```

in which, the options are the same as before except:

- *scores group 1* is a variable that contains the scores for the first group.

- *scores group 2* is a variable that contains the scores for the second group. (If you want to do a *one-sample t-test* then simply exclude this second variable.)

In both forms of the function, there are additional options that can be specified, but do not need to be if you are happy to use the defaults. These are:

- *alternative = "two.sided"/"less"/"greater"*: This option determines whether you're doing a two-tailed test, and if not the direction of your hypothesis. It has three possible values: the default value is to do a two-tailed test (*alternative = "two.sided"*, or don't include the option). If you want to do a one-tailed test then you can specify either *alternative = "less"* (you predict that the difference between means will be less than zero) or *alternative = "greater"* (you predict that the difference between means will be greater than zero).

- *mu = 0*: A difference between means of zero is the default null hypothesis, but can be changed. For example, including *mu = 3* in the function would test the null hypothesis that the difference between means is different to 3.

- *var.equal*: By default the function assumes that variances are unequal (*var.equal = FALSE*). If for some reason you want to assume equal variances (we can't think why you would), then include the option *var.equal = TRUE*.

- *conf.level = 0.95*: This determines the alpha level for the *p*-value and confidence intervals. By default it is 0.95 (for 95% confidence intervals) and usually you'd exclude this option, but if you want to use a different value, say 99%, you could include *conf.level = 0.99*.

- *na.action*: If you have complete data (as we have here) you can exclude this option, but if you have missing values (i.e., 'NA's in the dataframe) then it can be useful to use *na.action = na.exclude*, which will exclude all cases with missing values – see R's Souls' Tip 7.1.

Therefore, we could carry out an independent *t*-test on the data in the *spiderLong* dataframe (which looks like this):

```
          Group Anxiety
1         Picture      30
2         Picture      35
3         Picture      45
4         Picture      40
5         Picture      50
6         Picture      35
7         Picture      55
8         Picture      25
9         Picture      30
10        Picture      45
11        Picture      40
12        Picture      50
13  Real Spider        40
14  Real Spider        35
15  Real Spider        50
16  Real Spider        55
17  Real Spider        65
18  Real Spider        55
19  Real Spider        50
20  Real Spider        35
21  Real Spider        30
22  Real Spider        50
23  Real Spider        60
24  Real Spider        39
```

by executing:

```
ind.t.test<-t.test(Anxiety ~ Group, data = spiderLong)
ind.t.test
```

which creates a model called *ind.t.test* based on predicting anxiety scores (**Anxiety**) from group membership (**Group**). We can view this model by executing its name (hence the second command).

Alternatively, if we'd input the data as in *spiderWide*, which looks like this:

```
    picture real
1        30    40
2        35    35
3        45    50
4        40    55
5        50    65
6        35    55
7        55    50
8        25    35
9        30    30
10       45    50
11       40    60
12       50    39
```

we would need to run the *t*-test by executing:

```
ind.t.test<-t.test(spiderWide$real, spiderWide$picture)
ind.t.test
```

These commands create a model called *ind.t.test* based on the variables **real** and **picture** in the *spiderWide* dataframe. As before, we view this model by executing its name.

9.5.2.6. Output from the independent *t*-test ①

Regardless of how you enter the data or specify the *t.test()* function, the output is basically identical: see Output 9.3. First we are given the value for *t*, the degrees of freedom and the *p*-value. The *p*-value is greater than .05, and hence we cannot reject the null hypothesis of no difference between the groups. Note that the *t*-value and *p*-value are the same as when we ran the analysis as a linear model in section 9.4.2 (Output 9.1). The *p*-value is a little bit different, because the degrees of freedom have been adjusted to correct for heteroscedasticity.[4]

The confidence intervals give the range of the difference that we would expect to include the true difference on 95% of occasions. The interval ranges from −15.6 to +1.65, which indicates a quite wide range of possible values for the true difference. Finally, we're given the means of the two groups: −40 and 47 (we knew these already from the descriptive statistics).

You might notice that the degrees of freedom are weird. Earlier on we said that the degrees of freedom are calculated by adding the two sample sizes and then subtracting the number of samples ($df = N_1 + N_2 - 2 = 12 + 12 - 2 = 22$); however, the output reports 21.39. This discrepancy is because this function uses a **Welch's *t*-test,** which does not make the assumption of homogeneity of variance. The Welch uses a correction which adjusts the degrees of freedom based on the homogeneity of variance, so rather than 22 degrees of freedom (as we'd expect) we have 21.39 degrees of freedom. This has had the effect of changing the *p*-value from 0.1068 to 0.107, both of which we would report as 0.107 anyway. When the sample sizes are equal, the adjustment will not make very much difference. (The formula is really big and complicated, and doesn't make much sense to me anyway, but if you're interested, Wikipedia has it: http://en.wikipedia.org/wiki/Welch's_t_test.)

```
        Welch Two Sample t-test

data:  Anxiety by Group

t = -1.6813, df = 21.385, p-value = 0.1072

alternative hypothesis: true difference in means is not equal to 0

95 percent confidence interval:
 -15.648641    1.648641

sample estimates:
   mean in group Picture mean in group Real Spider
                      40                        47
```

Output 9.3

9.5.2.7. Robust methods to compare independent means ②

Wilcox (2005) describes some robust procedures for comparing two means from independent groups. Load these functions using the instructions in section 5.8.4. Having done this,

[4] It's possible to make the same adjustment with the *lm()* function to correct for heteroscedasticity, but it's much more complicated. The approach is called a 'sandwhich' estimator, and it's done using the **sandwich()** function. The sandwich function takes the arguments *bread* and *meat*. (Some descriptions written by vegetarians use bread and tofu.) (Really, we're not joking: see http://www.bsos.umd.edu/gvpt/uslaner/robustregression.pdf.)

we now have access to Wilcox's functions. Regardless of whether your data come from the same or different entities, these functions require the data to be in two different columns (one for each experimental condition). We already have the data in this format in the *spiderWide* dataframe.

This is the format that Wilcox's functions expect. The first robust function, **yuen()**, is based on a trimmed mean. It takes the general form:

```
yuen(scores group 1, scores group 2,  tr = .2, alpha = .05)
```

in which

- *scores group 1* is a variable that contains the scores for the first group.

- *scores group 2* is a variable that contains the scores for the second group.

- *tr* is the proportion of trimming to be done. The default is .2 or 20%, and you need to use this option only if you want to specify an amount other than 20%.

- *alpha* sets the alpha level for the test. You need to include this option only if you don't want to use the conventional level of .05.

As such, for a test of independent means based on 20% trimming we simply execute:

```
yuen(spiderWide$real, spiderWide$picture)
```

If we wanted to trim only 10% of the data then we could execute:

```
yuen(spiderWide$real, spiderWide$picture, tr = .1)
```

If you execute this command you will see Output 9.4, which shows that based on this robust test there is not a significant difference in anxiety scores across the two spider groups, $T_y(13.91) = 1.296$, $p = .216$.

We can also compare trimmed means but include a bootstrap by using **yuenbt()**, which takes the general form:

```
yuenbt(scores group 1, scores group 2,  tr = .2, nboot = 599, alpha = .05,
side = F)
```

As you can see, this function takes the same form as *yuen()*, but has two additional instructions:

- *nboot = 599*: This specifies the number of bootstrap samples to be used. If you exclude this option then the default is 599, which, if anything, you might want to increase (but it's probably not necessary to use more than 2000).

- *side = F*: By default the function bootstraps confidence intervals as is, which means that they can be asymmetric. If you want to force the confidence intervals to be symmetrical then include *side = T* in the function. If you do this you will get a *p*-value, but by default you won't (although you can infer significance from whether the confidence interval crosses zero).

For a bootstrap test of independent means based on 20% trimming we simply execute:

```
yuenbt(spiderWide$real, spiderWide$picture, nboot = 2000)
```

If you execute this command you will see Output 9.4, which shows that based on this robust test there is not a significant difference (because the confidence interval crosses zero) in anxiety scores across the two spider groups, $Y_t = 1.19$ (−5.40, 17.87).

yuen() output	*yuenbt()* output	*pb2gen()* output
$ci [1] -4.429 17.929	$ci [1]-5.399 17.869	$ci [1] -2.25 20.00
$p.value [1] 0.2161433	$test.stat [1] 1.193625	$p.value [1] 0.16
$dif [1] 6.75	$p.value [1] NA	$sq.se [1] 21.96355
$se [1] 5.209309		
$teststat [1] 1.295757		
$crit [1] 2.146035		
$df [1] 13.91372		

Output 9.4

A final method is to use a bootstrap and an M-estimator (rather than trimmed mean) by applying **pb2gen()** function. This function has the general form:

```
pb2gen(spiderWide$real, spiderWide$picture, alpha=.05, nboot=2000, est = mom)
```

which is the same as *yuenbt()* except that we can chose an estimator (the default of *mom* is fine). As such, for a bootstrap test of independent M-estimators we execute:

```
pb2gen(spiderWide$real, spiderWide$picture, nboot=2000)
```

If you execute the *pb2gen()* function with the default settings you will see Output 9.4, which shows that based on this robust test there is not a significant difference (because the confidence interval crosses zero) in anxiety scores across the two spider groups, $p = .16$. In short, all three robust methods suggest that the type of spider stimulus does not affect anxiety.

9.5.2.8. Calculating the effect size ②

Even though our *t*-statistic is not statistically significant, this doesn't necessarily mean that our effect is unimportant in practical terms. To discover whether the effect is substantive we need to use what we know about effect sizes (see section 2.6.4). I'm going to stick with the effect size *r* because it's widely understood and frequently used. Converting a *t*-value into an *r*-value is actually really easy; we can use the following equation (e.g. Rosenthal, 1991; Rosnow & Rosenthal, 2005):

$$r = \sqrt{\frac{t^2}{t^2 + df}}$$

We know the value of t and the df from the **R** output and so we can compute r as follows:

$$r = \sqrt{\frac{(-1.681)^2}{(-1.681)^2 + 21.39}} = \sqrt{\frac{2.826}{24.22}} = .34$$

We can also calculate r (the effect size) using **R**. The value of t is stored in our model as a variable called **statistic[[1]]** and the degrees of freedom are stored as **parameter[[1]]**. (Actually **statistic** and **parameter** can contain many things and so the '[[1]]' tells **R** that we want the first value only.) We can access these values just as we would any other variable, we tell **R** where to find them (i.e., the name of the model, in this case *ind.t.test*) and then append a dollar sign and the name of the variable. Therefore, we can create a variable **t** that contains the value of t by executing:

```
t<-ind.t.test$statistic[[1]]
```

We can similarly create a variable called **df** containing the degrees of freedom by executing:

```
df<-ind.t.test$parameter[[1]]
```

We can then calculate r by executing:

```
r <- sqrt(t^2/(t^2+df))
```

This command is simply the equation above but in R-speak, and it creates a variable called **r**. If we want to see the value we could execute the variable name, or use the *round()* function to display it rounded off to, say 3 decimal places:

```
round(r, 3)
```

The result is the same as if we calculated by hand ($r = .342$). If you think back to our benchmarks for effect sizes, this represents a medium effect (it is around .3, the threshold for a medium effect). Therefore, even though the effect was non-significant, it still represented a fairly substantial effect.

9.5.2.9. Reporting the independent *t*-test ①

There is a fairly standard way to report any test statistic: you usually state the finding to which the test relates and then report the test statistic, its degrees of freedom and the probability value of that test statistic. There has also been a recent move (by the American Psychological Association among others) to recommend that an estimate of the effect size is routinely reported. Although effect sizes are still rather sporadically used, I want to get you into good habits so we'll start thinking about effect sizes now. The **R** output tells us that the value of t was -1.68, that the number of degrees of freedom on which this was based was 21.39, and that it was not significant at $p < .05$. We can also see the means for each group. We could write this as:

✓ On average, participants experienced greater anxiety from real spiders ($M = 47.00$, $SE = 3.18$), than from pictures of spiders ($M = 40.00$, $SE = 2.68$). This difference was not significant $t(21.39) = -1.68$, $p > .05$; however, it did represent a medium-sized effect $r = .34$.

Note how we've reported the means in each group (and standard errors) as before. For the test statistic everything is much the same as before except that I've had to report that p was greater than (>) .05 rather than less than (<). Finally, note that I've commented on the effect size at the end.

9.6. The dependent *t*-test ①

As with the independent *t*-test, the dependent *t*-test is a numeric version of equation (9.1):

$$t = \frac{\overline{D} - \mu_D}{s_D / \sqrt{N}} \tag{9.6}$$

Equation (9.6) compares the mean difference between our samples ($\overline{D}$) to the difference that we would expect to find between population means (μ_D), and then takes into account the standard error of the differences ($s_D / \sqrt{N}$). If the null hypothesis is true, then we expect there to be no difference between the population means (hence $\mu_D = 0$).

9.6.1. Sampling distributions and the standard error ①

In equation (9.1) I referred to the lower half of the equation as the standard error of differences. The standard error was introduced in section 2.5.1 and is simply the standard deviation of the sampling distribution. Have a look back at this section now to refresh your memory about sampling distributions and the standard error. Sampling distributions have several properties that are important. For one thing, if the population is normally distributed then so is the sampling distribution; in fact, if the samples contain more than about 50 scores the sampling distribution should be normally distributed. The mean of the sampling distribution is equal to the mean of the population, so the average of all possible sample means should be the same as the population mean. This property makes sense because if a sample is representative of the population then you would expect its mean to be equal to that of the population. However, sometimes samples are unrepresentative and their means differ from the population mean. On average, though, a sample mean will be very close to the population mean and only rarely will the sample mean be substantially different from that of the population. A final property of a sampling distribution is that its standard deviation is equal to the standard deviation of the population divided by the square root of the number of observations in the sample. As I mentioned before, this standard deviation is known as the standard error.

We can extend this idea to look at the *differences* between sample means. If you were to take several pairs of samples from a population and calculate their means, then you could also calculate the difference between their means. I mentioned earlier that *on average* sample means will be very similar to the population mean: as such, most samples will have very similar means. Therefore, most of the time the difference between sample means from the same population will be zero, or close to zero. However, sometimes one or both of the samples could have a mean very deviant from the population mean and so it is possible to obtain large differences between sample means by chance alone. However, this would happen less frequently.

In fact, if you plotted these differences between sample means as a histogram, you would again have a sampling distribution with all of the properties previously described. The standard deviation of this sampling distribution is called the **standard error of differences**. A small standard error tells us that most pairs of samples from a population will have very similar means (i.e., the difference between sample means should normally be very small). A large standard error tells us that sample means can deviate quite a lot from the population mean and so differences between pairs of samples can be quite large by chance alone.

9.6.2. The dependent *t*-test equation explained ①

In an experiment, a person's score in condition 1 will be different from their score in condition 2, and this difference could be very large or very small. If we calculate the differences between each person's score in each condition and add up these differences we would get the total amount of difference. If we then divide this total by the number of participants we get the average difference (thus how much, on average, a person's score differed in condition 1 compared to condition 2). This average difference is $\bar{D}$ in equation (9.6) and it is an indicator of the systematic variation in the data (i.e., it represents the experimental effect). We need to compare this systematic variation against some kind of measure of the 'systematic variation that we could naturally expect to find'. In Chapter 2 we saw that the standard deviation was a measure of the 'fit' of the mean to the observed data (i.e., it measures the error in the model when the model is the mean), but it is does not measure the fit of the mean to the population. To do this we need the standard error (see the previous section, where we revised this idea).

How does the t-test actually work?

The standard error is a measure of the error in the mean as a model of the population. In this context, we know that if we had taken two random samples from a population (and not done anything to these samples) then the means could be different just by chance. The standard error tells us by how much these samples could differ. A small standard error means that sample means should be quite similar, so a big difference between two sample means is unlikely. In contrast, a large standard error tells us that big differences between the means of two random samples are more likely. Therefore it makes sense to compare the average difference between means against the standard error of these differences. This gives us a test statistic that, as I've said numerous times in previous chapters, represents model/error. Our model is the average difference between condition means, and we divide by the standard error which represents the error associated with this model (i.e., how similar two random samples are likely to be from this population).

To clarify, imagine that an alien came down and cloned me millions of times. This population is known as Landy of the Andys (this would be possibly the most dreary and strangely terrifying place I could imagine). Imagine the alien was interested in arachnophobia in this population (because I am petrified of spiders). Everyone in this population (my clones) will be the same as me, and would behave in an identical way to me. If you took two samples from this population and measured their fear of spiders, then the means of these samples would be the same (we are clones), so the difference between sample means would be zero. Also, because we are all identical, then all samples from the population will be perfect reflections of the population (the standard error would be zero also). Therefore, if we were to get two samples that differed even very slightly then this would be very unlikely indeed (because our population is full of cloned Andys). Therefore, a difference between samples must mean that they have come from different populations. Of course, in reality we don't have samples that perfectly reflect the population, but the standard error gives an idea of how well samples reflect the population from which they came.

Therefore, by dividing by the standard error we are doing two things: (1) standardizing the average difference between conditions (this just means that we can compare values of *t* without having to worry about the scale of measurement used to measure the outcome variable); and (2) contrasting the difference between means that we have against the difference that we could *expect* to get based on how well the samples represent the populations from which they came. If the standard error is large, then large differences between samples are more common (because the distribution of differences is more spread out). Conversely, if the standard error is small, then large differences between sample means are uncommon (because the distribution is very narrow and centred around zero). Therefore, if the average difference between our samples is large, and the standard error of differences is small, then we can be confident that the difference we observed in our sample is not a chance result. If the difference is not a chance result then it must have been caused by the experimental manipulation.

In a perfect world, we could calculate the standard error by taking all possible pairs of samples from a population, calculating the differences between their means, and then working out the standard deviation of these differences. However, in reality this is impossible. Therefore, we estimate the standard error from the standard deviation of differences obtained within the sample (s_D) and the sample size (N). Think back to section 2.5.1 where we saw that the standard error is simply the standard deviation divided by the square root of the sample size; likewise the standard error of differences ($\sigma_{\bar{D}}$) is simply the standard deviation of differences divided by the square root of the sample size:

$$\sigma_{\bar{D}} \frac{s_D}{\sqrt{N}}$$

If the standard error of differences is a measure of the unsystematic variation within the data, and the sum of difference scores represents the systematic variation, then it should be clear that the *t*-statistic is simply the ratio of the systematic variation in the experiment to the unsystematic variation. If the experimental manipulation creates any kind of effect, then we would expect the systematic variation to be much greater than the unsystematic variation (so at the very least, *t* should be greater than 1). If the experimental manipulation is unsuccessful then we might expect the variation caused by individual differences to be much greater than that caused by the experiment (so *t* will be less than 1). We can compare the obtained value of *t* against the maximum value we would expect to get by chance alone in a *t*-distribution with the same degrees of freedom (these values can be found in the Appendix); if the value we obtain exceeds this critical value we can be confident that this reflects an effect of our independent variable.

9.6.3. Dependent *t*-tests using R ①

Using our spider data again, we'll now assume that the data were collected using the same participants (**spiderWide.dat**): we have 12 arachnophobes who were exposed to a picture of a spider (**picture**) and on a separate occasion a real live tarantula (**real**). Their anxiety was measured in each condition (half of the participants were exposed to the picture before the real spider while the other half were exposed to the real spider first).

9.6.3.1. General procedure for the dependent *t*-test ①

To conduct a dependent *t*-test you should follow the same general procedure as for the independent *t*-test:

1 *Enter data*.

2 *Explore your data*: begin by graphing your data and computing some descriptive statistics. You should also check distributional assumptions (see Chapter 5). We have done this already so we won't do it again – the data are the same as the previous example.

3 *Compute the test*: you can then run the *t*-test. Depending on what you found in the previous step, you might need to run a robust version of the test.

4 *Calculate an effect size*: it is useful to quantify your effect with an effect size.

We will work through these steps in turn.

9.6.3.2. Entering data ①

As I mentioned before, **R** does not expect your data in a particular format for the *t*-test, though R Commander does. For the dependent *t*-test it expects data in the wide format. You should have already entered the data in the dataframe *spiderWide*, if not, you can enter the data as:

```
picture<-c(30, 35, 45, 40, 50, 35, 55, 25, 30, 45, 40, 50)
real<-c(40, 35, 50, 55, 65, 55, 50, 35, 30, 50, 60, 39)
```

These commands create a variable called **picture** which contains the anxiety scores when a picture was used and a variable called **real** which contains the corresponding anxiety scores when faced with the real spider. We can merge these variables into a dataframe called *spiderWide* by executing:

```
spiderWide<-data.frame(picture, real)
```

9.6.3.3. The dependent *t*-test using R Commander ①

As always, import the data, using **Data⇒Import data⇒from text file, clipboard, or URL...** (see section 3.7.3) click on [OK] and choose the file **spiderWide.dat**.

To run a dependent *t*-test, choose **Statistics⇒Means⇒Paired t-test....** Figure 9.6 shows the dialog box that appears. On the left-hand side, in the list labelled *First variable (pick one)* choose a variable representing your first experimental group (I've chosen **picture**). On the right-hand side, in the list labelled *Second variable (pick one)*, choose the variable representing your second experimental group (I've chosen **real**).

Our hypothesis is two-sided (or two-tailed), so that option can be left as it is, and we'd like 95% confidence intervals – although if we'd like a different confidence level, we can change .95 to a different value (.99 to get 99% confidence intervals, for example). To run the analysis click on [OK]. The output is described in section 9.6.3.6.

FIGURE 9.6
The dependent
t-test using R
Commander

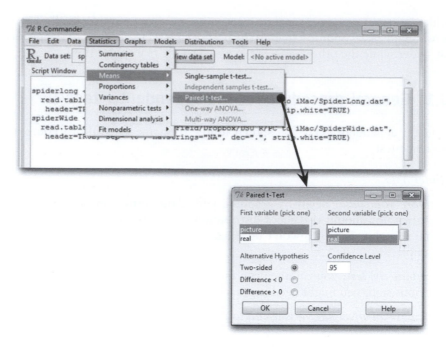

9.6.3.4. Exploring data and testing assumptions ①

We've explored these data already in section 9.5.2.4. I'll just remind you that with the data in this format you can get descriptive statistics by executing the following command:

```
stat.desc(spiderWide, basic = FALSE, norm = TRUE)
```

We talked about the assumption of normality in Chapter 5 and discovered that parametric tests (like the dependent *t*-test) assume that the sampling distribution is normal. This should be true in large samples, but in small samples people often check the normality of their data because if the data themselves are normal then the sampling distribution is likely to be also. With the dependent *t*-test we analyse the *differences* between scores because we're interested in the sampling distribution of these differences (not the raw data). Therefore, if you want to test for normality before a dependent *t*-test then what you should do is compute the differences between scores, and then check if this new variable is normally distributed (or use a big sample and not worry about normality). It is possible to have two measures that are highly non-normal that produce beautifully distributed differences.

SELF-TEST

✓ Using the **spiderWide.dat** data, compute the differences between the picture and real condition and check the assumption of normality for these differences.

9.6.3.5. The dependent *t*-test using R ①

To do a dependent *t*-test we again use the function *t.test()* but this time include the option *paired = TRUE*. In section 9.5.2.5 we saw that the form of the command depends on the format of the data. In this case we have scores from different groups stored in different columns, so we could execute:

```
dep.t.test<-t.test(spiderWide$real, spiderWide$picture, paired = TRUE)
dep.t.test
```

Note that this command is identical to one of the ones we used in section 9.5.2.5 for the independent *t*-test, except that we have included *paired = TRUE* so that **R** knows to treat the scores as dependent. These commands create a model called *dep.t.test* based on the variables **real** and **picture** in the *spiderWide* dataframe. We view this model by executing its name (hence the second command).

   If we had our data stored in long format so that our group scores are in a single column and group membership is expressed in a second column (as they are in **spiderLong.dat**), we can still run a dependent *t*-test. Again, we run it in the same way that we did for an independent *t*-test but we include the *paired = TRUE* option:

```
dep.t.test<-t.test(Anxiety ~ Group, data = spiderLong, paired = TRUE)
dep.t.test
```

which creates a model called *dep.t.test* based on predicting anxiety scores (**Anxiety**) from group membership (**Group**). We can view this model by executing its name.

9.6.3.6. Output from the dependent *t*-test ①

Regardless of how you enter the data or specify the *t.test()* function, the output is identical: see Output 9.5. The test statistic, *t*, is calculated by dividing the mean of differences by the standard error of differences (see equation (9.6): $t = 2.47$). The size of *t* is compared against known values based on the degrees of freedom. When the same participants have been used, the degrees of freedom are simply the sample size minus 1 ($df = N - 1 = 11$) – you should check this value is what you expect it to be, to ensure you haven't made a mistake. **R** uses the degrees of freedom to calculate the exact probability that a value of *t* as big as the one obtained could occur if the null hypothesis were true (i.e., there was no difference between these means). The probability for the spider data is very low ($p = .031$) and in fact it tells us that there is only a 3.1% chance that a value of *t* this big could happen if the null hypothesis were true. We saw in Chapter 2 that we generally accept a $p < .05$ as statistically meaningful; therefore, this *t* is significant because .031 is smaller than .05. The fact that the *t*-value is a positive number tells us that the first condition (the **real** condition) had a larger mean than the second (the **picture** condition) and so the real spider led to greater anxiety than the picture. Therefore, we can conclude that exposure to a real spider caused significantly more reported anxiety in arachnophobes than exposure to a picture, $t(11) = 2.47, p < .05$.

```
        Paired t-test
data:   spiderWide$real and spiderWide$picture
t = 2.4725, df = 11, p-value = 0.03098

alternative hypothesis: true difference in means is not equal to 0

95 percent confidence interval:
  0.7687815 13.2312185

sample estimates:
mean of the differences
                7
```

Output 9.5

This output provides a 95% confidence interval for the mean difference. Imagine we took 100 samples from a population of difference scores and calculated their means ($\bar{D}$) and a confidence interval for that mean. In 95 of those samples the constructed confidence intervals contains the true value of the mean difference. The confidence interval tells us the boundaries within which the true mean difference is likely to lie. So, assuming this sample's confidence interval is one of the 95 out of 100 that contains the population value, we can say that the true mean difference lies between 0.77 and 13.23. The importance of this interval is that it does not contain zero (i.e., both limits are positive) because this tells us that the true value of the mean difference is unlikely to be zero. Crucially, if we were to compare pairs of random samples from a population we would expect most of the differences between sample means to be zero. But since our interval, based on our two samples, does not contain zero, we can be confident that our two samples do not represent random samples from the same population. Instead they represent samples from different populations induced by the experimental manipulation.

9.6.3.7. Robust methods to compare dependent means ②

As with independent means, there are equivalent robust functions to test dependent groups in Rand Wilcox's (2005) book. Load these functions using the instructions in section 5.8.4. As with the functions for independent designs, the data need to be in two different columns (one for each experimental condition). We already have the data in this format in the *spiderWide* dataframe.

The first robust function, **yuend()**, is based on a trimmed mean. It takes the general form:

```
yuend(scores group 1, scores group 2,  tr = .2, alpha = .05)
```

In other words, it works in exactly the same way as the *yuen()* function in section 9.5.2.7. Refer back to that section for a more detailed description of the format of these functions. As such, for a test of dependent means based on 20% trimming we simply execute:

```
yuend(spiderWide$real, spiderWide$picture)
```

If you execute this command you will see Output 9.6, which shows that based on this robust test there is not a significant difference in anxiety scores across the two spider groups, $T_y(7) = 1.86$, $p = .106$.

yuend() output	*ydbt()* output
$ci [1] -1.843818 15.343818	$ci [1]-1.6298 15.1298
$siglevel [1] 0.1056308	$dif [1] 6.75
$dif [1] 6.75	$p.value [1] 0.105 [1] NA
$se [1] 3.634327	
$teststat [1] 1.85729	
$df [1] 7	

Output 9.6

We can also compare trimmed means but include a bootstrap by using **ydbt()**, which takes the general form:

```
ydbt(scores group 1, scores group 2,  tr = .2, nboot = 599, alpha = .05, side = F)
```

As you can see, this function takes the same form as *yuenbt()* in section 9.5.2.7. As such, for a bootstrap test of dependent means based on 20% trimming we simply execute:

```
ydbt(spiderWide$real, spiderWide$picture, nboot = 2000)
```

If you execute this command you will see Output 9.6, which shows that based on this robust test there is not a significant difference (because the confidence interval crosses zero) in anxiety scores across the two spider groups, $Y_t = 6.75$ (−1.63, 15.13), $p = .105$.

A final method is to use a bootstrap and an M-estimator (rather than trimmed mean) by applying **bootdpci()** function. This function has the general form:

```
bootdpci(scores group 1, scores group 2, alpha=.05, nboot=2000, est = tmean)
```

For a bootstrap test of dependent M-estimators we execute:

```
bootdpci(spiderWide$real, spiderWide$picture, est=tmean, nboot=2000)
```

If you execute the *bootdpci()* function with the default settings you will see Output 9.7, which shows that based on this robust test there is a significant difference (because the confidence interval does not cross zero and p is less than .05) in anxiety scores across the two spider groups, $\bar{\psi} = 7.5$ (0.50, 13.13), $p = .037$. In short, the robust methods disagree about whether the type of spider stimulus does not affect anxiety.

```
$output
      con.num psihat p.value p.crit ci.lower ci.upper
[1,]        1    7.5   0.037   0.05      0.5   13.125
```

Output 9.7

9.6.3.8. Calculating the effect size ②

Even though our *t*-statistic is statistically significant, this doesn't mean our effect is important in practical terms. To discover whether the effect is substantive we need to use what we know about effect sizes (see section 2.6.4). We can compute this value in the same way that we did for the independent *t*-test (section 9.5.2.8) by executing:[5]

```
t<-dep.t.test$statistic[[1]]
df<-dep.t.test$parameter[[1]]
r <- sqrt(t^2/(t^2+df))
round(r, 3)
```

```
[1] 0.598
```

Notice that the code is identical to last time we used it except that we have used the *dep.t.test* model to get the values of t and the degrees of freedom. You may also notice that the effect has grown. If you think back to our benchmarks for effect sizes this represents a very large effect (it is above .5, the threshold for a large effect). Therefore, as well as being statistically significant, this effect is large and probably substantive finding. This growth in the effect size might seem slightly odd given that we used exactly the same data (but see section 9.7).

[5]Actually, this will overestimate the effect size because of the correlation between the two conditions. This is quite a technical issue and I'm trying to keep things simple here, but bear this in mind and if you're interested read Dunlap, Cortina, Vaslow, and Burke (1996).

9.6.3.9. Reporting the dependent *t*-test ①

The rules that I made up – erm, I mean, reported – for the independent *t*-test pretty much apply for the dependent *t*-test. In this example the **R** output tells us that the value of *t* was 2.47, that this was based on 11 degrees of freedom, and that it was significant at *p* = .031. We can also see the means for each group. We could write this as:

✓ On average, participants experienced significantly greater anxiety from real spiders (*M* = 47.00, *SE* = 3.18) than from pictures of spiders (*M* = 40.00, *SE* = 2.68), *t*(11) = 2.47, *p* < .05, *r* = .60.

Note how we've reported the means in each group (and standard errors) in the standard format. For the test statistic, note that we've used an italic *t* to denote the fact that we've calculated a *t*-statistic, then in brackets we've put the degrees of freedom and then stated the value of the test statistic. The probability can be expressed in several ways: often people report things to a standard level of significance (such as .05) as I have done here, but sometimes people will report the exact significance. Finally, note that I've reported the effect size at the end – you won't always see this in published papers but that's no excuse for you not to report it!

Try to avoid writing vague, unsubstantiated things like this:

✗ People were more scared of real spiders (*t* = 2.47).

More scared than what? Where are the degrees of freedom? Was the result statistically significant? Was the effect important (what was the effect size)?

CRAMMING SAM'S TIPS   **The dependent *t*-test**

- The dependent *t*-test compares two means, when those means have come from the same entities; for example, if you have used the same participants in each of two experimental conditions.
- Look at the *p*-value. If the value is less than .05 then the means of the two conditions are significantly different.
- Look at the values of the means to tell you how the conditions differ.
- Report the *t*-statistic, the degrees of freedom and the significance value. Also report the means and their corresponding standard errors.
- If you're feeling brave, calculate and report the effect size too.

9.7. Between groups or repeated measures? ①

The two examples in this chapter are interesting (honestly!) because they illustrate the difference between data collected using the same participants and data collected using different participants. The examples use the same scores in each condition. When analysed as though the data came from the same participants the result was a significant difference between means, but when analysed as though the data came from different participants there was no significant difference between group means. This may seem like a puzzling finding – after all the numbers were identical in both examples. What this illustrates is the relative *power* of repeated-measures designs. When the same participants are used across conditions the unsystematic variance (often called the error variance) is reduced dramatically, making it

Labcoat Leni's Real Research 9.1

You don't have to be mad to work here, but it helps③

Board, B. J., & Fritzon, K. (2005). *Psychology, Crime & Law*, 11, 17–32.

In the UK you often see the 'humorous' slogan 'You don't have to be mad to work here, but it helps' displayed in work places. Well, Board and Fritzon (2005) took this a step further by measuring whether 39 senior business managers and chief executives from leading UK companies were mad (well, had personality disorders). They tested them with the Minnesota Multiphasic Personality Inventory Scales for DSM III Personality Disorders (MMPI-PD), which is a well-validated measure of 11 personality disorders: Histrionic, Narcissistic, Antisocial, Borderline, Dependent, Compulsive, Passive-aggressive, Paranoid, Schizotypal, Schizoid and Avoidant. They needed a comparison group, and what better one to choose than 317 legally classified psychopaths at Broadmoor Hospital (a high-security psychiatric hospital in the UK).

The authors report the means and standard deviations for these two groups in Table 2 of their paper. Using these values we can run *t*-tests on these means. The data from Board and Fritzon's Table 2 are in the file **Board&Fritzon2005.dat**. Use this file to run *t*-tests to see whether managers score higher on personality disorder questionnaires than legally classified psychopaths.

Report these results. What do you conclude?

Answers are in the additional material on the companion website (or look at Table 2 in the original article).

easier to detect any systematic variance. It is often assumed that the way in which you collect data is irrelevant, but I hope to have illustrated that it can make the difference between detecting a difference and not detecting one. In fact, researchers have carried out studies using the same participants in experimental conditions, then repeated the study using different participants in experimental conditions, and then used the method of data collection as an independent variable in the analysis. Typically, they have found that the method of data collection interacts significantly with the results found (see Erlebacher, 1977).

What have I discovered about statistics? ①

We started this chapter by looking at my relative failures as a human being compared to Simon Hudson before investigating some problems with the way **R** produces error bars for repeated-measures designs. We then had a look at some general conceptual features of the *t*-test, a parametric test that's used to test differences between two means. After this general taster, we moved onto look specifically at the dependent *t*-test (used when your conditions involve the same entities). I explained how it was calculated, how to do it in **R** and how to interpret the results. We then discovered much the same for the independent *t*-test (used when your conditions involve different entities). I also rattled on excitedly about how a situation with two conditions can be conceptualized as a general linear model, by which point those of you who have a life had gone to the pub for a stiff drink. My excitement about things like general linear models could explain why Clair Sparks chose Simon Hudson all those years ago. Perhaps she could see the writing on the wall! Fortunately, I was a ruthless pragmatist at the age of 10, and the Clair Sparks episode didn't seem to concern me unduly; I just set my sights elsewhere during the obligatory lunchtime game of kiss chase. These games were the last I would see of women for quite some time ...

R packages used in this chapter

ggplot2	Rcmdr
pastecs	WRS

R functions used in this chapter

bootdpci()	round()
by()	sandwich()
data.frame()	sd()
head()	sqrt()
length()	stat.desc()
lm()	summary()
mean()	t.test()
names()	ydbt()
paste()	yuen()
pb2gen()	yuenbt()
return()	yuend()

Key terms that I've discovered

Dependent *t*-test	Standard error of differences
Grand mean	Variance sum law
Independent *t*-test	Welch's *t*-test

Smart Alex's tasks

These scenarios are taken from Field and Hole (2003). In each case analyse the data in **R**.

- **Task 1:** One of my pet hates is 'pop psychology' books. Along with banishing Freud from all bookshops, it is my avowed ambition to rid the world of these rancid putre-faction-ridden wastes of trees. Not only do they give psychology a very bad name by stating the bloody obvious and charging people for the privilege, but they are also considerably less enjoyable to look at than the trees killed to produce them (admittedly the same could be said for the turgid tripe that I produce in the name of education, but let's not go there just for now). Anyway, as part of my plan to rid the world of popular psychology I did a little experiment. I took two groups of people who were in relationships and randomly assigned them to one of two conditions. One group read the famous popular psychology book *Women Are from Bras, Men Are from Penis*, whereas another group read *Marie Claire*. I tested only 10 people in each of these groups, and the dependent variable was an objective measure of their happiness with their relationship after reading the book. I didn't make any specific prediction about which reading material would improve relationship happiness. The data are in the file **Penis.dat**. Analyse them with the appropriate *t*-test. ①

- **Task 2**: Imagine Twaddle and Sons, the publishers of *Women are from Bras, Men are from Penis*, were upset about my claims that their book was about as useful as a paper umbrella. They decided to take me to task and design their own experiment in which participants read their book and one of my books (Field and Hole) at different times. Relationship happiness was measured after reading each book. To maximize their chances of finding a difference they used a sample of 500 participants, but got each participant to take part in both conditions (they read both books). The order in which books were read was counterbalanced and there was a delay of 6 months between reading the books. They predicted that reading their wonderful contribution to popular psychology would lead to greater relationship happiness than reading some dull and tedious book about experiments. The data are in **FieldHole.dat**. Analyse them using the appropriate *t*-test. ①

Answers can be found on the companion website (or for more detail see Field and Hole, 2003).

Further reading

Field, A. P., & Hole, G. (2003). *How to design and report experiments*. London: Sage. (In my completely unbiased opinion this is a useful book to get some more background on experimental methods.)

Miles, J. N. V., & Banyard, P. (2007). *Understanding and using statistics in psychology: A practical introduction*. London: Sage. (A fantastic and amusing introduction to statistical theory.)

Rosnow, R. L., & Rosenthal, R. (2005). *Beginning behavioral research: A conceptual primer* (5th ed.). Upper Saddle River, NJ: Pearson/Prentice Hall.

Wright, D. B., & London, K. (2009). *First steps in statistics* (2nd ed.). London: Sage. (This book has very clear introductions to the *t*-test.)

Interesting real research

Board, B. J., & Fritzon, K. (2005). Disordered personalities at work. *Psychology, Crime & Law, 11*(1), 17–32.

10

Comparing several means: ANOVA (GLM 1)

FIGURE 10.1
My brother Paul
(left) and I (right)
in our very fetching
school uniforms.

10.1. What will this chapter tell me? ①

There are pivotal moments in everyone's life, and one of mine was at the age of 11. Where I grew up in England there were three choices when leaving primary school and moving onto secondary school: (1) state school (where most people go); (2) grammar school (where clever people who pass an exam called the 11+ go); and (3) private school (where rich people go). My parents were not rich and I am not clever and consequently I failed my 11+, so private school and grammar school (where my clever older brother had gone) were out.

This left me to join all of my friends at the local state school. I could not have been happier. Imagine everyone's shock when my parents received a letter saying that some extra spaces had become available at the grammar school; although the local authority could scarcely believe it and had checked the 11+ papers several million times to confirm their findings, I was next on their list. I could not have been unhappier. So, I waved goodbye to all of my friends and trundled off to join my brother at Ilford County High School for Boys (a school that still hit students with a cane if they were particularly bad and that, for some considerable time and with good reason, had 'H.M. Prison' painted in huge white letters on its roof). It was goodbye to normality, and hello to 6 years of learning how not to function in society. I often wonder how my life would have turned out had I not gone to this school; in the parallel universes where the letter didn't arrive and Andy went to state school, or where my parents were rich and Andy went to private school, what became of him? If we wanted to compare these three situations we couldn't use a *t*-test because there are more than two conditions.[1] However, this chapter tells us all about the statistical models that we use to analyse situations in which we want to compare more than two conditions: **analysis of variance** (or **ANOVA** to its friends). This chapter will begin by explaining the theory of ANOVA when different participants are used (*independent ANOVA*). We'll then look at how to carry out the analysis in **R** and interpret the results.

10.2. The theory behind ANOVA ②

10.2.1 Inflated error rates ②

Before explaining how ANOVA works, it is worth mentioning why we don't simply carry out several *t*-tests to compare all combinations of groups that have been tested. Imagine a situation in which there were three experimental conditions and we were interested in differences between these three groups. If we were to carry out *t*-tests on every pair of groups, then that would involve doing three separate tests: one to compare groups 1 and 2, one to compare groups 1 and 3, and one to compare groups 2 and 3. If each of these *t*-tests uses a .05 level of significance then for each test the probability of falsely rejecting the null hypothesis (known as a Type I error) is only 5%. Therefore, the probability of no Type I errors is .95 (95%) for each test. If we assume that each test is independent (hence, we can multiply the probabilities) then the overall probability of no Type I errors is $.95^3 = .95 \times .95 \times .95 = .857$, because the probability of no Type I errors is .95 for each test and there are three tests. Given that the probability of no Type I errors is .857, then we can calculate the probability of making at least one Type I error by subtracting this number from 1 (remember that the maximum probability of any event occurring is 1). So, the probability of at least one Type I error is $1 - .857 = .143$, or 14.3%. Therefore, across this group of tests, the probability of making a Type I error has increased from 5% to 14.3%, a value greater than the criterion accepted by scientists. This error rate across statistical tests conducted on the same experimental data is known as the **familywise** or **experimentwise error rate**. An experiment with three conditions is a relatively simple design, and so the effect of carrying out several tests is not severe. If you imagine that we now increase the number of experimental conditions from three to five (which is only two more groups) then the

Why not do lots of *t*-tests?

---

[1] Really, this is the least of our problems: there's the small issue of needing access to parallel universes.

number of t-tests that would need to done increases to 10.[2] The familywise error rate can be calculated using the following general equation:

$$\text{familywise error} = 1 - (0.95)^n \tag{10.1}$$

in which n is the number of tests carried out on the data. With 10 tests carried out, the familywise error rate is $1 - .95^{10} = .40$, which means that there is a 40% chance of having made at least one Type I error. For this reason we use ANOVA rather than conducting lots of t-tests.

10.2.2.   Interpreting F ②

When we perform a t-test, we test the hypothesis that the two samples have the same mean. Similarly, ANOVA tells us whether three or more means are the same, so it tests the null hypothesis that all group means are equal. An ANOVA produces an F-statistic or F-ratio, which is similar to the t-statistic in that it compares the amount of systematic variance in the data to the amount of unsystematic variance. In other words, F is the ratio of the model to its error.

ANOVA is an *omnibus* test, which means that it tests for an overall effect: so, it does not provide specific information about which groups were affected. Suppose an experiment was conducted with three different groups, and the F-ratio tells us that the means of these three samples are not equal (i.e., that $\overline{X}_1 = \overline{X}_2 = \overline{X}_3$ is *not* true). There are several ways in which the means can differ. The first possibility is that all three sample means are significantly different ($\overline{X}_1 \neq \overline{X}_2 \neq \overline{X}_3$). A second possibility is that the means of groups 1 and 2 are the same but group 3 has a significantly different mean from both of the other groups ($\overline{X}_1 = \overline{X}_2 \neq \overline{X}_3$). Another possibility is that groups 2 and 3 have similar means but group 1 has a significantly different mean ($\overline{X}_1 \neq \overline{X}_2 = \overline{X}_3$). Finally, groups 1 and 3 could have similar means but group 2 has a significantly different mean from both ($\overline{X}_1 = \overline{X}_3 \neq \overline{X}_2$). So, in an experiment, the F-ratio tells us only that the experimental manipulation has had some effect, but it doesn't tell us specifically what the effect was.

10.2.3.   ANOVA as regression ②

I've hinted several times that all statistical tests boil down to variants on regression. In fact, ANOVA is just a special case of regression. This surprises many scientists because ANOVA and regression are usually used in different situations. The reason is largely historical in that

---

[2] These comparisons are group 1 vs. 2, 1 vs. 3, 1 vs. 4, 1 vs. 5, 2 vs. 3, 2 vs. 4, 2 vs. 5, 3 vs. 4, 3 vs. 5 and 4 vs. 5. The number of tests required – let's call it C – is calculated using this equation:

$$C = \frac{k!}{2(k-2)!}$$

in which k is the number of experimental conditions. The ! symbol stands for *factorial*, which means that you multiply the value preceding the symbol by all of the whole numbers between zero and that value (so $5! = 5 \times 4 \times 3 \times 2 \times 1 = 120$). Thus, with five conditions we find that:

$$C = \frac{5!}{2(5-2)!} = \frac{120}{2 \times 6} = 10$$

two distinct branches of methodology developed in the sciences: correlational research and experimental research. Researchers interested in controlled experiments adopted ANOVA as their procedure of choice, whereas those looking for real-world relationships adopted multiple regression. As we all know, scientists are intelligent, mature and rational people, and so neither group was tempted to slag off the other and claim that their own choice of methodology was far superior to the other (yeah, right!). With the divide in methodologies came a chasm between the statistical methods adopted by the two opposing camps (Cronbach, 1957, documents this divide in a lovely article). This divide has lasted many decades, to the extent that now students are generally taught regression and ANOVA in very different contexts and many textbooks teach ANOVA and regression in entirely different ways.

Although many considerably more intelligent people than me have attempted to redress the balance (notably the great Jacob Cohen, 1968), I am passionate about making my own small, feeble-minded attempt to enlighten you (and I set the ball rolling in sections 7.12 and 9.4.2). There are several good reasons why I think ANOVA should be taught within the context of regression. First, it provides a familiar context: I wasted many trees trying to explain regression, so why not use this base of knowledge to explain a new concept? (It should make it easier to understand.) Second, the traditional method of teaching ANOVA (known as the variance-ratio method) is fine for simple designs, but becomes impossibly cumbersome in more complex situations (such as analysis of covariance). The regression model extends very logically to these more complex designs without anyone needing to get bogged down in mathematics. Finally, the variance-ratio method becomes extremely unmanageable in unusual circumstances such as when you have unequal sample sizes.[3] The regression method makes these situations considerably simpler. Although these reasons are good enough, it is also the case that **R** very much deals with ANOVA in a regression-y sort of way (known as the general linear model, or GLM).

I have mentioned that ANOVA is a way of comparing the ratio of systematic variance to unsystematic variance in an experimental study. The ratio of these variances is known as the *F*-ratio. However, any of you who have read Chapter 7 should recognize the *F*-ratio (see section 7.2.3) as a way to assess how well a regression model can predict an outcome compared to the error within that model. If you haven't read Chapter 7 (surely not!), have a look before you carry on (it should only take you a couple of weeks to read). How can the *F*-ratio be used to test differences between means *and* whether a regression model fits the data? The answer is that when we test differences between means we *are* fitting a regression model and using *F* to see how well it fits the data, but the regression model contains only categorical predictors (i.e., grouping variables). So, just as the *t*-test could be represented by the linear regression equation (see section 9.4.2), ANOVA can be represented by the multiple regression equation in which the number of predictors is one less than the number of categories of the independent variable.

Let's take an example. There was a lot of controversy, when I wrote the first edition of my SPSS book, surrounding the drug Viagra. Admittedly there's less controversy now, but the controversy has been replaced by an alarming number of spam emails on the subject (for which I'll no doubt be grateful in 20 years' time), so I'm going to stick with the example. Viagra is a sexual stimulant (used to treat impotence) that broke into the black market under the belief that it will make someone a better lover (oddly enough, there was a glut of journalists taking the stuff at the time in the name of 'investigative journalism'… hmmm!). In the psychology literature, sexual performance issues have been linked to a loss of libido (Hawton, 1989). Suppose we tested this hypothesis by taking three groups of participants and administering one group with a placebo (such as a sugar pill), one group with a low dose of Viagra and one with a high dose. The dependent variable was an objective measure

---

[3] Having said this, it is well worth the effort in trying to obtain equal sample sizes in your different conditions because unbalanced designs do cause statistical complications (see section 10.3).

Table 10.1   Data in **Viagra.dat**

	Placebo	Low Dose	High Dose
	3	5	7
	2	2	4
	1	4	5
	1	2	3
	4	3	6
$\bar{X}$	2.20	3.20	5.00
s	1.30	1.30	1.58
s^2	1.70	1.70	2.50
Grand mean = **3.467** Grand SD = **1.767** Grand variance = **3.124**			

of libido (I will tell you only that it was measured over the course of a week – the rest I will leave to your own imagination). The data can be found in the file **Viagra.dat** (which is described in detail later in this chapter) and are in Table 10.1.

If we want to predict levels of libido from the different levels of Viagra then we can use the general equation that keeps popping up:

$$\text{outcome}_i = (\text{model}) + \text{error}_i$$

If we want to use a linear model, then we saw in section 9.4.2 that when there are only two groups we could replace the 'model' in this equation with a linear regression equation with one dummy variable to describe two groups. This dummy variable was a categorical variable with two numeric codes (0 for one group and 1 for the other). With three groups, however, we can extend this idea and use a multiple regression model with two dummy variables. In fact, as a general rule we can extend the model to any number of groups and the number of dummy variables needed will be one less than the number of categories of the independent variable. In the two-group case, we assigned one category as a base category (remember that in section 9.4.2 we chose the picture condition to act as a base) and this category was coded 0. When there are three categories we also need a base category and you should choose the condition to which you intend to compare the other groups. Usually this category will be the control group. In most well-designed science experiments there will be a group of participants who act as a baseline for other categories. This baseline group should act as the reference or base category, although the group you choose will depend upon the particular hypotheses that you want to test. In unbalanced designs (in which the group sizes are unequal) it is important that the base category contains a fairly large number of cases to ensure that the estimates of the regression coefficients are reliable. In the Viagra example, we can take the placebo group as the base category because this group was a placebo control. We are interested in comparing both the high- and low-dose groups to the group that received no Viagra at all. If the placebo group is the base category then the two dummy variables that we have to create represent the other two conditions: so, we should have one dummy variable called **high** and the other one called **low**). The resulting equation is described as:

$$\text{libido}_i = b_0 + b_2 \text{high}_i + b_1 \text{low}_i + \varepsilon_i \tag{10.2}$$

In equation (10.2), a person's libido can be predicted from knowing their group code (i.e., the code for the **high** and **low** dummy variables) and the intercept (b_0) of the model. The dummy variables in equation (10.2) can be coded in several ways, but the simplest way is to use a similar technique to that of the *t*-test. The base category is always coded 0. If a participant was given a high dose of Viagra then they are coded 1 for the **high** dummy variable and 0 for all other variables. If a participant was given a low dose of Viagra then they are coded 1 for the **low** dummy variable and 0 for all other variables (this is the same type of scheme we used in section 7.12). Using this coding scheme we can express each group by combining the codes of the two dummy variables (see Table 10.2).

Table 10.2   Dummy coding for the three-group experimental design

Group	Dummy Variable 1 (high)	Dummy Variable 2 (low)
Placebo	0	0
Low Dose Viagra	0	1
High Dose Viagra	1	0

Placebo group: Let's examine the model for the placebo group. In the placebo group both the **high** and **low** dummy variables are coded 0. Therefore, if we ignore the error term (ε_i), the regression equation becomes:

$$\text{libido}_i = b_0 + (b_1 \times 0) + (b_2 \times 0) = b_0$$
$$\overline{X}_{\text{placebo}} = b_0$$

This is a situation in which the high- and low-dose groups have both been excluded (because they are coded with 0). We are looking at predicting the level of libido when both doses of Viagra are ignored, and so the predicted value will be the mean of the placebo group (because this group is the only one included in the model). Hence, the intercept of the regression model, b_0, is always the mean of the base category (in this case the mean of the placebo group).

High-dose group: If we examine the high-dose group, the dummy variable **high** will be coded 1 and the dummy variable **low** will be coded 0. If we replace the values of these codes into equation (10.2) the model becomes:

$$\text{libido}_i = b_0 + (b_1 \times 0) + (b_2 \times 1) = b_0 + b_2$$

We know already that b_0 is the mean of the placebo group. If we are interested in only the high-dose group then the model should predict that the value of libido for a given participant equals the mean of the high-dose group. Given this information, the equation becomes:

$$\text{libido}_i = b_0 + b_2$$
$$\overline{X}_{\text{high}} = \overline{X}_{\text{placebo}} + b_2$$
$$b_2 = \overline{X}_{\text{high}} - \overline{X}_{\text{placebo}}$$

Hence, b_2 represents the difference between the means of the high-dose group and the placebo group.

Low-dose group: Finally, if we look at the model when a low dose of Viagra has been taken, the dummy variable **low** is coded 1 (and hence **high** is coded as 0). Therefore, the regression equation becomes:

$$\text{libido}_i = b_0 + (b_1 \times 1) + (b_2 \times 0) = b_0 + b_1$$

We know that the intercept is equal to the mean of the base category and that for the low-dose group the predicted value should be the mean libido for a low dose. Therefore the model can be reduced to:

$$\text{libido}_i = b_0 + b_1$$
$$\overline{X}_{\text{low}} = \overline{X}_{\text{placebo}} + b_1$$
$$b_1 = \overline{X}_{\text{low}} - \overline{X}_{\text{placebo}}$$

Hence, b_1 represents the difference between the means of the low-dose group and the placebo group. This form of dummy variable coding is the simplest form, but as we will see later, there are other ways in which variables can be coded to test specific hypotheses. These alternative coding schemes are known as *contrasts* (see section 10.4.2). The idea behind contrasts is that you code the dummy variables in such a way that the b-values represent differences between groups that you are interested in testing.

SELF-TEST

✓ To illustrate exactly what is going on I have created a file called **dummy.dat**. This file contains the Viagra data but with two additional variables (**dummy1** and **dummy2**) that specify to which group a data point belongs (as in Table 10.2). Access this file and run multiple regression analysis using libido as the outcome and **dummy1** and **dummy2** as the predictors. If you're stuck on how to run the regression then read Chapter 7 again (these chapters are ordered for a reason).

The resulting analysis is shown in Output 10.1. It might be a good idea to remind yourself of the group means from Table 10.1. The first thing to notice is that, just as in the regression chapter, an ANOVA has been used to test the overall fit of the model. This test is significant, $F(2, 12) = 5.12$, $p < .05$. Given that our model represents the group differences, this ANOVA tells us that using group means to predict scores is significantly better than using the overall mean: in other words, the group means are significantly different.

In terms of the regression coefficients, bs, the constant is equal to the mean of the base category (the placebo group). The regression coefficient for the first dummy variable (b_2) is equal to the difference between the means of the high-dose group and the placebo group ($5.0 - 2.2 = 2.8$). Finally, the regression coefficient for the second dummy variable (b_1) is equal to the difference between the means of the low-dose group and the placebo group ($3.2 - 2.2 = 1$). This analysis demonstrates how the regression model represents the three-group situation. We can see from the significance values of the t-tests that the difference between the high-dose group and the placebo group (b_2) is significant because $p < .05$. The difference between the low-dose and the placebo group is not, however, significant ($p = .282$).

```
Coefficients:
            Estimate Std. Error t value Pr(>|t|)
(Intercept)   2.2000     0.6272   3.508  0.00432 **
dummy1        2.8000     0.8869   3.157  0.00827 **
dummy2        1.0000     0.8869   1.127  0.28158
---
```

```
Signif. codes:   0 '***' 0.001 '**' 0.01 '*' 0.05 '.' 0.1 ' ' 1

Residual standard error: 1.402 on 12 degrees of freedom
Multiple R-squared: 0.4604,        Adjusted R-squared: 0.3704
F-statistic: 5.119 on 2 and 12 DF,   p-value: 0.02469
```

Output 10.1

A four-group experiment can be described by extending the three-group scenario. I mentioned earlier that you will always need one less dummy variable than the number of groups in the experiment: therefore, this model requires three dummy variables. As before, we need to specify one category as a base category (a control group). This base category should have a code of 0 for all three dummy variables. The remaining three conditions will have a code of 1 for the dummy variable that described that condition and a code of 0 for the other two dummy variables. Table 10.3 illustrates how the coding scheme would work.

Table 10.3 Dummy coding for the four-group experimental design

	Dummy variable 1	Dummy variable 2	Dummy variable 3
Group 1	1	0	0
Group 2	0	1	0
Group 3	0	0	1
Group 4 (base)	0	0	0

10.2.4. Logic of the F-ratio ②

In Chapter 7 we learnt a little about the F-ratio and its calculation. To recap, we learnt that the F-ratio is used to test the overall fit of a regression model to a set of observed data. In other words, it is the ratio of how good the model is compared to how bad it is (its error). I have just explained how ANOVA can be represented as a regression equation, and this should help you to understand what the F-ratio tells you about your data. Figure 10.2 shows the Viagra data in graphical form (including the group means, the overall mean and the difference between each case and the group mean). In this example, there were three groups; therefore, we want to test the hypothesis that the means of three groups are different (so the null hypothesis is that the group means are the same). If the group means were all the same, then we would not expect the placebo group to differ from the low-dose group or the high-dose group, and we would not expect the low-dose group to differ from the high-dose group. Therefore, on the diagram, the three shaded blue lines would be in the same vertical position (the exact position would be the grand mean – the solid horizontal line in the figure). We can see from the diagram that the group means are actually different because the horizontal blue lines (the group means) are in different vertical positions. We have just found out that in the regression model, b_2 represents the difference between the means of the placebo and the high-dose group, and b_1 represents the difference in means between the placebo and the low-dose groups. These two distances are represented in Figure 10.2 by the vertical arrows. If the null hypothesis is true and all the groups have the same means, then these b coefficients should be zero (because if the group means are equal then the difference between them will be zero).

FIGURE 10.2
The Viagra data
in graphical form.
The shaded blue
horizontal lines
represent the
mean libido of
each group. The
shapes represent
the libido of
individual
participants
(different shapes
indicate different
experimental
groups). The
black horizontal
line is the
average libido of
all participants

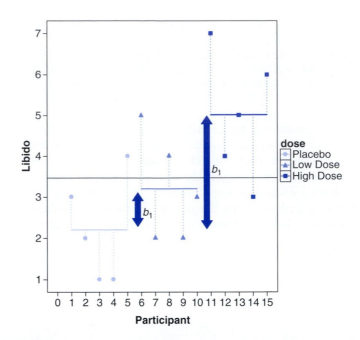

The logic of ANOVA follows from what we understand about regression:

- The simplest model we can fit to a set of data is the grand mean (the mean of the outcome variable). This basic model represents 'no effect' or 'no relationship between the predictor variable and the outcome'.

- We can fit a different model to the data collected that represents our hypotheses. If this model fits the data well then it must be better than using the grand mean. Sometimes we fit a linear model (the line of best fit), but in experimental research we often fit a model based on the means of different conditions.

- The intercept and one or more regression coefficients can describe the chosen model.

- The regression coefficients determine the shape of the model that we have fitted; therefore, the bigger the coefficients, the greater the deviation between the line and the grand mean.

- In correlational research, the regression coefficients represent the slope of the line, but in experimental research they represent the differences between group means.

- The bigger the differences between group means, the greater the difference between the model and the grand mean.

- If the differences between group means are large enough, then the resulting model will be a better fit of the data than the grand mean.

- If this is the case we can infer that our model (i.e., predicting scores from the group means) is better than not using a model (i.e., predicting scores from the grand mean). Put another way, our group means are significantly different.

Just like when we used ANOVA to test a regression model, we can compare the improvement in fit due to using the model (rather than the grand mean) to the error that still remains. Another way of saying this is that when the grand mean is used as a model, there will be a certain amount of variation between the data and the grand mean. When a model is fitted it will explain some of this variation, but some will be left unexplained. The F-ratio is the ratio of the explained to the unexplained variation. Look back at section 7.2.3 to refresh you memory on these concepts before reading on. This may all sound quite complicated, but actually most of it boils down to variations on one simple equation (see Jane Superbrain Box 10.1).

JANE SUPERBRAIN 10.1

You might be surprised to know that ANOVA boils down to one equation (well, sort of) ②

At every stage of the ANOVA we're assessing variation (or deviance) from a particular model (be that the most basic model, or the most sophisticated model). We saw back in section 2.4.1 that the extent to which a model deviates from the observed data can be expressed, in

general, in the form of equation (10.3). So, in ANOVA, as in regression, we use equation (10.3) to calculate the fit of the most basic model, and then the fit of the best model (the line of best fit). If the best model is any good then it should fit the data significantly better than our basic model:

$$\text{deviation} = \sum(\text{observed} - \text{model})^2 \qquad (10.3)$$

The interesting point is that all of the sums of squares in ANOVA are variations on this one basic equation. All that changes is what we use as the model, and what the corresponding observed data are. Look through the various sections on the sums of squares and compare the resulting equations to equation (10.3); hopefully, you can see that they are all basically variations on this general form of the equation!

10.2.5. Total sum of squares (SS_T) ②

To find the total amount of variation within our data we calculate the difference between each observed data point and the grand mean. We then square these differences and add them together to give us the total sum of squares (SS_T):

$$SS_T = \sum_{i=1}^{N}(x_i - \bar{x}_{\text{grand}})^2 \qquad (10.4)$$

We also saw in section 2.4.1 that the variance and the sums of squares are related such that variance, $s^2 = SS/(N-1)$, where N is the number of observations. Therefore, we can calculate the total sums of squares from the variance of all observations (the **grand variance**) by rearranging the relationship ($SS = s^2(N-1)$). The grand variance is the variation between all scores, regardless of the experimental condition from which the scores come. Figure 10.3 shows the different sums of squares graphically (note the similarity to Figure 7.4 which we looked at when we learnt about regression). The top left panel shows the total sum of squares: it is the sum of the squared distances between each point and the solid horizontal line (which represents the mean of all scores).

The grand variance for the Viagra data is given in Table 10.1, and if we count the number of observations we find that there were 15 in all. Therefore, SS_T is calculated as follows:

$$SS_T = s^2_{\text{grand}}(n-1)$$
$$= 3.124(15-1) = 3.124 \times 14 = 43.74$$

Before we move on, it is important to understand degrees of freedom, so have a look back at Jane Superbrain Box 2.2 to refresh your memory. We saw before that when we estimate population values, the degrees of freedom are typically one less than the number of scores used to calculate the population value. This is because to get these estimates we have to hold something constant in the population (in this case the mean), which leaves all but one of the scores free to vary (see Jane Superbrain Box 2.2). For SS_T, we used the entire sample (i.e., 15 scores) to calculate the sums of squares and so the total degrees of freedom (df_T) are one less than the total sample size ($N - 1$). For the Viagra data, this value is 14.

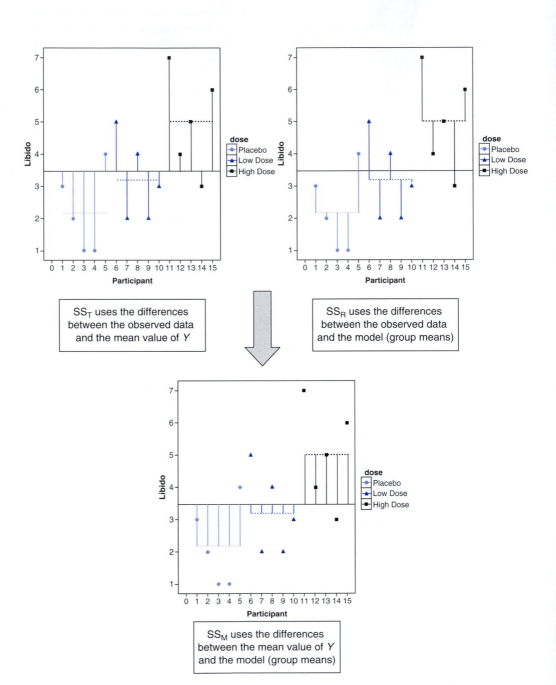

FIGURE 10.3
Graphical representation of the different sums of squares in ANOVA designs

SS_T uses the differences between the observed data and the mean value of Y

SS_R uses the differences between the observed data and the model (group means)

SS_M uses the differences between the mean value of Y and the model (group means)

10.2.6.   Model sum of squares (SS_M) ②

So far, we know that the total amount of variation within the data is 43.74 units. We now need to know how much of this variation the regression model can explain. In the ANOVA scenario, the model is based upon differences between group means, and so the model sums of squares tell us how much of the total variation can be explained by the fact that different data points come from different groups.

In section 7.2.3 we saw that the model sum of squares is calculated by taking the difference between the values predicted by the model and the grand mean (see Figure 7.4). In ANOVA, the values predicted by the model are the group means (the dashed horizontal lines in Figure 10.3). The bottom panel in Figure 10.3 shows the model sum of squared error: it is the sum of the squared distances between what the model predicts for each data point (i.e., the dotted horizontal line for the group to which the data point belongs) and the overall mean of the data (the solid horizontal line).

For each participant the value predicted by the model is the mean for the group to which the participant belongs. In the Viagra example, the predicted value for the five participants in the placebo group will be 2.2, for the five participants in the low-dose condition it will be 3.2, and for the five participants in the high-dose condition it will be 5. The model sum of squares requires us to calculate the differences between each participant's predicted value and the grand mean. These differences are then squared and added together (for reasons that should be clear in your mind by now). We know that the predicted value for participants in a particular group is the mean of that group. Therefore, the easiest way to calculate SS_M is to do the following:

1   Calculate the difference between the mean of each group and the grand mean.

2   Square each of these differences.

3   Multiply each result by the number of participants within that group (n_k).

4   Add the values for each group together.

The mathematical expression for this process is:

$$SS_M = \sum_{n=1}^{k} n_k (\bar{x}_k - \bar{x}_{grand})^2 \qquad (10.5)$$

Using the means from the Viagra data, we can calculate SS_M as follows:

$$
\begin{aligned}
SS_M &= 5(2.200 - 3.467)^2 + 5(3.200 - 3.467)^2 + 5(5.00 - 3.467)^2 \\
&= 5(-1.267)^2 + 5(-0.267)^2 + 5(1.533)^2 \\
&= 8.025 + 0.335 + 11.755 \\
&= 20.135
\end{aligned}
$$

For SS_M, the degrees of freedom (df_M) will always be one less than the number of parameters estimated. In short, this value will be the number of groups minus one (which you'll see denoted as $k - 1$). So, in the three-group case the degrees of freedom will always be 2 (because the calculation of the sums of squares is based on the group means, two of which will be free to vary in the population if the third is held constant).

10.2.7. Residual sum of squares (SS_R) ②

We now know that there are 43.74 units of variation to be explained in our data, and that our model can explain 20.14 of these units (nearly half). The final sum of squares is the residual sum of squares (SS_R), which tells us how much of the variation cannot be explained by the model. This value is the amount of variation caused by extraneous factors such as individual differences in weight, testosterone or whatever. Knowing SS_T and SS_M already, the simplest way to calculate SS_R is to subtract SS_M from SS_T ($SS_R = SS_T - SS_M$); however, telling you to do this provides little insight into what is being calculated and, of course, if you've messed up the calculations of either SS_M or SS_T (or indeed both!) then SS_R will be incorrect also.

We saw in section 7.2.3 that the residual sum of squares is the difference between what the model predicts and what was actually observed. In ANOVA, the values predicted by the model are the group means (the dashed horizontal lines in Figure 10.3). The top left panel shows the residual sum of squared error: it is the sum of the squared distances between each point and the dotted horizontal line for the group to which the data point belongs.

We already know that for a given participant, the model predicts the mean of the group to which that person belongs. Therefore, SS_R is calculated by looking at the difference between the score obtained by a person and the mean of the group to which the person belongs. In graphical terms the vertical lines in Figure 10.3 represent this sum of squares. These distances between each data point and the group mean are squared and then added together to give the residual sum of squares, SS_R, thus:

$$SS_R = \sum_{i=1}^{n} (x_{ik} - \bar{x}_k)^2 \tag{10.6}$$

Now, the sum of squares for each group represents the sum of squared differences between each participant's score in that group and the group mean. Therefore, we can express SS_R as $SS_R = SS_{group1} + SS_{group2} + SS_{group3} + \ldots$. Given that we know the relationship between the variance and the sums of squares, we can use the variances for each group in the Viagra data to create an equation like we did for the total sum of squares. As such, SS_R can be expressed as:

$$SS_R = \sum s_k^2 (n_k - 1) \tag{10.7}$$

This just means take the variance from each group (s_k^2) and multiply it by one less than the number of people in that group ($n_k - 1$). When you've done this for each group, add them all up. For the Viagra data, this gives us:

$$
\begin{aligned}
SS_R &= s_{group1}^2 (n_1 - 1) + s_{group2}^2 (n_2 - 1) + s_{group3}^2 (n_3 - 1) \\
&= (1.70)(5 - 1) + (1.70)(5 - 1) + (2.50)(5 - 1) \\
&= (1.70 \times 4) + (1.70 \times 4) + (2.50 \times 4) \\
&= 6.8 + 6.8 + 10 \\
&= 23.60
\end{aligned}
$$

The degrees of freedom for SS_R (df_R) are the total degrees of freedom minus the degrees of freedom for the model ($df_R = df_T - df_M = 14 - 2 = 12$). Put another way, it's $N - k$: the total sample size, N, minus the number of groups, k.

10.2.8.   Mean squares ②

SS_M tells us the *total* variation that the regression model (e.g., the experimental manip-ulation) explains, and SS_R tells us the *total* variation that is due to extraneous factors. However, because both of these values are summed values they will be influenced by the number of scores that were summed; for example, SS_M used the sum of only 3 different values (the group means) compared to SS_R and SS_T, which used the sum of 12 and 15 val-ues, respectively. To eliminate this bias we can calculate the average sum of squares (known as the *mean squares*, MS), which is simply the sum of squares divided by the degrees of freedom. The reason why we divide by the degrees of freedom rather than the number of parameters used to calculate the SS is because we are trying to extrapolate to a population and so some parameters within that populations will be held constant (this is the same rea-son why we divide by $N - 1$ when calculating the variance; see Jane Superbrain Box 2.2). So, for the Viagra data we find the following mean squares:

$$MS_M = \frac{SS_M}{df_M} = \frac{20.135}{2} = 10.067$$

$$MS_R = \frac{SS_R}{df_R} = \frac{23.60}{12} = 1.967$$

MS_M represents the average amount of variation explained by the model (e.g., the system-atic variation), whereas MS_R is a gauge of the average amount of variation explained by extraneous variables (the unsystematic variation).

10.2.9.   The *F*-ratio ②

The *F*-ratio is a measure of the ratio of the variation explained by the model and the varia-tion explained by unsystematic factors. In other words, it is the ratio of how good the model is against how bad it is (how much error there is). It can be calculated by dividing the model mean squares by the residual mean squares.

$$F = \frac{MS_M}{MS_R} \qquad\qquad (10.8)$$

As with the independent *t*-test, the *F*-ratio is, therefore, a measure of the ratio of sys-tematic variation to unsystematic variation. In experimental research, it is the ratio of the experimental effect to the individual differences in performance. An interesting point about the *F*-ratio is that because it is the ratio of systematic variance to unsystematic variance, if its value is less than 1 then it must, by definition, represent a non-significant effect. The reason why this statement is true is because if the *F*-ratio is less than 1 it means that MS_R is greater than MS_M, which in real terms means that there is more unsystematic than systematic vari-ance. You can think of this in terms of the effect of natural differences in ability being greater than differences brought about by the experiment. In this scenario, we can, therefore, be sure that our experimental manipulation has been unsuccessful (because it has brought about less change than if we left our participants alone!). For the Viagra data, the *F*-ratio is:

$$F = \frac{MS_M}{MS_R} = \frac{10.067}{1.967} = 5.12$$

This value is greater than 1, which indicates that the experimental manipulation had some effect above and beyond the effect of individual differences in performance. However, it doesn't yet tell us whether the F-ratio is large enough to not be a chance result. To discover this we can compare the obtained value of F against the maximum value we would expect to get by chance if the group means were equal in an F-distribution with the same degrees of freedom (these values can be found in the Appendix); if the value we obtain exceeds this critical value we can be confident that this reflects an effect of our independent variable (because this value would be very unlikely if there were no effect in the population). In this case, with 2 and 12 degrees of freedom the critical values are 3.89 ($p = .05$) and 6.93 ($p = .01$). The observed value, 5.12, is, therefore, significant at a .05 level of significance but not significant at a .01 level. The exact significance produced by **R** should, therefore, fall somewhere between .05 and .01 (which, incidentally, it does).

10.3. Assumptions of ANOVA ③

The assumptions under which the F-statistic is reliable are the same as for all parametric tests based on the normal distribution (see section 5.2). That is, the variances in each experimental condition need to be fairly similar (*homogeneity of variance*), observations should be independent and the dependent variable should be measured on at least an interval scale. In terms of normality, what matters is that distributions *within groups* are normally distributed.

10.3.1.   Homogeneity of variance ②

As with the t-test, there is an assumption that the variances of the groups are equal. This assumption can be tested using Levene's test, which tests the null hypothesis that the variances of the groups are the same (see section 5.7.1). Basically, it is an ANOVA test conducted on the absolute differences between the observed data and the mean or median from which the data came (see Oliver Twisted). If Levene's test is significant (i.e., the p-value is less than .05) then we can say that the variances are significantly different. This would mean that we had violated one of the assumptions of ANOVA and we would have to take steps to rectify this matter.

OLIVER TWISTED

Please Sir, can I have some more … Levene's test?

'Liar! Liar! Pants on fire!' screams Oliver, his cheeks red and his eyes about to explode, 'You promised in Chapter 5 to explain Levene's test properly and you haven't, you spatula head'. True enough, Oliver, I do have a spatula for a head. I also have a very nifty little demonstration of Levene's test in the additional material for this chapter on the companion website. It will tell you more than you could possibly want to know. Let's go fry an egg …

10.3.2.   Is ANOVA robust? ③

You often hear people say 'ANOVA is a robust test', which means that it doesn't matter much if we break the assumptions of the test: the F-ratio will still be accurate. There is some truth to this statement, but it is also an oversimplification of the situation. For one thing, the term *ANOVA* covers many different situations and the performance of *F* has been investigated in only some of those situations. There are two issues to consider. First, does *F* control the Type I error rate or is it significant even when there are no differences between means? Second, does *F* have enough power (i.e., is it able to detect differences when they are there)? Let's have a look at the evidence.

Looking at normality first, Glass et al. (1972) reviewed a lot of evidence that suggests that *F* controls the Type I error rate well under conditions of skew, kurtosis and non-normality. Skewed distributions seem to have little effect on the error rate and power for two-tailed tests (but can have serious consequences for one-tailed tests). However, some of this evidence has been questioned (see Jane Superbrain Box 5.1). In terms of kurtosis, leptokurtic distributions make the Type I error rate too low (too many null effects are significant) and consequently the power is too high; platykurtic distributions have the opposite effect. The effects of kurtosis seem unaffected by whether sample sizes are equal or not. One study that is worth mentioning in a bit of detail is by Lunney (1970) who investigated the use of ANOVA in just about the most non-normal situation you could imagine: when the dependent variable is binary (it could have values of only 0 or 1). The results showed that when the group sizes were equal, ANOVA was accurate when there were at least 20 degrees of freedom and the smallest response category contained at least 20% of all responses. If the smaller response category contained less than 20% of all responses then ANOVA performed accurately only when there were 40 or more degrees of freedom. The power of *F* also appears to be relatively unaffected by non-normality (Donaldson, 1968). This evidence suggests that *when group sizes are equal* the *F*-statistic can be quite robust to violations of normality.

However, when group sizes are not equal the accuracy of *F* is affected by skew, and non-normality also affects the power of *F* in quite unpredictable ways (Wilcox, 2005). One situation that Wilcox describes shows that when means are equal the error rate (which should be 5%) can be as high as 18%. If you make the differences between means bigger you should find that power increases, but actually he found that initially power *decreased* (although it increased when he made the group differences bigger still). As such *F* can be biased when normality is violated.

Turning to violations of the assumption of homogeneity of variance, ANOVA is fairly robust in terms of the error rate when sample sizes are equal. However, when sample sizes are unequal, ANOVA is not robust to violations of homogeneity of variance (this is why earlier on I said it's worth trying to collect equal-sized samples of data across conditions!). When groups with larger sample sizes have larger variances than the groups with smaller sample sizes, the resulting *F*-ratio tends to be conservative. That is, it's more likely to produce a non-significant result when a genuine difference does exist in the population. Conversely, when the groups with larger sample sizes have smaller variances than the groups with smaller samples sizes, the resulting *F*-ratio tends to be liberal. That is, it is more likely to produce a significant result when there is no difference between groups in the population (put another way, the Type I error rate is not controlled) – see Glass et al. (1972) for a review. When variances are proportional to the means then the power of *F* seems to be unaffected by the heterogeneity of variance and trying to stabilize variances does not substantially improve power (Budescu, 1982; Budescu & Appelbaum, 1981).

Violations of the assumption of independence are very serious indeed. Scariano and Davenport (1987) showed that when this assumption is broken (i.e., observations across groups are correlated) then the Type I error rate is substantially inflated. For example, using the conventional .05 Type I error rate when observations are independent, if these observations are made to correlate moderately (say, with a Pearson coefficient of .5), when comparing three groups, each of 10 observations, the actual Type I error rate is .74 (a substantial inflation!). Therefore, if observations are correlated you might think that you are working with the accepted .05 error rate (i.e., you'll incorrectly find a significant result only 5% of the time) when in fact your error rate is closer to .75 (i.e., you'll find a significant result on 75% of occasions when, in reality, there is no effect in the population).

There are various things that can be done to combat the litany of woe that you have just read. To find out more see Jane Superbrain Box 10.2.

JANE SUPERBRAIN 10.2

What do I do in ANOVA when assumptions are broken? ③

As we saw in Chapter 5, one common way to rectify problems with assumptions is to transform all of the data and then reanalyse these transformed values (see Chapter 5). When homogeneity of variance is the problem there are versions of the *F*-ratio that have been derived to be robust when homogeneity of variance has been violated. One that can be implemented in **R** is **Welch's F** (1951) – see Oliver Twisted.

If you have distributional problems, then there are robust (see section 5.8.4) variants of ANOVA that have been implemented in **R** by Wilcox (2005). These methods are based on bootstrapping or trimmed means and M-estimators (both of which can also include a bootstrap). We'll cover these methods later in the chapter.

On balance, if you have the stomach for it, Wilcox's robust methods are probably the best approach to dealing with violations of assumptions. If you don't have the stomach for it, there are a group of tests (often called assumption-free, distribution-free or non-parametric tests, none of which are particularly accurate names) that you can use instead. The one-way independent ANOVA has a non-parametric counterpart called the Kruskal–Wallis test. If you have non-normally distributed data, or have violated some other assumption, then this test can be a useful way around the problem. This test is described in Chapter 15.

OLIVER TWISTED

Please Sir, can I have some more … Welch's F?

'You don't understand Welch's *F*,' taunts Oliver, 'Andy, Andy, brains all sandy ….' Whatever, Oliver. Welch's *F* adjusts *F* and the residual degrees of freedom to combat problems arising from violations of the homogeneity of variance assumption. There is a lengthy explanation about Welch's *F* in the additional material available on the companion website. Oh, and Oliver, microchips are made of sand.

10.4. Planned contrasts ②

The *F*-ratio tells us only whether the model fitted to the data accounts for more variation than extraneous factors, but it doesn't tell us where the differences between groups lie. So, if the *F*-ratio is large enough to be statistically significant, then we know only that one or more of the differences between means are statistically significant (e.g., either b_2 or b_1 is statistically significant). It is, therefore, necessary after conducting an ANOVA to carry out further analysis to find out which groups differ. In multiple regression, each *b* coefficient is tested individually using a *t*-test and we could do the same for ANOVA. However, we would need to carry out two *t*-tests, which would inflate the familywise error rate (see section 10.2). Therefore, we need a way to contrast the different groups without inflating the Type I error rate. There are two ways in which to achieve this goal: the first is to break down the variance accounted for by the model into component parts: the second is to compare every group (as if conducting several *t*-tests) but to use a stricter acceptance criterion such that the familywise error rate does not rise above .05. The first option can be done using planned comparisons (also known as **planned contrasts**),[4] whereas the latter option is done using *post hoc* comparisons (see next section). The difference between planned comparisons and **post hoc tests** can be likened to the difference between one- and two-tailed tests in that planned comparisons are done when you have specific hypotheses that you want to test, whereas *post hoc* tests are done when you have no specific hypotheses. Let's first look at planned contrasts.

10.4.1. Choosing which contrasts to do ②

In the Viagra example we could have had very specific hypotheses. For one thing, we would expect any dose of Viagra to change libido compared to the placebo group. As a second hypothesis we might believe that a high dose should increase libido more than a low dose. To do planned comparisons, these hypotheses must be derived *before* the data are collected. It is fairly standard in science to want to compare experimental conditions to the control conditions as the first contrast, and then to see where the differences lie between the experimental groups. ANOVA is based upon splitting the total variation into two component parts: the variation due to the experimental manipulation (SS_M) and the variation due to unsystematic factors (SS_R) (see Figure 10.4).

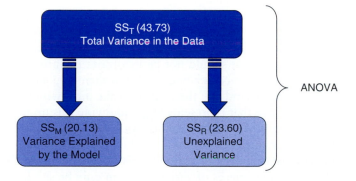

FIGURE 10.4
Partitioning variance for ANOVA

Planned comparisons take this logic a step further by breaking down the variation due to the experiment into component parts (see Figure 10.5). The exact comparisons that are carried out depend upon the hypotheses you want to test. Figure 10.5 shows a situation in which the experimental variance is broken down to look at how much variation is created by the two drug conditions compared to the placebo condition (contrast 1). Then the variation explained by taking Viagra is broken down to see how much is explained by taking a high dose relative to a low dose (contrast 2).

---

[4] The terms *comparison and contrast* are used interchangeably.

FIGURE 10.5
Partitioning of
experimental
variance into
component
comparisons

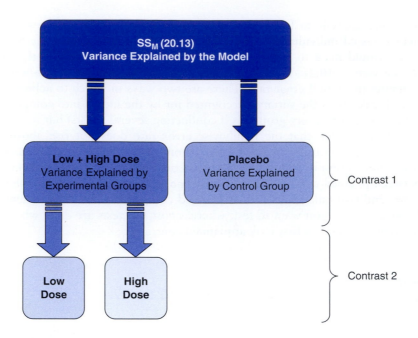

Typically, students struggle with the notion of planned comparisons, but there are three rules that can help you to work out what to do:

1   If we have a control group, this is usually because we want to compare it against the other groups.

2   Each contrast must compare only two 'chunks' of variation.

3   Once a group has been singled out in a contrast it can't be used in another contrast.

Let's look at these rules in detail. First, if a group is singled out in one comparison, then it should not reappear in another comparison. The important thing to remember is that we are breaking down one chunk of variation into smaller independent chunks. So, in Figure 10.5 contrast 1 involved comparing the placebo group to the experimental groups; because the placebo group is singled out, it should not be incorporated into any other contrasts. You can think of partitioning variance as being similar to slicing up a cake. You begin with a cake (the total sum of squares) and you then cut this cake into two pieces (SS_M and SS_R). You then take the piece of cake that represents SS_M and divide this up into smaller pieces. Once you have cut off a piece of cake you cannot stick that piece back onto the original slice, and you cannot stick it onto other pieces of cake, but you can divide it into smaller pieces of cake. Likewise, once a slice of variance has been split from a larger chunk, it cannot be attached to any other pieces of variance, it can only be subdivided into smaller chunks of variance. Now, all of this talk of cake is making me hungry, but hopefully it illustrates a point.

If you follow the independence of contrasts rule that I've just explained (the cake slicing!), and always compare only two pieces of variance, then you should always end up with one less contrast than the number of groups; there will be $k - 1$ contrasts (where k is the number of conditions you're comparing).

Second, each contrast must compare only two chunks of variance. This rule is so that we can draw firm conclusions about what the contrast tells us. The F-ratio tells us that some of our means differ, but not which ones, and if we were to perform a contrast on more than two chunks of variance we would have the same problem. By comparing only two chunks of variance we can be sure that a significant result represents a difference between these two portions of experimental variation.

Finally, in most social science research we use at least one control condition, and in the vast majority of experimental designs we predict that the experimental conditions will differ from the control condition (or conditions). As such, the biggest hint that I can give you is that when planning comparisons the chances are that your first contrast should be one that compares all of the experimental groups with the control group (or groups). Once you have done this first comparison, any remaining comparisons will depend upon which of the experimental groups you predict will differ.

To illustrate these principles, Figures 10.6 and 10.7 show the contrasts that might be done in a four-group experiment. The first thing to notice is that in both scenarios there are three possible comparisons (one less than the number of groups). Also, every contrast compares only two chunks of variance. What's more, in both scenarios the first contrast is the same: the experimental groups are compared against the control group or groups. In Figure 10.6 there was only one control condition and so this portion of variance is used only in the first contrast (because it cannot be broken down any further). In Figure 10.7 there were two control groups, and so the portion of variance due to the control conditions (contrast 1) can be broken down again so as to see whether or not the scores in the control groups differ from each other (contrast 3).

In Figure 10.6, the first contrast contains a chunk of variance that is due to the three experimental groups and this chunk of variance is broken down by first looking at whether groups E1 and E2 differ from E3 (contrast 2). It is equally valid to use contrast 2 to compare groups E1 and E3 to E2, or to compare groups E2 and E3 to E1. The exact comparison that you choose depends upon your hypotheses. For contrast 2 in Figure 10.6 to be valid we need to have a good reason to expect group E3 to be different from the other two groups. The third comparison in Figure 10.6 depends on the comparison chosen for

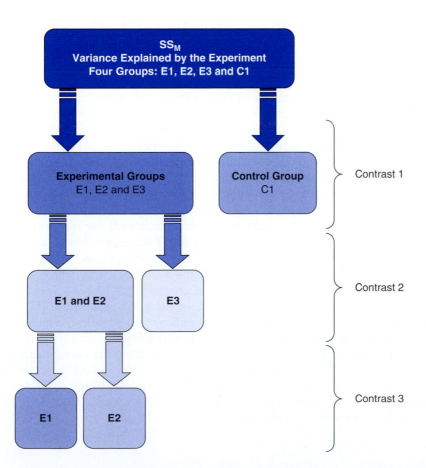

FIGURE 10.6

Partitioning variance for planned comparisons in a four-group experiment using one control group

FIGURE 10.7

Partitioning
variance
for planned
comparisons
in a four-group
experiment using
two control
groups

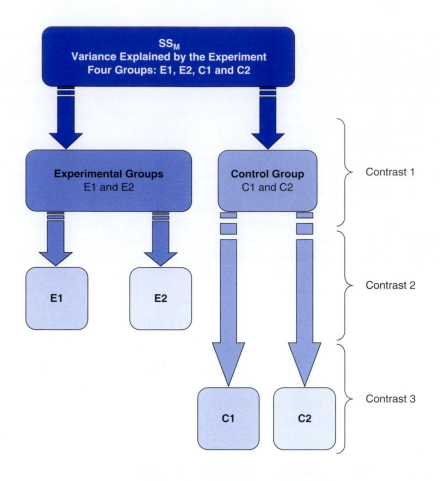

What does a planned
contrast tell me?

contrast 2. Contrast 2 necessarily had to involve comparing two experimental groups against a third, and the experimental groups chosen to be combined must be separated in the final comparison. As a final point, you'll notice that in Figures 10.6 and 10.7, once a group has been singled out in a comparison, it is never used in any subsequent contrasts.

When we carry out a planned contrast we compare 'chunks' of variance, and these chunks often consist of several groups. It is perhaps confusing to understand exactly what these contrasts tell us. Well, when you design a contrast that compares several groups to one other group, you are comparing the means of the groups in one chunk with the mean of the group in the other chunk. As an example, for the Viagra data I suggested that an appropriate first contrast would be to compare the two dose groups with the placebo group. The means of the groups are 2.20 (placebo), 3.20 (low dose) and 5.00 (high dose) and so the first comparison, which compared the two experimental groups to the placebo, is comparing 2.20 (the mean of the placebo group) to the average of the other two groups ((3.20 + 5.00)/2 = 4.10). If this first contrast turns out to be significant, then we can conclude that 4.10 is significantly greater than 2.20, which in terms of the experiment tells us that the average of the experimental groups is significantly different from the average of the controls. You can probably see that logically this means that, if the standard errors are the same, the experimental group with the highest mean (the high-dose group) will be significantly different from the mean of the placebo group. However, the experimental group with the lower mean (the low-dose group) might not necessarily differ from the placebo group;

we have to use the final comparison to make sense of the experimental conditions. For the Viagra data the final comparison looked at whether the two experimental groups differ (i.e., is the mean of the high-dose group significantly different from the mean of the low-dose group?). If this comparison turns out to be significant then we can conclude that having a high dose of Viagra significantly affected libido compared to having a low dose. If the comparison is non-significant then we have to conclude that the dosage of Viagra made no significant difference to libido. In this latter scenario it is likely that both doses affect libido more than placebo, whereas the former case implies that having a low dose may be no different than having a placebo. However, the word *implies* is important here: it is possible that the low-dose group might not differ from the placebo. To be completely sure we must carry out *post hoc* tests.

10.4.2. Defining contrasts using weights ②

Hopefully by now you have got some idea of how to plan which comparisons to do (i.e., if your brain hasn't exploded by now). Much as I'd love to tell you that all of the hard work is now over and **R** will magically carry out the comparisons that you've selected, it won't. To get **R** to carry out planned comparisons we need to tell it which groups we would like to compare, and doing this can be quite complex. In fact, when we carry out contrasts we assign values to certain variables in the regression model (sorry, I'm afraid that I have to start talking about regression again) – just as we did when we used dummy coding for the main ANOVA. To carry out contrasts we assign certain values to the dummy variables in the regression model. Whereas before we defined the experimental groups by assigning the dummy variables values of 1 or 0, when we perform contrasts we use different values to specify which groups we would like to compare. The resulting coefficients in the regression model (b_2 and b_1) represent the comparisons in which we are interested. The values assigned to the dummy variables are known as **weights**.

This procedure can seem horribly confusing, but there are a few basic rules for assigning values to the dummy variables to obtain the comparisons you want. I will explain these simple rules before showing how the process actually works. Remember the previous section when you read through these rules, and remind yourself of what I mean by a 'chunk' of variation.

- **Rule 1**: Choose sensible comparisons. Remember that you want to compare only two chunks of variation and that if a group is singled out in one comparison, that group should be excluded from any subsequent contrasts.

- **Rule 2**: Groups coded with positive weights will be compared against groups coded with negative weights. So, assign one chunk of variation positive weights and the opposite chunk negative weights.

- **Rule 3**: The sum of weights for a comparison should be zero. If you add up the weights for a given contrast the result should be zero.

- **Rule 4**: If a group is not involved in a comparison, automatically assign it a weight of 0. If we give a group a weight of 0 then this eliminates that group from all calculations.

- **Rule 5**: For a given contrast, the weights assigned to the group(s) in one chunk of variation should be equal to the number of groups in the opposite chunk of variation.

OK, let's follow some of these rules to derive the weights for the Viagra data. The first comparison we chose was to compare the two experimental groups against the control:

Therefore, the first chunk of variation contains the two experimental groups, and the second chunk contains only the placebo group. Rule 2 states that we should assign one chunk positive weights, and the other negative. It doesn't matter which way round we do this, but for convenience let's assign chunk 1 positive weights, and chunk 2 negative weights:

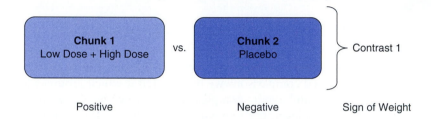

Using rule 5, the weight we assign to the groups in chunk 1 should be equivalent to the number of groups in chunk 2. There is only one group in chunk 2 and so we assign each group in chunk 1 a weight of 1. Likewise, we assign a weight to the group in chunk 2 that is equal to the number of groups in chunk 1. There are two groups in chunk 1 so we give the placebo group a weight of 2. Then we combine the sign of the weights with the magnitude to give us weights of −2 (placebo), 1 (low dose) and 1 (high dose):

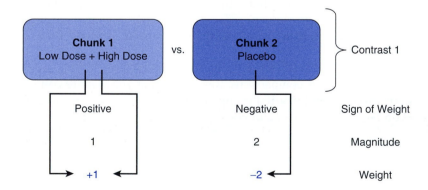

Rule 3 states that for a given contrast, the weights should add up to zero, and by following rules 2 and 5 this rule will always be followed (if you haven't followed these rules properly then this will become clear when you add the weights). So, let's check by adding the weights: sum of weights = 1 + 1 − 2 = 0.

The second contrast was to compare the two experimental groups and so we want to ignore the placebo group. Rule 4 tells us that we should automatically assign this group a weight of 0 (because this will eliminate this group from any calculations). We are left with two chunks of variation: chunk 1 contains the low-dose group and chunk 2 contains the high-dose group. By following rules 2 and 5 it should be obvious that one group is assigned a weight of +1 while the other is assigned a weight of −1. The control group is ignored (and so given a weight of 0). If we add the weights for contrast 2 we should find that they again add up to zero: sum of weights = 1 − 1 + 0 = 0.

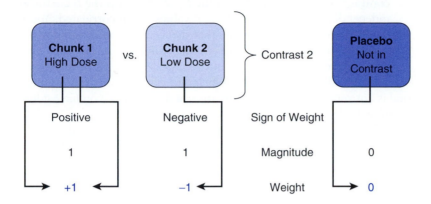

The weights for each contrast are codings for the two dummy variables in equation (10.2). Hence, these codings can be used in a multiple regression model in which b_2 represents contrast 1 (comparing the experimental groups to the control), b_1 represents contrast 2 (comparing the high-dose group to the low-dose group), and b_0 is the grand mean:

$$\text{libido}_i = b_0 + b_1\text{contrast}_{1i} + b_2\text{contrast}_{2i} \tag{10.9}$$

Each group is specified now not by the 0 and 1 coding scheme that we initially used, but by the coding scheme for the two contrasts. A code of −2 for contrast 1 and a code of 0 for contrast 2 identifies participants in the placebo group. Likewise, the high-dose group is identified by a code of 1 for both variables, and the low-dose group has a code of 1 for one contrast and a code of −1 for the other (see Table 10.4).

Table 10.4   Orthogonal contrasts for the Viagra data

Group	Dummy variable 1 (contrast₁)	Dummy variable 2 (contrast₂)	Product contrast₁ × contrast₂
Placebo	−2	0	0
Low dose	1	−1	−1
High dose	1	1	1
Total	0	0	0

It is important that the weights for a comparison sum to zero because it ensures that you are comparing two unique chunks of variation. Therefore, we can perform a *t*-test. A more important consideration is that when you multiply the weights for a particular group, these products should also add up to zero (see the final column of Table 10.4). If the products add to zero then we can be sure that the contrasts are *independent* or **orthogonal**. It is important

What are orthogonal contrasts?

for interpretation that contrasts are orthogonal. When we used dummy variable coding and ran a regression on the Viagra data, I commented that we couldn't look at the individual t-tests done on the regression coefficients because the familywise error rate is inflated (see section 10.4). However, if the contrasts are independent then the t-tests done on the b coefficients are also independent and so the resulting p-values are uncorrelated. You might think that it is very difficult to ensure that the weights you choose for your contrasts conform to the requirements for independence but, provided you follow the rules I have laid out, you should always derive a set of *orthogonal* comparisons. You should double-check by looking at the sum of the multiplied weights and if this total is not zero then go back to the rules and see where you have gone wrong (see the final column of Table 10.4).

Earlier on, I mentioned that when you used contrast codings in dummy variables in a regression model the b-values represented the differences between the means that the contrasts were designed to test. Although it is reasonable for you to trust me on this issue, for the more advanced students I'd like to take the trouble to show you how the regression model works (this next part is not for the faint-hearted and so those with an equation phobia should move onto the next section!). When we do planned contrasts, the intercept b_0 is equal to the grand mean (i.e., the value predicted by the model when group membership is not known), which when group sizes are equal is:

$$b_0 = \text{grand mean} = \frac{\bar{X}_{high} + \bar{X}_{low} + \bar{X}_{placebo}}{3}$$

Placebo group: If we use the contrast codings for the placebo group (see Table 10.4), the predicted value of libido equals the mean of the placebo group. The regression equation can, therefore, be expressed as:

$$\text{libido}_i = b_0 + b_1\text{contrast}_1 + b_2\text{contrast}_2$$
$$\bar{X}_{placebo} = \left(\frac{\bar{X}_{high} + \bar{X}_{low} + \bar{X}_{placebo}}{3}\right) + (-2b_1) + (b_2 \times 0)$$

Now, if we rearrange this equation and then multiply everything by 3 (to get rid of the fraction) we get:

$$2b_1 = \left(\frac{\bar{X}_{high} + \bar{X}_{low} + \bar{X}_{placebo}}{3}\right) - \bar{X}_{placebo}$$
$$6b_1 = \bar{X}_{high} + \bar{X}_{low} + \bar{X}_{placebo} - 3\bar{X}_{placebo}$$
$$6b_1 = \bar{X}_{high} + \bar{X}_{low} - 2\bar{X}_{placebo}$$

We can then divide everything by 2 to reduce the equation to its simplest form:

$$3b_1 = \left(\frac{\bar{X}_{high} + \bar{X}_{low}}{2}\right) - \bar{X}_{placebo}$$
$$b_1 = \frac{1}{3}\left[\left(\frac{\bar{X}_{high} + \bar{X}_{low}}{2}\right) - \bar{X}_{placebo}\right]$$

This equation shows that b_1 represents the difference between the average of the two experimental groups and the control group:

$$3b_1 = \left(\frac{\overline{X}_{high} + \overline{X}_{low}}{2}\right) - \overline{X}_{placebo}$$
$$= \frac{5 + 3.2}{2} - 2.2$$
$$= 1.9$$

We planned contrast 1 to look at the difference between the average of the experimental groups and the control, and so it should now be clear how b_1 represents this difference. The observant among you will notice that rather than being the true value of the difference between experimental and control groups, b_1 is actually a third of this difference ($b_1 = 1.9/3 = 0.633$). The reason for this division is that the familywise error is controlled by making the regression coefficient equal to the actual difference divided by the number of groups in the contrast (in this case 3).

High-dose group: For the situation in which the codings for the high-dose group (see Table 10.4) are used, the predicted value of libido is the mean for the high-dose group, and so the regression equation becomes:

$$libido_i = b_0 + b_1 contrast_1 + b_2 contrast_2$$
$$\overline{X}_{high} = b_0 + (b_1 \times 1) + (b_2 \times 1)$$
$$b_2 = \overline{X}_{high} - b_1 - b_0$$

We know already what b_1 and b_0 represent, so we place these values into the equation and then multiply by 3 to get rid of some of the fractions:

$$b_2 = \overline{X}_{high} - b_1 - b_0$$
$$b_2 = \overline{X}_{high} - \left\{\frac{1}{3}\left[\left(\frac{\overline{X}_{high} + \overline{X}_{low}}{2}\right) - \overline{X}_{placebo}\right]\right\} - \left(\frac{\overline{X}_{high} + \overline{X}_{low} + \overline{X}_{placebo}}{3}\right)$$
$$3b_2 = 3\overline{X}_{high} - \left[\left(\frac{\overline{X}_{high} + \overline{X}_{low}}{2}\right) - \overline{X}_{placebo}\right] - (\overline{X}_{high} + \overline{X}_{low} + \overline{X}_{placebo})$$

If we multiply everything by 2 to get rid of the other fraction, expand all of the brackets and then simplify the equation we get:

$$6b_2 = 6\overline{X}_{high} - (\overline{X}_{high} + \overline{X}_{low} - 2\overline{X}_{placebo}) - 2(\overline{X}_{high} + \overline{X}_{low} + \overline{X}_{placebo})$$
$$= 6\overline{X}_{high} - \overline{X}_{high} - \overline{X}_{low} + 2\overline{X}_{placebo} - 2\overline{X}_{high} - 2\overline{X}_{low} - 2\overline{X}_{placebo}$$
$$= 3\overline{X}_{high} - 3\overline{X}_{low}$$

Finally, we can divide the equation by 6 to find out what b_2 represents (remember that $3/6 = 1/2$):

$$b_2 = \frac{1}{2}(\overline{X}_{high} - \overline{X}_{low})$$

We planned contrast 2 to look at the difference between the experimental groups:

$$\overline{X}_{high} - \overline{X}_{low} = 5 - 3.2 = 1.8$$

It should now be clear how b_2 represents this difference. Again, rather than being the absolute value of the difference between the experimental groups, b_2 is actually half of this difference ($1.8/2 = 0.9$). The familywise error is again controlled, by making the regression coefficient equal to the actual difference divided by the number of groups in the contrast (in this case 2).

SELF-TEST

✓ To illustrate these principles, I have created a file called **Contrast.dat** in which the Viagra data are coded using the contrast coding scheme used in this section. Run multiple regression analyses on these data using **libido** as the outcome and using **dummy1** and **dummy2** as the predictor variables (leave all default options).

Output 10.2 shows the result of this regression. The F-statistic for the model is the same as when dummy coding was used (compare it to Output 10.1), showing that the model fit is the same (it should be because the model represents the group means and these have not changed); however, the regression coefficients have now changed. The first thing to notice is that the intercept is the grand mean, 3.467 (see, I wasn't telling lies). Second, the regression coefficient for contrast 1 is one-third of the difference between the average of the experimental conditions and the control condition (see above). Finally, the regression coefficient for contrast 2 is half of the difference between the experimental groups (see above). So, when a planned comparison is done in ANOVA a t-test is conducted comparing the mean of one chunk of variation with the mean of a different chunk. From the significance values of the t-tests we can see that our experimental groups were significantly different from the control ($p < .05$) but that the experimental groups were not significantly different ($p > .05$).

```
Coefficients:
            Estimate Std. Error t value Pr(>|t|)
(Intercept)   3.4667     0.3621   9.574 5.72e-07 ***
dummy1        0.6333     0.2560   2.474   0.0293 *
dummy2        0.9000     0.4435   2.029   0.0652 .
---
Signif. codes:  0 '***' 0.001 '**' 0.01 '*' 0.05 '.' 0.1 ' ' 1

Residual standard error: 1.402 on 12 degrees of freedom
Multiple R-squared: 0.4604,      Adjusted R-squared: 0.3704
F-statistic: 5.119 on 2 and 12 DF,  p-value: 0.02469
```

Output 10.2

CRAMMING SAM'S TIPS   Planned contrasts

- After an ANOVA you need more analysis to find out which groups differ.
- When you have generated specific hypotheses before the experiment, use *planned contrasts*.
- Each contrast compares two 'chunks' of variance. (A chunk can contain one or more groups.)
- The first contrast will usually be experimental groups vs. control groups.
- The next contrast will be to take one of the chunks that contained more than one group (if there were any) and divide it in to two chunks.
- You then repeat this process: if there are any chunks in previous contrasts that contained more than one group that haven't already been broken down into smaller chunks, then create a new contrast that breaks it down into smaller chunks.
- Carry on creating contrasts until each group has appeared in a chunk on its own in one of your contrasts.
- You should end up with one less contrast than the number of experimental conditions. If not, you've done it wrong.
- In each contrast assign a 'weight' to each group that is the value of the number of groups in the opposite chunk in that contrast.
- For a given contrast, randomly select one chunk, and for the groups in that chunk change their weights to be negative numbers.
- Breathe a sigh of relief.

10.4.3.   Non-orthogonal comparisons ②

I have spent a lot of time labouring how to design appropriate orthogonal comparisons without mentioning the possibilities that non-orthogonal contrasts provide. Non-orthogonal contrasts are comparisons that are in some way related, and the best way to get them is to disobey Rule 1 in the previous section. Using my cake analogy again, non-orthogonal comparisons are where you slice up your cake and then try to stick slices of cake together again. So, for the Viagra data a set of non-orthogonal contrasts might be to have the same initial contrast (comparing experimental groups against the placebo), but then to compare the high-dose group to the placebo. This disobeys rule 1 because the placebo group is singled out in the first contrast but used again in the second contrast. The coding for this set of contrasts is shown in Table 10.5, and by looking at the last column it is clear that when you multiply and add the codings from the two contrasts the sum is not zero. This tells us that the contrasts are not orthogonal.

Table 10.5   Non-orthogonal contrasts for the Viagra data

Group	Dummy variable 1 (Contrast₁)	Dummy variable 2 (Contrast₂)	Product Contrast₁ × Contrast₂
Placebo	−2	−1	2
Low dose	1	0	0
High dose	1	1	1
Total	0	0	3

There is nothing intrinsically wrong with performing non-orthogonal contrasts. However, if you choose to perform this type of contrast you must be very careful about how you interpret the results. With non-orthogonal contrasts, the comparisons you do are related and so the resulting test statistics and p-values will be correlated to some extent. For this reason you should use a more conservative probability level to accept that a given contrast is statistically meaningful (see section 10.5).

10.4.4.   Standard contrasts ②

Although under most circumstances you will design your own contrasts, there are special contrasts that have been designed to compare certain situations. Some of these contrasts are orthogonal, whereas others are non-orthogonal.

Table 10.6 shows the contrasts that are available in **R** using the **contrasts()** function. This function is used to code any categorical variable and the resulting codings can be used in pretty much any linear model (ANOVA, regression, logistic regression, etc.). Although the exact codings are not provided in Table 10.6, examples of the comparisons done in a three- and four-group situation are given (where the groups are labelled 1, 2, 3 and 1, 2, 3, 4, respectively). When you code variables **R** will treat the lowest-value code as group 1, the next highest code as group 2, and so on. Therefore, depending on which comparisons you want to make you should code your grouping variable appropriately (and then use Table 10.6 as a guide to which comparisons **R** will carry out). One thing that clever readers might notice about the contrasts in Table 10.6 is that some are orthogonal (i.e., Helmert contrasts) while others are non-orthogonal (e.g., treatment). You might also notice that the comparisons calculated using treatment contrasts are the same as those given by using the dummy variable coding described in Table 10.2).

Table 10.6   Standard contrasts available in **R**

Name	Definition	Contrast	Three Groups		Four Groups	
Dummy (default)	The default is dummy coding in which each category is compared to the first category	1	1 vs. 2		1 vs. 2	
		2	1 vs. 3		1 vs. 3	
		3			1 vs. 4	
contr. treatment()	Each category is compared to a user-defined baseline category (in this case I chose the second category)	1	2 vs. 1		2 vs. 1	
		2	2 vs. 3		2 vs. 3	
		3			2 vs. 4	
contr. SAS()	Each category is compared to the last category	1	1 vs. 3		1 vs. 4	
		2	2 vs. 3		2 vs. 4	
		3			3 vs. 4	
contr. helmert()	Each category (except the last) is compared to the mean effect of all subsequent categories	1	1 vs. (2, 3)		1 vs. (2, 3, 4)	
		2	2 vs. 3		2 vs. (3, 4)	
		3			3 vs. 4	

10.4.5.   Polynomial contrasts: trend analysis ②

One type of contrast deliberately omitted from Table 10.6 is the **polynomial contrast**, which can be obtained using **contr.poly()**. This contrast tests for trends in the data, and in its most basic form it looks for a linear trend (i.e., that the group means increase proportionately). However, there are other trends such as quadratic, cubic and quartic trends that can be examined. Figure 10.8 shows examples of the types of trend that can exist in data sets. The *linear* trend should be familiar to you all by now and represents a simple proportionate change in the value of the dependent variable across ordered categories (the diagram shows a positive linear trend, but of course it could be negative). A **quadratic trend** is where there is one change in the direction of the line (e.g., the line is curved in one place). An example of this might be a situation in which a drug enhances performance on a task at first, but then as the dose increases the performance drops again. To find a quadratic trend you need at least three groups (because in the two-group situation there are not enough categories of the independent variable for the means of the dependent variable to change one way and then another). A **cubic trend** is where there are two changes in the direction of the trend. So, for example, the mean of the dependent variable at first goes up across the first couple of categories of the independent variable, then across the succeeding categories the means go down, but then across the last few categories the means rise again. To have two changes in the direction of the mean you must have at least four categories of the independent variable. The final trend that you are likely to come across is the **quartic trend**, and this trend has three changes of direction (so you need at least five categories of the independent variable).

Polynomial trends should be examined in data sets in which it makes sense to order the categories of the independent variable (so, for example, if you have administered five doses of a drug it makes sense to examine the five doses in order of magnitude). For the Viagra data there are only three groups and so we can expect to find only a linear or quadratic trend (and it would be pointless to test for any higher-order trends).

Each of these trends has a set of codes for the dummy variables in the regression model, so we are doing the same thing that we did for planned contrasts except that the codings have already been devised to represent the type of trend of interest. In fact, the graphs in Figure 10.8

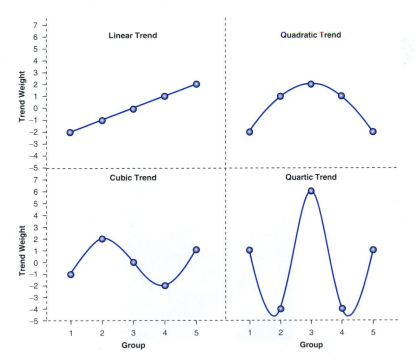

FIGURE 10.8

Linear, quadratic, cubic and quartic trends across five groups

have been constructed by plotting the coding values for the five groups. Also, if you add the codes for a given trend the sum will equal zero and if you multiply the codes you will find that the sum of the products also equals zero. Hence, these contrasts are orthogonal. The great thing about these contrasts is that you don't need to construct your own coding values to do them, because the codings already exist.

10.5. *Post* hoc procedures ②

Often it is the case that you have no specific *a priori* predictions about the data you have collected and instead you are interested in exploring the data for any between-group differences between means that exist. This procedure is sometimes called *data mining* or *exploring data*. Now, personally I have always thought that these two terms have certain 'rigging the data' connotations to them and so I prefer to think of these procedures as 'finding the differences that I should have predicted if only I'd been clever enough'.

Post hoc tests consist of **pairwise comparisons** that are designed to compare all different combinations of the treatment groups. So, it is rather like taking every pair of groups and then performing a *t*-test on each pair of groups. Now, this might seem like a particularly stupid thing to say in the light of what I have already told you about the problems of inflated familywise error rates. However, pairwise comparisons control the familywise error by correcting the level of significance for each test such that the overall Type I error rate (α) across all comparisons remains at .05. There are several ways in which the familywise error rate can be controlled. The most popular (and easiest) way is to divide α by the number of comparisons, k, thus ensuring that the cumulative Type I error is below .05:

$$p_{crit} = \frac{\alpha}{k}$$

Therefore, if we conduct 10 tests, we use .005 as our criterion for significance. This method is known as the **Bonferroni correction** (Figure 10.9). There is a trade-off for controlling the familywise error rate, and that is a loss of statistical power. This means that the probability of rejecting an effect that does actually exist is increased (this is called a Type II error). By being more conservative in the Type I error rate for each comparison, we increase the chance that we will miss a genuine difference in the data.

FIGURE 10.9
Carlo Bonferroni before the celebrity of his correction led to drink, drugs and statistics groupies

Let's look at this method, and some variations, using an example. Some research has suggested that children wearing superhero costumes might be more likely to harm themselves because of the unrealistic impression of invincibility that these costumes could create. For example, there are case studies of children reporting to hospital with severe injuries because of falling from windows or trying 'to initiate flight without having planned for landing strategies' (Davies, Surridge, Hole, & Munro-Davies, 2007). Having spent a lot of my childhood dressed in various costumes, I can relate to the imagined power that it bestows upon you; even now, I have been known to dress up as Fisher by donning a beard and glasses and trailing a goat around on a lead in the hope that it might make me more knowledgeable about statistics.

Imagine that we wanted to see whether different *types* of superhero costumes led to more severe injuries. We measured the severity of injury on a scale from 0 to 100 (0 = not at all injured, 100 = dead), and made a note of the type of costume a child was wearing. Let's also entertain the possibility that children fell (probably because of trying to fly) into four groups: Spiderman, Superman, the Hulk, and Teenage Mutant Ninja Turtles (let's face it, who wouldn't want to dress up as a ninja turtle?). These entirely fabricated data are in **Superhero.dat**. There is a task at the end of the chapter to analyse these data, but for now, let's look at comparing all of these groups; we would end up with the six comparisons in Table 10.7. The table shows the unadjusted p-value that you get for each comparison. The critical value of p_{crit} based on a Bonferroni correction for each comparison is the Type I error rate divided by the number of comparisons, $\alpha/k = .05/6 = .0083$. If the observed p is smaller than the critical value then the comparison is significant (at $\alpha = .05$). In this case, there is a significant difference between ninja turtle and Superman costumes (because .0000 is less than .0083) and between Superman and Hulk costumes (because .0014 is smaller than .0083). In all other cases p is bigger than the critical value so the difference is not significant.

Table 10.7 Critical values for p based on variations on Bonferroni (* indicates that a comparison is significant)

	p	Bonferroni $p_{crit}=\frac{\alpha}{k}$		j	Holm $p_{crit}=\frac{\alpha}{j}$		j	Benjamini–Hochberg $p_{crit}=\left(\frac{j}{k}\right)\alpha$	
NT–Super	.0000	.0083	*	6	.0083	*	1	.0083	*
Super–Hulk	.0014	.0083	*	5	.0100	*	2	.0167	*
Spider–Super	.0127	.0083		4	.0125		3	.0250	*
NT–Spider	.0252	.0083		3	.0167		4	.0333	*
NT–Hulk	.1704	.0083		2	.0250		5	.0417	
Spider–Hulk	.3431	.0083		1	.0500		6	.0500	

There are various improvements that have been made to the Bonferroni correction over the years and the general principle behind them is easy to understand so it's worth explaining. In an attempt to make the Bonferroni correction less conservative (i.e., to make it better at detecting differences that actually exist), authors such as Hommel, Hochberg and Holm[5] have suggested stepped approaches (Hochberg, 1988; Holm, 1979; Hommel,

---

[5] Their names all begin with 'Ho', which I find a strange coincidence. If your surname begins with 'Ho' too, beware: a life in multiple comparison research could await you.

1988). Holm's method is very simple to explain. You begin by computing the p-value for all of the pairs of groups in your data, you then order them from smallest to largest. We assign each p in the list an index (I've labelled it j) that tells us where in the list it falls. Table 10.7 shows this process: for the largest p we assign an index of 1, the next largest 2, and so on until the smallest one, which will be indexed as the number of comparisons (k), in this case 6. The critical value for a given comparison is the Type I error rate divided by the index variable (j):

$$p_{\text{crit}} = \frac{\alpha}{j}$$

Starting from the smallest p-value, this means that you begin with the normal Bonferroni correction because $j = k$ for this first comparison. However, notice that in subsequent comparisons we do not correct for every comparison made, instead we correct *only for the remaining comparisons*. Unlike the standard Bonferroni correction, the critical value of p gets bigger (and less conservative) for each comparison. The key idea behind this method is it is *stepped*. This means that as long as a comparison is significant, we proceed to the next one, but at the point that we encounter a non-significant comparison we *stop and assume that all remaining comparisons are non-significant also*. In Table 10.7, we see a significant difference between Ninja Turtle and Superman costumes (because .0000 is less than .0083); therefore, we move onto the next one down and see a significant difference between Superman and Hulk costumes (because .0014 is smaller than .01); therefore we move down again but find a non-significant difference between Spiderman and Superman costumes (because .0127 is larger than .0125); because of this non-significance we stop and do not consider any further comparisons.

A more modern take on this kind of sequential approach to multiple comparisons is to worry not about the familywise error rate, but to focus on the *false discovery rate (FDR)*. By focusing on the familywise error rate we are obsessing (in some people, literally) about the possibility of making one or more Type I errors. The corresponding belief system can be summed up as 'if I make even one Type I error then my entire set of conclusions is meaningless'. With a belief system like that it's no wonder people look depressed when they're analysing data. Benjamini and Hochberg think about things differently. Their belief system can be summed up as the rather more joyful 'let's try to estimate how many Type I errors (or false discoveries) we have made'. The FDR is simply the proportion of falsely rejected null hypotheses:

$$\text{FDR} = \frac{\text{number of falsely rejected null hypotheses}}{\text{total number of rejected null hypotheses}}$$

As such, the FDR approach to multiple comparisons is less strict than Bonferroni-based methods because it is concerned with keeping the FDR rather than the familywise error rate under control. In Benjamini and Hochberg's method (Benjamini & Hochberg, 1995, 2000) you start by computing the p-value for all of the pairs of groups in your data. You then order them and, as with Holm's method, index the order with the letter j (notice we order them the opposite way around to Holm's method). For each comparison you deem it significant if the observed p is smaller than a critical value defined as:

$$p_{\text{crit}} = \frac{j}{k}\alpha$$

Table 10.7 again shows this process. For the largest p-value we again have the normal Bonferroni correction (i.e., α/k), for the other comparisons we use a more liberal criterion.

Like Holm's method this procedure is stepped; however, rather than working down the table we work up (hence it is known as a 'step-up' procedure). So, we begin at the bottom and conclude a non-significant difference between Spiderman and Hulk costumes (because .3431 is greater than .05); given this non-significance we move up the table and see a non-significant difference between Ninja Turtle and Hulk costumes (because .1704 is greater than .0417); given this non-significance we again move up the table and see a significant difference between Ninja Turtle and Spiderman costumes (because .0252 is less than the critical value of .0333); because of this significance we stop and *assume that all other comparisons are also significant*. Procedurally this step-up approach is the opposite of Holm's step-down procedure.

There are many other *post hoc* procedures. I have explained only a few of the main ones that can be implemented in **R**. I could go into all of the other methods in tedious detail but there are some excellent texts already available for those who wish to know (Klockars & Sax, 1986; Toothaker, 1993) and **R** does not implement most of them anyway. (That said, the nice thing about **R** of course is that you could write your own function to do them if you had a few spare hours, a maths degree, and a bottle of gin.) However, it *is* important that you have an idea of which *post hoc* tests perform best. 'Best' is a word that can mean many things. For *post hoc* procedures, deciding on what's 'best' requires us to consider three things: whether the test controls the Type I error rate; whether the test controls the Type II error rate (i.e., has good statistical power); and whether the test is reliable when the test assumptions of ANOVA have been violated.

10.5.1. *Post hoc* procedures and Type I (α) and Type II error rates ②

The Type I error rate and the statistical power of a test are linked. Therefore, there is always a trade-off: if a test is conservative (the probability of a Type I error is small) then it is likely to lack statistical power (the probability of a Type II error will be high). So, it is important that multiple comparison procedures control the Type I error rate but without a substantial loss in power. If a test is too conservative then we are likely to reject differences between means that are, in reality, meaningful.

Bonferroni's and *Tukey's* HSD[6] tests both control the Type I error rate very well but are conservative tests (they lack statistical power). Of the two, Bonferroni has more power when the number of comparisons is small, whereas Tukey is more powerful when testing large numbers of means. Tukey generally has greater power than other tests of which you might have heard such as *Dunn* and *Scheffé*. Holm's method should have more power than Bonferroni, and the Benjamini–Hochberg method should have more power than Holm's procedure. If you are obsessed with controlling the Type I error rate, it is worth remembering that the Benjamini–Hochberg method does not attempt to do this: it controls the FDR.

10.5.2. *Post hoc* procedures and violations of test assumptions ②

Most research on *post hoc* tests has looked at whether the test performs well when the group sizes are different (an unbalanced design), when the population variances are very

---

[6] HSD stands for 'honest significant difference', which has a slightly dodgy ring to it if you ask me!

different, and when data are not normally distributed. The good news is that most multiple comparison procedures perform relatively well under small deviations from normality. The bad news is that they perform badly when group sizes are unequal and when population variances are different.

There are a variety of tests designed to deal with these situations, none of which are implemented in **R**. *Hochberg's GT2* is one such test and is worth mentioning because it is not implemented in **R** and is completely different than the Hochberg and Benjamini–Hochberg methods that I have already mentioned. Therefore, don't use the Hochberg option in **R** thinking it can cope with unequal variances: it is a different test.

Instead of telling you what can't be done, it might be more helpful to tell you what *can* be done. There are some robust methods that have been implemented in **R** by Wilcox (2005). As with methods for the ANOVA itself, these methods are based on bootstrapping or trimmed means and M-estimators (both of which can also include a bootstrap). All of these methods are very new and so there is very little on which to base advice on what to do for the best. However, all methods have been shown to control the Type I error well when applied to some very extreme distributions. If Type I error control is your main concern then the bootstrap seems to offer a small advantage, and if power is your concern then there are some benefits to methods based on M-estimators (Wilcox, 2003). However, the bottom line is that using any of these methods is undoubtedly better than using a non-robust method.

10.5.3.   Summary of *post hoc* procedures ②

The choice of comparison procedure will depend on the exact situation you have and whether it is more important for you to keep strict control over the familywise error rate, the FDR, or to have greater statistical power. However, some general guidelines can be drawn (Toothaker, 1993). When you have equal sample sizes and you are confident that your population variances are similar then Tukey has good power and tight control over the Type I error rate. Bonferroni is generally conservative, but if you want guaranteed control over the Type I error rate then this is the test to use. If there is any doubt over the underlying assumptions (e.g., unequal population variances) then use a robust method based on a bootstrap, trimmed means, or M-estimators.

CRAMMING SAM'S TIPS   *Post hoc* tests

- After an ANOVA you need a further analysis to find out which groups differ.
- When you have no specific hypotheses before the experiment, use *post hoc tests*.
- When you have equal sample sizes and group variances are similar, use Tukey.
- If you want guaranteed control over the Type I error rate, then use Bonferroni.
- If there is any doubt that group variances are equal, then use a robust method (e.g., bootstrap or trimmed means).

10.6. One-way ANOVA using R ②

Hopefully you should all have some appreciation for the theory behind ANOVA, so let's put that theory into practice by conducting an ANOVA test on the Viagra data.

10.6.1. Packages for one-way ANOVA in R ①

There are several packages that we will use in this chapter. If you're using R Commander (see the next section) then you don't need to worry: it will load everything it needs automatically. If you're using commands (which we recommend), you will need the packages *car* (for Levene's test), *compute.es* (for effect sizes) *ggplot2* (for graphs), *multcomp* (for *post hoc* tests), *pastecs* (for descriptive statistics), and *WRS* (for robust tests). If you do not have these packages installed (some should be installed from previous chapters), you can install them by executing the following commands:

```
install.packages("compute.es"); install.packages("car"); install.packages
("ggplot2");install.packages("multcomp");install.packages("pastecs");install.
packages("WRS", repos="http://R-Forge.R-project.org")
```

You then need to load these packages by executing these commands:

```
library(compute.es);  library(car);  library(ggplot2);  library(multcomp);
library(pastecs); library(WRS)
```

10.6.2. General procedure for one-way ANOVA ①

To conduct one-way ANOVA you should follow this general procedure:

1 *Enter data*: obviously you need to enter your data.

2 *Explore your data*: as with any analysis, it's a good idea to begin by graphing your data and computing some descriptive statistics. You should also check distributional assumptions and use Levene's test to check for homogeneity of variance (see Chapter 5).

3 *Compute the basic ANOVA*: you can then run the main analysis of variance. Depending on what you found in the previous step, you might need to run a robust version of the test.

4 *Compute contrasts or post hoc tests*: having conducted the main ANOVA you can follow it up with either contrasts or *post hoc* tests. Again, the exact methods you choose will depend upon what you unearth in step 2.

We will work through these steps in turn.

10.6.3. Entering data ①

As with the independent *t*-test, we need to enter the data into **R** using a coding variable to specify to which of the three groups the data belong. So, the data must be entered in two columns (one called **dose** which specifies how much Viagra the participant was given and one called **libido** which indicates the person's libido over the following week). The data are in the file **Viagra.dat**, but I recommend entering them by hand to gain practice in data entry. I have coded the grouping variable so that 1 = placebo, 2 = low dose and 3 = high dose (see section 3.5.4.3).

This data set is small (only 15 cases); therefore, we could enter the data directly into **R** by executing the following code:

```
libido<-c(3,2,1,1,4,5,2,4,2,3,7,4,5,3,6)
dose<-gl(3,5, labels = c("Placebo", "Low Dose", "High Dose"))
viagraData<-data.frame(dose, libido)
```

These commands create a variable called **libido** with the 15 libido scores contained within it, and a variable called **dose**, which uses the *gl()* function to create a factor variable with three groups each containing five participants. These variables are merged into a dataframe called *viagraData*. We can look at the contents of the dataframe by executing:

```
viagraData
```

You will see the following displayed in the console:

```
          dose libido
1      Placebo      3
2      Placebo      2
3      Placebo      1
4      Placebo      1
5      Placebo      4
6     Low Dose      5
7     Low Dose      2
8     Low Dose      4
9     Low Dose      2
10    Low Dose      3
11   High Dose      7
12   High Dose      4
13   High Dose      5
14   High Dose      3
15   High Dose      6
```

10.6.4. One-way ANOVA using R Commander ②

Running ANOVA using commands gives you much more versatility than R Commander. However, you can do a basic one-way ANOVA using R Commander. First load the data from the file **Viagra.dat** by using the **Data⇒Import data⇒from text file, clipboard, or URL...** menu (see section 3.7.3). This data set has two variables: **dose**, which is the grouping variable (1 = placebo, 2 = low dose, 3 = high dose); and **libido**, which is each participant's libido score. Once the data are loaded in a dataframe (I have called the dataframe *viagraData*), you need to convert the variable **dose** into a factor – see section 3.6.2 to remind yourself how to do that.

Once you have done that, you need to explore the data: get some descriptive statistics and test the assumptions. This is explained in Chapter 5. Levene's test looks at whether variances across conditions are equal – in other words, it tests the assumption of homogeneity of variance (see section 10.3.1). Use the **Statistics⇒Variances⇒Levene's test...** menu to run the analysis. The resulting dialog box is fairly self-explanatory (Figure 10.10): select a factor from the list labelled *Groups* (in this case we have only one factor, **dose**) and select the outcome variable from the list labelled *Response Variable* (in this case **libido**). By default, R Commander will base Levene's test on deviations from the median, which is a better measure than using deviations from the mean, but you can change this option if you like. Click on [OK] to run the analysis. The resulting output is described in section 10.6.5.

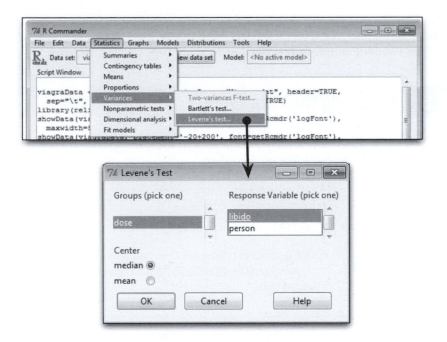

FIGURE 10.10
Levene's test using R Commander

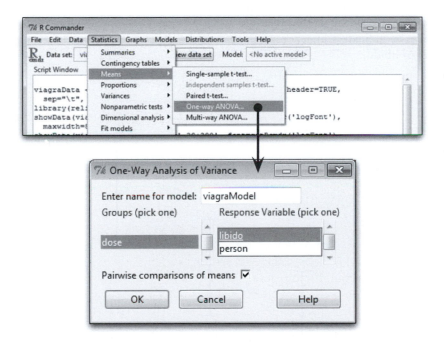

FIGURE 10.11
One-way ANOVA using R Commander

To do the ANOVA, use the **Statistics⇒Means⇒One-way ANOVA...** menu.[7] The result-ing dialog box is fairly self-explanatory (Figure 10.11). You need to enter a name for the model that you're going to create (I have chosen *viagraModel*) in the box labelled *Enter name for model:*, select a factor from the list labelled *Groups* (in this case we have only one factor, **dose**) and select the outcome variable (in this case **libido**) from the list labelled

---

[7] If this menu isn't active it could be because you haven't converted **dose** into a factor. You need to have at least one factor in the dataframe for this menu to be active.

Response Variable. You cannot do planned comparisons using R Commander, but if you want a basic set of *post hoc* tests then select Pairwise comparisons of means ☑ . Click on ⬚OK⬚ to run the analysis. The resulting output is described in sections 10.6.6.1 and 10.6.8.2.

10.6.5. Exploring the data ②

In Chapter 4 we saw that it is always a good idea to look at a graph of your data. In this case we will produce a line graph with error bars.

SELF-TEST

✓ Use *ggplot2* to produce a line chart with error bars showing bootstrapped confidence intervals for the Viagra data.

Figure 10.12 shows a line chart with error bars of the Viagra data. It's clear from this chart that all of the error bars overlap, indicating that, at face value, there are no between-group differences (although this measure is only approximate). The line that joins the means seems to indicate a linear trend in that, as the dose of Viagra increases, so does the mean level of libido.

FIGURE 10.12
Error bar chart of the Viagra data (95% bootstrapped confidence intervals)

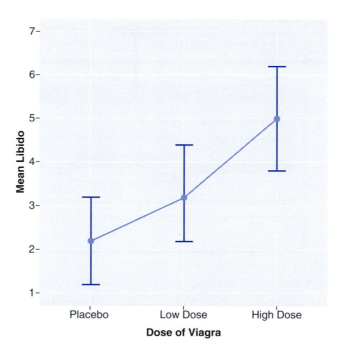

To get some descriptive statistics for each group we can use the *by()* function that we encountered in Chapter 5. Remember that this function takes the general form:

```
by(variable, group, output)
```

in which *variable* is the thing that you want to summarize (in this case **libido**), *group* is the variable that defines the groups by which you want to organize the output (in this case **dose**), and *output* is a function that tells **R** what output you would like to see (i.e., the mean). If we use the function **stat.desc()** from the package *pastecs* then **R** will output a host of useful descriptive statistics. Therefore, by combining *by()* and *stat.desc()*, we can get a table of descriptives for each group in a single line of code:

```
by(viagraData$libido, viagraData$dose, stat.desc)
```

Output 10.3 shows the resulting descriptive statistics (I have edited the output slightly to fit the page so you will see more decimal places and a few extra variables). Most of the variables are self-explanatory: we have the number of valid cases (*nbr.val*), minimum (*min*) and maximum (*max*) **libido**, the range, median, mean and variance (*var*), standard deviation (*std.dev*), standard error (*SE.mean*) and confidence interval (*CI.mean.0.95*).

```
viagraData$dose: Placebo
nbr.val   min   max   range    sum    median   mean    SE.mean
5.000    1.00  4.00  3.00    11.00   2.00     2.2000   0.5831

CI.mean.0.95              var          std.dev       coef.var
   1.6189318      1.7000000      1.3038405      0.5926548
-----------------------------------------------------------------
viagraData$dose: Low Dose

 nbr.val   min   max   range    sum    median   mean    SE.mean
5.000    2.00  5.00  3.00    16.00   3.00     3.200   0.5831

CI.mean.0.95              var          std.dev       coef.var
   1.6189318      1.7000000      1.3038405      0.4074502
-----------------------------------------------------------------
viagraData$dose: High Dose

nbr.val   min   max   range    sum    median   mean    SE.mean
5.00     3.00  7.00  4.00    25.00   5.0      5.0000   0.7071

CI.mean.0.95              var          std.dev       coef.var
   1.9632432      2.5000000      1.5811388      0.3162278
```

Output 10.3

The first thing to notice from Output 10.3 is that the means and standard deviations correspond to those shown in Table 10.1. In addition, we are told the standard error. You should remember that the standard error is the standard deviation of the sampling distribution of these data (so for the placebo group, if you took lots of samples from the population from which these data come, the means of these samples would have a standard deviation of 0.5831).

We are also given confidence intervals for the mean. By now, you should be familiar with what a confidence interval tells us, and that is that if we took 100 samples from the population from which the placebo group came and constructed confidence intervals for the mean, then 95 of these intervals would contain the true value of the mean. *CI.mean.0.95* doesn't give you the interval itself, but the value to add or subtract from the mean to create the interval. For example, in the placebo group the lower bound of the CI would be the mean minus *CI.mean.0.95* (i.e., $2.2000 - 1.6189 = 0.5811$) and the upper bound of the CI would be the mean plus *CI.mean.0.95* (i.e., $2.2000 + 1.6189 = 3.8189$). In other words, the true value of the mean is likely to be between 0.5811 and 3.8189. Although these diagnostics are not immediately important, we will refer back to them throughout the analysis.

The final thing before we get to the ANOVA itself is to compute Levene's test (see Chapter 5 and section 10.3.1). We encountered the *levene.Test()* function from the *car* package in Chapter 5, and we can again use it here. Just to remind you, it takes the general form:

```
leveneTest(outcome variable, group, center = median/mean)
```

So, if we want to do a Levene's test to see whether the variance in libido (the outcome) varies across groups that received different doses of the drug (**dose**), we can execute:

```
leveneTest(viagraData$libido, viagraData$dose, center = median)
```

The output (Output 10.4) shows that Levene's test is very non-significant, $F(2, 12) = 0.118$, $p = .89$. This means that for these data the variances are very similar (hence the high probability value); in fact, if you look at Output 10.3 you'll see that the variances of the placebo and low-dose groups are identical. Had this test been significant, we could instead conduct and report the results of Welch's F or a robust version of ANOVA, which we'll cover in the next section.

```
Levene's Test for Homogeneity of Variance
      Df F value Pr(>F)
group  2  0.1176   0.89
      12
```

Output 10.4

<h2>10.6.6. The main analysis ②</h2>

<h3>10.6.6.1. When the test assumptions are met ②</h3>

There are two functions that can be used for ANOVA: *lm()*, which we used in Chapter 7, and **aov()**. As I explained earlier in the chapter, ANOVA is just a special case of the general linear model; therefore, we can use the linear model function, *lm()*, to run the analysis. For the current example, we are predicting **libido** from group membership (i.e., **dose** of Viagra) so our model is:

$$\text{libido}_i = \text{dose}_i + \text{error}_i$$

Therefore, we can create a model (which I've called *viagraModel*) using *lm()* by executing:

```
viagraModel<-lm(libido~dose, data = viagraData)
```

where *libido~dose* simply creates the model 'libido predicted from dose'.

The other function we can use is *aov()*, which stands for analysis of variance. Actually, *aov()* and *lm()* are exactly the same as each other. However, *aov()* takes the output from *lm()* and returns it to us in a way that is more in keeping with a traditional ANOVA approach. It's what is known as a 'wrapper': it is *lm()* but 'wrapped' up differently. I'm going to stick with the *aov()* function because it yields output that maps onto traditional ANOVA methods, but be clear that underneath we're actually using *lm()* to do the hard work.

The *aov()* function has the following general format:

```
newModel<-aov(outcome ~ predictor(s), data = dataFrame, na.action = an
action))
```

in which:

- *newModel* is an object created that contains information about the model. We can get summary statistics for this model by executing *summary(newModel)* for the main ANOVA summary and *summary.lm(newModel)* for specific parameters of the model.

- *outcome* is the variable that you're trying to predict, also known as the dependent variable. In this example it will be the variable **libido**.

- *predictor(s)* lists the variable or variables from which you're trying to predict the outcome variable, also known as the independent variable(s). In this example it will be the variable **dose**. In more complex designs we can specify several predictors or independent variables, but we'll come to that in subsequent chapters.

- *dataFrame* is the name of the dataframe from which your outcome and predictor variables come.

- *na.action* is an optional command. If you have complete data (as we have here) you can ignore it, but if you have missing values (i.e., NAs in the dataframe) then it can be useful to use *na.action = na.exclude*, which will exclude all cases with missing values – see R's Souls' Tip 7.1).

For the current example, then, we could execute the following command:

```
viagraModel<-aov(libido ~ dose, data = viagraData)
```

to generate the model (note that the command is basically identical to when we used *lm()* to run an ANOVA above). We now have an object called *viagraModel* that contains information about how well **dose** predicts **libido**. To see the summary statistics execute:

```
summary(viagraModel)
```

Executing this command generates Output 10.5. The output is divided into effects due to the model (the experimental effect) and residuals (this is the unsystematic variation in the data). The effect labelled *dose* is the overall experimental effect. In this row we are told the sums of squares for the model (SS_M = 20.13) and this value corresponds to the value calculated in section 10.2.6. The degrees of freedom are equal to 2 and the mean squares value for the model corresponds to that calculated in section 10.2.8 (10.067). The sum of squares and mean squares represent the experimental effect. The row labelled *Residuals* gives details of the unsystematic variation within the data (the variation due to natural individual differences in libido and different reactions to Viagra). The table tells us how much unsystematic variation exists (the residual sum of squares, SS_R) and this value (23.60) corresponds to the value calculated in section 10.2.7. The table then gives the average amount of unsystematic variation, the mean squares (MS_R), which corresponds to the value (1.967) calculated in section 10.2.8. The test of whether the group means are the same is represented by the *F*-ratio for the effect of **dose**. The value of this ratio is 5.12, which is the same as was calculated in section 10.2.9. Finally, **R** tells us whether this value is likely to have happened by chance. The final column labelled *Pr(>F)* indicates the likelihood of an *F*-ratio the size of the one obtained occurring if there was no effect in the population (see also R's Souls' Tip 10.1). In this case, there is a probability of .025 that an *F*-ratio of this size would occur if in reality there was no effect (that's only a 2.5% chance!). We have seen in previous chapters that we use a cut-off point of .05 as a criterion for statistical significance. Hence, because the observed significance value is less than .05 we can say that there was a significant effect of Viagra. However, at this stage we still do not know exactly what the effect of Viagra was (we don't know which groups differed). One thing that is interesting here is that we obtained a significant experimental effect, yet our error bar plot indicated that no significant difference would be found. This contradiction illustrates how the error bar chart can act only as a rough guide to the data.

```
             Df  Sum Sq  Mean Sq  F value  Pr(>F)
dose          2  20.133  10.0667   5.1186  0.02469 *
Residuals    12  23.600   1.9667
---
Signif. codes:  0 '***' 0.001 '**' 0.01 '*' 0.05 '.' 0.1 ' ' 1
```

Output 10.5

R's Souls' Tip 10.1   One- and two-tailed tests in ANOVA ②

A question I get asked a lot by students is 'is the significance of the ANOVA one- or two-tailed, and if it's two-tailed can I divide by 2 to get the one-tailed value?' The answer is that to do a one-tailed test you have to be making a directional hypothesis (i.e., the mean for cats is greater than for dogs). ANOVA is a non-specific test, so it just tells us generally whether there is a difference or not, and because there are several means you can't possibly make a directional hypothesis. As such, it's invalid to halve the significance value.

The *aov()* function also automatically generates some plots that we can use to test the assumptions. We can see these graphs by executing:

```
plot(viagraModel)
```

The results are in Figure 10.13. You will actually see four graphs, but the first two are the most important for ANOVA. The first graph (on the left of the figure) can be used for testing homogeneity of variance. We encountered this kind of plot in Chapter 7: essentially, if it has a funnel shape then we're in trouble. The plot we have shows points that are equally spread for the three groups, which implies that variances are similar across groups (which was also the conclusion reached by Levene's test). The second plot (on the right) is a Q-Q plot (see Chapter 5), which tells us something about the normality of residuals in the model. We want our residuals to be normally distributed, which means that the dots on the graph should cling lovingly to the diagonal line. Ours look like they have had a bit of an argument with the diagonal line, which suggests that we may not be able to assume normality of errors and should perhaps use a robust version of ANOVA instead (which will be explained sooner than you might like).

10.6.6.2. When variances are not equal across groups ②

If Levene's test is significant then it is reasonable to assume that population variances are different across groups.[8] In this case, if our distributions are as they should be, we can apply

---

[8] It's worth reminding you that any significance test depends on sample size: in small samples there won't be power to detect differences across groups, and in large samples even small differences in variances might be deemed significant. As such, don't place too much weight on Levene's test if it's non-significant in a small sample, or significant in a large sample.

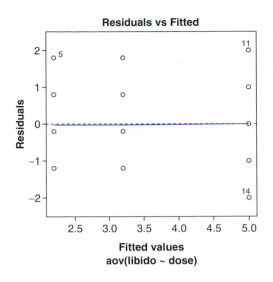

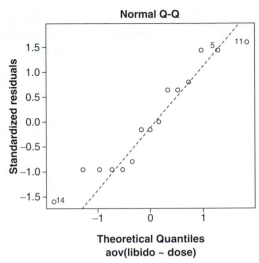

FIGURE 10.13
Plots of an
ANOVA model

Welch's F to the data, which makes adjustments for differences in group variances. This test is produced by the *oneway.test()* function, which is built into **R**. The format of this test is the same as *aov()*:

```
oneway.test(outcome ~ predictor, data = dataframe)
```

Therefore, we can get the output for Welch's F for the current data by executing:

```
oneway.test(libido ~ dose, data = viagraData)
```

Output 10.6 shows Welch's F-ratio. For our data we didn't need this test because our Levene's test was not significant, indicating that our population variances were similar. However, when homogeneity of variance has been violated you should look at this F-ratio *instead* of the ones in the previous section. If you're interested in how these values are calculated then look at Oliver Twisted, but to be honest it's not that much fun and you'd probably enjoy yourself more if you spent the time sticking jellyfish down your pants. You're much better off just trusting that **R** has done what it was supposed to do. Note that the error degrees of freedom have been adjusted – you should remember this when you report the values. For these data, Welch's $F(2, 7.94) = 4.23$, $p = .054$, which is just about non-significant. If we were using this test it would imply that the mean libido did not differ significantly across different doses of Viagra.

```
        One-way analysis of means (not assuming equal variances)

data:  libido and dose
F = 4.3205, num df = 2.000, denom df = 7.943, p-value = 0.05374
```

Output 10.6

10.6.6.3. Robust ANOVA – it's not for the weak of heart ③

Wilcox (2005) describes a set of robust procedures for conducting one-way ANOVA. Load these functions using the instructions in section 5.8.4. Having done this, we now have access to Wilcox's functions. The first issue with using these functions is that most of them require the data to be in wide format rather than the long format that we have been using so far in this chapter. We can convert the data to wide format using the *unstack()* command (see section 3.9.4), which has the general form:

```
newDataFrame<-unstack(oldDataFrame, scores ~ columns)
```

In this case our scores are stored in the variable **libido** and we want to make different columns for each group, so our columns variable is **dose**. Therefore, we can reformat the data by executing:

```
viagraWide<-unstack(viagraData, libido ~ dose)
```

This command creates a new dataframe called *viagraWide*, which is our Viagra data but in wide format, so each column represents a different group:

```
  Placebo Low.Dose High.Dose
1       3        5         7
2       2        2         4
3       1        4         5
4       1        2         3
5       4        3         6
```

This is the format that Wilcox's functions expect. The first robust function, **t1way()**, is based on a trimmed mean. It takes the general form:

```
t1way(dataFrame, tr = .2, grp = c(x, y, …, z))
```

in which,

- *dataFrame* is the name of the dataframe to be analysed.

- *tr* is the proportion of trimming to be done. The default is .2 or 20%, and you need to use this option only if you want to specify an amount other than 20%.

- *grp* can be used to specify particular groups by referring to their column in the dataframe; for example, if we wanted to analyse only the placebo and high-dose group, we could do this using *grp = c(1,3)*.

As such, for an ANOVA of the Viagra data based on 20% trimmed means we simply execute:

```
t1way(viagraWide)
```

If we wanted to trim only 10% of the data then we could execute:

```
t1way(viagraWide, tr = .1)
```

If you execute this command you will see Output 10.7, which shows that, based on this robust test, there is not a significant difference in libido scores across the three dose groups, $F_t(2, 7.94) = 4.32$, $p = .054$.

We can also compare medians rather than means using **med1way()**, which takes the general form:

```
med1way(dataFrame, grp = c(x, y, …, z))
```

in which, *dataFrame* is the name of the dataframe to be analysed and *grp* is used in the same way as in *t1way()*. As such, for an ANOVA of the Viagra data based on medians we simply execute:

```
med1way(viagraWide)
```

If you execute this command you will see Output 10.7, which shows that, based on this robust test, there is not a significant difference in median libido scores across the three dose groups, $F_m = 4.78$, $p = .07$.

A final method is to add a bootstrap to the trimmed mean method using **t1waybt()**. This function has the general form:

```
t1waybt(dataFrame, tr = .2, alpha = .05, grp = c(x, y, …, z), nboot = 599)
```

which is the same as *t1way()* except that we have two additional options. The first is *alpha*, which sets the Type I error rate. The default is .05, which is fairly standard, so unless you want something different you don't need to use this option. The second is *nboot*, which specifies the number of bootstrap samples to be used. The default is 599, which, if anything, you might want to increase (but it's probably not necessary to use more than 2000). As such, for an ANOVA of the Viagra data based on 20% trimmed means, with 599 bootstrap samples, we execute:

```
t1waybt(viagraWide)
```

However, if we wanted, for example, a 5% trimmed mean with 2000 bootstrap samples we would execute:

```
t1waybt(viagraWide, tr = .05, nboot = 2000)
```

If you execute the *t1waybt()* function with the default settings you will see Output 10.7, which shows that, based on this robust test, there is not a significant difference in trimmed mean libido scores across the three dose groups, $F_t = 3$, $p = .089$. In short, all three robust methods suggest that dose does not have a significant impact on libido.

t1way() output	*med1way()* output	*t1waybt()* output
$TEST [1] 4.320451	$TEST [1] 4.782879	$test [1] 3
$nu1 [1] 2	$crit.val [1] 5.472958	$p.value [1] 0.0886076
$nu2 [1] 7.943375	$p.value [1] 0.07	
$siglevel [1] 0.05373847		

Output 10.7

10.6.7. Planned contrasts using R ②

To do planned comparisons in **R** we have to set the contrast attribute of our grouping variable using the *contrast()* function and then re-create our ANOVA model using *aov()*. By default, dummy coding is used, which was explained in section 10.2.3. We can see this if we summarize our existing *viagraModel* using the *summary.lm()* function rather than *summary()*. By using *summary.lm()* we are asking for a summary of the parameters of the linear model (rather than the overall ANOVA). Assuming you still have the *viagraModel* object (if not, re-create it) execute this command:

```
summary.lm(viagraModel)
```

You should get Output 10.8. Note that this is basically the same as Output 10.1, which we used to explain how dummy coding works. So, the 'low dose' effect is the effect of low dose compared to placebo and is non-significant ($t = 1.13$, $p = .282$), whereas the effect of high dose compared to the placebo group is significant ($t = 3.16$, $p = .008$).

```
Coefficients:
             Estimate Std. Error t value Pr(>|t|)
(Intercept)    2.2000     0.6272   3.508  0.00432 **
doseLow Dose   1.0000     0.8869   1.127  0.28158
doseHigh Dose  2.8000     0.8869   3.157  0.00827 **
---
Signif. codes:  0 '***' 0.001 '**' 0.01 '*' 0.05 '.' 0.1 ' ' 1

Residual standard error: 1.402 on 12 degrees of freedom
Multiple R-squared: 0.4604,      Adjusted R-squared: 0.3704
F-statistic: 5.119 on 2 and 12 DF,  p-value: 0.02469
```

Output 10.8

This is all very well, but what if we do not want dummy coding, but want to use our own planned comparisons, use another built-in comparison, or do a trend analysis? In general, we do this by resetting the contrast attribute associated with our predictor variable (in this case **dose**), using the following general command:

```
contrasts(predictor variable)<-contrast instructions
```

The *contrast instructions* can be either a set of weights for the contrasts that you want to do, or one of the built-in contrasts listed in Table 10.6. These built in functions can be:

```
contr.helmert(n)
contr.poly(n)
contr.treatment(n, base = x)
contr.SAS(n)
```

In all cases, *n* is the number of groups in the predictor variable (for **dose**, this value will be 3). The *contr.treatment()* function has an additional option, *base*, which allows you to specify the group that you want to use as a baseline. Therefore, if you want dummy coding (i.e., the first category is the baseline) you would use *contr.treatment(n, base = 1)*. The function *contr. SAS()* is the same as using *contr.treatment()* when you select the last category as the baseline.

To put this all together, if we wanted to set the contrast property of **dose** to be a Helmert contrast then we would execute:

```
contrasts(viagraData$dose)<-contr.helmert(3)
```

Note that the *3* is the number of groups present in the **dose** variable. We're not going to use this contrast, though, we're going to specify our own.

10.6.7.1. Your own contrasts ②

To conduct the planned comparisons described in section 10.4, we follow the general procedure just described. We need to tell **R** what weights to assign to each group. The first step is to decide which comparisons you want to do and then what weights must be assigned to each group for each of the contrasts. We have already gone through this process in section 10.4.2, so we know that the weights for contrast 1 were −2 (placebo group), +1 (low-dose group) and +1 (high-dose group). If we wanted to express these weights we could create a new object called *contrast1* and use the function *c()* to list the weights:

```
contrast1<-c(-2,1,1)
```

This variable indicates that the first group has a weight of –2, and the second and third groups a weight of 1. The order of the numbers is important because it corresponds to the order of groups in your predictor variable. In the Viagra data, remember that the order of groups was: placebo (because it was coded with the lowest value, 1), low dose (because it was coded using the next lowest number, 2), and high dose (because it was coded with the highest number, 3). As such, *contrast1* has the weights for placebo, low dose and high dose, in that order.

We can do the same for the second contrast. We know from section 10.4.2 that the weights for contrast 2 were: 0 (placebo group), −1 (low-dose group) and +1 (high-dose group). Remembering that the first weight we enter will be for the placebo group, we must enter the value 0 as the first weight, then –1 for the low-dose group and finally 1 for the high-dose group. It is imperative that you remember to input zero weights for any groups that are not in the contrast. We can specify this contrast by executing:

```
contrast2<-c(0,-1,1)
```

which creates a variable called *contrast2* that contains the weights for the second contrast.

Having created these variables we now need to bind them together using **cbind()**, which literally binds two columns of data together, and set them as the contrast attached to our predictor variable, **dose**. We can do this by executing:

```
contrasts(viagraData$dose)<-cbind(contrast1, contrast2)
```

This command sets the contrast property of **dose** to contain the weights for the two contrasts that we want to conduct.[9] If you have a look at the **dose** variable by executing:

```
viagraData$dose
```

You'll see this:

```
[1] Placebo     Placebo     Placebo     Placebo     Placebo     Low Dose   Low
Dose   Low Dose   Low Dose   Low Dose   High Dose High Dose High Dose
[14] High Dose High Dose
attr(,"contrasts")
          contrast1 contrast2
Placebo        -2         0
Low Dose        1        -1
High Dose       1         1
Levels: Placebo Low Dose High Dose
```

Note that the variable now has a contrast attribute that contains the weights that we just specified. This is very useful to look at to check that you have entered the weights correctly. Remember that when we do planned comparisons we arrange the weights such that we compare any group with a positive weight against any group with a negative weight. Therefore, the table of weights shows that contrast 1 compares the placebo group against the two experimental groups, and contrast 2 compares the low-dose group to the high-dose group. These are the contrasts we wanted. Happy days.

Once we have set the contrast attribute we create a new model using *aov()*, in exactly the same way as we did before, by executing:

```
viagraPlanned<-aov(libido ~ dose, data = viagraData)
```

If you use the *summary()* command you'll see that the model is the same as the *viagraModel* that we created earlier. However, to access the contrasts we need the model parameters, which are obtained by executing:

```
summary.lm(viagraPlanned)
```

---

[9] I think that creating the *contrast1* and *contrast2* variables makes what we're doing a bit easier to understand, but in reality I would normally create these contrasts by executing this single command:

```
contrasts(viagraData$dose)<-cbind(c(-2,1,1), c(0,-1,1))
```

The resulting Output 10.9 is the same as Output 10.2, which we looked at earlier when explaining how these contrasts work. Re-read that earlier material to see from where the values of the parameters come. The table gives the standard error of each contrast and a *t*-statistic. The significance value of the contrast is given in the final column, and this value is two-tailed. Using the first contrast as an example, if we had used this contrast to test the general hypothesis that the experimental groups would differ from the placebo group, then we should use this two-tailed value. However, in reality we tested the hypothesis that the experimental groups would increase libido above the levels seen in the placebo group: this hypothesis is one-tailed. Provided the means for the groups bear out the hypothesis we can divide the significance values by 2 to obtain the one-tailed probability (i.e., .0293/2 = .0147). Hence, for contrast 1, we can say that taking Viagra significantly increased libido compared to the control group (p = .0147). For contrast 2 we also had a one-tailed hypothesis (that a high dose of Viagra would increase libido significantly more than a low dose) and the means bear this hypothesis out. The significance of contrast 2 tells us that a high dose of Viagra increased libido significantly more than a low dose (p(one-tailed) = .0652/2 = .0326). Notice that had we not had a specific hypothesis regarding which group would have the highest mean, then we would have had to conclude that the dose of Viagra had no significant effect on libido. For this reason it can be important as scientists that we generate hypotheses before collecting any data, because this method of scientific discovery is more powerful.

In summary, the planned contrasts revealed that taking Viagra significantly increased libido compared to a control group, $t(12) = 2.47$, $p < .05$, and taking a high dose significantly increased libido compared to a low dose, $t(12) = 2.03$, $p < .05$ (one-tailed).

```
Coefficients:
            Estimate Std. Error t value Pr(>|t|)
(Intercept)   3.4667     0.3621   9.574 5.72e-07 ***
dose1         0.6333     0.2560   2.474   0.0293 *
dose2         0.9000     0.4435   2.029   0.0652 .
---
Signif. codes:  0 '***' 0.001 '**' 0.01 '*' 0.05 '.' 0.1 ' ' 1

Residual standard error: 1.402 on 12 degrees of freedom
Multiple R-squared: 0.4604,      Adjusted R-squared: 0.3704
F-statistic: 5.119 on 2 and 12 DF,  p-value: 0.02469
```

Output 10.9

10.6.7.2. Trend analysis ②

To conduct a trend analysis we can use *contr.poly()*. It is important that we have coded the predictor variable groups in a meaningful order. We expect libido to be smallest in the placebo group, to increase in the low-dose group and then to increase again in the high-dose group. To detect a meaningful trend, we need to have coded these groups in ascending order. We have done this by coding the placebo group with the lowest value 1, the low-dose group with the middle value 2 and the high-dose group with the highest coding value of 3. If we coded the groups differently, this would influence both whether a trend is detected and, if a trend is detected, whether it is statistically meaningful.

To obtain a trend analysis we follow the general procedure of setting the contrast attribute of the predictor variable, which in this case we can do by executing:

```
contrasts(viagraData$dose)<-contr.poly(3)
```

The '3' just tells *contr.poly()* how many groups there are in the predictor variable. Having set the contrast we again create a new model using *aov()*, by executing:

```
viagraTrend<-aov(libido ~ dose, data = viagraData)
```

To access the contrasts we need the model parameters, which are obtained by executing:

```
summary.lm(viagraTrend)
```

The resulting Output 10.10 breaks down the experimental effect to see whether it can be explained by either a linear (*dose.L*) or a quadratic (*dose.Q*) relationship in the data. First, let's look at the linear component. This comparison tests whether the means increase across groups in a linear way. The most important things to note are the value of the t and the corresponding significance value. For the linear trend $t = 3.16$ and this value is significant at $p = .008$. Therefore, we can say that as the dose of Viagra increased from nothing to a low dose to a high dose, libido increased proportionately.

Moving onto the quadratic trend, this comparison is testing whether the pattern of means is curvilinear (i.e., is represented by a curve that has one bend). The error bar graph of the data suggests that the means cannot be represented by a curve and the results for the quadratic trend bear this out: $t = 0.52$ and this value is significant at $p = .612$, which is not very significant at all.

```
Coefficients:
            Estimate Std. Error t value Pr(>|t|)
(Intercept)   3.4667     0.3621   9.574 5.72e-07 ***
dose.L        1.9799     0.6272   3.157  0.00827 **
dose.Q        0.3266     0.6272   0.521  0.61201
---
Signif. codes:  0 '***' 0.001 '**' 0.01 '*' 0.05 '.' 0.1 ' ' 1

Residual standard error: 1.402 on 12 degrees of freedom
Multiple R-squared: 0.4604,     Adjusted R-squared: 0.3704
F-statistic: 5.119 on 2 and 12 DF,  p-value: 0.02469
```

Output 10.10

10.6.8. *Post hoc* tests using R ②

How you conduct *post hoc* tests in **R** depends on which test you'd like to do. Bonferroni and related methods (such as Holm and Benjamini–Hochberg) are done using the *pairwise.t.test()* function, which is part of the **R** base system. However, Tukey and Dunnett's test (and some others that we're not going to look at) can be done using the *glht()* function in the *multcomp()* package. Finally, Wilcox (2005) has some robust methods implemented in his functions *lincon()* and *mcpp20()*. This section is divided according to these different methods.

10.6.8.1. Bonferroni and related methods ②

Bonferroni and related methods (e.g., Holm, Benjamini–Hochberg, Hommel, Hochberg) can be implemented using the *pairwise.t.test()* function that is built into **R**. This function takes the general form:

```
pairwise.t.test(outcome, predictor, paired = FALSE, p.adjust.method = "method")
```

in which:

- *outcome* is the name of your outcome variable (in this case it will be **libido** (*viagraData$libido*).

- *predictor* is the name of your grouping variable (in this case it will be **dose** (*viagraData$dose*).

- *paired* is a logical statement that by default is FALSE but can be set to TRUE (the capital letters matter). This specifies whether you want paired *t*-tests or not. For these data we have independent groups so we do not want paired *t*-tests and the default of FALSE is fine, but we'll revisit this option in Chapter 13.

- *p.adjust.method* is a string that specifies which correction you would like to apply to your *p*-values. You can replace *"method"* in the command above with *"bonferroni"*, *"holm"*, *"hochberg"*, *"hommel"*, *"BH"* (which produces the Benjamini–Hochberg method), *"BY"* (which produces the more recent Benjamini–Yekutieli method), *"fdr"* (the general false discovery rate method), and *"none"* (you don't correct the *p*-value at all, you just do lots of *t*-tests – not advisable).

As such, we can obtain Bonferroni and Benjamini–Hochberg *post hoc* tests for the current data by executing these two commands:

```
pairwise.t.test(viagraData$libido,    viagraData$dose,    p.adjust.method    =
"bonferroni")
```

```
pairwise.t.test(viagraData$libido, viagraData$dose, p.adjust.method = "BH")
```

Both commands specify **libido** as the outcome variable, and **dose** as the grouping variable, but they differ in the method that is set for correcting the *p*-values. The results can be seen in Output 10.11. Both methods produce a grid of *p*-values for all combinations of the groups. First of all, let's look at the Bonferroni corrected values: the placebo group is compared to the low-dose group and reveals a non-significant difference (.845 is greater than .05), but when compared to the high-dose group there is a significant difference (.025 is less than .05).

SELF-TEST

✓ Our planned comparison showed that any dose of Viagra produced a significant increase in libido, yet the *post hoc* tests indicate that a low dose does not. Why is there this contradiction?

In section 10.4.2, I explained that the first planned comparison would compare the experimental groups to the placebo group. Specifically, it would compare the average of the two group means of the experimental groups ((3.2 + 5.0)/2 = 4.1) to the mean of the placebo group (2.2). So, it was assessing whether the difference between these values (4.1 − 2.2 = 1.9) was significant. In the *post hoc* tests, when the low dose is compared to the placebo, the contrast is testing whether the difference between the means of these two groups is significant. The difference in this case is only 1, compared to a difference of 1.9 for the planned comparison. This explanation illustrates how it is possible to have apparently contradictory results from planned contrasts and *post hoc* comparisons. More important, it illustrates how careful we must be in interpreting planned contrasts.

The final comparison is the low-dose group compared to the high-dose group, which is not significant (because 0.196 is greater than .05). This result contradicts the planned comparisons (remember that contrast 2 compared these groups and found a significant difference).

SELF-TEST

✓ Why does the *post hoc* test show a non-significant difference between high and low dose, when the planned comparison showed a significant difference?

This contradiction occurs for two possible reasons. First, *post hoc* tests by their nature are two-tailed (you use them when you have made no specific hypotheses and you cannot predict the direction of hypotheses that don't exist!) and contrast 2 was significant only when considered as a one-tailed hypothesis. However, even at the two-tailed level the planned comparison was closer to significance than the *post hoc* test and this fact illustrates that *post hoc* procedures are more conservative (i.e., have less power to detect true effects) than planned comparisons.

Looking now at the BH corrected tests, we find the same pattern of results as for Bonferroni: placebo is significantly different from a high dose (because .025 is less than .05), but not a low dose (.282 is greater than .05) and low and high doses did not significantly differ (.098 is greater than .05).

Bonferroni	BH
Pairwise comparisons using t tests with pooled SD	Pairwise comparisons using t tests with pooled SD
data: viagraData$libido and viagraData$dose	data: viagraData$libido and viagraData$dose
Placebo Low Dose Low Dose 0.845 – High Dose 0.025 0.196	Placebo Low Dose Low Dose 0.282 – High Dose 0.025 0.098
P value adjustment method: bonferroni	P value adjustment method: BH

Output 10.11

10.6.8.2. Tukey and Dunnett ②

Tukey and Dunnett can be implemented using the *glht()* function that is part of the *multcomp* package (so remember to install and load it). This function takes the general form:

```
newModel<-glht(aov.Model, linfct = mcp(predictor = "method"), base = x)
```

in which:

- *newModel* is an object containing the information from the *post hoc* tests. To see this information we can use *summary(newModel)* for the basic *post hoc* tests and *confint(newModel)* to see the confidence intervals.

- *aov.Model* is the name of a model that has already been created with the *aov()* function (in this case it will be *viagraModel*).

- *predictor* is the name of your grouping variable (in this case it will be **dose** (*viagraData$dose*).

- *linfct = mcp(predictor = "method")* specifies which correction you would like to apply to your *p*-values. You can replace "*method*" in the command above with "*Dunnett*", "*Tukey*", "*Sequen*", "*AVE*", "*Changepoint*", "*Williams*", "*Marcus*", "*McDermott*", "*UmbrellaWilliams*", and "*GrandMean*".

- *base* is used only when "*Dunnett*" is specified. This option allows you to specify the baseline group using a group number. In this case if we wanted the placebo as the baseline we would use *base = 1*, but if we wanted the high-dose group we could specify *base = 3*.

For the Viagra data, we can obtain Tukey *post hoc* tests by executing:

```
postHocs<-glht(viagraModel, linfct = mcp(dose = "Tukey"))
summary(postHocs)
confint(postHocs)
```

The first command creates an object (which I've called *postHocs*) that is based on the *viagraModel* that we created in section 10.6.6.1. The *linfct* command is set to perform Tukey tests on the variable dose (the reason why we can type 'dose' rather than 'viagraData$dose' is because the function will look for 'dose' within *viagraModel*, which has been specified within the function). To access the information within *postHocs* we execute *summary()* to get the *post hoc* tests (Output 10.12) and *confint()* to get the corresponding confidence intervals (Output 10.13).

Output 10.12 shows the three comparisons (low dose vs. placebo, high dose vs. placebo, high dose vs. low dose), the estimate (which is the difference between the group means), the standard error associated with the difference between means, the *t*-test (which is simply the difference between means divided by the standard error, so for the first contrast it is 1/0.8869 = 1.127), and its associated *p*-value. As with the tests in the previous section, this output confirms significant differences between the high dose and placebo groups, $t = 3.16$, $p < .05$, but not between the low-dose group and the placebo, $t = 1.13$, $p = .52$, and high dose, $t = 2.03$, $p = .15$, groups. The confidence intervals (Output 10.13) also confirm this because they do not cross zero for the comparison of the high dose and placebo group, which means that the true difference between group means is likely not to be zero (i.e., no difference); conversely, for the other contrasts the confidence intervals cross zero, implying that the true difference between means could be zero.

```
Simultaneous Tests for General Linear Hypotheses

Multiple Comparisons of Means: Tukey Contrasts

Fit: aov(formula = libido ~ dose, data = viagraData)

Linear Hypotheses:
                         Estimate Std. Error t value Pr(>|t|)
Low Dose  - Placebo == 0   1.0000     0.8869   1.127   0.5162
High Dose - Placebo == 0   2.8000     0.8869   3.157   0.0208 *
High Dose - Low Dose == 0  1.8000     0.8869   2.029   0.1474
---
Signif. codes:  0 '***' 0.001 '**' 0.01 '*' 0.05 '.' 0.1 ' ' 1
(Adjusted p values reported -- single-step method)
```

Output 10.12

```
Simultaneous Confidence Intervals

Multiple Comparisons of Means: Tukey Contrasts

Fit: aov(formula = libido ~ dose, data = viagraData)

Quantile = 2.6671
95% family-wise confidence level

Linear Hypotheses:
                          Estimate lwr      upr
Low Dose - Placebo == 0     1.0000  -1.3656   3.3656
High Dose - Placebo == 0    2.8000   0.4344   5.1656
High Dose - Low Dose == 0   1.8000  -0.5656   4.1656
```

Output 10.13

We can obtain Dunnett *post hoc* tests for the Viagra data by executing:

```
postHocs<-glht(viagraModel, linfct = mcp(dose = "Dunnett"), base = 1)
summary(postHocs)
confint(postHocs)
```

The first command is the same as before, except that we have replaced "Tukey" with "Dunnett". We have also added the base command (because we're using Dunnett) to specify which group to use as the control group. We have used *base = 1*, which means 'use the first group', which in this case is the placebo group. To access the information we again execute *summary()* and *confint()*. The results are in Output 10.14. I won't labour the point because the conclusions are the same as for Tukey; all I will say is that you should note that Dunnett's test compares groups to a baseline so we end up with two tests rather than three. In this case we asked every group to be compared to the placebo group, so there is no comparison of the high and low-dose groups.

```
Simultaneous Tests for General Linear Hypotheses

Multiple Comparisons of Means: Dunnett Contrasts

Fit: aov(formula = libido ~ dose, data = viagraData)

Linear Hypotheses:
                          Estimate Std. Error t value Pr(>|t|)
Low Dose - Placebo == 0     1.0000      0.8869   1.127   0.4459
High Dose - Placebo == 0    2.8000      0.8869   3.157   0.0152 *
---
Signif. codes:  0 '***' 0.001 '**' 0.01 '*' 0.05 '.' 0.1 ' ' 1
(Adjusted p values reported -- single-step method)

Simultaneous Confidence Intervals

Multiple Comparisons of Means: Dunnett Contrasts

Fit: aov(formula = libido ~ dose, data = viagraData)

Quantile = 2.5023
95% family-wise confidence level

Linear Hypotheses:
                          Estimate lwr      upr
Low Dose - Placebo == 0     1.0000  -1.2194   3.2194
High Dose - Placebo == 0    2.8000   0.5806   5.0194
```

Output 10.14

10.6.8.3. Run for cover – it's robust *post hoc* tests ③

As with the robust ANOVA, to run robust *post hoc* tests we need to (1) source Rand Wilcox's functions (see section 10.6.6.3 for how to do this); and (2) input data in the wide format – therefore, we'll use the object *viagraWide* that we created in section 10.6.6.3. We are going to use two functions: *lincon()*, which is based on trimmed means; and *mcppb20()*, which uses a percentile bootstrap to compute *p*-values as well as trimming the group means. The latter method, in particular, seems good at controlling the Type I error rate. The general forms of these functions are similar to *t1way()* and *t1waybt()*, which we encountered earlier in the chapter:[10]

```
lincon(dataframe, tr = .2, grp = c(x, y, …, z))
mcppb20(dataframe, tr = .2, nboot = 2000, grp = c(x, y, …, z))
```

The options for each function are the same as described in section 10.6.6.3. Note that these functions take the same parameters, except that *mcppb20()* has an additional *nboot* command to control the number of bootstrap samples (the default is 2000, which is fine). Trimming on the means defaults to 20% (*tr* = .2). If you are happy with the default values then we can execute these commands on the *viagraWide* dataframe as follows:

```
lincon(viagraWide)
mcppb20(viagraWide)
```

It's as easy as that. Output 10.15 comes from *lincon()*. Note that the confidence intervals are corrected for the number of tests, but the *p*-values are not. As such, we should ascertain significance from whether or not the confidence intervals cross zero. In this case they all do, which implies that none of the groups are significantly different. This is different from what we found when we did not trim the means (see the previous two sections).

SELF-TEST

✓ Repeat the analysis with 10% trimmed means. How do your conclusions differ?

```
[1] "Note: confidence intervals are adjusted to control FWE"
[1] "But p-values are not adjusted to control FWE"
$test
      Group Group      test crit       se df
[1,]      1     2 0.8660254 3.74 1.154701  4
[2,]      1     3 2.5980762 3.74 1.154701  4
[3,]      2     3 1.7320508 3.74 1.154701  4
$psihat
      Group Group psihat ci.lower ci.upper    p.value
[1,]      1     2     -1 -5.31858  3.31858 0.43533094
[2,]      1     3     -3 -7.31858  1.31858 0.06016985
[3,]      2     3     -2 -6.31858  2.31858 0.15830242
```

Output 10.15

[10] They actually have a few extra options, but I'm keeping things simple.

Output 10.16 comes from *mcpp20()*. Unlike *lincon()*, both the confidence intervals and *p*-values are corrected for the number of tests. The main table lists three contrasts. To make sense of these we have to look at the contrast codes listed under *$con*. These are like the contrast weights that we looked at earlier in the chapter, so groups with positive weights are compared to those with negative weights. From the contrast codes we can see that contrast 1 compares groups 1 and 2 (i.e., placebo vs. low dose), contrast 2 compares groups 1 and 3 (i.e., placebo vs. high dose), and contrast 3 compares groups 2 and 3 (i.e., low dose vs. high dose).

Looking at the confidence intervals, it's clear that only the interval for contrast 2 does not cross zero, implying a significance difference between the high dose and placebo group (which is confirmed by the associated *p*-value, which is smaller than .05). For the other two comparisons the confidence intervals cross zero (and the *ps* are greater than .05), implying non-significant differences in libido between the low-dose group and both placebo (contrast 1) and high-dose (contrast 3) groups. Essentially, this profile of results is consistent with what we found using non-robust *post hoc* tests.

```
[1] "Taking bootstrap samples. Please wait."
$psihat
     con.num psihat         se  ci.lower    ci.upper p-value
[1,]       1     -1 1.154701 -3.333333   1.3333333  0.3250
[2,]       2     -3 1.154701 -5.333333  -0.3333333  0.0055
[3,]       3     -2 1.154701 -4.333333   0.6666667  0.0840


$crit.p.value
[1] 0.017


$con
     [,1] [,2] [,3]
[1,]    1    1    0
[2,]   -1    0    1
[3,]    0   -1   -1
```

Output 10.16

CRAMMING SAM'S TIPS One-way ANOVA

- The one-way independent ANOVA compares several means, when those means have come from different groups of people; for example, if you have several experimental conditions and have used different participants in each condition.
- When you have generated specific hypotheses before the experiment use *planned comparisons*, but if you don't have specific hypotheses use *post hoc* tests.
- There are lots of different *post hoc* tests: when you have equal sample sizes and homogeneity of variance is met, use Tukey's HSD. If there is any doubt about the underlying assumptions then use a robust method.
- Test for homogeneity of variance using Levene's test. Find the table with this label: if the *p*-value is less than .05 then the assumption is violated. If homogeneity of variance has been met (the significance of Levene's test is greater than .05), run a normal ANOVA. If, however, the assumption is violated (the significance of Levene's test is less than .05) compute Welch's *F* instead of the normal ANOVA, or use a robust method based on trimmed means and/or a bootstrap.
- In the main ANOVA, if the value of *p* is less than .05 then the means of the groups are significantly different.
- For contrasts and *post hoc* tests, look at the confidence intervals and *p*-values to discover if your comparisons are significant. If the confidence intervals do not contain zero or the *p*-value is less than .05 then the effect is significant.

Labcoat Leni's Real Research 10.1   Scraping the barrel? ①

Gallup, G. G. J., et al. (2003). *Evolution and Human Behavior, 24,* 277–289.

Evolution has endowed us with many beautiful things (cats, dolphins, the Great Barrier Reef, etc.), all selected to fit their ecological niche. Given evolution's seemingly limitless capacity to produce beauty, it's something of a wonder how it managed to produce such a monstrosity as the human penis. One theory is that the penis evolved into the shape that it is because of sperm competition. Specifically, the human penis has an unusually large glans (the 'bell end', as it's affectionately known) compared to other primates, and this may have evolved so that the penis can displace seminal fluid from other males by 'scooping it out' during intercourse. To put this idea to the test, Gordon Gallup and his colleagues came up with an ingenious study (Gallup et al., 2003). Armed with various female masturbatory devices from Hollywood Exotic Novelties, an artificial vagina from California Exotic Novelties, and some water and cornstarch to make fake sperm, they loaded the artificial vagina with 2.6 ml of fake sperm and inserted one of three female sex toys into it before withdrawing it. Over several trials, three different female sex toys were used: a control phallus that had no coronal ridge (i.e., no bell end), a phallus with a minimal coronal ridge (small bell end) and a phallus with a coronal ridge.

They measured sperm displacement as a percentage using the following equation (included here because it is more interesting than all of the other equations in this book):

$$\frac{\text{weight of vagina with semen} - \text{weight of vagina following insertion and removal of phallus}}{\text{weight of vagina with semen} - \text{weight of empty vagina}} \times 100$$

As such, 100% means that all of the sperm was displaced by the phallus, and 0% means that none of the sperm was displaced. If the human penis evolved as a sperm displacement device, then Gallup et al. predicted: (1) that having a bell end would displace more sperm than not; and (2) the phallus with the larger coronal ridge would displace more sperm than the phallus with the minimal coronal ridge. The conditions are ordered (no ridge, minimal ridge, normal ridge) so we might also predict a linear trend. The data can be found in the file **Gallup et al.csv**. Draw an error bar graph of the means of the three conditions. Conduct a one-way ANOVA with planned comparisons to test the two hypotheses above. What did Gallup et al. find?

Answers are in the additional material on the companion website (or look at pages 280–281 in the original article).

10.7. Calculating the effect size ②

One thing you will notice is that **R** doesn't routinely provide an effect size for one-way independent ANOVA. However, we saw in equation (7.4) that:

$$R^2 = \frac{SS_M}{SS_T}$$

We can actually get this value from the main ANOVA by using *summary.lm()* on the object you create with *aov()*. For example, for the *viagraModel* this function gives us Output 10.8, at the bottom of which we see that $r^2 = .46$. For some bizarre reason, in the context of ANOVA, r^2 is usually called **eta squared, η^2**. It is then a simple matter to take the square root of this value to give us the effect size, r ($\sqrt{.46} = .68$). Using the benchmarks for effect sizes this represents a large effect (it is above the .5 threshold for a large effect). Therefore, the effect of Viagra on libido is a substantive finding.

However, this measure of effect size is slightly biased because it is based purely on sums of squares from the sample and no adjustment is made for the fact that we're trying to estimate the effect size in the population. Therefore, we often use a slightly more complex measure called **omega squared (ω^2)**. This effect size estimate is still based on the sums of squares that we've met in this chapter, but like the F-ratio it uses the variance explained by the model, and the error variance (in both cases the average variance, or mean squared error, is used):

$$\omega^2 = \frac{SS_M - (df_M)MS_R}{SS_T + MS_R}$$

All of these values can be found in Output 10.5 (although SS_T is not in the output, it is easily calculated as $SS_T = SS_M + SS_R$). In this example we'd get:

$$\omega^2 = \frac{20.13 - (2 \times 1.97), \text{ or } 20.13 - (2)1.97}{43.73 + 1.97}$$

$$= \frac{16.19}{45.70}$$

$$= .35$$

$$\omega = .60$$

As you can see, this has led to a slightly lower estimate than using r, and in general ω is a more accurate measure. Although in the sections on ANOVA I will use ω as my effect size measure, think of it as you would r (because it's basically an unbiased estimate of r anyway). People normally report ω^2, and it has been suggested that values of .01, .06 and .14 represent small, medium and large effects respectively (Kirk, 1996). Remember, though, that these are rough guidelines and that effect sizes need to be interpreted within the context of the research literature.

OLIVER TWISTED

Please Sir, can I have some more … omega?

'There's no place like omega', chants Oliver as he clicks the heels of his red shoes together. Much as you want to wake up in Kansas, Oliver, you're going to find yourself in bubo-infested Dickensian London. If you'd like to join him there, read the online material, which shows you how to write a function to calculate ω^2 in **R**. I think you'll agree it's not entirely different from a bubo infestation.

Most of the time it isn't that interesting to have effect sizes for the overall ANOVA because it's testing a general hypothesis. Instead, we really want effect sizes for the differences between pairs of groups. We can obtain these using the *mes()* function of the *calculate.es* package. This function takes the general form:

```
mes(mean_group1, mean_group2, sd_group1, sd_group2, n_group1, n_group2)
```

In other words, we simply input the mean, standard deviation (*sd*) and sample size (*n*) of the two groups that we want to compare. We have this information in Output 10.3. For example, if we want to compare the placebo and low-dose group we would execute:

```
mes(2.2, 3.2, 1.3038405, 1.3038405, 5, 5)
```

We have entered the mean of the placebo group (2.2), the mean of the low-dose group (3.2), the standard deviation of the placebo group (1.3038), the standard deviation of the low-dose group (also 1.3038), and both groups have a sample size of 5. Similarly, we can get effect sizes for the difference between the placebo and high-dose group by executing:

```
mes(2.2, 5, 1.3038405, 1.5811388, 5, 5)
```

Finally, the difference between the low- and high-dose groups can be quantified by executing:

```
mes(3.2, 5, 1.3038405, 1.5811388, 5, 5)
```

The outputs of these commands are shown in Output 10.17 (I have edited them to show only the effect sizes d and r). The difference between the placebo and low-dose group is a medium-sized effect (the means are about three-quarters of a standard deviation different), $d = -0.77$, $r = -.36$; the difference between the placebo and high-dose group is a very large effect (a difference between the group means of almost 2 standard deviations), $d = -1.93$, $r = -.69$; finally, the difference between the low- and high-dose groups is a largish effect (more than a standard deviation difference between the group means), $d = -1.24$, $r = -.53$.

```
Placebo vs. Low Dose:

$MeanDifference
         d        var.d                g         var.g
-0.7669650   0.4294118  -0.6927426   0.3503214


$Correlation
          r        var.r
-0.35805743   0.07113067


Placebo vs. High Dose:

$MeanDifference
         d        var.d                g         var.g
-1.9321836   0.5866667  -1.7451981   0.4786126


$Correlation
          r        var.r
-0.69480834   0.02029603


Low Dose vs. High Dose:

$MeanDifference
         d        var.d                g         var.g
-1.2421180   0.4771429  -1.1219130   0.3892612


$Correlation
          r        var.r
-0.52758935   0.04482986
```

Output 10.17

An alternative is to compute effect sizes for the orthogonal contrasts. We can use the same equation as in section 9.5.2.8:

$$r_{contrast} = \sqrt{\frac{t^2}{t^2 + 26}}$$

We could write a function (see R's Souls' Tip 6.2) to do this computation for us in **R**:

```
rcontrast<-function(t, df)
{r<-sqrt(t^2/(t^2 + df))
       print(paste("r = ", r))
       }
```

Executing this command creates a function called *rcontrast*. First, we tell **R** that we want to be able to input *t* and *df* into the function (these are specified in brackets). This means that to use the function we have to input these values in brackets in the correct order. The rest of the function uses these values to compute *r* and then print the result. The first command takes the value of *t* and *df* entered into the function and places them into the equation written above in **R**-speak (because of how I have labelled everything in the function you should be able to compare directly the command with the equation above) to get a value of *r*. The command prints some text (in speech marks) followed by the value of *r*. If you can't be bothered to write out the command, you should be able to use it directly if you have the package associated with this book, *DSUR*, loaded (see section 3.4.5).

   Having executed this function, we can use it to calculate *r* for the contrasts. Output 10.9 gives us the value of *t* for each contrast (2.474 and 2.029). The degrees of freedom can be calculated as in normal regression (see section 7.2.4) as $N - p - 1$, in which *N* is the total sample size (in this case 15), and *p* is the number of predictors (in this case 2, the two contrast variables). Therefore, the degrees of freedom are $15 - 2 - 1 = 12$. Therefore, we can execute the following commands:

```
rcontrast(2.474, 12)
rcontrast(2.029, 12)
```

The resulting values of *r* are

```
[1] "r =   0.581182458413787"
[1] "r =   0.505407970122564"
```

Both effects are fairly large.

10.8. Reporting results from one-way independent ANOVA ②

When we report an ANOVA, we have to give details of the *F*-ratio and the degrees of freedom from which it was calculated. For the experimental effect in these data the *F*-ratio was derived by dividing the mean squares for the effect by the mean squares for the residual. Therefore, the degrees of freedom used to assess the *F*-ratio are the degrees of freedom for the effect of the model ($df_M = 2$) and the degrees of freedom for the residuals of the model ($df_R = 12$). Therefore, the correct way to report the main finding would be:

✓ There was a significant effect of Viagra on levels of libido, $F(2, 12) = 5.12$, $p < .05$, $\omega = .60$.

Notice that the value of the *F*-ratio is preceded by the values of the degrees of freedom for that effect. Also, we rarely state the exact significance value of the *F*-ratio: instead we report that the significance value, *p*, was less than the criterion value of .05 and include an effect size measure. The linear contrast can be reported in much the same way:

• There was a significant linear trend, $F(1, 12) = 9.97$, $p < .01$, $\omega = .62$, indicating that as the dose of Viagra increased, libido increased proportionately.

Notice that the degrees of freedom have changed to reflect how the *F*-ratio was calculated. I've also included an effect size measure (have a go at calculating this as we did for the main *F*-ratio and see if you get the same value). Also, we have now reported that the *F*-value was significant at a value less than the criterion value of .01. We can also report our planned contrasts or group comparisons:

- Planned contrasts revealed that taking any dose of Viagra significantly increased libido compared to having a placebo, $t(12) = 2.47$, $p < .05$ (one-tailed), and that taking a high dose significantly increased libido compared to taking a low dose, $t(12) = 2.03$, $p < .05$ (one-tailed).

- Despite fairly large effect sizes, Bonferroni tests revealed non-significant differences between the low-dose group and both the placebo, $p = .845$, $d = -0.77$, and high-dose, $p = .196$, $d = -1.24$, groups. The high-dose group, however, had a mean almost 2 standard deviations bigger than the placebo group, $p = .025$, $d = -1.93$.

What have I discovered about statistics? ①

This chapter has introduced you to analysis of variance (ANOVA), which is the topic of the next few chapters also. One-way independent ANOVA is used in situations when you want to compare several means, and you've collected your data using different participants in each condition. I started off explaining that if we just do lots of *t*-tests on the same data then our Type I error rate becomes inflated. Hence we use ANOVA instead. I looked at how ANOVA can be conceptualized as a general linear model (GLM) and so is in fact the same as multiple regression. Like multiple regression, there are three important measures that we use in ANOVA: the total sum of squares, SS_T (a measure of the variability in our data), the model sum of squares, SS_M (a measure of how much of that variability can be explained by our experimental manipulation), and SS_R (a measure of how much variability can't be explained by our experimental manipulation). We discovered that, crudely speaking, the *F*-ratio is just the ratio of variance that we can explain to the variance that we can't. We also discovered that a significant *F*-ratio tells us only that our groups differ, not how they differ. To find out where the differences lie we have two options: specify specific contrasts to test hypotheses (*planned contrasts*), or test every group against every other group (*post hoc tests*). The former are used when we have generated hypotheses before the experiment, whereas the latter are for exploring data when no hypotheses have been made. Finally, we discovered how to implement these procedures in **R**.

We also saw that my life was changed by a letter that popped through the letterbox one day saying only that I could go to the local grammar school if I wanted to. When my parents told me, rather than being in celebratory mood, they were very downbeat; they knew how much it meant to me to be with my friends and how I had got used to my apparent failure. Sure enough, my initial reaction was to say that I wanted to go to the local school. I was unwavering in this view. Unwavering, that is, until my brother convinced me that being at the same school as him would be really cool. It's hard to measure how much I looked up to him, and still do, but the fact that I willingly subjected myself to a lifetime of social dysfunction just to be with him is a measure of sorts. As it turned out, being at school with him was not always cool – he was bullied for being a boffin (in a school of boffins) and being the younger brother of a boffin made me a target. Luckily, unlike my brother, I was not a boffin and played football, which seemed to be good enough reasons for them to leave me alone. Most of the time.

R packages used in this chapter

car	pastecs
compute.es	Rcmdr
ggplot2	WRS
multcomp	

R functions used in this chapter

aov()	mcppb20()
by()	med1way()
cbind()	mes()
contrasts()	oneway.test()
contr.helmert()	pairwise.t.test()
contr.poly()	read.csv()
contr.SAS()	read.delim()
contr.treatment()	stat.desc()
gl()	summary()
glht()	summary.lm()
levene.test()	t1way()
lincon()	t1waybt()
lm()	unstack()

Key terms that I've discovered

Analysis of variance (ANOVA)	Orthogonal
Bonferroni correction	Pairwise comparisons
Cubic trend	Planned contrasts
Eta squared, η^2	Polynomial contrast
Experimentwise error rate	*Post hoc* tests
Familywise error rate	Quadratic trend
Grand variance	Quartic trend
Harmonic mean	Treatment contrast
Helmert contrast	Weights
Independent ANOVA	Welch's *F*
Omega squared (ω^2)	

Smart Alex's tasks

- **Task 1:** Imagine that I was interested in how different teaching methods affected students' knowledge. I noticed that some lecturers were aloof and arrogant in their teaching style and humiliated anyone who asked them a question, while others were encouraging and supporting of questions and comments. I took three statistics courses where I taught the same material. For one group of students I wandered around with a large cane and beat anyone who asked daft questions or got questions wrong (*punish*). In the second group I used my normal teaching style, which is to encourage students to discuss things that they find difficult and to give anyone working hard a nice sweet (*reward*). The final group I remained indifferent to and neither punished nor rewarded students' efforts (*indifferent*). As the dependent measure I took the students' exam marks (*percentage*). Based on theories of operant conditioning, we expect punishment to be a very unsuccessful way of reinforcing learning, but we expect reward to be very successful. Therefore, one prediction is that reward will produce the best learning. A second hypothesis is that punishment should actually retard learning such that it is worse than an indifferent approach to learning. The data are in the file **Teach.dat**. Carry out a one-way ANOVA and use planned comparisons to test the hypotheses that: (1) reward results in better exam results than either punishment or indifference; and (2) indifference will lead to significantly better exam results than punishment. ②

- **Task 2**: Earlier in this chapter we encountered some data relating to children's injuries while wearing superhero costumes. Children reporting to the emergency centre at hospitals had the severity of their injury (**injury**) assessed (on a scale from 0, no injury, to 100, death). In addition, a note was taken of which superhero costume they were wearing (**hero**): Spiderman, Superman, the Hulk or a Teenage Mutant Ninja Turtle. Use one-way ANOVA and multiple comparisons to test the hypotheses that different costumes are associated with more severe injuries. ②

- **Task 3**: In Chapter 15 (section 15.6) there are some data looking at whether eating soya meals reduces your sperm count. Have a look at this section, access the data for that example, but analyse them with ANOVA. What's the difference between what you find and what is found in section 15.6.4? Why do you think this difference has arisen? ②

- **Task 4**: Students (and lecturers for that matter) love their mobile phones, which is rather worrying given some recent controversy about links between mobile phone use and brain tumours. The basic idea is that mobile phones emit microwaves, and so holding one next to your brain for large parts of the day is a bit like sticking your brain in a microwave oven and hitting the 'cook until well done' button. If we wanted to test this experimentally, we could get six groups of people and strap a mobile phone to their heads (so that they can't remove it). Then, by remote control, we turn the phones on for a certain amount of time each day. After 6 months, we measure the size of any tumour (in mm³) close to the site of the phone antenna (just behind the ear). The six groups experienced 0, 1, 2, 3, 4 or 5 hours per day of phone microwaves for 6 months. The data are in **Tumour.dat** (from Field & Hole, 2003, so there is a very detailed answer in there). ②

- **Task 5**: Using the Glastonbury data from Chapter 7 (**GlastonburyFestivalRegression. dat**), carry out a one-way ANOVA on the data to see if the change in hygiene (**change**) is significantly different across people with different musical tastes (**music**). Do a contrast to compare each group against 'No Affiliation'. Compare the results to those described in section 7.12. ②

- **Task 6**: Labcoat Leni's Real Research 15.2 describes an experiment (Çetinkaya & Domjan, 2006) on quails with fetishes for terrycloth objects (really, it does). In this example, you are asked to analyse two of the variables that they measured with a Kruskal–Wallis test. However, there were two other outcome variables (time spent near the terrycloth object and copulatory efficiency). These data can be analysed with one-way ANOVA. Read Labcoat Leni's Real Research 15.2 to get the full story, then carry out two one-way ANOVAs and Bonferroni *post hoc* tests on the aforementioned outcome variables. ②

Answers can be found on the companion website.

Further reading

Howell, D. C. (2006). *Statistical methods for psychology* (6th ed.). Belmont, CA: Duxbury. (Or you might prefer his *Fundamental statistics for the behavioral sciences,* also in its 6th edition, 2007. Both are excellent texts that provide very detailed coverage of the standard variance approach to ANOVA but also the GLM approach that I have discussed.)

Iversen, G. R., & Norpoth, H. (1987). *ANOVA* (2nd ed.). Sage University Paper Series on Quantitative Applications in the Social Sciences, 07-001. Newbury Park, CA: Sage. (Quite high level, but a good read for those with a mathematical brain.)

Klockars, A. J., & Sax, G. (1986). *Multiple comparisons.* Sage University Paper Series on Quantitative Applications in the Social Sciences, 07-061. Newbury Park, CA: Sage. (High-level but thorough coverage of multiple comparisons – in my opinion this book is better than Toothaker for planned comparisons.)

Rosenthal, R., Rosnow, R. L., & Rubin, D. B. (2000). *Contrasts and effect sizes in behavioural research: A correlational approach.* Cambridge: Cambridge University Press. (Fantastic book on planned comparisons by three of the great writers on statistics.)

Rosnow, R. L., & Rosenthal, R. (2005). *Beginning behavioral research: A conceptual primer* (5th ed.). Upper Saddle River, NJ: Pearson/Prentice Hall. (Look, they wrote another great book!)

Toothaker, L. E. (1993). *Multiple comparison procedures.* Sage University Paper Series on Quantitative Applications in the Social Sciences, 07-089. Newbury Park, CA: Sage. (Also high level, but gives an excellent précis of *post hoc* procedures.)

Wright, D. B.,& London, K. (2009). *First steps in statistics* (2nd ed.). London: Sage. (If this chapter is too complex then Wright and London's book is a very readable basic introduction to ANOVA.)

Interesting real research

Davies, P., Surridge, J., Hole, L., & Munro-Davies, L. (2007). Superhero-related injuries in paediatrics: A case series. *Archives of Disease in Childhood, 92*(3), 242–243.

Gallup, G. G. J., Burch, R. L., Zappieri, M. L., Parvez, R., Stockwell, M., & Davis, J. A. (2003). The human penis as a semen displacement device. *Evolution and Human Behavior, 24,* 277–289.

11 Analysis of covariance, ANCOVA (GLM 2)

11.1. What will this chapter tell me? ②

My road to rock stardom had taken a bit of a knock with my unexpected entry to an all-boys grammar school (rock bands and grammar schools really didn't go together). I needed to be inspired and I turned to the masters: Iron Maiden. I first heard Iron Maiden at the age of 11 when a friend of mine lent me *Piece of Mind* and told me to listen to 'The Trooper'. It was, to put it mildly, an epiphany. I became their smallest (I was 11) biggest fan and started to obsess about them in the unhealthiest way possible. I started stalking the man who ran their fan club with letters, and, bless him, he replied. Eventually this stalking paid off and he arranged for me to go backstage when they played the Hammersmith Odeon in London (now the Apollo Hammersmith) on 5 November 1986 (*Somewhere on Tour*, in case you're interested). Not only was it the first time that I had seen them live, but also I got to meet them. It's hard to put into words how bladder-splittingly exciting this was. I was so utterly awe-struck that I managed to say precisely no words to them. As usual, then, a social situation provoked me to make an utter fool of myself.[1] When it was over I was in no doubt that this was the best day of my life. In fact, I thought, I should just kill myself there and then because nothing would ever be as good as that again.[2] This may be true, but I have subsequently had many other very nice experiences, so who is to say that they were not better? I could compare experiences to see which one is the best, but there is an important confound: my age. At the age of 13, meeting Iron Maiden was bowel-weakeningly exciting, but adulthood (sadly) dulls your capacity for this kind of unqualified joy of life. Therefore, to really see which experience was best, I would have to take account of the variance in enjoyment that is attributable to my age at the time. This will give me a purer measure of how much variance in my enjoyment is attributable to the event itself. This chapter describes analysis of covariance, which extends the basic idea of ANOVA from the previous chapter to situations when we want to factor in other variables that influence the outcome variable.

11.2. What is ANCOVA? ②

In the previous chapter we saw how one-way ANOVA could be characterized in terms of a multiple regression equation that used dummy variables to code group membership. In addition, in Chapter 7 we saw how multiple regression could incorporate several continuous predictor variables. It should, therefore, be no surprise that the regression equation for ANOVA can be extended to include one or more continuous variables that predict the outcome (or dependent variable). Continuous variables such as these, that are not part of the main experimental manipulation but have an influence on the dependent variable, are known as **covariates** and they can be included in an ANOVA analysis. When we measure covariates and include them in an analysis of variance we call it analysis of covariance (or *ANCOVA* for short). This chapter focuses on this technique.

In the previous chapter we used an example looking at the effects of Viagra on libido. Let's think about things other than Viagra that might influence libido: well, the obvious one is the libido of the participant's sexual partner (after all, 'it takes two to tango'), but there are other things too such as medication (antidepressants or the contraceptive pill) and fatigue that suppress libido. If these variables (the *covariates*) are measured, then it is possible to control for the influence they have on the dependent variable by including them in the regression model. From what we know of hierarchical regression (see Chapter 7), it should be clear that if we enter the covariate into the regression model first, and then enter the dummy variables representing the experimental manipulation, we can see what effect an independent variable has *after* the effect of the covariate. As such, we *partial out* the effect of the covariate. There are two reasons for including covariates in ANOVA:

- **To reduce within-group error variance**: In the discussion of ANOVA and *t*-tests we got used to the idea that we assess the effect of an experiment by comparing the amount of variability in the data that the experiment can explain against the variability that it cannot explain. If we can explain some of this 'unexplained' variance (SS_R) in terms of other variables (covariates), then we reduce the error variance, allowing us to more accurately assess the effect of the independent variable (SS_M).

---

[1] In my teens I stalked many bands, and Iron Maiden are by far the nicest of the bands I've met.

[2] Apart from my wedding day as it turned out.

- **Elimination of confounds**: In any experiment, there may be unmeasured variables that confound the results (i.e., variables other than the experimental manipulation that affect the outcome variable). If any variables are known to influence the dependent variable being measured, then ANCOVA is ideally suited to remove the bias of these variables. Once a possible confounding variable has been identified, it can be measured and entered into the analysis as a covariate.

There are other reasons for including covariates in ANOVA but because I do not intend to describe the computation of ANCOVA in any detail I recommend that the interested reader consult my favourite sources on the topic (Stevens, 2002; Wildt & Ahtola, 1978).

Imagine that the researcher who conducted the Viagra study in the previous chapter suddenly realized that the libido of the participants' sexual partners would affect the participants' own libido (especially because the measure of libido was behavioural). Therefore, they repeated the study on a different set of participants, but this time took a measure of the partners' libido. The partners' libido was measured in terms of how often they tried to initiate sexual contact. In the previous chapter, we saw that this experimental scenario could be characterized in terms of equation (10.2). Think back to what we know about multiple regression (Chapter 7) and you can hopefully see that this equation can be extended to include this covariate as follows:

$$\text{libido}_i = b_0 + b_3 \text{covariate}_i + b_2 \text{high}_i + b_1 \text{low}_i + \varepsilon_i$$
$$\text{libido}_i = b_0 + b_3 \text{partner's libido}_i + b_2 \text{high}_i + b_1 \text{low}_i + \varepsilon_i$$

(11.1)

11.3. Assumptions and issues in ANCOVA ③

ANCOVA has the same assumptions as ANOVA except that there are two important additional considerations: (1) independence of the covariate and treatment effect, and (2) homogeneity of regression slopes.

11.3.1. Independence of the covariate and treatment effect ③

I said in the previous section that one use of ANCOVA is to reduce within-group error variance by allowing the covariate to explain some of this error variance. However, for this to be true the covariate must be independent of the experimental effect.

Figure 11.2 shows three different scenarios. Part A shows a basic ANOVA and is similar to Figure 10.4; it shows that the experimental effect (in our example, libido) can be partitioned into two parts that represent the experimental or treatment effect (in this case the administration of Viagra) and the error or unexplained variance (i.e., factors that affect libido that we haven't measured). Part B shows the ideal scenario for ANCOVA in which the covariate shares its variance only with the bit of libido that is currently unexplained. In other words, it is completely independent of the treatment effect (it does not overlap with the effect of Viagra at all). This scenario is the only one in which ANCOVA is appropriate. Part C shows a situation in which people often use ANCOVA when they should not. In this situation the effect of the covariate overlaps with the experimental effect. In other words, the experimental effect is confounded with the effect of the covariate. In this situation, the covariate will reduce (statistically speaking) the experimental effect because it explains some of the variance that would otherwise be attributable to the experiment.

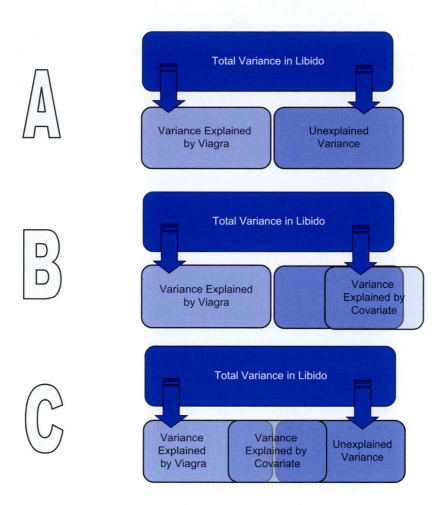

FIGURE 11.2
The role of the
covariate in
ANCOVA (see text
for details)

When the covariate and the experimental effect (independent variable) are not independent, the treatment effect is obscured, spurious treatment effects can arise and at the very least the interpretation of the ANCOVA is seriously compromised (Wildt & Ahtola, 1978).

The problem of the covariate and treatment sharing variance is common and is ignored or misunderstood by many people (Miller & Chapman, 2001). In a very readable review, Miller and Chapman cite many situations in which people misapply ANCOVA, and I recommend reading this paper. To summarize the main issue, when treatment groups differ on the covariate, putting the covariate into the analysis will not 'control for' or 'balance out' those differences (Lord, 1967, 1969). This situation arises mostly when participants are not randomly assigned to experimental treatment conditions. For example, anxiety and depression are closely correlated (anxious people tend to be depressed) so if you wanted to compare an anxious group of people against a non-anxious group on some task, the chances are that the anxious group would also be more depressed than the non-anxious group. You might think that by adding depression as a covariate into the analysis you can look at the 'pure' effect of anxiety, but you can't. This would be the situation in part C of Figure 11.2; the effect of the covariate (depression) would contain some of the variance from the effect of anxiety. Statistically speaking all that we know is that anxiety and depression share variance; we cannot separate this shared variance into 'anxiety variance' and 'depression variance', it will always just be 'shared'. Another common example is if you happen to find that your experimental groups differ in their ages. Placing age into the analysis as a covariate will not solve this problem – it is still confounded with the experimental manipulation. ANCOVA is not a magic solution to this problem.

This problem can be avoided by randomizing participants to experimental groups, or by matching experimental groups on the covariate (in our anxiety example, you could try to find participants for the low anxious group who score high on depression). We can check whether this problem is likely to be an issue by checking whether experimental groups differ on the covariate before we run the ANCOVA. To use our anxiety example again, we could test whether our high and low anxious groups differ on levels of depression (with a *t*-test or ANOVA). If the groups do not significantly differ then we can use depression as a covariate.

11.3.2. Homogeneity of regression slopes ③

When an ANCOVA is conducted we look at the overall relationship between the outcome (dependent variable) and the covariate: we fit a regression line to the entire data set, ignoring to which group a person belongs. In fitting this overall model we, therefore, assume that this overall relationship is true for all groups of participants. For example, if there's a positive relationship between the covariate and the outcome in one group, we assume that there is a positive relationship in all of the other groups too. If, however, the relationship between the outcome (dependent variable) and covariate differs across the groups then the overall regression model is inaccurate (it does not represent all of the groups). This assumption is very important and is called the assumption of *homogeneity of regression slopes*. The best way to think of this assumption is to imagine plotting a scatterplot for each experimental condition with the covariate on one axis and the outcome on the other. If you then calculated, and drew, the regression line for each of these scatterplots you should find that the regression lines look more or less the same (i.e., the values of *b* in each group should be equal).

Let's try to make this concept a bit more concrete. The main example in this chapter leads on from the example in the previous chapter in which we explored whether different doses of Viagra affect libido. Imagine that we repeated this experiment, but measured partner's libido as well and wanted to include this variable as a covariate. The homogeneity of regression slopes assumption means that we assume that the relationship between the outcome (dependent variable) and the covariate is the same in each of our treatment groups. Figure 11.3 shows a scatterplot that displays this relationship (i.e., the relationship between partner's libido, the covariate, and participant's libido, the outcome) for each of the three experimental conditions. Each symbol represents the data from a particular participant, and the type of symbol tells us the group (circles = placebo, triangles = low dose, squares = high dose). The lines are the regression slopes for the particular group; they summarize the relationship between libido and partner's libido shown by the dots (black = placebo group, light blue = low-dose group, dark blue = high-dose group).

It should be clear that there is a positive relationship (the regression line slopes upwards from left to right) between partner's libido and participant's libido in both the placebo and low-dose conditions. In fact, the slopes of the lines for these two groups (black and light blue) are very similar, showing that the relationship between libido and partner's libido is very similar in these two groups. This situation is an example of homogeneity of regression slopes (the regression slopes in the two groups are similar). However, in the high-dose condition there appears to be no relationship at all between participant's libido and that of their partner (the squares are fairly randomly scattered and the regression line is very flat and shows a slightly negative relationship). The slope of this line is very different from the other two, and this difference gives us cause to doubt whether there is homogeneity of regression slopes (because the relationship between participant's

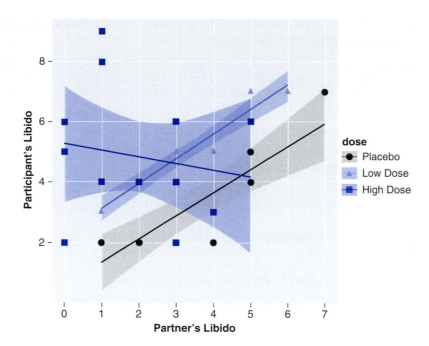

FIGURE 11.3
Scatterplot and regression lines of libido against partner's libido for each of the experimental conditions

libido and that of their partner is different in the high-dose group than in the other two groups).

Although, in a traditional ANCOVA, heterogeneity of regression slopes is a bad thing, there are situations where you might actually expect regression slopes to differ across groups and that this is, in itself, an interesting hypothesis. When research is conducted across different locations, you might reasonably expect the effects you get to differ slightly across those locations. For example, if you had a new treatment for backache, you might get several physiotherapists to try it out in different hospitals. You might expect the effect of the treatment to differ across these hospitals (because therapists will differ in expertise, the patients they see will have different problems and so on). Heterogeneity of regression slopes is not a bad thing *per se*. If you have violated the assumption of homogeneity of regression slopes, or if the variability in regression slopes is an interesting hypothesis in itself, then you can explicitly model this variation using multilevel linear models (see Chapter 19).

11.4. ANCOVA using R ②

In the previous section I said that we would develop the example from the previous chapter (which looked at the effect of Viagra on libido), but covary the effect of partner's libido. Let's now look at the data and run the analysis.

11.4.1. Packages for ANCOVA in R ①

In this chapter, you will need the packages *car* (for Levene's test, Type III sums of squares), *compute.es* (for effect sizes), *effects* (for adjusted means), *ggplot2* (for graphs), *multcomp* (for *post hoc* tests), *pastecs* (for descriptive statistics), and *WRS* (for robust tests). If you do not have these packages installed (some should be installed from previous chapters), you can install them by executing the following commands:

```
install.packages("car"); install.packages("compute.es"); install.packages
("effects");install.packages("ggplot2");install.packages("multcomp");install.
packages("pastecs"); install.packages("WRS", repos="http://R-Forge.R-project.
org")
```

You then need to load these packages by executing these commands:

```
library(car); library(compute.es); library(effects); library(ggplot2);
library(multcomp); library(pastecs); library(WRS)
```

11.4.2. General procedure for ANCOVA ①

To conduct ANCOVA you should follow this general procedure:

1 *Enter data*: I'm stating the obvious again.

2 *Explore your data*: begin by graphing your data and computing some descriptive statistics. You should also check distributional assumptions and use Levene's test to check for homogeneity of variance (see Chapter 5).

3 *Check that the covariate and any independent variables are independent*: you need to run an ANOVA with the covariate as the outcome and any independent variables as predictors to check that the covariate does not differ significantly across levels of these variables. If you get a significant result then stop the analysis here. You have basically entered a bottomless pit of despair from which there is no escape.

4 *Do the ANCOVA*: assuming all was fine in steps 2 and 3, run the main analysis of covariance. Depending on what you found with step 2, you might need to run a robust version of the test.

5 *Compute contrasts or post hoc tests*: you can try to follow up the analysis to see which groups differ.

6 *Check for homogeneity of regression slopes*: rerun the ANCOVA, including the interaction between the independent variable and the covariate. If this interaction is significant then you cannot assume homogeneity of regression slopes.

We will work through these steps in turn.

11.4.3. Entering data ①

The data for the main example are in Table 11.1 and can be found in the file **ViagraCovariate.dat**. Table 11.1 shows the participant's libido and their partner's libido, and Table 11.2 shows the means and standard deviations of these data. You can load this data file by setting your working directory to the location of the file (see section 3.4.4) and executing:

```
viagraData<-read.delim("ViagraCovariate.dat", header = TRUE)
```

In essence, if you're entering the data in an external package such as Excel then the data should be laid out more or less as they are in Table 11.1. So, create a coding variable called **Dose** and, as in Chapter 10, let's use 1 = placebo, 2 = low dose, 3 = high dose. There were different numbers of participants in each condition, so you need to enter nine values of 1 into this column (so that the first nine rows contain the value 1), followed by eight rows containing the value 2, followed by 13 rows containing the value 3. At this point, you should have one column with 30 rows of data entered. Next, create a second variable called **libido** and enter the 30 scores that correspond to the person's libido. Finally, create a third variable called **partnerLibido**. Then, enter the 30 scores that correspond to the partner's libido.

TABLE 11.1   Data from **ViagraCovariate.dat**

Dose	Participant's libido	Partner's libido
Placebo	3	4
	2	1
	5	5
	2	1
	2	2
	2	2
	7	7
	2	4
	4	5
Low dose	7	5
	5	3
	3	1
	4	2
	4	2
	7	6
	5	4
	4	2
High dose	9	1
	2	3
	6	5
	3	4
	4	3
	4	3
	4	2
	6	0
	4	1
	6	3
	2	0
	8	1
	5	0

We could enter the data directly into **R** by executing the following code:

```
libido<-c(3,2,5,2,2,2,7,2,4,7,5,3,4,4,7,5,4,9,2,6,3,4,4,4,6,4,6,2,8,5)
partnerLibido<-c(4,1,5,1,2,2,7,4,5,5,3,1,2,2,6,4,2,1,3,5,
4,3,3,2,0,1,3,0,1,0)
dose<-c(rep(1,9),rep(2,8), rep(3,13))
```

These commands create a variable called **libido** with the 30 libido scores contained within it, a variable called **partnerLibido** containing the libido scores for the corresponding partners, and a variable called **dose** which uses the *rep()* function to repeat the number 1 nine times, the number 2 eight times and the number 3 thirteen times (see the data below). We need to convert the numeric variable **dose** into a factor (i.e., categorical variable) and we can do this, as we did in the last chapter, by executing:

```
dose<-factor(dose, levels = c(1:3), labels = c("Placebo", "Low Dose", "High
Dose"))
```

Remember that we have specified that the levels of **dose** are 1, 2 and 3 *(levels = c(1:3))*, and that we want to label these levels as Placebo, Low Dose and High Dose *(labels = c("Placebo", "Low Dose", "High Dose"))*. Finally, we can merge these variables into a dataframe called *viagraData* by executing:

```
viagraData<-data.frame(dose, libido, partnerLibido)
```

The resulting data look like this:

```
        dose libido partnerLibido
1    Placebo      3             4
2    Placebo      2             1
3    Placebo      5             5
4    Placebo      2             1
5    Placebo      2             2
6    Placebo      2             2
7    Placebo      7             7
8    Placebo      2             4
9    Placebo      4             5
10  Low Dose      7             5
11  Low Dose      5             3
12  Low Dose      3             1
13  Low Dose      4             2
14  Low Dose      4             2
15  Low Dose      7             6
16  Low Dose      5             4
17  Low Dose      4             2
18 High Dose      9             1
19 High Dose      2             3
20 High Dose      6             5
21 High Dose      3             4
22 High Dose      4             3
23 High Dose      4             3
24 High Dose      4             2
25 High Dose      6             0
26 High Dose      4             1
27 High Dose      6             3
28 High Dose      2             0
29 High Dose      8             1
30 High Dose      5             0
```

SELF-TEST

✓ Use **R** to find out the means and standard deviations of both the participant's libido and the partner's libido in the three groups. (Answers are in Table 11.2.)

Table 11.2 Means (and standard deviations) from **ViagraCovariate.dat**

Dose	Participant's libido	Partner's libido
Placebo	3.22 (1.79)	3.44 (2.07)
Low dose	4.88 (1.46)	3.12 (1.73)
High dose	4.85 (2.12)	2.00 (1.63)

11.4.4. ANCOVA using R Commander ②

There is no menu in R Commander that relates directly to ANCOVA. However, because ANCOVA is simply regression, you could theoretically run it through the **Statistics⇒Fit models⇒Linear regression…** menu. However, I don't recommend using R Commander for ANCOVA because it doesn't deal very well with categorical predictors, and you can't control the order in which variables are entered (which is pretty important as we shall see). For these reasons I'm going to force you to use commands in this chapter. You could, however, use R Commander for some of the preliminary analyses; if you want to do this then see the previous chapter (section 10.6.4).

11.4.5. Exploring the data ②

We'll begin with some graphs. To look at the spread of data it's useful to look at boxplots for each group both for libido and partner's libido. In addition, it is helpful to look at the relationship between the outcome variable and the covariate within each group (this tells us about homogeneity of regression slopes). In this section, we'll look at some boxplots.

SELF-TEST

✓ Use *ggplot2* to produce boxplots for the Viagra data. Try to re-create Figure 11.4.

Figure 11.4 shows boxplots for the levels of libido in both participants and their partners across the three doses of Viagra. Levels of libido seem to increase for participants as

FIGURE 11.4
Boxplots of the
Viagra data

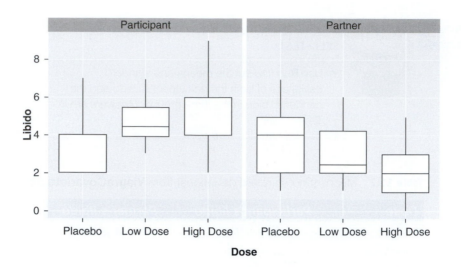

the dose of Viagra increases but the opposite is true for their partners. Also, the spread of scores is more variable for the participants than their partners.

If you completed the earlier self-test, then you will already have some descriptive statistics for the data; if not, we can use the *by()* function and combine it with the *stat.desc()* function in the *pastecs* package to get descriptive statistics for each group separately (see Chapter 5 for more detail). Execute this command for both **libido** and **partnerLibido**:

```
by(viagraData$libido, viagraData$dose, stat.desc)
by(viagraData$partnerLibido, viagraData$dose, stat.desc)
```

The resulting output should confirm the means and standard deviations in Table 11.2 (amongst other things).

The final thing to do at this stage is to compute Levene's test (see Chapter 5 and section 10.3.1). We encountered the *leveneTest()* function from the *car* package in Chapter 5, and we can again use it here. If we want to do Levene's test to see whether the variance in **libido** (the outcome) varies across groups that received different doses of the drug (**dose**), we can execute:

```
leveneTest(viagraData$libido, viagraData$dose, center = median)
```

The output (Output 11.1) shows that Levene's test is very non-significant, $F(2, 27) = 0.33$, $p = .72$. This means that for these data the variances are very similar (hence the high probability value). Had this test been significant, we could instead conduct and report a robust version of ANOVA, which we'll cover later in this chapter.

```
Levene's Test for Homogeneity of Variance
      Df F value Pr(>F)
group  2  0.3256 0.7249
      27
```

Output 11.1

A good double-check of Levene's test is to look at the highest and lowest variances. For our three groups we have standard deviations of 1.79 (placebo), 1.46 (low dose) and 2.12 (high dose) – see Table 11.1. If we square these values we get variances of 3.20 (placebo), 2.13 (low dose) and 4.49 (high dose). We then take the largest variance and divide it by the smallest: in this case 4.49/2.13 = 2.11. If we look at Figure 5.8 we can get the approximate critical value when comparing three variances and with 10 people per group (we have unequal groups, but this will do as an approximation). The critical value in this situation is approximately 5. Our observed value of 2.11 is less than this critical value of 5 so we probably don't need to worry too much about the differences in variances.

11.4.6.   Are the predictor variable and covariate independent? ②

In section 11.3.1, I mentioned that before including a covariate in an analysis we should check that it is independent of the experimental manipulation. In this case, the proposed covariate is partner's libido, and we need to check that this variable was roughly equal across levels of our independent variable. In other words, is the mean level of partner's libido roughly equal across our three Viagra groups? We can test this by running an ANOVA with **partnerLibido** as the outcome and **dose** as the predictor.

SELF-TEST

✓ Conduct an ANOVA to test whether partner's libido (our covariate) is independent of the dose of Viagra (our independent variable).

Output 11.2 shows the results of such an ANOVA. The main effect of **dose** is not significant, $F(2, 27) = 1.98$, $p = .16$, which shows that the average level of partner's libido was roughly the same in the three Viagra groups. In other words, the means for partner's libido in Table 11.2 are not significantly different in the placebo, low- and high-dose groups. This result means that it is appropriate to use partner's libido as a covariate in the analysis.

```
          Df Sum Sq Mean Sq F value Pr(>F)
dose       2 12.769  6.3847  1.9793 0.1577
Residuals 27 87.097  3.2258
```

Output 11.2

11.4.7.   Fitting an ANCOVA model ②

To create an ANCOVA model we can use the *aov()* function that we discovered in the previous chapter (see section 10.6.6.1). Remember that the *aov()* function is just the *lm()* function in disguise, so we can use what we learnt in Chapter 7 to add new variables into our ANOVA model. Remember that to add a predictor, we simply write '+ variableName' into the model. So, in Chapter 10 our ANOVA model was:

```
viagraModel<-aov(libido ~ dose, data = viagraData)
```

To add the predictor **partnerLibido**, we could simply change the model to this:

```
viagraModel<-aov(libido ~ dose + partnerLibido, data = viagraData)
```

Note that we have simply added '+ partnerLibido' to the list of predictors. In essence, this is all there is to it. We could simply execute this command, sit back, crack open a cool drink and admire our handiwork. However, just as we were starting to enjoy a wave of smugness at having conducted an ANCOVA, the sinister shadow of humility would slap us on the face and point out that we need to think about the order of our predictors. If we use the *aov()* function alone then we'll get different results if we specify our model as 'libido ~ dose + partnerLibido' than if we specify 'libido ~ partnerLibido + dose' (note the order of predictors). This is curious and is something to which we need to give some thought (see R's Souls' Tip 11.1).

R's Souls' Tip 11.1 Order matters ②

The order in which we enter predictors into a model makes a difference to the effects in the overall ANOVA – which is very confusing. Luckily it does not affect the model parameters (i.e., the *b*s). Let's look at an example.

First, let's fit the ANCOVA model with **partnerLibido** entered first and then **dose**. To create this model (called *covariateFirst*), we specify the model as *libido ~ partnerLibido + dose*. We can see the ANOVA table for this model by executing the following commands:

```
covariateFirst<-aov(libido ~ partnerLibido + dose, data = viagraData)
summary(covariateFirst)
```

The resulting ANOVA table is:

```
              Df Sum Sq Mean Sq F value  Pr(>F)
partnerLibido  1  6.734  6.7344  2.2150 0.14870
dose           2 25.185 12.5926  4.1419 0.02745 *
Residuals     26 79.047  3.0403
```

This model implies a non-significant effect of the covariate (**partnerLibido**) on the participant's libido, but a significant effect of **dose**.

Let's now redo the model but specifying the predictors in the opposite order. To create this model (called *doseFirst*), we specify the model as *libido ~ dose + partnerLibido*. Note that all we have done is change the order of the predictors. We can see the ANOVA table for this model by executing the following commands:

```
doseFirst<-aov(libido ~ dose + partnerLibido, data = viagraData)
summary(doseFirst)
```

The resulting ANOVA table is:

```
              Df Sum Sq Mean Sq F value  Pr(>F)
dose           2 16.844  8.4219  2.7701 0.08117 .
partnerLibido  1 15.076 15.0757  4.9587 0.03483 *
Residuals     26 79.047  3.0403
```

This model implies the complete opposite of the previous one: a *significant* effect of the covariate (**partnerLibido**) on the participant's libido, but a *non-significant* effect of **dose**.

This is strange, isn't it? The reason is that when **R** computes the fit of the model it uses Type I, or sequential, sums of squares by default. This means that any predictor entered into the model is evaluated after predictors before it in the model. Hence, order matters: in our first model **partnerLibido** is evaluated as the only term in the model, whereas in the second model it is evaluated after **dose** has already been entered and evaluated.

An alternative (adopted by many statistics packages) is to use Type III sums of squares. For our first model (*covariateFirst*), we could get the Type III sums of squares by executing (see text for details):

```
Anova(covariateFirst, type = "III")
```

For our second model (*doseFirst*), we could execute:

```
Anova(doseFirst, type = "III")
```

The outputs for both models are below:

```
libido ~ partnerLibido + dose
               Df Sum of Sq      RSS     AIC F value   Pr(F)
<none>                        79.047 37.065
partnerLibido  1    15.076   94.123 40.302  4.9587 0.03483 *
dose           2    25.185  104.232 41.363  4.1419 0.02745 *
---

Model: libido ~ dose + partnerLibido
               Df Sum of Sq      RSS     AIC F value   Pr(F)
<none>                        79.047 37.065
dose           2    25.185  104.232 41.363  4.1419 0.02745 *
partnerLibido  1    15.076   94.123 40.302  4.9587 0.03483 *
```

Note that even though the predictors have been entered in the opposite order the results are now consistent in the two models.

Before we get carried away creating our ANCOVA model, we need to think about two related questions. First, how should we compute the sums of squares? Second, which contrasts do we want to do? The answer to the second question depends, to some extent, on the answer to the first. The first issue is complex. Essentially we have the choice between evaluating our model using Type I, II or III sums of squares. For an explanation of the difference between these sums of squares and their relative merits, see Jane Superbrain Box 11.1.

JANE SUPERBRAIN 11.1

Types of sums of squares ③

We can compute sums of squares in four different ways, which gives rise to what are known as Type I, II, III and IV sums of squares. To explain these, we need an example. Let's imagine that we're predicting **libido** from **partnerLibido** (the covariate), **dose** (the independent variable) and their interaction (**partnerLibido × dose**).

The simplest explanation of Type I sums of squares is that they are like doing a hierarchical regression in which we put one predictor into the model first, and then enter the second predictor. This second predictor will be evaluated after the first. If we entered a third predictor then this would be evaluated after the first and second, and so on. In other words the order that we enter the predictors matters. Therefore, if we entered our variables in the order **partnerLibido**, **dose** and then **partnerLibido × dose**, then **dose** would be evaluated after the effect of **partnerLibido** and **partnerLibido × dose** would be evaluated after the effects of *both* **partnerLibido** and **dose**. R's Souls' Tip 11.1 demonstrates Type I sums of squares in more detail.

Type III sums of squares differ from Type I in that all effects are evaluated taking into consideration *all other effects in the model* (not just the ones entered before). This process is comparable to doing a forced entry regression including the covariate(s) and predictor(s) in the same block. Therefore, in our example, the effect of **dose** would be evaluated after the effects of both **partnerLibido** and **partnerLibido × dose**, the effect of **partnerLibido** would be evaluated after the effects of both **dose** and **partnerLibido × dose**, finally, **partnerLibido × dose** would be evaluated after the effects of both **dose** and **partnerLibido**.

(Continued)

(Continued)

Type II sums of squares are somewhere in between Type I and III in that all effects are evaluated taking into consideration all other effects in the model *except for higher-order effects that include the effect being evaluated.* In our example, this would mean that the effect of **dose** would be evaluated after the effect of **partnerLibido** (note that unlike Type III sums of squares, the interaction term is not considered); similarly, the effect of **partnerLibido** would be evaluated after only the effect of **dose**. Finally, because there is no higher-order interaction that includes **partnerLibido × dose,** this effect would be evaluated after the effects of both **dose** and **partnerLibido**. In other words, for the highest-order term Type II and Type III sums of squares are the same. Type IV sums of squares are essentially the same as Type III but are designed for situations in which there are missing data.

The obvious question is which type of sums of squares should you use:

- **Type I**: Unless the variables are completely independent of each other (which is unlikely to be the case) then Type I sums of squares cannot really evaluate the true main effect of each variable. For example, if we enter **partnerLibido** first, its sums of squares are computed ignoring **dose**; therefore any variance in **libido** that is shared by **dose** and **partnerLibido** will be attributed to **partnerLibido** (i.e., variance that it shares with **dose** is attributed solely to it). The sums of squares for **dose** will then be computed excluding any variance that has already been 'given over' to **partnerLibido**. As such the sums of squares won't reflect the true effect of **dose** because variance in libido that **dose** shares with **partnerLibido** is not attributed to it because it has already been 'assigned' to **partnerLibido**. Consequently, Type I sums of squares tend not to be used to evaluate hypotheses about main effects and interactions because the order of predictors will affect the results.
- **Type II**: If you're interested in main effects then you should use Type II sums of squares. Unlike Type III sums of squares, Type IIs give you an accurate picture of a main effect because they are evaluated ignoring

the effect of any interactions involving the main effect under consideration. Therefore, variance from a main effect is not 'lost' to any interaction terms containing that effect. If you are interested in main effects and do not predict an interaction between your main effects then these tests will be the most powerful. However, *if an interaction is present*, then Type II sums of squares cannot reasonably evaluate main effects (because variance from the interaction term is attributed to them). However, if there is an interaction then you shouldn't really be interested in main effects anyway. One advantage of Type II sums of squares is that they are not affected by the type of contrast coding used to specify the predictor variables.

- **Type III**: Type III sums of squares tend to get used as the default in many statistical packages. They have the advantage over Type IIs that when an interaction is present, the main effects associated with that interaction are still meaningful (because they are computed taking the interaction into account). Perversely, this advantage is a disadvantage too because it's pretty silly to entertain 'main effects' as meaningful in the presence of an interaction. Type III sums of squares encourage people to do daft things like get excited about main effects that are superseded by a higher-order interaction. Type III sums of squares are preferable to other types when sample sizes are unequal; however, they work only when predictors are encoded with orthogonal contrasts.

Hopefully, it should be clear that the main choice in ANOVA designs is between Type II and Type III sums of squares. The choice depends on your hypotheses and which effects are important in your particular situation. If your main hypothesis is around the highest-order interaction then it doesn't matter which you choose (you'll get the same results); if you don't predict an interaction and are interested in main effects then Type II will be most powerful; and if you have an unbalanced design then use Type III. This advice is, of course, a simplified version of reality; be aware that there is (often heated) debate about which sums of squares are appropriate to a given situation.

If we want Type I sums of squares, then in ANCOVA we enter the covariate(s) first, and the independent variable(s) second. So, we would need to specify the model not as we did above, but as:

```
viagraModel<-aov(libido ~ partnerLibido + dose, data = viagraData)
```

Note that the order of predictors in the model is the covariate (**partnerLibido**) followed by the independent variable (**dose**), which means that the effect of **dose** is evaluated *after* the effect of **partnerLibido**. If we specify the predictors in the opposite order we could get completely different results (R's Souls' Tip 11.1).

We can get Type II and III sums of squares by using the *Anova()* function in the *car* package.[3] This function takes the general form:

```
Anova(modelName, type = "III")
```

Note that the function needs a capital letter at the beginning (otherwise you'll use a function that does something different than what you want), and we replace *modelName* with the name of the model for which we want Type III sums of squares. The *type* option defaults to *type = "II"* (Type II sums of squares), but we can change it to *type = "III"* to get Type III sums of squares.

The second question we asked was about which contrasts to select. This issue goes back to our discussion of planned comparisons in Chapter 10. By default, **R** will use dummy coding on the **dose** variable (it will compare each group to the first group). This is a non-orthogonal contrast. If we want to use an orthogonal contrast such as a Helmert contrast or set our own contrast then we need to use the *contrast()* function to set the contrast for **dose** before we create the model (see section 10.6.7). The reason why the answer to this question depends on which sums of squares we use is because to calculate Type III sums of squares properly we *must* specify orthogonal contrasts. By default **R** will use a non-orthogonal contrast (dummy coding), therefore, if we do not change the contrast or contrasts to be orthogonal the Type III sums of squares computed will be wrong. We must, therefore, either set a Helmert contrast by executing:

```
contrasts(viagraData$dose)<-contr.helmert(3)
```

or set our own contrast codes as we did in section 10.4. To remind you, we chose some planned contrasts in Chapter 10, in which the first contrast compared the placebo group to all doses of Viagra, and the second contrast then compared the high and low doses (see section 10.4). We saw in sections 10.4 and 10.6.7 that to do this in **R** we had to enter certain numbers to code these contrasts. For the first contrast we discovered an appropriate set of codes would be −2 for the placebo group and then 1 for both the high- and low-dose groups. For the second contrast the codes would be 0 for the placebo group, −1 for the low-dose group and 1 for the high-dose group (see Table 10.4). If you want to do these contrasts for ANCOVA, then you enter these codes into the *contrasts()* function for **dose** just as we did in section 10.6.7:

```
contrasts(viagraData$dose)<-cbind(c(-2,1,1), c(0,-1,1))
```

We will use these contrasts; therefore, to run the ANCOVA (with Type III sums of squares) we would execute:

```
contrasts(viagraData$dose)<-cbind(c(-2,1,1), c(0,-1,1))

viagraModel<-aov(libido ~ partnerLibido + dose, data = viagraData)

Anova(viagraModel, type="III")
```

The first line sets the contrasts for **dose**, the second line creates the ANCOVA model, and the third line prints the model summary with Type III sums of squares.

11.4.8. Interpreting the main ANCOVA model ②

Output 11.3 shows the main ANCOVA. Looking first at the significance values, it is clear that the covariate significantly predicts the dependent variable, because the significance value is less than .05. Therefore, the person's libido is influenced by their partner's libido.

---

[3] You can also use the *drop1()* function to get Type III sums of squares. For ANOVA and ANCOVA, this takes the form:

```
drop1(modelName, ~., test="F")
```

What's more interesting is that when the effect of partner's libido is removed, the effect of Viagra is significant (*p* is .027, which is less than .05).

```
Anova Table (Type III tests)

Response: libido
              Sum Sq Df F value    Pr(>F)
(Intercept)   76.069  1 25.0205 3.342e-05 ***
partnerLibido 15.076  1  4.9587   0.03483 *
dose          25.185  2  4.1419   0.02745 *
Residuals     79.047 26
```

Output 11.3

Looking back at the group means from Table 11.2 for the libido data, it seems pretty clear that the significant ANOVA reflects a difference between the placebo group and the two experimental groups (because the low- and high-dose groups have very similar means, 4.88 and 4.85, whereas the placebo group mean is much lower at 3.22). Actually we can't interpret these group means because they have not been adjusted for the effect of the covariate. These original means tell us nothing about the group differences reflected by the significant ANCOVA. To get the **adjusted means** we need to use the *effect()* function in the *effects* package. This produces a summary table of means for a specified effect in a model created by *aov()* or *lm()*, but adjusted for other variables in the model (so called *marginal means*). The function takes the general form:

```
object<-effect("name of effect", modelName, se=TRUE)
summary(object)
object$se
```

How do I interpret ANCOVA?

Note that we create an object that contains information about a given effect. The "name of effect" should be replaced with the effect in the model that interests you (in the current example we want the effect of **dose**). We also have to tell the function the name of the model (so we would replace *modelName* with the name of the ANCOVA model, in this case, *viagraModel*). Finally, if we want to see the standard errors associated with each mean, then we need to include the option *se=TRUE*.

The effect object we created with this command contains various bits of information, but to print the adjusted means and confidence intervals we can just apply the *summary()* function to the newly created object. The standard errors are stored as a variable called *se* within the effect object; therefore, to see the standard errors we need to execute *object$se*.

To put all of this into practice for the Viagra data, to see the adjusted means we should execute:

```
adjustedMeans<-effect("dose", viagraModel, se=TRUE)
summary(adjustedMeans)
adjustedMeans$se
```

Output 11.4 shows the adjusted means (and their confidence intervals) and also the standard errors. Unlike the means in Table 11.2, these adjusted means for the low-dose and high-dose groups are fairly different. In other words, when the means are adjusted for the effect of the covariate it looks very much like as dose increases, libido increases (from 2.93 in the placebo group, to 4.71 in the low-dose group and 5.15 in the high-dose group). The standard errors for each group appear after the *adjustedMeans$se* command: 0.59 for the placebo group, 0.62 for the low-dose group and 0.50 for the high-dose group.

```
dose effect
dose
  Placebo   Low Dose High Dose
 2.926370   4.712050  5.151251


 Lower 95 Percent Confidence Limits
dose
  Placebo   Low Dose High Dose
 1.700854   3.435984  4.118076


 Upper 95 Percent Confidence Limits
dose
  Placebo   Low Dose High Dose
 4.151886   5.988117  6.184427
> adjustedMeans$se

        31          32          33
0.5962045  0.6207971  0.5026323
```

Output 11.4

11.4.9. Planned contrasts in ANCOVA ②

The overall ANCOVA does not tell us which means differ, so to break down the overall effect of **dose** we need to look at the contrasts that we specified before we created the ANCOVA model. To see these contrasts we can use the *summary.lm()* function on the ANCOVA model (*viagraModel*):

```
summary.lm(viagraModel)
```

Output 11.5 shows the model parameters, which correspond to the contrasts that we specified for the variable **dose**. The first dummy variable (**dose1**) compares the placebo group with the low- and high-dose groups. As such, it compares the adjusted mean of the placebo group (2.93) with the average of the adjusted means for the low- and high-dose groups ((4.71+5.15)/2 = 4.93). The *b*-value for the first dummy variable should therefore be the difference between these values: 4.93−2.93 = 2. However, we also discovered in a rather complex and boring bit of section 10.4.2 that this value gets divided by the number of groups within the contrast (i.e., 3) and so will be 2/3 = .67 (as it is in the output). The associated *t*-statistic is significant, indicating that the placebo group was significantly different from the combined mean of the Viagra groups.

The second dummy variable (**dose2**) compares the low- and high-dose groups, and so the *b*-value should be the difference between the adjusted means of these groups: 5.15−4.71 = 0.44. We again discovered in section 10.4.2 that this value also gets divided by the number of groups within the contrast (i.e., 2) and so will be 0.44/2 = 0.22 (as in the output). The associated *t*-statistic is not significant (its significance is .59 which is greater than .05), indicating that the high-dose group did not produce a significantly higher libido than the low-dose group.

The final thing to notice is the value of *b* for the covariate (0.416). This value tells us that, other things being equal, if a partner's libido increases by one unit, then the person's libido should increase by just under half a unit (although there is nothing to suggest a causal link between the two). The sign of this coefficient tells us the direction of the relationship between the covariate and the outcome. So, in this example, because the coefficient is positive it means that partner's libido has a positive relationship with the participant's libido: as one increases so does the other. A negative coefficient would mean the opposite: as one increases, the other decreases.

```
Coefficients:
              Estimate Std. Error t value Pr(>|t|)
(Intercept)     3.1260     0.6250   5.002 3.34e-05 ***
partnerLibido   0.4160     0.1868   2.227  0.03483 *
dose1           0.6684     0.2400   2.785  0.00985 **
dose2           0.2196     0.4056   0.541  0.59284
```

Output 11.5

11.4.10. Interpreting the covariate ②

I've already mentioned that the parameter estimates tell us how to interpret the covariate. If the *b*-value for the covariate is positive then it means that the covariate and the outcome variable have a positive relationship (as the covariate increases, so does the outcome). If the *b*-value is negative it means the opposite: that the covariate and the outcome variable have a negative relationship (as the covariate increases, the outcome decreases). For these data the *b*-value was positive, indicating that as the partner's libido increases, so does the participant's libido. Another way to discover the same thing is simply to draw a scatterplot of the covariate against the outcome.

SELF-TEST

✓ Plot a scatterplot of **partnerLibido** against **libido**.

FIGURE 11.5
Scatterplot of partner's libido against libido

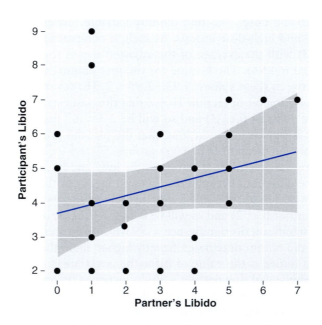

Figure 11.5 shows the resulting scatterplot for these data and confirms what we already know: the effect of the covariate is that as partner's libido increases, so does the participant's libido (as shown by the slope of the regression line).

11.4.11.   *Post hoc* tests in ANCOVA ②

It is also possible to obtain *post hoc* tests as we did for ANOVA (see section 10.6.8). However, because we want to test differences between the *adjusted* means, we can use only the *glht()* function; the *pairwise.t.test()* function will not test the adjusted means. As such, we are limited to using Tukey or Dunnett's *post hoc* tests. Remember from Chapter 10 that to use this function we enter our model (in this case the ANCOVA model) into it and then use the *summary()* and *confint()* functions to see the *post hoc* tests in the console. For the *viagraModel*, we could therefore execute:

```
postHocs<-glht(viagraModel, linfct = mcp(dose = "Tukey"))
summary(postHocs)
confint(postHocs)
```

Output 11.6 shows the three comparisons (low dose vs. placebo, high dose vs. placebo, high dose vs. low dose). Note that the estimate in each case is the difference between the *adjusted* group means (Output 11.4): the estimate for the low dose vs. placebo is $4.71 - 2.93 = 1.78$; for high dose vs. placebo it is $5.15 - 2.93 = 2.22$; and for the low vs. high is $5.15 - 4.71 = 0.44$. The output also gives us the standard error associated with the difference between adjusted means, the *t*-test (which is simply the difference between means divided by the standard error), and its associated *p*-value. This output suggests significant differences between the high-dose and placebo groups ($t = 2.77$, $p < .05$), but not between the low-dose group and the placebo ($t = 2.10$, $p = .12$), and high-dose ($t = 0.54$, $p = .85$) groups. The confidence intervals (Output 11.7) also confirm this conclusion because they do not cross zero for the comparison of the high dose and placebo groups, which means that the true difference between group means is likely not to be zero; conversely, for the other contrasts the confidence intervals cross zero, implying that the true difference between means could be zero.

```
          Simultaneous Tests for General Linear Hypotheses

Multiple Comparisons of Means: Tukey Contrasts


Fit: aov(formula = libido ~ partnerLibido + dose, data = viagraData)


Linear Hypotheses:
                         Estimate Std. Error t value Pr(>|t|)
Low Dose - Placebo == 0    1.7857     0.8494   2.102   0.1088
High Dose - Placebo == 0   2.2249     0.8028   2.771   0.0264 *
High Dose - Low Dose == 0  0.4392     0.8112   0.541   0.8516
---
Signif. codes:  0 '***' 0.001 '**' 0.01 '*' 0.05 '.' 0.1 ' ' 1
(Adjusted p values reported -- single-step method)
```

Output 11.6

```
        Simultaneous Confidence Intervals

Multiple Comparisons of Means: Tukey Contrasts


Fit: aov(formula = libido ~ partnerLibido + dose, data = viagraData)


Quantile = 2.4856
95% family-wise confidence level
```

```
Linear Hypotheses:
                             Estimate lwr      upr
Low Dose - Placebo == 0    1.7857  -0.3255   3.8968
High Dose - Placebo == 0   2.2249   0.2294   4.2204
High Dose - Low Dose == 0  0.4392  -1.5772   2.4556
```

Output 11.7

11.4.12.   Plots in ANCOVA ②

We saw in the previous chapter that the *aov()* function automatically generates some plots that we can use to test the assumptions. We can see these graphs by executing:

`plots(viagraModel)`

The results are in Figure 11.6. You will actually see four graphs, but the first two are the most important. The first graph (on the left of the figure) can be used for testing homogeneity of variance. We encountered this kind of plot in Chapter 7: if it has a funnel shape then we're in trouble. The plot we have does show funnelling (the spread of scores is wider at some points than at others), which implies that the residuals might be heteroscedastic (a bad thing). The second plot (on the right) is a Q-Q plot (see Chapter 5), which tells us about the normality of residuals in the model. We want our residuals to be normally distributed, which means that the dots on the graph should hover around the diagonal line. On ours, it looks like the diagonal line has not washed for several weeks and the dots are running away from the smell. Again, this is not good news for the model. These plots suggest that a robust version of ANCOVA might be in order.

FIGURE 11.6
Plots of an
ANCOVA model

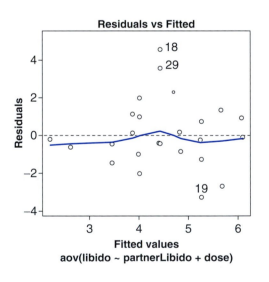

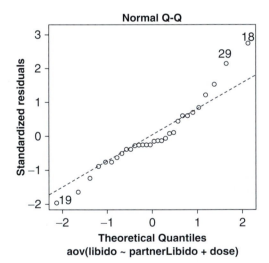

11.4.13.   Some final remarks ②

This example illustrates how ANCOVA can help us to exert stricter experimental control by taking account of confounding variables to give us a 'purer' measure of effect of the experimental manipulation.

SELF-TEST

✓ Run a one-way ANOVA to see whether the three groups differ in their levels of libido.

Output 11.8 shows (for illustrative purposes) the ANOVA table for these data when the covariate is not included. It is clear from the significance value, which is greater than .05, that Viagra seems to have no significant effect on libido. Therefore, without taking account of the libido of the participants' partners we would have concluded that Viagra had no significant effect on libido, yet it does.

```
          Df Sum Sq Mean Sq F value Pr(>F)
dose       2 16.844  8.4219  2.4159 0.1083
Residuals 27 94.123  3.4860
```

Output 11.8

11.4.14.   Testing for homogeneity of regression slopes ③

We saw earlier in the chapter that the assumption of homogeneity of regression slopes means that the relationship between the covariate and outcome variable (in this case **partnerLibido** and **libido**) should be similar at different levels of the predictor variable (in this case in the three **dose** groups). Figure 11.3 showed scatterplots of the relationship between **partnerLibido** and **libido** in the three groups. This scatterplot showed that although this relationship was comparable in the low-dose and placebo groups, it appeared different in the high-dose group.

SELF-TEST

✓ Use *ggplot2* to re-create Figure 11.3.

To test the assumption of homogeneity of regression slopes we need to run the ANCOVA again, but include the interaction between the covariate and predictor variable. We can do this in three ways. The first is to re-specify the whole model from scratch. We can include interaction terms by linking variable names with a colon. For example, the interaction of **partnerLibido** and **dose** would be written in **R** as *partnerLibido:dose* (or indeed *dose:partnerLibido*, it doesn't matter). Therefore, to include this interaction in an ANCOVA model we could execute:

```
hoRS<-aov(libido ~ partnerLibido + dose + dose:partnerLibido, data = viagraData)
```

This command creates a model called *hoRS* (short for homogeneity of regression slopes), which includes the covariate, the independent variable and their interaction.

The second way is to use the fact that you can include variables and their interactions in the same model by specifying *variable1*variable2* as the predictor. Doing so will enter not just the interaction but also the effects of the individual variables as well. So, for example, this command:

```
hoRS<-aov(libido ~ partnerLibido*dose, data = viagraData)
```

does exactly the same thing as the previous command.

The final method is to update our original ANCOVA model (*viagraModel*) to include the interaction term using the *update()* function (see R's Souls' Tip 7.2). The *viagraModel* already includes **partnerLibido** and **dose**, so all we need to do is add the interaction term by including '+ dose:partnerLibido' as follows:

```
hoRS<-update(viagraModel, .~. + partnerLibido:dose)
```

The .~. simply means 'keep the same outcome variable and predictor as before' and the '+ partnerLibido: dose' means 'add the interaction term'. This method is, as you can see, the quickest. Execute one of these commands to create the *hoRS* object and then use the *anova()* function to get the Type III sums of squares by executing:[4]

```
Anova(hoRS, type="III")
```

Output 11.9 shows the main summary table for the ANCOVA including the interaction term. The effects of the dose of Viagra and the partner's libido are still significant, but the main thing in which we're interested is the interaction term, so look at the significance value of the covariate by outcome interaction (**partnerLibido:dose**), if this effect is significant then the assumption of homogeneity of regression slopes has been broken. The effect here is significant ($p < .05$); therefore the assumption is not tenable. Although this finding is not surprising given the pattern of relationships shown in Figure 11.3, it does raise concern about the main analysis. This example illustrates why it is important to test assumptions and not to just blindly accept the results of an analysis.

```
Anova Table (Type III tests)

Response: libido
                      Sum Sq Df F value    Pr(>F)
(Intercept)          53.542  1 21.9207 9.323e-05 ***
partnerLibido        17.182  1  7.0346  0.013947 *
dose                 36.558  2  7.4836  0.002980 **
partnerLibido:dose   20.427  2  4.1815  0.027667 *
Residuals            58.621 24
```

Output 11.9

11.5. Robust ANCOVA ③

As with one-way ANOVA, Wilcox (2005) describes a set of robust procedures for conducting one-way ANCOVA. To access these we again need to load the *WRS* package (see section 5.8.4.). There are two functions that we will look at which can be used to compare trimmed means between two groups including a covariate: **ancova()** and **ancboot()**. These methods all work on the same principle. To free the analysis from the restrictions of homogeneity of regression slopes, as well as the other distributional assumptions, these tests compare trimmed means at different points along the covariate. In other words, rather than assume that the relationship between the covariate and outcome variable is constant in the two groups, it finds five points where the slopes are the same (i.e., five values of the covariate for which the relationship between the outcome and covariate is roughly the same in both groups). It then compares the trimmed means at these five points to see whether

---

[4] We could also use Type II sums of squares here: because we're interested only in the highest-order interaction, Type II and III sums of squares will give us exactly the same results (see Jane Superbrain Box 11.1.).

they differ. This process is quite useful because it gives you an idea of how the differences between group means changes as a function of the covariate.

The function *ancova()* does the analysis just described, and *ancboot()* does the same but uses a bootstrap-*t* method to compute confidence intervals. These functions have the following basic form:

```
ancova(covGrp1, dvGrp1, covGrp2, dvGrp2, tr = .2)
ancboot(covGrp1, dvGrp1, covGrp2, dvGrp2, tr = .2, nboot = 599)
```

In these commands *covGrp1* is a variable that contains the data for the covariate from the first group, *dvGrp1* is a variable that contains the data for the outcome variable (i.e., dependent variable) from the first group; *covGrp2* is a variable that contains the data for the covariate from the second group; and *dvGrp2* is a variable that contains the data for the outcome variable from the second group. The level of trimming is by default 20%, but can be changed by including the *tr* = option. The second command also includes the *nboot* option to control the number of bootstrap samples (the default is 599).

Let's take a look at a new example. Two news stories caught my eye that related to some physics research (Di Falco, Ploschner, & Krauss, 2010). In the first headline (November 2010) the *Daily Mirror* (a UK newspaper) reported 'Scientists make Harry Potter's invisible cloak'. I'm not really a Harry Potter aficionado,[5] so it wasn't his mention that caught my attention, but the idea of being able to don a cloak that would render me invisible and able to get up to mischief was very exciting indeed. Where could I buy one? By February 2011 the same newspaper was reporting on a different piece of research (Chen et al., 2011), but it came with a slightly more sedate headline: 'Harry Potter-style "invisibility cloak" built by scientists'.

Needless to say, scientists hadn't actually made Harry Potter's cloak of invisibility. Di Falco et al. had created a flexible material (Metaflex) that had optical properties that meant that if you layered it up you might be able to create something around which light would bend. Not exactly a cloak in the clothing sense of the word, but easier to wear than, say, a slab of granite. Chen et al. also hadn't made a 'cloak of invisibility' in the clothing sense, but had created a calcite lump of invisibility. This could hide small objects (centimetres and millimeters in scale): you could conceal my brain but little else. Nevertheless, with a suitably large piece of calcite in tow, I could theoretically hide my whole body (although people might get suspicious of the apparently autonomous block of calcite manoeuvring itself around the room on a trolley).

Although the newspapers probably overstated the case a little, these are two very exciting pieces of research that bring the possibility of a cloak of invisibility closer to a reality. So, I imagine a future in which we have some cloaks of invisibility to test out. As a psychologist (with his own slightly mischievous streak) I might be interested in the effect that wearing a cloak of invisibility has on people's tendency to mischief. I took 80 participants and placed them in an enclosed community. The community was riddled with hidden cameras so that we could record mischievous acts. We recorded how many mischievous acts everyone conducted in the first 3 weeks (**mischief1**). After 3 weeks we told about half of the sample (*n* = 34) that we were switching the cameras off so that no one would be able to see what they were getting up to; the remainder (*n* = 46) were given a cloak of invisibility. These people with cloaks were told not to tell anyone else about their cloak and that they could wear it whenever they liked. We recorded the number of mischievous acts over the next 3 weeks (**mischief2**). The variable **cloak** records whether or not a person was given a cloak (**cloak** = 2) or not (**cloak** = 1). These data are in the file **CloakofInvisibility.dat**. Load this file into a dataframe called *invisibilityData* by setting your working directory to the correct folder and executing:

```
invisibilityData<-read.delim("CloakofInvisibility.dat", header = TRUE)
```

---

[5] Though perhaps I should be, given that another UK newspaper once dubbed me 'the Harry Potter of the social sciences' (http://www.discoveringstatistics.com/docs/thes_170909.pdf). I wasn't sure whether this made me a heroic wizard battling against the evil forces of statistics, or an adult with a mental age of 11.

We can convert the numeric variable **cloak** into a factor (i.e., categorical variable) by executing:

```
invisibilityData$cloak<-factor(invisibilityData$cloak,   levels   =   c(1:2),
labels = c("No Cloak", "Cloak"))
```

We have specified that the levels of **cloak** are 1 and 2 (*levels = c(1:2)*), and that we want to label these levels as No Cloak and Cloak (*labels = c("No Cloak", "Cloak")*).

SELF-TEST

✓ Use *ggplot2* to produce boxplots for the invisibility data. Try to re-create Figure 11.7.

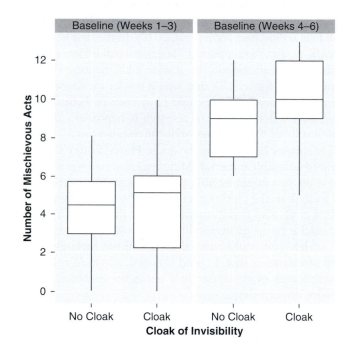

Figure 11.7 shows boxplots for the number of mischievous acts before and after the cloaks were given out by whether or not the person was given a cloak. Levels of mischief are comparable at baseline, and increase in both groups (not surprising given that those without cloaks were told that the cameras were being switched off). The whiskers show that the spread of scores is greater for the participants who received cloaks.

SELF-TEST

✓ Create a standard ANCOVA model of these data. What conclusions can you draw?

The main difficulty in running robust regression is getting the data into the right format. Figure 11.8 shows the data from the *invisibilityData* dataframe (edited to save space). You can see that the groups have been stacked and the covariates and dependent variable (outcome) are in different columns. The functions for robust ANCOVA require us to create four variables, which I have labelled as follows in the functions:

- *covGrp1*: This variable contains scores for the covariate (**mischief1**) for the first group (in this case the 'No Cloak' group of the **cloak** variable). This is the upper left block of data in Figure 11.8.

- *dvGrp1*: This variable contains scores for the dependent variable/outcome (**mischief2**) for the first group (in this case the 'No Cloak' group of the **cloak** variable). This is the upper right block of data in Figure 11.8.

- *covGrp2*: This variable contains scores for the covariate (**mischief1**) for the second group (in this case the 'Cloak' group of the **cloak** variable). This is the lower left block of data in Figure 11.8.

- *dvGrp2*: This variable contains scores for the dependent variable/outcome (**mischief2**) for the second group (in this case the 'Cloak' group of the **cloak** variable). This is the lower right block of data in Figure 11.8.

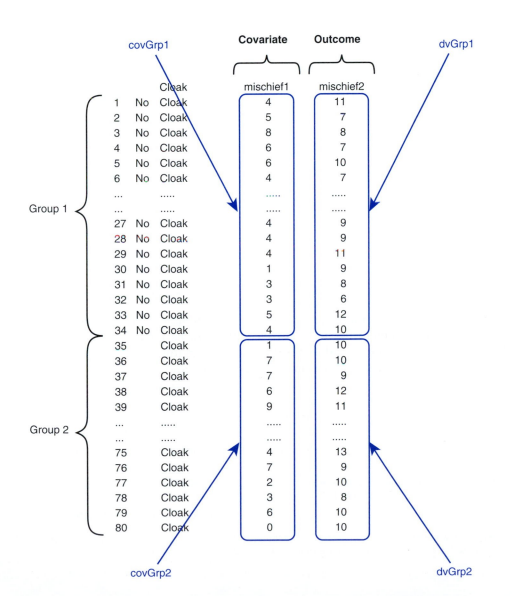

FIGURE 11.8
Extracting data for robust ANCOVA

SELF-TEST

✓ Can you use what you have learnt about **R** to create
   the four variables **covGrp1**, **dvGrp1**, **covGrp2**,
   dvGrp2?

To create these variables, we could start by splitting the dataframe into two new dataframes: one for the cloak group and the other for the no-cloak group. We can achieve this by executing these commands:

```
noCloak<-subset(invisibilityData, cloak=="No Cloak")
invisCloak<-subset(invisibilityData, cloak=="Cloak")
```

Note that we have created two new dataframes (named *noCloak* and *invisCloak*). In both cases we have used the *subset()* function (section 3.9.2), specified the original dataframe (*invisibilityData*), set a condition on which to select rows (this condition is that the value of the variable **cloak** is equal to 'Cloak' for the first dataframe and 'No Cloak' for the second).

We can now create the four variables by selecting the appropriate columns (i.e., variables) from these new dataframes. Execute these four commands:

```
covGrp1<-invisCloak$mischief1
dvGrp1<-invisCloak$mischief2
covGrp2<-noCloak$mischief1
dvGrp2<-noCloak$mischief2
```

The first command creates a variable called *covGrp1* which contains the values of the **mischief1** variable within the *invisCloak* dataframe; the second creates a variable called *dvGrp1* which contains the values of the **mischief2** variable within the *invisCloak* dataframe; the third and fourth commands do the same but using the *noCloak* dataframe.[6]

Having created these variables, we can input them into the robust ANCOVA commands (note that I have also changed the number of bootstrap samples to 2000) and execute them:

```
ancova(covGrp1, dvGrp1, covGrp2, dvGrp2)
ancboot(covGrp1, dvGrp1, covGrp2, dvGrp2, nboot = 2000)
```

Output 11.10 shows the results of the *ancova()* function and Output 11.11 shows the results from *ancboot()*. Both of these outputs can be interpreted in the same way. The *X* column indicates five values for the covariate (in this case 2, 4, 5, 6, 7) for which the relationship between baseline mischief and post-cloak mischief are comparable in the two groups. At these points we are told the number of cases in the data for the two groups (*n1* and *n2*) that have a covariate value close to *x* (not exactly *x*, but close to it). Based on these two samples, trimmed means (20% by default) are computed and the difference between them tested. This difference is stored in the column *DIF* and its estimates standard error in the *se* column. The test statistic comparing the difference is

---

[6] The astute amongst you might wonder why we don't create these variables directly from the original dataframe. For example, we could create *covGrp1* by executing:

```
covGrp1<-subset(invisibilityData, cloak=="Cloak", select = mischief1)
```

However, if we used this command, *covGrp1* would be a dataframe and not a variable. The robust ANCOVA commands don't seem to like dataframes, which is why we don't use this quicker method.

in the *TEST* column (and is just the difference divided by the standard error). The confidence interval of the difference between trimmed means is included (these are corrected to control for the fact that we have done five tests). Note that the confidence intervals are the first things to be different in the two outputs: this is because in the output from *ancboot()* these confidence intervals are based on bootstrapping. Finally, we are told a *p*-value for the test of the difference between trimmed means. If this value is less that .05 we conclude that there is a significant difference between the trimmed means when adjusting for the covariate.

```
[1] "NOTE: Confidence intervals are adjusted to control the probability"
[1] "of at least one Type I error."
[1] "But p-values are not"
$output
  X n1 n2   DIF    TEST     se     ci.low   ci.hi  p.value  crit.val
  2 21 17 1.4056 1.8882 0.74441 -0.673383 3.4846 0.072261 2.79278
  4 31 26 1.7336 3.1302 0.55382  0.226996 3.2401 0.003720 2.72031
  5 32 26 1.0125 1.6767 0.60388 -0.639430 2.6644 0.104360 2.73551
  6 29 24 1.1711 2.3109 0.50675 -0.205854 2.5480 0.027304 2.71716
  7 24 17 1.3750 2.6145 0.52591 -0.079079 2.8291 0.015021 2.76490
```

Output 11.10

```
[1] "Note: confidence intervals are adjusted to control FWE"
[1] "But p-values are not adjusted to control FWE"
[1] "Taking bootstrap samples. Please wait."
$output
        X n1 n2      DIF      TEST        ci.low      ci.hi p.value
[1,]  2 21 17 1.405594 1.888193 -0.63118033 3.442369  0.0800
[2,]  4 31 26 1.733553 3.130180  0.21825768 3.248848  0.0050
[3,]  5 32 26 1.012500 1.676646 -0.63977784 2.664778  0.1140
[4,]  6 29 24 1.171053 2.310930 -0.21544474 2.557550  0.0270
[5,]  7 24 17 1.375000 2.614530 -0.06392599 2.813926  0.0115

$crit
[1] 2.736084
```

Output 11.11

Outputs 11.10 and 11.11 show significant differences between trimmed means for four of the five design points. In other words, in most cases the groups differ significantly in their mean level of mischief after the intervention (adjusted for baseline levels of mischievousness). We didn't get a significant difference for values of the covariate around 5 (the middle of the five design points tested), which seems to suggest that having an invisibility cloak increased mischievousness in those who were ordinarily not very mischievous (baseline scores around 2 and 4) or ordinarily highly mischievous (baseline scores around 6 and 7), but not in the 'averagely mischievous' person.

The robust ANCOVA function also produces a plot (Figure 11.9) of the covariate plotted against the outcome variable. Two regression splines are fitted (one for each group) but note that these are not straight lines (i.e., the slopes are not assumed to be linear). We can use this graph to help interpret the results by looking at the spread of data points for the two groups at each of the design points in the robust analysis (i.e., values of x = 2, 4, 5, 6, 7). Notice that the circles are usually higher than the crosses. The one exception is when X = 5, where there is a cross at the highest point and a circle at the lowest point. This probably explains why we found no significant group differences at this design point in the robust analysis (it is the one point where it is not obvious that the circles are generally higher than the crosses).

FIGURE 11.9
Plot of baseline
mischievousness
(*X*) against
post-cloak
mischievousness
(*Y*) from the
ancova() function

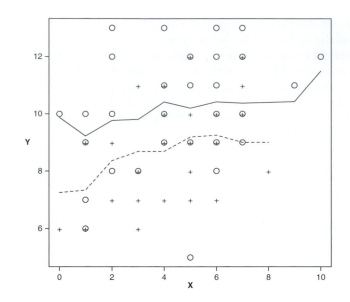

Labcoat Leni's Real Research 11.1   Space invaders ②

Muris, P., et al. (2008). *Child Psychiatry and Human Development*, *39*, 469–480.

Anxious people tend to interpret ambiguous information in a negative way. For example, being highly anxious myself, if I overheard a student saying 'Andy Field's lectures are really *different*' I would assume that 'different' meant 'rubbish', but it could also mean 'refreshing' or 'innovative'. One current mystery is how these interpretational biases develop in children. Peter Muris and his colleagues addressed this issue in an ingenious study. Children did a task in which they imagined that they were astronauts who had discovered a new planet. Although the planet was similar to Earth, some things were different. They were given some scenarios about their time on the planet (e.g., 'On the street, you encounter a spaceman. He has a sort of toy handgun and he fires at you …') and the child had to decide which of two outcomes occurred. One outcome was positive ('You laugh: it is a water pistol and the weather is fine anyway') and the other negative ('Oops, this hurts! The pistol produces a red beam which burns your skin!'). After each response the child was told whether their choice was correct. Half of the children were *always* told that the negative interpretation was correct, and the remainder were told that the positive interpretation was correct.

Over 30 scenarios children were trained to interpret their experiences on the planet as negative or positive. Muris et al. then gave children a standard measure of interpretational biases in everyday life to see whether the training had created a bias to interpret things negatively. In doing so, they could ascertain whether children learn interpretational biases through feedback (e.g., from parents) about how to disambiguate ambiguous situations.

The data from this study are in the file **Muris et al (2008).dat**. The independent variable is **Training** (positive or negative) and the outcome was the child's interpretational bias score (**Interpretational_Bias**) – a high score reflects a tendency to interpret situations negatively. It is important to factor in the **Age** and **Gender** of the child and also their natural anxiety level (which they measured with a standard questionnaire of child anxiety called the **SCARED**) because these things affect interpretational biases also. Labcoat Leni wants you to carry out a one-way ANCOVA on these data to see whether **Training** significantly affected children's **Interpretational_Bias** using **Age**, **Gender** and **SCARED** as covariates. What can you conclude?

Answers are in the additional material on the companion website (or look at pages 475–476 in the original article).

CRAMMING SAM'S TIPS   ANCOVA

- Analysis of covariance (ANCOVA) compares several means, but adjusting for the effect of one or more other variables (called *covariates*); for example, if you have several experimental conditions and want to adjust for the age of the participants.
- Before the analysis you should check that the independent variables and covariate(s) are independent. You can do this using ANOVA or a *t*-test to check that levels of the covariate do not differ significantly across groups.
- You need to decide whether to use Type I or Type III sums of squares. If you use Type III you must do an orthogonal contrast rather than a non-orthogonal one.
- If you have generated specific hypotheses before the experiment use planned comparisons. You obtain these contrasts using the *contrast()* function.
- In the resulting output from the ANCOVA, look at the *p*-value for both the covariate and the independent variable. If the value is less than .05 then for the covariate it means that this variable has a significant relationship to the outcome variable; for the independent variable it means that the means are significantly different across the experimental conditions after partialling out the effect that the covariate has on the outcome.
- If you don't have specific hypotheses you can use *post hoc* tests by using the *glht()* function.
- For contrasts and *post hoc* tests, again look to the *p*-values to discover if your comparisons are significant (they will be if the significance value is less than .05).
- Test the same assumptions as for ANOVA, but in addition you should test the assumption of *homogeneity of regression slopes*. This has to be done by customizing the ANCOVA model to look at the independent variable × covariate interaction.

11.6. Calculating the effect size ②

We saw in the previous chapter that we can use eta squared, η^2, as an effect size measure in ANOVA. This effect size is just r^2 by another name and is calculated by dividing the effect of interest, SS_M, by the total amount of variance in the data, SS_T. As such, it is the proportion of total variance explained by an effect. In ANCOVA (and some of the more complex ANOVAs that we'll encounter in future chapters), we have more than one effect; therefore, we could calculate eta squared for each effect. However, we can also use an effect size measure called **partial eta squared** (*partial η^2*). This differs from eta squared in that it looks not at the proportion of total variance that a variable explains, but at the proportion of variance that a variable explains that *is not explained by other variables in the analysis*. Let's look at this with our example; say we want to know the effect size of the dose of Viagra. Partial eta squared is the proportion of variance in libido that the dose of Viagra shares that is not attributed to partner's libido (the covariate). If you think about the variance that the covariate cannot explain, there are two sources: it cannot explain the variance attributable to the dose of Viagra, SS_{Viagra} and it cannot explain the error variability, SS_R. Therefore, we use these two sources of variance instead of the total variability, SS_T, in the calculation. The difference between eta squared and partial eta squared is shown as:

$$\eta^2 = \frac{SS_{\text{Effect}}}{SS_{\text{Total}}} \qquad\qquad \text{partial}\,\eta^2 = \frac{SS_{\text{Effect}}}{SS_{\text{Effect}} + SS_{\text{Residual}}} \qquad\qquad (11.2)$$

To calculate it for our Viagra example, we need to use the sums of squares in Output 11.3 for the effect of dose (25.19), the covariate (15.08) and the error (79.05):

$$\text{partial } \eta^2_{\text{Dose}} = \frac{SS_{\text{Dose}}}{SS_{\text{Dose}} + SS_{\text{Residual}}}$$

$$= \frac{25.19}{25.19 + 79.05}$$

$$= \frac{25.19}{104.24}$$

$$= .24$$

$$\text{partial } \eta^2_{\text{Partner Libido}} = \frac{SS_{\text{Partner Libido}}}{SS_{\text{Partner Libido}} + SS_{\text{Residual}}}$$

$$= \frac{15.08}{15.08 + 79.05}$$

$$= \frac{15.08}{94.13}$$

$$= .16$$

These values show that **dose** explained a bigger proportion of the variance not attributable to other variables than **partnerLibido**.

As with ANOVA, you can also use omega squared (ω^2). However, as we saw in section 10.7, this measure can be calculated only when we have equal numbers of participants in each group (which is not the case in this example). So, we're a bit stumped.

However, all is not lost because, as I've said many times already, the overall effect size is not nearly as interesting as the effect size for more focused comparisons. If we think about the planned contrasts that we did, we can use the same equation as in section 9.6.3.8:

$$r_{\text{Contrast}} = \sqrt{\frac{t^2}{t^2 + 26}}$$

Remember that in section 10.7 we wrote a function to compute this for us called *rcontrast()*, which you should be able to use if you have the package associated with this book, DSUR, loaded – see section 3.4.5). All we need are the values of t and df.

Output 11.5 gives us the value of *t* for the covariate (2.227) and our contrasts comparing different groups.[7] The degrees of freedom can be calculated as in normal regression (see section 7.2.4) as $N - p - 1$, in which N is the total sample size (in this case 30), and p is the number of predictors (in this case 3, the two contrast variables and the covariate). Therefore, the degrees of freedom are 26.

Therefore, first, create a variable (I've called it *t*) containing the three values of *t* from Output 11.5, and another called *df* that is the value of the degrees of freedom:

```
t<-c(2.227, 2.785, 0.541)
df<-26
```

We can print the corresponding effect sizes for the three *t*-values to the console by placing these variables **t** and **df** into the *rcontrast()* function and executing:

```
rcontrast(t, df)
```

Having executed this command **R** will print the resulting values to the console:

```
  effect_size        r
1          r =   0.400
2          r =   0.479
3          r =   0.106
```

If you think back to our benchmarks for effect sizes, the effect of the covariate (.400) and the difference between the combined dose groups and the placebo (.479) both represent medium to large effect sizes (they're both between .4 and .5). Therefore, as well as being

---

[7] We should use a slightly more elaborate procedure when groups are unequal. It's a bit beyond the scope of this book, but Rosnow, Rosenthal, and Rubin (2000) give a very clear account.

statistically significant, these effects are substantive findings. The difference between the high- and low-dose groups (.106) was a fairly small effect.

An alternative is to calculate effect sizes between all combinations of groups, just as we did for ANOVA. We could again use the *mes()* function from the *calculate.es* package:

$$mes(mean_{group1}, mean_{group2}, sd_{group1}, sd_{group2}, n_{group1}, n_{group2})$$

We know the adjusted means (Output 11.4) and sample sizes, the problem is that we don't know the adjusted standard deviations. We could either use the unadjusted standard deviations as an approximation, or we could estimate them from the standard errors of the adjusted means (Output 11.4). We discovered in Chapter 2 that the standard error is the standard deviation divided by the square root of the sample size on which the mean is based. If we rearrange this equation we get:

$$s = \sigma_{\bar{x}} \sqrt{N}$$

In other words, the standard deviation is the standard error multiplied by the square root of the sample size.[8] We already have the standard errors for the adjusted means stored in the variable *adjustedMeans$se* (see section 11.4.8). If we create a variable, *n*, containing the three group's sample sizes by executing:

```
n<-c(9,8,13)
```

then we can approximate the standard deviations by multiplying the square root of this variable (*sqrt(n)* in **R**-speak) by the corresponding standard errors (stored in *adjustedMeans$se*). Therefore, to print the standard deviations to the console, execute:

```
adjustedMeans$se*sqrt(n)
```

You should find that the values are:

```
1.788613 1.755879 1.812267
```

Now we have all the information we need to use the *mes()* function. For example, if we want to compare the low-dose group with the placebo we would execute:

```
mes(5.988117, 4.151886, 1.755879, 1.788613, 8, 9)
```

We have entered the mean of the low-dose group (5.988117), the mean of the placebo group (4.151886), the corresponding standard deviations (1.755879 and 1.788613), and the sample sizes (8 and 9).

Similarly we can get effect sizes for the difference between the high-dose and placebo groups by executing:

```
mes(6.184427, 4.151886, 1.812267, 1.788613, 13, 9)
```

Finally, the difference between the high- and low-dose groups can be quantified by executing:

```
mes(6.184427, 5.988117, 1.812267, 1.755879, 13, 8)
```

The outputs of these commands are shown in Output 11.12 (I have edited the outputs to show only the effect sizes *d* and *r*). The difference between the low-dose and placebo group is a large effect (the adjusted means are about a standard deviation different), $d = 1.04$, $r = .46$; the difference between the high-dose and placebo groups is also a large effect (over a standard deviation difference between the adjusted group means), $d = 1.13$, $r = .48$; finally,

---

[8] Strictly speaking, this is true only when the sample size is greater than about 30, which is not the case here.

the difference between the high- and low-dose groups is a very small effect (the adjusted means are about a tenth of standard deviation different), $d = 0.11$, $r = .05$.

```
Low Dose vs. Placebo:
$MeanDifference
        d      var.d          g      var.g
1.0354225 0.2676435 0.9827739 0.2411175


$Correlation
        r      var.r
0.45912390 0.03277639

High Dose vs. Placebo:

$MeanDifference
        d      var.d          g      var.g
1.1274090 0.2169217 1.0845960 0.2007595


$Correlation
        r      var.r
0.48480943 0.02347250

High Dose vs. Low Dose:

$MeanDifference
        d      var.d          g      var.g
0.1095664 0.2022089 0.1051837 0.1863557


$Correlation
        r      var.r
0.05313258 0.04728373
```

Output 11.12

11.7. Reporting results ②

Reporting ANCOVA is much the same as reporting ANOVA, except we now have to report the effect of the covariate as well. For the covariate and the experimental effect we give details of the F-ratio and the degrees of freedom from which it was calculated. In both cases, the F-ratio was derived from dividing the mean squares for the effect by the mean squares for the residual. Therefore, the degrees of freedom used to assess the F-ratio are the degrees of freedom for the effect of the model ($df_M = 1$ for the covariate and 2 for the experimental effect) and the degrees of freedom for the residuals of the model ($df_R = 26$ for both the covariate and the experimental effect) – see Output 11.3. Therefore, the correct way to report the main findings would be:

- The covariate, partner's libido, was significantly related to the participant's libido, $F(1, 26) = 4.96$, $p < .05$, $r = .40$. There was also a significant effect of the dose of Viagra on levels of libido after controlling for the effect of partner's libido, $F(2, 26) = 4.14$, $p < .05$, partial $\eta^2 = .24$.

We can also report some contrasts (see Output 11.5):

- Planned contrasts revealed that taking a high or low dose of Viagra significantly increased libido compared to taking a placebo, $t(26) = 2.79$, $p < .01$, $r = .48$; there was no significant difference between the high and low doses of Viagra, $t(26) = 0.54$, $p = .59$, $r = .11$.

Post hoc tests could be reported as follows (see Output 11.6):

- Tukey *post hoc* tests revealed that the covariate adjusted mean of the high-dose group was significantly greater than that of the placebo (difference = 2.22, $t = 2.77$, $p < .05$, $d = 1.13$). However, there was no significant difference between the low-dose and placebo groups (difference = 1.79, $t = 2.10$, $p = .11$, $d = 1.04$) and between the low-dose and high-dose groups (difference = 0.44, $t = 0.54$, $p = .85$, $d = 0.11$). Despite the lack of significance between the low-dose and placebo groups, the effect size was quite large.

What have I discovered about statistics? ②

This chapter has shown you how the general linear model that was described in Chapter 10 can be extended to include additional variables. The advantages of doing so are that we can remove the variance in our outcome that is attributable to factors other than our experimental manipulation. This gives us tighter experimental control, and may also help us to explain some of our error variance, and, therefore, give us a purer measure of the experimental manipulation. We didn't go into too much theory about ANCOVA, we just looked conceptually at how the regression model can be expanded to include these additional variables (*covariates*). Instead we jumped straight into an example, which was to look at the effect of Viagra on libido (as in Chapter 10) but including partner's libido as a covariate. I explained how to do the analysis using **R** and interpret the results. We also looked at an additional assumption that has to be considered when doing ANCOVA: the assumption of homogeneity of regression slopes. This just means that the relationship between the covariate and the outcome variable should be the same in all of your experimental groups. We finished off by looking at some very state-of-the-art robust versions of ANCOVA for when our data are up to mischief; we also learnt that this would be more likely if they possessed an invisibility cloak. The moral here is never to give your data set an invisibility cloak.

Having seen Iron Maiden in all of their glory, I was inspired. Although I had briefly been deflected from my destiny by the shock of grammar school, I was back on track. I *had* to form a band. There was just one issue: no one else played a musical instrument. The solution was easy: through several months of covert subliminal persuasion I convinced my two best friends (both called Mark, oddly enough) that they wanted nothing more than to start learning the drums and bass guitar. A power trio was in the making!

R packages used in this chapter

car	multcomp
compute.es	pastecs
effects	WRS
ggplot2	

R functions used in this chapter

ancboot()	glht()
ancova()	leveneTest()
Anova()	lm()
aov()	mes()
by()	plot()
confint()	reshape()
contrasts()	stat.desc()
drop1()	subset()
effect()	summary()
factor()	summary.lm()
ggplot()	update()

Key terms that I've discovered

Adjusted mean	Homogeneity of regression slopes
Analysis of covariance (ANCOVA)	Partial eta squared (partial η^2)
Covariate	Partial out

Smart Alex's tasks

- **Task 1**: Stalking is a very disruptive and upsetting (for the person being stalked) experience in which someone (the stalker) constantly harasses or obsesses about another person. It can take many forms, from being sent intensely disturbing letters threatening to boil your cat if you don't reciprocate the stalker's undeniable love for you, to following you around your local area in a desperate attempt to see which CD you buy on a Saturday. A psychologist, who'd had enough of being stalked by people, decided to try two different therapies on different groups of stalkers (25 stalkers in each group – this variable is called **Group**). To the first group of stalkers he gave what he termed cruel-to-be-kind therapy. This therapy was based on punishment for stalking behaviours: every time the stalkers followed him around, or sent him a letter, the psychologist attacked them with a cattle prod. The second therapy was psychodyshamic therapy, which is a recent development on psychodynamic therapy that acknowledges its limited empirical support (you could say it's based on Fraudian theory). In keeping with Freud's ideas the therapist would discuss the stalker's penis (or lack of it if they were a woman), the penis of their father, their dog's penis, the penis of the cat down the road and anyone else's penis that sprang to mind. At the end of therapy, the psychologist measured the number of hours in the week that the stalker spent stalking their prey (**stalk2**). The therapist believed that the success of therapy might well depend on how bad the problem was to begin with, so had measured the number of hours that the patient spent stalking prior to treatment (**stalk1**). The data are in the file **Stalker.dat**. Analyse the effect of therapy on stalking behaviour after therapy, controlling for the amount of stalking behaviour before therapy. Also try conducting a robust ANCOVA. ②
- **Task 2**: A marketing manager for a certain well-known drinks manufacturer was interested in the therapeutic benefit of certain soft drinks for curing hangovers. He took 15 people out on the town one night and got them drunk. The next morning as they awoke, dehydrated and feeling as though they'd licked a camel's sandy feet clean

with their tongue, he gave five of them water to drink, five of them Lucozade (in case this isn't sold outside the UK, it's a very nice glucose-based drink) and the remaining five a leading brand of cola (this variable is called **drink**). He then measured how well they felt (on a scale from 0 = I feel like death to 10 = I feel really full of beans and healthy) two hours later (this variable is called **well**). He wanted to know which drink produced the greatest level of wellness. However, he realized it was important to control for how drunk the person got the night before, and so he measured this on a scale from 0 = as sober as a nun to 10 = flapping about like a haddock out of water on the floor in a puddle of their own vomit. The data are in the file **HangoverCure. dat**. Conduct an ANCOVA to see whether people felt better after different drinks when controlling for how drunk they were the night before. ②

- **Task 3**: The annual elephant football (soccer) event in Nepal[9] is the highlight of the elephant calendar. However, in recent years a heated argument has arisen between the African and Asian elephants. It started in 2010 when the president of the Asian Elephant Football Association, an elephant named Boji, claimed that Asian elephants were more talented than their African counterparts. The head of the African Elephant Soccer Association, an elephant called Tunc, replied in a press statement that read 'I make it a matter of personal pride never to take seriously any remark made by something that looks like an enormous scrotum'. I was called in to settle things. I collected data from the two types of elephants (**elephant**) over a season. For each elephant, I measured how many goals they scored in the season (**goals**) and how many years of experience they had (**experience**). The data are in **Elephant Football.dat**. Analyse the effect of the type of elephant on goal scoring, controlling for the amount of football experience the elephant has. Also try conducting a robust ANCOVA. ③

The answers are on the companion website, and task 1 has a full interpretation in Field and Hole (2003).

Further reading

Howell, D. C. (2006). *Statistical methods for psychology* (6th ed.). Belmont, CA: Duxbury. (Or you might prefer his *Fundamental statistics for the behavioral sciences,* also in its 6th edition, 2007.)

Miller, G. A., & Chapman, J. P. (2001). Misunderstanding analysis of covariance. *Journal of Abnormal Psychology, 110,* 40–48.

Rutherford, A. (2000). *Introducing ANOVA and ANCOVA: A GLM approach*. London: Sage.

Wildt, A. R. & Ahtola, O. (1978). *Analysis of covariance*. Sage University Paper Series on Quantitative Applications in the Social Sciences, 07-012. Newbury Park, CA: Sage. (This text is pretty high level but very comprehensive if you want to know the maths behind ANCOVA.)

Interesting real research

Chen, X. Z., Luo, Y., Zhang, J. J., Jiang, K., Pendry, J. B., & Zhang, S. A. (2011). Macroscopic invisibility cloaking of visible light. *Nature Communications, 2,* art. 176. doi: 17610.1038/ ncomms1176.

Di Falco, A., Ploschner, M., & Krauss, T. F. (2010). Flexible metamaterials at visible wavelengths. *New Journal of Physics, 12,* 113006. doi: 11300610.1088/1367-2630/12/11/113006.

Muris, P., Huijding, J., Mayer, B., & Hameetman, M. (2008). A space odyssey: Experimental manipulation of threat perception and anxiety-related interpretation bias in children. *Child Psychiatry and Human Development, 39(4),* 469–480.

[9] http://news.bbc.co.uk/1/hi/8435112.stm

12 Factorial ANOVA (GLM 3)

FIGURE 12.1
Andromeda coming to a living room near you in 1988 (from left to right: Malcolm, me and the two Marks)

12.1. What will this chapter tell me? ②

After persuading my two friends (Mark and Mark) to learn the bass and drums, I took the rather odd decision to *stop* playing the guitar. I didn't stop, as such, but I focused on singing instead. In retrospect, I'm not sure why because I am *not* a good singer. Mind you, I'm not a good guitarist either. The upshot was that a classmate, Malcolm, ended up as our guitarist. I really can't remember how or why we ended up in this configuration, but we called ourselves Andromeda, we learnt several Queen and Iron Maiden songs and we were truly awful. I have some tapes somewhere to prove just what a cacophony of tuneless drivel

498

we produced, but the chances of these recordings appearing on the companion website are slim at best. Suffice it to say, you'd be hard pushed to recognize *which* Iron Maiden and Queen songs we were trying to play. I try to comfort myself with the fact that we were only 14 or 15 at the time, but even youth does not excuse the depths of ineptitude to which we sank. Still, we garnered a reputation for being too loud in school assembly and we did a successful tour of our friends' houses (much to their parents' amusement I'm sure). We even started to write a few songs (I wrote one called 'Escape from Inside', about the film *The Fly*, that contained the wonderful rhyming couplet of 'I am a fly, I want to die': genius!). The only thing that we did that resembled the activities of a 'proper' band was to split up due to 'musical differences'; these differences being that Malcolm wanted to write 15-part symphonies about a boy's journey to worship electricity pylons and discover a mythical beast called the cuteasauros, whereas I wanted to write songs about flies and dying (preferably both). When we could not agree on a musical direction the split became inevitable. We could have tested empirically the best musical direction for the band by writing and performing two songs: Malcolm his 15-part symphony and me my 3-minute song about a fly. If we played these songs to various people and measured their screams of agony then we could ascertain the best musical direction to gain popularity. We have two variables that predict screams: whether Malcolm or I wrote the song (songwriter), and whether the song was a 15-part symphony or a song about a fly (song type). The one-way ANOVA that we encountered in Chapter 10 cannot deal with two predictor variables – this is a job for factorial ANOVA.

12.2. Theory of factorial ANOVA (independent design) ②

In the previous two chapters we have looked at situations in which we've tried to test for differences between groups when there has been a single independent variable (i.e., one variable has been manipulated). However, at the beginning of Chapter 10 I said that one of the advantages of ANOVA was that we could look at the effects of more than one independent variable (and how these variables interact). This chapter extends what we already know about ANOVA to look at situations where there are two (or more) independent variables. We've already seen in the previous chapter that it's very easy to incorporate a second variable into the ANOVA framework when that variable is a continuous variable (i.e., not split into groups), but now we'll move on to situations where there is a second independent variable that has been systematically manipulated by assigning people to different conditions.

12.2.1. Factorial designs ②

In Chapters 10 and 11 we have looked at the effects of a single independent variable on some outcome. However, independent variables often get lonely and want to have friends. Scientists are obliging individuals and often put a second (or third) independent variable into their designs to keep the others company. When an experiment has two or more independent variables it is known as a *factorial design* (this is because, as we have seen, variables are sometimes referred to as *factors*). There are several types of factorial design:

- **Independent factorial design**: In this type of experiment there are several independent variables or predictors and each has been measured using different entities (between groups). We discuss this design in this chapter.

What is a factorial design?

- **Repeated-measures (related) factorial design:** This is an experiment in which several independent variables or predictors have been measured, but the same entities have been used in all conditions. This design is discussed in Chapter 13.

- **Mixed design:** This is a design in which several independent variables or predictors have been measured; some have been measured with different entities, whereas others used the same entities. This design is discussed in Chapter 14.

As you might imagine, analysing these types of experiments can get quite complicated. Fortunately, we can extend the ANOVA model that we encountered in the previous two chapters to deal with these more complicated situations. When we use ANOVA to analyse a situation in which there are two or more independent variables it is sometimes called **factorial ANOVA**; however, the specific names attached to different ANOVAs reflect the experimental design that they are being used to analyse (see Jane Superbrain Box 12.1). This section extends the one-way ANOVA model to the factorial case (specifically when there are two independent variables). In subsequent chapters we will look at repeated-measures designs, factorial repeated-measures designs and finally mixed designs.

JANE SUPERBRAIN 12.1

Naming ANOVAs ②

ANOVAs can be quite confusing because there appear to be lots of them. When you read research articles you'll quite often come across phrases like 'a two-way independent ANOVA was conducted', or 'a three-way repeated-measures ANOVA was conducted'. These names may look confusing but they are quite easy if you break them down. All ANOVAs have two things in common: they involve some quantity of independent variables, and these variables can be measured using either the same or different participants. If the same participants are used we typically use the term *repeated measures*, and if different participants are used we use the term *independent*. When there are two or more independent variables, it's possible that some variables use the same participants whereas others use different

participants. In this case we use the term *mixed*. When we name an ANOVA, we are simply telling the reader how many independent variables we used and how they were measured. In general terms we could write the name of an ANOVA as:

- (number of independent variables)-way (how these variables were measured) ANOVA.

By remembering this you can understand the name of any ANOVA you come across. Look at these examples and try to work out how many variables were used and how they were measured:

- one-way independent ANOVA;
- two-way repeated-measures ANOVA;
- two-way mixed ANOVA;
- three-way independent ANOVA.

The answers you should get are:

- one independent variable measured using different participants;
- two independent variables both measured using the same participants;
- two independent variables: one measured using different participants and the other measured using the same participants;
- three independent variables all of which are measured using different participants.

12.3. Factorial ANOVA as regression ③

12.3.1. An example with two independent variables ②

Throughout this chapter we'll use an example that has two independent variables. This is known as a two-way ANOVA (see Jane Superbrain Box 12.1). I'll look at an example with two independent variables because this is the simplest extension of the ANOVAs that we have already encountered.

An anthropologist was interested in the effects of alcohol on mate selection at nightclubs. Her rationale was that after alcohol had been consumed, subjective perceptions of physical attractiveness would become more inaccurate (the well-known **beer-goggles effect**). She was also interested in whether this effect was different for men and women. She picked 48 students: 24 male and 24 female. She then took groups of eight participants to a nightclub and gave them no alcohol (participants received placebo drinks of alcohol-free lager), 2 pints of strong lager, or 4 pints of strong lager. At the end of the evening she took a photograph of the person that the participant was chatting up. She then got a pool of independent judges to assess the attractiveness of the person in each photograph (out of 100). The data are in Table 12.1 and **goggles.csv**.

Table 12.1 Data for the beer-goggles effect

Alcohol	None		2 Pints		4 Pints	
Gender	Female	Male	Female	Male	Female	Male
	65	50	70	45	55	30
	70	55	65	60	65	30
	60	80	60	85	70	30
	60	65	70	65	55	55
	60	70	65	70	55	35
	55	75	60	70	60	20
	60	75	60	80	50	45
	55	65	50	60	50	40
Total	485	535	500	535	460	285
Mean	60.625	66.875	62.50	66.875	57.50	35.625
Variance	24.55	106.70	42.86	156.70	50.00	117.41

12.3.2. Extending the regression model ③

We saw in section 10.2.3 that one-way ANOVA could be conceptualized as a regression equation (a general linear model). In this section we'll consider how we extend this linear model to incorporate two independent variables. To keep things as simple as possible I want you to imagine that we have only two levels of the alcohol variable in our example (none and 4 pints). As such, we have two predictor variables, each with two levels. All of the general linear models we've considered in this book take the general form of:

$$\text{outcome}_i = (\text{model}) + \text{error}_i$$

For example, when we encountered multiple regression in Chapter 7 we saw that this model was written as (see equation (7.9)):

$$Y_i = (b_0 + b_1 X_{1i} + b_2 X_{2i} + \ldots + b_n X_{ni}) + \varepsilon_i$$

Also, when we came across one-way ANOVA, we adapted this regression model to conceptualize our Viagra example, as (see equation (10.2)):

$$\text{libido}_i = (b_0 + b_2 \text{high}_i + b_1 \text{low}_i) + \varepsilon_i$$

In this model, the high and low variables were dummy variables (i.e., variables that can take only values of 0 or 1). In our current example, we have two variables: **gender** (male or female) and **alcohol** (none and 4 pints). We can code each of these with zeros and ones; for example, we could code gender as male = 0, female = 1, and we could code the alcohol variable as 0 = none, 1 = 4 pints. We could then directly copy the model we had in one-way ANOVA:

$$\text{attractiveness}_i = (b_0 + b_1 \text{gender}_i + b_2 \text{alcohol}_i) + \varepsilon_i$$

However, this model does not consider the interaction between gender and alcohol. If we want to include this term too, then the model simply extends to become (first expressed generally and then in terms of this specific example):

$$\text{attractiveness}_i = (b_0 + b_1 A_i + b_2 B_i + b_3 AB_i) + \varepsilon_i$$
$$\text{attractiveness}_i = (b_0 + b_1 \text{gender}_i + b_2 \text{alcohol}_i + b_3 \text{ interaction}_i) + \varepsilon_i \tag{12.1}$$

The question is: how do we code the interaction term? The interaction term represents the combined effect of **alcohol** and **gender**; to get any interaction term in regression you simply multiply the variables involved. This is why you see interaction terms written as **gender × alcohol**, because in regression terms the interaction variable literally is the two variables multiplied by each other. Table 12.2 shows the resulting variables for the regression (note that the interaction variable is simply the value of the gender dummy variable multiplied by the value of the alcohol dummy variable). So, for example, a male receiving 4 pints of alcohol would have a value of 0 for the gender variable, 1 for the alcohol variable and 0 for the interaction variable. The group means for the various combinations of gender and alcohol are also included because they'll come in useful in due course.

Table 12.2 Coding scheme for factorial ANOVA

Gender	Alcohol	Dummy (Gender)	Dummy (Alcohol)	Interaction	Mean
Male	None	0	0	0	66.875
Male	4 Pints	0	1	0	35.625
Female	None	1	0	0	60.625
Female	4 Pints	1	1	1	57.500

To work out what the b-values represent in this model we can do the same as we did for the t-test and one-way ANOVA; that is, look at what happens when we insert values of our predictors (**gender** and **alcohol**). To begin with, let's see what happens when we look at men who had no alcohol. In this case, the value of **gender** is 0, the value of **alcohol** is 0 and the value of **interaction** is also 0. The outcome we predict (as with one-way ANOVA) is the mean of this group (66.875), so our model becomes:

$$\text{attractiveness}_i = (b_0 + b_1\text{gender}_i + b_2\text{alcohol}_i + b_3 \text{interaction}_i) + \varepsilon_i$$
$$\bar{X}_{\text{Men,None}} = b_0 + (b_1 \times 0) + (b_2 \times 0) + (b_3 \times 0)$$
$$b_0 = \bar{X}_{\text{Men,None}}$$
$$b_0 = 66.875$$

So, the constant b_0 in the model represents the mean of the group for which all variables are coded as 0. As such it's the mean value of the base category (in this case men who had no alcohol).

Now, let's see what happens when we look at females who had no alcohol. In this case, the **gender** variable is 1 and the **alcohol** and **interaction** variables are still 0. Also remember that b_0 is the mean of the men who had no alcohol. The outcome is the mean for women who had no alcohol. Therefore, the equation becomes:

$$\bar{X}_{\text{Women,None}} = b_0 + (b_1 \times 1) + (b_2 \times 0) + (b_3 \times 0)$$
$$\bar{X}_{\text{Women,None}} = b_0 + b_1$$
$$\bar{X}_{\text{Women,None}} = \bar{X}_{\text{Men,None}} + b_1$$
$$b_1 = \bar{X}_{\text{Women,None}} - \bar{X}_{\text{Men,None}}$$
$$b_1 = 60.625 - 66.875$$
$$b_1 = -6.25$$

So, b_1 in the model represents the difference between men and women who had no alcohol. More generally we can say it's the effect of **gender** for the base category of **alcohol** (the base category being the one coded with 0, in this case no alcohol).

Now let's look at males who had 4 pints of alcohol. In this case, the **gender** variable is 0, the **alcohol** variable is 1 and the **interaction** variable is still 0. We can also replace b_0 with the mean of the men who had no alcohol. The outcome is the mean for men who had 4 pints. Therefore, the equation becomes:

$$\bar{X}_{\text{Men,4 Pints}} = b_0 + (b_1 \times 0) + (b_2 \times 1) + (b_3 \times 0)$$
$$\bar{X}_{\text{Men,4 Pints}} = b_0 + b_2$$
$$\bar{X}_{\text{Men,4 Pints}} = \bar{X}_{\text{Men,None}} + b_2$$
$$b_2 = \bar{X}_{\text{Men,4 Pints}} - \bar{X}_{\text{Men,None}}$$
$$b_2 = 35.625 - 66.875$$
$$b_2 = -31.25$$

So, b_2 in the model represents the difference between having no alcohol and 4 pints in men. Put more generally, it's the effect of **alcohol** in the base category of **gender** (i.e., the category of **gender** that was coded with a 0, in this case men).

Finally, we can look at females who had 4 pints of alcohol. In this case, **gender** is 1, **alcohol** is 1 and **interaction** is also 1. We can also replace b_0, b_1 and b_2 with what we now know they represent. The outcome is the mean for women who had 4 pints. Therefore, the equation becomes:

$$\bar{X}_{\text{Women, 4 Pints}} = b_0 + (b_1 \times 1) + (b_2 \times 1) + (b_3 \times 1)$$

$$\bar{X}_{\text{Women, 4 Pints}} = b_0 + b_1 + b_2 + b_3$$

$$\bar{X}_{\text{Women, 4 Pints}} = \bar{X}_{\text{Men, None}} + (\bar{X}_{\text{Women, None}} - \bar{X}_{\text{Men, None}})$$
$$+ (\bar{X}_{\text{Men, 4 Pints}} - \bar{X}_{\text{Men, None}}) + b_3$$

$$\bar{X}_{\text{Women, 4 Pints}} = \bar{X}_{\text{Women, None}} + \bar{X}_{\text{Men, 4 Pints}} - \bar{X}_{\text{Men, None}} + b_3$$

$$b_3 = \bar{X}_{\text{Men, None}} - \bar{X}_{\text{Women, None}} + \bar{X}_{\text{Women, 4 Pints}} - \bar{X}_{\text{Men, 4 Pints}}$$

$$b_3 = 66.875 - 60.625 + 57.500 - 35.625$$

$$b_3 = 28.125$$

So, b_3 in the model really compares the difference between men and women in the no-alcohol condition to the difference between men and women in the 4 pints condition. Put another way, it compares the effect of gender after no-alcohol to the effect of gender after 4 pints.[1] If you think about it in terms of an interaction graph, this makes perfect sense. For example, the top left-hand side of Figure 12.2 shows the interaction graph for these data. Now imagine we calculated the difference between men and women for the no-alcohol groups. This would

FIGURE 12.2
Breaking down what an interaction represents

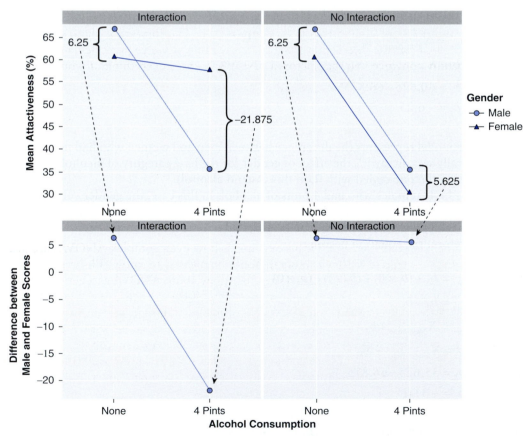

[1] In fact, if you rearrange the terms in the equation you'll see that you can also phrase the interaction the opposite way around: it represents the effect of alcohol in men compared to women.

be the difference between the lines on the graph for the no-alcohol group (the difference between group means, which is 6.25). If we then do the same for the 4 pints group, we find that the difference between men and women is −21.875. If we plotted these two values as a new graph we'd get a line connecting 6.25 to −21.875 (see the bottom left-hand side of Figure 12.2). This reflects the difference between the effect of gender after no alcohol compared to after 4 pints. We know that beta values represent gradients of lines, and in fact b_3 in our model is the gradient of this line (this is 6.25 − (−21.875) = 28.125).

Let's also see what happens if there isn't an interaction effect: the right-hand side of Figure 12.2 shows the same data except that the mean for the females who had 4 pints has been changed to 30. If we calculate the difference between men and women after no alcohol we get the same as before: 6.25. If we calculate the difference between men and women after 4 pints we now get 5.625. If we again plot these differences on a new graph, we find a virtually horizontal line. So, when there's no interaction, the line connecting the effect of gender after no alcohol and after 4 pints is flat and the resulting b_3 in our model would be close to 0 (remember that a zero gradient means a flat line). In fact its actual value would be 6.25−5.625 = 0.625.

SELF-TEST

✓ The file **GogglesRegression.dat** contains the dummy variables used in this example. Just to prove that all of this works, use this file and run a multiple regression on the data.

The resulting table of coefficients is in Output 12.1. The important thing to note is that the beta value for the interaction (28.125) is the same as we've just calculated, which should hopefully convince you that factorial ANOVA is – as is everything, it would seem – just regression dressed up in a different costume.

```
Coefficients:
             Estimate Std. Error t value Pr(>|t|)
(Intercept)   66.875      3.055   21.890   < 2e-16 ***
gender        -6.250      4.320   -1.447     0.159
alcohol      -31.250      4.320   -7.233  7.13e-08 ***
interaction   28.125      6.110    4.603  8.20e-05 ***
---
```

Output 12.1

What I hope to have shown you in this example is how even complex ANOVAs are just forms of regression (a general linear model). You'll be pleased to know (I'll be pleased to know for that matter) that this is the last I'm going to say about ANOVA as a general linear model. I hope I've given you enough background so that you get a sense of the fact that we can just keep adding independent variables into our model. All that happens is these new variables just get added into a multiple regression equation with an associated beta value (just like the regression chapter). Interaction terms can also be added simply by multiplying the variables that interact. These interaction terms will also have an associated beta value. So, any ANOVA (no matter how complex) is just a form of multiple regression.

12.4. Two-way ANOVA: behind the scenes ②

Now that we have a good conceptual understanding of factorial ANOVA as an extension of the basic idea of a linear model, we will turn our attention to some of the specific calculations that go on behind the scenes. The reason for doing this is that it should help you to understand what the output of the analysis means.

Two-way ANOVA is conceptually very similar to one-way ANOVA. Basically, we still find the total sum of squared errors (SS_T) and break this variance down into variance that can be explained by the experiment (SS_M) and variance that cannot be explained (SS_R). However, in two-way ANOVA, the variance explained by the experiment is made up of not one experimental manipulation but two. Therefore, we break the model sum of squares down into variance explained by the first independent variable (SS_A), variance explained by the second independent variable (SS_B) and variance explained by the interaction of these two variables ($SS_{A \times B}$) – see Figure 12.3.

FIGURE 12.3

Breaking down the variance in two-way ANOVA

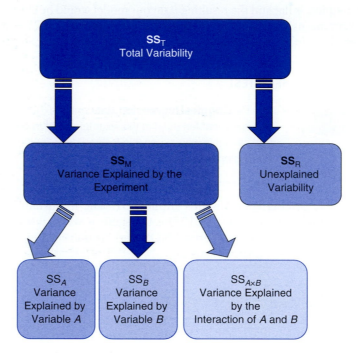

12.4.1.   Total sums of squares (SS_T) ②

We start off in the same way as we did for a one-way ANOVA. That is, we calculate how much variability there is between scores when we ignore the experimental condition from which they came. Remember from one-way ANOVA (equation (10.4)) that SS_T is calculated using the following equation:

$$SS_T = \sum_{i=1}^{N}(x_i - \bar{x}_{grand})^2$$
$$= s_{grand}^2(N-1)$$

The grand variance is simply the variance of all scores when we ignore the group to which they belong. So if we treated the data as one big group it would look as follows:

65	50	70	45	55	30
70	55	65	60	65	30
60	80	60	85	70	30
60	65	70	65	55	55
60	70	65	70	55	35
55	75	60	70	60	20
60	75	60	80	50	45
55	65	50	60	50	40

Grand mean = 58.33

If we calculate the variance of all of these scores, we get 190.78 (try this on your calculator if you don't trust me). We used 48 scores to generate this value, and so N is 48. As such the equation becomes:

$$SS_T = s_{grand}^2(N-1)$$
$$= 190.78(48-1)$$
$$= 8966.66$$

The degrees of freedom for this SS will be $N-1$, or 47.

12.4.2. The model sum of squares (SS_M) ②

The next step is to work out the model sum of squares. As I suggested earlier, this sum of squares is then further broken into three components: variance explained by the first independent variable (SS_A), variance explained by the second independent variable (SS_B) and variance explained by the interaction of these two variables ($SS_{A \times B}$).

Before we break down the model sum of squares into its component parts, we must first calculate its value. We know we have 8966.66 units of variance to be explained, and our first step is to calculate how much of that variance is explained by our experimental manipulations overall (ignoring which of the two independent variables is responsible). When we did one-way ANOVA we worked out the model sum of squares by looking at the difference between each group mean and the overall mean (see section 10.2.6). We can do the same here. We effectively have six experimental groups if we combine all levels of the two independent variables (three doses for the male participants and three doses for the females). So, given that we have six groups of different people we can then apply the equation for the model sum of squares that we used for one-way ANOVA (equation (10.5)):

$$SS_M = \sum_{n=1}^{k} n_k(\bar{x}_k - \bar{x}_{grand})^2$$

The grand mean is the mean of all scores (we calculated this above as 58.33) and n is the number of scores in each group (i.e., the number of participants in each of the six experimental groups; eight in this case). Therefore, the equation becomes:

$$
\begin{aligned}
SS_M &= 8(60.625 - 58.33)^2 + 8(66.875 - 58.33)^2 + 8(62.5 - 58.33)^2 + \ldots \\
&\quad + 8(66.875 - 58.33)^2 + 8(57.5 - 58.33)^2 + 8(35.625 - 58.33)^2 \\
&= 8(2.295)^2 + 8(8.545)^2 + 8(4.17)^2 + 8(8.545)^2 + 8(-0.83)^2 + 8(-22.705)^2 \\
&= 42.1362 + 584.1362 + 139.1112 + 584.1362 + 5.5112 + 4124.1362 \\
&= 5479.167
\end{aligned}
$$

The degrees of freedom for this SS will be the number of groups used, k, minus 1. We used six groups and so $df = 5$.

At this stage we know that the model (our experimental manipulations) can explain 5479.167 units of variance out of the total of 8966.66 units. The next stage is to further break down this model sum of squares to see how much variance is explained by our independent variables separately.

12.4.2.1. The main effect of gender (SS$_A$) ②

To work out the variance accounted for by the first independent variable (in this case, **gender**) we need to group the scores in the data set according to the gender to which they belong. So, basically we ignore the amount of drink that has been drunk, and we just place all of the male scores into one group and all of the female scores into another. So, the data will look like this (note that the first box contains the three female columns from our original table and the second box contains the male columns):

A_1: Female				A_2: Male		
65	70	55		50	45	30
70	65	65		55	60	30
60	60	70		80	85	30
60	70	55		65	65	55
60	65	55		70	70	35
55	60	60		75	70	20
60	60	50		75	80	45
55	50	50		65	60	40
Mean Female = 60.21				Mean Male = 56.46		

We can then apply the equation for the model sum of squares that we used to calculate the overall model sum of squares:

$$
SS_A = \sum_{n=1}^{k} n_k (\bar{x}_k - \bar{x}_{grand})^2
$$

The grand mean is the mean of all scores (above) and n is the number of scores in each group (i.e., the number of males and females; 24 in this case). Therefore, the equation becomes:

$$\begin{aligned} SS_{gender} &= 24(60.21 - 58.33)^2 + 24(56.46 - 58.33)^2 \\ &= 24(1.88)^2 + 24(-1.87)^2 \\ &= 84.8256 + 83.9256 \\ &= 168.75 \end{aligned}$$

The degrees of freedom for this SS will be the number of groups used, k, minus 1. We used two groups (males and females) and so $df = 1$. To sum up, the main effect of gender compares the mean of all males against the mean of all females (regardless of which alcohol group they were in).

12.4.2.2. The main effect of alcohol (SS_B) ②

To work out the variance accounted for by the second independent variable (in this case, **alcohol**) we need to group the scores in the data set according to how much alcohol was consumed. So, basically we ignore the gender of the participant, and we just place all of the scores after no drinks in one group, the scores after 2 pints in another group and the scores after 4 pints in a third group. So, the data will look like this:

B_1: None		B_2: 2 Pints		B_3: 4 Pints	
65	50	70	45	55	30
70	55	65	60	65	30
60	80	60	85	70	30
60	65	70	65	55	55
60	70	65	70	55	35
55	75	60	70	60	20
60	75	60	80	50	45
55	65	50	60	50	40
Mean None = 63.75		Mean 2 pints = 64.6875		Mean 4 pints = 46.5625	

We can then apply the same equation for the model sum of squares that we used for the overall model sum of squares and for the main effect of gender:

$$SS_B = \sum_{n=1}^{k} n_k (\bar{x}_k - \bar{x}_{grand})^2$$

The grand mean is the mean of all scores (58.33 as before) and n is the number of scores in each group (i.e., the number of scores in each of the boxes above, in this case 16). Therefore, the equation becomes:

$$\begin{aligned} SS_{alcohol} &= 16(63.75 - 58.33)^2 + 16(64.6875 - 58.33)^2 + 16(46.5625 - 58.33)^2 \\ &= 16(5.42)^2 + 16(6.3575)^2 + 16(-11.7675)^2 \\ &= 470.0224 + 646.6849 + 2215.5849 \\ &= 3332.292 \end{aligned}$$

The degrees of freedom for this SS will be the number of groups used, k, minus 1 (see section 10.2.6). We used three groups and so $df = 2$. To sum up, the main effect of alcohol compares the means of the no-alcohol, 2-pints and 4-pints groups (regardless of whether the scores come from men or women).

12.4.2.3. The interaction effect ($SS_{A \times B}$) ②

The final stage is to calculate how much variance is explained by the interaction of the two variables. The simplest way to do this is to remember that the SS_M is made up of three components (SS_A, SS_B and $SS_{A \times B}$). Therefore, given that we know SS_A and SS_B we can calculate the interaction term using subtraction:

$$SS_{A \times B} = SS_M - SS_A - SS_B$$

Therefore, for these data, the value is:

$$\begin{aligned} SS_{A \times B} &= SS_M - SS_A - SS_B \\ &= 5479.167 - 168.75 - 3332.292 \\ &= 1978.125 \end{aligned}$$

The degrees of freedom can be calculated in the same way, but are also the product of the degrees of freedom for the main effects (either method works):

$$\begin{aligned} df_{A \times B} &= df_M - df_A - df_B \\ &= 5 - 1 - 2 \\ &= 2 \end{aligned} \qquad\qquad \begin{aligned} df_{A \times B} &= df_A \times df_B \\ &= 1 \times 2 \\ &= 2 \end{aligned}$$

12.4.3. The residual sum of squares (SS_R) ②

The residual sum of squares is calculated in the same way as for one-way ANOVA (see section 10.2.7) and again represents individual differences in performance or the variance that can't be explained by factors that were systematically manipulated. We saw in one-way ANOVA that the value is calculated by taking the squared error between each data point and its corresponding group mean. An alternative way to express this was as (see equation (10.7)):

$$\begin{aligned} SS_R &= \sum s_k^2 (n_k - 1) \\ &= s_{\text{group 1}}^2 (n_1 - 1) + s_{\text{group 2}}^2 (n_2 - 1) + s_{\text{group 3}}^2 (n_3 - 1) + \ldots + s_{\text{group } n}^2 (n_n - 1) \end{aligned}$$

So, we use the individual variances of each group and multiply them by one less than the number of people within the group (n). We have the individual group variances in our original table of data (Table 12.1) and there were eight people in each group (therefore, $n = 8$) and so the equation becomes:

$$\begin{aligned} SS_R &= s_{\text{group1}}^2 (n_1 - 1) + s_{\text{group2}}^2 (n_2 - 1) + s_{\text{group3}}^2 (n_3 - 1) + s_{\text{group4}}^2 (n_4 - 1) + \ldots \\ &\quad + s_{\text{group5}}^2 (n_5 - 1) + s_{\text{group6}}^2 (n_6 - 1) \\ &= 24.55(8 - 1) + 106.7(8 - 1) + 42.86(8 - 1) + 156.7(8 - 1) + 50(8 - 1) + 117.41(8 - 1) \\ &= (24.55 \times 7) + (106.7 \times 7) + (42.86 \times 7) + (156.7 \times 7) + (50 \times 7) + (117.41 \times 7) \\ &= 171.85 + 746.9 + 300 + 1096.9 + 350 + 821.87 \\ &= 3487.52 \end{aligned}$$

The degrees of freedom for each group will be one less than the number of scores per group (i.e., 7). Therefore, if we add the degrees of freedom for each group, we get a total of $6 \times 7 = 42$.

12.4.4. The *F*-ratios ②

Each effect in a two-way ANOVA (the two main effects and the interaction) has its own *F*-ratio. To calculate these we have to first calculate the mean squares for each effect by taking the sum of squares and dividing by the respective degrees of freedom (think back to section 10.2.8). We also need the mean squares for the residual term. So, for this example we'd have four mean squares calculated as follows:

$$MS_A = \frac{SS_A}{df_A} = \frac{168.75}{1} = 168.75$$

$$MS_B = \frac{SS_B}{df_B} = \frac{3332.292}{2} = 1666.146$$

$$MS_{A \times B} = \frac{SS_{A \times B}}{df_{A \times B}} = \frac{1978.125}{2} = 989.062$$

$$MS_R = \frac{SS_R}{df_R} = \frac{3487.52}{42} = 83.036$$

The *F*-ratios for the two independent variables and their interactions are then calculated by dividing their mean squares by the residual mean squares. Again, if you think back to one-way ANOVA this is exactly the same process.

$$F_A = \frac{MS_A}{MS_R} = \frac{168.75}{83.036} = 2.032$$

$$F_B = \frac{MS_B}{MS_R} = \frac{1666.146}{83.036} = 20.065$$

$$F_{A \times B} = \frac{MS_{A \times B}}{MS_R} = \frac{989.062}{83.036} = 11.911$$

Each of these *F*-ratios can be compared against critical values (based on their degrees of freedom, which can be different for each effect) to tell us whether these effects are likely to reflect data that have arisen by chance, or reflect an effect of our experimental manipulations (these critical values can be found in the Appendix). If an observed *F* exceeds the corresponding critical values then it is significant. **R** will calculate each of these *F*-ratios and their exact significance, but what I hope to have shown you in this section is that two-way ANOVA is basically the same as one-way ANOVA except that the model sum of squares is partitioned into three parts: the effect of each of the independent variables and the effect of how these variables interact.

12.5.   Factorial ANOVA using R ②

12.5.1. Packages for factorial ANOVA in R ①

If you're using commands (which we recommend), then you will need the packages *car* (for Levene's test), *compute.es* (for effect sizes), *ggplot2* (for graphs), *multcomp* (for *post hoc* tests), *pastecs* (for descriptive statistics), *reshape* (for reshaping the data) and *WRS* (for robust tests). If you do not have these packages installed (some should be installed from previous chapters), you can install them by executing the following commands:

```
install.packages("car"); install.packages("compute.es"); install.packages
("ggplot2");install.packages("multcomp");install.packages("pastecs");install.
packages("reshape"); install.packages("WRS", repos="http://R-Forge.R-project.
org")
```

You then need to load these packages by executing these commands:

```
library(car); library(compute.es); library(ggplot2); library(multcomp);
library(pastecs); library(reshape); library(WRS)
```

12.5.2.   General procedure for factorial ANOVA ①

To conduct factorial ANOVA you should follow this general procedure:

1 *Enter data*: you've probably gathered this much by now.

2 *Explore your data*: as always, we'll begin by graphing the data and computing descriptive statistics. You should check distributional assumptions and use Levene's test to check for homogeneity of variance (see Chapter 5).

3 *Construct or choose contrasts*: you need to decide what contrasts to do and to specify them appropriately for all of the independent variables in your analysis. If you want to use Type III sums of squares, *these contrasts must be orthogonal*.

4 *Compute the ANOVA*: you can then run the main analysis of variance. Depending on what you found in the previous step, you might need to run a robust version of the test.

5 *Compute contrasts or post hoc tests*: having conducted the main ANOVA, you can follow it up with *post hoc* tests or look at the results of your contrasts. Again, the exact methods you choose will depend upon what you unearth in step 2.

We will work through these steps in turn.

12.5.3.   Factorial ANOVA using R Commander ②

Running factorial ANOVA using commands gives you much more versatility than R Commander. However, you can do a basic factorial ANOVA using R Commander. First load the data from the file **goggles.csv** by using the **Data⇒Import data⇒from text file, clipboard, or URL...** menu (see section 3.7.3). Note that this file is a comma-separated (not a tab-delimited) file. This data set has three variables: **gender**, which is entered as text ('Male' and 'Female'), **alcohol**, which is also entered as text ('None', '2 Pints' and '4 Pints'), and **attractiveness**, which is the outcome variable. I have called the dataframe *gogglesData*. Note that because **gender** and **alcohol** contained text strings, rather than numbers, **R** has assumed that these variables are factors.

We can explore the data by getting some descriptive statistics and testing the assumptions. This is explained in Chapter 5. Levene's test looks at whether variances across conditions are equal. Use the **Statistics⇒Variances⇒Levene's test...** menu to run the analysis as in Chapters 5 and 10. You will need to run separate tests for **alcohol** and **gender** (as you will see, by using commands we can also run the test for the interaction of these variables).

To do the ANOVA, use the **Statistics⇒Means⇒Multi-way ANOVA...** menu. The resulting dialog box is fairly self-explanatory (Figure 12.4). You need to enter a name for the model that you're going to create (I have chosen *gogglesModel*) in the box labelled *Enter name for model*, select any factors from the list labelled *Factors* (in this case we have two factors, **alcohol** and **gender**) and select the outcome variable (in this case **attractiveness**) from the list labelled *Response Variable*. You cannot do planned comparisons or *post hoc* tests using this menu. Click on ⌷ OK ⌷ to run the analysis. The resulting output is described in sections 12.5.8. Note that R Commander uses Type II sums of squares when computing a factorial ANOVA, which may or may not be what you want (see Jane Superbrain Box 11.1 in the previous chapter).

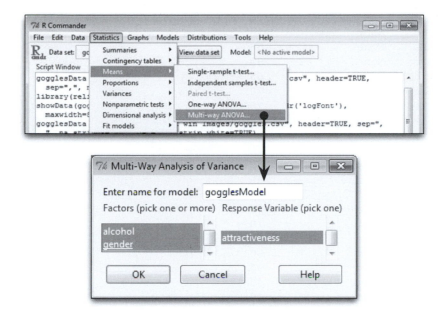

FIGURE 12.4
Factorial-way
ANOVA using R
Commander

12.5.4. Entering the data ②

The data for the example can be found in the file **goggles.csv**. You can load this data file by setting your working directory and executing:

```
gogglesData<-read.csv("goggles.csv", header = TRUE)
```

Note that we have used the *read.csv()* function because the data are stored in a comma-separated values file (.csv). If we look at the data in **R** we will see that levels of the between-group variables have been entered in single columns.

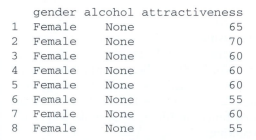

```
  gender alcohol attractiveness
1 Female   None              65
2 Female   None              70
3 Female   None              60
4 Female   None              60
5 Female   None              60
6 Female   None              55
7 Female   None              60
8 Female   None              55
```

```
9   Female 2 Pints              70
10  Female 2 Pints              65
11  Female 2 Pints              60
12  Female 2 Pints              70
13  Female 2 Pints              65
14  Female 2 Pints              60
15  Female 2 Pints              60
16  Female 2 Pints              50
17  Female 4 Pints              55
18  Female 4 Pints              65
19  Female 4 Pints              70
20  Female 4 Pints              55
21  Female 4 Pints              55
22  Female 4 Pints              60
23  Female 4 Pints              50
24  Female 4 Pints              50
25    Male     None             50
26    Male     None             55
27    Male     None             80
28    Male     None             65
29    Male     None             70
30    Male     None             75
31    Male     None             75
32    Male     None             65
33    Male   2 Pints            45
34    Male   2 Pints            60
35    Male   2 Pints            85
36    Male   2 Pints            65
37    Male   2 Pints            70
38    Male   2 Pints            70
39    Male   2 Pints            80
40    Male   2 Pints            60
41    Male   4 Pints            30
42    Male   4 Pints            30
43    Male   4 Pints            30
44    Male   4 Pints            55
45    Male   4 Pints            35
46    Male   4 Pints            20
47    Male   4 Pints            45
48    Male   4 Pints            40
```

These data were originally entered in Excel, and as you can see we need two different coding variables to represent gender and alcohol consumption. Therefore, in Excel, I created a variable called **gender** into which I typed 'Female' or 'Male'; because I have used words rather than numbers, when **R** imports the data it guesses that this variable is a factor (i.e., we don't need to explicitly convert it to a factor like we would had I used numbers to represent males and females). **R** will code this factor with the levels in alphabetical order (so, females will be level 1 and males level 2 of gender, which coincidentally is the same order as in the data file).

Next, I created a variable called **alcohol** and entered 'None', '2 Pints' or '4 Pints'. Again, **R** guesses that this variable is a factor when it imports the data, and organizes the levels of this variable alphabetically. The alphabetic ordering means that **R** has imported this factor with the groups ordered as '2 Pints', '4 Pints' and 'None'. This is because numbers (e.g., 2 and 4) are deemed to come before letters in the alphabet. Ideally, we might like the groups to be ordreed as they are in the data (i.e., 'None', '2 Pints' and '4 Pints'). To reorder the groups, we can use the *levels* option of the *factor()* function. All we need to do is type the levels in the order that we want them. So, by executing:

```
gogglesData$alcohol<-factor(gogglesData$alcohol, levels = c("None", "2
Pints", "4 Pints"))
```

we take the variable **alcohol** from the *gogglesData* dataframe, and we reorder the levels of the factor as 'None', '2 Pints' and '4 Pints' (*levels = c("None", "2 Pints", "4 Pints")*).

You can see from the data that there are 24 females followed by 24 males, and within these groups there are 8 people who had no alcohol, 8 who had two pints and 8 who consumed four pints. Finally, I created a variable called **attractiveness** into which I put the scores (out of 100) representing the attractiveness of the each participant's date.

If we wanted to enter the data directly into **R**, we would need to assign group codes for the **gender** and **alcohol** variables. We might code **gender** as 1 for females and 2 for males, and we might code **alcohol** as no alcohol = 1, 2 pints = 2 and 4 pints = 3. The way this coding works is as follows:

Gender	Alcohol	Participant was
1	1	Male who consumed no alcohol
1	2	Male who consumed 2 pints
1	3	Male who consumed 4 pints
2	1	Female who consumed no alcohol
2	2	Female who consumed 2 pints
2	3	Female who consumed 4 pints

We can create these two coding variables very quickly by using the *gl()* function (Chapter 3). Remember that this function takes the general form:

```
factor<-gl(number of levels, cases in each level, total cases, labels =
c("label1", "label2"…))
```

This function creates a factor variable called *factor*; you specify the number of levels or groups of the factor, how many cases are in each level/group, optionally the total number of cases (the default is to multiply the number of groups by the number of cases per group), and you can also use the *labels* option to list names for each level/group. For gender, we want 24 females followed by 24 males, so we can specify it as:

```
gender<-gl(2, 24, labels = c("Female", "Male"))
```

The numbers in the function tell **R** that we want 2 groups of 24 cases, the labels option then specifies the names to attach to these two groups. To create the alcohol variable we want 3 groups that each contain 8 cases. This will create 24 cases ($3 \times 8 = 24$), or, put another way, it will create the codes for the first gender group (i.e., females). However, we want this pattern to be repeated for the second gender group also; we can do this by adding a third value to the function that is the total number of cases (i.e., 48). By specifying the total number of cases, the *gl()* function will repeat the pattern of 24 codes until it reaches this total number of cases – in other words if we specify 48 as the limit, it will repeat the pattern twice.

```
alcohol<-gl(3, 8, 48, labels = c("None", "2 Pints", "4 Pints"))
```

We can add the attractiveness values by creating a numeric variable in the usual way:

```
attractiveness<-c(65,70,60,60,60,55,60,55,70,65,60,70,65,60,
60,50,55,65,70,55,55,60,50,50,50,55,80,65,70,75,75,65,45,60,85,65,70,
70,80,60,30,30,30,55,35,20,45,40)
```

Finally, we can merge these variables into a dataframe called *gogglesData* by executing:

```
gogglesData<-data.frame(gender, alcohol, attractiveness)
```

12.5.5. Exploring the data ②

As ever, we'll look at some graphs first. Let's start with the means across the different conditions.

SELF-TEST

✓ Use *ggplot2* to plot a line graph (with error bars) of the attractiveness of the date with alcohol consumption on the *x*-axis and different-coloured lines to represent males and females.

The resulting plot (shown later in the chapter in Figure 12.8) is what is known as an **interaction graph**. These graphs are useful for interpreting significant interaction effects (should the analysis throw one up).

We can also look at boxplots for attractiveness scores for men and women at each level of alcohol consumption.

SELF-TEST

✓ Use *ggplot2* to plot boxplots of the attractiveness of the date at each level of alcohol consumption on the *x*-axis and different panels to represent males and females.

Figure 12.5 shows boxplots for these data. For females, the median score (the horizontal line in the middle of each box) does not change much across the doses of alcohol, and also the spread of their scores is relatively narrow; however, for males, the spread of scores is wider than for females, and the median attractiveness seems to fall dramatically after 4 pints.

FIGURE 12.5

Boxplots of the beer-goggles data

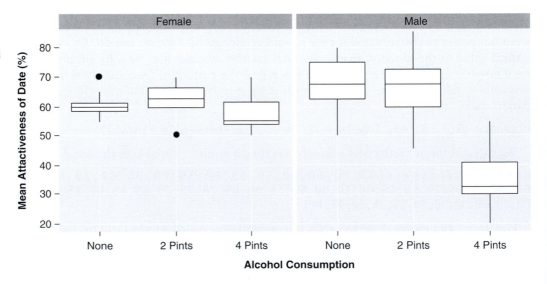

We have used the *by()* and *stat.desc()* functions before to get descriptive statistics for separate groups (see section 10.6.5 for more detail). Therefore, if we wanted to explore the effects of alcohol and gender on the attractiveness of the dates selected, we could do so by executing separate commands:

```
by(gogglesData$attractiveness, gogglesData$gender, stat.desc)
by(gogglesData$attractiveness, gogglesData$alcohol, stat.desc)
```

The resulting output is useful for interpreting the main effects of alcohol and gender on the attractiveness of mates. However, we are also interested in how these variables interact. This requires obtaining statistics for all combinations of **alcohol** and **gender**. To do this we need to use the *list()* function to create a list of variables that we can then feed into the *by()* function. If, for example, we execute *list(gogglesData$alcohol, gogglesData$gender)* we create a list (just like a shopping list) that contains the variables **alcohol** and **gender**. If we place this list within the *by()* function, then we will get descriptive statistics for all combinations of levels of the variables within the list. To see what I mean, execute:

```
by(gogglesData$attractiveness, list(gogglesData$alcohol,
gogglesData$gender), stat.desc)
```

The resulting (edited) output is in Output 12.2. Notice that the descriptive statistics are split by every combination of **gender** and **alcohol**, resulting in six different groups of information. So, for example, we can see that in the no-alcohol condition, males typically chatted up a female who was rated at about 67% on the attractiveness scale, whereas females selected a male who was rated as 61% on that scale. These means will be useful in interpreting the direction of any effects that emerge in the analysis.

```
: None
: Female
      median    mean    SE.mean CI.mean.0.95  var   std.dev   coef.var
      60.000   60.625   1.752     4.143      24.554 4.9551    0.0817
------------------------------------------------------------------
: 2 Pints
: Female
      median    mean    SE.mean CI.mean.0.95  var   std.dev   coef.var
      62.500   62.500  2.315     5.473       42.857 6.547     0.105
------------------------------------------------------------------
: 4 Pints
: Female
      median    mean    SE.mean CI.mean.0.95  var   std.dev   coef.var
      55.000   57.500  2.500     5.912       50.000 7.071     0.123
------------------------------------------------------------------
: None
: Male
      median    mean    SE.mean CI.mean.0.95  var   std.dev   coef.var
      67.500   66.875  3.652     8.636       106.696 10.329 0.154
------------------------------------------------------------------
: 2 Pints
: Male
median   mean    SE.mean CI.mean.0.95  var   std.dev   coef.var        67.500
66.875     4.426    10.465          156.696 12.518      0.187
------------------------------------------------------------------
: 4 Pints
: Male
      median   mean    SE.mean CI.mean.0.95  var   std.dev   coef.var
      32.500 35.625   3.831     9.059       117.411 10.836 0.304
```

Output 12.2

The final thing to do at this stage is to compute Levene's test (see Chapter 5 and section 10.3.1). We can again use the *leveneTest()* function from the *car* package here. If we want to do a Levene's test to see whether the variance in **attractiveness** differs across different gender and alcohol groups seperately, we can simply execute:

```
leveneTest(gogglesData$attractiveness, gogglesData$gender, center = median)
leveneTest(gogglesData$attractiveness, gogglesData$alcohol, center =
median)
```

However, as with the descriptive statistics, we're primarily interested in the interaction of these variables, so we would ideally like to know whether the variances differ across all six groups (not just the two gender groups and three alcohol groups). To do this, we can add the *interaction()* option to the *leveneTest()* function, which will compute Levene's test across any combination of groups for the variables specified within *interaction()*. In this case, we want to know whether the variances differ across all six groups that result from the combination of **gender** and **alcohol** (i.e., female_none, female_2 pints, female_4 pints, male_none, male_2 pints, male_4 pints). Therefore, we specify both variables within *interaction()*, that is, *interaction(gogglesData$alcohol, gogglesData$gender)*. The resulting command that we need to execute is therefore:

```
leveneTest(gogglesData$attractiveness,     interaction(gogglesData$alcohol,
gogglesData$gender), center = median)
```

Output 12.3 shows the results of Levene's test. We have encountered Levene's test numerous times before, so you should know that it tests whether there are any significant differences between group variances and so a non-significant result like the one we have here, $F(5, 42) = 1.425$, $p = .235$, is indicative of the assumption being met.

```
Levene's Test for Homogeneity of Variance
      Df F value Pr(>F)
group  5  1.4252 0.2351
      42
```

Output 12.3

12.5.6.   Choosing contrasts ②

We saw in Chapter 10 that it's useful to follow up ANOVA with contrasts that break down the main effects and tell us where the differences between groups lie. For one-way ANOVA, we entered codes that define the contrasts we want to do. We can follow the same procedure for factorial ANOVA except that we have to define contrasts for *all* of the independent variables. One very important consideration here is that if we want to look at Type III sums of squares (see Jane Superbrain Box 11.1) then *we must use an orthogonal contrast for these sums of squares to be computed correctly*.

We encountered an orthogonal contrast in Table 10.6: the Helmert contrast. This contrast will give you what you want in many different situations; however, if it doesn't and you want to define your own contrasts then this can be done in the same way as we discussed in Chapter 10 (see Oliver Twisted).

The effect of **gender** has only two levels, so we could code an orthogonal contrast as simply −1 (females) and 1 (males). Remember that when we code contrasts anything with a positive sign is compared to anything with a negative sign, so this contrast will compare males to females.

OLIVER TWISTED

Please Sir, can I have some more ... contrasts?

'This example is too similar to the one in Chapter 10', sulks Oliver as he stamps his feet on the floor. 'It smells of rotting cabbage.' I think actually, Oliver, the stench of rotting cabbage is probably because you stood your Dickensian self under a window when someone emptied his or her toilet bucket into the street. On the website I've prepared a different (slightly more complicated) example of how to specify your own contrasts to give you a bit more practice.

The effect of **alcohol** has three levels: none, 2 pints and 4 pints. The no-alcohol group is a control, so, following the advice from Chapter 10, our first contrast might compare the no-alcohol group to the remaining categories (that is, all of the groups that had some alcohol). We need a second contrast then to separate the two alcohol groups. The resulting codes are in Table 12.3; this scenario is basically the same as the Viagra data in Chapter 10 so reread that chapter if you don't understand the values in the table.

Table 12.3 Orthogonal contrasts for the **alcohol** variable

Group	$Contrast_1$	$Contrast_2$
No Alcohol	−2	0
2 Pints	1	−1
4 Pints	1	1

Setting contrasts for the two variables will also produce parameter estimates for the interaction term. So, in this case, we'll get not only a contrast comparing no alcohol to the combined effect of 2 and 4 pints, but also one that tests whether this effect is different in men and women. Similarly, contrast 2 tests whether the 2- and 4-pints groups differ, but we will also get a parameter estimate that tests whether the difference between the 2- and 4-pints groups is affected by the gender of the participant. To set the orthogonal contrasts we execute:

```
contrasts(gogglesData$alcohol)<-cbind(c(-2, 1, 1), c(0, -1, 1))
contrasts(gogglesData$gender)<-c(-1, 1)
```

The first command sets the two contrasts for **alcohol**, just as we did in Chapter 10; the second sets a single contrast for **gender**. We can check that we have set the contrast correctly by executing the name of the variable and looking at the contrast attribute:

```
> gogglesData$alcohol

attr(,"contrasts")
         [,1] [,2]
None       -2    0
2 Pints     1   -1
4 Pints     1    1
Levels: None 2 Pints 4 Pints

> gogglesData$gender
```

```
attr(,"contrasts")
        [,1]
Female   -1
Male      1
Levels: Female Male
```

Remembering that positive numbers are compared with negative and a zero means that the group is not involved at all, we can see that for alcohol we have set the first contrast to compare 'none' with the 2- and 4-pints groups (combined) and a second contrast that ignores the no-alcohol group and compares only the 2-pints against the 4-pints group.

12.5.7. Fitting a factorial ANOVA model ②

To create a factorial ANOVA model we can use the *aov()* function that we have used in the previous two chapters (see section 10.6.6.1). Remember that the *aov()* function is just the *lm()* function in disguise, so we can use what we learnt in Chapter 7 to add new variables into our ANOVA model. Remember, that to add a predictor, we simply write '+ variableName' into the model. In the current model we wish to predict **attractiveness** scores from both **gender** and **alcohol** so our model is simply 'attractiveness ~ gender + alcohol', isn't it? Actually, it's not, because we also need to include the interaction term. To specify an interaction term we link variable names with a colon. For example, the interaction of **gender** and **alcohol** would be written in **R** as *gender:alcohol* (or indeed *alcohol:gender*, it doesn't matter). Therefore, to specify the model including the interaction term, we could execute:

```
gogglesModel<-aov(attractiveness ~ gender + alcohol + gender:alcohol, data = gogglesData)
```

This command creates a model called *gogglesModel*, which includes the two independent variables and their interaction.

The above method is good because it makes very explicit the predictors in the model (and is a useful reminder that we're simply using a linear model, as we have throughout the book so far). However, there is a quicker method. You can include two variables and their interactions in a model by specifying *variable1*variable2* as the predictor. Doing so will enter not just the interaction but also the effects of the individual variables as well. So, for example, this command:

```
gogglesModel<-aov(attractiveness ~ alcohol*gender, data = gogglesData)
```

does exactly the same thing as the previous command (see R's Souls' Tip 12.1).

We had a fairly lengthy discussion about sums of squares in the previous chapter (see Jane Superbrain Box 11.1) and I refer you back there if what I'm about to say doesn't make any sense. If we want to look at the Type III sums of squares for the model, we need to also execute this command after we have created the model:

```
Anova(gogglesModel, type="III")
```

This takes the model that we have just created (*gogglesModel*) but, rather than displaying the Type I sums of squares (the default), it will show us the Type III sums of squares.

12.5.8. Interpreting factorial ANOVA ②

Output 12.4 tells us whether any of the independent variables have had an effect on the dependent variable. The important things to look at in the table are the significance values

R's Souls' Tip 12.1 Specifying more complex designs

It follows that if you have three independent variables then you can simply add the third variable into the model in the same way. For example, if we had also measured whether the **lighting** at the club was dim or bright (which would affect how well you could see your date), then we could specify the model as:

`gogglesModel<-aov(attractiveness ~ gender*alcohol*lighting, data = gogglesData)`

Note that we have used 'gender*alcohol*lighting' as the predictors, which will add in the three main effects but also all of the interactions between these variables.

of the independent variables. The first thing to notice is that there is a significant main effect of **alcohol** (because the significance value is less than .05). The F-ratio is highly significant, indicating that the amount of alcohol consumed significantly affected whom the participant would try to chat up. This means that overall, when we ignore whether the participant was male or female, the amount of alcohol influenced their mate selection. The best way to see what this means is to look at a bar chart of the average attractiveness at each level of alcohol (ignore gender completely). This graph displays the means in Output 12.2 that we calculated in section 12.4.2.2.

```
Anova Table (Type III tests)

Response: attractiveness
                Sum Sq Df    F value      Pr(>F)
(Intercept)     163333  1 1967.0251  < 2.2e-16 ***
gender             169  1    2.0323     0.1614
alcohol           3332  2   20.0654 7.649e-07 ***
gender:alcohol    1978  2   11.9113 7.987e-05 ***
Residuals         3488 42
```

Output 12.4

SELF-TEST

✓ Plot error bar graphs of the main effects of **alcohol** and **gender**.

Figure 12.6 clearly shows that when you ignore gender the overall attractiveness of the selected mate is very similar when no alcohol has been drunk and when 2 pints have been drunk (the means of these groups are approximately equal). Hence, this significant main effect is *likely* to reflect the drop in the attractiveness of the selected mates when 4 pints have been drunk. This finding seems to indicate that a person is willing to accept a less attractive mate after 4 pints.

Output 12.4 also tells us about the main effect of gender. This time the F-ratio is not significant ($p = .161$, which is larger than .05). This effect means that overall, when we ignore how much alcohol had been drunk, the gender of the participant did not influence the attractiveness of the partner that the participant selected. In other words, other things being equal, males and females selected equally attractive mates. The bar chart (that you have hopefully produced from the self-test) of the average attractiveness of mates for men and

FIGURE 12.6
Graph showing
the main effect of
alcohol

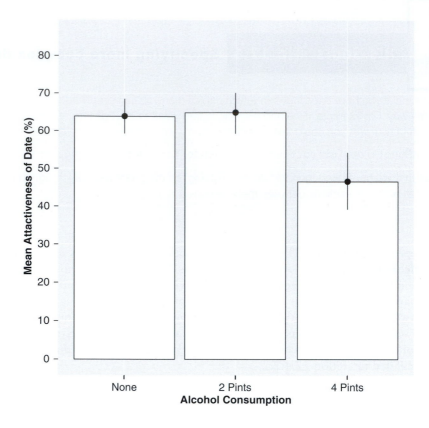

women (ignoring how much alcohol had been consumed) reveals the meaning of this main effect. Figure 12.7 plots the means in Output 12.2 that we calculated in section 12.4.2.1. This graph shows that the average attractiveness of the partners of male and female participants was fairly similar (the means are different by only 4%). Therefore, this non-significant effect reflects the fact that the mean attractiveness was similar. We can conclude from this that, other things being equal, men and women chose equally attractive partners.

Finally, Output 12.4 tells us about the interaction between the effect of **gender** and the effect of **alcohol**. The F-value is highly significant (because the p-value is less than .05). What this actually means is that the effect of alcohol on mate selection was different for male participants than it was for females. *In the presence of this significant interaction it makes no sense to interpret the main effects.* Figure 12.8 shows the plot that we produced earlier as a self-test task; this graph tells us something about the nature of this interaction effect.

Figure 12.8 shows that for women, alcohol has very little effect: the attractiveness of their selected partners is quite stable across the three conditions (as shown by the near-horizontal line). However, for the men, the attractiveness of their partners is stable when only a small amount has been drunk, but rapidly declines when 4 pints have been drunk. Non-parallel lines usually indicate a significant interaction effect. In this particular graph the lines actually cross, which indicates a fairly large interaction between independent variables. The lines tell us that alcohol has little effect on mate selection until 4 pints have been drunk and that the effect of alcohol is prevalent only in male participants. In short, the results show that women maintain high standards in their mate selection regardless of alcohol, whereas men have a few beers and then try to get off with anything on legs. One interesting point that these data demonstrate is that we earlier concluded that alcohol significantly affected how attractive a mate was selected (the **alcohol** main effect);

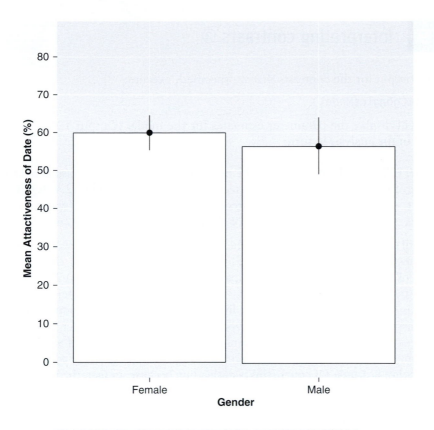

FIGURE 12.7
Graph to show the main effect of gender on mate selection

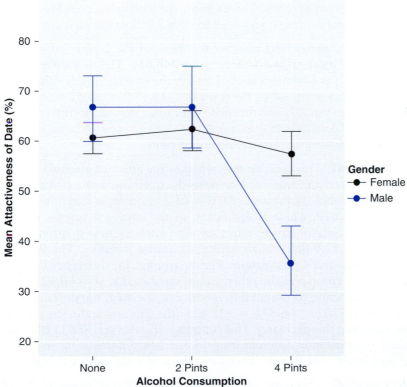

FIGURE 12.8
Graph of the interaction of gender and alcohol consumption in mate selection

however, the interaction effect tells us that this is true only in males (females appear unaffected). This shows why main effects should not be interpretted when a significant interaction involving those main effects exists.

12.5.9. Interpreting contrasts ②

To see the output for the contrasts that we specified, execute:

```
summary.lm(gogglesModel)
```

Doing so will display the parameter estimates for the model (Output 12.5). Let's look at each effect in the analysis in turn:

- **gender1**: This is the contrast for the main effect of gender; because gender has only two groups this is the same as the effect of **gender** from Output 12.4. (Quite literally, in fact: the t- and F-statistics are directly related by $F = t^2$. Our t-value for this contrast is -1.426, and the value of F for the effect of gender is $-1.426^2 = 2.03$).

- **alcohol1**: This contrast compares the no-alcohol group to the two alcohol groups. This tests whether the mean of the no-alcohol group (63.75) is different than the mean of the 2-pints and 4-pints groups combined $((64.69 + 46.56)/2 = 55.625)$. This is a difference of -8.125 ($55.63 - 63.75$). As explained in Chapter 10, the estimate for this difference is this difference divided by the number of groups involved in the contrast ($-8.125/3 = -2.708$). The p-value is .006, which is smaller than .05, indicating a significant difference. So we could conclude that the effect of alcohol is that any amount of alcohol reduces the attractiveness of the dates selected compared to when no alcohol is drunk. Of course this is misleading because, in fact, the means for the no-alcohol and 2-pints groups are fairly similar (63.75 and 64.69), so 2 pints of alcohol don't reduce the attractiveness of selected dates. The comparison is significant because it's testing the combined effect of 2 and 4 pints; 4 pints has such a drastic effect that it drags down the overall mean. This example shows why you need to be careful about how you interpret contrasts: you need to have a look at the next contrast as well.

- **alcohol2**: This contrast tests whether the mean of the 2-pints group (64.69) is different than the mean of the 4-pints group (46.56). This is a difference of -18.13 ($46.56 - 64.69$); as explained in Chapter 10, the estimate is this value divided by the number of groups involved in the contrast ($-18.13/2 = 9.06$). The p-value is .000, which is smaller than .05, and therefore indicates a significant difference between the groups. We can conclude that having 4 pints significantly reduced the attractiveness of selected dates compared to having only 2 pints.

- **gender1:alcohol1**: This contrast tests whether the effect of **alcohol1** described above is different in men and women. It answers the question: is the effect of alcohol compared to no alcohol on the attractiveness of dates comparable in men and women? The p-value is .010, which is significant, so the answer is no, the extent to which alcohol vs. no alcohol has an effect on date attractiveness is different in men and women. Figure 12.9 (left) shows what this contrast is testing. The 'Alcohol' group is the combined 2- and 4-pints groups. For the women, the difference in means between the no-alcohol group and the other groups combined is $60 - 60.625 = -0.625$ (the line is flat, reflecting this small difference). For the men, the difference between the two means is $51.25 - 66.875 = -15.625$ (the line for males on the graph slopes down, reflecting this decrease). This contrast tests whether -0.625 (the difference for females) is significantly different from 15.625 (the difference for males). In terms of the graph, it tests whether the lines for males and females have different slopes.

- **gender1:alcohol2**: This contrast tests whether the effect of **alcohol2** described above is different in men and women. It answers the question: is the effect of 2 pints compared to 4 pints on the attractiveness of dates comparable in men and women? The p-value is .000, which is significant, so the answer is no, the extent to which 2 vs. 4

pints has an effect on date attractiveness is different in men and women). Figure 12.9 (right) shows what this contrast is testing. For the women, the difference in means between the 2- and 4-pints groups is 57.50 – 62.50 = –5 (the line slopes down slightly). For the men, the difference between the two means is 35.625 – 66.875 = –31.25 (the line for males on the graph slopes down much more than for females). This contrast tests whether –5 (the difference for females) is significantly different from –31.25 (the difference for males). In terms of the graph, it tests whether the lines for males and females have different slopes.

```
Coefficients:
                  Estimate Std. Error t value Pr(>|t|)
(Intercept)         58.333      1.315  44.351  < 2e-16  ***
gender1             -1.875      1.315  -1.426 0.161382
alcohol1            -2.708      0.930  -2.912 0.005727  **
alcohol2            -9.062      1.611  -5.626 1.37e-06 ***
gender1:alcohol1    -2.500      0.930  -2.688 0.010258  *
gender1:alcohol2    -6.562      1.611  -4.074 0.000201 ***
```

Output 12.5

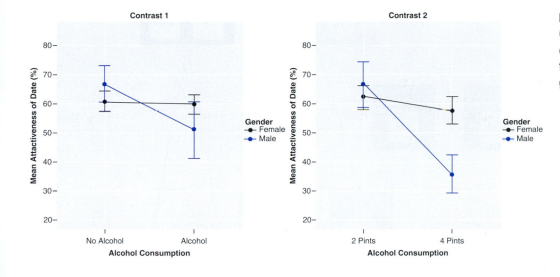

FIGURE 12.9
Graphical displays of the contrasts for the beer-goggles data

12.5.10. Simple effects analysis ③

A popular way to break down an interaction term is to use a technique called **simple effects analysis.** This analysis looks at the effect of one independent variable at individual levels of the other independent variable. So, for example, in our beer-goggles data we could do simple effects analysis looking at the effect of gender at each level of alcohol. This would mean taking the average attractiveness of the date selected by men and comparing it to that for women after no drinks, then making the same comparison for 2 pints and then finally for 4 pints. Another way of looking at this is to say we would compare each black dot to the corresponding blue dot in Figure 12.8: based on the graph, we might expect to find no difference after no alcohol and after 2 pints (in both cases the black and blue dots are located in about the same position) but we would expect a difference after 4 pints (because the black and blue dots are quite far apart). The alternative way to do it would be to compare the mean attractiveness after no alcohol, 2 pints and 4 pints for men and then in a separate analysis do the same but for women. (This would be a bit like doing a one-way ANOVA on the effect of alcohol in men, and then doing a different one-way ANOVA for the effect of alcohol in women.)

OLIVER TWISTED

Please Sir, can I have some more … simple effects?

'I want to impress my friends by doing a simple effects analysis by hand', boasts Oliver. You don't really need to know how simple effects analyses are calculated to run them, Oliver, but seeing as you asked, it is explained in the additional material available from the companion website.

FIGURE 12.10
Schematic representation of the contrasts and codes for simple effects analysis on the goggles data

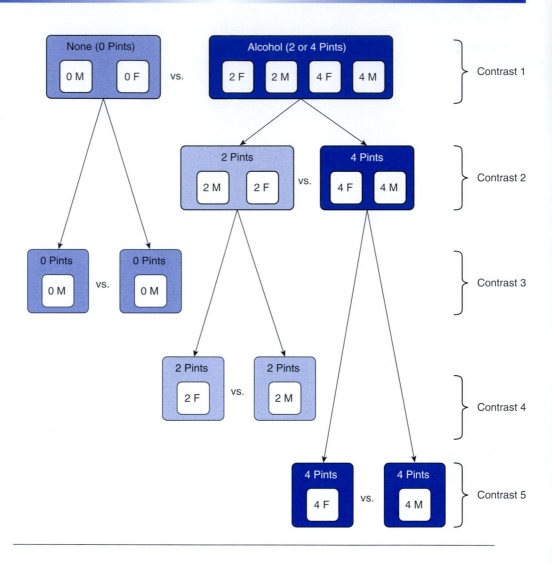

	0 M	0 F	2 F	2 M	4 F	4 M
Contrast 1	−2	−2	1	1	1	1
Contrast 2	0	0	−1	−1	1	1
Contrast 3	−1	1	0	0	0	0
Contrast 4	0	0	1	−1	0	0
Contrast 5	0	0	0	0	−1	1

Simple effect of Gender { Contrast 3, Contrast 4, Contrast 5

R's Souls' Tip 12.2   Simple effects analysis in R ③

Unfortunately, simple effects are not that easy to do in **R**. The first thing we need to do is create a variable in the dataframe that merges the variables of interest into a single factor. In other words, rather than have **alcohol** and **gender** as separate variables, we want a new variable that simply codes the six groups that result from combining all levels of **alcohol** and **gender**. We can do this using the *gl()* function to add a variable (*simple*) to the dataframe that is six groups each containing eight observations:

```
gogglesData$simple<-gl(6,8)
```

We can then use the *factor()* function to specify labels for these six groups:

```
gogglesData$simple<-factor(gogglesData$simple, levels = c(1:6), labels = c("F_
None","F_2pints", "F_4pints","M_None","M_2pints", "M_4pints"))
```

The data now look like this (I've edited out cases to save space):

```
   gender alcohol  alcohol2 attractiveness    simple
1  Female    None No Alcohol             65   F_None
2  Female    None No Alcohol             70   F_None
...   ...     ...       ...             ...      ...
9  Female 2 Pints    Alcohol             70 F_2pints
10 Female 2 Pints    Alcohol             65 F_2pints
...   ...     ...       ...             ...      ...
17 Female 4 Pints    Alcohol             55 F_4pints
18 Female 4 Pints    Alcohol             65 F_4pints
...   ...     ...       ...             ...      ...
25   Male    None No Alcohol             50   M_None
26   Male    None No Alcohol             55   M_None
...   ...     ...       ...             ...      ...
33   Male 2 Pints    Alcohol             45 M_2pints
34   Male 2 Pints    Alcohol             60 M_2pints
...   ...     ...       ...             ...      ...
47   Male 4 Pints    Alcohol             45 M_4pints
48   Male 4 Pints    Alcohol             40 M_4pints
```

Note that we have added the variable *simple*, which codes whether a person was male or female and how much alcohol they had in a single variable.

Next, we create contrasts that break these six groups up using the standard rules for planned contrasts. Figure 12.10 shows how we would break the groups up into five contrasts to do a simple effects analysis of **gender**. The first contrast compares no alcohol to alcohol (2 or 4 pints combined). Remember that these two 'chunks' of variation are made up of the different gender groups and so need to be broken down further. For example, the no-alcohol group is made up of the males that had no alcohol ('0 M') and the females that had no alcohol ('0 F'), and the alcohol chunk contains the males and females that had 2 pints ('2 M' and '2 F') and the males and females that had 4 pints ('4 M' and '4 F'). The second contrast breaks down the 'alcohol' chunk to compare 2 pints against 4 pints. Again, remember that both chunks at this stage are made up of the two corresponding gender groups. The third contrast takes the no-alcohol 'chunk' and compares the two gender groups contained within it. This contrast is the simple effect of gender when no alcohol was consumed. The fourth contrast takes the 2-pint 'chunk' and breaks the variance down to compare the two gender groups contained within it. This contrast is the simple effect of gender when 2 pints were consumed. Finally, the fifth contrast takes the 4-pint 'chunk' and compares the two gender groups contained within it. This contrast is the simple effect of gender

(Continued)

(Continued)

when 4 pints were consumed. If you look back to Chapter 10 you'll see that these contrasts conform to the rules of orthogonal contrasts, and that the codes in Figure 12.10 specify the contrasts.

To create these contrasts in **R** we can create five variables (one for each contrast) that contain the codes for the respective groups. (Bear in mind that in the dataframe the groups are ordered as: female none, female 2 pints, female 4 pints, male none, male 2 pints, male 4 pints, and we have to order the codes accordingly.) I have also labelled the contrasts in a way that tells us something about what they represent:

```
alcEffect1<-c(-2, 1, 1, -2, 1, 1)
alcEffect2<-c(0, -1, 1, 0, -1, 1)
gender_none<-c(-1, 0, 0, 1, 0, 0)
gender_twoPint<-c(0, -1, 0, 0, 1, 0)
gender_fourPint<-c(0, 0, -1, 0, 0, 1)
```

To tidy things up lets merge these variables into an object called *simpleEff*:

```
simpleEff<-cbind(alcEffect1, alcEffect2, gender_none, gender_twoPint, gender_fourPint)
```

We can now set the contrasts for the variable **simple** to be this object:

```
contrasts(gogglesData$simple)<-simpleEff
```

We then create a new model in which **attractiveness** is predicted from **simple** (which, remember, contains both the effects of alcohol and gender but coded so that the contrasts give us simple effects):

```
simpleEffectModel<-aov(attractiveness ~ simple, data = gogglesData)
```

To see the contrasts we use *summary.lm()* on the newly created model:

```
summary.lm(simpleEffectModel)
```

The resulting output contains the parameter estimates for the five contrasts. Looking at the significance values for each simple effect, it appears that there was no significant difference between men and women when they drank no alcohol, $p = .177$, or when they drank 2 pints, $p = .34$, but there was a very significant difference, $p < .001$, when 4 pints were consumed (which, judging from the interaction graph, reflects the fact that the mean for men is considerably lower than for women).

```
Coefficients:
                      Estimate Std. Error t value Pr(>|t|)
(Intercept)             58.333      1.315  44.351  < 2e-16 ***
simplealcEffect1        -2.708      0.930  -2.912  0.00573 **
simplealcEffect2        -9.062      1.611  -5.626 1.37e-06 ***
simplegender_none        3.125      2.278   1.372  0.17742
simplegender_twoPint     2.188      2.278   0.960  0.34243
simplegender_fourPint  -10.938      2.278  -4.801 2.02e-05 ***
```

12.5.11. *Post hoc* analysis ②

The variable **alcohol** has three levels and so you might want to perform *post hoc* tests to see where the differences between groups lie. I want to stress again that the significant main effect of alcohol that we observed should not be interpreted given the significant interaction with gender. Therefore, I'm covering *post hoc* tests here for illustrative purposes: if this was a real piece of research I would focus on the interaction effect and not perform *post hoc* tests on **alcohol**.

We saw in Chapter 10 that we can specify Bonferroni *post hoc* tests using the *pairwise.t.test()* function and Tukey tests using *glht()*. Refer back to that chapter for details of these functions, but for the present example we could obtain *post hoc* tests for alcohol by executing either of these commands:

```
pairwise.t.test(gogglesData$attractiveness, gogglesData$alcohol, p.adjust.
method = "bonferroni")
postHocs<-glht(gogglesModel, linfct = mcp(alcohol = "Tukey"))
summary(postHocs)
confint(postHocs)
```

The resulting *post hoc* tests are shown in Outputs 12.6 (Bonferroni) and 12.7 (Tukey); they both break down the main effect of **alcohol** and can be interpreted as if a one-way ANOVA had been conducted on the **alcohol** variable (i.e., the reported effects for alcohol are collapsed with regard to gender). The Bonferroni and Tukey tests show the same pattern of results: when participants had drunk no alcohol or 2 pints of alcohol, they selected equally attractive mates. However, after 4 pints had been consumed, participants selected significantly less attractive mates than after both 2 pints ($p < .001$) and no alcohol ($p < .001$). It is interesting to note that the mean attractiveness of partners after no alcohol and 2 pints was so similar that the probability of the obtained difference between those means is 1 (i.e., completely probable).

```
        Pairwise comparisons using t tests with pooled SD
data:   gogglesData$attractiveness and gogglesData$alcohol

        None     2 Pints
2 Pints 1.00000  -
4 Pints 0.00024  0.00011

P value adjustment method: bonferroni
```

Output 12.6

```
        Simultaneous Tests for General Linear Hypotheses

Multiple Comparisons of Means: Tukey Contrasts

Fit: aov(formula = attractiveness ~ gender + alcohol + gender:alcohol,
    data = gogglesData)

Linear Hypotheses:
                    Estimate Std. Error t value Pr(>|t|)
2 Pints - None == 0   0.9375     3.2217   0.291    0.954
4 Pints - None == 0 -17.1875     3.2217  -5.335 1.01e-05 ***
4 Pints - 2 Pints == 0 -18.1250  3.2217  -5.626  < 1e-05 ***
---
Signif. codes:  0 '***' 0.001 '**' 0.01 '*' 0.05 '.' 0.1 ' ' 1
(Adjusted p values reported -- single-step method)


> confint(postHocs)

        Simultaneous Confidence Intervals

Multiple Comparisons of Means: Tukey Contrasts

Fit: aov(formula = attractiveness ~ gender + alcohol + gender:alcohol,
    data = gogglesData)
```

```
Quantile = 2.4303
95% family-wise confidence level


Linear Hypotheses:
                        Estimate  lwr       upr
2 Pints - None == 0      0.9375   -6.8921    8.7671
4 Pints - None == 0    -17.1875  -25.0171   -9.3579
4 Pints - 2 Pints == 0 -18.1250  -25.9546  -10.2954
```

Output 12.7

12.5.12.　Overall conclusions ②

In summary, we should conclude that alcohol has an effect on the attractiveness of selected mates. Overall, after a relatively small dose of alcohol (2 pints) humans are still in control of their judgements and the attractiveness levels of chosen partners are consistent with a control group (no alcohol consumed). However, after a greater dose of alcohol, the attractiveness of chosen mates decreases significantly. This effect is what is referred to as the 'beer-goggles effect'. More interesting, the interaction shows a gender difference in the beer-goggles effect. Specifically, it looks as though men are significantly more likely to pick less attractive mates when drunk. Women, in comparison, manage to maintain their standards despite being drunk. What we still don't know is whether women will become susceptible to the beer-goggles effect at higher doses of alcohol.

12.5.13.　Plots in factorial ANOVA ②

We saw in the previous two chapters that the *aov()* function automatically generates some plots that we can use to test the assumptions. We can see these graphs by executing:

`plot(gogglesModel)`

The results are in Figure 12.11. The first graph (on the left) can be used for testing homogeneity of variance: if it has a funnel shape then we're in trouble. The plot we have does show funnelling (the spread of scores is wider at some points than at others), which implies that the residuals might be heteroscedastic (a bad thing). The second plot (on the right) is a Q-Q plot (see Chapter 5), which tells us about the normality of residuals in the model. We want our residuals to be normally distributed, which means that the dots on the graph should hover around the diagonal line. On our plot this is the case, suggesting that we can assume normality of our residuals/errors.

12.6.　Interpreting interaction graphs ②

Interactions are very important, and the key to understanding them is being able to interpret interaction graphs. We've already had a look at one interaction graph when we interpreted the analysis in this chapter. We used Figure 12.8 to conclude that the interaction probably reflected the fact that men and women chose equally attractive dates after no alcohol and 2 pints, but that at 4 pints men's standards dropped significantly more than

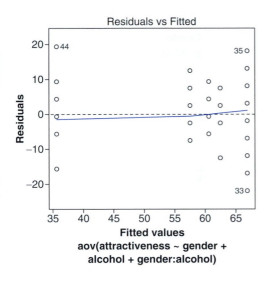

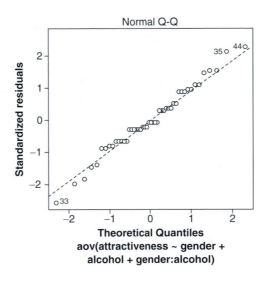

FIGURE 12.11
Plots of the beer-goggles model

CRAMMING SAM'S TIPS   Two-way independent ANOVA

- Two-way independent ANOVA compares several means when there are two independent variables and different participants have been used in all experimental conditions. For example, if you wanted to know whether different teaching methods worked better for different subjects, you could take students from four courses (Psychology, Geography, Management and Statistics) and assign them to either lecture-based or book-based teaching. The two variables are course and method of teaching. The outcome might be the end of year mark (as a percentage).

- Test for homogeneity of variance using *Levene's test*. If the *p*-value is less than .05 then the assumption is violated.

- A 'main effect' is the effect of a variable in isolation, whereas an 'interaction' represents the combined effect of two or more variables.

- In the main analysis you'll get a summary table containing a main effect of each predictor variable and an effect of the interaction between the two variables; if the *p*-value is less than .05 then the effect is significant. For main effects consult *post hoc* tests to see which groups differ, and for the interaction look at contrasts, an interaction graph or conduct simple effects analysis. If the interaction effect is significant it makes little sense to interpret or do further analysis on the main effects.

- For *post hoc* tests, look at the *p*-value of each test to discover if your comparisons are significant (they will be if the significance value is less than .05).

- Test the same assumptions as for one-way independent ANOVA (see Chapter 10).

women's. Imagine we'd got the profile of results shown in Figure 12.12; do you think we would've still got a significant interaction effect?

This profile of data probably would also give rise to a significant interaction term because, although the attractiveness of men and women's dates is similar after no alcohol and 4 pints of alcohol, there is a big difference after 2 pints. This reflects a scenario in which the beer-goggles effect is equally big in men and women after 4 pints (and doesn't exist after no alcohol) but kicks in quicker for men: the attractiveness of their dates plummets after 2 pints, whereas women maintain their standards until 4 pints (at which point they'd happily date an unwashed skunk). Let's try another example. Is there a significant interaction in Figure 12.13?

FIGURE 12.12
Another interaction
graph

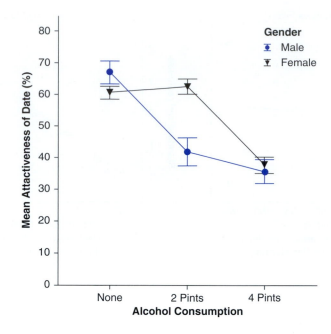

FIGURE 12.13
A 'lack of'
interaction graph

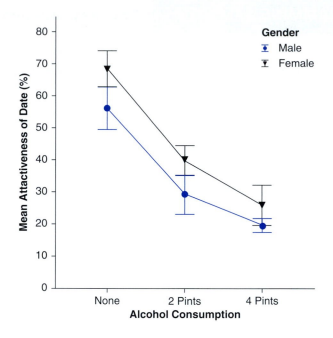

For the data in Figure 12.13 there is unlikely to be a significant interaction because the effect of alcohol is the same for men and women. So, for both men and women, the attractiveness of their dates after no alcohol is quite high, but after 2 pints all types drop by a similar amount (the slope of the male and female lines is about the same). After 4 pints there is a further drop and, again, this drop is about the same in men and women (the lines again slope at about the same angle). The fact that the line for males is lower than for females just reflects the fact that across all conditions, men have lower standards than their female counterparts: this reflects a main effect of gender (i.e., males generally chose less attractive dates than females at all levels of alcohol). There are two general points that we can make from these examples:

- Non-parallel lines on an interaction graph imply significant interactions. However, it's important to remember that this doesn't mean that non-parallel lines automatically mean that the interaction is significant: whether the interaction is significant will depend on the degree to which the lines are not parallel.

- If the lines on an interaction graph cross then obviously they are not parallel and this can give away a possible significant interaction. However, contrary to popular belief, it isn't *always* the case that if the lines of the interaction graph cross then the interaction is significant.

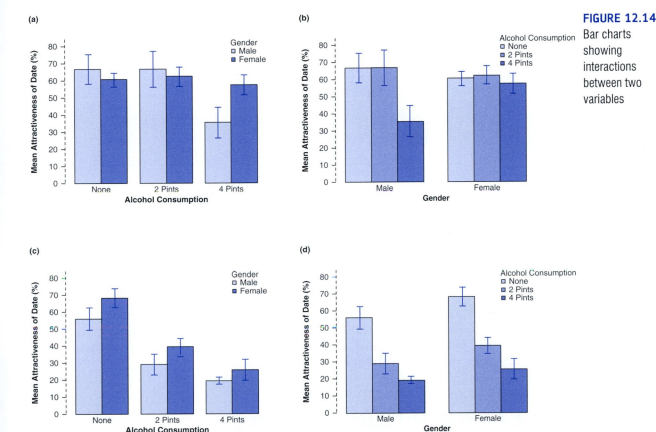

FIGURE 12.14
Bar charts showing interactions between two variables

A further complication is that sometimes people draw bar charts rather than line charts. Figure 12.14 shows some bar charts of interactions between two independent variables. Panels (a) and (b) actually display the data from the example used in this chapter (in fact, why not have a go at plotting them). As you can see, there are two ways to present the same data: panel (a) shows the data when levels of alcohol are placed along the *x*-axis and different-coloured bars are used to show means for males and females, and panel (b) shows the opposite scenario in which gender is plotted on the *x*-axis and different colours distinguish the dose of alcohol. Both of these graphs show an interaction effect.

What you're looking for is for the differences between coloured bars to be different at different points along the *x*-axis. So, for panel (a) you'd look at the difference between the light and dark blue bars for no alcohol, and then look to 2 pints and ask, 'Is the difference between the bars different than when I looked at no alcohol?' In this case the dark and light blue bars look the same at no alcohol as they do at 2 pints – hence, no interaction. However, we'd then move on to look at 4 pints, and we'd again ask, 'Is the difference between the light and dark blue bars different than what it has been in any of the other conditions?' In this case the answer is yes: for no alcohol and 2 pints, the light and dark blue bars were about the same height, but at 4 pints the dark blue bar is much higher than the light one. This shows an interaction: the pattern of responses changes at 4 pints. Panel (b) shows the same thing but plotted the other way around. Again we look at the pattern of responses. So, first we look at the men and see that the pattern is that the first two bars are the same height, but the last bar is much shorter. The interaction effect is shown up by the fact that for the women there is a different pattern: all three bars are about the same height.

SELF-TEST

✓ What about panels (c) and (d): do you think there is an interaction?

Again, they display the same data in two different ways, but it's different data than what we've used in this chapter. First let's look at panel (c): for the no-alcohol data, the dark bar is a little bit bigger than the light one; moving on to the 2-pints data, the dark bar is also a little bit taller than the light bar; and finally for the 4-pints data the dark bar is again higher than the light one. In all conditions the same pattern is shown – the dark blue bar is a bit higher than the light blue one (i.e., females pick more attractive dates than men regardless of alcohol consumption) – therefore, there is no interaction. Looking at panel (d), we see a similar result. For men, the pattern is that attractiveness ratings fall as more alcohol is drunk (the bars decrease in height) and then for the women we see the same pattern: ratings fall as more is drunk. This again is indicative of no interaction: the change in attractiveness due to alcohol is similar in men and women.

12.7. Robust factorial ANOVA ③

As with one-way ANOVA, Wilcox (2005) describes robust procedures for conducting factorial ANOVA. To access these we need to load the *WRS* package (see section 5.8.4.). There are four functions that we will look at:

- **t2way()**: This performs a two-way independent ANOVA on trimmed means.
- **mcp2atm()**: This performs *post hoc* tests for a two-way independent design based on trimmed means.
- **pbad2way()**: This performs a two-way independent ANOVA using M-measures of location (e.g., the median) and a bootstrap.
- **mcp2a()**: This performs *post hoc* tests for the above function.

The first problem we have is that these functions need the data to be in wide format rather than long (see Chapter 3). Figure 12.15 shows the existing data format (long) and how we need it to look (wide). Essentially we want levels of our two factors to be represented in different columns. Therefore, rather than a dataframe with three columns and 48 rows, we want one with six columns and eight rows.

We could re-enter the data in the wide format (which is very tempting when you've spent half an hour trying to work out how to get **R** to restructure it for you), but we're going to look at how to use *melt()* and *cast()* to do the restructuring for us. To get the restructuring to work, we need to add a variable to our dataframe that identifies the rows in the wide format. Notice in Figure 12.15 that the data are made up of six chunks that represent the combinations of **gender** and **alcohol**, and each chunk contains eight rows. We want to move these chunks from being stacked on top of each other to being beside each other. To do this, **R** needs to know what row a particular score will end up in when we move each block of scores from the stack into the columns. The easiest approach is simply to create a variable (called **row**) that identifies within each chunk the row number of a given score. In other words, it will be a value from 1 to 8 telling us whether the score is the first, second, third, etc. score within the chunk. At the moment, the chunks are stacked on top of each other so we want a variable that is the sequence of numbers 1 to 8 repeated for each of the six chunks. We can add this variable to the dataframe by executing:

```
gogglesData$row<-rep(1:8, 6)
```

This command uses the *rep()* function to create a variable **row** in the dataframe *gogglesData*, that is, the numbers 1 to 8 repeated six times (*rep(1:8, 6)*). The dataframe now looks like this (edited):

```
   gender alcohol attractiveness row
1  Female    None             65   1
2  Female    None             70   2
3  Female    None             60   3
4  Female    None             60   4
5  Female    None             60   5
6  Female    None             55   6
7  Female    None             60   7
8  Female    None             55   8
9  Female 2 Pints             70   1
10 Female 2 Pints             65   2
11 Female 2 Pints             60   3
12 Female 2 Pints             70   4
13 Female 2 Pints             65   5
14 Female 2 Pints             60   6
15 Female 2 Pints             60   7
16 Female 2 Pints             50   8
```

Note that the structure is the same as before – it's just that we have a new variable called **row** that identifies the scores within each combination of **gender** and **alcohol** as a value from 1 to 8.

Now we have changed the data set we need to make it molten so that we can cast the data into the wide format. To do this we use the *melt()* function (see section 3.9.4). Remember that in this function we differentiate variables that identify attributes of the scores (in this case, **gender**, **alcohol**, and **row** all tell us about a given attractiveness score, for example, that it was the first score in the male group who drank 2 pints) from the scores or measured variables themselves. Attributes are specified with the *id* option, and scores with the *measured* option. Therefore, we can create a molten dataframe called *gogglesMelt* by executing:

```
gogglesMelt<-melt(gogglesData, id = c("row", "gender", "alcohol"), measured =
c("attractiveness"))
```

FIGURE 12.15
Restructuring the
data for robust
factorial ANOVA

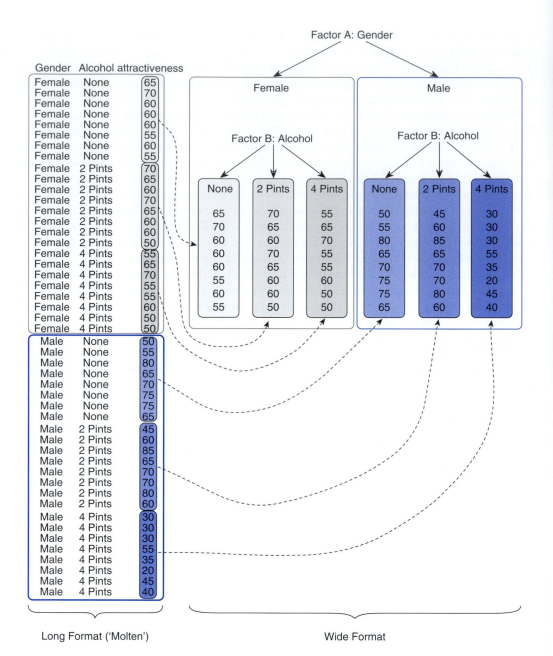

FIGURE 12.15
Restructuring the data for robust factorial ANOVA

Having melted the data, we want to cast it in the wide format using *cast()*. To do this we use a formula in the form: *variables specifying the rows ~ variables specifying the columns*. In this case, **row** tells us in which row to place a score, and we want the alcohol and gender variables split across different columns, so we'd use the formula: *row ~ gender + alcohol*. Therefore, we can make a wide dataframe called *gogglesWide* by executing:

```
gogglesWide<-cast(gogglesMelt,  row ~ gender + alcohol)
```

Note that we have applied this command to the molten data set (*gogglesMelt*). The result is that the data have been transformed from the long format to the wide format. However, because we added the variable **row** to the dataframe, our new dataframe also contains this variable, and for the analysis we want only the **alcohol** and **gender** variables, therefore, we want to remove **row**. We can do this by executing:

```
gogglesWide$row<-NULL
```

which basically zaps the variable **row** into oblivion. If you look at the dataframe you'll see a lovely wide format set of data:

```
gogglesWide
```

F_None	F_2 Pints	F_4 Pints	M_None	M_2 Pints	M_4 Pints
65	70	55	50	45	30
70	65	65	55	60	30
60	60	70	80	85	30
60	70	55	65	65	55
60	65	55	70	70	35
55	60	60	75	70	20
60	60	50	75	80	45
55	50	50	65	60	40

It's important to note the order of the columns because this affects how we specify the robust analysis. In this case, the hierarchy of the independent variables is **gender** followed by **alcohol**. In other words, we have taken the six groups and first divided them into male and female, then within the male and female groups we have subdivided according to the amount of alcohol they drank. We would say that **gender** is factor A and **alcohol** factor B. If this idea is not clear then Figure 12.15 might help you to visualize it. As such, the order of the columns reflects a 2 × 3 design (2 levels of gender divided up into 3 levels of alcohol). If the columns were ordered as F_None, M_None, F 2 Pints, M 2 Pints, F 4 Pints, M 4 Pints, then we would have a 3 × 2 design (3 levels of alcohol each divided up into 2 levels of gender). In this case factor A would be **alcohol** and factor B **gender**.

The function *t2way()* takes the general form:

```
t2way(levels of factor A, levels of factor B, data, tr = .2, alpha = .05)
```

As with other functions we've encountered, the level of trimming is by default 20% (*tr* = .2) but can be changed by including the *tr* = option. Also the default alpha level is .05 but can be changed by including the *alpha* = option. Assuming we are happy with the default level of trimming, we need only specify the dataframe (*gogglesWide*) and the levels of factor A (2 in this case as explained above) and factor B (3 in this case). Therefore, we can do a robust two-way factorial ANOVA based on trimmed means by executing:

```
t2way(2,3, gogglesWide)
```

The function *pbad2way()* has a similar format:

```
pbad2way(levels of factor A, levels of factor B, data, est = mom, nboot = 2000)
```

The main differences are an option to control the number of bootstrap samples (*nboot*), although the default of 2000 is fine, and an option *est* to control the M-estimator that you want to use. You can use *est = median* (to use the median) or *est = mom* (to use a method based on identifying and removing outliers). In smaller samples you might find that *est = mom* throws up an error message, in which case switch to *est = median*. If we're happy with 2000 bootstrap samples and using *mom* rather than *median* then we can run the analysis for the current data by executing:[2]

```
pbad2way(2,3, gogglesWide)
```

The output of both of these commands is shown in Output 12.8. For *t2way()* (left-hand side of Output 12.8) we are given a test statistic for factor A (*$Qa*), factor B (*$Qb*) and their interaction (*$Qab*) as well as the corresponding *p*-value (*$A.p.value*, *$B.p.value*, and

---

[2] If you want to compare medians then execute:
```
pbad2way(2,3, gogglesWide, est = median)
```

$AB.p.value respectively). Remember that factor A was gender and factor B alcohol; therefore, we could conclude that there was no significant main effect of gender, $Q = 1.67$, $p = .209$, but there was a significant main effect of alcohol, $Q = 48.28$, $p = .001$, and a significant gender × alcohol interaction, $Q = 26.26$, $p = .001$. The bottom of the output shows the trimmed means on which these results are based: factor A (gender) is represented by rows, and factor B (alcohol) by columns. So, for example, the trimmed mean of the attractiveness score for females who drank 2 pints was 63.3.

The output of *pbad2way()* (right-hand side of Output 12.8) tells us much the same things but we get only *p*-values and no test statistics: there was no significant main effect of gender, $p = .171$, but there was a significant main effect of alcohol, $p < .001$, and a significant gender × alcohol interaction, $p < .001$.

t2way()	pbad2way()

`$Qa      $sig.levelA`
`[1] 1.666667  [1] 0.171`
 	
`$A.p.value     $sig.levelB`
`[1] 0.209      [1] 0`
 	
`$Qb     $sig.levelAB`
`[1] 48.2845   [1] 5e-04`
 	
`$B.p.value`
`[1] 0.001`
 	
`$Qab`
`[1] 26.25718`
 	
`$AB.p.value`
`[1] 0.001`
 	
`$means`
`      [,1]      [,2]       [,3]`
`[1,] 60.0 63.33333 56.66667`
`[2,] 67.5 67.50000 35.00000`	

Output 12.8

The *post hoc* tests for each analysis are conducted using the same command structure. That is, we define the number of levels of factor A, then factor B, then indicate the dataframe. Therefore, to run *post hoc* tests based on a 20% trimmed mean, we execute:[3]

```
mcp2atm(2,3, gogglesWide)
```

To conduct *post hoc* tests based on an M-estimator we execute:[4]

```
mcp2a(2,3, gogglesWide)
```

Output 12.9 shows the *post hoc* tests based on trimmed means (*mcp2atm*). The main effect of gender is tested by *$Factor.A$test* and *$Factor.A$psihat*. We have two choices.

---

[3] Obviously if you changed the level of trim for the main analysis you would need to do the same here. For example, for 10% trimmed means:

```
t2way(2,3, gogglesWide, tr = .1)
```
```
mcp2atm(2,3, gogglesWide, tr = .1)
```

[4] Remember that if you chose the median as your M-estimator then you would need to execute:

```
mcp2a(2,3, gogglesWide, est = median)
```

The first is to interpret the value in the column labelled *test* against the critical value (*crit*): if the test value is larger than the critical value then the test is significant (at $p < .05$). In this case, 1.29 is smaller than 2.06 so the result is non-significant. The second choice is to interpret *psihat* and its confidence interval and *p*-value. We should focus on interpreting the confidence interval because (unlike the *p*-value) it is corrected for the number of tests. In this case the confidence interval crosses zero, which indicates a non-significant result. These tests of gender, because it contains only two levels, basically just confirm what we already know from the main analysis.

The effect of alcohol (*$Factor.B$test* and *$Factor.B$psihat*) is more interesting because it breaks down the main effect of alcohol. There are three contrasts to interpret, but how do we know what they mean? To interpret these contrasts we need to look at the contrast codes for factor A, B and the interaction at the bottom of the output. The rows labelled [1,] … [6,] relate to the six columns of data. In other words they are: F_None, F_2 Pints, F_4 Pints, M_None, M_2 Pints, M_4 Pints. Remembering that groups with positive codes are compared against groups with negative codes, *$conA* tells us that A was the effect of gender (you have the three female groups coded with 1 and the three male groups coded with −1). Similarly, *$conB* tells us that B was the effect of alcohol split into three contrasts. Each contrast is in a separate column. We could rewrite this matrix as:

	Con1	Con2	Con3
F_None	1	1	0
F_2 Pints	-1	0	1
F_4 Pints	0	-1	-1
M_None	1	1	0
M_2 Pints	-1	0	1
M_4 Pints	0	-1	-1

Remembering that 0 means that the group is not involved, and that positives are compared to negatives, the first contrast (column 1) compares 2 pints to none, the second contrast (column 2) is 4 pints compared to none, and the third (column 3) is 2 pints compared to 4 pints).

Finally, the codes for the interaction (*$conAB*) are the same as for the main effect of alcohol except that the plus and minus signs are reversed for males and females, which tests whether the effect of alcohol differs across gender. In other words, contrast 1 compares whether the difference between 2 pints and no alcohol is different in men and women.

For the main effect of alcohol, contrast 1 is not significant (−0.52 is smaller than 2.68 and the confidence interval for *psihat* crosses zero), but contrasts 2 (5.75 is greater than 2.65 and the confidence interval for *psihat* does not contain zero) and 3 (6.18 is greater than 2.64 and the confidence interval for *psihat* does not contain zero) are. This indicates a significant difference in attractiveness scores for 4 pints compared to both no alcohol and 2 pints, but not between 2 pints and no alcohol.

For the interaction term, we get the same profile of results: contrast 1 is not significant (−0.52 is smaller than 2.68 and the confidence interval for *psihat* crosses zero), but contrasts 2 (−4.68 is greater than 2.65 – you can ignore the minus sign – and the confidence interval for *psihat* does not contain zero) and 3 (−4.08 is greater than 2.64 and the confidence interval for *psihat* does not contain zero) are. These findings indicate that the difference in attractiveness scores for 4 pints compared to both no alcohol and 2 pints differed in men and women, but that the lack of difference between 2 pints and no alcohol was similar for males and females. This profile of results tells the same story as the factorial ANOVA that we interpreted in the main part of the chapter.

```
$Factor.A
$Factor.A$test
     con.num     test     crit       se       df
[1,]       1 1.290994 2.065879 7.745967 23.57301

$Factor.A$psihat
     con.num psihat  ci.lower ci.upper   p.value
[1,]       1     10 -6.002228 26.00223 0.2092233

$Factor.B
$Factor.B$test
     con.num      test     crit       se       df
[1,]       1 -0.5203149 2.678921 6.406377 14.50207
[2,]       2  5.7486837 2.647995 6.233311 16.11968
[3,]       3  6.1847459 2.636865 6.332785 16.81814

$Factor.B$psihat
     con.num    psihat  ci.lower ci.upper     p.value
[1,]       1 -3.333333 -20.49551 13.82885 6.106962e-01
[2,]       2 35.833333  19.32755 52.33911 2.905447e-05
[3,]       3 39.166667  22.46796 55.86537 1.047835e-05

$Factor.AB
$Factor.AB$test
     con.num      test     crit       se       df
[1,]       1 -0.5203149 2.678921 6.406377 14.50207
[2,]       2 -4.6791611 2.647995 6.233311 16.11968
[3,]       3 -4.0793005 2.636865 6.332785 16.81814

$Factor.AB$psihat
     con.num     psihat  ci.lower  ci.upper     p.value
[1,]       1  -3.333333 -20.49551  13.82885 0.6106961628
[2,]       2 -29.166667 -45.67245 -12.66089 0.0002466289
[3,]       3 -25.833333 -42.53204  -9.13463 0.0007964981


$All.Tests
[1] NA

$conA
     [,1]
[1,]    1
[2,]    1
[3,]    1
[4,]   -1
[5,]   -1
[6,]   -1

$conB
     [,1] [,2] [,3]
[1,]    1    1    0
[2,]   -1    0    1
[3,]    0   -1   -1
[4,]    1    1    0
[5,]   -1    0    1
[6,]    0   -1   -1
```

```
$conAB
     [,1] [,2] [,3]
[1,]    1    1    0
[2,]   -1    0    1
[3,]    0   -1   -1
[4,]   -1   -1    0
[5,]    1    0   -1
[6,]    0    1    1
```

Output 12.9

Output 12.10 shows the *post hoc* tests based on an M-estimator (*mcp2a*). The interpretation of these results is exactly the same as for the trimmed means. If the value of *sig.test* is less than the critical value (*sig.crit*) and the confidence interval does not cross zero then the contrast is significant. For the main effect of alcohol we find a significant difference in attractiveness scores for 4 pints compared to both no alcohol, $\hat{\psi} = 35.80$, $p < .001$, and 2 pints, $\hat{\psi} = 40.80$, $p < .001$, but not between 2 pints and no alcohol, $\hat{\psi} = -5$, $p = .383$. Similarly, for the interaction term, males and females were comparable in terms of the difference in attractiveness ratings between 4 pints compared to both no alcohol, $\hat{\psi} = -32.23$, $p < .001$, and 2 pints, $\hat{\psi} = -27.23$, $p < .01$, but not between 2 pints and no alcohol, $\hat{\psi} = -5$, $p = .318$.

```
$FactorA
     con.num    psihat sig.test sig.crit  ci.lower ci.upper
[1,]       1  14.46429   0.1515    0.025 -10.08929 28.23214

$FactorB
     con.num    psihat sig.test sig.crit  ci.lower ci.upper
[1,]       1  -5.00000   0.3825    0.025 -18.83929 13.24405
[2,]       2  35.80357   0.0000    0.025  20.62500 51.84524
[3,]       3  40.80357   0.0000    0.025  21.25000 55.20833

$Interactions
     con.num    psihat sig.test sig.crit  ci.lower    ci.upper
[1,]       1  -5.00000   0.3180    0.025 -19.37500  12.500000
[2,]       2 -32.23214   0.0005    0.025 -45.20833 -13.750000
[3,]       3 -27.23214   0.0015    0.025 -41.96429  -9.583333
```

Output 12.10

OLIVER TWISTED

Please Sir, can I have some more … robust methods?

'These robust tests are not nearly complicated enough', salivates Oliver with a maniacal look in his eye and suspiciously empty bowl of additive-ridden sweets by his side. 'I want to add in a third independent variable, and then I want the magic number ferret to lick the brains from my skull.' Oh dear, he's lost it. You can lose it too by finding out how to do a robust three-way independent ANOVA on the companion website. If you're lucky you might get a brain licking too or, at the very least, a headache.

12.8. Calculating effect sizes ③

As we saw in previous chapters (e.g., section 11.6), we can use omega squared (ω^2) as an effect size measure. The calculation of ω^2 becomes somewhat more cumbersome in factorial designs ('somewhat' being one of my characteristic understatements!). Howell (2006), as ever, does a wonderful job of explaining the complexities of it all (and has a nice table summarizing the various components for a variety of situations). Condensing all of this down, I'll just say that we need to first compute a variance component for each of the effects (the two main effects and the interaction term) and the error, and then use these to calculate effect sizes for each. If we call the first main effect A, the second main effect B and the interaction effect $A \times B$, then the variance components for each of these are based on the mean squares of each effect and the sample sizes on which they're based:

$$\hat{\sigma}^2_\alpha = \frac{(a-1)(\text{MS}_A - \text{MS}_R)}{nab}$$

$$\hat{\sigma}^2_\beta = \frac{(b-1)(\text{MS}_B - \text{MS}_R)}{nab}$$

$$\hat{\sigma}^2_{\alpha\beta} = \frac{(a-1)(b-1)(\text{MS}_{A \times B} - \text{MS}_R)}{nab}$$

In these equations, a is the number of levels of the first independent variable, b is the number of levels of the second independent variable and n is the number of people per condition.

We also need to estimate the total variability, and this is just the sum of these other variables plus the residual mean squares:

$$\hat{\sigma}^2_{total} = \hat{\sigma}^2_\alpha + \hat{\sigma}^2_\beta + \hat{\sigma}^2_{\alpha\beta} + \text{MS}_R$$

The effect size is then the variance estimate for the effect in which you're interested divided by the total variance estimate:

$$\omega^2_{effect} = \frac{\hat{\sigma}^2_{effect}}{\hat{\sigma}^2_{total}}$$

We can write a function in **R** to compute the effect sizes for us (see R's Souls' Tip 6.2). This process might seem like a faff, but remember that once you have the function written, you can use it again and again. Output 12.4 gives us the sums of squares for each effect and the interaction, so it would be nice to be able to enter these values to get the resulting omega squared. We can write and execute this function:

```
omega_factorial<-function(n, a, b, SSa, SSb, SSab, SSr)
{
        MSa<-SSa/(a-1)
        MSb<-SSb/(b-1)
        MSab<-SSab/((a-1)*(b-1))
        MSr<-SSr/(a*b*(n-1))
        varA<-((a-1)*(MSa-MSr))/(n*a*b)
        varB<-((b-1)*(MSb-MSr))/(n*a*b)
        varAB<-((a-1)*(b-1)*(MSab-MSr))/(n*a*b)
        varTotal<-varA + varB + varAB + MSr
        print(paste("Omega-Squared A: ", varA/varTotal))
        print(paste("Omega-Squared B: ", varB/varTotal))
        print(paste("Omega-Squared AB: ", varAB/varTotal))
        }
```

This creates a function called *omega_factorial*.[5] First, we tell **R** that we want to be able to input n, a, b, SSa, SSb, SSab, and SSr into the function (these are specified in brackets). This means that to use the function we have to input these values in brackets in the correct order. The rest of the function uses these values to compute the various values of ω^2. The first four commands take the sums of squares and convert them to mean squares by dividing by the degrees of freedom (rather than have you input the degrees of freedom by hand, we calculate them from *a* and *b*, the number of levels of the two independent variables). The next four lines calculate the variance estimates in the equations above; for example, *varA* computes $\hat{\sigma}^2_\alpha$ by writing out the equation above in **R**-speak (because of how I have labelled everything in the function you should be able to compare directly the command in the function with the equation above). The final three lines print some text (in speech marks) that describes which ω^2 we're calculating followed by each variance estimate divided by the total variance estimate (i.e., $\hat{\sigma}^2_{effect}/\hat{\sigma}^2_{total}$).

Having executed this function we can use it to calculate ω^2 in the current data by using the values of *n* (8 people per group), *a* (levels of gender = 2), *b* (levels of alcohol = 3) and the four sums of squares from Output 12.4:

```
omega_factorial(8, 2, 3, 169, 3332, 1978, 3488)
```

Executing this command will print the following to the console:

```
[1] "Omega-Squared A:   0.00949745068429"
[1] "Omega-Squared B:   0.34982188991376"
[1] "Omega-Squared AB:  0.200209417472152"
```

For the main effect of gender we get $\omega^2_{gender} = 0.009$; for the main effect of alcohol we get $\omega^2_{alcohol} = 0.350$; and for the interaction $\omega^2_{gender \times alcohol} = 0.200$.

I have mentioned several times that it is perhaps more useful to quantify focused differences (i.e., between two things) than overall effects. In the case of a factorial ANOVA when there is a significant interaction, we might compute effect sizes for the simple effects (section 12.5.10). In other words, compute the differences between means for one independent variable at different levels of the other independent variable. In the current example, we might compute effect sizes for the effect of gender at different levels of alcohol. We could again use the *mes()* function from the *calculate.es* package:

```
mes(mean_males, mean_females, sd_males, sd_females, n_males, n_females)
```

We have all the information we need to use the *mes()* function in Output 12.2. For example, if we want to compare men and women who drank no alcohol we would execute:

```
mes(66.875, 60.625, 10.3293963, 4.95515604, 8, 8)
```

We have entered the mean of the men who drank no alcohol (66.875), the mean of women who drank no alcohol (60.625), the corresponding standard deviations (10.329 and 4.955), and the sample sizes (both 8).

Similarly we can get effect sizes for the difference between men and women who drank 2 pints by executing:

```
mes(66.875, 62.5, 12.5178444, 6.5465367, 8, 8)
```

Finally, the difference between men and women who drank 4 pints can be quantified by executing:

```
mes(35.625, 57.5, 10.8356225, 7.0710678, 8, 8)
```

The (edited) outputs of these commands are shown in Output 12.11. The difference in attractiveness scores between males and females who drank no alcohol is a medium effect

---

[5] If you install the package *DSUR*, which we produced for this book, you can use this function without executing these commands.

(the means are under a standard deviation different), $d = 0.77$, $r = .36$; the difference between males and females who drank 2 pints is a fairly small effect (there is less than half a standard deviation difference between the group means), $d = 0.44$, $r = .21$; finally, the difference between males and females who drank 4 pints is a very large effect (the means are more than 2 standard deviation apart), $d = -2.39$, $r = -.77$.

```
No Alcohol: Males vs. Females

$MeanDifference
        d      var.d          g      var.g
0.7715168 0.2686012 0.7294340 0.2400984


$Correlation
         r       var.r
0.35990788 0.04428981


2 Pints: Males vs. Females

$MeanDifference
        d      var.d          g      var.g
0.4379891 0.2559948 0.4140988 0.2288298


$Correlation
         r       var.r
0.2139249 0.0556082


4 Pints: Males vs. Females

$MeanDifference
         d       var.d           g       var.g
-2.3909552   0.4286458 -2.2605394   0.3831598


$Correlation
          r        var.r
-0.767030763   0.007475955
```

Output 12.11

12.9. Reporting the results of two-way ANOVA ②

As with the other ANOVAs we've encountered, we have to report the details of the F-ratio and the degrees of freedom from which it was calculated. For the various effects in these data the F-ratio will be based on different degrees of freedom: it was derived from dividing the mean squares for the effect by the mean squares for the residual. For the effects of alcohol and the alcohol × gender interaction, the model degrees of freedom were 2 ($df_M = 2$), but for the effect of gender the degrees of freedom were only 1 ($df_M = 1$). For all effects, the degrees of freedom for the residuals were 42 ($df_R = 42$). We can, therefore, report the three effects from this analysis as follows:

✓ There was a significant main effect of the amount of alcohol consumed at the night-club, on the attractiveness of the mate they selected, $F(2, 42) = 20.07$, $p < .001$, $\omega^2 = .35$. The Bonferroni *post hoc* tests revealed that the attractiveness of selected dates was significantly lower after 4 pints than both after 2 pints and no alcohol (both $ps < .001$). The attractiveness of dates after 2 pints and no alcohol were not significantly different.

✓ There was a non-significant main effect of gender on the attractiveness of selected mates, $F(1, 42) = 2.03$, $p = .161$, $\omega^2 = .009$.

✓ There was a significant interaction effect between the amount of alcohol consumed and the gender of the person selecting a mate, on the attractiveness of the partner selected, $F(2, 42) = 11.91$, $p < .001$, $\omega^2 = .20$. This indicates that male and female genders were affected differently by alcohol. Specifically, the attractiveness of partners was similar in males ($M = 66.88$, $SD = 10.33$) and females ($M = 60.63$, $SD = 4.96$) after no alcohol, $d = 0.77$; the attractiveness of partners was also similar in males ($M = 66.88$, $SD = 12.52$) and females ($M = 62.50$, $SD = 6.55$) after 2 pints, $d = 0.44$; however, attractiveness of partners selected by males ($M = 35.63$, $SD = 10.84$) was significantly lower than those selected by females ($M = 57.50$, $SD = 7.07$) after 4 pints, $d = -2.39$.

Labcoat Leni's Real Research 12.1   Don't forget your toothbrush? ②

Davey, G. C. L., et al. (2003). *Journal of Behavior Therapy & Experimental Psychiatry, 34*, 141–160.

We have all experienced that feeling after we have left the house of wondering whether we locked the door, or closed the window, or whether we remembered to remove the bodies from the fridge in case the police turn up. This behaviour is normal; however, people with obsessive compulsive disorder (OCD) tend to check things excessively. They might, for example, check whether they have locked the door so often that it takes them an hour to leave their house. It is a very debilitating problem.

One theory of this checking behaviour in OCD suggests that it is caused by a combination of the mood you are in (positive or negative) interacting with the rules you use to decide when to stop a task (do you continue until you feel like stopping, or until you have done the task as best as you can?). Davey, Startup, Zara, MacDonald, and Field (2003) tested this hypothesis by inducing a negative, positive or no mood in different people and then asking them to imagine that they were going on holiday and to generate as many things as they could that they should check before they went away. Within each mood group, half of the participants were instructed to generate as many items as they could (known as an 'as many as can' stop rule), whereas the remainder were asked to generate items for as long as they felt like continuing the task (known as a 'feel like continuing' stop rule). The data are in the file **Davey2003.dat**.

Davey et al. hypothesized that people in negative moods, using an 'as many as can' stop rule, would generate more items than those using a 'feel like continuing' stop rule. Conversely, people in a positive mood would generate more items when using a 'feel like continuing' stop rule compared to an 'as many as can' stop rule. Finally, in neutral moods, the stop rule used shouldn't affect the number of items generated. Draw an error bar chart of the data and then conduct the appropriate analysis to test Davey et al.'s hypotheses.

Answers are in the additional material on the companion website (or look at pages 148–149 in the original article).

What have I discovered about statistics? ②

This chapter has been a whistle-stop tour of factorial ANOVA. In fact we'll come across more factorial ANOVAs in the next two chapters, but for the time being we've just looked at the situation where there are two independent variables, and different people have been used in all experimental conditions. We started off by discovering that even complex ANOVAs are simply regression analyses in disguise. We moved on to look at how to calculate the various sums of squares in this analysis, but, most important, we saw that we get three effects: two main effects (the effect of each of the independent variables) and an interaction effect. We moved on to see how this analysis is done using **R** and how the output is interpreted. Much of this was similar to the ANOVAs we've come across in previous chapters, but one big difference was the interaction term. We spent a bit of time exploring interactions (and especially interaction graphs) to see what an interaction looks like and how to spot it. The brave readers also found out how to follow up an interaction with simple effects analysis. Finally, we discovered that calculating effect sizes in factorial designs is a complete headache and should be attempted only by the criminally insane. So far we've steered clear of repeated-measures designs, but in the next chapter I have to resign myself to the fact that I can't avoid explaining them for the rest of my life.☹

We also discovered that no sooner had I started my first band than it disintegrated. I went with drummer Mark to sing in a band called the Outlanders, who were much better musically but were not, if the truth were told, metal enough for me. They also sacked me after a very short period of time for not being able to sing like Bono (an insult at the time, but in retrospect …).

R packages used in this chapter

car	multcomp
compute.es	pastecs
ggplot2	reshape
	WRS

R functions used in this chapter

Anova()	list()
aov()	lm()
by()	melt()
cast()	mes()
contrasts()	pairwise.t.test()
confint()	pbad2way()
factor()	plot()
ggplot()	read.csv()
gl()	rep()
glht()	stat.desc()
mcp2a()	summary()
mcp2atm()	summary.lm()
leveneTest()	t2way()

Key terms that I've discovered

Beer-goggles effect	Interaction graph
Factorial ANOVA	Mixed design
Independent factorial design	Related factorial design
	Simple effects analysis

Smart Alex's tasks

- **Task 1**: People's musical tastes change as they get older (my parents, for example, after years of listening to relatively cool music when I was a kid, subsequently hit their mid-forties and developed a worrying obsession with country and western music). This worries me immensely because the future seems bleak if it is spent listening to Garth Brooks and thinking 'oh boy, did I underestimate Garth's immense talent when I was in my 20s'. So, I did some imaginary research to find out whether my fate really was sealed, or whether it's possible to be old and like good music too. First, I got two groups of people (45 people in each group): one group contained young people (which I arbitrarily decided was under 40 years of age) and the other group contained more mature individuals (above 40 years of age). This is my first independent variable, **age**. I then split each of these groups of 45 into three smaller groups of 15 and assigned them to listen to Fugazi (who everyone knows are the coolest band on the planet),[6] ABBA or Barf Grooks (a less well-known country and western musician not to be confused with anyone real who produces music that makes me want to barf). This is my second independent variable, **music**. After listening to the music I got each person to rate it on a scale ranging from −100 (please poke a pencil through my eardrum so I don't have to listen any more) through 0 (I am completely indifferent) to +100 (I love this music so much, it gives me a tingle down my spine). This variable is called **liking**. The data are in the file **fugazi.dat**. Conduct a two-way independent ANOVA on them. ②

- **Task 2**: In Chapter 3 we used some data that related to men and women's psychological arousal levels when watching either *Bridget Jones's Diary* or *Memento* (**ChickFlick.dat**). Analyse these data to see whether men and women differ in their reactions to different types of films. ②

- **Task 3**: At the start of this chapter I described a way of empirically researching whether I wrote better songs than my old band mate Malcolm, and whether this depended on the type of song (a symphony or song about flies). The outcome variable would be the number of screams elicited by audience members during the songs. These data are in the file **Escape From Inside.dat**. Draw an error bar graph (lines) and analyse and interpret these data. ②

- **Task 4**: Using R's Souls' Tip 12.2, conduct a simple effects analysis of the effect of alcohol at different levels of gender (which is the opposite to the example in the chapter). ③

- **Task 5**: Back in 2008, hospitals were reporting an increase in injuries related to playing Nintendo Wii (http://www.telegraph.co.uk/news/uknews/1576244/Spate-of-injuries-blamed-on-Nintendo-Wii.html). These injuries were attributed mainly to

[6] See http://www.dischord.com

muscle and tendon strains. A researcher was interested to see whether these injuries could be prevented. She hypothesized that a stretching warm-up before playing Wii would help lower injuries, and that athletes would be less susceptible to injuries because their regular activity makes them more flexible. She took 60 athletes and 60 non-athletes (**athlete**), half of them played Wii and half watched others playing as a control (**wii**), and within these groups half did a 5-minute stretch routine before playing/watching whereas the other half did not (**stretch**). The outcome was a pain score out of 10 (where 0 is no pain, and 10 is severe pain) after playing for 4 hours (**injury**). The data are in the file **Wii.dat**. Conduct a three-way ANOVA to test whether athletes are less prone to injury, and whether the prevention programme worked. ③

The answers are on the companion website. Task 1 is an example from Field and Hole (2003) and so has a more detailed answer if you feel like you want it.

Further reading

Howell, D. C. (2006). *Statistical methods for psychology* (6th ed.). Belmont, CA: Duxbury. (Or you might prefer his *Fundamental Statistics for the Behavioral Sciences,* also in its 6th edition, 2007.)

Rosenthal, R., Rosnow, R. L., & Rubin, D. B. (2000). *Contrasts and effect sizes in behavioural research: A correlational approach.* Cambridge: Cambridge University Press. (This is quite advanced but really cannot be bettered for contrasts and effect size estimation.)

Rosnow, R. L., & Rosenthal, R. (2005). *Beginning behavioral research: A conceptual primer* (5th ed.). Upper Saddle River, NJ: Pearson/Prentice Hall. (Has some wonderful chapters on ANOVA, with a particular focus on effect size estimation, and some very insightful comments on what interactions actually mean.)

Interesting real research

Davey, G. C. L., Startup, H. M., Zara, A., MacDonald, C. B., & Field, A. P. (2003). Perseveration of checking thoughts and mood-as-input hypothesis. *Journal of Behavior Therapy & Experimental Psychiatry, 34,* 141–160.

Repeated-measures designs (GLM 4)

13

FIGURE 13.1
Scansion in the early days; I used to stare a lot (from left to right: me, Mark and Mark)

13.1. What will this chapter tell me? ②

At the age of 15, I was on holiday with my friend Mark (the drummer) in Cornwall. I had a pretty decent mullet by this stage (nowadays I just wish I had enough hair to grow a mullet) and had acquired a respectable collection of heavy metal T-shirts from going to various gigs. We were walking along the cliff tops one evening at dusk reminiscing about our times in Andromeda. We came to the conclusion that the only thing we hadn't enjoyed about that band was Malcolm and that maybe we should reform it with a different guitarist.[1] As I

[1] I feel bad about saying this because Malcolm was a very nice guy and, to be honest, at that age (and some would argue beyond) I could be a bit of a cock.

was wondering who we could get to play guitar, Mark pointed out the blindingly obvious: I played guitar. So, when we got home Scansion was born.[2] As the singer, guitarist and song-writer, I set about writing some songs. I moved away from writing about flies and set my sights on the pointlessness of existence, death, betrayal and so on. We had the dubious hon-our of being reviewed in the music magazine *Kerrang!* (in a live review they called us 'twee', which is really not what you want to be called if you're trying to make music so heavy that it ruptures the bowels of Satan). Our highlight, however, was playing a gig at the famous Marquee Club in London (this club has closed now, not as a result of us playing there I has-ten to add, but in its day it started the careers of people like Jimi Hendrix, The Who, Iron Maiden and Led Zeppelin).[3] This was the biggest gig of our career and it was essential that we played like we never had before. As it turned out, we did: I ran on stage, fell over and in the process detuned my guitar beyond recognition and broke the zip on my trousers. I spent the whole gig out of tune and spread-eagled to prevent my trousers falling down. Like I said, I'd never played like *that* before. We used to get quite obsessed with comparing how we played at different gigs. I didn't know about statistics then (happy days) but if I had I would have realized that we could rate ourselves and compare the mean ratings for different gigs; because we would always be the ones doing the rating, this would be a repeated-measures design, so we would need a repeated-measures ANOVA to compare these means. That's what this chapter is about; hopefully it won't make our trousers fall down.

13.2. Introduction to repeated-measures designs ②

Over the last three chapters we have looked at a procedure called ANOVA, which is used for testing differences between several means. So far we've concentrated on situations in which different entities contribute to different means; put another way, different people take part in different experimental conditions. Actually, it doesn't have to be different peo-ple (I tend to say people because I'm a psychologist and so spend my life torturing, I mean testing, people in the name of science), it could be different plants, different companies, different plots of land, different viral strains, different goats or even different duck-billed platypuses (or whatever the plural is). Anyway, the point is that I've completely ignored situations in which the same people (plants, goats, hamsters, seven-eyed green galactic leaders from space, or whatever) contribute to the different means because explaining how to do it in **R** is a bit of an R-se. I've put it off long enough, and now I'm going to take you through what happens when we do ANOVA on repeated-measures data.

SELF-TEST

✓ What is a repeated-measures design? (Clue: it is described in Chapter 1.)

'Repeated measures' is a term used when the same entities participate in all conditions of an experiment or provide data at multiple time points. For example, you might test the effects of alcohol on enjoyment of a party. Some people can drink a lot of alcohol with-out really feeling the consequences, whereas others, like myself, have only to sniff a pint of lager and they start flapping around on the floor waving their arms and legs around shouting 'Look at me, I'm Andy, King of the lost world of the Haddocks'. Therefore, it

[2] Scansion is a term for the rhythm of poetry. We got the name by searching through a dictionary until we found a word that we liked. Originally we didn't think it was 'metal' enough, and we decided that any self-respecting heavy metal band needed to have a big spiky 'X' in their name. So, for the first couple of years we spelt it 'Scanxion'. Like I said, I could be a bit of a cock back then.

[3] http://www.themarqueeclub.net

is important to control for individual differences in tolerance to alcohol, and this can be achieved by testing the same people in all conditions of the experiment: participants could be given a questionnaire assessing their enjoyment of the party after they had consumed 1 pint, 2 pints, 3 pints and 4 pints of lager.

We saw in Chapter 1 that this type of design has several advantages; however, there is a big disadvantage if you're going to use ANOVA to analyse your data. In Chapter 10 we saw that the accuracy of the *F*-test in ANOVA depends upon the assumption that scores in different conditions are independent (see section 10.3). When repeated measures are used this assumption is violated: scores taken under different experimental conditions are likely to be related because they come from the same participants. As such, the conventional *F*-test will lack accuracy. The relationship between scores in different treatment conditions means that an additional assumption has to be made and, put simplistically, we assume that the relationship between pairs of experimental conditions is similar (i.e., the level of dependence between experimental conditions is roughly equal). This assumption is called the assumption of **sphericity**, which, trust me, is a pain in the neck to try to pronounce when you're giving statistics lectures at 9 a.m.

13.2.1. The assumption of sphericity ②

The assumption of sphericity can be likened to the assumption of homogeneity of variance in between-group ANOVA. Sphericity (denoted by ε and sometimes referred to as *circularity*) is a more general condition of **compound symmetry**. Compound symmetry holds true when both the variances across conditions are equal (this is the same as the homogeneity of variance assumption in between-group designs) and the covariances between pairs of conditions are equal. So, we assume that the variation within experimental conditions is fairly similar and that no two conditions are any more dependent than any other two. Although compound symmetry has been shown to be a sufficient condition for ANOVA using repeated-measures data, it is not a necessary condition. Sphericity is a less restrictive form of compound symmetry (in fact, much of the early research into repeated-measures ANOVA confused compound symmetry with sphericity). Sphericity refers to the equality of variances of the *differences* between treatment levels. So, if you were to take each pair of treatment levels, and calculate the differences between each pair of scores, then it is necessary that these differences have approximately equal variances. As such, *you need at least three conditions for sphericity to be an issue.*

What is sphericity?

13.2.2. How is sphericity measured? ②

If we were going to check the assumption of sphericity by hand, which incidentally only a complete lunatic would do, then we could start by calculating the differences between pairs of scores in all combinations of the treatment levels. Once this has been done, we could calculate the variance of these differences. Table 13.1 shows data from an experiment with three conditions. The differences between pairs of scores are computed for each participant and the variance for each set of differences is calculated. We saw above that sphericity is met when these variances are roughly equal. For these data, sphericity will hold when:

$$\text{Variance}_{A-B} \approx \text{Variance}_{A-C} \approx \text{Variance}_{B-C}$$

In these data there is some deviation from sphericity because the variance of the differences between conditions A and B (15.7) is greater than the variance of the differences between A and C (10.3) and between B and C (10.7). However, these data have *local circularity* (or local sphericity) because two of the variances of differences are very similar. Therefore, the sphericity assumption has been met for any multiple comparisons involving these conditions (for a discussion of local circularity see Rouanet & Lépine, 1970). The deviation from sphericity in the data in Table 13.1 does not seem too severe (all variances are *roughly* equal), but can we assess whether a deviation is severe enough to warrant action?

Table 13.1 Hypothetical data to illustrate the calculation of the variance of the differences between conditions

Group A	Group B	Group C	A−B	A−C	B−C
10	12	8	−2	2	4
15	15	12	0	3	3
25	30	20	−5	5	10
35	30	28	5	7	2
30	27	20	3	10	7
		Variance:	15.7	10.3	10.7

13.2.3. Assessing the severity of departures from sphericity ②

Sphericity can be assessed using a test known as **Mauchly's test**, which tests the hypothesis that the variances of the differences between conditions are equal. Therefore, if Mauchly's test statistic is significant (i.e., has a probability value less than .05) we should conclude that there are significant differences between the variances of differences and, therefore, the condition of sphericity is not met. If, however, Mauchly's test statistic is non-significant (i.e., $p > .05$) then it is reasonable to conclude that the variances of differences are not significantly different (i.e., they are roughly equal). So, in short, if Mauchly's test is significant then we must be wary of the resulting *F*-ratios. However, like any significance test, it is dependent on sample size: in big samples small deviations from sphericity can be significant, and in small samples large violations can be non-significant.

13.2.4. What is the effect of violating the assumption of sphericity? ③

Rouanet and Lépine (1970) provided a detailed account of the validity of the *F*-ratio under violations of the sphericity assumption. They argued that there are two different *F*-ratios that can be used to assess treatment comparisons, labelled *F′* and *F″*, respectively. *F′* refers to an *F*-ratio derived from the mean squares of the comparison in question and the specific error term for the comparison of interest – this is the *F*-ratio normally used. *F″* is derived not from the specific error mean square but from the total error mean squares for *all* repeated-measures comparisons. Rouanet and Lépine (1970) showed that for *F″* to be valid, *overall* sphericity must hold (i.e., the whole data set must be spherical), but for *F′* to be valid, sphericity must hold for the *specific comparison in question* (see also Mendoza, Toothaker, & Crain, 1976). *F′* is the statistic generally used, and the effect of violating sphericity is a loss of power (compared to when *F″* is used) and a test statistic (*F*-ratio) that simply cannot be compared to tabulated values of the *F*-distribution (see Oliver Twisted).

OLIVER TWISTED

Please Sir, can I have some more … sphericity?

'Balls' says Oliver, 'are spherical, and I like balls. Maybe I'll like sphericity too if only you could explain it to me in more detail.' Be careful what you wish for, Oliver. In my youth I wrote an article called 'A bluffer's guide to sphericity', which I used to cite in this book, roughly on this page. Occasionally people ask me for it, so I thought I might as well reproduce it in the additional material for this chapter.

Not only does sphericity create problems for the F in repeated-measures ANOVA, but also it causes some amusing complications for *post hoc* tests (Jane Superbrain Box 13.1). If you don't want to worry about what these complications are then the take-home message is that when sphericity is violated, the Bonferroni method seems to be generally the most robust of the univariate techniques, especially in terms of power and control of the Type I error rate. When sphericity is definitely not violated, Tukey's test can be used.

JANE SUPERBRAIN 13.1

Sphericity and post hoc tests ③

The violation of sphericity has implications for multiple comparisons. Boik (1981) provided an estimable account of the effects of non-sphericity on *post hoc* tests in repeated-measures designs, and concluded that even very small departures from sphericity produce large biases in the F-test. He recommends against using these tests for repeated-measure contrasts. When experimental error terms are small, the power to detect relatively strong effects can be as low as .05 (when sphericity = .80). Boik argues that the situation for *multiple* comparisons cannot be improved and concludes by recommending a multivariate analogue. Mitzel and Games (1981) found that when sphericity does not hold ($\varepsilon < 1$) the pooled error term conventionally employed in pairwise comparisons resulted in non-significant differences between two means declared significant (i.e., a lenient Type I error rate) or undetected differences (a conservative Type I error rate). Mitzel and Games, therefore, recommended the use of separate error terms for each comparison.

Maxwell (1980) systematically tested the power and alpha levels for five *post hoc* tests under repeated-measures conditions. The tests assessed were Tukey's wholly significant difference (WSD) test, which uses a pooled error term; Tukey's procedure but with a separate error term with either $n-1$ degrees of freeedom (labelled SEP1) or $(n-1)(k-1)$ degrees of freeedom (labelled SEP2); Bonferroni's procedure (BON); and a multivariate approach, the Roy–Bose simultaneous confidence interval (SCI). Maxwell (1980) tested these *a priori* procedures, varying the sample size, number of levels of the repeated factor and departure from sphericity. He found that the multivariate approach was always 'too conservative for practical use' (p. 277), and this was most extreme when n (the number of participants) is small relative to k (the number of conditions). Tukey's test inflated the alpha rate unacceptably with increasing departures from sphericity even when a separate error term was used (SEP1 and SEP2). The Bonferroni method, however, was extremely robust (although *slightly* conservative) and controlled alpha levels regardless of the manipulation. Therefore, in terms of Type I error rates, the Bonferroni method was best.

In terms of test power (the Type II error rate) for a small sample ($n = 8$) Maxwell found WSD to be most powerful under conditions of non-sphericity, but this advantage was severely reduced when $n = 15$.

Keselman and Keselman (1988) extended Maxwell's work within unbalanced designs. They too used Tukey's WSD, a modified WSD (with non-pooled error variance), Bonferroni t-statistics and a multivariate approach, and found that when unweighted means were used (with unbalanced designs) none of the four tests could control the Type I error rate. When weighted means were used only the multivariate tests could limit alpha rates, although Bonferroni t-statistics were considerably better than the two Tukey methods. In terms of power, Keselman and Keselman (1988) concluded that 'as the number of repeated treatment levels increases, BON is substantially more powerful than SCI' (p. 223).

13.2.5. What do you do if you violate sphericity? ②

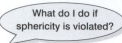

If data violate the sphericity assumption, there are several corrections that can be applied to produce a valid F-ratio. There are three commonly used corrections based upon the estimates of sphericity advocated by Greenhouse and Geisser (1959) and Huynh and Feldt (1976). Both of these estimates give rise to a correction factor that is applied to the degrees of freedom used to assess the observed F-ratio. The calculation of these estimates is beyond the scope of this book (interested readers should consult Girden, 1992); we need know only that the three estimates differ. The **Greenhouse–Geisser correction** (usually denoted as $\hat{\varepsilon}$) varies between $1/(k-1)$, where k is the number of repeated-measures conditions, and 1. The closer $\hat{\varepsilon}$ is to 1, the more homogeneous the variances of differences, and hence the closer the data are to being spherical. For example, in a situation in which there are five conditions the lower limit of $\hat{\varepsilon}$ will be $1/(5-1)$, or .25 (known as the **lower-bound estimate** of sphericity).

Huynh and Feldt (1976) reported that when the Greenhouse–Geisser estimate is greater than .75 too many false null hypotheses fail to be rejected (i.e., the correction is too conservative) and Collier, Baker, Mandeville, and Hayes (1967) showed that this was also true when the sphericity estimate was as high as .90. Huynh and Feldt, therefore, proposed their own less conservative correction (usually denoted as $\widetilde{\varepsilon}$). However, Maxwell and Delaney (1990) report that $\widetilde{\varepsilon}$ overestimates sphericity. Stevens (2002) therefore recommends taking an average of the two and adjusting df by this averaged value. Girden (1992) recommends that when estimates of sphericity are greater than .75 the **Huynh–Feldt correction** should be used, but when sphericity estimates are less than .75 or nothing is known about sphericity at all, then the Greenhouse–Geisser correction should be used instead. We will see how these values are used in due course.

Given that violations of sphericity affect the accuracy of F, a second option when you have data that violate sphericity is to use a test other than F. The first possibility is to use multivariate test statistics (multivariate analysis of variance, MANOVA), because they are not dependent upon the assumption of sphericity (see O'Brien & Kaiser, 1985). MANOVA is covered in depth in Chapter 16, but we can get **R** to produce multivariate test statistics in the context of repeated-measures ANOVA. However, there may be trade-offs in power between these univariate and multivariate tests (see Jane Superbrain Box 13.2). A second possibility is to analyse the data as a multilevel model (described in detail in Chapter 19). This idea probably sounds a bit scary, but it is simply a regression in which we can include multiple observations from the same entities. If we analyse the data in this way then we can interpret the model coefficients without worrying about sphericity because dummy-coding our grouping variables ensures that these coefficients only ever compare two things (and sphericity is only an issue when comparing three or more means). Also, the model fit can be tested without an F-ratio, and if we're feeling really brave we can explicitly model the assumed relationship between observations at different time points (this is called the *covariance structure* and is described in Chapter 19). Although we cover a basic ANOVA approach to be consistent with what you might well be taught, we recommend the multilevel approach and demonstrate that as well for all of the examples.

13.3. Theory of one-way repeated-measures ANOVA ②

In a repeated-measures ANOVA the effect of our experiment is shown up in the within-participant variance (rather than in the between-group variance). Remember that in

JANE SUPERBRAIN 13.2

Power in ANOVA and MANOVA ③

There is a trade-off in test power between univariate and multivariate approaches (although some authors argue that this can be overcome with suitable mastery of the techniques – O'Brien and Kaiser, 1985). Davidson (1972) compared the power of adjusted univariate techniques with those of Hotelling's T^2 (a MANOVA test statistic) and found that the univariate technique was relatively powerless to detect small reliable changes between highly correlated conditions when other less correlated conditions were also present. Mendoza, Toothaker, and

Nicewander (1974) conducted a Monte Carlo study comparing univariate and multivariate techniques under violations of compound symmetry and normality and found that 'as the degree of violation of compound symmetry increased, the empirical power for the multivariate tests also increased. In contrast, the power for the univariate tests generally decreased' (p. 174). Maxwell and Delaney (1990) noted that the univariate test is relatively more powerful than the multivariate test as n decreases and proposed that 'the multivariate approach should probably not be used if n is less than $a + 10$ (a is the number of levels for repeated measures)' (p. 602). As a rule it seems that when you have a large violation of sphericity ($\varepsilon < .7$) and your sample size is greater than ($a + 10$) then multivariate procedures are more powerful, but with small sample sizes or when sphericity holds ($\varepsilon > .7$) the univariate approach is preferred (Stevens, 2002). It is also worth noting that the power of MANOVA increases and decreases as a function of the correlations between dependent variables (see Jane Superbrain Box 16.1) and so the relationship between treatment conditions must be considered.

independent ANOVA (section 10.2) the within-participant variance is our residual variance (SS_R); it is the variance created by individual differences in performance. This variance is not contaminated by the experimental effect, because whatever manipulation we've carried out has been done on different people. However, when we carry out our experimental manipulation on the same people, the within-participant variance will be made up of two things: the effect of our manipulation and, as before, individual differences in performance. So, some of the within-subject variation comes from the effects of our experimental manipulation: we did different things in each experimental condition to the participants, and so variation in an individual's scores will partly be due to these manipulations. For example, if everyone scores higher in one condition than another, it's reasonable to assume that this happened not by chance, but because we did something different to the participants in one of the conditions compared to any other one. *Because* we did the *same* thing to everyone within a particular condition, any variation that cannot be explained by the manipulation we've carried out must be due to random factors outside our control, unrelated to our experimental manipulations (we could call this 'error'). As in independent ANOVA, we use an F-ratio that compares the size of the variation due to our experimental manipulations to the size of the variation due to random factors, the only difference being how we calculate these variances. If the variance due to our manipulations is big relative to the variation due to random factors, we get a big value of F, and we can conclude that the observed results are unlikely to have occurred if there was no effect in the population.

Figure 13.2 shows how the variance is partitioned in a repeated-measures ANOVA. The important thing to note is that we have the same types of variances as in independent ANOVA: we have a total sum of squares (SS_T), a model sum of squares (SS_M) and a residual sum of squares (SS_R). The *only* difference between repeated-measures and independent

FIGURE 13.2
Partitioning
variance for
repeated-
measures ANOVA

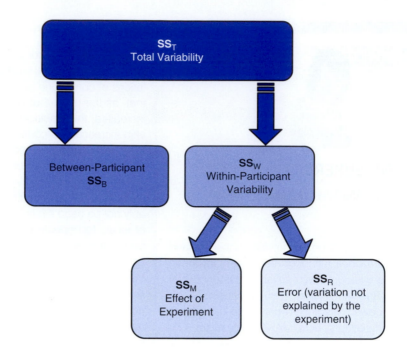

ANOVA is from where those sums of squares come: in repeated-measures ANOVA the model and residual sums of squares are both part of the within-participant variance. Let's have a look at an example.

I'm a Celebrity, Get Me Out of Here! is a TV show in which celebrities (well, they're not really celebrities as such, more like ex-celebrities), in a pitiful attempt to salvage their careers (or just have careers in the first place), go and live in the jungle in Australia for a few weeks. During the show these contestants have to do various humiliating and degrading tasks to win food for their camp mates. These tasks invariably involve creepy-crawlies in places where creepy-crawlies shouldn't go; for example, you might be locked in a coffin full of rats, forced to put your head in a bowl of large spiders, or have eels and cockroaches poured onto you. It's cruel, voyeuristic, gratuitous, car-crash TV, and I love it. As a vegetarian, a particular favourite task for me is the bushtucker trials in which the celebrities have to eat things like live stick insects, witchetty grubs, fish eyes and kangaroo testicles/penises. Honestly, seeing a fish eye exploding in someone's mouth forever scars your mental image of them. I've often wondered (perhaps a little too much) which of the bushtucker foods is the most revolting. Imagine that I tested this by getting eight celebrities, and forced them to eat four different animals (the aforementioned stick insect, kangaroo testicle, fish eye and witchetty grub) in counterbalanced order. On each occasion I measured the time it took the celebrity to retch, in seconds. This is a repeated-measures design because every celebrity eats every food. The independent variable was the type of food eaten and the dependent variable was the time taken to retch.

The data for this example are in Table 13.2. There were four foods, each eaten by eight different celebrities. Their times taken to retch are shown. In addition, the mean amount of time to retch for each celebrity is shown in the table (and the variance in the time taken to retch), and also the mean time to retch for each item eaten. The total variance in retching time will, in part, be caused by the fact that different animals are more or less palatable (the manipulation), and will, in part, be caused by the fact that the celebrities themselves will differ in their constitution (individual differences).

Table 13.2 Data for the bushtucker example

Celebrity	Stick insect	Kangaroo testicle	Fish eye	Witchetty grub	Mean	s^2
1	8	7	1	6	5.50	9.67
2	9	5	2	5	5.25	8.25
3	6	2	3	8	4.75	7.58
4	5	3	1	9	4.50	11.67
5	8	4	5	8	6.25	4.25
6	7	5	6	7	6.25	0.92
7	10	2	7	2	5.25	15.58
8	12	6	8	1	6.75	20.92
Mean	8.13	4.25	4.13	5.75		

13.3.1. The total sum of squares (SS_T) ②

Remember from one-way independent ANOVA that SS_T is calculated using the following equation (see equation (10.4)):

$$SS_T = s^2_{grand}(N-1)$$

Well, in repeated-measures designs the total sum of squares is calculated in exactly the same way. The grand variance in the equation is simply the variance of all scores when we ignore the group to which they belong. So if we treated the data as one big group it would look as follows:

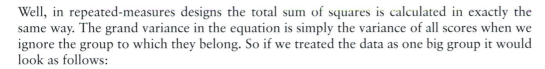

8	7	1	6
9	5	2	5
6	2	3	8
5	3	1	9
8	4	5	8
7	5	6	7
10	2	7	2
12	6	8	1

Grand Mean = 5.56
Grand Variance = 8.19

The variance of these scores is 8.19 (try this on your calculator). We used 32 scores to generate this value, so N is 32. As such the equation becomes:

$$SS_T = s^2_{grand}(N-1)$$
$$= 8.19(32-1)$$
$$= 253.89$$

The degrees of freedom for this sum of squares, as with the independent ANOVA, will be $N-1$, or 31.

13.3.2. The within-participant sum of squares (SS_W) ②

The crucial difference in this design is that there is a variance component called the within-participant variance (this arises because we've manipulated our independent variable within each participant). This is calculated using a sum of squares. Generally speaking, when we calculate any sum of squares we look at the squared difference between the mean and individual scores. This can be expressed in terms of the variance across scores and the number of scores on which that variance is based. For example, when we calculated the residual sum of squares in independent ANOVA (SS_R) we used the following equation (look back to equation (10.7)):

$$SS_R = \sum_{i=1}^{n} (x_i - \bar{x}_i)^2$$
$$= s^2(n-1)$$

This equation gave us the variance between individuals within a particular group, and so is an estimate of individual differences within a particular group. Therefore, to get the total value of individual differences we have to calculate the sum of squares within each group and then add them up:

$$SS_R = s_{\text{group}1}^2(n_1 - 1) + s_{\text{group}2}^2(n_2 - 1) + s_{\text{group}3}^2(n_3 - 1) + \ldots s_{\text{group}n}^2(n_n - 1)$$

This is all well and good when we have different people in each group, but in repeated-measures designs we've subjected people to more than one experimental condition, and, therefore, we're interested in the variation not within a group of people (as in independent ANOVA) but within an actual person. That is, how much variability is there within an individual? To find this out we actually use the same equation but we adapt it to look at people rather than groups. So, if we call this sum of squares SS_W (for within-participant SS) we could write it as:

$$SS_W = s_{\text{person}1}^2(n_1 - 1) + s_{\text{person}2}^2(n_2 - 1) + \ldots + s_{\text{person}n}^2(n_n - 1)$$

This equation simply means that we are looking at the variation in an individual's scores and then adding these variances for all the people in the study. The ns simply represent the number of scores on which the variances are based (i.e., the number of experimental conditions, or in this case the number of foods).

All of the variances we need are in Table 13.2, so we can calculate SS_W as:

$$SS_W = s_{\text{celebrity}1}^2(n_1 - 1) + s_{\text{celebrity}2}^2(n_2 - 1) + \ldots + s_{\text{celebrity n}}^2(n_n - 1)$$
$$= 9.67(4-1) + 8.25(4-1) + 7.58(4-1) + 11.67(4-1) + 4.25(4-1) +$$
$$\quad 0.92(4-1) + 15.58(4-1) + 20.92(4-1)$$
$$= 29 + 24.75 + 22.75 + 35 + 12.75 + 2.75 + 46.75 + 62.75$$
$$= 236.50$$

The degrees of freedom for each person are $n - 1$ (i.e., the number of conditions minus 1). To get the total degrees of freedom we add the *df*s for all participants. So, with eight participants (celebrities) and four conditions (i.e., $n = 4$), there are 3 degrees of freedom for each celebrity and $8 \times 3 = 24$ degrees of freedom in total.

13.3.3. The model sum of squares (SS_M) ②

So far, we know that the total amount of variation within the data is 253.58 units. We also know that 236.50 of those units are explained by the variance created by individuals' (celebrities') performances under different conditions. Now some of this variation is the result of our experimental manipulation and some of this variation is simply random fluctuation. The next step is to work out how much variance is explained by our manipulation and how much is not.

In independent ANOVA, we worked out how much variation could be explained by our experiment (the model SS) by looking at the means for each group and comparing these to the overall mean. So, we measured the variance resulting from the differences between group means and the overall mean (see equation (10.5)). We do exactly the same thing with a repeated-measures design. First we calculate the mean for each level of the independent variable (in this case the mean time to retch for each food) and compare these values to the overall mean of all foods.

So, we calculate this SS in the same way as for independent ANOVA:

1 Calculate the difference between the mean of each group and the grand mean.

2 Square each of these differences.

3 Multiply each result by the number of participants that contribute to that mean (n_i).

4 Add the values for each group together:

$$SS_M = \sum_{n=1}^{k} n_k (\bar{x}_k - \bar{x}_{grand})^2$$

Using the means from the bushtucker data (see Table 13.2), we can calculate SS_M as follows:

$$\begin{aligned}
SS_M &= 8(8.13 - 5.56)^2 + 8(4.25 - 5.56)^2 + 8(4.13 - 5.56)^2 + 8(5.75 - 5.56)^2 \\
&= 8(2.57)^2 + 8(-1.31)^2 + 8(-1.44)^2 + 8(0.19)^2 \\
&= 83.13
\end{aligned}$$

For SS_M, the degrees of freedom (df_M) are again one less than the number of things used to calculate the sum of squares. For the model sums of squares we calculated the sum of squared errors between the four means and the grand mean. Hence, we used four things to calculate these sums of squares. Therefore, the degrees of freedom will be 3. So, as with independent ANOVA the model degrees of freedom are always the number of conditions (k) minus 1:

$$df_M = k - 1 = 3$$

13.3.4. The residual sum of squares (SS_R) ②

We now know that there are 253.58 units of variation to be explained in our data, and that the variation across our conditions accounts for 236.50 units. Of these 236.50 units, our experimental manipulation can explain 83.13 units. The final sum of squares is the residual sum of squares (SS_R), which tells us how much of the variation cannot be explained by the model. This value is the amount of variation caused by extraneous factors outside of experimental control. Knowing SS_W and SS_M already, the simplest way to calculate SS_R is to subtract SS_M from SS_W ($SS_R = SS_W - SS_M$):

$$\begin{aligned} SS_R &= SS_W - SS_M \\ &= 236.50 - 83.13 \\ &= 153.37 \end{aligned}$$

The degrees of freedom are calculated in a similar way:

$$\begin{aligned} df_R &= df_W - df_M \\ &= 24 - 3 \\ &= 21 \end{aligned}$$

13.3.5. The mean squares ②

SS_M tells us how much variation the model (e.g., the experimental manipulation) explains and SS_R tells us how much variation is due to extraneous factors. However, because both of these values are summed values the number of scores that were summed influences them. As with independent ANOVA we eliminate this bias by calculating the average sum of squares (known as the *mean squares*, MS), which is simply the sum of squares divided by the degrees of freedom:

$$MS_M = \frac{SS_M}{df_M} = \frac{83.13}{3} = 27.71$$

$$MS_R = \frac{SS_R}{df_R} = \frac{153.37}{21} = 7.30$$

MS_M represents the average amount of variation explained by the model (e.g., the systematic variation), whereas MS_R is a gauge of the average amount of variation explained by extraneous variables (the unsystematic variation).

13.3.6. The *F*-ratio ②

The *F*-ratio is a measure of the ratio of the variation explained by the model and the variation explained by unsystematic factors. It can be calculated by dividing the model mean squares by the residual mean squares. You should recall that this is exactly the same as for independent ANOVA:

$$F = \frac{MS_M}{MS_R}$$

So, as with the independent ANOVA, the F-ratio is still the ratio of systematic variation to unsystematic variation. As such, it is the ratio of the experimental effect to the effect on performance of unexplained factors. For the bushtucker data, the F-ratio is:

$$F = \frac{MS_M}{MS_R} = \frac{27.71}{7.30} = 3.79$$

This value is greater than 1, which indicates that the experimental manipulation had some effect above and beyond the effect of extraneous factors. As with independent ANOVA, this value can be compared against a critical value based on its degrees of freedom (which are df_M and df_R, which are 3 and 21 in this case).

13.3.7. The between-participant sum of squares ②

I mentioned that the total variation is broken down into a within-participant variation and a between-participant variation. We sort of forgot about the between-participant variation because we didn't need it to calculate the F-ratio. However, I will just briefly mention what it represents. The easiest way to calculate this term is by subtraction, because we know from Figure 13.2 that:

$$SS_T = SS_B + SS_W$$

Now, we have already calculated SS_T and SS_W so by rearranging the equation and replacing the values of these terms, we get:

$$\begin{aligned} SS_B &= SS_T - SS_W \\ &= 253.89 - 236.50 \\ &= 17.39 \end{aligned}$$

This term represents individual differences between cases. So, in this example, different celebrities will have different tolerances of eating these sorts of food. This is shown by the means for the celebrities in Table 13.2. For example, celebrity 4 ($M = 4.50$) was, on average, more than 2 seconds quicker to retch than participant 8 ($M = 6.75$). Celebrity 8 had a better constitution than celebrity 4. The between-participant sum of squares reflects these differences between individuals. In this case only 17.08 units of variation in the times to retch can be explained by individual differences between our celebrities.

13.4. One-way repeated-measures designs using R ②

13.4.1. Packages for repeated measures designs in R ①

I've discovered four ways of doing repeated-measures designs of the sort that you might analyse with ANOVA; there might be more, but once you've found four there really isn't much incentive to keep checking. These methods are:

- *Anova()*: We've used this function in other chapters, and it is good in that it produces sphericity tests and corrections like you might be used to seeing in other statistics packages. However, the process involved in using the function doesn't follow naturally from the way I have taught ANOVA thus far, so I decided not to cover this method. If you're curious though then a search engine is your friend.

- *lm()* or *aov()*: These functions follow most naturally from how we have done ANOVAs in the previous chapters. However, they don't produce sphericity test. Also, if you're going to take this linear model approach you're better off doing it using *lme()*. So, I will mention this method for continuity but mainly I use it as a stepping stone to describe *lme()*.

- **lme()**: This function enables you to do a regression in which observations can be correlated (which happens in repeated-measures designs). This form of regression is known as a multilevel model and is covered in more detail in Chapter 19. Therefore, this method naturally develops what we have already learnt about the *lm()* function. Using *lme()* has the benefit that we can forget about sphericity, and it's also how 'proper' statisticians would deal with repeated-measures data. The downside is that this approach is a little different from what you might be used to if you have ever analysed repeated-measures designs (i.e., you are not using ANOVA) with other packages such as SPSS or SAS.

- **ezANOVA()**: In case *lme()* freaks you out we'll also look at a function called *ezANOVA*, which as the name suggests enables you to do ANOVA easily (and in a way that closely matches other statistics packages that you might have used).

If you're using commands (which actually you have to), then you will need the packages *ez* (if you're going to use ANOVA), *ggplot2* (for graphs), *multcomp* (for *post hoc* tests), *nlme* (if you decide to use a multilevel model), *pastecs* (for descriptive statistics), *reshape* (for reshaping the data) and *WRS* (for robust tests). If you do not have these packages installed (some should be installed from previous chapters), you can install them by executing the following commands:

```
install.packages("ez"); install.packages("ggplot2"); install.packages
("multcomp"); install.packages("nlme"); install.packages("pastecs");
install.packages("reshape"); install.packages("WRS", repos="http://R-Forge.
R-project.org")
```

You then need to load these packages by executing these commands:

```
library(ez); library(ggplot2); library(multcomp); library(nlme);
library(pastecs); library(reshape); library(WRS)
```

13.4.2. General procedure for repeated-measures designs ①

To conduct repeated-measures analysis you should follow this general procedure:

1 *Enter data*: which turns out not to be as straightforward as you might think.
2 *Explore your data*: you know the routine by now – graphs, descriptive statistics and maybe even a bit of sphericity checking if you're not going to use *lme()*.
3 *Construct or choose contrasts*: you need to decide what contrasts to do and to specify them appropriately for all of the independent variables in your analysis.
4 *Compute the ANOVA/multilevel model*: you can then run the main analysis. Depending on what you found in the previous step, you might need to run a robust test.
5 *Compute contrasts or post hoc tests*: having conducted the main analysis you can follow it up with *post hoc* tests or look at the results of your contrasts. Again, the exact methods you choose will depend upon what you unearth in step 2.

We will work through these steps in turn.

13.4.3.   Repeated-measures ANOVA using R Commander ②

Figure 13.3 shows how to do repeated-measures ANOVA using R Commander: you can't, sad faces all round.

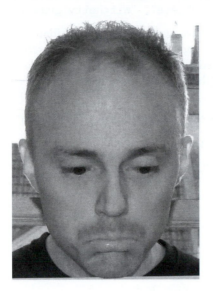

FIGURE 13.3
Repeated-measures ANOVA using R Commander

13.4.4.   Entering the data ②

The data for the example can be found in the file **Bushtucker.dat**. You can load this data file by setting your working directory to the appropriate location and executing:

```
bushData<-read.delim("Bushtucker.dat", header = TRUE)
```

I have structured the data in the format that you'd be most likely to use if you had entered the data in another software package and followed the usual conventions. The data have been entered in 'wide' format; that is, *levels of the repeated-measures variable are spread across different columns*.

```
participant stick_insect kangaroo_testicle fish_eye witchetty_grub
P1              8                 7                1              6
P2              9                 5                2              5
P3              6                 2                3              8
P4              5                 3                1              9
P5              8                 4                5              8
P6              7                 5                6              7
P7             10                 2                7              2
P8             12                 6                8              1
```

These data were originally entered in Excel, and, as you can see, I created a column in which I entered text that identifies each participant (P1, P2 etc.). The remaining four columns represent each participant's time to retch after consuming each of the four food types. For example, participant 7 took 10 seconds to retch after the stick insect, 2 after the kangaroo testicle and witchetty grub and 7 after the fish eye.

Although the format of the data follows typical conventions, to run the analysis in **R** we need the data to be in the long format. We can do this using the *melt()* function, which we've used many times before (e.g., Chapter 3). Remember that in this function we specify columns in the data that identify characteristics of the scores (such as from whom they originate) using the *id* option, and columns that identify the scores themselves using the *measured* option. In this case our scores are split over four columns (*stick_insect*, *kangaroo_testicle*, *fish_eye*, *witchetty_grub*), so these are our measured variables, and *participant* tells us from whom the scores originate, so this is our *id* variable. We can create a new dataframe (called *longBush*) by executing:

```
longBush<-melt(bushData, id = "participant", measured = c("stick_insect",
"kangaroo_testicle", "fish_eye", "witchetty_grub"))
```

This dataframe contains three columns: the first identifies the participant, the second identifies the type of food, and the third contains the scores (time to retch). By default, these columns will be named *participant*, *variable*, and *value*, which are not the most helpful of labels. Let's rename these columns so that we actually know what they represent by executing:

```
names(longBush)<-c("Participant", "Animal", "Retch")
```

Finally, let's convert the **Animal** variable to a factor with suitable labels by executing:

```
longBush$Animal<-factor(longBush$Animal, labels = c("Stick Insect", "Kangaroo
Testicle", "Fish Eye", "Witchetty Grub"))
```

The data now look like this:[4]

```
   Participant            Animal Retch
1           P1       Stick Insect     8
9           P1  Kangaroo Testicle     7
17          P1           Fish Eye     1
25          P1     Witchetty Grub     6
2           P2       Stick Insect     9
10          P2  Kangaroo Testicle     5
18          P2           Fish Eye     2
26          P2     Witchetty Grub     5
3           P3       Stick Insect     6
11          P3  Kangaroo Testicle     2
19          P3           Fish Eye     3
27          P3     Witchetty Grub     8
4           P4       Stick Insect     5
12          P4  Kangaroo Testicle     3
20          P4           Fish Eye     1
28          P4     Witchetty Grub     9
5           P5       Stick Insect     8
13          P5  Kangaroo Testicle     4
21          P5           Fish Eye     5
29          P5     Witchetty Grub     8
6           P6       Stick Insect     7
14          P6  Kangaroo Testicle     5
22          P6           Fish Eye     6
30          P6     Witchetty Grub     7
7           P7       Stick Insect    10
15          P7  Kangaroo Testicle     2
23          P7           Fish Eye     7
31          P7     Witchetty Grub     2
8           P8       Stick Insect    12
16          P8  Kangaroo Testicle     6
24          P8           Fish Eye     8
32          P8     Witchetty Grub     1
```

[4] To make it clearer that there are four observations for each person I have sorted the data by participant by executing:

```
longBush<-longBush[order(longBush$Participant),]
```

Notice that each participant (identified by the **Participant** variable) has four scores (distinguished by the variable **Animal**). These four scores are now represented by four different rows rather than four columns as they were before.

If we wanted to enter the data directly into **R**, we would first need to create the variable that identifies participants by using the *gl()* function (Chapter 3). Remember that this function takes the general form:

```
factor<-gl(number of levels, cases in each level, total cases, labels = c("label1", "label2"…))
```

This function creates a factor variable called *factor*; you specify the number of levels or groups of the factor, how many cases are in each level/group, optionally the total number of cases (the default is to multiply the number of groups by the number of cases per group), and you can also use the *labels* option to list names eight participants, so we can specify it as:

```
Participant<-gl(8, 4, labels = c("P1", "P2", "P3", "P4", "P5", "P6", "P7", "P8" ))
```

The numbers in the function tell **R** that we had eight sets of four scores, and the *labels* option then specifies the names to attach to these eight sets, which correspond to their participant number. To create the **Animal** variable we want four groups, each containing one score. This will create four cases (4 × 1 = 4), or, put another way, it will create the codes for the first participant. However, we want this pattern to be repeated for the remaining participants; we can do this by adding a third value to the function that is the total number of cases (i.e., 32). By specifying the total number of cases the *gl()* function will repeat the pattern of four codes until it reaches this total number of cases:

```
Animal<-gl(4, 1, 32, labels = c("Stick Insect", "Kangaroo Testicle", "Fish Eye", "Witchetty Grub"))
```

We can add the times to retch by creating a numeric variable in the usual way:

```
Retch<-c(8, 7, 1, 6, 9, 5, 2, 5, 6, 2, 3, 8, 5, 3, 1, 9, 8, 4, 5, 8, 7, 5, 6, 7, 10, 2, 7, 2, 12, 6, 8, 1)
```

Finally, we can merge these variables into a dataframe called *longBush* by executing:

```
longBush<-data.frame(Participant, Animal, Retch)
```

13.4.5. Exploring the data ②

As ever, we'll look at some graphs first. Let's start with the means across the different conditions.

SELF-TEST

✓ Use *ggplot2* to plot a bar graph (with error bars) of the time to retch with the type of animal eaten on the *x*-axis.

The resulting plot (Figure 13.4) shows that on average celebrities were quickest to retch after eating a testicle or eyeball (the means are lowest). Comparatively speaking, the stick insect was the most palatable because it took the longest time to induce retching.

FIGURE 13.4
Mean time to retch
after eating four
different animals

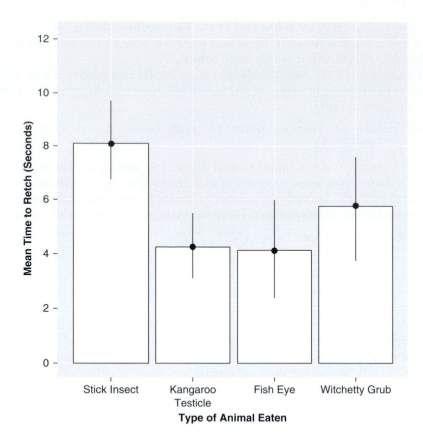

We can also look at boxplots for the time taken to retch after eating the different animals.

SELF-TEST

✓ Use *ggplot2* to plot boxplots of the time to retch after
  eating each animal (*x*-axis).

Figure 13.5 shows boxplots for these data. These show a similar profile to the bar chart: the median time to retch is highest for the stick insect and lowest for the testicle and eyeball. In addition, we can see that the middle part of the distribution of scores is a little more spread out for the fish eye and witchetty grub (the 'boxes' are longer) than the testicle and stick insect.

We have previously used the *by()* function and the *stat.desc()* function in the *pastecs* package to get descriptive statistics for separate groups (see Chapter 5 for more detail). Therefore, if we wanted to explore the effects of the type of animal on retching times, we could do so by executing:

```
by(longBush$Retch, longBush$Animal, stat.desc)
longBush$Animal: Stick Insect
```

```
median    mean    SE.mean  CI.mean.0.95   var   std.dev coef.var
8.0000   8.1250   0.7892       1.8661    4.9821  2.2320  0.2747
-------------------------------------------------------------
longBush$Animal: Kangaroo Testicle

median    mean    SE.mean  CI.mean.0.95   var   std.dev coef.var
4.5000   4.2500   0.6478       1.5318    3.3571  1.8323  0.4311
-------------------------------------------------------------
longBush$Animal: Fish Eye

median    mean    SE.mean  CI.mean.0.95   var   std.dev coef.var
4.0000   4.1250   0.9717       2.2977    7.5536  2.7484  0.6663
-------------------------------------------------------------
longBush$Animal: Witchetty Grub

median    mean    SE.mean  CI.mean.0.95   var   std.dev coef.var
6.5000   5.7500  1.0308       2.4374    8.5000  2.9155  0.5070
```

Output 13.1

The resulting (edited) output is in Output 13.1. From this table we can see that, on average, the time taken to retch was longest after eating the stick insect, and shortest after eating a testicle or eyeball. These mean values are useful for interpreting any significant effects that the main analysis throws up (pun intended).

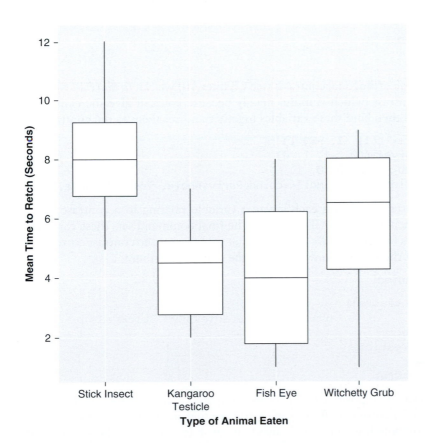

FIGURE 13.5
Boxplots of the bushtucker data

13.4.6.   Choosing contrasts ②

It's useful to follow up the main analysis with contrasts that break down the main effect (or effects) and tell us where the differences between groups lie. For one-way independent ANOVA, we entered codes that defined the contrasts we want to do. We can follow the same procedure for repeated-measures designs. As we have seen before, if we want to look at Type III sums of squares (see Jane Superbrain Box 11.1) then *we must specify contrasts, and the contrasts must also be orthogonal*, otherwise the resulting sums of squares will not be the Type III ones that we're expecting.

Let's imagine that we predicted that because eyes and testicles resemble human body parts, celebrities would be more disgusted by eating them than witchetty grubs and stick insects (which are eaten whole and don't resemble anything very human). Our first contrast might, therefore, compare the fish eye and kangaroo testicle (combined) to the witchetty grub and stick insect (combined). We need a second contrast then to separate the fish eye from the kangaroo testicle, and a third contrast to separate the witchetty grub from the stick insect. The resulting codes are in Table 13.3.

Table 13.3   Orthogonal contrasts for the **Animal** variable

Group	Contrast$_1$	Contrast$_2$	Contrast$_3$
Stick insect	1	0	−1
Kangaroo testicle	−1	−1	0
Fish eye	−1	1	0
Witchetty grub	1	0	1

To set these orthogonal contrasts (see Chapter 10) we can first create variables representing each contrast (which is useful mainly because you can give the contrasts informative names), and then bind these variables together and set them as the contrast for **Animal**:

```
PartvsWhole<-c(1, -1, -1, 1)
TesticlevsEye<-c(0, -1, 1, 0)
StickvsGrub<-c(-1, 0, 0, 1)
contrasts(longBush$Animal)<-cbind(PartvsWhole, TesticlevsEye, StickvsGrub)
```

The first three commands each create a variable relating to a contrast that contains the codes for each group from Table 13.3. The final command sets these three variables to be the contrasts for **Animal**. We can check that we have set the contrast correctly by executing the name of the variable and looking at the contrast attribute:

```
longBush$Animal
```

```
attr(,"contrasts")
                  PartvsWhole TesticlevsEye StickvsGrub
Stick Insect               1             0          -1
Kangaroo Testicle         -1            -1           0
Fish Eye                  -1             1           0
Witchetty Grub             1             0           1
```

Remembering that positive numbers are compared with negative and a zero means that the group is not involved at all, we can clearly see that the first contrast compares the eye and testicle (combined) with the stick insect and grub (combined). The second contrast ignores the stick insect and witchetty grub and compares the testicle to the eye (not a sentence I'd ever envisaged using in a statistics textbook). The third contrast ignores the testicle and eye and compares the stick insect to the witchetty grub.

13.4.7. Analysing repeated measures: two ways to skin a .dat ②

13.4.7.1. The easier (but slightly limited) way: repeated-measures ANOVA ②

To conduct an ANOVA using a repeated-measures design we can use the function *ezANOVA()* in the package *ez*. The advantage of this method is that it produces an output that resembles what you'll be used to seeing if you have ever attempted repeated-measures ANOVA using a different package (such as SPSS or SAS). It will also compute sphericity estimates and the aforementioned corrections for sphericity. The general format of this function is:

```
newModel<-ezANOVA(data = dataFrame, dv = .(outcome variable), wid = .(variable
that identifies participants),  within = .(repeated measures predictors),
between = .(between-group predictors), detailed = FALSE, type = 2)
```

This creates a model (*newModel*) from your dataframe (*dataFrame*). You can then set the following options:

- *dv*: This is the variable containing the scores (i.e., the outcome variable). In this case the outcome was the time to retch, which is represented by the variable **Retch**.

- *wid*: *ezANOVA* requires a variable that identifies the participants so that it can ascertain from which participant a given score came. In our current dataframe this is the variable **Participant**.

- *within*: This is a variable or list of variables representing the independent variables or predictors that were manipulated as repeated measures. In the current data this would be the variable **Animal**, which represents the type of food that was eaten.

- *between*: This is a variable or list of variables representing the independent variables or predictors that were manipulated as between-group variables. In the current data we don't have a variable manipulated in this way, but if you have a mixed design (as in the next chapter) you will need this option.

- *detailed*: This option is set to FALSE by default, but setting it to TRUE gives you a slightly more detailed (and in my opinion useful) output.

- *type*: This option determines the type of sums of squares. If omitted it defaults to *type = 2*, which produces Type II sums of squares. If you want Type III sums of squares (Jane Superbrain Box 11.1) then change this option to *type = 3*.

Note that some of these options take the form *option = .()*. Placing lists of variables within *.()* is just a convention of this function. It does not have any special significance, and does not have the power to turn you into a dragon.

Based on this description, hopefully you can see that we can run the ANOVA by executing:

```
bushModel<-ezANOVA(data = longBush, dv = .(Retch), wid = .(Participant),
within = .(Animal), detailed = TRUE, type = 3)
```

To see the output execute the model name:

bushModel

```
$ANOVA
Effect        DFn DFd  SSn      SSd        F         p          p<.05   ges
(Intercept)  1    7  990.125  17.375  398.899  1.973536e-07    *     0.8529
Animal       3   21   83.125 153.375    3.794  2.557030e-02    *     0.3274


$'Mauchly's Test for Sphericity'

  Effect       W         p          p<.05
2 Animal 0.136248 0.04684581       *


$'Sphericity Corrections'

Effect     GGe        p[GG]      p[GG]<.05  HFe         p[HF]       p[HF]<.05
Animal 0.5328456 0.06258412                0.6657636 0.04833061       *
```

Output 13.2

Output 13.2 shows the results from *ezANOVA()*. We'll begin with the sphericity information. Mauchly's test for sphericity (see also R's Souls' Tip 13.1) should be non-significant if we are to assume that the condition of sphericity has been met. The important column is the one containing the significance value (p) and in this case the value, .047, is less than the critical value of .05 (which is why there is an asterisk next to the p-value), so we reject the assumption that the variances of the differences between levels are equal. In other words, the assumption of sphericity has been violated, $W = 0.14$, $p = .047$. Knowing that we have violated this assumption a pertinent question is: how should we proceed?

We discovered earlier that there are two corrections based upon the estimates of sphericity advocated by Greenhouse and Geisser (1959) and Huynh and Feldt (1976). Both of these estimates give rise to a correction factor that is applied to the degrees of freedom used to assess the observed *F*-ratio. The closer the *Greenhouse–Geisser* correction, $\hat{\varepsilon}$, is to 1, the more homogeneous the variances of differences, and hence the closer the data are to being spherical. In a situation in which there are four conditions (as with our data) the lower limit of $\hat{\varepsilon}$ will be $1/(4-1)$, or .33. Output 13.2 shows that the calculated value of $\hat{\varepsilon}$ is .533 (*GGe* in the output). This is closer to the lower limit of .33 than it is to the upper limit of 1 and it therefore represents a substantial deviation from sphericity. The output also contains the Huynh–Feldt estimate (*HFe* in the output), which is slightly closer to 1

R's Souls' Tip 13.1 My Mauchly's test has vanished ②

Sometimes the output for Mauchly's test is nowhere to be found. It has gone, vanished, been sucked into the void. 'I must have done something wrong', you think to yourself. You check your commands, rerun them, perhaps you reinstall **R** and try it all again. Still they will not return. Perhaps you rob a bank and buy a new computer, but still nothing. In despair, you turn to alcohol. Eventually a budding research career has evaporated like the alcohol on your breath.

Actually, you haven't done anything wrong, so hold off on buying the gin, just for a while. The reason for the missing output is that (as I mentioned in section 13.2.1) you need at least three conditions for sphericity to be an issue (read that section if you want to know why). Therefore, if you have a repeated-measures variable that has only two levels then sphericity is met. Hence, the estimates of sphericity will be 1 (perfect sphericity) and the resulting significance test cannot be computed. Therefore, no output is generated. Maybe, a nice touch would be for it to print 'Hooray! Hooray! Sphericity has gone away!' We can dream.

than the Greenhouse–Geisser estimate (worryingly, it's value is .666, which could be proof that our data are evil). We will come back to these estimates very shortly.

Output 13.2 also shows the results of the ANOVA for the within-subject variable. This table can be read in much the same way as for one-way between-group ANOVA (see Chapter 10). There is a sum of squares for the repeated-measures effect of **Animal**, which tells us how much of the total variability is explained by the experimental effect. Note the value of 83.13, which is the model sum of squares (SS_M) that we calculated in section 13.3.3. There is also an error term (*SSd* in the output), which is the amount of unexplained variation across the conditions of the repeated-measures variable. This is the residual sum of squares (SS_R) that was calculated in section 13.3.4, and note that the value is 153.38 (which is the same value as we calculated). As I explained earlier, these sums of squares are converted into mean squares by dividing by the degrees of freedom. As we saw before, the *df* for the effect of **Animal** (*DFn* in the output) is simply $k - 1$, where k is the number of levels of the independent variable. The error *df* (*DFd* in the output) is $(n - 1)(k - 1)$, where n is the number of participants (or in this case, the number of celebrities) and k is as before. The *F*-ratio is obtained by dividing the mean squares for the experimental effect (27.71) by the error mean squares (7.30). As with between-group ANOVA, this test statistic represents the ratio of systematic variance to unsystematic variance. The value of $F = 3.79$ (the same as we calculated earlier) is then compared against a critical value for 3 and 21 degrees of freedom. **R** displays the exact significance level for the *F*-ratio. The significance of *F* is .026, which is significant because it is less than the criterion value of .05: the output help-fully places an asterisk next to any values that are significant at .05 in the column labelled *p*<.05. We can, therefore, conclude that there was a significant difference between the four animals in their capacity to induce retching when eaten. However, this main test does not tell us which animals differed from each other.

Although this result seems very plausible, we have learnt that the violation of the sphericity assumption makes the *F*-test inaccurate. We know from Output 13.2 that these data were non-spherical and so we need to make allowances for this violation. Output 13.2 also contains *p*-values that have been corrected using the Greenhouse–Geisser and Huynh–Feldt corrections (Jane Superbrain Box 13.3); these are labelled *p[GG]* and *p[HF]*, respectively. For these data the corrections result in the observed *F* being non-significant when using the Greenhouse–Geisser correction (because $p = .063$, which is greater than .05). However, it was noted earlier that this correction is quite conservative, and so can miss effects that genuinely exist. It is, therefore, useful to consult the Huynh–Feldt corrected *p*-value as well.

JANE SUPERBRAIN 13.3

Adjusting for sphericity ③

The Greenhouse–Geisser and Huynh–Feldt adjusted *p*-values are calculated by making an adjustment to the degrees of freedom associated with the *F*-statistic (therefore, the critical value against which the obtained *F*-statistic is compared changes). The *F*-ratio itself remains unchanged. The degrees of freedom are adjusted by multiplying them by the estimate of sphericity shown in Output 13.2 (see the previous Oliver Twisted). For example, the Greenhouse–Geisser estimate of sphericity was .533. The original degrees of freedom for the model were 3; this value is corrected by multiplying by the estimate of sphericity ($3 \times .533 = 1.599$). Likewise the error *df* was 21; this value is corrected in the same way ($21 \times .533 = 11.19$). The *F*-ratio is then tested against a critical value with these new degrees of freedom (1.599, 11.19). The Huynh–Feldt correction is applied in the same way.

Using this correction, the F-value is still significant because the probability value of .048 is just below the criterion value of .05. So, by this correction, we would accept the hypothesis that the type of animal eaten affected the time to retch. However, it was also noted earlier that this correction is quite liberal and so tends to accept values as significant when, in reality, they are not significant. This leaves us with the puzzling dilemma of whether or not to accept this F-statistic as significant (and also illustrates how ridiculous it is to have a fixed criterion like .05 against which to determine significance).

I mentioned earlier that Stevens (2002) recommends taking an average of the two estimates, and certainly when the two corrections give different results (as is the case here) this can be useful. If the two corrections give rise to the same conclusion it makes little difference which you choose to report (although if you accept the F-statistic as significant you might as well report the more conservative Greenhouse–Geisser estimate to avoid criticism). Although it is easy to calculate the average of the two correction factors and to correct the degrees of freedom accordingly, it is not so easy to then calculate an exact probability for those degrees of freedom. Therefore, should you ever be faced with this perplexing situation (and to be honest that's fairly unlikely) I recommend taking an average of the two significance values to give you a rough idea of which correction is giving the most accurate answer. In this case, the average of the two p-values is $(.063 + .048)/2 = .056$. Therefore, we should probably go with the Greenhouse–Geisser correction and conclude that the F-ratio is non-significant.

These data illustrate how important it is to use a valid critical value of F: it can potentially mean the difference between making a Type I error and not. However, it also highlights how arbitrary it is that we use a .05 level of significance. These two corrections produce significance values that differ by only .015 and yet they lead to completely opposite conclusions. The decision about 'significance' has, in some ways, become rather arbitrary. The F, and hence the size of effect, is unaffected by these corrections and so whether the p falls slightly above or slightly below .05 is less important than how big the effect is. We might be well advised to look at an effect size to see whether the effect is substantive regardless of its significance.

In terms of *post hoc* tests, we can use the *pairwise.t.test()* function that we have used in previous chapters (see Chapter 10 in particular). The format of this option is exactly the same as before except that we need to add the option *paired = TRUE* to reflect the fact that means are dependent (so, we're asking for paired t-tests rather than independent t-tests). To get *post hoc* tests for the current data, execute:

```
pairwise.t.test(longBush$Retch, longBush$Animal, paired = TRUE, p.adjust.
method = "bonferroni")


Pairwise comparisons using paired t tests

data:  longBush$Retch and longBush$Animal

                  Stick Insect Kangaroo Testicle Fish Eye
Kangaroo Testicle 0.0121       -                 -
Fish Eye          0.0056       1.0000            -
Witchetty Grub    1.0000       1.0000            1.0000

P value adjustment method: bonferroni
```

Output 13.3

Output 13.3 shows the results of the *post hoc* tests. We can see that the time to retch was significantly longer after eating a stick insect compared to a kangaroo testicle ($p = .012$) and a fish eye ($p = .006$) but not compared to a witchetty grub. The time to retch after eating a kangaroo testicle was not significantly different than after eating a fish eyeball or witchetty grub (both $ps > .05$). Finally, the time to retch was not significantly different after eating a fish eyeball compared to a witchetty grub ($p > .05$).

13.4.7.2. The slightly more complicated way: the multilevel approach ②

The most complicated thing about the slightly more complicated way is trying to explain it; it is not actually that hard to do. The method we will use is known as a multilevel linear model, and the whole of Chapter 19 is dedicated to explaining these models. Therefore, I'm going to gloss over some of the details and refer you to that chapter if you want to get a better understanding of what we're doing. In short, a multilevel model is simply a regression or linear model that considers dependency in the data. We learnt in Chapter 7 that one of the assumptions of regression was that residuals (errors) needed to be independent. If they're not, demons will rise from statistics hell and waggle their reproductive organs at us. Repeated-measures designs, as we have seen, have dependent data, therefore dependent residuals; if we try to analyse them with an ordinary regression, we need to prepare ourselves to run screaming from the demons' ....

A multilevel model is an extension of regression that handles dependent data by explicitly modelling the dependency. It is, therefore, very well suited to repeated-measures experimental designs. One advantage of this approach is that we can continue to think about the analysis as a linear model; we just use a different function, *lme()*, rather than *aov()*, which will allow us to model the fact that some scores come from the same entities and are, therefore, correlated.

We saw in Chapter 10 that we can write a one-way ANOVA as a linear model in **R** as:

```
newModel<-aov(outcome ~ predictor, data = dataFrame)
```

In the current example we're trying to predict the time taken to retch (**Retch**) from the type of animal eaten (**Animal**), and our dataframe is called *longBush*. Therefore, we could write our model as:

```
bushModel<-aov(Retch ~ Animal, data = longBush)
```

However, this model takes no account of the fact that the predictor (**Animal**) is made up of data from the same people (and thus dependent). As it stands, we would violate an assumption of our linear model. We need to factor this dependency into the model.[5] We can do this using *lme()*, which has an option *random* that enables us to specify that there is variability in participants' propensities to retch within the variable **Animal**.

The general format of *lme()* is as follows:

```
newModel  <-lme(outcome ~ predictor(s), random = random effects, data =
dataFrame, method = "ML")
```

The key thing to focus on is that this command is basically exactly the same as if we had used the *lm()* and *aov()* functions. We simply specify our outcome and predictor variables. However, there are two additional options. The first is to specify a method. The default is something known as restricted maximum-likelihood estimation (REML), but – for various reasons that we'll get into in Chapter 19 – it's preferable to use maximum likelihood (ML), so always set the method to be "ML" when doing repeated-measures ANOVA. The second option is *random =*, which allows us to specify any random effects. Again, we'll get into what random effects are in Chapter 19, because it's quite complicated. However, for

---

[5] We can do this using *aov()* by adding an error term to the model that is based on within-participant variability across different animals, *Error(Participant/Animal)*:

```
bushModel<-aov(Retch ~ Animal + Error(Participant/Animal), data = longBush)
```

However, the resulting model would still be assessed using an *F*-ratio which means that we need to worry about sphericity, which is slightly irritating because *aov()* won't throw out sphericity-corrected estimates, or indeed the estimates themselves. For this reason, I favour using *lme()* and forgetting that sphercity even exists.

now I'll just say that in the current context a random effect is an effect that can vary across different entities. For example, if we want to model the fact that people's overall threshold to retch will vary, we can write this as *random = ~1|Participant/Animal*. All this means is that if you look at the variable **Participant** within the variable **Animal** (that's what the 'Participant/Animal' bit means), then overall levels (that's represented by 1) of the outcome (time to retch) vary. By including this term, we're telling the model that data with the same value of **Participant** within different levels of **Animal** are dependent (i.e., from the same person). I know, it's a bit of a head crusher.

Whether any of that made sense or not, trust me that we can specify our model as

```
bushModel<-lme(Retch ~ Animal, random = ~1|Participant/Animal, data = long-
Bush, method = "ML")
```

Notice that we have defined the model in exactly the same was as for *aov()*, we have simply added in a term that lets the model know that the variable **Animal** is made up of the same participants repeated multiple times across the variable **Animal** (*random = ~1|Participant/Animal*). If we execute this model and ask for a summary, we will get a set of parameters that relate to the contrasts that we set earlier for **Animal**. If we want to test whether **Animal** had an overall effect, then we need to compare the model that we have just created to one in which the predictor is absent. To do this, we create another model, but rather than include **Animal** as a predictor, we include only the intercept (which we denote with '1'). As such we create the baseline model as follows:

```
baseline<-lme(Retch ~ 1, random = ~1|Participant/Animal, data = longBush,
method = "ML")
```

Notice that this command is exactly the same as before except that the model is 'Retch ~ 1' rather than 'Retch ~ Animal'.[6] By comparing these models we can see whether adding the variable **Animal** as a predictor significantly improves the model (in other words, by using group means to predict the speed of retching, does the model fit the data better than when we don't include this predictor?). To compare the models (see section 7.8.4.2) execute:

```
anova(baseline, bushModel)
```

Output 13.5 shows the comparison of the baseline model and the model that includes **Animal** as a predictor (*bushModel*). The degrees of freedom change from 4 for the baseline model to 7 for *bushModel*, which is a difference of 3. This is because **Animal** has been coded with three contrasts, which means that three parameters (one for each contrast) have been added to the model. The AIC and BIC tell us about the fit of the model (smaller values mean a better fit). The fact that these values are smaller in the final model than the baseline tells us that the fit of the model has got better. The likelihood ratio (*L.Ratio* in the output) tells us whether this improvement in fit is significant, and because the *p*-value of .0054 is less than .05 it is. Therefore, **Animal** is a significant predictor of **Retch**. We can conclude, then, that the type of animal consumed had a significant effect on the time taken to retch, $\chi^2(3) = 12.69$, $p = .005$.

```
         Model df    AIC      BIC      logLik    Test  L.Ratio p-value
baseline   1    4 165.0875 170.9504 -78.54373
bushModel  2    7 158.3949 168.6551 -72.19747 1 vs 2 12.69253  0.0054
```

Output 13.4

[6] In actual fact when we write 'Retch ~ Animal' the model that we get is 'Retch ~ 1 + Animal'. The '1' is the intercept and **R** incudes it automatically (which is why we don't have to explicitly mention the '1' when we start including predictors in the model). You can see, then, that the baseline and final models differ only in the inclusion of **Animal** as a predictor; therefore, if the final model is a significantly better fit of the data than the baseline then this finding tells us that **Animal** is a significant predictor of **Retch**.

We can further explore the model by executing:

summary(bushModel)

Output 13.5 shows the parameter estimates for the model. Most important, these include the parameters for the three contrasts that we set. First, when we compare whole animals (stick insect and witchetty grub combined) to animal parts (testicle and eye) retching times were significantly different, $b = 1.38$, $t(21) = 3.15$, $p = .005$. From the descriptive statistics (Output 13.1) it looks as though people retched more quickly after eating parts of animals $((4.25 + 4.125)/2 = 4.188)$ than whole animals $((8.125 + 5.75)/2 = 6.938)$. The second contrast tells us that there was no significant difference in the time to retch after eating a kangaroo testicle and a fish eye, $b = -0.063$, $t(21) = -0.101$, $p = .920$. The final contrast tells us that there was a trend for retching times to be shorter after eating a witchetty grub $(M = 5.75)$ than a stick insect $(M = 8.125)$, $b = -1.188$, $t(21) = -1.924$, $p = .068$.

```
Formula: ~1 | Animal %in% Participant
        (Intercept)   Residual
StdDev:   2.309935 0.01176165

Fixed effects: Retch ~ Animal
                      Value Std.Error DF   t-value p-value
(Intercept)          5.5625 0.4365423 21 12.742178  0.0000
AnimalPartvsWhole    1.3750 0.4365423 21  3.149752  0.0048
AnimalTesticlevsEye -0.0625 0.6173641 21 -0.101237  0.9203
AnimalStickvsGrub   -1.1875 0.6173641 21 -1.923500  0.0681
```

Output 13.5

Although the contrasts tell us everything we need to know, if there had not been a logical set of contrasts to do we might have done *post hoc* tests. We can, of course, use the *pairwise.t.test()* function as explained in the previous section. However, by doing the analysis in the slightly more complicated way, we also have the option to use the *glht()* function that we have used in previous chapters (see Chapter 10 in particular). The format of this option is exactly the same as when we have used this function before; therefore, to get *post hoc* tests for the current data, execute:

postHocs<-glht(bushModel, linfct = mcp(Animal = "Tukey"))

summary(postHocs)

confint(postHocs)

```
Linear Hypotheses:
                              Estimate Std. Error z value Pr(>|z|)
Testicle - Stick Insect == 0   -3.875      1.155  -3.355  0.00444 **
Fish Eye - Stick Insect == 0   -4.000      1.155  -3.463  0.00319 **
Witchetty - Stick Insect == 0  -2.375      1.155  -2.056  0.16759
Fish Eye - Testicle == 0       -0.125      1.155  -0.108  0.99955
Witchetty - Testicle == 0       1.500      1.155   1.299  0.56371
Witchetty - Fish Eye == 0       1.625      1.155   1.407  0.49492

        Simultaneous Confidence Intervals

Multiple Comparisons of Means: Tukey Contrasts

Linear Hypotheses:
                                      Estimate lwr      upr
Kangaroo Testicle - Stick Insect == 0  -3.8750  -6.8401 -0.9099
Fish Eye - Stick Insect == 0           -4.0000  -6.9651 -1.0349
```

```
Witchetty Grub - Stick Insect == 0           -2.3750   -5.3401   0.5901
Fish Eye - Kangaroo Testicle == 0            -0.1250   -3.0901   2.8401
Witchetty Grub - Kangaroo Testicle == 0   1.5000   -1.4651   4.4651
Witchetty Grub - Fish Eye == 0               1.6250   -1.3401   4.5901
```

Output 13.6

Output 13.6 shows the results of the *post hoc* tests. We can see that the time to retch was significantly longer after eating a stick insect compared to a kangaroo testicle ($p = .004$) and a fish eye ($p = .003$) but not compared to a witchetty grub. The time to retch after eating a kangaroo testicle was not significantly different to after eating a fish eyeball or witchetty grub (both $ps > .05$). Finally, the time to retch was not significantly different after eating a fish eyeball compared to a witchetty grub ($p > .05$).

CRAMMING SAM'S TIPS   Repeated-measures ANOVA

- The one-way repeated-measures ANOVA compares several means, when those means have come from the same participants; for example, if you measured people's statistical ability each month over a year-long course.
- There are several ways to do repeated-measures ANOVA. One is a conventional ANOVA approach using the *ezANOVA()* function; the other is to use a multilevel linear model using the *lme()* function.
- In repeated-measures ANOVA there is an additional assumption: *sphericity*. This assumption needs to be considered only when you have three or more repeated-measures conditions. If you use the *ezANOVA()* function then test for sphericity using *Mauchly's test*. If the *p*-value is less than .05 then the assumption is violated. If the significance of Mauchly's test is greater than .05 then the assumption of sphericity has been met.
- If the assumption of sphericity has been met then use the *p*-value for the main ANOVA. If the assumption was violated then read the *p*-value corrected using either the *Greenhouse–Geisser* (*p[GG]*) or *Huynh–Feldt* (*p[HF]*) estimate of sphericity (read this chapter to find out the relative merits of the two procedures). If the *p*-value is less than .05 then the means of the groups are significantly different.
- If you use *lme()* then you can forget about sphericity.
- For contrasts and *post hoc* tests, again look to the *p*-values to discover if your comparisons are significant (they will be if the significance value is less than .05).

13.4.8.   Robust one-way repeated-measures ANOVA ③

As with the other ANOVAs we have encountered, Wilcox (2005) describes robust procedures for conducting one-way repeated-measures ANOVA. To access these we need to again load the *WRS* package (see section 5.8.4.). There are four functions that we will look at:

- **rmanova()**: This performs one-way repeated-measures ANOVA on trimmed means.
- **rmmcp()**: This performs *post hoc* tests for one-way repeated-measures design based on trimmed means.
- **rmanovab()**: This performs one-way repeated-measures ANOVA using a bootstrap procedure.
- **pairdepb()**: This performs *post hoc* tests for the above function.

These functions need the data to be in wide format rather than long (see Chapter 3). However, the data were originally in this format so we can simply reuse these (remember they are stored in an object called *bushData*). The data look like this:

```
participant stick_insect kangaroo_testicle fish_eye witchetty_grub
P1              8                  7            1               6
P2              9                  5            2               5
P3              6                  2            3               8
P4              5                  3            1               9
P5              8                  4            5               8
P6              7                  5            6               7
P7             10                  2            7               2
P8             12                  6            8               1
```

We want only the scores so we need to get rid of the **participant** variable. The participant variable is in the first column, so we could create a new dataframe (*bushData2*) that excludes this first column by executing:

```
bushData2<-bushData[, -c(1)]
```

This command takes the *bushData* object and retains all of the rows (hence no command before the comma) but drops column 1 by specifying *–c(1)*, the minus sign means 'delete' in this context. The new dataframe now contains only the scores:

```
bushData2
```

```
stick_insect kangaroo_testicle fish_eye witchetty_grub
    8                  7            1               6
    9                  5            2               5
    6                  2            3               8
    5                  3            1               9
    8                  4            5               8
    7                  5            6               7
   10                  2            7               2
   12                  6            8               1
```

The function *rmanova()* takes the general form:

```
rmanova(data, tr = .2)
```

As with other functions we've encountered, the level of trimming is by default 20% (*tr = .2*), but can be changed by including the *tr =* option. Also, the default alpha level is .05. Assuming we are happy with the default level of trimming, we need only specify the dataframe (*bushData2*); therefore, we can do one-way repeated-measures ANOVA based on trimmed means by executing:

```
rmanova(bushData2)
```

The function *rmanovab()* has the format:

```
rmanovab(data, tr = .2, alpha = .05, nboot = 599)
```

The main differences are an option to control the number of bootstrap samples (*nboot*), and an option to change the level of significance (the default of .05 is fine though). I would normally use 2000 bootstrap samples, so if we wanted to change this option, but leave the default level of trim (20%) and alpha (.05) then we can run the analysis for the current data by executing:

```
rmanovab(bushData2, nboot = 2000)
```

The output of both of these commands is shown in Output 13.7. For *rmanova()* (left-hand side of Output 13.7) we are given a test statistic, F, for the effect of animal (*$test*), the degrees of freedom (*$df*), the p-value (*$siglevel*), the group means (*$tmeans*). Given that the significance level (.1002) is greater than .05, we can say that there were no significant differences in retch times after eating different animals, $F(2.31, 11.55) = 2.75$, $p = .100$. (Note that I have reported the test statistic, its degrees of freedom and the p-value, which you can find in the output.)

rmanova()	*rmanovab()*
[1] "The number of groups to be compared is"	1] "The number of groups to be compared is"
[1] 4	[1] 4
$test	$teststat
[1] 2.752794	[1] 2.752794
$df	$crit
[1] 2.309193 11.545964	[1] 4.841391
$siglevel	
[1] 0.1002	
$tmeans	
[1] 8.000000 4.166667 4.000000 6.000000	
$ehat	
[1] 0.5873188	
$etil	
[1] 0.7697309	

Output 13.7

The output of *rmanovab()* (right-hand side of Output 13.7) tells us much the same things, but we get only a test statistic (*$teststat*) and the critical value for this statistic at a .05 level of significance (*$crit*). If the test statistic is significant at $p < .05$ (or whatever alpha you specified if you didn't use the default value) then the test statistic should be greater than the critical value. In this case, the test statistic (2.75) is less than the critical value (4.84) indicating no significant differences in retch times after eating different animals, $F = 2.75$, $F_{crit} = 4.84$, $p > .05$. Both of these robust methods yield non-significant results (unlike the multilevel models).

The *post hoc* tests for each analysis are conducted using the same command structure. Assuming you leave the default options, to run *post hoc* tests based on a 20% trimmed mean, execute:[7]

```
rmmcp(bushData2)
```

To conduct *post hoc* tests based on trimmed means and a bootstrap:

```
pairdepb(bushData2, nboot = 2000)
```

Output 13.8 shows the *post hoc* tests based on trimmed means (*rmmcp*). If the value of *p.value* is less than the critical value (*p.crit*) and the confidence interval does not cross zero then the comparison is significant. The columns labelled *group* tell you which groups are being compared (the numbers relate to the columns in the dataframe).

- [1,] tests the difference between the stick insect and kangaroo testicle. This contrast is not significant because *p.value* (.014) is greater than *p.crit* (.010) and the confidence interval crosses zero.

---

[7] Obviously if you changed the level of trim for the main analysis you would need to do the same here. For example, for 15% trimmed means:

```
rmanova(bushData2, tr = .15)
rmmcp(bushData2, tr = .15)
```

- [2,] tests the difference between the stick insect and fish eye. This difference is not significant because *p.value* (.012) is greater than *p.crit* (.009) and the confidence interval crosses zero.

- [3,] tests the difference between the stick insect and witchetty grub. This difference is not significant because *p.value* (.441) is greater than *p.crit* (.017) and the confidence interval crosses zero.

- [4,] tests the difference between the kangaroo testicle and fish eye. This difference is not significant because *p.value* (1) is greater than *p.crit* (.05) and the confidence interval crosses zero.

- [5,] tests the difference between the kangaroo testicle and witchetty grub. This difference is not significant because *p.value* (.344) is greater than *p.crit* (.013) and the confidence interval crosses zero.

- [6,] tests the difference between the fish eye and witchetty grub. This difference is not significant because *p.value* (.460) is greater than *p.crit* (.025) and the confidence interval crosses zero.

We could report that there was no significant difference between the time to retch after eating a stick insect compared to a kangaroo testicle, $\hat{\Psi} = 3.67$ (−0.48, 7.82), $p > .05$, fish eye $\hat{\Psi} = 4.00$ (−0.36, 8.36), $p > .05$, or witchetty grub $\hat{\Psi} = 2.00$ (−8.10, 12.10), $p > .05$; or a kangaroo testicle compared to a fish eye $\hat{\Psi} = 0$ (−5.39, 5.39), $p > .05$, or witchetty grub $\hat{\Psi} = -1.83$ (−9.23, 5.57), $p > .05$; or a fish eye compared to a witchetty grub $\hat{\Psi} = -2.00$ (−12.55, 8.55), $p > .05$. Note that in each case I have reported *psihat* and its confidence interval.

```
$test
      Group Group       test    p.value  p.crit         se
[1,]      1     2  3.7282016 0.01359625 0.01020 0.9834947
[2,]      1     3  3.8733436 0.01172054 0.00851 1.0326995
[3,]      1     4  0.8355727 0.44148206 0.01690 2.3935678
[4,]      2     3  0.0000000 1.00000000 0.05000 1.2769904
[5,]      2     4 -1.0454201 0.34371248 0.01270 1.7536809
[6,]      3     4 -0.8000000 0.46001407 0.02500 2.5000000


$psihat
      Group Group     psihat    ci.lower    ci.upper
[1,]      1     2   3.666667  -0.4830017    7.816335
[2,]      1     3   4.000000  -0.3572784    8.357278
[3,]      1     4   2.000000  -8.0992023   12.099202
[4,]      2     3   0.000000  -5.3880170    5.388017
[5,]      2     4  -1.833333  -9.2326553    5.565989
[6,]      3     4  -2.000000 -12.5482728    8.548273


$con
      [,1]
[1,]     0


$num.sig
[1] 0
```

Output 13.8

Output 13.9 shows the *post hoc* tests based on trimmed means and a bootstrap (*pairdepb*). The interpretation of these results is similar to that for the trimmed means. If the value of *test* is greater than the critical value (*$crit*) and the confidence interval does not cross zero then the contrast is significant. Therefore, we're comparing each value of test against 4.98; as you can see, all values of test are smaller than this value and their confidence intervals cross zero, so we can conclude that none of the groups differ significantly.

We could again report that (note that the values and confidence intervals for *psihat* have changed): there was no significant difference between the time to retch after eating a stick insect compared to a kangaroo testicle, $\hat{\Psi} = 3.83$ (−0.70, 8.37), $p > .05$, fish eye $\hat{\Psi} = 4.00$ (−1.15, 9.15), $p > .05$, or witchetty grub $\hat{\Psi} = 2.00$ (−7.78, 11.78), $p > .05$; or a kangaroo testicle compared to a fish eye $\hat{\Psi} = 0.17$ (−7.27, 7.61), $p > .05$, or witchetty grub $\hat{\Psi} = -1.83$ (−9.76, 6.09), $p > .05$; or a fish eye compared to a witchetty grub $\hat{\Psi} = -2.00$ (−12.90, 8.90), $p > .05$.

```
[1] "Taking bootstrap samples. Please wait."
$test
      Group Group         test          se
[1,]     1     2   4.2097438  0.9105859
[2,]     1     3   3.8729833  1.0327956
[3,]     1     4   1.0192944  1.9621417
[4,]     2     3   0.1116291  1.4930394
[5,]     2     4  -1.1527967  1.5903354
[6,]     3     4  -0.9144599  2.1870833


$psihat
      Group Group      psihat      ci.lower    ci.upper
[1,]     1     2   3.8333333  -0.7038692    8.370536
[2,]     1     3   4.0000000  -1.1461402    9.146140
[3,]     1     4   2.0000000  -7.7768199   11.776820
[4,]     2     3   0.1666667  -7.2727438    7.606077
[5,]     2     4  -1.8333333  -9.7575433    6.090877
[6,]     3     4  -2.0000000 -12.8976429    8.897643


$crit
[1] 4.982729
```

Output 13.9

13.5. Effect sizes for repeated-measures designs ③

As with independent ANOVA, the best measure of the overall effect size is omega squared (ω^2). However, just to make life even more complicated than it already is, the equations we've previously used for omega squared can't be used for repeated-measures data. If you do use the same equation on repeated-measures data it will slightly overestimate the effect size. For the sake of simplicity some people do use the same equation for one-way independent and repeated-measures ANOVAs (and I'm guilty of this in another book), but if you want to hit simplicity in the face with Stingy the particularly poison-ridden jellyfish, and embrace complexity like a particularly hot date, then the equation is (hang onto your hats):

$$\omega^2 = \frac{\left[\dfrac{k-1}{nk}(MS_M - MS_R)\right]}{MS_R + \dfrac{MS_B - MS_R}{k} + \left[\dfrac{k-1}{nk}(MS_M - MS_R)\right]} \tag{13.1}$$

I know what you're thinking, and it's something along the lines of 'are you having a laugh?'. Well, no, I'm not, but really the equation isn't too bad if you break it down. First, there are some mean squares that we've come across before (and calculated before). There's the mean square for the model (MS_M) and the residual mean square (MS_R) both of which we calculated earlier in the chapter. There's also k, the number of conditions in the experiment, which for these data would be 4 (there were four animals), and there's n, the number of people who took part (in this case, the number of celebrities, 8). The main problem is that we have all of these values from calculating everything by hand, but why would you ever calculate an ANOVA by hand except if you were writing a competing textbook?

A practical solution is to use generalized eta-squared (Bakeman, 2005) because it is produced by *ezANOVA()* in the column labelled *ges*. We can see from Output 13.2 that the value for **Animal** is .3274.

I've mentioned at various other points that it's actually more useful to have effect size measures for focused comparisons anyway (rather than the main ANOVA), and so a slightly easier approach to calculating effect sizes is to calculate them for the contrasts we did (see Output 13.5). We can use the equation that we've seen before to convert the *t*-values to *r*:

$$r = \sqrt{\frac{t^2}{t^2 + df}}$$

Remember in section 10.7 we wrote a function to compute this called *rcontrast()*, which you should be able to use if you have the package associated with this book, *DSUR*, loaded – see section 3.4.5. We can use this function to calculate *r* for the contrasts we did by executing these commands (the values of *t* and *df* come from Output 13.5):

```
rcontrast(3.149752, 21)
rcontrast(-0.101237, 21)
rcontrast(-1.923500, 21)
```

The resulting values of *r* are

```
[1] "r =  0.566434937677424"
[1] "r =  0.0220863356562026"
[1] "r =  0.387030341310243"
```

which show that the difference between body parts and whole animals was a large effect ($r = .57$), between the stick insect and witchetty grub a medium effect ($r = .39$), but between the testicle and eyeball a very small effect ($r = .02$).

13.6. Reporting one-way repeated-measures designs ②

What we report when we conduct repeated-measures ANOVA depends on how we do it. If you have used a traditional ANOVA approach (e.g., using *ezANOVA*) then you report the same details as with an independent ANOVA. The only additional thing we should concern ourselves with is reporting the corrected degrees of freedom if sphericity was violated. Personally, I'm also keen on reporting the results of sphericity tests as well. As with the independent ANOVA, the degrees of freedom used to assess the *F*-ratio are the degrees of freedom for the effect of the model ($df_M = 1.60$) and the degrees of freedom for the residuals of the model ($df_R = 11.19$). Remember that in this example we corrected both using the

Greenhouse–Geisser estimates of sphericity, which is why the degrees of freedom are as they are. Therefore, we could report the main finding as:

✓ Mauchly's test indicated that the assumption of sphericity had been violated, $\chi^2(5) = 11.41$, $p < .05$, therefore Greenhouse–Geisser corrected tests are reported ($\varepsilon = .53$). The results show that the time to retch was not significantly affected by the type of animal eaten, $F(1.60, 11.19) = 3.79$, $p > .05$, $\eta^2 = .327$.

Alternatively, we could report the Huynh–Feldt corrected values:

✓ Mauchly's test indicated that the assumption of sphericity had been violated, $\chi^2(5) = 11.41$, $p < .05$, therefore degrees of freedom were corrected using Huynh–Feldt estimates of sphericity ($\varepsilon = .67$). The results show that the time to retch was significantly affected by the type of animal eaten, $F(2, 13.98) = 3.79$, $p < .05$, $\eta^2 = .327$.

If you have done a multilevel model then you would write your results differently (you could also put the results in a table as in section 19.8):

✓ The type of animal consumed had a significant effect on the time taken to retch, $\chi^2(3) = 12.69$, $p = .005$. Orthogonal contrasts revealed that retching times were significantly quicker for animal parts (testicle and eye) compared to whole animals (stick insect and witchetty grub), $b = 1.38$, $t(21) = 3.15$, $p = .005$; there was no significant difference in the time to retch after eating a kangaroo testicle and a fish eye, $b = -0.063$, $t(21) = -0.101$, $p = .920$, or between eating a witchetty grub or a stick insect, $b = -1.188$, $t(21) = -1.924$, $p = .068$.

Labcoat Leni's Real Research 13.1   Who's afraid of the big bad wolf? ②

Field, A. P. (2006). *Journal of Abnormal Psychology*, 115(4), 742–752.

I'm going to let my ego get the better of me and talk about some of my own research. When I'm not scaring my students with statistics, I scare small children with Australian marsupials. There is a good reason for doing this, which is to try to discover how children develop fears (which will help us to prevent them). Most of my research looks at the effect of giving children information about animals or situations that are novel to them (rather like a parent, teacher or TV show would do). In one particular study (Field, 2006), I used three novel animals (the quoll, quokka and cuscus) and children were told negative things about one of the animals, positive things about another, and were given no information about the third (our control). I then asked the children to place their hands in three wooden boxes, each of which they believed contained one of the aforementioned animals. My hypothesis was that they would take longer to place their hand in the box containing the animal about which they had heard negative information.

The data from this part of the study are in the file **Field(2006).dat**. Labcoat Leni wants you to carry out a one-way repeated-measures ANOVA on the times taken for children to place their hands in the three boxes (negative information, positive information, no information). First, draw an error bar graph of the means, then do some normality tests on the data, then do a log transformation on the scores, and do the ANOVA on these log-transformed scores (if you read the paper, you'll notice that I found that the data were not normal, so I log-transformed them before doing the ANOVA). Do children take longer to put their hands in a box that they believe contains an animal about which they have been told nasty things?

Answers are in the additional material on the companion website (or look at page 748 in the original article).

13.7. Factorial repeated-measures designs ②

We have seen already that simple between-group designs can be extended to incorporate a second (or third) independent variable. It is equally easy to incorporate a second, third or even fourth independent variable into a repeated-measures analysis.

There is evidence from advertising research that attitudes towards stimuli can be changed using positive imagery (e.g., Stuart, Shimp, & Engle, 1987). As part of an initiative to stop binge drinking in teenagers, the government funded some scientists to look at whether negative imagery could be used to make teenagers' attitudes towards alcohol more negative. The scientists designed a study to address this issue by comparing the effects of negative imagery against positive and neutral imagery for different types of drinks. Table 13.4 illustrates the experimental design and contains the data for this example (each row represents a single participant).

Participants viewed a total of nine mock adverts over three sessions. In one session, they saw three adverts: (1) a brand of beer (Brain Death) presented with a negative image (a dead body with the slogan 'drinking Brain Death makes your liver explode'); (2) a brand of wine (Dangleberry) presented in the context of a positive image (a sexy naked man or woman – depending on the participant's preference – and the slogan 'drinking Dangleberry wine makes you irresistible'); and (3) a brand of water (Puritan) presented alongside a neutral image (a person watching television accompanied by the slogan 'drinking Puritan water makes you behave completely normally'). In a second session (a week later), the participants

Table 13.4 Data from **Attitude.dat**

Drink		Beer			Wine			Water		
Imagery	+ve	−ve	Neut	+ve	−ve	Neut	+ve	−ve	Neut
Male	1	6	5	38	−5	4	10	−14	−2
	43	30	8	20	−12	4	9	−10	−13
	15	15	12	20	−15	6	6	−16	1
	40	30	19	28	−4	0	20	−10	2
	8	12	8	11	−2	6	27	5	−5
	17	17	15	17	−6	6	9	−6	−13
	30	21	21	15	−2	16	19	−20	3
	34	23	28	27	−7	7	12	−12	2
	34	20	26	24	−10	12	12	−9	4
	26	27	27	23	−15	14	21	−6	0
Female	1	−19	−10	28	−13	13	33	−2	9
	7	−18	6	26	−16	19	23	−17	5
	22	−8	4	34	−23	14	21	−19	0
	30	−6	3	32	−22	21	17	−11	4
	40	−6	0	24	−9	19	15	−10	2
	15	−9	4	29	−18	7	13	−17	8
	20	−17	9	30	−17	12	16	−4	10
	9	−12	−5	24	−15	18	17	−4	8
	14	−11	7	34	−14	20	19	−1	12
	15	−6	13	23	−15	15	29	−1	10

saw the same three brands, but this time Brain Death was accompanied by the positive imagery, Dangleberry by the neutral image and Puritan by the negative. In a third session, the participants saw Brain Death accompanied by the neutral image, Dangleberry by the negative image and Puritan by the positive. After each advert participants were asked to rate the drinks on a scale ranging from −100 (dislike very much) through 0 (neutral) to 100 (like very much). The order of adverts was randomized, as was the order in which people participated in the three sessions. This design is quite complex. There are two independent variables: the type of drink (beer, wine or water) and the type of imagery used (positive, negative or neutral). These two variables completely cross over, producing nine experimental conditions.

13.7.1. Entering the data ②

The data for the example can be found in the file **Attitude.dat**. You can load this data file by setting your working directory to the appropriate location and executing:

```
attitudeData<-read.delim("Attitude.dat", header = TRUE)
```

I have again structured the data in the format that you'd be most likely to use if you had entered the data in another software package and followed the usual conventions. The data have been entered in 'wide' format; that is, *levels of the repeated-measures variable are spread across different columns.*

In this experiment there are nine experimental conditions and so the data have been entered in nine columns (so the format is identical to Table 13.4):

beerpos	Beer	+	Sexy Person
beerneg	Beer	+	Corpse
beerneut	Beer	+	Person in Armchair
winepos	Wine	+	Sexy Person
wineneg	Wine	+	Corpse
wineneut	Wine	+	Person in Armchair
waterpos	Water	+	Sexy Person
waterneg	Water	+	Corpse
waterneut	Water	+	Person in Armchair

There is also a column to indicate to which person each row of data belongs (called **participant**).

As with the previous example, although the format of the data follows typical conventions, because of the way **R** handles repeated-measures designs we need the data to be in the long format. We can again do this using the *melt()* function. We specify columns in the data that identify characteristics of the scores (such as, from whom they originate) using the *id* option, and columns that identify the scores themselves using the *measured* option. In this case our scores are split over nine columns (*beerpos, beerneg, beerneut, winepos, wineneg, wineneut, waterpos, waterneg, waterneut*), so these are our measured variables, and *participant* tells us from whom the scores originate so this is our *id* variable. We can create a new dataframe (called *longAttitude*) by executing:

```
longAttitude <-melt(attitudeData, id = "participant", measured = c( "beerpos",
"beerneg", "beerneut", "winepos", "wineneg", "wineneut", "waterpos", "waterneg",
"waterneut"))
```

This dataframe contains three columns: the first identifies the participant, the second identifies the name of the column from which the data originate, and the third contains the attitude scores. By default, these columns will be named *participant*, *variable*, and *value*, which are not the most helpful of labels. Let's rename these columns so that we actually know what they represent by executing:

```
names(longAttitude)<-c("participant", "groups", "attitude")
```

The variable **groups** is a mixture of our two predictor variables (imagery and type of drink). Note for example, that the first 60 rows are scores for the drink beer and within these 60 rows, 20 are positive imagery, 20 negative imagery and 20 neutral imagery. We therefore, need to create two variables that dissociate the type of imagery from the type of drink; these two variables will be the two predictors in our model. First, let's create a variable called **drink**, which specifies whether beer, wine or water was in the advert. We can do this using the *gl()* function that we used earlier in the chapter. Execute this command:

```
longAttitude$drink<-gl(3, 60, labels = c("Beer", "Wine", "Water"))
```

This creates a variable **drink** in the dataframe *longAttitude*. The numbers in the function tell **R** that we had three sets three sets, which correspond to the type of drink. Essentially, this will create 60 rows with the label *Beer* then 60 labelled *Wine* then 60 labelled *Water*.

We also need a variable that tells us the type of imagery that was used. To do this we want three groups that each contain 20 scores. This will create 60 cases ($3 \times 20 = 60$), or, put another way, it will create the codes for the first level (beer) of the **drink** variable. We want this pattern to be repeated for the remaining 2 levels of **drink** (i.e., wine and water). We can do this by adding a third value to the function that is the total number of cases (i.e., 180). By specifying the total number of cases the *gl()* function will repeat the pattern of codes until it reaches this total number of cases

```
longAttitude$imagery<-gl(3, 20, 180, labels = c("Positive", "Negative", "Neutral"))
```

The data now look like this (edited and ordered by participant):

```
    participant groups  attitude drink  imagery
1            P1 beerpos        1  Beer Positive
21           P1 beerneg        6  Beer Negative
41           P1 beerneut       5  Beer  Neutral
61           P1 winepos       38  Wine Positive
81           P1 wineneg       -5  Wine Negative
101          P1 wineneut       4  Wine  Neutral
121          P1 waterpos      10 Water Positive
141          P1 waterneg     -14 Water Negative
161          P1 waterneu      -2 Water  Neutral
...          ...    ...       ...  ...     ...
10          P10 beerpos       26  Beer Positive
30          P10 beerneg       27  Beer Negative
50          P10 beerneut      27  Beer  Neutral
70          P10 winepos       23  Wine Positive
90          P10 wineneg      -15  Wine Negative
110         P10 wineneut      14  Wine  Neutral
130         P10 waterpos      21 Water Positive
150         P10 waterneg      -6 Water Negative
170         P10 waterneu       0 Water  Neutrall
```

Notice that each participant (identified by the **participant** variable) has nine scores (distinguished by the variables **drink** and **imagery**). In the reformatted data the nine scores within each participant are now represented by nine different rows rather than nine columns as they were before.

SELF-TEST

✓ Using what you learnt earlier in the chapter and the commands that we have just used to create **drink** and **imagery**, can you work out how to enter the data into **R** directly?

13.7.2. Exploring the data ②

As ever, we'll look at some graphs first. To save space we'll look just at the boxplots at this stage.

SELF-TEST

✓ Use *ggplot2* to plot boxplots of the attitude scores for each type of drink (*x*-axis) after adverts using different imagery (different plots).

The resulting plot (Figure 13.6) shows that the median scores are highest (in general) after positive imagery, and lowest after negative. Scores are most spread out for beer (the box and whiskers are longest).

FIGURE 13.6
Boxplots of the attitude data

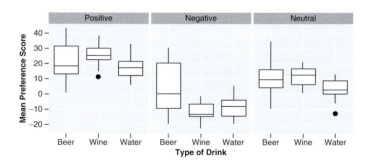

We have previously used the *by()* function and the *stat.desc()* function in the *pastecs* package to get descriptive statistics for separate groups (see Chapter 5 for more detail). We also saw in the previous chapter that if we want to create descriptives for a combination of variables we can simply list all of the variables in the *list()* function; therefore, to get descriptive statistics for the combined levels of **drink** and **imagery** we execute:

```
by(longAttitude$attitude, list(longAttitude$drink, longAttitude$imagery),
stat.desc, basic = FALSE)
```

The resulting (edited) output is in Output 13.10. From this table we can see that the variability among scores was greatest when beer was used as a product (compare the standard deviations of the beer variables against the others). Also, when a corpse image was used (negative imagery), the ratings given to the products were negative (as expected) for wine and water but not for beer (so for some reason, negative imagery didn't seem to work when beer was used as a stimulus). The values in this table will help us later to interpret the main effects of the analysis.

```
: Beer
: Positive

median    mean    SE.mean   CI.mean.0.95    var     std.dev   coef.var
18.500   21.050   2.909       6.088      169.208   13.008     0.618
-----------------------------------------------------------------
: Wine
: Positive

median    mean    SE.mean   CI.mean.0.95    var     std.dev   coef.var
25.000   25.350   1.507       3.153       45.397    6.738     0.266
-----------------------------------------------------------------
: Water
: Positive

median    mean    SE.mean   CI.mean.0.95    var     std.dev   coef.var
17.000   17.400   1.582       3.311       50.042    7.074     0.407
-----------------------------------------------------------------
: Beer
: Negative

median    mean    SE.mean   CI.mean.0.95    var     std.dev   coef.var
 0.00     4.45    3.87        8.10        299.42    17.30     3.89
-----------------------------------------------------------------
: Wine
: Negative

median     mean    SE.mean   CI.mean.0.95    var     std.dev   coef.var
-13.500  -12.000   1.382       2.893       38.211    6.181    -0.515
-----------------------------------------------------------------
: Water
: Negative

median    mean    SE.mean   CI.mean.0.95    var     std.dev   coef.var
-10.000  -9.200   1.521       3.184       46.274    6.802    -0.739
-----------------------------------------------------------------
: Beer
: Neutral

median    mean    SE.mean   CI.mean.0.95    var     std.dev   coef.var
 8.00    10.00    2.30        4.82        106.00    10.30     1.03
-----------------------------------------------------------------
: Wine
: Neutral

median    mean    SE.mean   CI.mean.0.95    var     std.dev   coef.var
12.500   11.650   1.396       2.922       38.976    6.243     0.536
-----------------------------------------------------------------
: Water
: Neutral

median    mean    SE.mean   CI.mean.0.95    var     std.dev   coef.var
 2.50     2.35    1.53        3.20         46.77     6.84      2.91
```

Output 13.10

13.7.3.   Setting contrasts ②

As with one-way repeated-measures designs, we need to set contrasts before proceeding to the main analysis. Just to remind you, these contrasts are important because (1) they help us to break down any main effects or interactions into more interpretable effects, and (2) if you use Type III sums of squares then you must first set (orthogonal) contrasts for these to be computed correctly. In this example, we need to set contrasts for both **drink** and **imagery**.

For **drink**, we have two alcoholic drinks (beer and wine) and one non-alcoholic (water). The government is interested in preventing binge drinking, so water is an obvious control group. Therefore, our first contrast should compare the alcoholic drinks (beer and wine) to water (the control). We need a second contrast then to separate the beer and wine. Therefore, contrast 1 answers the question 'are the effects different for alcoholic and non-alcoholic drinks?' and contrast 2 answers the question 'are the effects different for different types of alcoholic drink?' The resulting codes are in Table 13.5.

Table 13.5   Orthogonal contrasts for the **drink** variable

Group	Contrast$_1$	Contrast$_2$
Beer	1	−1
Wine	1	1
Water	−2	0

To set these orthogonal contrasts (see Chapter 10) we can first create variables representing each contrast (which is useful because you can give the contrasts informative names), and then bind these variables together and set them as the contrast for **drink**:

```
AlcoholvsWater<-c(1, 1, -2)
BeervsWine<-c(-1, 1, 0)
contrasts(longAttitude$drink)<-cbind(AlcoholvsWater, BeervsWine)
```

The first two commands each create a variable relating to a contrast that contains the codes for each group from Table 13.5. The final command sets these variables to be the contrasts for **drink**.

For **imagery**, the government is interested in preventing binge drinking and so their main hypothesis is about whether negative imagery is effective compared to other forms usually used in advertising (i.e., positive or neutral). Therefore, our first contrast should compare negative imagery to other forms (positive and neutral combined). We need a second contrast then to separate the positive and neutral imagery. Therefore, contrast 1 answers the question 'are the effects different for negative imagery compared to other forms?' and contrast 2 answers the question 'are the effects different for positive and neutral imagery?' The resulting codes are in Table 13.6.

Table 13.6   Orthogonal contrasts for the **imagery** variable

Group	Contrast$_1$	Contrast$_2$
Positive	1	−1
Negative	−2	0
Neutral	1	1

We can set these contrasts in the same way as for **drink**. We first create variables representing each contrast, and then bind these variables together and set them as the contrast for **imagery**:

```
NegativevsOther<-c(1, -2, 1)
PositivevsNeutral<-c(-1, 0, 1)
contrasts(longAttitude$imagery)<-cbind(NegativevsOther, PositivevsNeutral)
```

The first two commands each create a variable relating to a contrast that contains the codes for each group from in Table 13.6. The final command sets these variables to be the contrasts for **drink**.

We can check that we have set the contrast correctly by executing the name of the variable and looking at the contrast attribute:

```
longAttitude$drink
```

```
attr(,"contrasts")
      AlcoholvsWater BeervsWine
Beer               1         -1
Wine               1          1
Water             -2          0

Levels: Beer Wine Water
```

```
longAttitude$imagery
```

```
         NegativevsOther PositivevsNeutral
Positive               1                -1
Negative              -2                 0
Neutral                1                 1
Levels:  Positive Negative Neutral
```

Remembering that positive numbers are compared with negative and a zero means that the group is not involved at all, we can see that for **drink**, contrast 1 compares water to the other drinks and contrast 2 compares wine and beer; for **imagery**, contrast 1 compares negative imagery to other forms, and contrast 2 compares positive and neutral imagery.

13.7.4. Factorial repeated-measures ANOVA ②

As with one-way repeated-measures ANOVA, we can do a fairly easy analysis using the *ezANOVA()* function. Earlier in the chapter we saw that all we need to do is to specify our repeated-measures predictor within the option labelled *within = .()*. In the previous example, we specified a single variable within the brackets, but when we have several predictors we can simply list the predictors separated by commas. The rest of the function is similar to the previous example. For these data, therefore, we would execute these commands:

```
attitudeModel<-ezANOVA(data = longAttitude, dv = .(attitude), wid = .(par-
ticipant),  within = .(imagery, drink), type = 3, detailed = TRUE)
attitudeModel
```

This creates a model (*attitudeModel*) from our dataframe (*longAttitude*). Note that we have set the variable **attitude** as the outcome (*dv = .(attitude)*), we have told the function that participants can be identified by the variable **participants** (*wid = .(participant)*), the predictors are **drink** and **imagery** (*within = .(imagery, drink)*), that we want Type III sums of squares (*type = 3*), and that we want to see the sums of squares in the output (*detailed = TRUE*). Executing the second command (*attitudeModel*) simply prints the model to the console.

```
$ANOVA
         Effect DFn DFd   SSn  SSd      F         p p<.05   ges
1    (Intercept)  1  19 11218 1920 111.01 2.26e-09     * 0.413
2          drink  2  38  2092 7786   5.11 1.09e-02     * 0.116
3        imagery  2  38 21629 3353 122.56 2.68e-17     * 0.575
4  drink:imagery  4  76  2624 2907  17.15 4.59e-10     * 0.141

$'Mauchly's Test for Sphericity'
         Effect     W        p p<.05
2          drink 0.267 6.95e-06     *
3        imagery 0.662 2.45e-02     *
4  drink:imagery 0.595 4.36e-01

$'Sphericity Corrections'
         Effect   GGe     p[GG] p[GG]<.05   HFe     p[HF] p[HF]<.05
2          drink 0.577 2.98e-02         * 0.591 2.88e-02         *
3        imagery 0.747 1.76e-13         * 0.797 3.14e-14         *
4  drink:imagery 0.798 1.90e-08         * 0.979 6.81e-10         *
```

Output 13.11

Output 13.11 shows the results from *ezANOVA()*. Mauchly's sphericity test (see section 13.2.3) is computed for each of the three effects in the model (two main effects and one interaction). The significance values of these tests indicate that both the main effects of **drink** ($p < .001$) and **imagery** ($p = .025$) have violated this assumption and so the *F*-values should be corrected (see Jane Superbrain Box 13.3). For the interaction the assumption of sphericity is met (because $p = .436$) and so we need not correct the *F*-ratio for this effect.

Output 13.11 also shows the results of the ANOVA (and whether each effect is significant after correcting the *F*-values for sphericity). Looking at the significance values, it is clear that there is a significant effect of the type of drink used as a stimulus (sphericity was violated, so for this effect we look at *p[GG]* or *p[HF]*, both of which are significant because they are less than .05), a significant main effect of the type of imagery used (again sphericity was violated, so we look at *p[GG]* or *p[HF]*, both of which are significant), and a significant interaction between these two variables (sphericity was not violated, so we can look at *p* in the table labelled *$ANOVA*). I will examine each of these effects in turn.

13.7.4.1. The effect of drink ②

Output 13.11 told us that the effect of the type of drink used in the advert was significant. For this effect we looked at one of the corrected significance values because sphericity was violated (see above). Both of the corrected values were significant and so we may as well report the conservative Greenhouse–Geisser corrected values of the degrees of freedom. This effect tells us that if we ignore the type of imagery that was used, participants still rated some types of drink significantly differently.

To interpret this effect we should plot the means and look at some descriptive statistics.

SELF-TEST

✓ Using *ggplot2* and *stat.desc*, plot an error bar graph and get the means for the main effect of **drink**.

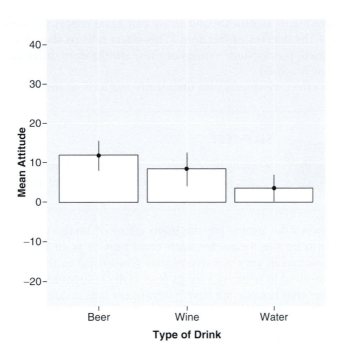

FIGURE 13.7
Error bar graph of
the main effect of
drink

Output 13.12 shows the means for the main effect of **drink**.[8] Figure 13.7 uses this information to display the means for each condition. It is clear from this graph that beer and wine were rated higher than water (with beer being rated most highly). To see the nature of this effect we could look at the *post hoc* tests (see below) and the contrasts. However, because we have a significant interaction effect it does not make sense (despite the fact that Type III sums of squares make you think that it does) to interpret this main effect because it is superseded by the interaction with **imagery**.

```
longAttitude$drink: Beer
median     mean      SE.mean    CI.mean.0.95     var      std.dev    coef.var
12.50     11.83       1.97         3.95        233.46     15.28        1.29
-------------------------------------------------------------------------------
longAttitude$drink: Wine
median     mean      SE.mean    CI.mean.0.95     var      std.dev    coef.var
12.00      8.33       2.17         4.33        281.51     16.78        2.01
-------------------------------------------------------------------------------
longAttitude$drink: Water
median     mean      SE.mean    CI.mean.0.95     var      std.dev    coef.var
 3.50      3.52       1.67         3.34        166.69     12.91        3.67
```

Output 13.12

13.7.4.2. The effect of imagery ②

Output 13.11 also indicates that the effect of the type of imagery used in the advert had a significant influence on participants' ratings of the stimuli. Again, we must look at one of the corrected significance values because sphericity was violated (see above). Both of the

[8] These means are obtained by taking the average of the means in Output 13.10 for a given condition. For example, the mean for the beer condition (ignoring imagery) is

$$\bar{X}_{\text{Beer}} = \frac{\bar{X}_{\text{Beer + Sexy}} + \bar{X}_{\text{Beer + Corpse}} + \bar{X}_{\text{Beer + Neutral}}}{3} = \frac{21.05 + 4.45 + 10.00}{3} = 11.83.$$

corrected values are highly significant and so we can again report the Greenhouse–Geisser corrected values of the degrees of freedom. This effect tells us that if we ignore the type of drink that was used, participants' ratings of those drinks were different according to the type of imagery that was used.

To interpret this effect we should plot the means and look at some descriptive statistics.

SELF-TEST

✓ Using *ggplot2* and *stat.desc*, plot an error bar graph and get the means for the main effect of **imagery**.

Output 13.13 shows the means for the main effect of **imagery**. Figure 13.8 uses this information to illustrate the means for each condition. It is clear from this graph that positive imagery resulted in very positive ratings (compared to the neutral imagery) and negative imagery resulted in negative ratings (especially compared to the effect of neutral imagery). Remember that because we have a significant interaction effect it does not make sense to interpret this main effect because it is superseded by the interaction with **drink**.

```
longAttitude$imagery: Positive
median    mean    SE.mean   CI.mean.0.95     var      std.dev   coef.var
20.500    21.267  1.265     2.531            95.962   9.796     0.461
-------------------------------------------------------------------------
longAttitude$imagery: Negative
median    mean    SE.mean   CI.mean.0.95     var      std.dev   coef.var
-9.00     -5.58   1.71      3.43             176.15   13.27     -2.38
-------------------------------------------------------------------------
longAttitude$imagery: Neutral
median    mean    SE.mean   CI.mean.0.95     var      std.dev   coef.var
7.00      8.00    1.14      2.29             78.44    8.86      1.11
```

Output 13.13

FIGURE 13.8

Error bar graph of the main effect of imagery

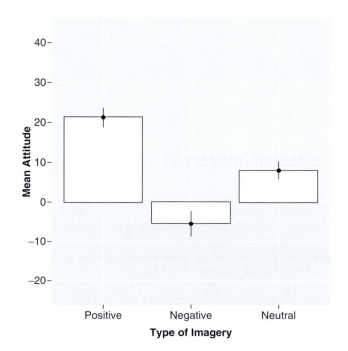

13.7.4.3. The interaction effect (drink × imagery) ②

Output 13.11 indicated that imagery interacted in some way with the type of drink used as a stimulus. From the output we should report that there was a significant interaction between the type of drink used and imagery associated with it, $F(4, 76) = 17.16$, $p < .001$. This effect tells us that the type of imagery used had a different effect depending on which type of drink it was presented alongside. We can use the means in Output 13.10 to determine the nature of this interaction.

SELF-TEST

✔ Using *ggplot2*, plot a line graph with error bars of the means for the **drink** × **imagery** interaction.

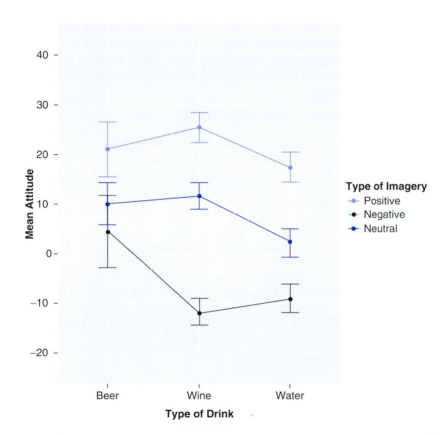

FIGURE 13.9
Interaction graph for the attitude data. The three lines represent the type of imagery: positive imagery (light blue), negative imagery (black) and neutral imagery (dark blue)

Figure 13.9 shows the interaction graph, and we are looking for non-parallel lines. The graph shows that the pattern of responding across drinks was similar when positive and neutral imagery were used. That is, ratings were positive for beer, they were slightly higher for wine and then they went down slightly for water. The fact that the line representing positive imagery is higher than the neutral line indicates that positive imagery gave rise to higher ratings than neutral imagery across all drinks. The bottom line (representing negative imagery) shows a different effect: ratings were lower for wine and water but not for beer. Therefore, negative imagery had the desired effect on attitudes towards wine and water, but for some reason attitudes towards beer remained fairly neutral. Therefore, the interaction is likely to reflect the fact that negative imagery has a different effect than both positive and neutral imagery (because it decreases ratings rather than increasing them). This interaction is completely in line with the experimental predictions. To verify the interpretation of the interaction effect, we can look at some *post hoc* tests or the contrasts (we'll get to those later).

To get *post hoc* tests for the interaction term we need to use a variable that combines **imagery** and **drink** into a single coding variable. Fortunately we already have such a variable in the data set; it's called **groups** and it was created when we converted our original data set from wide format to long. We can use this variable in the *pairwise.t.test()* function to get comparisons between all nine groups that the interaction term encompasses. The format of this option is exactly the same as we used earlier in the chapter, and we execute:

```
pairwise.t.test(longAttitude$attitude, longAttitude$groups, paired = TRUE,
p.adjust.method = "bonferroni")
```

Output 13.14 shows the results of the *post hoc* tests. We can see (in bold in the output) that for beer there are significant differences between positive imagery and both negative ($p = .002$) and neutral ($p = .020$), but not between negative and neutral ($p = 1.00$); for wine, there are significant differences between positive imagery and both negative ($p < .001$) and neutral ($p < .001$), and between negative and neutral ($p < .001$); and for water, there are significant differences between positive imagery and both negative ($p < .001$) and neutral ($p < .001$), and between negative and neutral ($p < .001$). These findings support our earlier conclusion that beer is unusual in that negative imagery does appear to reduce attitudes compared to neutral imagery.

```
        Pairwise comparisons using paired t tests

data:  longAttitude$attitude and longAttitude$groups

         beerpos beerneg beerneut winepos wineneg wineneut waterpos waterneg
beerneg  0.00217 -       -        -       -       -        -        -
beerneut 0.01982 1.00000 -        -       -       -        -        -
winepos  1.00000 0.01105 0.00310  -       -       -        -        -
wineneg  5.6e-08 0.00265 2.0e-07  1.9e-10 -       -        -        -
wineneut 0.39905 1.00000 1.00000  2.2e-05 2.3e-07 -        -        -
waterpos 1.00000 0.47584 1.00000  0.07300 1.3e-09 0.10547  -        -
waterneg 2.9e-06 0.18860 0.00010  3.2e-10 1.00000 1.1e-07  4.9e-11  -
waterneut 0.00212 1.00000 0.74838 4.3e-10 0.00041 8.1e-05  9.0e-07  0.00068

P value adjustment method: bonferroni
```

Output 13.14

13.7.5. Factorial repeated-measures designs as a GLM ③

Earlier in the chapter we used *lme()*, which looks at repeated-measures data in a linear model. I have already outlined various advantages to this method. It is a simple matter to extend what we have already learnt to a situation that includes more than one predictor or independent variable. All we do is extend the model to include each predictor and any interactions. We saw earlier that if we want to look at individual effects then we should build up the model from a baseline that includes no predictors other than the intercept.

```
baseline<-lme(attitude ~ 1, random = ~1|participant/drink/imagery, data =
longAttitude, method = "ML")
```

Compare this model with the one that we used for the one-way repeated-measures design earlier in the chapter. We have specified the model as the outcome predicted only from the intercept (*attitude ~ 1*), specified the relevant dataframe (*data = longAttitude*), and asked to use maximum likelihood to estimate the model (*method = "ML"*). The main thing that has changed is the random part of the model, which is slightly more complex than before to reflect the fact that there are now two predictors. The random part of model (*random = ~1/participant/drink/imagery*) simply tells **R** that the variables **drink** and **imagery** are nested within the variable **participant** (in other words, scores for levels of these variables can be found within each participant). Execute the above command to create the baseline model.

If we want to see the overall effect of each predictor then we need to add them one at a time. To add drink to the model we could just change the model from *attitude ~ 1* to *attitude ~ drink*. In other words, execute:

```
baseline<-lme(attitude ~ drink, random = ~1|participant/drink/imagery, data = longAttitude, method = "ML")
```

However, it is quicker to use the *update()* function (see R's Souls' Tip 7.2):

```
drinkModel<-update(baseline, .~. + drink)
```

This command takes the model called *baseline* (which we have already created), and the .~. means keep the outcome and predictors the same as the baseline model (the dots mean 'keep the same', so the fact that we put dots on both sides of the ~ means that we want to keep both the outcome and predictors the same as in the baseline model). The '+ drink' means 'add **drink** as a predictor'. Therefore, '.~. + drink' can be interpreted as 'keep the same outcomes and predictors as the baseline model but add **drink** as a predictor'. Executing this command creates a model called *drinkModel* that includes only **drink** as a predictor.

In a similar way we can add **imagery** to the model as a predictor.

```
imageryModel<-update(drinkModel, .~. + imagery)
```

This command takes the model called *drinkModel* (which we have just created), as before, the .~. means keep the outcome and predictors the same as in *drinkModel* and the '+ imagery' adds **imagery** as a predictor. Therefore, '.~. + imagery' can be interpreted as 'keep the same outcomes and predictors as *drinkModel* but add **imagery** as a predictor'. Executing this command creates a model called *imageryModel* that includes both **drink** and **imagery** as predictor.

Finally, we can add the interaction term by executing:

```
attitudeModel<-update(imageryModel, .~. + drink:imagery)
```

This command takes the model called *imageryModel* (which we have just created), as before, the .~. means keep the outcome and predictors the same as in *imageryModel*, and the '+ drink:imagery' adds the **drink** × **imagery** interaction as a predictor. Executing this command, therefore, creates a model called *attitudeModel* that includes the main effects of **drink** and **imagery** as well as their interaction as predictors.

To compare these models we can list them in the order in which we want them compared in the *anova()* function (see 7.8.4.2):

```
anova(baseline, drinkModel, imageryModel, attitudeModel)
```

Executing the above command produces Output 13.15, which first compares the effect of **drink** to the baseline (i.e., no predictors). By adding **drink** as a predictor we increase the degrees of freedom by 2 (the two contrasts that we used to code this variable) and significantly improve the model. In other words, the type of drink had a significant effect on attitudes, $\chi^2(2) = 9.1$, $p = .010$. Next, we see the effect of adding the main effect of **imagery** into the model (compared to the previous model that contained only the effect of drink). Again the degrees of freedom are increased by 2 (the two contrasts used to code this variable) and the fit of the model is significantly improved; the type of imagery used in the advert had a significant effect on attitudes, $\chi^2(2) = 151.9$, $p < .001$. The final model (which includes both main effects and the interaction between them) is then compared to the previous model (that includes only the two main effects). The interaction term is made up of four contrasts (the number of contrasts for each variable in the interaction multiplied) and significantly improves the model fit; therefore, attitudes were significantly affected by the combined effect of the type of drink and type of imagery, $\chi^2(4) = 42.0$, $p < .001$. These results confirm the overall effects that we looked at with *ezANOVA()* in the previous section, and you should look back at that section to remind yourself of how we interpreted these effects.

```
             Model df  AIC  BIC logLik   Test L.Ratio p-value
baseline         1  5 1504 1520   -747
drinkModel       2  7 1498 1521   -742 1 vs 2     9.1  0.0104
imageryModel     3  9 1351 1379   -666 2 vs 3   151.9  <.0001
attitudeModel    4 13 1317 1358   -645 3 vs 4    42.0  <.0001
```

Output 13.15

We can further explore the model by executing:

summary(attitudeModel)

Output 13.16 shows the parameter estimates for the model (I've edited some of the names to save space). Most important, these include the parameters for the contrasts that we set for each variable. First, we get the two contrasts for **drink**, which show a significant effect on attitudes when comparing alcoholic drinks to water, $b = 2.19$, $t(38) = 3.18$, $p = .003$, but not when comparing beer with wine $b = -1.75$, $t(38) = -1.47$, $p = .150$. next, we get the two contrasts for **imagery**, which show a significant effect on attitudes when comparing negative imagery to other types, $b = 6.74$, $t(114) = 17.26$, $p < .001$, and when comparing positive to neutral imagery, $b = -6.63$, $t(114) = -9.81$, $p < .001$. The next four effects are the contrasts for the interaction term and we'll look at these in turn.

```
Linear mixed-effects model fit by maximum likelihood
 Data: longAttitude
  AIC  BIC logLik
 1317 1358   -645


Fixed effects: attitude ~ drink + imagery + drink:imagery
                               Value Std.Error  DF t-value p-value
(Intercept)                     7.89     0.973 114    8.12  0.0000
AlcoholvsWater                  2.19     0.688  38    3.18  0.0029
BeervsWine                     -1.75     1.191  38   -1.47  0.1500
NegativevsOther                 6.74     0.391 114   17.26  0.0000
PositivevsNeutral              -6.63     0.676 114   -9.81  0.0000
AlcoholvsWater:NegativevsOther  0.19     0.276 114    0.69  0.4922
BeervsWine:NegativevsOther      3.24     0.478 114    6.77  0.0000
AlcoholvsWater:PositivevsNeut   0.45     0.478 114    0.93  0.3533
BeervsWine:positivevsNeut      -0.66     0.828 114   -0.80  0.4256
```

Output 13.16

13.7.5.1. Alcohol vs. water, negative vs. other imagery ②

The first interaction term looks at the effect of alcoholic drinks (i.e., wine and beer combined) relative to water when comparing negative imagery with other types of imagery (i.e., positive and neutral combined). This contrast is non-significant. This result tells us that the decreased liking found when negative imagery is used (compared to other forms) is the same for both alcoholic drinks and water. The top left panel of Figure 13.10 shows the means being compared. The gap between the lines, which represents the effect of negative imagery compared to other forms, is roughly the same for alcoholic drinks and water. This finding indicates that the effect of negative imagery (compared to other forms) in lowering attitudes is comparable in alcoholic and non-alcoholic drinks, $b = 0.19$, $t(114) = 0.69$, $p = .492$.

13.7.5.2. Beer vs. wine, negative vs. other imagery ②

The second interaction term looks at whether the effect of negative imagery compared to other types of imagery (i.e., positive and neutral combined) is comparable in beer and wine. This contrast is significant. This result tells us that the decreased liking found when negative imagery is used (compared to other forms) is different in beer and wine. The top right panel of Figure 13.10 shows the means being compared. The gap between the lines, which represents the effect of negative imagery compared to other forms, is much bigger for wine than it is for beer. This finding suggests that the effect of negative imagery (compared to other forms) in lowering attitudes to beer was significantly smaller than for wine, $b = 3.24$, $t(114) = 6.77$, $p < .001$.

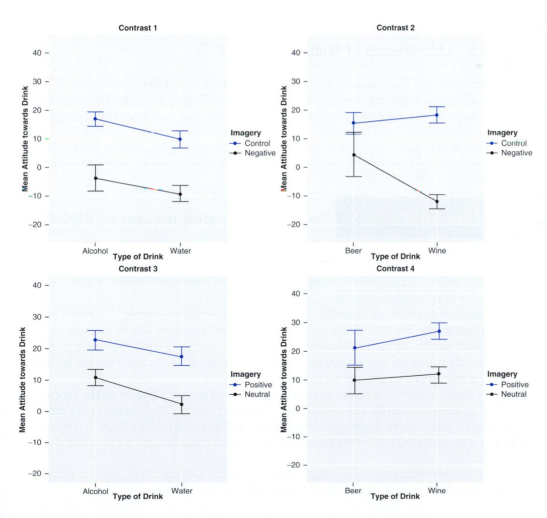

FIGURE 13.10
Graphs to show the four contrasts in the **drink × imagery** interaction

13.7.5.3. Alcohol vs. water, positive vs. neutral imagery ②

The third interaction term looks at whether the effect of positive imagery (compared to neutral) is comparable in alcoholic drinks (i.e., wine and beer combined) relative to water. This contrast is non-significant. This result tells us that the increased liking found when positive imagery is used (compared to neutral) is similar for both alcoholic drinks and water. The bottom left panel of Figure 13.10 shows the means being compared. The distance between the lines, which represents the effect of positive imagery compared to neutral, is roughly the same for beer as it is for wine. This finding suggests that positive imagery has a similar effect in increasing attitudes (compared to neutral imagery) in both alcoholic and non-alcoholic drinks, $b = 0.45$, $t(114) = 0.93$, $p = .353$.

13.7.5.4. Beer vs. wine, positive vs. neutral imagery ②

The final interaction term looks at whether the effect of positive imagery compared to neutral is comparable in beer and wine. This contrast is not significant. This result tells us that the increased liking found when positive imagery is used (compared to neutral) is comparable in beer and wine. The bottom right panel of Figure 13.10 shows the means being compared. Note that the distance between the lines (i.e., the effect of positive imagery compared to neutral) is roughly the same for beer as it is for wine. In summary, the effect of positive imagery (compared to neutral) in increasing attitudes to beer was not significantly different to that for wine, $b = -0.66$, $t(114) = -0.80$, $p = .426$.

13.7.5.5. Limitations of these contrasts ②

These contrasts, by their nature, tell us nothing about the differences between water and beer and wine separately, or the effect of negative imagery compared to, say, neutral imagery alone. If you need more comparisons, you could run *post hoc* tests (as explained earlier in the chapter).

Although it may seem tiresome to spend so long interpreting an analysis so thoroughly, you are well advised to take such a systematic approach if you want to truly understand the

CRAMMING SAM'S TIPS   **Two-way repeated-measures ANOVA**

- Two-way repeated-measures ANOVA compares several means when there are two independent variables, and the same participants have been used in all experimental conditions.
- We recommend treating your data as a multilevel model (i.e., repeated-measures regression). However, if you don't then test the assumption of *sphericity* when you have three or more repeated-measures conditions. Test for sphericity using *Mauchly's test*. If the *p*-value is less than .05 then the assumption is violated. If the significance of Mauchly's test is greater than .05 then the assumption of sphericity has been met. You should test this assumption for all effects (in a two-way ANOVA this means you test it for the effect of both variables and the interaction term).
- In a two-way ANOVA you will have three effects: a main effect of each variable and the interaction between the two. For *each* effect, if the assumption of sphericity has been met then use the *p*-value for the main ANOVA. If the assumption was violated then read the *p*-value corrected using either the *Greenhouse–Geisser* (*p[GG]*) or *Huynh–Feldt* (*p[HF]*) estimate of sphericity (read this chapter to find out the relative merits of the two procedures). If the *p*-value is less than .05 then the means of the groups are significantly different.
- Break down the main effects and interaction terms using contrasts and *post hoc* tests; again look to the *p*-values to discover if your comparisons are significant (they will be if the significance value is less than .05).

effects that you obtain. Interpreting interaction terms is complex, and I can think of a few well-respected researchers who still struggle with them, so don't feel disheartened if you find them hard. Try to be thorough, and break each effect down as much as possible using contrasts, and hopefully you will find enlightenment.

13.7.6.   Robust factorial repeated-measures ANOVA ③

At the time of writing there aren't any functions (that I can find) that deal with factorial repeated-measures designs. This is a blessing for me (I don't have to work out how to use them and then write about them) but a curse for you (if you happen to have misbehaving data).

13.8. Effect sizes for factorial repeated-measures designs ③

Calculating omega squared for one-way repeated-measures ANOVA was hair-raising enough, so we'll definitely leave it alone for factorial designs (you can read this as 'I don't know how to do it'). However, *ezANOVA* produces generalized eta-squared (Output 13.11); in this case the values were .575 for the main effect of imagery, .116 for the main effect of drink and .141 for the interaction term. This shows a relatively strong effect of imagery, but fairly modest effects of drink and the interaction.

   As I keep saying, effect sizes are really more useful when they describe a focused effect, so I'd advise calculating effect sizes for your contrasts when you've got a factorial design (and any main effects that compare only two groups). We can use the *rcontrast()* function that we used for one-way ANOVA: simply input each value of *t* and its associated degrees of freedom for each of the eight effects in Output 13.16 (remember that you have to load the DSUR package first). For drink there were two contrasts: alcohol vs. water

```
> rcontrast(3.18, 38)
[1] "r =  0.458457001137587"
```

and beer vs. wine

```
> rcontrast(-1.47, 38)
[1] "r =  0.231961343984559"
```

For imagery we contasted negative vs. other

```
> rcontrast(17.26, 114)
[1] "r =  0.850434536664415"
```

and positive vs. neutral

```
> rcontrast(-9.81, 114)
[1] "r =  0.676574089263451"
```

Finally, we had four interaction contrasts: alcohol vs. water with negative vs. other imagery

```
> rcontrast(0.69, 114)
[1] "r =  0.0644898962213597"
```

beer vs. wine with negative vs. other imagery

```
> rcontrast(6.77, 114)
[1] "r =  0.535495195928629"
```

alcohol vs. water with positive vs. neutral imagery

```
> rcontrast(0.93, 114)
[1] "r =  0.0867739323982253"
```

and beer vs. wine with positive vs. neutral imagery

```
> rcontrast(-0.80, 114)
[1] "r =  0.0747174253416562"
```

As such, the effect in the interaction that was significant (beer vs. wine, negative vs. other imagery) yields a fairly large effect size. The remaining effects in the interaction, which were not significant, yield fairly small effect sizes (all under .1).

13.9. Reporting the results from factorial repeated-measures designs ②

As we saw before, how you report repeated-measures ANOVA depends on how you do it. If you have used a traditional ANOVA approach (e.g., using *ezANOVA*) then report it as you would any factorial ANOVA: remember that you've got three effects to report, and these effects might have different degrees of freedom. For the main effects of drink and imagery, the assumption of sphericity was violated so we'd have to report the Greenhouse–Geisser corrected degrees of freedom. We can, therefore, begin by reporting the violation of sphericity:

✓ Mauchly's test indicated that the assumption of sphericity had been violated for the main effects of drink, $W = 0.267$, $p < .001$, $\varepsilon = .58$, and imagery, $W = 0.662$, $p < .05$, $\varepsilon = .75$. Therefore degrees of freedom were corrected using Greenhouse–Geisser estimates of sphericity.

We can then report the three effects from this analysis as follows:

✓ All effects are reported as significant at $p < .05$. There was a significant main effect of the type of drink on ratings of the drink, $F(1.15, 21.93) = 5.11$.

✓ There was also a significant main effect of the type of imagery on ratings of the drinks, $F(1.50, 28.40) = 122.57$.

✓ There was a significant interaction effect between the type of drink and the type of imagery used, $F(4, 76) = 17.16$. This indicates that imagery had different effects on people's ratings, depending on which type of drink was used. Bonferroni *post hoc* tests revealed that for beer there were significant differences between positive imagery and both negative ($p = .002$) and neutral ($p = .020$), but not between negative and neutral ($p = 1.00$); for wine, there were significant differences between positive imagery and both negative ($p < .001$) and neutral ($p < .001$), and between negative and neutral ($p < .001$); and for water, there were significant differences between positive imagery and both negative ($p < .001$) and neutral ($p < .001$), and between negative and neutral ($p < .001$). These findings suggest that beer is unusual in that negative imagery does appear to reduce attitudes compared to neutral imagery.

If you have done a multilevel model then you would write your results differently (you could also put the results in a Table as in section 19.8):

✓ The type of drink had a significant effect on attitudes, $\chi^2(2) = 9.1$, $p = .010$, as did the type of imagery used in the advert, $\chi^2(2) = 151.9$, $p < .001$. Most important, the drink × imagery interaction was significant, $\chi^2(4) = 42.0$, $p < .001$. Contrasts revealed that (1) the effect of negative imagery (compared to other forms) in lowering attitudes is comparable in alcoholic and non-alcoholic drinks, $b = 0.19$, $t(114) = 0.69$, $p = .492$; (2) the effect of negative imagery (compared to other forms) in lowering attitudes to beer was significantly smaller than for wine, $b = 3.24$, $t(114) = 6.77$, $p < .001$; (3) positive imagery has a similar effect in increasing attitudes (compared to neutral imagery) in both alcoholic and non-alcoholic drinks, $b = 0.45$, $t(114) = 0.93$, $p = .353$; and (4) the effect of positive imagery (compared to neutral) in increasing attitudes to beer was not significantly different from that for wine, $b = -0.66$, $t(114) = -0.80$, $p = .426$.

What have I discovered about statistics? ②

This chapter has helped us to walk through the murky swamp of repeated-measures designs. We discovered that is was infested with rabid leg-eating crocodiles. The first thing we learnt was that with repeated-measures designs there is yet another assumption to worry about: *sphericity*. Having recovered from this shock revelation, we were fortunate to discover that this assumption, if violated, can be easily remedied. It can also be remedied by doing a multilevel model; not so easy, but as rewarding as a cocktail on a hot beach. We then moved on to look at the theory of repeated-measures ANOVA for one independent variable. Although not essential by any stretch of the imagination, this was a useful exercise to demonstrate that basically it's exactly the same as when we have an independent design (well, there are a few subtle differences, but I was trying to emphasize the similarities). We then worked through an example using **R**, before tackling the particularly foul-tempered, starving hungry, and mad as Stabby the mercury-sniffing hatter, piranha fish of omega squared. That's a road I kind of regretted going down after I'd started, but, stubborn as ever, I persevered. This led us ungracefully on to factorial repeated-measures designs and, specifically, the situation where we have two independent variables. We learnt that, as with other factorial designs, we have to worry about interaction terms. But, we also discovered some useful ways to break these terms down using contrasts. I kept going on about multilevel models a lot as well, which is a topic to which we shall return, but not until I've taken a three-month trip to the aforementioned hot beach.

By 16 I had started my first 'serious' band. We actually stayed together for about 7 years (with the same line-up, and we're still friends now) before Mark (drummer) moved to Oxford, I moved to Brighton to do my Ph.D., and rehearsing became a mammoth feat of organization. We had a track on a CD, some radio play and transformed from a thrash metal band to a blend of Fugazi, Nirvana and metal. I never split my trousers during a gig again (although I did once split my head open). Why didn't we make it? Well, Mark was an astonishingly good drummer so it wasn't his fault, the other Mark was an extremely good bassist too (of the three of us he is the one that has always been in a band since we split up), so the weak link was me. This was especially unfortunate given that I had three roles in the band (guitar, singing, songs) – my poor band mates never stood a chance.☺ I stopped playing music for quite a few years after we split. I still wrote songs (for personal consumption) but the three of us were such close friends that I couldn't bear the thought of playing with other people. At least not for a few years …

R packages used in this chapter

compute.es	nlme
ez	pastecs
ggplot2	reshape
multcomp	WRS

R functions used in this chapter

Anova()	lme()
aov()	melt()
by()	pairdepb()
cast()	rmanova()
contrasts()	rmanovab()
ezANOVA()	rmmcp()
ggplot()	stat.desc()
gl()	summary()
glht()	update()
lm()	

Key terms that I've discovered

Compound symmetry	Mauchly's test
Greenhouse–Geisser correction	Repeated-measures ANOVA
Huynh–Feldt correction	Sphericity
Lower bound	

Smart Alex's tasks

- **Task 1**: Students often worry about the consistency of marking between lecturers. Lecturers obtain reputations for being 'hard' or 'light' markers (or to use the students' terminology, 'evil manifestations from Beelzebub's bowels' and 'nice people'), but there is often little to substantiate these reputations. A group of students put the idea to the test by submitting the same essays to four different lecturers. The mark given by each lecturer was recorded for each of the eight essays. This design is repeated measures because every lecturer marked every essay. The independent variable was the lecturer who marked the report and the dependent variable was the percentage mark given. The data are in the file **TutorMarks.dat**. Conduct a one-way ANOVA on these data by hand. ②

- **Task 2**: Repeat the analysis above using **R** and interpret the results. ②

- **Task 3**: Imagine I wanted to look at the effect alcohol has on the roving eye. The 'roving eye' effect is the propensity of people in relationships to 'eye up' members of the opposite sex. I took 20 men and fitted them with incredibly sophisticated glasses that could track their eye movements and record both the movement and the object being observed (this is the point at which it should be apparent that I'm making it up as I go along). Over four different nights I plied these poor souls with 1, 2, 3 or 4 pints of strong lager in a nightclub. Each night I measured how many different women they eyed up (a woman was categorized as having been eyed up if the man's eye moved from her head to her toe and back up again). To validate this measure we also collected the amount of dribble on the man's chin while looking at a woman. The data are in the file **RovingEye.dat**. Analyse them with a one-way ANOVA. ②

- **Task 4**: In the previous chapter we came across the beer-goggles effect, a severe perceptual distortion after imbibing alcohol that makes previously unattractive people suddenly become the hottest thing since Spicy Gonzalez's extra-hot Tabasco-marinated chillies. One minute you're standing in a zoo admiring the orang-utans, and 2 pints later you're wondering why someone would put the adorable Zoë Field in a cage. Imagine we followed up the fabricated example from the previous chapter to look at whether the beer-goggles effect is made worse by the fact that it usually occurs in clubs that have dim lighting. We took a sample of 26 men (because the effect is stronger in men) and gave them various doses of alcohol over four different weeks (0 pints, 2 pints, 4 pints and 6 pints of lager). This is our first independent variable. Each week (and, therefore, in each state of drunkenness) participants were asked to select a mate in a normal club (that had dim lighting) and then select a second mate in a specially designed club that had bright lighting. As such, the second independent variable was whether the club had dim or bright lighting. The outcome measure was the attractiveness of each mate as assessed by a panel of independent judges. To recap, all participants took part in all levels of the alcohol consumption variable, and selected mates in both brightly and dimly lit clubs. The data are in the file **BeerGogglesLighting.dat**. Analyse them with a two-way repeated-measures ANOVA. ②

Answers can be found on the companion website.

Further reading

Field, A. P. (1998). A bluffer's guide to sphericity. *Newsletter of the Mathematical, Statistical and Computing Section of the British Psychological Society*, 6(1), 13–22. (Available in the additional material for this chapter.)

Howell, D. C. (2006). *Statistical methods for psychology* (6th ed.). Belmont, CA: Duxbury. (Or you might prefer his *Fundamental Statistics for the Behavioral Sciences,* also in its 6th edition, 2007.)

Rosenthal, R., Rosnow, R. L., & Rubin, D. B. (2000). *Contrasts and effect sizes in behavioural research: A correlational approach*. (Cambridge: Cambridge University Press. This is quite advanced but really cannot be bettered for contrasts and effect size estimation.)

Interesting real research

Field, A. P. (2006). The behavioral inhibition system and the verbal information pathway to children's fears. *Journal of Abnormal Psychology*, 115(4), 742–752.

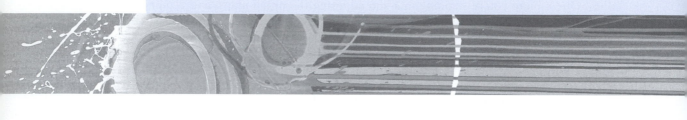

14

Mixed designs (GLM 5)

FIGURE 14.1
My 18th birthday
cake

14.1. What will this chapter tell me? ①

Most teenagers are anxious and depressed, but I probably had more than my fair share.
The parasitic leech that was the all-boys grammar school that I attended had feasted on my
social skills, leaving in its wake a terrified husk. Although I had no real problem with playing my guitar and shouting in front of people, speaking to them was another matter entirely.
In the band I felt at ease, in the real world I did not. Your 18th birthday is a time of great
joy, where (in the UK at any rate) you cast aside the shackles of childhood and embrace the
exciting new world of adult life. Your birthday cake might symbolize this happy transition
by reflecting one of your great passions. Mine had a picture on it of a longhaired person

who looked somewhat like me, slitting his wrists. That pretty much sums it up. Still, you can't lock yourself in your bedroom with your Iron Maiden albums for ever, and soon enough I tried to integrate with society. Between the ages of 16 and 18 this pretty much involved getting drunk. I quickly discovered that getting drunk made it much easier to speak to people, and getting *really* drunk made you unconscious and then the problem of speaking to people went away entirely. This situation was exacerbated by the sudden presence of girls in my social circle. I hadn't seen a girl since Clair Sparks; they were particularly problematic because not only had you to talk to them, but what you said had to be really impressive because then they might become your girlfriend. Also, in 1990, girls didn't like to talk about Iron Maiden – they probably still don't. Speed dating[1] didn't exist back then, but if it had it would have been a sick and twisted manifestation of hell on earth for me. The idea of having a highly pressured social situation where you *have* to think of something witty and amusing to say or be thrown to the baying vultures of eternal loneliness would have had me injecting pure alcohol into my eyeballs; at least that way I could be in a coma and unable to see the disappointment on the faces of those forced to spend 3 minutes in my company. That's what this chapter is all about: speed dating, oh, and mixed ANOVA too, but if I mention that you'll move swiftly onto the next chapter when the bell rings.

14.2. Mixed designs ②

If you thought that the previous chapter was bad, well, I'm about to throw an added complication into the mix. We can combine repeated-measures and independent designs, and this chapter looks at this situation. As if this wasn't bad enough, I'm also going to use it as an excuse to show you a design with three independent variables (at this point you should imagine me leaning back in my chair, cross-eyed, dribbling and laughing maniacally). A mixture of between-group and repeated-measures variables is called a **mixed design**. It should be obvious that you need at least two independent variables for this type of design to be possible, but you can have more complex scenarios too (e.g., two between-group and one repeated-measures, one between-group and two repeated-measures, or even two of each). **R** allows you to test almost any design you might want to, and of virtually any degree of complexity. However, interaction terms are difficult enough to interpret with only two variables, so imagine how difficult they are if you include four. The best advice I can offer is to stick to three or fewer independent variables if you want to be able to interpret your interaction terms,[2] and certainly don't exceed four unless you want to give yourself a migraine.

What is a mixed design?

This chapter will go through an example of a **mixed ANOVA**. There won't be any theory because really and truly you've probably had enough ANOVA theory by now to have a good idea of what's going on (you can read this as 'it's too complex for me and I'm going to cover up my own incompetence by pretending you don't need to know about it'). Essentially though, as we have seen, any ANOVA is a linear model, so when we have three independent variables or predictors we simply add this third predictor into the

---

[1] In case speed dating goes out of fashion and no one knows what I'm going on about, the basic idea is that lots of men and women turn up to a venue (or just men or just women if it's a gay night), one-half of the group sit individually at small tables and the remainder choose a table, get 3 minutes to impress the other person at the table with their tales of heteroscedastic data, then a bell rings and they get up and move to the next table. Having worked around all of the tables, the end of the evening is spent either stalking the person whom you fancied or avoiding the hideous mutant who was going on about hetero... something or other.

[2] Fans of irony will enjoy the four-way ANOVAs that I conducted in Field and Davey (1999) and Field and Moore (2005), to name but two examples.

linear model, give it a *b* and remember to also include any interactions involving the new predictor.

This chapter is spent looking at an example using **R** and then interpreting the output. In the process you'll hopefully develop your understanding of interactions and how to break them down using contrasts.

14.3. What do men and women look for in a partner? ②

The example we're going to use in this chapter stays with the dating theme. It seems that lots of magazines (or perhaps it's just my wife's copies of *Marie Claire*, which I don't read – honestly) go on all the time about how men and women want different things from relationships. The big question seems to be: are looks or personality more important? Imagine you wanted to put this to the test. You devised a cunning plan whereby you'd set up a speed-dating night. Little did the people who came along know that you'd got some of your friends to act as the dates. Each date varied in their attractiveness (attractive, average or ugly) and their charisma (charismatic, average and dull). By combining these characteristics you get nine different combinations and each combination was represented by one of your stooge dates. As such, your stooge dates were made up of nine different people. Three were extremely attractive people but differed in their personality: one had tons of charisma,[3] one had some charisma and the other was as dull as this book. Another three people were of average attractiveness, and again differed in their personality: one was highly charismatic, one had average charisma and the third was a dullard. The final three were, with no offence intended to pigs, pig-ugly, and again one was charismatic, one had some charisma and the final poor soul was mind-numbingly tedious. Obviously you had two sets of stooge dates: one set was male and the other female, so that your participants could match up with dates of the appropriate sex.

The participants themselves were not these nine stooges, but 10 men and 10 women who came to the speed-dating event that you had set up. Over the course of the evening they speed-dated all nine stooges of the gender that they'd normally date. After their 3-minute date, they rated how much they'd like to have a proper date with the person as a percentage (100% = 'I'd pay large sums of money for their phone number', 0% = 'I'd pay a large sum of money for a plane ticket to get me as far away from them as possible'). As such, each participant rated nine different people who varied in their attractiveness and personality. So, there are two repeated-measures variables: **looks** (with three levels because the person could be attractive, average or ugly) and **personality** (again with three levels because the person could have lots of charisma, have some charisma or be a dullard). The people giving the ratings could be male or female, so we should also include the **gender** of the person making the ratings (male or female), and this, of course, will be a between-group variable. The data are in Table 14.1.

14.4. Entering and exploring your data ②

14.4.1. Packages for mixed designs in R ①

You can analyse a mixed design using any of the four methods that I outlined in the previous chapter for doing a repeated-measures designs. As with the previous chapter, we're

---

[3] The highly attractive people with tons of charisma were, of course, taken to a remote cliff top and shot after the experiment because life is hard enough without having people like that floating around making you feel inadequate.

Table 14.1 Data from **LooksOrPersonality.dat** (Att = attractive, Av = average, Ug = ugly)

Looks	High Charisma			Some Charisma			Dullard		
	Att	Av	Ug	Att	Av	Ug	Att	Av	Ug
Male	86	84	67	88	69	50	97	48	47
	91	83	53	83	74	48	86	50	46
	89	88	48	99	70	48	90	45	48
	89	69	58	86	77	40	87	47	53
	80	81	57	88	71	50	82	50	45
	80	84	51	96	63	42	92	48	43
	89	85	61	87	79	44	86	50	45
	100	94	56	86	71	54	84	54	47
	90	74	54	92	71	58	78	38	45
	89	86	63	80	73	49	91	48	39
Female	89	91	93	88	65	54	55	48	52
	84	90	85	95	70	60	50	44	45
	99	100	89	80	79	53	51	48	44
	86	89	83	86	74	58	52	48	47
	89	87	80	83	74	43	58	50	48
	80	81	79	86	59	47	51	47	40
	82	92	85	81	66	47	50	45	47
	97	69	87	95	72	51	45	48	46
	95	92	90	98	64	53	54	53	45
	95	93	96	79	66	46	52	39	47

going to stick with *ezANOVA()* for those of you who want to adopt an ANOVA approach to the data, and *lme()* for those of you who want to use a multilevel model (which we recommend).

As with fully repeated-measures designs, you have to use commands because R Commander doesn't have an interface for repeated-measures designs. You will need the packages *ez* (if you're going to use ANOVA), *ggplot2* (for graphs), *nlme* (if you use a multilevel model), *pastecs* (for descriptive statistics), *reshape* (for reshaping the data) and *WRS* (for robust tests). If you do not have these packages installed (some should be installed from previous chapters), you can install them by executing the following commands:

```
install.packages("ez"); install.packages("ggplot2"); install.packages("nlme");
install.packages("pastecs"); install.packages("reshape"); install.packages
("WRS", repos="http://R-Forge.R-project.org")
```

You then need to load these packages by executing these commands:

```
library(ez); library(ggplot2); library(nlme); library(pastecs);
library(reshape); library(WRS)
```

14.4.2.   General procedure for mixed designs ①

To analyse research with a mixed design you should follow this general procedure:

1 *Enter data*: which is about as awkward as it was for repeated-measures designs.

2 *Explore your data*: as with repeated-measures designs, look at graphs, descriptive statistics and check sphericity if you're using ANOVA (boo, hiss) rather than a multilevel model (hooray!).

3 *Construct or choose contrasts*: you need to decide what contrasts to do and to specify them appropriately for all of the independent variables in your analysis.

4 *Compute the main model*: you can then run the main analysis. Depending on what you found in the previous step, you might need to run a robust version of the test.

5 *Compute contrasts or post hoc tests*: having conducted the main analysis, you can follow it up with *post hoc* tests or look at the results of your contrasts.

We will work through these steps in turn.

14.4.3.   Entering the data ②

The data for the example can be found in the file **LooksOrPersonality.dat**. You can load this data file by setting your working directory to the appropriate location and executing:

```
dateData<-read.delim("LooksOrPersonality.dat", header = TRUE)
```

I have again structured the data in the format that you'd be most likely to use if you had entered the data in another software package and followed the usual conventions. The data have been entered in 'wide' format; that is, *levels of the repeated-measures variable are spread across different columns.*

In this experiment there are nine experimental conditions and so the data have been entered in nine columns (so the format is identical to Table 14.1):

att_high	Attractive	+	High Charisma
av_high	Average Looks	+	High Charisma
ug_high	Ugly	+	High Charisma
att_some	Attractive	+	Some Charisma
av_some	Average Looks	+	Some Charisma
ug_some	Ugly	+	Some Charisma
att_none	Attractive	+	Dullard
av_none	Average Looks	+	Dullard
ug_none	Ugly	+	Dullard

There is also a column to indicate to which person each row of data belongs (called **participant**) and a column to indicate their gender (**gender**).

As with the example in the previous chapter, although the format of the data follows typical conventions, because of the way **R** handles repeated-measures designs we need the data to be in the long format. We can again use the *melt()* function. We specify columns in the data that identify characteristics of the scores (such as from whom they originate and characteristics of that person) using the *id* option, and columns that identify the scores themselves using the *measured* option. In this case our scores are split over nine columns (*att_high, av_high, ug_high, att_some, av_some, ug_some, att_none, av_none, ug_none*), so these are our measured variables. We have two variables that remain constant for each of the nine scores: the participant from which the score comes and their gender. These are our *id* variables. We can create a new dataframe (called *speedData*) by executing:

```
speedData<-melt(dateData, id = c("participant","gender"), measured = c("att_
high", "av_high", "ug_high", "att_some", "av_some", "ug_some", "att_none",
"av_none", "ug_none"))
```

This dataframe contains four columns: the first identifies the participant, the second identifies their gender, the third identifies the name of the column from which the data originate, and the fourth contains the rating of the date. By default, these columns will be named *participant, gender, variable,* and *value.* The latter two labels are not helpful, so we'll rename these columns so that we know what they represent by executing:

```
names(speedData)<-c("participant", "gender", "groups", "dateRating")
```

The variable **groups** is a mixture of our two predictor variables (**looks** and **personality**). Note, for example, that the first 60 rows are scores for the high-charisma dates and, within these 60 rows, the first 20 are the scores for the attractive stooges, the next 20 are the scores for the average looking stooges, and the final 20 are the scores for the ugly stooges. We therefore, need to create two variables that dissociate the attractiveness of the stooge from their charisma level; these two variables will be the two predictors in our model.

First, let's create a variable called **personality**, which specifies whether the date being rated had high, average or low charisma. We can do this using the *gl()* function that we have used in previous chapters. Execute this command:

```
speedData$personality<-gl(3,  60,  labels  =  c("Charismatic",  "Average",
"Dullard"))
```

This creates a variable **personality** in the dataframe *speedData.* The numbers in the function tell **R** that we want to create three sets of 60 scores, the labels option then specifies the names to attach to these three sets, which correspond to the levels of charisma. Essentially, this will create 60 rows with the label *Charismatic* then 60 labelled *Average* then 60 labelled *Dullard.*

We also need a variable (called **looks**) that tells us how attractive the date was. To do this we want three groups that each contain 20 scores. This will create 60 cases (3 × 20 = 60), or, put another way, it will create the codes for the first level (*Charismatic*) of the **personality** variable. We want this pattern to be repeated for the remaining two levels of **personality** (i.e., *Average* and *Dullard*). We can do this by adding a third value to the function that is the total number of cases (i.e., 180). By specifying the total number of cases, the *gl()* function will repeat the pattern of codes until it reaches this total number of cases

```
speedData$looks<-gl(3, 20, 180, labels = c("Attractive", "Average", "Ugly"))
```

The data now look like this (edited and ordered by participant):

```
   participant gender    groups dateRating personality       looks
1          P01   Male  att_high         86 Charismatic  Attractive
21         P01   Male   av_high         84 Charismatic     Average
41         P01   Male   ug_high         67 Charismatic        Ugly
61         P01   Male  att_some         88     Average  Attractive
81         P01   Male   av_some         69     Average     Average
101        P01   Male   ug_some         50     Average        Ugly
```

121	P01	Male	att_none	97	Dullard	Attractive
141	P01	Male	av_none	48	Dullard	Average
161	P01	Male	ug_none	47	Dullard	Ugly
...	...	...	...	...	...	
20	P20	Female	att_high	95	Charismatic	Attractive
40	P20	Female	av_high	93	Charismatic	Average
60	P20	Female	ug_high	96	Charismatic	Ugly
80	P20	Female	att_some	79	Average	Attractive
100	P20	Female	av_some	66	Average	Average
120	P20	Female	ug_some	46	Average	Ugly
140	P20	Female	att_none	52	Dullard	Attractive
160	P20	Female	av_none	39	Dullard	Average
180	P20	Female	ug_none	47	Dullard	Ugly

Notice that each participant (identified by the **participant** variable) has a value indicating their gender and then nine scores (distinguished by the variables **looks** and **personality**). In the reformatted data the nine scores within each participant are now represented by nine different rows rather than nine columns as they were before.

SELF-TEST

✓ Using what you learnt earlier in the chapter and the commands that we have just used to create **looks** and **personality**, can you work out how to enter the data into **R** directly?

14.4.4. Exploring the data ②

As ever, we'll look at some graphs first. To save space we'll look just at the boxplots at this stage.

SELF-TEST

✓ Use *ggplot2* to plot boxplots of the rating of the dates according to their level of attractiveness (*x*-axis), and level of charisma (different colours) for men and women (different plots).

The resulting plot (Figure 14.2) shows that the pattern of scores for average-looking dates was quite similar for males and females (their ratings decreased as the dates varied from charismatic to dullards). For attractive dates, males and females gave similar ratings except for when the date was dull (when males' ratings remained high but females' ratings dropped). For ugly dates, again the ratings were similar for men and women, except that women rated the charismatic dates higher than males did.

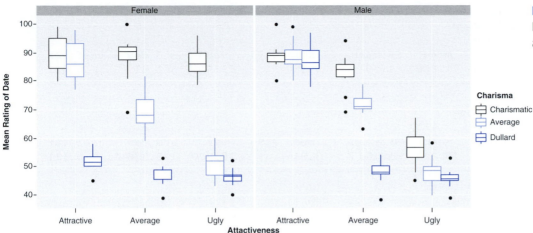

FIGURE 14.2
Boxplots of the
attitude data

We have previously used the *by()* function and the *stat.desc()* function in the *pastecs* package to get descriptive statistics for separate groups (see Chapter 5 for more detail). We also saw in the previous chapter that if we want to create descriptives for a combination of variables we can simply list all of the variables in the *list()* function; therefore, to get descriptive statistics for the combined levels of **gender**, **looks** and **personality** we execute:

```
by(speedData$dateRating, list(speedData$looks, speedData$personality,
speedData$gender), stat.desc, basic = FALSE)
```

The resulting (edited) output is in Output 14.1. The output contains descriptive statistics (means, standard deviations, etc.) for each of the nine conditions split according to whether participants were male or female. These descriptive statistics are interesting because they show us the pattern of means across all experimental conditions (so we use these means to produce the graphs of the three-way interaction).

```
: Attractive
: Charismatic
: Male
median    mean    SE.mean   CI.mean.0.95    var     std.dev    coef.var
89.000   88.300    1.802      4.075       32.456     5.697      0.065
-----------------------------------------------------------------------
: Average
: Charismatic
: Male
median    mean    SE.mean   CI.mean.0.95    var     std.dev    coef.var
84.000   82.800    2.215      5.011       49.0667    7.005      0.085
-----------------------------------------------------------------------
: Ugly
: Charismatic
: Male
median    mean    SE.mean   CI.mean.0.95    var     std.dev    coef.var
56.500   56.800    1.812      4.100       32.844     5.731      0.101
-----------------------------------------------------------------------
: Attractive
: Average
: Male
median    mean    SE.mean   CI.mean.0.95    var     std.dev    coef.var
87.500   88.500    1.815      4.106       32.944     5.740      0.065
-----------------------------------------------------------------------
```

```
: Average
: Average
: Male
median    mean    SE.mean   CI.mean.0.95    var     std.dev   coef.var
71.000   71.800   1.397       3.160       19.5111   4.417      0.061
-----------------------------------------------------------------------
: Ugly
: Average
: Male
median    mean    SE.mean   CI.mean.0.95    var     std.dev   coef.var
48.500   48.300   1.700       3.846       28.900    5.376      0.111
-----------------------------------------------------------------------
: Attractive
: Dullard
: Male
median    mean    SE.mean   CI.mean.0.95    var     std.dev   coef.var
86.500   87.300   1.720       3.890       29.567    5.438      0.062
-----------------------------------------------------------------------
: Average
: Dullard
: Male
median    mean    SE.mean   CI.mean.0.95    var     std.dev   coef.var
48.000   47.800   1.323       2.994       17.511    4.185      0.088
-----------------------------------------------------------------------
: Ugly
: Dullard
: Male
median    mean    SE.mean   CI.mean.0.95    var     std.dev   coef.var
45.500   45.800   1.133       2.564       12.844    3.584      0.078
-----------------------------------------------------------------------
: Attractive
: Charismatic
: Female
median    mean    SE.mean   CI.mean.0.95    var     std.dev   coef.var
89.000   89.600   2.099       4.748       44.044    6.637      0.074
-----------------------------------------------------------------------
: Average
: Charismatic
: Female
median    mean    SE.mean   CI.mean.0.95    var     std.dev   coef.var
90.500   88.400   2.634       5.958       69.378    8.329      0.094
-----------------------------------------------------------------------
: Ugly
: Charismatic
: Female
median    mean    SE.mean   CI.mean.0.95    var     std.dev   coef.var
86.000   86.700   1.720       3.890       29.567    5.438      0.063
-----------------------------------------------------------------------
: Attractive
: Average
: Female
median    mean    SE.mean   CI.mean.0.95    var     std.dev   coef.var
86.000   87.100   2.152       4.869       46.322    6.81       0.078
-----------------------------------------------------------------------
: Average
: Average
: Female
median    mean    SE.mean   CI.mean.0.95    var     std.dev   coef.var
68.000   68.900   1.882       4.258       35.433    5.953      0.086
-----------------------------------------------------------------------
```

```
: Ugly
: Average
: Female
median    mean    SE.mean   CI.mean.0.95    var     std.dev    coef.var
52.000   51.200    1.724       3.901      29.733     5.453      0.107
-------------------------------------------------------------------
: Attractive
: Dullard
: Female
median    mean    SE.mean   CI.mean.0.95    var     std.dev    coef.var
51.500   51.800    1.093       2.474      11.956     3.458      0.067
-------------------------------------------------------------------
: Average
: Dullard
: Female
median    mean    SE.mean   CI.mean.0.95    var     std.dev    coef.var
48.000   47.000    1.183       2.677      14.000     3.742      0.080
-------------------------------------------------------------------
: Ugly
: Dullard
: Female
median    mean    SE.mean   CI.mean.0.95    var     std.dev    coef.var
46.500   46.100    0.971       2.197       9.433     3.07       0.067
```

Output 14.1

14.5. Mixed ANOVA ②

As with repeated-measures ANOVA, we can do a fairly easy analysis using the *ezANOVA()* function. If you want to approach the analysis in this way and you plan to use Type III sums of squares (see Jane Superbrain Box 11.1) then you have to set an orthogonal contrast for your predictor variables, otherwise you might think you're getting type III sums of squares, but actually you won't be. Let's do this first.

For both **personality** and **looks** we could consider the lowest categories (*Dullard* and *Ugly*) as useful control conditions. Therefore, for **personality**, we could create contrasts that compare some charisma (i.e., average and charismatic) to being a dullard, and then compare the charismatic with the average date (Table 14.2). Likewise, for **looks**, we could create a contrast that compares some attractiveness (i.e., average and attractive combined) to being ugly, and then a second contrast that compares the attractive with the average date (Table 14.3). These contrasts would be orthogonal (the rationale is basically the same as for the contrasts that we encountered in Chapter 10).

To set these orthogonal contrasts (see Chapter 10) we can first create variables representing each contrast (which is useful mainly because you can give the contrasts informative names), and then bind these variables together and set them as the contrast for **personality**:

```
SomevsNone<-c(1, 1, -2)
HivsAv<-c(1, -1, 0)
contrasts(speedData$personality)<-cbind(SomevsNone, HivsAv)
```

The first two commands each create a variable relating to a contrast that contains the codes for each group from Table 14.2. The final command sets these variables to be the contrasts for **personality**.

Table 14.2 Orthogonal contrasts for the **personality** variable

Group	Contrast$_1$	Contrast$_2$
Charismatic	1	−1
Average	1	1
Dullard	−2	0

Table 14.3 Orthogonal contrasts for the **looks** variable

Group	Contrast$_1$	Contrast$_2$
Attractive	1	−1
Average	1	1
Ugly	−2	0

We can set the contrasts for **looks** in the same way as for **personality**: we first create variables representing each contrast, and then bind these variables together and set them as the contrast for **looks**:

```
AttractivevsUgly<-c(1, 1, -2)
AttractvsAv<-c(1, -1, 0)
contrasts(speedData$looks)<-cbind(AttractivevsUgly, AttractvsAv)
```

The first two commands each create a variable relating to a contrast that contains the codes for each group from in Table 14.3. The final command sets these variables to be the contrasts for **looks**.

Having set the contrasts, we can use the *ezANOVA()* function in much the same way as for a repeated-measures design. The only difference is that we can add our between-group variable (**gender**) by using the *between = .()* option. Have a quick look back to section 13.4.7.1 to remind yourself of the format of the function, and how the *between = .()* option fits into it. We can run the analysis by executing the following command:

```
speedModel<-ezANOVA(data = speedData, dv = .(dateRating), wid =
.(participant),  between = .(gender), within = .(looks, personality), type
= 3, detailed = TRUE)
speedModel
```

Executing these commands creates a model called *speedModel*; within the *ezANOVA()* function we have the following commands:

- *data = speedData*: This tells *ezANOVA* that the data are in the dataframe called *speedData*.
- *dv = .(dateRating)*: This tells *ezANOVA* that the outcome variable is **dateRating**.
- *wid = .(participant)*: This tells *ezANOVA* that participants can be identified using the variable **participant**.
- *between = .(gender)*: This tells *ezANOVA* that **gender** was measured using different entities/participants (i.e., it is a between-group variable).
- *within = .(looks, personality)*: This tells *ezANOVA* that **looks** and **personality** were measured using the same entities/participants (i.e., they are repeated-measures variables).

- *type = 3*: This tells *ezANOVA* that we want Type III sums of squares.

- *detailed = TRUE*: This tells *ezANOVA* to produced a detailed output (i.e., one that includes sums of squares).

Executing the second command (*speedModel*) simply prints the model to the console.

```
$ANOVA
                 Effect DFn DFd      SSn  SSd       F        p p<.05      ges
            (Intercept) 1  18   846249.8 760  2.00e+04 7.01e-29 * 9.94e-01
                 gender 1  18        0.2 760  4.74e-03 9.46e-01   4.07e-05
                  looks 2  36    20779.6 883  4.24e+02 9.59e-26 * 8.09e-01
           gender:looks 2  36     3944.1 883  8.04e+01 5.23e-14 * 4.45e-01
            personality 2  36    23233.6 1274 3.28e+02 7.69e-24 * 8.26e-01
     gender:personality 2  36     4420.1 1274 6.24e+01 1.97e-12 * 4.74e-01
      looks:personality 4  72     4055.3 1993 3.66e+01 1.10e-16 * 4.52e-01
      gender:looks:pers 4  72     2669.7 1993 2.41e+01 1.11e-12 * 3.52e-01


$'Mauchly's Test for Sphericity'
                       Effect     W     p p<.05
3                       looks 0.960 0.708
4                gender:looks 0.960 0.708
5                 personality 0.929 0.536
6          gender:personality 0.929 0.536
7           looks:personality 0.613 0.534
8 gender:looks:personality 0.613 0.534


$'Sphericity Corrections'
                       Effect   GGe    p[GG] p[GG]<.05 HFe   p[HF] p[HF]<.05
                        looks 0.962 7.62e-25    *      1.074 9.59e-26    *
                 gender:looks 0.962 1.49e-13    *      1.074 5.23e-14    *
                  personality 0.934 2.06e-22    *      1.038 7.69e-24    *
           gender:personality 0.934 9.44e-12    *      1.038 1.97e-12    *
            looks:personality 0.799 9.00e-14    *      0.992 1.43e-16    *
     gender:looks:personality 0.799 1.47e-10    *      0.992 1.34e-12    *
```

Output 14.2

SELF-TEST

✓ Output 14.2 shows the results of Mauchly's
  sphericity test. Based on what you have already
  learnt, was sphericity violated?

Output 14.2 shows the results of Mauchly's sphericity test for each of the three repeated-measures effects in the model and their interaction with **gender**. None of the effects violate the assumption of sphericity because all of the values in the column labelled *p* are above .05 (there are also no asterisks in the column labelled *p < .05* for Mauchley's test); therefore, we can assume sphericity when we look at our *F*-statistics.

Output 14.2 shows the summary table (labelled *$ANOVA*) of the effects in the ANOVA. There are the three main effects of our predictor variables, but also three interaction effects involving two variables and another interaction that includes all three variables.

Again, we need to look at the column labelled *p* and if the values in this column are less than .05 for a particular effect then it is statistically significant. Working down from the top of the table we find a non-significant effect of **gender**, which means that if we ignore the attractiveness and charisma levels of the data, male and female participants did not differ in the ratings they gave. There is a significant effect of **looks**, which means that if we ignore whether the date was charismatic, and whether the rating was from a man or a woman, then the attractiveness of a person significantly affected the ratings they received. The **looks** × **gender** interaction is also significant, which means that although the ratings were affected by whether the date was attractive, average or ugly, the way in which ratings were affected by attractiveness was different in male and female raters.

Next, we find a significant effect of **personality**, which means that if we ignore whether the date was attractive, and whether the rating was from a man or a woman, then the charisma of a person significantly affected the ratings they received. The **personality** × **gender** interaction is also significant, indicating that this effect of charisma differed in male and female raters.

There is a significant interaction between **looks** and **personality**, which means that if we ignore the gender of the rater, the profile of ratings across different levels of attractiveness was different for highly charismatic dates, charismatic dates and dullards. (It is equally true to say this the opposite way around: the profile of ratings across different levels of charisma was different for attractive, average and ugly dates.) Just to add to the mounting confusion, the **looks** × **personality** × **gender** interaction is also significant, meaning that the **looks** × **personality** interaction was significantly different in male and female participants.

This is all a lot to take in, so we'll look at each of these effects in turn in subsequent sections. First, though, we will look at how to analyse the data as a multilevel model.

SELF-TEST

✓ What is the difference between a main effect and an interaction?

CRAMMING SAM'S TIPS   **Mixed ANOVA**

- Mixed designs are where you compare several means when there are two or more independent variables, and at least one of them has been measured using the same participants and at least one other has been measured using different participants.
- You can analyse these designs using a traditional ANOVA framework, or as a multilevel model.
- If you plan to look at Type III sums of squares then you must set an orthogonal contrast for all predictors before constructing the model.
- If you use an ANOVA approach, then test the assumption of sphericity for the repeated-measures variable(s) when they have three or more conditions using Mauchly's test. If the value in the column labelled *p* is less than .05 then the assumption is violated. You should test this assumption for all effects (if there are two or more repeated-measures variables, this means you test the assumption for all variables and the corresponding interaction terms).
- For each effect in the ANOVA, if the assumption of sphericity has been met then use the *p*-value for the main ANOVA. If the assumption was violated then read the *p*-value corrected using either the Greenhouse–Geisser (*p[GG]*) or Huynh–Feldt (*p[HF]*) estimate of sphericity. If the *p*-value is less than .05 then the means of the groups are significantly different.
- Look at the means, or better still draw graphs, to help you interpret the contrasts.

14.6. Mixed designs as a GLM ③

I outlined various advantages to analysing repeated-measures data with a multilevel model in the previous chapter. We can extend the repeated-measures designs from the previous chapter by simply adding the between-group variable (and any interaction terms) as an additional predictor. Remember that when we use a multilevel model, the repeated measures are specified in the random part of the model, so adding in a between-group predictor does not affect this part of the model (because it is not a repeated measure). We can literally just set up the model as we would for a repeated-measures design, but then add the between-group predictor.

14.6.1. Setting contrasts ②

Before we build the model, we need to set contrasts. You might find this weird because we already set some contrasts for using *ezANOVA*. However, the contrasts we set before were simply so that we could get Type III sums of squares, and we were constrained to use orthogonal contrasts. However, if we use a multilevel model we don't have to worry about orthogonal contrasts because we don't need to concern ourselves with types of sums of squares in the same way that we do for ANOVA. Therefore, I'm going to use different contrasts to highlight how, despite the steeper learning curve, multilevel models are worth using for repeated-measures data because they offer a much more flexible framework for analysing your data.

If we look at the first variable, **looks**, there were three conditions: attractive, average and ugly. In many ways it makes sense to compare the attractive and ugly conditions to the average, because the average person represents the norm. This would not make sense as an orthogonal contrast because it would mean grouping the attractive and ugly groups together in a contrast and these groups are polar opposites (i.e., we might expect their ratings to cancel out because presumably attractive dates receive higher ratings than ugly dates). However, we can set up this contrast as a non-orthogonal contrast. Table 14.4 shows how this would be done. The key is that the baseline category is coded as 0 for all contrasts (that's how **R** knows it is the baseline). So, we give our baseline group (average attractiveness) a value of 0 in both contrasts. Then for one of the contrasts we assign a 1 to attractive and in the other we assign a 1 to ugly. Contrast 1 compares the attractive condition to the average condition (we can tell this because the attractive group is assigned a 1 for this contrast), and contrast 2 compares the ugly condition to the average condition (we can tell this because the ugly group is assigned a 1 for this contrast).

To set these contrasts (see Chapter 10) we can first create variables representing each contrast (which is useful in giving the contrasts informative names), and then bind these variables together and set them as the contrast for **looks**:

```
AttractivevsAv<-c(1, 0, 0)
UglyvsAv<-c(0, 0, 1)
contrasts(speedData$looks)<-cbind(AttractivevsAv, UglyvsAv)
```

The first two commands each create a variable relating to a contrast that contains the codes for each group from Table 14.4. The final command sets these variables to be the contrasts for **looks**.

Now, let's think about the second predictor. The **personality** variable also has a category that represents the norm, and that is the dates with the average amount of charisma. Again we could use this condition as a control against which to compare our two extremes (lots

Table 14.4 Non-orthogonal contrasts for the **looks** variable

Group	Contrast$_1$	Contrast$_2$
Attractive	1	0
Average	0	0
Ugly	0	1

Table 14.5 Non-orthogonal contrasts for the **personality** variable

Group	Contrast$_1$	Contrast$_2$
Charismatic	1	0
Average	0	0
Dullard	0	1

of charisma and none whatsoever). Therefore, we could again set the contrasts codes such that charismatic is compared to average charisma in contrast 1 and dullard is compared to average charisma in contrast 2. The codes are in Table 14.5 and you should note that we have used the same codes that we did for **looks**.

To set these contrasts we can first create variables representing each contrast and set them as the contrast for **personality**:

```
HighvsAv<-c(1, 0, 0)
DullvsAv<-c(0, 0, 1)
contrasts(speedData$personality)<-cbind(HighvsAv, DullvsAv)
```

The first two commands each create a variable relating to a contrast that contains the codes for each group from Table 14.5. The final command sets these variables to be the contrasts for **personality**.

We also have a third variable **gender**. We don't need to set an explicit contrast for this variable because it has only two levels (male or female) therefore the default contrast will be fine. (With only two groups any contrast we set can only compare these two groups, therefore setting a contrast is pointless.) If your third variable had more than two levels then you should also set a contrast for this variable that tests the hypotheses that you have.

We can check that we have set the contrast correctly by executing the name of the variable and looking at the contrast attribute:

```
speedData$looks
```

```
attr(,"contrasts")
          AttractivevsAv UglyvsAv
Attractive              1        0
Average                 0        0
Ugly                    0        1
Levels: Attractive Average Ugly
```

```
speedData$personality
```

```
attr(,"contrasts")
           HighvsAv DullvsAv
Charismatic        1        0
Average            0        0
Dullard            0        1
Levels: Charismatic Average Dullard
```

As you can see the codes match those in Tables 14.4 and 14.5.

14.6.2. Building the model ②

We saw in the previous chapter that if we want to look at the overall main effects and interactions then we should build up the model one predictor at a time from a baseline that includes no predictors other than the intercept. We can specify the baseline model as we did in the previous chapter:

```
baseline<-lme(dateRating ~ 1, random = ~1|participant/looks/personality,
data = speedData, method = "ML")
```

Compare this model with the one that we used for a factorial repeated-measures design in the previous chapter. Apart from the variables we're using, it is exactly the same: we have specified the model as the outcome predicted only from the intercept (*dateRating* ~ *1*), specified the relevant dataframe (*data* = *speedData*), and asked to use maximum likelihood to estimate the model (*method* = "*ML*"). The random part of the model reflects the fact that there are two repeated-measures predictors: *random* = ~*1*|*participant/looks/personality* tells **R** that the variables **looks** and **personality** are nested within the variable **participant** (in other words, scores for levels of these variables can be found within each participant). Execute the above command to create the baseline model.

To see the overall effect of each main effect and interaction we need to add them to the model one at a time. To add **looks** to the model we could just change the model from *dateRating* ~ *1* to *dateRating* ~ *looks*. In other words, execute:

```
looksM<-lme(dateRating ~ looks, random = ~1|participant/looks/personality,
data = speedData, method = "ML")
```

However, it is quicker to use the *update()* function (see R's Souls' Tip 7.2):

```
looksM<-update(baseline, .~. + looks)
```

This command takes the model called *baseline* (which we have already created), and the .~. means keep the outcome and predictors the same as the baseline model (the dots mean 'keep the same', so the fact that we put dots on both sides of the ~ means that we want to keep both the outcome and predictors the same as in the baseline model). The '+ looks' means 'add **looks** as a predictor'. Therefore, '.~. + looks' can be interpreted as 'keep the same outcomes and predictors as the baseline model but add **looks** as a predictor'. Executing this command creates a model called *looksM* that includes only **looks** as a predictor.

In a similar way we can add **personality** to the model as a predictor.

```
personalityM<-update(looksM, .~. + personality)
```

This command takes the model called *looksM* (which we have just created), as before, the .~. means keep the outcome and predictors the same as in *looksM*, and the '+ personality' adds **personality** as a predictor. Therefore, '.~. + personality' can be interpreted as 'keep the same outcomes and predictors as *looksM* but add **personality** as a predictor'. Executing this command creates a model called *personalityM* that includes both **looks** and **personality** as predictors.

We can add **gender** to the model in exactly the same way:

```
genderM<-update(personalityM, .~. + gender)
```

This command takes the previous model (*personalityM*), keeps all of the same predictors and outcomes (.~.) and adds **gender** (+ *gender*). Therefore, executing this command creates a model called *genderM* that includes **looks**, **personality** and **gender** as predictors.

We also need to add in the interactions between pairs of variables (the two-way interactions). There are three of these interactions made up from all of the combinations of the three main effects: **looks** × **personality**, **looks** × **gender**, and **personality** × **gender**.

Remember that in **R** an interaction is written using a colon, so the **looks** × **personality** interaction can be specified as *looks:personality*.

We can add these interactions one at a time using the update command. Each time we create a new model that contains all of the terms from the previous model but adds in an interaction:

```
looks_gender<-update(genderM, .~. + looks:gender)
personality_gender<-update(looks_gender, .~. + personality:gender)
looks_personality<-update(personality_gender, .~. + looks:personality)
```

Note that the model called *looks_gender* is created by taking the *genderM* model (which contains all of the main effects) and adding the **looks** × **gender** interaction to it. Similarly, the *personality_gender* model is created by taking the *looks_gender* model and adding the **personality** × **gender** interaction to it. Hopefully you get the gist.

We also need to include the interaction of all three variables, which would be written in **R** as *looks:personality:gender*. Again, we do this with the update command. We take the model with all of the main effects and two-way interactions (*looks_personality*) and add in the three-way interaction:

```
speedDateModel<-update(looks_personality, .~. + looks:personality:gender)
```

Executing this command creates a model called *speedDateModel*, which contains all main effects and interactions. This is the final model.

To compare these models we can list them in the order in which we want them compared in the *anova()* function:

```
anova(baseline, looksM, personalityM, genderM, looks_gender, personality_
gender, looks_personality, speedDateModel)
```

Executing the above command produces Output 14.3, which first compares the effect of **looks** to the baseline (i.e., no predictors). By adding **looks** as a predictor we increase the degrees of freedom by 2 (the two contrasts that we used to code this variable) and significantly improve the model. In other words, the attractiveness of the date had a significant effect on ratings, $\chi^2(2) = 68.30$, $p < .0001$. Next, we see the effect of adding the main effect of **personality** into the model (compared to the previous model that contained only the effect of **looks**). Again the degrees of freedom are increased by 2 (the two contrasts used to code this variable) and the fit of the model is significantly improved; the personality of the date had a significant effect on attitudes, $\chi^2(2) = 138.76$, $p < .0001$. The next model tells us whether adding **gender** improved the fit of the model; it did not, indicating that gender did not have a significant overall effect on ratings $\chi^2(1) = 0.002$, $p = .966$. This effect adds only 1 degree of freedom because it was coded with a single contrast.

	Model	df	AIC	BIC	logLik	Test	L.Ratio	p-value
baseline	1	5	1575.766	1591.730	-782.8829			
looksM	2	7	1511.468	1533.819	-748.7343	1 vs 2	68.29719	<.0001
personalityM	3	9	1376.704	1405.441	-679.3520	2 vs 3	138.76442	<.0001
genderM	4	10	1378.702	1410.632	-679.3511	3 vs 4	0.00180	0.9662
looks_gender	5	12	1343.161	1381.477	-659.5808	4 vs 5	39.54079	<.0001
personality_gender	6	14	1289.198	1333.899	-630.5988	5 vs 6	57.96394	<.0001
looks_personality	7	18	1220.057	1277.530	-592.0283	6 vs 7	77.14102	<.0001
speedDateModel	8	22	1148.462	1218.707	-552.2309	7 vs 8	79.59473	<.0001

Output 14.3

The next model (*looks_gender*) shows that the **looks** × **gender** interaction is also significant, $\chi^2(2) = 39.54$, $p < .0001$. This interaction adds 2 degrees of freedom (because **looks** is coded with two contrasts and **gender** only one, so we get $2 \times 1 = 2$ *df*). This significant interaction means that although the ratings were affected by whether the date was attractive, average or ugly, the way in which ratings were affected by attractiveness was different in male and female raters.

The next model (*personality_gender*) shows that the **personality** × **gender** interaction is also significant, $\chi^2(2) = 57.96$, $p < .0001$, indicating that this effect of charisma differed in male and female raters. This interaction adds 2 degrees of freedom (because **personality** is coded with two contrasts and **gender** only one, so we get $2 \times 1 = 2$ *df*).

The next model (*looks_personality*) tells us that there is a significant interaction between **looks** and **personality**, $\chi^2(4) = 77.14$, $p < .0001$. This interaction adds 4 degrees of freedom (because it is made up of two variables each coded with two contrasts, so we get $2 \times 2 = 4$ *df*). This interaction term means that if we ignore the gender of the rater, the profile of ratings across different levels of attractiveness was different for highly charismatic dates, charismatic dates and dullards. (It is equally true to say this the opposite way around: the profile of ratings across different levels of charisma was different for attractive, average and ugly dates.)

The final model (*speedDateModel*) shows that the **looks** × **personality** × **gender** interaction is also significant, $\chi^2(4) = 79.59$, $p < .0001$, meaning that the **looks** × **personality** interaction was significantly different in male and female participants. This interaction adds 4 degrees of freedom (because **personality** is coded with two contrasts, **looks** is also coded with two contrasts, and **gender** with only one, so we get $2 \times 2 \times 1 = 4$ *df*).

These results confirm the findings from the ANOVA and just demonstrate really that there are two ways to skin this data analysis cat. The end results are the same. However, the multilevel model approach has the advantages that (1) we don't need to concern ourselves with sphericity, and (2) we can now break down these very complicated effects by looking at the model parameters (which reflect the contrasts that we used to code the predictor variables). We can see the model parameters by executing:

```
summary(speedDateModel)
```

Output 14.4 shows the parameter estimates for the model (I've edited some of the names to save space and put some spaces in the table to try to group related contrasts together).

```
Linear mixed-effects model fit by maximum likelihood

Fixed effects: dateRating ~ looks + personality + gender +
looks:personality +      looks:gender + personality:gender +
looks:personality:gender
                         Value Std.Error  DF  t-value p-value
(Intercept)               68.9 1.740866  108 39.57800  0.0000

AttractivevsAv            18.2 2.400632   36  7.58134  0.0000
UglyvsAv                 -17.7 2.400632   36 -7.37306  0.0000

HighvsAv                  19.5 2.400632  108  8.12286  0.0000
DullvsAv                 -21.9 2.400632  108 -9.12260  0.0000

gender                     2.9 2.461957   18  1.17792  0.2542

AttractivevsAv:gender     -1.5 3.395006   36 -0.44183  0.6613
UglyvsAv:gender           -5.8 3.395006   36 -1.70839  0.0962

HighvsAv:gender           -8.5 3.395006  108 -2.50368  0.0138
DullvsAv:gender           -2.1 3.395006  108 -0.61856  0.5375

AttractivevsAv:HighvsAv  -17.0 3.395006  108 -5.00736  0.0000
UglyvsAv:HighvsAv         16.0 3.395006  108  4.71280  0.0000
AttractivevsAv:DullvsAv  -13.4 3.395006  108 -3.94697  0.0001
UglyvsAv:DullvsAv         16.8 3.395006  108  4.94845  0.0000
```

```
AttractivevsAv:HighvsAv:gender      5.8   4.801263  108   1.20802   0.2297
UglyvsAv:HighvsAv:gender          -18.5   4.801263  108  -3.85315   0.0002
AttractivevsAv:DullvsAv:gender     36.2   4.801263  108   7.53968   0.0000
UglyvsAv:DullvsAv:gender            4.7   4.801263  108   0.97891   0.3298
```

Output 14.4

14.6.3.   The main effect of gender ②

We saw in Output 14.3 that gender did not have a significant overall effect on ratings of the dates, $\chi^2(1) = 0.002$, $p = .966$. This effect tells us that if we ignore all other variables, male participants' ratings were basically the same as those of female participants.

SELF-TEST

✓ Using *ggplot2* and *stat.desc*, plot an error bar graph and get the means for the main effect of **gender**.

FIGURE 14.3
Error bar graph of the main effect of gender

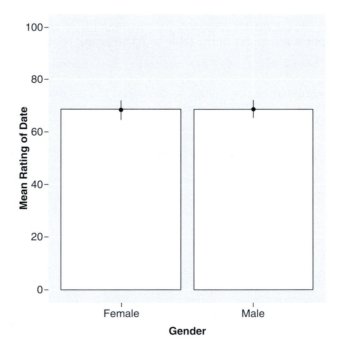

Output 14.5 is a table of means for the main effect of **gender** with the associated standard errors. This information is plotted in Figure 14.3. It is clear from this graph that men and women's ratings were generally the same when we ignore the other predictors. However, remember that because there are significant interactions involving this main effect we shouldn't really interpret it (because the higher-order interactions supersede it).

```
speedData$gender: Male
median     mean    SE.mean   CI.mean.0.95     var      std.dev    coef.var
71.000    68.600   1.961        3.896        346.018   18.602      0.271
-----------------------------------------------------------------------------
speedData$gender: Female
median     mean    SE.mean   CI.mean.0.95     var      std.dev    coef.var
67.500    68.533   2.036        4.046        373.218   19.319      0.282
```

Output 14.5

SELF-TEST

✓ Based on the previous section and what you have
learned in previous chapters, can you interpret the
main effect of **looks**?

We came across the main effect of **looks** in Output 14.3. Now we're going to have a look
at what this effect means. We can report that the attractiveness of the date had a significant
effect on ratings, $\chi^2(2) = 68.30$, $p < .0001$. This effect tells us that if we ignore all other
variables, ratings were different for attractive, average and unattractive dates.

SELF-TEST

✓ Using *ggplot2* and *stat.desc*, plot an error bar graph
and get the means for the main effect of **looks**.

```
speedData$looks: Attractive
median     mean    SE.mean   CI.mean.0.95     var      std.dev    coef.var
86.00     82.10    1.90         3.81         217.52    14.75       0.18
-----------------------------------------------------------------------------
speedData$looks: Average
median     mean    SE.mean   CI.mean.0.95     var      std.dev    coef.var
70.000    67.783   2.181        4.364        285.359   16.893      0.249
-----------------------------------------------------------------------------
speedData$looks: Ugly
median     mean    SE.mean   CI.mean.0.95     var      std.dev    coef.var
50.000    55.817   1.957        3.917        229.881   15.162      0.272
```

Output 14.6

Output 14.6 is a table of means for the main effect of **looks** with the associated standard
errors. To make things easier, this information is plotted in Figure 14.4. You can see that
as attractiveness falls, the mean rating falls too. So this main effect seems to reflect that
the raters were more likely to express a greater interest in going out with attractive people
than average or ugly people. However, we really need to look at some contrasts to find out
exactly what's going on.

FIGURE 14.4
Error bar graph of the main effect of looks

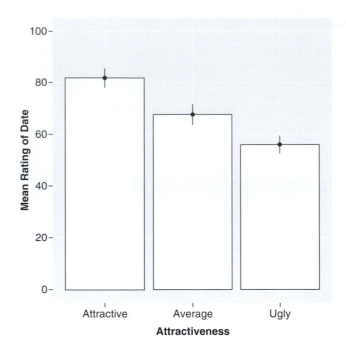

Output 14.4 shows the contrasts that we requested. The first contrast that we set (*AttractivevsAv*) shows that attractive dates were rated significantly higher than average dates, $b = 18.2$, $t(36) = 7.58$, $p < .001$. The second contrast (*UglyvsAv*) shows that average dates were rated significantly higher than ugly ones, -17.7, $t(36) = -7.37$, $p < .001$. Remember that because there are significant interactions involving **looks**, we shouldn't really interpret the main effect (because the higher-order interactions supersede it).

14.6.5. The main effect of **personality** ②

The main effect of **personality** is in Output 14.3. We can report that there was a significant main effect of charisma, $\chi^2(2) = 138.76$, $p < .0001$. This effect tells us that if we ignore all other variables, ratings were different for highly charismatic, averagely charismatic and dullard people.

SELF-TEST

✓ Using *ggplot2* and *stat.desc*, plot an error bar graph and get the means for the main effect of **personality**.

Output 14.7 and Figure 14.5 show that as charisma declines, the mean rating falls too. So this main effect seems to reflect that the raters were more likely to express a greater interest in going out with charismatic people than average people or dullards.

```
speedData$personality: Charismatic
median      mean      SE.mean    CI.mean.0.95      var       std.dev    coef.var
86.000     82.100     1.704         3.409        174.193     13.198      0.161
-----------------------------------------------------------------------------
speedData$personality: Average
median      mean      SE.mean    CI.mean.0.95      var       std.dev    coef.var
71.00      69.30       2.15         4.30         276.96      16.64       0.24
-----------------------------------------------------------------------------
speedData$personality: Dullard
median      mean      SE.mean    CI.mean.0.95      var       std.dev    coef.var
48.000     54.300     2.000         4.002        240.010     15.492      0.285
```

Output 14.7

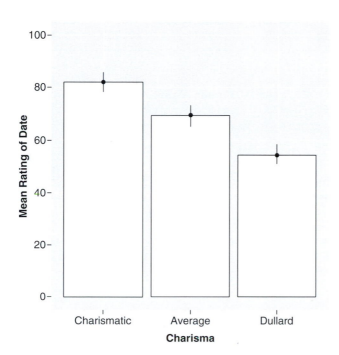

FIGURE 14.5
Error bar graph of
the main effect of
personality

Output 14.4 shows the contrasts that we requested. The first contrast that we set (*HighvsAv*) shows that highly charismatic dates were rated significantly higher than dates with average charisma, $b = 19.5$, $t(108) = 8.12$, $p < .001$. The second contrast (*DullvsAv*) shows that dates with average charisma were rated significantly higher than dullards, $b = -21.9$, $t(108) = -9.12$, $p < .001$. Remember that because there are significant interactions involving **personality,** we shouldn't really interpret the main effect (because the higher-order interactions supersede it).

14.6.6. The interaction between **gender** and **looks** ②

Output 14.3 indicated that gender interacted in some way with the attractiveness of the date. We can report that there was a significant interaction between the attractiveness of the date and the gender of the participant, $\chi^2(2) = 39.54$, $p < .0001$. This effect tells us that the profile of ratings across dates of different attractiveness was different for men and women.

SELF-TEST

✓ Using *ggplot2* and *stat.desc*, plot a line graph and get the means for the **looks** × **gender** interaction.

```
: Attractive
: Male
median    mean    SE.mean    CI.mean.0.95    var       std.dev    coef.var
88.000    88.033  0.996      2.037           29.757    5.455      0.062
-------------------------------------------------------------------------------
: Average
: Male
median    mean    SE.mean    CI.mean.0.95    var       std.dev    coef.var
71.000    67.467  2.873      5.876           247.637   15.736     0.233
-------------------------------------------------------------------------------
: Ugly
: Male
median    mean    SE.mean    CI.mean.0.95    var       std.dev    coef.var
48.500    50.300  1.239      2.535           46.079    6.788      0.135
-------------------------------------------------------------------------------
: Attractive
: Female
median    mean    SE.mean    CI.mean.0.95    var       std.dev    coef.var
82.500    76.167  3.366      6.885           339.937   18.437     0.242
-------------------------------------------------------------------------------
: Average
: Female
median    mean    SE.mean    CI.mean.0.95    var       std.dev    coef.var
67.500    68.100  3.330      6.811           332.714   18.240     0.268
-------------------------------------------------------------------------------
: Ugly
: Female
median    mean    SE.mean    CI.mean.0.95    var       std.dev    coef.var
52.500    61.333  3.458      7.072           358.644   18.938     0.309
```

Output 14.8

The means and interaction graph (Figure 14.6 and Output 14.8) shows the meaning of this result. The graph shows the average male ratings of dates of different attractiveness ignoring how charismatic the date was (blue line). The women's scores are shown as a black line. The graph clearly shows that male and female ratings are very similar for average-looking dates, but men give higher ratings (i.e., they're really keen to go out with these people) than women for attractive dates, but women express more interest in going out with ugly people than men do. In general, this interaction seems to suggest that men's interest in dating a person is more influenced by their looks than for females. Although both males' and females' interest decreases as attractiveness decreases, this decrease is more pronounced for men. This interaction can be clarified using the contrasts in Output 14.4. However, we wouldn't normally interpret this interaction because the significant higher-order three-way interaction supersedes it.

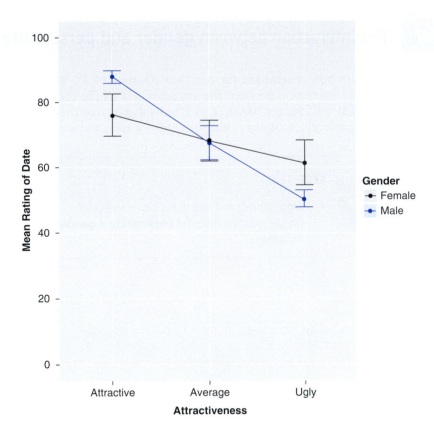

FIGURE 14.6
Graph of the
interaction
between looks and
gender

14.6.6.1. Looks × gender interaction 1: attractive vs. average, male vs. female ②

The first contrast for the **looks** × **gender** interaction term (*AttractivevsAv:gender*) compares male and female ratings of attractive relative to average-looking dates. This contrast is not significant, $b = -1.5$, $t(36) = -0.44$, $p = .661$. This result tells us that the increased interest in attractive dates compared to average-looking dates found for men is not significantly more than for women. So, in Figure 14.6 the slope of the blue line (men) between the attractive dates and average dates is not steeper than the black line (females). We can conclude that the preferences for attractive dates, compared to average-looking dates, are similar for males and females.

14.6.6.2. Looks × gender interaction 2: ugly vs. average, male vs. female ②

The second contrast (*UglyvsAv:gender*) compares male and female ratings of ugly relative to average-looking dates. This contrast is not significant, $b = -5.8$, $t(36) = -1.71$, $p = .096$, which suggests that the decreased interest in ugly dates compared to average-looking dates found for male raters is not significantly different than for female raters. In Figure 14.6 the slope of the blue line (men) between the ugly dates and average dates is not steeper than the black line (females). We can conclude that the preferences for average-looking dates, compared to ugly dates, are similar for males and females.

14.6.7. The interaction between **gender** and **personality** ②

Gender interacted with how charismatic the date was (Output 14.3). We can report that there was a significant interaction between the attractiveness of the date and the gender of the participant, $\chi^2(2) = 57.96$, $p < .0001$. This effect suggests that the profile of ratings across dates of different levels of charisma was different for men and women.

SELF-TEST

✓ Using *ggplot2* and *stat.desc*, plot a line graph and get the means for the **personality** × **gender** interaction.

```
: Charismatic
: Male
median    mean    SE.mean   CI.mean.0.95    var      std.dev    coef.var
82.00    75.97    2.77        5.67        230.72     15.19       0.20
-------------------------------------------------------------------------
: Average : Male
median    mean    SE.mean   CI.mean.0.95    var      std.dev    coef.var
71.000   69.533   3.197       6.538       306.533    17.508      0.252
-------------------------------------------------------------------------
: Dullard
: Male
median    mean    SE.mean   CI.mean.0.95    var      std.dev    coef.var
49.00    60.30    3.63        7.43        396.36     19.91       0.33
-------------------------------------------------------------------------
: Charismatic
: Female
median    mean    SE.mean   CI.mean.0.95    var      std.dev    coef.var
89.0000  88.2333  1.2361      2.5282      45.8402    6.7705      0.0767
-------------------------------------------------------------------------
: Average
: Female
median    mean    SE.mean   CI.mean.0.95    var      std.dev    coef.var
68.000   69.067   2.926       5.984       256.823    16.026      0.232
-------------------------------------------------------------------------
: Dullard
: Female
median    mean    SE.mean   CI.mean.0.95    var      std.dev    coef.var
48.0000  48.3000  0.7629      1.5602      17.4586    4.1784      0.0865
```

Output 14.9

The means tell us the meaning of this interaction (see Figure 14.7 and Output 14.9). The graph shows the average male ratings of dates of different levels of charisma, ignoring how attractive they were (blue line). The women's scores are shown as a black line. The graph shows almost the reverse pattern as for the attractiveness data; again male and female ratings are very similar for dates with average amounts of charisma, but this time men show more interest in dates who are dullards than women do, and women show slightly more interest in very charismatic dates than men do. In general, this interaction seems to suggest than women's interest in dating a person is more influenced by their charisma than

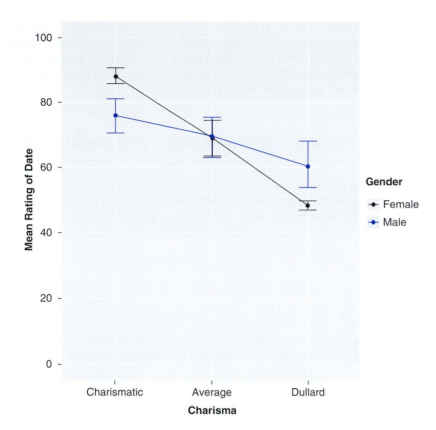

FIGURE 14.7
Graph of the interaction between charisma and gender

for men. Although both males' and females' interest decreases as charisma decreases, this decrease is more pronounced for females. This interaction can be clarified using the contrasts in Output 14.4. However, we wouldn't normally interpret this interaction because the significant higher-order three-way interaction supersedes it.

14.6.7.1. Personality × gender interaction 1: high vs. some charisma, male vs. female ②

The first contrast for this interaction term (*HighvsAv:gender*) looks at high charisma compared to average charisma, comparing male and female scores. This contrast is significant, $b = -8.5$, $t(108) = -2.50$, $p = .014$. This result tells us that the increased interest in highly charismatic dates compared to averagely charismatic dates found for women is significantly more than for men. So, in Figure 14.7 the slope of the black line (women) between the charismatic dates and dates with average charisma is steeper than the equivalent blue line (men). We can conclude that the preferences for very charismatic dates, compared to averagely charismatic dates, are significantly greater for females than males.

14.6.7.2. Personality × gender interaction 2: dullard vs. some charisma, male vs. female ②

The second contrast for this interaction term (*DullvsAv:gender*) looks at differences in male and female ratings of dullards compared to dates with average charisma. This contrast is not significant, $b = -2.1$, $t(108) = -0.62$, $p = .538$. This result tells us that the decreased interest in dull dates compared to averagely charismatic dates found for women is not significantly more than for men. So, in Figure 14.7 the slope of the black line (females) between dates with some charisma and dullard dates is not significantly steeper than the corresponding blue line (males). We can conclude that the preferences for dates with some charisma over dullards are similar for females than males.

14.6.8.   The interaction between **looks** and **personality** ②

Output 14.3 indicated that the attractiveness of the date interacted in some way with how charismatic the date was. We can report that there was a significant interaction between the attractiveness of the date and the charisma of the date, $\chi^2(4) = 77.14$, $p < .0001$. This effect tells us that the profile of ratings across dates of different levels of charisma was different for attractive, average and ugly dates.

SELF-TEST

✓ Using *ggplot2* and *stat.desc*, plot a line graph and get the means for the **looks** × **personality** interaction.

The means tell us the meaning of this interaction (see Output 14.10 and Figure 14.8). The graph shows the average ratings of dates of different levels of attractiveness when the date also had high levels of charisma (black), some charisma (light blue) and no charisma (blue). Look first at the difference between attractive and average-looking dates. The interest in highly charismatic dates doesn't change (the line is more or less flat between these two points), but for dates with some charisma or no charisma interest levels decline. So, if you have lots of charisma you can get away with being average-looking and people will still want to date you. Now, if we look at the difference between average-looking and ugly dates, a different pattern is observed. For dates with no charisma (blue) there is little difference between ugly and average people (so if you're a dullard you have to be really attractive before people want to date you). However, for those with charisma, there is a decline in interest if you're ugly (so if you're ugly, having charisma won't help you much). This interaction is very complex, but we can break it down using the contrasts in Output 14.4. However, we wouldn't normally interpret this interaction because the significant higher-order three-way interaction supersedes it.

```
: Attractive
: Charismatic
median     mean    SE.mean   CI.mean.0.95    var       std.dev    coef.var
89.0000   88.9500  1.3543      2.8345     36.6816      6.0565      0.0681
-------------------------------------------------------------------------
: Average
: Charismatic
median     mean    SE.mean   CI.mean.0.95    var       std.dev    coef.var
86.5000   85.6000  1.7938      3.7546     64.3579      8.0223      0.0937
-------------------------------------------------------------------------
: Ugly
: Charismatic
median     mean    SE.mean   CI.mean.0.95    var       std.dev    coef.var
73.000    71.750    3.639       7.616     264.829     16.274       0.227
-------------------------------------------------------------------------
```

```
: Attractive
: Average
median     mean    SE.mean  CI.mean.0.95   var      std.dev   coef.var
86.5000   87.8000  1.3795    2.8874       38.0632   6.1695     0.0703
---------------------------------------------------------------------
: Average
: Average
median     mean    SE.mean  CI.mean.0.95   var      std.dev   coef.var
71.0000   70.3500  1.1883    2.4871       28.2395   5.3141     0.0755
---------------------------------------------------------------------
: Ugly
: Average
median     mean    SE.mean  CI.mean.0.95   var      std.dev   coef.var
49.50     49.75    1.22      2.56         29.99     5.48       0.11
---------------------------------------------------------------------
: Attractive
: Dullard
median     mean    SE.mean  CI.mean.0.95   var      std.dev   coef.var
68.000    69.550   4.191     8.772        351.313   18.743     0.269
---------------------------------------------------------------------
: Average
: Dullard
median     mean    SE.mean  CI.mean.0.95   var      std.dev   coef.var
48.000    47.400   0.869     1.818        15.095    3.885      0.082
---------------------------------------------------------------------
: Ugly
: Dullard
median     mean    SE.mean  CI.mean.0.95   var      std.dev   coef.var
46.0000   45.9500  0.7272    1.5220       10.5763   3.2521     0.0708
```

Output 14.10

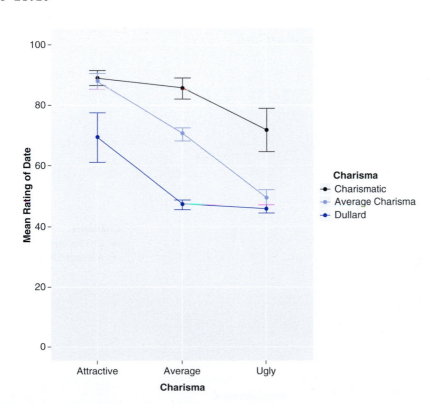

FIGURE 14.8
Graph of the interaction between looks and personality

14.6.8.1. Looks × personality interaction 1: attractive vs. average, high charisma vs. some charisma ②

The first contrast for this interaction term (*AttractivevsAv:HighvsAv*) investigates ratings of attractive compared to average-looking dates, when comparing charismatic dates to those with average charisma. This is like asking: is the difference between high charisma and average charisma the same for attractive people and average-looking people? The best way to understand what this contrast is testing is to extract the relevant bit of the interaction graph, which I have done in Figure 14.9. If you look at this you can see that the interest (as indicated by high ratings) in attractive dates was the same regardless of whether they had high or average charisma. However, for average-looking dates, there was more interest when that person had high charisma rather than average. The contrast is highly significant, $b = -17.0, t(108) = -5.01, p < .001$, and tells us that as dates become less attractive there is a greater decline in interest when charisma is average compared to when charisma is high.

14.6.8.2. Looks × personality interaction 2: ugly vs. average, high charisma vs. some charisma ②

The second contrast for this interaction term (*UglyvsAv:HighvsAv*) investigates ratings of ugly compared to average looking dates when comparing charismatic to average-charisma dates. This is like asking: is the difference between high charisma and average charisma the same for ugly people and average-looking people? I have again extracted the relevant bit of the interaction graph (Figure 14.10). You can see that the interest (as indicated by high ratings) decreases from average-looking dates to ugly ones in both high- and some-charisma dates; however, this fall is slightly greater in the average-charisma dates (the light blue line is slightly steeper). The contrast is significant, $b = 16.0, t(108) = 4.71, p < .001$, and tells us that as dates become less attractive there is a greater decline in interest when charisma is low compared to when charisma is high.

FIGURE 14.9

Graph displaying looks × personality interaction 1: attractive vs. average, high charisma vs. some charisma

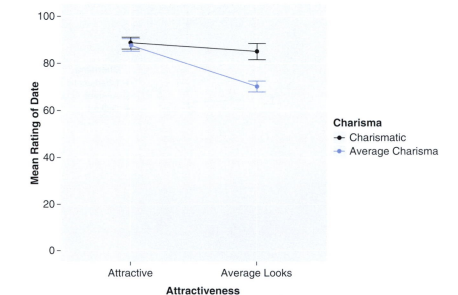

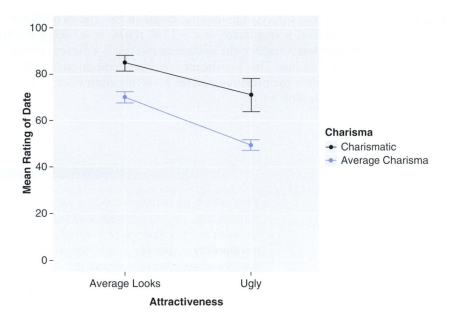

FIGURE 14.10
Graph displaying
looks × personality
interaction 2:
ugly vs. average,
high charisma vs.
some charisma

14.6.8.3. Looks × personality interaction 3: attractive vs. average, dullard vs. some charisma ②

The third contrast for this interaction term (*AttractivevsAv:DullvsAv*) investigates ratings of attractive compared to average looking dates, when comparing dullards to dates with average charisma. This is like asking: is the difference between no charisma and average charisma the same for attractive people and average-looking people? Again, the best way to understand what this contrast is testing is to extract the relevant bit of the interaction graph (see Figure 14.11). If you look at this you can see that the interest (as indicated by high ratings) in attractive dates was higher when they had some charisma than when they were

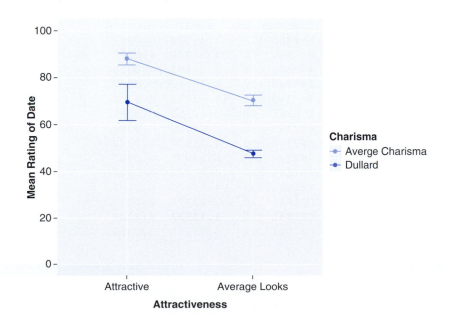

FIGURE 14.11
Graph displaying
looks × personality
interaction
3: attractive
vs. average,
dullard vs. some
charisma

a dullard. The same is also true for average-looking dates. In fact the two lines are fairly parallel. The contrast, however, is significant, $b = -13.4$, $t(108) = -3.95$, $p < .001$, and tells us that as dates become less attractive the decline in interest is different depending on whether charisma is average or low. This significant contrast seems at odds with what the graph shows (as was the case for the previous contrast) – if this contradiction is bothering you then read Jane Superbrain Box 14.1.

JANE SUPERBRAIN 14.1

Contrasts that are significant when the graphs don't seem to show an interaction ③

The parameters in the model will depend on what else is included in the model. I have said many times in this chapter (and others) that you should not interpret main effects and interactions when a higher-order interaction is significant. These data are a good illustration of why. Contrast 3 of the **looks × personality** interaction had a graph that showed parallel lines, which we usually associate with non-significant interactions, yet the contrast was significant. This is because of the influence of the higher-order **looks × personality × gender** interaction. When we built up the model we created a model that contained everything apart from the three-way interaction (this is the model called *looks_personality*). Let's have a look at the parameter estimates for this model by using the *summary()* function:

The contrast in bold is contrast 3 of the **looks × personality** interaction, which, from the graph, looked non-significant. This contrast looks at the effect of attractive dates compared to average ones in dull dates relative to those with average charisma. When the three-way interaction was included this contrast was highly significant, but in its absence the contrast reflects the non-significant result that we'd expect from the graph. This example highlights the reason why you should interpret the highest-order significant effect and not worry about interpreting lower-order effects in the model.

`summary(looks_personality)`

	Value	Std.Error	DF	t-value	p-value
(Intercept)	70.46667	1.884462	112	37.39353	0.0000
AttractivevsAv	11.20000	2.467340	36	4.53930	0.0001
UglyvsAv	-15.40000	2.467340	36	-6.24154	0.0000
HighvsAv	21.61667	2.467340	112	8.76112	0.0000
DullvsAv	-28.71667	2.467340	112	-11.63872	0.0000
genderMale	-0.23333	2.252362	18	-0.10359	0.9186
AttractivevsAv:gender	12.50000	2.467340	36	5.06619	0.0000
UglyvsAv:gender	-10.40000	2.467340	36	-4.21507	0.0002
HighvsAv:gender	-12.73333	2.467340	112	-5.16075	0.0000
DullvsAv:gender	11.53333	2.467340	112	4.67440	0.0000
AttractivevsAv:HighvsAv	-14.10000	3.021861	112	-4.66600	0.0000
looksUglyvsAv:HighvsAv	6.75000	3.021861	112	2.23372	0.0275
AttractivevsAv:DullvsAv	**4.70000**	**3.021861**	**112**	**1.55533**	**0.1227**
UglyvsAv:DullvsAv	19.15000	3.021861	112	6.33715	0.0000

14.6.8.4. Looks × personality interaction 4: ugly vs. average, dullard vs. some charisma ②

The final contrast for this interaction term (*UglyvsAv:DullvsAv*) investigates ratings of ugly compared to average-looking dates, when comparing dullards to dates with average charisma. This is like asking: is the difference between no charisma and some charisma the same for ugly people and average-looking people? Figure 14.12 shows the relevant bits of the interaction graph; you can see that the interest (as indicated by high ratings) in average-looking dates was higher when they had some charisma than when they were a dullard, but for ugly dates the ratings were roughly the same regardless of the level of charisma. This contrast is highly significant, $b = 16.8$, $t(108) = 4.95$, $p < .001$, and tells us that as dates become less attractive the decline in interest in dates with a bit of charisma is significantly greater than for dullards.

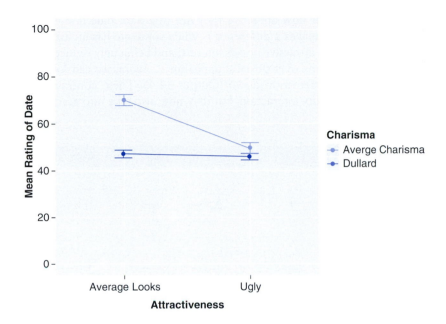

FIGURE 14.12
Graph displaying looks × personality interaction 4: ugly vs. average, dullard vs. some charisma

14.6.9. The interaction between **looks, personality** and **gender** ③

The three-way interaction tells us whether the **looks** × **personality** interaction described above is the same for men and women (i.e., whether the combined effect of attractiveness of the date and their level of charisma is the same for male participants as for female subjects). Output 14.3 tells us that there is a significant three-way **looks** × **personality** × **gender** interaction, $\chi^2(4) = 79.59$, $p < .0001$. This is the highest-order effect that is significant, and consequently, we would ordinarily focus on interpreting this effect and not all the lower-order ones (which I have interpreted only for illustrative purposes).

SELF-TEST

✓ Using *ggplot2* and *stat.desc*, plot a line graph and get the means for the **looks** × **personality** × **gender** interaction.

How do I interpret a three-way interaction?

The nature of this interaction is revealed in Figure 14.13, which shows the looks × personality interaction for men and women separately (the means on which this graph is based appear in Output 14.1). The male graph shows that when dates are attractive, men will express a high interest regardless of charisma levels (the different coloured data points overlap). At the opposite end of the attractiveness scale, when a date is ugly, men will express very little interest (ratings are all low), regardless of the date's charisma. The only time charisma makes any difference to a man is if the date is average-looking, in which case high charisma boosts interest, being a dullard reduces interest, and having a bit of charisma leaves things somewhere in between. The take-home message is that men are superficial cretins who are more interested in physical attributes.

The picture for women is very different. If someone has high levels of charisma then it doesn't really matter what they look like, women will express an interest in them (the black line is relatively flat). At the other extreme, if the date is a dullard, then they will express no interest in them, regardless of how attractive they are (the dark blue line is relatively flat). The only time attractiveness makes a difference is when someone has an average amount of charisma, in which case being attractive boosts interest, and being ugly reduces it. Put another way, women prioritize charisma over physical appearance. Again, we can look at some contrasts to further break this interaction down (Output 14.4). These contrasts are similar to those for the **looks** × **personality** interaction, but they now also take into account the effect of gender as well.

FIGURE 14.13
Graphs showing the looks by charisma interaction for men and women. Lines represent high charisma (black), some charisma (light blue) and no charisma (dark blue)

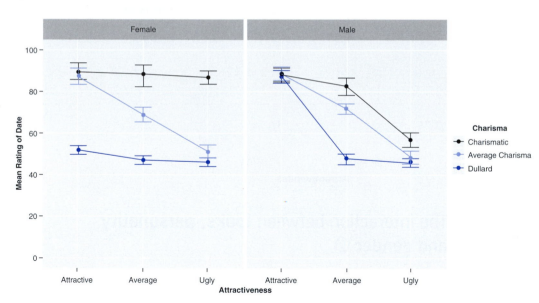

14.6.9.1. Looks × personality × gender interaction 1: attractive vs. average, high charisma vs. some charisma, male vs. female ③

The first contrast for this interaction term compares ratings for attractive dates to average-looking dates, when high charisma is compared to average charisma in males compared to females, $b = 5.8$, $t(108) = 1.21$, $p = .230$. The interaction graph in Figure 14.14 shows that interest (as indicated by high ratings) in attractive dates was the same regardless of whether they had high or average charisma. However, for average-looking dates, there was more interest when that person had high charisma rather than some charisma. Most important,

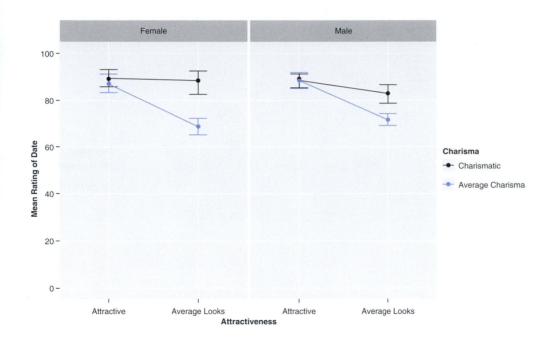

FIGURE 14.14
Graph displaying looks × personality × gender interaction 1: attractive vs. average, high charisma vs. some charisma, males vs. females

this pattern of results is the same in males and females, and this is reflected in the non-significance of this contrast.

14.6.9.2. Looks × personality × gender interaction 2: ugly vs. average, high charisma vs. some charisma, males vs. females ③

The second contrast for this interaction term compares interest in ugly compared to average-looking dates, when high charisma is compared to average charisma, in men compared to women. The interaction graph in Figure 14.15 shows that the patterns are different for men and women. This is reflected by the fact that the contrast is significant, $b = -18.5$, $t(108) = -3.85$, $p < .001$. To unpick this we need to look at the graph. First, let's look at the men. For men, as attractiveness goes down, so does interest when the date has high charisma and when they have average charisma. In fact the lines are parallel. So, regardless of charisma, there is a similar reduction in interest as attractiveness declines. For women the picture is quite different. When charisma is high, there is no decline in interest as attractiveness falls (the black line is flat); however, when charisma is average, the attractiveness of the date does matter and interest is lower in an ugly date than in an average-looking date. Another way to look at it is that for dates with average charisma, the reduction in interest as attractiveness goes down is about the same in men and women (the light blue lines have the same slope). However, for dates who have high charisma, the decrease in interest if these dates are ugly rather than average looking is much more dramatic in men than women (the black line is much steeper for men than it is for women). This is what the significant contrast tells us.

14.6.9.3. Looks × personality × gender interaction 3: attractive vs. average, dullard vs. some charisma, male vs. female ③

The third contrast for this interaction term compares interest in attractive compared to average-looking dates, when dullards are compared to average charisma, in men compared

FIGURE 14.15
Graph displaying looks × personality × gender interaction 2: ugly vs. average, high charisma vs. some charisma, males vs. females

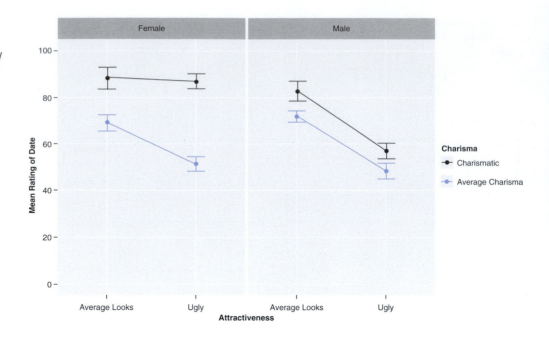

FIGURE 14.16
Graph displaying looks × personality × gender interaction 4: ugly vs. average, dullard vs. some charisma, males vs. females

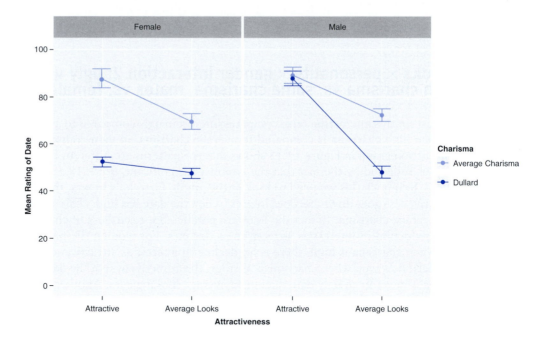

to women. The interaction graph in Figure 14.16 shows that the patterns are different for men and women. This is reflected by the fact that the contrast is significant, $b = 36.2$, $t(108) = 7.54$, $p < .001$. To unpick this effect we need to look at the graph. First, if we look at average-looking dates, for both men and women more interest is expressed when the date has average charisma than when they are a dullard (and the distance between the lines is about the same). So the difference doesn't appear to be here. If we now look at attractive dates, we see that men are equally interested in their dates regardless of their charisma, but women are much less interested in an attractive person if they are a dullard. Put another way, for attractive dates, the distance between the lines is much smaller for men than it is for women. Another way to look at it is that for dates with average charisma, the reduction in interest as attractiveness goes down is about the same in men and women (the black lines have the same slope). However, for dates who are dullards, the decrease in interest if these dates are average-looking rather than attractive is much more dramatic in men than women (the light blue line is much steeper for men than it is for women).

14.6.9.4. Looks × personality × gender interaction 4: ugly vs. average, dullard vs. some charisma, male vs. female ③

The final contrast for this interaction term compares interest in ugly compared to average-looking dates, when comparing dullards to average charisma, in men compared to women. The interaction graph in Figure 14.17 shows that interest (as indicated by high ratings) in ugly dates was the same regardless of whether they had average charisma or were a dullard. However, for average-looking dates, there was more interest when that person had some charisma rather than if they were a dullard. Most important, this pattern of results is similar in males and females, and this is reflected in the non-significance of this contrast, $b = 4.7$, $t(108) = 0.98$, $p = .330$.

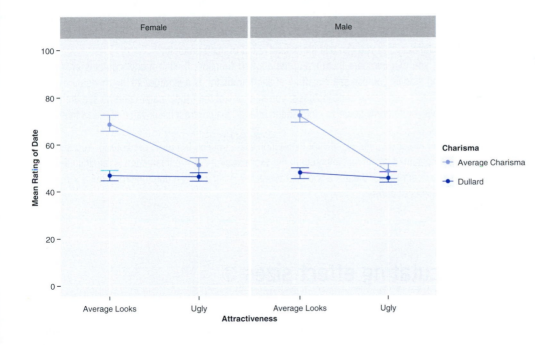

FIGURE 14.17
Graph displaying looks × personality × gender interaction 4: ugly vs. average, dullard vs. some charisma, males vs. females

14.6.10. Conclusions ③

These contrasts tell us nothing about the differences between the attractive and ugly conditions, or the high-charisma and dullard conditions, because these were never compared. We could rerun the analysis and specify our contrasts differently to get these effects. However, what is clear from our data is that differences exist between men and women in terms of how they're affected by the looks and personality of potential dates. Men appear to be enthusiastic about dating anyone who is attractive, regardless of how awful their personality. Women are almost completely the opposite: they are enthusiastic about dating anyone with a lot of charisma, regardless of how they look (and are unenthusiastic about dating people without charisma regardless of how attractive they look). The only consistency between men and women is when there is some charisma (but not lots), in which case for both genders the attractiveness influences how enthusiastic they are about dating the person.

What should be even clearer from this chapter is that when more than two independent variables are used in a model, it yields complex interaction effects that require a great deal of concentration to interpret (imagine interpreting a four-way interaction). Therefore, it is essential to take a systematic approach to interpretation, and plotting graphs is a particularly useful way to proceed. It is also advisable to think carefully about the appropriate contrasts to use to answer the questions you have about your data. It is these contrasts that will help you to interpret interactions, so make sure you select sensible ones.

CRAMMING SAM'S TIPS   Multilevel models

- The multilevel model approach is a more flexible approach to analysing mixed designs. You can also forget about sphericity.
- It makes it easy to include contrasts to break apart interaction effects. Set appropriate contrasts for all predictors before you begin.
- Build the model up one predictor at a time so that you can test the overall effect of each predictor.
- If you build models up hierarchically, you can compare them using the *anova()* function. If each model contains only one additional predictor then by comparing models you can see the effect of each predictor as it is added to the model.
- When you have a model with all predictors and interactions included, you can look at the model parameters to see the contrasts that you have set. These will help you to break down any interaction effects. If a contrast has a value of p less than .05 we consider it significant.
- Begin by interpreting the highest-order effect (i.e., the significant interaction that contains the most predictors). You should not interpret any lower order effects contained within that interaction. For example, if the $a \times b$ interaction is significant then don't interpret the main effects of a or b; similarly if the $a \times b \times c$ interaction is significant then don't interpret the $a \times b$, $a \times c$, or $b \times c$ interactions or the main effects of a, b or c.

14.7. Calculating effect sizes ③

I keep emphasizing the fact that effect sizes are really more useful when they summarize a focused effect. This also gives me a useful excuse to circumvent the complexities of omega squared in mixed designs (it's the road to madness, I assure you). Therefore, just calculate effect sizes for your contrasts when you've got a factorial design (and any main effects that compare only two groups).[4] Output 14.4 shows the values for several contrasts, all of which have a t-value and associated degrees of freedom. We can compute approximate effect sizes in the same way that we did for repeated-measures designs, using:

$$r = \sqrt{\frac{t^2}{t^2 + df}}$$

[4] Of course if you have used *ezANOVA()* then you could report generalized eta squared for your effects (*ges* in Output 14.2); however, I question how useful this kind of effect size is for effects with more than two groups, and for interaction terms.

Remember that in section 10.7 we wrote a function to compute this called *rcontrast()*, which you should be able to use if you have the package associated with this book, *DSUR*, loaded – see section 3.4.5). We can get the effect sizes simply by executing:

```
rcontrast(t, df)
```

in which *t* is the value of *t* for the effect that you want to quantify and *df* is its associated degrees of freedom. We should really only quantify the highest-order interaction because other effects in Output 14.4 are not interesting, given that the three-way interaction is significant.

Therefore, we can get the effect sizes by executing *rcontrast()* for each of the four contrasts for the three-way interaction:

```
rcontrast(-1.20802, 108)

[1] "r =  0.115464310595437"

rcontrast(3.85315, 108)

[1] "r =  0.347643452246021"

rcontrast(-7.53968, 108)

[1] "r =  0.587236020509728"

rcontrast(-0.97891, 108)

[1] "r =  0.0937805285056477"
```

In other words, we get:

- $r_{\text{Attractive vs. Average, High vs. Average, Male vs. Female}} = .12$,
- $r_{\text{Ugly vs. Average, High vs. Average, Male vs. Female}} = .35$,
- $r_{\text{Attractive vs. Average, Dull vs. Average, Male vs. Female}} = .59$,
- $r_{\text{Ugly vs. Average, Dull vs. Average, Male vs. Female}} = .09$.

The two effects that were significant (attractive vs. average, dullard vs. some, male vs. female and ugly vs. average, high vs. some, male vs. female) yielded fairly substantial effect sizes. The two effects that were not significant yielded fairly small effect sizes.

14.8. Reporting the results of mixed ANOVA ②

As you've probably gathered, when you have more than two independent variables there's a hell of a lot of information that people tend to report. They report all of the main effects, all of the interactions and any contrasts they may have done. This can take up a lot of space and one good tip is: reserve the detail for the effects that actually matter (e.g., main effects and lower-order interactions should not be interpreted if you've got significant higher-order interactions that include those variables). I'm a big fan of giving brief explanations of results in the results section to really get the message across about what a particular effect is telling us, and so I tend to not just report results, but offer some interpretation as well. Having said that, some journal editors are big fans of telling me my results sections are too long. So, you should probably ignore everything I say.

If you've taken the ANOVA approach, then, you could report something like this (although not as a list!):

✓ All effects are reported as significant at $p < .05$. There were significant main effects of the attractiveness of the date, $F(2, 36) = 423.73$, and the amount of charisma the date possessed, $F(2, 36) = 328.25$ on interest expressed by the participant. However, the ratings from male and female participants were, in general, the same, $F(1, 18) < 1$, $r = .02$.

✓ There were significant interaction effects of the attractiveness of the date and the gender of the participant, $F(2, 36) = 80.43$, the level of charisma of the date and the gender of the participant, $F(2, 36) = 62.45$, and the level of charisma of the date and the attractiveness of the date, $F(4, 72) = 36.63$.

✓ Most important, the looks × personality × gender interaction was significant, $F(4, 72) = 24.12$. This indicates that the looks × personality interaction described previously was different in male and female participants.

If you have used a multilevel model then you'd report something like this:

✓ There were significant main effects of the attractiveness of the date, $\chi^2(2) = 68.30$, $p < .0001$, and the amount of charisma the date possessed, $\chi^2(2) = 138.76$, $p < .0001$, on interest expressed by the participant. However, the ratings from male and female participants were, in general, the same, $\chi^2(1) = 0.002$, $p = .966$.

✓ There were significant interaction effects of the attractiveness of the date and the gender of the participant, $\chi^2(2) = 39.54$, $p < .0001$, the level of charisma of the date and the gender of the participant, $\chi^2(2) = 57.96$, $p < .0001$, and the level of charisma of the date and the attractiveness of the date, $\chi^2(4) = 77.14$, $p < .0001$.

✓ Most important, the looks × personality × gender interaction was significant, $\chi^2(4) = 79.59$, $p < .0001$. This indicates that the looks × personality interaction described previously was different in male and female participants. Contrasts were used to break down this interaction; these contrasts compared male and females scores at each level of charisma compared to the middle category of 'average charisma' across each level of attractiveness compared to the category of average attractiveness. The first contrast revealed a non-significant difference between male and female responses when comparing attractive dates to average-looking dates when the date had high charisma compared to some charisma, $b = 5.8$, $t(108) = 1.21$, $p = .230$, $r = .12$, and tells us that for both males and females, as dates become less attractive there is a greater decline in interest when charisma is average compared to when it is high. The second contrast looked for differences between males and females when comparing ugly dates to average-looking dates when the date had high charisma compared to average charisma. This contrast was significant, $b = -18.5$, $t(108) = -3.85$, $p < .001$, $r = .35$, and tells us that for dates with average charisma, the reduction in interest as attractiveness goes down is about the same in men and women, but for dates who have high charisma, the decrease in interest if these dates are ugly rather than average-looking is much more dramatic in men than women. The third contrast investigated differences between males and females when comparing attractive dates to average-looking dates when the date was a dullard compared to when they had average charisma. This contrast was significant, $b = 6.2$, $t(108) = 7.54$, $p < .001$, $r = .59$, and tells us that for dates with average charisma, the reduction in interest as attractiveness goes down is about the same in men and women, but for dates who are dullards, the decrease in interest if these dates are average-looking rather than attractive is much more dramatic in men than women. The final contrast looked for differences between men and women when comparing ugly dates to average-looking dates when the date was a dullard compared to when they had average charisma. This contrast was not significant, $b = 4.7$, $t(108) = 0.98$, $p = .330$, $r = .09$, and tells us that for both men and women, as dates become less attractive the decline in interest in dates with average charisma is greater than for dullards.

Labcoat Leni's Real Research 14.1   Keep the faith(ful)? ③

Schützwohl, A. (2008). *Personality and Individual Differences*, 44, 633–644.

People can be jealous. People can be especially jealous when they think that their partner is being unfaithful. An evolutionary view of jealousy suggests that men and women have evolved distinctive types of jealousy because male and female reproductive success is threatened by different types of infidelity. Specifically, a woman's sexual infidelity deprives her mate of a reproductive opportunity and in some cases burdens him with years investing in a child that is not his. Conversely, a man's sexual infidelity does not burden his mate with unrelated children, but may divert his resources from his mate's progeny. This diversion of resources is signalled by emotional attachment to another female. Consequently, men's jealousy mechanism should have evolved to prevent a mate's *sexual* infidelity, whereas in women it has evolved to prevent *emotional* infidelity. If this is the case then men and women should divert their attentional resources towards different cues to infidelity: women should be 'on the lookout' for emotional infidelity, whereas men should be watching out for sexual infidelity.

Achim Schützwohl put this theory to the test in a unique study in which men and women saw sentences presented on a computer screen (Schützwohl, 2008). On each trial, participants saw a target sentence that was always emotionally neutral (e.g., 'The gas station is at the other side of the street'). However, the trick was that before each of these targets, a distractor sentence was presented that could also be affectively neutral, or could indicate sexual infidelity (e.g., 'Your partner suddenly has difficulty becoming sexually aroused when he and you want to have sex') or emotional infidelity (e.g., 'Your partner doesn't say "I love you" to you anymore'). The idea was that if these distractor sentences grabbed a person's attention then (1) they would remember them, and (2) they would not remember the target sentence that came afterwards (because their attentional resources were still focused on the distractor). These effects should show up only in people currently in a relationship. The outcome was the number of sentences that a participant could remember (out of 6), and the predictors were whether the person had a partner or not (**Relationship**), whether the trial used a neutral distractor, an emotional infidelity distractor or a sexual infidelity distractor, and whether the sentence was a distractor or the target following the distractor. Schützwohl analysed men and women's data separately (presumably to avoid having to interpret a hideous four-way interaction). The predictions are that women should remember more emotional infidelity sentences (distractors) but fewer of the targets that followed those sentences (target). For men, the same effect should be found but for sexual infidelity sentences.

The data from this study are in the file **Schützwohl(2008).dat**. Labcoat Leni wants you to carry out two three-way mixed ANOVAs (one for men and the other for women) to test these hypotheses. Answers are in the additional material on the companion website (or look at pages 638–642 in the original article).

14.9. Robust analysis for mixed designs ③

If I had £1 (or $1, €1 or whatever currency you fancy) for every time someone had told me with 100% confidence that there was no 'non-parametric' equivalent of mixed ANOVA, then I'd have a nice shiny new drum kit. Contrary to this popular assertion, there are robust methods that can be used (see section 5.8.4) based on trimmed means and M-estimators that are described in Rand Wilcox's book (Wilcox, 2005). Wilcox also makes available functions to do these tests in **R**. To access these tests we need to load the *WRS* package (see section 5.8.4.). There are four functions that we will look at:

- **tsplit()**: This performs a two-way mixed ANOVA on trimmed means.

- **sppba()**: This computes the main effect of factor *A* of a two-way mixed design using an M-estimator and bootstrap.

- **sppbb()**: This computes the main effect of factor *B* of a two-way mixed design using an M-estimator and bootstrap .

- **sppbi()**: This computes the *A* × *B* interaction of a two-way mixed design using an M-estimator and bootstrap.

There is not a function for analysing a three-way mixed design like the main example in the chapter, so we'll use a different example.

My wife has a theory that she has received fewer friend requests from random men on Facebook since she changed her profile picture to a photo of us both. Like the geeky boffin couple we are, we decided to think about ways you could test her theory scientifically. We could systemmatically manipulate how people present themselves on social networking sites, and measure how many friend request they get from people they don't know. In our fertile imaginations, we took 40 women who had profiles on a social networking website; 17 of them had a relationship status of 'single' and the remaining 23 had their status as 'in a relationship'. We asked them not to change this status and this acted as a between-group variable (**relationship_status**). We believed that people would get fewer requests from strangers if they were in a relationship. Over a 6-week period we asked these women to set their profile picture to a photo of them on their own (**alone**) and to count how many friend requests they got from men they didn't know, then to switch it to a photo of them with a man (**couple**) and again record their friend requests from random men. Each profile picture was up for 3 weeks, and the order in which women displayed the two types of picture was randomized. This is a mixed design with relationship status as the between-group variable, type of profile picture as the repeated-measures variable, and the number of friend requests from strange men the outcome.

The data are in the file **ProfilePicture.dat**. Set your working directory to the location of this file and load the data into a dataframe by executing:

```
pictureData<-read.delim("ProfilePicture.dat", header = TRUE)
```

The data are currently in this format (I've edited out some cases):

```
   case relationship_status couple alone
1    1    In a Relationship    4     4
2    2    In a Relationship    4     6
3    3    In a Relationship    4     7
4    4    In a Relationship    3     5
...  ...        ...           ...   ...
36  36               Single    5    10
37  37               Single    4     8
38  38               Single    6     9
39  39               Single    7    10
40  40               Single    3     5
```

The variables in each column are described above.

SELF-TEST

✓ Using *ggplot2* and *stat.desc*, plot a line graph and get the means for the **relationship_status** × **profile picture** interaction.

The first problem we have is that the robust functions need the data to be in wide format rather than long (see Chapter 3). Figure 14.18 shows the existing data format and how we need it to look (wide). Essentially we want levels of our two factors to be represented in different columns. Our repeated measure (type of picture) is already spread across different columns (**couple** and **alone**), but relationship status is differentiated by different rows of data (rows 1–17 are those in a relationship whereas 18–40 are single). Therefore, we need to take the rows representing people who are single and shift them into two columns alongside the columns currently labelled **couple** and **single**.

We can do this restructuring using the *melt()* and *cast()* functions from the *reshape* package. To get the restructuring to work, we need to add a variable to our dataframe that identifies the rows in the wide format. Notice in Figure 14.18 that the data are made up of four chunks that represent the combinations of the type of picture and **relationship_status,** and each chunk contains several rows. We want to move the chunks that are currently stacked on top of each other so that they are beside each other (Figure 14.18). To do this, **R** needs to know what row a particular score will end up in when we move each block of scores from the stacks into the columns. The easiest approach is simply to create a variable (called **row**) that identifies within each chunk the row number of a given score. In other

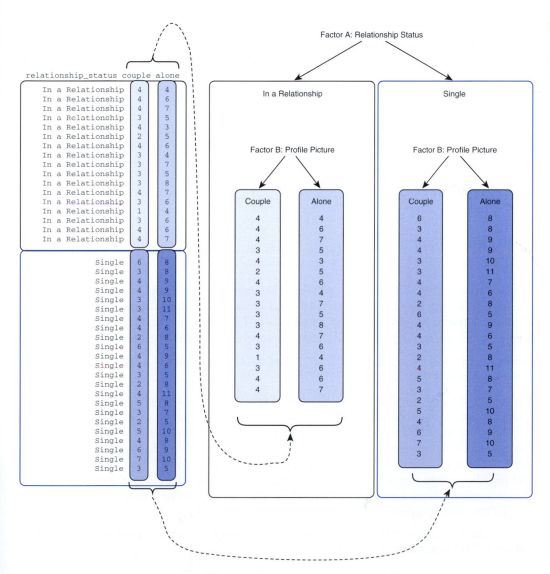

FIGURE 14.18
Restructuring the data for robust mixed ANOVA

words, it will be a value telling us whether the score is the first, second, third, etc. score within the chunk. At the moment the chunks are stacked on top of each other, so we want a variable that is the sequence of numbers 1 to 17 for the first chunk and 1 to 23 for the second (because the relationship status groups contain 17 and 23 people, respectively). We can add this variable to the dataframe by executing:

```
pictureData$row<-c(1:17, 1:23)
```

This command creates a variable *row* in the dataframe *pictureData*, that is, the numbers 1 to 17 followed by the numbers 1 to 23. The structure of the data will be the same as before, it's just that we have a new variable called **row** that identifies the scores within each relationship status group.

Next we need to make it molten so that we can cast the data into the wide format. To do this we use the *melt()* function (see section 3.9.4). Remember that in this function we differentiate variables that identify attributes of the scores (in this case, **case**, **relationship_status** and **row** all tell us about a given score, for example, that it was the third score in the 'single' group) from the scores or measured variables themselves (in this case the columns labelled **couple** and **alone** both contain scores). Attributes are specified with the *id* option, and scores with the *measured* option. Therefore, we can create a molten dataframe called *profileMelt* by executing:

```
profileMelt<-melt(pictureData, id = c("case", "row", "relationship_status"),
measured = c("couple", "alone"))
```

The data now look like this (I have edited out many cases to save space):

```
   case row relationship_status variable value
1     1   1    In a Relationship   couple     4
2     2   2    In a Relationship   couple     4
...  ...  ...           ...          ...     ...
18   18   1               Single   couple     6
19   19   2               Single   couple     3
...  ...  ...           ...          ...     ...
41    1   1    In a Relationship    alone     4
42    2   2    In a Relationship    alone     6
...  ...  ...           ...          ...     ...
79   39  22               Single    alone    10
80   40  23               Single    alone     5
```

The variable that differentiates whether the profile picture was the person alone, or the person alongside a man, has been labelled *variable* and the variable that contains the number of friend requests is called *value*. These labels are not that informative, so let's rename them as *profile_picture* and *friend_requests* using the *names()* function.

```
names(profileMelt)<-c("case", "row", "relationship_status", "profile_picture",
"friend_requests")
```

Executing this command takes the dataframe *profileMelt* and assigns the names in *c()* to each column. As such, our variables all now have names that relate to what they represent.

Finally, we want to cast our data into the wide format using *cast()*. To do this we use a formula in the form: *variables specifying the rows ~ variables specifying the columns*. In this case, **row** tells us in which row to place a score, and we want the **relationship_status** and **profile_picture** variables split across different columns, so we'd use the formula: *row ~ relationship_status + profile_picture*. Therefore, we can make a wide dataframe called *profileData* by executing:

```
profileData<-cast(profileMelt, row ~ relationship_status + profile_picture,
value = "friend_requests")
```

Note that we have applied this command to the molten data set (*profileMelt*). The *value =* "*friend_requests*" explicitly tells the function in which column to find the outcome variables. (The function will work without this command because it will take an educated guess at which columns contains the scores, but it's good practice to specify the outcome variable in the function.)

The result is that the data have been transformed to the wide format. However, because we added the variable **row** to the dataframe, our new dataframe also contains this variable, and for the analysis we don't want it. We can remove this variable by executing:

```
profileData$row<-NULL
```

If you look at the dataframe you'll see a lovely wide format set of data (I have abbreviated 'in a relationship' to 'IAR'):

```
profileData
```

IAR_With Man	IAR_Alone	Single_With Man	Single_Alone
4	4	6	8
4	6	3	8
4	7	4	9
3	5	4	9
4	3	3	10
2	5	3	11
4	6	4	7
3	4	4	6
3	7	2	8
3	5	6	5
3	8	4	9
4	7	4	6
3	6	3	5
1	4	2	8
3	6	4	11
4	6	5	8
4	7	3	7
NA	NA	2	5
NA	NA	5	10
NA	NA	4	8
NA	NA	6	9
NA	NA	7	10
NA	NA	3	5

Note that because the in 'a relationship' group contained fewer cases (17 rather than 23) there are NAs in the data set. These won't affect the functions for robust analyses.

It's important to note the order of the columns because this affects how we specify the robust analysis. In this case, the hierarchy of the independent variables is **relationship_status** followed by **profile_picture**. In other words, we have taken the four groups of scores and first divided them into in a relationship and single, then within these groups we have subdivided according to the type of profile picture that was used. We would say that **relationship_status** is factor *A* and **profile_picture** factor *B* (Figure 14.18). As such, the order of the columns reflects a 2 × 2 design (two levels of relationship status divided up into two levels of profile picture).

The function *tsplit()* takes the general form:

```
tsplit(levels of factor A, levels of factor B, data, tr = .2)
```

As with other functions we've encountered, the level of trimming is by default 20% (*tr* = .2), but can be changed by including the *tr* = option. Assuming we are happy with the default level of trimming, we need only specify the dataframe (*profileData*) and the levels of factor *A* (two in this case as explained above) and factor *B* (two in this case). Therefore, we can do a robust two-way factorial ANOVA based on trimmed means by executing:

```
tsplit(2, 2, profileData)
```

The functions *sppba()*, *sppbb()*, *sppbi()* all have the same format:

```
sppba(levels of factor A, levels of factor B, data, est = mom, nboot = 2000)
```

The main differences are an option to control the number of bootstrap samples (*nboot*), and an option *est* = to control the M-estimator that you want to use. You can use *est* = *median* (to use the median) or *est* = *mom* (to use a method based on identifying and removing outliers). In smaller samples you might find that *est* = *mom* throws up an error message, in which case switch to *est* = *median*. The default number of bootstrap samples is 599; let's increase that to 2000 and run the analysis by executing:[5]

```
sppba(2, 2, profileData, est = mom, nboot = 2000)
sppbb(2, 2, profileData, est = mom, nboot = 2000)
sppbi(2, 2, profileData, est = mom, nboot = 2000)
```

tsplit()	*sppba(), sppbb(), sppbi()*

$Qa
[1] 10.78843
 	
$Qa.siglevel
         [,1]
[1,] 0.002795259
 	
$Qb
[1] 92.12093
 	
$Qb.siglevel
         [,1]
[1,] 2.618876e-10
 	
$Qab
[1] 8.167141
 	
$Qab.siglevel
         [,1]
[1,] 0.008003836
	sppba
	
	$p.value
	[1] 0.001
	
	$psihat
	[1] -1.464194
	
	$con
	      [,1]
	[1,] 1
	[2,] -1
	
	sppbb
	
	$p.value
	[1] 0.0004997501
	
	$center
	[1] -3.171429
	
	sppbi
	
	$p.value
	[1] 0.015
	
	$psihat
	[1] 1.4375
	
	$con
	      [,1]
	[1,] 1
	[2,] -1

Output 14.11

[5] If you want to compare medians then execute:
```
sppba(2, 2, profileData, est = median, nboot = 2000)
```

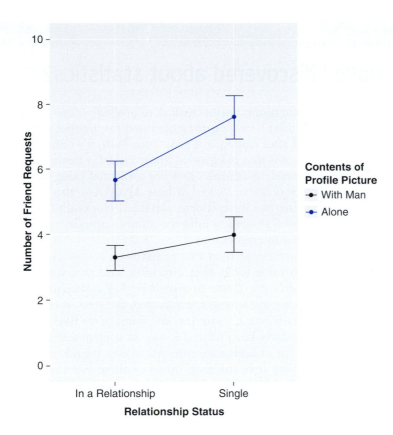

FIGURE 14.19
Graph showing the mean number of friend requests on a social networking site from weird men as a function of a woman's relationship status and whether their profile picture shows them alone or with a man

The output of these commands is shown in Output 14.11. For *tsplit()* (left-hand side of Output 14.11) we are given a test statistic for factor *A* (*$Qa*), factor *B* (*$Qb*) and their interaction (*$Qab*) as well as the corresponding *p*-value (*$Qa.siglevel*, *$Qb.siglevel* and *$Qab.siglevel*, respectively). Remember that factor *A* was relationship status and factor *B* the profile picture used; therefore, we could conclude that there were significant main effects of relationship status, $Q = 10.79$, $p = .003$, and type of profile picture, $Q = 92.13$, $p < .001$, and a significant relationship status × type of profile picture interaction, $Q = 8.17$, $p = .008$.

The *sppba()*, *sppbb()* and *sppbi()* outputs (right-hand side of Output 12.8) tell us much the same things, and in each case we get a test statistic (*$psihat*) and an associated *p*-value (*$p.value*). There were significant main effects of relationship status, $\hat{\Psi} = -1.46$, $p = .001$, and type of profile picture, $\hat{\Psi} = -3.17$, $p < .001$, and a significant relationship status × type of profile picture interaction, $\hat{\Psi} = 1.44$, $p = .015$.

These results are shown in Figure 14.19. The main effect of profile picture reflects the fact that more friend requests generally are made when the picture shows the woman on her own (the blue line is higher than the black), the main effect of relationship status reflects the fact that for both lines the number of requests is higher when the person's status is 'single' than when it says 'in a relationship'. The significant interaction seems to reflect the fact that the blue line is steeper than the black. In other words, the increases in friend requests obtained when your relationship status is 'single' (compared to 'in a relationship') is more when your profile picture shows you alone. Basically, in terms of attracting friend requests from strange men you've never met, your best bet is to say you're single and put a picture of you alone on your profile. The weirdos will come in droves.

What have I discovered about statistics? ②

Three-way ANOVA is a confusing nut to crack. I've probably done hundreds of three-way ANOVAs in my life and still I kept getting confused throughout writing this chapter (and so if you're confused after reading it it's not your fault, it's mine). Hopefully, what you should have discovered is that the general linear model is flexible enough that you can mix and match independent variables that are measured using the same or different participants. In addition, we've looked at how ANOVA is also flexible enough to go beyond merely including two independent variables. Hopefully, you've also started to realize why there are good reasons to limit the number of independent variables that you include (for the sake of interpretation).

Of course, far more interesting than that is that you've discovered that men are superficial creatures who value looks over charisma, and that women are prepared to date the hunchback of Notre Dame provided he has sufficient charisma. This is why as a 16–18-year-old my life was so complicated, because where on earth do you discover your hidden charisma? Luckily for me, some girls find alcoholics appealing. The girl I was particularly keen on at 16 was, as it turned out, keen on me too. I refused to believe this for at least a month. All of our friends were getting bored of us declaring our undying love for each other to them but then not speaking to each other; they eventually intervened. There was a party one evening and all of her friends had spent hours convincing me to ask her on a date, guaranteeing me that she would say 'yes'. I had psyched myself up, I was going to do it: I was actually going to ask a girl out on a date. My whole life had been leading up to this moment and I must not do anything to ruin it. By the time she arrived my nerves had got the better of me and she had to step over my paralytic corpse to get into the house. Later on, my friend Paul Spreckley (see Figure 9.1) physically carried the girl in question from another room and put her next to me and then said something to the effect of 'Andy, I'm going to sit here until you ask her out'. He had a long wait but eventually, miraculously, the words came out of my mouth. Like the undying love of many a 16-year-old, our love died about 2 years later.

R packages used in this chapter

ez	pastecs
ggplot2	reshape
multcomp	WRS
nlme	

R functions used in this chapter

by()	melt()
c()	names()
cast()	rcontrast()
cbind()	sppba()
contrasts()	sppbb()
ezANOVA()	sppbi()
ggplot()	stat.desc()
gl()	summary()
list()	tsplit()
lme()	update()

Key terms that I've discovered

Mixed ANOVA	Mixed design

Smart Alex's tasks

- **Task 1**: I am going to extend the example from the previous chapter (advertising and different imagery) by adding a between-group variable into the design.[6] To recap, participants viewed a total of nine mock adverts over three sessions. In these adverts there were three products (a brand of beer, a brand of wine, and a brand of water). These could be presented alongside positive, negative or neutral imagery. Over the three sessions and nine adverts, each type of product was paired with each type of imagery (read the previous chapter if you need more detail). After each advert participants rated the drinks on a scale ranging from −100 (dislike very much) through 0 (neutral) to 100 (like very much). The design, thus far, has two independent variables: the type of drink (beer, wine or water) and the type of imagery used (positive, negative or neutral). I also took note of each person's gender. It occurred to me that men and women might respond differently to the products (because, in keeping with stereotypes, men might mostly drink lager whereas women might drink wine). Therefore, I wanted to analyse the data taking this additional variable into account. Now, gender is a between-group variable because a participant can be only male or female: they cannot participate as a male and then change into a female and participate again! The data are the same as in the previous chapter (Table 13.4) and can be found in the file **MixedAttitude.dat**. Run a mixed ANOVA on these data. ③

- **Task 2**: Text messaging is very popular among mobile phone owners, to the point that books have been published on how to write in text speak (BTW, hope u no wat I mean by txt spk). One concern is that children may use this form of communication so much that it will hinder their ability to learn correct written English. One

---

[6] Previously the example contained two repeated-measures variables (drink type and imagery type), but now it will include three variables (two repeated measures and one between-group).

concerned researcher conducted an experiment in which one group of children was encouraged to send text messages on their mobile phones over a six-month period. A second group was forbidden from sending text messages for the same period. To ensure that kids in this latter group didn't use their phones, this group was given armbands that administered painful shocks in the presence of microwaves (like those emitted from phones). There were 50 different participants: 25 were encouraged to send text messages, and 25 were forbidden. The outcome was a score on a grammatical test (as a percentage) that was measured both before and after the experiment. The first independent variable was, therefore, text message use (text messagers versus controls) and the second independent variable was the time at which grammatical ability was assessed (before or after the experiment). The data are in the file **TextMessages.dat**. ③

- **Task 3**: A researcher was interested in the effects on people's mental health of participating in *Big Brother* (see Chapter 1 if you don't know what *Big Brother* is). The researcher hypothesized that they start off with personality disorders that are exacerbated by being forced to live with people as attention seeking as them. To test this hypothesis, she gave eight contestants a questionnaire measuring personality disorders before they entered the house, and again when they left the house. A second group of eight people acted as a waiting list control. These people were short-listed to go into the house, but never actually made it. They too were given the questionnaire at the same points in time as the contestants. The data are in **BigBrother.dat**. Conduct a mixed ANOVA on the data. ②

- **Task 4**: In this chapter we did a robust analysis on some data about how people's profile pictures on social networking sites affect their friend requests. Reanalyse these data using a non-robust analysis. The data are in the file **ProfilePicture.dat**. ②

Answers can be found on the companion website. Some more detailed comments about task 2 can be found in Field and Hole (2003).

Further reading

Field, A. P. (1998). A bluffer's guide to sphericity. *Newsletter of the Mathematical, Statistical and Computing Section of the British Psychological Society*, 6(1), 13–22. (Available in the additional material on the companion website.)

Howell, D. C. (2006). *Statistical methods for psychology* (6th ed.). Belmont, CA: Duxbury. (Or you might prefer his *Fundamental Statistics for the Behavioral Sciences*, also in its 6th edition, 2007.)

Interesting real research

Schützwohl, A. (2008). The disengagement of attentive resources from task-irrelevant cues to sexual and emotional infidelity. *Personality and Individual Differences*, 44, 633–644.

Non-parametric tests

15

FIGURE 15.1
In my office during my Ph.D., probably preparing some teaching – I had quite long hair back then because it hadn't started falling out at that point

15.1. What will this chapter tell me? ①

After my psychology degree (at City University, London) I went to the University of Sussex to do my Ph.D. (also in psychology) and, like many people, I had to teach to survive. Much to my dread, I was allocated to teach second-year undergraduate statistics. This was possibly the worst combination of events that I could ever imagine. I was still very shy at the time, and I didn't have a clue about statistics. Standing in front of a room full of strangers and trying to teach them ANOVA was only marginally more appealing than dislocating my knees and running a marathon – with broken glass in my trainers (sneakers). I obsessively prepared for my first session so that it would go well; I created handouts, I invented examples, I rehearsed what I would say. I went in terrified but at least knowing that if preparation was any predictor of success then I would be OK. About half way through the first session as I was mumbling on to a room of bored students, one of them rose majestically from her seat. She walked slowly towards me, and I'm convinced that she was surrounded by an aura of bright white light and dry ice. Surely she had been chosen by her peers to impart a message of gratitude for the hours of preparation I had done and the skill with which I was unclouding their brains of the mysteries of ANOVA. She stopped beside me. We stood inches apart and my eyes raced around the floor looking for the reassurance of my shoelaces: 'No one in this room has a rabbit[1] clue what you're going on about', she spat before storming out. Scales have not been invented yet to measure how much I wished I'd ran the dislocated-knees marathon that morning and then taken the day off. I was absolutely mortified. To this day I have intrusive thoughts about groups of students in my lectures walking zombie-like towards the front of the lecture theatre chanting 'No one knows what you're going on about' before devouring my brain in a rabid feeding frenzy. The point is that sometimes our lives, like data, go horribly, horribly wrong. This chapter is about data that are as wrong as dressing a cat in a pink tutu.

15.2. When to use non-parametric tests ①

We've seen in the last few chapters how we can use various techniques to look for differences between means. However, all of these tests rely on parametric assumptions (see Chapter 5). Data are often unfriendly and don't always turn up in nice normally distributed packages! Just to add insult to injury, it's not always possible to correct for problems with the distribution of a data set – so, what do we do in these cases? The answer is that we can use special kinds of statistical procedures known as **non-parametric tests**.[2] Non-parametric tests are sometimes known as assumption-free tests because they make fewer assumptions about the type of data on which they can be used.[3] Most of these tests work on the principle of **ranking** the data: that is, finding the lowest score and giving it a rank of 1, then finding the next highest score and giving it a rank of 2, and so on. This process results in high scores being represented by large ranks, and low scores being represented by small ranks. The analysis is then carried out on the ranks rather than the actual data. This process is an ingenious way around the problem of using data that break the parametric assumptions. Some people believe that non-parametric tests have less power than their parametric counterparts, but as we will see in Jane Superbrain Box 15.2 below this is not always true. In this chapter we'll look at four of the most common non-parametric procedures: the Wilcoxon rank-sum test (which is also known as the Mann–Whitney test), the Wilcoxon signed-rank test, Friedman's test and the Kruskal–Wallis test. For each of these we'll discover how to carry out the analysis in **R** and how to interpret and report the results.

What are non-parametric tests?

---

[1] She didn't say 'rabbit', but she did say a word that describes what rabbits do a lot; it begins with an 'f' and the publishers think that it will offend you.

[2] Having said which, with the advent of the kinds of robust procedures we have used throughout this book, I'm not sure for how much longer people will use these tests.

[3] Non-parametric tests sometimes get referred to as distribution-free tests, with an explanation that they make *no* assumptions about the distribution of the data. Technically, this isn't true: they do make distributional assumptions (e.g., the ones in this chapter all assume a continuous distribution), but they are less restrictive ones than their parametric counterparts.

15.3. Packages used in this chapter ①

Most of the tests used in this chapter are in the *stats* package, which is installed and loaded automatically. However, we will need the packages *clinfun* (for the Jonckheere test), *pastecs* (for descriptive statistics), *pgirmess* (for *post hoc* tests), *ggplot2* (for graphs), and *Rcmdr* (R Commander) if you're going to use that rather than commands (see section 3.6). If you don't have these packages installed you'll need to install them by executing:

```
install.packages("clinfun"); install.packages("ggplot2"); install.packages
("pastecs"); install.packages("pgirmess");
```

Then you need to load the packages by executing these commands:

```
library(clinfun); library(ggplot2); library(pastecs); library(pgirmess)
```

15.4. Comparing two independent conditions: the Wilcoxon rank-sum test ①

When you want to test differences between two conditions and different participants have been used in each condition then you have two choices: the **Mann–Whitney test** (Mann & Whitney, 1947) and the **Wilcoxon's rank-sum test** (Wilcoxon, 1945; Figure 15.2). These tests are the non-parametric equivalent of the independent *t*-test. In fact both tests are equivalent, and there's another, more famous, Wilcoxon test, so it gets extremely confusing for most of us. **R** does the Wilcoxon rank-sum test, but if you read about the Mann–Whitney test, it's the same. (I'd prefer it if **R** did the Mann–Whitney test, that way we'd only have one Wilcoxon test to worry about. But that's not the way it is, so we'll have to get used to it.)

For example, a neurologist might collect data to investigate the depressant effects of certain recreational drugs. She tested 20 clubbers in all: 10 were given an ecstasy tablet to take on a Saturday night and 10 were allowed to drink only alcohol. Levels of depression were measured using the Beck Depression Inventory (BDI) the day after and midweek. The data are in Table 15.1 and in the file **Drug.dat**.

15.4.1.   Theory of the Wilcoxon rank-sum test ②

The logic behind the Wilcoxon rank-sum test is incredibly elegant. First, let's imagine a scenario in which there is no difference in depression levels between ecstasy and alcohol users. If we were to rank the data *ignoring the group to which a person belonged* from lowest to highest (i.e., give the lowest score a rank of 1 and the next lowest a rank of 2, etc.), then what should we find? Well, if there's no difference between the groups then we would expect to find a similar number of high and low ranks in each group; specifically, if we added up the ranks, then we'd expect the summed total of ranks in each group to be about the same. Now think about what would happen if there was a difference between the groups. Let's imagine that the ecstasy group is more depressed than the alcohol group. If we ranked the scores as before, then we would expect the higher ranks to be in the ecstasy group and the lower ranks to be in the alcohol group. Again, if we summed the ranks in each group, we'd expect the sum of ranks to be higher in the ecstasy group than in the alcohol group.

FIGURE 15.2
Frank Wilcoxon

Table 15.1 Data for drug experiment

Participant	Drug	BDI (Sunday)	BDI (Wednesday)
1	Ecstasy	15	28
2	Ecstasy	35	35
3	Ecstasy	16	35
4	Ecstasy	18	24
5	Ecstasy	19	39
6	Ecstasy	17	32
7	Ecstasy	27	27
8	Ecstasy	16	29
9	Ecstasy	13	36
10	Ecstasy	20	35
11	Alcohol	16	5
12	Alcohol	15	6
13	Alcohol	20	30
14	Alcohol	15	8
15	Alcohol	16	9
16	Alcohol	13	7
17	Alcohol	14	6
18	Alcohol	19	17
19	Alcohol	18	3
20	Alcohol	18	10

How do I rank data?

The Wilcoxon rank-sum test works on this principle. Let's have a look at how ranking works in practice. Figure 15.3 shows the ranking process for both the Wednesday and Sunday data. To begin with, let's use our data for Wednesday, because it's more straightforward. First, just arrange the scores in ascending order, attach a label to remind you which group they came from (I've used A for alcohol and E for ecstasy), then assign potential ranks starting with 1 for the lowest score and going up to the number of scores you have. The reason why I've called these 'potential' ranks is that sometimes the

Wednesday Data

Score	3	5	6	6	7	8	9	10	17	24	27	28	29	30	32	35	35	35	36	39
Potential Rank	1	2	3	4	5	6	7	8	9	10	11	12	13	14	15	16	17	18	19	20
Actual Rank	1	2	3.5	3.5	5	6	7	8	9	10	11	12	13	14	15	17	17	17	19	20
Group	A	A	A	A	A	A	A	A	A	E	E	E	E	A	E	E	E	E	E	E

Sum of Ranks for Alcohol (A) = 59 **Sum of Ranks for Ecstasy (E) = 151**

Sunday Data

Score	13	13	14	15	15	15	16	16	16	16	17	18	18	18	19	19	20	20	27	35
Potential Rank	1	2	3	4	5	6	7	8	9	10	11	12	13	14	15	16	17	18	19	20
Actual Rank	1.5	1.5	3	5	5	5	8.5	8.5	8.5	8.5	11	13	13	13	15.5	15.5	17.5	17.5	19	20
Group	A	E	A	A	A	E	A	A	E	E	E	E	A	A	E	A	E	A	E	E

Sum of Ranks for Alcohol (A) = 90.5 **Sum of Ranks for Ecstasy (E) = 119.5**

FIGURE 15.3
Ranking the depression scores for Wednesday

same score occurs more than once in a data set (e.g., in these data a score of 6 occurs twice, and a score of 35 occurs three times). These are called *tied ranks* and these values need to be given the same rank, so all we do is assign a rank that is the average of the potential ranks for those scores. So, with our two scores of 6, because they would've been ranked 3 and 4, we take an average of these values (3.5) and use this value as a rank for both occurrences of the score. Likewise, with the three scores of 35, we have potential ranks of 16, 17 and 18; we actually use the average of these three ranks, (16 + 17 + 18)/3 = 17. When we've ranked the data, we add up all of the ranks for the two groups. So, add the ranks for the scores that came from the alcohol group (you should find the sum is 59) and then add the ranks for the scores that came from the ecstasy group (this value should be 151). We're almost at the answer.

For each of these values, we need to correct for the number of people in the group, by subtracting the mean rank of the group for a group of that many people (because otherwise larger groups would have larger ranks). The mean rank is the mean of the numbers from 1 to 10:

$$\text{mean rank} = 1 + 2 + 3 + 4 + 5 + 6 + 7 + 8 + 9 + 10$$

There's a slightly easier formula, especially if you have a lot of numbers:

$$\begin{aligned}\text{mean rank} &= \frac{N(N+1)}{2} \\ &= \frac{10 \times 11}{2} \\ &= 55\end{aligned}$$

We therefore calculate two potential values for W, one for each group:

$$W = \text{sum of ranks} - \text{mean rank}$$
$$W_1 = 59 - 55 = 4$$
$$W_2 = 151 - 55 = 96$$

Typically, we take the smallest of these values to be our test statistic, therefore the test statistic for the Wednesday data is $W = 4$. However, which of the two values of W is reported by **R** depends on which way around you input variables into the function, which is a little confusing, but don't worry about it – it makes no difference to the significance.

SELF-TEST

✓ Based on what you have just learnt, try ranking the Sunday data. (The answers are in Figure 15.3 – there are lots of tied ranks and the data are generally horrible.)

You should find that when you've ranked the data, and added the ranks for the two groups, the sum of ranks for the alcohol group is 90.5 and for the ecstasy group it is 119.5. These are the sums of the ranks. We take the smaller of the two (90.5) and subtract 55, thereby obtaining a value of W of 35.5.

Having computed the test statistic, **R** then calculates the associated *p*-value, which can be done in two ways. First, there is the *exact* approach, which is the best one to take. The exact approach uses a **Monte Carlo method** to obtain the significance level.[4] This basically involves creating lots of data sets that match the sample, but instead of putting people into the correct groups, it puts them into a random group. Because the people were assigned to a group randomly, we know that the null hypothesis is true – so it calculates the value for W, based on these data in which the null hypothesis is true. Let's think about this – if the null hypothesis is true, and the results of this analysis look like your analysis, well, that's not so good for your hypothesis. However, **R** doesn't just put the people into a random group and analyse them once, it then repeats it, and looks at the results again … and again … and again. It does this thousands of times and looks at how often the difference that appears in the data when the null hypothesis is true is as large as the difference in your data.

This method is great, because we don't need to make any assumptions about the distribution,[5] but it's not so great because it takes a long time; and as the sample size increases, the length of time it takes increases more and more. If your sample is big enough you might actually die before you get an answer. In addition, if you have ties in the data, you cannot use the exact method.

With large sample sizes, you are better off using a normal approximation to calculate the p-value. The normal approximation doesn't assume that the data are normal. Instead it assumes that the sampling distribution of the W statistic is normal, which means that a standard error can be computed that is used to calculate a z and hence a p-value. The default in **R** is to use a normal approximation if the sample size is larger than 40; and if you have ties, you have to use a normal approximation whether you like it or not.

If you use a normal approximation to calculate the p-value, you also have the option to use a continuity correction.[6] The reason for the continuity correction is that we're using a normal distribution, which is smooth, but a person can change in rank only by 1 (or 0.5, if there are ties), which is not smooth. Therefore, the p-value using the normal approximation is a little too small; the continuity correction attempts to rectify this problem but can make your p-value a little too high instead. The difference that the correction makes is pretty small – there is no consensus on the best thing to do. If you don't specify, **R** will include the correction.

15.4.2. Inputting data and provisional analysis ①

SELF-TEST

✓ See whether you can use what you have learnt about data entry to enter the data in Table 15.1 into **R**.

---

[4] If you're wondering why it's called the Monte Carlo method, it's because back in the late nineteenth century when Karl Pearson was trying to simulate data he didn't have a computer to do it for him. So he used to toss coins. A lot. That is, until a friend suggested that roulette wheels, if unbiased, were excellent random number generators. Rather than trying to persuade the Royal Society to fund trips to Monte Carlo casinos to collect data from their roulette wheels, he purchased copies of *Le Monaco*, a weekly Paris periodical that published exactly the data that he required, at the cost of 1 franc (Pearson, 1894; Plackett, 1983). When simulated data are used to test a statistical method, or to estimate a statistic, it is known as the Monte Carlo method even though we use computers now and not roulette wheels.

[5] Actually it does make an assumption, but it's a good one: it assumes that the distribution in your sample looks exactly like the distribution in your sample. This assumption is, of course, true. It also explains why it has to do this analysis every time you run the test, because it's different for every sample (unlike tests like the *t*-test, where it is assumed that the distribution is normal).

[6] If you're reading this book out of order, the continuity correction is the same as the Yates correction that you came across in Chapter 18. Or if you're reading it in order, that you will come across in Chapter 18.

When the data are collected using different participants in each group, we need to input the data using a factor variable. So, the data editor will have three columns of data. The first column is a coding variable (called something like **drug**), which, in this case, will have only two levels (ecstasy group and alcohol group). We can create this variable using the *gl()* function (see section 3.5.4.3), by executing:

```
drug<-gl(2, 10, labels = c("Ecstasy", "Alcohol"))
```

This command creates a variable called **drug**, which contains two blocks of 10 rows of data: the first block will be labelled *Ecstasy* and the second block *Alcohol*.

The second column will have values for the dependent variable (BDI) measured the day after (call this variable **sundayBDI**) and the third will have the midweek scores on the same questionnaire (call this variable **wedsBDI**). We can, therefore, create these variables by executing:

```
sundayBDI<-c(15, 35, 16, 18, 19, 17, 27, 16, 13, 20, 16, 15, 20, 15, 16, 13,
14, 19, 18, 18)
wedsBDI<-c(28, 35, 35, 24, 39, 32, 27, 29, 36, 35, 5, 6, 30, 8, 9, 7, 6, 17,
3, 10)
```

Finally, we can tie these variables together in a dataframe called *drugData* by executing:

```
drugData<-data.frame(drug, sundayBDI, wedsBDI)
```

If you don't want to do that, you'll find the data in the file called **Drug.dat**, which you can load by executing:

```
drugData<-read.delim("Drug.dat", header = TRUE)
```

First, we would run some exploratory analyses on the data and because we're going to be looking for group differences we need to run these exploratory analyses for each group.

SELF-TEST

✓ Carry out some analyses to test for normality and homogeneity of variance in these data (see sections 5.6 and 5.7).

The results of these exploratory analyses are shown in Outputs 15.1 and 15.2. Output 15.1 shows that for the Sunday data the distribution for ecstasy, $p < .05$, appears to be non-normal whereas the alcohol data, $W = 0.96$, *ns*, are normal; we can tell this by whether the significance of the Shapiro–Wilk test is less than .05 (and, therefore, significant) or greater than .05 (and, therefore, non-significant, *ns*). For the Wednesday data, although the data for ecstasy are normal, $W = 0.94$, *ns*, the data for alcohol appear to be significantly non-normal, $W = 0.75$, $p < .01$. This finding would alert us to the fact that the sampling distribution might also be non-normal for the Sunday and Wednesday data and that a non-parametric test should be used.

Output 15.2 shows the results of Levene's test. For the Sunday data, $F(1, 18) = 3.64$, *ns*, and for Wednesday, $F(1, 18) = 0.51$, *ns*, the variances are not significantly different, indicating that the assumption of homogeneity has been met.

```
drug: Ecstasy
               Sunday_BDI Wednesday_BDI
median         17.50000000    33.5000000
mean           19.60000000    32.0000000
SE.mean         2.08806130     1.5129074
CI.mean.0.95    4.72352283     3.4224344
```

```
var            43.60000000    22.8888889
std.dev         6.60302961     4.7842334
coef.var        0.33688927     0.1495073
skewness        1.23571300    -0.2191665
skew.2SE        0.89929826    -0.1594999
kurtosis        0.26030385    -1.4810114
kurt.2SE        0.09754697    -0.5549982
normtest.W      0.81064005     0.9411414
normtest.p      0.01952069     0.5657834
-----------------------------------------------------------------
drug: Alcohol
              Sunday_BDI  Wednesday_BDI
median       16.00000000    7.500000000
mean         16.40000000   10.100000000
SE.mean       0.71802197    2.514181996
CI.mean.0.95  1.62427855    5.687474812
var           5.15555556   63.211111111
std.dev       2.27058485    7.950541561
coef.var      0.13845030    0.787182333
skewness      0.11686189    1.500374383
skew.2SE      0.08504701    1.091907319
kurtosis     -1.49015904    1.079109997
kurt.2SE     -0.55842624    0.404388605
normtest.W    0.95946594    0.753466710
normtest.p    0.77976592    0.003933045
```

Output 15.1

```
Levene's Test for Homogeneity of Variance (center = "mean")
      Df F value  Pr(>F)
group  1   3.6436 0.07236 .
      18
---
Signif. codes:  0 '***' 0.001 '**' 0.01 '*' 0.05 '.' 0.1 ' ' 1

Levene's Test for Homogeneity of Variance (center = «mean»)
      Df F value Pr(>F)
group  1   0.5081 0.4851
      18
```

Output 15.2

<h3>15.4.3.   Running the analysis using R Commander ①</h3>

As always, import the data, using **Data⇒Import data⇒from text file, clipboard, or URL…** (see section 3.7.3) click on `OK` and choose the file **Drug.dat**.

   To run the Wilcoxon test on independent samples, select **Statistics⇒Nonparametric tests⇒Two-sample Wilcoxon test…** to activate the dialog box in Figure 15.4. In the box on the left, labelled *Groups (pick one)*, select the variable that defines the groups that you want to compare; this variable must be a factor with two levels. In our case we want to select the variable **drug**. On the right, in the list labelled *Response Variable (pick one)*, choose the outcome variable on which you want to compare groups. In this case, we'll pick **sundayBDI** first.

FIGURE 15.4
The non-parametric tests menu in R Commander and the dialog box for the Wilcoxon test for independent samples

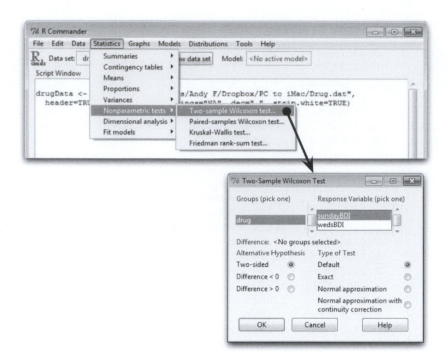

The Wilcoxon test offers two main different ways to calculate a *p*-value. The first option is the default. The default depends on the sample size and the presence of ties. If the sample size is 40 or fewer, then the default will be to do an exact test, as long as there are no ties. If the sample is larger than 40, the default will be to use a normal approximation with continuity correction. You can override this default if you like, but remember that if you have ties the exact test won't work, and if you have a large sample the exact test may not finish before your funeral.

You should probably leave the default option of a two-sided test as it is (although if you have predicted a direction of the effect you could choose to test whether or not the difference will be bigger (*Difference > 0*) or smaller (*Difference < 0*) than zero. When you have selected your variables, click on ⬚ OK ⬚ to run the analysis. The output will be discussed in due course.

15.4.4.   Running the analysis using R ①

The function for the Wilcoxon test is called **wilcox.test()** and works in a very similar way to the *t.test()* function (see section 9.5.2). That is, there are two different ways that you can use this function and it depends on whether your group data are in a single column or if they are in two different columns.

If you have the data for different groups stored in a single column, then the *wilcox.test()* function is used like the *lm()* function (in other words, like a regression):

```
newModel<-wilcox.test(outcome ~ predictor, data = dataFrame, paired = FALSE/
TRUE)
```

in which:

- *newModel* is an object created that contains information about the model. We can get summary statistics for this model by executing the name of the model.

- *outcome* is a variable that contains the scores for the outcome measure (in this case **drug**).

- *predictor* is a variable that tells us to which group a score belongs (in this case **sundayBDI** or **wedsBDI**).

- *dataFrame* is the name of the dataframe containing the aforementioned variables.

- *paired = FALSE* determines whether or not you want to do the Wilcoxon test on matched (in which case include *paired = TRUE*) or independent samples (in which case exclude the option because this is the default or include *paired = FALSE*).

However, if you have the data for different groups stored in two columns, then the *wilcox.test()* function takes this form:

```
newModel<-wilcox.test(scores group 1, scores group 2, paired = FALSE/TRUE)
```

in which the options are the same as before except that:

- *scores group 1* is a variable that contains the scores for the first group.

- *scores group 2* is a variable that contains the scores for the second group.

In both forms of the function, there are additional options that can be specified (but do not need to be). These are:

- *alternative = c("two.sided"/"less"/"greater")*: This option determines whether you're doing a two-tailed test, which is the default and happens if we don't include this option. If you want to do a one-tailed test then you need to include the option *alternative = "less"* (if you predict that the difference between means will be less than zero) or *alternative = "greater"* (if you predict that the difference between means will be greater than zero).

- *mu = 0*: A difference between groups of zero is the default null hypothesis, but can be changed. For example, including *mu = 5* would test the null hypothesis that the difference between groups is different to 5.

- *exact*: By default the function does an exact test (*exact = TRUE*). You can switch this option off by including *exact = FALSE*.

- *correct*: By default the function does a continuity correction (*correct = TRUE*); but if you don't want one include *correct = FALSE*.

- *conf.level = 0.95*: This determines the alpha level for the *p*-value and confidence intervals. By default it is 0.95 (for 95% confidence intervals), but if you want to use a different value, say 99%, you could include *conf.level = 0.99*.

- *na.action*: If you have complete data (as we have here) you can exclude this option, but if you have missing values (i.e., NAs in the dataframe) then it can be useful to use *na.action = na.exclude*, which will exclude all cases with missing values – see R's Souls' Tip 7.1.

Therefore, to compute a basic Wilcoxon test for our Sunday data we could execute:

```
sunModel<-wilcox.test(sundayBDI ~ drug, data = drugData)
sunModel
```

For the Wednesday data we need only change the name of the outcome variable:

```
wedModel<-wilcox.test(wedsBDI ~ drug, data = drugData)
wedModel
```

These commands create models called *sunModel* and *wedModel* that predict Sunday and Wednesday depression levels from group membership (**drug**). We execute the name of the model to see the output.[7] Having left all of the default options as they are, **R** will calculate the *p*-value, using the exact approach if *N* is less than 40 and there are no ties, or the normal approximation approach if *N* is more than 40 or if there are any ties. It will also use a continuity correction. To use a normal approximation rather than exact *p*, and to get rid of the continuity correction we can exclude *exact = FALSE* and *correct = FALSE* respectively:

```
sunModel<-wilcox.test(sundayBDI ~ drug, data = drugData, exact = FALSE,
correct= FALSE)
wedModel<-wilcox.test(wedsBDI ~ drug, data = drugData, exact = FALSE,
correct= FALSE)
```

15.4.5.   Output from the Wilcoxon rank-sum test ①

The output from the Wilcoxon tests is shown in Output 15.3 (Sunday) and Output 15.4 (Wednesday). For the BDI score on Sunday, you will find the *p*-value is 0.286 with the continuity correction (the default − if you rerun the test without this correction, you'll find the *p*-value is 0.269). We could say that the type of drug did not significantly affect depression levels the day after, $W = 35.5$, $p = .286$.

```
Wilcoxon rank sum test with continuity correction

data:  sundayBDI by drug
W = 35.5, p-value = 0.2861
alternative hypothesis: true location shift is not equal to 0
```

Output 15.3

```
Wilcoxon rank sum test with continuity correction

data:  wedsBDI by drug
W = 4, p-value = 0.000569
alternative hypothesis: true location shift is not equal to 0
```

Output 15.4

For the Wednesday data, however, the type of drug did significantly affect depression levels the day after, $W = 4$, $p < .001$. Note that because we left the default of an exact test, **R** gives us a warning message that it cannot do this, because of the ties.

15.4.6.   Calculating an effect size ②

As we've seen throughout this book, it's important to report effect sizes so that people have a standardized measure of the size of the effect you observed, which they can compare to other studies. **R** doesn't calculate an effect size for us, but we can calculate approximate effect sizes fairly easily. First, we take the *p*-value. Recall that **R** used a normal approximation to calculate the *p*-value; it did this via calculating a *z* for the data. It doesn't report, or store, the *z*-value, but we can recover it from the *p*-value using the **qnorm()** function. We

[7] We could run the commands without creating a model to get the output in a single command, but having the models is useful later for computing effect sizes.

JANE SUPERBRAIN 15.1

Doing it from scratch ②

The Wilcoxon rank-sum test is a good example of something you could easily program yourself, if there wasn't already a function in **R**. In addition, you can get some useful information, and learn a little about **R**. Here's the code to do the Wilcoxon test:

```
g1 <- drugData$sundayBDI[drugData$drug ==
"Alcohol"]
g2 <- drugData$sundayBDI[drugData$drug ==
"Ecstasy"]
n1 <- length(g1); n2 <- length(g2)
w <- rank(c(g1, g2))
r1 <- w[1:n1]; r2 <- w[(n1+1):(n1+n2)]
w1 <- sum(r1); w2 <- sum(r2)
```

```
wilc1 <- w1-n1*(n1+1)/2; wilc2
<- w2-n2*(n2+1)/2
wilc = min(wilc1, wilc2)
wilc
m1 <- mean(r1); m2 <- mean(r2)
m1; m2
```

First, we create **g1** and **g2**. These are the BDI scores on Sunday for the alcohol group (**g1**) and ecstasy group (**g2**). We count the number of people in each group, using the *length()* function, and call these values **n1** and **n2**.

Then we put **g1** and **g2** back together, using *c(g1, g2)*, into one long variable, which we convert to ranks, with the *rank()* function.

We get the ranks out again, and put these into **r1** and **r2**. The ranks for group 1 are the numbers from 1 to the number of people in group 1 (10). The ranks for group 2 are the number in group 1, plus 1 (11), to the number in both groups (20). We find the sums of these ranks, with the *sum()* function, and correct for the number of people; we call these **wilc1** and **wilc2**. The Wilcoxon W is the smaller of these two. In addition, we calculate the mean rank for each group, which can be a useful descriptive statistic. These are given as **m1** and **m2**.

can then convert the z-value into an effect size estimate. The equation to convert a z-score into the effect size estimate, r, is as follows (from Rosenthal, 1991, p. 19):

$$r = \frac{z}{\sqrt{N}}$$

in which z is the z-score and N is the size of the study (i.e., the number of total observations) on which z is based.

We can write ourselves a function (or access the function directly from our DSUR package – see section 3.4.5) to get the effect size from the models we created earlier. The function looks like this:

```
rFromWilcox<-function(wilcoxModel, N){
    z<- qnorm(wilcoxModel$p.value/2)
    r<- z/ sqrt(N)
    cat(wilcoxModel$data.name, "Effect Size, r = ", r)
}
```

Executing these commands creates a function called *rFromWilcox()*, which takes a model computed using *wilcox.test()* and the total sample size (N) as input. The first command within the function calculates the value of z using the *qnorm()* function. The p-value for a *wilcox.test()* model is stored in an object with the name *p.value*, so we can refer to it directly by appending *$p.value* to the name of the model. Therefore, the command takes the p-value associated with the model entered into the function, divides it by 2 so that we're looking at only one end of the normal distribution, and then applies *qnorm* to it (which gives us the *z* associated with that value of *p*). The second command computes *r* using the equation above by dividing *z* (which we've just computed) by the square root of *N* (which we know because it is entered into the function). The final command prints to the console the object *data.name* from the original model (this tells us what the model represents) then a text string that tells us what the output shows, and then the value of *r* computed in the previous command.

For the current example, we could apply this function by executing:

```
rFromWilcox(sunModel, 20)
rFromWilcox(wedModel, 20)
```

In both cases we enter the model name and the total sample size. The resulting output shows us that the *r* values are −0.25 for Sunday and −0.78 for Wednesday:

```
sundayBDI by drug Effect Size, r =  -0.2470529
wedsBDI by drug Effect Size, r =  -0.7790076
```

This represents a small to medium effect for the Sunday data (it is below the .3 criterion for a medium effect size) and a huge effect for the Wednesday data (the effect size is well above the .5 threshold for a large effect). The Sunday data show how a moderately large effect size can still be non-significant in a small sample.

15.4.7.   Writing the results ①

For the Wilcoxon rank-sum test, we need to report only the test statistic (which is denoted by *W*) and its significance. Of course, we really ought to include the effect size as well. So, we could report something like:

> ✓ Depression levels in ecstasy users (*Mdn* = 17.50) did not differ significantly from alcohol users (*Mdn* = 16.00) the day after the drugs were taken, *W* = 35.5, *p* = 0.286, *r* = −.25. However, by Wednesday, ecstasy users (*Mdn* = 33.50) were significantly more depressed than alcohol users (*Mdn* = 7.50), *W* = 4, *p* < .001, *r* = −.78.

Note that I've reported the median for each condition – this statistic is more appropriate than the mean for non-parametric tests.

CRAMMING SAM'S TIPS   **Some important terms**

- The Wilcoxon rank-sum test compares two conditions when different participants take part in each condition and the resulting data violate any assumption of the independent *t*-test.
- Look at the *p*-value. If the value is less than .05 then the two groups are significantly different.
- You might want to calculate the mean rank.
- Report the *W*-statistic and the significance value. Also report the medians and their corresponding ranges (or draw a boxplot).
- You should calculate the effect size and report this too.

JANE SUPERBRAIN 15.2

Non-parametric tests and statistical power ②

Ranking the data is a useful way around the distributional assumptions of parametric tests, but there is a price to pay: by ranking the data we lose some information about the magnitude of differences between scores. Consequently, non-parametric tests can be less powerful than their parametric counterparts. Statistical power (section 2.6.5) refers to the ability of a test to find an effect that genuinely exists. So, by saying that non-parametric tests are less powerful, we mean that if there is a genuine effect in our data then a parametric test is more likely to detect it than a non-parametric one. However, this statement is true only *if the assumptions of the parametric test are met*. So, if we use a parametric test and

a non-parametric test on the same data, and those data meet the appropriate assumptions, then the parametric test will have greater power to detect the effect than the non-parametric test.

The problem is that to define the power of a test we need to be sure that it controls the Type I error rate (the number of times a test will find a significant effect when in reality there is no effect to find – see section 2.6.2). We saw in Chapter 2 that this error rate is normally set at 5%. We know that when the sampling distribution is normally distributed then the Type I error rate of tests based on this distribution is indeed 5%, and so we can work out the power. However, when data are not normal the Type I error rate of tests based on this distribution won't be 5% (in fact we don't know what it is for sure as it will depend on the shape of the distribution) and so we have no way of calculating power (because power is linked to the Type I error rate – see section 2.6.5). So, although you often hear (in the first edition of my SPSS book, for example!) of non-parametric tests having an increased chance of a Type II error (i.e., more chance of accepting that there is no difference between groups when, in reality, a difference exists), this is true only if the sampling distribution is normally distributed.

15.5. Comparing two related conditions: the Wilcoxon signed-rank test ①

The **Wilcoxon signed-rank test** (Wilcoxon, 1945), not to be confused with the rank-sum test in the previous section, is used in situations in which there are two sets of scores to compare, but these scores come from the same participants. As such, think of it as the non-parametric equivalent of the dependent *t*-test.

Imagine the experimenter in the previous section was now interested in the *change* in depression levels, within people, for each of the two drugs. We now want to compare the BDI scores on Sunday to those on Wednesday. When testing the differences between related scores, we assume normality of the differences (see Chapter 9). Let's first test this assumption.

SELF-TEST

✓ Compute the change in BDI scores from Sunday to Wednesday and then compute normality tests for this change score separately for the alcohol and ecstasy groups.

Output 15.5 shows the results of a descriptive analysis. For the alcohol group we have a non-normal distribution, $W = 0.83$, $p < .05$, in the change scores, but for the ecstasy group the difference scores are approximately normal, $W = 0.91$, $p = .273$. Therefore, we need to use a non-parametric test for the alcohol group (although we'll do one for the ecstasy group too, just to get some practice).

```
drugData$drug: Alcohol
median    mean   SE.mean CI.mean  var    std.dev coef.var
-7.500   -6.300   2.098   4.746  44.011   6.634   -1.053

skewness  skew.2SE  kurtosis  kurt.2SE   normtest.W  normtest.p
   1.239     0.902     0.987     0.370        0.828       0.032
-----------------------------------------------------------------
drugData$drug: Ecstasy
median    mean   SE.mean CI.mean  var    std.dev coef.var
14.000   12.400   2.531   5.724  64.044   8.002    0.645

skewness  skew.2SE  kurtosis  kurt.2SE   normtest.W  normtest.p
  -0.414    -0.301    -1.369    -0.513        0.909       0.273
```

Output 15.5

15.5.1. Theory of the Wilcoxon signed-rank test ②

The Wilcoxon signed-rank test works in a fairly similar way to the dependent t-test (Chapter 9) in that it is based on the differences between scores in the two conditions you're comparing. Once these differences have been calculated they are ranked (just like in section 15.4.1) but the sign of the difference (positive or negative) is assigned to the rank. If we use the same data as before, we can compare depression scores on Sunday to those on Wednesday for the two drugs separately.

Table 15.2 shows the ranking for these data. Remember that we're ranking the two drugs separately. First, we calculate the difference between Sunday and Wednesday (that's just Sunday's score subtracted from Wednesday's). If the difference is zero (i.e., the scores are the same on Sunday and Wednesday) then we exclude these data from the ranking. We make a note of the sign of the difference (positive or negative) and then rank the differences (starting with the smallest) ignoring whether they are positive or negative. The ranking is the same as in section 15.4.1, and we deal with tied scores in exactly the same way. Finally, we collect together the ranks that came from a positive difference between the conditions, and add them up to get the sum of positive ranks (T_+). We also add up the ranks that came from negative differences between the conditions to get the sum of negative ranks (T_-). So, for ecstasy, $T_+ = 36$ and $T_- = 0$ (in fact there were no negative ranks), and for alcohol, $T_+ = 8$ and $T_- = 47$. The test statistic, T, is the smaller of the two values, and so is 0 for ecstasy and 8 for alcohol.

To calculate the significance of the test statistic (T), we again look at the mean ($\bar{T}$) and standard error ($SE_{\bar{T}}$), which, like the rank-sum test in the previous section, are functions of the sample size, n (because we used the same participants, there is only one sample size):

$$\bar{T} = \frac{n(n+1)}{4}$$

$$SE_{\bar{T}} = \sqrt{\frac{n(n+1)(2n+1)}{24}}$$

Table 15.2 Ranking data in the Wilcoxon signed-rank test

BDI Sunday	BDI Wednesday	Difference	Sign	Rank	Positive ranks	Negative ranks
Ecstasy						
15	28	13	+	2.5	2.5	
35	35	0	Exclude			
16	35	19	+	6	6	
18	24	6	+	1	1	
19	39	20	+	7	7	
17	32	15	+	4.5	4.5	
27	27	0	Exclude			
16	29	13	+	2.5	2.5	
13	36	23	+	8	8	
20	35	15	+	4.5	4.5	
Total =					36	0
Alcohol						
16	5	−11	−	9		9
15	6	−9	−	7		7
20	30	10	+	8	8	
15	8	−7	−	3.5		3.5
16	9	−7	−	3.5		3.5
13	7	−6	−	2		2
14	6	−8	−	5.5		5.5
19	17	−2	−	1		1
18	3	−15	−	10		10
18	10	−8	−	5.5		5.5
Total =					8	47

In both groups, n is simply 10 (because that's how many participants were used). However, remember that for our ecstasy group we excluded two people because they had differences of zero, therefore the sample size we use is 8, not 10. This gives us:

$$\bar{T}_{\text{Ecstasy}} = \frac{8(8+1)}{4} = 18$$

$$SE_{\bar{T}_{\text{Ecstasy}}} = \sqrt{\frac{8(8+1)(16+1)}{24}} = 7.14$$

For the alcohol group there were no exclusions so we get:

$$\bar{T}_{\text{Alcohol}} = \frac{10(10+1)}{4} = 27.50$$

$$SE_{\bar{T}_{\text{Alcohol}}} = \sqrt{\frac{10(10+1)(20+1)}{24}} = 9.81$$

As before, if we know the test statistic, the mean of test statistics and the standard error, then we can easily convert the test statistic to a *z*-score using the equation that we came across way back in Chapter 1:

$$z = \frac{X - \bar{X}}{s} = \frac{T - \bar{T}}{SE_{\bar{T}}}$$

If we calculate this value for the ecstasy and alcohol depression scores we get:

$$z_{\text{Ecstasy}} = \frac{T - \bar{T}}{SE_{\bar{T}}} = \frac{0 - 18}{7.14} = -2.52$$

$$z_{\text{Alcohol}} = \frac{T - \bar{T}}{SE_{\bar{T}}} = \frac{8 - 27.5}{9.81} = -1.99$$

If these values are bigger than 1.96 (ignoring the minus sign) then the test is significant at $p < .05$. So, it looks as though there is a significant difference between depression scores on Wednesday and Sunday for both ecstasy and alcohol.

15.5.2.   Running the analysis with R Commander ①

To do the same analysis using R Commander we can use the same dataframe as before, but because we want to look at the change for each drug *separately*, we need to use the *subset* command and ask **R** to split the file by the variable **drug**. This process ensures that any subsequent analysis is done for the ecstasy group and the alcohol group separately. To do this in R Commander, select **Data⇒Active data set⇒Subset active data set...** to open the dialog box shown in Figure 15.5. We want to keep all of the variables, so we leave the box at the top checked.

For the *Subset expression*, remember that you need to use a double equals sign for 'is equal to' in **R**, so we write *"drug==Alcohol"*. Finally, we give the data set a new name; we'll call it *alcoholData*. Click on ⬚ OK ⬚ to create the dataframe. Repeat the process to create a dataframe called *ecstasyData* that contains only the data from the ecstasy group.

Now we have the data prepared, we can use R Commander to run the Wilcoxon signed-rank test. Make sure you have the *alcoholData* data set as the active data set in R Commander, and select **Statistics ⇒ Nonparametric tests ⇒ Paired-samples Wilcoxon test...** to open the dialog box in Figure 15.6.

FIGURE 15.5

R Commander menu and dialog box for subset

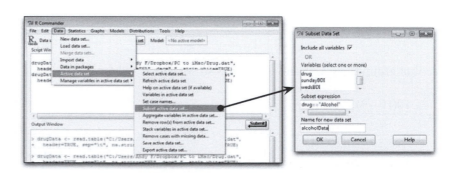

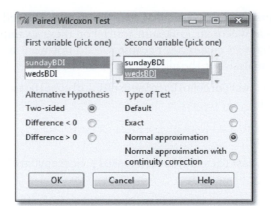

FIGURE 15.6
Dialog box for
the Wilcoxon
signed-rank test

Pick the two variables that you would like to compare: in our case, there are only two to select from, so choose one in the left-hand box, and the other in the right-hand box (it doesn't matter which way around you do it).

You can choose a *p*-value calculation method. As with the rank-sum test (section 15.4.3), you can leave this as the default, in which case **R** will use the exact method to calculate the *p*-value if your sample size is less than 40, and the normal approximation if larger than 40. You can choose the exact method, which is often better than the normal approximation, but cannot be used if you have ties in the data, and can be slow if your sample size is large. If you choose the normal approximation method, you can do this with or without the continuity correction. If you choose the default, the continuity correction will be used. We will select the normal approximation (we have ties, so we cannot use the exact method anyway) and we will choose not to use the continuity correction.

You can leave the default option of a two-sided test as it is (although if you have predicted a direction of the effect you could choose to test whether or not the difference will be bigger (*Difference > 0*) or smaller (*Difference < 0*) than zero. When you have selected your variables, click on OK to run the analysis. The output will be discussed very soon.

15.5.3. Running the analysis using R ①

We want to run our analysis on the alcohol and ecstasy groups separately; therefore, our first job is to split the dataframe into two.

SELF-TEST

✓ Use the *subset()* function to create separate dataframes for the different drugs called *alcoholData* and *ecstasyData*.

If you completed the self-test then you should now have two dataframes called *alcohol Data* and *ecstasyData*. We can again use the *wilcox.test()* function, but this time because our data are stored in different columns (**wedsBDI** and **sundayBDI**) we need to enter the names of the two variables we want to compare rather than a formula, and we need to include the option *paired = TRUE* to tell **R** that the data are paired. (If we don't include this option **R** will do a Wilcoxon rank-sum test.) For these examples, we're also going to include the option *correct = FALSE*, because we do not want a continuity correction. Therefore, to run the analysis for the alcohol group execute:

```
alcoholModel<-wilcox.test(alcoholData$wedsBDI, alcoholData$sundayBDI, paired =
TRUE, correct= FALSE)
alcoholModel
```

and for the ecstasy group:

```
ecstasyModel<-wilcox.test(ecstasyData$wedsBDI, ecstasyData$sundayBDI, paired =
TRUE, correct= FALSE)
ecstasyModel
```

In both cases we create a model (*alcoholModel* and *ecstasyModel*) based on a Wilcoxon test between the *sundayBDI* and *wedsBDI* variables.

15.5.4. Wilcoxon signed-rank test output ①

What are the effects of ecstasy?

Output 15.6 shows the output for the alcohol group. You will get a warning when the function runs, telling you that it couldn't do an exact test, because there are ties. We didn't ask for an exact test, but when the sample size is less than 40 **R** tries to do one anyway. It reports the value of T_+ (which it calls V)[8] and that this value is significant at $p = .047$. Therefore, we should conclude (based on the medians) that when taking alcohol there was a significant decline in depression (as measured by the BDI) from the morning after to midweek ($p = .047$).

Output 15.7 shows the results for the ecstasy group. We should conclude that when taking ecstasy there was a significant increase in depression (as measured by the BDI) from the morning after to midweek, $p = .012$.

```
        Wilcoxon signed rank test
data:  alcoholData$wedsBDI and alcoholData$sundayBDI
V = 8, p-value = 0.04657
alternative hypothesis: true location shift is not equal to 0
```

Output 15.6

```
        Wilcoxon signed rank test

data:  ecstacy$bdi.wednesday and ecstacy$bdi.sunday
V = 36, p-value = 0.01151
alternative hypothesis: true location shift is not equal to 0
```

Output 15.7

From the results of the two different groups, we can see that there is an opposite effect when alcohol is taken to that when ecstasy is taken. Alcohol makes you slightly depressed the morning after, but this depression has dropped by midweek. Ecstasy also causes some depression the morning after consumption; however, this depression increases towards the

---

[8] The order in which you input variables into the function will affect the value of V because it is T_+ and whether ranks are positive or negative depends on which way around you subtract scores. In Table 15.2 we subtracted Sunday BDI scores from those on the Wednesday and $T_+ = 36$ and $T_- = 0$ for the ecstasy group, but if we had subtracted Wednesday scores from Sunday scores these would have been the opposite way around ($T_+ = 0$ and $T_- = 36$). So the order that you put variables into the functions affects the value of T_+ (and, therefore, V). You don't need to worry about this little quirk: the *p*-value will be the same whichever way around you specify the variables.

middle of the week. Of course, to see the true effect of the morning after we would have had to take measures of depression before the drugs were administered. This opposite effect between groups of people is known as an interaction (i.e., you get one effect under certain circumstances and a different effect under other circumstances) and we came across this in Chapters 12–14.

15.5.5.   Calculating an effect size ②

The effect size can be calculated in the same way as for the Wilcoxon rank-sum test (see the equation in section 15.4.6); therefore, we can reuse the *rFromWilcox()* function. In both the alcohol and ecstasy groups we had 20 observations (although we only used 10 people and tested them twice, it is the number of observations, not the number of people, that is important here). Therefore, we can get the effect sizes by inputting the model names and the number of observations into the function:

```
rFromWilcox(alcoholModel, 20)
rFromWilcox(ecstasyModel, 20)
```

The resulting output is:

```
alcoholData$wedsBDI and alcoholData$sundayBDI Effect Size, r =  -0.4450246

ecstasyData$wedsBDI and ecstasyData$sundayBDI Effect Size, r =  -0.5649883
```

For the alcohol group we find a medium to large change in depression when alcohol is taken, $r = -.45$, which is between Cohen's criteria of .3 and .5 for a medium and large effect, respectively. For the ecstasy group, $r = -.56$, which represents a large change in levels of depression when ecstasy is taken (it is above Cohen's benchmark of .5).

15.5.6.   Writing the results ①

For the Wilcoxon test, we need only report the significance of the test and preferably an effect size. So, we could report something like:

✓ For ecstasy users, depression levels were significantly higher on Wednesday (*Mdn* = 33.50) than on Sunday (*Mdn* = 17.50), $p = .047$, $r = -.56$. However, for alcohol users the opposite was true: depression levels were significantly lower on Wednesday (*Mdn* = 7.50) than on Sunday (*Mdn* = 16.0), $p = .012$, $r = -.45$.

CRAMMING SAM'S TIPS   The Wilcoxon signed-rank test

- The Wilcoxon signed-rank test compares two conditions when the same participants take part in each condition and the resulting data violate an assumption of the dependent *t*-test.
- Look at the *p*-value. If the value is less than .05 then the two groups are significantly different.
- Report the significance value of the test and an effect size if possible. Also report the medians and their corresponding ranges (or draw a boxplot).

Labcoat Leni's Real Research 15.1   Having a quail of a time? ①

Matthews, R. C., et al. (2007). *Psychological Science*, *18*(9), 758–762.

We encountered some research in Chapter 2 in which we discovered that you can influence aspects of male quail sperm production through 'conditioning'. The basic idea is that the male is granted access to a female for copulation in a certain chamber (e.g., one that is coloured green) but gains no access to a female in a different context (e.g., a chamber with a tilted floor). The male, therefore, learns that when he is in the green chamber his luck is in, but if the floor is tilted then frustration awaits. For other males the chambers will be reversed (i.e., they get sex only when in the chamber with the tilted floor). The human equivalent (well, sort of) would be if you always managed to pull in the Pussycat Club but never in the Honey Club.[9] During the test phase, males get to mate in both chambers. The question is: after the males have learnt that they will get a mating opportunity in a certain context, do they produce more sperm or better-quality sperm when mating in that context compared to the control context? (That is, are you more of a stud in the Pussycat Club? OK, I'm going to stop this analogy now.)

Mike Domjan and his colleagues predicted that if conditioning evolved because it increases reproductive fitness then males who mated in the context that had previously signalled a mating opportunity would fertilize a significantly greater number of eggs than quails that mated in their control context (Matthews, Domjan, Ramsey, & Crews, 2007). They put this hypothesis to the test in an experiment that is utter genius. After training, they allowed 14 females to copulate with two males (counterbalanced): one male copulated with the female in the chamber that had previously signalled a reproductive opportunity (**Signalled**), whereas the second male copulated with the same female but in the chamber that had not previously signalled a mating opportunity (**Control**). Eggs were collected from the females for 10 days after the mating and a genetic analysis was used to determine the father of any fertilized eggs.

The data from this study are in the file **Matthews et al. (2007).dat**. Labcoat Leni wants you to carry out a Wilcoxon signed-rank test to see whether more eggs were fertilized by males mating in their signalled context compared to males in their control context.

Answers are in the additional material on the companion website (or look at page 760 in the original article).

15.6. Differences between several independent groups: the Kruskal–Wallis test ①

In Chapter 10 we discovered a technique called one-way independent ANOVA that could be used to test for differences between several independent groups. I mentioned several times in that chapter that the *F*-statistic can be robust to violations of its assumptions (section 10.3). We also saw that there are measures that can be taken when you have heterogeneity of variance (Jane Superbrain Box 10.2). However, there is another alternative: the one-way independent ANOVA has a non-parametric counterpart called the Kruskal–Wallis test (Kruskal & Wallis, 1952). If you have data that have violated an assumption then this test can be a useful way around the problem. If you'd like to know a bit more about William Kruskal (Figure 15.7) then there is a lovely biography by Fienberg, Stigler, and Tanur (2007).

I read a story in a newspaper claiming that scientists had discovered that the chemical genistein, which occurs naturally in soya, was linked to lowered sperm counts in Western

[9] These are both clubs in Brighton that I've never been to because I don't like that sort of thing.

FIGURE 15.7
William Kruskal

males. In fact, when you read the actual study, it had been conducted on rats, it found no link to lowered sperm counts, but there was evidence of abnormal sexual development in male rats (probably because this chemical acts like oestrogen). The journalist naturally interpreted this as a clear link to apparently declining sperm counts in Western males (never trust what you read in the newspapers). Anyway, as a vegetarian who eats lots of soya products and probably would like to have kids one day, I might want to test this idea in humans rather than rats. I took 80 males and split them into four groups that varied in the number of soya meals they ate per week over a year-long period. The first group was a control group and had no soya meals at all per week (i.e., none in the whole year); the second group had one soya meal per week (that's 52 over the year); the third group had four soya meals per week (that's 208 over the year); and the final group had seven soya meals a week (that's 364 over the year). At the end of the year, all of the participants were sent away to produce some sperm that I could count (when I say 'I', I mean someone else in a laboratory as far away from me as humanly possible).[10]

15.6.1.   Theory of the Kruskal–Wallis test ②

The theory for the Kruskal–Wallis test is very similar to that of the Mann–Whitney (and Wilcoxon rank-sum) test, so before reading on look back at section 15.4.1. Like the Wilcoxon rank-sum test, the Kruskal–Wallis test is based on ranked data. So, to begin with, you simply order the scores from lowest to highest, ignoring the group to which the score belongs, and then assign the lowest score a rank of 1, the next highest a rank of 2 and so

---

[10] In case any medics are reading this chapter, these data are made up and, because I have absolutely no idea what a typical sperm count is, they're probably ridiculous. I apologize and you can laugh at my ignorance.

Table 15.3 Data for the soya example with ranks

No Soya Sperm (millions)	Rank	1 Soya Meal Sperm (millions)	Rank	4 Soya Meals Sperm (millions)	Rank	7 Soya Meals Sperm (millions)	Rank
0.35	4	0.33	3	0.40	6	0.31	1
0.58	9	0.36	5	0.60	10	0.32	2
0.88	17	0.63	11	0.96	19	0.56	7
0.92	18	0.64	12	1.20	21	0.57	8
1.22	22	0.77	14	1.31	24	0.71	13
1.51	30	1.53	32	1.35	27	0.81	15
1.52	31	1.62	34	1.68	35	0.87	16
1.57	33	1.71	36	1.83	37	1.18	20
2.43	41	1.94	38	2.10	40	1.25	23
2.79	46	2.48	42	2.93	48	1.33	25
3.40	55	2.71	44	2.96	49	1.34	26
4.52	59	4.12	57	3.00	50	1.49	28
4.72	60	5.65	61	3.09	52	1.50	29
6.90	65	6.76	64	3.36	54	2.09	39
7.58	68	7.08	66	4.34	58	2.70	43
7.78	69	7.26	67	5.81	62	2.75	45
9.62	72	7.92	70	5.94	63	2.83	47
10.05	73	8.04	71	10.16	74	3.07	51
10.32	75	12.10	77	10.98	76	3.28	53
21.08	80	18.47	79	18.21	78	4.11	56
Total (R_i)	**927**		**883**		**883**		**547**

on (see section 15.4.1 for more detail). When you've ranked the data you collect the scores back into their groups and simply add up the ranks for each group. The sum of ranks for each group is denoted by R_i (where i is used to denote the particular group). Table 15.3 shows the raw data for this example along with the ranks.

SELF-TEST

✓ Have a go at ranking the data and see if you get the same results as me.

Once the sum of ranks has been calculated for each group, the test statistic, H, is calculated as:

$$H = \frac{12}{N(N+1)} \sum_{i=1}^{k} \frac{R_i^2}{n_i} - 3(N+1)$$

(15.1)

In this equation, R_i is the sum of ranks for each group, N is the total sample size (in this case 80) and n_i is the sample size of a particular group (in this case we have equal sample sizes and they are all 20). Therefore, all we really need to do for each group is square the sum of ranks and divide this value by the sample size for that group. We then add up these values. That deals with the middle part of the equation; the rest of it involves calculating various values based on the total sample size. For these data we get:

$$H = \frac{12}{80(81)}\left(\frac{927^2}{20} + \frac{883^2}{20} + \frac{883^2}{20} + \frac{547^2}{20}\right) - 3(81)$$

$$= \frac{12}{6480}(42966.45 + 38984.45 + 38384.45 + 14960.45) - 243$$

$$= 0.0019(135895.8) - 243$$

$$= 251.66 - 243$$

$$= 8.659$$

This test statistic has a special kind of distribution known as the chi-square distribution (see Chapter 18) and for this distribution there is one value for the degrees of freedom, which is one less than the number of groups ($k - 1$), in this case 3.

15.6.2. Inputting data and provisional analysis ①

SELF-TEST

✓ See whether you can enter the data in Table 15.3 into **R** (you don't need to enter the ranks). Then conduct some exploratory analyses on the data (see sections 5.6 and 5.7).

When the data are collected using different participants in each group, we input the data using a coding variable. So, the data editor will have two columns of data. The first column is a factor (called something like **Soya**), which, in this case, will have four levels. We can create this variable using the *gl()* function by executing:

```
Soya<-gl(4, 20, labels = c("No Soya", "1 Soya Meal", "4 Soya Meals", "7 Soya Meals"))
```

This command creates a variable called **Soya**, which contains four blocks of 20 rows of data; the first block will be labelled *No Soya*, the second block *1 Soya Meal*, and so on. The second variable will have values for the dependent variable (sperm count) measured at the end of the year (call this variable **Sperm**) – see the online materials for a fuller description. Finally, we can tie these variables together in a dataframe called *soyaData* by executing:

```
soyaData<-data.frame(Sperm, Soya)
```

The data can also be found in the file **Soya.dat**. If you prefer, load this file into a dataframe called *soyaData* by executing:

```
soyaData<-read.delim("Soya.dat", header = TRUE)
```

Then the variable **Soya**, which contains text, will be imported as a factor. This is fine, except that whereas when we created this factor ourselves we could specify the order of the groups, when we import the data the order of the groups will be alphabetic. For these data they will be:

1 1 soya meal per week

2 4 soya meals per week

3 7 soya meals per week

4 No soya meals per week

For reasons that will become apparent, it's useful to have the first level as our control category (i.e., no soya), which is how we ordered the groups when entering the data by hand. Therefore, we need to reorder the factor levels (look back to R's Souls' Tip 3.13). We can do this by executing:

```
soyaData$Soya<-factor(soyaData$Soya, levels = levels(soyaData$Soya)[c(4, 1, 2, 3)])
```

This command uses the *factor()* function to reorder the levels of the **Soya** variable. It re-creates the variable **Soya** in the *soyaData* dataframe (*soyaData$Soya*) based on itself, but then uses the *levels()* function to reorder the groups. We simply put the order of the levels that we'd like in the *c()* function, so in this case we have asked for the levels to be ordered 4, 1, 2, 3, which means that the current fourth group (no soya) will become the first group, the current first group will become the second group, and so on. Having executed this command, our groups will be ordered:

1 No soya meals per week

2 1 soya meal per week

3 4 soya meals per week

4 7 soya meals per week

Having got the data loaded, we would run some exploratory analyses and because we're going to be looking for group differences we need to run these exploratory analyses for each group. If you do these analyses (as requested in the self help test) you should find the same results shown in Outputs 15.8 and 15.9.

Output 15.8 shows that the Kruskal–Wallis test is significant for the group that ate no soya, $W(20) = 0.805$, $p = .001$, one soya meal per week $W(20) = .826$, $p = .002$), and four soya meals, $W(20) = 0.743$, $p < .001$. The test for those who ate seven meals per week is not quite significant, $W(20) = 0.912$, $p = .07$. As such, the data for all of the groups are significantly (or close to being) different from normal.

Output 15.9 shows the results of Levene's test (section 5.7.1). The assumption of homogeneity of variance has been violated, $F(3, 76) = 2.86$, $p = .042$. As such, these data are not normally distributed, and the groups have heterogeneous variances.

```
soyaData$Soya: No Soya
skewness    skew.2SE    kurtosis    kurt.2SE    normtest.W  normtest.p
1.546141    1.509598    2.328051    1.172959    0.805256    0.001036
-----------------------------------------------------------------
soyaData$Soya: 1 Soya Meal
skewness    skew.2SE    kurtosis    kurt.2SE    normtest.W  normtest.p
1.350566    1.318646    1.422732    0.716825    0.825832    0.002154
```

```
soyaData$Soya: 4 Soya Meals
skewness    skew.2SE    kurtosis    kurt.2SE   normtest.W  normtest.p
1.822237    1.779169    2.792615    1.407024   0.742743    0.000136


soyaData$Soya: 7 Soya Meals
 skewness    skew.2SE    kurtosis    kurt.2SE normtest.W normtest.p
 0.608671    0.594286    -0.916165   -0.461598 0.912261   0.070391
```

Output 15.8

```
Levene's Test for Homogeneity of Variance (center = median)
      Df F value  Pr(>F)
group  3  2.8606 0.04237 *
      76
---
Signif. codes:  0 '***' 0.001 '**' 0.01 '*' 0.05 '.' 0.1 ' ' 1
```

Output 15.9

15.6.3. Doing the Kruskal–Wallis test using R Commander ①

Import the data, using **Data⇒Import data⇒from text file, clipboard, or URL...** (see section 3.7.3), click on OK and choose the file **Soya.dat**. To run the Kruskal–Wallis test, select **Statistics⇒Nonparametric tests⇒Kruskal-Wallis test** to activate the dialog box in Figure 15.8. In the box on the left, labelled *Groups (pick one)*, select the variable that defines the groups that you want to compare; this variable must be a factor. In our case we want to select the variable **Soya**. On the right, in the list labelled *Response variable (pick one)*, choose the outcome variable on which you want to compare groups. In this case, we'll pick **Sperm**. To run the analysis click on OK. We'll examine the output shortly.

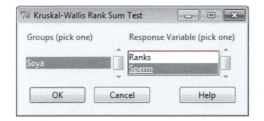

FIGURE 15.8
Dialog box for the Kruskal–Wallis test

15.6.4. Doing the Kruskal–Wallis test using R ①

The Kruskal–Wallis test is done using the **kruskal.test()** function, which works in the same way as the *wilcox.test()* function that we used for the rank-sum test. The general form of the function is:

```
newModel<-kruskal.test(outcome ~ predictor, data = dataFrame, na.action = "an.action")
```

For the current data, we could, therefore execute:

```
kruskal.test(Sperm ~ Soya, data = soyaData)
```

This command does the Kruskal–Wallis test on sperm scores predicted from the soya group to which a person belonged. Note that we have executed the command directly, without creating a model, which is fine because we don't really need to use the output of the function for any reason other than interpretation.

To interpret the Kruskal–Wallis test, it is useful to obtain the mean rank for each group. We can do this by adding a variable called **Ranks** to the dataframe with the *rank()* function:

```
soyaData$Ranks<-rank(soyaData$Sperm)
```

This command creates a variable **Ranks** in the *soyaData* dataframe that is the ranks for the variable **Sperm**. We can then obtain the mean rank for each group using the *by()* and *mean()* functions:

```
by(soyaData$Ranks, soyaData$Soya, mean)
```

15.6.5.   Output from the Kruskal–Wallis test ①

Output 15.10 shows the test statistic, *H*, for the Kruskal–Wallis test (although **R** labels it *chi-squared*, because of its distribution, rather than *H*), its associated degrees of freedom (in this case we had 4 groups so the degrees of freedom are 4 − 1, or 3) and the significance. The crucial thing to look at is the significance value, which is .034; because this value is less than .05 we could conclude that the amount of soya meals eaten per week does significantly affect sperm counts. Like a one-way ANOVA, though, this test tells us only that a difference exists; it doesn't tell us exactly where the differences lie. One way to get an idea is to look at the mean ranks (Output 15.11). These show that the ranks were lowest (27.35) in the group that had seven soya meals per week, but fairly similar in the other three groups, which implies that any differences might be between the seven soya meals group and the other three groups.

```
        Kruskal-Wallis rank sum test
data:  Sperm by Soya
Kruskal-Wallis chi-squared = 8.6589, df = 3, p-value = 0.03419
Output 15.10
soyaData$Soya: No Soya Meals
[1] 46.35
------------------------------------------------------------------
soyaData$Soya: 1 Soya Meal
[1] 44.15
------------------------------------------------------------------
soyaData$Soya: 4 Soya Meals
[1] 44.15
------------------------------------------------------------------
soyaData$Soya: 7 Soya Meals
[1] 27.35
```

Output 15.11

SELF-TEST

✓ Use *ggplot2* to draw a boxplot of these data

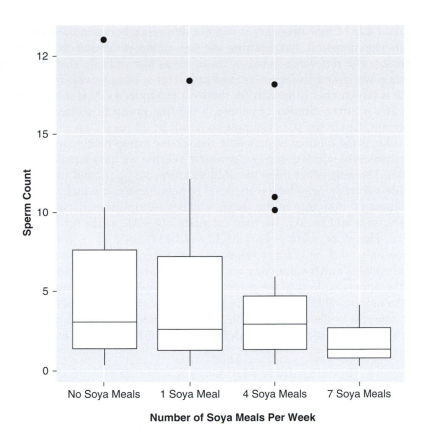

FIGURE 15.9
Boxplot for the sperm counts of individuals eating different numbers of soya meals per week

One way to see which groups differ is to look at a boxplot (see section 4.7) of the groups (see Figure 15.9). The first thing to note is that there are some outliers (note the circles and asterisks that lie above the top whiskers) – these are men who produced a particularly rampant amount of sperm. Using the control as our baseline, the medians of the first three groups seem quite similar; however, the median of the group that ate seven soya meals per week does seem a little lower, so perhaps this is where the difference lies. However, these conclusions are subjective. What we really need are some contrasts or *post hoc* tests like we used in ANOVA (see sections 10.4 and 10.5).

15.6.6.   *Post hoc* tests for the Kruskal–Wallis test ②

One way to do non-parametric *post hoc* procedures is essentially the same as doing Wilcoxon rank-sum tests on all possible comparisons. This method is described by Siegel and Castellan (1988) and involves taking the difference between the mean ranks of the different groups and comparing this to a value based on the value of z (corrected for the number of comparisons being done) and a constant based on the total sample size and the sample size in the two groups being compared. The inequality is:

Can I do non-parametric *post hoc* tests?

$$\left| \bar{R}_u - \bar{R}_v \right| \geq z_{\alpha/k(k-1)} \sqrt{\frac{N(N+1)}{12}\left(\frac{1}{n_u} + \frac{1}{n_v}\right)} \qquad (15.2)$$

The left-hand side of this inequality is just the difference between the mean rank of the two groups being compared, but ignoring the sign of the difference (so the two vertical lines that enclose the difference between mean ranks just indicate that if the difference is negative then we ignore the negative sign and treat it as positive). For the rest of the expression, k is the number of groups (in the soya example, 4), N is the total sample size (in this case 80), n_u is the number of people in the first group that's being compared (we have equal group sizes in the soya example so it will be 20 regardless of which groups we compare), and n_v is the number of people in the second group being compared (again this will be 20 regardless of which groups we compare because we have equal group sizes in the soya example). The only other thing we need to know is $z_{\alpha/k(k-1)}$, and to get this value we need to decide a level for α, which is the level of significance at which we want to work. You should know by now that in the social sciences we traditionally work at a .05 level of significance, so α will be .05. We then calculate $k(k-1)$, which for these data will be $4(4-1) = 12$. Therefore, $\alpha/k(k-1) = .05/12 = .00417$. So, $z_{\alpha/k(k-1)}$ just means 'the value of z for which only $\alpha/k(k-1)$ other values of z are bigger' (or in this case 'the value of z for which only .00417 other values of z are bigger'). In practical terms this means we go to the table in the Appendix, look at the column labelled *Smaller Portion* and find the number .00417 (or the nearest value to this, which, if you look at the table, is .00415), and we then look in the same row at the column labelled z. In this case, you should find that the value of z is 2.64. The next thing to do is to calculate the right-hand side of inequality (15.2):

$$\text{critical difference} = z_{\alpha/k(k-1)}\sqrt{\frac{N(N+1)}{12}\left(\frac{1}{n_u}+\frac{1}{n_v}\right)}$$

$$= 2.64\sqrt{\frac{80(80+1)}{12}\left(\frac{1}{20}+\frac{1}{20}\right)}$$

$$= 2.64\sqrt{540(0.1)}$$

$$= 2.64\sqrt{54}$$

$$= 19.40$$

For this example, because the sample sizes across groups are equal, this critical difference can be used for all comparisons. However, when sample sizes differ across groups, the critical difference will have to be calculated for each comparison individually. The next step is simply to calculate all of the differences between the mean ranks of all of the groups (the mean ranks can be found in Output 15.11), as in Table 15.4.

Inequality (15.2) basically means that if the difference between mean ranks is bigger than or equal to the critical difference for that comparison, then that difference is significant. In this case, because we have only one critical difference, it means that if any difference is

Table 15.4 Differences between mean ranks for the soya data

Comparison	$\bar{R}_u$	$\bar{R}_v$	$\bar{R}_u - \bar{R}_v$	$\lvert\bar{R}_u - \bar{R}_v\rvert$
No Meals − 1 Meal	46.35	44.15	2.20	2.20
No Meals − 4 Meals	46.35	44.15	2.20	2.20
No Meals − 7 Meals	46.35	27.35	19.00	19.00
1 Meal − 4 Meals	44.15	44.15	0.00	0.00
1 Meal − 7 Meals	44.15	27.35	16.80	16.80
4 Meals − 7 Meals	44.15	27.35	16.80	16.80

bigger than 19.40, then it is significant. As you can see, all differences are below this value, so we would have to conclude that none of the groups were significantly different.

We can do all of these calculations using the *kruskalmc()* function from the *pgirmess* package. You use this function in exactly the same way as the *kruskal.test* function, so for the current example, we can do the *post hoc* tests by executing:

```
kruskalmc(Sperm ~ Soya, data = soyaData)
```

Output 15.12 shows the output of the function and, as you can see, it lists all of the possible pairs of groups, along with the critical difference that we calculated above, and the absolute difference between mean ranks that we calculated in Table 15.4. Conveniently, there is also a column labelled *difference* that tells us whether the observed difference is greater than the critical difference (TRUE) or not (FALSE). In other words, it tells us whether or not the difference is significant. In the current example, none of the differences are bigger than the critical difference; hence they all say *FALSE*, which means that the differences are all non-significant.

```
Multiple comparison test after Kruskal-Wallis
p.value: 0.05
Comparisons
                           obs.dif critical.dif difference
No Soya Meals-1 Soya Meal      2.2     19.38715        FALSE
No Soya Meals-4 Soya Meals     2.2     19.38715        FALSE
No Soya Meals-7 Soya Meals    19.0     19.38715        FALSE
1 Soya Meal-4 Soya Meals       0.0     19.38715        FALSE
1 Soya Meal-7 Soya Meals      16.8     19.38715        FALSE
4 Soya Meals-7 Soya Meals     16.8     19.38715        FALSE
```

Output 15.12

One of the problems with comparing every group against all others is that we have to be quite strict about accepting a difference as significant, otherwise we will inflate the Type I error rate (section 10.2.1). To reduce this problem we could use more focused comparisons.

In this example, we have a control group that had no soya meals. As such, a nice succinct set of comparisons would be to compare each group against the control:

- Test 1: one soya meal per week compared to no soya meals

- Test 2: four soya meals per week compared to no soya meals

- Test 3: seven soya meals per week compared to no soya meals

This results in three tests, rather than six, so these tests can be less strict than if we compare all groups. Fortunately, we can implement this analysis using the *kruskalmc()* function by using the *cont* option. This option takes the form of *cont* = '*one-tailed*' or '*two-tailed*' and, if included, will compare all levels against the first. Therefore, the only complication is that we need to make sure that the no-soya group is the first level of the **Soya** factor. Fortunately, we thought ahead and made the no-soya group the first level when we loaded/entered the data into **R**; however, in other situations you can reorder factor levels if necessary (see R's Souls' Tip 3.13). Therefore, to compare each group to the no-soya group (using a two-tailed test) we simply execute:

```
kruskalmc(Sperm ~ Soya, data = soyaData, cont = 'two-tailed')
```

Note that the command is exactly the same as before, except that we have added *cont* = '*two-tailed*' to it, which will make it compare all groups to the first group only.

Output 15.13 shows the results of this test. Note that we have only three tests now and consequently our critical difference has decreased (the observed differences between the mean ranks of groups are the same as for the corresponding parts of the previous output). Looking at the column labelled *difference*, we can see that there was a significant difference between the no-soya and seven soya meals a week group. This result contradicts our earlier finding (Output 15.12) in which the test for the no-soya group compared to the seven meals group was deemed non-significant; why do you think that is? Well, for our current tests, we have done three comparisons and so corrected the critical difference for only these three tests. However, our earlier tests corrected for six tests, which resulted in a stricter (therefore, larger) critical difference. This example illustrates the benefits of choosing selective comparisons over blindly comparing everything and anything.

```
Multiple comparison test after Kruskal-Wallis, treatment vs control
(two-tailed)
p.value: 0.05
Comparisons
                            obs.dif critical.dif difference
No Soya Meals-1 Soya Meal       2.2     15.63787      FALSE
No Soya Meals-4 Soya Meals      2.2     15.63787      FALSE
No Soya Meals-7 Soya Meals     19.0     15.63787       TRUE
```

Output 15.13

15.6.7. Testing for trends: the Jonckheere–Terpstra test ②

Sometimes we don't think that groups will just be different, but we want to hypothesize a trend. The Jonckheere–Terpstra statistic tests for an ordered pattern to the medians of the groups you're comparing. Essentially it does the same thing as the Kruskal–Wallis test (i.e., test for a difference between the medians of the groups) but it incorporates information about whether the order of the groups is meaningful. As such, you should use this test when you expect the groups you're comparing to produce a meaningful order of medians. So, in the current example we expect that the more soya a person eats, the more their sperm count will go down. Therefore, the control group should have the highest sperm count, those having one soya meal per week should have a lower sperm count, the sperm count in the four meals per week group should be lower still, and the seven meals per week group should have the lowest sperm count. Therefore, there is an order to our medians: they should decrease across the groups. Conversely, there might be situations where you expect your medians to increase. For example, there's a phenomenon in psychology known as the 'mere exposure effect', which basically means that the more you're exposed to something, the more you'll like it. Record companies use this to good effect by making sure songs are played on radio for about two months prior to their release, so on the day of release, everyone loves the song and is dying to have it and rushes out to buy it, sending it to number one.[11] Anyway, if you took three groups and exposed them to a song 10 times, 20 times and 30 times respectively and then measured how much people liked the song, you'd expect the medians to increase. Those who heard it 10 times would like it a bit, but those who heard it 20 times would like it more, and those who heard it 30 times would like it the most.

The Jonckheere–Terpstra test (actually referred to more often just as the Jonckheere test) was designed for these situations. In **R**, it works on the principle that your coding variable

[11] In most cases the mere exposure effect seems to have the reverse effect on me: the more I hear the manufactured rubbish that gets into the charts, the more I want to rid my brain of the mental anguish it creates by making myself deaf by ramming hot irons into my ears.

(the one that defines the groups) specifies the order in which you expect the medians to change (it doesn't matter whether you expect them to increase or decrease). For our soya example, our groups are in the correct order because we entered them that way and if you loaded the data from the file, I showed you already how to change the order (see R's Souls' Tip 3.13). The test determines whether the medians of the groups ascend or descend in the *order specified by the coding variable*; therefore, given the order of levels for the variable **Soya**, it will test whether the median sperm count increases or decreases across the groups. The Jonckheere–Terpstra test is carried out using the **jonckheere.test()** function, which is found in the *clinfun* package. This function takes the general form:

```
jonckheere.test(outcome variable, group variable (as numbers))
```

In other words we only need to specify the name of the outcome variable and the name of the grouping variable. The only slight complication is that for the grouping variable we need to use the numeric codes rather than the names of the groups (because the function uses the numbers to determine the order of the groups). However, we can do this by putting our grouping variable inside the *as.numeric()* function, which will return the group codes. Therefore, we can conduct a Jonckheere test by executing:

```
jonckheere.test(soyaData$Sperm, as.numeric(soyaData$Soya))
```

The results are shown in Output 15.14, which tells us the value of the test statistic, *JT*, which is 912. In large samples (more than about eight per group) this test statistic has a sampling distribution that is normal, and a mean and standard deviation that are easily defined and calculated (the mean is 1200 and the standard deviation is 116.33). **R** has calculated the *p*-value for us, which is .013; because this value is less than .05 we have a statistically significant trend in the data. We can use the mean ranks (Output 15.11) to see that it is a decreasing trend: sperm counts go down as more soya is eaten.

```
        Jonckheere-Terpstra test
data:
JT = 912, p-value = 0.0133
alternative hypothesis: two.sided
```

Output 15.14

OLIVER TWISTED

Please Sir, can I have some more … Jonck?

'I want to know how the Jonckheere–Terpstra test actually works', complains Oliver. Of course you do, Oliver, sleep is hard to come by these days. I am only too happy to oblige, my little syphilitic friend. The additional material for this chapter on the companion website has a complete explanation of the test and how it works. I bet you're glad you asked.

15.6.8.   Calculating an effect size ②

Unfortunately there isn't an easy way to convert a chi-square statistic that has more than one degree of freedom to an effect size *r*. You could use the significance value of the Kruskal–Wallis test statistic to find an associated value of *z* from a table of probability values for the normal distribution (like that in the Appendix). From this you could use the conversion to *r* that we used in section 15.4.6. However, this kind of effect size is rarely that useful (because it's summarizing a general effect).

15.6.9.   Writing and interpreting the results ①

For the Kruskal–Wallis test, we need only report the test statistic (which, as we saw earlier, is denoted by H), its degrees of freedom and its significance. So, we could report something like:

> ✓ Sperm counts were significantly affected by eating soya meals, $H(3) = 8.66$, $p = .034$.

However, we need to report the follow-up tests as well (including their effect sizes):

> ✓ Sperm counts were significantly affected by eating soya meals, $H(3) = 8.66$, $p = .034$. Focused comparisons of the mean ranks between groups showed that sperm counts were not significantly different when one soya meal (*difference* = 2.2) or four soya meals (*difference* = 2.2) were eaten per week compared to none. However, when seven soya meals were eaten per week sperm counts were significantly lower than when no soya was eaten (*difference* = 19). In all cases, the critical difference ($\alpha = .05$ corrected for the number of tests) was 15.64. We can conclude that if soya is eaten every day it significantly reduces sperm counts compared to eating none; however, eating soya less frequently than every day has no significant effect on sperm counts ('phew!' says the vegetarian man!).

We might also want to report our trend:

> ✓ Jonckheere's test revealed a significant trend in the data: as more soya was eaten, the median sperm count decreased, $J = 912$, $p = .013$.

CRAMMING SAM'S TIPS   The Kruskal–Wallis test

- The Kruskal–Wallis test compares several conditions when different participants take part in each condition and the resulting data violate an assumption of one-way independent ANOVA.
- Look at the *p*-value. If the value is less than .05 then the groups are significantly different.
- You can follow up the main analysis with *post hoc* tests (ideally, focused ones). If the column labelled *difference* in the output says 'true' then the groups differ significantly.
- If you predict that the means will increase or decrease across your groups in a certain order then do Jonckheere's trend test.
- Report the *H*-statistic, the degrees of freedom and the significance value for the main analysis. Also report the medians and their corresponding ranges (or draw a boxplot).

15.7. Differences between several related groups: Friedman's ANOVA ①

In Chapter 13 we discovered a technique called one-way related ANOVA that could be used to test for differences between several related groups. Although, as we've seen, robust versions

Labcoat Leni's Real Research 15.2 Eggs-traordinary! ①

Çetinkaya, H., & Domjan, M. (2006). *Journal of Comparative Psychology, 120*(4), 427–432.

There seems to be a lot of sperm in this book (not literally, I hope) – it's possible that I have a mild obsession. We saw in Labcoat Leni's Real Research 15.1 that male quail fertilized more eggs if they had been trained to be able to predict when a mating opportunity would arise. However, some quail develop fetishes. Really. In the previous example the type of compartment acted as a predictor of an opportunity to mate, but in studies where a terrycloth object acts as a sign that a mate will shortly become available, some quail start to direct their sexual behaviour towards the terrycloth object. (I may regret this anology, but, in human terms, if you imagine that every time you were going to have sex with your boyfriend you gave him a green towel a few moments before seducing him, then after enough seductions he would start rubbing his crotch against any green towel he saw. If you've ever wondered why you boyfriend rubs his crotch on green towels, then I hope this explanation has been enlightening.) In evolutionary terms, this fetishistic behaviour seems counterproductive because sexual behaviour becomes directed towards something that cannot provide reproductive success. However, perhaps this behaviour serves to prepare the organism for the 'real' mating behaviour.

Hakan Çetinkaya and Mike Domjan conducted a brilliant study in which they sexually conditioned male quail (Çetinkaya & Domjan, 2006). All quail experienced the terrycloth stimulus and an opportunity to mate, but for some the terrycloth stimulus immediately preceded the mating opportunity (paired group) whereas others experienced it 2 hours after the mating opportunity (this was the control group because the terrycloth stimulus did not predict a mating opportunity). In the paired group, quail were classified as fetishistic or not depending on whether they engaged in sexual behaviour with the terrycloth object.

During a test trial the quail mated with a female and the researchers measured the percentage of eggs fertilized, the time spent near the terrycloth object, the latency to initiate copulation, and copulatory efficiency. If this fetishistic behaviour provides an evolutionary advantage then we would expect the fetishistic quail to fertilize more eggs, initiate copulation faster and be more efficient in their copulations.

The data from this study are in the file **Cetinkaya & Domjan (2006).dat**. Labcoat Leni wants you to carry out a Kruskal–Wallis test to see whether fetishist quail produced a higher percentage of fertilized eggs and initiated sex more quickly.

Answers are in the additional material on the companion website (or look at pages 429–430 in the original article).

of ANOVA exist, there is another alternative to the repeated-measures case: **Friedman's ANOVA** (Friedman, 1937). As such, it is used for testing differences between conditions when there are more than two conditions and the same participants have been used in all conditions (each case contributes several scores to the data). If you have violated some assumption of parametric tests then this test can be a useful way around the problem.

Young people (women especially) can become obsessed with body weight and diets, and, because the media are insistent on ramming ridiculous images of stick-thin celebrities down our throats (should that be 'into our eyes'?) and brainwashing us into believing that these emaciated corpses are actually attractive, we all end up terribly depressed that we're not perfect (because we don't have a couple of slugs stuck to our faces instead of lips). Then corporate parasites jump on our vulnerability by making loads of money on diets that will help us attain the body beautiful. Well, not wishing to miss out on this great opportunity to exploit people's insecurities, I came up with my own diet called the Andikins diet.[12] The principle is that you follow my lifestyle: you eat no meat, drink lots of Darjeeling tea, eat shedloads of lovely European cheese, lots of fresh crusty bread, pasta, chocolate at every available opportunity

[12] Not to be confused with the Atkins diet, obviously.☺

(especially when writing books), then enjoy a few beers at the weekend, play football twice a week and play your drum kit for an hour a day or until your neighbour threatens to saw your arms off and beat you around the head with them for making so much noise. To test the efficacy of my wonderful new diet, I took 10 women who considered themselves to be in need of losing weight and put them on this diet for two months. Their weight was measured in kilograms at the start of the diet and then after one month and two months.

15.7.1. Theory of Friedman's ANOVA ②

The theory for Friedman's ANOVA is much the same as the other tests we've seen in this chapter: it is based on ranked data. To begin with, you simply place your data for different conditions into different columns (in this case there were three conditions, so we have three columns). The data for the diet example are in Table 15.5; note that the data are in different columns, and so each row represents the weight of a different person. The next thing we have to do is rank the data *for each person*. So, we start with person 1, we look at their scores (in this case person 1 weighed 63.75 kg at the start, 65.38 kg after one month on the diet, and 81.34 kg after two months on the diet), and then we give the lowest one a rank of 1, the next highest a rank of 2 and so on (see section 15.4.1 for more detail). When you've ranked the data for the first person, you move onto the next person, and starting at 1 again, rank their lowest score, then rank the next highest as 2 and so on. You do this for all people from whom you've collected data. You then simply add up the ranks for each condition (R_i, where i is used to denote the particular group).

SELF-TEST

✓ Have a go at ranking the data and see if you get the same results as in Table 15.5.

Table 15.5   Data for the diet example with ranks

	Weight			Weight		
	Start	Month 1	Month 2	Start (Ranks)	Month 1 (Ranks)	Month 2 (Ranks)
Person 1	63.75	65.38	81.34	1	2	3
Person 2	62.98	66.24	69.31	1	2	3
Person 3	65.98	67.70	77.89	1	2	3
Person 4	107.27	102.72	91.33	3	2	1
Person 5	66.58	69.45	72.87	1	2	3
Person 6	120.46	119.96	114.26	3	2	1
Person 7	62.01	66.09	68.01	1	2	3
Person 8	71.87	73.62	55.43	2	3	1
Person 9	83.01	75.81	71.63	3	2	1
Person 10	76.62	67.66	68.60	3	1	2
			R_i	19	20	21

Once the sum of ranks has been calculated for each group, the test statistic, F_r, is calculated as:

$$F_r = \left[\frac{12}{Nk(k+1)} \sum_{i=1}^{k} R_i^2 \right] - 3N(k+1) \qquad (15.3)$$

In this equation, R_i is the sum of ranks for each group, N is the total sample size (in this case 10) and k is the number of conditions (in this case 3). This equation is very similar to that for the Kruskal–Wallis test (compare equations (15.1) and (15.3)). All we need to do for each condition is square the sum of ranks and then add up these values. That deals with the middle part of the equation; the rest of it involves calculating various values based on the total sample size and the number of conditions. For these data we get:

$$F_r = \left[\frac{12}{(10 \times 3)(3+1)}(19^2 + 20^2 + 21^2) \right] - (3 \times 10)(3+1)$$

$$= \frac{12}{120}(361 + 400 + 441) - 120$$

$$= 0.1(1202) - 120$$

$$= 120.2 - 120$$

$$= 0.2$$

When the number of people tested is large (bigger than about 10) this test statistic, like the Kruskal–Wallis test in the previous section, has a chi-square distribution (see Chapter 18) and for this distribution there is one value for the degrees of freedom, which is one less than the number of groups $(k-1)$, in this case 2.

15.7.2. Inputting data and provisional analysis ①

SELF-TEST

✓ Using what you know about inputting data, try to enter these data into **R** and run some exploratory analyses (see Chapter 5).

When the data are collected using the same participants in each condition, the data are entered using different columns. So, the data editor will have three columns of data. The first column is for the data from the start of the diet (called something like **Start**), the second column will have values for the weights after one month (called **Month1**) and the final column will have the weights at the end of the diet (called **Month2**). The data can be found in the file **Diet.dat**.

Output 15.15 shows the results of some exploratory analysis (using the *stat.desc* function from Chapter 5). With a bit of luck you'll get the same results, which shows that the Friedman's ANOVA is significant for the baseline data (**Start**), $W(10) = 0.78$, $p = .009$, and one month into the diet, $W(10) = 0.68$, $p < .001$. Therefore the variables **Start** and **Month1** deviate significantly from normal. The data at the end of the diet do not appear to differ from normal, though, $W(10) = 0.87$, $p = .121$.

	Start	Month1	Month2
median	69.225000000	6.857500e+01	72.25000000
mean	78.053000000	7.746300e+01	77.06700000
SE.mean	6.397375860	5.886269e+00	5.09347536
CI.mean.0.95	14.471869624	1.331567e+01	11.52224176
var	409.264178889	3.464817e+02	259.43491222
std.dev	20.230278764	1.861402e+01	16.10698334
coef.var	0.259186434	2.402956e-01	0.20899974
skewness	1.054846022	1.329796e+00	1.01105333
skew.2SE	0.767671126	9.677677e-01	0.73580071
kurtosis	-0.514513976	1.196569e-01	0.25546331
kurt.2SE	-0.192810362	4.484056e-02	0.09573301
normtest.W	0.784370035	6.849797e-01	0.87721476
normtest.p	0.009357858	5.796060e-04	0.12120786

Output 15.15

15.7.3. Doing Friedman's ANOVA in R Commander ①

As always, import the data, using **Data⇒Import data⇒from text file, clipboard, or URL…**
(see section 3.7.3), click on OK and choose the file **Diet.dat**. To run Friedman's ANOVA,
select **Statistics⇒Nonparametric tests⇒Friedman rank-sum test…** to activate the dialog box
in Figure 15.10. Once the dialog box is activated, select the three variables that represent
the dependent variable at the different levels of the independent variable from the list. This
is very straightforward: we have only three variables, so select them all and click on OK.

FIGURE 15.10
Dialog box for
Friedman's ANOVA

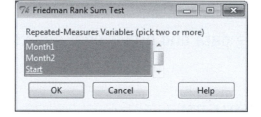

15.7.4. Friedman's ANOVA using R ①

We can do Friedman's ANOVA using the **friedman.test()** function. This function is a bit of
a prima donna because, in order to work, it demands that (1) you give it a matrix rather
than a dataframe, because it thinks dataframes smell of rotting brains, and (2) it wants all
of the variables of interest in one data set, and there mustn't be any additional variables. To
combat the first issue we need to convert our dataframe into a matrix by putting it into the
as.matrix() function (see section 3.9.3). As for the second, in the current example our dataframe does contain only the variables of interest. However, for other analyses you can use
what you learnt in section 3.9 to extract only the data that you need for the Friedman test.

The other complication is that the function gets confused by missing data. Again, we
have a complete data set in this example so we don't need to do anything, but if you have
missing data you need to delete any cases that don't have a complete set of scores. We can
do this easily using the **na.omit()** function. If we put our dataframe name into that function

and execute we'll get back the same dataframe but with cases that have any missing data deleted. Therefore, we could execute:

```
dietCompleteCases <- na.omit(dietData)
```

This would create a dataframe called *dietCompleteCases*, which is the same as the *dietData* dataframe except that it will have deleted any case (row) for which there is missing data in any column.

To run the Friedman test we simply input the name of our dataframe, but within the *as.matrix()* function, which converts it to a matrix. In this example, we would execute:

```
friedman.test(as.matrix(dietData))
```

15.7.5.   Output from Friedman's ANOVA ①

Output 15.16 shows the result of the Friedman test: the main part is the test statistic, which **R** calls *chi-squared* rather that F_r because F_r has a chi-square distribution). The value of this statistic is 0.2, the same value that we calculated earlier. We're also told the test statistic's degrees of freedom (in this case we had three groups so the degrees of freedom are $3-1$, or 2), and the significance. The significance value is .905, which is well above .05, therefore we could conclude that the there is no evidence that the Andikins diet has any effect: the weights didn't significantly change over the course of the diet.

```
Friedman rank sum test

data:  just.diet
Friedman chi-squared = 0.2, df = 2, p-value = 0.9048
```

Output 15.16

15.7.6.   *Post hoc* tests for Friedman's ANOVA ②

In normal circumstances we wouldn't do any follow-up tests because the overall effect from Friedman's ANOVA was not significant. However, in case you get a result that is significant we will have a look at what options you have. As with the Kruskal–Wallis test, there is a function that enables us to compare all groups, or to compare groups to a baseline. This function, **friedmanmc()**, requires the data to be in exactly the same format as the *friedman.test()* function and we use it in exactly the same way. Therefore, for the current data we would execute:

```
friedmanmc(as.matrix(dietData))
```

The results are in Output 15.17. As with the Kruskal–Wallis test, you need to look at the column labelled *differences*; if this says *TRUE* then the groups differ significantly, but if it says *FALSE*, they don't. In this case, we have a clean sweep of non-significant results (which, given the main test was ragingly non-significant, isn't a surprise).

```
Multiple comparisons between groups after Friedman test
p.value: 0.05
Comparisons
     obs.dif critical.dif difference
1-2     1       10.7062       FALSE
1-3     2       10.7062       FALSE
2-3     1       10.7062       FALSE
```

Output 15.17

15.7.7.   Calculating an effect size ②

As I mentioned before, there isn't an easy way to convert a chi-square statistic that has more than one degree of freedom to an effect size r and, in any case, it's not always that helpful to have an effect size for a general effect like that tested by Friedman's ANOVA.[13] Therefore, it's more sensible (in my opinion at least) to calculate effect sizes for any comparisons you've done after the ANOVA. As we saw in section 15.5.5, it's straightforward to get an effect size r from the Wilcoxon signed-rank test. Therefore, you could conduct some Wilcoxon tests and get the effect sizes using the *rFromWilcox()* function.

15.7.8.   Writing and interpreting the results ①

For Friedman's ANOVA we need only report the test statistic (which we saw earlier is denoted by χ^2),[14] its degrees of freedom and its significance. So, we could report something like:

✓ The weight of participants did not significantly change over the two months of the diet, $\chi^2(2) = 0.20$, $p > .05$.

Although with no significant initial analysis we wouldn't report *post hoc* tests for these data, in case you need to, you should say something like this:

✓ The weight of participants did not significantly change over the two months of the diet, $\chi^2(2) = 0.20$, $p > .05$. *Post hoc* tests were used with Bonferroni correction applied. It appeared that weight didn't significantly change from the start of the diet to one month, (*difference* = 1), from the start of the diet to two months, (*difference* = 2), or from one month to two months, (*difference* = 1). In all cases, the critical difference ($\alpha = .05$ corrected for the number of tests) was 10.71. We can conclude that the Andikins diet, like its creator, is a complete failure.

CRAMMING SAM'S TIPS   Friedman's ANOVA

- Friedman's ANOVA compares several conditions when the same participants take part in each condition and the resulting data violate an assumption of one-way repeated-measures ANOVA.
- Look at the row labelled *p-value*. If the value is less than .05 then the conditions are significantly different.
- You can follow up the main analysis with *post hoc* tests using the *friedmanmc()* function. Look at the column labelled *differences*: if it says *TRUE* then the groups differ significantly.
- Report the χ^2 statistic, its degrees of freedom and significance.
- Report the medians and their ranges (or draw a boxplot).

---

[13] If you really want to, though, you can (as with the Kruskal–Wallis test) use the significance value of the chi-square test statistic to find an associated value of z from a table of probability values for the normal distribution (see Appendix) and then use the conversion to r that we've seen throughout this chapter.

[14] You might also see it denoted as χ^2_F.

What have I discovered about statistics? ①

This chapter has dealt with an alternative approach to violations of parametric assumptions, which is to use tests based on ranking the data. We started with the Wilcoxon rank-sum test, which is used for comparing two independent groups. This test allowed us to look in some detail at the process of ranking data. We then moved on to look at the Wilcoxon signed-rank test, which is used to compare two related conditions. We moved onto more complex situations in which there are several conditions (the Kruskal–Wallis test for independent conditions and Friedman's ANOVA for related conditions). For each of these tests we looked at the theory of the test (although these sections could be ignored) and then focused on how to conduct them using **R**, how to interpret the results and how to report the results of the test. In the process we discovered that drugs make you depressed, soya reduces your sperm count, and my lifestyle is not conducive to losing weight.

We also discovered that my teaching career got off to an inauspicious start. As it turned out, one of the reasons why the class did not have a clue what I was talking about was that I hadn't been shown their course handouts and I was trying to teach them ANOVA using completely different equations than their lecturer (there are many ways to compute an ANOVA). The other reason was that I was a rubbish teacher. This event did change my life, though, because the experience was so awful that I did everything in my power to make sure that it didn't happen again. After years of experimentation I can now pass on the secret of avoiding students telling you how awful your ANOVA classes are: the more penis jokes you tell, the less likely you are to be emotionally crushed by dissatisfied students.

R packages used in this chapter

clinfun	pgirmess
ggplot2	Rcmdr
pastecs	

R functions used in this chapter

as.matrix()	mean()
as.numeric()	min()
by()	na.omit()
data.frame()	qnorm()
friedmanmc()	rank()
friedman.test()	rFromWilcox()
gl()	sqrt()
kruskalmc()	stat.desc()
kruskal.test()	subset()
length()	sum()
leveneTest()	wilcox.test()
jonckheere.test()	

Key terms that I've discovered

Friedman's ANOVA
Jonckheere–Terpstra test
Kruskal–Wallis test
Mann–Whitney test
Monte Carlo method

Non-parametric tests
Ranking
Wilcoxon rank-sum test
Wilcoxon signed-rank test

Smart Alex's tasks

- **Task 1**: A psychologist was interested in the cross-species differences between men and dogs. She observed a group of dogs and a group of men in a naturalistic setting (20 of each). She classified several behaviours as being dog-like (urinating against trees and lampposts, attempts to copulate with anything that moved, and attempts to lick their own genitals). For each man and dog she counted the number of dog-like behaviours displayed in a 24-hour period. It was hypothesized that dogs would display more dog-like behaviours than men. The data are in the file **MenLikeDogs.dat**. Analyse them with a Wilcoxon rank-sum test. ①

- **Task 2**: There's been much speculation over the years about the influence of subliminal messages on records. To name a few cases, both Ozzy Osbourne and Judas Priest have been accused of putting backward masked messages on their albums that subliminally influence poor unsuspecting teenagers into doing things like blowing their heads off with shotguns. A psychologist was interested in whether backward masked messages really did have an effect. He took the master tapes of Britney Spears' 'Baby One More Time' and created a second version that had the masked message 'deliver your soul to the dark lord' repeated in the chorus. He took this version, and the original, and played one version (randomly) to a group of 32 people. He took the same group six months later and played them whatever version they hadn't heard the time before. So each person heard both the original, and the version with the masked message, but at different points in time. The psychologist measured the number of goats that were sacrificed in the week after listening to each version. It was hypothesized that the backward message would lead to more goats being sacrificed. The data are in the file **DarkLord.dat**. Analyse them with a Wilcoxon signed-rank test. ①

- **Task 3**: A psychologist was interested in the effects of television programmes on domestic life. She hypothesized that through 'learning by watching', certain programmes might actually encourage people to behave like the characters within them. This in turn could affect the viewer's own relationships (depending on whether the programme depicted harmonious or dysfunctional relationships). She took episodes of three popular TV shows and showed them to 54 couples, after which the couple were left alone in the room for an hour. The experimenter measured the number of times the couple argued. Each couple viewed all three of the TV programmes at different points in time (a week apart) and the order in which the programmes were viewed was counterbalanced over couples. The TV programmes selected were *EastEnders* (which typically portrays the lives of extremely miserable, argumentative, London folk who like nothing more than to beat each other up, lie to each other, sleep with each other's wives and generally show no evidence of any consideration to their fellow humans!), *Friends* (which portrays a group of unrealistically considerate and nice people who love each other oh so very much – but for some reason I love it anyway!), and a National Geographic programme about whales (this was supposed to act as a control). The data are in the file **Eastenders.dat**. Access the file and conduct Friedman's ANOVA on the data. ①

- **Task 4**: A researcher was interested in trying to prevent coulrophobia (fear of clowns) in children. She decided to do an experiment in which different groups of children (15 in each) were exposed to different forms of positive information about clowns. The first group watched some adverts for McDonald's in which their mascot Ronald McDonald is seen cavorting about with children going on about how they should love their mums. A second group was told a story about a clown who helped some children when they got lost in a forest (although what on earth a clown was doing in a forest remains a mystery). A third group was entertained by a real clown, who came into the classroom and made balloon animals for the children.[15] A final group acted as a control condition and they had nothing done to them at all. The researcher took self-report ratings of how much the children liked clowns, resulting in a score for each child that could range from 0 (not scared of clowns at all) to 5 (very scared of clowns). The data are in the file **coulrophobia.dat**. Access them and conduct a Kruskal–Wallis test. ①

Answers can be found on the companion website and, because these examples are used in Field and Hole (2003), you could steal this book or photocopy Chapter 7 to get some very detailed answers.

Further reading

Siegel, S., & Castellan, N. J. (1988). *Nonparametric statistics for the behavioral sciences* (2nd ed.). New York: McGraw-Hill. (This has become the definitive text on non-parametric statistics, and is the only book seriously worth recommending as 'further' reading. It is probably not a good book for anyone with a statistics phobia, but if you've coped with my chapter then this book will be an excellent next step.)

Wilcox, R. R. (2005). *Introduction to robust estimation and hypothesis testing* (2nd ed.). Burlington, MA: Elsevier. (Wilcox's book is quite technical compared to this one, but really is a wonderful resource. Wilcox describes how to use an astonishing range of robust tests, many of which we discuss throughout this book.)

Interesting real research

Çetinkaya, H., & Domjan, M. (2006). Sexual fetishism in a quail (*Coturnix japonica*) model system: Test of reproductive success. *Journal of Comparative Psychology*, 120(4), 427–432.

Matthews, R. C., Domjan, M., Ramsey, M., & Crews, D. (2007). Learning effects on sperm competition and reproductive fitness. *Psychological Science*, 18(9), 758–762.

---

[15] Unfortunately, the first time they attempted the study the clown accidentally burst one of the balloons. The noise frightened the children and they associated that fear response with the clown. All 15 children are currently in therapy for coulrophobia!

16

Multivariate analysis of variance (MANOVA)

FIGURE 16.1
Fuzzy doing some
light reading

16.1. What will this chapter tell me? ②

Having had what little confidence I had squeezed out of me by my formative teaching experiences, I decided that I could either kill myself, or get a cat. I'd wanted to do both for years, but when I was introduced to a little 4-week-old bundle of gingerness the choice was made. Fuzzy (as I named him) was born on 8 April 1996 and has been my right-hand feline ever since. He is like the Cheshire cat in Lewis Carroll's *Alice's Adventures in Wonderland*[1] in that

[1] This is one of my favourite books from my childhood. For those that haven't read it, the Cheshire cat is a big fat cat mainly remembered for vanishing and reappearing out of nowhere; on one occasion it vanished leaving only its smile behind.

he seemingly vanishes and reappears at will: I go to find clothes in my wardrobe and notice a ginger face peering out at me, I put my pants in the laundry basket and he looks up at me from a pile of smelly socks, I go to have a bath and he's sitting in it, and I shut the bedroom door yet wake up to find him asleep next to me. His best vanishing act was a few years ago when I moved house. He'd been locked up in his travel basket (which he hates) during the move, so once we were in our new house I thought I'd let him out as soon as possible. I found a quiet room, checked the doors and windows to make sure he couldn't escape, opened the basket, gave him a cuddle and left him to get to know his new house. When I returned five minutes later, he was gone. The door had been shut, the windows closed and the walls were solid (I checked). He had literally vanished into thin air and he didn't even leave behind his smile. Before his dramatic disappearance, Fuzzy had stopped my suicidal tendencies, and there is lots of research showing that having a pet is good for your mental health. If you wanted to test this you could compare people with pets against those without to see if they had better mental health. However, the term *mental health* covers a wide range of concepts, including (to name a few) anxiety, depression, general distress and psychosis. As such, we have four outcome measures and all the tests we have encountered allow us to look at one. Fear not, when we want to compare groups on several outcome variables we can extend ANOVA to become MANOVA. That's what this chapter is all about.

16.2. When to use MANOVA ②

Over Chapters 9–14, we have seen how the general linear model (GLM) can be used to detect group differences on a single dependent variable. However, there may be circumstances in which we are interested in several dependent variables, and in these cases the simple ANOVA model is inadequate. Instead, we can use an extension of this technique known as **multivariate analysis of variance** (or **MANOVA**). MANOVA can be thought of as ANOVA for situations in which there are several dependent variables. The principles of ANOVA extend to MANOVA in that we can use MANOVA when there is only one independent variable or when there are several, we can look at interactions between independent variables, and we can even do contrasts to see which groups differ from each other. ANOVA can be used only in situations in which there is one dependent variable (or outcome) and so is known as a **univariate** test (univariate quite obviously means 'one variable'); MANOVA is designed to look at several dependent variables (outcomes) simultaneously and so is a **multivariate** test (multivariate means 'many variables'). This chapter will explain some basics about MANOVA for those of you who want to skip the fairly tedious theory sections and just get on with the test. However, for those who want to know more there is a fairly lengthy theory section to try to explain the workings of MANOVA. We then look at an example using **R** and see how the output from MANOVA can be interpreted. This leads us to look at another statistical test known as **discriminant function analysis**.

What is MANOVA?

16.3. Introduction: similarities to and differences from ANOVA ②

If we have collected data about several dependent variables then we could simply conduct a separate ANOVA for each dependent variable (and if you read research articles you'll find that it is not unusual for researchers to do this). Think back to Chapter 10, and you should remember that a similar question was posed regarding why ANOVA was used in preference to multiple *t*-tests. The reason why MANOVA is used instead of multiple ANOVAs is

Why not do lots of ANOVAs?

the same: the more tests we conduct on the same data, the more we inflate the familywise error rate (see section 10.2.1). The more dependent variables we have measured, the more ANOVAs we would need to conduct and the greater the chance of making a Type I error.

However, there are other reasons for preferring MANOVA to several ANOVAs. For one thing, there is important additional information that is gained from a MANOVA. If separate ANOVAs are conducted on each dependent variable, then any relationship between dependent variables is ignored. As such, we lose information about any correlations that might exist between the dependent variables. MANOVA, by including all dependent variables in the same analysis, takes account of the relationship between outcome variables. Related to this point, ANOVA can tell us only whether groups differ along a single dimension, whereas MANOVA has the power to detect whether groups differ along a combination of dimensions. For example, ANOVA tells us how scores on a single dependent variable distinguish groups of participants (so, for example, we might be able to distinguish people who are married, living together or single by their happiness). MANOVA incorporates information about several outcome measures and, therefore, informs us of whether groups of participants can be distinguished by a combination of scores on several dependent measures. For example, 'happiness' is a complex construct, so we might want to measure participants' happiness with work, socially, sexually and within themselves (self-esteem). It may not be possible to distinguish people who are married, living together or single only by their happiness at work, but they might be distinguished by *a combination* of their happiness across all four domains: work, social, sexual, and the self. So, in this sense MANOVA has greater

JANE SUPERBRAIN 16.1

The power of MANOVA ③

I mentioned in the previous section that MANOVA had greater power than ANOVA to detect effects because it could take account of the correlations between dependent variables (Huberty & Morris, 1989). However, the issue of power is more complex than alluded to by my simple statement. Ramsey (1982) found that as the correlation between dependent variables increased, the power of MANOVA decreased. This led Tabachnick and Fidell (2007) to recommend that MANOVA 'works best with highly negatively correlated DVs, and acceptably well with moderately correlated DVs in either direction' and that 'MANOVA also is wasteful when DVs are uncorrelated' (p. 268). In contrast, Stevens's (1980) investigation of the effect of dependent variable correlations on test power revealed that 'the power with

high intercorrelations is in most cases greater than that for moderate intercorrelations, and in some cases it is dramatically higher' (p. 736). These findings are slightly contradictory, which leaves us with the puzzling conundrum of what, exactly, the relationship is between power and intercorrelation of the dependent variables. Luckily, Cole, Maxwell, Arvey, and Salas (1994) have done a great deal to illuminate this relationship. They found that the power of MANOVA depends on a combination of the correlation between dependent variables and the effect size to be detected. In short, if you are expecting to find a large effect, then MANOVA will have greater power if the measures are somewhat different (even negatively correlated) and if the group differences are in the same direction for each measure. If you have two dependent variables, one of which exhibits a large group difference, and one of which exhibits a small or no group difference, then power will be increased if these variables are highly correlated. The take-home message from Cole et al.'s work is that if you are interested in how powerful the MANOVA is likely to be you should consider not just the intercorrelation of dependent variables but also the size and pattern of group differences that you expect to get. However, it should be noted that Cole et al.'s work is limited to the case where two groups are being compared, and power considerations are more complex in multiple-group situations.

power to detect an effect, because it can detect whether groups differ along a combination of variables, whereas ANOVA can detect only if groups differ along a single variable (see Jane Superbrain Box 16.1). For these reasons, MANOVA is preferable to conducting several ANOVAs.

16.3.1.   Words of warning ②

From my description of MANOVA it is probably looking like a pretty groovy little test that allows you to measure hundreds of dependent variables and then just sling them into the analysis. This is not the case. It is not a good idea to lump all of your dependent variables together in a MANOVA unless you have a good theoretical or empirical basis for doing so. I mentioned way back at the beginning of this book that statistical procedures are just a way of number crunching and so even if you put rubbish into an analysis you will still reach conclusions that are statistically meaningful, but are unlikely to be empirically meaningful. In circumstances where there is a good theoretical basis for including some but not all of your dependent variables, you should run separate analyses: one for the variables being tested on a heuristic basis and one for the theoretically meaningful variables. The point to take on board here is not to include lots of dependent variables in a MANOVA just because you have measured them.

16.3.2.   The example for this chapter ②

Throughout the rest of this chapter we're going to use a single example to look at how MANOVA works and then how to conduct one using **R**. Imagine that we were interested in the effects of cognitive behaviour therapy (CBT) on obsessive compulsive disorder (OCD). OCD is a disorder characterized by intrusive images or thoughts that the sufferer finds abhorrent (in my case this might be the thought of someone carrying out a t-test on data that are not normally distributed, but in normal people it could be something like imagining your parents have died). These thoughts lead the sufferer to engage in activities to neutralize the unpleasantness of these thoughts (these activities can be mental, such as doing a MANOVA in my head to make me feel better about the t-test thought, or physical, such as touching the floor 23 times so that your parents won't die). Now, we could compare a group of OCD sufferers after CBT and after behaviour therapy (BT) with a group of OCD sufferers who are still awaiting treatment (a no-treatment condition, NT).[2] There are both behavioural and cognitive elements to most psychopathologies. For example, in OCD if someone had an obsession with germs and contamination, this disorder might manifest itself in obsessive hand-washing and would influence not just how many times they actually wash their hands (behaviour), but also the number of times they think about washing their hands (cognitions). If we are interested in seeing how successful a therapy is, it is not enough to look only at behavioural outcomes (such as whether obsessive behaviours are reduced); it is important to establish whether cognitions are being changed also. Hence, in this example two dependent measures were taken: the occurrence of obsession-related behaviours (**Actions**) and the occurrence of obsession-related cognitions (**Thoughts**). These dependent variables were measured on a single day and so represent the number of obsession-related behaviours/thoughts in a normal day.

---

[2] The non-psychologists out there should note that behaviour therapy works on the basis that if you stop the maladaptive behaviours the disorder will go away, whereas cognitive therapy is based on the idea that treating the maladaptive cognitions will stop the disorder.

Table 16.1 Data from **OCD.dat**

Group:	DV 1: Actions			DV 2: Thoughts		
	CBT (1)	BT (2)	NT (3)	CBT (1)	BT (2)	NT (3)
	5	4	4	14	14	13
	5	4	5	11	15	15
	4	1	5	16	13	14
	4	1	4	13	14	14
	5	4	6	12	15	13
	3	6	4	14	19	20
	7	5	7	12	13	13
	6	5	4	15	18	16
	6	2	6	16	14	14
	4	5	5	11	17	18
$\overline{X}$	4.90	3.70	5.00	13.40	15.20	15.00
s	1.20	1.77	1.05	1.90	2.10	2.36
s^2	1.43	3.12	1.11	3.60	4.40	5.56

$$\overline{X}_{grand(Actions)} = 4.53 \qquad \overline{X}_{grand(Thoughts)} = 14.53$$
$$s^2_{grand(Actions)} = 2.1195 \qquad s^2_{grand(Thoughts)} = 4.8780$$

The data are in Table 16.1 and can be found in the file **OCD.dat**. Participants belonged to group 1 (CBT), group 2 (BT) or group 3 (NT), and within these groups all participants had both actions and thoughts measured.

16.4. Theory of MANOVA ③

The theory of MANOVA is very complex to understand without knowing matrix algebra, and frankly matrix algebra is way beyond the scope of this book (those with maths brains can consult Namboodiri, 1984; Stevens, 2002). However, I intend to give a flavour of the conceptual basis of MANOVA, using matrices, without requiring you to understand exactly how those matrices are used. Those interested in the exact underlying theory of MANOVA should read Bray and Maxwell's (1985) superb monograph.

16.4.1. Introduction to matrices ③

A matrix is simply a collection of numbers arranged in columns and rows. In fact, throughout this book you have been using matrices: every dataframe you have created is a matrix but with names for each column. In dataframes we have numbers arranged in columns and rows and this is a matrix. A matrix can have many columns and many rows and we usually specify the dimensions of the matrix using numbers. So, a 2×3 matrix is a matrix with two rows and three columns, and a 5×4 matrix is one with five rows and four columns (examples below):

$$\begin{pmatrix} 2 & 5 & 6 \\ 3 & 5 & 8 \end{pmatrix} \qquad \begin{pmatrix} 2 & 4 & 6 & 8 \\ 3 & 4 & 6 & 7 \\ 4 & 3 & 5 & 8 \\ 2 & 5 & 7 & 9 \\ 4 & 6 & 6 & 9 \end{pmatrix}$$

2×3 matrix $\qquad$ 5×4 matrix

In many of our dataframes we have thought of each row as representing the data from a single participant and each column as representing data relating to a particular variable. So, for the 5×4 matrix, we can imagine a situation where five participants were tested on four variables: the first participant scored 2 on the first variable and 8 on the fourth variable. The values within a matrix are typically referred to as *components* or *elements*.

A **square matrix** is one in which there are equal numbers of columns and rows. In this type of matrix it is sometimes useful to distinguish between the diagonal components (i.e., the values that lie on the diagonal line from the top left component to the bottom right component) and the off-diagonal components (the values that do not lie on the diagonal). In the matrix below, the diagonal components are 5, 12, 2 and 6 because they lie along the diagonal line. The off-diagonal components are all of the other values. A square matrix in which the diagonal elements are equal to 1 and the off-diagonal elements are equal to 0 is known as an **identity matrix**:

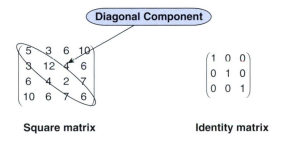

Square matrix $\qquad\qquad$ Identity matrix

Hopefully, the concept of a matrix should now be slightly less scary than it was previously: it is not some magical mathematical entity, merely a way of representing a data set – just like a spreadsheet.

Now, there is a special case of a matrix where there are data from only one entity, and this is known as a *row vector*. Likewise, if there is only one column in a matrix this is known as a *column vector*. In the examples below, the row vector can be thought of as a single person's score on four different variables, whereas the column vector can be thought of as five participants' scores on one variable:

$$\begin{pmatrix} 2 & 6 & 4 & 8 \end{pmatrix} \qquad \begin{pmatrix} 8 \\ 6 \\ 10 \\ 15 \\ 6 \end{pmatrix}$$

Row vector $\qquad$ Column vector

Armed with this knowledge of what vectors are, we can have a brief look at how they are used to conduct MANOVA.

16.4.2.   Some important matrices and their functions ③

As with ANOVA, we are primarily interested in how much variance can be explained by the experimental manipulation (which in real terms means how much variance is explained by the fact that certain scores appear in certain groups). Therefore, we need to know the sum of squares due to the grouping variable (the systematic variation, SS_M), the sum of squares due to natural differences between participants (the residual variation, SS_R) and of course the total amount of variation that needs to be explained (SS_T); for more details about these sources of variation reread Chapters 7 and 10. However, I mentioned that MANOVA also takes into account several dependent variables simultaneously and it does this by using a matrix that contains information about the variance accounted for by each dependent variable. For the univariate F-test (e.g., ANOVA) we calculated the ratio of systematic variance to unsystematic variance for a single dependent variable. In MANOVA, the test statistic is derived by comparing the ratio of systematic to unsystematic variance for several dependent variables. This comparison is made by using the ratio of a matrix representing the systematic variance of all dependent variables to a matrix representing the unsystematic variance of all dependent variables. To sum up, the test statistic in both ANOVA and MANOVA represents the ratio of the effect of the systematic variance to the unsystematic variance; in ANOVA these variances are single values, but in MANOVA each is a matrix containing many variances and covariances.

The matrix that represents the systematic variance (or the model sum of squares for all variables) is denoted by the letter **H** and is called the **hypothesis sum of squares and cross-products matrix** (or **hypothesis SSCP**). The matrix that represents the unsystematic variance (the residual sums of squares for all variables) is denoted by the letter **E** and is called the **error sum of squares and cross-products matrix** (or **error SSCP**). Finally, there is a matrix that represents the total amount of variance present for each dependent variable (the total sums of squares for each dependent variable) and this is denoted by **T** and is called the **total sum of squares and cross-products matrix** (or **total SSCP**).

Later, I will show how these matrices are used in exactly the same way as the simple sums of squares (SS_M, SS_R and SS_T) in ANOVA to derive a test statistic representing the ratio of systematic to unsystematic variance in the model. The observant among you may have noticed that the matrices I have described are all called **sum of squares and cross-products (SSCP) matrices**. It should be obvious why these matrices are referred to as sum of squares matrices, but why is there a reference to cross-products in their name?

SELF-TEST

✓ Can you remember (from Chapter 6) what a cross-product is?

Cross-products represent a total value for the combined error between two variables (so in some sense they represent an unstandardized estimate of the total correlation between two variables). As such, whereas the sum of squares of a variable is the total squared difference between the observed values and the mean value, the cross-product is the total combined error between two variables. I mentioned earlier that MANOVA had the power to account for any correlation between dependent variables, and it does this by using these cross-products.

16.4.3.   Calculating MANOVA by hand: a worked example ③

To begin with, let's carry out univariate ANOVAs on each of the two dependent variables in our OCD example (see Table 16.1). A description of the ANOVA model can be found in Chapter 10, and I will draw heavily on the assumption that you have read this chapter; if you are hazy on the details of Chapter 10 then now would be a good time to (re)read sections 10.2.5–10.2.9.

16.4.3.1. Univariate ANOVA for DV 1 (Actions) ②

There are three sums of squares that need to be calculated. First, we need to assess how much variability there is to be explained within the data (SS_T). Next, we need to see how much of this variability can be explained by the model (SS_M). Finally, we have to assess how much error there is in the model (SS_R). From Chapter 10 we can calculate each of these values:

- $SS_{T(Actions)}$: The total sum of squares is obtained by calculating the difference between each of the 20 scores and the mean of those scores, then squaring these differences and adding these squared values up. Alternatively, you can get **R** to calculate the variance for the action data (regardless of which group the score falls into) and then multiplying this value by the number of scores minus 1:

$$SS_T = s_{grand}^2(n-1)$$
$$= 2.1195(30-1)$$
$$= 2.1195 \times 29$$
$$= 61.47$$

- $SS_{M(Actions)}$: This value is calculated by taking the difference between each group mean and the grand mean and then squaring them. Multiply these values by the number of scores in the group and then add them together:

$$SS_M = 10(4.90-4.53)^2 + 10(3.70-4.53)^2 + 10(5.00-4.53)^2$$
$$= 10(0.37)^2 + 10(-0.83)^2 + 10(0.47)^2$$
$$= 1.37 + 6.89 + 2.21$$
$$= 10.47$$

- $SS_{R(Actions)}$: This value is calculated by taking the difference between each score and the mean of the group from which it came. These differences are then squared and then added together. Alternatively we can get **R** to calculate the variance within each group, multiply each group variance by the number of scores minus 1 and then add them together:

$$SS_R = s_{CBT}^2(n_{CBT}-1) + s_{BT}^2(n_{BT}-1) + s_{NT}^2(n_{NT}-1)$$
$$= (1.433)(10-1) + (3.122)(10-1) + (1.111)(10-1)$$
$$= (1.433 \times 9) + (3.122 \times 9) + (1.111 \times 9)$$
$$= 12.9 + 28.1 + 10.0$$
$$= 51.00$$

The next step is to calculate the average sums of squares (the mean square) of each by dividing by the degrees of freedom (see section 10.2.8):

SS	df	MS
$SS_{M(Actions)} = 10.47$	2	5.235
$SS_{R(Actions)} = 51.00$	27	1.889

The final stage is calculate F by dividing the mean squares for the model by the mean squares for the error in the model:

$$F = \frac{MS_M}{MS_R} = \frac{5.235}{1.889} = 2.771$$

This value can then be evaluated against critical values of F. The point to take home here is the calculation of the various sums of squares and to what each one relates.

16.4.3.2. Univariate ANOVA for DV 2 (Thoughts) ②

As with the data for dependent variable 1, there are three sums of squares that need to be calculated:

- $SS_{T(Thoughts)}$:

$$\begin{aligned} SS_T &= s^2_{grand}(n-1) \\ &= 4.878(30-1) \\ &= 4.878 \times 29 \\ &= 141.46 \end{aligned}$$

- $SS_{M(Thoughts)}$:

$$\begin{aligned} SS_M &= 10(13.40-14.53)^2 + 10(15.2-14.53)^2 + 10(15.0-14.53)^2 \\ &= 10(-1.13)^2 + 10(0.67)^2 + 10(0.47)^2 \\ &= 12.77 + 4.49 + 2.21 \\ &= 19.47 \end{aligned}$$

- $SS_{R(Thoughts)}$:

$$\begin{aligned} SS_R &= s^2_{CBT}(n_{CBT}-1) + s^2_{BT}(n_{BT}-1) + s^2_{NT}(n_{NT}-1) \\ &= (3.6)(10-1) + (4.4)(10-1) + (5.56)(10-1) \\ &= (3.6 \times 9) + (4.4 \times 9) + (5.56 \times 9) \\ &= 32.4 + 39.6 + 50.0 \\ &= 122 \end{aligned}$$

The next step is to calculate the average sums of squares (the mean square) of each by dividing by the degrees of freedom (see section 10.2.8):

SS	df	MS
$SS_{M(Thoughts)} = 19.47$	2	9.735
$SS_{R(Thoughts)} = 122.00$	27	4.519

The final stage is to calculate F by dividing the mean squares for the model by the mean squares for the error in the model:

$$F = \frac{MS_M}{MS_R} = \frac{9.735}{4.519} = 2.154$$

This value can then be evaluated against critical values of F. Again, the point to take home here is the calculation of the various sums of squares and to what each one relates.

16.4.3.3. The relationship between DVs: cross-products ②

We know already that MANOVA uses the same sums of squares as ANOVA, and in the next section we will see exactly how it uses these values. However, I have also mentioned that MANOVA takes account of the relationship between dependent variables by using the cross-products. There are three different cross-products that are of interest, and these three cross-products relate to the three sums of squares that we calculated for the univariate ANOVAs: that is, there is a total cross-product, a cross-product due to the model and a residual cross-product. Let's look at the total cross-product (CP_T) first.

I mentioned in Chapter 6 that the cross-product was the difference between the scores and the mean in one group multiplied by the difference between the scores and the mean in the other group. In the case of the total cross-product, the mean of interest is the grand mean for each dependent variable (see Table 16.2). Hence, we can adapt the cross-product equation described in Chapter 6 using the two dependent variables. The resulting equation for the total cross-product is as follows:

$$CP_T = \sum_{i=1}^{n} \left(x_{i(\text{Actions})} - \overline{X}_{\text{grand (Actions)}} \right)\left(x_{i(\text{Thoughts})} - \overline{X}_{\text{grand (Thoughts)}} \right) \tag{16.1}$$

Therefore, for each dependent variable you take each score and subtract from it the grand mean for that variable. This leaves you with two values per participant (one for each dependent variable), which should be multiplied together to get the cross-product for each participant. The total can then be found by adding the cross-products of all participants. Table 16.2 illustrates this process.

The total cross-product is a gauge of the overall relationship between the two variables. However, we are also interested in how the relationship between the dependent variables is influenced by our experimental manipulation, and this relationship is measured by the model cross-product (CP_M). The CP_M is calculated in a similar way to the model sum of squares. First, the difference between each group mean and the grand mean is calculated for each dependent variable. The cross-product is calculated by multiplying the differences found for each group. Each product is then multiplied by the number of scores within the

Table 16.2 Calculation of the total cross-product

Group	Actions	Thoughts	Actions $-\overline{X}_{grand(Actions)}$ (D_1)	Thoughts $-\overline{X}_{grand(Thoughts)}$ (D_2)	$D_1 \times D_2$
CBT	5	14	0.47	−0.53	−0.25
	5	11	0.47	−3.53	−1.66
	4	16	−0.53	1.47	−0.78
	4	13	−0.53	−1.53	0.81
	5	12	0.47	−2.53	−1.19
	3	14	−1.53	−0.53	0.81
	7	12	2.47	−2.53	−6.25
	6	15	1.47	0.47	0.69
	6	16	1.47	1.47	2.16
	4	11	−0.53	−3.53	1.87
BT	4	14	−0.53	−0.53	0.28
	4	15	−0.53	0.47	−0.25
	1	13	−3.53	−1.53	5.40
	1	14	−3.53	−0.53	1.87
	4	15	−0.53	0.47	−0.25
	6	19	1.47	4.47	6.57
	5	13	0.47	−1.53	−0.72
	5	18	0.47	3.47	1.63
	2	14	−2.53	−0.53	1.34
	5	17	0.47	2.47	1.16
NT	4	13	−0.53	−1.53	0.81
	5	15	0.47	0.47	0.22
	5	14	0.47	−0.53	−0.25
	4	14	−0.53	−0.53	0.28
	6	13	1.47	−1.53	−2.25
	4	20	−0.53	5.47	−2.90
	7	13	2.47	−1.53	−3.78
	4	16	−0.53	1.47	−0.78
	6	14	1.47	−0.53	−0.78
	5	18	0.47	3.47	1.63
$\overline{X}_{grand}$	4.53	14.53		$CP_T = \sum N(D_1 \times D_2) = -5.47$	

group (as was done with the sum of squares). This principle is illustrated in the following equation and Table 16.3:

$$CP_M = \sum_{grp=1}^{k} n\left[\left(\overline{x}_{grp\,(Actions)} - \overline{X}_{grand\,(Actions)}\right)\left(\overline{x}_{grp\,(Thoughts)} - \overline{X}_{grand\,(Thoughts)}\right)\right] \qquad (16.2)$$

Table 16.3 Calculating the model cross-product

	$\overline{X}_{group}$	$\overline{X}_{group} - \overline{X}_{grand}$	$\overline{X}_{group}$	$\overline{X}_{group} - \overline{X}_{grand}$		
	Actions	(D_1)	**Thoughts**	(D_2)	$D_1 \times D_2$	$N(D_1 \times D)_2$
CBT	4.9	0.37	13.4	−1.13	−0.418	−4.18
BT	3.7	−0.83	15.2	0.67	−0.556	−5.56
NT	5.0	0.47	15.0	0.47	0.221	2.21
$\overline{X}_{grand}$	4.53		14.53		$CP_M = \sum N(D_1 \times D_2) = -7.53$	

Finally, we also need to know how the relationship between the two dependent variables is influenced by individual differences in participants' performances. The residual cross-product (CP_R) tells us about how the relationship between the dependent variables is affected by individual differences, or error in the model. CP_R is calculated in a similar way to the total cross-product, except that the group means are used rather than the grand mean (see equation (16.3)). So, to calculate each of the difference scores, we take each score and subtract from it the mean of the group to which it belongs (see Table 16.4):

$$CP_R = \sum_{i=1}^{n} \left(x_{i(\text{Actions})} - \overline{x}_{\text{group (Actions)}} \right) \left(x_{i(\text{Thoughts})} - \overline{x}_{\text{group (Thoughts)}} \right) \tag{16.3}$$

The observant among you may notice that the residual cross-product can also be calculated by subtracting the model cross-product from the total cross-product:

$$CP_R = CP_T - CP_M$$
$$= 5.47 - (-7.53) = 13$$

However, it is useful to calculate the residual cross-product manually in case of mistakes in the calculation of the other two cross-products. The fact that the residual and model cross-products should sum to the value of the total cross-product can be used as a useful double-check.

Each of the different cross-products tells us something important about the relationship between the two dependent variables. Although I have used a simple scenario to keep the maths relatively simple, these principles can be easily extended to more complex scenarios. For example, if we had measured three dependent variables then the cross-products between pairs of dependent variables are calculated (as they were in this example) and entered into the appropriate SSCP matrix (see next section). As the complexity of the situation increases, so does the amount of calculation that needs to be done. At times such as these the benefit of software like **R** becomes ever more apparent.

16.4.3.4. The total SSCP matrix (T) ③

In this example we have only two dependent variables, and so all of the SSCP matrices will be 2×2 matrices. If there had been three dependent variables then the resulting matrices would all be 3×3 matrices. The total SSCP matrix, T, contains the total sums of squares for each dependent variable and the total cross-product between the two dependent variables.

Table 16.4 Calculation of CP_R

Group	Actions	Actions $-\bar{X}_{group(Actions)}$ (D_1)	Thoughts	Thoughts $-\bar{X}_{group(Thoughts)}$ (D_2)	$D_1 \times D_2$
CBT	5	0.10	14	0.60	0.06
	5	0.10	11	−2.40	−0.24
	4	−0.90	16	2.60	−2.34
	4	−0.90	13	−0.40	0.36
	5	0.10	12	−1.40	−0.14
	3	−1.90	14	0.60	−1.14
	7	2.10	12	−1.40	−2.94
	6	1.10	15	1.60	1.76
	6	1.10	16	2.60	2.86
	4	−0.90	11	−2.40	2.16
$\bar{X}_{CBT}$	4.9		13.4		$\Sigma = 0.40$
BT	4	0.30	14	−1.20	−0.36
	4	0.30	15	−0.20	−0.06
	1	−2.70	13	−2.20	5.94
	1	−2.70	14	−1.20	3.24
	4	0.30	15	−0.20	−0.06
	6	2.30	19	3.80	8.74
	5	1.30	13	−2.20	−2.86
	5	1.30	18	2.80	3.64
	2	−1.70	14	−1.20	2.04
	5	1.30	17	1.80	2.34
$\bar{X}_{BT}$	3.7		15.2		$\Sigma = 22.60$
NT	4	−1.00	13	−2.00	2.00
	5	0.00	15	0	0.00
	5	0.00	14	−1.00	0.00
	4	−1.00	14	−1.00	1.00
	6	1.00	13	−2.00	−2.00
	4	−1.00	20	5.00	−5.00
	7	2.00	13	−2.00	−4.00
	4	−1.00	16	1.00	−1.00
	6	1.00	14	−1.00	−1.00
	5	0.00	18	3.00	0.00
$\bar{X}_{NT}$	5		15		$\Sigma = -10.00$

$$CP_R = \sum(D_1 \times D_2) = 13$$

You can think of the first column and first row as representing one dependent variable and the second column and row as representing the second dependent variable:

	Column 1 Actions	Column 2 Thoughts
Row 1 Actions	$SS_{T(Actions)}$	CP_T
Row 2 Thoughts	CP_T	$SS_{T(Thoughts)}$

We calculated these values in the previous sections and so we can simply place the appropriate values in the appropriate cell of the matrix:

$$T = \begin{pmatrix} 61.47 & 5.47 \\ 5.47 & 141.47 \end{pmatrix}$$

From the values in the matrix (and what they represent) it should be clear that the total SSCP represents both the total amount of variation that exists within the data and the total co-dependence that exists between the dependent variables. You should also note that the off-diagonal elements are the same (they are both the total cross-product) because this value is equally important for both of the dependent variables.

16.4.3.5. The residual SSCP matrix (E) ③

The residual (or error) sum of squares and cross-product matrix, E, contains the residual sums of squares for each dependent variable and the residual cross-product between the two dependent variables. This SSCP matrix is similar to the total SSCP, except that the information relates to the error in the model:

	Column 1 Actions	Column 2 Thoughts
Row 1 Actions	$SS_{R(Actions)}$	CP_R
Row 2 Thoughts	CP_R	$SS_{R(Thoughts)}$

We calculated these values in the previous sections and so we can simply place the appropriate values in the appropriate cell of the matrix:

$$E = \begin{pmatrix} 51 & 13 \\ 13 & 122 \end{pmatrix}$$

From the values in the matrix (and what they represent) it should be clear that the residual SSCP represents both the unsystematic variation that exists for each dependent variable and the co-dependence between the dependent variables that is due to chance factors alone. As before, the off-diagonal elements are the same (they are both the residual cross-product).

16.4.3.6. The model SSCP matrix (H) ③

The model (or hypothesis) sum of squares and cross-product matrix, H, contains the model sums of squares for each dependent variable and the model cross-product between the two dependent variables:

	Column 1 Actions	Column 2 Thoughts
Row 1 Actions	$SS_{M(Actions)}$	CP_M
Row 2 Thoughts	CP_M	$SS_{M(Thoughts)}$

We calculated these values in the previous sections and so we can simply place the appropriate values in the appropriate cell of the matrix:

$$H = \begin{pmatrix} 10.47 & -7.53 \\ -7.53 & 19.47 \end{pmatrix}$$

From the values in the matrix (and what they represent) it should be clear that the model SSCP represents both the systematic variation that exists for each dependent variable and the co-dependence between the dependent variables that is due to the model (i.e., is due to the experimental manipulation). As before, the off-diagonal elements are the same (they are both the model cross-product).

Matrices are additive, which means that you can add (or subtract) two matrices together by adding (or subtracting) corresponding elements. Now, when we calculated univariate ANOVA we saw that the total sum of squares was the sum of the model sum of squares and the residual sum of squares (i.e., $SS_T = SS_M + SS_R$). The same is true in MANOVA except that we are adding matrices rather than single values:

$$T = H + E$$
$$T = \begin{pmatrix} 10.47 & -7.53 \\ -7.53 & 19.47 \end{pmatrix} + \begin{pmatrix} 51 & 13 \\ 13 & 122 \end{pmatrix}$$
$$= \begin{pmatrix} 10.47+51 & -7.53+13 \\ -7.53+13 & 19.47+122 \end{pmatrix}$$
$$= \begin{pmatrix} 61.47 & 5.47 \\ 5.47 & 141.47 \end{pmatrix}$$

The demonstration that these matrices add up should (hopefully) help you to understand that the MANOVA calculations are conceptually the same as for univariate ANOVA – the difference is that matrices are used rather than single values.

16.4.4. Principle of the MANOVA test statistic ④

In univariate ANOVA we calculate the ratio of the systematic variance to the unsystematic variance (i.e., we divide SS_M by SS_R).[3] The conceptual equivalent would therefore be to divide the matrix H by the matrix E. There is, however, a problem in that matrices are not divisible by other matrices. However, there is a matrix equivalent to division, which is to multiply by what's known as the inverse of a matrix. So, if we want to divide H by E we have to multiply H by the inverse of E (denoted as E^{-1}). So, therefore, the test statistic is based upon the matrix that results from multiplying the model SSCP with the inverse of the residual SSCP. This matrix is called **HE⁻¹**.

[3] In reality we use the mean squares, but these values are merely the sums of squares corrected for the degrees of freedom.

Calculating the inverse of a matrix is incredibly difficult, and there is no need for you to understand how it is done because **R** will do it for you. However, the interested reader should consult either Stevens (2002) or Namboodiri (1984) – these texts provide very accessible accounts of how to derive an inverse matrix. For readers who do consult these sources, see Oliver Twisted. For the uninterested reader, you'll have to trust me on the following:

$$E^{-1} = \begin{pmatrix} 0.0202 & -0.0021 \\ -0.0021 & 0.0084 \end{pmatrix}$$

$$HE^{-1} = \begin{pmatrix} 0.2273 & -0.0852 \\ -0.1930 & 0.1794 \end{pmatrix}$$

Remember that HE^{-1} represents the ratio of systematic variance in the model to the unsystematic variance in the model, and so the resulting matrix is conceptually the same as the F-ratio in univariate ANOVA. There is another problem, though. In ANOVA, when we divide the systematic variance by the unsystematic variance we get a single figure: the F-ratio. In MANOVA, when we divide the systematic variance by the unsystematic variance we get a matrix containing several values. In this example, the matrix contains four values, but had there been three dependent variables the matrix would have had nine values. In fact, the resulting matrix will always contain p^2 values, where p is the number of dependent variables. The problem is how to convert these matrix values into a meaningful single value. This is the point at which we have to abandon any hope of understanding the maths behind the test and talk conceptually instead.

16.4.4.1. Discriminant function variates ④

The problem of having several values with which to assess statistical significance can be simplified considerably by converting the dependent variables into underlying dimensions or factors (this process will be discussed in more detail in Chapter 17). In Chapter 7, we saw how multiple regression worked on the principle of fitting a linear model to a set of data to predict an outcome variable (the dependent variable in ANOVA terminology). This linear model was made up of a combination of predictor variables (or independent variables) each of which had a unique contribution to this linear model. We can do a similar thing here, except that we are interested in the opposite problem (i.e., predicting an independent variable from a set of dependent variables). So, it is possible to calculate underlying linear dimensions of the dependent variables. These linear combinations of the dependent variables are known as *variates* (or sometimes called *latent variables* or *factors*). In this context we wish to use these linear variates to predict which group a person belongs to (i.e., whether they were given CBT, BT or no treatment), so we are using them to discriminate groups of people. Therefore, these variates are called *discriminant functions* or **discriminant function variates**. Although I have drawn a parallel between these discriminant functions and the model in multiple regression, there is a difference in that we can extract several discriminant functions from a set of dependent variables, whereas in multiple regression all independent variables are included in a single model.

That's the theory in simplistic terms, but how do we discover these discriminant functions? Well, without going into too much detail, we use a mathematical procedure of maximization, such that the first discriminant function (V_1) is the linear combination of dependent variables that maximizes the differences between groups.

It follows from this that the ratio of systematic to unsystematic variance (SS_M/SS_R) will be maximized for this first variate, but subsequent variates will have smaller values of this ratio. Remember that this ratio is an analogue of what the F-ratio represents in univariate ANOVA, and so in effect we obtain the maximum possible value of the F-ratio when we look at the first discriminant function. This variate can be described in terms of a linear regression equation (because it is a linear combination of the dependent variables):

$$y_i = b_0 + b_1 X_{1i} + b_2 X_{2i}$$
$$V_{1i} = b_0 + b_1 DV_{1i} + b_2 DV_{2i}$$
$$\qquad = b_0 + b_1 \text{Actions}_i + b_2 \text{Thoughts}_i \qquad\qquad (16.4)$$

Equation (16.4) shows the multiple regression equation for two predictors and then extends this to show how a comparable form of this equation can describe discriminant functions. The b-values in the equation are weights (just as in regression) that tell us something about the contribution of each dependent variable to the variate in question. In regression, the values of b are obtained by the method of least squares; in discriminant function analysis the values of b are obtained from the *eigenvectors* (see Jane Superbrain Box 16.2) of the matrix HE^{-1}. We can actually ignore b_0 because this serves only to locate the variate in geometric space, which isn't necessary when we're using it to discriminate groups.

In a situation in which there are only two dependent variables and two groups for the independent variable, there will be only one variate. This makes the scenario very simple: by looking at the discriminant function of the dependent variables, rather than looking at the dependent variables themselves, we can obtain a single value of SS_M/SS_R for the discriminant function, and then assess this value for significance. However, in more complex cases where there are more than two dependent variables or more than three levels of the independent variable (as is the case in our example), there will be more than one variate. The number of variates obtained will be the smaller of p (the number of dependent variables) and $k-1$ (where k is the number of levels of the independent variable). In our example, both p and $k-1$ are 2, so we should be able to find two variates. I mentioned earlier that the b-values that describe the variates are obtained by calculating the eigenvectors of the matrix HE^{-1}, and in fact there will be two eigenvectors derived from this matrix: one with the b-values for the first variate, and one with the b-values of the second variate. Conceptually speaking, eigenvectors are the vectors associated with a given matrix that are unchanged by transformation of that matrix to a diagonal matrix (look at Jane Superbrain Box 16.2 for a visual explanation of eigenvectors and eigenvalues). A diagonal matrix is simply a matrix in which the off-diagonal elements are zero and by changing HE^{-1} to a diagonal matrix we eliminate all of the off-diagonal elements (thus reducing the number of values that we must consider for significance testing). Therefore, by calculating the eigenvectors and eigenvalues, we still end up with values that represent the ratio of systematic to unsystematic variance (because they are unchanged by the transformation), but there are considerably less of them. The calculation of eigenvectors is extremely complex (insane students can consider reading Namboodiri, 1984), so you can trust me that for the matrix HE^{-1} the eigenvectors obtained are:

$$\text{eigenvector}_1 = \begin{pmatrix} 0.603 \\ -0.335 \end{pmatrix}$$

$$\text{eigenvector}_2 = \begin{pmatrix} 0.425 \\ 0.339 \end{pmatrix}$$

JANE SUPERBRAIN 16.2

What are eigenvectors and eigenvalues? ④

The definitions and mathematics of eigenvalues and eigenvectors are very complicated and most of us need not worry about them (although they do crop up again in this chapter and the next). However, although the mathematics is hard, they are quite easy to visualize! Imagine we have two variables: the salary a supermodel earns in a year, and how attractive she is. Also imagine these two variables are normally distributed and so can be considered together as a bivariate

at 90 degrees, which means that they are independent of one another). So, with two variables, eigenvectors are just lines measuring the length and height of the ellipse that surrounds the scatterplot of data for those variables. If we add a third variable (e.g., experience of the supermodel) then all that happens is our scatterplot gets a third dimension, the ellipse turns into something shaped like a rugby ball (or American football), and because we now have a third dimension (height, width and depth) we get an extra eigenvector to measure this extra dimension. If we add a fourth variable, a similar logic applies (although it's harder to visualize): we get an extra dimension, and an eigenvector to measure that dimension. Now, each eigenvector has an *eigenvalue* that tells us its length (i.e., the distance from one end of the eigenvector to the other). So, by looking at all of the eigenvalues for a data set, we know the dimensions of the ellipse or rugby ball: put more generally, we know the dimensions of the data. Therefore, the eigenvalues show how evenly (or otherwise) the variances of the matrix are distributed.

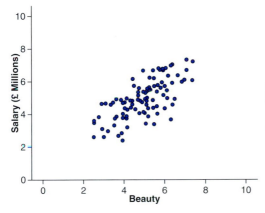

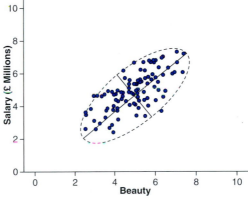

normal distribution. If these variables are correlated, then their scatterplot forms an ellipse. This is shown in the scatterplots above: if we draw a dashed line around the outer values of the scatterplot we get something oval shaped. Now, we can draw two lines to measure the length and height of this ellipse. These lines are the *eigenvectors* of the original correlation matrix for these two variables (a vector is just a set of numbers that tells us the location of a line in geometric space). Note that the two lines we've drawn (one for height and one for width of the oval) are perpendicular; that is, they are

In the case of two variables, the *condition* of the data is related to the ratio of the larger eigenvalue to the smaller. Let's look at the two extremes: when there is no relationship at all between variables, and when there is a perfect relationship. When there is no relationship, the scatterplot will, more or less, be contained within a circle (or a sphere if we had three variables). If we again draw lines that measure the height and width of this circle we'll find that these lines are the same length. The eigenvalues measure the length, therefore the eigenvalues will also be the same. So, when we divide the largest eigenvalue

(Continued)

(Continued)

by the smallest we'll get a value of 1 (because the eigenvalues are the same). When the variables are perfectly correlated (i.e., there is perfect collinearity) then the scatterplot forms a straight line and the ellipse surrounding it will also collapse to a straight line. Therefore, the height of the ellipse will be very small indeed (it will approach zero). Therefore, when we divide the largest eigenvalue by the smallest we'll get a value that tends to infinity (because the smallest eigenvalue is close to zero). Therefore, an infinite condition index is a sign of deep trouble.

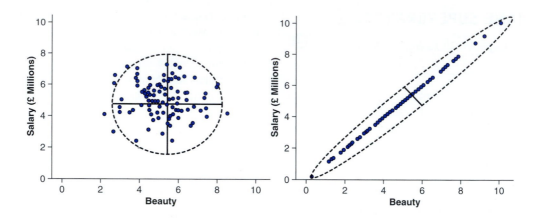

Replacing these values into the two equations for the variates and bearing in mind we can ignore b_0, we obtain the models described in the following equation:

$$V_{1i} = b_0 + 0.603\text{Actions}_i - 0.335\text{Thoughts}_i$$
$$V_{2i} = b_0 + 0.425\text{Actions}_i + 0.339\text{Thoughts}_i$$

(16.5)

It is possible to use the equations for each variate to calculate a score for each person on the variate. For example, the first participant in the CBT group carried out 5 obsessive actions, and had 14 obsessive thoughts. Therefore, this participant's score on variate 1 would be −1.675:

$$V_1 = (0.603 \times 5) - (0.335 \times 14) = -1.675$$

The score for variate 2 would be 6.87:

$$V_2 = (0.425 \times 5) + (0.339 \times 14) = 6.871$$

If we calculated these variate scores for each participant and then calculated the SSCP matrices (e.g., H, E, T and HE^{-1}) that we used previously, we would find that all of them have cross-products of zero. The reason for this is that the variates extracted from the data are orthogonal, which means that they are uncorrelated. In short, the variates extracted are independent dimensions constructed from a linear combination of the dependent variables that were measured.

This data reduction has a very useful property in that if we look at the matrix HE^{-1} calculated from the variate scores (rather than the dependent variables) we find that all of the off-diagonal elements (the cross-products) are zero. The diagonal elements of this matrix represent the ratio of the systematic variance to the unsystematic variance (i.e., SS_M/SS_R) for each of the underlying variates. So, for the data in this example, this means that instead of having four values representing the ratio of systematic to unsystematic variance, we now have only two. This reduction may not seem a lot. However, in general if we have p dependent variables, then ordinarily we would end up with p^2 values representing the ratio of systematic to unsystematic variance; by looking at discriminant functions, we reduce this number to p. If there were four dependent variables we would end up with four values rather than 16 (which highlights the benefit of this process).

For the data in our example, the matrix HE^{-1} calculated from the variate scores is:

$$HE^{-1}_{variates} = \begin{pmatrix} 0.335 & 0.000 \\ 0.000 & 0.073 \end{pmatrix}$$

It is clear from this matrix that we have two values to consider when assessing the significance of the group differences. It probably seems like a complex procedure to reduce the data down in this way: however, it transpires that the values along the diagonal of the matrix for the variates (namely 0.335 and 0.073) are the *eigenvalues* of the original HE^{-1} matrix. Therefore, these values can be calculated directly from the data collected without first forming the eigenvectors. If you have lost all sense of rationality and want to see how these eigenvalues are calculated then see Oliver Twisted. These eigenvalues are conceptually equivalent to the F-ratio in ANOVA and so the final step is to assess how large these values are compared to what we would expect by chance alone. There are four ways in which the values are assessed.

OLIVER TWISTED

Please Sir, can I have some more … maths?

'You are a bit stupid. I think it would be fun to check your maths so that we can see exactly how much of a village idiot you are', mocks Oliver. Luckily you can. Never one to shy from public humiliation on a mass scale, I have provided the matrix calculations for this example on the companion website. Find a mistake, go on, you know that you can …

16.4.4.2. Pillai–Bartlett trace (V) ④

The **Pillai–Bartlett trace** (also known as Pillai's trace) is given by

$$V = \sum_{i=1}^{s} \frac{\lambda_i}{1+\lambda_i} \tag{16.6}$$

in which λ represents the eigenvalues for each of the discriminant variates and s represents the number of variates. Pillai's trace is the sum of the proportion of explained variance on the discriminant functions. As such, it is similar to the ratio of SS_M/SS_T, which is known as R^2.

For our data, Pillai's trace turns out to be 0.319, which can be transformed to a value that has an approximate F-distribution:

$$V = \frac{0.335}{1+0.335} + \frac{0.073}{1+0.073} = 0.319$$

16.4.4.3. Hotelling's T^2 ④

The **Hotelling–Lawley trace** (also known as Hotelling's T^2; Figure 16.2) is simply the sum of the eigenvalues for each variate:

$$T = \sum_{i=1}^{s} \lambda_i \tag{16.7}$$

So for these data its value is 0.408 (0.335 + 0.073). This test statistic is the sum of SS_M/SS_R for each of the variates and so it compares directly to the F-ratio in ANOVA.

FIGURE 16.2
Harold Hotelling enjoying my favourite activity of drinking tea

16.4.4.4. Wilks's lambda (Λ) ④

Wilks's lambda is the product of the *unexplained* variance on each of the variates:

$$\Lambda = \prod_{i=1}^{s} \frac{1}{1+\lambda_i} \tag{16.8}$$

The $\prod$ symbol is similar to the summation symbol (Σ) that we have encountered already except that it means *multiply* rather than add up. So, Wilks's lambda represents the ratio of error variance to total variance (SS_R/SS_T) for each variate.

For the data in this example the value is

$$\Lambda = \left(\frac{1}{1+0.335}\right)\left(\frac{1}{1+0.073}\right) = 0.698$$

and it should be clear that large eigenvalues (which in themselves represent a large experimental effect) lead to small values of Wilks's lambda – hence statistical significance is found when Wilks's lambda is small.

16.4.4.5. Roy's largest root ④

Roy's largest root always makes me think of some bearded statistician with a garden spade digging up an enormous parsnip (or similar root vegetable); however, it isn't a parsnip but, as the name suggests, is the eigenvalue for the first variate. So, in a sense it is the same as the Hotelling–Lawley trace but for the first variate only, that is:

$$\theta = \lambda_{\text{largest}} \qquad\qquad (16.9)$$

As such, Roy's largest root represents the proportion of explained variance to unexplained variance (SS_M/SS_R) for the first discriminant function.[4] For the data in this example, the value of Roy's largest root is simply 0.335 (the eigenvalue for the first variate). So, this value is conceptually the same as the *F*-ratio in univariate ANOVA. It should be apparent, from what we have learnt about the maximizing properties of these discriminant variates, that Roy's root represents the maximum possible between-group difference given the data collected. Therefore, this statistic should in many cases be the most powerful.

16.5. Practical issues when conducting MANOVA ③

There are three main practical issues to be considered before running MANOVA. First of all, as always, we have to consider the assumptions of the test. Next, for the main analysis there are four commonly used ways of assessing the overall significance of a MANOVA, and debate exists about which method is best in terms of power and sample size considerations. Finally, we also need to think about what analysis to do *after* the MANOVA: like ANOVA, MANOVA is a two-stage test in which an overall (or omnibus) test is first performed before more specific procedures are applied to tease apart group differences. As you will see, there is substantial debate over how best to further analyse and interpret group differences when the overall MANOVA is significant. We will look at these issues in turn.

16.5.1. Assumptions and how to check them ③

MANOVA has similar assumptions to ANOVA but extended to the multivariate case:

- **Independence**: Observations should be statistically independent.
- **Random sampling**: Data should be randomly sampled from the population of interest and measured at an interval level.
- **Multivariate normality**: In ANOVA, we assume that our dependent variable is normally distributed within each group. In the case of MANOVA, we assume that the dependent variables (collectively) have multivariate normality within groups.
- **Homogeneity of covariance matrices**: In ANOVA, it is assumed that the variances in each group are roughly equal (homogeneity of variance). In MANOVA we must assume that this is true for each dependent variable, but also that the correlation between any two dependent variables is the same in all groups. This assumption is examined by testing whether the population **variance–covariance matrices** of the different groups in the analysis are equal.[5]

---

[4] This statistic is sometimes characterized as $\lambda_{\text{largest}}/(1+\lambda_{\text{largest}})$ but this is not the statistic reported by **R**.

[5] For those of you who read about SSCP matrices, if you think about the relationship between sums of squares and variance, and cross-products and correlations, it should be clear that a variance–covariance matrix is basically a standardized form of an SSCP matrix.

Most of the assumptions can be checked in the same way as for univariate tests (see Chapter 10); the additional assumptions of multivariate normality and equality of covariance matrices require different procedures. The assumption of multivariate normality can be tested using **R** with a test known as the Shapiro test that we used to test for univariate normality; however, this version of the test looks for multivariate normality. We can also look at some graphical displays of multivariate outliers produced by the **aq.plot()** function of the *mvoutlier* package.

The assumption of equality of covariance matrices is often tested using **Box's test**. This test should be non-significant if the matrices are the same. The effect of violating this assumption is unclear, except that Hotelling's T^2 is robust in the two-group situation when sample sizes are equal (Hakstian, Roed, & Lind, 1979). Box's test is notoriously susceptible to deviations from multivariate normality and so can be non-significant not because the matrices are similar, but because the assumption of multivariate normality is not tenable. Also, as with any significance test, in large samples Box's test could be significant even when covariance matrices are relatively similar. As a general rule, if sample sizes are equal then people tend to disregard Box's test, because (1) it is unstable, and (2) in this situation we can assume that Hotelling's and Pillai's statistics are robust (see section 16.5.2). For these reasons Box's test has yet to be implemented in **R** because it is of questionable use given its inaccuracy.

However, if group sizes are different, then robustness of the MANOVA cannot be assumed. The more dependent variables you have measured, and the greater the differences in sample sizes, the more distorted the probability values become. Tabachnick and Fidell (2007) suggest that if the larger samples produce greater variances and covariances then the probability values will be conservative (and so significant findings can be trusted). However, if it is the smaller samples that produce the larger variances and covariances then the probability values will be liberal and so significant differences should be treated with caution (although non-significant effects can be trusted). Therefore, the variance–covariance matrices for samples should be inspected to assess whether the printed probabilities for the multivariate test statistics are likely to be conservative or liberal. In the event that you cannot trust the printed probabilities, there is little you can do except equalize the samples by randomly deleting cases in the larger groups (although with this loss of information comes a loss of power). Of course, if you like a belt and braces approach, you can always check your results by using a robust MANOVA too.

16.5.2.   Choosing a test statistic ③

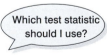

Which test statistic should I use?

Only when there is one underlying variate will the four test statistics necessarily be the same. Therefore, it is important to know which test statistic is best in terms of test power and robustness. A lot of research has investigated the power of the four MANOVA test statistics (Olson, 1974, 1976, 1979; Stevens, 1980). Olson (1974) observed that for small and moderate sample sizes the four statistics differ little in terms of power. If group differences are concentrated on the first variate (as will often be the case in social science research) Roy's statistic should prove most powerful (because it takes account of only that first variate), followed by Hotelling's trace, Wilks's lambda and Pillai's trace. However, when groups differ along more than one variate, the power ordering is the reverse (i.e., Pillai's trace is most powerful and Roy's root is least). One final issue pertinent to test power is that of sample size and the number of dependent variables. Stevens (1980) recommends using fewer than 10 dependent variables unless sample sizes are large.

In terms of robustness, all four test statistics are relatively robust to violations of multivariate normality (although Roy's root is affected by platykurtic distributions – see Olson, 1976). Roy's root is also not robust when the homogeneity of covariance matrix assumption is untenable (Stevens, 1979). The work of Olson and Stevens led Bray and Maxwell (1985) to conclude that when sample sizes are equal the Pillai–Bartlett trace is the most robust to violations of assumptions. However, when sample sizes are unequal this statistic is affected by violations of the assumption of equal covariance matrices. As a rule, with unequal group sizes, check the homogeneity of covariance matrices; if they seem homogeneous and if the assumption of multivariate normality is tenable, then assume that Pillai's trace is accurate.

16.5.3. Follow-up analysis ③

There is some controversy over how best to follow up the main MANOVA. The traditional approach is to follow a significant MANOVA with separate ANOVAs on each of the dependent variables. If this approach is taken, you might well wonder why we bother with the MANOVA in the first place (earlier on I said that multiple ANOVAs were a bad thing to do). Well, the ANOVAs that follow a significant MANOVA are said to be 'protected' by the initial MANOVA (Bock, 1975). The idea is that the overall multivariate test protects against inflated Type I error rates because if that initial test is non-significant (i.e., the null hypothesis is true) then any subsequent tests are ignored (any significance must be a Type I error because the null hypothesis is true). However, the notion of protection is somewhat fallacious because a significant MANOVA, more often than not, reflects a significant difference for one, but not all, of the dependent variables. Subsequent ANOVAs are then carried out on all of the dependent variables, but the MANOVA protects only the dependent variable for which group differences genuinely exist (see Bray and Maxwell, 1985, pp. 40–41). Therefore, you might want to consider applying a Bonferroni correction to the subsequent ANOVAs (Harris, 1975).

By following up a MANOVA with ANOVAs you assume that the significant MANOVA is not due to the dependent variables representing a set of underlying dimensions that differentiate the groups. Therefore, some researchers advocate the use of discriminant analysis, which finds the linear combination(s) of the dependent variables that best *separates* (or discriminates) the groups. This procedure is more in keeping with the ethos of MANOVA because it embraces the relationships that exist between dependent variables and it is certainly useful for illuminating the relationship between the dependent variables and group membership. The major advantage of this approach over multiple ANOVAs is that it reduces and explains the dependent variables in terms of a set of underlying dimensions thought to reflect substantive theoretical dimensions. We will consider both approaches.

16.6. MANOVA using R ②

In the remainder of this chapter we will use the OCD data to illustrate how MANOVA is done (those of you who skipped the theory section should refer to Table 16.1).

16.6.1. Packages for factorial ANOVA in R ①

You will need the packages *car* (for looking at Type III sums of squares), *ggplot2* (for graphs), *MASS* (for discriminant function analysis), *mvoutlier* (for plots to look for multivariate outliers), *mvnormtest* (to test for multivariate normality), *pastecs* (for descriptive statistics), *reshape* (for reshaping the data) and *WRS* (for robust tests). The *MASS* package is automatically installed, but you can install any of the others that you don't already have by executing the following commands:

```
install.packages("car"); install.packages("ggplot2"); install.
packages("mvoutlier"); install.packages("mvnormtest"); install.
packages("pastecs"); install.packages("reshape"); install.
packages("WRS", repos="http://R-Forge.R-project.org")
```

You then need to load these packages by executing these commands:

```
library(car); library(ggplot2); library(MASS); library(mvoutlier);
library(mvnormtest); library(pastecs); library(reshape); library(WRS)
```

16.6.2.   General procedure for MANOVA ①

To conduct factorial MANOVA you should follow this general procedure:

1 *Enter data.*

2 *Explore your data*: begin by graphing the data and computing descriptive statistics. You should check multivariate normality and take a look at the variance–covariance matrices for each group.

3 *Set contrasts for all predictor variables*: you need to decide what contrasts to do and to specify them appropriately for all of the independent variables in your analysis.

4 *Compute the MANOVA*: you can then run the main multivariate analysis of variance. Depending on what you found in the previous step, you might need to run a robust version of the test.

5 *Run univariate ANOVAs*: having conducted the MANOVA, you can follow it up with separate ANOVAs for each dependent variable.

6 *Discriminant function analysis*: better than the option above, consider running a discriminant function analysis.

We will work through these steps in turn.

16.6.3.   MANOVA using R Commander ②

You cannot directly do a MANOVA using R Commander. It's not all bad news, though, because if you've reached this point in the book without giving up or hurling yourself or the book out of the window, then MANOVA will be easy: the commands are pretty straightforward compared to some of the things we've covered.

16.6.4.   Entering the data ②

The data for the example can be found in the file **OCD.dat**. You can load this data file by setting your working directory and executing:

```
ocdData<-read.delim("OCD.dat", header = TRUE)
```

If we look at the data (by executing *ocdData*) we will see that it has been entered in 'wide' format; that is, *levels of a between-group variable go in a single column.*

		Group	Actions	Thoughts
1		CBT	5	14
2		CBT	5	11
3		CBT	4	16
4		CBT	4	13
5		CBT	5	12
6		CBT	3	14
7		CBT	7	12
8		CBT	6	15
9		CBT	6	16
10		CBT	4	11
11		BT	4	14
12		BT	4	15
13		BT	1	13
14		BT	1	14
15		BT	4	15
16		BT	6	19
17		BT	5	13
18		BT	5	18
19		BT	2	14
20		BT	5	17
21	No Treatment Control		4	13
22	No Treatment Control		5	15
23	No Treatment Control		5	14
24	No Treatment Control		4	14
25	No Treatment Control		6	13
26	No Treatment Control		4	20
27	No Treatment Control		7	13
28	No Treatment Control		4	16
29	No Treatment Control		6	14
30	No Treatment Control		5	18

These data were originally entered in Excel, and, as you can see, we have a coding variable to represent the treatment condition. Therefore, in Excel, I created a variable called **Group** into which I typed 'CBT', 'BT' or 'No Treatment Control'; because I have used words rather than numbers, when **R** imports the data it guesses that this variable is a factor (i.e., we don't need to explicitly convert it to a factor). It will treat the order of categories as alphabetic; in other words the factor levels are treated as BT, CBT and No Treatment Control rather than the order they were entered into Excel (which was CBT, BT, No Treatment Condition). Let's reorder the levels so that the order matches the original data using the *levels* option of the *factor()* function. While we're at it, I want to rename 'No Treatment Control' as 'NT' for various reasons. We can do this using the *labels* option of the *factor()* function.

```
ocdData$Group<-factor(ocdData$Group, levels = c("CBT", "BT", "No Treatment
Control"), labels = c("CBT", "BT", "NT"))
```

By executing the above command we take the **Group** variable from the *ocdData* dataframe and reorder the levels as 'CBT', 'BT' and 'No Treatment Control' (*levels = c("CBT", "BT", "No Treatment Control")*). We then relabel these levels as 'CBT', 'BT' and 'NT' (*labels = c("CBT", "BT", "NT")*).

The scores for each outcome measure are stored in two columns labelled **Actions** and **Thoughts**. From this, we can tell, for example, that participant 15 had behaviour therapy (BT) and had four obsession-related actions and 15 obsession-related thoughts.

If we wanted to enter the data directly into **R**, we would create a coding variable called **Group** using the *gl()* function (Chapter 3). This function creates a coding variable based on the number of groups you want and how many cases are in each group. You can use the *labels* option to list names for each group. For **Group**, we want three treatment groups each containing 10 participants, so we can specify it as:

```
Group<-gl(3, 10, labels = c("CBT", "BT", "NT"))
```

The numbers in the function tell **R** that we want three groups of 10 cases, and the *labels* option then specifies the names to attach to these three groups.

We can create numeric variables containing the number of obsession-related **Actions** and **Thoughts** in the usual way:

```
Actions<-c(5, 5, 4, 4, 5, 3, 7, 6, 6, 4, 4, 4, 1, 1, 4, 6, 5, 5, 2, 5, 4, 5,
5, 4, 6, 4, 7, 4, 6, 5)
Thoughts<-c(14, 11, 16, 13, 12, 14, 12, 15, 16, 11, 14, 15, 13, 14, 15, 19,
13, 18, 14, 17, 13, 15, 14, 14, 13, 20, 13, 16, 14, 18)
```

Finally, we can merge these variables into a dataframe called *ocdData* by executing:

```
ocdData<-data.frame(Group, Actions, Thoughts)
```

16.6.5.   Exploring the data ②

Let's start by looking at the relationship between thoughts and actions for the different conditions. The resulting plot (Figure 16.3) shows no relationship between obsession-related thoughts and behaviours in the CBT group, a positive relationship in the BT group and a negative relationship in the NT group.

SELF-TEST

✓ Use *ggplot2* to plot a scatterplot of the number of obsession-related actions (*x*-axis) against obsession-related thoughts (*y*-axis) for each treatment group (as separate panels).

FIGURE 16.3
Scatterplot of the relationship between obsession-related thoughts and actions in different treatment conditions

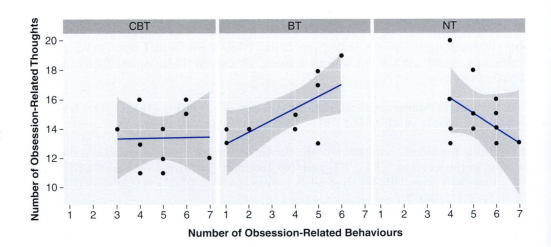

Let's look now at the mean number of obsession-related thoughts and behaviours across the three groups.

Figure 16.4 shows the resulting plot. For actions, BT appears to reduce the number of obsessive behaviours compared to CBT and NT. For thoughts, CBT reduces the number of obsessive thoughts compared to BT and NT.

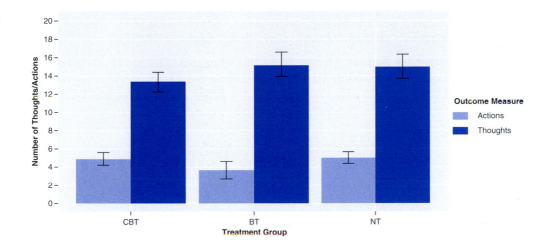

FIGURE 16.4
Error bar chart showing the mean numbers of obsession-related thoughts and actions across the different treatment conditions

Finally, we can also look at boxplots to see the distribution of scores for the number of obsession-related thoughts and actions across the different treatment groups.

Figure 16.5 shows the resulting graph. It is fairly clear that the range and distribution of scores are reasonably similar across groups and across measures (all of the boxes and whiskers are a similar vertical length. The only noteworthy point really is that there is some evidence of an outlier in the no-treatment group (for **Thoughts**) and, in the same group, scores for **Actions** seem like they might be a little skewed (there is no lower tail).

FIGURE 16.5
Boxplots of the
OCD data

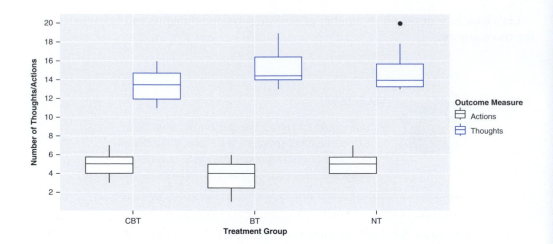

Next, we can use the *by()* function and the *stat.desc()* function in the *pastecs* package to get descriptive statistics for separate groups (see Chapter 5 for more detail). We execute separate commands for **Thoughts** and **Actions**:

```
by(ocdData$Actions, ocdData$Group, stat.desc, basic = FALSE)
by(ocdData$Thoughts, ocdData$Group, stat.desc, basic = FALSE)
```

The resulting output for **Actions** (Output 16.1) and **Thoughts** (Output 16.2) corresponds to the values calculated by hand in Table 16.1 and shows much the same as Figure 16.4: that BT seemed to lower behaviours compared to the other groups whereas CBT resulted in lower numbers of thoughts than the other groups.

```
ocdData$Group: CBT
median   mean    SE.mean CI.mean.0.95  var    std.dev   coef.var
5.000    4.900   0.379   0.856         1.433  1.197     0.244
-----------------------------------------------------------------
ocdData$Group: BT
median   mean    SE.mean CI.mean.0.95  var    std.dev   coef.var
4.000    3.700   0.559   1.264         3.122  1.767     0.478
-----------------------------------------------------------------
ocdData$Group: NT
median   mean    SE.mean CI.mean.0.95  var    std.dev   coef.var
5.000    5.000   0.333   0.754         1.111  1.054     0.211
```

Output 16.1

```
ocdData$Group: CBT
median   mean    SE.mean CI.mean.0.95  var    std.dev   coef.var
13.500   13.400  0.600   1.357         3.600  1.897     0.142
-----------------------------------------------------------------
ocdData$Group: BT
median   mean    SE.mean CI.mean.0.95  var    std.dev   coef.var
14.500   15.200  0.663   1.501         4.400  2.098     0.138
-----------------------------------------------------------------
ocdData$Group: NT
median   mean    SE.mean CI.mean.0.95  var    std.dev   coef.var
14.000   15.000  0.745   1.686         5.556  2.357     0.157
```

Output 16.2

Having looked at the data in summary form, we can start to look at assumptions. To check the homogeneity of covariance matrices we don't do a formal test, but simply compare the values within them. To get the variance–covariance matrices for each group we can again use the *by()* function but in combination with the *cov()* function, which can be used to print the covariance matrix to the console.

```
by(ocdData[, 2:3], ocdData$Group, cov)
```

The above command takes columns 2 and 3 of the *ocdData* dataframe (*ocdData[, 2:3]*), which means that we're selecting the columns that contain the variables **Actions** and **Thoughts**. The command then applies the function *cov()* to these columns, but splits the output by the variable *Group* (*ocdData$Group*).

Output 16.3 shows the variance–covariances matrices for each group. The diagonal elements represent the variances for each outcome measure and the off-diagonals are the covariances (i.e., the relationship between thoughts and actions). The variances for actions are a little different across groups (1.43, 3.12 and 1.11), with the largest variance being nearly three times as big as the smallest. The variances for thoughts are really quite similar (3.60, 4.40, and 5.56), with a variance ratio (the largest variance relative to smallest) of about 1.5, which is below the threshold of 2. Looking at the covariances, these are also reasonably different (0.04, 2.51, and −1.11) reflecting the different relationships between thoughts and actions across the groups that we saw in Figure 16.3. On balance, there is evidence to suggest that the matrices are different across groups; however, given the group sizes are equal we probably don't need to worry too much about these differences. However, if we had different group sizes then remember that: (1) if the larger samples produce greater variances and covariances then the probability values will be conservative (and so significant findings can be trusted); and (2) if it is the smaller samples that produce the larger variances and covariances then the probability values will be liberal and so significant differences in the MANOVA should be treated with caution. In any case, for the current data it would be sensible to carry out a robust analysis as well as the normal one.

```
ocdData$Group: CBT
            Actions    Thoughts
Actions   1.43333333 0.04444444
Thoughts 0.04444444 3.60000000
-----------------------------------------------------------------
ocdData$Group: BT
          Actions Thoughts
Actions   3.122222 2.511111
Thoughts 2.511111 4.400000
-----------------------------------------------------------------
ocdData$Group: NT
            Actions   Thoughts
Actions    1.111111 -1.111111
Thoughts -1.111111  5.555556
```

Output 16.3

The final assumption that we need to test is multivariate normality. We can do this using the *mshapiro.test()* function in the *mvnormtest* package. We need to apply this test to the groups individually, so the first thing to do is to extract the data for each group. We learnt how to do this in section 3.9.1. For example, to get the CBT group data we could execute:

```
cbt<-ocdData[1:10, 2:3]
```

This command creates a variable called *cbt* that is a subset of the *ocdData* dataframe. The square brackets indicate that we want a selection of the data, the *1:10* indicates the rows that we want to select (i.e., rows 1 to 10 inclusive), and *2:3* indicates the columns that we want to select (i.e., columns 2 and 3). This gives us the following data:

```
   Actions Thoughts
1        5        14
2        5        11
3        4        16
4        4        13
5        5        12
6        3        14
7        7        12
8        6        15
9        6        16
10       4        11
```

The *mshapiro.test()* function needs these data in a format such that actions and thoughts appear in rows rather than columns, and the participants appear in columns rather than rows. Fortunately this can be done easily using the transpose function *t()*. This function simply transposes the rows and columns; so, by executing:

```
cbt<-t(cbt)
```

we change the variable cbt so that it is a transposed version of the original variable:

```
          1  2  3  4  5  6  7  8  9 10
Actions   5  5  4  4  5  3  7  6  6  4
Thoughts 14 11 16 13 12 14 12 15 16 11
```

We can do the same for the BT and NT groups. However, it is quicker if we do the transpose at the same time as creating the variable (for *cbt* I split the process into two stages only so you could see what was happening). Therefore, executing:

```
bt<-t(ocdData[11:20, 2:3])
nt<-t(ocdData[21:30, 2:3])
```

creates a variable *bt*, which is rows 11 to 20 and columns 2 and 3 of the original dataframe, and *nt*, which is rows 21 to 30 and columns 2 and 3 of the original dataframe. In both cases we apply the transform function, *t()*, to get the extracted data in the correct format for *mshapiro.test()*. To apply the test, we simply execute the function on each of the three variables that we have just created:

```
mshapiro.test(cbt)
mshapiro.test(bt)
mshapiro.test(nt)
```

Output 16.4 shows the results of the three tests: if the *p* value is less than .05 then our data deviate from multivariate normality. It's clear that for the CBT ($p = .777$) and BT ($p = .175$) groups there is no problem because both results are non-significant; however, for the NT group ($p = .03$) the data deviate significantly from multivariate normality.

```
> mshapiro.test(cbt)
        Shapiro-Wilk normality test
data:   Z
W = 0.9592, p-value = 0.7767
> mshapiro.test(bt)
        Shapiro-Wilk normality test
data:   Z
W = 0.8912, p-value = 0.175
> mshapiro.test(nt)
        Shapiro-Wilk normality test
data:   Z
W = 0.826, p-value = 0.02998
```

Output 16.4

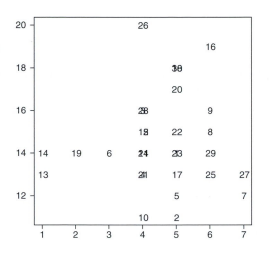

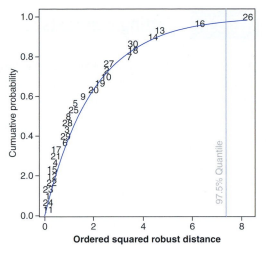

FIGURE 16.6
AQ plot of the OCD data

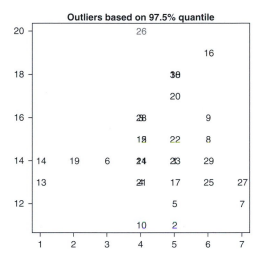

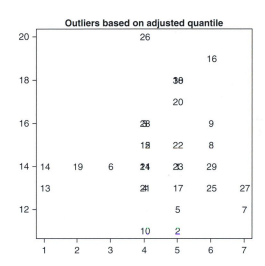

We can also look for multivariate outliers using the *aq.plot()* function from the *mvoutlier* package. All we need to do is enter the columns of the dataframe containing the outcome measures into the function. For example, executing:

```
aq.plot(ocdData[, 2:3])
```

will produce the plot for the current data; remember that *ocdData[, 2:3]* means 'select all of the rows (because there is nothing before the comma) but only columns 2 to 3 (because we have specified *2:3* after the comma)'. In other words, we're selecting only the variables **Actions** (column 2) and **Thoughts** (column 3). The resulting plot is shown in Figure 16.6. These plots show the case numbers (i.e., the row number in the dataframe) and you need to look for values in red (or, because this book isn't in colour, blue in Figure 16.6) in all but the top right graph. You can see that row 26 might be an outlier. In the top right plot, you are looking for any cases that fall to the right of the vertical line labelled *97.5% Quantile*. Again, row 26 of the dataframe has been identified. These plots, therefore, suggest that row 26 might be an outlier. You could consider deleting this case to see if it makes the data multivariate normal, or leave the case in and conduct a robust MANOVA to combat the effects of the outlier.

SELF-TEST

✓ Delete case 26 from the dataframe and redo the Shapiro test of multivariate normality.

16.6.6.   Setting contrasts ②

One way to follow up a MANOVA is to look at individual univariate ANOVAs for each dependent variable. For these tests, you can specify contrasts just as we have in several other chapters (see, for example, section 10.6.7). For this example it makes sense to compare each of the treatment groups to the no-treatment control group. This is the treatment contrast described in Table 10.6. The no-treatment control group was coded as the last category, so we could set this contrast by executing:

```
contrasts(ocdData$Group)<-contr.treatment(3, base = 3)
```

The *contrasts(ocdData$Group)* just tells **R** that we want to set the contrast for the **Group** variable, then *contr.treatment* sets the contrast to be a treatment contrast. The *3* indicates that **Group** has three levels, and *base = 3* sets level 3 (i.e., NT) as the baseline category.

I like to set the contrasts manually so that I can give them names that will help me to interpret the output, so alternatively, we could set the contrasts by executing:

```
CBT_vs_NT<-c(1, 0, 0)
BT_vs_NT <-c(0, 1, 0)
contrasts(ocdData$Group)<-cbind(CBT_vs_NT, BT_vs_NT)
```

One important point here is that we're using a non-orthogonal contrast, which means that we can't look at Type III sums of squares because their computation requires orthogonal contrasts. However, we have only one predictor (**Group**) so this doesn't matter, because the Type I sums of squares produced by **R** will be the same as the Type III when there is only one variable in the model (refer back to Jane Superbrain Box 11.1 for an explanation of why).

16.6.7.   The MANOVA model ②

To create a MANOVA model we use the **manova()** function, which is just the *lm()* function in disguise. Therefore, we can use what we learnt in Chapter 7 to understand how the function works. The function takes exactly the same form as *aov()*, which we used in Chapter 10. It has the general form:

```
newModel<-manova(outcome ~ predictor(s), data = dataFrame, na.action = an
action))
```

in which:

- *newModel* is an object created that contains information about the model. We can get summary statistics for this model by executing *summary(newModel)* for the main MANOVA summary.

- *outcome* is a single object containing the variables that you're trying to predict (i.e., the dependent variables). In this example it will be **Actions** and **Thoughts**.

- *predictor(s)* lists the variable or variables from which you're trying to predict the outcome variables (i.e., the independent variable(s)). In this example it will be the variable **Group**. In more complex designs we can specify several predictors or independent variables, just as we have in previous chapters.

- *dataFrame* is the name of the dataframe from which your outcome and predictor variables come.

- *na.action* is an optional command. If you have complete data (as we have here) you can ignore it, but if you have missing values (i.e., NAs in the dataframe) then it can be useful to use *na.action* = *na.exclude*, which will exclude all cases with missing values).

As with most of the models in this book, we specify a model in the function of the form 'outcome ~ predictor(s)'. In the case of MANOVA there are several outcomes, so the model becomes 'outcomes ~ predictor(s)'. To put multiple outcomes into the model, we have to bind the variables together into a single entity using the *cbind()* function that we have encountered many times before. In the current example, we want to combine **Thoughts** and **Actions**, so we can create a single outcome object by executing:

```
outcome<-cbind(ocdData$Actions, ocdData$Thoughts)
```

This command creates an object called *outcome*, which contains the **Actions** and **Thoughts** variables of the *ocdData* dataframe pasted together in columns. We use this new object as the outcome in our model, and specify any predictors as we have in previous chapters. Therefore, for this example, we could estimate the model by executing:

```
ocdModel<-manova(outcome ~ Group, data = ocdData)
```

This command creates a model called *ocdModel*, which predicts the object called *outcome* (which, remember, includes the variables **Thoughts** and **Actions**) from the independent variable **Group**. If you had several independent variables you could add them in by using a plus symbol (remember to also add in the interaction), for example, 'outcome ~ Group + IV2 + Group:IV2', or by using an asterisk to automatically include all main effects and interactions, for example, 'outcome ~ Group*IV2'.

To see the output of the model we use the summary command; by default, **R** produces Pillai's trace (which is a sensible choice), but we can see the other test statistics by including the *test* = option. For example, to see all four test statistics we would need to execute:

```
summary(ocdModel, intercept = TRUE)
summary(ocdModel, intercept = TRUE, test = "Wilks")
summary(ocdModel, intercept = TRUE, test = "Hotelling")
summary(ocdModel, intercept = TRUE, test = "Roy")
```

The first command produces Pillai's trace (because *test* = is omitted), and the rest produce the others by overriding the default. Output 16.5 shows the main table of results. Test statistics are quoted for the intercept of the model (even MANOVA can be characterized as a regression model, although how this is done is beyond the scope of my brain) and for the **Group** variable. For our purposes, the group effects are of interest because they tell us whether or not the therapies had an effect on the OCD clients. You'll see that the four multivariate test statistics and their values correspond to those calculated in sections 16.4.4.2–16.4.4.5. In the next column these values are transformed into an *F*-ratio with 2 degrees of freedom. The column of real interest, however, is the one containing the significance values of these *F*-ratios. For these data, Pillai's trace ($p = .049$), Wilks's lambda ($p = .050$) and Roy's largest root ($p = .020$) all reach the criterion for significance of .05. However, Hotelling's trace ($p = .051$) is non-significant by this criterion. This scenario is interesting, because the test statistic we choose determines whether or not we reject the null hypothesis that there are no between-group differences. However, given what we know about the robustness of Pillai's trace when sample sizes are equal, we might be well advised to trust the result of that test statistic, which indicates a significant difference. This example highlights the additional power associated with Roy's root (you should note how this statistic is considerably more significant than all others) when the test assumptions have been met and when the group differences are focused on one variate (which they are in this example, as we will see later).

Pillai's trace:

```
              Df  Pillai approx F num Df den Df  Pr(>F)
(Intercept)    1 0.98285   745.23      2     26 < 2e-16 ***
Group          2 0.31845     2.56      4     54 0.04904 *
Residuals     27
---
Signif. codes:  0 '***' 0.001 '**' 0.01 '*' 0.05 '.' 0.1 ' ' 1
```

Wilk's lambda:

```
              Df   Wilks approx F num Df den Df  Pr(>F)
(Intercept)    1 0.01715   745.23      2     26 < 2e-16 ***
Group          2 0.69851     2.55      4     52 0.04966 *
Residuals     27
---
Signif. codes:  0 '***' 0.001 '**' 0.01 '*' 0.05 '.' 0.1 ' ' 1
```

Hotelling's trace:

```
              Df Hotelling-Lawley approx F num Df den Df Pr(>F)
(Intercept)    1           57.325   745.23      2     26 <2e-16 ***
Group          2            0.407     2.55      4     50 0.0508 .
Residuals     27
---
Signif. codes:  0 '***' 0.001 '**' 0.01 '*' 0.05 '.' 0.1 ' ' 1
```

Roy's largest root:

```
              Df     Roy approx F num Df den Df  Pr(>F)
(Intercept)    1 57.325   745.23      2     26 < 2e-16 ***
Group          2  0.335     4.52      2     27 0.02027 *
Residuals     27
---
Signif. codes:  0 '***' 0.001 '**' 0.01 '*' 0.05 '.' 0.1 ' ' 1
```

Output 16.5

R's Souls' Tip 16.1 Type II and III sums of squares ③

As with other times we have used the *lm()* function, or some variant of it, **R** will, by default, produce Type I sums of squares but it is usually preferable in (M)ANOVA to look at Type II (or even Type III) sums of squares. The differences are explained in Jane Superbrain Box 11.1. When you have one predictor in the model, as we have in the current example, Type I, II and III sums of squares will give the same results so it doesn't matter. However, with two or more predictors in the model you might prefer Type II or III sums of squares because they do not depend upon the order in which you enter variables into the model. In which case we can use the *Anova()* function from the *car* package, as we have in previous chapters, to obtain these sums of squares. In the current example, having created a model, *ocdModel*, we could display the Type II or III sums of squares by executing:

```
Anova(ocdModel, type = "II")
```

```
Anova(ocdModel, type = "III")
```

It's also worth bearing in mind that Type I, II and III sums of squares yield the same results when you have a balanced design (i.e., equal numbers of cases in all combinations of your predictor variables).

From this result we should probably conclude that the type of therapy employed had a significant effect on OCD. The nature of this effect is not clear from the multivariate test statistic: first, it tells us nothing about which groups differed from which; and second it tells us nothing about whether the effect of therapy was on the obsession-related thoughts, the obsession-related behaviours, or a combination of both. To determine the nature of the effect, we can look at univariate tests.

16.6.8. Follow-up analysis: univariate test statistics ②

If we want to follow up the analysis with univariate analyses of the individual outcome measures, then we can simply execute:

```
summary.aov(ocdModel)
```

This produces Output 16.6, which shows the ANOVA summary table for the dependent variables. The table labelled *Response 1* is for the **Actions** variable and *Response 2* is for the **Thoughts** variable. The rows labelled *Group* show the values of the sums of squares for both actions and thoughts (these values correspond to the values of SS_M calculated in sections 16.4.3.1 and 16.4.3.2, respectively). The row labelled *Residuals* contains information about the residual sums of squares and mean squares for each of the dependent variables: these values of SS_R were calculated in sections 16.4.3.1 and 16.4.3.2, and I urge you to look back to these sections to consolidate what these values mean.

```
Response 1 :
            Df Sum Sq Mean Sq F value  Pr(>F)
Group        2 10.467  5.2333  2.7706 0.08046 .
Residuals   27 51.000  1.8889
---
Signif. codes:  0 '***' 0.001 '**' 0.01 '*' 0.05 '.' 0.1 ' ' 1

Response 2 :
            Df  Sum Sq Mean Sq F value Pr(>F)
Group        2  19.467  9.7333  2.1541 0.1355
Residuals   27 122.000  4.5185
```

Output 16.6

The important parts of this table are the columns labelled *F value* and *Pr(>F)* in which the *F*-ratios for each univariate ANOVA and their significance values are listed. What should be clear from Output 16.6, and the calculations made in sections 16.4.3.1 and 16.4.3.2, is that the values associated with the univariate ANOVAs conducted after the MANOVA are *identical* to those obtained if one-way ANOVA was conducted on each dependent variable. This fact illustrates that MANOVA offers only hypothetical protection of inflated Type I error rates: there is no real-life adjustment made to the values obtained.

The values of *p* in Output 16.6 indicate that there was a non-significant difference between therapy groups in terms of both obsession-related thoughts ($p = .136$) and obsession-related behaviours ($p = .080$). These two results should lead us to conclude that the type of therapy has had no significant effect on the levels of OCD experienced by clients. Those of you who are still awake may have noticed something odd about this example: the multivariate test statistics led us to conclude that therapy had a significant impact on OCD, yet the univariate results indicate that therapy has not been successful.

SELF-TEST

✓ Why might the univariate tests be non-significant when the multivariate tests were significant?

The reason for the anomaly in these data is simple: the multivariate test takes account of the correlation between dependent variables, and so for these data it has more power to detect group differences. With this knowledge in mind, the univariate tests are not particularly useful for interpretation, because the groups differ along a combination of the dependent variables. To see how the dependent variables interact we need to carry out a discriminant function analysis, which will be described in due course.

16.6.9. Contrasts ③

I need to begin this section by reminding you that because the univariate ANOVAs were both non-significant we should not interpret these contrasts. However, purely to give you an example to follow for when your main analysis is significant, we'll look at the contrasts. The contrasts are not part of the MANOVA model, and so to generate the output for them you have to create separate linear models for each outcome measure. This is basically the same as doing a one-way ANOVA on each outcome measure. So, for **Thoughts** and **Actions** we could create the following models using the *aov()* function (see Chapter 10):

```
actionModel<-lm(Actions ~ Group, data = ocdData)
thoughtsModel<-lm(Thoughts ~ Group, data = ocdData)
```

The first command creates a model, *actionModel*, based on predicting the variable **Actions** from Group (Actions ~ Group) and the second command does much the same but predicting **Thoughts**. We can get the contrast parameters by using *summary.lm()*, just as we did in Chapter 10:

```
summary.lm(actionModel)
summary.lm(thoughtsModel)
```

In section 16.6.6 I suggested carrying out a contrast that compares each of the therapy groups to the no-treatment control group. The results of these contrasts are shown in Output 16.7 (for **Actions**) and Output 16.8 (for **Thoughts**). The contrasts will be labelled helpfully if, like I did, you set the contrasts manually and give them sensible names. The main thing to notice (from the values of $Pr(>|t|)$) is that when we compare CBT to NT there are no significant differences in thoughts ($p = .104$) or behaviours ($p = .872$), because both values are above the .05 threshold. However, comparing BT to NT, there is no significant difference in thoughts ($p = .835$) but there is a significant difference in behaviours between the groups ($p = .044$, which is less than .05). This is a little unexpected because the univariate ANOVA for behaviours was non-significant and so we would not expect there to be group differences.

```
Coefficients:
              Estimate Std. Error t value Pr(>|t|)
(Intercept)     5.0000     0.4346  11.504 6.47e-12 ***
GroupCBT_vs_NT -0.1000     0.6146  -0.163   0.8720
GroupBT_vs_NT  -1.3000     0.6146  -2.115   0.0438 *
---
Signif. codes:  0 '***' 0.001 '**' 0.01 '*' 0.05 '.' 0.1 ' ' 1
```

Output 16.7

```
Coefficients:
                Estimate Std. Error t value Pr(>|t|)
(Intercept)      15.0000     0.6722  22.315   <2e-16 ***
GroupCBT_vs_NT   -1.6000     0.9506  -1.683    0.104
GroupBT_vs_NT     0.2000     0.9506   0.210    0.835
---
Signif. codes:  0 '***' 0.001 '**' 0.01 '*' 0.05 '.' 0.1 ' ' 1
```

Output 16.8

CRAMMING SAM'S TIPS   MANOVA

- MANOVA is used to test the difference between groups across several dependent variables simultaneously.
- The test assumed multivariate normality and homogeneity of covariance matrices. This latter assumption can be ignored when sample sizes are equal because some MANOVA test statistics are robust to violations of this assumption. Multivariate normality can be tested with a multivariate version of the Shapiro–Wilk test: if it is significant ($p < .05$) then the assumption is violated.
- There are four test statistics that can be used in MANOVA (*Pillai's trace, Wilks's lambda, Hotelling's trace* and *Roy's largest root*). I recommend using Pillai's trace. If the p-value of this statistic is less than .05 then the groups differ significantly with respect to the dependent variables.
- ANOVAs can be used to follow up the MANOVA (a different ANOVA for each dependent variable). These ANOVAs can in turn be followed up using contrasts (see Chapters 10–14). Personally I don't recommend this approach and suggest conducting a *discriminant function analysis*.

16.7. Robust MANOVA ③

Wilcox provides functions for two robust methods for MANOVA (Wilcox, 2005), both of which are based on ranking the data (see Chapter 15). To access these tests we need to load the *WRS* package (see section 5.8.4.). There are two functions that we will look at:

- **mulrank()**: This performs a MANOVA on the ranked data using Munzel and Brunner's method (Munzel & Brunner, 2000).

- **cmanova()**: This performs Choi and Marden's (1997) robust test based on the ranked data. It is an extension of the Kruskal–Wallis test that was described in the Chapter 15.

Both of these functions can be used only when you have one predictor (i.e., one independent variable). For more complex designs you should accept defeat. Remember that our data are currently in this format (I've edited out some cases):

```
   Group Actions Thoughts
1    CBT       5       14
...  ...      ...      ...
10   CBT       4       11
11    BT       4       14
...  ...      ...      ...
20    BT       5       17
21    NT       4       13
...  ...      ...      ...
30    NT       5       18
```

The robust functions need the data to be in wide format rather than long (see Chapter 3). Figure 16.7 shows the existing data format and how we need it to look (wide). Essentially we want levels of the independent variable (**Group**) and outcome measures (**Thoughts** and **Actions**) to be represented in different columns. The outcome measures are already spread across different columns (**Thoughts** and **Actions**), but the treatment group is differentiated by different rows of data (rows 1–10 are those in a CBT group, rows 11–20 are the BT group, and so on). Therefore, we need to take the rows representing people who were in the BT and NT groups and shift them into columns alongside the columns currently labelled **Thoughts** and **Actions**.

We can do this restructuring using the *melt()* and *cast()* functions from the *reshape* package. To get the restructuring to work, we need to add a variable to our dataframe that identifies the rows in the wide format. Notice in Figure 16.7 that the data are made up of six chunks that represent the three treatment groups and the two outcome measures. We want to move the chunks that are currently stacked on top of each other so that they are beside each other (Figure 16.7). To do this, **R** needs to know what row a particular score will end up in when we move each block of scores from the stacks into the columns. The easiest approach is simply to create a variable (called **row**) that identifies within each chunk the row number of a given score. In other words, it will be a value telling us whether the score is the first, second, third, etc. score within the chunk. At the moment, the chunks are stacked on top of each other, so we want a variable that is the sequence of numbers 1 to 10 repeated for the three different treatment groups (because they all contain 10 rows of data). We can add this variable to the dataframe by executing:

```
ocdData$row<-rep(1:10, 3)
```

Executing this command creates a variable *row* in the dataframe *ocdData*, that is the numbers 1 to 10 repeated three times. The structure of the data will be the same as before – it's just that we have a new variable called **row** that identifies the scores within each treatment group.

FIGURE 16.7
Restructuring the OCD data for robust MANOVA

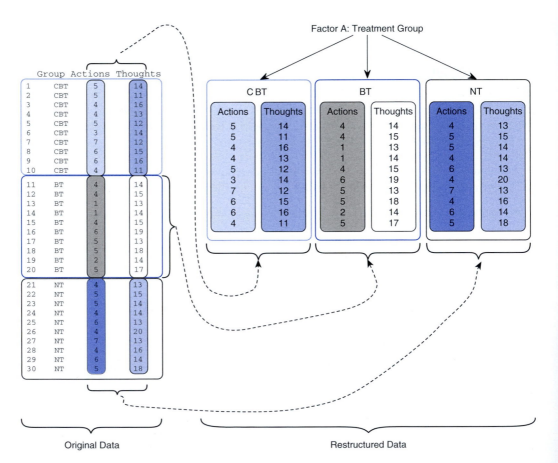

Next we need to make the data molten so that we can cast them into the wide format. To do this we use the *melt()* function (see section 3.9.4). Remember that in this function we differentiate variables that identify attributes of the scores (in this example, **Group** and **row** tell us about a given score, for example, that it was the fifth score in the CBT group) from the scores themselves (in this case the columns labelled **Actions** and **Thoughts** both contain scores). Attributes are specified with the *id* option, and scores with the *measured* option. Therefore, we can create a molten dataframe called *ocdMelt* by executing:

```
ocdMelt<-melt(ocdData, id = c("Group", "row"), measured = c("Actions", "Thoughts"))
```

The data now look like this (I have edited out many cases to save space):

```
    Group row        variable        value
1    CBT   1          Actions           5
...  ...  ...           ...            ...
10   CBT   10         Actions           4
11   BT    1          Actions           4
...  ...  ...           ...            ...
19   BT    9          Actions           2
...  ...  ...           ...            ...
26   NT    6          Actions           4
27   NT    7          Actions           7
...  ...  ...           ...            ...
33   CBT   3         Thoughts          16
34   CBT   4         Thoughts          13
...  ...  ...           ...            ...
41   BT    1         Thoughts          14
42   BT    2         Thoughts          15
...  ...  ...           ...            ...
51   NT    1         Thoughts          13
...  ...  ...           ...            ...
60   NT    10        Thoughts          18
```

The variable that differentiates whether the outcome measure was thoughts or actions has been labelled *variable* and the variable that contains the frequencies of thoughts/behaviours is called *value*. These labels are not that informative, so let's rename them as *Outcome_Measure* and *Frequency* using the *names()* function.

```
names(ocdMelt)<-c("Group", "row", "Outcome_Measure", "Frequency")
```

Executing this command takes the dataframe *ocdMelt* and assigns the names in *c()* to each column. As such, our variables all now have names that relate to what they represent.

Finally, we want to cast our data into the wide format using *cast()*. To do this we use a formula in the form: *variables specifying the rows ~ variables specifying the columns*. In this case, **row** tells us which row to place a score, and we want the **Group** and **Outcome_Measures** variables split across different columns, so we'd use the formula:[6] *row ~ Group + Outcome_Measures*. Therefore, we can make a wide dataframe called *ocdRobust* by executing:

```
ocdRobust<-cast(ocdMelt, row ~ Group + Outcome_Measure, value = "Frequency")
```

Note that we have applied this command to the molten data set (*ocdMelt*). The *value = "Frequency"* explicitly tells the function in which column to find the outcome variable (without this command the function will take an educated guess, but it's good practice to be specific).

---

[6] It's important that you specify **Group** and **Outcome_Measure** in this order becaue this arranges the data correctly for Wilcox's functions. If you use *row ~ Outcome_Measures + Group* then the resulting data would be structured as *CBT_Action, BT_Action, NT_Action, CBT_Thoughts, BT_Thoughts, NT_Thoughts*.

The result is that the data have been transformed to the wide format. However, because we added the variable **row** to the dataframe, our new dataframe also contains this variable, and for the analysis we don't want it. We can remove this variable by executing:

```
ocdRobust$row<-NULL
```

You should find that you now have a wide format set of data:

```
ocdRobust
```

CBT_Action	CBT_Thoughts	BT_Action	BT_Thoughts	NT_Action	NT_Thoughts
5	14	4	14	4	13
5	11	4	15	5	15
4	16	1	13	5	14
4	13	1	14	4	14
5	12	4	15	6	13
3	14	6	19	4	20
7	12	5	13	7	13
6	15	5	18	4	16
6	16	2	14	6	14
4	11	5	17	5	18

It's important to note the order of the columns: the hierarchy of the independent variables is **Group** followed by **Outcome_Measures**. In other words, we have taken the six groups of scores and first divided them into CBT, BT and NT, then within these groups we have subdivided according to which outcome measure was used.

The functions *mulrank()* and *cmanova()* both take the same general form:

```
mulrank(number of groups, number of outcome measures, data)
cmanova(number of groups, number of outcome measures, data)
```

We need only specify the dataframe (*ocdRobust*) and then the number of groups (three in this case) and the number of outcome measures (two in this case). Therefore, we can do a robust MANOVA based on ranks by executing:

```
mulrank(3, 2, ocdRobust)
cmanova(3, 2, ocdRobust)
```

mulrank()	*cmanova()*
`$test.stat` `[1] 1.637357`	`$test.stat` `[1] 9.057746`
`$nu1` `[1] 3.643484`	`$df` `[1] 4`

`$p.value`
`        [,1]`
`[1,] 0.1675409`
	`$p.value`
	`           [,1]`
	`[1,] 0.0596722`

`$N` `[1] 30`	

`$q.hat`
`          [,1]        [,2]`
`[1,] 0.5533333 0.3666667`
`[2,] 0.3750000 0.5900000`
`[3,] 0.5716667 0.5433333`	

Output 16.9

The output of both of these commands is shown in Output 16.9. For *mulrank()* (left-hand side of Output 16.9) we are given a test statistic for the type of treatment (*$test.stat*) as well as the corresponding *p*-value (*$p.value*). We could conclude that there was no significant main effect of the type of treatment on outcomes of OCD, $F = 1.64$, $p = .168$. The numbers under *$q.hat* tell us the relative effects (i.e., the typical ranks across the combinations of groups in the rows and outcome measures in the columns). We could relabel this grid as:

```
        [Actions] [Thoughts]
[CBT] 0.5533333 0.3666667
[ BT] 0.3750000 0.5900000
[ NT] 0.5716667 0.5433333
```

This shows that in the NT groups the ranks were fairly similar for thoughts and actions (0.57 and 0.54). For BT the ranks were lower for actions (0.38) than thoughts (0.59), and for CBT the reverse was true: ranks were lower for thoughts (0.37) than actions (0.55). In other words, CBT affected thoughts more than actions, and BT affected actions more than thoughts. However, the overall effect was not significant.

The output of *cmanova()* (right-hand side of Output 16.9) tells us much the same things: we get a test statistic (*$test.stat*), the degrees of freedom (*$df*) and an associated *p*-value (*$p.value*). We could conclude that there was no significant main effect of the type of treatment on outcomes of OCD, $H(4) = 9.06$, $p = .060$.

16.8. Reporting results from MANOVA ②

Reporting a MANOVA is much like reporting an ANOVA. As you can see in Output 16.5, the multivariate tests are converted into approximate *F*s, and people often just report these *F*s just as they would for ANOVA (i.e., they give details of the *F*-ratio and the degrees of freedom from which it was calculated). For our effect of group, we would report the hypothesis *df* and the error *df*. Therefore, we could report these analyses as:

✓ There was a significant effect of therapy on the number of obsessive thoughts and behaviours, $F(4, 54) = 2.56$, $p < .05$.

However, in my opinion, the multivariate test statistic should be quoted as well. There are four different multivariate tests reported in Output 16.5; I'll report each one in turn (note that the degrees of freedom and value of *F* change), but in reality you would just report one of the four:

✓ Using Pillai's trace, there was a significant effect of therapy on the number of obsessive thoughts and behaviours, $V = 0.32$, $F(4, 54) = 2.56$, $p < .05$.

✓ Using Wilks's lambda statistic, there was a significant effect of therapy on the number of obsessive thoughts and behaviours, $\Lambda = 0.70$, $F(4, 52) = 2.56$, $p < .05$.

✓ Using Hotelling's trace statistic, there was not a significant effect of therapy on the number of obsessive thoughts and behaviours, $T = 0.41$, $F(4, 50) = 2.55$, $p > .05$.

✓ Using Roy's largest root, there was a significant effect of therapy on the number of obsessive thoughts and behaviours, $\Theta = 0.35$, $F(2, 27) = 4.52$, $p < .05$.

We can also report the follow-up ANOVAs in the usual way (see Output 16.6):

✓ Using Pillai's trace, there was a significant effect of therapy on the number of obsessive thoughts and behaviours, $V = 0.32$, $F(4, 54) = 2.56$, $p < .05$. However, separate univariate ANOVAs on the outcome variables revealed non-significant treatment effects on obsessive thoughts, $F(2, 27) = 2.15$, $p > .05$, and behaviours, $F(2, 27) = 2.77$, $p > .05$.

If you have used a robust MANOVA (Output 16.9) then you might report this as follows:

✓ A MANOVA was conducted on the ranked data using Munzel and Brunner's (2000) method, implemented in **R** using the *mulrank()* function (Wilcox, 2005). There was no significant main effect of the type of treatment on outcomes of OCD, $F = 1.64$, $p = .168$.

✓ A MANOVA was conducted on the ranked data using Choi and Marden's (1997) method, implemented in **R** using the *cmanova()* function (Wilcox, 2005). There was no significant main effect of the type of treatment on outcomes of OCD, $H(4) = 9.06$, $p = .060$.

16.9. Following up MANOVA with discriminant analysis ③

I mentioned earlier on that a significant MANOVA could be followed up using either univariate ANOVA or **discriminant analysis** (sometimes called discriminant function analysis or DFA for short). In the example in this chapter, the univariate ANOVAs were not a useful way of looking at what the multivariate tests showed because the relationship between dependent variables is obviously having an effect. However, these data were designed especially to illustrate how the univariate ANOVAs should be treated cautiously and in real life a significant MANOVA is likely to be accompanied by at least one significant ANOVA. However, this does not mean that the relationship between dependent variables is not important, and it is still vital to investigate the nature of this relationship. Discriminant analysis is the best way to achieve this, and I strongly recommend that you follow up a MANOVA with both univariate tests and discriminant analysis if you want to fully understand your data.

In discriminant analysis we look to see how we can best separate (or discriminate) a set of groups using several predictors (so it is a little like logistic regression but where there are several groups rather than two).[7] In some senses it might seem as though we're doing the reverse of the MANOVA: in MANOVA we predicted a set of outcome measures from a grouping variable, whereas in DFA we predict a grouping variable from a set of outcome measures. However, the basic underlying principles of these tests are the same: remember that when we looked at the theory of MANOVA we saw that it works by identifying linear variates that best differentiate the groups, and these 'linear variates' are the 'functions' in discriminant function analysis.

Discriminant analysis is quite straightforward in **R**: you use the *lda()* function from the *MASS* package. The basic format of this function is:

```
newModel<-lda(Group ~ Predictor(s), data = dataFrame, prior = prior probabilities,
na.action = "na.omit")
```

There are a host of other options that you can use (execute *?lda* for more information), but within the context of MANOVA this is all we really need. Within the function, *Group* is the name of the variable in your dataframe that contains the groups that you're trying to discriminate, and *Predictor(s)* is a list of continuous variables from which you are trying to make the discrimination. This creates a formula for a linear model (just as we have seen many times in this book). So, if you're using a single predictor your model might be specified as *Group ~ Predictor*, but with two or more predictors you simply add each predictor

---

[7] In fact, I could have just as easily described discriminant analysis rather than logistic regression in Chapter 8 because they are different ways of achieving the same end result. However, logistic regression has far fewer restrictive assumptions and is generally more robust, which is why I have limited the coverage of discriminant analysis to this chapter.

in using the '+' symbol; for example, *Group ~ Predictor1 + Predictor2 + Predictor3*. In our case we want to predict the variable **Group** from the variables **Thoughts** and **Actions** so our model is *Group ~ Actions + Thoughts*. The *data* option just lets you specify the name of your dataframe (in this case *ocdData*). The *na.action* option determines how missing data are handled. By default the function will simply fail, but you can set the option to *na.omit* (as shown above) to delete missing cases instead (R's Souls' Tip 7.1). We can ignore this option altogether because we have no missing data. There is also an option to set the prior probabilities but when our groups have equal sample sizes we can omit this option (R's Souls' Tip 16.2). For the current data, we could, therefore, execute:

```
ocdDFA<-lda(Group ~ Actions + Thoughts, data = ocdData)
```

This creates a model called *ocdDFA*. To see this model execute the name of the model:

```
ocdDFA
```

R's Souls' Tip 16.2 Prior probabilities ③

To do a DFA, you should set the prior probabilities, that is, the probability of belonging to a particular group. This value is simply the 'chance' of a case being in a particular group. In our OCD example there are 30 cases. If we wanted to know the probability that a case was in the CBT group, then we can look at the number of cases in that group. There were 10 cases, and 30 in total, therefore the probability of being in the CBT group is 10/30 = .33. In other words, a third of the whole sample was in the CBT group. Therefore, in general, the prior probability is:

$$\text{prior probability of group} = \frac{n_{\text{group}}}{N}$$

When group sizes are equal (as they are in our OCD example) then the prior probability is the same for every group. The *lda()* function assumes this scenario and so when you have equal sized groups you don't need to worry or think about prior probabilities unless you have a good theoretical reason not to base them on the sample size of the group.

However, when you have unequal group sizes it is a good idea to base the prior probabilities on the sample size of the group. We can do this using the *prior* option of *lda()*. If you're basing prior probabilities on sample sizes, then you can set this option, in general, as:

```
prior = c(n₁, n₂, n₃)/N
```

in which the *n*s refer to group sample sizes, and *N* is the total sample size. Imagine, in our OCD example, that the CBT group contained 20 people, the BT group 18, and the NT group 12. This is 40 cases in total. Therefore, we would write:

```
prior = c(20, 18, 12)/40
```

Note that you must be careful to put the sample sizes in the correct order (i.e., 20 will be assumed to be the sample size of level 1 of the grouping variable, and 18 the sample size for level 2 and so on). In the context of the *lda()* function, we would execute:

```
ocdDFA<-lda(Group ~ Actions + Thoughts, data = ocdData, prior = c(20, 18, 12)/40)
```

You can extend this idea to more than three groups. For example, with five groups with sample sizes of 5, 10, 5, 20, 10 (and, therefore, a total of 50) the prior option would be:

```
prior = c(5, 10, 5, 20, 10)/50
```

```
Call:
lda(Group ~ Actions + Thoughts, data = ocdData, na.action = "na.omit")

Prior probabilities of groups:
      CBT          BT          NT
0.3333333 0.3333333 0.3333333

Group means:
    Actions Thoughts
CBT     4.9     13.4
BT      3.7     15.2
NT      5.0     15.0

Coefficients of linear discriminants:
                LD1        LD2
Actions   0.6030047 -0.4249451
Thoughts -0.3352478 -0.3392631

Proportion of trace:
   LD1    LD2
0.8219 0.1781
```

Output 16.10

Output 16.10 shows us first the prior probabilities, which are .33 for each group; these are the group sample size divided by the total sample size (i.e., 10/30 = .33), and because the sample sizes of the three groups are equal, the prior probabilities are the same for each group too (R's Souls' Tip 16.2). Next we are given the group means, which we have already computed before running the main analysis so are not particularly interesting to revisit.

The main part of the output tells us the coefficients of the linear discriminants, which in plain English are the values of b in equation (16.4). You'll notice that these values correspond to the values in the eigenvectors derived in section 16.4.4.1 and used in equation (16.5). Given that the variates can be expressed in terms of a linear regression equation (see equation (16.4)), the coefficients of the linear discriminants are equivalent to the unstandardized betas in regression. Hence, the coefficients tell us the relative contribution of each variable to the variates. If we look at variate 1 first, thoughts and behaviours have the opposite effect (behaviour has a positive relationship with this variate, whereas thoughts have a negative relationship). The first variate, then, could be seen as one that differentiates thoughts and behaviours (it affects thoughts and behaviours in the opposite way). Both thoughts and behaviours have a strong relationship with the second variate. This tells us that this variate represents something that affects thoughts and behaviours in a similar way. Remembering that ultimately these variates are used to differentiate groups, we could say that the first variate differentiates groups by some factor that affects thoughts and behaviours differently, whereas the second variate differentiates groups on some dimension that affects thoughts and behaviours in the same way.

Finally the proportion of trace shows us that the first variate accounts for 82.2% of variance compared to the second variate, which accounts for only 17.8%. These proportions are the eigenvalues for each variate (i.e., the values of the diagonal elements of the matrix HE^{-1}) expressed as a proportion.

```
$x
          LD1         LD2
1   0.4602010 -0.01736741
2   1.4659443  1.00042182
3  -0.8132992 -0.27094845
4   0.1924441  0.74684078
```

```
 5    1.1306965   0.66115874
 6   -0.7458083   0.83252282
 7    2.3367058  -0.18873149
 8    0.7279579  -0.78157561
 9    0.3927101  -1.12083868
10    0.8629396   1.42536694
11   -0.1428037   0.40757770
12   -0.4780514   0.06831463
13   -1.6165699   2.02167613
14   -1.9518176   1.68241305
15   -0.4780514   0.06831463
16   -0.6130332  -2.13862792
17    0.7954487   0.32189566
18   -0.8807901  -1.37441972
19   -1.3488130   1.25746794
20   -0.5455423  -1.03515665
21    0.1924441   0.74684078
22    0.1249532  -0.35663049
23    0.4602010  -0.01736741
24   -0.1428037   0.40757770
25    1.3984534  -0.10304945
26   -2.1542903  -1.62800076
27    2.0014580  -0.52799457
28   -0.8132992  -0.27094845
29    1.0632056  -0.44231253
30   -0.8807901  -1.37441972
```

Output 16.11

It is sometimes useful to look at the **discriminant scores**. These are the scores for each person, on each variate, obtained from equation (16.5). These scores can be useful because the variates that the analysis identifies may represent underlying social or psychological constructs. If these constructs are identifiable, then it is useful for interpretation to know what a participant scores on each dimension. To obtain these scores execute:

```
predict(ocdDFA)
```

The resulting Output 16.11 shows each participant's score on the first (LD1) and second (LD2) variate.

Perhaps more useful than the scores themselves is a plot of the scores broken down by group membership. This can be obtained by using the *plot()* function on our model:

```
plot(ocdDFA)
```

By executing this command you will produce the plot at the top of Figure 16.8. This graph plots the variate scores for each person, grouped according to the experimental condition to which that person belonged. To interpret this plot, I have broken it down to look at the first variate (bottom left of Figure 16.8) separate from the second variate (bottom right of Figure 16.8). To discover which groups variate 1 discriminates we need to try to ignore variate 2 (that's why I have blanked out the axis for LD2) and look at how the groups change as we move along variate 1. In other words, we ignore the vertical position of each point on the plot, and look at how the groups are distributed along the horizontal axis (LD1). A crude, but simple, way to do this is to split the vertical axis down the middle (as I have done with a vertical blue line at 0 on the scale) and ask yourself which groups cluster on either side of the line. I have circled the BT groups in light blue and the CBT groups in black. Hopefully, this will make clear that to the left of the blue vertical line there are a lot of cases from the BT group, but to the right of the blue vertical line there are lots of cases from the CBT group. In other words, the blue vertical line seems to separate the BT group from the CBT group. This tells us that variate 1 discriminates the BT group from the CBT.

Moving on to the second variate (bottom right of Figure 16.8), we now need to focus on LD2 and try to ignore LD1 (I have blanked out the axis to help). In other words, we ignore the horizontal position of each point on the plot, and look at how the groups are distributed along the vertical axis (LD2). Again, you can get a rough idea of what's happening by splitting the vertical axis down the middle (as I have done with a horizontal blue line at 0, the midpoint of the scale) and ask yourself which groups cluster on either side of the line. The picture is not as clear as for variate 1, but it seems to me that there are a lot of cases from the NT group below the line, but hardly any above. I have highlighted these cases with dark blue circles to help you to see. Looking at the BT and CBT cases they tend to fall above the line (although not always). This pattern suggests that the second variate differentiates the no-treatment group (cases are below the blue horizontal line) from the two interventions (the cases are typically above the blue horizontal line), but this difference is not as dramatic as for the first variate. Remember that the variates significantly discriminate the groups in combination (i.e., when both are considered).

FIGURE 16.8
Combined-groups plot

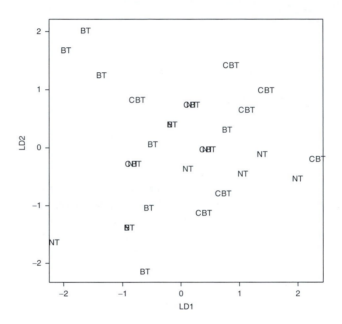

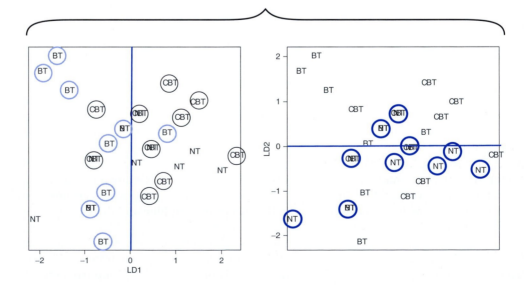

CRAMMING SAM'S TIPS **Discriminant function analysis**

- Discriminant function analysis can be used after MANOVA to see how the dependent variables discriminate the groups.
- DFA identifies variates (combinations of the dependent variables) that discriminate groups of cases.
- Look at the *Coefficients of linear discriminants* to find out how the dependent variables contribute to the variates. High scores indicate that a dependent variable is important for a variate, and variables with positive and negative coefficients are contributing to the variate in opposite ways.
- Finally, to find out which groups are discriminated by a variate, look at the plot of discriminant scores. Split the vertical and horizontal axes at the midpoint and look at which groups tend to fall on either side of the line. The variate plotted on a given axis is discriminating between groups that fall on different sides of the line (i.e., the midpoint).

16.10. Reporting results from discriminant analysis ②

The guiding principle in presenting data is to give the readers enough information to be able to judge for themselves what your data mean. Personally, I would suggest reporting the percentage of variance explained (which gives the reader the same information as the eigenvalue but in a more palatable form) and the coefficients of linear discriminants. All of these values can be found in Output 16.10. Finally, although I won't reproduce it below, you could consider including a copy of the discriminant scores plot (Figure 16.8), which will help readers to determine how the variates contribute to distinguishing your groups. We could, therefore, write something like this:

✓ The MANOVA was followed up with discriminant analysis, which revealed two discriminant functions. The first explained 82.2% of the variance, whereas the second explained only 17.8%. The coefficients of the discriminant functions revealed that function 1 differentiated obsessive behaviours ($b = 0.603$) and thoughts ($b = -0.335$). The second variate produced similar coefficients for actions (-0.425) and thoughts (-0.339). The discriminant function plot showed that the first function discriminated the BT group from the CBT group, and the second function differentiated the no-treatment group from the two interventions.

16.11. Some final remarks ④

16.11.1. The final interpretation ④

So far we have gathered an awful lot of information about our data, but how can we bring all of it together to answer our research question: can therapy improve OCD and, if so, which therapy is best? Well, the MANOVA tells us that therapy can have a significant effect on OCD symptoms, but the non-significant univariate ANOVAs suggested that this improvement is not simply in terms of either thoughts or behaviours. The discriminant

Labcoat Leni's Real Research 16.1   A lot of hot air! ④

Marzillier, S. L., & Davey, G. C. L. (2005). *Cognition and Emotion*, 19, 729–750.

Have you ever wondered what researchers do in their spare time? Well, some of them spend it tracking down the sounds of people burping and farting! It has long been established that anxiety and disgust are linked. Anxious people are, typically, easily disgusted. Throughout this book I have talked about how you cannot infer causality from relationships between variables. This has been a bit of a conundrum for anxiety researchers: does anxiety cause feelings of digust or does a low threshold for being disgusted cause anxiety? Two colleagues of mine at Sussex addressed this in an unusual study in which they induced feelings of anxiety, feelings of disgust, or a neutral mood, and they looked at the effect that these induced moods had on feelings of anxiety, sadness, happiness, anger, disgust and contempt. To induce these moods, they used three different types of manipulation: vignettes (e.g., 'You're swimming in a dark lake and something brushes your leg' for anxiety, and 'You go into a public toilet and find it has not been flushed. The bowl of the toilet is full of diarrhoea' for disgust), music (e.g., some scary music for anxiety, and a tape of burps, farts and vomitting for disgust), videos (e.g., a clip from *Silence of the Lambs* for anxiety and a scene from *Pink Flamingos* in which Divine eats dog faeces for disgust) and memory (remembering events from the past that had made the person anxious, disgusted or neutral).

Different people underwent anxious, disgust and neutral mood inductions. Within these groups, the induction was done using either vignettes and music, videos, or memory recall and music for different people. The outcome variables were the change (from before to after the induction) in six moods: anxiety, sadness, happiness, anger, disgust and contempt.

The data are in the file **Marzillier and Davey (2005).dat**. Draw an error bar graph of the changes in moods in the different conditions, then conduct a 3 (Mood: anxiety, disgust, neutral) × 3 (Induction: vignettes + music, videos, memory recall + music) MANOVA on these data. Whatever you do, don't imagine what their fart tape sounded like while you do the analysis!

Answers are in the additional material on the companion website (or look at page 738 of the original article).

analysis suggests that the group separation can be best explained in terms of one underlying dimension. In this context the dimension is likely to be OCD itself (which we can realistically presume is made up of both thoughts and behaviours). So, therapy doesn't necessarily change behaviours or thoughts *per se*, but it does influence the underlying dimension of OCD. So, the answer to the first question seems to be: yes, therapy can influence OCD, but the nature of this influence is unclear.

The next question is more complex: which therapy is best? Figures 16.3 and 16.4 show the relationships between the dependent variables and the group means of the original data. The graph of the means (Figure 16.4) shows that for actions, BT reduces the number of obsessive behaviours, whereas CBT and NT do not. For thoughts, CBT reduces the number of obsessive thoughts, whereas BT and NT do not (check the pattern of the bars). Looking now at the relationships between thoughts and actions (Figure 16.3), in the BT group there is a positive relationship between thoughts and actions, so the more obsessive thoughts a person has, the more obsessive behaviours they carry out. In the CBT group there is no relationship at all (thoughts and actions vary quite independently). In the no-treatment group there is a negative (and non-significant incidentally) relationship between thoughts and actions.

What we have discovered from the discriminant analysis is that BT and CBT can be differentiated from the control group based on variate 2, a variate that has a similar effect on both thoughts and behaviours. We could say then that BT and CBT are both better than a no-treatment group at changing obsessive thoughts and behaviours. We also discovered that BT and CBT could be distinguished by variate 1, a variate that had the opposite effects on thoughts and behaviours.

We could conclude that BT is better at changing behaviours and CBT is better at changing thoughts. So, the NT group can be distinguished from the CBT and BT graphs using a variable that affects both thoughts and behaviours. Also, the CBT and BT groups can be distinguished by a variate that has opposite effects on thoughts and behaviours. So, some therapy is better than none, but the choice of CBT or BT depends on whether you think it's more important to target thoughts (CBT) or behaviours (BT).

16.11.2. Univariate ANOVA or discriminant analysis? ②

This example should have made clear that univariate ANOVA and discriminant analysis are ways of answering different questions arising from a significant MANOVA. If univariate ANOVAs are chosen, Bonferroni corrections should be applied to the level at which you accept significance. The truth is that you should run both analyses to get a full picture of what is happening in your data. The advantage of discriminant analysis is that it tells you something about the underlying dimensions within your data (which is especially useful if you have employed several dependent measures in an attempt to capture some social or psychological construct). Even if univariate ANOVAs are significant, the discriminant analysis provides useful insight into your data and should be used. I hope that this chapter will convince you of this recommendation.

What have I discovered about statistics? ②

In this chapter we've cackled maniacally in the ear of MANOVA, force-fed discriminant function analysis cod-liver oil, and discovered to our horror that Roy has a large root. There are sometimes situations in which several outcomes have been measured in different groups, and we discovered that in these situations the ANOVA technique can be extended and is called MANOVA (multivariate analysis of variance). The reasons for using this technique rather than running lots of ANOVAs are that we retain control over the Type I error rate, and we can incorporate the relationships between outcome variables into the analysis. Some of you will have then discovered that MANOVA works in very similar ways to ANOVA, but just with matrices rather than single values. Others will have discovered that it's best to ignore the theory sections of this book. We had a look at an example of MANOVA and discovered that, just to make life as confusing as possible, you get four test statistics relating to the same effect! Of these, I tried to convince you that Pillai's trace was the safest option. Finally, we had a look at the two options for following up MANOVA: running lots of ANOVAs, or doing a discriminant function analysis. Of these, discriminant function analysis gives us the most information, but can be a bit of a nightmare to interpret.

We also discovered that pets can be therapeutic. I left the whereabouts of Fuzzy a mystery. Now admit it, how many of you thought he was dead? He's not: he is lying next to me as I type this sentence. After frantically searching the house I went back to the room that he had vanished from to check again whether there was a hole that he could have wriggled through. As I scuttled around on my hands and knees tapping the walls, a little ginger (and sooty) face popped out from the fireplace with a look as if to say 'have you lost something?' (see Figure 16.9). Yep, freaked out by the whole moving experience, he had done the only sensible thing and hidden up the chimney! Cats, you gotta love 'em.

FIGURE 16.9
Fuzzy hiding up a fireplace

R packages used in this chapter

car	pastecs
ggplot2	reshape
mvnormtest	WRS
mvoutlier	

R functions used in this chapter

aov()	lm()
aq.plot()	manova()
by()	melt()
c()	mshapiro.test()
cast()	mulrank()
cbind()	names()
cmanova()	plot()
contrasts()	predict()
cov()	stat.desc()
factor()	summary()
ggplot()	summary.aov()
gl()	summary.lm()
lda()	t()

Key terms that I've discovered

Box's test	Multivariate analysis of variance (MANOVA)
Discriminant function analysis (DFA)	Multivariate normality
Discriminant function variates	Pillai–Bartlett trace (V)
Discriminant scores	Random sampling
Error SSCP (E)	Roy's largest root
HE^{-1}	Square matrix
Homogeneity of covariance matrices	Sum of squares and cross-products
Hotelling–Lawley trace (T^2)	matrix (SSCP)
Hypothesis SSCP (H)	Total SSCP (T)
Identity matrix	Univariate
Independence	Variance–covariance matrix
Multivariate	Wilks's lambda (Λ)

Smart Alex's tasks

- **Task 1:** A clinical psychologist noticed that several of his manic psychotic patients did chicken impersonations in public. He wondered whether this behaviour could be used to diagnose this disorder and so compared 10 of his patients against 10 of the most normal people he could find: naturally he chose to observe lecturers at the University of Sussex. He measured how many chicken impersonations they did over the course of a day, and how good their impersonations were (as scored out of 10 by an independent farmyard noise expert). The data are in the file **chicken.dat**. Use MANOVA and DFA to find out whether these variables could be used to distinguish manic psychotic patients from those without the disorder. ③

- **Task 2:** I was intrigued by a news story claiming that children who lie would become successful citizens (http://bit.ly/ammQNT). I was particularly intrigued because although the article cited a lot of well-conducted work by Dr Khang Lee that shows that children lie, I couldn't find anything at all in that well-conducted work that supported the journalist's claim that children who lie become successful citizens. However, let's imagine a Huxleyesque parallel universe in which the government is stupid enough to believe the contents of this newspaper story and decides to implement a systematic programme of infant conditioning. Some infants were trained not to lie, others were bought up as normal, and a final group was trained in the art of lying. Thirty years later, they collected data on how successful these children were as adults. They measured their **salary**, and two indices of how successful they were in their **family** and **work** life, on a 0–10 scale (10 = as successful as could possibly be, 0 = better luck in your next life). The data are in **lying.dat**. Use MANOVA and DFA to find out whether, in this completely fabricated parallel universe, lying really does make you a better citizen. ③

- **Task 3:** I was interested in whether students' knowledge of different aspects of psychology improved throughout their degree. I took a sample of first years, second years and third years and gave them five tests (scored out of 15) representing different aspects of psychology: **exper** (experimental psychology, such as cognitive and neuropsychology); **stats** (statistics); **social** (social psychology); **develop** (developmental psychology); **person** (personality). Your task is to: (1) carry out an appropriate general analysis to determine whether there are overall group differences along these five measures; (2) look at the scale-by-scale analyses of group differences produced in the output and interpret the results accordingly; (3) select contrasts that test the hypothesis that second and third years will score higher than first years on all scales; (4) select tests that compare all groups to each other and briefly compare these results with the contrasts; and (5) carry out a separate analysis in which you test whether a combination of the measures can successfully discriminate the groups (comment only briefly on this analysis). Include only those scales that revealed group differences for the contrasts. How do the results help you to explain the findings of your initial analysis? The data are in the file **psychology.dat**. ④

Answers can be found on the companion website.

Further reading

Bray, J. H., & Maxwell, S. E. (1985). *Multivariate analysis of variance*. Sage University Paper Series on Quantitative Applications in the social Sciences, 07-054. Newbury Park, CA: Sage. (This monograph on MANOVA is superb: I cannot recommend anything better.)

Huberty, C. J., & Morris, J. D. (1989). Multivariate analysis versus multiple univariate analysis. *Psychological Bulletin*, *105*(2), 302–308.

Interesting real research

Marzillier, S. L., & Davey, G. C. L. (2005). Anxiety and disgust: Evidence for a unidirectional relationship. *Cognition and Emotion*, *19*(5), 729–750.

Exploratory factor analysis

17

FIGURE 17.1
Me at Niagara
Falls in 1998. I
was in the middle
of writing the first
edition of the SPSS
version of this
book at the time.
Note how fresh-
faced I look

17.1. What will this chapter tell me? ①

I was a year or so into my Ph.D., and, thanks to my initial terrible teaching experiences, I had developed a bit of an obsession with over-preparing for classes. I wrote detailed hand-outs and started using funny examples. Through my girlfriend at the time I met Dan Wright (a psychologist, who was in my department but sadly moved to Florida). He had published a statistics book of his own and was helping his publishers to sign up new authors. On the basis that my handouts were quirky and that I was too young to realize that writing a text-book at the age of 23 was academic suicide (really, textbooks take a long time to write and they are not at all valued compared to research articles), I was duly signed up. The commissioning editor was a man constantly on the verge of spontaneously combusting with intellectual energy. He can start a philosophical debate about literally anything: should he ever be trapped in a elevator he will be compelled to attempt to penetrate the occupants' minds with probing arguments that the elevator doesn't exist, that they don't exist, and that their entrapment is an illusory construct generated by their erroneous beliefs in the physical world. Ultimately, though, he'd still be a man trapped in an elevator (with several exhausted corpses). A combination of his unfaltering self-confidence, my fear of social interactions with people I don't know, and my utter bemusement that anyone would want me to write a book made me incapable of saying anything sensible to him. Ever. He must have thought that he had signed up an imbecile. He was probably right. (I find him less intimidating since thinking up the elevator scenario.) The trouble with agreeing to write books is that you then have to write them. For the next two years or so I found myself trying to juggle my research, a lectureship at the University of London, and writing a book. Had I been writing a book on heavy metal it would have been fine because all of the information was moshing away in my memory waiting to stage-dive out. Sadly, however, I had agreed to write a book on something that I new nothing about: statistics. I soon discovered that writing the book was like doing a factor analysis: in factor analysis we take a lot of information (variables) and the **R** program effortlessly reduces this mass of confusion into a simple message (fewer variables) that is easier to digest. The program does this (sort of) by filtering out the bits of the information overload that we don't need to know about. It takes a few seconds. Similarly, my younger self took a mass of information about statistics that I didn't understand and filtered it down into a simple message that I *could* understand: I became a living, breathing factor analysis … except that, unlike **R**, it took me two years and some considerable effort.

17.2. When to use factor analysis ②

In the social sciences we are often trying to measure things that cannot directly be measured (so-called **latent variables**). For example, management researchers (or psychologists even) might be interested in measuring 'burnout', which is when someone who has been working very hard on a project (a book, for example) for a prolonged period of time suddenly finds themselves devoid of motivation, inspiration, and wants to repeatedly headbutt their computer screaming 'please Mike, unlock the door, let me out of the basement, I need to feel the soft warmth of sunlight on my skin!'. You can't measure burnout directly: it has many facets. However, you can measure different aspects of burnout: you could get some idea of motivation, stress levels, whether the person has any new ideas and so on. Having done this, it would be helpful to know whether these differences really do reflect a single variable. Put another way, are these different variables driven by the same underlying variable? This chapter will look at factor analysis (and principal components analysis) – a technique for identifying groups or clusters of variables. This technique has three main uses: (1) to understand the structure of a set of variables (e.g., pioneers of intelligence such as Spearman and Thurstone used factor analysis to try to understand the structure of the latent variable 'intelligence'); (2) to construct a questionnaire to measure an underlying variable (e.g., you might design a questionnaire to measure burnout); and (3) to reduce a data set to a more manageable size while retaining as much of the original information as possible (e.g., we saw in Chapter 7 that multicollinearity can be a problem in multiple regression, and factor analysis can be used to solve this problem by combining variables that are collinear). Through this chapter we'll discover what factors are, how we find them, and what they tell us (if anything) about the relationship between the variables we've measured.

17.3. Factors ②

If we measure several variables, or ask someone several questions about themselves, the correlation between each pair of variables (or questions) can be arranged in what's known as an *R-matrix*. An *R-matrix* is just a correlation matrix: a table of correlation coefficients between variables (in fact, we saw small versions of these matrices in Chapter 6). The diagonal elements of an *R-matrix* are all ones because each variable will correlate perfectly with itself. The off-diagonal elements are the correlation coefficients between pairs of variables, or questions.[1] The existence of clusters of large correlation coefficients between subsets of variables suggests that those variables could be measuring aspects of the same underlying dimension. These underlying dimensions are known as **factors** (or *latent variables*). By reducing a data set from a group of interrelated variables into a smaller set of factors, factor analysis achieves parsimony by explaining the maximum amount of common variance in a correlation matrix using the smallest number of explanatory constructs.

What is a factor?

There are numerous examples of the use of factor analysis in the social sciences. The trait theorists in psychology used factor analysis endlessly to assess personality traits. Most readers will be familiar with the extroversion–introversion and neuroticism traits measured by Eysenck (1953). Most other personality questionnaires are based on factor analysis – notably Cattell's (1966a) 16 personality factors questionnaire – and these inventories are frequently used for recruiting purposes in industry (and even by some religious groups). However, although factor analysis is probably most famous for being adopted by psychologists, its use is by no means restricted to measuring dimensions of personality. Economists, for example, might use factor analysis to see whether productivity, profits and workforce can be reduced down to an underlying dimension of company growth.

Let's put some of these ideas into practice by imagining that we wanted to measure different aspects of what might make a person popular. We could administer several measures that we believe tap different aspects of popularity. So, we might measure a person's social skills (Social Skills), their selfishness (Selfish), how interesting others find them (Interest), the proportion of time they spend talking about the other person during a conversation (Talk1), the proportion of time they spend talking about themselves (Talk2), and their propensity to lie to people (the Liar scale). We can then calculate the correlation coefficients for each pair of variables and create an *R-matrix*. Figure 17.2 shows this matrix. Any significant correlation coefficients are shown in bold type. It is clear that there are two clusters of interrelating variables. Therefore, these variables might be measuring some common underlying dimension. The amount that someone talks about the other person during a conversation seems to correlate highly with both the level of social skills and how interesting the other finds that person. Also, social skills correlate well with how interesting others perceive a person to be. These relationships indicate that the better your social skills, the more interesting and talkative you are likely to be. However, there is a second cluster of variables. The amount that people talk about themselves within a conversation correlates with how selfish they are and how much they lie. Being selfish also correlates with the degree to which a person tells lies. In short, selfish people are likely to lie and talk about themselves.

In factor analysis we strive to reduce this *R-matrix* down into its underlying dimensions by looking at which variables seem to cluster together in a meaningful way. This data

---

[1] This matrix is called an *R-matrix*, or just *R*, because it contains correlation coefficients and *r* usually denotes Pearson's correlation (see Chapter 6) – the *r* turns into a capital letter when it denotes a matrix. Given that this book is about some software called **R**, this is slightly confusing, so be careful – it should be obvious when we are talking about the program, and when I'm talking about the correlation matrix, and when it's not, I'll tell you.

FIGURE 17.2
An *R*-matrix

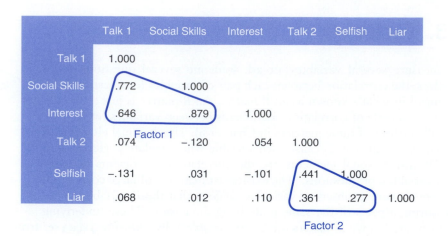

reduction is achieved by looking for variables that correlate highly with a group of other variables, but do not correlate with variables outside of that group. In this example, there appear to be two clusters that fit the bill. The first factor seems to relate to general sociability, whereas the second factor seems to relate to the way in which a person treats others socially (we might call it 'consideration'). It might, therefore, be assumed that popularity depends not only on your ability to socialize, but also on whether you are genuine towards others.

17.3.1.   Graphical representation of factors ②

Factors (not to be confused with independent variables in factorial ANOVA) are statistical entities that can be visualized as classification axes along which measurement variables can be plotted. In plain English, this statement means that if you imagine factors as being the axis of a graph, then we can plot variables along these axes. The coordinates of variables along each axis represent the strength of relationship between that variable and each factor. Figure 17.3 shows such a plot for the popularity data (in which there were only two factors). The first thing to notice is that for both factors, the axis line ranges from −1 to 1, which are the outer limits of a correlation coefficient. Therefore, the position of a given variable depends on its correlation with the two factors. The circles represent the three variables that correlate highly with factor 1 (Sociability: horizontal axis) but have a low correlation with factor 2 (Consideration: vertical axis). Conversely, the triangles represent variables that correlate highly with consideration to others but have a low correlation with sociability. From this plot, we can tell that selfishness, the amount a person talks about themselves and their propensity to lie all contribute to a factor that could be called consideration of others. Conversely, how much a person takes an interest in other people, how interesting they are and their level of social skills contribute to a second factor, sociability. This diagram therefore supports the structure that was apparent in the *R*-matrix. Of course, if a third factor existed within these data it could be represented by a third axis (creating a 3-D graph). It should also be apparent that if more than three factors exist in a data set, then a 2-D drawing cannot represent them all.

  If each axis on the graph represents a factor, then the variables that go to make up a factor can be plotted according to the extent to which they relate to a given factor. The coordinates of a variable, therefore, represent its relationship to the factors. In an ideal world a variable should have a large coordinate for one of the axes, and low coordinates for any other factors. This scenario would indicate that this particular variable related to only one

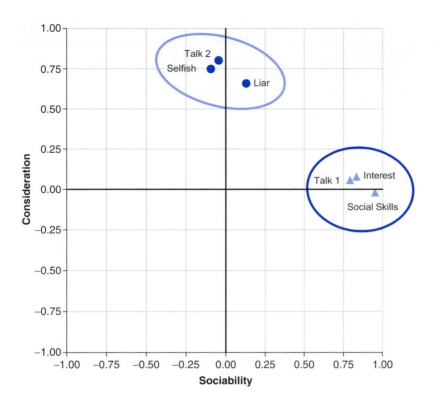

FIGURE 17.3
Example of a factor plot

factor. Variables that have large coordinates on the same axis are assumed to measure different aspects of some common underlying dimension. The coordinate of a variable along a classification axis is known as a **factor loading**. The factor loading can be thought of as the Pearson correlation between a factor and a variable (see Jane Superbrain Box 17.1). From what we know about interpreting correlation coefficients (see section 6.5.4.3) it should be clear that if we square the factor loading we obtain a measure of the substantive importance of a particular variable to a factor.

17.3.2. Mathematical representation of factors ②

The axes drawn in Figure 17.3 are straight lines and so can be described mathematically by the equation of a straight line. Therefore, factors can also be described in terms of this equation.

SELF-TEST

✓ What is the equation of a straight line?

The following equation reminds us of the equation describing a linear model and then applies this to the scenario of describing a factor:

$$Y_i = b_1 X_{1i} + b_2 X_{2i} + \ldots + b_n X_{ni} + \varepsilon_i$$

$$\text{Factor}_i = b_1 \text{ Variable}_{1i} + b_2 \text{ Variable}_{2i} + \ldots + b_n \text{ Variable}_{ni} + \varepsilon_i \tag{17.1}$$

You'll notice that there is no intercept in the equation, the reason being that the lines intersect at zero (hence the intercept is also zero). The bs in the equation represent the factor loadings.

Sticking with our example of popularity, we found that there were two factors underlying this construct: general sociability and consideration. We can, therefore, construct an equation that describes each factor in terms of the variables that have been measured. The equations are as follows:

$$Y_i = b_1 X_{1i} + b_2 X_{2i} + \ldots + b_n X_{ni} + \varepsilon_i$$
$$\text{Sociability}_i = b_1 \text{Talk1}_i + b_2 \text{Social Skills}_i + b_3 \text{Interest}_i$$
$$+ b_4 \text{Talk2}_i + b_5 \text{Selfish}_i + b_6 \text{Liar}_i + \varepsilon_i$$
$$\text{Consideration}_i = b_1 \text{Talk1}_i + b_2 \text{Social Skills}_i + b_3 \text{Interest}_i$$
$$+ b_4 \text{Talk2}_i + b_5 \text{Selfish}_i + b_6 \text{Liar}_i + \varepsilon_i$$

(17.2)

Notice that the equations are identical in form: they both include all of the variables that were measured. However, the values of b in the two equations will be different (depending on the relative importance of each variable to the particular factor). In fact, we can replace each value of b with the coordinate of that variable on the graph in Figure 17.3 (i.e., replace the values of b with the factor loading). The resulting equations are as follows:

$$Y_i = b_1 X_{1i} + b_2 X_{2i} + \ldots + b_n X_{ni} + \varepsilon_i$$
$$\text{Sociability}_i = 0.87 \text{Talk1}_i + 0.96 \text{Social Skills}_i + 0.92 \text{Interest}_i$$
$$+ 0.00 \text{Talk2}_i - 0.10 \text{Selfish}_i + 0.09 \text{Liar}_i + \varepsilon_i$$
$$\text{Consideration}_i = 0.01 \text{Talk1}_i - 0.03 \text{Social Skills}_i + 0.04 \text{Interest}_i$$
$$+ 0.82 \text{Talk2}_i + 0.75 \text{Selfish}_i + 0.70 \text{Liar}_i + \varepsilon_i$$

(17.3)

Observe that, for the sociability factor, the values of b are high for Talk1, Social Skills and Interest. For the remaining variables (Talk2, Selfish and Liar) the values of b are very low (close to 0). This tells us that three of the variables are very important for that factor (the ones with high values of b) and three are very unimportant (the ones with low values of b). We saw that this point is true because of the way that three variables clustered highly on the factor plot. The point to take on board here is that the factor plot and these equations represent the same thing: the factor loadings in the plot are simply the b-values in these equations (but see Jane Superbrain Box 17.1). For the second factor, inconsideration to others, the opposite pattern can be seen in that Talk2, Selfish and Liar all have high values of b whereas the remaining three variables have b-values close to 0. In an ideal world, variables would have very high b-values for one factor and very low b-values for all other factors.

These factor loadings can be placed in a matrix in which the columns represent each factor and the rows represent the loadings of each variable on each factor. For the popularity data this matrix would have two columns (one for each factor) and six rows (one for each variable). This matrix, usually denoted A, is given by:

$$A = \begin{pmatrix} 0.87 & 0.01 \\ 0.96 & -0.03 \\ 0.92 & 0.04 \\ 0.00 & 0.82 \\ -0.10 & 0.75 \\ 0.09 & 0.70 \end{pmatrix}$$

To understand what the matrix means, try relating the elements to the loadings in equation (17.3). For example, the top row represents the first variable, Talk1, which had a loading of .87 for the first factor (Sociability) and a loading of .01 for the second factor (Consideration). This matrix is called the **factor matrix** or **component matrix** (if doing **principal components analysis**) – see Jane Superbrain Box 17.1 to find out about the different forms of this matrix.

The major assumption in factor analysis is that these algebraic factors represent real-world dimensions, the nature of which must be *guessed at* by inspecting which variables have high loads on the same factor. So, psychologists might believe that factors represent dimensions of the psyche, education researchers might believe they represent abilities, and sociologists might believe they represent races or social classes. However, it is an extremely contentious point whether this assumption is tenable, and some believe that the dimensions derived from factor analysis are real only in the statistical sense – and are real-world fictions.

JANE SUPERBRAIN 17.1

What's the difference between a pattern matrix and a structure matrix? ③

Throughout my discussion of factor loadings I've been quite vague. Sometimes I've said that these loadings can be thought of as the correlation between a variable and a given factor, then at other times I've described these loadings in terms of regression coefficients (*b*). Now, it should be obvious from what we discovered in Chapters 6 and 7 that correlation coefficients and regression coefficients are quite different things, so what the hell am I going on about: shouldn't I make up my mind what the factor loadings actually are?

Well, in vague terms (the best terms for my brain) both correlation coefficients and regression coefficients represent the relationship between a variable and linear model in a broad sense, so the key take-home message is that

factor loadings tell us about the relative contribution that a variable makes to a factor. As long as you understand that much, you have no problems.

However, the factor loadings in a given analysis can be both correlation coefficients and regression coefficients. Soon we'll discover that the interpretation of factor analysis is helped greatly by a technique known as *rotation*. Without going into details, there are two types: orthogonal and oblique rotation (see section 17.3.9). When orthogonal rotation is used, any underlying factors are assumed to be independent, and the factor loading *is* the correlation between the factor and the variable, but is also the regression coefficient. Put another way, the values of the correlation coefficients are the same as the values of the regression coefficients. However, there are situations in which the underlying factors are assumed to be related or correlated to each other. In these situations, oblique rotation is used and the resulting correlations between variables and factors will differ from the corresponding regression coefficients. In this case, there are, in effect, two different sets of factor loadings: the correlation coefficients between each variable and factor (which are put in the factor **structure matrix**) and the regression coefficients for each variable on each factor (which are put in the factor **pattern matrix**). These coefficients can have quite different interpretations (see Graham, Guthrie, & Thompson, 2003).

17.3.3. Factor scores ②

A factor can be described in terms of the variables measured and the relative importance of them for that factor (represented by the value of *b*). Therefore, having discovered which factors exist, and estimated the equation that describes them, it should be possible to also estimate a person's score on a factor, based on their scores for the constituent variables. These scores are known as **factor scores**. As such, if we wanted to derive a score of sociability for a particular person, we could place their scores on the various measures into equation (17.3). This method is known as a *weighted average*. In fact, this method is overly simplistic and rarely used, but it is probably the easiest way to explain the principle. For example, imagine the six scales all range from 1 to 10 and that someone scored the following: Talk1 (4), Social Skills (9), Interest (8), Talk2 (6), Selfish (8), and Liar (6). We could put these values into equation (17.3) to get a score for this person's sociability and their consideration to others:

$$
\begin{aligned}
\text{Sociability} &= 0.87\text{Talk1} + 0.96\text{Social Skills} + 0.92\text{Interest} \\
&\quad + 0.00\text{Talk2} - 0.10\text{Selfish} + 0.09\text{Liar} \\
&= (0.87 \times 4) + (0.96 \times 9) + (0.92 \times 8) + (0.00 \times 6) \\
&\quad - (0.10 \times 8) + (0.09 \times 6) \\
&= 19.22 \\
\text{Consideration} &= 0.01\text{Talk1} - 0.03\text{Social Skills} + 0.04\text{Interest} \\
&\quad + 0.82\text{Talk2} + 0.75\text{Selfish} + 0.70\text{Liar} \\
&= (0.01 \times 4) - (0.03 \times 9) + (0.04 \times 8) + (0.82 \times 6) \\
&\quad + (0.75 \times 8) + (0.70 \times 6) \\
&= 15.21
\end{aligned}
\tag{17.4}
$$

The resulting scores of 19.22 and 15.21 reflect the degree to which this person is sociable and their inconsideration to others, respectively. This person scores higher on sociability than inconsideration. However, the scales of measurement used will influence the resulting scores, and if different variables use different measurement scales, then factor scores for different factors cannot be compared. As such, this method of calculating factor scores is poor and more sophisticated methods are usually used.

17.3.3.1. The regression method ④

There are several sophisticated techniques for calculating factor scores that use factor score coefficients as weights in equation (17.1) rather than using the factor loadings. The form of the equation remains the same, but the bs in the equation are replaced with these factor score coefficients. Factor score coefficients can be calculated in several ways. The simplest way is the regression method. In this method the factor loadings are adjusted to take account of the initial correlations between variables; in doing so, differences in units of measurement and variable variances are stabilized.

To obtain the matrix of factor score coefficients (B) we multiply the matrix of factor loadings by the inverse (R^{-1}) of the original correlation or R-matrix. You might remember from the previous chapter that matrices cannot be divided (see section 16.4.4.1). Therefore, if we want to divide by a matrix it cannot be done directly and instead we multiply by its inverse. Therefore, by multiplying the matrix of factor loadings by the inverse of the correlation matrix we are, conceptually speaking, dividing the factor loadings by the correlation coefficients. The resulting factor score matrix, therefore, represents the relationship between each variable and each factor, taking into account the original relationships between pairs of variables. As such, this matrix represents a purer measure of the *unique* relationship between variables and factors.

The matrices for the popularity data are shown below. The resulting matrix of factor score coefficients, B, comes from the **R** (the program) output. The matrices R^{-1} and A can be multiplied by hand to get the matrix B, and those familiar with matrix algebra – or who have consulted Namboodiri, (1984) or Stevens (2002) – might like to verify the result (see Oliver Twisted). To get the same degree of accuracy as $\mathbf{R}$ you should work to at least five decimal places:

$$B = R^{-1}A$$

$$B = \begin{pmatrix} 4.76 & -7.46 & 3.91 & -2.35 & 2.42 & -0.49 \\ -7.46 & 18.49 & -12.42 & 5.45 & -5.54 & 1.22 \\ 3.91 & -12.42 & 10.07 & -3.65 & 3.79 & -0.96 \\ -2.35 & 5.45 & -3.65 & 2.97 & -2.16 & 0.02 \\ 2.42 & -5.54 & 3.79 & -2.16 & 2.98 & -0.56 \\ -0.49 & 1.22 & -0.96 & 0.02 & -0.56 & 1.27 \end{pmatrix} \begin{pmatrix} 0.87 & 0.01 \\ 0.96 & -0.03 \\ 0.92 & 0.04 \\ 0.00 & 0.82 \\ -0.10 & 0.75 \\ 0.09 & 0.70 \end{pmatrix}$$

$$B = \begin{pmatrix} 0.343 & 0.006 \\ 0.376 & -0.020 \\ 0.362 & 0.020 \\ 0.000 & 0.473 \\ -0.037 & 0.437 \\ 0.039 & 0.405 \end{pmatrix}$$

The pattern of the loadings is the same for the factor score coefficients: that is, the first three variables have high loadings for the first factor and low loadings for the second, whereas the pattern is reversed for the last three variables. The difference is only in the actual value of the weightings, which are smaller because the correlations between variables are now accounted for. These factor score coefficients can be used to replace the b-values in equation (17.2):

$$\begin{aligned} \text{Sociability} &= 0.343\text{Talk1} + 0.376\text{Social Skills} + 0.362\text{Interest} \\ &\quad + 0.000\text{Talk2} - 0.037\text{Selfish} + 0.039\text{Liar} \\ &= (0.343 \times 4) + (0.376 \times 9) + (0.362 \times 8) + (0.000 \times 6) \\ &\quad - (0.037 \times 8) + (0.039 \times 6) \\ &= 7.59 \end{aligned}$$

$$\begin{aligned} \text{Consideration} &= 0.006\text{Talk1} - 0.020\text{Social Skills} + 0.020\text{Interest} \quad\quad (17.5) \\ &\quad + 0.473\text{Talk2} + 0.437\text{Selfish} + 0.405\text{Liar} \\ &= (0.006 \times 4) - (0.020 \times 9) + (0.020 \times 8) + (0.473 \times 6) \\ &\quad + (0.437 \times 8) + (0.405 \times 6) \\ &= 8.768 \end{aligned}$$

Equation (17.5) shows how these coefficient scores are used to produce two factor scores for each person. In this case, the participant had the same scores on each variable as were used in equation (17.4). The resulting scores are much more similar than when the factor loadings were used as weights because the different variances among the six variables have now been controlled for. The fact that the values are very similar reflects the fact that this person not only scores highly on variables relating to sociability, but is also inconsiderate (i.e., they score equally highly on both factors). This technique for producing factor scores ensures that the resulting scores have a mean of 0 and a variance equal to the squared multiple correlation between the estimated factor scores and the true factor values. However, the downside of the regression method is that the scores can correlate not only with factors other than the one on which they are based, but also with other factor scores from a different orthogonal factor.

OLIVER TWISTED

Please Sir, can I have some more … matrix algebra?

'*The Matrix* …', enthuses Oliver, '… that was a good film. I want to dress in black and glide through the air as though time has stood still. Maybe the matrix of factor scores is as cool as the film.' I think you might be disappointed, Oliver, but we'll give it a shot. The matrix calculations of factor scores are detailed in the additional material for this chapter on the companion website. Be afraid, be very afraid …

17.3.3.2. Uses of factor scores ②

There are several uses of factor scores. First, if the purpose of the factor analysis is to reduce a large set of data into a smaller subset of measurement variables, then the factor scores tell us an individual's score on this subset of measures. Therefore, any further analysis can be carried out on the factor scores rather than the original data. For example, we could carry out a *t*-test to see whether females are significantly more sociable than males using the factor scores for *sociability*. A second use is in overcoming collinearity problems in regression. If, following a multiple regression analysis, we have identified sources of multicollinearity then the interpretation of the analysis is questioned (see section 7.7.2.3). In this situation, we can carry out a principal components analysis on the predictor variables to reduce them down to a subset of uncorrelated factors. The variables causing the multicollinearity will combine to form a factor. If we then rerun the regression but using the factor scores as predictor variables then the problem of multicollinearity should vanish (because the variables are now combined into a single factor).

By now, you should have some grasp of the concept of what a factor is, how it is represented graphically, how it is represented algebraically, and how we can calculate composite scores representing an individual's 'performance' on a single factor. I have deliberately restricted the discussion to a conceptual level, without delving into how we actually find these mythical beasts known as factors. This section will look at how we find factors. Specifically, we will examine different types of method, look at the maths behind one method (principal components), investigate the criteria for determining whether factors are important, and discover how to improve the interpretation of a given solution.

17.3.4. Choosing a method ②

The first thing you need to know is that there are several methods for unearthing factors in your data. The method you chose will depend on what you hope to do with the analysis. Tinsley and Tinsley (1987) give an excellent account of the different methods available. There are two things to consider: whether you want to generalize the findings from your sample to a population and whether you are exploring your data or testing a specific hypothesis. This chapter describes techniques for exploring data using factor analysis. Testing hypotheses about the structures of latent variables and their relationships to each other requires considerable complexity and can be done with packages such as *sem* or *Lavaan* in **R**.[2] Those interested in hypothesis testing techniques (known as **confirmatory**

---

[2] The *sem* package is the more straightforward, but is slightly less capable of handling unusual situations than *Lavaan* (*sem* was written by John Fox, who also wrote *R Commander*).

factor analysis) are advised to read Pedhazur and Schmelkin (1991, Chapter 23) for an introduction.

Assuming we want to explore our data, we then need to consider whether we want to apply our findings to the sample collected (descriptive method) or to generalize our findings to a population (inferential methods). When factor analysis was originally developed it was assumed that it would be used to explore data to generate future hypotheses. As such, it was assumed that the technique would be applied to the entire population of interest. Therefore, certain techniques assume that the sample used is the population, and so results cannot be extrapolated beyond that particular sample. Principal components analysis is an example of one of these techniques, as is principal factors analysis (*principal axis factoring*). Principal components analysis and principal factors analysis are the preferred methods and usually result in similar solutions (see section 17.3.6). When these methods are used, conclusions are restricted to the sample collected and generalization of the results can be achieved only if analysis using different samples reveals the same factor structure.

Another approach has been to assume that participants are randomly selected and that the variables measured constitute the population of variables in which we're interested. By assuming this, it is possible to develop techniques from which the results can be generalized from the sample participants to a larger population. However, a constraint is that any findings hold true only for the set of variables measured (because we've assumed this set constitutes the entire population of variables). Techniques in this category include the maximum-likelihood method (see Harman, 1976) and Kaiser's alpha factoring. The choice of method depends largely on what generalizations, if any, you want to make from your data.[3]

17.3.5. Communality ②

Before continuing, it is important that you understand some basic things about the variance within an *R*-matrix. It is possible to calculate the variability in scores (the variance) for any given measure (or variable). You should be familiar with the idea of variance by now and comfortable with how it can be calculated (if not, see Chapter 2). The total variance for a particular variable will have two components: some of it will be shared with other variables or measures (**common variance**) and some of it will be specific to that measure (**unique variance**). We tend to use the term *unique variance* to refer to variance that can be reliably attributed to only one measure. However, there is also variance that is specific to one measure but not reliably so; this variance is called error or **random variance**. The proportion of common variance present in a variable is known as the **communality**. As such, a variable that has no specific variance (or random variance) would have a communality of 1; a variable that shares none of its variance with any other variable would have a communality of 0.

In factor analysis we are interested in finding common underlying dimensions within the data and so we are primarily interested only in the common variance. Therefore, when we run a factor analysis it is fundamental that we know how much of the variance present in our data is common variance. This presents us with a logical impasse: to do the factor analysis we need to know the proportion of common variance present in the data, yet the only way to find out the extent of the common variance is by carrying out a factor analysis. There are two ways to approach this problem. The first is to assume that all of the variance is common variance. As such, we assume that the communality of every variable is 1. By making this assumption we merely transpose our original data into constituent linear components (known as principal components analysis). The second approach is to estimate the

---

[3] It's worth noting at this point that principal component analysis is not in fact the same as factor analysis. This doesn't stop idiots like me from discussing them as though they are, but more on that later.

amount of common variance by estimating communality values for each variable. There are various methods of estimating communalities, but the most widely used (including **alpha factoring**) is to use the squared multiple correlation (SMC) of each variable with all others. So, for the popularity data, imagine you ran a multiple regression using one measure (Selfish) as the outcome and the other five measures as predictors: the resulting multiple R^2 (see section 7.6.2) would be used as an estimate of the communality for the variable Selfish. This second approach is used in factor analysis. These estimates allow the factor analysis to be done. Once the underlying factors have been extracted, new communalities can be calculated that represent the multiple correlation between each variable and the factors extracted. Therefore, the communality is a measure of the proportion of variance explained by the extracted factors.

17.3.6. Factor analysis vs. principal components analysis ②

I have just explained that there are two approaches to locating underlying dimensions of a data set: factor analysis and principal components analysis. These techniques differ in the communality estimates that are used. Simplistically, though, factor analysis derives a mathematical model from which factors are estimated, whereas principal components analysis merely decomposes the original data into a set of linear variates – see Dunteman, (1989) and Widaman (2007) for more detail on the differences between the procedures. As such, only factor analysis can estimate the underlying factors, and it relies on various assumptions for these estimates to be accurate. Principal components analysis is concerned only with establishing which linear components exist within the data and how a particular variable might contribute to that component. In terms of theory, this chapter is dedicated to principal components analysis rather than factor analysis. The reasons are that principal components analysis is a psychometrically sound procedure, is conceptually less complex than factor analysis, and bears numerous similarities to discriminant analysis (described in the previous chapter).

However, we should consider whether the techniques provide different solutions to the same problem. Based on an extensive literature review, Guadagnoli and Velicer (1988) concluded that the solutions generated from principal components analysis differ little from those derived from factor analysis techniques. In reality, there are some circumstances for which this statement is untrue. Stevens (2002) summarizes the evidence and concludes that, with 30 or more variables and communalities greater than .7 for all variables, different solutions are unlikely; however, with fewer than 20 variables and any low communalities (< .4), differences can occur.

The flip-side of this argument is eloquently described by Cliff (1987) who observed that proponents of factor analysis 'insist that components analysis is at best a common factor analysis with some error added and at worst an unrecognizable hodgepodge of things from which nothing can be determined' (p. 349). Indeed, feeling is strong on this issue, with some arguing that when principal components analysis is used it should not be described as a factor analysis and that you should not impute substantive meaning to the resulting components. However, to non-statisticians the difference between a principal component and a factor may be difficult to conceptualize (they are both linear models), and the differences arise largely from the calculation.[4]

---

[4] For this reason I have used the terms *components* and *factors* interchangeably throughout this chapter. Although this use of terms will reduce some statisticians (and psychologists) to tears, I'm banking on these people not needing to read this book. I acknowledge the methodological differences, but I think it's easier for students if I dwell on the similarities between the techniques and not the differences.

17.3.7.   Theory behind principal components analysis ③

Principal components analysis works in a very similar way to MANOVA and discriminant function analysis (see previous chapter). Although it isn't necessary to understand the mathematical principles in any detail, readers of the previous chapter may benefit from some comparisons between the two techniques. For those who haven't read that chapter, I suggest you flick through it before moving ahead!

In MANOVA, various sum of squares and cross-product matrices were calculated that contained information about the relationships between dependent variables. I mentioned before that these SSCP matrices could be easily converted to variance–covariance matrices, which represent the same information but in averaged form (i.e., taking account of the number of observations). I also said that by dividing each element by the relevant standard deviation the variance–covariance matrices become standardized. The result is a correlation matrix. In principal components analysis we usually deal with correlation matrices (although it is possible to analyse a variance–covariance matrix too), and the point to note is that this matrix pretty much represents the same information as an SSCP matrix in MANOVA. The difference is just that the correlation matrix is an averaged version of the SSCP that has been standardized.

In MANOVA, we used several SSCP matrices that represented different components of experimental variation (the model variation and the residual variation). In principal components analysis the covariance (or correlation) matrix cannot be broken down in this way (because all data come from the same group of participants). In MANOVA, we ended up looking at the variates or components of the SSCP matrix that represented the ratio of the model variance to the error variance. These variates were linear dimensions that separated the groups tested, and we saw that the dependent variables mapped onto these underlying components. In short, we looked at whether the groups could be separated by some linear combination of the dependent variables. These variates were found by calculating the eigenvectors of the SSCP. The number of variates obtained was the smaller of p (the number of dependent variables) and $k - 1$ (where k is the number of groups). In component analysis we do something similar (I'm simplifying things a little, but it will give you the basic idea). That is, we take a correlation matrix and calculate the variates. There are no groups of observations, and so the number of variates calculated will always equal the number of variables measured (p). The variates are described, as for MANOVA, by the eigenvectors associated with the correlation matrix. The elements of the eigenvectors are the weights of each variable on the variate (see equation (16.5)). These values are the factor loadings described earlier. The largest eigenvalue associated with each of the eigenvectors provides a single indicator of the substantive importance of each variate (or component). The basic idea is that we retain factors with relatively large eigenvalues and ignore those with relatively small eigenvalues.

The eigenvalue for a factor can also be calculated by summing the square of the loadings for that factor. This isn't much use if you're calculating factor analysis, because you need to calculate the eigenvalues to calculate the loadings. But it can be a useful way to help understand the eigenvalues – the higher the loadings on a factor, the more of the variance in the variables that the factor explains.

In summary, component analysis works in a similar way to MANOVA. We begin with a matrix representing the relationships between variables. The linear components (also called variates, or factors) of that matrix are then calculated by determining the eigenvalues of the matrix. These eigenvalues are used to calculate eigenvectors, the elements of which provide the loading of a particular variable on a particular factor (i.e., they are the b-values in equation (17.1)). The eigenvalue is also a measure of the substantive importance of the eigenvector with which it is associated.

17.3.8.   Factor extraction: eigenvalues and the scree plot ②

How many factors should I extract?

Not all factors are retained in an analysis, and there is debate over the criterion used to decide whether a factor is statistically important. I mentioned above that the eigenvalues associated with a variate indicate the substantive importance of that factor. Therefore, it seems logical that we should retain only factors with large eigenvalues. Retaining factors is known as factor **extraction**. How do we decide whether or not an eigenvalue is large enough to represent a meaningful factor? Well, one technique advocated by Cattell (1966b) is to plot a graph of each eigenvalue (Y-axis) against the factor with which it is associated (X-axis). This graph is known as a **scree plot** (because it looks like a rock face with a pile of debris, or scree, at the bottom). I mentioned earlier that it is possible to obtain as many factors as there are variables and that each has an associated eigenvalue. By graphing the eigenvalues, the relative importance of each factor becomes apparent. Typically there will be a few factors with quite high eigenvalues, and many factors with relatively low eigenvalues, and so this graph has a very characteristic shape: there is a sharp descent in the curve followed by a tailing off (see Figure 17.4). Cattell (1966b) argued that the cut-off point for selecting factors should be at the point of inflexion of this curve. The point of inflexion is where the slope of the line changes dramatically: so, in Figure 17.4, imagine drawing a straight line that summarizes the vertical part of the plot and another that summarizes the horizontal part (the blue dashed lines); then the point of inflexion is the data point at which these two lines meet. In both examples in Figure 17.4 the point of inflexion occurs at the third data point (factor); therefore, we would extract two factors. Thus, you retain (or extract) only factors to the left of the point of inflexion (and do not include the factor at the point of inflexion itself).[5] With a sample of more than 200 participants, the scree plot provides a fairly reliable criterion for factor selection (Stevens, 2002).

Although scree plots are very useful, factor selection should not be based on this criterion alone. Kaiser (1960) recommended retaining all factors with eigenvalues greater than 1. This criterion is based on the idea that the eigenvalues represent the amount of variation explained by a factor and that an eigenvalue of 1 represents a substantial amount of variation. Jolliffe (1972, 1986) reports that **Kaiser's criterion** is too strict and suggests the third option of retaining all factors with eigenvalues greater than .7. The difference between how many factors are retained using Kaiser's methods compared to Jolliffe's can be dramatic.

You might well wonder how the methods compare. Generally speaking, Kaiser's criterion overestimates the number of factors to retain (see Jane Superbrain Box 17.2) but there is some evidence that it is accurate when the number of variables is less than 30 and the resulting communalities (after extraction) are all greater than .7. Kaiser's criterion can also be accurate when the sample size exceeds 250 and the average communality is greater than or equal to .6. In any other circumstances you are best advised to use a scree plot provided the sample size is greater than 200 (see Stevens, 2002, for more detail).

---

[5] Actually, in his original paper, Cattell advised including the factor at the point of inflexion as well because it is 'desirable to include at least one common error factor as a "garbage can"'. The idea is that the point of inflexion represents an error factor. However, in practice this garbage can factor is rarely retained; also Thurstone argued that it is better to retain too few than too many factors, so most people do *not* retain the factor at the point of inflexion.

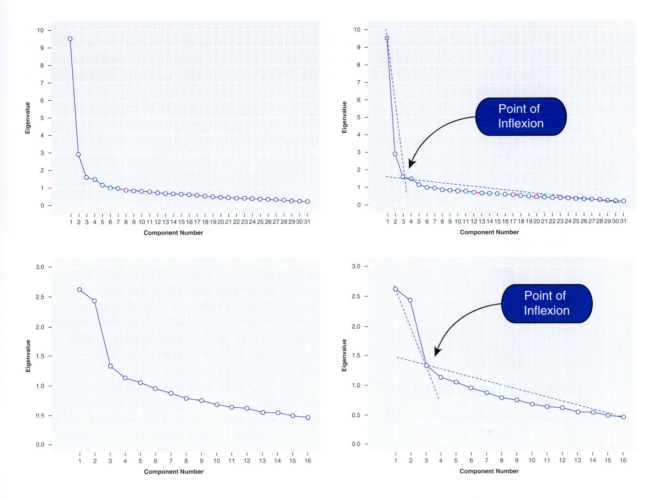

FIGURE 17.4
Examples of scree plots for data that probably have two underlying factors

However, as is often the case in statistics, the three criteria often provide different solutions. In these situations the communalities of the factors need to be considered. In principal components analysis we begin with communalities of 1 with all factors retained (because we assume that all variance is common variance). At this stage all we have done is to find the linear variates that exist in the data – so we have just transformed the data without discarding any information. However, to discover what common variance *really* exists between variables we must decide which factors are meaningful and discard any that are too trivial to consider. Therefore, we discard some information. The factors we retain will not explain all of the variance in the data (because we have discarded some information) and so the communalities after extraction will always be less than 1. The factors retained do not map perfectly onto the original variables – they merely reflect the common variance present in the data. If the communalities represent a loss of information then they are important statistics. The closer the communalities are to 1, the better our factors are at explaining the original data. It is logical that the greater the number of factors retained, the greater the communalities will be (because less information is discarded); therefore, the communalities are good indices of whether too few factors have been retained. In fact, with generalized least-squares factor analysis and maximum-likelihood factor analysis you can get a statistical measure of the goodness of fit of the factor solution (see the next chapter for more on goodness-of-fit tests). This basically measures the proportion of variance that the factor solution explains (so can be thought of as comparing communalities before and after extraction).

As a final word of advice, your decision on how many factors to extract will depend also on why you're doing the analysis; for example, if you're trying to overcome multicollinearity problems in regression, then it might be better to extract too many factors than too few.

JANE SUPERBRAIN 17.2

How many factors do I retain? ③

The discussion of factor extraction in the text is somewhat simplified. In fact, there are fundamental problems with Kaiser's criterion (Nunnally & Bernstein, 1994; Preacher & MacCallum, 2003). For one thing an eigenvalue of 1 means different things in different analyses: with 100 variables it means that a factor explains 1% of the variance, but with 10 variables it means that a factor explains 10% of the variance. Clearly, these two situations are very different and a single rule that covers both is inappropriate. An eigenvalue of 1 also means only that the factor explains as much variance as a variable, which rather defeats the original intention of the analysis to reduce variables down to 'more substantive' underlying factors (Nunnally & Bernstein, 1994). Consequently, Kaiser's criterion often overestimates the number of factors. On this basis Jolliffe's criterion is even worse (a factor explains less variance than a variable!).

There are other ways to determine how many factors to retain, but they are more complex (which is why I'm discussing them outside of the main text). The best is probably parallel analysis (Horn, 1965). Essentially each eigenvalue (which represents the size of the factor) is compared against an eigenvalue for the corresponding factor in many randomly generated data sets that have the same characteristics as the data being analysed. In doing so, each eigenvalue is being compared to an eigenvalue from a data set that has no underlying factors. This is a bit like asking whether our observed factor is bigger than a non-existing factor. Factors that are bigger than their 'random' counterparts are retained. Of parallel analysis, the scree plot and Kaiser's criterion, Kaiser's criterion is, in general, worst and parallel analysis best (Zwick & Velicer, 1986).

17.3.9. Improving interpretation: factor rotation ③

Once factors have been extracted, it is possible to calculate to what degree variables load on these factors (i.e., calculate the loading of the variable on each factor). Generally, you will find that most variables have high loadings on the most important factor and small loadings on all other factors. This characteristic makes interpretation difficult, and so a technique called factor rotation is used to discriminate between factors. If a factor is a classification axis along which variables can be plotted, then factor **rotation** effectively rotates these factor axes such that variables are loaded maximally on only one factor. Figure 17.5 demonstrates how this process works using an example in which there are only two factors.

Imagine that a sociologist was interested in classifying university lecturers as a demographic group. She discovered that two underlying dimensions best describe this group: alcoholism and achievement (go to any academic conference and you'll see that academics drink heavily). The first factor, alcoholism, has a cluster of variables associated with it (dark blue circles), and these could be measures such as the number of units drunk in a week, dependency and obsessive personality. The second factor, achievement, also has a cluster of variables associated with it (light blue circles), and these could be measures relating to salary, job status and number of research publications. Initially, the full lines represent the factors, and by looking at the coordinates it should be clear that the light blue circles have high loadings for factor 2 (they are a long way up this axis) and medium loadings for factor 1 (they are not very far up this axis). Conversely, the dark blue circles have high loadings for factor 1 and medium loadings for factor 2. By rotating the axes (dashed lines), we ensure that both clusters of variables are intersected by the factor to which they relate most. So, after rotation, the loadings of the variables are maximized on one factor (the factor that intersects the cluster) and minimized on the remaining factor(s). If an axis passes through a cluster of variables, then these variables will have a loading of approximately zero on the opposite axis. If this idea is confusing, then look at Figure 17.5 and think about the values of the coordinates before and after rotation (this is best achieved by turning the book when you look at the rotated axes).

There are two types of rotation that can be done. The first is **orthogonal rotation**, and the left-hand side of Figure 17.5 represents this method. In Chapter 10 we saw that the term *orthogonal* means unrelated, and in this context it means that we rotate factors while keeping them independent, or unrelated. Before rotation, all factors are independent (i.e., they do not correlate at all) and orthogonal rotation ensures that the factors remain uncorrelated. That is why in Figure 17.5 the axes are turned while remaining perpendicular.[6] The other form of rotation is **oblique rotation**. The difference with oblique rotation is that the factors are allowed to correlate (hence, the axes of the right-hand diagram of Figure 17.5 do not remain perpendicular).

The choice of rotation depends on whether there is a good theoretical reason to suppose that the factors should be related or independent (but see my later comments on this), and also how the variables cluster on the factors before rotation. On the first point, we might not expect alcoholism to be completely independent of achievement (after all, high achievement leads to high stress, which can lead to the drinks cabinet!). Therefore, on theoretical grounds, we might choose oblique rotation. On the second point, Figure 17.5 demonstrates how the positioning of clusters is important in determining how successful the rotation will be (note the position of the light blue circles). Specifically, if an orthogonal rotation was carried out on the right-hand diagram it would be considerably less successful in maximizing loadings than the oblique rotation that is displayed. One approach is to run the analysis using both types of rotation. Pedhazur and Schmelkin (1991) suggest that if the oblique rotation demonstrates a negligible correlation between the extracted factors then it is reasonable to use the orthogonally rotated solution. If the oblique rotation reveals a correlated factor structure, then the orthogonally rotated solution should be discarded. In

---

[6] This term means that the axes are at right angles to one another.

FIGURE 17.5
Schematic representations of factor rotation. The left graph displays orthogonal rotation whereas the right graph displays oblique rotation (see text for more details). θ is the angle through which the axes are rotated

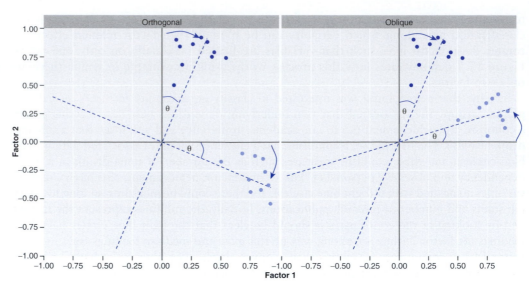

any case, an oblique rotation should be used only if there are good reasons to suppose that the underlying factors *could* be related in theoretical terms.

The mathematics behind factor rotation is complex (especially oblique rotation). However, in oblique rotation, because each factor can be rotated by different amounts, a **factor transformation matrix,** Λ is needed. The factor transformation matrix is a square matrix and its size depends on how many factors were extracted from the data. If two factors are extracted then it will be a 2×2 matrix, but if four factors are extracted then it becomes a 4×4 matrix. The values in the factor transformation matrix consist of sines and cosines of the angle of axis rotation (θ). This matrix is multiplied by the matrix of unrotated factor loadings, A, to obtain a matrix of rotated factor loadings.

For the case of two factors the factor transformation matrix would be:

$$\Lambda = \begin{pmatrix} \cos\theta & -\sin\theta \\ \sin\theta & \cos\theta \end{pmatrix}$$

Therefore, you should think of this matrix as representing the angle through which the axes have been rotated, or the degree to which factors have been rotated. The angle of rotation necessary to optimize the factor solution is found in an iterative way (see R's Souls' Tip 8.1) and different methods can be used.

17.3.9.1. Choosing a method of factor rotation ③

The **R** function that we will use has four methods of orthogonal rotation (**varimax, quartimax,** BentlerT and geominT) and five methods of oblique rotation (oblimin, **promax,** simplimax, BentlerQ and geominQ). These methods differ in how they rotate the factors and, therefore, the resulting output depends on which method you select.

The most important orthogonal rotations are quartimax and varimax. Quartimax rotation attempts to maximize the spread of factor loadings for a variable across all factors.

Therefore, interpreting variables becomes easier. However, this often results in lots of variables loading highly on a single factor. Varimax is the opposite in that it attempts to maximize the dispersion of loadings within factors. Therefore, it tries to load a smaller number of variables highly on each factor, resulting in more interpretable clusters of factors. For a first analysis, you should probably select varimax because it is a good general approach that simplifies the interpretation of factors.

The two important oblique rotations are promax and oblimin. Promax is a faster procedure designed for very large data sets. (If you are interested in adjustments that can be made to these rotations, other rotations, and even hand rotations, you can consult the *GPARotate()* function, found in the *psych* package.)

In theory, the exact choice of rotation will depend largely on whether or not you think that the underlying factors should be related. If you expect the factors to be independent then you should choose one of the orthogonal rotations (I recommend varimax). If, however, there are theoretical grounds for supposing that your factors might correlate, then **direct oblimin** should be selected. In practice, there are strong grounds to believe that orthogonal rotations are a complete nonsense for naturalistic data, and certainly for any data involving humans (can you think of any psychological construct that is not in any way correlated with some other psychological construct?). As such, some argue that orthogonal rotations should never be used.

17.3.9.2. Substantive importance of factor loadings ②

Once a factor structure has been found, it is important to decide which variables make up which factors. Earlier I said that the factor loadings were a gauge of the substantive importance of a given variable to a given factor. Therefore, it makes sense that we use these values to place variables with factors. It is possible to assess the statistical significance of a factor loading (after all, it is simply a correlation coefficient or regression coefficient); however, there are various reasons why this option is not as easy as it seems (see Stevens, 2002, p. 393). Typically, researchers take a loading of an absolute value of more than 0.3 to be important. However, the significance of a factor loading will depend on the sample size. Stevens (2002) produced a table of critical values against which loadings can be compared. To summarize, he recommends that for a sample size of 50 a loading of 0.722 can be considered significant, for 100 the loading should be greater than 0.512, for 200 it should be greater than 0.364, for 300 it should be greater than 0.298, for 600 it should be greater than 0.21, and for 1000 it should be greater than 0.162. These values are based on an alpha level of .01 (two-tailed), which allows for the fact that several loadings will need to be tested (see Stevens, 2002, for further detail). Therefore, in very large samples, small loadings can be considered statistically meaningful. (**R** can provide significance tests of factor loadings, but these get rather complex and are rarely used. By applying Stevens's guidelines you should gain some insight into the structure of variables and factors.)

The significance of a loading gives little indication of the substantive importance of a variable to a factor. This value can be found by squaring the factor loading to give an estimate of the amount of variance in a factor accounted for by a variable (like R^2). In this respect Stevens (2002) recommends interpreting only factor loadings with an absolute value greater than 0.4 (which explain around 16% of the variance in the variable).

17.4. Research example ②

One of the uses of factor analysis is to develop questionnaires: after all, if you want to measure an ability or trait, you need to ensure that the questions asked relate to the construct

FIGURE 17.6

The **R** anxiety questionnaire (RAQ)

SD = Strongly Disagree, D = Disagree, N = Neither, A = Agree, SA = Strongly Agree

		SD	D	N	A	SA
1	Statistics make me cry	O	O	O	O	O
2	My friends will think I'm stupid for not being able to cope with R	O	O	O	O	O
3	Standard deviations excite me	O	O	O	O	O
4	I dream that Pearson is attacking me with correlation coefficients	O	O	O	O	O
5	I don't understand statistics	O	O	O	O	O
6	I have little experience of computers	O	O	O	O	O
7	All computers hate me	O	O	O	O	O
8	I have never been good at mathematics	O	O	O	O	O
9	My friends are better at statistics than me	O	O	O	O	O
10	Computers are useful only for playing games	O	O	O	O	O
11	I did badly at mathematics at school	O	O	O	O	O
12	People try to tell you that R makes statistics easier to understand but it doesn't	O	O	O	O	O
13	I worry that I will cause irreparable damage because of my incompetence with computers	O	O	O	O	O
14	Computers have minds of their own and deliberately go wrong whenever I use them	O	O	O	O	O
15	Computers are out to get me	O	O	O	O	O
16	I weep openly at the mention of central tendency	O	O	O	O	O
17	I slip into a coma whenever I see an equation	O	O	O	O	O
18	R always crashes when I try to use it	O	O	O	O	O
19	Everybody looks at me when I use R	O	O	O	O	O
20	I can't sleep for thoughts of eigenvectors	O	O	O	O	O
21	I wake up under my duvet thinking that I am trapped under a normal distribution	O	O	O	O	O
22	My friends are better at R than I am	O	O	O	O	O
23	If I am good at statistics people will think I am a nerd	O	O	O	O	O

that you intend to measure. I have noticed that a lot of students become very stressed about **R**. Therefore I wanted to design a questionnaire to measure a trait that I termed '**R** anxiety'. I decided to devise a questionnaire to measure various aspects of students' anxiety towards learning **R**. I generated questions based on interviews with anxious and non-anxious students and came up with 23 possible questions to include. Each question was a statement followed by a five-point Likert scale ranging from 'strongly disagree' through 'neither agree nor disagree' to 'strongly agree'. The questionnaire is printed in Figure 17.6.

The questionnaire was designed to predict how anxious a given individual would be about learning how to use **R**. What's more, I wanted to know whether anxiety about **R** could be broken down into specific forms of anxiety. In other words, what latent variables contribute to anxiety about **R**? With a little help from a few lecturer friends I collected 2571 completed questionnaires (at this point it should become apparent that this example is fictitious). The data are stored in the file **RAQ.dat**. Load this file into **R** and have a look at the data. We know that in **R**, cases (or people's data) are typically stored in rows and variables are stored in columns and so this layout is consistent with past chapters. The second thing to notice is that there are 23 variables labelled **Q01** to **Q23**.

OLIVER TWISTED

*Please Sir, can I have some more …
questionnaires?*

'I'm going to design a questionnaire to measure one's propensity to pick a pocket or two', says Oliver, 'but how would I go about doing it?' You'd read the useful information about the dos and don'ts of questionnaire design in the additional material for this chapter on the companion website, that's how. Rate how useful it is on a Likert scale from 1 = not useful at all, to 5 = very useful.

17.4.1.   Sample size ②

Correlation coefficients fluctuate from sample to sample, much more so in small samples than in large. Therefore, the reliability of factor analysis is also dependent on sample size. Much has been written about the necessary sample size for factor analysis, resulting in many 'rules of thumb'. The common rule is to suggest that a researcher has at least 10–15 participants per variable. Although I've heard this rule bandied about on numerous occasions, its empirical basis is unclear (although Nunnally, 1978, did recommend having 10 times as many participants as variables). Kass and Tinsley (1979) recommended having between 5 and 10 participants per variable up to a total of 300 (beyond which test parameters tend to be stable regardless of the participant to variable ratio). Indeed, Tabachnick and Fidell (2007) agree that 'it is comforting to have at least 300 cases for factor analysis' (p. 613), and Comrey and Lee (1992) class 300 as a good sample size, 100 as poor and 1000 as excellent.

Fortunately, recent years have seen empirical research done in the form of experiments using simulated data (so-called Monte Carlo studies). Arrindell and van der Ende (1985) used real-life data to investigate the effect of different participant to variable ratios. They concluded that changes in this ratio made little difference to the stability of factor solutions. Guadagnoli and Velicer (1988) found that the most important factors in determining reliable factor solutions were the absolute sample size and the absolute magnitude of factor loadings. In short, they argue that if a factor has four or more loadings greater than .6 then it is reliable regardless of sample size. Furthermore, factors with 10 or more loadings greater than .40 are reliable if the sample size is greater than 150. Finally, factors with a few low loadings should not be interpreted unless the sample size is 300 or more. MacCallum, Widaman, Zhang, and Hong (1999) have shown that the minimum sample size or sample to variable ratio depends on other aspects of the design of the study. In short, their study indicated that as communalities become lower the importance of sample size increases. With all communalities above .6, relatively small samples (less than 100) may be perfectly adequate. With communalities in the .5 range, samples between 100 and 200 can be good enough provided there are relatively few factors each with only a small number of indicator variables. In the worst scenario of low communalities (well below .5) and a larger number of underlying factors they recommend samples above 500.

What's clear from this work is that a sample of 300 or more will probably provide a stable factor solution, but that a wise researcher will measure enough variables to adequately measure all of the factors that theoretically they would expect to find.

Another alternative is to use the **Kaiser–Meyer–Olkin (KMO) measure of sampling adequacy** (Kaiser, 1970). The KMO can be calculated for individual and multiple variables and represents the ratio of the squared correlation between variables to the squared partial correlation between variables. The KMO statistic varies between 0 and 1. A value of 0 indicates that the sum of partial correlations is large relative to the sum of correlations, indicating diffusion in the pattern of correlations (hence, factor analysis is likely to be inappropriate). A value close to 1 indicates that patterns of correlations are relatively compact and so factor analysis should yield distinct and reliable factors. Kaiser (1974) recommends accepting values greater than .5 as barely acceptable (values below this should lead you to either collect more data or rethink which variables to include). Furthermore, values between .5 and .7 are mediocre, values between .7 and .8 are good, values between .8 and .9 are great and values above .9 are superb (Hutcheson & Sofroniou, 1999).

17.4.2. Correlations between variables ③

When I was an undergraduate, my statistics lecturer always used to say 'if you put garbage in, you get garbage out'. This saying applies particularly to factor analysis, because **R** will usually find a factor solution for a set of variables. However, the solution is unlikely to have any real meaning if the variables analysed are not sensible. The first thing to do when conducting a factor analysis or principal components analysis is to look at the correlations of the variables. There are essentially two potential problems: (1) correlations that are not high enough; and (2) correlations that are too high. The correlations between variables can be checked using the *cor()* function (see Chapter 6) to create a correlation matrix of all variables. In both cases the remedy is to remove variables from the analysis. We will look at each problem in turn.

If our test questions measure the same underlying dimension (or dimensions) then we would expect them to correlate with each other (because they are measuring the same thing). Even if questions measure different aspects of the same things (e.g., we could measure overall anxiety in terms of sub-components such as worry, intrusive thoughts and physiological arousal), there should still be high correlations between the variables relating to these sub-traits. We can test for this problem first by visually scanning the correlation matrix and looking for correlations below about .3: if any variables have lots of correlations below this value then consider excluding them. It should be immediately clear that this approach is very subjective: I've used fuzzy terms such as 'about .3' and 'lots of', but I have to because every data set is different. Analysing data really is a skill, not a matter of following a recipe book.

If you want an objective test of whether correlations (overall) are too small then you can test for a very extreme scenario. If the variables in our correlation matrix did not correlate at all, then our correlation matrix would be an identity matrix (i.e., the off-diagonal components are zero – see section 16.4.2). **Bartlett's test** examines whether the population correlation matrix resembles an identity matrix. If the population correlation matrix resembles an identity matrix then it means that every variable correlates very badly with all other variables (i.e., all correlation coefficients are close to zero). If it *were* an identity matrix then it would mean that all variables are perfectly independent of one another (all correlation coefficients are zero). Given that we are looking for clusters of variables that measure similar things, it should be obvious why this scenario is problematic: if no variables correlate then there are no clusters to find. Bartlett's test tells us whether our correlation matrix is significantly different from an identity matrix. Therefore, if it is significant then it means that the correlations between variables are (overall) significantly different from zero. So, if Bartlett's test is significant then it is good news. However, as with any significance test, it depends on sample sizes and in factor analysis we typically use very large samples. Therefore, although a non-significant Bartlett's test is certainly cause for concern, a significant test does not necessarily mean that correlations are big enough to make the analysis meaningful. If you do identify any variables that seem to have very low correlations with lots of other variables, then exclude them from the factor analysis.

The opposite problem is when variables correlate too highly. Although mild multicollinearity is not a problem for factor analysis it is important to avoid extreme multicollinearity (i.e., variables that are very highly correlated) and **singularity** (variables that are perfectly correlated). As with regression, multicollinearity causes problems in factor analysis because it becomes impossible to determine the unique contribution to a factor of the variables that are highly correlated (as was the case for multiple regression). Multicollinearity does not cause a problem for principal components analysis. Therefore, as well as scanning the correlation matrix for low correlations, we could also look out for very high correlations $(r > .8)$. The problem with a heuristic such as this is that the effect of two variables correlating with $r = .9$ might be less than the effect of, say, three variables that all correlate at $r = .6$. In other words, eliminating such highly correlating variables might not be getting at the cause of the multicollinearity (Rockwell, 1975).

Multicollinearity can be detected by looking at the determinant of the R-matrix, denoted $|R|$ (see Jane Superbrain Box 17.3). One simple heuristic is that the determinant of the R-matrix should be greater than 0.00001.

If you have reason to believe that the correlation matrix has multicollinearity then you could look through the correlation matrix for variables that correlate very highly $(R > .8)$ and consider eliminating one of the variables (or more, depending on the extent of the

JANE SUPERBRAIN 17.3

What is the determinant? ③

The determinant of a matrix is an important diagnostic tool in factor analysis, but the question of what it is is not easy to answer because it has a mathematical definition and I'm not a mathematician. Rather than pretending that I understand the maths, all I'll say is that a good explanation of how the determinant is derived can be found at http://mathworld.wolfram.com. However, we can bypass the maths and think about the determinant conceptually.

The way that I think of the determinant is as describing the 'area' of the data. In Jane Superbrain Box 16.2 we saw the two diagrams below.

At the time I used these to describe eigenvectors and eigenvalues (which describe the shape of the data). The determinant is related to eigenvalues and eigenvectors, but instead of describing the height and width of the data it describes the overall area. So, in the left diagram below, the determinant of those data would represent the area inside the dashed ellipse. These variables have a low correlation so the determinant (area) is big; the biggest value it can be is 1. In the right diagram, the variables are perfectly correlated or singular, and the ellipse (dashed line) has been squashed down to basically a straight line. In other words, the opposite sides of the ellipse have actually met each other and there is no distance between them at all. Put another way, the area, or determinant, is zero. Therefore, the determinant tells us whether the correlation matrix is singular (determinant is 0), or if all variables are completely unrelated (determinant is 1), or somewhere in between.

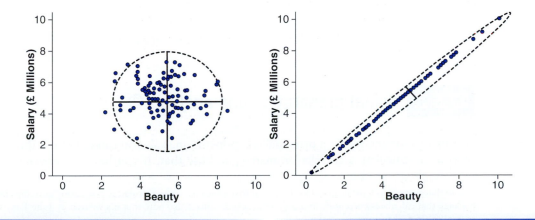

problem) before proceeding. You may have to try some trial and error to work out which variables are creating the problem (it's not always the two with the highest correlation, it could be a larger number of variables with correlations that are not obviously too large).

17.4.3. The distribution of data ②

As well as looking for interrelations, you should ensure that variables have roughly normal distributions and are measured at an interval level (which Likert scales are, perhaps wrongly, assumed to be). The assumption of normality is most important if you wish to generalize the results of your analysis beyond the sample collected. You can do factor analysis on non-continuous data; for example, if you had dichotomous variables you should construct the correlation matrix from polychoric correlation coefficients (these can be calculated using the *polychor()* function, found in the polycor package, which we used in Chapter 6).[7]

17.5. Running the analysis with R Commander ①

If you look through the menus, you'll find 'factor analysis'. The factor analysis that's available in R Commander is a little limited: it does only one kind of extraction (maximum likelihood) and, although this is a good method when it works, if often doesn't work. Understanding why it didn't work and what to do about it is difficult (and the solution is often to just use a different sort of extraction). For this reason, we don't recommend factor analysis with R Commander.

17.6. Running the analysis with R ②

17.6.1. Packages used in this chapter ①

There are several packages we will use in this chapter. You will need the packages *corpcor*, *GPArotation* (for rotating) and *psych* (for the factor analysis). If you don't have these packages installed you'll need to install them and load them.

```
install.packages("corpcor"); install.packages("GPArotation"); install.packages("psych")
```

Then you need to load the packages by executing these commands:

```
library(corpcor); library(GPArotation); library(psych)
```

17.6.2. Initial preparation and analysis ②

To run a factor analysis or a principal components analysis you can either use the raw data, or you can calculate a correlation matrix, and use that. If you have a *massive* number of

[7] Note that there is an h in the polychor function, that's because we're calculating *polychoric* correlations, using a package that calculates *poly*choric and *poly*serial *cor*relations. (Also note that it's written by John Fox, author of several other packages we use in this book.)

cases (and by massive, I mean at least 100,000, and probably closer to 1,000,000) you're better off calculating a correlation matrix first, and then factor-analysing that. If you don't have a massive number of cases, it doesn't matter which you do. It's also worth noting at this stage that sometimes the analysis doesn't work, usually because the correlation matrix that you're trying to analyse is weird (R's Souls' Tip 17.1).

First, we'll load the data into a dataframe called *raqData*. Set your working directory to the location of the file (see section 3.4.4) and execute:

```
raqData<-read.delim("raq.dat", header = TRUE)
```

We want to include all of the variables in our data set in our factor analysis. We can calculate the correlation matrix, using the *cor()* function (see Chapter 6):

```
raqMatrix<-cor(raqData)
```

R's Souls' Tip 17.1   Warning messages about non-positive definite matrix ④

On rare occasions, you might have a non-positive definite matrix. When you have this, **R** will give unhelpful warnings, such as:

```
Warning messages:
1: In log(det(m.inv.r)) : NaNs produced
2: In log(det(r)) : NaNs produced
```

What **R** is trying to tell you, in it's own friendly way, is that the determinant of the R (correlation) matrix is negative, and hence it cannot find the log of the determinant ('NaN' is **R**'s way of saying "not a number"). This problem is usually described as a non-positive definite matrix.

What is a non-positive definite matrix? As we have seen, factor analysis works by looking at your correlation matrix. This matrix has to be 'positive definite' for the analysis to work. What does that mean in plain English? It means lots of horrible things mathematically (e.g., the eigenvalues and determinant of the matrix have to be positive) and about the best explanation I've seen is at http://www2.gsu.edu/~mkteer/npdmatri.html. In more basic terms, factors are like lines floating in space, and eigenvalues measure the length of those lines. If your eigenvalue is negative then it means that the length of your line/factor is negative too. It's a bit like me asking you how tall you are, and you responding 'I'm minus 175 cm tall'. That would be nonsense. By analogy, if a factor has negative length, then that too is nonsense. When **R** decomposes the correlation matrix to look for factors, if it comes across a negative eigenvalue it starts thinking 'oh dear, I've entered some weird parallel universe where the usual rules of maths no longer apply and things can have negative lengths, and this probably means that time runs backwards, my mum is my dad, my sister is a dog, my head is a fish, and my toe is a frog called Gerald'. It still has a go at producing results, but those results probably won't make much sense. (We'd like it if it said 'these results are probably nonsense', rather than being a bit subtle about it, so you have to be *really* careful.)

Things like the KMO test and the determinant rely on a positive definite matrix; if you don't have one they can't be computed.

Why have I got a non-positive definite matrix? The most likely answer is that you have too many variables and too few cases of data, which makes the correlation matrix a bit unstable. It could also be that you have too many highly correlated items in your matrix (singularity, for example, tends to mess things up). In any case it means that your data are bad, naughty data, and not to be trusted; if you let them loose then you have only yourself to blame for the consequences.

What can I do? Other than cry, there's not that much you can do. You could try to limit your items, or selectively remove items (especially highly correlated ones) to see if that helps. Collecting more data can help too. There are some mathematical fudges you can do, but they're not as tasty as vanilla fudge and they are hard to implement easily.

Executing this command creates a matrix of correlation coefficients called *raqMatrix*. We can use this matrix in the analysis (although we don't have to). It's a good idea to have a look at the correlation matrix, for the reasons we discussed earlier. To make our eyes hurt a little less, let's use the *round()* function to display only 2 decimal places of the correlation matrix that we have just created:

```
round(raqMatrix, 2)
```

The *R*-matrix (or correlation matrix) produced using the *cor()* function is displayed in Output 17.1. You should be comfortable with the idea that to do a factor analysis we need to have variables that correlate fairly well, but not perfectly. Also, any variables that correlate with no others should be eliminated. Therefore, we can use this correlation matrix to check the pattern of relationships. First, scan the matrix for correlations greater than .3, then look for variables that only have a small number of correlations greater than this value. Then scan the correlation coefficients themselves and look for any greater than .9. If any are found then you should be aware that a problem could arise because of multicollinearity in the data.

	Q01	Q02	Q03	Q04	Q05	Q06	Q07	Q08
Q01	1.00	-0.10	-0.34	0.44	0.40	0.22	0.31	0.33
Q02	-0.10	1.00	0.32	-0.11	-0.12	-0.07	-0.16	-0.05
Q03	-0.34	0.32	1.00	-0.38	-0.31	-0.23	-0.38	-0.26
Q04	0.44	-0.11	-0.38	1.00	0.40	0.28	0.41	0.35
Q05	0.40	-0.12	-0.31	0.40	1.00	0.26	0.34	0.27
Q06	0.22	-0.07	-0.23	0.28	0.26	1.00	0.51	0.22
Q07	0.31	-0.16	-0.38	0.41	0.34	0.51	1.00	0.30
Q08	0.33	-0.05	-0.26	0.35	0.27	0.22	0.30	1.00
Q09	-0.09	0.31	0.30	-0.12	-0.10	-0.11	-0.13	0.02
Q10	0.21	-0.08	-0.19	0.22	0.26	0.32	0.28	0.16
Q11	0.36	-0.14	-0.35	0.37	0.30	0.33	0.34	0.63
Q12	0.35	-0.19	-0.41	0.44	0.35	0.31	0.42	0.25
Q13	0.35	-0.14	-0.32	0.34	0.30	0.47	0.44	0.31
Q14	0.34	-0.16	-0.37	0.35	0.32	0.40	0.44	0.28
Q15	0.25	-0.16	-0.31	0.33	0.26	0.36	0.39	0.30
Q16	0.50	-0.17	-0.42	0.42	0.39	0.24	0.39	0.32
Q17	0.37	-0.09	-0.33	0.38	0.31	0.28	0.39	0.59
Q18	0.35	-0.16	-0.38	0.38	0.32	0.51	0.50	0.28
Q19	-0.19	0.20	0.34	-0.19	-0.17	-0.17	-0.27	-0.16
Q20	0.21	-0.20	-0.32	0.24	0.20	0.10	0.22	0.18
Q21	0.33	-0.20	-0.42	0.41	0.33	0.27	0.48	0.30
Q22	-0.10	0.23	0.20	-0.10	-0.13	-0.17	-0.17	-0.08
Q23	0.00	0.10	0.15	-0.03	-0.04	-0.07	-0.07	-0.05

	Q09	Q10	Q11	Q12	Q13	Q14	Q15	Q16
Q01	-0.09	0.21	0.36	0.35	0.35	0.34	0.25	0.50
Q02	0.31	-0.08	-0.14	-0.19	-0.14	-0.16	-0.16	-0.17
Q03	0.30	-0.19	-0.35	-0.41	-0.32	-0.37	-0.31	-0.42
Q04	-0.12	0.22	0.37	0.44	0.34	0.35	0.33	0.42
Q05	-0.10	0.26	0.30	0.35	0.30	0.32	0.26	0.39
Q06	-0.11	0.32	0.33	0.31	0.47	0.40	0.36	0.24
Q07	-0.13	0.28	0.34	0.42	0.44	0.44	0.39	0.39
Q08	0.02	0.16	0.63	0.25	0.31	0.28	0.30	0.32
Q09	1.00	-0.13	-0.12	-0.17	-0.17	-0.12	-0.19	-0.19
Q10	-0.13	1.00	0.27	0.25	0.30	0.25	0.30	0.29
Q11	-0.12	0.27	1.00	0.34	0.42	0.33	0.36	0.37
Q12	-0.17	0.25	0.34	1.00	0.49	0.43	0.33	0.41
Q13	-0.17	0.30	0.42	0.49	1.00	0.45	0.34	0.36

```
Q14 -0.12   0.25   0.33   0.43   0.45   1.00   0.38   0.42
Q15 -0.19   0.30   0.36   0.33   0.34   0.38   1.00   0.45
Q16 -0.19   0.29   0.37   0.41   0.36   0.42   0.45   1.00
Q17 -0.04   0.22   0.59   0.33   0.41   0.35   0.37   0.41
Q18 -0.15   0.29   0.37   0.49   0.53   0.50   0.34   0.42
Q19  0.25  -0.13  -0.20  -0.27  -0.23  -0.25  -0.21  -0.27
Q20 -0.16   0.08   0.26   0.30   0.20   0.23   0.21   0.27

         Q17    Q18    Q19    Q20    Q21    Q22    Q23
Q01   0.37   0.35  -0.19   0.21   0.33  -0.10   0.00
Q02  -0.09  -0.16   0.20  -0.20  -0.20   0.23   0.10
Q03  -0.33  -0.38   0.34  -0.32  -0.42   0.20   0.15
Q04   0.38   0.38  -0.19   0.24   0.41  -0.10  -0.03
Q05   0.31   0.32  -0.17   0.20   0.33  -0.13  -0.04
Q06   0.28   0.51  -0.17   0.10   0.27  -0.17  -0.07
Q07   0.39   0.50  -0.27   0.22   0.48  -0.17  -0.07
Q08   0.59   0.28  -0.16   0.18   0.30  -0.08  -0.05
Q09  -0.04  -0.15   0.25  -0.16  -0.14   0.26   0.17
Q10   0.22   0.29  -0.13   0.08   0.19  -0.13  -0.06
Q11   0.59   0.37  -0.20   0.26   0.35  -0.16  -0.09
Q12   0.33   0.49  -0.27   0.30   0.44  -0.17  -0.05
Q13   0.41   0.53  -0.23   0.20   0.37  -0.20  -0.05
Q14   0.35   0.50  -0.25   0.23   0.40  -0.17  -0.05
Q15   0.37   0.34  -0.21   0.21   0.30  -0.17  -0.06
Q16   0.41   0.42  -0.27   0.27   0.42  -0.16  -0.08
Q17   1.00   0.38  -0.16   0.21   0.36  -0.13  -0.09
Q18   0.38   1.00  -0.26   0.24   0.43  -0.16  -0.08
Q19  -0.16  -0.26   1.00  -0.25  -0.27   0.23   0.12
Q20   0.21   0.24  -0.25   1.00   0.47  -0.10  -0.03
Q21   0.36   0.43  -0.27   0.47   1.00  -0.13  -0.07
Q22  -0.13  -0.16   0.23  -0.10  -0.13   1.00   0.23
Q23  -0.09  -0.08   0.12  -0.03  -0.07   0.23   1.00
```

Output 17.1

As well as looking at the correlation matrix, we should run Bartlett's test and the KMO on the correlation matrix. Bartlett's test is run using the **cortest.bartlett()** function from the *psych* package. We can run this test either on the raw data or on the correlation matrix. To run it from the raw data simply input the dataframe (in this case *raqData*) into the function:

```
cortest.bartlett(raqData)
```

To run it from the correlation matrix (in this case *raqMatrix*), input the name of the correlation matrix but also provide the sample size (in this case 2751):

```
cortest.bartlett(raqMatrix, n = 2571)
```

Both methods will give you the results in Output 17.2. If you ran the test from the raw data, you'll get the warning *R was not square, finding R from data*, which is nothing to worry about it just means that because we didn't give the function a correlation matrix, it's calculating it from the raw data (that's what we expect it to do). For factor analysis to work we need some relationships between variables and if the *R*-matrix were an identity matrix then all correlation coefficients would be zero. Therefore, we want this test to be *significant* (i.e., have a significance value less than .05). A significant test tells us that the *R*-matrix is not an identity matrix; therefore, there are some relationships between the variables we hope to include in the analysis. For these data, Bartlett's test is highly significant, $\chi^2(253) = 19,334$, $p < .001$, and therefore factor analysis is appropriate.

```
R was not square, finding R from data
$chisq
[1] 19334.49

$p.value
[1] 0

$df
[1] 253
```
Output 17.2

Next we'd also like the KMO. None of the packages in **R** currently have a straight-forward way to calculate the KMO. However, one of the nice things about **R** is that people can write programs to do anything that **R** doesn't currently do, and G. Jay Kerns, from Youngstown State University (see http://tolstoy.newcastle.edu.au/R/e2/help/07/08/22816.html) has written one called **kmo()**, which calculates the KMO and a variety of other things. The function itself is easy to use manually (see Oliver Twisted), but because it is not part of a package we have included it in our DSUR package so that you can use it directly (assuming you have loaded the DSUR package). You can use the function by simply entering the name of your dataframe into it and executing.

kmo(raqData)

The results of the KMO test are shown in Output 17.3. We came across the KMO statistic in section 17.4.1 and saw that Kaiser (1974) recommends a bare minimum of .5 and that values between .5 and .7 are mediocre, values between .7 and .8 are good, values between .8 and .9 are great and values above .9 are superb (Hutcheson & Sofroniou, 1999). For these data the overall value is .93, which falls into the range of being superb (or 'marvellous' as the report puts it), so we should be confident that the sample size and the data are adequate for factor analysis.

OLIVER TWISTED

Please Sir, can I have some more … kmo?

'Stop spanking my monkey!', cries an hysterical Oliver, 'it's never done you any harm, and it's orange.' I was talking about the Kaiser–Meyer–Olkin test, Oliver. 'Oh, sorry', he says with a sigh of relief, 'I thought KMO stood for Kill My Orang-utan'. Erm, OK, Oliver has finally lost the plot, which I'm fairly sure is what you'll do if you inspect the *kmo()* function on the companion website. Although we have included it in our DSUR package, you can also copy it and execute it manually.

KMO can be calculated for multiple and individual variables. The value of KMO should be above the bare minimum of .5 for all variables (and preferably higher) as well as overall. The KMO values for individual variables are produced by the *kmo()* function too. For these data all values are well above .5, which is good news. If you find any variables with values below .5 then you should consider excluding them from the analysis (or run the analysis with and without that variable and note the difference). Removal of a variable affects the KMO statistics, so if you do remove a variable be sure to rerun the *kmo()* function on the new data.

```
$overall
[1] 0.9302245

$report
[1] "The KMO test yields a degree of common variance marvelous."

$individual

Q01       Q02       Q03       Q04       Q05       Q06       Q07
0.9297    0.8748    0.9510    0.9553    0.9601    0.8913    0.9417

Q08       Q09       Q10       Q11       Q12       Q13       Q14
0.8713    0.8337    0.9487    0.9059    0.9548    0.9482    0.9672

Q15       Q16       Q17       Q18       Q19       Q20       Q21
0.9404    0.9336    0.9306    0.9479    0.9407    0.8891    0.9293

Q22       Q23
0.8784    0.7664
```

Output 17.3

Finally, we'd like the determinant of the correlation matrix. To find the determinant, we use the **det()** function, into which we place the name of a correlation matrix. We have computed this matrix already for the current data (*raqMatrix*) so we can execute:

```
det(raqMatrix)
```

If we hadn't already created the matrix, we could get the determinant by putting the *cor()* function for the raw data into the *det()* function:

```
det(cor(raqData))
```

Either method produces the same value:

```
[1]  0.0005271037
```

This value is greater than the necessary value of 0.00001 (see section 17.5). As such, our determinant does not seem problematic. After checking the determinant, you can, if necessary, eliminate variables that you think are causing the problem. In summary, all questions in the RAQ correlate reasonably well with all others and none of the correlation coefficients are excessively large; therefore, we won't eliminate any questions at this stage.

CRAMMING SAM'S TIPS   Preliminary analysis

- Scan the *correlation matrix*; look for variables that don't correlate with any other variables, or correlate very highly ($r = .9$) with one or more other variables. In factor analysis, check that the determinant of this matrix is bigger than 0.00001; if it is then multicollinearity isn't a problem.
- Check the *KMO and Bartlett's test*; the KMO statistic should be greater than .5 as a bare minimum; if it isn't collect more data. Bartlett's test of sphericity should be significant (the significance value should be less than .05).

17.6.3.   Factor extraction using R ②

For our present purposes we will use *principal components analysis*, which strictly speaking isn't factor analysis; however, the two procedures may often yield similar results (see section 17.3.6). Principal component analysis is carried out using the **principal()** function, in the *psych* package. This function takes the general form:

```
pcModel<-principal(dataframe/R-matrix, nfactors = number of factors, rotate =
"method of rotation", scores = TRUE/FALSE)
```

This command creates a principal components model called *pcModel*, by specifying either a dataframe of raw data or a correlation matrix. There are three main options:

- *nfactors* allows you to specify how many factors/components you want to extract (see section 17.3.8) as a number. If you don't specify *nfactors*, then one component is extracted.

- *rotate* allows you to specify a method of factor rotation (see section 17.3.9) using a text string. If you don't declare a method of rotation, the default of varimax rotation is used.

- *scores* allows you to obtain factor scores (TRUE) or not (FALSE). The default is FALSE.

I mentioned earlier that when conducting principal components analysis we begin by establishing the linear variates within the data and then decide how many of these variates to retain (or 'extract'). Therefore, our starting point is to create a principal components model that has the same number of factors as there are variables in the data: by doing this we are just reducing the data set down to its underlying factors. By extracting as many factors as there are variables we can inspect their eigenvalues and make decisions about which factors to extract. (Note that if you use factor analysis, rather than principal components analysis, you need to extract fewer factors than you have variables – so if you have 23 variables, extracting 18, or so, factors should be OK.)

To create this model we execute one of these commands:

```
pc1 <-  principal(raqData, nfactors = 23, rotate = "none")
pc1 <- principal(raqMatrix, nfactors = 23, rotate = "none")
```

The first command creates the model from the raw data and the second from the correlation matrix: both methods will give you identical results, but we will show both throughout. These commands create a model called *pc1*, which extracts 23 factors – the same as

R's Souls' Tip 17.2   A cure for lazy-itis ②

Sometimes, I'm too lazy to count the variables in my data set, in which case I can ask **R** to count them for me, using the *length()* function, which counts the number of items in an object. Therefore, we can obtain the number of variables in a dataframe using:

```
length(dataFrame)
```

Similarly, we can apply this function to a matrix to find out the number of rows in a column of a matrix:

```
length(matrix[,1])
```

Therefore, we can use these commands within the *principal()* function to automatically specify the number of factors as the number of variables in the dataframe/matrix by executing:

```
pc2 <-  principal(raq, nfactors=length(raqData), rotate="none")
pc2 <- principal(raqmatrix, nfactors=length(raqMatrix[,1]), rotate="none")
```

the number of variables. If you have a large data set or are just too lazy to remember how many variables you have then you can change the command slightly to get **R** to calculate the number of variables in the dataframe or correlation matrix automatically (see R's Souls' Tip 17.2). A final thing to note is that we have set the rotation method to *"none"*, which means that we won't carry out factor rotation because we don't need to at this stage.

We can look at the results of the principal components analysis by executing its name:

pc1

Output 17.4 shows the results of the first principal components model. The first part of this is the unrotated loadings. Currently these are not interesting, but they represent the loading from each factor or component to each variable.

```
Principal Components Analysis
Call: principal(r = raq, nfactors = 23, rotate = "none")
Standardized loadings based upon correlation matrix
       PC1    PC2    PC3    PC4    PC5    PC6    PC7    PC8
Q01    0.59   0.18  -0.22   0.12  -0.40  -0.11  -0.22  -0.08
Q02   -0.30   0.55   0.15   0.01  -0.03  -0.38   0.19  -0.39
Q03   -0.63   0.29   0.21  -0.07   0.02   0.00   0.01  -0.05
Q04    0.63   0.14  -0.15   0.15  -0.20  -0.12  -0.06   0.11
Q05    0.56   0.10  -0.07   0.14  -0.42  -0.17  -0.06   0.11
Q06    0.56   0.10   0.57  -0.05   0.17   0.01   0.00   0.05
Q07    0.69   0.04   0.25   0.10   0.17  -0.08   0.05   0.03
Q08    0.55   0.40  -0.32  -0.42   0.15   0.10  -0.07  -0.04
Q09   -0.28   0.63  -0.01   0.10   0.17  -0.27  -0.01  -0.03
Q10    0.44   0.03   0.36  -0.10  -0.34   0.22   0.44  -0.03
Q11    0.65   0.25  -0.21  -0.40   0.13   0.18  -0.01   0.03
Q12    0.67  -0.05   0.05   0.25   0.04  -0.08  -0.14   0.08
Q13    0.67   0.08   0.28  -0.01   0.13   0.03  -0.21   0.05
Q14    0.66   0.02   0.20   0.14   0.08  -0.03  -0.10  -0.06
Q15    0.59   0.01   0.12  -0.11  -0.07   0.29   0.32  -0.12
Q16    0.68   0.01  -0.14   0.08  -0.32   0.00   0.12  -0.14
Q17    0.64   0.33  -0.21  -0.34   0.10   0.05  -0.02   0.03
Q18    0.70   0.03   0.30   0.13   0.15  -0.09  -0.10   0.06
Q19   -0.43   0.39   0.10  -0.01  -0.15   0.07   0.05   0.68
Q20    0.44  -0.21  -0.40   0.30   0.33  -0.01   0.34   0.03
Q21    0.66  -0.06  -0.19   0.28   0.24  -0.15   0.18   0.10
Q22   -0.30   0.47  -0.12   0.38   0.07   0.12   0.31   0.12
Q23   -0.14   0.37  -0.02   0.51   0.02   0.62  -0.28  -0.22

...

       PC17   PC18   PC19   PC20   PC21   PC22   PC23 h2       u2
Q01   -0.05  -0.17   0.16  -0.01  -0.21   0.05   0.01  1   0.0e+00
Q02   -0.08   0.00   0.01  -0.02  -0.02   0.03   0.02  1  -3.1e-15
Q03    0.43   0.08   0.09   0.05   0.01   0.00   0.05  1  -1.6e-15
Q04    0.19   0.05  -0.21   0.04   0.09  -0.02   0.02  1  -1.1e-15
Q05   -0.04   0.01  -0.04   0.00  -0.02   0.02   0.01  1  -2.0e-15
Q06   -0.14   0.05   0.09  -0.07   0.04  -0.32  -0.11  1   0.0e+00
Q07    0.03  -0.15   0.20   0.16   0.14   0.24   0.09  1   1.1e-16
Q08    0.10   0.07   0.12  -0.15   0.06   0.16  -0.36  1  -2.2e-16
Q09   -0.19  -0.02  -0.08  -0.03   0.04  -0.01   0.03  1  -4.4e-16
Q10    0.07  -0.01   0.00   0.04  -0.03   0.02  -0.04  1  -4.4e-16
Q11   -0.05   0.07   0.07  -0.18   0.06   0.00   0.41  1  -8.9e-16
Q12   -0.08   0.04   0.36   0.00  -0.04  -0.10  -0.02  1  -2.2e-16
Q13   -0.06  -0.32  -0.30  -0.06   0.16   0.08  -0.05  1   0.0e+00
Q14    0.34  -0.09   0.06   0.02   0.03  -0.01   0.05  1  -4.4e-16
Q15   -0.12  -0.10  -0.04  -0.07  -0.19   0.10   0.00  1  -4.4e-16
Q16   -0.03   0.22  -0.02  -0.04   0.35  -0.12  -0.01  1  -2.0e-15
```

```
Q17                 0.04 -0.04 -0.10   0.42 -0.15 -0.23 -0.01   1 -4.4e-16
Q18                -0.06  0.45 -0.15   0.08 -0.18  0.23  0.01   1 -8.9e-16
Q19                -0.06  0.01  0.05  -0.02  0.02  0.04 -0.02   1 -6.7e-16
Q20                -0.09  0.00  0.04   0.18  0.10  0.06 -0.04   1 -8.9e-16
Q21                 0.20 -0.03 -0.11  -0.31 -0.20 -0.13 -0.01   1 -2.0e-15
Q22                 0.04 -0.06  0.02   0.00  0.01 -0.01  0.01   1  0.0e+00
Q23                -0.03  0.05 -0.03   0.01 -0.01 -0.02  0.00   1  0.0e+00


                    PC1  PC2  PC3  PC4  PC5  PC6  PC7  PC8  PC9
SS loadings        7.29 1.74 1.32 1.23 0.99 0.90 0.81 0.78 0.75
Proportion Var     0.32 0.08 0.06 0.05 0.04 0.04 0.04 0.03 0.03
Cumulative Var     0.32 0.39 0.45 0.50 0.55 0.59 0.62 0.65 0.69


                    PC10 PC11 PC12 PC13 PC14 PC15 PC16 PC17 PC18
SS loadings         0.72 0.68 0.67 0.61 0.58 0.55 0.52 0.51 0.46
Proportion Var      0.03 0.03 0.03 0.03 0.03 0.02 0.02 0.02 0.02
Cumulative Var      0.72 0.75 0.78 0.80 0.83 0.85 0.88 0.90 0.92


                    PC19 PC20 PC21 PC22 PC23
SS loadings         0.42 0.41 0.38 0.36 0.33
Proportion Var      0.02 0.02 0.02 0.02 0.01
Cumulative Var      0.94 0.95 0.97 0.99 1.00


Test of the hypothesis that 23 factors are sufficient.

The degrees of freedom for the null model are 253 and the objective
function was 7.55
The degrees of freedom for the model are -23  and the objective
function was 0
The number of observations was 2571 with Chi Square =  0 with prob < NA

Fit based upon off diagonal values = 1
```

Output 17.4

On the far right of the factor loading matrix are two columns, labelled *h2* and *u2*. *h2* is the communalities (which are sometimes called h^2). These communalities are all equal to 1 because we have extracted 23 items, the same as the number of variables: we've explained all of the variance in every variable. When we extract fewer factors (or components) we'll have lower communalities. Next to the communality column is the uniqueness column, labelled *u2*. This is the amount of unique variance for each variable, and it's 1 minus the communality; because all of the communalities are 1, all of the uniquenesses are 0.[8]

The next thing to look at after the factor loading matrix is the eigenvalues. The eigenvalues associated with each factor represent the variance explained by that particular linear component. **R** calls these SS loadings (sums of squared loadings), because they are the sum of the squared loadings. (You can also find them in a variable associated with the model called *values*, so in our case we could access this variable using *pc1$values*).

R also displays the eigenvalues in terms of the proportion of variance explained. Factor 1 explains 7.29 units of variance out of a possible 23 (the number of factors) so as a proportion this is 7.29/23 = 0.32; this is the value that **R** reports. We can convert these proportions to percentages by multiplying by 100; so, factor 1 explains 32% of the total variance.

---

[8] Some of them are very, very slightly different from zero; for example, question 2 has a uniqueness, which is reported as −3.1e-15, which means .0000000000000031. This is caused by a rounding error (because **R** stores variables to only 15 decimal places).

It should be clear that the first few factors explain relatively large amounts of variance (especially factor 1) whereas subsequent factors explain only small amounts of variance.

The eigenvalues show us that four components (or factors) have eigenvalues greater than 1, suggesting that we extract four components if we use Kaiser's criterion. By Jolliffe's criterion (retain factors with eigenvalues greater than 0.7) we should retain 10 factors, but there is little to recommend this criterion over Kaiser's. We should also consider the scree plot. As mentioned above, the eigenvalues are stored in a variable called *pc1$values*, and we can draw a quick scree plot using the *plot()* function, by executing:

```
plot(pc1$values, type = "b")
```

This command simply plots the eigenvalues (*y*) against the factor number (*x*). By default, the *plot()* function will plot points (*type= "p"*). We want to see a line so that we can look at the trend (we could ask for this by specifying *type="l"*), but ideally we want to look at both a line and points on the same graph, which is why we specify *type="b"*.

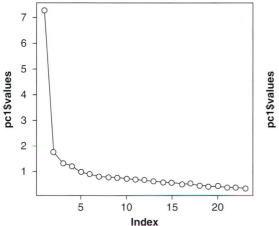 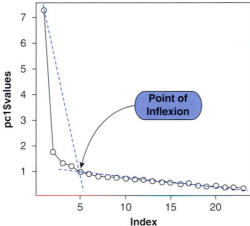

FIGURE 17.7
Scree plot from principal components analysis of RAQ data. The second plot shows the point of inflexion at the fourth component.

Figure 17.7 shows the scree plot; I show it once as **R** produces it and then again with lines showing a plateau and (what I consider to be) the point of inflexion. This curve is difficult to interpret because it begins to tail off after three factors, but there is another drop after four factors before a stable plateau is reached. Therefore, we could probably justify retaining either two or four factors. Given the large sample, it is probably safe to assume Kaiser's criterion. The evidence from the scree plot and from the eigenvalues suggests a four-component solution may be the best.

Now that we know how many components we want to extract, we can rerun the analysis, specifying that number. To do this, we use an identical command to the previous model but we change *nfactors = 23* to be *nfactors = 4* because we now want only four factors. (We should also change the name of the resulting model so that we don't overwrite the previous one):

```
pc2 <-  principal(raqData, nfactors = 4, rotate = "none")
pc2 <- principal(raqMatrix, nfactors = 4, rotate = "none")
```

Again, the first command is to run the analysis from the raw data and the second is if you're using the correlation matrix. In both cases the commands create a model called *pc2* that is the same as before except that we've extracted only 4 factors (not 23). We can look at this model by executing its name:

```
pc2
```

Output 17.5 shows the second principal components model. Again, the output contains the unrotated factor loadings, but only for the first four factors. Notice that these are unchanged from the previous factor loading matrix. Also notice that the eigenvalues (SS loadings), proportions of variance explained and cumulative proportion of variance explained are also unchanged (except now there are only four of them, because we only have four components). However, the communalities (the $h2$ column) and uniquenesses (the $u2$ column) are changed. Remember that the communality is the proportion of common variance within a variable (see section 17.3.4). Principal components analysis works on the initial assumption that all variance is common; therefore, before extraction the communalities are all 1. In effect, all of the variance associated with a variable is assumed to be common variance. Once factors have been extracted, we have a better idea of how much variance is, in reality, common. The communalities in the output reflect this common variance. So, for example, we can say that 43% of the variance associated with question 1 is common, or shared, variance. Another way to look at these communalities is in terms of the proportion of variance explained by the underlying factors. Before extraction, there were as many factors as there are variables, so all variance is explained by the factors and communalities are all 1. However, after extraction some of the factors are discarded and so some information is lost. The retained factors cannot explain all of the variance present in the data, but they can explain some. The amount of variance in each variable that can be explained by the retained factors is represented by the communalities after extraction.

Now that we have the communalities, we can go back to Kaiser's criterion to see whether we still think that four factors should have been extracted. In section 17.3.8 we saw that Kaiser's criterion is accurate when there are fewer than 30 variables and communalities after extraction are greater than .7 or when the sample size exceeds 250 and the average communality is greater than .6. Of the communalities in Output 17.5, only one exceeds .7. The average of these communalities can be found by adding them up and dividing by the number of communalities (11.573/23 = .503). So, on both grounds Kaiser's rule may not be accurate. However, in this instance we should consider the huge sample that we have, because the research into Kaiser's criterion gives recommendations for much smaller samples. It's also worth remembering that we have already inspected the scree plot, which should be a good guide in a sample as large as ours. However, given the ambiguity in the scree plot (there was also a case for retaining only two factors) you might like to rerun the analysis specifying that **R** extract only two factors and compare the results.

```
Principal Components Analysis
Call: principal(r = raq, nfactors = 4, rotate = "none")
Standardized loadings based upon correlation matrix
      PC1    PC2    PC3    PC4   h2    u2
Q01   0.59   0.18  -0.22   0.12  0.43  0.57
Q02  -0.30   0.55   0.15   0.01  0.41  0.59
Q03  -0.63   0.29   0.21  -0.07  0.53  0.47
Q04   0.63   0.14  -0.15   0.15  0.47  0.53
Q05   0.56   0.10  -0.07   0.14  0.34  0.66
Q06   0.56   0.10   0.57  -0.05  0.65  0.35
Q07   0.69   0.04   0.25   0.10  0.55  0.45
Q08   0.55   0.40  -0.32  -0.42  0.74  0.26
Q09  -0.28   0.63  -0.01   0.10  0.48  0.52
Q10   0.44   0.03   0.36  -0.10  0.33  0.67
Q11   0.65   0.25  -0.21  -0.40  0.69  0.31
Q12   0.67  -0.05   0.05   0.25  0.51  0.49
Q13   0.67   0.08   0.28  -0.01  0.54  0.46
Q14   0.66   0.02   0.20   0.14  0.49  0.51
Q15   0.59   0.01   0.12  -0.11  0.38  0.62
Q16   0.68   0.01  -0.14   0.08  0.49  0.51
Q17   0.64   0.33  -0.21  -0.34  0.68  0.32
```

```
Q18   0.70   0.03   0.30   0.13 0.60 0.40
Q19  -0.43   0.39   0.10  -0.01 0.34 0.66
Q20   0.44  -0.21  -0.40   0.30 0.48 0.52
Q21   0.66  -0.06  -0.19   0.28 0.55 0.45
Q22  -0.30   0.47  -0.12   0.38 0.46 0.54
Q23  -0.14   0.37  -0.02   0.51 0.41 0.59


                    PC1   PC2   PC3   PC4
SS loadings         7.29 1.74 1.32 1.23
Proportion Var 0.32 0.08 0.06 0.05
Cumulative Var 0.32 0.39 0.45 0.50


Test of the hypothesis that 4 factors are sufficient.

The degrees of freedom for the null model are 253 and the objective
function was 7.55
The degrees of freedom for the model are 167  and the objective
function was 1.03
The number of observations was 2571 with Chi Square = 2634.37 with prob
< 0


Fit based upon off diagonal values = 0.96
```

Output 17.5

There's another thing that we can look at to see if we've extracted the correct number of factors: this is the reproduced correlation matrix and the difference between the reproduced correlation matrix and the correlation matrix in the data.

The reproduced correlations are obtained with the **factor.model()** function. The *factor. model()* function, needs to know the factor loading matrix. The factor loading matrix is labelled as an object called *loadings* in the principal components model; therefore we can access it by specifying *pc2$loadings* (which translates as 'the *loadings* object associated with the *pc2* model). Therefore, we can get the reproduced correlations by executing:

```
factor.model(pc2$loadings)
```

The difference between the reproduced and actual correlation matrices is referred to as the residuals, and these are obtained with the **factor.residuals()** function. You again need to provide the factor loading matrix but also the correlation matrix to which you want to compare it (in this case the original correlation matrix, *raqMatrix*). We can, therefore, obtain the residuals by executing:

```
factor.residuals(raqMatrix, pc2$loadings)
         Q01    Q02    Q03    Q04    Q05    Q06    Q07    Q08    Q09
Q01   0.435 -0.112 -0.372  0.447  0.376  0.218  0.366  0.412 -0.042
Q02  -0.112  0.414  0.380 -0.134 -0.122 -0.033 -0.148  0.002  0.430
Q03  -0.372  0.380  0.530 -0.399 -0.345 -0.200 -0.373 -0.270  0.352
Q04   0.447 -0.134 -0.399  0.469  0.399  0.278  0.419  0.390 -0.073
Q05   0.376 -0.122 -0.345  0.399  0.343  0.273  0.380  0.312 -0.080
Q06   0.218 -0.033 -0.200  0.278  0.273  0.654  0.528  0.183 -0.108
Q07   0.366 -0.148 -0.373  0.419  0.380  0.528  0.545  0.267 -0.161
Q08   0.412  0.002 -0.270  0.390  0.312  0.183  0.267  0.739  0.055
Q09  -0.042  0.430  0.352 -0.073 -0.080 -0.108 -0.161  0.055  0.484
Q10   0.172 -0.061 -0.181  0.212  0.205  0.461  0.382  0.180 -0.116
Q11   0.423 -0.097 -0.357  0.419  0.348  0.290  0.363  0.691 -0.071
Q12   0.402 -0.219 -0.440  0.448  0.397  0.388  0.495  0.228 -0.195
Q13   0.347 -0.122 -0.342  0.395  0.360  0.545  0.533  0.313 -0.147
Q14   0.362 -0.155 -0.373  0.411  0.370  0.477  0.514  0.249 -0.159
```

```
Q15   0.311 -0.158 -0.337  0.343  0.306  0.406  0.425  0.339 -0.174
Q16   0.440 -0.217 -0.458  0.466  0.400  0.300  0.439  0.390 -0.175
Q17   0.439 -0.048 -0.331  0.434  0.359  0.290  0.365  0.695 -0.009
Q18   0.368 -0.149 -0.376  0.424  0.388  0.562  0.570  0.250 -0.168
Q19  -0.204  0.357  0.403 -0.231 -0.207 -0.147 -0.254 -0.104  0.363
Q20   0.342 -0.301 -0.440  0.353  0.292 -0.021  0.219  0.164 -0.218
Q21   0.449 -0.254 -0.488  0.480  0.412  0.244  0.430  0.282 -0.191
Q22  -0.025  0.333  0.275 -0.050 -0.060 -0.209 -0.179 -0.099  0.417
Q23   0.045  0.246  0.158  0.042  0.028 -0.082 -0.037 -0.136  0.323
```

Output 17.6

Output 17.6 shows an edited version of the reproduced correlation matrix that was requested using the *factor.model()* function in the first table. The diagonal of this matrix contains the communalities after extraction for each variable (you can check the values against Output 17.5). Output 17.7 contains an extract from the matrix of residuals: the difference between the fitted model and the real data. The diagonal of this matrix is the uniquenesses.

```
        Q01     Q02     Q03     Q04     Q05     Q06     Q07     Q08     Q09
Q01   0.565   0.013   0.035  -0.011   0.027  -0.001  -0.061  -0.081  -0.050
Q02   0.013   0.586  -0.062   0.022   0.003  -0.041  -0.011  -0.052  -0.115
Q03   0.035  -0.062   0.470   0.019   0.035  -0.027  -0.009   0.011  -0.052
Q04  -0.011   0.022   0.019   0.531   0.002   0.000  -0.010  -0.041  -0.051
Q05   0.027   0.003   0.035   0.002   0.657  -0.016  -0.041  -0.044  -0.016
Q06  -0.001  -0.041  -0.027   0.000  -0.016   0.346  -0.014   0.040  -0.005
Q07  -0.061  -0.011  -0.009  -0.010  -0.041  -0.014   0.455   0.030   0.033
Q08  -0.081  -0.052   0.011  -0.041  -0.044   0.040   0.030   0.261  -0.039
Q09  -0.050  -0.115  -0.052  -0.051  -0.016  -0.005   0.033  -0.039   0.516
Q10   0.042  -0.023  -0.013   0.003   0.053  -0.139  -0.098  -0.021  -0.018
Q11  -0.066  -0.046   0.006  -0.051  -0.050   0.038  -0.018  -0.061  -0.045
Q12  -0.057   0.024   0.030  -0.006  -0.050  -0.076  -0.072   0.024   0.027
Q13   0.008  -0.021   0.024  -0.051  -0.058  -0.078  -0.091   0.001  -0.021
Q14  -0.024  -0.009   0.002  -0.060  -0.055  -0.075  -0.074   0.032   0.038
Q15  -0.065  -0.007   0.025  -0.009  -0.045  -0.047  -0.033  -0.039  -0.012
Q16   0.059   0.050   0.039  -0.050  -0.005  -0.056  -0.051  -0.068  -0.014
Q17  -0.069  -0.039   0.003  -0.052  -0.049  -0.008   0.025  -0.105  -0.027
Q18  -0.020  -0.015   0.001  -0.042  -0.066  -0.048  -0.069   0.030   0.018
Q19   0.015  -0.153  -0.061   0.045   0.041  -0.020  -0.015  -0.056  -0.114
Q20  -0.128   0.099   0.115  -0.110  -0.092   0.122   0.002   0.011   0.060
Q21  -0.120   0.049   0.071  -0.070  -0.078   0.029   0.053   0.014   0.055
Q22  -0.079  -0.102  -0.071  -0.049  -0.072   0.043   0.010   0.020  -0.161
Q23  -0.049  -0.147  -0.008  -0.076  -0.070   0.013  -0.033   0.086  -0.152
```

Output 17.7

The correlations in the reproduced matrix differ from those in the *R*-matrix because they stem from the model rather than the observed data. If the model were a perfect fit to the data then we would expect the reproduced correlation coefficients to be the same as the original correlation coefficients. Therefore, to assess the fit of the model we can look at the differences between the observed correlations and the correlations based on the model. For example, if we take the correlation between questions 1 and 2, the correlation based on the observed data is −.099 (taken from Output 17.1). The correlation based on the model is −.112, which is slightly higher. We can calculate the difference as follows :

$$\text{residual} = r_{\text{observed}} - r_{\text{from model}}$$
$$\text{residual}_{Q_1 Q_2} = (-0.099) - (-0.112)$$
$$= 0.013$$

You should notice that this difference is the value quoted in Output 17.7 for questions 1 and 2. Therefore, Output 17.7 contains the differences between the observed correlation coefficients and the ones predicted from the model. For a good model these values will all be small. There are several ways we can define how small we want the residuals to be.

One approach is to see how large the residuals are, compared to the original correlations. The very worst the model could be (if we extracted no factors at all) would be the size of the correlations in the original data. Thus one approach is to compare the size of the residuals with the size of the correlations. If the correlations were small to start with, we'd expect very small residuals. If the correlations were large to start with, we wouldn't mind if the residuals were relatively larger. So one measure of the residuals is to compare the residuals with the original correlations – because residuals are positive and negative, they should be squared before doing that. A measure of the fit of the model is therefore the sum of the squared residuals divided by the sum of the squared correlations. As this is considered a measure of fit and sometimes people like measures of fit to go from 0 to 1, we subtract the value from 1. This statistic is given at the bottom of the main output (Output 17.5) as:

```
Fit based upon off diagonal values = 0.96
```

Values over 0.95 are often considered indicators of good fit, and as our value is 0.96, this indicates that four factors are sufficient.

There are many other ways of looking at residuals, which we'll now explore. We couldn't find an R function to do these other things, but we will write one as we go along.[9] A simple approach to residuals is just to say that we want the residuals to be small. In fact, we want most values to be less than 0.05. We can work out how many residuals are large by this criterion fairly easily in R. First, we need to extract the residuals into a new object. We need to do this because at the moment the matrix of residuals is symmetrical (so the residuals are repeated above and below the diagonal of the matrix), and also the diagonal of the matrix does not contain residuals. First let's create an object called *residuals* that contains the factor residuals by executing:

```
residuals<-factor.residuals(raqMatrix, pc2$loadings)
```

We can then extract the upper triangle of this matrix using the **upper.tri()** function. This has the effect of extracting only the elements above the diagonal (so we discard the diagonal elements and the elements below the diagonal):

```
residuals<-as.matrix(residuals[upper.tri(residuals)])
```

This command re-creates the object *residuals* by using only the upper triangle of the original matrix. The *as.matrix()* function just makes sure that the residuals are stored as a matrix (they're actually stored as a single column of data). We now have an object called *residuals* that contains the residuals stored in a column. This is handy because it makes it easy to calculate various things. For example, if we want to know how many large residuals there are (i.e., residuals with absolute values greater than 0.05) then we can execute:

```
large.resid<-abs(residuals) > 0.05
```

which uses the *abs()* function to first compute the absolute value of the column of residuals (this is so we ignore whether the residual is positive or negative). The > 0.05 in the command means that *large.resid* will be TRUE (or 1) if the residual is greater than 0.05, and false (or 0) if the residual is less than or equal to 0.05. We end up with a column the same length as the matrix of factor residuals but containing values of TRUE (if the residual is large) or FALSE (if it is small). We can then use the *sum()* function to add up the number of TRUE responses in the matrix:

```
sum(large.resid)
```

[9] R has over 3000 packages. For relatively simple things, it's often easier to write a small function yourself than try to find whether a function already exists. Or, you can find a friend that can write a function for you. We will show you how, because we're your friends.

The result is 91. If we want to know this as a proportion of the total number of residuals we can simply execute:

```
sum(large.resid)/nrow(residuals)
```

Executing this command will return the number of large residuals (*sum(large.resid)*) divided by the total number of residuals: *nrows()* tells us how many items (i.e., residuals) there are in total. This will return a value of 0.3596, or 36%. There are no hard and fast rules about what proportion of residuals should be below 0.05; however, if more than 50% are greater than 0.05 you probably have grounds for concern. For our data, we have 36% so we need not worry.

Another way to look at the residuals is to look at their mean. Rather than looking at the mean, we should square the residuals, find the mean, and then find the square root. This is the root-mean-square residual. Again, this is easy to calculate from our *residuals* object. We can execute:

```
sqrt(mean(residuals^2))
```

This command squares each item in the residuals object (*residuals ^ 2*), then uses the *mean()* function to compute the mean of these squared residuals. The *sqrt()* function is then used to compute the square root of that mean. The resulting value is 0.055, that's our mean residual. A little lower would have been nice, but this is not dreadful. If this were much higher (say 0.08) we might want to consider extracting more factors.

Finally, it's worth looking at the distributions of the residuals – we expect the residuals to be approximately normally distributed – if there are any serious outliers, even if the other values are all good, we should probably look further into that. We can again use our *residuals* object to plot a quick histogram using the *hist()* function:

```
hist(residuals)
```

Figure 17.8 shows the histogram of the residuals. They do seem approximately normal and there are no outliers. We could wrap these commands up in a nice function called *residual. stats ()* so that we can use it again in other factor analyses (R's Souls' Tip 17.3).

FIGURE 17.8
Histogram of the model residuals

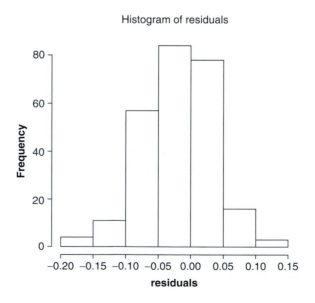

R's Souls' Tip 17.3 Creating a *residual.stats()* function

We saw (in R's Souls' Tip 6.2) that you can write your own functions in **R**. If we wanted to wrap all of the factor analysis residual commands into a function we can do this fairly easily by executing:

```
residual.stats<-function(matrix){
        residuals<-as.matrix(matrix[upper.tri(matrix)])
        large.resid<-abs(residuals) > 0.05
        numberLargeResids<-sum(large.resid)
        propLargeResid<-numberLargeResids/nrow(residuals)
        rmsr<-sqrt(mean(residuals^2))

        cat("Root means squared residual = ", rmsr, "\n")
        cat("Number of absolute residuals > 0.05 = ", numberLargeResids, "\n")
        cat("Proportion of absolute residuals > 0.05 = ", propLargeResid, "\n")
        hist(residuals)
}
```

The first line creates the function by naming it *residual.stats* and telling it to expect a matrix as input. The commands within { } are explained within the main text: they extract the residuals from the matrix entered into the function, compute the number (*numberLargeResids*) and proportion (*propLargeResid*) of absolute values greater than 0.05, compute the root mean squared residual (*rmsr*), and plot a histogram. The commands using the *cat()* function simply specify the text and values to appear in the output.

Having executed the function, we could use it on our residual matrix in one of two ways. First, we could calculate the residual matrix using the *factor.residuals()* function, and label the resulting matrix *resids*. Then pop this matrix into the *residual.stats()* function:

```
resids <- factor.residuals(raqMatrix, pc2$loadings)
residual.stats(resids)
```

The second way is to combine these steps and calculate the residuals matrix directly inside the *residual.stats()* function:

```
residual.stats(factor.residuals(raqMatrix, pc2$loadings))
```

The output would be as follows (and the histogram in Figure 17.8):

```
Root means squared residual =  0.05549286
Number of absolute residuals > 0.05 =  91
Proportion of absolute residuals > 0.05 =  0.3596838
```

CRAMMING SAM'S TIPS   Factor extraction

- To decide how many factors to extract, look at the eigenvalues and the scree plot.
- If you have fewer than 30 variables then using eigenvalues greater than 1 is OK (Kaiser's criterion) as long as your communalities are all over .7. Likewise, if your sample size exceeds 250 and the average of the communalities is .6 or greater then this is also fine. Alternatively, with 200 or more participants the scree plot can be used.
- Check the residuals and make sure that fewer than 50% have absolute values greater than 0.05, and that the model fit is greater than 0.90.

17.6.4.   Rotation ②

We have already seen that the interpretability of factors can be improved through rotation. Rotation maximizes the loading of each variable on one of the extracted factors while minimizing the loading on all other factors. This process makes it much clearer which variables relate to which factors. Rotation works through changing the absolute values of the variables while keeping their differential values constant. I've discussed the various rotation options in section 17.3.9.1, but, to summarize, the exact choice of rotation will depend on whether or not you think that the underlying factors should be related. If there are theoretical grounds to think that the factors are independent (unrelated) then you should choose one of the orthogonal rotations (I recommend varimax). However, if theory suggests that your factors might correlate then one of the oblique rotations (oblimin or promax) should be selected.

17.6.4.1. Orthogonal rotation (varimax) ②

To carry out a varimax rotation, we change the *rotate* option in the *principal()* function from *"none"* to *"varimax"* (we could also exclude it altogether because varimax is the default if the option is not specified):

```
pc3 <-  principal(raqData, nfactors = 4, rotate = "varimax")
pc3 <-  principal(raqMatrix, nfactors = 4, rotate = "varimax")
```

The first command is to run the analysis from the raw data and the second is if you're using the correlation matrix. In both cases the commands create a model called *pc3* that is the same as the previous model (*pc2*) except that we have used varimax rotation on the model. We can look at this model by executing its name:

```
pc2
```

   Output 17.8 shows the first part of the rotated component matrix (also called the rotated factor matrix), which is a matrix of the factor loadings for each variable on each factor. This matrix contains the same information as the component matrix in Output 17.5, except that it is calculated *after* rotation. Notice that the loadings have changed, but the *h2* (communality) and *u2* (uniqueness) columns have not. Rotation changes factors to distribute the variance differently, but it cannot account for more or less variance in the variables than it could before rotation. Also notice that the eigenvalues (SS loadings) have changed. One of the aims of rotation is to even up the eigenvalues; however, the sum of the eigenvalues (and the proportion of variance accounted for) cannot change during rotation.

   Interpreting the factor loading matrix is a little complex, and we can make it easier by using the **print.psych()** function. This does two things: first, it removes loadings that are below a certain value that we specify (by using the *cut* option); and second, it reorders the items to try to put them into their factors, which we request using the *sort* option. Generally you should be very careful with the cut-off value – if you think that a loading of .4 will be interesting, you should use a lower cut-off (say, .3), because you don't want to miss a loading that was .39. Execute this command:

```
print.psych(pc3, cut = 0.3, sort = TRUE)
```

This command prints the factor loading matrix associated with the model *pc3*, but displaying only loadings above .3 (*cut = 0.3*) and sorting items by the size of their loadings (*sort = TRUE*).

```
Principal Components Analysis
Call: principal(r = raqData, nfactors = 4, residuals = TRUE, rotate =
"varimax")
```

```
Standardized loadings based upon correlation matrix
       RC3    RC1    RC4    RC2    h2    u2
Q01   0.24   0.50   0.36   0.06  0.43  0.57
Q02  -0.01  -0.34   0.07   0.54  0.41  0.59
Q03  -0.20  -0.57  -0.18   0.37  0.53  0.47
Q04   0.32   0.52   0.31   0.04  0.47  0.53
Q05   0.32   0.43   0.24   0.01  0.34  0.66
Q06   0.80  -0.01   0.10  -0.07  0.65  0.35
Q07   0.64   0.33   0.16  -0.08  0.55  0.45
...
                    RC3    RC1    RC4    RC2
SS loadings         3.73   3.34   2.55   1.95
```

Output 17.8

The resulting matrix is in Output 17.9. Compare this matrix to the unrotated solution (Output 17.5). Before rotation, most variables loaded highly on the first factor and the remaining factors didn't really get a look in. However, the rotation of the factor structure has clarified things considerably: there are four factors and variables load very highly onto only one factor (with the exception of one question). The suppression of loadings less than .3 and ordering variables by loading size also make interpretation considerably easier (because you don't have to scan the matrix to identify substantive loadings).

The next step is to look at the content of questions that load onto the same factor to try to identify common themes. If the mathematical factor produced by the analysis represents some real-world construct then common themes among highly loading questions can help us identify what the construct might be. The questions that load highly on factor 1 are Q6 (I have little experience of computers) with the highest loading of .80, Q18 (**R** always crashes when I try to use it), Q13 (I worry I will cause irreparable damage …), Q7 (All computers hate me), Q14 (Computers have minds of their own …), Q10 (Computers are only for games), and Q15 (Computers are out to get me) with the lowest loading of .46. All these items seem to relate to using computers or **R**. Therefore we might label this factor *fear of computers*.

Looking at factor 2, we have Q20 (Everybody looks at me when I use **R**), with a loading of .68, Q21 (I wake up under my duvet …), Q3 (Standard deviations excite me),[10] Q12 (People try to tell you that **R** makes statistics easier …), Q4 (I dream that Pearson is attacking me), Q16 (I weep openly at the mention of central tendency), Q1 (Statistics makes me cry) and Q5 (I don't understand statistics), with the lowest loading of .52 – this item also loads moderately on some of the other factors. The questions that load highly on factor 2 all seem to relate to different aspects of statistics; therefore, we might label this factor *fear of statistics*.

```
Principal Components Analysis
Call: principal(r = raqData, nfactors = 4, rotate = "varimax")
Standardized loadings based upon correlation matrix
      item   RC3    RC1    RC4    RC2    h2    u2
Q06      6  0.80                       0.65  0.35
Q18     18  0.68   0.33                0.60  0.40
Q13     13  0.65                       0.54  0.46
Q07      7  0.64   0.33                0.55  0.45
Q14     14  0.58   0.36                0.49  0.51
Q10     10  0.55                       0.33  0.67
Q15     15  0.46                       0.38  0.62
Q20     20         0.68                0.48  0.52
Q21     21         0.66                0.55  0.45
```

[10] Note that this variable has a negative loading – this means that a high score on the factor is associated with a lower score on this item.

```
Q03     3          -0.57           0.37 0.53 0.47
Q12    12    0.47   0.52                0.51 0.49
Q04     4    0.32   0.52   0.31         0.47 0.53
Q16    16    0.33   0.51   0.31         0.49 0.51
Q01     1           0.50   0.36         0.43 0.57
Q05     5    0.32   0.43                0.34 0.66
Q08     8                  0.83         0.74 0.26
Q17    17                  0.75         0.68 0.32
Q11    11                  0.75         0.69 0.31
Q09     9                        0.65 0.48 0.52
Q22    22                        0.65 0.46 0.54
Q23    23                        0.59 0.41 0.59
Q02     2          -0.34         0.54 0.41 0.59
Q19    19          -0.37         0.43 0.34 0.66

                   RC3   RC1   RC4   RC2
SS loadings        3.73 3.34 2.55 1.95
Proportion Var     0.16 0.15 0.11 0.08
Cumulative Var     0.16 0.31 0.42 0.50
```

Test of the hypothesis that 4 factors are sufficient.

The degrees of freedom for the null model are 253 and the
objective function was 7.55
The degrees of freedom for the model are 167 and the objective
function was 1.03
The number of observations was 2571 with Chi Square = 2634.37
with prob < 0

Fit based upon off diagonal values = 0.96

Output 17.9

Factor 3 has only three items loading on it. Q8 (I have never been good at mathematics), Q17 (I slip into a coma when I see an equation), and Q11 (I did badly at mathematics at school). The three questions that load highly on factor 3 all seem to relate to mathematics; therefore, we might label this factor *fear of mathematics*.

Finally, the questions that load highly on factor 4 are Q9 (My friends are better at statistics than me), Q22 (My friends are better at **R**), Q2 (My friends will think I'm stupid) and Q19 (Everybody looks at me). All these items contain some component of social evaluation from friends; therefore, we might label this factor *peer evaluation*.

This analysis seems to reveal that the initial questionnaire, in reality, is composed of four subscales: fear of computers, fear of statistics, fear of maths and fear of negative peer evaluation. There are two possibilities here. The first is that the RAQ failed to measure what it set out to (namely, **R** anxiety) but does measure some related constructs. The second is that these four constructs are sub-components of **R** anxiety; however, the factor analysis does not indicate which of these possibilities is true.

17.6.4.2. Oblique rotation ②

When we did the orthogonal rotation, we told **R** that we expected the components that we extracted to be uncorrelated. This was a bit of a strange thing to say. All of our factors related to fear: fear of computers, fear of statistics, fear of negative peer evaluation and feed of mathematics. It's likely that these will be correlated: people with fear of one thing might have fear of other things. If this is the case an oblique rotation is called for.

The command for an oblique rotation is very similar to that for an orthogonal rotation, we just change the *rotate* option, from *"varimax"* to *"oblimin"*:

```
pc4 <- principal(raqData, nfactors = 4, rotate = "oblimin")
pc4 <- principal(raqMatrix, nfactors = 4, rotate = "oblimin")
```

The first command is to run the analysis from the raw data and the second is if you're using the correlation matrix. In both cases the commands create a model called *pc4* that is the same as the model *pc2* except that we have used oblimin rotation on the model. As with the previous model, we can look at the factor loadings from this model in a nice easy-to-digest format by executing:

```
print.psych(pc4, cut = 0.3, sort = TRUE)
```

The output from this analysis is shown in Output 17.10. The same four factors seem to have emerged although they are in a different order. Factor 1 seems to represent fear of computers, factor 2 represents fear of peer evaluation, factor 3 represents fear of statistics and factor 4 represents fear of mathematics.

```
Principal Components Analysis
Call: principal(r = raqData, nfactors = 4, rotate = "oblimin")
Standardized loadings based upon correlation matrix
      item   TC1   TC4   TC3   TC2    h2   u2
Q06    6    0.87                     0.65 0.35
Q18   18    0.70                     0.60 0.40
Q07    7    0.64                     0.55 0.45
Q13   13    0.64                     0.54 0.46
Q10   10    0.57                     0.33 0.67
Q14   14    0.57                     0.49 0.51
Q12   12    0.45        0.43         0.51 0.49
Q15   15    0.40                     0.38 0.62
Q08    8          0.90               0.74 0.26
Q11   11          0.78               0.69 0.31
Q17   17          0.78               0.68 0.32
Q20   20                0.71         0.48 0.52
Q21   21                0.60         0.55 0.45
Q03    3               -0.51         0.53 0.47
Q04    4                0.41         0.47 0.53
Q16   16                0.41         0.49 0.51
Q01    1          0.33  0.40         0.43 0.57
Q05    5                0.34         0.34 0.66
Q22   22                      0.65   0.46 0.54
Q09    9                      0.63   0.48 0.52
Q23   23                      0.61   0.41 0.59
Q02    2               -0.36  0.51   0.41 0.59
Q19   19               -0.35  0.38   0.34 0.66

                 TC1   TC4   TC3   TC2
SS loadings     3.90  2.88  2.94  1.85
Proportion Var  0.17  0.13  0.13  0.08
Cumulative Var  0.17  0.29  0.42  0.50

 With factor correlations of
        TC1    TC4    TC3    TC2
TC1    1.00   0.44   0.36  -0.18
TC4    0.44   1.00   0.31  -0.10
TC3    0.36   0.31   1.00  -0.17
TC2   -0.18  -0.10  -0.17   1.00
```

```
Test of the hypothesis that 4 factors are sufficient.
The degrees of freedom for the null model are  253 and the
objective function was 7.55
The degrees of freedom for the model are 167 and the objective
function was 1.03
The number of observations was 2571 with Chi Square = 2634.37
with prob < 0

Fit based upon off diagonal values = 0.96
```

Output 17.10

Also in this output you'll find a correlation matrix between the factors. This matrix contains the correlation coefficients between factors – **R** didn't bother to show this to us when it did an orthogonal rotation, because the correlations were all zero. Factor 2 (*TC2*) has little relationship with any other factors (the correlation coefficients are low), but all other factors are interrelated to some degree (notably *TC3* with both *TC1* and *TC4*, and *TC4* with *TC1*). The fact that these correlations exist tell us that the constructs measured can be interrelated. If the constructs were independent then we would expect oblique rotation to provide an identical solution to an orthogonal rotation and the component correlation matrix should be an identity matrix (i.e., all factors have correlation coefficients of 0). Therefore, this final matrix gives us a guide to whether it is reasonable to assume independence between factors: for these data it appears that we cannot assume independence. Therefore, the results of the orthogonal rotation should not be trusted: the obliquely rotated solution is probably more meaningful.

When an oblique rotation is conducted the factor matrix is split into two matrices: the *pattern matrix* and the *structure matrix* (see Jane Superbrain Box 17.1). For orthogonal rotation these matrices are the same. The pattern matrix contains the factor loadings and is comparable to the factor matrix that we interpreted for the orthogonal rotation. The structure matrix takes into account the relationship between factors (in fact it is a product of the pattern matrix and the matrix containing the correlation coefficients between factors). Most researchers interpret the pattern matrix, because it is usually simpler; however, there are situations in which values in the pattern matrix are suppressed because of relationships between the factors. Therefore, the structure matrix is a useful double-check and Graham et al. (2003) recommend reporting both (with some useful examples of why this can be important).

Getting the structure matrix out of **R** is a little bit more complex than getting the pattern matrix. You need to multiply the factor loading matrix by the correlation matrix of the factors. We've come across the loadings, these are called *pc4$loadings*. The correlations of the factors are called the Phi (Greek letter ϕ, which rhymes with pie) and so are stored in *pc4$Phi*. Given that we have these two matrices, we can get the structure matrix by multiplying them; however, this is not a regular multiplication, this is a matrix multiplication, so instead of writing * we write %*%. The structure matrix is therefore given by executing:

```
pc4$loadings %*% pc4$Phi
```

The kind of people that write **R** think that this is straightforward, but we realize it's not, especially when you're starting out. Also, doing this calculation produces a rather unfriendly looking structure matrix that isn't sorted by the size of factor loadings. So, we've written a function for you, called **factor.structure()**; you can source it from our DSUR package. The function takes this general form:

```
factor.structure(pcModel, cut = 0.2, decimals = 2)
```

All you need to do is enter the name of the principal components model into the function and execute. Just like the *print.psych()* function we have included an option (*cut*) so you can specify a value below which you don't want to see the loading (the default is .2), and also an option, *decimals*, that allows you to change the number of decimal places you see (the default is 2). For our current model we could execute:

```
factor.structure(pc4, cut = 0.3)
```

Output 17.11 shows the structure matrix. The picture becomes more complicated in the structure matrix because with the exception of factor 2, several variables load quite highly onto more than one factor. This has occurred because of the relationship between factors 1 and 3 and between factors 3 and 4. This example should highlight why the pattern matrix is preferable for interpretative reasons: because it contains information about the *unique* contribution of a variable to a factor.

	TC1	TC4	TC3	TC2
Q06	0.78			
Q18	0.76	0.36	0.42	
Q13	0.72	0.43	0.33	
Q07	0.72	0.38	0.42	
Q14	0.67	0.35	0.44	
Q12	0.6	0.33	0.59	
Q10	0.56			
Q15	0.55	0.44	0.31	
Q08		0.85		
Q17	0.44	0.82	0.3	
Q11	0.43	0.82		
Q21	0.46	0.37	0.7	
Q20			0.68	
Q03	-0.39	-0.36	-0.64	0.41
Q16	0.5	0.5	0.58	
Q04	0.47	0.49	0.56	
Q01	0.4	0.5	0.53	
Q05	0.44	0.4	0.47	
Q22				0.66
Q09				0.66
Q23				0.58
Q02			-0.39	0.55
Q19			-0.44	0.45

Output 17.11

On a theoretical level the dependence between our factors does not cause concern; we might expect a fairly strong relationship between fear of maths, fear of statistics and fear of computers. Generally, the less mathematically and technically minded people struggle with statistics. However, we would not expect these constructs to correlate with fear of peer evaluation (because this construct is more socially based). In fact, this factor is the one that correlates fairly badly with all others – so on a theoretical level, things have turned out rather well!

17.6.5. Factor scores ②

Having reached a suitable solution and rotated that solution, we can look at the factor scores. Factor scores are obtained by adding *scores = TRUE* to the *principal()* function. Therefore, to get factor scores for our model *pc4*, we would rerun the analysis using by executing:

```
pc5 <- principal(raqData, nfactors = 4, rotate = "oblimin", scores = TRUE)
```

CRAMMING SAM'S TIPS   Interpretation

- If you've conducted orthogonal rotation then look at the table labelled *rotated component matrix*. For each variable, note the component for which the variable has the highest loading. Also, for each component, note the variables that load highly onto it (by 'high' I mean loadings should be above .4 when you ignore the plus or minus sign). Try to make sense of what the factors represent by looking for common themes in the items that load onto them.
- If you've conducted oblique rotation then calculate and look at the *pattern matrix*. For each variable, note the component for which the variable has the highest loading. Also, for each component, note the variables that load highly onto it (by 'high' I mean loadings should be above .4 when you ignore the plus or minus sign). Double-check what you find by doing the same thing for the *structure matrix*. Try to make sense of what the factors represents by looking for common themes in the items that load onto them.

By setting the *scores* option to *TRUE* the factor scores are added to the principal component model in an object called *scores*; therefore, we can access these scores by using *pc5$scores* (which translates as the *scores* object attached to the model *pc5* that we just created). To view the factor scores, you could execute:

```
pc5$scores
```

However, there are rather a lot of them (2571 actually), so let's look at the first 10 rows, by using the *head()* function and executing:

```
head(pc5$scores, 10)
```

SELF-TEST

✓ Using what you learnt in Chapter 6, or Section 17.6.2, calculate the correlation matrix for the factor scores. Compare this to the correlations of the factors in Output 17.10.

	TC1	TC4	TC3	TC2
[1,]	0.37296709	1.8808424	0.95979596	0.3910711
[2,]	0.63334164	0.2374679	0.29090777	-0.3504080
[3,]	0.39712768	-0.1056263	-0.09333769	0.9249353
[4,]	-0.78741595	0.2956628	-0.77703307	0.2605666
[5,]	0.04425942	0.6815179	0.59786611	-0.6912687
[6,]	-1.70018648	0.2091685	0.02784164	0.6653081
[7,]	0.66139239	0.4224096	1.52552021	-0.9805434
[8,]	0.59491329	0.4060248	1.06465956	-1.0932598
[9,]	-2.34971189	-3.6134797	-1.42999472	-0.5443773
[10,]	0.93504597	0.2285419	0.96735727	-1.5712753

Output 17.12

Output 17.12 shows the factor scores for the first 10 participants. Factor scores can be used in this way to assess the relative fear of one person compared to another. We can also use factor scores in regression when groups of predictors correlate so highly that there is multicollinearity.

Before we can do any analysis with our factor scores, we need to add the factor scores into our dataframe. To do this, we use the *cbind()* function, which we have used numerous times before:

```
raqData <- cbind(raqData, pc5$scores)
```

SELF-TEST

✓ Can you think of another way of obtaining the structure matrix (the correlations between factors and items) now you've learned about factor scores?

17.6.6. Summary ②

To sum up, the analyses revealed four underlying scales in our questionnaire that may, or may not, relate to genuine sub-components of **R** anxiety. It also seems as though an obliquely rotated solution was preferred due to the interrelationships between factors. The use of factor analysis is purely exploratory; it should be used only to guide future hypotheses, or to inform researchers about patterns within data sets. A great many decisions are left to the researcher using factor analysis, and I urge you to make informed decisions, rather than basing decisions on the outcomes you would like to get. In section 17.9 we consider whether or not our scale is reliable.

17.7. How to report factor analysis ①

As with any analysis, when reporting factor analysis we need to provide our readers with enough information to make an informed opinion about our data. As a bare minimum we should be very clear about our criteria for extracting factors and the method of rotation used. We must also produce a table of the rotated factor loadings of all items and flag (in bold) values above a criterion level (I would personally choose .40, but I discussed the various criteria you could use in section 17.3.9.2). You should also report the percentage of variance that each factor explains and possibly the eigenvalue too. Table 17.1 shows an example of such a table for the RAQ data; note that I have also reported the sample size in the title.

In my opinion, a table of factor loadings and a description of the analysis are a bare minimum, though. You could consider (if it's not too large) including the table of correlations from which someone could reproduce your analysis (should they want to). You could also consider including some information on sample size adequacy.

For this example we might write something like this:

✓ A principal components analysis (PCA) was conducted on the 23 items with orthogonal rotation (varimax). The Kaiser–Meyer–Olkin measure verified the sampling adequacy for the analysis KMO = .93 ('superb' according to Kaiser, 1974), and all KMO values for individual items were > .77, which is well above the acceptable limit of .5. Bartlett's test of sphericity, χ^2 (253) = 19,334, $p < .001$, indicated that correlations between items were sufficiently large for PCA. An initial analysis was run to obtain eigenvalues for each component in the data. Four components had eigenvalues over Kaiser's criterion of 1 and in combination explained 50.32% of the variance. The scree plot was slightly ambiguous and showed inflexions that would justify retaining both two and four components. Given the large sample size, and the convergence of the scree plot and Kaiser's criterion on four components, four components were retained in the final analysis. Table 17.1 shows the factor loadings after rotation. The items that cluster on the same components suggest that component 1 represents a fear of computers, component 2 a fear of statistics, component 3 a fear of maths and component 4 peer evaluation concerns.

Table 17.1 Summary of exploratory factor analysis results for the **R** anxiety questionnaire (*N* = 2571)

Item	Varimax rotated factor loadings			
	Fear of computers	*Fear of statistics*	*Peer evaluation*	*Fear of maths*
I have little experience of computers	**.80**	−.01	−.07	.10
R always crashes when I try to use it	**.68**	.33	−.08	.13
I worry that I will cause irreparable damage because of my incompetence with computers	**.65**	.23	−.10	.23
All computers hate me	**.64**	.33	−.08	.16
Computers have minds of their own and deliberately go wrong whenever I use them	**.58**	.36	−.07	.14
Computers are useful only for playing games	**.55**	.00	−.12	.13
Computers are out to get me	**.46**	.22	−.19	.29
I can't sleep for thoughts of eigen vectors	−.04	**.68**	−.14	.08
I wake up under my duvet thinking that I am trapped under a normal distribution	.29	**.66**	−.07	.16
Standard deviations excite me	−.20	**−.57**	.37	−.18
People try to tell you that R makes statistics easier to understand but it doesn't	**.47**	**.52**	−.08	.10
I dream that Pearson is attacking me with correlation coefficients	.32	**.52**	.04	.31
I weep openly at the mention of central tendency	.33	**.51**	−.12	.31
Statistics makes me cry	.24	**.50**	.06	.36
I don't understand statistics	.32	**.43**	.02	.24
I have never been good at mathematics	.13	.17	.01	**.83**
I slip into a coma whenever I see an equation	.27	.22	−.04	**.75**
I did badly at mathematics at school	.26	.21	−.14	**.75**
My friends are better at statistics than me	−.09	−.20	**.65**	.12
My friends are better at R than I am	−.19	.03	**.65**	−.10
If I'm good at statistics my friends will think I'm a nerd	−.02	.17	**.59**	−.20
My friends will think I'm stupid for not being able to cope with R	−.01	−.34	**.54**	.07
Everybody looks at me when I use R	−.15	−.37	**.43**	−.03
Eigenvalues	3.73	3.34	1.95	2.55
% of variance	16.22	14.52	8.48	11.10
α	.82	.82	.57	.82

Note: Factor loadings over .40 appear in bold.

Finally, if you have used oblique rotation you should consider reporting a table of both the structure and pattern matrix because the loadings in these tables have different interpretations (see Jane Superbrain Box 17.1).

Labcoat Leni's Real Research 17.1 World wide addiction?

Nichols, L. A., & Nicki, R. (2004). *Psychology of Addictive Behaviors*, *18*(4), 381–384.

The Internet is now a houshold tool. In 2007 it was estimated that around 179 million people worldwide used the Internet (over 100 million of those were in the USA and Canada). From the increasing popularity (and usefulness) of the Internet has emerged a new phenomenon: Internet addiction. This is now a serious and recognized problem, but until very recently it was very difficult to research this topic because there was not a psychometrically sound measure of Internet addition. That is, until Laura Nichols and Richard Nicki developed the Internet Addiction Scale, IAS (Nichols & Nicki, 2004). (Incidentally, while doing some research on this topic I encountered an Internet addiction recovery website that I won't name but that offered a whole host of resources that would keep you online for ages, such as questionnaires, an online support group, videos, articles, a recovery blog and podcasts. It struck me that this was a bit like having a recovery centre for heroin addiction where the addict arrives to be greeted by a nice-looking counsellor who says 'there's a huge pile of heroin in the corner over there, just help yourself'.)

Anyway, Nichols and Nicki developed a 36-item questionnaire to measure internet addiction. It contained items such as 'I have stayed on the Internet longer than I intended to' and 'My grades/work have suffered because of my Internet use', which could be responded to on a 5-point scale (Never, Rarely, Sometimes, Frequently, Always). They collected data from 207 people to validate this measure.

The data from this study are in the file **Nichols & Nicki (2004).dat**. The authors dropped two items because they had low means and variances, and dropped three others because of relatively low correlations with other items. They performed a principal components analysis on the remaining 31 items. Labcoat Leni wants you to run

 some descriptive statistics to work out which two items were dropped for having low means/variances, then inspect a correlation matrix to find the three items that were dropped for having low correlations. Finally, he wants you to run a principal components analysis on the data.

Answers are in the additional material on the companion website (or look at the original article).

17.8. Reliability analysis ②

17.8.1. Measures of reliability ③

If you're using factor analysis to validate a questionnaire, it is useful to check the reliability of your scale.

SELF-TEST

✓ Thinking back to Chapter 1, what are reliability and test–retest reliability?

How do I tell if my questionnaire is reliable?

Reliability means that a measure (or in this case questionnaire) should consistently reflect the construct that it is measuring. One way to think of this is that, other things being equal, a person should get the same score on a questionnaire if they complete it at two different points in time (we have already discovered that this is called test–retest reliability). So, someone who is terrified of statistics and who scores highly on our RAQ should score similarly highly if we tested them a month later (assuming they hadn't gone into some kind of statistics-anxiety therapy in that month). Another way to look at reliability is to say that two people who are the same in terms of the construct being measured should get the same score. So, if we took two people who were equally statistics-phobic, then they should get more or less identical scores on the RAQ. Likewise, if we took two people who loved statistics, they should both get equally low scores. It should be apparent that if we took someone who loved statistics and someone who was terrified of it, and they got the same score on our questionnaire, then it wouldn't be an accurate measure of statistical anxiety. In statistical terms, the usual way to look at reliability is based on the idea that individual items (or sets of items) should produce results consistent with the overall questionnaire. So, if we take someone scared of statistics, then their overall score on the RAQ will be high; if the RAQ is reliable then if we randomly select some items from it the person's score on those items should also be high.

The simplest way to do this in practice is to use **split-half reliability**. This method randomly splits the data set into two. A score for each participant is then calculated based on each half of the scale. If a scale is very reliable a person's score on one half of the scale should be the same (or similar) to their score on the other half: therefore, across several participants, scores from the two halves of the questionnaire should correlate perfectly (well, very highly). The correlation between the two halves is the statistic computed in the split-half method, with large correlations being a sign of reliability. The problem with this method is that there are several ways in which a set of data can be split into two and so the results could be a product of the way in which the data were split. To overcome this problem, Cronbach (1951) came up with a measure that is loosely equivalent to splitting data in two in every possible way and computing the correlation coefficient for each split. The average of these values is equivalent to **Cronbach's alpha**, α, which is the most common measure of scale reliability.[11]

Cronbach's α is:

$$\alpha = \frac{N^2 \overline{Cov}}{\sum s_{item}^2 + \sum Cov_{item}} \tag{17.6}$$

which may look complicated, but actually isn't. The first thing to note is that for each item on our scale we can calculate two things: the variance within the item, and the covariance between a particular item and any other item on the scale. Put another way, we can construct a variance–covariance matrix of all items. In this matrix the diagonal elements will be the variance within a particular item, and the off-diagonal elements will be covariances between pairs of items. The top half of the equation is simply the number of items (N) squared multiplied by the average covariance between items (the average of the off-diagonal elements in the aforementioned variance–covariance matrix). The bottom half is

[11] Although this is the easiest way to conceptualize Cronbach's α, whether or not it is exactly equal to the average of all possible split-half reliabilities depends on exactly how you calculate the split-half reliability (see the glossary for computational details). If you use the Spearman–Brown formula, which takes no account of item standard deviations, then Cronbach's α will be equal to the average split-half reliability only when the item standard deviations are equal; otherwise α will be smaller than the average. However, if you use a formula for split-half reliability that does account for item standard deviations (such as Flanagan, 1937; Rulon, 1939) then α will always equal the average split-half reliability (see Cortina, 1993).

just the sum of all the item variances and item covariances (i.e., the sum of everything in the variance–covariance matrix).

There is a standardized version of the coefficient too, which essentially uses the same equation except that correlations are used rather than covariances, and the bottom half of the equation uses the sum of the elements in the correlation matrix of items (including the ones that appear on the diagonal of that matrix). The normal alpha is appropriate when items on a scale are summed to produce a single score for that scale (the standardized alpha is not appropriate in these cases). The standardized alpha is useful, though, when items on a scale are standardized before being summed.

17.8.2. Interpreting Cronbach's α (some cautionary tales ...) ②

You'll often see in books, journal articles, or be told by people that a value of .7 to .8 is an acceptable value for Cronbach's α; values substantially lower indicate an unreliable scale. Kline (1999) notes that although the generally accepted value of .8 is appropriate for cognitive tests such as intelligence tests, for ability tests a cut-off point of .7 is more suitable. He goes on to say that when dealing with psychological constructs values below even .7 can, realistically, be expected because of the diversity of the constructs being measured.

However, Cortina (1993) notes that such general guidelines need to be used with caution because the value of α depends on the number of items on the scale. You'll notice that the top half of the equation for α includes the number of items squared. Therefore, as the number of items on the scale increases, α will increase. Therefore, it's possible to get a large value of α because you have a lot of items on the scale! For example, Cortina reports data from two scales, both of which have $\alpha = .8$. The first scale has only three items, and the average correlation between items was a respectable .57; however, the second scale had 10 items, with an average correlation between these items of a less respectable .28. Clearly the internal consistency of these scales differs enormously, yet they are both equally reliable

A second common interpretation of alpha is that it measures 'unidimensionality', or the extent to which the scale measures one underlying factor or construct. This interpretation stems from the fact that when there is one factor underlying the data, α is a measure of the strength of that factor (see Cortina, 1993). However, Grayson (2004) demonstrates that data sets with the same α can have very different structures. He showed that $\alpha = .8$ can be achieved in a scale with one underlying factor, with two moderately correlated factors and with two uncorrelated factors. Cortina (1993) has also shown that with more than 12 items, and fairly high correlations between items ($r > .5$), α can reach values around and above .7 (.65 to .84). These results compellingly show that α should not be used as a measure of 'unidimensionality'. Indeed, Cronbach (1951) suggested that if several factors exist then the formula should be applied separately to items relating to different factors. In other words, if your questionnaire has subscales, α should be applied separately to these subscales.

The final warning is about items that have a reverse phrasing. For example, in our RAQ that we used in the factor analysis part of this chapter, we had one item (question 3) that was phrased the opposite way around to all other items. The item was 'standard deviations excite me'. Compare this to any other item and you'll see it requires the opposite response. For example, item 1 is 'statistics make me cry'. Now, if you don't like statistics then you'll strongly agree with this statement and so will get a score of 5 on our scale. For item 3, if you hate statistics then standard deviations are unlikely to excite you so you'll strongly disagree and get a score of 1 on the scale. These reverse-phrased items are important for reducing response bias; participants will actually have to read the items in case they are phrased the other way around. For factor analysis, this reverse phrasing doesn't matter, all that happens is you get a negative factor loading for any reversed items (in fact, look

Eek! My alpha is negative: is that correct?

at Output 17.10 and you'll see that item 3 has a negative factor loading). However, in reliability analysis these reverse-scored items do make a difference. To see why, think about the equation for Cronbach's α. In this equation, the top half incorporates the *average* covariance between items. If an item is reverse-phrased then it will have a negative relationship with other items, hence the covariances between this item and other items will be negative. The average covariance is obviously the sum of covariances divided by the number of covariances, and by including a bunch of negative values we reduce the sum of covariances, and hence we also reduce Cronbach's α, because the top half of the equation gets smaller. In extreme cases, it is even possible to get a negative value for Cronbach's α, simply because the magnitude of negative covariances is bigger than the magnitude of positive ones. A negative Cronbach's α doesn't make much sense, but it does happen, and if it does, ask yourself whether you included any reverse-phrased items.

17.8.3. Reliability analysis with R Commander ①

As with factor analysis, it's possible to use R Commander to obtain reliability estimates. However, the procedure is not as flexible as the *alpha()* function in the psych package, so that's the one we use.

17.8.4. Reliability analysis using R ②

Let's test the reliability of the RAQ using the data in **RAQ.dat**. Remember also that I said we should conduct reliability analysis on any subscales individually. If we use the results from our orthogonal rotation (look back at), then we have four subscales:

1 Subscale 1 (*Fear of computers*): items 6, 7, 10, 13, 14, 15, 18

2 Subscale 2 (*Fear of statistics*): items 1, 3, 4, 5, 12, 16, 20, 21

3 Subscale 3 (*Fear of mathematics*): items 8, 11, 17

4 Subscale 4 (*Peer evaluation*): items 2, 9, 19, 22, 23

(Don't forget that question 3 has a negative sign; we'll need to remember to deal with that.) First, we'll create four new data sets, containing the subscales for the items. We don't need to do that, but it saves a lot of typing later on. We can create these data sets by simply selecting the appropriate columns of the full dataframe (*raqData*) as described in section 3.9.1.

```
computerFear<-raqData[, c(6, 7, 10, 13, 14, 15, 18)]
statisticsFear <- raqData[, c(1, 3, 4, 5, 12, 16, 20, 21)]
mathFear <- raqData[, c(8, 11, 17)]
peerEvaluation <- raqData[, c(2, 9, 19, 22, 23)]
```

This command takes the *raqData* dataframe and retains all of the rows (hence no command before the comma), and any columns specified in the *c()* function after the comma. For example, the first command creates an object called *computerFear* that contains only columns 6, 7, 10, 13, 14, 15, and 18 of the dataframe *raqData*.

Reliability analysis is done with the **alpha()** function, which is found in the *psych* package. You might have a problem here, because there is also a function in *ggplot2* called alpha, and if you've loaded *ggplot2* first, that version will have priority. This was covered in R's Souls' Tip 3.4, but to remind you, if you get the wrong *alpha()* function, you can specify the package, using:

```
psych::alpha()
```

An additional complication that we need to deal with is that pesky item 3, which is negatively scored. We can do one of two things with this item. We can reverse the variable in the data set, or we can tell *alpha()* that it is negative, using the *keys* option. This latter option is better because we leave the initial data unchanged (which is useful because we don't get into awkward situations in which we save the data and then can't recall at a later date whether or not the data contains the reverse scored or original scores).

To use the keys option we give *alpha()* a vector of 1s and −1s, which matches the number of variables in the data set, using a 1 for a positively score item and a −1 for a negatively scored item. So for *computerFear*, which has only positively scored items, we would use:

```
keys = c(1, 1, 1, 1, 1, 1, 1)
```

but for *statisticsFear*, which has item 3 (the negatively scored item) as its second item, we would use:

```
keys = c(1, -1, 1, 1, 1, 1, 1, 1)
```

For three of our four subscales we don't need to use the *keys* option because all items are positively scored, but for *statisticsFear* we need to. To use the *alpha()* function we simply input the name of the dataframe for each subscale, and, where necessary, include the *keys* option. Therefore, we could run the reliability analysis for our four subscales by executing:

```
alpha(computerFear)
alpha(statisticsFear, keys = c(1, -1, 1, 1, 1, 1, 1, 1))
alpha(mathFear)
alpha(peerEvaluation)
```

17.8.5. Interpreting the output ②

Output 17.13 shows the results of this basic reliability analysis for the fear of computing subscale. First, and perhaps most important, the value of *alpha* at the very top is Cronbach's α: the overall reliability of the scale (you should look at the raw alpha, they're usually very similar though). To reiterate, we're looking for values in the range of .7 to .8 (or thereabouts) bearing in mind what we've already noted about effects from the number of items. In this case α is slightly above .8, and is certainly in the region indicated by Kline (1999), so this probably indicates good reliability.

Along with alpha, there is a measure labelled G6, short for Guttman's lambda 6; this can be calculated from the squared multiple correlation (hence it's labelled *smc*).[12] The *average_r* is the average inter-item correlation (from which we can calculate standardized alpha).

Also in this top section are some scale characteristics. If we calculated someone's score by taking the average of all of their items (which is the same as adding up the score and dividing by the number of items), we would have a variable with an overall mean of 3.4 and standard deviation of 0.71.[13]

---

[12] Fact fiends might be interested to know that Guttman came up with Cronbach's alpha before Cronbach, and called it lambda 3.

[13] You can test this by running:
```
describe(apply((raq[c(6, 7, 10, 13, 14, 15, 18)]), 1, mean))
```
which gives you a mean of 3.42 and *sd* = 0.71.

Next, we get a table giving the statistics for the scale if we deleted each item in turn. The values in the column labelled *raw_alpha* are the values of the overall α if that item isn't included in the calculation. As such, they reflect the change in Cronbach's α that would be seen if a particular item were deleted. The overall α is .82, and so all values in this column should be around that same value. What we're actually looking for is values of alpha greater than the overall α. If you think about it, if the deletion of an item increases Cronbach's α then this means that the deletion of that item improves reliability (remembering that scales with more items are more reliable, so removing an item should always lower alpha). Therefore, any items that have values of α in this column greater than the overall α may need to be deleted from the scale to improve its reliability. None of the items here would substantially affect reliability if they were deleted. None of the items increase alpha by being deleted. This table also contains the standardized alpha if the item is removed, the G6 if the item is removed and the mean correlation if the item is removed.

The next table in the output is labelled *item statistics*. The values in the first column labelled *r* are the correlations between each item and the total score from the questionnaire – sometimes called item–total correlations. There's a problem with this statistic, and that is that the item is included in the total. That is, if we correlate item 6 with the mean of all items, we're correlating the item with itself, so of course it will correlate. We can correct this by correlating each item with all of the other items. Two versions of this are presented, *r.cor* and *r.drop*: *r.cor* is a little complex, so we won't go into it (but the help file for alpha explains it), *r.drop* is the correlation of that item with the scale total if that item isn't included in the scale total. Sometimes this is called the item–rest correlation (because it's how the item correlates with the rest of the items) and sometimes it's called the corrected item–total correlation.

```
Reliability analysis
Call: alpha(x = computerFear)

 raw_alpha std.alpha G6(smc) average_r mean    sd
     0.82      0.82    0.81       0.4  3.4  0.71


 Reliability if an item is dropped:
     raw_alpha std.alpha G6(smc) average_r
Q06       0.79      0.79    0.77      0.38
Q07       0.79      0.79    0.77      0.38
Q10       0.82      0.82    0.80      0.44
Q13       0.79      0.79    0.77      0.39
Q14       0.80      0.80    0.77      0.39
Q15       0.81      0.81    0.79      0.41
Q18       0.79      0.78    0.76      0.38


 Item statistics
        n    r r.cor r.drop mean    sd
Q06 2571 0.74  0.68   0.62  3.8  1.12
Q07 2571 0.73  0.68   0.62  3.1  1.10
Q10 2571 0.57  0.44   0.40  3.7  0.88
Q13 2571 0.73  0.67   0.61  3.6  0.95
Q14 2571 0.70  0.64   0.58  3.1  1.00
Q15 2571 0.64  0.54   0.49  3.2  1.01
Q18 2571 0.76  0.72   0.65  3.4  1.05


Non missing response frequency for each item
        1    2    3    4    5 miss
Q06 0.06 0.10 0.13 0.44 0.27    0
Q07 0.09 0.24 0.26 0.34 0.07    0
```

```
Q10 0.02 0.10 0.18 0.57 0.14    0
Q13 0.03 0.12 0.25 0.48 0.12    0
Q14 0.07 0.18 0.38 0.31 0.06    0
Q15 0.06 0.18 0.30 0.39 0.07    0
Q18 0.06 0.12 0.31 0.37 0.14    0
```

Output 17.13

In a reliable scale all items should correlate with the total. So, we're looking for items that don't correlate with the overall score from the scale: if any of these values of *r.drop* are less than about .3 then we've got problems, because it means that a particular item does not correlate very well with the scale overall. Items with low correlations may have to be dropped. For these data, all data have corrected item–total correlations above .3, which is encouraging. The table also shows the mean and standard deviation of the scale if the item is omitted.

The final table in the alpha output is a table of frequencies. It tells us what percentage of people gave each response to each of the items. This is useful to make sure that everyone in your sample is not giving the same response. It is usually the case that an item where everyone (or almost everyone) gives the same response will almost certainly have poor reliability statistics.

As a final point, it's worth noting that if items do need to be removed at this stage then you should rerun your factor analysis as well to make sure that the deletion of the item has not affected the factor structure.

```
Reliability analysis
Call: alpha(x = statisticsFear, keys = c(1, -1, 1, 1, 1, 1, 1, 1))

  raw_alpha std.alpha G6(smc) average_r mean   sd
     0.82      0.82     0.81      0.37   3.1  0.5

 Reliability if an item is dropped:
     raw_alpha std.alpha G6(smc) average_r
Q01      0.80      0.80     0.79      0.37
Q03      0.80      0.80     0.79      0.37
Q04      0.80      0.80     0.78      0.36
Q05      0.81      0.81     0.80      0.38
Q12      0.80      0.80     0.79      0.36
Q16      0.79      0.80     0.78      0.36
Q20      0.82      0.82     0.80      0.40
Q21      0.79      0.80     0.78      0.36

 Item statistics
        n    r r.cor r.drop mean   sd
Q01 2571 0.67  0.60   0.54  3.6 0.83
Q03 2571 0.67  0.60   0.55  3.4 1.08
Q04 2571 0.70  0.64   0.58  3.2 0.95
Q05 2571 0.63  0.55   0.49  3.3 0.96
Q12 2571 0.69  0.63   0.57  2.8 0.92
Q16 2571 0.71  0.67   0.60  3.1 0.92
Q20 2571 0.56  0.47   0.42  2.4 1.04
Q21 2571 0.71  0.67   0.61  2.8 0.98

Non missing response frequency for each item
        1    2    3    4    5 miss
Q01 0.02 0.07 0.29 0.52 0.11    0
Q03 0.03 0.17 0.34 0.26 0.19    0
Q04 0.05 0.17 0.36 0.37 0.05    0
```

```
Q05 0.04 0.18 0.29 0.43 0.06    0
Q12 0.09 0.23 0.46 0.20 0.02    0
Q16 0.06 0.16 0.42 0.33 0.04    0
Q20 0.22 0.37 0.25 0.15 0.02    0
Q21 0.09 0.29 0.34 0.26 0.02    0
```

Output 17.14

OK, let's move on to the fear of statistics subscale (items 1, 3, 4, 5, 12, 16, 20 and 21). I won't go through the **R** output in detail again, but it is shown in Output 17.14. The overall α is .82, and none of the items here would increase the reliability if they were deleted. The values in the column labelled *r.drop* are again all above .3, which is good. In all, this indicates that all items are positively contributing to the overall reliability. The overall α is also excellent (.82) because it is above .8, and indicates good reliability.

```
Reliability analysis
Call: alpha(x = statisticsFear)

  raw_alpha std.alpha G6(smc) average_r mean  sd
     0.61      0.64     0.71     0.18   3.1 0.5

 Reliability if an item is dropped:
     raw_alpha std.alpha G6(smc) average_r
Q01      0.52      0.56    0.64      0.15
Q03      0.80      0.80    0.79      0.37
Q04      0.50      0.55    0.64      0.15
Q05      0.52      0.57    0.66      0.16
Q12      0.52      0.56    0.65      0.15
Q16      0.51      0.55    0.63      0.15
Q20      0.56      0.60    0.68      0.18
Q21      0.50      0.55    0.63      0.15

 Item statistics
          n     r r.cor r.drop mean   sd
Q01 2571  0.68  0.62   0.51   3.6 0.83
Q03 2571 -0.37 -0.64  -0.55   3.4 1.08
Q04 2571  0.69  0.65   0.53   3.2 0.95
Q05 2571  0.65  0.57   0.47   3.3 0.96
Q12 2571  0.67  0.62   0.50   2.8 0.92
Q16 2571  0.70  0.66   0.53   3.1 0.92
Q20 2571  0.55  0.45   0.35   2.4 1.04
Q21 2571  0.70  0.66   0.54   2.8 0.98

Non missing response frequency for each item
           1    2    3    4    5 miss
Q01 0.02 0.07 0.29 0.52 0.11    0
Q03 0.03 0.17 0.34 0.26 0.19    0
Q04 0.05 0.17 0.36 0.37 0.05    0
Q05 0.04 0.18 0.29 0.43 0.06    0
Q12 0.09 0.23 0.46 0.20 0.02    0
Q16 0.06 0.16 0.42 0.33 0.04    0
Q20 0.22 0.37 0.25 0.15 0.02    0
Q21 0.09 0.29 0.34 0.26 0.02    0
```

Output 17.15

Just to illustrate the importance of reverse-scoring items before running reliability analysis, Output 17.15 shows the reliability analysis for the fear of statistics subscale but done on the original data (i.e., without item 3 being reverse scored by using the *keys* option). Note that the overall α is considerably lower (.61 rather than .82). Also, note that this item has a negative item–total correlation (which is a good way to spot if you have a potential reverse-scored item in the data that hasn't been reverse scored). Finally, note that for item 3, the α if item deleted is .8. That is, if this item were deleted then the reliability would improve from about .6 to about .8. This, I hope, illustrates that failing to reverse-score items that have been phrased oppositely to other items on the scale will mess up your reliability analysis.

Moving swiftly on to the fear of maths subscale (items 8, 11 and 17), Output 17.16 shows the output from the analysis. As with the previous two subscales, the overall α is around .8, which indicates good reliability. The values of alpha if the item were deleted indicate that none of the items here would increase the reliability if they were deleted because all values in this column are less than the overall reliability of .82. The values of the corrected item–total correlations (*r.drop*) are again all above .3, which is good,

```
Reliability analysis
Call: alpha(x = mathFear)

  raw_alpha std.alpha G6(smc) average_r mean    sd
     0.82       0.82    0.75        0.6  3.7  0.75


 Reliability if an item is dropped:
     raw_alpha std.alpha G6(smc) average_r
Q08       0.74      0.74    0.59       0.59
Q11       0.74      0.74    0.59       0.59
Q17       0.77      0.77    0.63       0.63


 Item statistics
        n     r r.cor r.drop mean    sd
Q08 2571 0.86  0.76   0.68  3.8  0.87
Q11 2571 0.86  0.75   0.68  3.7  0.88
Q17 2571 0.85  0.72   0.65  3.5  0.88


Non missing response frequency for each item
       1    2    3    4    5 miss
Q08 0.03 0.06 0.19 0.58 0.15    0
Q11 0.02 0.06 0.22 0.53 0.16    0
Q17 0.03 0.10 0.27 0.52 0.08    0
```

Output 17.16

Finally, if you run the analysis for the final subscale of peer evaluation, you should get Output 17.17. Unlike the previous subscales, the overall α is quite low at .57 and although this is in keeping with what Kline says we should expect for this kind of social science data, it is well below the other scales. The values of alpha if the item is dropped indicate that none of the items here would increase the reliability if they were deleted because all values in this column are less than the overall reliability of .57. The values of *r.drop* are all around .3, and in fact for item 23 the value is below .3. This indicates fairly bad internal consistency and identifies item 23 as a potential problem. The scale has five items, compared to seven, eight and three on the other scales, so its reduced reliability is not going to be dramatically affected by the number of items (in fact, it has more items than the fear of maths subscale). If you look at the items on this subscale, they cover quite diverse themes of peer evaluation, and this might explain the relative lack of consistency. This might lead us to rethink this subscale.

```
Reliability analysis
Call: alpha(x = peerEvaluation)
  raw_alpha std.alpha G6(smc) average_r mean   sd
      0.57      0.57    0.53      0.21  3.4 0.65

 Reliability if an item is dropped:
     raw_alpha std.alpha G6(smc) average_r
Q02       0.52      0.52    0.45      0.21
Q09       0.48      0.48    0.41      0.19
Q19       0.52      0.53    0.46      0.22
Q22       0.49      0.49    0.43      0.19
Q23       0.56      0.57    0.50      0.25

 Item statistics
        n    r r.cor r.drop mean   sd
Q02 2571 0.61  0.45   0.34  4.4 0.85
Q09 2571 0.66  0.53   0.39  3.2 1.26
Q19 2571 0.60  0.42   0.32  3.7 1.10
Q22 2571 0.64  0.50   0.38  3.1 1.04
Q23 2571 0.53  0.31   0.24  2.6 1.04

Non missing response frequency for each item
       1    2    3    4    5 miss
Q02 0.01 0.04 0.08 0.31 0.56    0
Q09 0.08 0.28 0.23 0.20 0.20    0
Q19 0.02 0.15 0.22 0.33 0.29    0
Q22 0.05 0.26 0.34 0.26 0.10    0
Q23 0.12 0.42 0.27 0.12 0.06    0
```

Output 17.17

CRAMMING SAM'S TIPS   Reliability

- Reliability is really the consistency of a measure.
- Reliability analysis can be used to measure the consistency of a questionnaire.
- Remember to deal with reverse-scored items. Use the keys option when you run the analysis.
- Run separate reliability analyses for all subscales of your questionnaire.
- Cronbach's α indicates the overall reliability of a questionnaire and values around .8 are good (or .7 for ability tests and such like).
- The *raw alpha* when an item is dropped tells you whether removing an item will improve the overall reliability: values greater than the overall reliability indicate that removing that item will improve the overall reliability of the scale. Look for items that dramatically increase the value of α.
- If you do remove items, rerun your factor analysis to check that the factor structure still holds!

17.9. Reporting reliability analysis ②

You can report the reliabilities in the text using the symbol α and remembering that because Cronbach's α can't be larger than 1 then we drop the zero before the decimal place (if we are following APA format):

- The fear of computers, fear of statistics and fear of maths subscales of the RAQ all had high reliabilities, all Cronbach's α = .82. However, the fear of negative peer evaluation subscale had relatively low reliability, Cronbach's α = .57.

However, the most common way to report reliability analysis when it follows a factor analysis is to report the values of Cronbach's α as part of the table of factor loadings. For example, in Table 17.1 notice that in the last row of the table I have quoted the value of Cronbach's α for each subscale in turn.

What have I discovered about statistics? ②

This chapter has made us tiptoe along the craggy rock face that is factor analysis. This is a technique for identifying clusters of variables that relate to each other. One of the difficult things with statistics is realizing that they are subjective: many books (this one included, I suspect) create the impression that statistics are like a cook book and if you follow the instructions you'll get a nice tasty chocolate cake (yum!). Factor analysis perhaps more than any other test in this book illustrates how incorrect this is. The world of statistics is full of arbitrary rules that we probably shouldn't follow (.05 being the classic example) and nearly all of the time, whether you realize it or not, we should act upon our own discretion. So, if nothing else, I hope you've discovered enough to give you sufficient discretion about factor analysis to act upon! We saw that the first stage of factor analysis is to scan your variables to check that they relate to each other to some degree but not too strongly. The factor analysis itself has several stages: check some initial issues (e.g., sample size adequacy), decide how many factors to retain, and finally decide which items load on which factors (and try to make sense of the meaning of the factors). Having done all that, you can consider whether the items you have are reliable measures of what you're trying to measure.

We also discovered that at the age of 23 I took it upon myself to become a living homage to the digestive system. I furiously devoured articles and books on statistics (some of them I even understood), I mentally chewed over them, I broke them down with the stomach acid of my intellect, I stripped them of their goodness and nutrients, I compacted them down, and after about two years I forced the smelly brown remnants of those intellectual meals out of me in the form of a book. I was mentally exhausted at the end of it; 'It's a good job I'll never have to do that again', I thought.

R packages used in this chapter

corpcor	psych
GPArotation	

R functions used in this chapter

abs()	hist()
alpha()	kmo()
as.matrix()	mean()
c()	nrow()
cat()	plot()
cbind()	polychor()
cor()	principal()
cortest.bartlett()	print.psych()
det()	residual.stats()
factor.model()	round()
factor.residuals()	sqrt()
factor.structure()	sum()
ggplot2()	upper.tri()

Key terms that I've discovered

Alpha factoring	Kaiser–Meyer–Olkin (KMO) measure of
Bartlett's test of sphericity	sampling adequacy
Common variance	Latent variable
Communality	Oblique rotation
Component matrix	Orthogonal rotation
Confirmatory factor analysis (CFA)	Pattern matrix
Cronbach's α	Principal components analysis (PCA)
Direct oblimin	Promax
Extraction	Quartimax
Factor	Random variance
Factor analysis	Rotation
Factor loading	Scree plot
Factor matrix	Singularity
Factor scores	Split-half reliability
Factor transformation matrix,	Structure matrix
Kaiser's criterion	Unique variance
	Varimax

Smart Alex's tasks

- **Task 1**: The University of Sussex is constantly seeking to employ the best people possible as lecturers (no, really, it is). Anyway, they wanted to revise a questionnaire based on Bland's theory of research methods lecturers. This theory predicts that good research methods lecturers should have four characteristics: (1) a profound love of statistics; (2) an enthusiasm for experimental design; (3) a love of teaching; and (4) a complete absence of normal interpersonal skills. These characteristics should be related (i.e., correlated). The 'Teaching of Statistics for Scientific Experiments' (TOSSE) already existed, but the university revised this questionnaire and it became the 'Teaching of Statistics for Scientific Experiments – Revised' (TOSSE–R). They gave this questionnaire to 239 research methods lecturers around the world to see if it supported Bland's theory. The questionnaire is in Figure 17.9, and the data are in **TOSSE.R.dat.** Conduct a factor analysis (with appropriate rotation) to see the factor structure of the data. ②

FIGURE 17.9

The Teaching of Statistics for Scientific Experiments – Revised (TOSSE–R)

SD = Strongly Disagree, D = Disagree, N = Neither, A = Agree, SA = Strongly Agree						
		SD	D	N	A	SA
1	I once woke up in the middle of a vegetable patch hugging a turnip that I'd mistakenly dug up thinking it was Roy's largest root	O	O	O	O	O
2	If I had a big gun I'd shoot all the students I have to teach	O	O	O	O	O
3	I memorize probability values for the F-distribution	O	O	O	O	O
4	I worship at the shrine of Pearson	O	O	O	O	O
5	I still live with my mother and have little personal hygiene	O	O	O	O	O
6	Teaching others makes me want to swallow a large bottle of bleach because the pain of my burning oesophagus would be light relief in comparison	O	O	O	O	O
7	Helping others to understand sums of squares is a great feeling	O	O	O	O	O
8	I like control conditions	O	O	O	O	O
9	I calculate three ANOVAs in my head before getting out of bed every morning	O	O	O	O	O
10	I could spend all day explaining statistics to people	O	O	O	O	O
11	I like it when people tell me I've helped them to understand factor rotation	O	O	O	O	O
12	People fall asleep as soon as I open my mouth to speak	O	O	O	O	O
13	Designing experiments is fun	O	O	O	O	O
14	I'd rather think about appropriate dependent variables than go to the pub	O	O	O	O	O
15	I soil my pants with excitement at the mere mention of factor analysis	O	O	O	O	O
16	Thinking about whether to use repeated or independent measures thrills me	O	O	O	O	O
17	I enjoy sitting in the park contemplating whether to use participant observation in my next experiment	O	O	O	O	O
18	Standing in front of 300 people in no way makes me lose control of my bowels	O	O	O	O	O
19	I like to help students	O	O	O	O	O
20	Passing on knowledge is the greatest gift you can bestow on an individual	O	O	O	O	O
21	Thinking about Bonferroni corrections gives me a tingly feeling in my groin	O	O	O	O	O
22	I quiver with excitement when thinking about designing my next experiment	O	O	O	O	O
23	I often spend my spare time talking to the pigeons ... and even they die of boredom	O	O	O	O	O
24	I tried to build myself a time machine so that I could go back to the 1930s and follow Fisher around on my hands and knees licking the floor on which he'd just trodden	O	O	O	O	O
25	I love teaching	O	O	O	O	O
26	I spend lots of time helping students	O	O	O	O	O
27	I love teaching because students have to pretend to like me or they'll get bad marks	O	O	O	O	O
28	My cat is my only friend	O	O	O	O	O

• **Task 2:** Dr Sian Williams (University of Brighton) devised a questionnaire to measure organizational ability. She predicted five factors to do with organizational ability: (1) preference for organization; (2) goal achievement; (3) planning approach; (4) acceptance of delays; and (5) preference for routine. These dimensions are theoretically independent. Williams's questionnaire (Figure 17.10) contains 28 items using a 7-point Likert scale (1 = strongly disagree, 4 = neither, 7 = strongly agree). She gave it to 239 people. Run a principal components analysis on the data in **Williams.dat.** ②

Answers can be found on the companion website.

FIGURE 17.10
Williams's organizational ability questionnaire

1	I like to have a plan to work to in everyday life
2	I feel frustrated when things don't go to plan
3	I get most things done in a day that I want to
4	I stick to a plan once I have made it
5	I enjoy spontaneity and uncertainty
6	I feel frustrated if I can't find something I need
7	I find it difficult to follow a plan through
8	I am an organized person
9	I like to know what I have to do in a day
10	Disorganized people annoy me
11	I leave things to the last minute
12	I have many different plans relating to the same goal
13	I like to have my documents filed and in order
14	I find it easy to work in a disorganized environment
15	I make 'to do' lists and achieve most of the things on it
16	My workspace is messy and disorganized
17	I like to be organized
18	Interruptions to my daily routine annoy me
19	I feel that I am wasting my time
20	I forget the plans I have made
21	I prioritize the things I have to do
22	I like to work in an organized environment
23	I feel relaxed when I don't have a routine
24	I set deadlines for myself and achieve them
25	I change rather aimlessly from one activity to another during the day
26	I have trouble organizing the things I have to do
27	I put tasks off to another day
28	I feel restricted by schedules and plans

Further reading

Cortina, J. M. (1993). What is coefficient alpha? An examination of theory and applications. *Journal of Applied Psychology*, 78, 98–104. (A very readable paper on Cronbach's α.)

Dunteman, G. E. (1989). *Principal components analysis*. Sage University Paper Series on Quantitative Applications in the Social Sciences, 07-069. Newbury Park, CA: Sage. (This monograph is quite high level but comprehensive.)

Pedhazur, E., & Schmelkin, L. (1991). *Measurement, design and analysis*. Hillsdale, NJ: Erlbaum. (Chapter 22 is an excellent introduction to the theory of factor analysis.)

Tabachnick, B. G. & Fidell, L. S. (2007). *Using multivariate statistics* (5th ed.). Boston: Allyn & Bacon. (Chapter 13 is a technical but wonderful overview of factor analysis.)

Interesting real research

Nichols, L. A., & Nicki, R. (2004). Development of a psychometrically sound internet addiction scale: A preliminary step. *Psychology of Addictive Behaviors*, *18*(4), 381–384.

18

Categorical data

FIGURE 18.1
Midway through
writing the second
edition of my
SPSS book, things
had gone a little
strange

18.1. What will this chapter tell me? ①

We discovered in the previous chapter that I wrote a book. An earlier edition of this book, which focused on SPSS. There are a lot of good things about writing books. The main benefit is that your parents are impressed. Well, they're not *that* impressed actually, because they think that a good book sells as many copies as *Harry Potter* and that people should queue outside bookshops for the latest enthralling instalment of *Discovering Statistics* .... My parents are, consequently, quite baffled about how this book is seen as reasonably successful, yet I don't get invited to dinner by the Queen. Nevertheless, given that my family don't really understand what I do, books are tangible proof that I do *something*. The size of this book and the fact it has equations in it is an added bonus because it makes me look cleverer than I actually am. However, there is a price to pay, which is immeasurable mental anguish. In England we don't talk about our emotions, because we fear that if they get out into the open, civilization as we know it will collapse, so I definitely will not mention that the writing process for the second edition of my SPSS book was so stressful that I came within one of Fuzzy's whiskers of a total meltdown. It took me two years to recover, just in time to start thinking about the third edition and an adaptation for **R**. Still, it was worth it because the feedback suggests that some people find the books vaguely useful. Of course, the publishers don't care about helping people, they care only about raking in as much cash as possible to feed their cocaine habits and champagne addictions. Therefore, they are obsessed with sales figures and comparisons with other books. They have databases that have sales figures of this book and its competitors in different 'markets' (you are not a person, you are a 'consumer', and you don't live in a country, you live in a 'market') and they gibber and twitch at their consoles creating frequency distributions (with 3-D effects) of these values. The data they get are frequency data (the number of books sold in a certain timeframe). Therefore, if they wanted to compare sales of this book to its competitors, in different countries, they would need to read this chapter because it's all about analysing data, for which we know only the frequency with which events occur. Of course, they won't read this chapter, but they should …

18.2. Packages used in this chapter ①

We'll use the *gmodels* package in this chapter to do chi-square, and *MASS* for loglinear analysis. *MASS* should be installed by default in **R** so you should only need to install *gmodels* by executing:

```
install.packages("gmodels")
```

However, you will need to load both packages by executing:

```
library(gmodels); library(MASS)
```

18.3. Analysing categorical data ①

Sometimes, we are interested not in test scores, or continuous measures, but in *categorical variables*. These are not variables involving cats (although the examples in this chapter might convince you otherwise), but are what we have mainly used as grouping variables. They are variables that describe categories of entities (see section 1.5.1.2). We've come across these types of variables in virtually every chapter of this book. There are different types of categorical variable (see section 6.5.7), but in theory a person, or case, should fall into only one category. Good examples of categorical variables are gender (with few exceptions, people can be only biologically male or biologically female),[1] pregnancy (a woman can be only pregnant or not pregnant) and voting in an election (as a general rule you are allowed to vote for only one candidate). In all cases (except logistic regression) so far, we've used such categorical variables to predict some kind of continuous outcome, but there are times when we want to look at relationships between lots of categorical variables.

---

[1] Before anyone rips my arms from their sockets and beats me around the head with them, I am aware that numerous chromosomal and hormonal conditions exist that complicate the matter. Also, people can have a different gender identity than their biological gender.

This chapter looks at two techniques for doing this. We begin with the simple case of two categorical variables and discover the chi-square statistic (which we're not really discovering because we've unwittingly come across it countless times before). We then extend this model to look at relationships between several categorical variables.

18.4. Theory of analysing categorical data ①

We will begin by looking at the simplest situation that you could encounter; that is, analysing two categorical variables. If we want to look at the relationship between two categorical variables then we can't use the mean or any similar statistic because we don't have any variables that have been measured continuously. Trying to calculate the mean of a categorical variable is completely meaningless because the numeric values you attach to different categories are arbitrary, and the mean of those numeric values will depend on how many members each category has. Therefore, when we've measured only categorical variables, we analyse frequencies. That is, we analyse the number of things that fall into each combination of categories. If we take an example, a researcher was interested in whether animals could be trained to line-dance. He took 200 cats and tried to train them to line-dance by giving them either food or affection as a reward for dance-like behaviour. At the end of the week he counted how many animals could line-dance and how many could not. There are two categorical variables here: **Training** (the animal was trained using either food or affection, not both) and **Dance** (the animal either learnt to line-dance or it did not). By combining categories, we end up with four different categories. All we then need to do is to count how many cats fall into each category. We can tabulate these frequencies as in Table 18.1 (which shows the data for this example), and this is known as a **contingency table.**

Table 18.1 Contingency table showing how many cats will line-dance after being trained with different rewards

		Training		
		Food as reward	**Affection as reward**	**Total**
Could they dance?	Yes	28	48	76
	No	10	114	124
	Total	38	162	200

18.4.1. Pearson's chi-square test ①

If we want to see whether there's a relationship between two categorical variables (i.e., does the number of cats that line-dance relate to the type of training used?) we can use the Pearson's **chi-square test** (Fisher, 1922; Pearson, 1900). This is an extremely elegant statistic based on the simple idea of comparing the frequencies you observe in certain categories to the frequencies you might expect to get in those categories by chance. All the way back in Chapters 2, 7 and 10 we saw that if we fit a model to any set of data we can evaluate that model using a very simple equation (or some variant of it):

$$\text{Deviation} = \sum (\text{observed} - \text{model})^2$$

This equation was the basis of our sums of squares in regression and ANOVA. Now, when we have categorical data we can use the same equation. There is a slight variation in that we divide by the model scores as well, which is actually much the same process as dividing the sum of squares by the degrees of freedom in ANOVA. So, basically, what we're doing is standardizing the deviation for each observation. If we add all of these standardized deviations together the resulting statistic is Pearson's chi-square (χ^2) given by:

$$\chi^2 = \Sigma \frac{\left(\text{observed}_{ij} - \text{model}_{ij}\right)^2}{\text{model}_{ij}} \tag{18.1}$$

in which i represents the rows in the contingency table and j represents the columns. The observed data are, obviously, the frequencies in Table 18.1, but we need to work out what the model is. In ANOVA the model we use is group means, but as I've mentioned we can't work with means when we have only categorical variables so we work with frequencies instead. Therefore, we use 'expected frequencies'. One way to estimate the expected frequencies would be to say 'well, we've got 200 cats in total, and four categories, so the expected value is simply 200/4 = 50'. This would be fine if, for example, we had the same number of cats that had affection as a reward and food as a reward; however, we didn't: 38 got food and 162 got affection as a reward. Likewise there are not equal numbers that could and couldn't dance. To take account of this, we calculate expected frequencies for each of the cells in the table (in this case there are four cells) and we use the column and row totals for a particular cell to calculate the expected value:

$$\text{Model}_{ij} = E_{ij} = \frac{\text{row total}_i \times \text{column total}_j}{n}$$

where n is simply the total number of observations (in this case 200). We can calculate these expected frequencies for the four cells within our table (row total and column total are abbreviated to RT and CT respectively):

$$\text{Model}_{\text{Food, Yes}} = \frac{\text{RT}_{\text{Yes}} \times \text{CT}_{\text{Food}}}{n} = \frac{76 \times 38}{200} = 14.44$$

$$\text{Model}_{\text{Food, No}} = \frac{\text{RT}_{\text{No}} \times \text{CT}_{\text{Food}}}{n} = \frac{124 \times 38}{200} = 23.56$$

$$\text{Model}_{\text{Affection, Yes}} = \frac{\text{RT}_{\text{Yes}} \times \text{CT}_{\text{Affection}}}{n} = \frac{76 \times 162}{200} = 61.56$$

$$\text{Model}_{\text{Affection, No}} = \frac{\text{RT}_{\text{No}} \times \text{CT}_{\text{Affection}}}{n} = \frac{124 \times 162}{200} = 100.44$$

Given that we now have these model values, all we need to do is take each value in each cell of our data table, subtract from it the corresponding model value, square the result, and then divide by the corresponding model value. Once we've done this for each cell in the table, we just add them up!

$$\begin{aligned}
\chi^2 &= \frac{(28 - 14.44)^2}{14.44} + \frac{(10 - 23.56)^2}{23.56} + \frac{(48 - 61.56)^2}{61.56} + \frac{(114 - 100.44)^2}{100.44} \\
&= \frac{(13.56)^2}{14.44} + \frac{(-13.56)^2}{23.56} + \frac{(-13.568)^2}{61.56} + \frac{(13.56)^2}{100.44} \\
&= 12.73 + 7.80 + 2.99 + 1.83 \\
&= 25.35
\end{aligned}$$

This statistic can then be checked against a distribution with known properties. All we need to know is the degrees of freedom and these are calculated as $(r - 1)(c - 1)$ in which r is the number of rows and c is the number of columns. Another way to think of it is the number of levels of each variable minus one multiplied. In this case we get $df = (2 - 1)(2 - 1) = 1$. If you were doing the test by hand, you would find a critical value for the chi-square distribution with $df = 1$ and if the observed value was bigger than this critical value you would say that there was a significant relationship between the two variables. These critical values are produced in the Appendix, and for $df = 1$ the critical values are 3.84 ($p = .05$) and 6.63 ($p = .01$), and so because the observed chi-square is bigger than these values it is significant at $p < .01$. However, if you use **R**, it will simply produce an estimate of the precise probability of obtaining a chi-square statistic at least as big as (in this case) 25.35 if there were no association in the population between the variables.

18.4.2.   Fisher's exact test ①

There is one problem with the chi-square test, which is that the sampling distribution of the test statistic has an *approximate* chi-square distribution. The larger the sample is, the better this approximation becomes, and in large samples the approximation is good enough to not worry about the fact that it is an approximation. However, in small samples the approximation is not good enough, making significance tests of the chi-square distribution inaccurate. This is why you often read that to use the chi-square test the expected frequencies in each cell must be greater than 5 (see section 18.5). When the expected frequencies are greater than 5, the sampling distribution is probably close enough to a perfect chi-square distribution for us not to worry. However, when the expected frequencies are too low, it probably means that the sample size is too small and that the sampling distribution of the test statistic is too deviant from a chi-square distribution to be of any use.

Fisher came up with a method for computing the exact probability of the chi-square statistic that is accurate when sample sizes are small. This method is called **Fisher's exact test** (Fisher, 1922) even though it's not so much a test as a way of computing the exact probability of the chi-square statistic. This procedure is normally used on 2×2 contingency tables (i.e., two variables each with two options) and with small samples. However, it can be used on larger contingency tables and with large samples, but on larger contingency tables it becomes computationally intensive and you might find **R** taking a long time to give you an answer. In large samples there is really no point because it was designed to overcome the problem of small samples, so you don't need to use it when samples are large.

18.4.3.   The likelihood ratio ②

An alternative to Pearson's chi-square is the likelihood ratio statistic, which is based on maximum-likelihood theory. The general idea behind this theory is that you collect some data and create a model for which the probability of obtaining the observed set of data is maximized, then you compare this model to the probability of obtaining those data under the null hypothesis. The resulting statistic is, therefore, based on comparing observed frequencies with those predicted by the model:

$$L\chi^2 = 2 \sum \text{observed}_{ij} \ln\left(\frac{\text{observed}_{ij}}{\text{model}_{ij}} \right)$$

(18.2)

in which i and j are the rows and columns of the contingency table and ln is the natural logarithm (this is the standard mathematical function that we came across in Chapter 8, and you can find it on your calculator, usually labelled as ln or $\log_e$). Using the same model and observed values as in the previous section, this would give us:

$$L\chi^2 = 2\left[28 \times \ln\left(\frac{28}{14.44}\right) + 10 \times \ln\left(\frac{10}{23.56}\right) + 48 \times \ln\left(\frac{48}{61.56}\right) + 114 \times \ln\left(\frac{114}{100.44}\right)\right]$$

$$= 2[28 \times 0.662 + 10 \times -0.857 + 48 \times -0.249 + 114 \times 0.127]$$

$$= 2[18.54 - 8.57 - 11.94 + 14.44]$$

$$= 24.94$$

As with Pearson's chi-square, this statistic has a chi-square distribution with the same degrees of freedom (in this case 1). As such, it is tested in the same way: we could look up the critical value of chi-square for the number of degrees of freedom that we have. As before, the value we have here will be significant because it is bigger than the critical values of 3.84 ($p = .05$) and 6.63 ($p = .01$). For large samples this statistic will be roughly the same as Pearson's chi-square, but is preferred when samples are small.

18.4.4. Yates's correction ②

When you have a 2×2 contingency table (i.e., two categorical variables each with two categories) then Pearson's chi-square tends to produce significance values that are too small (in other words, it tends to make a Type I error). Therefore, Yates suggested a correction to the Pearson formula (usually referred to as **Yates's continuity correction**). The basic idea is that when you calculate the deviation from the model (the observed$_{ij}$ − model$_{ij}$ in equation (18.1)) you subtract 0.5 from the absolute value of this deviation before you square it. In plain English, this means you calculate the deviation, ignore whether it is positive or negative, subtract 0.5 from the value and then square it. Pearson's equation then becomes:

$$\chi^2 = \sum \frac{(|\text{observed}_{ij} - \text{model}_{ij}| - 0.5)^2}{\text{model}_{ij}}$$

For the data in our example this just translates into :

$$\chi^2 = \frac{(13.56 - 0.5)^2}{14.44} + \frac{(13.56 - 0.5)^2}{23.56} + \frac{(13.56 - 0.5)^2}{61.56} + \frac{(13.56 - 0.5)^2}{100.44}$$

$$= 11.81 + 7.24 + 2.77 + 1.70$$

$$= 23.52$$

The key thing to note is that it lowers the value of the chi-square statistic and, therefore, makes it less significant. Although this seems like a nice solution to the problem there is a fair bit of evidence that this overcorrects and produces chi-square values that are too small! Howell (2006) provides an excellent discussion of the problem with Yates's correction for continuity, if you're interested; all I will say is that, although it's worth knowing about, it's probably best ignored.

18.5. Assumptions of the chi-square test ①

It should be obvious that the chi-square test does not rely on assumptions such as having continuous normally distributed data like most of the other tests in this book (categorical data cannot be normally distributed because they aren't continuous). However, the chi-square test still has two important assumptions:

- Pretty much all of the tests we have encountered in this book have made an assumption about the independence of data and the chi-square test is no exception. For the chi-square test to be meaningful it is imperative that each person, item or entity contributes to only one cell of the contingency table. Therefore, you cannot use a chi-square test on a repeated-measures design (e.g., if we had trained some cats with food to see if they would dance and then trained the same cats with affection to see if they would dance, we couldn't analyse the resulting data with Pearson's chi-square test).

- The expected frequencies should be greater than 5. Although it is acceptable in larger contingency tables to have up to 20% of expected frequencies below 5, the result is a loss of statistical power (so the test may fail to detect a genuine effect). Even in larger contingency tables no expected frequencies should be below 1. Howell (2006) gives a nice explanation of why violating this assumption creates problems. If you find yourself in this situation consider using Fisher's exact test (section 18.4.2).

Finally, although it's not an assumption, it seems fitting to mention in a section in which a gloomy and foreboding tone is being used that proportionately small differences in cell frequencies can result in statistically significant associations between variables if the sample is large enough (although it might need to be very large indeed). Therefore, we must look at row and column percentages to interpret any effects we get. These percentages will reflect the patterns of data far better than the frequencies themselves (because these frequencies will be dependent on the sample sizes in different categories.

18.6. Doing the chi-square test using R ①

There are two ways in which categorical data can be entered: enter the raw scores, or enter weighted cases. We'll look at both in turn.

18.6.1. Entering data: raw scores ①

If we input the raw scores, it means that every row of the data editor represents each entity about which we have data (in this example, each row represents a cat). So, you would create two codings (**Training** and **Dance**). Training would contain two values – one to indicate food was a reward, and one to indicate affection was a reward. Dance would contain Yes, or No, depending on whether the cat danced. There were 200 cats in all and so there are 200 rows of data. This is how the data are stored in **cats.dat**. You can load this data file by setting your working directory to the location of the file (see section 3.4.4) and executing:

```
catData<-read.delim("cats.dat", header = TRUE)
```

The resulting data look like this (heavily edited because you don't need to see all 200 rows to get the idea):

```
          Training Dance
1       Food as Reward    Yes
2       Food as Reward    Yes
3       Food as Reward    Yes
4       Food as Reward    Yes
5       Food as Reward    Yes
...          ...          ...
29      Food as Reward    No
30      Food as Reward    No
31      Food as Reward    No
32      Food as Reward    No
33      Food as Reward    No
...          ...          ...
39   Affection as Reward  Yes
40   Affection as Reward  Yes
41   Affection as Reward  Yes
42   Affection as Reward  Yes
43   Affection as Reward  Yes
...          ...          ...
87   Affection as Reward  No
88   Affection as Reward  No
89   Affection as Reward  No
90   Affection as Reward  No
91   Affection as Reward  No
```

SELF-TEST

✓ Using what you have learnt about data entry in **R**, can you work out how you would enter these data directly into **R**?

18.6.2.   Entering data: the contingency table ①

An alternative method of data entry is to enter the contingency table directly. This is much easier if someone tells you that there were 38 cats that were given food as a reward, and 28 of them danced, and 162 cats given affection as a reward, and 48 of them danced. There are several ways to enter frequency data in this way, one of which is to create two variables, one of which contains the two values for those given food, and one of which contains the two values for those given affection, and then combine them together, using the *cbind()* function. For example, for the current data we would execute:

```
food <- c(10, 28)
affection <- c(114, 48)
catsTable <- cbind(food, affection)
```

The resulting data look like this:

```
     food affection
[1,]   10       114
[2,]   28        48
```

The columns represent whether the training was done using food or affection, and the rows show whether the animal danced (the second row) or not (the first row). As you can see, this method of data entry is a fair bit easier than entering the raw data.

18.6.3. Running the analysis with R Commander ①

As always, import the data, using **Data⇒Import data⇒from text file, clipboard, or URL...** (see section 3.7.3) click on ⬜ OK ⬜ and choose the file **cats.dat**. To do a chi-square test, select **Statistics⇒Proportions⇒Two-sample proportions test...** to open the dialog box in Figure 18.2. Pick the variable in the list labelled *Groups (pick one)* that defines the difference between the groups (in our case, that's **Training**), and the outcome variable from the list labelled *Response Variable (pick one)* (in our case, that's whether or not the cat danced, **Dance**).

You should probably leave the default option of a two-sided test as it is (although if you have predicted a direction of the effect you could choose to test whether or not the difference will be bigger (*Difference > 0*) or smaller (*Difference < 0*) than zero. You can choose the type of test: *Normal approximation* produces the Pearson chi-square test whereas *Normal approximation with continuity correction* produces the Yates correction to the chi-square test.

When you click on ⬜ OK ⬜ Output 18.1 is produced. The first part of the output shows a table that gives the percentages for each of the types of training; so when affection was used as a reward, 29.6% of the cats danced, but when food was used as a reward, 73.7% of the cats danced.

The second part of the output shows the chi-squared test. The chi-square value of 25.36, with 1 degree of freedom, is highly significant because the *p*-value is less than .05 (in fact, it is .000000477). You can rerun the analysis with Yates's correction.

FIGURE 18.2

The chi-square test using R Commander

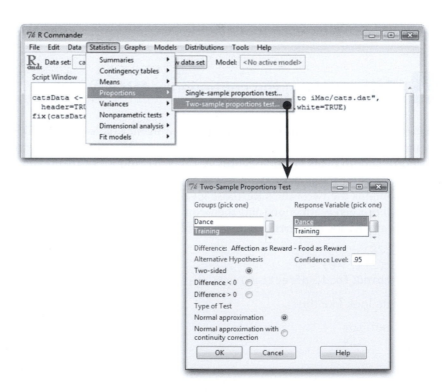

```
                       Dance
Training               No   Yes Total Count
  Affection as Reward 70.4 29.6  100   162
  Food as Reward      26.3 73.7  100    38
```

```
        2-sample test for equality of proportions without
continuity
        correction
```

```
data:  .Table
X-squared = 25.3557, df = 1, p-value = 4.767e-07
alternative hypothesis: two.sided
95 percent confidence interval:
 0.2838731 0.5972186
sample estimates:
   prop 1     prop 2
0.7037037 0.2631579
```

Output 18.1

18.6.4. Running the analysis using R ①

To run a chi-square analysis we can use the **CrossTable()** function (note the capital letters), in the *gmodels* package. This function takes two general forms depending on whether or not we're inputting the raw data or a contingency table. For raw data, the function takes the basic form:

```
CrossTable(predictor, outcome, fisher = TRUE, chisq = TRUE, expected = TRUE,
sresid = TRUE, format = "SAS"/"SPSS")
```

and for a contingency table:

```
CrossTable(contingencyTable, fisher = TRUE, chisq = TRUE, expected = TRUE,
sresid = TRUE, format = "SAS"/"SPSS")
```

These commands are identical except for how the variables are specified. In the first case we enter the name of the predictor (in this case **Training**) and the outcome (in this case **Dance**) variables and in the second case we enter the name of the contingency table dataframe (in this case *catsTable*). There are several other options we can ask for: we obtain the chi-square test by adding *chisq = TRUE*, and the Fisher exact test by adding *fisher = TRUE*. We can also add *expected = TRUE* to see the expected values of each cell of the contingency table, which is useful to ensure that the related assumption has been satisfied. We use the *sresiduals* option to obtain standardized residuals, which are useful for breaking down a significant effect if we get one, and for these residuals to be displayed we need to include the option *format = "SPSS"*. These options and some others are described in R's Souls' Tip 17.2.

Therefore, to run the chi-square test on our cat data, we could execute:

```
CrossTable(catsData$Training, catsData$Dance, fisher = TRUE, chisq = TRUE,
expected = TRUE, sresid = TRUE, format = "SPSS")
```

on the raw scores (i.e., the *catsData* dataframe), or:

```
CrossTable(catsTable, fisher = TRUE, chisq = TRUE, expected = TRUE, sresid =
TRUE, format = "SPSS")
```

on the contingency table data (i.e., the *catsTable* dataframe). These options will give us the basic chi-square test (*chisq = TRUE*), Fisher's exact test (*fisher = TRUE*), expected values

R's Souls' Tip 18.1 Other *CrossTable()* options ②

The *CrossTable()* function has several other options that you might find useful (execute *?CrossTable* to investigate further):

- *digits = x*: You can specify the number of digits after the decimal point for cell proportions in the output.
- *mcnemar = TRUE*: This option will produce the results of **McNemar's test**. This tests differences between two related groups when nominal data have been collected. It's typically used when we're looking for changes in people's scores and it compares the proportion of people who changed their response in one direction (i.e., scores increased) to those who changed in the opposite direction (scores decreased). So, this test needs to be used when we've got two related dichotomous variables.
- *prop.c = FALSE*: This stops the column proportions being displayed in the output.
- *prop.t = FALSE*: This stops the total proportions being displayed in the output.
- *prop.chisq = FALSE*: This stops the chi-square proportions being displayed in the output.
- *resid = TRUE*: This produces Pearson residuals in the resulting contingency table.
- *sresid = TRUE*: This produces standardized residuals in the resulting contingency table.
- *asresid = TRUE*: This produces adjusted standardized residuals in the resulting contingency table.
- *Format = "SAS"/"SPSS"*: This sets the output to mimic that of SAS (default) or SPSS. To see residuals you need to set the format to SPSS.

(*expected = TRUE*) and standardized residuals (*sresid = TRUE* in combination with *format = "SPSS"*).

18.6.5. Output from the *CrossTable()* function ①

The output produced by **R** first shows the contingency table (Output 18.2). For each combination of training (food or affection) we are given (in this order) the number of cats, the expected frequency, the chi-square contribution of the cell, the row proportion, the column proportion, the total proportion, and the standardized residual. You can adapt the command you execute to produce a slightly simpler version of this table if you prefer – see R's Souls' Tip 18.2.

R's Souls' Tip 18.2 Simplifying the contingency table ②

The table in Output 18.2 has rather more information than we want: we probably need only the numbers, and the proportion of cats that danced for each type of training. That is, we probably don't need the column proportion, total proportion and chi-square contribution. We can remove these by adding *prop.c=FALSE, prop.t=FALSE, prop.chisq=FALSE* to the command (R's Souls' Tip 18.1), so if you find the table confusing execute:

```
CrossTable(catsData$Training, catsData$Dance, fisher = TRUE, chisq = TRUE, expected = TRUE, prop.c = FALSE, prop.t = FALSE, prop.chisq = FALSE  sresid = TRUE, format = "SPSS")
```

This version of the command will result in a simpler table in the output.

```
 Cell Contents
|-------------------------|
|                   Count |
|         Expected Values |
| Chi-square contribution |
|             Row Percent |
|          Column Percent |
|           Total Percent |
|            Std Residual |
|-------------------------|
```

Total Observations in Table: 200

| | catsData$Dance | | |
catsData$Training	Yes	No	Row Total
Food as Reward	28	10	38
	14.440	23.560	
	12.734	7.804	
	73.684%	26.316%	19.000%
	36.842%	8.065%	
	14.000%	5.000%	
	3.568	-2.794	
Affection as Reward	48	114	162
	61.560	100.440	
	2.987	1.831	
	29.630%	70.370%	81.000%
	63.158%	91.935%	
	24.000%	57.000%	
	-1.728	1.353	
Column Total	76	124	200
	38.000%	62.000%	

Output 18.2

   The column totals contain the number of cases that fall into each combination of categories and are rather like our original contingency table. We can see that in total 76 cats danced (38% of the total) and of these 28 were trained using food (36.8% of the total that danced) and 48 were trained with affection (63.2% of the total that danced). Further, 124 cats didn't dance at all (62% of the total) and of those that didn't dance, 10 were trained using food as a reward (8.1% of the total that didn't dance) and a massive 114 were trained using affection (91.9% of the total that didn't dance). The proportion of cats within the **Dance** variable (i.e., the column proportions) can be read from the fifth row in each cell. We can also look at the percentages within the training categories by looking at the fourth rows within each cell of the table. These values tell us, for example, that of those trained with food as a reward, 73.7% danced and 26.3% did not. Similarly, for those trained with affection only 29.6% danced compared to 70.4% that didn't. In summary, when food was used as a reward most cats would dance, but when affection was used most cats refused to dance.

   Before moving on to look at the test statistics itself it is vital that we check that the assumption for chi-square has been met. The assumption is that in 2 × 2 tables (which is what we have here), all expected frequencies should be greater than 5. The second row of each cell shows the expected frequencies, which incidentally are the same as we calculated earlier; it should be clear that the smallest expected count is 14.44 (for cats that were trained with food and did dance). This value exceeds 5 and so the assumption has been met. If you found an expected count lower than 5 the best remedy is to collect more data to try to boost the proportion of cases falling into each category.

```
Statistics for All Table Factors


Pearson's Chi-squared test
------------------------------------------------------------
Chi^2 =   25.35569      d.f. =  1      p =   4.767434e-07


Pearson's Chi-squared test with Yates' continuity correction
------------------------------------------------------------
Chi^2 =   23.52028      d.f. =  1      p =   1.236041e-06


Fisher's Exact Test for Count Data
------------------------------------------------------------
Sample estimate odds ratio:   6.579265


Alternative hypothesis: true odds ratio is not equal to 1
p =   1.311709e-06
95% confidence interval:   2.837773 16.42969


Alternative hypothesis: true odds ratio is less than 1
p =   0.9999999
95% confidence interval:   0 14.25436


Alternative hypothesis: true odds ratio is greater than 1
p =   7.7122e-07
95% confidence interval:   3.193221 Inf



        Minimum expected frequency: 14.44
```

Output 18.3

As we saw earlier, Pearson's chi-square test examines whether there is an association between two categorical variables (in this case the type of training and whether the animal danced or not). The next part of the output produced by the *CrossTable()* function is the chi-square statistic and its significance value (Output 18.3). The Pearson chi-square statistic tests whether the two variables are independent. If the *p*-value is small enough (conventionally less than .05) then we reject the null hypothesis that the variables are independent and gain confidence in the hypothesis that they are in some way related. The value of the chi-square statistic is given in the output (and the degrees of freedom) as is the significance value. The value of the chi-square statistic is 25.356, which is within rounding error of what we calculated in section 18.4.1. This value is highly significant ($p < .001$), indicating

How do I interpret chi-square?

that the type of training used had a significant effect on whether an animal would dance. The table included the chi-square contribution for each cell. If we were to add these up, we would find that they would sum to the total for chi-square, so: $1.831 + 2.987 + 7.804 + 12.734 = 25.356$.

A series of other statistics are also included in the output. The next part is the chi-square with Yates's correction (see section 18.4.4) and its value is the same as the value we calculated earlier (23.52). As I mentioned earlier, this test is probably best ignored anyway, but it does confirm the result from the main chi-square test.

The final test is the Fisher's exact test. You only need to look at the first version of this, labelled *Alternative hypothesis: true odds ratio is not equal to 1*, where it gets a *p*-value of .0000013, which is less than < .001, and therefore the Fisher's exact test also shows that we should reject the null hypothesis.

(You might notice that the *p*-value for the Fisher's exact test is in between the Pearson chi-square and Yates's corrected chi-square – this is usually the case.)

The highly significant result indicates that there is an association between the type of training and whether the cat danced or not. What we mean by an association is that the pattern of responses (i.e., the proportion of cats that danced to the proportion that did not) in the two training conditions is significantly different. This significant finding reflects the fact that when food is used as a reward, about 74% of cats learn to dance and 26% do not, whereas when affection is used, the opposite is true (about 70% refuse to dance and 30% do dance). Therefore, we can conclude that the type of training used significantly influences the cats: they will dance for food but not for love! Having lived with a lovely cat for many years now, this supports my cynical view that they will do nothing unless there is a bowl of cat-food waiting for them at the end of it!

18.6.6. Breaking down a significant chi-square test with standardized residuals ②

Although in a 2 × 2 contingency table like the one we have in this example, where the nature of the association can be quite clear from just the cell percentages or counts, in larger contingency tables it can be useful to do a finer-grained investigation of the table. In a way, you can think of a significant chi-square test in much the same way as a significant interaction in ANOVA: it is an effect that needs to be broken down further. One very easy way to break down a significant chi-square test is to use data that we already have – the standardized residual.

Just like regression, the residual is simply the error between what the model predicts (the expected frequency) and the data actually observed (the observed frequency):

$$\text{residual}_{ij} = \text{observed}_{ij} - \text{model}_{ij}$$

in which *i* and *j* represent the two variables (i.e., the rows and columns in the contingency table). This is the same as every other residual or deviation that we have encountered in this book (compare this equation to, for example, equation (2.4)). To standardize this equation, we simply divide by the square root of the expected frequency:

$$\text{standardized residual} = \frac{\text{observed}_{ij} - \text{model}_{ij}}{\sqrt{\text{model}_{ij}}}$$

Does this equation look familiar? Well, it's basically part of equation (18.1). The only difference is that rather than looking at squared deviations, we're looking at the pure deviation. Remember that the rationale for squaring deviations in the first place is simply to make them positive so that they don't cancel out when we add them. The chi-square statistic is based on adding together values, so it is important that the deviations are squared so that they don't cancel out. However, if we're not planning to add up the deviations or residuals then we can inspect them in their unsquared form. There are two important things about these standardized residuals:

1 Given that the chi-square statistic is the sum of these standardized residuals (sort of), then if we want to decompose what contributes to the overall association that the chi-square statistic measures, then looking at the individual standardized residuals is a good idea because they have a direct relationship with the test statistic.

2   These standardized residuals behave like any other (see section 7.7.1.1) in the sense that each one is a z-score. This is very useful because it means that just by looking at a standardized residual we can assess its significance (see section 1.7.4). As we have learnt many times before, if the value lies outside of ± 1.96 then it is significant at $p < .05$, if it lies outside ± 2.58 then it is significant at $p < .01$ and if it lies outside ± 3.29 then it is significant at $p < .001$.

If you included the *sresid = TRUE* option in the *CrossTable()* function (which we encouraged you do to) you will find these standardized residuals in each cell in the contingency table. In Output 18.2 these residuals are the bottom value within each cell. As such, there are four residuals: one for each combination of the type of training and whether the cats danced. When food was used as a reward the standardized residual was significant for both those that danced ($z = 3.57$) and those that didn't dance ($z = -2.79$) because both values are bigger than 1.96 (when you ignore the minus sign). The plus or minus sign tells us something about the direction of the effect, as do the counts and expected counts within the cells. We can interpret these standardized residuals as follows: when food was used as a reward significantly more cats than expected danced, and significantly fewer cats than expected did not dance. When affection was used as a reward the standardized residual was not significant for both those that danced ($z = -1.73$) and those that didn't dance ($z = 1.35$) because they are both smaller than 1.96 (when you ignore the minus sign). This tells us that when affection was used as a reward as many cats as expected danced and did not dance. In a nutshell, the cells for when food was used as a reward both significantly contribute to the overall chi-square statistic. Put another way, the association between the type of reward and dancing is mainly driven by when food is a reward.

18.6.7.   Calculating an effect size ②

The most common and possibly most useful measure of effect size for categorical data is the *odds ratio*, which we encountered in Chapter 8. Odds ratios are most interpretable in 2×2 contingency tables and are probably not useful for larger contingency tables. However, this isn't as restrictive as you might think because, as I've said more times than I care to recall in the GLM chapters, effect sizes are only ever useful when they summarize a focused comparison. A 2×2 contingency table is the categorical data equivalent of a focused comparison!

The odds ratio in its basic form is simple enough to calculate. If we look at our example, we can first calculate the odds that a cat danced given that they had food as a reward. This is simply the number of cats that were given food and danced, divided by the number of cats given food that didn't dance:

$$\text{odds}_{\text{dancing after food}} = \frac{\text{number that had food and danced}}{\text{number that had food but didn't dance}}$$
$$= \frac{28}{10}$$
$$= 2.8$$

Next we calculate the odds that a cat danced given that they had affection as a reward. This is simply the number of cats that were given affection and danced, divided by the number of cats given affection that didn't dance:

$$\text{odds}_{\text{dancing after affection}} = \frac{\text{number that had affection and danced}}{\text{number that had affection but didn't dance}}$$

$$= \frac{48}{114}$$

$$= 0.421$$

The odds ratio is simply the odds of dancing after food divided by the odds of dancing after affection:

$$\text{odds ratio} = \frac{\text{odds}_{\text{dancing after food}}}{\text{odds}_{\text{dancing after affection}}}$$

$$= \frac{2.8}{0.421}$$

$$= 6.65$$

What this tells us is that if a cat was trained with food the odds of their dancing were 6.65 times higher than if they had been trained with affection. As you can see, this is an extremely elegant and easily understood metric for expressing the effect you've got.

The above description shows the basic odds ratio, which is particularly useful for getting a sense of what the measure represents; however, there are other more sophisticated ways to estimate the odds ratio and its associated confidence interval. Luckily, if we include *fisher = TRUE* in our *CrossTable()* function then the output will include one such method. In Output 18.3 we are told that the odds ratio is 6.58 (note that this is slightly smaller than our calculation), and that it has a confidence interval of 2.84 to 16.43. Remember from Chapter 8 that the important thing is that the confidence interval does not cross 1. Remember that a value of 1 means that the odds of dancing after food would be exactly the same as dancing after affection, a value less than 1 means that the odds of dancing are smaller after food than after affection, and a value greater than 1 means that the odds of dancing are greater after food than after affection. Therefore, a 1 is the point at which the direction of the effect changes. Therefore, if the confidence interval crosses 1 it means that the population value of the observed effect might be in the same direction as in your sample, but it could also be in the opposite direction.

18.6.8. Reporting the results of chi-square ①

When reporting Pearson's chi-square we simply state the value of the test statistic with its associated degrees of freedom and the significance value. The test statistic, as we've seen, is denoted by χ^2. The output tells us that the value of χ^2 was 25.36, that the degrees of freedom on which this was based were 1, and that it was significant at $p < .001$. It's also useful to reproduce the contingency table, and my vote would go to quoting the odds ratio and its confidence interval too. As such, we could report:

✓ There was a significant association between the type of training and whether or not cats would dance $\chi^2(1) = 25.36$, $p < .001$. This seems to represent the fact that, based on the odds ratio, the odds of cats dancing were 6.58 (2.84, 16.43) times higher if they were trained with food than if trained with affection.

CRAMMING SAM'S TIPS   The chi-square test

- If you want to test the relationship between two categorical variables you can do this with the *chi-square test*.
- Look at the value of the chi-squared test; if the *p*-value is less than .05 then there is a significant relationship between your two variables.
- Check to make sure that no expected frequencies are less than 5.
- Look at the crosstabulation table to work out what the relationship between the variables is. Better still, look out for significant standardized residuals (values outside of ±1.96), and calculate the *odds ratio*.
- Report the χ^2 statistic, the degrees of freedom and the significance value. Also report the contingency table.

Labcoat Leni's Real Research 18.1   Is the black American happy? ①

Beckham, A. S. (1929). *Journal of Abnormal and Social Psychology*, 24, 186–190.

When I was doing my psychology degree I spent a lot of time reading about the civil rights movement in the USA. Although I was supposed to be reading psychology, I became more interested in Malcolm X and Martin Luther King Jr. This is why I find Beckham's 1929 study of black Americans such an interesting piece of research. Beckham was a black American academic who founded the psychology laboratory at Howard University, Washington, DC, and his wife Ruth was the first black woman ever to be awarded a Ph.D. (also in psychology) at the University of Minnesota. The article needs to be placed within the era in which it was published. To put some context on the study, it was published 36 years before the Jim Crow laws were finally overthrown by the Civil Rights Act of 1964, and in a time when black Americans were segregated, openly discriminated against and were victims of the most abominable violations of civil liberties and human rights. For a richer context I suggest reading James Baldwin's superb novel *The Fire Next Time*. Even the language of the study and the data from it are an uncomfortable reminder of the era in which it was conducted.

Beckham sought to measure the psychological state of black Americans with three questions put to 3443 black Americans from different walks of life. He asked them whether they thought black Americans were happy, whether they personally were happy as a black American, and whether black Americans *should* be happy. They could answer only *yes* or *no* to each question. By today's standards the study is quite simple, and he did no formal statistical analysis of his data (Fisher's article containing the popularized version of the chi-square test was published only 7 years earlier in a statistics journal that would not have been read by psychologists). I love this study, though, because it demonstrates that you do not need elaborate methods to answer important and far-reaching questions; with just three questions, Beckham told the world an enormous amount about very real and important psychological and sociological phenomena.

The frequency data (number of yes and no responses within each employment category) from this study are in the file **Beckham1929.dat**. Labcoat Leni wants you to carry out three chi-square tests (one for each question that was asked). What conclusions can you draw?

Answers are in the additional material on the companion website.

18.7. Several categorical variables: loglinear analysis ③

So far we've looked at situations in which there are only two categorical variables. However, often we want to analyse more complex contingency tables in which there are three or more variables. For example, what about if we took the example we've just used but also collected data from a sample of 70 dogs? We might want to compare the behaviour in dogs to that in cats. We would now have three variables: **Animal** (dog or cat), **Training** (food as reward or affection as reward) and **Dance** (did they dance or not?). This couldn't be analysed with the Pearson chi-square and instead has to be analysed with a technique called **loglinear analysis.**

18.7.1. Chi-square as regression ④

To begin with, let's have a look at how our simple chi-square example can be expressed as a regression model. Although we already know about as much as we need to about the chi-square test, if we want to understand more complex situations life becomes considerably easier if we consider our model as a general linear model (i.e., regression). All of the general linear models we've considered in this book take the general form of:

$$\text{outcome}_i = (\text{model}) + \text{error}_i$$

For example, when we encountered multiple regression in Chapter 7 we saw that this model was written as (see equation (7.9)):

$$Y_i = (b_0 + b_1 X_{1i} + b_2 X_{2i} + \ldots + b_n X_{ni}) + \varepsilon_i$$

Also, when we came across one-way ANOVA, we adapted this regression model to conceptualize our Viagra example, as (see equation (10.2)):

$$\text{libido}_i = b_0 + b_2\,\text{high}_i + b_1\,\text{low}_i + \varepsilon_i$$

The t-test was conceptualized in a similar way. In all cases the same basic equation is used; it's just the complexity of the model that changes. With categorical data we can use the same model in much the same way as with regression to produce a linear model. In our current example we have two categorical variables: **Training** (food or affection) and **Dance** (yes they did dance or no they didn't dance). Both variables have two categories and so we can represent each one with a single dummy variable (see section 7.12.1) in which one category is coded as 0 and the other as 1. So for training, we could code 'food' as 0 and 'affection' as 1, and we could code the dancing variable as 0 for 'yes' and 1 for 'no' (see Table 18.2).

Table 18.2 Coding scheme for dancing cats

Training	Dance	Dummy (Training)	Dummy (Dance)	Interaction	Frequency
Food	Yes	0	0	0	28
Food	No	0	1	0	10
Affection	Yes	1	0	0	48
Affection	No	1	1	1	114

This situation might be familiar if you think back to factorial ANOVA (section 12.3) in which we also had two variables as predictors. In that situation we saw that when there are two variables the general linear model became (think back to equation (12.1)):

$$\text{outcome}_i = (b_0 + b_1 A_i + b_2 B_i + b_3 AB_i) + \varepsilon_i$$

in which A represents the first variable, B represents the second and AB represents the interaction between the two variables. Therefore, we can construct a linear model using these dummy variables that is exactly the same as the one we used for factorial ANOVA (above). The interaction term will simply be the training variable multiplied by the **Dance** variable (look at Table 18.2, and if it doesn't make sense look back to section 12.3 because the coding is exactly the same as this example):

$$\text{outcome}_i = (\text{Model}) + \text{error}_i$$
$$\text{outcome}_{ij} = (b_0 + b_1 \text{Training}_i + b_2 \text{Dance}_j + b_3 \text{Interaction}_{ij}) + \varepsilon_{ij} \tag{18.3}$$

However, because we're using categorical data, to make this model linear we have to actually use log values (see Chapter 8) and so the actual model becomes:[2]

$$\ln(O_i) = \ln(\text{model}) + \ln(\varepsilon_i)$$
$$\ln(O_{ij}) = (b_0 + b_1 \text{Training}_i + b_2 \text{Dance}_j + b_3 \text{Interaction}_{ij}) + \ln(\varepsilon_{ij}) \tag{18.4}$$

Training, Dance and **Interaction** can take the values 0 and 1, depending on which combination of categories we're looking at (Table 18.2). Therefore, to work out what the b-values represent in this model we can do the same as we did for the t-test and ANOVA and look at what happens when we replace **Training** and **Dance** with values of 0 and 1. To begin with, let's see what happens when we look at when **Training** and **Dance** are both zero. This represents the category of cats that got food reward and did line-dance. When we used this sort of model for the t-test and ANOVA the outcomes we used were taken from the observed data: we used the group means (e.g., see sections 9.4.2 and 10.2.3). However, with categorical variables, means are rather meaningless because we haven't measured anything on an ordinal or interval scale, instead we merely have frequency data. Therefore, we use the observed frequencies (rather than observed means) as our outcome instead. In Table 18.1 we saw that there were 28 cats that had food for a reward and did line-dance. If we use this as the observed outcome then the model can be written as (if we ignore the error term for the time being):

$$\ln(O_{ij}) = b_0 + b_1 \text{Training}_i + b_2 \text{Dance}_j + b_3 \text{Interaction}_{ij}$$

For cats that had food reward and did dance, the **Training** and **Dance** variables and the interaction will all be 0 and so the equation reduces down to:

$$\ln(O_{\text{Food,Yes}}) = b_0 + (b_1 \times 0) + (b_2 \times 0) + (b_3 \times 0)$$
$$\ln(O_{\text{Food,Yes}}) = b_0$$
$$\ln(28) = b_0$$
$$b_0 = 3.332$$

---

[2] Actually, the convention is to denote b_0 as θ and the b-values as λ, but I think these notational changes serve only to confuse people so I'm sticking with b because I want to emphasize the similarities to regression and ANOVA.

Therefore, b_0 in the model represents the log of the observed value when all of the categories are zero. As such it's the log of the observed value of the base category (in this case cats that got food and danced).

Now, let's see what happens when we look at cats that had affection as a reward and danced. In this case, the **Training** variable is 1 and the **Dance** variable and the interaction are still 0. Also, our outcome now changes to be the observed value for cats that received affection and danced (from Table 18.1 we can see the value is 48). Therefore, the equation becomes:

$$\ln(O_{Affection,Yes}) = b_0 + (b_1 \times 1) + (b_2 \times 0) + (b_3 \times 0)$$
$$\ln(O_{Affection,Yes}) = b_0 + b_1$$
$$b_1 = \ln(O_{Affection,Yes}) - b_0$$

Remembering that b_0 is the expected value for cats that had food and danced, we get:

$$b_1 = \ln(O_{Affection,Yes}) - \ln(O_{Food,Yes})$$
$$= \ln(48) - \ln(28)$$
$$= 3.871 - 3.332$$
$$= 0.539$$

The important thing is that b_1 is the difference between the log of the observed frequency for cats that received affection and danced, and the log of the observed values for cats that received food and danced. Put another way, within the group of cats that danced it represents the difference between those trained using food and those trained using affection.

Now, let's see what happens when we look at cats that had food as a reward and did not dance. In this case, the **Training** variable is 0, the **Dance** variable is 1 and the interaction is again 0. Our outcome now changes to be the observed frequency for cats that received food but did not dance (from Table 18.1 we can see the value is 10). Therefore, the equation becomes:

$$\ln(O_{Food,No}) = b_0 + (b_1 \times 0) + (b_2 \times 1) + (b_3 \times 0)$$
$$\ln(O_{Food,No}) = b_0 + b_2$$
$$b_2 = \ln(O_{Food,No}) - b_0$$

Remembering that b_0 is the expected value for cats that had food and danced, we get:

$$b_2 = \ln(O_{Food,No}) - \ln(O_{Food,Yes})$$
$$= \ln(10) - \ln(28)$$
$$= 2.303 - 3.332$$
$$= -1.029$$

The important thing is that b_2 is the difference between the log of the observed frequency for cats that received food and danced, and the log of the observed frequency for cats that received food and didn't dance. Put another way, within the group of cats that received food as a reward it represents the difference between cats that didn't dance and those that did.

Finally, we can look at cats that had affection and danced. In this case, the **Training** and **Dance** variables are both 1 and the interaction (which is the value of **Training** multiplied by the value of **Dance**) is also 1. We can also replace b_0, b_1, and b_2, with what we now know they represent. The outcome is the log of the observed frequency for cats that received affection but didn't dance (this expected value is 114 – see Table 18.1). Therefore, the equation becomes (I've used the shorthand of A for affection, F for food, Y for yes, and N for no):

$$\ln(O_{A,N}) = b_0 + (b_1 \times 1) + (b_2 \times 1) + (b_3 \times 1)$$

$$\ln(O_{A,N}) = b_0 + b_1 + b_2 + b_3$$

$$\ln(O_{A,N}) = \ln(O_{F,Y}) + (\ln(O_{A,Y}) - \ln(O_{F,Y})) + (\ln(O_{F,N}) - \ln(O_{F,Y})) + b_3$$

$$\ln(O_{A,N}) = \ln(O_{A,Y}) + \ln(O_{F,N}) - \ln(O_{F,Y}) + b_3$$

$$b_3 = \ln(O_{A,N}) - \ln(O_{F,N}) + \ln(O_{F,Y}) - \ln(O_{A,Y})$$

$$= \ln(114) - \ln(10) + \ln(28) - \ln(48)$$

$$= 1.895$$

So, b_3 in the model really compares the difference between affection and food when the cats didn't dance to the difference between food and affection when the cats did dance. Put another way, it compares the effect of **Training** when cats didn't dance to the effect of **Training** when they did dance.

The final model is therefore:

$$\ln(O_{ij}) = 3.332 + 0.539\text{Training} - 1.029\text{Dance} + 1.895\text{Interaction} + \ln(\varepsilon_{ij})$$

The important thing to note here is that everything is exactly the same as factorial ANOVA except that we dealt with log-transformed values (in fact compare this section to section 12.3 to see just how similar everything is). In case you still don't believe me that this works as a general linear model, I've prepared a file called **CatRegression.dat**, which contains the two variables **Dance** (0 = no, 1 = yes) and **Training** (0 = food, 1 = affection) and the interaction (**Interaction**). There is also a variable called **Observed** that contains the observed frequencies in Table 18.1 for each combination of **Dance** and **Training**. Finally, there is a variable called **LnObserved**, which is the natural logarithm of these observed frequencies (remember that throughout this section we've dealt with the log observed values).

SELF-TEST

✓ Run a multiple regression analysis using **CatRegression.dat** with **LnObserved** as the outcome, and **Training**, **Dance** and **Interaction** as your three predictors.

Output 18.4 shows the resulting coefficients table from this regression. The important thing to note is that the constant, b_0, is 3.332 as calculated above, the beta value for type of training, b_1, is 0.539 and for dance, b_2, is –1.030, both of which are within rounding error of what was calculated above. Also the coefficient for the interaction, b_3, is 1.895 as predicted. There is one interesting point, though: all of the standard errors are zero (or very, very close to zero), or, put differently, there is *no* error at all in this model (which is also why there are no significance tests). This is because the various combinations of coding variables completely explain the observed values. This is known as a **saturated model**, and I will return to this point later, so bear it in mind. For the time being, I hope this convinces you that chi-square can be conceptualized as a linear model.

```
Coefficients:
              Estimate Std. Error   t value Pr(>|t|)
(Intercept)   3.332e+00  1.289e-15  2.585e+15   <2e-16 ***
Training      5.390e-01  1.622e-15  3.322e+14   <2e-16 ***
Dance        -1.030e+00  2.513e-15 -4.097e+14   <2e-16 ***
Interaction   1.895e+00  2.774e-15  6.830e+14   <2e-16 ***
```

Output 18.4

OK, this is all very well, but the heading of this section did rather imply that I would show you how the chi-square test can be conceptualized as a linear model. Well, basically, the chi-square test looks at whether two variables are independent; therefore, it has no interest in the combined effect of the two variables, only their unique effect. Thus, we can conceptualize chi-square in much the same way as the saturated model, except that we don't include the interaction term. If we remove the interaction term, our model becomes:

$$\ln(\text{Model}_{ij}) = b_0 + b_1\text{Training} + b_2\text{Dance}_j$$

With this new model, we cannot predict the observed values like we did for the saturated model because we've lost some information (namely, the interaction term). Therefore, the outcome from the model changes, and therefore the beta-values change too. We saw earlier that the chi-square test is based on 'expected frequencies'. Therefore, if we're conceptualizing the chi-square test as a linear model, our outcomes will be these expected values. If you look back to the beginning of this chapter you'll see we already have the expected frequencies based on this model. We can recalculate the beta values based on these expected values:

$$\ln(E_{ij}) = b_0 + b_1\text{Training} + b_2\text{Dance}_j$$

For cats that had food reward and did dance, the **Training** and **Dance** variables will be 0 and so the equation reduces down to:

$$\ln(E_{\text{Food,Yes}}) = b_0 + (b_1 \times 0) + (b_2 \times 0)$$
$$\ln(E_{\text{Food,Yes}}) = b_0$$
$$b_0 = \ln(14.44)$$
$$= 2.67$$

Therefore, b_0 in the model represents the log of the expected value when all of the categories are zero.

When we look at cats that had affection as a reward and danced, the **Training** variable is 1 and the **Dance** variable is still 0. Also, our outcome now changes to be the expected value for cats that received affection and danced:

$$\ln(E_{\text{Affection,Yes}}) = b_0 + (b_1 \times 1) + (b_2 \times 0)$$
$$\ln(E_{\text{Affection,Yes}}) = b_0 + b_1$$
$$b_1 = \ln(E_{\text{Affection,Yes}}) - b_0$$
$$= \ln(E_{\text{Affection,Yes}}) - \ln(E_{\text{Food,Yes}})$$
$$= \ln(61.56) - \ln(14.44)$$
$$= 1.45$$

The important thing is that b_1 is the difference between the log of the expected frequency for cats that received affection and did dance and the log of the expected values for cats that received food and danced. In fact, the value is the same as the column marginal, that is the difference between the total number of cats getting affection and the total number of cats getting food: $\ln(162) - \ln(38) = 1.45$. Put simply, it represents the main effect of the type of **Training**.

When we look at cats that had food as a reward and did not dance, the **Training** variable is 0 and the **Dance** variable is 1. Our outcome now changes to be the expected frequency for cats that received food but did not dance:

$$\ln(E_{\text{Food,No}}) = b_0 + (b_1 \times 0) + (b_2 \times 1)$$
$$\ln(E_{\text{Food,No}}) = b_0 + b_2$$
$$b_2 = \ln(O_{\text{Food,No}}) - b_0$$
$$= \ln(O_{\text{Food,No}}) - \ln(O_{\text{Food,Yes}})$$
$$= \ln(23.56) - \ln(14.44)$$
$$= 0.49$$

Therefore, b_2 is the difference between the log of the expected frequencies for cats that received food and didn't or did dance. In fact, the value is the same as the row marginal, that is the difference between the total number of cats that did and didn't dance: $\ln(124) - \ln(76) = 0.49$. In simpler terms, it is the main effect of whether or not the cat danced.

We can double-check all of this by looking at the final cell:

$$\ln(E_{\text{Affection,No}}) = b_0 + (b_1 \times 1) + (b_2 \times 1)$$
$$\ln(E_{\text{Affection,No}}) = b_0 + b_1 + b_2$$
$$\ln(100.44) = 2.67 + 1.45 + 0.49$$
$$4.61 = 4.61$$

The final chi-square model is therefore:

$$\ln(O_i) = \ln(\text{model}) + \ln(\varepsilon_i)$$

$$\ln(O_i) = 2.67 + 1.45\text{Training} + 0.49\text{Dance} + \ln(\varepsilon_i)$$

We can rearrange this to get some residuals (the error term):

$$\ln(s_i) = \ln(O_i) - \ln(\text{model})$$

In this case, the model is merely the expected frequencies that were calculated for the chi-square test, so the residuals are the differences between the observed and expected frequencies.

SELF-TEST

✓ To show that this all actually works, run another multiple regression analysis using **CatRegression.dat**. This time the outcome is the log of expected frequencies (**LnExpected**) and **Training** and **Dance** are the predictors (the interaction is not included).

This demonstrates how chi-square can work as a linear model, just like regression and ANOVA, in which the beta values tell us something about the relative differences in frequencies across categories of our two variables. If nothing else made sense, I want you to leave this section aware that chi-square (and analysis of categorical data generally) can be expressed as a linear model (although we have to use log values). We can express categories of a variable using dummy variables, just as we did with regression and ANOVA, and the resulting beta values can be calculated in exactly the same way as for regression and ANOVA. In ANOVA, these beta values represented differences between the means of a particular category compared against a baseline category. With categorical data, the beta values represent the same thing, the only difference being that rather than dealing with means, we're dealing with expected values. Grasping this idea (that regression, t-tests, ANOVAs and categorical data analysis are basically the same) will help (me) considerably in the next section.

18.7.2. Loglinear analysis ③

In the previous section, after nearly reducing my brain to even more of a rotting vegetable than it already is trying to explain how categorical data analysis is just another form of regression, I ran the data through an ordinary regression in **R** to prove that I wasn't talking complete gibberish. At the time I rather glibly said 'oh, by the way, there's no error in the model, that's odd isn't it?' and sort of passed this off by telling you that it was a 'saturated' model and not to worry too much about it because I'd explain it all later just as soon as I'd worked out what the hell was going on. That seemed like a good avoidance tactic at the time, but unfortunately I now have to explain what I was going on about.

To begin with, I hope you're now happy with the idea that categorical data can be expressed in the form of a linear model provided that we use log values (this, incidentally, is why the technique we're discussing is called loglinear analysis). From what you hopefully already know about ANOVA and linear models generally, you should also be cosily tucked up in bed with the idea that we can extend any linear model to include any amount of predictors and any resulting interaction terms between predictors. Therefore, if we can represent a simple two-variable categorical analysis in terms of a linear model, then it shouldn't amaze you to discover that if we have more than two variables this is no problem: we can extend the simple model by adding whatever variables and the resulting interaction terms. This is all you really need to know. So, just as in multiple regression and ANOVA, if we think of things in terms of a linear model, then conceptually it becomes very easy to understand how the model expands to incorporate new variables. So, for example, if we have three predictors (A, B and C) in ANOVA (think back to section 14.4) we end up with three two-way interactions (AB, AC, BC) and one three-way interaction (ABC). Therefore, the resulting linear model of this is just:

$$\text{outcome}_{ijk} = (b_0 + b_1 A_i + b_2 B_j + b_3 C_k + b_4 AB_{ij} + b_5 AC_{ik} + b_6 BC_{jk} + b_7 ABC_{ijk}) + \varepsilon_{ij}$$

In exactly the same way, if we have three variables in a categorical data analysis we get an identical model, but with an outcome in terms of logs :

$$\ln(O_{ijk}) = (b_0 + b_1 A_i + b_2 B_j + b_3 C_k + b_4 AB_{ij} + b_5 AC_{ik} + b_6 BC_{jk} + b_7 ABC_{ijk}) + \ln(\varepsilon_{ij})$$

Obviously the calculation of beta values and expected values from the model becomes considerably more cumbersome and confusing, but that's why we invented computers – so that we don't have to worry about it. Loglinear analysis works on these principles. However, as we've seen in the two-variable case, when our data are categorical and we include all of the available terms (main effects and interactions) we get no error: our predictors can perfectly predict our outcome (the expected values). So, if we start with the most complex model possible, we will get no error. The job of loglinear analysis is to try to fit a simpler model to the data without any substantial loss of predictive power. Therefore, loglinear analysis typically works on a principle of backward elimination (yes, the same kind of backward elimination that we can use in multiple regression – see section 7.6.4.3). So we begin with the saturated model, and then we remove a predictor from the model and, using this new model, we predict our data (calculate expected frequencies, just like the chi-square test) and then see how well the model fits the data (i.e., are the expected frequencies close to the observed frequencies?). If the fit of the new model is not very different from the more complex model, then we abandon the complex model in favour of the new one. Put another way, we assume the term we removed was not having a significant impact on the ability of our model to predict the observed data.

However, we don't just remove terms randomly, we do it hierarchically. So, we start with the saturated model and then remove the highest-order interaction, and assess the effect that this has. If removing the interaction term has no effect on the model then it's obviously not having much of an effect; therefore, we get rid of it and move on to remove any lower-order interactions. If removing these interactions has no effect then we carry on to any main effects until we find an effect that does affect the fit of the model if it is removed.

To put this in more concrete terms, at the beginning of the section on loglinear analysis I asked you to imagine we'd extended our training and line-dancing example to incorporate a sample of dogs. So, we now have three variables: **Animal** (dog or cat), **Training** (food or affection) and **Dance** (did they dance or not?). Just as in ANOVA this results in three main effects:

- Animal
- Training
- Dance

three interactions involving two variables:

- Animal × Training
- Animal × Dance
- Training × Dance

and one interaction involving all three variables:

- Animal × Training × Dance

When I talk about backward elimination, all I mean is that loglinear analysis starts by including all of these effects; we then take the highest-order interaction (in this case the three-way interaction of **Animal** × **Training** × **Dance**) and remove it. We construct a new model without this interaction, and from the model calculate expected frequencies. We (well, the computer) then compares these expected frequencies (or model frequencies) to the observed frequencies using the standard equation for the likelihood ratio statistic (see section 18.4.3). If the new model significantly changes the likelihood ratio statistic, then removing this interaction term has a significant effect on the fit of the model and we know that this effect is statistically important. If this is the case then we will stop there and say that we have a significant three-way interaction! We won't test any other effects because with categorical data all lower-order effects are consumed within higher-order effects. If, however, removing the three-way interaction doesn't significantly affect the fit of the model then we move on to lower-order interactions. Therefore, we look at the **Animal** × **Training**, **Animal** × **Dance** and **Training** × **Dance** interactions in turn and construct models in which these terms are not present. For each model we again calculate expected values and compare them to the observed data using a likelihood ratio statistic.[3] Again, if any one of these models does result in a significant change in the likelihood ratio then the term is retained and we won't move on to look at any main effects involved in that interaction (so if the **Animal** × **Training** interaction is significant it won't look at the main effects of **Animal** or **Training**). However, if the likelihood ratio is unchanged then the analysis removes the offending interaction term and moves on to look at main effects.

I mentioned that the likelihood ratio statistic (see section 18.4.3) is used to assess each model. From the equation it should be clear how this equation can be adapted to fit any model: the observed values are the same throughout, and the model frequencies are simply the expected frequencies from the model being tested. For the saturated model, this statistic will always be 0 (because the observed and model frequencies are the same so the ratio of observed to model frequencies will be 1, and $\ln(1) = 0$), but as we've seen, in other cases it will provide a measure of how well the model fits the observed frequencies. To test whether a new model has changed the likelihood ratio, all we need do is to take the likelihood ratio for a model and subtract from it the likelihood statistic for the previous model (provided the models are hierarchically structured):

$$L\chi^2_{\text{change}} = L\chi^2_{\text{current model}} - L\chi^2_{\text{previous model}} \qquad (18.5)$$

I've tried in this section to give you a flavour of how loglinear analysis works, without actually getting too much into the nitty-gritty of the calculations. I've tried to show you how we can conceptualize a chi-square analysis as a linear model and then relied on what I've previously told you about ANOVA to hope that you can extrapolate these conceptual ideas to understand roughly what's going on. The curious among you might want to know exactly how everything is calculated and to these people I have two things to say: 'I don't know' and 'I know a really good place where you can buy a straitjacket'. If you're that interested then Tabachnick and Fidell (2007) have, as ever, written a wonderfully detailed and lucid chapter on the subject, which frankly puts this feeble attempt to shame. Still, assuming you're happy to live in relative ignorance, we'll now have a look at how to do a loglinear analysis.

18.8. Assumptions in loglinear analysis ②

Loglinear analysis is an extension of the chi-square test and so has similar assumptions; that is, an entity should fall into only one cell of the contingency table (i.e., cells of the table must be independent) and the expected frequencies should be large enough for a reliable analysis. In loglinear analysis with more than two variables it's all right to have up to 20% of cells with expected frequencies less than 5; however, all cells must have expected frequencies greater than 1. If this assumption is broken the result is a radical reduction in test power – so dramatic in fact that it may not be worth bothering with the analysis at all. Remedies for problems with expected frequencies are: (1) collapse the data across one of the variables (preferably the one you least expect to have an effect!); (2) collapse levels of one of the variables; (3) collect more data; or (4) accept the loss of power.

---

[3] It's worth mentioning that for every model, the computation of expected values differs, and as the designs get more complex, the computation gets increasingly tedious and incomprehensible (at least to me); however, you don't need to know the calculations to get a feel for what is going on.

If you want to collapse data across one of the variables then certain things have to be considered:

1 The highest-order interaction should be non-significant.

2 At least one of the lower-order interaction terms involving the variable to be deleted should be non-significant.

Let's take the example we've been using. Say we wanted to delete the **Animal** variable. Then for this to be valid, the **Animal** × **Training** × **Dance** variable should be non-significant, and either the **Animal** × **Training** or the **Animal** × **Dance** interaction should also be non-significant. You can also collapse categories within a variable. So, if you had a variable of 'season' relating to spring, summer, autumn and winter, and you had very few observations in winter, you could consider reducing the variable to three categories: spring, summer, autumn/winter perhaps. However, you should really only combine categories that it makes theoretical sense to combine. Finally, some people overcome the problem by simply adding a constant to all cells of the table, but there really is no point in doing this because it doesn't address the issue of power.

18.9. Loglinear analysis using R ②

18.9.1. Initial considerations ②

Data are entered for loglinear analysis in the same way as for the chi-square test (see sections 18.6.1 and 18.6.2). The data for the cat and dog example are in the file **CatsandDogs. dat**; load and open this file by setting your working directory to the location of the file and executing:

```
catsDogs<-read.delim("CatsandDogs.dat", header = TRUE)
catsDogs
```

Notice that the data set has three variables (**Animal**, **Training** and **Dance**) and each one contains text representing the different categories of these variables. To begin with, we should produce a contingency table of the data.

The *CrossTable()* function cannot cope with three variables in a table. There are a couple of ways to deal with this limitation. One way is to use a *subset* function (section 3.9.2) to create two dataframes, and run *CrossTable()* on each. This is the most useful thing to do if you want row and/or column percentages and so we'll cover that here. However, you can also use the **table()** and **xtabs()** functions (see Oliver Twisted).

OLIVER TWISTED

Please Sir, can I have some more … tables?

'Fagin has challenged me to steal a gold-coated table from under a rich gent's nose while he eats roast goose from it. I wonder how I can do it?' ponders Oliver. 'Perhaps the *table()* function will help me, or maybe *xtabs()* although that's probably best for tables with adult content.' OK, Oliver, I'll explain them to you on the companion website, but I think you'll be disappointed with them as aids to your criminal activities. If you ever need to cross-tabulate some frequencies though, you'll be glad you asked.

To create the separate dataframes for cats and dogs, we execute:

```
justCats = subset(catsDogs, Animal=="Cat")
justDogs = subset(catsDogs, Animal=="Dog")
```

The first command creates a dataframe called *justCats* which is based on the whole dataframe (*catsDogs*) but includes only cases for which the variable **Animal** is exactly equal to the word 'Cat'. The second command does much the same but selects only dogs.

Having created these two new dataframes, we can use the *CrossTable()* command to generate contingency tables for each of them by executing:

```
CrossTable(justCats$Training, justCats$Dance, sresid = TRUE, prop.t = FALSE,
prop.c = FALSE, prop.chisq = FALSE, format = "SPSS")
CrossTable(justDogs$Training, justDogs$Dance, sresid = TRUE, prop.t = FALSE,
prop.c = FALSE, prop.chisq = FALSE, format = "SPSS")
```

These commands produce a contingency table of the variables **Training** and **Dance** for cats (first command) and dogs (second command). These commands probably look quite long, but this is only because we have asked to suppress the total proportions (*prop.t = FALSE*), the column proportions (*prop.c = FALSE*) and chi-square proportions (*prop.chisq = FALSE*), so that they don't appear in the output (see R's Souls' Tip 18.2). We have also asked for standardized residuals (*sresid = TRUE* in combination with *format = "SPSS"*) because these might come in handy for interpretation.

```
   Cell Contents
|-------------------------|
|                   Count |
|             Row Percent |
|            Std Residual |
|-------------------------|

Total Observations in Table:  200

                       | justCats$Dance
   justCats$Training   |      No    |      Yes    | Row Total |
-----------------------|------------|------------|-----------|
  Affection as Reward  |      114   |       48   |      162  |
                       |  70.370%   |   29.630%  |  81.000%  |
                       |    1.353   |   -1.728   |           |
-----------------------|------------|------------|-----------|
      Food as Reward   |       10   |       28   |       38  |
                       |  26.316%   |   73.684%  |  19.000%  |
                       |   -2.794   |    3.568   |           |
-----------------------|------------|------------|-----------|
        Column Total   |      124   |       76   |      200  |
-----------------------|------------|------------|-----------|
```

Output 18.5

The crosstabulation table produced by the *CrossTable()* function contains the number of cases that fall into each combination of categories. The first table (Output 18.5) contains the information for cats and is the same information as in Output 18.3, because the data are the same (we just added some dogs to the data). Output 18.6 shows the frequencies for the dogs; we can summarize the data in a similar way as we did for the cats. In total 49 dogs danced and of these 20 were trained using food and 29 were trained with affection. Further, 21 dogs didn't dance at all. In summary, a lot more dogs danced than didn't. Of those that had affection as a reward, 80.56% danced compared to 19.44% that didn't, but for those rewarded with food only 58.82% danced compared to 41.18% that didn't. In short, dogs seem more willing to dance than cats (70% compared to 38%), and seem more motivated by affection than cats (81% danced compared to 30% of cats).

```
   Cell Contents
|-------------------------|
|                   Count |
|             Row Percent |
|            Std Residual |
|-------------------------|

Total Observations in Table:   70

                    | justDogs$Dance
   justDogs$Training |        No |       Yes | Row Total |
--------------------|-----------|-----------|-----------|
Affection as Reward |         7 |        29 |        36 |
                    |   19.444% |   80.556% |   51.429% |
                    |    -1.156 |     0.757 |           |
--------------------|-----------|-----------|-----------|
     Food as Reward |        14 |        20 |        34 |
                    |   41.176% |   58.824% |   48.571% |
                    |     1.190 |    -0.779 |           |
--------------------|-----------|-----------|-----------|
       Column Total |        21 |        49 |        70 |
--------------------|-----------|-----------|-----------|
```

Output 18.6

18.9.2.   Loglinear analysis as a chi-square test ②

First we'll do a loglinear analysis that involves only the cats, and we'll ignore the dogs. We'll see that loglinear analysis gives the same results as the chi-square test, then we'll generalize the model to dogs and cats, and show how you can do things with the loglinear analysis that you can't do with the chi-square test.

To do the loglinear analysis, we can use the **loglm()** function. The easiest way to use this function is by entering a contingency table into it; in which case it takes the general form:

```
newModel<-loglm( ~ predictors, data = contingencyTable, fit = TRUE)
```

In other words, it creates a model object called *newModel* based on a contingency table (*contingencyTable*), with a specified list of variables and/or interactions (*predictors*). In other words, the format is very much like the *lm()* function that we have used throughout the book.

The first stage, therefore, is to create a contingency table to put into the *loglm()* function; we can do this using the *xtabs()* function. This function takes the general form:

```
newTable<-xtabs(~ classifying variables, data = dataFrame)
```

In other words, we create a new dataframe called *newTable*, which is based on an existing dataframe, and we simply list the variables by which we want to classify cases. In this case, we want to look at only the cats, so we'll use the *justCats* dataframe that we generated in the previous section, and we want to classify cases based on **Training** and whether they danced or not (**Dance**). Therefore, we could execute:

```
catTable<-xtabs(~ Training + Dance, data = justCats)
```

This command will create an object called *catTable*, which takes the *justCats* dataframe and classifies cases based on levels of the variables Training and Dance. If you look at *catTable* by executing its name, you'll see that it is a very simple table of counts:

```
                       Dance
Training               No Yes
   Affection as Reward 114  48
   Food as Reward       10  28
```

We input this object into *loglm()*. We are going to run two loglinear analyses. First, we'll run the saturated model. As explained earlier in this chapter, this model will be able to reproduce the proportions exactly and hence the chi-square test will be zero, with a *p*-value equal to 1. In the second model, we will remove the interaction effect leaving only the effects of **Dance** and **Training**.

When creating loglinear models, we use a formula, in the same way that we have throughout this book when using functions like *lm()* and *glm()*. We have seen that usually we write models as '*outcome ~ predictor(s)*'; however, in loglinear analysis there is no outcome (dependent) variable because we're predicting the frequency of cases in different combinations of the predictors. Therefore, we don't include anything on the left of the tilde. In general, we'd write something like '*~ a + b*' in which *a* and *b* are predictor variables; because we want all of the effects in the saturated model, our model will be *~Dance + Training + Training:Dance*. We can, therefore create this model by executing:[4]

```
catSaturated<-loglm(~ Training + Dance + Training:Dance, data = catTable,
fit = TRUE)
```

In the second model, we remove the interaction effect and have only **Training** and **Dance** as predictors. In doing so we should be able to predict the proportion of individuals in each category by knowing the proportion of cats who were trained each way, and the proportion of cats who danced. So if 19% of the cats were trained with food, and 38% of the cats danced, we would expect to know how many cats had food as training and danced, how many had food as training and did not dance, how many had affection and danced, and how many had affection and did not dance. In fact, we'd expect 38% of the cats that had food as training to have danced, and 38% of the cats that had affection as training to have danced. We can obtain these expected values by adding *fit = TRUE* to the *loglm()* function, which tells the command to also calculate the fitted (expected) values. We'll compare these values with the proportions that we have, and we'll do a significance test to see if they differ. (That's exactly what we do in the chi-square test.) We create this new model in the same way as the saturated model, except that we change the name of the model, and we omit the interaction term:

```
catNoInteraction<-loglm(~ Training + Dance, data = catTable, fit = TRUE)
```

Finally, we can create a **mosaic plot**. A mosaic plot is a graphical representation of frequency data. Essentially, a square is divided up into portions, where the size of each portion represents the number of cases (or expected frequencies) relative to the total. Figure 18.3 shows some examples of mosaic plots. In the top left the big square has been divided up into four shaded squares of equal size: the fact the squares are equal size tells us that there are an equal number of cats who danced and didn't dance and were trained with food and affection. In the top right, the two squares under 'affection' are wider than those under 'food', but the height of the squares on the dance/no dance dimension are equal. This tells us that there were more cats trained with affection than food (because on this dimension

---

[4] Given what you have already learnt about specifying models it should be clear that you could specify the full model as follows (because *Training*Dance* will include the main effects automatically):
```
catSaturated<-loglm(~Training*Dance, data = catTable, fit = TRUE)
```

the squares are wider for affection than food), but the same number of cats danced and didn't dance (because the squares are the same height). In the bottom left we can see that an equal number of cats were trained with food and affection (because the boxes are equally wide), but more cats danced than didn't (the boxes are longer for the 'yes' category than the 'no'). Finally, the bottom right shows a situation in which more cats were trained with affection than food (we can tell because the boxes under 'affection' are wider than for 'food'), but also for food training more cats danced than not (the box is longer for 'yes') and for affection training equal numbers of cats danced and did not (the boxes for this category are of equal size). Therefore, by looking at mosaic plots we can get an idea of the relative frequency of different categories. To do a mosaic plot in **R**, we can use the **mosaicplot()** function, which takes the general form:

```
mosaicplot(contingencyTable, shade = TRUE, main = "Title")
```

Therefore, we need only input a contingency table, then we can optionally provide a title by using the *main =* option, and ask for shading to show which areas of the plot are significant by including the *shade =* option.

We can create plots of the expected values from our two models: these are stored in a variable called *fit* that is attached to each model, so we can access them using *model$fit*

FIGURE 18.3
Examples of mosaic plots

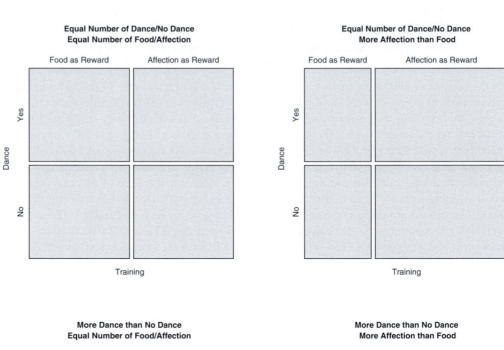

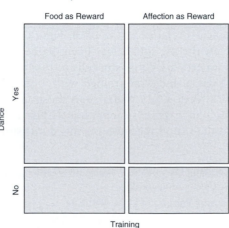
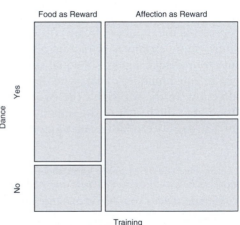

(in which *model* is the name of the model). For the saturated model, the expected values will be the same as the raw data (because the model is a perfect fit of the data), but for the second model these expected values will be the same as the expected cell values for the chi-square test that we computed at the beginning of the chapter (i.e., 14.44, 23.56, 61.56, and 100.44).

To create a mosaic plot for the saturated model we can simply execute:

```
mosaicplot(catSaturated$fit, shade = TRUE, main = "Cats: Saturated Model")
```

This command will create a plot of the expected values from the catSaturated model, it gives it a title of 'Cats: Saturated Model', and shades it to highlight significant areas. Similarly, the expected values for the second model can be plotted by executing:

```
mosaicplot(catNoInteraction$fit, shade = TRUE, main = "Cats: Expected Values")
```

18.9.3. Output from loglinear analysis as a chi-square test ②

Output 18.7 shows the output of the saturated model and Output 18.8 the model without the interaction term – I've cut out some of the boring details that you don't need to worry about. The summary of the saturated model shows that the model is not significant. In fact, the chi-square is zero, and the *p*-value is 1. Remember that these are goodness-of-fit tests, which means that they test whether the expected values from the model deviate from the observed data. A non-significant result therefore means a good fit. In fact, the statistic is 0 (and *p*-value is 1) because this model fits the data perfectly: the expected values are the same as the actual data.

```
Formula:
~Training + Dance + Training:Dance

Statistics:
                  X^2 df P(> X^2)
Likelihood Ratio   0   0        1
Pearson            0   0        1
```

Output 18.7

In the second model, we drop the interaction term. This term allowed the proportion of cats that danced to vary across conditions. In other words, it allowed an association between the **Dance** and **Training** variables. When this association is removed from the model, the model does not fit the data well any more: likelihood ratio and Pearson chi-square test are very similar, and both are highly significant, which means that the model deviates significantly from the data. In other words, when we remove the association between **Dance** and **Training**, the model becomes a poor fit to the data. This is what the chi-square test that we did at the beginning of the chapter measures: what is the effect of the association or interaction between **Dance** and **Training** on cell frequencies. Note that the values of the likelihood ratio and chi-square test in Output 18.8 are the same as those we computed at the start of the chapter.

```
Formula:
~Training + Dance

Statistics:
                        X^2 df      P(> X^2)
Likelihood Ratio 24.93159  1 5.940113e-07
Pearson          25.35569  1 4.767434e-07
```

Output 18.8

FIGURE 18.4
Mosaic plot
summarizing the
Cat Saturated
Model

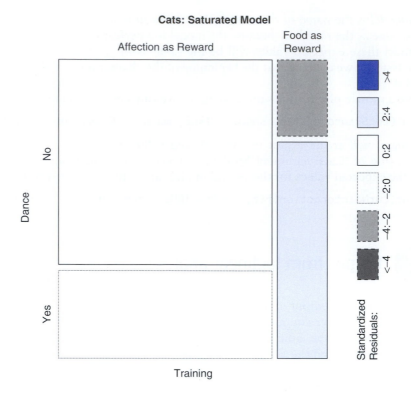

Ultimately, we're trying to find the most parsimonious model that does not deviate significantly from the data; in this case this is the saturated model, because the other model is significant (and hence a poor fit of the data). Therefore, we interpret the saturated model.

Figure 18.4 shows the mosaic plot, which summarizes the saturated model for us. The size of each rectangle represents the number of cats. The colour and the boundary of each rectangle tells us about the residuals. A blue residual with a solid boundary means the residual is positive, a red rectangle (on your screen, but dark grey in Figure 18.4) or a dashed boundary means the residual is negative. A rectangle gets coloured only if the standardized residual is higher than 2, or lower than −2. Recall that a standardized residual is significant if it is (approximately) higher than 2, or lower than −2, so the coloured rectangles are significant.

What the graph shows is that more cats than we would have expected (given the null hypothesis) failed to dance when given affection, as shown by the large rectangle on the top left with the solid boundary, but that the residual (i.e., the difference between the number we found and the number we expect, given the null hypothesis) was not significant: because the rectangle is white. Similarly, fewer cats than we expected danced, when given affection as a reward, as shown by the rectangle on the bottom left. We know it's fewer, because it has a dashed boundary, and we know it's not significant, because it's white.

When it comes to those cats that were rewarded with food, a different story emerges. Fewer cats failed to dance when rewarded with food than we would have expected. We can see this from the light grey rectangle (pink on your screen) on the top right. We know that it's fewer, because of the dashed boundary, and it is coloured, so it is significant.

Similarly, more cats danced when rewarded with food than we would have expected, given the null hypothesis. We can see this, because the lower right rectangle has a solid boundary, and because it is shaded blue, we know that the residual is positive.

Figure 18.5 shows the mosaic plot of the fitted values for the model without the interaction term: here all the residuals are zero (they are all white boxes with solid boundaries). The plot shows that it doesn't matter what sort of training the cat had, the same proportion danced in both groups.

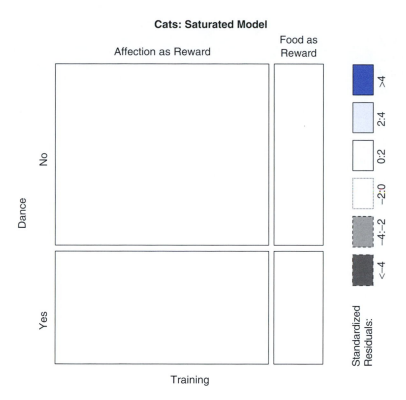

Cats: Saturated Model

18.9.4. Loglinear analysis ②

Usually when we do a loglinear analysis we have more than two variables – we can do it with two (as we've seen), but there's no point, because a chi-square test does the job for us and it's easier and less confusing. When we have more than two variables, we have more possible effects than before. Recall that if we have two variables, then we have the main effects: **Training + Dance**, and the interaction effect (**Training × Dance**). With three variables, we have:

1 Main effects: **Training + Dance + Animal**

2 Two-way interactions: Because we have three variables, there are three two-way interactions:
   a **Training × Dance**
   b **Dance × Animal**
   c **Training × Animal**

3 Three-way interaction: **Training × Dance × Animal**

You can see that as the number of variables increases, the number of effects increases even more. With four variables (which I'll call a, b, c and d because I have no imagination whatsoever), we have:

1 Main effects:
   a $a + b + c + d$

2 Two-way interactions:
   a $a \times b$

  b $a \times c$
  c $a \times d$
  d $b \times c$
  e $b \times d$
  f $c \times d$

3 Three-way interactions:
  a $a \times b \times c$
  b $a \times b \times d$
  c $a \times c \times d$
  d $b \times c \times d$

4 Four-way interaction:
  a $a \times b \times c \times d$

The principle is the same however many effects you have: you start with the saturated model, and remove effects until the model becomes significant (i.e., significantly deviates from the original data). When the model is significant, you go back to the last model that was not significant and interpret it (because it will be the best fit you can achieve given the available predictor variables).

First of all we need to generate our contingency table using *xtabs()*, and we can do this by executing:

```
CatDogContingencyTable<-xtabs(~ Animal + Training + Dance, data = catsDogs)
```

This takes the original dataframe (*catsDogs*) and creates a contingency table based on the variables **Animal**, **Training** and **Dance**. The resulting contingency table is stored as *CatDogContingencyTable*, which is what we'll use in the loglinear analysis; it looks like this:

```
, , Dance = No

       Training
Animal Affection as Reward Food as Reward
   Cat                 114              10
   Dog                   7              14

, , Dance = Yes

       Training
Animal Affection as Reward Food as Reward
   Cat                  48              28
   Dog                  29              20
```

We start by estimating the saturated model, which we know will fit the data perfectly with a chi-square equal to zero. We'll call the model *caturated* because I feel the need for a rubbish cat-related pun. We can create this model in the same way as before:[5]

```
caturated<-loglm(~ Animal*Training*Dance, data = CatDogContingencyTable)
summary(caturated)
```

The first command creates the model called *caturated* based on all main effects and interactions in the contingency table called *CatDogContingencyTable*. The second command

---

[5] I've chosen to specify the model as *~Animal*Training*Dance* because this will automatically include all of the main effects and lower-order interactions, and is less typing than ~ *Animal* + *Training* + *Dance* + *Animal:Training* + *Animal:Dance* + *Dance:Training* + *Dance:Training:Animal*

summarizes this model; Output 18.9 shows the main statistics, and as we expect it has a likelihood ratio of 0, and a *p*-value of 1, because it is a perfect fit of the data.

```
Formula:
~Animal * Training * Dance

Statistics:
                   X^2 df P(> X^2)
Likelihood Ratio    0  0         1
Pearson             0  0         1
```

Output 18.9

Next we'll fit the model with all of the main effects and two-way interactions. In other words, we'll remove the three-way interaction; because this model tells us the effect of removing the three-way interaction we'll call it *threeWay*. We could create this model by respecifying the model with all terms except the three-way interaction:

```
threeWay <- loglm(~ Animal + Training + Dance + Animal:Training + Animal:Dance
+ Dance:Training, data = CatDogContingencyTable)
```

This command uses the same format as before to create a model called *threeWay*. The only difference (apart from that we have changed the name of the model) is that the three-way interaction isn't included. This is a lot of typing, so you could also consider using the *update()* function (see R's Souls' Tip 7.2). Remember that this function allows us to take an existing model and 'update' it. In the past we have updated models by adding in new variables, but we can also remove them using this function. For example, to remove the three-way interaction from the saturated model we would execute:

```
threeWay<-update(caturated, .~. -Animal:Training:Dance)
```

Remember that the .~. simply means 'keep the same outcome variable and predictor as before'; so, we've specified that we want to take the model called *caturated*, we want to keep the same outcomes and predictors as before, but by including '–*Animal:Training:Dance*' we ask to remove the three-way interaction (the minus sign means 'remove'). We can summarize this model by executing:

```
summary(threeWay)
```

The pertinent parts of the resulting output are in Output 18.10. The model has a likelihood ratio of 20.30, with 1 *df* and *p* < .001. It seems as though this model is a poor fit to the data.

```
Formula:
. ~ Animal + Training + Dance + Animal:Training + Animal:Dance +
    Training:Dance

Statistics:
                      X^2 df       P(> X^2)
Likelihood Ratio 20.30491  1 6.603088e-06
Pearson          20.77759  1 5.158318e-06
```

Output 18.10

To compare models is very easy, we just subtract the likelihood ratios, and the degrees of freedom. But we're kind of lazy, and so we'll use the *anova()* function, which will do this for us (see section 7.8.4). We can compare the saturated model to the one without the three-way interaction by executing:

```
anova(caturated, threeWay)
```

The resulting Output 18.11 shows the difference between these models. We're interested in the part called Delta: delta is Greek letter Δ, which is the equivalent of D, and is often used in statistics to mean 'difference'.[6] The *anova()* function calculates the difference in the likelihoods for the two models, which is 20.30 – 0 = 20.30, and the difference in df, which is 1 – 0 = 1. You can see that this is a useful function, because it has done some literally brain-melting sums for us: I did warn you we were being lazy.

In the column labelled *P(> Delta(Dev)* we see the *p*-value of the difference between the models. This value is less than .001 and, therefore, highly significant. This significant result tells us that removing the three-way interaction has made the model a significantly worse fit to the data. In other words, the three-way interaction is a significant factor in making the model a good fit. It also means that for interpretation purposes we need to stick with the saturated model. We should now stop and conclude that the three-way interaction is significant, and interpret the effect.

```
LR tests for hierarchical log-linear models

Model 1:
 . ~ Training + Animal + Dance
Model 2:
 ~Animal * Training * Dance


          Deviance df Delta(Dev) Delta(df) P(> Delta(Dev)
Model 1    20.30491  1
Model 2     0.00000  0   20.30491            1               1e-05
Saturated   0.00000  0    0.00000            0               1e+00
```

Output 18.11

For illustrative purposes let's pretend that we don't need to stop, and carry on. Let's create models that systematically remove the two-way interactions:

```
trainingDance<-update(threeWay, .~. -Training:Dance)
animalDance<-update(threeWay, .~. -Animal:Dance)
animalTraining<-update(threeWay, .~. -Animal:Training)
```

The first command creates a model called *trainingDance* that takes that *threeWay* model and removes the **Training × Dance** interaction (i.e., it does not include either this interaction or the three-way interaction). The second does the same but removes the **Animal × Dance** interaction. The final command again takes the *threeWay* model but this time removes the **Training × Animal** interaction. We can compare all of these models to the model without the three-way interaction using the *anova()* function:

```
anova(threeWay, trainingDance)
anova(threeWay, animalDance)
anova(threeWay, animalTraining)
```

Output 18.12 shows the result of the first comparison, which shows us the effect of removing the **Training × Dance** interaction: the likelihood ratio difference (or delta) is 8.6 (28.9 – 20.3) with 2 – 1 = 1 degrees of freedom. This difference is significant, at *p* = .003, and therefore we cannot remove the Training × Dance interaction from the model without the fit getting worse (in other words, this interaction is significant too).

```
          Deviance df Delta(Dev) Delta(df) P(> Delta(Dev)
Model 1    28.91551  2
Model 2    20.30491  1  8.610596            1              0.00334
Saturated   0.00000  0 20.304911            1              0.00001
```

Output 18.12

[6] Sometimes people say 'What's the delta?' when they mean 'What's the difference?' If you ever meet anyone who says this, you'll know what they mean (and you'll know that they are a pretentious prig).

Output 18.13 shows the effect of removing the **Animal** × **Dance** effect. Now we get a likelihood ratio difference of 13.75, with 1 *df*. The *p*-value is < .001, and therefore we cannot remove the **Animal** × **Dance** effect without making the fit of the model worse.

```
          Deviance df Delta(Dev) Delta(df) P(> Delta(Dev)
Model 1   34.05329  2
Model 2   20.30491  1   13.74838          1         0.00021
Saturated 0.00000   0   20.30491          1         0.00001
```

Output 18.13

Output 18.14 shows the effect of removing the **Animal** × **Training** interaction. The difference here is 13.76, with 1 *df*. Again this is highly significant, and therefore this effect cannot be removed from the model without making the fit worse.

```
          Deviance df Delta(Dev) Delta(df) P(> Delta(Dev)
Model 1   34.06486  2
Model 2   20.30491  1   13.75995          1         0.00021
Saturated 0.00000   0   20.30491          1         0.00001
```

Output 18.14

The next step is to try to interpret the three-way interaction (remember we looked at the two-way interactions only for illustrative purposes). The first useful thing we can do is to plot the frequencies across all of the different categories. You should plot the frequencies in terms of the percentages. You should also look at the mosaic plot. We can obtain this plot by using the *mosaicplot()* function and applying it to our contingency table:

```
mosaicplot(CatDogContingencyTable, shade = TRUE, main = "Cats and Dogs")
```

> I don't need a loglinear analysis to tell me that cats are vastly superior to dogs!

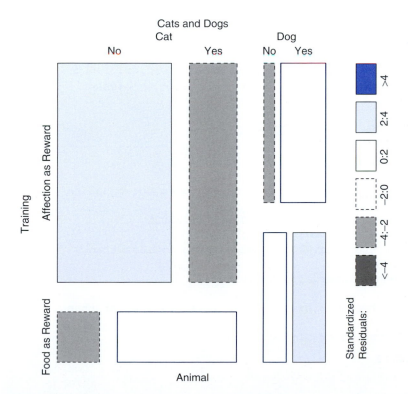

FIGURE 18.6

Mosaic plot of the cat and dog data

Executing this command creates the mosaic plot in Figure 18.6. This plot shows what we already know about cats: they will dance (or do anything else for that matter) when there is food involved but if you train them with affection they're not interested. Dogs on the other hand will dance when there's affection involved (actually more dogs danced than didn't dance regardless of the type of reward, but the effect is more pronounced when affection was the training method). In fact, both animals show similar responses to food training, it's just that cats won't do anything for affection. So cats are sensible creatures that only do stupid stuff when there's something in it for them (i.e., food), whereas dogs are just plain stupid.

18.10. Following up loglinear analysis ②

An alternative way to interpret a three-way interaction is to conduct chi-square analysis at different levels of one of your variables. For example, to interpret our **Animal** × **Training** × **Dance** interaction, we could perform a chi-square test on **Training** and **Dance** but do this separately for dogs and cats (in fact the analysis for cats will be the same as the example we used for chi-square). You can then compare the results in the different animals.

SELF-TEST

✓ Use the *subset()* function to run a chi-square test on **Dance** and **Training** for dogs and cats separately.

```
Pearson's Chi-squared test
----------------------------------------------------------
Chi^2 =  3.932462      d.f. =  1      p =  0.04736256

Pearson's Chi-squared test with Yates' continuity correction
----------------------------------------------------------
Chi^2 =  2.965686      d.f. =  1      p =  0.08504836


Fisher's Exact Test for Count Data
----------------------------------------------------------
Sample estimate odds ratio:  0.3502677

Alternative hypothesis: true odds ratio is not equal to 1
p =  0.06797422
95% confidence interval:  0.1001861 1.127025

Alternative hypothesis: true odds ratio is less than 1
p =  0.04208209
95% confidence interval:  0 0.9586623

Alternative hypothesis: true odds ratio is greater than 1
p =  0.9880647
95% confidence interval:  0.1208492 Inf
```

Output 18.15

The results and interpretation for cats are in Output 18.3 and for dogs the output is shown in Output 18.15. For dogs there is still a significant relationship between the types of training and whether they danced but it is weaker (the chi-square is 3.93 compared to 25.4 in the cats).[7] This reflects the fact that dogs are more likely to dance if given affection than if given food, the opposite of cats.

18.11. Effect sizes in loglinear analysis ②

As with Pearson's chi-square, one of the most elegant ways to report your effects is in terms of **odds ratios**. Odds ratios are easiest to understand for 2×2 contingency tables and so if you have significant higher-order interactions, or your variables have more than two categories, it is worth trying to break these effects down into logical 2×2 tables and calculating odds ratios that reflect the nature of the interaction. So, for example, in this example we could calculate odds ratios for dogs and cats separately. We have the odds ratios for cats already (section 18.6.7), and for dogs we would get 0.35 as reported in Output 18.15.

SELF-TEST

✓ Calculate the odds ratio for dogs by hand.

This tells us that if a dog was trained with food the odds of their dancing were 0.35 times the odds if they were rewarded with affection (i.e., they were less likely to dance). Another way to say this is that the odds of their dancing were 1/0.35 = 2.90 times lower if they were trained with food instead of affection. Compare this to cats where the odds of dancing were 6.58 higher if they were trained with food rather than affection. As you can see, comparing the odds ratios for dogs and cats is an extremely elegant way to present the three-way interaction term in the model.

18.12. Reporting the results of loglinear analysis ②

When reporting loglinear analysis you need to report the likelihood ratio statistic for the final model, usually denoted just by χ^2. For any terms that are significant you should report the chi-square change. For this example we could report:

✓ The three-way loglinear analysis produced a final model that retained all effects. The likelihood ratio of this model was $\chi^2 (0) = 0$, $p = 1$. This indicated that the highest order interaction (the Animal × Training × Dance interaction) was significant, $\chi^2 (1) = 20.31$, $p < .001$. To break down this effect, separate chi-square tests on the Training and Dance variables were performed separately for dogs and cats. For cats, there was

---

[7] The chi-square statistic depends on the sample size, so really you need to calculate effect sizes and compare them to make this kind of statement (unless you had equal numbers of dogs and cats).

a significant association between the type of training and whether or not cats would dance, $\chi^2(1) = 25.36$, $p < .001$; this was true in dogs also, $\chi^2(1) = 3.93$, $p < .05$. Odds ratios indicated that the odds of dancing were 6.58 higher after food than affection in cats, but only 0.35 in dogs (i.e., in dogs, the odds of dancing were 2.90 times lower if trained with food compared to affection). Therefore, the analysis seems to reveal a fundamental difference between dogs and cats: cats are more likely to dance for food rather than affection, whereas dogs are more likely to dance for affection than food.

CRAMMING SAM'S TIPS   Loglinear analysis

- If you want to test the relationship between more than two categorical variables you can do this with *loglinear analysis*.
- Loglinear analysis is hierarchical: start with a model containing all main effects and interactions. Starting with the highest-order interaction, remove terms to see whether their removal significantly affects the fit of the model. If it does then this term is not removed, it is interpreted and all lower-order effects are ignored.
- Look at the crosstabulation table to interpret any significant effects (the percentage of total for cells is the best thing to look at).

What have I discovered about statistics? ①

When I wrote the first edition of the SPSS version of this book I had always intended to do a chapter on loglinear analysis, but by the time I got to that chapter I had already written 300 pages more than I was contracted to do, and had put so much effort into the rest of it that, well, the thought of that extra chapter was making me think of large cliffs and jumping. When the second edition needed to be written, I wanted to make sure that at the very least I did a loglinear chapter. However, when I came to it, I'd already written 200 pages more than I was supposed to for this new edition, and with deadlines fading into the distance, history was repeating itself. It won't surprise you to know then that I was really happy to have written the damn thing! This chapter has taken a very brief look at analysing categorical data. What I've tried to do is to show you how we approach categorical data in much the same way as any other kind of data: we fit a model, we calculate the deviation between our model and the observed data, and we use that to evaluate the model we've fitted. I've also tried to show that the model we fit is the same one that we've come across throughout this book: it's a linear model (regression). When we have only two variables we can use Pearson's chi-square test or the likelihood ratio test to look at whether those two variables are associated. In more complex situations, we simply extend these models into something known as a loglinear model. This is a bit like ANOVA for categorical data: for every variable we have, we get a main effect but we also get interactions between variables. Loglinear analysis simply evaluates all of these effects hierarchically to tell us which ones best predict our outcome.

Fortunately the experience of this loglinear chapter taught me a valuable lesson, which is never to agree to write a chapter about something that you know very little about, and if you do then definitely don't leave it until the very end of the writing process when you're under pressure and mentally exhausted. It's lucky that we learn from our mistakes, isn't it …?

R packages used in this chapter

gmodels | MASS

R functions used in this chapter

anova()	mosaicplot()
c()	rep()
cbind()	subset()
CrossTable()	summary()
factor()	table()
glm()	update()
loglm()	xtabs()
lm()	

Key terms that I've discovered

Chi-square test	Mosaic plot
Contingency table	Odds ratio
Fisher's exact test	Phi
Loglinear analysis	Saturated model
McNemar's test	Yates's continuity correction

Smart Alex's tasks ③

- **Task 1**: Certain editors at Sage like to think they're a bit of a whiz at football (soccer if you prefer). To see whether they are better than Sussex lecturers and postgraduates we invited various employees of Sage to join in our football matches (oh, sorry, I mean we invited them down for important meetings about books). Every player was allowed to play in only one match. Over many matches, we counted the number of players who scored goals. The data are in the file **SageEditorsCan'tPlayFootball.dat**. Do a chi-square test to see whether more publishers or academics scored goals. We predict that Sussex people will score more than Sage people. ③

- **Task 2**: In 2008 I had a sabbatical in the Netherlands (I have a real soft spot for Holland). However, living there for three months did enable me to notice certain cultural differences between Holland and England. The Dutch are famous for travelling by bike; they do it much more than the English. However, I noticed that many more Dutch people cycle while steering with only one hand. I pointed this out to one of my friends, Birgit Mayer, and she said that I was being a crazy English fool and that Dutch people did not cycle one-handed. Several weeks of me pointing at one-handed cyclists and her pointing at two-handed cyclists ensued. To put it to the test I counted the number of Dutch and English cyclists who ride with one or two hands on the handlebars (**Handlebars.dat**). Can you work out which one of us is right? ①

- **Task 3**: I was interested in whether horoscopes are just a figment of people's minds. Therefore, I got 2201 people, made a note of their star sign (this variable, obviously, has 12 categories: Capricorn, Aquarius, Pisces, Aries, Taurus, Gemini, Cancer, Leo,

Virgo, Libra, Scorpio and Sagittarius) and whether they believed in horoscopes (this variable has two categories: believer or unbeliever). I then sent them a horoscope in the post of what would happen over the next month: everybody, regardless of their star sign, received the same horoscope, which read *'August is an exciting month for you. You will make friends with a tramp in the first week of the month and cook him a cheese omelette. Curiosity is your greatest virtue, and in the second week, you'll discover knowledge of a subject that you previously thought was boring, statistics perhaps. You might purchase a book around this time that guides you towards this knowledge. Your new wisdom leads to a change in career around the third week, when you ditch your current job and become an accountant. By the final week you find yourself free from the constraints of having friends, your boy/girlfriend has left you for a Russian ballet dancer with a glass eye, and you now spend your weekends doing loglinear analysis by hand with a pigeon called Hephzibah for company.'* At the end of August I interviewed all of these people and I classified the horoscope as having come true, or not, based on how closely their lives had matched the fictitious horoscope. The data are in the file **Horoscope.dat**. Conduct a loglinear analysis to see whether there is a relationship between the person's star sign, whether they believe in horoscopes and whether the horoscope came true. ③

- **Task 4**: On my statistics course students have weekly classes in a computer laboratory. Postgraduate tutors run these classes but I often pop in to help out. I've noticed in these sessions that many students are studying Facebook rather more than they are studying the very interesting statistics assignments that I have set them. I wanted to see the impact that this behaviour had on their exam performance. I collected data from all 260 students on my course. First I checked their **Attendance** and classified them as having attended either more or less than 50% of their lab classes. Next, I classified them as being either someone who looked at **Facebook** during their lab class, or someone who never did. Lastly, after the Research Methods in Psychology exam, I classified them as having either passed or failed (**Exam**). The data are in **Facebook.dat**. Do a loglinear analysis on the data to see if there is an association between studying Facebook and failing your exam. ③

Answers can be found on the companion website.

Further reading

Hutcheson, G., & Sofroniou, N. (1999). *The multivariate social scientist*. London: Sage.

Tabachnick, B. G. & Fidell, L. S. (2007). *Using multivariate statistics* (4th ed.). Boston: Allyn & Bacon. (Chapter 16 is a fantastic account of loglinear analysis.)

Interesting real research

Beckham, A. S. (1929). Is the Negro happy? A psychological analysis. *Journal of Abnormal and Social Psychology, 24*, 186–190.

Multilevel linear models

19

FIGURE 19.1
Having a therapy
session in 2007

19.1. What will this chapter tell me? ①

Over the last couple of chapters we saw that I had gone from a child having dreams and aspirations of being a rock star, to becoming a living (barely) statistical test. A more dramatic demonstration of my complete failure to achieve my life's ambitions I can scarcely imagine. Having devoted far too much of my life to statistics, it was time to unlock the latent rock star once more. The second edition of the SPSS version of this book had left me in desperate need for some therapy and, therefore, at the age of 29 I decided to start playing the drums (there's a joke in there somewhere about it being the perfect instrument for a failed musician, but really they're much harder to play than people think). A couple of years later I had a call from an old friend of mine, Doug, who used to be in a band that my old band Scansion used to play with a lot: 'Remember the last time I saw you we talked about you coming and having a jam with us?' I had absolutely no recollection whatsoever of him saying this, so I responded 'Yes'. 'Well, how about it then?' he said. 'OK,' I said, 'you arrange it and I'll bring my guitar.' 'No, you whelk,' he said, 'we want you to drum and maybe you could learn some of the songs on the CD I gave you last year?' I'd played his band's CD and I liked it, but there was no way on this earth that I could play the drums as well as their drummer. 'Sure, no problem', I lied. I spent the next two weeks playing along to this CD as if my life depended on it and when the rehearsal came, much as I'd love to report that I drummed like a lord, I didn't. I did, however, nearly have a heart attack and herniate everything in my body that it's possible to herniate (really, the music is pretty fast!). Still, we had another rehearsal, and then another and, well, many years down the line we're still having them. The only difference is that now I can play the songs at a speed that makes their old recordings seem as though a sedated snail was on the drums (www.myspace.com/fracturepattern). The point is that it's never too late to learn something new. This is just as well because, as a man who clearly doesn't learn from his mistakes, I agreed to write a chapter on multilevel linear models, a subject about which I know absolutely nothing. I'm writing it last, when I feel mentally exhausted and stressed. Hopefully at some point between now and the end of writing the chapter I will learn something. With a bit of luck you will too.

19.2. Hierarchical data ②

In all of the analyses in this book so far we have treated data as though they are organized at a single level. However, in the real world, data are often hierarchical. This just means that some variables are clustered or *nested* within other variables. For example, when I'm not writing statistics books I spend most of my time researching how anxiety develops in children below the age of 10. This typically involves my running experiments in schools. When I run research in a school, I test children who have been assigned to different classes, and who are taught by different teachers. The classroom that a child is in could conceivably affect my results. Let's imagine I test in two different classrooms. The first class is taught by Mr. Nervous. Mr. Nervous is very anxious and often when he supervises children he tells them to be careful, or that things that they do are dangerous, or that they might hurt themselves. The second class is taught by Little Miss Daredevil.[1] She is very carefree and she believes that children in her class should have the freedom to explore new experiences. Therefore, she is always telling them not to be scared of things and to explore new situations. One day I go into the school to test the children. I take in a big animal carrier, which I tell them has an animal inside. I measure whether they will put their hand in the carrier to stroke the animal. Children taught by Mr. Nervous have grown up in an environment where their teacher reinforces caution, whereas children taught by Miss Daredevil have been encouraged to embrace new experiences. Therefore, we might expect Mr. Nervous's children to be more reluctant to put their hand in the box because of the classroom experiences that they have had. The classroom is, therefore, known as a *contextual variable*. In reality, as an experimenter I would be interested in a much more complicated situation. For example, I might tell some of the children that the animal is a bloodthirsty beast, whereas I tell others that the animal is

---

[1] Those of you who don't spot the Mr. Men references here, check out http://www.mrmen.com. Mr. Nervous used to be called Mr. Jelly and was a pink jelly-shaped blob, which in my humble opinion was better than his current incarnation.

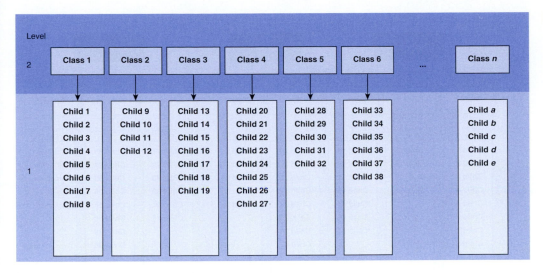

FIGURE 19.2
An example
of a two-level
hierarchical data
structure: children
(level 1) are
organized within
classrooms
(level 2)

friendly. Now obviously I'm expecting the information I give the children to affect their enthusiasm for stroking the animal. However, it's also possible that their classroom has an effect. Therefore, my manipulation of the information that I give the children also has to be placed within the context of the classroom to which the child belongs. My threat information is likely to have more impact on Mr. Nervous's children than it will on Miss Daredevil's children. One consequence of this is that children within Mr. Nervous's class will be more similar to each other than they are to children in Miss Daredevil's class and vice versa.

Figure 19.2 illustrates this scenario more generally. In a big data set, we might have collected data from lots of children. This is the bottom of the hierarchy and is known as a *level 1* variable. So, children (or cases) are our level 1 variable. However, these children are organized by classroom (children are said to be *nested* within classes). The class to which a child belongs is a level up from the participant in the hierarchy and is said to be a level 2 variable.

The situation that I have just described is the simplest hierarchy that you can have because there are just two levels. However, you can have other layers to your hierarchy. The easiest way to explain this is to stick with our example of my testing children in different classes and then to point out the obvious fact that classrooms are themselves nested within schools. Therefore, if I ran a study incorporating lots of different schools, as well as different classrooms within those schools, then I would have to add another level to the hierarchy. We can apply the same logic as before, in that children in particular schools will be more similar to each other than to children in different schools. This is because schools tend to reflect their social demographic (which can differ from school to school) and they may differ in their policies also. Figure 19.3 shows this scenario. There are now three levels in the hierarchy: the child (level 1), the class to which the child belongs (level 2) and the school within which that class exists (level 3). In this situation we have two contextual variables: school and classroom.

Hierarchical data structures need not apply only to between-participant situations. We can also think of data as being nested within people. In this situation the case, or person, is not at the bottom of the hierarchy (level 1), but is further up. A good example is memory. Imagine that after giving children threat information about my caged animal I asked them a week later to recall everything they could about the animal. For each child there are many facts that they could recall. Let's say that I originally gave them 15 pieces of information; some children might recall all 15 pieces of information, but others might remember only

FIGURE 19.3

An example of a three-level hierarchical data structure

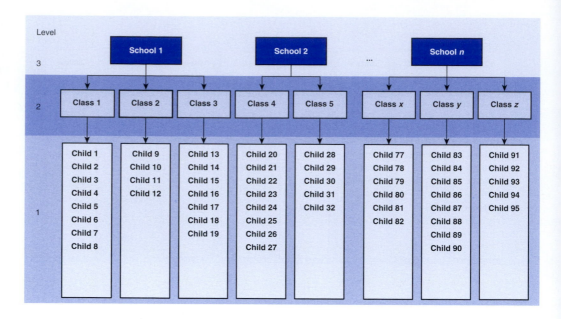

two or three bits of information. The bits of information, or memories, are nested within the person and their recall depends on the person. The probability of a given memory being recalled depends on what other memories are available, and the recall of one memory may have knock-on effects for what other memories are recalled. Therefore, memories are not independent units. As such, the person acts as a context within which memories are recalled (Wright, 1998).

Figure 19.4 shows the structure of the situation that I have just described. The child is our level 2 variable, and within each child there are several memories (our level 1 variable). Of course we can also have levels of the hierarchy above the child. So, we could still, for example, factor in the context of the class from which they came (as I have done in Figure 19.4) as a level 3 variable. Indeed, we could even include the school again as a level 4 variable.

FIGURE 19.4

An example of a three-level hierarchical data structure, where the level 1 variable is a repeated measure (memories recalled)

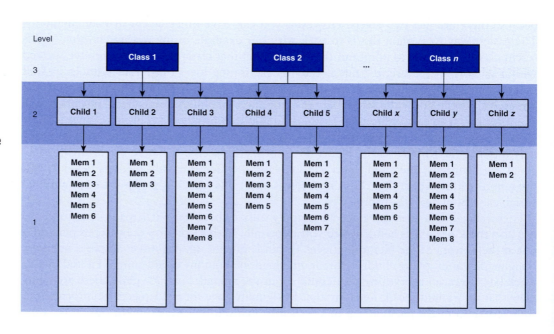

19.2.1. The intraclass correlation ②

You might well wonder why it matters that data are hierarchical (or not). The main problem is that the contextual variables in the hierarchy introduce dependency in the data. In plain English, this means that residuals will be correlated. I have alluded to this fact already when I noted that children in Mr. Nervous's class would be more similar to each other than to children in Miss Daredevil's class. In some sense, having the same teacher makes children more similar to each other. This similarity is a problem because in nearly every test we have covered in this book we assume that cases are independent. In other words, there is absolutely no correlation between residual scores of one child and another. However, when entities are sampled from similar contexts, this independence is unlikely to be true. For example, Charlotte and Emily's responses to the animal in the carrier have both been influenced by Mr. Nervous's cautious manner, so their behaviour will be similar. Likewise, Kiki and Jip's responses to the animal in the box have both been influenced by Miss Daredevil's carefree manner, so their behaviour will be similar too. We have seen before that in ANOVA, for example, a lack of independence between cases is a huge problem that really affects the resulting test statistic – and not in a good way! (See section 10.3.)

By thinking about contextual variables and factoring them into the analysis we can overcome this problem of non-independent observations. One way that we can do this is to use the intraclass correlation (ICC). We came across this measure in section 17.9.3 as a measure of inter-rater reliability, but it can also be used as a measure of dependency between scores. We'll skip the formalities of calculating the ICC (but see Oliver Twisted if you're keen to know), and we'll just give a conceptual grasp of what it represents. In our two-level example of children within classes, the ICC represents the proportion of the total variability in the outcome that is attributable to the classes. It follows that if a class has had a big effect on the children within it then the variability within the class will be small (the children will behave similarly). As such, variability in the outcome within classes is minimized, and variability in the outcome between classes is maximized; therefore, the ICC is large. Conversely, if the class has little effect on the children then the outcome will vary a lot within classes, which will make differences between classes relatively small. Therefore, the ICC is small too. Thus, the ICC tells us that variability within levels of a contextual variable (in this case the class to which a child belongs) is small, but between levels of a contextual variable (comparing classes) is large. As such, the ICC is a good gauge of whether a contextual variable has an effect on the outcome.

OLIVER TWISTED

Please Sir, can I have some more … ICC?

'I have a dependency on gruel', whines Oliver. 'Maybe I could measure this dependency if I knew more about the ICC.' Well, you're so high on gruel, Oliver, that you have rather missed the point. Still, I did write an article on the ICC once upon a time (Field, 2005a) and it's reproduced in the additional web material for your delight and amusement.

19.2.2. Benefits of multilevel models ②

Multilevel linear models have numerous uses. To convince you that trawling through this chapter is going to reward you with statistical possibilities beyond your wildest dreams, here are just a few (slightly overstated) benefits of multilevel models:

- **Cast aside the assumption of homogeneity of regression slopes.** We saw in Chapter 11 that when we use analysis of covariance we have to assume that the relationship between our covariate and our outcome is the same across the different groups that make up our predictor variable. However, this doesn't always happen. Luckily, in multilevel models we can explicitly model this variability in regression slopes, thus overcoming this inconvenient problem.

- **Say 'bye bye' to the assumption of independence.** We saw in Chapter 10 that when we use independent ANOVA we have to assume that the different cases of data are independent. If this is not true, little lizards climb out of your mattress while you're asleep and eat you. Again, multilevel models are specifically designed to allow you to model these relationships between cases. Also, in Chapter 7 we saw that multiple regression relies on having independent observations. However, there are situations in which you might want to measure someone on more than one occasion (i.e., over time). Ordinary regression turns itself into cheese and hides in the fridge at the prospect of cases of data that are related. Multilevel models eat these data for breakfast, with a piece of regression-flavoured cheese.

- **Laugh in the face of missing data.** I've spent a lot of this book extolling the virtues of balanced designs and not having missing data. Regression, ANOVA, ANCOVA and most of the other tests we have covered do strange things when data are missing or the design is not balanced. This can be a real pain. Missing data are a particular problem within clinical trials because it is common to attempt to collect follow-up data, often many months after treatment has ended when patients might be difficult to track down. Of course, there are ways to correct for and impute missing data, but these techniques are often quite complicated (Yang, Li, & Shoptaw, 2008), therefore, often when using repeated-measures designs if a single time point is missing the whole case usually needs to be deleted; missing data leads to more data being deleted. Multilevel models do not require complete data sets and so when data are missing for one time point they do not need to be imputed, nor does the whole case need to be deleted. Instead parameters can be estimated successfully with the available data, which offers a relatively easy solution to dealing with missing data. It is important to stress that no statistical procedure can overcome data that are missing. Good methods, designs and research execution should be used to minimize missing values, and reasons for missing values should always be explored. It is just that when using traditional statistical procedures for repeated-measures data additional procedures to account for missing data are usually necessary and can be problematic.

I think you'll agree that multilevel models are pretty funky. 'Is there anything they can't do?' I hear you cry. Well, no, not really.

19.3. Theory of multilevel linear models ③

The underlying theory of multilevel models is very complicated indeed – far too complicated for my little peanut of a brain to comprehend. Fortunately, the advent of computers and software like **R** makes it possible for feeble-minded individuals such as myself to take advantage of this wonderful tool without actually needing to know the maths. Better still, this means I can get away with not explaining the maths (and really, I'm not kidding, I don't understand any of it). What I will do, though, is try to give you a flavour of what multi-level models are and what they do by describing the key concepts within the framework of linear models that has permeated this whole book. I also want to remind you that if you have worked through Chapters 13 and 14 then you have already done a multilevel model and used the *lme()* function that we discuss in this chapter, because we used it to analyse repeated-measures designs. In these repeated-measures designs can be thought of as a two-level hierarchy in which scores (level 1) are nested within participants (level 2).

19.3.1. An example ②

Throughout the first part of the chapter we will use an example to illustrate some of the concepts in multilevel models. Cosmetic surgery is on the increase at the moment. In the USA, there was a 1600% increase in cosmetic surgical and non-surgical treatments between 1992 and 2002, and in 2004, 65,000 people in the UK underwent privately and publicly funded operations (Kellett, Clarke, & McGill, 2008). With the increasing popularity of this surgery, many people are starting to question the motives of those who want to go under the knife. There are two main reasons to have cosmetic surgery: (1) to help a physical problem such as having breast reduction surgery to relieve backache; and (2) to change your external appearance, for example by having a face lift. Related to this second point, there is even some case for arguing that cosmetic surgery could be performed as a psychological intervention: to improve self-esteem (Cook, Rosser, & Salmon, 2006; Kellett et al., 2008). The main example for this chapter looks at the effects of cosmetic surgery on quality of life. The variables in the data file are (**Cosmetic Surgery.dat**):

- **Post_QoL**: This is a measure of quality of life after the cosmetic surgery. This is our outcome variable.

- **Base_QoL**: We need to adjust our outcome for quality of life before the surgery.

- **Surgery**: This variable is a dummy variable that specifies whether the person has undergone cosmetic surgery (1) or whether they are on the waiting list (0), which acts as our control group.

- **Surgery_Text**: This variable is the same as above but specifies group membership as text (we will use this variable when we create graphs but not for the main analysis).

- **Clinic**: This variable specifies which of 10 clinics the person attended to have their surgery.

- **Age**: This variable tells us the person's age in years.

- **BDI**: It is becoming increasingly apparent that people volunteering for cosmetic surgery (especially when the surgery is purely for vanity) might have very different personality profiles than the general public (Cook, Rossera, Toone, James, & Salmon, 2006). In particular, these people might have low self-esteem or be depressed. When looking at quality of life it is important to assess natural levels of depression, and this variable used the Beck Depression Inventory (BDI) to do just that.

- **Reason**: This dummy variable specifies whether the person had/is waiting to have surgery purely to change their appearance (0), or because of a physical reason (1).

- **Reason_Text**: This variable is the same as above but contains text to define each group rather than a number.

- **Gender**: This variable simply specifies whether the person was a man (1) or a woman (0).

When conducting hierarchical models we generally work up from a very simple model to more complicated models, and we will take that approach in this chapter. In doing so I hope to illustrate multilevel modelling by attaching it to frameworks that you already understand, such as ANOVA and ANCOVA.

FIGURE 19.5
Diagram to show
the hierarchical
structure of
the cosmetic
surgery data
set. People are
clustered within
clinics. Note that
for each person
there would be a
series of variables
measured:
surgery, BDI, age,
gender, reason
and pre-surgery
quality of life

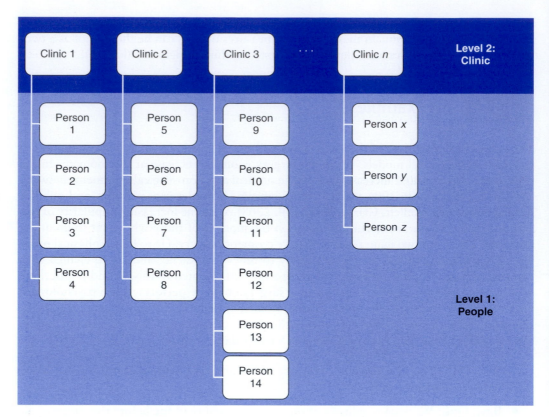

Figure 19.5 shows the hierarchical structure of the data. Essentially, people being treated in the same surgeries are not independent of each other because they will have had surgery from the same surgeon. Surgeons will vary in how good they are, and quality of life will to some extent depend on how well the surgery went (if they did a nice neat job then quality of life should be higher than if they left you with unpleasant scars). Therefore, people within clinics will be more similar to each other than people in different clinics. As such, the person undergoing surgery is the level 1 variable, but there is a level 2 variable, a variable higher in the hierarchy, which is the clinic attended.

19.3.2. Fixed and random coefficients ③

Throughout this book we have discussed effects and variables, and these concepts should be very familiar to you by now. However, we have viewed these effects and variables in a relatively simple way: we have not distinguished between whether something is fixed or random.

What we mean by 'fixed' and 'random' can be a bit confusing because the terms are used in a variety of contexts. You hear people talk about **fixed effects** and **random effects**. An effect in an experiment is said to be a fixed effect if all possible treatment conditions that a researcher is interested in are present in the experiment. An effect is said to be random if the experiment contains only a random sample of possible treatment conditions. This distinction is important because fixed effects can be generalized only to the situations in your experiment, whereas random effects can be generalized beyond the treatment conditions in the experiment (provided that the treatment conditions are representative). For example, in our Viagra example from Chapter 10, the effect is fixed if we say that we are interested only in the three conditions that we had (placebo, low dose and high dose) and we can generalize our findings only to the situation of a placebo, low dose and high dose. However, if we were to say that the three doses were only a sample of possible doses (maybe we could have tried a very high dose), then it is a random effect and we can generalize beyond just placebos, low doses and high doses. All of the effects in this book so far we have treated as fixed effects. The vast majority of academic research that you read will treat variables as fixed effects.

People also talk about **fixed variables** and **random variables**. A fixed variable is one that is not supposed to change over time (e.g., for most people their gender is a fixed variable – it never changes), whereas a random one varies over time (e.g., your weight is likely to fluctuate over time).

In the context of multilevel models we need to make a distinction between **fixed coefficients** and **random coefficients**. In the regressions, ANOVAs and ANCOVAs throughout this book we have assumed that the regression parameters are fixed. We have seen numerous times that a linear model is characterized by two things: the intercept, b_0, and the slope, b_1:

$$Y_i = b_0 + b_1 X_{1i} + \varepsilon_i$$

Note that the outcome (Y), the predictor (X) and the error (ε) all vary as a function of i, which normally represents a particular case of data. In other words, it represents the level 1 variable. If, for example, we wanted to predict Sam's score, we could replace the is with her name:

$$Y_{Sam} = b_0 + b_1 X_{1,Sam} + \varepsilon_{Sam}$$

This is just some basic revision. Now, when we do a regression like this we assume that the bs are fixed and we estimate them from the data. In other words, we're assuming that the model holds true across the entire sample and that for every case of data in the sample we can predict a score using the same values of the gradient and intercept. However, we can also conceptualize these parameters as being random.[2] If we say that a parameter is random then we assume not that it is a fixed value, but that its value can vary. Up until now we have thought of regression models as having **fixed intercepts** and **fixed slopes**, but this opens up three new possibilities for us that are shown in Figure 19.6. This figure uses the data from our ANCOVA example in Chapter 11 and shows the relationship between a person's libido and that of their partner overall (the dashed line) and separately for the three groups in the study (a placebo group, a group that had a low dose of Viagra and a group that had a high dose).

19.3.2.1. The random intercept model ③

The simplest way to introduce random parameters into the model is to assume that the intercepts vary across contexts (or groups) – because the intercepts vary, we call them **random intercepts**. For our libido data this is like assuming that the relationship between libido and partner's libido is the same in the placebo, low- and high-dose groups (i.e., the slope is the same), but that the models for each group are in different locations (i.e., the intercepts are different). This is shown in the top panel of Figure 19.6, in which the models within the different contexts (colours) have the same shape (slope) but are located in different geometric space (they have different intercepts).

[2] In a sense 'random' isn't an intuitive term for us non-statisticians because it implies that values are plucked out of thin air (randomly selected). However, this is not the case – they are carefully estimated just as fixed parameters are.

FIGURE 19.6
Data sets showing
an overall model
(dashed line) and
the models for
separate contexts
within the data
(i.e., groups of
cases)

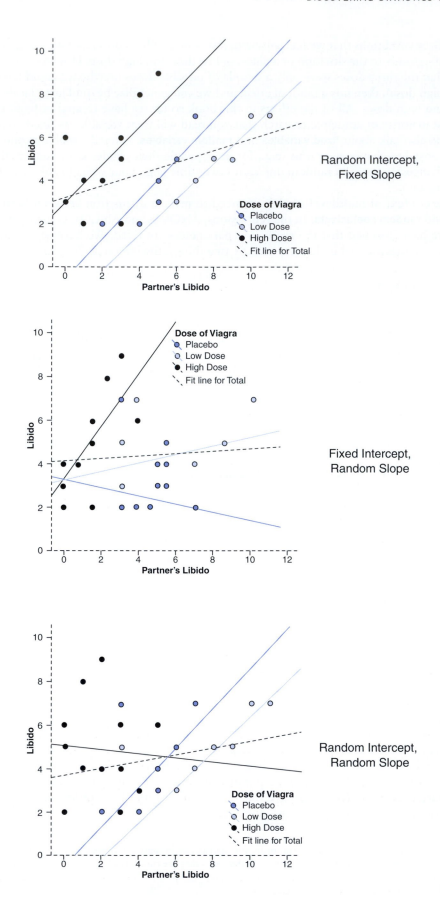

19.3.2.2. Random slope model ③

We can also assume that the slopes vary across contexts – i.e., we assume **random slopes**. For our libido data this is like assuming that the relationship between libido and partner's libido is different in the placebo, low- and high-dose groups (i.e., the slopes are different), but that the models for each group are fixed at the same geometric location (i.e., the intercepts are the same). This is what happens when we violate the assumption of homogeneity of regression slopes in ANCOVA. Homogeneity of regression slopes is the assumption that regression slopes are the same across contexts. If this assumption is not tenable then we can use a multilevel model to explicitly estimate that variability in slopes. This is shown in the middle panel of Figure 19.6 in which the models within the different contexts (colours) converge on a single intercept but have different slopes. It's worth noting that it would be unusual in reality to assume random slopes without also assuming random intercepts because variability in the nature of the relationship (slopes) would normally create variability in the overall level of the outcome variable (intercepts). Therefore, if you assume that slopes are random you would normally also assume that intercepts are random.

19.3.2.3. The random intercept and slope model ③

The most realistic situation is to assume that both intercepts and slopes vary around the overall model. This is shown in the bottom panel of Figure 19.6 in which the models within the different contexts (colours) have different slopes but are also located in different geometric space and so have different intercepts.

19.4. The multilevel model ④

We have seen conceptually what a random intercept, random slope and random intercept and slope model looks like. Now let's look at how we actually represent the models. To keep things concrete, let's use our example. For the sake of simplicity, let's imagine first that we wanted to predict someone's quality of life (QoL) after cosmetic surgery. We can represent this as a linear model as follows:

$$\text{QoL After Surgery}_i = b_0 + b_1\text{Surgery}_i + \varepsilon_i \tag{19.1}$$

We have seen equations like this many times and it represents a linear model: regression, a t-test (in this case) and ANOVA. In this example, we had a contextual variable, which was the clinic in which the cosmetic surgery was conducted. We might expect the effect of surgery on quality of life to vary as a function of which clinic the surgery was conducted at because surgeons will differ in their skill. This variable is a level 2 variable. As such we could allow the model that represents the effect of surgery on quality of life to vary across the different contexts (clinics). We can do this by allowing the intercepts to vary across clinics, or by allowing the slopes to vary across clinics or by allowing both to vary across clinics.

To begin with, let's say we want to include a random intercept for quality of life. All we do is add a component to the intercept that measures the variability in intercepts, u_{0j}. Therefore, the intercept changes from b_0 to become $(b_0 + u_{0j})$. This term estimates the intercept of the overall model fitted to the data, b_0, and the variability of intercepts around that overall model, u_{0j}. The overall model becomes:[3]

$$Y_{ij} = (b_0 + u_{0j}) + b_1 X_{ij} + \varepsilon_{ij} \tag{19.2}$$

---

[3] Some people use gamma (γ), not b, to represent the parameters, but I prefer b because it makes the link to the other linear models that we have used in this book clearer.

The js in the equation reflect levels of the variable over which the intercept varies (in this case the clinic) – the level 2 variable. Another way that we could write this is to take out the error terms so that it looks like an ordinary regression equation except that the intercept has changed from a fixed, b_0, to a random one, b_{0j}, which is defined in a separate equation:

$$Y_{ij} = b_{0j} + b_1 X_{ij} + \varepsilon_{ij}$$
$$b_{0j} = b_0 + u_{0j} \tag{19.3}$$

Therefore, if we want to know the estimated intercept for clinic 7, we simply replace the j with 'clinic 7' in the second equation:

$$b_{0\text{Clinic 7}} = b_0 + u_{0\text{Clinic 7}}$$

If we want to include random slopes for the effect of surgery on quality of life, then all we do is add a component to the slope of the overall model that measures the variability in slopes, u_{1j}. Therefore, the gradient changes from b_1 to become $(b_1 + u_{1j})$. This term estimates the slope of the overall model fitted to the data, b_1, and the variability of slopes in different contexts around that overall model, u_{1j}. The overall model becomes (compare to the random intercept model above):

$$Y_{ij} = b_0 + (b_1 + u_{1j})X_{ij} + \varepsilon_{ij} \tag{19.4}$$

Again we can take the error terms out into a separate equation to make the link to a familiar linear model even clearer. It now looks like an ordinary regression equation except that the slope has changed from a fixed, b_1, to a random one, b_{1j}, which is defined in a separate equation:

$$Y_{ij} = b_{0i} + b_{1j} X_{ij} + \varepsilon_{ij}$$
$$b_{1j} = b_1 + u_{1j} \tag{19.5}$$

If we want to model a situation with random slopes *and* intercepts, then we combine the two models above. We still estimate the intercept and slope of the overall model (b_0 and b_1) but we also include the two terms that estimate the variability in intercepts, u_{0j}, and slopes, u_{1j}. The overall model becomes (compare to the two models above):

$$Y_{ij} = (b_0 + u_{0j}) + (b_1 + u_{1j})X_{ij} + \varepsilon_{ij} \tag{19.6}$$

We can link this more directly to a simple linear model if we take some of these extra terms out into separate equations. We could write this model as a basic linear model, except we've replaced our fixed intercept and slope (b_0 and b_1) with their random counterparts (b_{0j} and b_{1j}):

$$Y_{ij} = b_{0j} + b_{1j} X_{ij} + \varepsilon_{ij}$$
$$b_{0j} = b_0 + u_{0j}$$
$$b_{1j} = b_1 + u_{1j} \tag{19.7}$$

The take-home point is that we're not doing anything terribly different from the rest of the book: it's basically just a posh regression.

Now imagine we wanted to add in another predictor, for example quality of life before surgery. Knowing what we do about multiple regression, we shouldn't be invading the personal space of the idea that we can simply add this variable in with an associated beta:

$$\text{QoL After Surgery}_i = b_0 + b_1\text{Surgery}_i + b_2\text{QoL Before Surgery}_i + \varepsilon_i \qquad (19.8)$$

This is all just revision of ideas from earlier in the book. Remember also that the i represents the level 1 variable, in this case the people we tested. Therefore, we can predict a given person's quality of life after surgery by replacing the i with their name:

$$\text{QoL After}_\text{Sam} = b_0 + b_1\text{Surgery}_\text{Sam} + b_2\text{QoL Before}_\text{Sam} + \varepsilon_\text{Sam}$$

Now, if we want to allow the intercept of the effect of surgery on quality of life after surgery to vary across contexts then we simply replace b_0 with b_{0j}. If we want to allow the slope of the effect of surgery on quality of life after surgery to vary across contexts then we replace b_1 with b_{1j}. So, even with a random intercept and slope, our model stays much the same:

$$\begin{aligned}
\text{QoL After}_{ij} &= b_{0j} + b_{1j}\text{Surgery}_{ij} + b_2\text{QoL Before}_{ij} + \varepsilon_{ij} \\
b_{0j} &= b_0 + u_{0j} \\
b_{1j} &= b_1 + u_{1j}
\end{aligned} \qquad (19.9)$$

Remember that the j in the equation relates to the level 2 contextual variable (clinic in this case). So, if we wanted to predict someone's score we wouldn't just do it from their name, but also from the clinic they attended. Imagine our guinea pig Sam had her surgery done at clinic 7, then we could replace the is and js as follows:

$$\begin{aligned}
\text{QoL After Surgery}_{\text{Sam, Clinic 7}} \\
= b_{0\text{Clinic7}} + b_{1\text{Clinic7}}\text{Surgery}_{\text{Sam, Clinic7}} \\
+ b_2\text{QoL Before Surgery}_{\text{Sam, Clinic7}} + \varepsilon_{\text{Sam, Clinic7}}
\end{aligned}$$

I want to sum up by just reiterating that all we're really doing in a multilevel model is a fancy regression in which we allow either the intercepts or slopes, or both, to vary across different contexts. All that really changes is that for every parameter that we allow to be random, we get an estimate of the variability of that parameter as well as the parameter itself. So, there isn't anything terribly complicated; we can add new predictors to the model and for each one decide whether its regression parameter is fixed or random.

19.4.1. Assessing the fit and comparing multilevel models ④

As in logistic regression (Chapter 8) the overall fit of a multilevel model is tested using a chi-square likelihood ratio test (see section 18.4.3) and **R** reports the -2log-likelihood ($-2LL$, see section 8.3.1). Essentially, the smaller the value of the log-likelihood, the better. **R** also produces two adjusted versions of the log-likelihood value, both of which were described briefly in section 7.6.3. Both of these can be interpreted in the same way as the log-likelihood, but they have been corrected for various things:

- *Akaike's information criterion* (**AIC**): This is basically a goodness-of-fit measure that is corrected for model complexity. That just means that it takes into account how many parameters have been estimated.

- *Schwarz's Bayesian criterion* (**BIC**): This statistic is comparable to the AIC, although it is slightly more conservative (it corrects more harshly for the number of parameters being estimated). It should be used when sample sizes are large and the number of parameters is small.

Neither the AIC or BIC are intrinsically interpretable (it's not meaningful to talk about their values being large or small *per se*); however, they are useful as a way of comparing models. The value of AIC and BIC can be compared to their equivalent values in other models. In all cases smaller values mean better-fitting models.

Many writers recommend building up multilevel models starting with a 'basic' model in which all parameters are fixed and then adding in random coefficients as appropriate and exploring confounding variables (Raudenbush & Bryk, 2002; Twisk, 2006). One advantage of doing this is that you can compare the fit of the model as you make parameters random, or as you add in variables. To compare models we simply subtract the log-likelihood of the new model from the value for the old:

$$\chi^2_{\text{Change}} = (-2\text{Log-Likelihood}_{\text{Old}}) - (-2\text{Log-Likelihood}_{\text{New}})$$
$$df_{\text{Change}} = \text{Number of Parameters}_{\text{Old}} - \text{Number of Parameters}_{\text{New}}$$

(19.10)

This equation is the same as equations (18.5) and (8.6). There are two caveats to this equation: (1) it works only if full maximum-likelihood estimation is used (and not restricted maximal likelihood – see R's Souls' Tip 19.1); and (2) the new model must contain all of the effects of the older model.

19.4.2. Types of covariance structures ④

If you have any random effects or repeated measures in your multilevel model then you have to decide upon the *covariance structure* of your data. If you have random effects and repeated measures then you can specify different covariance structures for each. The covariance structure simply specifies the form of the variance–covariance matrix (a matrix in which the diagonal elements are variances and the off-diagonal elements are covariances). There are various forms that this matrix could take and we have to tell **R** what form we think it *does* take. Of course we might not know what form it takes (most of the time we'll be taking an educated guess), so it is sometimes useful to run the model with different covariance structures defined and use the goodness-of-fit indices (the AIC and BIC) to see whether changing the covariance structure improves the fit of the model (remember that a smaller value of these statistics means a better-fitting model).

The covariance structure is important because **R** uses it as a starting point to estimate the model parameters. As such, you will get different results depending on which covariance structure you choose. If you specify a covariance structure that is too simple then you are more likely to make a Type I error (finding a parameter is significant when in reality it is not), but if you specify one that is too complex then you run the risk of a Type II error (finding parameters to be non-significant when in reality they are). **R** can implement many different covariance structures. We will look at four of the commonest covariance structures to give you a feel for what they are and when they should be used. In each case I use a representation of the variance–covariance matrix to illustrate. With all of these matrices you could imagine that the rows and columns represents four different clinics in our cosmetic surgery data:

$$\begin{pmatrix} 1 & 0 & 0 & 0 \\ 0 & 1 & 0 & 0 \\ 0 & 0 & 1 & 0 \\ 0 & 0 & 0 & 1 \end{pmatrix}$$

Variance components: This covariance structure is very simple and assumes that all random effects are independent (this is why all of the covariances in the matrix are 0). Variances of random effects are assumed to be the same (hence why they are 1 in the matrix) and sum to the variance of the outcome variable. This covariance structure is sometimes called the independence model.

$$\begin{pmatrix} \sigma_1^2 & 0 & 0 & 0 \\ 0 & \sigma_2^2 & 0 & 0 \\ 0 & 0 & \sigma_3^2 & 0 \\ 0 & 0 & 0 & \sigma_4^2 \end{pmatrix}$$

Diagonal: This variance structure is like variance components except that variances are assumed to be heterogeneous (this is why the diagonal of the matrix is made up of different variance terms). This structure again assumes that variances are independent and, therefore, that all of the covariances are 0.

$$\begin{pmatrix} 1 & \rho & \rho^2 & \rho^3 \\ \rho & 1 & \rho & \rho^2 \\ \rho^2 & \rho & 1 & \rho \\ \rho^3 & \rho^2 & \rho & 1 \end{pmatrix}$$

AR(1): This stands for first-order autoregressive structure. In layman's terms this means that the relationship between variances changes in a systematic way. If you imagine the rows and columns of the matrix to be points in time, then it assumes that the correlation between repeated measurements is highest at adjacent time points. So, in the first column, the correlation between time points 1 and 2 is ρ; let's assume that this value is .3. As we move to time point 3, the correlation between time point 1 and 3 is ρ^2, or .09. In other words, it has decreased: scores at time point 1 are more related to scores at time 2 than they are to scores at time 3. At time 4, the correlation goes down again to ρ^3 or .027. So, the correlations between time points next to each other are assumed to be ρ, scores two intervals apart are assumed to have correlations of ρ^2, and scores three intervals apart are assumed to have correlations of ρ^3. So the correlation between scores gets smaller over time. Variances are assumed to be homogeneous, but there is a version of this covariance structure where variance can be heterogeneous. This structure is often used for repeated-measures data (especially when measurements are taken over time such as in growth models).

$$\begin{pmatrix} \sigma_1^2 & \sigma_{21} & \sigma_{31} & \sigma_{41} \\ \sigma_{21} & \sigma_2^2 & \sigma_{32} & \sigma_{42} \\ \sigma_{31} & \sigma_{32} & \sigma_3^2 & \sigma_{43} \\ \sigma_{41} & \sigma_{42} & \sigma_{43} & \sigma_4^2 \end{pmatrix}$$

Unstructured: This covariance structure is completely general. Covariances are assumed to be completely unpredictable: they do not conform to a systematic pattern.

19.5. Some practical issues ③

19.5.1. Assumptions ③

Multilevel linear models are an extension of regression, so all of the assumptions for regression apply to multilevel models (see section 7.7.2). There is a caveat, though, which is that the assumptions of independence and independent errors can sometimes be solved by a multilevel model because the purpose of this model is to factor in the correlations between cases caused by higher-level variables. As such, if a lack of independence is being caused by a level 2 or level 3 variable then a multilevel model should make this problem go away (although not always). As such, try to check the usual assumptions in the usual way.

There are two additional assumptions in multilevel models that relate to the random coefficients. These coefficients are assumed to be normally distributed around the overall model. So, in a random intercepts model the intercepts in the different contexts are assumed to be normally distributed around the overall model. Similarly, in a random slopes model, the slopes of the models in different contexts are assumed to be normally distributed.

Also it's worth mentioning that multicollinearity can be a particular problem in multilevel models if you have interactions that cross levels in the data hierarchy (cross-level interactions). However, centring predictors can help matters enormously (Kreft & de Leeuw, 1998), and we will see how to centre predictors in section 19.5.3.

19.5.2. Sample size and power ③

As you might well imagine, the situation with power and sample size is very complex indeed. One complexity is that we are trying to make decisions about our power to detect both fixed and random effects coefficients. Kreft and de Leeuw (1998) do a tremendous job of making sense of things for us. Essentially, the take-home message is the more data, the better. As more levels are introduced into the model, more parameters need to be estimated and the larger the sample sizes need to be. Kreft and de Leeuw conclude that if you are looking for cross-level interactions then you should aim to have more than 20 contexts (groups) in the higher-level variable, and that group sizes 'should not be too small'. They conclude by saying that there are so many factors involved in multilevel analysis that it is impossible to produce any meaningful rules of thumb.

Twisk (2006) agrees that the number of contexts relative to individuals within those contexts is important. He also points out that standard sample size and power calculations can be used but then 'corrected' for the multilevel component of the analysis (by factoring, among other things, the intraclass correlation). However, there are two corrections that he discusses that yield very different sample sizes! He recommends using sample size calculations with caution.

19.5.3. Centring variables ④

Centring refers to the process of transforming a variable into deviations around a fixed point. This fixed point can be any value that you choose, but typically we use the grand mean. We have already come across a form of centring way back in Chapter 1, when we discovered how to compute z-scores. When we calculate a z-score we take each score and subtract from it the mean of all scores (this centres the values at 0), and then divide by the standard deviation (this changes the units of measurement to standard deviations). When we centre a variable around the mean we simply subtract the mean from all of the scores: this centres the variables around 0.

There are two forms of centring that are typically used in multilevel modelling: **grand mean centring** and **group mean centring**. Grand mean centring means that for a given variable we take each score and subtract from it the mean of all scores (for that variable). Group mean centring means that for a given variable we take each score and subtract from it the mean of the scores (for that variable) within a given group. In both cases it is usually only level 1 predictors that are centred (in our cosmetic surgery example this would be predictors such as age, BDI and pre-surgery quality of life). If group mean centring is used then a level 1 variable is typically centred around means of a level 2 variable (in our cosmetic surgery data this would mean that, for example, the age of a person would be centred around the mean age for the clinic at which the person had their surgery).

Centring can be used in ordinary multiple regression too, and because this form of regression is already familiar to you I'd like to begin by looking at the effects of centring in regression. In multiple regression the intercept represents the value of the outcome when all of the predictors take a value of 0. There are some predictors for which a value of 0 makes little sense. For example, if you were using heart rate as a predictor variable then a value of 0 would be meaningless (no one will have a heart rate of 0 unless they are dead). As such, the intercept in this case has no real-world use: why would you want to know the value of the outcome when heart rate was 0 given than no alive person would even have a heart rate that low? Centring heart rate around its mean changes the meaning of the intercept. The intercept becomes the value of the outcome when heart rate is its average value. In more general terms, if all predictors are centred around their mean then the intercept is the value of the outcome when all predictors are the value of their mean. Centring can, therefore, be a useful tool for interpretation when a value of 0 for the predictor is meaningless.

The effect of centring in multilevel models, however, is much more complicated. There are some excellent reviews that look in detail at the effects of centring on multilevel models

(Enders & Tofighi, 2007; Kreft & de Leeuw, 1998; Kreft, de Leeuw, & Aiken, 1995), and here I will just give a very basic précis of what they say. Essentially if you fit a multilevel model using the raw score predictors and then fit the same model but with grand mean centred predictors then the resulting models are equivalent. By this, I mean that they will fit the data equally well, have the same predicted values, and the residuals will be the same. The parameters themselves (the *b*s) will, of course, be different but there will be a direct relationship between the parameters from the two models (i.e., they can be directly transformed into each other). Therefore, grand mean centring doesn't change the model, but it would change your interpretation of the parameters (you can't interpret them as though they are raw scores). When group mean centring is used the picture is much more complicated. In this situation the raw score model is not equivalent to the centred model in either the fixed part or the random part. One exception is when only the intercept is random (which arguably is an unusual situation), and the group means are reintroduced into the model as level 2 variables (Kreft & de Leeuw, 1998).

The decision about whether to centre or not is quite complicated and you really need to make the decision yourself in a given analysis. Centring can be a useful way to combat multicollinearity between predictor variables. It's also helpful when predictors do not have a meaningful zero point. Finally, multilevel models with centred predictors tend to be more stable, and estimates from these models can be treated as more or less independent of each other, which might be desirable. If group mean centring is used then the group means should be reintroduced as a level 2 variable unless you want to look at the effect of your 'group' or level 2 variable uncorrected for the mean effect of the centred level 1 predictor, such as when fitting a model when time is your main explanatory variable (Kreft & de Leeuw, 1998).

The question arises of whether grand mean or group mean centring is 'better'. People doing statistics often fixate on their being a 'best' way to do things, but the 'best' method often depends on what it is that you're actually trying to do. Centring is a good example. Some people make a decision about whether to use group or grand mean centring based on some statistical criterion; however, there is no statistically correct choice between not centring, group mean centring and grand mean centring (Kreft et al., 1995). Instead, Enders and Tofighi (2007) recommend making decisions based on the substantive research question. In short, they make four recommendations when analysing data with a two-level hierarchy: (1) group mean clustering should be used if the primary interest is in an association between variables measured at level 1 (i.e., the aforementioned relationship between surgery and quality of life after surgery); (2) grand mean centring is appropriate when the primary interest is in the level 2 variable but you want to control for the level 1 covariate (i.e., you want to look at the effect of clinic on quality of life after surgery while controlling for the type of surgery); (3) both types of centring can be used to look at the differential influence of a variable at level 1 and 2 (i.e., is the effect of surgery on quality of life post-surgery different at the clinic level to the client level?); and (4) group mean centring is preferable for examining cross-level interactions (e.g., the interactive effect of clinic and surgery on quality of life after surgery).

OLIVER TWISTED

Please Sir, can I have some more … centring?

'Recentgin', babbles Oliver as he stumbles drunk out of Mrs Moonshine's alcohol emporium. 'I've had some recent gin.' I think you mean *centring*, Oliver, not *recentgin*. If you want to know how to centre your variables using **R**, then the additional material for this chapter on the companion website will tell you.

19.6. Multilevel modelling in R ④

Multilevel modelling can be done with specialist software such as MLwiN and HLM. There are several excellent books that compare **R** with various other packages (Tabachnick & Fidell, 2001; Twisk, 2006). **R** is more versatile than packages such as SPSS in that it can do multilevel modelling when the outcome variable is categorical. However, the packages that do multilevel models in **R** do not currently produce bootstrap estimates of the model parameters, and these can be a very useful way to circumvent pesky distributional assumptions (see section 5.8.4).

We saw in section 19.4.1 that it is useful to build up models starting with a 'basic' model in which all parameters are fixed and then add random coefficients as appropriate before exploring confounding variables. We will take this approach in our example.

19.6.1. Packages for multilevel modelling in R ①

There are several packages that can be used for multilevel models. Two of the most used are: *nlme* (Pinheiro, Bates, DebRoy, Sarkar, & R Development Core Team, 2010) and *lme4* (Bates & Maechler, 2010). I am going to focus on the package *nlme* (*non linear mixed effect*) because, unlike *lme4*, it enables you to model the covariance structure, which will be useful when we come to look at growth models towards the end of the chapter.

For the examples in this chapter you will need the packages *car* (to recode variables), *nlme* (for the multilevel analysis), *ggplot2* (for graphs), and *reshape* (to restructure the data). If you do not have these packages installed, you can install them by executing the following commands:

```
install.packages("car"); install.packages("ggplot2"); install.
packages("nlme"); install.packages("reshape")
```

You then need to load these packages by executing the commands:

```
library(car); library(ggplot2); library(nlme); library(reshape)
```

19.6.2. Entering the data ②

Data entry depends a bit on the type of multilevel model that you wish to run: the data layout is slightly different when the same variables are measured at several points in time. However, we will look at the case of repeated-measures data in a second example. In this first example, the situation we have is very much like multiple regression in that data from each person who had surgery are not measured over multiple time points. Figure 19.7 shows the data layout. Each row represents a case of data (in this case a person who had surgery). Their scores on the various variables are simply entered in different columns. So, for example, the first person was 31 years old, had a BDI score of 12, was in the waiting list control group (**Surgery** = 0) at clinic 1, was female (**Gender** = 0) and was waiting for surgery to change her appearance (**Reason** = 0).

To access these data we need to create a dataframe, which I have called *surgeryData*, that contains the data from the file **CosmeticSurgery.dat**. This file stores the data as tab-delimited text, so we can import it into the dataframe using the following command (I'm assuming as always that you have set the working directory to be where the file is stored):

```
surgeryData = read.delim("Cosmetic Surgery.dat", header = TRUE)
```

FIGURE 19.7
Data layout
for multilevel
modelling with no
repeated measure

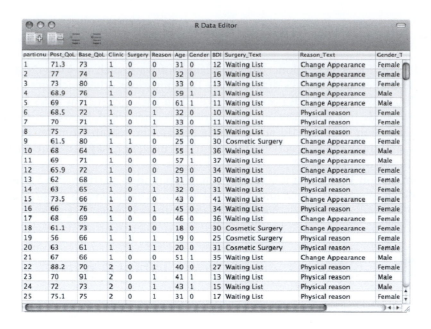

19.6.3.   Picturing the data ②

Before we begin the analysis it's a good idea to have a look at the data. Our main example looks at **Surgery** and baseline quality of life (**Base_QoL**) as a predictors of quality of life after surgery (**Post_QoL**). Remember that the surgery was conducted at one of 10 clinics. Therefore, to begin with we could simply look at the relationship between baseline quality of life and post-surgery quality of life separately for the two surgery conditions (cosmetic surgery vs. waiting list). We might also want to graph this separately for the 10 clinics. We can use what we learnt about *ggplot2* in Chapter 4 to produce this plot; the resulting graph is shown in Figure 19.8.

SELF-TEST

✓ Using what you know about *ggplot2*, produce
  the graph described above. Display the levels of
  Surgery_Text in colours, and use **Clinic** to produce
  different graphs within a grid.

19.6.4.   Ignoring the data structure: ANOVA ②

First of all, let's ground the example in something very familiar to us: ANOVA. Let's say for the time being that we were interested only in the effect that surgery has on post-operative quality of life. We could analyse this with a simple one-way independent ANOVA (or indeed a *t*-test), and the model is described by equation (19.1).

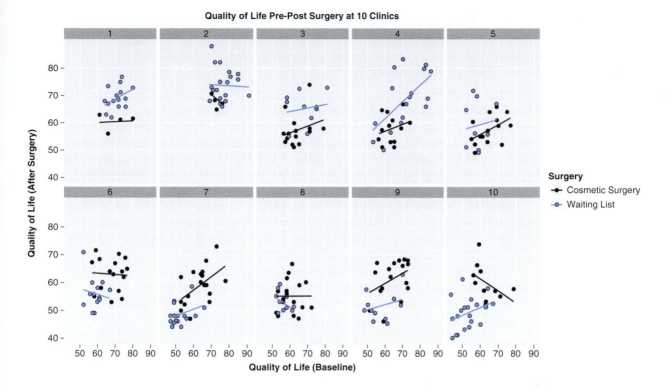

Quality of Life Pre-Post Surgery at 10 Clinics

FIGURE 19.8

Graph of the relationship between baseline and post-surgery quality of life for people who had cosmetic surgery compared to those on the waiting list at 10 different clinics.

SELF-TEST

✓ Using what you know about ANOVA, conduct a one-way ANOVA using **Surgery** as the predictor and **Post_QoL** as the outcome.

In reality we wouldn't do an ANOVA, I'm just using it as a way of showing you that multilevel models are not big and scary, but are simply extensions of what we have done before. Output 19.1 shows the results of the ANOVA that you should get if you did the self-test. We find a non-significant effect of surgery on quality of life, $F(1, 274) = 0.33$, $p > .05$.

```
           Df  Sum Sq Mean Sq F value Pr(>F)
Surgery     1    28.6  28.620  0.3302  0.566
Residuals 274 23747.9  86.671
```

Output 19.1

We have also seen that we can think of ANOVA as a general linear model in which an outcome (in this case **Post_QoL**) is predicted from group membership (in this case

Surgery). Therefore, we could fit the same model but using the *lm()* function that we first encountered in Chapter 7.

```
surgeryLinearModel<-lm(Post_QoL ~ Surgery, data = surgeryData)
summary(surgeryLinearModel)
```

We have used the function *lm* (linear model) to create an object called *surgeryLinearModel*. The commands in brackets tell *lm()* what model we want to fit; as we have seen elsewhere in this book, the '~' means 'predicted from'. So, we have specified that we want **Post_QoL** predicted from **Surgery**. In other words, we have simply written out the linear model in equation (19.1) but without the *b*s. The rest of the options simply tell *lm()* to fit the model on the dataframe that we just created (*data = surgeryData*). Finally *summary(surgeryLinearModel)* prints the model parameters to the **R** console.

Output 19.2 shows the main table for the model. Compare this table with Output 19.1 and you'll see that there is basically no difference: we get a non-significant effect of surgery with an *F* of 0.33, and a *p* of .56. The point I want you to absorb here is that if we ignore the hierarchical structure of the data then what we are left with is something very familiar: an ANOVA/regression. The numbers are more or less exactly the same; all that has changed is that we have used different commands to get to the same end point.

```
Coefficients:
                     Estimate Std. Error t value Pr(>|t|)
(Intercept)           59.2710     0.8134  72.869   <2e-16 ***
Surgery[T.Waiting List]  0.6449     1.1222   0.575    0.566
---
Signif. codes:  0 '***' 0.001 '**' 0.01 '*' 0.05 '.' 0.1 ' ' 1

Residual standard error: 9.31 on 274 degrees of freedom
Multiple R-squared: 0.001204,    Adjusted R-squared: -0.002442
F-statistic: 0.3302 on 1 and 274 DF,  p-value: 0.566
```

Output 19.2

19.6.5.   Ignoring the data structure: ANCOVA ②

We have seen that there is no effect of cosmetic surgery on quality of life, but we did not take into account the quality of life before surgery. Let's, therefore, extend the example a little to look at the effect of the surgery on quality of life while taking into account the quality of life scores before surgery. Our model is now described by equation (19.8). You could do this analysis with an ANCOVA, using the *aov()* function or as a linear model using the *lm()* function. As in the previous section we'll run the analysis both ways, just to illustrate that we're doing the same thing when we run a hierarchical model.

SELF-TEST

✓ Using what you know about ANCOVA, conduct a one-way ANCOVA using **Surgery** as the predictor, **Post_QoL** as the outcome and **Base_QoL** as the covariate.

Output 19.3 shows the results of the ANCOVA that you should get if you did the self-test. The top output shows the Type I sums of squares, whereas the bottom is the same model but with Type III sums of squares (they differ slightly for baseline quality of life because we have an unbalanced design). With baseline quality of life included we find a significant effect of surgery on quality of life, $F(1, 273) = 4.04$, $p < .05$. Baseline quality of life also predicted quality of life after surgery, $F(1, 273) = 214.89$, $p < .001$.

```
              Df  Sum Sq Mean Sq  F value  Pr(>F)
Base_QoL       1 10291.4 10291.4 211.4321 < 2e-16 ***
Surgery        1   196.8   196.8   4.0435 0.04533 *
Residuals    273 13288.3    48.7
---
Signif. codes:  0 '***' 0.001 '**' 0.01 '*' 0.05 '.' 0.1 ' ' 1


Model:
Post_QoL ~ Base_QoL + Surgery
         Df Sum of Sq   RSS    AIC  F value   Pr(F)
<none>               13288 1075.3
Base_QoL  1  10459.6 23748 1233.5 214.8876 < 2e-16 ***
Surgery   1    196.8 13485 1077.3   4.0435 0.04533 *
---
Signif. codes:  0 '***' 0.001 '**' 0.01 '*' 0.05 '.' 0.1 ' ' 1
```

Output 19.3

We can also think of ANCOVA within the general linear model framework: the outcome (in this case **Post_QoL**) is predicted from group membership (in this case **Surgery**) and the covariate (**Base_QoL**). As with before the covariate was added, we can fit the model but using the *lm()* function by simply adding the baseline quality of life variable to the equation.

```
surgeryLinearModel<-lm(Post_QoL ~ Surgery + Base_QoL, data = surgeryData)
summary(surgeryLinearModel)
```

As before, the *lm()* function creates an object called *surgeryLinearModel*. We have specified that **Post_QoL** is the outcome variable and that it is predicted from (the ~ symbol) **Surgery** and baseline quality of life (**Base_QoL**). Again, notice how the *Post_QoL~Surgery + Base_QoL* is basically just equation (19.8) without the *b*s. The rest of the function specifies the data (*data = surgeryData*) and prints a summary of the model (*summary(surgeryLinearModel)*).

Output 19.4 shows the main table for the model. Compare this table with Output 19.3 and you'll see that again there is no difference: we get a significant effect of surgery with a *t* of −2.011, $p < .05$, and a significant effect of baseline quality of life with a *t* of 14.66, $p < .001$. We can also see that the regression coefficient for surgery is −1.70.

Hopefully this exercise, as well as being good revision, has convinced you that we're just doing a regression here, something you have been doing throughout this book. Multilevel models are not radically different, and if you think about it as just an extension of what you already know, then it's really relatively easy to understand. So, having shown you that we can do basic analyses through the linear models function, let's now use its power to factor in the hierarchical structure of the data.

```
Call:
lm(formula = Post_QoL ~ Surgery + Base_QoL, data = surgeryData)

Residuals:
     Min       1Q   Median       3Q      Max
-13.4142  -5.1326  -0.6495   4.0540  23.5005
```

```
Coefficients:
             Estimate Std. Error t value Pr(>|t|)
(Intercept) 18.14702    2.90767   6.241 1.65e-09 ***
Surgery     -1.69723    0.84404  -2.011   0.0453 *
Base_QoL     0.66504    0.04537  14.659  < 2e-16 ***
---
Signif. codes:  0 '***' 0.001 '**' 0.01 '*' 0.05 '.' 0.1 ' ' 1

Residual standard error: 6.977 on 273 degrees of freedom
Multiple R-squared: 0.4411,      Adjusted R-squared: 0.437
F-statistic: 107.7 on 2 and 273 DF,  p-value: < 2.2e-16
```

Output 19.4

To sum up, we have seen that when we factor in the pre-surgery quality of life scores, which themselves significantly predict post-surgery quality of life scores, surgery seems to positively affect quality of life. However, at this stage we have ignored the fact that our data have a hierarchical structure. Essentially we have violated the independence assumption because scores from people who had their surgery at the same clinic are likely to be related to each other (and certainly more related than with people at different clinics). We have seen that violating the assumption of independence can have some quite drastic consequences (see section 10.3). However, rather than just panic and gibber about our *F*-ratio being inaccurate, we can model this covariation within clinics explicitly by including the hierarchical data structure in our analysis.

19.6.6. Assessing the need for a multilevel model ③

The first step in a multilevel analysis such as this is to assess the need to do it in the first place. If there is not significant variation across contexts in the first place then doing a multilevel model is simply a perverse exercise in mental flagellation. If there is little evidence of variation across contexts then save yourself a lot of pain and just do a regression/ANOVA/ whatever variant of the general linear model that you feel like doing.

Ascertaining whether there is variation over your contexts is fairly straightforward. First, we need to fit a baseline model in which we include only the intercept; next, we fit a model that allows intercepts to vary over contexts; finally we compare these two models to see whether the fit has improved as a result of allowing intercepts to vary. If it has, we jump on the runaway train to multilevel insanity; if it has not, we do a little dance of joy into the loving arms of a simpler life.

In our surgery example then, we first need to get **R** to fit a baseline model that includes only the intercept. This is done using the *gls()* function (*generalized least squares*).[4]

```
interceptOnly <-gls(Post_QoL ~ 1, data = surgeryData, method = "ML")
summary(interceptOnly)
```

The format of the *gls()* function is very much like the *lm()* function that we have encountered before. In this example, we have asked **R** to create an object called *interceptOnly*, and we have specified that **Post_QoL** is the outcome variable and that it is predicted from (~)

---

[4] You might wonder why we don't simply use the *lm()* command. To compare models we need them to be computed in the same way. Multilevel models are estimated using maximum likelihood methods and generalized least squares use this method too, so we can compare these models. However, *lm()* used ordinary least squares methods and so can't be compared to a model estimated using maximum likelihood.

only the intercept (the '1' in the function translates as 'intercept'). The rest of the function specifies the data (*data = surgeryData*) and how to estimate the model (*method = "ML"*). The *method* option is very important. If you do not include it (i.e., use the default option), then **R** will use restricted maximum-likelihood methods (these can also be applied explicitly by writing *method = "REML"*). However, we have chosen to use maximum-likelihood estimation (*method = "ML"*). There are pros and cons to both (see R's Souls' Tip 19.1) but if you want to compare models as you build them up, you should use maximum-likelihood estimation. The final option (*summary(interceptOnly)*) is optional and prints the summary of the model shown in Output 19.5.

R's Souls' Tip 19.1 Estimation ③

R gives you the choice of two methods for estimating the parameters in the analysis: maximum likelihood (ML), which we have encountered before, and restricted maximum likelihood (REML). The conventional wisdom seems to be that ML produces more accurate estimates of fixed regression parameters, whereas REML produces more accurate estimates of random variances (Twisk, 2006). As such, the choice of estimation procedure depends on whether your hypotheses are focused on the fixed regression parameters or on estimating variances of the random effects. However, in many situations the choice of ML or REML will make only small differences to the parameter estimates. Also, if you want to compare models you must use ML.

```
Generalized least squares fit by maximum likelihood
  Model: Post_QoL ~ 1
  Data: surgeryData
       AIC       BIC      logLik
  2017.124 2024.365  -1006.562

Coefficients:
               Value Std.Error   t-value p-value
(Intercept) 59.60978 0.5596972 106.5036       0

Standardized residuals:
       Min         Q1        Med        Q3       Max
-2.1127754 -0.7875625 -0.1734394 0.7962286 3.0803354

Residual standard error: 9.281527
Degrees of freedom: 276 total; 275 residual
```

Output 19.5

Next, we need to fit the same model, but this time allowing the intercepts to vary across contexts, in this case we want them to vary across clinics. We do this by using the *lme* (linear mixed effect) function. In fact, this is the function that you'll use throughout the rest of the chapter. The format of this function is much the same as *lm()* and *gls()*; the only difference is that we need to specify the random part of the model using the option $random = x|y$, in which x is an equation specifying the random parts of the model and y is the contextual variable or variables across which we want to model variance. In the current example, we are trying to model intercepts that vary across clinics; therefore, we could add the instruction $random = \sim1|Clinic$. Remember that we use '1' to denote the intercept, and that **Clinic** is the variable that contains information about the clinic that a given person attended. The resulting command is:

```
randomInterceptOnly <-lme(Post_QoL ~ 1, data = surgeryData, random =
~1|Clinic, method = "ML")
summary(randomInterceptOnly)
```

As before, executing this command creates a model (this time I've called it *random-InterceptOnly*), that predicts post-surgery quality of life from only the intercept (*Post_QoL~1*), but also allows intercepts to vary across clinics (*random = \sim1|Clinic*). We have again asked for maximum-likelihood estimation (*method = "ML"*). You can use *summary(randomInterceptOnly)* to view the model summary (Output 19.6).

```
Linear mixed-effects model fit by maximum likelihood
 Data: surgeryData
        AIC       BIC     logLik
  1911.473 1922.334 -952.7364

Random effects:
 Formula: ~1 | Clinic
         (Intercept) Residual
StdDev:    5.909691 7.238677

Fixed effects: Post_QoL ~ 1
              Value Std.Error  DF  t-value p-value
(Intercept) 60.08377  1.923283 266 31.24022       0

Standardized Within-Group Residuals:
       Min        Q1        Med        Q3        Max
-1.8828507 -0.7606631 -0.1378732  0.7075242  2.8607949

Number of Observations: 276
Number of Groups: 10
```

Output 19.6

To see whether allowing the intercepts to vary improves the model we can do several things. First, we can compare the fit of the model using indices such as AIC and BIC. If you compare Output 19.5 with Output 19.6 you'll see that the BIC when only the intercept was included is 2024.37 but decreases to 1922.33 when intercepts are allowed to vary. Remember that smaller values of BIC indicate a better fit of the data, so this gives us an indication that by allowing intercepts to vary the model fit has improved (BIC has decreased). This is all very well, but it does not give us an objective answer to whether the improvement in fit is 'significant' or big enough for us to continue down the multilevel path.

The second thing we can do is test the change in the $-2LL$ (equation (19.10)). We saw earlier that to be able to do this (1) full maximum-likelihood estimation must be used (and we have used this method); and (2) the new model contains all of the effects of the older model (this is true also, the models are identical except that we added a parameter reflecting the variability in intercepts across clinics). The log-likelihood is given in the outputs for each model and we could simply multiply these values by -2 to get the $-2LL$. We can also get **R** to do this for us for each model, and this has an advantage in that it will also tell us the degrees of freedom on which each log-liklihood is based. We can use the function *logLik()* for each model and then type '*−2*' to multiply by −2. To obtain the −2*LL* for our two models, we would therefore type:

```
logLik(interceptOnly)*-2
logLik(randomInterceptOnly)*-2
```

The resulting output should reveal that the model with random intercepts has a −2*LL* of 2013.12 based on three degrees of freedom, whereas the model with only the intercept had a −2*LL* of 19.05.47, based on two degrees of freedom. Therefore:

$$\chi^2_{change} = 2013.12 - 1905.47 = 107.65$$
$$df_{change} = 3 - 2 = 1$$

If we look at the critical values for the chi-square statistic with 1 degree of freedom in the Appendix, they are 3.84 ($p < .05$) and 6.63 ($p < .01$); therefore, this change is highly significant.

A simpler way to do much the same thing is to use the *anova()* function (section 7.8.4). For these types of models, this function compares the change in −2*LL* without you having to compute it and produces an exact significance for this change. The same caveats as before apply: you should have used maximum likelihood and the models should be nested (that is, models higher up the chain need to contain all of the effects that were in models earlier in the chain). We can use this function as follows to compare our two models:

```
anova(interceptOnly, randomInterceptOnly)
```

The resulting Output 19.7 shows the fit indices for each model, but most important shows the value of change in the −2*LL*, the likelihood ratio, that we computed above (we can feel fairly smug that the value of 107.65 matches our earlier calculations). It also shows the degrees of freedom for each model (so that we can verify that the change in degrees of freedom is 1 as we previously calculated). Finally, it shows a *p*-value, which is highly significant and verifies our earlier conclusion that it is important that we model the variability in intercepts because when we do the fit of our model is significantly improved. The change in the −2*LL* has a chi-square distribution, so we can report this statistic in the normal way, $\chi^2(1) = 107.65$, $p < .0001$. We can conclude then that the intercepts vary significantly across the different clinics. Multilevel madness must ensue.

```
Model df  AIC     BIC     logLik   Test  L.Ratio p-value
 1   2 2017.12 2024.36 -1006.56
 2   3 1911.47 1922.33  -952.73 1 vs 2 107.6517  <.0001
```

Output 19.7

19.6.7. Adding in fixed effects ③

We have seen that intercepts vary significantly across clinics. The model that we currently have is this:

$$\text{QoL After Surgery}_{ij} = b_{0j} + \varepsilon_{ij}$$
$$b_{0j} = b_0 + u_{0j}$$

However, we originally had hypotheses about how surgery and baseline quality of life will affect quality of life after surgery. Now that we have a baseline model with random intercepts, we can start to build up the final model by adding these predictors. Let's first add in the **Surgery** variable, which defines whether a person had surgery or was on the waiting list. Our model now becomes:

$$\text{QoL After Surgery}_{ij} = b_{0j} + b_1 \text{Surgery}_{ij} + \varepsilon_{ij}$$
$$b_{0j} = b_0 + u_{0j}$$

To add this predictor we again create a new object in **R** (which I have called *randomInterceptSurgery*) using the *lme()* function. This function is exactly the same as before except that we have replaced *Post_QoL~1* with *Post_QoL~Surgery*. As such, the model now predicts quality of life after surgery from the variable **Surgery** and the intercept.[5]

```
randomInterceptSurgery <-lme(Post_QoL ~ Surgery, data = surgeryData, random
= ~1|Clinic, method = "ML")
summary(randomInterceptSurgery)
```

The resulting Output 19.8 shows this model. Note that the BIC has actually increased from 1922.33 in the previous model to 1924.62 in this one, which suggests that adding **Surgery** has not improved the fit of the model (consistent with this interpretation the log-likelihood has increased also). This interpretation is also borne out by the fixed effect of **Surgery**, which is not significant, $b = 1.66$, $t(265) = -1.83$, $p = .068$.

Although **Surgery** does not appear to be a significant predictor, we had a final model that also included baseline quality of life, so we should add that fixed effect too. Our model is now described by:

$$\text{QoL After Surgery}_{ij} = b_{0j} + b_1 \text{Surgery}_{ij} + b_2 \text{QoL Before Surgery}_{ij} + \varepsilon_{ij}$$
$$b_{0j} = b_0 + u_{0j}$$

To add this predictor we again use *lme()* to create a new object (which I have called *randomInterceptSurgeryQoL*). This function is exactly the same as before except that we have replaced *Post_QoL~Surgery* with *Post_QoL~Surgery + Base_QoL*. Hopefully, you can see that each time we specify a model we simply write out the equation that describes the model, but without the *b*s. As such, the model now predicts quality of life after surgery from the variables **Surgery**, **Base_QoL** and the intercept, with intercepts varying across clinics.

```
randomInterceptSurgeryQoL <-lme(Post_QoL ~ Surgery + Base_QoL, data = sur-
geryData, random = ~1|Clinic, method = "ML")
summary(randomInterceptSurgeryQoL)
```

```
Linear mixed-effects model fit by maximum likelihood
 Data: surgeryData
       AIC       BIC      logLik
  1910.137 1924.619 -951.0686

Random effects:
 Formula: ~1 | Clinic
```

---

[5] You might wonder where the '1' representing the intercept has gone. The intercept is implied within the model so we don't need to specify it, although we could be explicit and write *Post_QoL ~ 1 + Surgery*. The end result would be the same. Similarly, we could write *Post_QoL ~ 0 + Surgery* if we wanted to remove the intercept from the model.

```
                 (Intercept) Residual
StdDev:      6.099513  7.18542

Fixed effects: Post_QoL ~ Surgery
                Value Std.Error   DF  t-value p-value
(Intercept) 59.30517 2.0299632  265 29.21490   0.000
Surgery      1.66583 0.9091314  265  1.83233   0.068
 Correlation:
          (Intr)
Surgery -0.21

Standardized Within-Group Residuals:
       Min          Q1          Med          Q3         Max
-1.8904290  -0.7191399  -0.1420998   0.7177762   2.8644538

Number of Observations: 276
Number of Groups: 10
```

Output 19.8

R's Souls' Tip 19.2 Missing data ③

We saw in R's Souls' Tip 7.1 that missing data create problems for linear models (i.e., regression). Unlike ordinary regresison, multilevel models do not require balanced data sets, so you can have missing data, but you still need to tell **R** what to do with missing cases: just like ordinary regression, if you try to do a multilevel model with missing values in the dataframe you will get an error because *lme()* does not know what to do with these values. As with ordinary regression, you should add *na.action = na.exclude* to the *lme()* function to let it know that it can ignore any NAs it finds in the dataframe. In the surgery data we don't have missing values so we haven't had to use this instruction, but we could easily insert it. For example, the command for our model with Surgery and Base_QoL would become:

```
randomInterceptSurgeryQoL <-lme(Post_QoL ~ Surgery + Base_QoL, data = surgeryData,
random = ~1|Clinic, method = "ML", na.action = na.exclude)
```

```
Linear mixed-effects model fit by maximum likelihood
 Data: surgeryData
      AIC      BIC    logLik
  1847.49 1865.592 -918.745

Random effects:
 Formula: ~1 | Clinic
        (Intercept) Residual
StdDev:    3.039264 6.518986

Fixed effects: Post_QoL ~ Surgery + Base_QoL
                Value Std.Error   DF   t-value p-value
(Intercept) 29.563601  3.471879  264  8.515160  0.0000
Surgery     -0.312999  0.843145  264 -0.371228  0.7108
Base_QoL     0.478630  0.052774  264  9.069465  0.0000
```

```
Correlation:
         (Intr) Surgry
Surgery   0.102
Base_QoL -0.947 -0.222

Standardized Within-Group Residuals:
       Min           Q1          Med          Q3          Max
-1.8872666  -0.7537675  -0.0954987   0.5657241   3.0020852

Number of Observations: 276
Number of Groups: 10
```

Output 19.9

Output 19.9 shows the summary of the final model. Note that the BIC and AIC have both decreased since the previous model (Output 19.8); for example, the BIC has reduced from 1924.62 to 1865.59. This implies a better fitting model. We can have a look at how the fit of the models has improved using the *anova()* function that we used before; the following will compare all three models that we have so far fitted):

```
anova(randomInterceptOnly, randomInterceptSurgery,
randomInterceptSurgeryQoL)
```

Output 19.10 shows the resulting analysis. We start with just varying intercepts (model 1), and we can see that by including surgery as a fixed effect (model 2) we got no significant improvement ($p > .05$). In fact the change in the $-2LL$ is only 3.34, which has a significance of $p = .068$ (note that this is the same significance as for the t that tests the regression parameter of the fixed effect of surgery in Output 19.8). In model 3, we added the effect of baseline quality of life, and this had a dramatic impact. The $-2LL$ changed by 64.65 and this change was highly significant, $\chi^2(1) = 64.65$, $p < .0001$. As we have already noted the AIC and BIC also decrease from model 2 to model 3 showing that the fit is improving.

```
Model df      AIC       BIC      logLik    Test  L.Ratio p-value
1   3 1911.473 1922.334 -952.7364
2   4 1910.137 1924.619 -951.0686 1 vs 2   3.33564  0.0678
3   5 1847.490 1865.592 -918.7450 2 vs 3  64.64721  <.0001
```

Output 19.10

Given that including baseline quality of life has improved the fit of our model so much, let's briefly take stock of the model (shown in Output 19.9). The regression parameter for the effect of **Surgery** is −0.31, which is not significant, $t(264) = -0.37$, $p > .05$. However, baseline quality of life has a regression parameter of 0.48, which is highly significant $t(264) = 9.07$, $p < .001$. The standard deviation of the intercepts is 3.04 (we can square this value to get the variance of intercepts across clinics, which in this case is 9.24).

19.6.8. Introducing random slopes ④

We have seen that including a random intercept is important for this model (it changes the log-likelihood significantly). Figure 19.9 suggests that different clinics have different slopes; therefore, we could now look at whether adding a random slope will benefit the model. The model is now described by equation (19.9), which we saw earlier on; it can be specified in **R** with only minor modifications to the *lme()* function. All we are doing is adding another random term to the model, so, whereas before we specified random part of the model as *random = ~1|Clinic*, we now need to change this to *random = ~Surgery|Clinic*. This change tells **R** that the model now allows the effect of **Surgery** (i.e., the slope) to vary across clinics. As when we specified the main model, the intercept is implied in this, so the change will give us both random intercepts over clinics, but also random slopes for the variable **Surgery**.[6]

```
addRandomSlope<-lme(Post_QoL ~ Surgery + Base_QoL, data = surgeryData, random
= ~Surgery|Clinic, method = "ML")
summary(addRandomSlope)
anova(randomInterceptSurgeryQoL,addRandomSlope)
```

The code above creates a new object called *addRandomSlope*, which is the same model as before but with a random slope added for the effect of **Surgery**. We then ask for a summary of this new model as we have done before, we then compare this new model to the previous one, using the *anova()* function, which we have used before. Output 19.11 shows the results of this model comparison. By allowing the effect of **Surgery** to vary across clinics we have reduced the BIC from 1865.59 to 1837.97, and the $-2LL$ has changed significantly,[7] $\chi^2(2) = 38.87$, $p < .0001$. In short, adding random slopes to the model has significantly improved its fit, which means there is significant variability in the effect of surgery across clinics.

Across this model and the previous one, we can conclude from the $-2LL$ as we built up the models that the intercepts, $\chi^2(1) = 64.65$, $p < .0001$, and slopes, $\chi^2(2) = 38.87$, $p < .0001$, for the relationship between surgery and quality of life (when controlling for baseline quality of life) vary significantly across the different clinics.

```
  Model df       AIC       BIC    logLik   Test  L.Ratio p-value
1     5 1847.490 1865.592 -918.7450
2     7 1812.624 1837.966 -899.3119 1 vs 2 38.86626  <.0001
```

Output 19.11

Output 19.12 shows the summary of the model that contains both random slopes and intercepts. The regression parameter for the effect of **Surgery** is now $b = -0.65$, which is still not significant, $t(264) = -0.31$, $p > .05$. Baseline quality of life is still highly significant, $b = 0.31$, $t(264) = 5.80$, $p < .001$. The standard deviation of the intercepts is 6.13, and the effect of **Surgery** has a standard deviation of 6.20 (which we can square to find the variance, which is 38.41). The slopes and intercepts are highly correlated also ($r = -.97$).

```
Linear mixed-effects model fit by maximum likelihood
 Data: surgeryData
       AIC       BIC    logLik
  1812.624 1837.967 -899.3119

Random effects:
 Formula: ~Surgery | Clinic
 Structure: General positive-definite, Log-Cholesky parametrization
            StdDev   Corr
(Intercept) 6.132655 (Intr)
Surgery     6.197489 -0.965
Residual    5.912335
```

---

[6] It would be pretty unusual to want random slopes but not intercepts, because variability in the effect of a variable across contexts will tend to create variability in the intercepts across contexts too. However, should you want to have a model with random slopes but not intercepts you simply change the random effect to ~0 + *Surgery*|*Clinic*; the 0 gets rid of the intercept.

[7] The observant among you will notice that even though we have added only one new term to the model (the random slope of surgery across clinics), the degrees of freedom have increased by 2 rather than 1. That's odd isn't it? Actually, it's not and it happens because by including random slopes we actually add *two* parameters to the model: the estimate of the variance of the effect of surgery across clinics, and also an estimate of the covariance between slopes and intercepts (i.e., the extent to which intercepts and slopes are dependent on each other).

```
Fixed effects: Post_QoL ~ Surgery + Base_QoL
                Value Std.Error  DF    t-value  p-value
(Intercept) 40.10253  3.892945 264 10.301334   0.0000
Surgery     -0.65453  2.110917 264 -0.310069   0.7568
Base_QoL     0.31022  0.053506 264  5.797812   0.0000
 Correlation:
         (Intr) Surgery
Surgery  -0.430
Base_QoL -0.855 -0.063

Standardized Within-Group Residuals:
      Min          Q1         Med         Q3         Max
-2.4114778  -0.6628574  -0.1138411  0.6833110  2.8334730

Number of Observations: 276
Number of Groups: 10
```

Output 19.12

FIGURE 19.9
Predicted values
from the model
(surgery predicting
quality of life after
controlling for
baseline quality
of life) plotted
against the
observed values

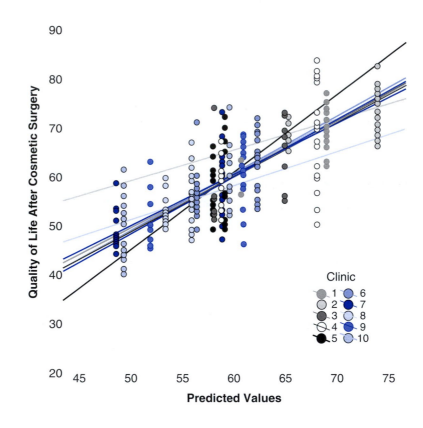

19.6.9. Adding an interaction term to the model ④

We can now build up the model by adding in another variable. One of the variables we
measured was the reason for the person having cosmetic surgery: was it to resolve a physical problem or was it purely for vanity? We can add this variable to the model, and also
look at whether it interacts with surgery in predicting quality of life. Our model will simply
expand to incorporate these new terms, and each term will have a regression coefficient

(which we select to be fixed). Therefore, our final model can be described as in the equation below (note that all that has changed is that there are two new predictors):

$$QoL\ After_{ij} = b_{0j} + b_{1j}Surgery_{ij} + b_2 QoL\ Before\ Surgery_{ij} + b_3 Reason_{ij}$$
$$+ b_4(Reason \times Surgery)_{ij} + \varepsilon_{ij}$$
$$b_{0j} = b_0 + u_{0j} \tag{19.1}$$
$$b_{1j} = b_1 + u_{1j}$$

To set up this model in **R** is very easy; it just requires some minor changes to the code. First, we'll add in the effect of **Reason**. To do this we create a new model, which I have called *addReason*, and we set it up in exactly the same way as before, except that we add **Reason** to the model. So, our model changes from *Post_QoL~Surgery + Base_QoL* to *Post_QoL~Surgery + Base_QoL + Reason*. It's as simple as that. In fact, it can be even simpler if you use the update function (see R's Souls' Tip 19.3).

```
addReason<-lme(Post_QoL ~ Surgery + Base_QoL + Reason, data = surgeryData,
random = ~Surgery|Clinic, method = "ML")
```

As we've seen before, to add an interaction term we use a colon (i.e., *Surgery:Reason*). I have called this model *finalModel* and we specify it exactly the same as the previous model except that we add in the interaction term. Again, we could simplify this process by using the update function (see R's Souls' Tip 19.3).

```
finalModel<-lme(Post_QoL ~ Surgery + Base_QoL + Reason + Surgery:Reason, data =
surgeryData, random = ~Surgery|Clinic, method = "ML")
```

R's Souls' Tip 19.3 The *update* function ③

Throughout the first example in this chapter I have built the models up piece by piece because I think it's useful to see how the code relates to the equation that describes the model. However, as we have seen before (see R's Souls' Tip 7.2) the *update()* function is a quicker way to add new things to old models. Let's start with the random slopes example from the main text. Our model is as follows:

```
addRandomSlope<-lme(Post_QoL ~ Surgery + Base_QoL, data = surgeryData, random =
~Surgery|Clinic, method = "ML")
```

In the text, we added the variable **Reason** to this model, using the longhand method:

```
addReason<-lme(Post_QoL ~ Surgery + Base_QoL + Reason, data = surgeryData, random =
~Surgery|Clinic, method = "ML")
```

Using the *update()* function we can do the same thing in much less text:

```
addReason<-update(addRandomSlope, .~. + Reason)
```

This function, like the longhand one, creates a new model called *addReason*, and it does this by updating an existing model. The first part of the parenthesis tells **R** that we want to update the model called *addRandomSlope*; the *.~. +* *Reason* tells **R** to keep the outcome variable and all of the previous predictors and to add **Reason** as a predictor.

Similarly, having created the model *addReason*, we can update this model to include the **Surgery × Reason** interaction (as we did in the main text). We can again use the update function as follows:

```
finalModel<-update(addReason, .~. + Reason:Surgery)
```

This command creates a new model called *finalModel*. Note that we have specified *addReason* in the *update()* function because we want to update the model that includes **Reason** as a predictor, and have added the interaction term typing + *Reason:Surgery*.

We need to see whether adding these new terms has improved the fit of the model and again we can simply use the *anova()* function. We have two new models (*addReason* and *finalModel*) that we want to compare to our previous model (*addRandomSlope*). We can do this comparison in a single function, remembering to order our models in the same order that they were built (so each time we have added only a single parameter):

```
anova(addRandomSlope, addReason, finalModel)
```

Output 19.13 presents the resulting output, which shows that adding **Reason** to the model reduces the $-2LL$ by 3.80, which is not quite a significant change, $p = .0513$; however, adding the **Surgery** $\times$ **Reason** interaction reduces the $-2LL$ by 5.78, which is a significant change, $p < .05$.

```
               Model df   AIC      BIC     logLik   Test   L.Ratio p-value
addRandomSlope  1    7 1812.62 1837.96 -899.31
addReason       2    8 1810.82 1839.78 -897.41 1 vs 2 3.7989  0.0513
finalModel      3    9 1807.04 1839.62 -894.52 2 vs 3 5.7795  0.0162
```

Output 19.13

Output 19.14 shows the summary of the final model. Quality of life before surgery significantly predicted quality of life after surgery, $t(262) = 5.75$, $p < .001$, surgery still did not significantly predict quality of life, $t(262) = -1.46$, $p = .15$, but the reason for surgery, $t(262) = -3.08$, $p < .01$, and the interaction of the reason for surgery and surgery, $t(262) = 2.48$, $p < .05$, both did significantly predict quality of life. The table of estimates also gives us the regression coefficients. However, if we want to get confidence intervals for these parameters we need to use the function *intervals()*, within which we simply specify the model for which we would like confidence intervals, and the level of the confidence intervals as a proportion (i.e., 0.99 produces 99% confidence intervals). For example:

```
intervals(finalModel, 0.90)
intervals(finalModel, 0.95)
intervals(finalModel, 0.99)
```

produce 90%, 95% and 99% intervals. If you insert only the model name into the function you will get 95% CIs by default.

Output 19.15 shows the 95% confidence intervals for our final model. We can see, for example, that **Surgery** had a $b = -3.19$, with a 95% confidence interval of -7.45 (lower) and 1.08 (upper). This interval crosses zero and so is not significant at $p < .05$, which of course we knew already from the main summary. These confidence intervals are very useful for establishing whether the variance of the intercepts and slopes is significant. For example, we can see that the standard deviation for intercepts was 5.48 with a 95% confidence interval from 3.31 to 9.07, for the slope of **Surgery** we get 5.42 (3.13, 9.37); because both confidence intervals do not cross zero we can see that the variability in both slopes and intercepts was significant, $p < .05$.

```
Linear mixed-effects model fit by maximum likelihood
 Data: surgeryData
       AIC       BIC       logLik
  1807.045 1839.629 -894.5226

Random effects:
 Formula: ~Surgery | Clinic
 Structure: General positive-definite, Log-Cholesky parametrization
            StdDev    Corr
(Intercept) 5.482366  (Intr)
Surgery     5.417501 -0.946
Residual    5.818910
```

```
Fixed effects: Post_QoL ~ Surgery + Base_QoL + Reason + Reason:Surgery
                    Value Std.Error  DF    t-value  p-value
(Intercept)      42.51782  3.875318 262 10.971440  0.0000
Surgery          -3.18768  2.185369 262 -1.458645  0.1459
Base_QoL          0.30536  0.053125 262  5.747833  0.0000
Reason           -3.51515  1.140934 262 -3.080938  0.0023
Surgery:Reason    4.22129  1.700269 262  2.482717  0.0137

Correlation:
                (Intr) Surgry Bas_QL Reason
Surgery         -0.356
Base_QoL        -0.865 -0.078
Reason          -0.233  0.306  0.065
Surgery:Reason   0.096 -0.505  0.024 -0.661

Standardized Within-Group Residuals:
      Min         Q1         Med        Q3        Max
-2.2331485 -0.6972193 -0.1541074 0.6326387 3.1641797

Number of Observations: 276
Number of Groups: 10
```

Output 19.14

```
Approximate 95% confidence intervals

 Fixed effects:
                   lower        est.      upper
(Intercept)    34.9565211 42.5178190 50.0791170
Surgery        -7.4516428 -3.1876767  1.0762895
Base_QoL        0.2017008  0.3053561  0.4090114
Reason         -5.7412731 -3.5151479 -1.2890227
Surgery:Reason  0.9038206  4.2212885  7.5387563
attr(,"label")
[1] "Fixed effects:"

 Random Effects:
  Level: Clinic
                            lower        est.      upper
sd((Intercept))         3.3138275  5.4823658  9.0699757
sd(Surgery)             3.1331192  5.4175011  9.3674439
cor((Intercept),Surgery) -0.9937813 -0.9455545 -0.5986153

 Within-group standard error:
   lower      est.     upper
5.331222  5.818910  6.351211
```

Output 19.15

As this is our final model, let's now give some thought to interpretation. The effect of the reason for surgery is easy to interpret. Given that we coded this predictor as 1 = physical reason and 0 = change appearance, the negative coefficient tells us that as reason increases (i.e., as a person goes from having surgery to change their appearance to having it for a physical reason) quality of life decreases. However, this effect in isolation isn't that interesting because it includes both people who had surgery and the waiting list controls. More interesting is the interaction term, because this takes account of whether or not the person had surgery. To break down this interaction we could rerun the analysis separately for the two 'reason groups'. Obviously we would remove the interaction term and the main effect of **Reason** from this analysis (because we are analysing the physical reason group separately from the group who wanted to change their appearance). As such, you need to fit the model in the previous section, but separately for those who had cosmetic surgery and those who had surgery for a physical reason.

Fortunately, this is fairly easy to do because *lme()* has a *subset* option that enables you to select a variable that specifies which rows of the data file that you want to use. First we need to create a variable that returns 'True' if the person had surgery for physical reasons and 'False' for those who had cosmetic surgery:

```
physicalSubset<- surgeryData$Reason==1
```

This function simply creates a variable called *physicalSubset* that will be set to TRUE only if the variable **Reason** is equal to 1. In our data set people who have a '1' for **Reason** are those who had surgery for a physical reason, so we are asking **R** to set *physicalSubset* to TRUE if the person had surgery for a physical reason. (Remember that *surgeryData$Reason* means 'the variable called *Reason* in the data set called *surgeryData*', and that in **R** '==' means 'equal to'.) We also create another variable called *cosmeticSubset* that returns TRUE for any people who had cosmetic surgery. We create this variable in much the same way (but now we specify that the variable **Reason** must be equal to 0, because in our data set 0 represents people who had cosmetic surgery):

```
cosmeticSubset<-surgeryData$Reason==0
```

Next, we create two new models that contain **Base_QoL** and **Surgery** as predictors and have random slopes and intercepts. The first one is for people who had surgery for a physical reason, so we set the subset option to be *physicalSubset*, which specifies all of the people who had surgery for this reason:

```
physicalModel<-lme(Post_QoL ~ Surgery + Base_QoL, data = surgeryData, random = ~Surgery|Clinic, subset= physicalSubset, method = "ML")
```

This creates a model (called *physicalModel*). Note that I have used *subset = physicalSubset*, which uses the variable **physicalSubset** to determine whether or not to include a particular case of data. By doing this our resulting model will include only those who had surgery for a physical reason. Similarly, we can use the variable **cosmeticSubset** to create another model that is fit using only those who had cosmetic surgery:

```
cosmeticModel<-lme(Post_QoL ~ Surgery + Base_QoL, data = surgeryData, random = ~Surgery|Clinic, subset= cosmeticSubset, method = "ML")
```

We can get a summary of these models in the usual way:

```
summary(physicalModel)
summary(cosmeticModel)

Linear mixed-effects model fit by maximum likelihood
 Data: surgeryData
  Subset: physicalSubset
       AIC      BIC    logLik
  1172.560 1194.832 -579.2798

Random effects:
 Formula: ~Surgery | Clinic
 Structure: General positive-definite, Log-Cholesky parametrization
            StdDev    Corr
(Intercept) 5.773827 (Intr)
Surgery     5.804865 -0.948
Residual    5.798764
```

```
Fixed effects: Post_QoL ~ Surgery + Base_QoL
                Value Std.Error  DF   t-value p-value
(Intercept) 38.02079  4.705980 166 8.079250  0.0000
Surgery      1.19655  2.099769 166 0.569848  0.5696
Base_QoL     0.31771  0.069471 166 4.573271  0.0000
 Correlation:
          (Intr)  Surgry
Surgery  -0.306
Base_QoL -0.908 -0.078


Standardized Within-Group Residuals:
       Min         Q1         Med          Q3         Max
-2.2447342 -0.6505340 -0.1264188  0.6111506  2.9472101


Number of Observations: 178
Number of Groups: 10
```

Output 19.16

```
Linear mixed-effects model fit by maximum likelihood
 Data: surgeryData
  Subset: cosmeticSubset
      AIC       BIC     logLik
  650.9469 669.0417 -318.4734


Random effects:
 Formula: ~Surgery | Clinic
  Structure: General positive-definite, Log-Cholesky parametrization
            StdDev   Corr
(Intercept) 5.006026 (Intr)
Surgery     5.292027 -0.969
Residual    5.738551


Fixed effects: Post_QoL ~ Surgery + Base_QoL
                Value Std.Error DF   t-value p-value
(Intercept) 41.78605  5.573849 87  7.496802  0.0000
Surgery     -4.30702  2.275002 87 -1.893193  0.0617
Base_QoL     0.33849  0.080274 87  4.216720  0.0001
 Correlation:
          (Intr)  Surgry
Surgery  -0.252
Base_QoL -0.937 -0.058
Standardized Within-Group Residuals:
       Min         Q1         Med          Q3         Max
-1.8945645 -0.6616222 -0.1461451  0.6460834  2.6741347
Number of Observations: 98
Number of Groups: 9
```

Output 19.17

The model for those who had surgery for a physical reason is shown in Output 19.16, whereas the model for those who had cosmetic surgery is in Output 19.17. It shows that for those operated on only to change their appearance, surgery almost significantly predicted quality of life after surgery, $b = -4.31$, $t(87) = -1.89$, $p = .06$. The negative gradient shows that for these people quality of life after surgery was lower compared to the control group. However, for those who had surgery to solve a physical problem surgery did not significantly predict quality of life, $b = 1.20$, $t(166) = 0.57$, $p = .57$. However, the slope was positive, indicating that people who had surgery scored higher on quality of life than those on the waiting list (although not significantly so!). The interaction effect, therefore, reflects the difference in slopes for surgery as a predictor of quality of life in those who had surgery for physical problems (slight positive slope) and those who had surgery purely for vanity (a negative slope).

We could sum up these results by saying that quality of life after surgery, after controlling for quality of life before surgery, was lower for those who had surgery to change their appearance than those who had surgery for a physical reason. This makes sense because for those having surgery to correct a physical problem, the surgery has probably brought relief and so their quality of life will improve. However, for those having surgery for vanity they might well discover that having a different appearance wasn't actually at the root of their unhappiness, so their quality of life is lower.

CRAMMING SAM'S TIPS   Multilevel models R output

- The *−2LL* and its significance can be used to compare models that are the same in all but one parameter. The AIC and BIC can also be compared across models (but not significance tested).
- The *fixed effects* tell you whether your predictors significantly predict the outcome. If the significance value is less than .05 then the effect is significant.
- Interpret the nature of the effect using the regression coefficient and its confidence interval. The direction of these coefficients tells us whether the relationship between each predictor and the outcome is positive or negative. To get the confidence intervals you need to use the *intervals()* function.
- The standard deviation of random effects can tell us how much intercepts and slopes varied over our level 1 variable. The significance of these estimates can be ascertained from their confidence intervals, obtained using the *intervals()* function.

19.7. Growth models ④

Growth models are extremely important in many areas of science, including psychology, medicine, physics, chemistry and economics. In a growth model the aim is to look at the rate of change of a variable over time: for example, we could look at white blood cell counts, attitudes, radioactive decay or profits. In all cases we're trying to see which model best describes the change over time.

19.7.1.   Growth curves (polynomials) ④

Figure 19.10 gives some examples of possible **growth curves**. This diagram shows three **polynomials** representing a linear trend (the dark blue line) otherwise known as a first-order polynomial, a quadratic trend (the light blue line) otherwise known as a second-order polynomial, and a cubic trend (the black line) otherwise known as a third-order polynomial. Notice first that the linear trend is a straight line, but as the polynomials increase they get more and more curved, indicating more rapid growth over time. Also, as polynomials increase, the change in the curve is quite dramatic (so dramatic that I adjusted the scale of

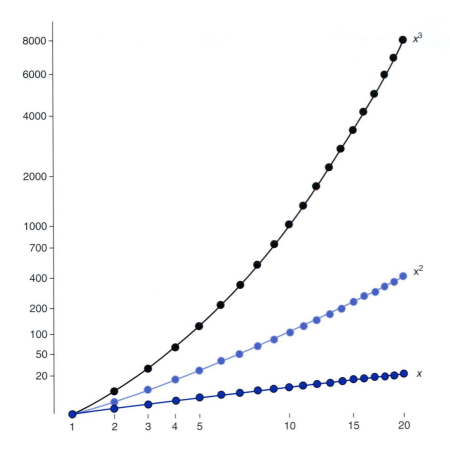

FIGURE 19.10

Illustration of a first-order (linear, blue), second-order (quadratic, light blue) and third-order (cubic, black) polynomial

the graph to fit all three curves on the same diagram). This observation highlights the fact that any growth curve higher than a quadratic (or possibly cubic) trend is very unrealistic in real data. By fitting a growth model to the data we can see which trend best describes the growth of an outcome variable over time (though no one will believe that a significant fifth-order polynomial is telling us anything meaningful about the real world!).

The growth curves that we have described might seem familiar to you: they are the same as the trends that we described for ordered means in section 10.4.5. What we are discussing now is really no different. There are just two important things to remember when fitting growth curves: (1) you can fit polynomials up to one less than the number of time points that you have; and (2) a polynomial is defined by a simple power function. On the first point, this means that with three time points you can fit a linear and quadratic growth curve (or a first- and second-order polynomial), but you cannot fit any higher-order growth curves. Similarly, if you have six time points you can fit up to a fifth-order polynomial. This is the same basic idea as having one less contrast than the number of groups in ANOVA (see section 10.4).

What is a growth curve?

On the second point, we have to define growth curves manually in multilevel models in R: there is not a convenient option that we can select to do it for us. However, this is quite easy to do. If *time* is our predictor variable, then a linear trend is tested by including this variable alone. A quadratic or second-order polynomial is tested by including a predictor that is $time^2$, a cubic or third-order polynomial is tested by including a predictor that is $time^3$ and so on. So any polynomial is tested by including a variable that is the predictor to the power of the order of polynomial that you want to test: for a fifth-order polynomial we need a predictor of $time^5$ and for an n-order polynomial we would have to include $time^n$ as a predictor. Hopefully you get the general idea.

19.7.2.   **An example: the honeymoon period ②**

I once saw a brilliant talk given by Professor Daniel Kahneman, who won the 2002 Nobel Prize for Economics. In this talk Kahneman brought together an enormous amount of research on life satisfaction (he explored questions such as whether people are happier if they are richer). There was one graph in this talk that particularly grabbed my attention. It showed that leading up to marriage people reported greater life satisfaction, but by about two years after marriage this life satisfaction decreased back to its baseline level. This graph perfectly illustrated what people talk about as the 'honeymoon period': a new relationship/marriage is great at first (no matter how ill suited you may be) but after six months or so the cracks start to appear and everything turns to elephant dung. Kahneman argued that people adapt to marriage; it does not make them happier in the long run (Kahneman & Krueger, 2006).[8] This got me thinking about relationships not involving marriage (is it marriage that makes you happy, or just being in a long-term relationship?). Therefore, in a completely fictitious parallel world where I don't research child anxiety, but instead concern myself with people's life satisfaction, I collected some data. I organized a massive speed-dating event (see Chapter 14). At the start of the night I measured everyone's life satisfaction (**Satisfaction_Baseline**) on a 10-point scale (0 = completely dissatisfied, 10 = completely satisfied) and their gender (**Gender**). After the speed dating I noted all of the people who had found dates. If they ended up in a relationship with the person that they met on the speed-dating night then I stalked these people over the next 18 months of that relationship. As such, I had measures of their life satisfaction at 6 months (**Satisfaction_6_Months**), 12 months (**Satisfaction_12_Months**) and 18 months (**Satisfaction_18_Months**), after they entered the relationship. None of the people measured were in the same relationship (i.e., I measured only life satisfaction from one of the people in the couple).[9] Also, as is often the case with longitudinal data, I didn't have scores for all people at all time points because not everyone was available at the follow-up sessions. One of the benefits of a multilevel approach is that these missing data do not pose a particular problem. The data are in the file **Honeymoon Period.dat**.

Load these data into **R** by executing the following command:

```
satisfactionData = read.delim("Honeymoon Period.dat", header = TRUE)
```

Figure 19.11 shows the data. Each dot is a data point and the line shows the average life satisfaction over time. Basically, from baseline, life satisfaction rises slightly at time 2 (6 months) but then starts to decrease over the next 12 months. There are two things to note about the data. First, time 0 is before the people enter into their new relationship, yet already there is a lot of variability in their responses (reflecting the fact that people will vary in their satisfaction due to other reasons such as finances, personality and so on). This suggests that intercepts for life satisfaction differ across people. Second, there is also a lot of variability in life satisfaction after the relationship has started (time 1) and at all subsequent time points, which suggests that the slope of the relationship between time and life satisfaction might vary across people also. If we think of the time points as a level 1 variable that is nested with people (a level 2 variable) then we can easily model this variability in intercepts and slopes within people. We have a situation similar to Figure 19.4 (except

[8] The romantics among you might be relieved to know that others have used the same data to argue the complete opposite: that married people are happier than non-married people in the long term (Easterlin, 2003).

[9] However, I could have measured both people in the couple because, using a multilevel model I could have treated people as being nested within 'couples' to take account of the dependency in their data.

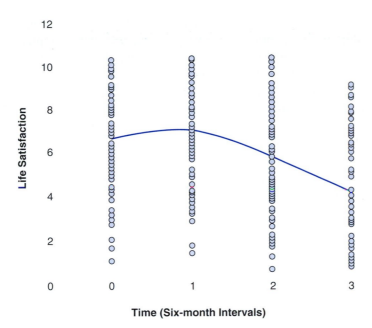

FIGURE 19.11
Life satisfaction
over time

with two levels instead of three, although we could add in the location of the speed dating event as a level three variable if we had that information).

19.7.3.   Restructuring the data ③

The first problem with having data measured over time is that to do a multilevel model the data need to be in a different format than what we are used to. For a repeated-measures design we normally set up the data with each row representing a person: in this case, the repeated-measures variable of time will be represented by four different columns (see section 3.9.4). We saw in Chapter 3 that this is called the 'wide' format. If we were going to run an ordinary repeated-measures ANOVA, this data layout would be fine; however, for a multilevel model we need the variable **Time** to be represented by a single column. We refer to this format as the 'long' format. As such we need to restructure the data.

SELF-TEST

✓ Thinking back to Chapter 3, use the *melt()* function to restructure the data into long format. If you get stuck, section 3.9.4 shows you how. Call your new dataframe *restructuredData*.

19.7.4.   Setting up the basic model ④

Now that we have our data set up, we can run the analysis. Essentially, we can set up this analysis in a very similar way to the previous example. There is only one important difference: because we are working with time series data we have to model the covariance structure (see section 19.4.2). The most common way to do this is to assume a first-order autoregressive covariance structure; to remind you, this means that data points close in time are assumed to be more highly correlated than data points distant in time. In all other respects we set up the model in the same way as in the previous example.

First we fit a baseline model in which we include only the intercept. As in the previous example, this is done using the *gls()* function:

```
intercept <-gls(Life_Satisfaction ~ 1, data = restructuredData, method =
"ML", na.action = na.exclude)
```

Note that we have asked **R** to create an object called *intercept*, and we have specified that **Life_Satisfaction** is the outcome variable and that it is predicted from only the intercept (the '~1' in the function). The rest of the function specifies the data (*data = restructuredData*) and how to estimate the model (*method = "ML"*). There is one important difference compared to the previous example. We have included a new option *na.action = na.exclude*. This is because the current data file (unlike the last example) has missing data and these missing values are specified as 'NA' in the data file. This option tells **R** what to do when it encounters an 'NA', and we have set it to exclude these cases (see R's Souls' Tip 19.2). Without this option the model would return an error.

Next, we need to fit the same model, but this time allowing the intercepts to vary across contexts (in this case we want them to vary across people). As in the previous example, we use the *lme()* function:

```
randomIntercept <-lme(Life_Satisfaction ~ 1, data = restructuredData,
random = ~1|Person, method = "ML",  na.action = na.exclude, control =
list(opt="optim"))
```

The format of this command is the same as the previous example. We create a model (called *randomIntercept*) that predicts life satisfaction from only the intercept (*Life_Satisfaction~1*), but also allows intercepts to vary across people (*random = ~1|Person*). Remember that the variable **Person** in the data set is a numeric variable that indicates whether data come from the same person. We have again asked for maximum-likelihood estimation (*method = "ML"*) and to exclude data points that are missing (*na.action = na.exclude*). However, note that there is a new option that we have not encountered before: *control = list(opt="optim")*. This option changes the optimizer that **R** uses to estimate the model. Normally the default optimizer is fine, but for these data some of the models cannot be computed using the default, so I have changed it to one that succeeds (see R's Souls' Tip 19.4).

R's Souls' Tip 19.4   Advanced options for *lme()* ③

You can use the control option in *lme()* to change the default options for the estimation procedure. A couple of the parameters you might want to change if your models won't converge are:

- *maxIter*: This sets the maximum number of iterations that **R** will use to reach a solution. The default is 50, but if your model fails to converge then you can increase this value, for example to 100, using *control = list(maxIter = 100)*.
- *opt*: This sets the optimizer that is used. The default (from **R** 2.2.0) is called *nlminb*, but there is an alternative optimizer called *optim*. If your model fails to converge it can be useful to try using a different optimizer. For example, some of the models in the honeymoon period example do not converge using the defaults, which is why we changed from the default optimizer by using *control = list(opt = "optim")*.

You can change both parameters using the same option by simply including both in the *list()* that you specify. For example, to increase the number of iterations to 2000 and to change the optimizer from *nlminb* to *opt* you would use *control = list(maxIter = 2000, opt = "optim")*. For a full list of advanced options execute *?lmeControl*.

19.7.5.   Adding in time as a fixed effect ③

In a growth curve analysis, we are primarily interested in one fixed effect: time. This variable in our data set is the index variable (**Time**), which specifies whether the life satisfaction score was recorded at baseline (0), 6 months (1), 12 months (2) or 18 months (3). In the previous example we built up our models individually using the *lme()* function; however, for this example our models have a lot of options (*method = "ML"*, *na.action = na.exclude*, *control = list(opt="optim")*), which we must specify in each new model. This typing would be tedious, so we will use the *update()* function to retain everything from a previous model (including options such as the method, how to deal with missing cases, and the optimization method) but add things to it (R's Souls' Tip 19.3). We can quickly update the previous model (*randomIntercept*) to include **Time** as a predictor by executing:

```
timeRI<-update(randomIntercept, .~. + Time)
```

This command creates a new object in **R** called *timeRI*. The first part of the parenthesis tells **R** *which* model to update (in this case we have updated *randomIntercept*). The remainder tells **R** *how* to update this model: .~. simply means 'keep the previous outcome and all of the previous predictors' and + *Time* means 'add **Time** as a predictor'. If you want to have a look at the new model you can use *summary(timeRI)*.

19.7.6.   Introducing random slopes ④

We can add a random slope to the model very simply using the *update()* function and respecifying the random part of the model. At the moment, the random part of the model is specified as *random = ~1|Person*, which means that intercepts (~1) vary across people (**Person**). If we want slopes to vary across people as well, then we're saying that the effect of **Time** is different in different people. This is a standard growth model scenario: the rate of development or growth over time differs within entities (in this case people, but it could be companies, mice, states, hospitals, schools, geographical areas, etc.). As such, we want to update the random part of the model to be *random = ~Time|Person*, which means that intercepts and the effect of time (~*Time*) vary across people (**Person**). We use the *update()* function to create a new model (called *timeRS*) which is identical to the previous model (*timeRI*) but updates the random part of the model to be *random = ~Time|Person*:

```
timeRS<-update(timeRI, random = ~Time|Person)
```

19.7.7.   Modelling the covariance structure ④

Now we have a basic random effects model, we can introduce a term that models the covariance structure or errors (see section 19.4.2). We do this by using the option *correlation = x*, in which *x* is one of several pre-defined covariance structures. The most likely covariance structures that'll you'll use will be (for a full list execute *?corClasses*):

- *corAR1()*: This is a first-order autoregressive covariance structure (see Jane Superbrain Box 19.1). It should be used when time points are equally spaced (as is the case in the current example).

- *corCAR1()*: This is similar to the above but for use with a continuous time covariate. Basically you should use this covariance structure if your time points are not equally spaced.

- *corARMA()*: Another autoregressive error structure, but this one allows the correlation structure to involve a moving average of error variance (see Jane Superbrain Box 19.1).

We can add a covariance structure to the model using the *update()* function to create a new model (called *ARModel*) which is identical to the previous model (*timeRS*) but adds in a first-order autoregressive covariance structure:

```
ARModel<-update(timeRS, correlation = corAR1(0, form = ~Time|Person))
```

Note that we have used *correlation = corAR1(0, form = ~Time|Person)*. We could have used the default setting, which would be to use *correlation = corAR1()*, but this would include only the random intercept (it would be the same as specifying *correlation = corAR1(0, form = ~1|Person)*.

JANE SUPERBRAIN 19.1

Autoregressive and moving average models ④

Autoregressive models (AR) are very difficult to understand. I do not really understand them, and I doubt I ever will. Imagine that we have a time series (Y_t) and we adjust this by subtracting the mean $(y_t = Y_t - \bar{Y})$. The t in these equations just represents different points in time. As far as I can gather, if we have a first-order autoregressive model, AR(1), then we predict these adjusted values from the adjusted *values at the previous time point* (i.e., $t - 1$). We can use a standard linear model to do this:

$$y_t = -a_1 y_{t-1} + e_t$$

The $-a$ is known as the lag or autoregressive coefficient, and e_t is the residual or error at time t. You can hopefully see that this is a simple linear model in which values at one time are predicted from values at a previous time (the word *autoregressive* reflects the fact that values are predicted from themselves).

A second-order autoregressive model. AR(2), is much the same except that we're interested not just in the previous time point, but in the previous two time points. The model simply expands to include this extra time point:

$$y_t = -a_1 y_{t-1} - a_2 y_{t-2} + e_t$$

You should be able to extend this basic logic to understand third- and fourth-order autoregressive models. In these models, residuals are assumed not to correlate; in other words, errors at one time point are not believed to correlate with errors at another time point. The data themselves correlate at different time points, but the errors don't.

However, we might want to assume that the residuals also correlate over time. In other words, our data at time t can be predicted not just from the data at the previous time point but also the error at previous time points. This is known as a moving average (MA) model. Like AR models, a first-order moving average model factors in residuals at the current time point (e_t) and also residuals from the previous time point (e_{t-1}). A second-order MA model would factor in residuals for the current time point, the previous time point, and two points back in time (e_{t-2}), and so on. So, for example, if we had an AR(1) and MA(1) our model becomes:

$$y_t = -a_1 y_{t-1} + e_t + c_1 e_{t-1}$$

Note that this is the same as the AR(1) model except that there is an extra term representing the error from the previous time point, e_{t-1}, which is multiplied by c_1, a coefficient representing the first-order moving average. Models that combine autoregressive and moving average models are known as ARMA models. ARMA models have two parameters: p defines the order of the autoregressive part of the model, q specifies the order of the moving average part of the model. In both cases 1 = first-order, 2 = second-order and so on. Therefore, ARMA($p = 2$, $q = 1$) would be a second-order autoregressive model with a first-order moving average, ARMA($p = 2$, $q = 2$) would be a second-order autoregressive model with a second-order moving average. Hopefully you get the general gist because my brain is literally about to explode all over my screen.

19.7.8. Comparing models ③

So far we have created five models: (1) a baseline model predicting life satisfaction from only the intercept (*interceptOnly*); (2) a model with random intercepts across people (*randomIntercept*); (3) a model with time as a predictor of life satisfaction and random intercepts across people (*timeRI*); (4) a model with time as a predictor, a random effect of time over people and random intercepts (*timeRS*); and (5) a model with time as a predictor, random effects of time across people, a random effect of intercepts across people, and a first-order autoregressive covariance structure (*ARModel*). Let's now look at how these models fit the data. Each time we have added only one new component to the model so we can compare them with the log-likelihood as we did in the previous example. We can compare all five models by executing:

```
anova(intercept, randomIntercept, timeRI, timeRS, ARModel)
```

```
            Model df  AIC      BIC      logLik    Test     L.Ratio p-value
intercept    1    2 2064.053 2072.217 -1030.026
randomInt    2    3 1991.396 2003.642  -992.698 1 vs 2    74.657  <.0001
timeRI       3    4 1871.728 1888.057  -931.864 2 vs 3   121.667  <.0001
timeRS       4    6 1874.626 1899.120  -931.313 3 vs 4     1.102  0.5763
ARModel      5    7 1872.891 1901.466  -929.445 4 vs 5     3.736  0.0533
```

Output 19.18

The resulting output, in Output 19.18, shows that adding a random intercept significantly improved the fit of the model, $\chi^2(1) = 74.66$, $p < .0001$. Similarly, adding the fixed effect of time to the model significantly improved the fit compared to the previous model, $\chi^2(1) = 121.67$, $p < .0001$. However, adding a random slope for the effect of time across participants did not significantly improve the model, $\chi^2(2) = 1.10$, $p = .576$. Finally, adding a first-order autoregressive covariance structure did more or less significantly improve the model, $\chi^2(1) = 3.74$, $p = .053$. Note that for each model the degrees of freedom change by 1 because we have added only a single parameter;[10] this change in degrees of freedom is used for the log-likelihood test.

We can take a quick look at the final model, and the confidence intervals for the parameter estimates within it by using:

```
Summary(ARModel); intervals(ARModel)
```

Output 19.19 shows the resulting model summary and Output 19.20 shows the 95% confidence intervals. The effect of time, $b = -0.87$ (-1.03, -0.71), $t(322) = -10.97$, $p < .001$, was highly significant, indicating that life satisfaction significantly changed over the 18 month period (see Figure 19.11). In addition, the standard deviation of intercepts was 1.62 (1.31, 2.02), and for the effect of time across people (slopes) was 0.05 (0.00, 41.83). Neither of the confidence intervals crosses zero, implying that this variance in slopes and intercepts was significant. Note that in the case of the slopes, this finding contradicts the results of the log-likelihood statistic, which implied that adding random slopes did not significantly improve the model (Output 19.18). The approximate confidence interval for slopes is very wide and not symmetrical, which implies that we might be wise to give more weight to the log-likelihood.

---

[10] The exception is the model where we add random slopes. See earlier for an explanation of why the change in degrees of freedom is 2 in this case.

```
Linear mixed-effects model fit by maximum likelihood
 Data: restructuredData
       AIC      BIC     logLik
  1872.891 1901.466 -929.4453

Random effects:
 Formula: ~Time | Person
 Structure: General positive-definite, Log-Cholesky parametrization
            StdDev      Corr
(Intercept) 1.62767553 (Intr)
Time        0.04782877 -0.062
Residual    1.74812486

Correlation Structure: AR(1)
 Formula: ~Time | Person
 Parameter estimate(s):
      Phi
0.2147812
Fixed effects: Life_Satisfaction ~ Time
               Value  Std.Error  DF   t-value p-value
(Intercept) 7.131470 0.21260192 322  33.54377       0
Time       -0.870087 0.07929275 322 -10.97310       0
 Correlation:
     (Intr)
Time -0.527

Standardized Within-Group Residuals:
        Min          Q1         Med          Q3         Max
-2.08400991 -0.62083911  0.06392492  0.59512953  2.49161500

Number of Observations: 438
Number of Groups: 115
```

Output 19.19

```
Approximate 95% confidence intervals

 Fixed effects:
                lower       est.      upper
(Intercept)  6.714162  7.1314700  7.5487782
Time        -1.025728 -0.8700874 -0.7144467
attr(,"label")
[1] "Fixed effects:"

 Random Effects:
  Level: Person
                              lower        est.      upper
sd((Intercept))        1.314720e+00  1.62767553  2.0151263
sd(Time)               5.468419e-05  0.04782877 41.8327717
cor((Intercept),Time) -6.937502e-01 -0.06192455  0.6237635

 Correlation structure:
          lower      est.     upper
Phi 0.002025179 0.2147812 0.408935
attr(,"label")
[1] "Correlation structure:"
```

```
Within-group standard error:
   lower     est.     upper
1.542913 1.748125 1.980630
```

Output 19.20

19.7.9.   Adding higher-order polynomials ③

We have seen that the main effect of time is significant. This main effect is the linear trend of time. However, Figure 19.11, seems to show a more curvilinear change over time (satisfaction first increases from baseline to 6 months before declining after 6 months). To capture this trend we would need to add a quadratic or perhaps even cubic trend (refer back to Figure 19.10). There are several ways in **R** to look for trends. One way to add quadratic trends is to do it manually. We saw in Figure 19.10 that a quadratic trend equates to *time²* and that a cubic trend is simply *time³*. We could, therefore, simply create new predictor variables in our dataframe that are time multiplied by itself (time²) or time multiplied by itself twice (time³). We could then enter these new variables as predictors into the model.

Fortunately, rather than computing new variables, **R** can create these new predictors 'on the fly'. To create the quadratic term we simply specify *I(Time ^ 2)* as a new predictor. 'Time ^ 2' is **R**'s way of writing 'time²' (the ^ means 'to the power of'); because arithmetic operators such as +, *, − and ^ can be used to define the form of a model (e.g., satisfaction~gender + age + age*gender) we need to enclose 'Time ^ 2' within the *I()* function so that **R** knows to treat it as an arithmetic operator rather than part of the model specification. The last model we looked at was called *ARModel*, and included the main effect of *Time* as a predctor. We can use *update()* to create a new model (*timeQuadratic*) that adds the quadratic term to this model:

```
timeQuadratic<-update(ARModel, .~. + I(Time^2))
```

We can create a model (*timeCubic*) that adds a cubic term in exactly the same way as for the quadratic trend. This time, we update the quadratic model (*timeQuadratic*) so that it includes *time³*, which is done the same as for the quadratic trend except that we specify time cubed rather than squared, 'I(Time ^ 3)'. We can compare these two new models with the model that included only the linear trend of time (*ARModel*) using the *anova()* function and ask for a summary of the final model using the *summary()* and *intervals()* functions.

```
timeCubic <-update(timeQuadratic, .~. + I(Time^3))
anova(ARModel, timeQuadratic, timeCubic)
summary(timeCubic)
intervals(timeCubic)
```

Output 19.21 shows the model comparison. It is clear from this that adding the quadratic term to the model significantly improves the fit, $\chi^2(1) = 57.35$, $p < .0001$; however, adding in the cubic trend does not, $\chi^2(1) = 3.38$, $p = .066$.

```
              Model  df  AIC      BIC      logLik    Test     L.Ratio p-value
ARModel         1    7  1872.89 1901.466 -929.445
timeQuadratic   2    8  1817.54 1850.202 -900.772 1 vs 2  57.347   <.0001
timeCubic       3    9  1816.16 1852.901 -899.081 2 vs 3   3.382   0.0659
```

Output 19.21

Looking at the summary of the final model, the fixed effects (Output 19.22) and the confidence intervals (Output 19.23) tell us that the linear, $b = 1.55$ (0.61, 2.48), $t(320) = 3.24$, $p < .01$, and quadratic, $b = -1.33$ (-2.15, -0.50), $t(320) = -3.15$, $p < .01$, both significantly described the pattern of the data over time; however, the cubic trend was not significant, $b = 0.17$ (-0.01, 0.35), $t(320) = 1.84$, $p > .05$. This confirms what we already know from comparing the fit of successive models. The trend in the data is best described by a second-order polynomial, or a quadratic trend. This reflects the initial increase in life satisfaction 6 months after finding a new partner but a subsequent reduction in life satisfaction at 12 and 18 months after the start of the relationship (Figure 19.11). It's worth remembering that this quadratic trend is only an *approximation*: if it were completely accurate then we would predict from the model that couples who had been together for 10 years would have negative life satisfaction, which is impossible given the scale we used to measure it.

```
Linear mixed-effects model fit by maximum likelihood
 Data: restructuredData
       AIC        BIC      logLik
  1816.162  1852.902  -899.0808

Random effects:
 Formula: ~Time | Person
 Structure: General positive-definite, Log-Cholesky parametrization
            StdDev     Corr
(Intercept) 1.8826725 (Intr)
Time        0.4051351 -0.346
Residual    1.4572374

Correlation Structure: AR(1)
 Formula: ~Time | Person
 Parameter estimate(s):
      Phi
0.1326346
Fixed effects: Life_Satisfaction ~ Time + I(Time^2) + I(Time^3)
                Value Std.Error  DF   t-value  p-value
(Intercept)  6.634783 0.2230273 320 29.748744  0.0000
Time         1.546635 0.4772221 320  3.240913  0.0013
I(Time^2)   -1.326426 0.4209411 320 -3.151098  0.0018
I(Time^3)    0.171096 0.0929297 320  1.841131  0.0665
 Correlation:
          (Intr) Time   I(T^2)
Time      -0.278
I(Time^2)  0.139 -0.951
I(Time^3) -0.098  0.896 -0.987

Standardized Within-Group Residuals:
        Min          Q1         Med          Q3         Max
-2.58597365 -0.54411056 -0.04373592  0.50525444  2.78413461

Number of Observations: 438
Number of Groups: 115
```

Output 19.22

The outputs for the final model also tell us about the random parameters in the model. First of all, the standard deviation of the random intercepts was 1.88 (1.49, 2.39). The fact that the 95% confidence interval doesn't cross zero suggests that we were correct to assume that life satisfaction at baseline varied significantly across people. Also, the variance of slope of time varied significantly across people, $SD = 0.41$ (0.17, 0.96). The confidence interval again does not cross zero, suggesting that the change in life satisfaction over time varied significantly across people too. Finally, the correlation between the slopes and intercepts, −0.35 (−0.67, 0.10) suggests that as intercepts increased, the slope decreased (although the confidence interval crosses zero so this trend is not significant).

```
Approximate 95% confidence intervals

 Fixed effects:
                  lower        est.        upper
(Intercept)   6.19800573   6.6347826   7.0715595
Time          0.61204293   1.5466350   2.4812271
I(Time^2)    -2.15079781  -1.3264264  -0.5020551
I(Time^3)    -0.01089790   0.1710958   0.3530895
attr(,"label")
[1] "Fixed effects:"

 Random Effects:
  Level: Person
                            lower        est.        upper
sd((Intercept))         1.4852030   1.8826725  2.38651276
sd(Time)                0.1705194   0.4051351  0.96255585
cor((Intercept),Time) -0.6738687  -0.3461486  0.09538264

 Correlation structure:
         lower        est.        upper
Phi -0.1856231 0.1326346 0.4257069
attr(,"label")
[1] "Correlation structure:"

 Within-group standard error:
   lower        est.       upper
1.173241 1.457237 1.809978
```
Output 19.23

Another way to test for trends over time is by converting **Time** to power polynomials. This is achieved with a simple function *poly()*. Within this function you specify the variable that you want to be converted, and the number of polynomials you want (up to the number of time points that you measured minus 1). For example, *poly(Time, 1)* will create a linear trend, *poly(Time, 2)* creates a linear and quadratic and *poly(Time, 3)* creates a linear, quadratic and cubic trend. In our current example we had four time points so a cubic trend is the highest order polynomial that we can have; if we, for example, specified *poly(Time, 4)* we would get an error.

```
Linear mixed-effects model fit by maximum likelihood
 Data: restructuredData
      AIC        BIC       logLik
  1816.162 1852.902 -899.0808

Random effects:
 Formula: ~Time | Person
 Structure: General positive-definite, Log-Cholesky parametrization
            StdDev     Corr
(Intercept) 1.8826725 (Intr)
Time        0.4051351 -0.346
Residual    1.4572374

Correlation Structure: AR(1)
 Formula: ~Time | Person
```

```
Parameter estimate(s):
      Phi
0.1326346
Fixed effects: Life_Satisfaction ~ poly(Time, 3)
                   Value Std.Error  DF   t-value  p-value
(Intercept)      5.938943  0.182953 320  32.46157  0.0000
poly(Time, 3)1 -20.615766  1.759420 320 -11.71736  0.0000
poly(Time, 3)2 -11.682913  1.418904 320  -8.23376  0.0000
poly(Time, 3)3   2.439191  1.324833 320   1.84113  0.0665
 Correlation:
                (Intr) p(T,3)1 p(T,3)2
poly(Time, 3)1 -0.009
poly(Time, 3)2 -0.016  0.027
poly(Time, 3)3  0.004 -0.035    0.014

Standardized Within-Group Residuals:
        Min           Q1          Med           Q3          Max
-2.58597365  -0.54411056  -0.04373592   0.50525444   2.78413461

Number of Observations: 438
Number of Groups: 115
```

Output 19.24

The advantage of this method of creating polynomials is that the resulting predictors are orthogonal (i.e., independent). By using *Time*, *Time²* and *Time³* we create predictors that are highly correlated, but by using *poly()* we create predictors that are completely uncorrelated. This means that we can evaluate one trend without it being affected by another. If we wanted to add our trends using this method we can again use the *update()* function to respecify the model with AR(1) covariance structure (*ARModel*). Remember that this model already has time as a predictor, and we need to get rid of this predictor and replace it with our polynomials. To do this we just respecify the outcome and predictors within the update function and this will overwrite the previous predictors:

```
polyModel<-update(ARModel, .~ poly(Time, 3))
```

Remember that '~' means 'predicted from'; the '.' means 'use the same thing as in the existing model'. As such, *.~ poly(Time, 3)* translates as 'use the same outcome as in the existing model but predict it from *poly(Time, 3)*'. In other words, the previous predictor of **Time** that was specified for the *ARModel* will be replaced by the linear, quadratic and cubic polynomials for **Time** that are created by the *poly()* function. All other parts of the *ARModel* (i.e., the random effects and covariance structure) remain unchanged.

Output 19.24 shows the model summary (*summary(polymodel)*) for the model including the polynomials. We won't dwell on this output other than to say that if you compare it to Output 19.22 it shows the same profile of results: the linear (*poly(Time, 3)1*) and quadratic (*poly(Time, 3)2*) trends are significant, whereas the cubic (*poly(Time, 3)3*) was just non-significant ($p = .067$). The regression coefficients are different (because these contrasts are orthogonal), but basically the same pattern or results emerges.

SELF-TEST

✓ We have used the *update()* function in this second example. To get some practice at specifying multilevel models, try building each of the models in this example but specifying each one in full.

19.7.10. Further analysis ④

It's worth pointing out that I've kept this growth curve analysis simple to give you the basic tools. In the example I allowed only the linear term to have a random intercept and slopes, but given that we discovered that a second-order polynomial described the change in responses, we could redo the analysis and allow random intercepts and slopes for the second-order polynomial also. To do these we would just have to specify these terms in the random part of the model. If we were to do this it would make sense to add the random components one at a time and test whether they have a significant impact on the model by comparing the log-likelihood values or other fit indices.

Also, the polynomials I have described are not the only ones that can be used. You could test for a logarithmic trend over time, or even an exponential one.

CRAMMING SAM'S TIPS   Growth models

- Growth models are multilevel models in which changes in an outcome over time are modelled using potential growth patterns.
- These growth patterns can be linear, quadratic, cubic, logarithmic, exponential, or anything you like really.
- The hierarchy in the data is that time points are nested within people (or other entities). As such, it's a way of analysing repeated-measures data that have a hierarchical structure.
- The *anova()* function can be used to compare the overall fit of hierarchical models. The resulting change in the log-likelihood and the significance of this change can be used to ascertain if the fit has been improved (a significant change equates to a significant improvement). The AIC and BIC can also be compared across models (but not significance tested).
- The *fixed effects* tell you whether the growth functions that you have entered into the model significantly predict the outcome. If the *p*-value is less than .05 then the effect is significant.
- The *intervals()* function can be used to get confidence intervals for model parameters. These intervals can tell us how much intercepts and slopes varied over our level 1 variable, and whether this variance is significant (if the interval does not cross zero, it is significant).
- An autoregressive covariance structure, AR(1), is often assumed in time course data such as that in growth models.

Labcoat Leni's Real Research 19.1   A fertile gesture ③

Miller, G., Tybur, J. M., & Jordan, D. B. (2007). *Evolution and Human Behavior, 28*, 375–381.

Most female mammals experience a phase of 'estrus' during which they are more sexually receptive, proceptive, selective and attractive. As such, the evolutionary benefit to this phase is believed to be to attract mates of superior genetic stock. However, some people have argued that this important phase became uniquely lost or hidden in human females. Testing these evolutionary ideas is exceptionally difficult, but Geoffrey Miller and his colleagues came up with an incredibly elegant piece of research that did just that. They reasoned that if the 'hidden-estrus' theory is incorrect then men should find women most attractive during the fertile phase of their menstrual cycle compared to the pre-fertile (menstrual) and post-fertile (luteal) phase.

(Continued)

(Continued)

To measure how attractive men found women in an ecologically valid way, they came up with the ingenious idea of collecting data from women working at lap-dancing clubs. These women maximize their tips from male visitors by attracting more dances. In effect the men 'try out' several dancers before choosing a dancer for a prolonged dance. For each dance the male pays a 'tip'. Therefore, the greater the number of men choosing a particular woman, the more her earnings will be. As such, each dancer's earnings are a good index of how attractive the male customers have found her. Miller and his colleagues argued, therefore, that if women do have an estrus phase then they will be more attractive during this phase and therefore earn more money. This study is a brilliant example of using a real-world phenomenon to address an important scientific question in an ecologically valid way.

The data for this study are in the file **Miller et al. (2007).dat**. The researchers collected data via a website from several dancers (**ID**), who provided data for multiple lap-dancing shifts (so for each person there are several rows of data). They also measured what phase of the menstrual cycle the women were in at a given shift (**Cyclephase**), and whether they were using hormonal contraceptives (**Contraceptive**) because this would affect their cycle. The outcome was their earnings on a given shift in dollars (**Tips**).

A multilevel model can be used here because the data are unbalanced: the women differed in the number of shifts they provided data for (the range was 9 to 29 shifts); multilevel models can handle this problem.

Labcoat Leni wants you to carry out a multilevel model to see whether **Tips** can be predicted from **Cyclephase**, **Contraceptive** and their interaction. Is the 'estrus-hidden' hypothesis supported? Answers are in the additional material on the companion website (or look at page 378 in the original article).

19.8. How to report a multilevel model ③

Specific advice on reporting multilevel models is hard to come by. Also, the models themselves can take on so many forms that giving standard advice is hard. If you have built up your model from one with only fixed parameters to one with a random intercept, and then random slope, it is advisable to report all stages of this process (or at the very least report the fixed-effects-only model and the final model). For any model you need to say something about the random effects. For the final model of the cosmetic surgery example you could write something like:

✓ The relationship between surgery and quality of life showed significant variance in intercepts across participants, $SD = 5.48$ (95% CI: 3.31, 9.07), $\chi^2(1) = 107.65$, $p < .0001$. In addition, the slopes varied across participants, $SD = 5.42$ (3.13, 9.37), $\chi^2(2) = 38.87$, $p < .0001$, and the slopes and intercepts were negatively and significantly correlated, cor $= -.95$ (−.99, −.60).

For the model itself, you have two choices. The first is to report the results in the text, with the *b*-values, *t*s and degrees of freedom for the fixed effects, and then report the parameters for the random effects in the text as well. The second is to produce a table of parameters as you would for regression. For example, we might report our cosmetic surgery example as follows:

✓ Quality of life before surgery significantly predicted quality of life after surgery, $b = 0.31$, $t(262) = 5.75$, $p < .001$, surgery did not significantly predict quality of life, $b = -3.19$, $t(262) = -1.46$, $p = .15$, but the reason for surgery, $b = -3.52$, $t(262) = -3.08$, $p < .01$, and the interaction of the reason for surgery and surgery, $b = 4.22$, $t(262) = 2.48$, $p < .05$, both did significantly predict quality of life. This interaction was broken down by conducting separate multilevel models on the 'physical reason' and 'attractiveness reason'. The models specified were the same as the main model but excluded the main effect and interaction term involving the reason for surgery. These analyses showed that for those operated on only to change their appearance, surgery almost significantly predicted quality of life after surgery, $b = -4.31$, $t(87) = -1.89$, $p = .06$:

quality of life was lower after surgery compared to the control group. However, for those who had surgery to solve a physical problem, surgery did not significantly predict quality of life, $b = 1.20$, $t(166) = 0.57$, $p = .57$. The interaction effect, therefore, reflects the difference in slopes for surgery as a predictor of quality of life in those who had surgery for physical problems (slight positive slope) and those who had surgery purely for vanity (a negative slope).

Alternatively we could present parameter information in a table:

	b	SE b	95% CI
Baseline QoL	0.31	0.05	0.20, 0.41
Surgery	−3.19	2.19	−7.45, 1.08
Reason	−3.52	1.14	−5.74, −1.29
Surgery × Reason	4.22	1.70	0.90, 7.54

What have I discovered about statistics? ②

Writing this chapter was quite a steep learning curve for me. I've been meaning to learn about multilevel modelling for ages, and now I finally feel like I know something. This is pretty amazing considering that the bulk of the reading and writing was done between 11pm and 3am over many nights. However, despite now feeling as though I understand them, I don't, and if you feel like you now understand them then you're wrong. This sounds harsh, but sadly multilevel modelling is very complicated and we have scratched only the surface of what there is to know. Multilevel models often fail to converge, with no apology or explanation, and trying to fathom out what's happening can feel like hammering nails into your head.

Needless to say, I didn't mention any of this at the start of the chapter because I wanted you to read it. Instead, I lulled you into a false sense of security by looking gently at how data can be hierarchical and how this hierarchical structure can be important. Most of the tests in this book simply ignore the hierarchy. We also saw that hierarchical models are just basically a fancy regression in which you can estimate the variability in the slopes and intercepts within entities. We saw that you should start with a model that ignores the hierarchy and then add in random intercepts and slopes to see if they improve the fit of the model. Having submerged ourselves in the warm bath of standard multilevel models, we moved on to the icy lake of growth curves. We saw that there are ways to model trends in the data over time (and that these trends can also have variable intercepts and slopes). We also discovered that these trends have long confusing names like fourth-order polynomial. We asked ourselves why they couldn't have a sensible name, like Kate. In fact, we decided to ourselves that we'd secretly call a linear trend Kate, a quadratic trend Benjamin, a cubic trend Zoë, and a fourth-order trend Doug. 'That will show the statisticians' we thought to ourselves, and felt a little bit self-satisfied too.

We also saw that after years of denial, my love of making a racket got the better of me. This brings my life story up to date. Admittedly I left out some of the more colourful bits, but only because I couldn't find an extremely tenuous way to link them to statistics. We saw that over my life I managed to completely fail to achieve any of my childhood dreams. It's OK, I have other ambitions now (a bit smaller scale than 'rock star') and I'm looking forward to failing to achieve them too. The question that remains is whether there is life after *Discovering Statistics*. What effect does writing a statistics book have on your life?

R packages used in this chapter

car	nlme
ggplot2	reshape

R functions used in this chapter

aov()	lme()
anova()	loglik()
ggplot()	melt()
gls()	poly()
I()	summary()
intervals()	update()
lm()	

Key terms that I've discovered

AIC	Group mean centring
AR(1)	Growth curve
BIC	Multilevel linear model
Centring	Polynomial
Diagonal	Random coefficient
Fixed coefficient	Random effect
Fixed effect	Random intercept
Fixed intercept	Random slope
Fixed slope	Random variable
Fixed variable	Unstructured
Grand mean centring	Variance components

Smart Alex's tasks

- **Task 1:** Using the cosmetic surgery example, run the analysis described in section 19.6.9 but also including **BDI, Age** and **Gender** as fixed effect predictors. What differences does including these predictors make? ④

- **Task 2:** Using our growth model example in this chapter, analyse the data but include **Gender** as an additional covariate. Does this change your conclusions? ④

- **Task 3: Getting kids to exercise (Hill, Abraham, & Wright, 2007):** The purpose of this research was to examine whether providing children with a leaflet based on the 'theory of planned behaviour' increases children's exercise. There were four different interventions (**Intervention**): a control group, a leaflet, a leaflet and quiz, and a leaflet and plan. A total of 503 children from 22 different classrooms were sampled (**Classroom**). It was not practical to have children in the same classrooms in different conditions, therefore the 22 classrooms were randomly assigned to the four different conditions. Children were asked 'On average over the last three weeks, I have exercised energetically for at least 30 minutes _____ times per week' after the intervention (**Post_Exercise**). Run a multilevel model analysis on these data (**Hill et al. (2007).dat**) to see whether the intervention affected the children's exercise levels (the hierarchy in the data is: children within classrooms within interventions). ④

- **Task 4**: Repeat the above analysis but include the pre-intervention exercise scores (**Pre_Exercise**) as a covariate. What difference does this make to the results? ④

Answers can be found on the companion website.

Further reading

Kreft, I., & de Leeuw, J. (1998). *Introducing multilevel modeling.* London: Sage. (This is a fantastic book that is easy to get into but has a lot of depth too.)

Tabachnick, B. G., & Fidell, L. S. (2001). *Using multivariate statistics* (4th ed.). Boston: Allyn & Bacon. (Chapter 15 is a fantastic account of multilevel linear models that goes a bit more in depth than I do.)

Twisk, J. W. R. (2006). *Applied multilevel analysis: A practical guide.* Cambridge: Cambridge University Press. (An absolutely superb introduction to multilevel modelling. This book is exceptionally clearly written and is aimed at novices. Without question, this is the best beginner's guide that I have read.)

Interesting real research

Cook, S. A., Rosser, R., & Salmon, P. (2006). Is cosmetic surgery an effective psychotherapeutic intervention? A systematic review of the evidence. *Journal of Plastic, Reconstructive & Aesthetic Surgery*, 59, 1133–1151.

Miller, G., Tybur, J. M., & Jordan, B. D. (2007). Ovulatory cycle effects on tip earnings by lap dancers: Economic evidence for human estrus? *Evolution and Human Behavior*, 28, 375–381.

Epilogue: life after discovering statistics

Here's some questions that the writer sent
Can an observer be a participant?
Have I seen too much?
Does it count if it doesn't touch?
If the view is all I can ascertain,
Pure understanding is out of range

(Fugazi, 'Ex Spectator', *The Argument*, 2001)

When I wrote the SPSS version of this book my main ambition was to write a statistics book that I would enjoy reading. Pretty selfish, I know. I thought that if I had a reference book that had a few examples that amused me then it would make life a lot easier when I needed to look something up. I honestly didn't think anyone would buy the thing (well, apart from my mum and dad) and I anticipated a glut of feedback along the lines of 'the whole of Chapter X is completely wrong and you're an arrant fool', or 'you should be ashamed of how many trees have died in the name of this rubbish, you brainless idiot'. In fact, even the publishers didn't think it would sell (they have only revealed this subsequently, I might add). There are several other things that I didn't expect to happen:

1 *Nice emails*: I didn't expect to receive hundreds of extremely nice emails from people who liked the book. To this day it still absolutely amazes me that anyone reads it, let alone takes the time to write me a nice email, and knowing that the book has helped people always puts a huge smile on my face. When the nice comments are followed by four pages of statistics questions the smile fades a bit …

2 *Everybody thinks that I'm a statistician*: I should have seen this one coming really, but since writing a statistics textbook everyone assumes that I'm a statistician. I'm not, I'm a psychologist. Consequently, I constantly disappoint people by not being able to answer their statistics questions. In fact, this book is the sum total of my knowledge about statistics; there is nothing else (statistics-wise) in my brain that isn't in this book. Actually, that's a lie: there is *more* in this book about statistics than in my brain. For example, in the logistic regression chapter there is an example on multinomial logistic regression. To write this new section I read a lot about multinomial logistic regression because I'd never used it. I wrote that section about three years ago, and I've now forgotten everything that I wrote. Should I ever need to do

910

a multinomial logistic regression I will read the chapter in this book and think to myself 'wow, it really sounds as though I know what I'm talking about'.

3   *Craziness on a grand scale*: The nicest thing about life after discovering statistics is the effort that people go to to demonstrate that they are even stranger than me. All of these people have made life after *Discovering statistics* a profoundly enjoyable experience.

- *Catistics*: I've had quite a few photographs of people's cats (and dogs) reading my book (check them out, or post some new ones, on my Facebook page at http://www.facebook.com/ProfAndyField). There has been many a week where one of these in my inbox has turned what was going to be a steaming turd of a day into a fragrant romp through fields of tulips. How can you not get a big stupid grin on your face when you see these?

- *Facebook*: Two particularly strange people from Exeter (UK) whom I have never met set up an 'Andy Field appreciation society' on Facebook. I don't go there much because it scares me a bit. But secretly I think it is quite cool. It's almost like being the rock star that I always wanted to be, except that when people join a rock star's appreciation society they mean it, but people join mine because it's funny. Nevertheless, beggars can't be choosers and I'm happy to overlook a technicality such as the truth if it means that I can believe that I'm popular.

- *Films*: Possibly the strangest thing to have happened is Julie-Renée Kabriel and her bonkers friends from Washburn University producing a video homage to 'Discovering Stats' (http://www.youtube.com/watch?v=oLsrt594Xxc). I was in equal parts crippled with laughter and utterly bemused watching this video. My parents liked it too. (Oddly enough, it's to the tune of 'Sweet Home Alabama' by Lynyrd Skynyrd; I once gave a talk at Aberdeen University (UK) after which I got taken to a bar and ended up (quite unexpectedly) playing drums to that song with a makeshift band of complete strangers.)

- *Invitation to an autopsy*: I got invited to an autopsy. Really! Some (very nice) forensic scientists in Leicester loved this book so much that they felt that I needed to be rewarded for my efforts. They felt that the most appropriate reward would be to offer to take me to see a dead body being carved up (or to spend a day visiting crime scenes). In a strange way, I can see their logic. I haven't been because I'm slightly scared that it's a cruel trick and that it will turn out to be my body on the slab. However, in the interests of having a good story for the next edition I might just go …

- *Befriended by Satan*: I got an email from the then manager of a black metal band, Abgott, who, while using my book for her studies, was impressed to see that I like black metal bands. My band was playing the next week in London and, never one to miss an opportunity, I invited her to come along. She not only turned up, but bought some of the band and some free CDs. They renamed me 'The Evil Statistic'. Buy their albums, buy their albums, buy their albums …

Life after *Discovering statistics* never ceases to amuse me. I never dreamed for a second that I'd be writing numerous editions and an adaptation of it for **R**. I would recommend writing a statistics book to anyone: it changes your life. You get a constant warm fuzzy feeling from being told that you've helped people, strangers send you photos of their pets, they make films about you, they give you CDs, you get an appreciation society, you can go to see corpses being cut up, join a black metal band (well, maybe not, but if my drumming improves and their drummer's arms and legs fall off, who knows?) and have people constantly overestimate your intelligence. Long may the craziness continue.

Troubleshooting R

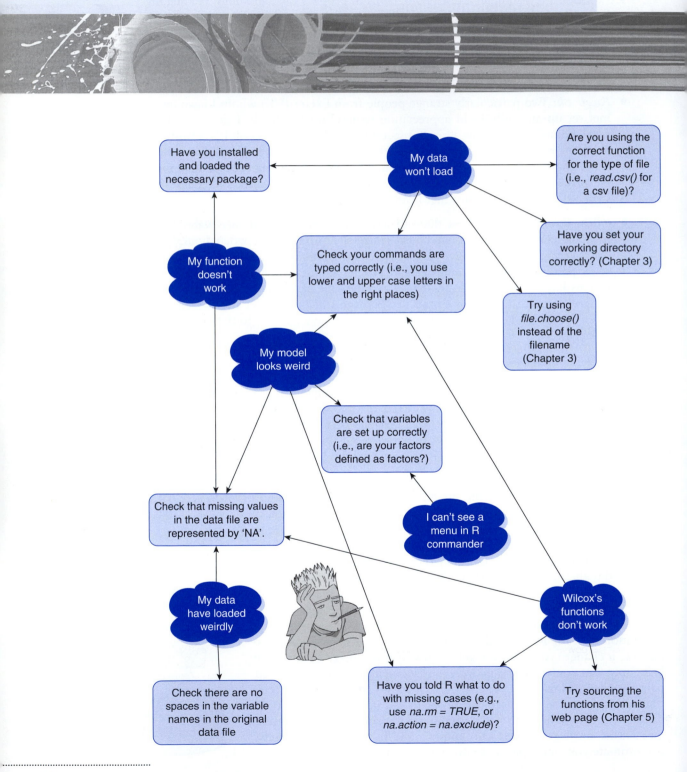

Have you installed and loaded the necessary package?

My data won't load

Are you using the correct function for the type of file (i.e., *read.csv()* for a csv file)?

My function doesn't work

Check your commands are typed correctly (i.e., you use lower and upper case letters in the right places)

Have you set your working directory correctly? (Chapter 3)

Try using *file.choose()* instead of the filename (Chapter 3)

My model looks weird

Check that variables are set up correctly (i.e., are your factors defined as factors?)

Check that missing values in the data file are represented by 'NA'.

I can't see a menu in R commander

My data have loaded weirdly

Wilcox's functions don't work

Check there are no spaces in the variable names in the original data file

Have you told R what to do with missing cases (e.g., use *na.rm = TRUE*, or *na.action = na.exclude*)?

Try sourcing the functions from his web page (Chapter 5)

Glossary

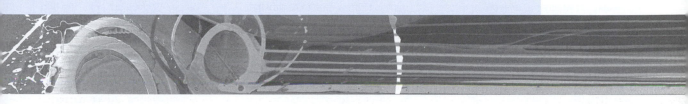

0: the amount of a clue that Sage have about how much effort I put into writing this book.

−2LL: the *log-likelihood* multiplied by minus 2. This version of the likelihood is used in *logistic regression*.

α-level: the probability of making a *Type I error* (usually this value is .05).

A life: what you don't have when writing statistics textbooks.

Adjusted mean: in the context of *analysis of covariance* this is the value of the group mean adjusted for the effect of the *covariate*.

Adjusted predicted value: a measure of the influence of a particular case of data. It is the predicted value of a case from a model estimated without that case included in the data. The value is calculated by re-estimating the model without the case in question, then using this new model to predict the value of the excluded case. If a case does not exert a large influence over the model then its predicted value should be similar regardless of whether the model was estimated including or excluding that case. The difference between the predicted value of a case from the model when that case was included and the predicted value from the model when it was excluded is the *DFFit*.

Adjusted R^2: a measure of the loss of predictive power or *shrinkage* in regression. The adjusted R^2 tells us how much variance in the outcome would be accounted for if the model had been derived from the population from which the sample was taken.

AIC (Akaike's information criterion): a *goodness-of-fit* measure that is corrected for model complexity. That just means that it takes into account how many parameters have been estimated. It is not intrinsically interpretable, but can be compared in different models to see how changing the model affects the fit. A small value represents a better fit of the data.

Alpha factoring: a method of *factor analysis*.

Alternative hypothesis: the prediction that there will be an effect (i.e., that your experimental manipulation will have some effect or that certain variables will relate to each other).

Analysis of covariance: a statistical procedure that uses the *F*-ratio to test the overall fit of a linear model, controlling for the effect that one or more *covariates* have on the *outcome variable*. In experimental research this linear model tends to be defined in terms of group means, and the resulting ANOVA is therefore an overall test of whether group means differ after the variance in the outcome variable explained by any *covariates* has been removed.

Analysis of variance: a statistical procedure that uses the *F*-ratio to test the overall fit of a linear model. In experimental research this linear model tends to be defined in terms of group means, and the resulting ANOVA is therefore an overall test of whether group means differ.

ANCOVA: acronym for *analysis of covariance*.

ANOVA: acronym for *analysis of variance*.

AR(1): this stands for first-order autoregressive structure. It is a covariance structure used in *multilevel models* in which the relationship between scores changes in a systematic way. It is assumed that the correlation between scores gets smaller over time and variances are assumed to be homogeneous. This structure is often used for repeated-measures data (especially when measurements are taken over time such as in growth models).

Autocorrelation: when the *residuals* of two observations in a regression model are correlated.

b_i: unstandardized regression coefficient. Indicates the strength of relationship between a given predictor, *i*, and an outcome in the units of measurement of the predictor. It is the change in the outcome associated with a unit change in the predictor.

β_i: standardized regression coefficient. Indicates the strength of relationship between a given predictor, *i*, and an outcome in a *standardized* form. It is the change in the outcome (in standard deviations) associated with a one standard deviation change in the predictor.

β-level: the probability of making a *Type II error* (Cohen, 1992, suggests a maximum value of .2).

Bar chart: a graph in which a summary statistic (usually the mean) is plotted on the *y*-axis against a categorical variable on the *x*-axis (this categorical variable could represent, for example, groups of people, different times or different experimental conditions). A bar shows the value of the mean for each category. Different-coloured bars may be used to represent levels of a second categorical variable.

Bartlett's test of sphericity: unsurprisingly this is a test of the assumption of *sphericity*. This test examines whether a *variance–covariance matrix* is proportional to an *identity matrix*. Therefore, it effectively tests whether the diagonal elements of the variance–covariance matrix are equal (i.e., group variances are the same), and that the off-diagonal elements are approximately zero (i.e., the *dependent variables* are not *correlated*). Jeremy Miles, who does a lot of multivariate stuff, claims he's never ever seen a matrix that reached non-significance using this test and, come to think of it, I've never seen one either (although I do less multivariate stuff) so you've got to wonder about its practical utility.

Beer-goggles effect: the phenomenon that people of the opposite gender (or the same, depending on your sexual orientation) appear much more attractive after a few alcoholic drinks.

Between-group design: another name for *independent design*.

Between-subject design: another name for *independent design*.

BIC (Schwarz's Bayesian criterion): a *goodness-of-fit* statistic comparable to the AIC, although it is slightly more conservative (it corrects more harshly for the number of parameters being estimated). It should be used when sample sizes are large and the number of parameters is small. It is not intrinsically interpretable, but can be compared in different models to see how changing the model affects the fit. A small value represents a better fit of the data.

Bimodal: a description of a distribution of observations that has two *modes*.

Binary logistic regression: *logistic regression* in which the outcome variable has exactly two categories.

Binary variable: a *categorical variable* that has only two mutually exclusive categories (e.g., being dead or alive).

Biserial correlation: a standardized measure of the strength of relationship between two variables when one of the two variables is *dichotomous*. The biserial correlation

coefficient is used when one variable is a continuous dichotomy (e.g., has an underlying continuum between the categories).

Bivariate correlation: a correlation between two variables.

Bonferroni correction: a correction applied to the *α-level* to control the overall *Type I error rate* when multiple significance tests are carried out. Each test conducted should use a criterion of significance of the *α-level* (normally .05) divided by the number of tests conducted. This is a simple but effective correction, but tends to be too strict when lots of tests are performed.

Bootstrap: a technique from which the sampling distribution of a statistic is estimated by taking repeated values (with replacement) from the data set (so in effect, treating the data as a population from which smaller samples are taken). The statistic of interest (e.g., the *mean* or the *b* coefficient) is calculated for each sample, from which the sampling distribution of the statistic is estimated. The standard error of the statistic is estimated as the standard deviation of the sampling distribution created from the bootstrap samples. From this, confidence intervals and significance tests can be computed.

Boredom effect: refers to the possibility that performance in tasks may be influenced (the assumption is a negative influence) by boredom or lack of concentration if there are many tasks or if the task goes on for a long period of time. In short, what you are experiencing reading this glossary is a boredom effect.

Box's test: a test of the assumption of *homogeneity of covariance matrices*. This test should be non-significant if the matrices are roughly the same. Box's test is very susceptible to deviations from *multivariate normality* and so can be non-significant, not because the *variance–covariance matrices* are similar across groups, but because the assumption of multivariate normality is not tenable. Hence, it is vital to have some idea of whether the data meet the multivariate normality assumption (which is extremely difficult) before interpreting the result of Box's test.

Boxplot (a.k.a. box–whisker diagram): a graphical representation of some important

characteristics of a set of observations. At the centre of the plot is the *median*, which is surrounded by a box, the top and bottom of which are the limits within which the middle 50% of observations fall (the *interquartile range*). Sticking out of the top and bottom of the box are two whiskers, which extend to the most and least extreme scores respectively.

Box–whisker plot: see *boxplot*.

Categorical variable: any variable made up of categories of objects/entities. The UK degree classifications are a good example because degrees are classified as 1, 2:1, 2:2, 3, pass or fail. Therefore, graduates form a categorical variable because they will fall into only one of these categories (hopefully the category of students receiving a first!).

Central limit theorem: this theorem states that when samples are large (above about 30) the *sampling distribution* will take the shape of a *normal distribution* regardless of the shape of the population from which the sample was drawn. For small samples the *t*-distribution better approximates the shape of the sampling distribution. We also know from this theorem that the *standard deviation* of the sampling distribution (i.e., the *standard error* of the sample *mean*) will be equal to the standard deviation of the sample (*s*) divided by the square root of the sample size (*N*).

Central tendency: a generic term describing the centre of a *frequency distribution* of observations as measured by the *mean*, *mode* and *median*.

Centring: the process of transforming a variable into deviations around a fixed point. This fixed point can be any value that is chosen, but typically a mean is used. To centre a variable the mean is subtracted from each score. See *grand mean centring*, *group mean centring*.

Chartjunk: superfluous material that distracts from the data being displayed on a graph.

Chi-square distribution: a *probability distribution* of the sum of squares of several normally distributed variables. It tends to be used to 1) test hypotheses about categorical data, and 2) test the fit of models to the observed data.

Chi-square test: although this term can apply to any *test statistic* having a *chi-square distribution*, it generally refers to Pearson's chi-square test of the independence of two categorical variables. Essentially it tests whether two categorical variables forming a *contingency table* are associated.

Cocaine: the drug of choice at Sage. They inject it into their eyeballs, you know.

Coefficient of determination: the proportion of variance in one variable explained by a second variable. It is the *Pearson correlation coefficient* squared.

Common variance: variance shared by two or more variables.

Communality: the proportion of a variable's variance that is *common variance*. This term is used primarily in *factor analysis*. A variable that has no *unique variance* (or *random variance*) would have a communality of 1, whereas a variable that shares none of its variance with any other variable would have a communality of 0.

Complete separation: a situation in *logistic regression* when the outcome variable can be perfectly predicted by one predictor or a combination of predictors. Suffice it to say this situation makes your computer have the equivalent of a nervous breakdown: it'll start gibbering, weeping and saying it doesn't know what to do.

Component matrix: general term for the *structure matrix* in **R** *principal components analysis*.

Compound symmetry: a condition that holds true when both the variances across conditions are equal (this is the same as the *homogeneity of variance* assumption) and the *covariances* between pairs of conditions are also equal.

Confidence interval: for a given statistic calculated for a sample of observations (e.g., the mean), the confidence interval is a range of values around that statistic that are believed to contain, with a certain probability (e.g., 95%), the true value of that statistic (i.e., the population value).

Confirmatory factor analysis (CFA): a version of *factor analysis* in which specific hypotheses about structure and relations between the *latent variables* that underlie the data are tested.

Confounding variable: a variable (that we may or may not have measured) other than the *predictor variables* in which we're interested that potentially affects an *outcome variable*.

Console window: The main window in **R**. This window contains the command line, which can be used to type and execute commands, but it is also the window in which text output from executed commands is displayed.

Content validity: evidence that the content of a test corresponds to the content of the construct it was designed to cover.

Contingency table: a table representing the cross-classification of two or more *categorical variables*. The levels of each variable are arranged in a grid, and the number of observations falling into each category is noted in the cells of the table. For example, if we took the categorical variables of **glossary** (with two categories: whether an author was made to write a glossary or not), and **mental state** (with three categories: normal, sobbing uncontrollably and utterly psychotic), we could construct a table as below. This instantly tells us that 127 authors who were made to write a glossary ended up as utterly psychotic, compared to only 2 who did not write a glossary.

Continuous variable: a variable that can be measured to any level of precision. (Time is a continuous variable, because there is in principle no limit on how finely it could be measured.)

Cook's distance: a measure of the overall influence of a case on a model. Cook and Weisberg (1982) have suggested that values greater than 1 may be cause for concern.

Correlation coefficient: a measure of the strength of association or relationship between two variables. See *Pearson's correlation coefficient*, *Spearman's correlation coefficient*, *Kendall's tau*.

Correlational research: a form of research in which you observe what naturally goes on in the world without directly interfering with it. This term implies that data will be analysed so as to look at relationships between naturally occurring variables rather than making statements about cause and effect. Compare with *cross-sectional research* and *experimental research*.

Counterbalancing: a process of systematically varying the order in which experimental conditions are conducted. In the simplest case of there being two conditions (A and B), counterbalancing simply implies that half of the participants complete condition A followed by condition B, whereas the remainder do condition B followed by condition A. The aim is to remove systematic bias caused by *practice effects* or *boredom effects*.

Covariance: a measure of the 'average' relationship between two variables. It is the average *cross-product deviation* (i.e., the cross-product divided by one less than the number of observations).

Covariance ratio (CVR): a measure of whether a case influences the variance of the parameters in a *regression model*. When this ratio

		Glossary		
		Author made to write glossary	**No glossary**	**Total**
Mental state	Normal	5	423	428
	Sobbing uncontrollably	23	46	69
	Utterly psychotic	127	2	129
	Total	155	471	626

is close to 1 the case is having very little influence on the variances of the model parameters. Belsey et al. (1980) recommend the following: if the CVR of a case is greater than $1 + [3(k + 1)/n]$ then deleting that case will damage the precision of some of the model's parameters, but if it is less than $1 - [3(k + 1)/n]$ then deleting the case will improve the precision of some of the model's parameters (k is the number of predictors and n is the sample size).

Covariate: a variable that has a relationship with (in terms of *covariance*), or has the potential to be related to, the *outcome variable* we've measured.

Cox and Snell's R^2_{cs}: a version of the *coefficient of determination* for logistic regression. It is based on the log-likelihood of a model (LL(new)) and the log-likelihood of the original model (LL(baseline)), and the sample size, n. However, it is notorious for not reaching its maximum value of 1 (see *Nagelkerke's R^2_N*).

CRAN (Comprehensive R Archive Network): a virtual warehouse that stores the R software, packages associated with it, documentation and code.

Criterion validity: evidence that scores from an instrument correspond with or predict concurrent external measures conceptually related to the measured construct.

Cronbach's α: a measure of the reliability of a scale defined by

$$\alpha = \frac{N^2 \overline{Cov}}{\sum s^2_{item} + \sum Cov_{item}}$$

in which the top half of the equation is simply the number of items (N) squared multiplied by the average covariance between items (the average of the off-diagonal elements in the *variance–covariance matrix*). The bottom half is the sum of all the elements in the *variance–covariance matrix*.

Cross-product deviations: a measure of the 'total' relationship between two variables. It is the deviation of one variable from its mean multiplied by the other variable's deviation from its mean.

Cross-sectional research: a form of research in which you observe what naturally goes on in the world without directly interfering with it. This term specifically implies that data come from people at different age points with different people representing each age point. See also *correlational research*.

Cross-validation: assessing the accuracy of a model across different samples. This is an important step in *generalization*. In a *regression model* there are two main methods of cross-validation: *adjusted R^2* or data splitting, in which the data are split randomly into two halves, and a regression model is estimated for each half and then compared.

Crying: what you feel like doing after writing statistics textbooks.

Cubic trend: if you connected the means in ordered conditions with a line then a cubic trend is shown by two changes in the direction of this line. You must have at least four ordered conditions.

Dataframe: an object containing variables. It differs from a matrix in that the variables can be of differing types (e.g., you can have string variables and numeric variables in the same dataframe but not in the same matrix).

Date variable: variables made up of dates. The data can take forms such as dd-mmm-yyyy (e.g., 21-Jun-1973), dd-mmm-yy (e.g., 21-Jun-73), mm/dd/yy (e.g., 06/21/73) or dd.mm.yyyy (e.g., 21.06.1973).

Degrees of freedom: an impossible thing to define in a few pages let alone a few lines. Essentially it is the number of 'entities' that are free to vary when estimating some kind of statistical parameter. In a more practical sense, it has a bearing on significance tests for many commonly used *test statistics* (such as the *F-ratio*, *t-test*, *chi-square statistic*) and determines the exact form of the *probability distribution* for these *test statistics*. The explanation involving rugby players in Chapter 2 is far more interesting…

Deleted residual: a measure of the influence of a particular case of data. It is the difference between the *adjusted predicted value* for a case and the original observed value for that case.

Density plot: similar to a *histogram* except that, rather than having a summary bar representing the frequency of scores, it shows each individual score as a dot. They can be useful for looking at the shape of a distribution of scores.

Dependent *t*-test: a test using the *t-statistic* that establishes whether two means collected from the same sample (or related observations) differ significantly.

Dependent variable: another name for *outcome variable*. This name is usually associated with experimental methodology (which is the only time it really makes sense) and is so called because it is the variable that is not manipulated by the experimenter and so its value depends on the variables that have been manipulated. To be honest I just use the term *outcome variable* all the time – it makes more sense (to me) and is less confusing.

Deviance: the difference between the observed value of a variable and the value of that variable predicted by a statistical model.

DFA: acronym for discriminant function analysis (see *discriminant analysis*).

DFBeta: a measure of the influence of a case on the values of b_i in a *regression model*. If we estimated a regression parameter b_i and then deleted a particular case and re-estimated the same regression parameter b_i, then the difference between these two estimates would be the DFBeta for the case that was deleted. By looking at the values of the DFBetas, it is possible to identify cases that have a large influence on the parameters of the regression model; however, the size of DFBeta will depend on the units of measurement of the regression parameter.

DFFit: a measure of the influence of a case. It is the difference between the *adjusted predicted value* and the original predicted value of a particular case. If a case is not influential then its DFFit should be zero – hence, we expect non-influential cases to have small DFFit values. However, we have the problem that this statistic depends on the units of measurement of the outcome and so a DFFit of 0.5 will be very small if the outcome ranges from 1 to 100, but very large if the outcome varies from 0 to 1.

Diagonal: a covariance structure used in *multilevel models*. In this variance structure variances are assumed to be heterogeneous and all of the covariances are 0.

Dichotomous: description of a variable that consists of only two categories (e.g., the variable gender is dichotomous because it consists of only two categories: male and female).

Direct oblimin: a method of *oblique rotation*.

Discrete variable: a variable that can only take on certain values (usually whole numbers) on the scale.

Discriminant analysis: also known as discriminant function analysis. This analysis identifies and describes the *discriminant function variates* of a set of variables and is useful as a follow-up test to *MANOVA* as a means of seeing how these variates allow groups of cases to be discriminated.

Discriminant function variate: a linear combination of variables created such that the differences between group means on the transformed variable are maximized. It takes the general form:

$$\text{variate}_{1i} = b_1 X_{1i} + b_2 X_{2i} + \dots + b_n X_{ni}$$

Discriminant score: a score for an individual case on a particular *discriminant function variate* obtained by replacing that case's scores on the measured variables into the equation that defines the variate in question.

Dummy variables: a way of recoding a categorical variable with more than two categories into a series of variables all of which are *dichotomous* and can take on values of only 0 or 1. There are seven basic steps to create such variables: (1) count the number of groups you want to recode and subtract 1; (2) create as many new variables as the value you calculated in step 1 (these are your dummy variables); (3) choose one of your groups as a baseline (i.e., a group against which all other groups should be compared, such as a control group); (4) assign that baseline group values of 0 for all of your dummy variables; (5) for your first dummy variable, assign the value 1 to the first group that you want to compare against the baseline group (assign all other

groups 0 for this variable); (6) for the second dummy variable assign the value 1 to the second group that you want to compare against the baseline group (assign all other groups 0 for this variable); (7) repeat this process until you run out of dummy variables.

Durbin–Watson test: tests for serial correlations between errors in *regression models*. Specifically, it tests whether adjacent residuals are correlated, which is useful in assessing the assumption of *independent errors*. The test statistic can vary between 0 and 4, with a value of 2 meaning that the residuals are uncorrelated. A value greater than 2 indicates a negative correlation between adjacent residuals, whereas a value below 2 indicates a positive correlation. The size of the Durbin–Watson statistic depends upon the number of predictors in the model and the number of observations. For accuracy, look up the exact acceptable values in Durbin and Watson's (1951) original paper. As a very conservative rule of thumb, values less than 1 or greater than 3 are definitely cause for concern; however, values closer to 2 may still be problematic depending on the sample and model.

Ecological validity: evidence that the results of a study, experiment or test can be applied, and allow inferences, to real-world conditions.

Eel: long, snakelike, scaleless fish that lacks pelvic fins. From the order Anguilliformes or Apodes, they should probably not be inserted into your anus to cure constipation (or for any other reason).

Editor window: The editor window in **R** is a basic text editor that enables you to collect together commands into a file rather than executing them individually through the command line in the *console window*.

Effect size: an objective and (usually) standardized measure of the magnitude of an observed effect. Measures include Cohen's *d*, Glass's *g* and Pearson's correlations coefficient, *r*.

Error bar chart: a graphical representation of the mean of a set of observations that includes the 95% confidence interval of the mean. The mean is usually

represented as a circle, square or rectangle at the value of the mean (or a bar extending to the value of the mean). The confidence interval is represented by a line protruding from the mean (upwards, downwards or both) to a short horizontal line representing the limits of the confidence interval. Error bars can be drawn using the standard error or standard deviation instead of the 95% confidence interval.

Error SSCP (E): the error sum of squares and cross-product matrix. This is a *sum of squares and cross-product matrix* for the error in a predictive *linear model* fitted to *multivariate* data. It represents the *unsystematic variance* and is the multivariate equivalent of the *residual sum of squares*.

Eta squared (η^2): an *effect size* measure that is the ratio of the *model sum of squares* to the *total sum of squares*. So, in essence, *the coefficient of determination* by another name. It doesn't have an awful lot going for it: not only is it biased, but it typically measures the overall effect of an ANOVA and effect sizes are more easily interpreted when they reflect specific comparisons (e.g., the difference between two means).

Experimental hypothesis: synonym for *alternative hypothesis*.

Experimental research: a form of research in which one or more variables is systematically manipulated to see their effect (alone or in combination) on an *outcome variable*. This term implies that data will be able to be used to make statements about cause and effect. Compare with *cross-sectional research* and *correlational research*.

Experimentwise error rate: the probability of making a *Type I error* in an experiment involving one or more statistical comparisons when the null hypothesis is true in each case.

Extraction: a term used for the process of deciding whether a *factor* in *factor analysis* is statistically important enough to 'extract' from the data and interpret. The decision is based on the magnitude of the eigenvalue associated with the factor. See *Kaiser's criterion, scree plot*.

F_{max}: see *Hartley's F_{max}*.

F-ratio: a test statistic with a known *probability distribution* (the *F*-distribution). It is the ratio of the average variability in the data that a given model can explain to the average variability unexplained by that same model. It is used to test the overall fit of the model in *simple regression* and *multiple regression*, and to test for overall differences between group means in experiments.

Factor: another name for an *independent variable* or *predictor* that's typically used when describing experimental designs. However, to add to the confusion, it is also used synonymously with *latent variable* in factor analysis.

Factor analysis: a *multivariate* technique for identifying whether the correlations between a set of observed variables stem from their relationship to one or more *latent variables* in the data, each of which takes the form of a *linear model*.

Factor matrix: general term for the *structure matrix* in *factor analysis*.

Factor loading: the *regression coefficient* of a variable for the *linear model* that describes a *latent variable* or *factor* in *factor analysis*.

Factor scores: a single score from an individual entity representing their performance on some *latent variable*. The score can be crudely conceptualized as follows: take an entity's score on each of the variables that make up the factor and multiply it by the corresponding *factor loading* for the variable, then add these values up (or average them).

Factor transformation matrix, Λ: a matrix used in *factor analysis*. It can be thought of as containing the angles through which factors are rotated in factor *rotation*.

Factorial ANOVA: an analysis of variance involving two or more *independent variables* or *predictors*.

Falsification: the act of disproving a hypothesis or theory.

Familywise error rate: the probability of making a *Type I error* in any family of tests when the null hypothesis is true in each case. The 'family of tests' can be loosely defined as a set of tests conducted on the same data set and addressing the same empirical question.

Fisher's exact test: Fisher's exact test (Fisher, 1922) is not so much a test as a way of computing the exact probability of a statistic. It was designed originally to overcome the problem that with small samples the sampling distribution of the chi-square statistic deviates substantially from a chi-square distribution. It should be used with small samples.

Fit: how sexually attractive you find a statistical test. Alternatively, it's the degree to which a statistical model is an accurate representation of some observed data. (Incidentally, it's just plain *wrong* to find statistical tests sexually attractive.)

Fixed coefficient: a coefficient or model parameter that is fixed; that is, it cannot vary over situations or contexts (cf. *random coefficient*).

Fixed effect: An effect in an experiment is said to be a fixed effect if all possible treatment conditions that a researcher is interested in are present in the experiment. Fixed effects can be generalized only to the situations in the experiment. For example, the effect is fixed if we say that we are interested only in the conditions that we had in our experiment (e.g., placebo, low dose and high dose) and we can generalize our findings only to the situation of a placebo, low dose and high dose.

Fixed intercept: A term used in *multilevel modelling* to denote when the intercept in the model is fixed. That is, it is not free to vary across different groups or contexts (cf. *random intercept*).

Fixed slope: A term used in *multilevel modelling* to denote when the slope of the model is fixed. That is, it is not free to vary across different groups or contexts (cf. *random slope*).

Fixed variable: A fixed variable is one that is not supposed to change over time (e.g., for most people their gender is a fixed variable – it never changes).

Frequency distribution: a graph plotting values of observations on the horizontal axis, and the frequency with which each value occurs in the data set on the vertical axis (a.k.a. *histogram*).

Friedman's ANOVA: a non-parametric test of whether more than two related groups differ. It is the non-parametric version of one-way *repeated-measures ANOVA*.

Generalization: the ability of a statistical model to say something beyond the set of observations that spawned it. If a model generalizes it is assumed that predictions from that model can be applied not just to the sample on which it is based, but to a wider population from which the sample came.

Glossary: a collection of grossly inaccurate definitions (written late at night when you really ought to be asleep) of things that you thought you understood until some evil book publisher forced you to try to define them.

Goodness of fit: an index of how well a model fits the data from which it was generated. It's usually based on how well the data predicted by the model correspond to the data that were actually collected.

Grand mean: the *mean* of an entire set of observations.

Grand mean centring: grand mean *centring* means the transformation of a variable by taking each score and subtracting the mean of all scores (for that variable) from it (cf. *group mean centring*).

Grand variance: the *variance* within an entire set of observations.

Graphics window: the window in which graphics or graphs appear (this window is labelled *Quartz* in MacOS).

Greenhouse–Geisser correction: an estimate of the departure from *sphericity*. The maximum value is 1 (the data completely meet the assumption of sphericity) and the minimum is the *lower bound*. Values below 1 indicate departures from sphericity and are used to correct the *degrees of freedom* associated with the corresponding *F-ratios* by multiplying them by the value of the estimate. Some say the Greenhouse–Geisser correction is too conservative (strict) and recommend the *Huynh–Feld correction* instead.

Group mean centring: group mean *centring* is to transform a variable by taking each score and subtracting from it the mean of the scores (for that variable) for the group to which that score belongs (cf. *grand mean centring*).

Growth curve: a curve that summarizes the change in some outcome over time. See *polynomial*.

Harmonic mean: a weighted version of the *mean* that takes account of the relationship between variance and sample size. It is calculated by summing the reciprocal of all observations, then dividing by the number of observations. The reciprocal of the end product is the harmonic mean:

$$H = \frac{1}{\frac{1}{n}\sum_{i=1}^{n}\frac{1}{x_i}}$$

Hartley's F_{max}: also known as the *variance ratio*, is the ratio of the variances between the group with the biggest variance and the group with the smallest variance. This ratio is compared to critical values in a table published by Hartley as a test of *homogeneity of variance*. Some general rules are that with sample sizes (n) of 10 per group, an F_{max} less than 10 is more or less always going to be non-significant, with 15–20 per group the ratio needs to be less than about 5, and with samples of 30–60 the ratio should be below about 2 or 3.

Hat values: another name for *leverage*.

HE^{-1}: this is a matrix that is functionally equivalent to the *hypothesis SSCP* divided by the *error SSCP* in *MANOVA*. Conceptually it represents the ratio of *systematic* to *unsystematic variance*, so is a *multivariate* analogue of the *F-ratio*.

Helmert contrast: a non-orthogonal *planned contrast* that compares the mean of each condition (except the last) to the overall mean of all subsequent conditions combined.

Heterogeneity of variance: the opposite of *homogeneity of variance*. This term means that the variance of one variable varies (i.e., is different) across levels of another variable.

Heteroscedasticity: the opposite of *homoscedasticity*. This occurs when the residuals at each level of the predictor variables(s) have unequal variances. Put another way, at each point along any predictor variable, the spread of residuals is different.

Hierarchical regression: a method of *multiple regression* in which the order in which predictors are entered into the regression model is determined by the researcher based on previous research: variables already known to be predictors are entered first, new variables are entered subsequently.

Histogram: a *frequency distribution*.

Homogeneity of covariance matrices: an assumption of some *multivariate* tests such as

MANOVA. It is an extension of the *homogeneity of variance assumption* in *univariate* analyses. However, as well as assuming that *variances* for each *dependent variable* are the same across groups, it assumes that relationships (*covariances*) between these dependent variables are roughly equal. It is tested by comparing the population *variance–covariance matrices* of the different groups in the analysis.

Homogeneity of regression slopes: an assumption of *analysis of covariance*. This is the assumption that the relationship between the *covariate* and *outcome variable* is constant across different treatment levels. So, if we had three treatment conditions, if there's a positive relationship between the covariate and the outcome in one group, we assume that there is a similar-sized positive relationship between the covariate and outcome in the other two groups too.

Homogeneity of variance: the assumption that the variance of one variable is stable (i.e., relatively similar) at all levels of another variable.

Homoscedasticity: an assumption in regression analysis that the residuals at each level of the predictor variables(s) have similar variances. Put another way, at each point along any predictor variable, the spread of residuals should be fairly constant.

Hosmer and Lemeshow's R_L^2: a version of the *coefficient of determination* for logistic regression. It is a fairly literal translation in that it is the $-2LL$ for the model divided by the original $-2LL$ – in other words, it's the ratio of what the model can explain compared to what there was to explain in the first place!

Hotelling–Lawley trace (T^2): a *test statistic* in *MANOVA*. It is the sum of the eigenvalues for each *discriminant function variate* of the data and so is conceptually the same as the *F-ratio* in *ANOVA*: it is the sum of the ratio of *systematic* and *unsystematic variance* (SS_M/SS_R) for each of the variates.

Huynh–Feldt correction: an estimate of the departure from *sphericity*. The maximum value is 1 (the data completely meet the assumption of sphericity). Values below this indicate departures from sphericity and are used to correct the *degrees*

of freedom associated with the corresponding *F-ratios* by multiplying them by the value of the estimate. It is less conservative than the *Greenhouse–Geisser estimate*, but some say it is too liberal.

Hypothesis: a prediction about the state of the world (see *experimental hypothesis* and *null hypothesis*).

Hypothesis SSCP (H): the hypothesis sum of squares and cross-product matrix. This is a *sum of squares and cross-product matrix* for a predictive *linear model* fitted to *multivariate* data. It represents the *systematic variance* and is the multivariate equivalent of the *model sum of squares*.

Identity matrix: a square matrix (i.e., with the same number of rows and columns) in which the diagonal elements are equal to 1, and the off-diagonal elements are equal to 0. The following are all examples:

$$\begin{pmatrix} 1 & 0 \\ 0 & 1 \end{pmatrix} \quad \begin{pmatrix} 1 & 0 & 0 \\ 0 & 1 & 0 \\ 0 & 0 & 1 \end{pmatrix} \quad \begin{pmatrix} 1 & 0 & 0 & 0 \\ 0 & 1 & 0 & 0 \\ 0 & 0 & 1 & 0 \\ 0 & 0 & 0 & 1 \end{pmatrix}$$

Independence: the assumption that one data point does not influence another. When data come from people, it basically means that the behaviour of one person does not influence the behaviour of another.

Independent ANOVA: *analysis of variance* conducted on any design in which all *independent variables* or *predictors* have been manipulated using different participants (i.e., all data come from different entities).

Independent design: an experimental design in which different treatment conditions utilize different organisms (e.g., in psychology, this would mean using different people in different treatment conditions) and so the resulting data are independent (a.k.a. between-group or between-subject designs).

Independent errors: for any two observations in regression the *residuals* should be uncorrelated (or independent).

Independent factorial design: an experimental design incorporating two or more *predictors* (or *independent variables*), all of which have been manipulated using different participants (or whatever entities are being tested).

Independent *t*-test: a test using the *t-statistic* that establishes whether two means collected from independent samples differ significantly.

Independent variable: another name for a *predictor variable*. This name is usually associated with experimental methodology (which is the only time it makes sense) and is so called because it is the variable that is manipulated by the experimenter and so its value does not depend on any other variables (just on the experimenter). I just use the term *predictor variable* all the time because the meaning of the term is not constrained to a particular methodology.

Interaction effect: the combined effect of two or more *predictor variables* on an *outcome variable*.

Interaction graph: a graph showing the means of two or more *independent variables* in which means of one variable are shown at different levels of the other variable. Unusually the means are connected with lines, or are displayed as bars. These graphs are used to help understand *interaction effects*.

Interquartile range: the limits within which the middle 50% of an ordered set of observations falls. It is the difference between the value of the *upper quartile* and *lower quartile*.

Interval data: data measured on a scale along the whole of which intervals are equal. For example, people's ratings of this book on Amazon.com can range from 1 to 5; for these data to be interval it should be true that the increase in appreciation for this book represented by a change from 3 to 4 along the scale should be the same as the change in appreciation represented by a change from 1 to 2, or 4 to 5.

Interval variable: a variable consisting of *interval data*.

Intraclass correlation (ICC): a *correlation coefficient* that assesses the consistency between measures of the same class (i.e., measures of the same thing). (Cf. *Pearson's correlation coefficient*, which measures the relationship between variables of a different class.) Two common uses are in comparing paired data (such as twins) on the same measure, and assessing the consistency between judges' ratings

of a set of objects. The calculation of these correlations depends on whether a measure of consistency (in which the order of scores from a source is considered, but not the actual value around which the scores are anchored) or absolute agreement (in which both the order of scores and the relative values are considered) is required, and whether the scores represent averages of many measures or just a single measure. This measure is also used in *multilevel linear models* to measure the dependency in data within the same context.

Jonckheere–Terpstra test: this statistic tests for an ordered pattern of medians across independent groups. Essentially it does the same thing as the *Kruskal–Wallis test* (i.e., test for a difference between the medians of the groups), but it incorporates information about whether the order of the groups is meaningful. As such, you should use this test when you expect the groups you're comparing to produce a meaningful order of medians.

Kaiser–Meyer–Olkin (KMO) measure of sampling adequacy: the KMO can be calculated for individual and multiple variables and represents the ratio of the squared correlation between variables to the squared *partial correlation* between variables. It varies between 0 and 1: a value of 0 indicates that the sum of partial correlations is large relative to the sum of correlations, indicating diffusion in the pattern of correlations (hence, *factor analysis* is likely to be inappropriate); a value close to 1 indicates that patterns of correlations are relatively compact and so factor analysis should yield distinct and reliable factors. Values between .5 and .7 are mediocre, values between .7 and .8 are good, values between .8 and .9 are great and values above .9 are superb (see Hutcheson & Sofroniou, 1999).

Kaiser's criterion: a method of *extraction* in *factor analysis* based on the idea of retaining factors with associated eigenvalues greater than 1. This method appears to be accurate when the number of variables in the analysis is less than 30 and the resulting *communalities* (after *extraction*) are all greater than .7, or when the sample size exceeds

250 and the average communality is greater than or equal to .6.

Kendall's tau: a non-parametric correlation coefficient similar to *Spearman's correlation coefficient*, but which should be used in preference for a small data set with a large number of tied ranks.

Kruskal–Wallis test: non-parametric test of whether more than two independent groups differ. It is the non-parametric version of one-way *independent ANOVA*.

Kurtosis: this measures the degree to which scores cluster in the tails of a frequency distribution. A distribution with positive kurtosis (*leptokurtic*, kurtosis > 0) has too many scores in the tails and is too peaked, whereas a distribution with negative kurtosis (*platykurtic*, kurtosis < 0) has too few scores in the tails and is quite flat.

Latent variable: a variable that cannot be directly measured, but is assumed to be related to several variables that can be measured.

Leptokurtic: see *kurtosis*.

Levels of measurement: the relationship between what is being measured and the numbers obtained on a scale.

Levene's test: tests the hypothesis that the variances in different groups are equal (i.e., the difference between the variances is zero). It basically does a one-way ANOVA on the *deviations* (i.e., the absolute value of the difference between each score and the mean of its group). A significant result indicates that the variances are significantly different – therefore, the assumption of *homogeneity of variances* has been violated. When samples sizes are large, small differences in group variances can produce a significant Levene's test and so the *variance ratio* is a useful double-check.

Leverage: leverage statistics (or hat values) gauge the influence of the observed value of the outcome variable over the predicted values. The average leverage value is $(k+1)/n$ in which k is the number of predictors in the model and n is the number of participants. Leverage values can lie between 0 (the case has no influence whatsoever) and 1 (the case has complete influence over prediction). If no cases exert undue influence over the model then we would expect all of the leverage value to be close to the average value. Hoaglin and Welsch (1978) recommend investigating cases with values greater than twice the average ($2(k + 1)/n$) and Stevens (2002) recommends using three times the average ($3(k + 1)/n$) as a cut-off point for identifying cases having undue influence.

Likelihood: the probability of obtaining a set of observations given the parameters of a model fitted to those observations.

Linear model: a model that is based upon a straight line.

Line chart: a graph in which a summary statistic (usually the mean) is plotted on the *y*-axis against a categorical variable on the *x*-axis (this categorical variable could represent, for example, groups of people, different times or different experimental conditions). The value of the mean for each category is shown by a symbol, and means across categories are connected by a line. Different-coloured lines may be used to represent levels of a second categorical variable.

Logistic regression: a version of *multiple regression* in which the outcome is a *categorical variable*. If the categorical variable has exactly two categories the analysis is called binary logistic regression, and when the outcome has more than two categories it is called multinomial logistic regression.

Log-likelihood: a measure of error, or unexplained variation, in categorical models. It is based on summing the probabilities associated with the predicted and actual outcomes and is analogous to the *residual sum of squares* in multiple regression in that it is an indicator of how much unexplained information there is after the model has been fitted. Large values of the log-likelihood statistic indicate poorly fitting statistical models, because the larger the value of the log-likelihood, the more unexplained observations there are. The log-likelihood is the logarithm of the *likelihood*.

Loglinear analysis: a procedure used as an extension of the *chi-square test* to analyse situations in which we have more than two *categorical variables* and we want to test for relationships between these variables. Essentially, a *linear model* is fitted to the data that predicts expected frequencies (i.e., the number of cases expected in a given category). In this respect it is much the same as *analysis of variance* but for entirely categorical data.

Long format data (a.k.a. 'molten' data): data that are arranged such that levels of independent or predictor variables are differentiated by different rows in a *dataframe*. As such, *outcome variable* scores are contained in a single column of data with rows containing information about the attributes of those scores.

Lower bound: the name given to the lowest possible value of the *Greenhouse–Geisser estimate* of *sphericity*. Its value is $1/(k−1)$, in which k is the number of treatment conditions.

Lower quartile: the value that cuts off the lowest 25% of the data. If the data are ordered and then divided into two halves at the median, then the lower quartile is the median of the lower half of the scores.

M-estimator: a robust measure of location. One example is the median. In some cases it is a measure of location computed after outliers have been removed: unlike the *trimmed mean*, the amount of trimming used to remove outliers is determined empirically.

Main effect: the unique effect of a *predictor variable* (or *independent variable*) on an *outcome variable*. The term is usually used in the context of *ANOVA*.

Mann–Whitney test: a *non-parametric test* that looks for differences between two independent samples. That is, it tests whether the populations from which two samples are drawn have the same location. It is functionally the same as *Wilcoxon's rank-sum test*, and both tests are non-parametric equivalents of the *independent t-test*.

MANOVA: acronym for *multivariate analysis of variance*.

Matrix: a collection of items (usually numbers) arranged in columns and rows. The values within a matrix are typically referred to as *components* or *elements*.

Mauchly's test: a test of the assumption of *sphericity*. If this test is significant then the assumption of *sphericity* has not been met and an appropriate correction must be applied to the *degrees of freedom* of the *F-ratio* in *repeated-measures ANOVA*. The test works by comparing the *variance–covariance matrix* of the data to an *identity matrix*; if the variance–covariance matrix is a scalar multiple of an *identity matrix* then sphericity is met.

Maximum-likelihood estimation: a way of estimating statistical parameters by choosing the parameters that make the data most likely to have happened. Imagine for a set of parameters that we calculated the probability (or likelihood) of getting the observed data; if this probability was high then these particular parameters yield a good fit of the data, but conversely if the probability was low, these parameters are a bad fit of our data. Maximum-likelihood estimation chooses the parameters that maximize the probability.

McNemar's test: This tests differences between two related groups (see *Wilcoxon signed-rank test* and *sign test*), when *nominal data* have been used. It's typically used when we're looking for changes in people's scores and it compares the proportion of people who changed their response in one direction (i.e., scores increased) to those who changed in the opposite direction (scores decreased). So, this test needs to be used when we've got two related dichotomous variables.

Mean: a simple statistical model of the centre of a distribution of scores. A hypothetical estimate of the 'typical' score.

Mean squares: a measure of average variability. For every *sum of squares* (which measure the total variability) it is possible to create mean squares by dividing by the number of things used to calculate the sum of squares (or some function of it).

Measurement error: the discrepancy between the numbers used to represent the thing that we're measuring and the actual value of the thing we're measuring (i.e., the value we would get if we could measure it directly).

Median: the middle score of a set of ordered observations. When there is an even number of observations the median is the average of the two scores that fall either side of what would be the middle value.

Meta-analysis: this is a statistical procedure for assimilating research findings. It is based on the simple idea that we can take effect sizes from individual studies that research the same question, quantify the observed effect in a standard way (using *effect sizes*) and then combine these effects to get a more accurate idea of the true effect in the population.

Mixed ANOVA: *analysis of variance* used for a *mixed design*.

Mixed design: an experimental design incorporating two or more *predictors* (or *independent variables*) at least one of which has been manipulated using different participants (or whatever entities are being tested) and at least one of which has been manipulated using the same participants (or entities). Also known as a split-plot design because Fisher developed ANOVA for analysing agricultural data involving 'plots' of land containing crops.

Mode: the most frequently occurring score in a set of data.

Model sum of squares: a measure of the total amount of variability for which a model can account. It is the difference between the *total sum of squares* and the *residual sum of squares*.

Molten data: see *long format data*.

Monte Carlo method: a term applied to the process of using data simulations to solve statistical problems. Its name comes from the use of Monte Carlo roulette tables to generate 'random' numbers in the pre-computer age. Karl Pearson, for example, purchased copies of *Le Monaco*, a weekly Paris periodical that published data from the Monte Carlo casinos' roulette wheels. He used these data as pseudo-random numbers in his statistical research.

Mosaic plot: A graphical display showing the relationship between two or more categorical variables.

Multicollinearity: a situation in which two or more variables are very closely linearly related.

Multilevel linear model: a linear model (just like regression, ANCOVA, ANOVA, etc.) in which the hierarchical structure of the data is explicitly considered. In this analysis regression parameters can be fixed (as in regression and ANOVA) but also random (i.e., free to vary across different contexts at a higher level of the hierarchy). This means that for each regression parameter there is a fixed component but also an estimate of how much the parameter

varies across contexts (see *fixed coefficient*, *random coefficient*).

Multimodal: description of a distribution of observations that has more than two *modes*.

Multinomial logistic regression: *logistic regression* in which the outcome variable has more than two categories.

Multiple R^2: the multiple correlation coefficient squared. It is the proportion of variance shared by the observed values of an outcome and the values of the outcome predicted by a multiple regression model.

Multiple regression: an extension of *simple regression* in which an outcome is predicted by a linear combination of two or more predictor variables. The form of the model is:

$$Y_i = (b_0 + b_1 X_{1i} + b_2 X_{2i} + \ldots + b_n X_{ni}) + \varepsilon_i$$

in which the outcome is denoted as Y, and each predictor is denoted as X. Each predictor has a regression coefficient b associated with it, and b_0 is the value of the outcome when all predictors are zero.

Multivariate: means 'many variables' and is usually used when referring to analyses in which there is more than one *outcome variable* (e.g., MANOVA, *principal components analysis*, etc.).

Multivariate analysis of variance: family of tests that extend the basic *analysis of variance* to situations in which more than one *outcome variable* has been measured.

Multivariate normality: an extension of a normal distribution to multiple variables. It is a *probability distribution* of a set of variables $v' = \begin{bmatrix} v_1, v_2 \ldots, v_n \end{bmatrix}$ given by:

$$f(v') = 2\pi^{-\frac{n}{2}} |\Sigma|^{-\frac{1}{2}} \exp\left\{ -\frac{1}{2}(v-\mu)' \Sigma^{-1}(v-\mu) \right\}$$

in which μ is the vector of means of the variables, and Σ is the *variance–covariance* matrix. If that made any sense to you then you're cleverer than I am.

Nagelkerke's R_N^2: a version of the *coefficient of determination* for logistic regression. It is a variation on *Cox and Snell's R_{CS}^2*, which overcomes the problem that this statistic has of not being able to reach its maximum value.

Negative skew: see *skew*.

Nominal variable: where numbers merely represent names. For

example, the numbers on sports players shirts: a player with the number 1 on her back is not necessarily worse than a player with a 2 on her back. The numbers have no meaning other than denoting the type of player (i.e., full back, centre forward, etc.).

Non-parametric tests: a family of statistical procedures that do not rely on the restrictive assumptions of parametric tests. In particular, they do not assume that the sampling distribution is normally distributed.

Normal distribution: a *probability distribution* of a random variable that is known to have certain properties. It is perfectly symmetrical (has a *skew* of 0), and has a *kurtosis* of 0.

Normally distributed data (as an assumption): when generalizing the findings of *parametric tests* there is typically an assumption made that something is normally distributed; in some cases it is the sampling distribution, in others the errors in the model. If this assumption is not true then robust tests should be applied.

Null hypothesis: the reverse of the *experimental hypothesis* that your prediction is wrong and the predicted effect doesn't exist.

Numeric variables: variables involving numbers.

Object: anything created in **R**. It could be a variable, a collection of variables, a statistical model, etc. Objects can be single values (such as the mean of a set of scores) or collections of information; for example, when you run an analysis, you create an object that contains the output of that analysis, which means that this object contains many different values and variables.

Oblique rotation: a method of *rotation* in *factor analysis* that allows the underlying factors to be correlated.

Odds: the probability of an event occurring divided by the probability of that event not occurring.

Odds ratio: the ratio of the *odds* of an event occurring in one group compared to another. So, for example, if the odds of dying after writing a glossary are 4, and the odds of dying after not writing a glossary are 0.25, then the odds ratio is 4/0.25 = 16. This means that the *odds* of dying if you write a glossary are 16 times higher than if you don't. An odds ratio of

1 would indicate that the *odds* of a particular outcome are equal in both groups.

Omega squared: an *effect size* measure associated with ANOVA that is less bias than *eta squared*. It is a (sometimes hideous) function of the *model sum of squares* and the *residual sum of squares* and isn't actually much use because it measures the overall effect of the ANOVA and so can't be interpreted in a meaningful way. In all other respects it's great though.

One-tailed test: a test of a directional hypothesis. For example, the hypothesis 'the longer I write this glossary, the more I want to place my editor's genitals in a starved crocodile's mouth' requires a one-tailed test because I've stated the direction of the relationship (see also *two-tailed test*).

Ordinal variable: data that tell us not only that things have occurred, but also the order in which they occurred. These data tell us nothing about the differences between values. For example, gold, silver and bronze medals are ordinal: they tell us that the gold medallist was better than the silver medallist, but they don't tell us how much better (was gold a lot better than silver, or were gold and silver very closely competed?).

Orthogonal: means perpendicular (at right angles) to something. It tends to be equated to *independence* in statistics because of the connotation that perpendicular *linear models* in geometric space are completely independent (one is not influenced by the other).

Orthogonal rotation: a method of *rotation* in *factor analysis* that keeps the underlying factors independent (i.e., not correlated).

Outcome variable: a variable whose values we are trying to predict from one or more *predictor variables*.

Outlier: an observation very different from most others. Outliers can bias statistics such as the mean.

Package: a collection of functions that, once the package is installed and loaded, can be used in **R**.

Pairwise comparisons: comparisons of pairs of means.

Parametric test: a test that requires data from one of the large catalogue of distributions that statisticians have described. Normally this term is used for parametric tests based on the *normal distribution*, which require four basic assumptions that must be met for the test to be accurate: a normally distributed sampling distribution (see *normal distribution*), *homogeneity of variance*, *interval* or *ratio data*, and *independence*.

Part correlation: another name for a *semi-partial correlation*.

Partial correlation: a measure of the relationship between two variables while 'controlling' the effect on both of one or more additional variables.

Partial eta squared (partial η^2): a version of *eta squared* that is the proportion of variance that a variable explains when excluding other variables in the analysis. Eta squared is the proportion of total variance explained by a variable, whereas partial eta squared is the proportion of variance that a variable explains that is not explained by other variables.

Partial out: to partial out the effect of a variable is to remove the variance that the variable shares with other variables in the analysis before looking at their relationships (see *partial correlation*).

Pattern matrix: a matrix in *factor analysis* containing the *regression coefficients* for each variable on each *factor* in the data. See also *structure matrix*.

Pearson's correlation coefficient: or Pearson's product-moment correlation coefficient to give it its full name, is a *standardized* measure of the strength of relationship between two variables. It can take any value from −1 (as one variable changes, the other changes in the opposite direction by the same amount), through 0 (as one variable changes the other doesn't change at all), to +1 (as one variable changes, the other changes in the same direction by the same amount).

Perfect collinearity: exists when at least one predictor in a *regression model* is a perfect linear combination of the others (the simplest example being two predictors that are perfectly correlated – they have a correlation coefficient of 1).

Phi: a measure of the strength of association between two *categorical variables*. Phi is used with 2×2 *contingency tables* (tables which have two categorical variables and each variable has only two categories). Phi is a variant of the *chi-square test*, χ^2: it is given by $\phi = \sqrt{\chi^2/n}$, in which n is the total number of observations.

Pillai–Bartlett trace (V): a *test statistic* in *MANOVA*. It is the sum of the proportion of explained variance on the *discriminant function variates* of the data. As such, it is similar to the ratio of SS_M/SS_T.

Planned comparisons: another name for *planned contrasts*.

Planned contrasts: a set of comparisons between group means that are constructed before any data are collected. These are theory-led comparisons and are based on the idea of partitioning the variance created by the overall effect of group differences into gradually smaller portions of variance. These tests have more power than *post hoc tests*.

Platykurtic: see *kurtosis*.

Point-biserial correlation: a standardized measure of the strength of relationship between two variables when one of the two variables is *dichotomous*. The point-biserial correlation coefficient is used when the dichotomy is discrete, or true, dichotomy (i.e., one for which there is no underlying continuum between the categories). An example of this is pregnancy: you can be either pregnant or not, there is no in-between state.

Polychotomous logistic regression: another name for *multinomial logistic regression*.

Polynomial: a posh name for a *growth curve* or trend over time. If *time* is our predictor variable, then any polynomial is tested by including a variable that is the predictor to the power of the order of polynomial that we want to test: a linear trend is tested by *time* alone, a quadratic or second-order polynomial is tested by including a predictor that is *time*^{2}, for a fifth-order polynomial we need a predictor of *time*^{5} and for an *n*th-order polynomial we would have to include *time*^{n} as a predictor.

Polynomial contrast: a contrast that tests for trends in the data. In its most basic form it looks for a linear trend (i.e., that the group means increase proportionately).

Population: in statistical terms this usually refers to the collection of units (be they people, plankton, plants, cities, suicidal authors, etc.)

to which we want to generalize a set of findings or a statistical model.

Positive skew: see *skew*.

Post hoc **tests:** a set of comparisons between group means that were not thought of before data were collected. Typically these tests involve comparing the means of all combinations of pairs of groups. To compensate for the number of tests conducted, each test uses a strict criterion for significance. As such, they tend to have less power than *planned contrasts*. They are usually used for exploratory work for which no firm hypotheses were available on which to base planned contrasts.

Power: the ability of a test to detect an effect of a particular size (a value of .8 is a good level to aim for).

Practice effect: refers to the possibility that participants' performance in a task may be influenced (positively or negatively) if they repeat the task because of familiarity with the experimental situation and/or the measures being used.

Predictor variable: a variable that is used to try to predict values of another variable known as an *outcome variable*.

Principal components analysis (PCA): a *multivariate* technique for identifying the linear components of a set of variables.

Probability distribution: a curve describing an idealized *frequency distribution* of a particular variable from which it is possible to ascertain the probability with which specific values of that variable will occur. For categorical variables it is simply a formula yielding the probability with which each category occurs.

Promax: a method of *oblique rotation* that is computationally faster than *direct oblimin* and so useful for large data sets.

Q-Q plot: Short for quantile–quantile plot. A graph plotting the *quantiles* of a variable against the quantiles of a particular distribution (often a *normal distribution*). If values fall on the diagonal of the plot then the variable shares the same distribution as the one specified. Deviations from the diagonal show deviations from the distribution of interest.

Quadratic trend: if the means in ordered conditions are connected with a line then a quadratic trend is shown by one change in the direction of this line (e.g., the line

is curved in one place); the line is, therefore, U-shaped. There must be at least three ordered conditions.

Qualitative methods: extrapolating evidence for a theory from what people say or write (contrast with *quantitative methods*).

Quantiles: values that split a data set into equal portions. *Quartiles*, for example, are a special case of quantiles that split the data into four equal parts. Similarly, *percentiles* are points that split the data into 100 equal parts and noniles are points that split the data into nine equal parts (you get the general idea).

Quantitative methods: inferring evidence for a theory through measurement of variables that produce numeric outcomes (contrast with *qualitative methods*).

Quartic trend: if the means in ordered conditions are connected with a line then a quartic trend is shown by three changes in the direction of this line. There must be at least five ordered conditions.

Quartiles: a generic term for the three values that cut an ordered data set into four equal parts. The three quartiles are known as the *lower quartile*, the second quartile (or *median*) and the *upper quartile*.

Quartimax: a method of *orthogonal rotation*. It attempts to maximize the spread of factor loadings for a variable across all *factors*. This often results in lots of variables loading highly on a single *factor*.

Quartz window: the name of the window in which graphics and graphs appear if you use MacOS.

Random coefficient: a coefficient or model parameter that is free to vary over situations or contexts (cf. *fixed coefficient*).

Random effect: an effect is said to be random if the experiment contains only a sample of possible treatment conditions. Random effects can be generalized beyond the treatment conditions in the experiment. For example, the effect is random if we say that the conditions in our experiment (e.g., placebo, low dose and high dose) are only a sample of possible conditions (maybe we could have tried a very high dose). We can generalize this random effect beyond just placebos, low doses and high doses.

Random intercept: A term used in *multilevel modelling* to denote when

the intercept in the model is free to vary across different groups or contexts (cf. *fixed intercept*).

Random slope: A term used in *multilevel modelling* to denote when the slope of the model is free to vary across different groups or contexts (cf. *fixed slope*).

Random variable: a random variable is one that varies over time (e.g., your weight is likely to fluctuate over time).

Random variance: variance that is unique to a particular variable but not reliably so.

Randomization: the process of doing things in an unsystematic or random way. In the context of experimental research the word usually applies to the random assignment of participants to different treatment conditions.

Range: the range of scores is value of the smallest score subtracted from the highest score. It is a measure of the dispersion of a set of scores. See also *variance*, *standard deviation*, and *interquartile range*.

Ranking: the process of transforming raw scores into numbers that represent their position in an ordered list of those scores. i.e., the raw scores are ordered from lowest to highest and the lowest score is assigned a rank of 1, the next highest score is assigned a rank of 2, and so on.

Ratio variable: an *interval variable* but with the additional property that ratios are meaningful. For example, people's ratings of this book on Amazon.com can range from 1 to 5; for these data to be ratio not only must they have the properties of *interval variables*, but in addition a rating of 4 should genuinely represent someone who enjoyed this book twice as much as someone who rated it as 2. Likewise, someone who rated it as 1 should be half as impressed as someone who rated it as 2.

Regression coefficient: see b_i and β_i.

Regression model: see *multiple regression* and *simple regression*.

Regression line: a line on a scatterplot representing the *regression model* of the relationship between the two variables plotted.

Related design: another name for a *repeated-measures design*.

Related factorial design: an experimental design incorporating two or more *predictors* (or *independent variables*), all of which have been manipulated using the same participants (or whatever entities are being tested).

Reliability: the ability of a measure to produce consistent results when the same entities are measured under different conditions.

Repeated-measures ANOVA: an *analysis of variance* conducted on any design in which the *independent variable* (*predictor*) or *variables* (*predictors*) have all been measured using the same participants in all conditions.

Repeated-measures design: an experimental design in which different treatment conditions utilize the same organisms (i.e., in psychology, this would mean the same people take part in all experimental conditions) and so the resulting data are related (a.k.a. related design or within-subject designs).

Residual: The difference between the value a model predicts and the value observed in the data on which the model is based. When the residual is calculated for each observation in a data set the resulting collection is referred to as the *residuals*.

Residual sum of squares: a measure of the variability that cannot be explained by the model fitted to the data. It is the total squared *deviance* between the observations, and the value of those observations predicted by whatever model is fitted to the data.

Residuals: see *residual*.

Robust test: A term applied to a family of procedures to estimate statistics that are reliable even when the normal assumptions of the statistic are not met.

Rotation: a process in *factor analysis* for improving the interpretability of factors. In essence, an attempt is made to transform the *factors* that emerge from the analysis in such a way as to maximize *factor loadings* that are already large, and minimize factor loadings that are already small. There are two general approaches: *orthogonal rotation* and *oblique rotation*.

Roy's largest root: a *test statistic* in *MANOVA*. It is the eigenvalue for the first *discriminant function variate* of a set of observations. So, it is the same as the *Hotelling–Lawley trace*, but for the first variate only.

It represents the proportion of explained variance to unexplained variance (SS_M/SS_R) for the first discriminant function.

Sample: a smaller (but hopefully representative) collection of units from a *population* used to determine truths about that population (e.g., how a given population behaves in certain conditions).

Sampling distribution: the *probability distribution* of a statistic. We can think of this as follows: if we take a *sample* from a *population* and calculate some statistic (e.g., the *mean*), the value of this statistic will depend somewhat on the sample we took. As such, the statistic will vary slightly from sample to sample. If, hypothetically, we took lots and lots of samples from the population and calculated the statistic of interest we could create a frequency distribution of the values we get. The resulting distribution is what the sampling distribution represents: the distribution of possible values of a given statistic that we could expect to get from a given population.

Sampling variation: the extent to which a statistic (the mean, median, *t*, *F*, etc.) varies in samples taken from the same population.

Saturated model: a model that perfectly fits the data and, therefore, has no error. It contains all possible *main effects* and *interactions* between variables.

Scatterplot: a graph that plots values of one variable against the corresponding value of another variable (and the corresponding value of a third variable can also be included on a 3-D scatterplot).

Scree plot: a graph plotting each *factor* in a *factor analysis* (X-axis) against its associated eigenvalue (Y-axis). It shows the relative importance of each factor. This graph has a very characteristic shape (there is a sharp descent in the curve followed by a tailing off) and the point of inflexion of this curve is often used as a means of *extraction*. With a sample of more than 200 participants, this provides a fairly reliable criterion for extraction (Stevens, 2002)

Second quartile: another name for the *median*.

Semi-partial correlation: a measure of the relationship between two variables while 'controlling' the effect that one or more additional variables

has on one of those variables. If we call our variables *x* and *y*, it gives us a measure of the variance in *y* that *x* alone shares.

Shapiro–Wilk test: a test of whether a distribution of scores is significantly different from a *normal distribution*. A significant value indicates a deviation from normality, but this test is notoriously affected by large samples in which small deviations from normality yield significant results.

Shrinkage: the loss of predictive power of a regression model if the model had been derived from the population from which the sample was taken, rather than the sample itself.

Simple effects analysis: this analysis looks at the effect of one *independent variable* (categorical *predictor variable*) at individual levels of another *independent variable*.

Simple regression: a *linear model* in which one variable or outcome is predicted from a single predictor variable. The model takes the form:

$$Y_i = (b_0 + b_1 X_i) + \varepsilon_i$$

in which *Y* is the outcome variable, *X* is the predictor, b_1 is the regression coefficient associated with the predictor and b_0 is the value of the outcome when the predictor is zero.

Singularity: a term used to describe variables that are perfectly correlated (i.e., the *correlation coefficient* is 1 or −1).

Skew: a measure of the symmetry of a *frequency distribution*. Symmetrical distributions have a skew of 0. When the frequent scores are clustered at the lower end of the distribution and the tail points towards the higher or more positive scores, the value of skew is positive. Conversely, when the frequent scores are clustered at the higher end of the distribution and the tail points towards the lower more negative scores, the value of skew is negative.

Spearman's correlation coefficient: a standardized measure of the strength of relationship between two variables that does not rely on the assumptions of a *parametric test*. It is *Pearson's correlation coefficient* performed on data that have been converted into ranked scores.

Sphericity: a less restrictive form of *compound symmetry*, which assumes that the variances of the differences between data taken from the same participant (or other entity being tested) are equal. This assumption is most commonly found in *repeated-measures ANOVA* but applies only where there are more than two points of data from the same participant (see also *Greenhouse–Geisser correction*, *Huynh–Feldt correction*).

Split-half reliability: a measure of *reliability* obtained by splitting items on a measure into two halves (in some random fashion) and obtaining a score from each half of the scale. The correlation between the two scores, corrected to take account of the fact the correlations are based on only half of the items, is used as a measure of reliability. There are two popular ways to do this. Spearman (1910) and Brown (1910) developed a formula that takes no account of the standard deviation of items:

$$r_{sh} = \frac{2r_{12}}{1 + r_{12}}$$

in which r_{12} is the correlation between the two halves of the scale. Flanagan (1937) and Rulon (1939), however, proposed a measure that does account for item variance:

$$r_{sh} = \frac{4r_{12} \times s_1 \times s_2}{s_T^2}$$

in which s_1 and s_2 are the standard deviations of each half of the scale, and s_T^2 is the variance of the whole test. See Cortina (1993) for more detail.

Square matrix: a *matrix* that has an equal number of columns and rows.

Standard deviation: an estimate of the average variability (spread) of a set of data measured in the same units of measurement as the original data. It is the square root of the *variance*.

Standard error: the standard deviation of the *sampling distribution* of a statistic. For a given statistic (e.g., the *mean*) it tells us how much variability there is in this statistic across *samples* from the same *population*. Large values, therefore, indicate that a statistic from a given sample may not be an accurate reflection of the population from which the sample came.

Standard error of differences: if we were to take several pairs of samples from a population and calculate their means, then we could also

calculate the difference between their means. If we plotted these differences between sample means as a *frequency distribution*, we would have the *sampling distribution* of differences. The standard deviation of this sampling distribution is the *standard error of differences*. As such it is a measure of the variability of differences between sample means.

Standard error of the mean (SE): the full name of the *standard error*.

Standardization: the process of converting a variable into a standard unit of measurement. The unit of measurement typically used is *standard deviation* units (see also *z-scores*). Standardization allows us to compare data when different units of measurement have been used (we could compare weight measured in kilograms to height measured in inches).

Standardized: see *standardization*.

Standardized DFBeta: a *standardized* version of *DFBeta*. These standardized values are easier to use than DFBeta because universal cut-off points can be applied. Stevens (2002) suggests looking at cases with absolute values greater than 2.

Standardized DFFit: a *standardized* version of *DFFit*.

Standardized residuals: the *residuals* of a model expressed in standard deviation units. Standardized residuals with an absolute value greater than 3.29 (actually, we usually just use 3) are cause for concern because in an average sample a value this high is unlikely to happen by chance; if more than 1% of our observations have standardized residuals with an absolute value greater than 2.58 (we usually just say 2.5), there is evidence that the level of error within our model is unacceptable (the model is a fairly poor fit of the sample data); and if more than 5% of observations have standardized residuals with an absolute value greater than 1.96 (or 2 for convenience), then there is also evidence that the model is a poor representation of the actual data.

Stepwise regression: a method of multiple regression in which variables are entered into the model based on a statistical criterion (the *semi-partial correlation* with the *outcome variable*). Once a new

variable is entered into the model, all variables in the model are assessed to see whether they should be removed.

String variables: variables involving words (i.e., letter strings). Such variables could include responses to open-ended questions such as 'how much do you like writing glossary entries?'; the response might be 'about as much as I like placing my gonads on hot coals'.

Structure matrix: a matrix in *factor analysis* containing the *correlation coefficients* for each variable on each *factor* in the data. When *orthogonal rotation* is used this is the same as the *pattern matrix*, but when oblique rotation is used these matrices are different.

Studentized deleted residual: a measure of the influence of a particular case of data. This is a standardized version of the *deleted residual*.

Studentized residuals: a variation on *standardized residuals*. Studentized residuals are the *unstandardized residual* divided by an estimate of its standard deviation that varies point by point. These residuals have the same properties as the *standardized residuals* but usually provide a more precise estimate of the error variance of a specific case.

Sum of squared errors: another name for the *sum of squares*.

Sum of squares (SS): an estimate of total variability (spread) of a set of data. First the *deviance* for each score is calculated, and then this value is squared. The SS is the sum of these squared deviances.

Sum of squares and cross-products matrix (SSCP matrix): a *square matrix* in which the diagonal elements represent the *sum of squares* for a particular variable, and the off-diagonal elements represent the *cross-products* between pairs of variables. The SSCP matrix is basically the same as the *variance–covariance matrix*, except the SSCP matrix expresses variability and between-variable relationships as total values, whereas the variance–covariance matrix expresses them as average values.

Suppressor effects: when a predictor has a significant effect but only when another variable is held constant.

Systematic variation: variation due to some genuine effect (be that the effect of an experimenter doing something to all of the participants in one sample but not in other samples, or natural variation between sets of variables). We can think of this as variation that can be explained by the model that we've fitted to the data.

t-statistic: Student's *t* is a *test statistic* with a known *probability distribution* (the *t*-distribution). In the context of regression it is used to test whether a regression coefficient *b* is significantly different from zero; in the context of experimental work it is used to test whether the differences between two means are significantly different from zero. See also *dependent t-test* and *independent t-test*.

Tertium quid: the possibility that an apparent relationship between two variables is actually caused by the effect of a third variable on them both (often called *the third-variable problem*).

Test–retest reliability: the ability of a measure to produce consistent results when the same entities are tested at two different points in time.

Test statistic: a statistic for which we know how frequently different values occur. The observed value of such a statistic is typically used to test *hypotheses*.

Theory: although it can be defined more formally, a theory is a hypothesized general principle or set of principles that explain known findings about a topic and from which new hypotheses can be generated.

Tolerance: tolerance statistics measure *multicollinearity* and are simply the reciprocal of the *variance inflation factor* (1/VIF). Values below 0.1 indicate serious problems, although Menard (1995) suggests that values below 0.2 are worthy of concern.

Total SSCP (*T*): the total sum of squares and cross-product matrix. This is a *sum of squares and cross-product matrix* for an entire set of observations. It is the *multivariate* equivalent of the *total sum of squares*.

Total sum of squares: a measure of the total variability within a set of observations. It is the total squared *deviance* between each observation and the overall mean of all observations.

Transformation: the process of applying a mathematical function to all observations in a data set, usually to correct some distributional abnormality such as *skew* or *kurtosis*.

Treatment contrast: a contrast in which each category is compared to a user-defined baseline category.

Trimmed mean: a statistic used in many *robust tests*. Imagine we had 20 scores representing the annual income of students (in thousands, rounded to the nearest thousand: 2, 2, 2, 2, 3, 3, 3, 3, 3, 4, 4, 4, 4, 4, 4, 4, 4, 4, 6, 35. The mean income is 5 (£5000). This value is biased by an outlier. A trimmed mean is simply a mean based on the distribution of scores after some percentage of scores has been removed from each extreme of the distribution. So, a 10% trimmed mean will remove 10% of scores from the top and bottom of ordered scores before the mean is calculated. With 20 scores, removing 10% of scores involves removing the top and bottom 2 scores. This gives us: 2, 2, 3, 3, 3, 3, 3, 4, 4, 4, 4, 4, 4, 4, 4, 4, the mean of which is 3.44. The mean depends on a symmetrical distribution to be accurate, but a trimmed mean produces accurate results even when the distribution is not symmetrical. There are more complex examples of robust methods such as the *bootstrap*.

Two-tailed test: a test of a non-directional hypothesis. For example, the hypothesis 'writing this glossary has some effect on what I want to do with my editor's genitals' requires a two-tailed test because it doesn't suggest the direction of the relationship. See also *one-tailed test*.

Type I error: occurs when we believe that there is a genuine effect in our population, when in fact there isn't.

Type II error: occurs when we believe that there is no effect in the population when, in reality, there is.

Unique variance: variance that is specific to a particular variable (i.e., is not shared with other variables). We tend to use the term 'unique variance' to refer to variance that can be reliably attributed to only one measure, otherwise it is called *random variance*.

Univariate: means 'one variable' and is usually used to refer to situations in which only one *outcome variable* has

been measured (i.e., *ANOVA*, *t-tests*, *Mann–Whitney tests*, etc.).

Unstructured: a covariance structure used in *multilevel models*. This covariance structure is completely general. Covariances are assumed to be completely unpredictable: they do not conform to a systematic pattern.

Unstandardized residuals: the *residuals* of a model expressed in the units in which the original outcome variable was measured.

Unsystematic variation: this is variation that isn't due to the effect in which we're interested (so could be due to natural differences between people in different samples such as differences in intelligence or motivation). We can think of this as variation that can't be explained by whatever model we've fitted to the data.

Upper quartile: the value that cuts off the highest 25% of ordered scores. If the scores are ordered and then divided into two halves at the median, then the upper quartile is the median of the top half of the scores.

Validity: evidence that a study allows correct inferences about the question it was aimed to answer or that a test measures what it set out to measure conceptually (see also *content validity*, *criterion validity*).

Variable view: there are two ways to view the contents of the data editor window. The variable view allows you to define properties of the variables for which you wish to enter data. See also *data view*.

Variables: anything that can be measured and can differ across entities or across time.

Variance: an estimate of average variability (spread) of a set of data. It is the sum of squares divided by the number of values on which the sum of squares is based minus 1.

Variance components: a covariance structure used in *multilevel models*. This covariance structure is very simple and assumes that all random effects are independent and variances of random effects are assumed to be the same and sum to the variance of the outcome variable.

Variance–covariance matrix: a square matrix (i.e., same number of columns and rows) representing the variables measured. The diagonals represent the *variances* within each variable, whereas the off-diagonals represent the *covariances* between pairs of variables.

Variance inflation factor (VIF): a measure of *multicollinearity*. The VIF indicates whether a predictor has a strong linear relationship with the other predictor(s). Myers (1990) suggests that a value of 10 is a good value at which to worry. Bowerman and O'Connell (1990) suggest that if the average VIF is greater than 1, then multicollinearity may be biasing the regression model.

Variance ratio: see *Hartley's F_{max}*.

Variance sum law: states that the variance of a difference between two independent variables is equal to the sum of their variances.

Varimax: a method of *orthogonal rotation*. It attempts to maximize the dispersion of *factor loadings* within *factors*. Therefore, it tries to load a smaller number of variables highly on each factor, resulting in more interpretable clusters of factors.

VIF: see *variance inflation factor*.

Wald statistic: a *test statistic* with a known *probability distribution* (a *chi-square distribution*) that is used to test whether the *b* coefficient for a predictor in a *logistic* regression model is significantly different from zero. It is analogous to the *t-statistic* in a *regression model* in that it is simply the *b* coefficient divided by its standard error. The Wald statistic is inaccurate when the regression coefficient (*b*) is large, because the standard error tends to become inflated, resulting in the Wald statistic being underestimated.

Weights: a number by which something (usually a variable in statistics) is multiplied. The weight assigned to a variable determines the influence that variable has within a mathematical equation: large weights give the variable a lot of influence.

Welch's *F*: a version of the *F*-ratio designed to be accurate when the assumption of *homogeneity of variance* has been violated. Not to be confused with the squelch test which is where you shake your head around after writing statistics books to see if you still have a brain.

Welch's *t*-test: a modification of the *independent t-test* that does not assume equal population variances. Therefore, it can be used as an adjustment to correct for violation of the assumption of homogeneity of variance.

Wide format data: data that are arranged such that levels of independent or predictor variables are differentiated by different columns in a *dataframe*. As such, *outcome variable* scores are contained in multiple columns of data each column representing a level of an independent variable.

Wilcoxon's rank-sum test: a *non-parametric test* that looks for differences between two independent samples. That is, it tests whether the populations from which two samples are drawn have the same location. It is functionally the same as the *Mann–Whitney test*, and both tests are non-parametric equivalents of the *independent t-test*.

Wilcoxon signed-rank test: a *non-parametric test* that looks for differences between two related samples. It is the non-parametric equivalent of the *related t-test*.

Wilks's lambda (λ): a *test statistic* in *MANOVA*. It is the product of the unexplained variance on each of the *discriminant function variates*, so it represents the ratio of error variance to total variance (SS_R/SS_T) for each variate.

Within-subject design: another name for a *repeated-measures design*.

Workspace: the collection of objects, models, dataframes and other things that you have created during an **R** session.

Working directory: a directory that **R** uses as the default location to open, save and 'look for' files. You should set the working directory to be the folder in which you have stored your data files, any scripts associated with the analysis or your workspace. Basically, anything to do with a session.

Writer's block: something I suffered from a lot while writing this edition. It's when you can't think of any decent examples and so end up talking about sperm the whole time. Seriously, look at this book, it's all sperm this, sperm that, quail sperm, human sperm. Frankly, I'm amazed donkey sperm didn't get in there somewhere. Oh, it just did.

Yates's continuity correction: an adjustment made to the *chi-square test* when the *contingency table* is 2 rows by 2 columns (i.e., there are two categorical variables, both of which consist of only two categories). In large samples the adjustment makes little difference and is slightly dubious anyway (see Howell, 2006).

z-score: the value of an observation expressed in standard deviation units. It is calculated by taking the observation, subtracting from it the mean of all observations, and dividing the result by the standard deviation of all observations. By converting a distribution of observations into z-scores a new distribution is created that has a mean of 0 and a standard deviation of 1.

Appendix

A.1 Table of the standard normal distribution

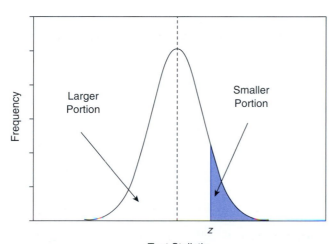

Test Stalistic

z	Larger Portion	Smaller Portion	y	z	Larger Portion	Smaller Portion	y
.00	.50000	.50000	.3989	.06	.52392	.47608	.3982
.01	.50399	.49601	.3989	.07	.52790	.47210	.3980
.02	.50798	.49202	.3989	.08	.53188	.46812	**.3977**
.03	.51197	.48803	.3988	.09	.53586	.46414	.3973
.04	.51595	.48405	.3986	.10	.53983	.46017	.3970
.05	.51994	.48006	.3984	.11	.54380	.45620	.3965

(Continued)

(Continued)

z	Larger Portion	Smaller Portion	y	z	Larger Portion	Smaller Portion	y
.12	.54776	.45224	.3961	.44	.67003	.32997	.3621
.13	.55172	.44828	.3956	.45	.67364	.32636	.3605
.14	.55567	.44433	.3951	.46	.67724	.32276	.3589
.15	.55962	.44038	.3945	.47	.68082	.31918	.3572
.16	.56356	.43644	.3939	.48	.68439	.31561	.3555
.17	.56749	.43251	.3932	.49	.68793	.31207	.3538
.18	.57142	.42858	.3925	.50	.69146	.30854	.3521
.19	.57535	.42465	.3918	.51	.69497	.30503	.3503
.20	.57926	.42074	.3910	.52	.69847	.30153	.3485
.21	.58317	.41683	.3902	.53	.70194	.29806	.3467
.22	.58706	.41294	.3894	.54	.70540	.29460	.3448
.23	.59095	.40905	.3885	.55	.70884	.29116	.3429
.24	.59483	.40517	.3876	.56	.71226	.28774	.3410
.25	.59871	.40129	.3867	.57	.71566	.28434	.3391
.26	.60257	.39743	.3857	.58	.71904	.28096	.3372
.27	.60642	.39358	.3847	.59	.72240	.27760	.3352
.28	.61026	.38974	.3836	.60	.72575	.27425	.3332
.29	.61409	.38591	.3825	.61	.72907	.27093	.3312
.30	.61791	.38209	.3814	.62	.73237	.26763	.3292
.31	.62172	.37828	.3802	.63	.73565	.26435	.3271
.32	.62552	.37448	.3790	.64	.73891	.26109	.3251
.33	.62930	.37070	.3778	.65	.74215	.25785	.3230
.34	.63307	.36693	.3765	.66	.74537	.25463	.3209
.35	.63683	.36317	.3752	.67	.74857	.25143	.3187
.36	.64058	.35942	.3739	.68	.75175	.24825	.3166
.37	.64431	.35569	.3725	.69	.75490	.24510	.3144
.38	.64803	.35197	.3712	.70	.75804	.24196	.3123
.39	.65173	.34827	.3697	.71	.76115	.23885	.3101
.40	.65542	.34458	.3683	.72	.76424	.23576	.3079
.41	.65910	.34090	.3668	.73	.76730	.23270	.3056
.42	.66276	.33724	.3653	.74	.77035	.22965	.3034
.43	.66640	.33360	.3637	.75	.77337	.22663	.3011

z	Larger Portion	Smaller Portion	y	z	Larger Portion	Smaller Portion	y
.76	.77637	.22363	.2989	1.07	.85769	.14231	.2251
.77	.77935	.22065	.2966	1.08	.85993	.14007	.2227
.78	.78230	.21770	.2943	1.09	.86214	.13786	.2203
.79	.78524	.21476	.2920	1.10	.86433	.13567	.2179
.80	.78814	.21186	.2897	1.11	.86650	.13350	.2155
.81	.79103	.20897	.2874	1.12	.86864	.13136	.2131
.82	.79389	.20611	.2850	1.13	.87076	.12924	.2107
.83	.79673	.20327	.2827	1.14	.87286	.12714	.2083
.84	.79955	.20045	.2803	1.15	.87493	.12507	.2059
.85	.80234	.19766	.2780	1.16	.87698	.12302	.2036
.86	.80511	.19489	.2756	1.17	.87900	.12100	.2012
.87	.80785	.19215	.2732	1.18	.88100	.11900	.1989
.88	.81057	.18943	.2709	1.19	.88298	.11702	.1965
.89	.81327	.18673	.2685	1.20	.88493	.11507	.1942
.90	.81594	.18406	.2661	1.21	.88686	.11314	.1919
.91	.81859	.18141	.2637	1.22	.88877	.11123	.1895
.92	.82121	.17879	.2613	1.23	.89065	.10935	.1872
.93	.82381	.17619	.2589	1.24	.89251	.10749	.1849
.94	.82639	.17361	.2565	1.25	.89435	.10565	.1826
.95	.82894	.17106	.2541	1.26	.89617	.10383	.1804
.96	.83147	.16853	.2516	1.27	.89796	.10204	.1781
.97	.83398	.16602	.2492	1.28	.89973	.10027	.1758
.98	.83646	.16354	.2468	1.29	.90147	.09853	.1736
.99	.83891	.16109	.2444	1.30	.90320	.09680	.1714
1.00	.84134	.15866	.2420	1.31	.90490	.09510	.1691
1.01	.84375	.15625	.2396	1.32	.90658	.09342	.1669
1.02	.84614	.15386	.2371	1.33	.90824	.09176	.1647
1.03	.84849	.15151	.2347	1.34	.90988	.09012	.1626
1.04	.85083	.14917	.2323	1.35	.91149	.08851	.1604
1.05	.85314	.14686	.2299	1.36	.91309	.08691	.1582
1.06	.85543	.14457	.2275	1.37	.91466	.08534	.1561

(Continued)

(Continued)

z	Larger Portion	Smaller Portion	y	z	Larger Portion	Smaller Portion	y
1.38	.91621	.08379	.1539	1.69	.95449	.04551	.0957
1.39	.91774	.08226	.1518	1.70	.95543	.04457	.0940
1.40	.91924	.08076	.1497	1.71	.95637	.04363	.0925
1.41	.92073	.07927	.1476	1.72	.95728	.04272	.0909
1.42	.92220	.07780	.1456	1.73	.95818	.04182	.0893
1.43	.92364	.07636	.1435	1.74	.95907	.04093	.0878
1.44	.92507	.07493	.1415	1.75	.95994	.04006	.0863
1.45	.92647	.07353	.1394	1.76	.96080	.03920	.0848
1.46	.92785	.07215	.1374	1.77	.96164	.03836	.0833
1.47	.92922	.07078	.1354	1.78	.96246	.03754	.0818
1.48	.93056	.06944	.1334	1.79	.96327	.03673	.0804
1.49	.93189	.06811	.1315	1.80	.96407	.03593	.0790
1.50	.93319	.06681	.1295	1.81	.96485	.03515	.0775
1.51	.93448	.06552	.1276	1.82	.96562	.03438	.0761
1.52	.93574	.06426	.1257	1.83	.96638	.03362	.0748
1.53	.93699	.06301	.1238	1.84	.96712	.03288	.0734
1.54	.93822	.06178	.1219	1.85	.96784	.03216	.0721
1.55	.93943	.06057	.1200	1.86	.96856	.03144	.0707
1.56	.94062	.05938	.1182	1.87	.96926	.03074	.0694
1.57	.94179	.05821	.1163	1.88	.96995	.03005	.0681
1.58	.94295	.05705	.1145	1.89	.97062	.02938	.0669
1.59	.94408	.05592	.1127	1.90	.97128	.02872	.0656
1.60	.94520	.05480	.1109	1.91	.97193	.02807	.0644
1.61	.94630	.05370	.1092	1.92	.97257	.02743	.0632
1.62	.94738	.05262	.1074	1.93	.97320	.02680	.0620
1.63	.94845	.05155	.1057	1.94	.97381	.02619	.0608
1.64	.94950	.05050	.1040	1.95	.97441	.02559	.0596
1.65	.95053	.04947	.1023	1.96	.97500	.02500	.0584
1.66	.95154	.04846	.1006	1.97	.97558	.02442	.0573
1.67	.95254	.04746	.0989	1.98	.97615	.02385	.0562
1.68	.95352	.04648	.0973	1.99	.97670	.02330	.0551

z	Larger Portion	Smaller Portion	y	z	Larger Portion	Smaller Portion	y
2.00	.97725	.02275	.0540	2.30	.98928	.01072	.0283
2.01	.97778	.02222	.0529	2.31	.98956	.01044	.0277
2.02	.97831	.02169	.0519	2.32	.98983	.01017	.0270
2.03	.97882	.02118	.0508	2.33	.99010	.00990	.0264
2.04	.97932	.02068	.0498	2.34	.99036	.00964	.0258
2.05	.97982	.02018	.0488	2.35	.99061	.00939	.0252
2.06	.98030	.01970	.0478	2.36	.99086	.00914	.0246
2.07	.98077	.01923	.0468	2.37	.99111	.00889	.0241
2.08	.98124	.01876	.0459	2.38	.99134	.00866	.0235
2.09	.98169	.01831	.0449	2.39	.99158	.00842	.0229
2.10	.98214	.01786	.0440	2.40	.99180	.00820	.0224
2.11	.98257	.01743	.0431	2.41	.99202	.00798	.0219
2.12	.98300	.01700	.0422	2.42	.99224	.00776	.0213
2.13	.98341	.01659	.0413	2.43	.99245	.00755	.0208
2.14	.98382	.01618	.0404	2.44	.99266	.00734	.0203
2.15	.98422	.01578	.0396	2.45	.99286	.00714	.0198
2.16	.98461	.01539	.0387	2.46	.99305	.00695	.0194
2.17	.98500	.01500	.0379	2.47	.99324	.00676	.0189
2.18	.98537	.01463	.0371	2.48	.99343	.00657	.0184
2.19	.98574	.01426	.0363	2.49	.99361	.00639	.0180
2.20	.98610	.01390	.0355	2.50	.99379	.00621	.0175
2.21	.98645	.01355	.0347	2.51	.99396	.00604	.0171
2.22	.98679	.01321	.0339	2.52	.99413	.00587	.0167
2.23	.98713	.01287	.0332	2.53	.99430	.00570	.0163
2.24	.98745	.01255	0325	2.54	.99446	.00554	.0158
2.25	.98778	.01222	.0317	2.55	.99461	.00539	.0154
2.26	.98809	.01191	.0310	2.56	.99477	.00523	.0151
2.27	.98840	.01160	.0303	2.57	.99492	.00508	.0147
2.28	.98870	.01130	.0297	2.58	.99506	.00494	.0143
2.29	.98899	.01101	.0290	2.59	.99520	.00480	.0139

(Continued)

(Continued)

z	Larger Portion	Smaller Portion	y	z	Larger Portion	Smaller Portion	y
2.60	.99534	.00466	.0136	2.84	.99774	.00226	.0071
2.61	.99547	.00453	.0132	2.85	.99781	.00219	.0069
2.62	.99560	.00440	.0129	2.86	.99788	.00212	.0067
2.63	.99573	.00427	.0126	2.87	.99795	.00205	.0065
2.64	.99585	.00415	.0122	2.88	.99801	.00199	.0063
2.65	.99598	.00402	.0119	2.89	.99807	.00193	.0061
2.66	.99609	.00391	.0116	2.90	.99813	.00187	.0060
2.67	.99621	.00379	.0113	2.91	.99819	.00181	.0058
2.68	.99632	.00368	.0110	2.92	.99825	.00175	.0056
2.69	.99643	.00357	.0107	2.93	.99831	.00169	.0055
2.70	.99653	.00347	.0104	2.94	.99836	.00164	.0053
2.71	.99664	.00336	.0101	2.95	.99841	.00159	.0051
2.72	.99674	.00326	.0099	2.96	.99846	.00154	.0050
2.73	.99683	.00317	.0096	2.97	.99851	.00149	.0048
2.74	.99693	.00307	.0093	2.98	.99856	.00144	.0047
2.75	.99702	.00298	.0091	2.99	.99861	.00139	.0046
2.76	.99711	.00289	.0088	3.00	.99865	.00135	.0044
2.77	.99720	.00280	.0086	…	…	…	…
2.78	.99728	.00272	.0084	3.25	.99942	.00058	.0020
2.79	.99736	.00264	.0081	…	…	…	…
2.80	.99744	.00256	.0079	3.50	.99977	.00023	.0009
2.81	.99752	.00248	.0077	…	…	…	…
2.82	.99760	.00240	.0075	4.00	.99997	.00003	.0001
2.83	.99767	.00233	.0073				

All values calculated by author using SPSS.

A.2   Critical values of the *t*-distribution

df	Two-Tailed Test		One-Tailed Test	
	0.05	0.01	0.05	0.01
1	12.71	63.66	6.31	31.82
2	4.30	9.92	2.92	6.96
3	3.18	5.84	2.35	4.54
4	2.78	4.60	2.13	3.75
5	2.57	4.03	2.02	3.36
6	2.45	3.71	1.94	3.14
7	2.36	3.50	1.89	3.00
8	2.31	3.36	1.86	2.90
9	2.26	3.25	1.83	2.82
10	2.23	3.17	1.81	2.76
11	2.20	3.11	1.80	2.72
12	2.18	3.05	1.78	2.68
13	2.16	3.01	1.77	2.65
14	2.14	2.98	1.76	2.62
15	2.13	2.95	1.75	2.60
16	2.12	2.92	1.75	2.58
17	2.11	2.90	1.74	2.57
18	2.10	2.88	1.73	2.55
19	2.09	2.86	1.73	2.54
20	2.09	2.85	1.72	2.53
21	2.08	2.83	1.72	2.52
22	2.07	2.82	1.72	2.51
23	2.07	2.81	1.71	2.50
24	2.06	2.80	1.71	2.49
25	2.06	2.79	1.71	2.49
26	2.06	2.78	1.71	2.48
27	2.05	2.77	1.70	2.47
28	2.05	2.76	1.70	2.47
29	2.05	2.76	1.70	2.46
30	2.04	2.75	1.70	2.46
35	2.03	2.72	1.69	2.44
40	2.02	2.70	1.68	2.42
45	2.01	2.69	1.68	2.41
50	2.01	2.68	1.68	2.40
60	2.00	2.66	1.67	2.39
70	1.99	2.65	1.67	2.38
80	1.99	2.64	1.66	2.37
90	1.99	2.63	1.66	2.37
100	1.98	2.63	1.66	2.36
∞ (z)	1.96	2.58	1.64	2.33

All values computed by the author using SPSS.

A.3 Critical values of the *F*-distribution

	p	df (Numerator)									
		1	2	3	4	5	6	7	8	9	10
1	0.05	161.45	199.50	215.71	224.58	230.16	233.99	236.77	238.88	240.54	241.88
	0.01	4052.18	4999.50	5403.35	5624.58	5763.65	5858.99	5928.36	5981.07	6022.47	6055.85
2	0.05	18.51	19.00	19.16	19.25	19.30	19.33	19.35	19.37	19.38	19.40
	0.01	98.50	99.00	99.17	99.25	99.30	99.33	99.36	99.37	99.39	99.40
3	0.05	10.13	9.55	9.28	9.12	9.01	8.94	8.89	8.85	8.81	8.79
	0.01	34.12	30.82	29.46	28.71	28.24	27.91	27.67	27.49	27.35	27.23
4	0.05	7.71	6.94	6.59	6.39	6.26	6.16	6.09	6.04	6.00	5.96
	0.01	21.20	18.00	16.69	15.98	15.52	15.21	14.98	14.80	14.66	14.55
5	0.05	6.61	5.79	5.41	5.19	5.05	4.95	4.88	4.82	4.77	4.74
	0.01	16.26	13.27	12.06	11.39	10.97	10.67	10.46	10.29	10.16	10.05
6	0.05	5.99	5.14	4.76	4.53	4.39	4.28	4.21	4.15	4.10	4.06
	0.01	13.75	10.92	9.78	9.15	8.75	8.47	8.26	8.10	7.98	7.87
7	0.05	5.59	4.74	4.35	4.12	3.97	3.87	3.79	3.73	3.68	3.64
	0.01	12.25	9.55	8.45	7.85	7.46	7.19	6.99	6.84	6.72	6.62
8	0.05	5.32	4.46	4.07	3.84	3.69	3.58	3.50	3.44	3.39	3.35
	0.01	11.26	8.65	7.59	7.01	6.63	6.37	6.18	6.03	5.91	5.81
9	0.05	5.12	4.26	3.86	3.63	3.48	3.37	3.29	3.23	3.18	3.14
	0.01	10.56	8.02	6.99	6.42	6.06	5.80	5.61	5.47	5.35	5.26
10	0.05	4.96	4.10	3.71	3.48	3.33	3.22	3.14	3.07	3.02	2.98
	0.01	10.04	7.56	6.55	5.99	5.64	5.39	5.20	5.06	4.94	4.85
11	0.05	4.84	3.98	3.59	3.36	3.20	3.09	3.01	2.95	2.90	2.85
	0.01	9.65	7.21	6.22	5.67	5.32	5.07	4.89	4.74	4.63	4.54
12	0.05	4.75	3.89	3.49	3.26	3.11	3.00	2.91	2.85	2.80	2.75
	0.01	9.33	6.93	5.95	5.41	5.06	4.82	4.64	4.50	4.39	4.30
13	0.05	4.67	3.81	3.41	3.18	3.03	2.92	2.83	2.77	2.71	2.67
	0.01	9.07	6.70	5.74	5.21	4.86	4.62	4.44	4.30	4.19	4.10
14	0.05	4.60	3.74	3.34	3.11	2.96	2.85	2.76	2.70	2.65	2.60
	0.01	8.86	6.51	5.56	5.04	4.69	4.46	4.28	4.14	4.03	3.94
15	0.05	4.54	3.68	3.29	3.06	2.90	2.79	2.71	2.64	2.59	2.54
	0.01	8.68	6.36	5.42	4.89	4.56	4.32	4.14	4.00	3.89	3.80
16	0.05	4.49	3.63	3.24	3.01	2.85	2.74	2.66	2.59	2.54	2.49
	0.01	8.53	6.23	5.29	4.77	4.44	4.20	4.03	3.89	3.78	3.69
17	0.05	4.45	3.59	3.20	2.96	2.81	2.70	2.61	2.55	2.49	2.45
	0.01	8.40	6.11	5.18	4.67	4.34	4.10	3.93	3.79	3.68	3.59
18	0.05	4.41	3.55	3.16	2.93	2.77	2.66	2.58	2.51	2.46	2.41
	0.01	8.29	6.01	5.09	4.58	4.25	4.01	3.84	3.71	3.60	3.51

df (Denominator)

		df (Numerator)									
	p	1	2	3	4	5	6	7	8	9	10
19	0.05	4.38	3.52	3.13	2.90	2.74	2.63	2.54	2.48	2.42	2.38
	0.01	8.18	5.93	5.01	4.50	4.17	3.94	3.77	3.63	3.52	3.43
20	0.05	4.35	3.49	3.10	2.87	2.71	2.60	2.51	2.45	2.39	2.35
	0.01	8.10	5.85	4.94	4.43	4.10	3.87	3.70	3.56	3.46	3.37
22	0.05	4.30	3.44	3.05	2.82	2.66	2.55	2.46	2.40	2.34	2.30
	0.01	7.95	5.72	4.82	4.31	3.99	3.76	3.59	3.45	3.35	3.26
24	0.05	4.26	3.40	3.01	2.78	2.62	2.51	2.42	2.36	2.30	2.25
	0.01	7.82	5.61	4.72	4.22	3.90	3.67	3.50	3.36	3.26	3.17
26	0.05	4.23	3.37	2.98	2.74	2.59	2.47	2.39	2.32	2.27	2.22
	0.01	7.72	5.53	4.64	4.14	3.82	3.59	3.42	3.29	3.18	3.09
28	0.05	4.20	3.34	2.95	2.71	2.56	2.45	2.36	2.29	2.24	2.19
	0.01	7.64	5.45	4.57	4.07	3.75	3.53	3.36	3.23	3.12	3.03
30	0.05	4.17	3.32	2.92	2.69	2.53	2.42	2.33	2.27	2.21	2.16
	0.01	7.56	5.39	4.51	4.02	3.70	3.47	3.30	3.17	3.07	2.98
35	0.05	4.12	3.27	2.87	2.64	2.49	2.37	2.29	2.22	2.16	2.11
	0.01	7.42	5.27	4.40	3.91	3.59	3.37	3.20	3.07	2.96	2.88
40	0.05	4.08	3.23	2.84	2.61	2.45	2.34	2.25	2.18	2.12	2.08
	0.01	7.31	5.18	4.31	3.83	3.51	3.29	3.12	2.99	2.89	2.80
45	0.05	4.06	3.20	2.81	2.58	2.42	2.31	2.22	2.15	2.10	2.05
	0.01	7.23	5.11	4.25	3.77	3.45	3.23	3.07	2.94	2.83	2.74
50	0.05	4.03	3.18	2.79	2.56	2.40	2.29	2.20	2.13	2.07	2.03
	0.01	7.17	5.06	4.20	3.72	3.41	3.19	3.02	2.89	2.78	2.70
60	0.05	4.00	3.15	2.76	2.53	2.37	2.25	2.17	2.10	2.04	1.99
	0.01	7.08	4.98	4.13	3.65	3.34	3.12	2.95	2.82	2.72	2.63
80	0.05	3.96	3.11	2.72	2.49	2.33	2.21	2.13	2.06	2.00	1.95
	0.01	6.96	4.88	4.04	3.56	3.26	3.04	2.87	2.74	2.64	2.55
100	0.05	3.94	3.09	2.70	2.46	2.31	2.19	2.10	2.03	1.97	1.93
	0.01	6.90	4.82	3.98	3.51	3.21	2.99	2.82	2.69	2.59	2.50
150	0.05	3.90	3.06	2.66	2.43	2.27	2.16	2.07	2.00	1.94	1.89
	0.01	6.81	4.75	3.91	3.45	3.14	2.92	2.76	2.63	2.53	2.44
300	0.05	3.87	3.03	2.63	2.40	2.24	2.13	2.04	1.97	1.91	1.86
	0.01	6.72	4.68	3.85	3.38	3.08	2.86	2.70	2.57	2.47	2.38
500	0.05	3.86	3.01	2.62	2.39	2.23	2.12	2.03	1.96	1.90	1.85
	0.01	6.69	4.65	3.82	3.36	3.05	2.84	2.68	2.55	2.44	2.36
1000	0.05	3.85	3.00	2.61	2.38	2.22	2.11	2.02	1.95	1.89	1.84
	0.01	6.66	4.63	3.80	3.34	3.04	2.82	2.66	2.53	2.43	2.34

df (Denominator)

(Continued)

(Continued)

	p	df (Numerator)						
		15	20	25	30	40	50	1000
1	0.05	245.95	248.01	249.26	250.10	251.14	251.77	254.19
	0.01	6157.31	6208.74	6239.83	6260.65	6286.79	6302.52	6362.70
2	0.05	19.43	19.45	19.46	19.46	19.47	19.48	19.49
	0.01	99.43	99.45	99.46	99.47	99.47	99.48	99.50
3	0.05	8.70	8.66	8.63	8.62	8.59	8.58	8.53
	0.01	26.87	26.69	26.58	26.50	26.41	26.35	26.14
4	0.05	5.86	5.80	5.77	5.75	5.72	5.70	5.63
	0.01	14.20	14.02	13.91	13.84	13.75	13.69	13.47
5	0.05	4.62	4.56	4.52	4.50	4.46	4.44	4.37
	0.01	9.72	9.55	9.45	9.38	9.29	9.24	9.03
6	0.05	3.94	3.87	3.83	3.81	3.77	3.75	3.67
	0.01	7.56	7.40	7.30	7.23	7.14	7.09	6.89
7	0.05	3.51	3.44	3.40	3.38	3.34	3.32	3.23
	0.01	6.31	6.16	6.06	5.99	5.91	5.86	5.66
8	0.05	3.22	3.15	3.11	3.08	3.04	3.02	2.93
	0.01	5.52	5.36	5.26	5.20	5.12	5.07	4.87
9	0.05	3.01	2.94	2.89	2.86	2.83	2.80	2.71
	0.01	4.96	4.81	4.71	4.65	4.57	4.52	4.32
10	0.05	2.85	2.77	2.73	2.70	2.66	2.64	2.54
	0.01	4.56	4.41	4.31	4.25	4.17	4.12	3.92
11	0.05	2.72	2.65	2.60	2.57	2.53	2.51	2.41
	0.01	4.25	4.10	4.01	3.94	3.86	3.81	3.61
12	0.05	2.62	2.54	2.50	2.47	2.43	2.40	2.30
	0.01	4.01	3.86	3.76	3.70	3.62	3.57	3.37
13	0.05	2.53	2.46	2.41	2.38	2.34	2.31	2.21
	0.01	3.82	3.66	3.57	3.51	3.43	3.38	3.18
14	0.05	2.46	2.39	2.34	2.31	2.27	2.24	2.14
	0.01	3.66	3.51	3.41	3.35	3.27	3.22	3.02
15	0.05	2.40	2.33	2.28	2.25	2.20	2.18	2.07
	0.01	3.52	3.37	3.28	3.21	3.13	3.08	2.88
16	0.05	2.35	2.28	2.23	2.19	2.15	2.12	2.02
	0.01	3.41	3.26	3.16	3.10	3.02	2.97	2.76
17	0.05	2.31	2.23	2.18	2.15	2.10	2.08	1.97
	0.01	3.31	3.16	3.07	3.00	2.92	2.87	2.66
18	0.05	2.27	2.19	2.14	2.11	2.06	2.04	1.92
	0.01	3.23	3.08	2.98	2.92	2.84	2.78	2.58

df (Denominator)

		df (Numerator)						
	p	15	20	25	30	40	50	1000
19	0.05	2.23	2.16	2.11	2.07	2.03	2.00	1.88
	0.01	3.15	3.00	2.91	2.84	2.76	2.71	2.50
20	0.05	2.20	2.12	2.07	2.04	1.99	1.97	1.85
	0.01	3.09	2.94	2.84	2.78	2.69	2.64	2.43
22	0.05	2.15	2.07	2.02	1.98	1.94	1.91	1.79
	0.01	2.98	2.83	2.73	2.67	2.58	2.53	2.32
24	0.05	2.11	2.03	1.97	1.94	1.89	1.86	1.74
	0.01	2.89	2.74	2.64	2.58	2.49	2.44	2.22
26	0.05	2.07	1.99	1.94	1.90	1.85	1.82	1.70
	0.01	2.81	2.66	2.57	2.50	2.42	2.36	2.14
28	0.05	2.04	1.96	1.91	1.87	1.82	1.79	1.66
	0.01	2.75	2.60	2.51	2.44	2.35	2.30	2.08
30	0.05	2.01	1.93	1.88	1.84	1.79	1.76	1.63
	0.01	2.70	2.55	2.45	2.39	2.30	2.25	2.02
35	0.05	1.96	1.88	1.82	1.79	1.74	1.70	1.57
	0.01	2.60	2.44	2.35	2.28	2.19	2.14	1.90
40	0.05	1.92	1.84	1.78	1.74	1.69	1.66	1.52
	0.01	2.52	2.37	2.27	2.20	2.11	2.06	1.82
45	0.05	1.89	1.81	1.75	1.71	1.66	1.63	1.48
	0.01	2.46	2.31	2.21	2.14	2.05	2.00	1.75
50	0.05	1.87	1.78	1.73	1.69	1.63	1.60	1.45
	0.01	2.42	2.27	2.17	2.10	2.01	1.95	1.70
60	0.05	1.84	1.75	1.69	1.65	1.59	1.56	1.40
	0.01	2.35	2.20	2.10	2.03	1.94	1.88	1.62
80	0.05	1.79	1.70	1.64	1.60	1.54	1.51	1.34
	0.01	2.27	2.12	2.01	1.94	1.85	1.79	1.51
100	0.05	1.77	1.68	1.62	1.57	1.52	1.48	1.30
	0.01	2.22	2.07	1.97	1.89	1.80	1.74	1.45
150	0.05	1.73	1.64	1.58	1.54	1.48	1.44	1.24
	0.01	2.16	2.00	1.90	1.83	1.73	1.66	1.35
300	0.05	1.70	1.61	1.54	1.50	1.43	1.39	1.17
	0.01	2.10	1.94	1.84	1.76	1.66	1.59	1.25
500	0.05	1.69	1.59	1.53	1.48	1.42	1.38	1.14
	0.01	2.07	1.92	1.81	1.74	1.63	1.57	1.20
1000	0.05	1.68	1.58	1.52	1.47	1.41	1.36	1.11
	0.01	2.06	1.90	1.79	1.72	1.61	1.54	1.16

df (Denominator)

All values computed by author using SPSS.

A.4 Critical values of the chi-square distribution

df	p 0.05	0.01	df	p 0.05	0.01
1	3.84	6.63	25	37.65	44.31
2	5.99	9.21	26	38.89	45.64
3	7.81	11.34	27	40.11	46.96
4	9.49	13.28	28	41.34	48.28
5	11.07	15.09	29	42.56	49.59
6	12.59	16.81	30	43.77	50.89
7	14.07	18.48	35	49.80	57.34
8	15.51	20.09	40	55.76	63.69
9	16.92	21.67	45	61.66	69.96
10	18.31	23.21	50	67.50	76.15
11	19.68	24.72	60	79.08	88.38
12	21.03	26.22	70	90.53	100.43
13	22.36	27.69	80	101.88	112.33
14	23.68	29.14	90	113.15	124.12
15	25.00	30.58	100	124.34	135.81
16	26.30	32.00	200	233.99	249.45
17	27.59	33.41	300	341.40	359.91
18	28.87	34.81	400	447.63	468.72
19	30.14	36.19	500	553.13	576.49
20	31.41	37.57	600	658.09	683.52
21	32.67	38.93	700	762.66	789.97
22	33.92	40.29	800	866.91	895.98
23	35.17	41.64	900	970.90	1001.63
24	36.42	42.98	1000	1074.68	1106.97

All values computed by author using SPSS.

References

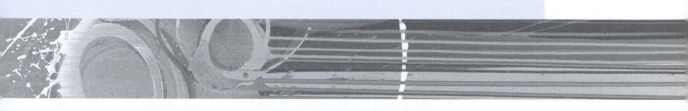

Agresti, A., & Finlay, B. (1986). *Statistical methods for the social sciences* (2nd ed.). San Francisco: Dellen.

Arrindell, W. A., & van der Ende, J. (1985). An empirical test of the utility of the observer-to-variables ratio in factor and components analysis. *Applied Psychological Measurement*, 9, 165–178.

Baguley, T. (2004). Understanding statistical power in the context of applied research. *Applied Ergonomics*, 35(2), 73–80.

Bakeman, R. (2005). Recommended effect size statistics for repeated measures designs. *Behavior Research Methods*, 37(3), 379–384.

Bale, C., Morrison, R., & Caryl, P. G. (2006). Chat-up lines as male sexual displays. *Personality and Individual Differences*, 40(4), 655–664.

Barnard, G. A. (1963). Ronald Aylmer Fisher, 1890–1962: Fisher's contributions to mathematical statistics. *Journal of the Royal Statistical Society, Series A*, 126, 162–166.

Bates, D., & Maechler, M. (2010). lme4: Linear mixed-effects models using S4 classes. R package (Version 0.999375–37). Retrieved from http://CRAN.R-project.org/package=lme4

Beckham, A. S. (1929). Is the Negro happy? A psychological analysis. *Journal of Abnormal and Social Psychology*, 24, 186–190.

Belsey, D. A., Kuh, E., & Welsch, R. (1980). *Regression diagnostics: Identifying influential data and sources of collinearity*. New York: Wiley.

Bemelman, M., & Hammacher, E. R. (2005). Rectal impalement by pirate ship: A case report. *Injury Extra*, 36, 508–510.

Benjamini, Y., & Hochberg, Y. (1995). Controlling the false discovery rate – a practical and powerful approach to multiple testing. *Journal of the Royal Statistical Society, Series B*, 57(1), 289–300.

Benjamini, Y., & Hochberg, Y. (2000). On the adaptive control of the false discovery fate in multiple testing with independent statistics. *Journal of Educational and Behavioral Statistics*, 25(1), 60–83.

Berger, J. O. (2003). Could Fisher, Jeffreys and Neyman have agreed on testing? *Statistical Science*, 18(1), 1–12.

Berry, W. D. (1993). *Understanding regression assumptions*. Sage University Paper Series on Quantitative Applications in the Social Sciences, 07-092. Newbury Park, CA: Sage.

Berry, W. D., & Feldman, S. (1985). *Multiple regression in practice*. Sage University Paper Series on Quantitative Applications in the Social Sciences, 07-050. Beverly Hills, CA: Sage.

Board, B. J., & Fritzon, K. (2005). Disordered personalities at work. *Psychology, Crime & Law*, 11(1), 17–32.

Bock, R. D. (1975). *Multivariate statistical methods in behavioral research*. New York: McGraw-Hill.

Boik, R. J. (1981). A priori tests in repeated measures designs: Effects of nonsphericity. *Psychometrika*, 46(3), 241–255.

Bowerman, B. L., & O'Connell, R. T. (1990). *Linear statistical models: An applied approach* (2nd ed.). Belmont, CA: Duxbury.

Bray, J. H., & Maxwell, S. E. (1985). *Multivariate analysis of variance*. Sage University Paper Series on Quantitative Applications in the Social Sciences, 07-054. Newbury Park, CA: Sage.

Brown, W. (1910). Some experimental results in the correlation of mental abilities. *British Journal of Psychology*, 3, 296–322.

Budescu, D. V. (1982). The power of the F test in normal populations with heterogeneous variances. *Educational and Psychological Measurement*, 42, 609–616.

Budescu, D. V., & Appelbaum, M. I. (1981). Variance stabilizing transformations and the power of the F test. *Journal of Educational Statistics*, 6(1), 55–74.

Cattell, R. B. (1966a). *The scientific analysis of personality*. Chicago: Aldine.

Cattell, R. B. (1966b). The scree test for the number of factors. *Multivariate Behavioral Research*, 1, 245–276.

Çetinkaya, H., & Domjan, M. (2006). Sexual fetishism in a quail (*Coturnix japonica*) model system: Test of reproductive success. *Journal of Comparative Psychology, 120*(4), 427–432.

Chamorro-Premuzic, T., Furnham, A., Christopher, A. N., Garwood, J., & Martin, N. (2008). Birds of a feather: Students' preferences for lecturers' personalities as predicted by their own personality and learning approaches. *Personality and Individual Differences, 44*, 965–976.

Chen, P. Y., & Popovich, P. M. (2002). *Correlation: Parametric and nonparametric measures.* Thousand Oaks, CA: Sage.

Chen, X. Z., Luo, Y., Zhang, J. J., Jiang, K., Pendry, J. B., & Zhang, S. A. (2011). Macroscopic invisibility cloaking of visible light. *Nature Communications, 2*, art. 176. doi: 10.1038/ncomms1176.

Choi, K., & Marden, J. (1997). An approach to multivariate rank tests in multivariate analysis of variance. *Journal of the American Statistical Association, 92*(440), 1581–1590.

Clarke, D. L., Buccimazza, I., Anderson, F. A., & Thomson, S. R. (2005). Colorectal foreign bodies. *Colorectal Disease, 7*(1), 98–103.

Cliff, N. (1987). *Analyzing multivariate data.* New York: Harcourt Brace Jovanovich.

Cohen, J. (1968). Multiple regression as a general data-analytic system. *Psychological Bulletin, 70*(6), 426–443.

Cohen, J. (1988). *Statistical power analysis for the behavioral sciences* (2nd ed.). New York: Academic Press.

Cohen, J. (1990). Things I have learned (so far). *American Psychologist, 45*(12), 1304–1312.

Cohen, J. (1992). A power primer. *Psychological Bulletin, 112*(1), 155–159.

Cohen, J. (1994). The earth is round (p < .05). *American Psychologist, 49*(12), 997–1003.

Cole, D. A., Maxwell, S. E., Arvey, R., & Salas, E. (1994). How the power of MANOVA can both increase and decrease as a function of the intercorrelations among the dependent variables. *Psychological Bulletin, 115*(3), 465–474.

Collier, R. O., Baker, F. B., Mandeville, G. K., & Hayes, T. F. (1967). Estimates of test size for several test procedures based on conventional variance ratios in the repeated measures design. *Psychometrika, 32*(2), 339–352.

Comrey, A. L., & Lee, H. B. (1992). *A first course in factor analysis* (2nd ed.). Hillsdale, NJ: Erlbaum.

Cook, R. D., & Weisberg, S. (1982). *Residuals and influence in regression.* New York: Chapman & Hall.

Cook, S. A., Rosser, R., & Salmon, P. (2006). Is cosmetic surgery an effective psychotherapeutic intervention? A systematic review of the evidence. *Journal of Plastic, Reconstructive & Aesthetic Surgery, 59*, 1133–1151.

Cook, S. A., Rossera, R., Toone, H., James, M. I., & Salmon, P. (2006). The psychological and social characteristics of patients referred for NHS cosmetic surgery: Quantifying clinical need. *Journal of Plastic, Reconstructive & Aesthetic Surgery, 59*, 54–64.

Cooper, C. L., Sloan, S. J., & Williams, S. (1988). *Occupational Stress Indicator management guide.* Windsor: NFER-Nelson.

Cooper, M., O'Donnell, D., Caryl, P. G., Morrison, R., & Bale, C. (2007). Chat-up lines as male displays: Effects of content, sex, and personality. *Personality and Individual Differences, 43*(5), 1075–1085.

Cortina, J. M. (1993). What is coefficient alpha? An examination of theory and applications. *Journal of Applied Psychology, 78*, 98–104.

Cox, D. R., & Snell, D. J. (1989). *The analysis of binary data* (2nd ed.). London: Chapman & Hall.

Cronbach, L. J. (1951). Coefficient alpha and the internal structure of tests. *Psychometrika, 16*, 297–334.

Cronbach, L. J. (1957). The two disciplines of scientific psychology. *American Psychologist, 12*, 671–684.

Davey, G. C. L., Startup, H. M., Zara, A., MacDonald, C. B., & Field, A. P. (2003). Perseveration of checking thoughts and mood-as-input hypothesis. *Journal of Behavior Therapy & Experimental Psychiatry, 34*, 141–160.

Davidson, M. L. (1972). Univariate versus multivariate tests in repeated-measures experiments. *Psychological Bulletin, 77*, 446–452.

Davies, P., Surridge, J., Hole, L., & Munro-Davies, L. (2007). Superhero-related injuries in paediatrics: a case series. *Archives of Disease in Childhood, 92*(3), 242–243.

DeCarlo, L. T. (1997). On the meaning and use of kurtosis. *Psychological Methods, 2*(3), 292–307.

Di Falco, A., Ploschner, M., & Krauss, T. F. (2010). Flexible metamaterials at visible wavelengths. *New Journal of Physics, 12*, 113006. doi: 11300610.1088/1367-2630/12/11/113006

Domjan, M., Blesbois, E., & Williams, J. (1998). The adaptive significance of sexual conditioning: Pavlovian control of sperm release. *Psychological Science, 9*(5), 411–415.

Donaldson, T. S. (1968). Robustness of the *F*-test to errors of both kinds and the correlation between the numerator and denominator of the *F*-ratio. *Journal of the American Statistical Association, 63*, 660–676.

Dunlap, W. P., Cortina, J. M., Vaslow, J. B., & Burke, M. J. (1996). Meta-analysis of experiments with matched groups or repeated measures designs. *Psychological Methods, 1*(2), 170–177.

Dunteman, G. E. (1989). *Principal components analysis.* Sage University Paper Series on Quantitative Applications in the Social Sciences, 07-069. Newbury Park, CA: Sage.

Durbin, J., & Watson, G. S. (1951). Testing for serial correlation in least squares regression, II. *Biometrika, 30*, 159–178.

Easterlin, R. A. (2003). Explaining happiness. *Proceedings of the National Academy of Sciences, 100*(19), 11176–11183.

Efron, B., & Tibshirani, R. (1993). *An introduction to the bootstrap*: Chapman & Hall.

Enders, C. K., & Tofighi, D. (2007). Centering predictor variables in cross-sectional multilevel models: A new look at an old issue. *Psychological Methods, 12*(2), 121–138.

Eriksson, S.-G., Beckham, D., & Vassell, D. (2004). Why are the English so shit at penalties? A review. *Journal of Sporting Ineptitude, 31*, 231–1072.

Erlebacher, A. (1977). Design and analysis of experiments contrasting the within- and between-subjects manipulations of the independent variable. *Psychological Bulletin, 84*, 212–219.

Eysenck, H. J. (1953). *The structure of human personality*. New York: Wiley.

Fesmire, F. M. (1988). Termination of intractable hiccups with digital rectal massage. *Annals of Emergency Medicine, 17*(8), 872.

Field, A. P. (2000). *Discovering statistics using SPSS for Windows: Advanced techniques for the beginner*. London: Sage.

Field, A. P. (2001). Meta-analysis of correlation coefficients: A Monte Carlo comparison of fixed- and random-effects methods. *Psychological Methods, 6*(2), 161–180.

Field, A. P. (2005a). Intraclass correlation. In B. Everitt & D. C. Howell (Eds.), *Encyclopedia of statistics in behavioral science* (Vol. 2, pp. 948–954). Hoboken. NJ: Wiley.

Field, A. P. (2005b). Is the meta-analysis of correlation coefficients accurate when population correlations vary? *Psychological Methods, 10*(4), 444–467.

Field, A. P. (2005c). Sir Ronald Aylmer Fisher. In B. S. Everitt & D. C. Howell (Eds.), *Encyclopedia of statistics in behavioral science* (Vol. 2, pp. 658–659). Hoboken. NJ: Wiley.

Field, A. P. (2006). The behavioral inhibition system and the verbal information pathway to children's fears. *Journal of Abnormal Psychology, 115*(4), 742–752.

Field, A. P. (2009). *Discovering statistics using SPSS: And sex and drugs and rock 'n' roll* (3rd ed.). London: Sage.

Field, A. P., & Davey, G. C. L. (1999). Reevaluating evaluative conditioning: A nonassociative explanation of conditioning effects in the visual evaluative conditioning paradigm. *Journal of Experimental Psychology – Animal Behavior Processes, 25*(2), 211–224.

Field, A. P., & Hole, G. J. (2003). *How to design and report experiments*. London: Sage.

Field, A. P., & Miles, J. N. V. (2010). *Discovering statistics using SAS: And sex and drugs and rock 'n' roll*. London: Sage.

Field, A. P., & Moore, A. C. (2005). Dissociating the effects of attention and contingency awareness on evaluative conditioning effects in the visual paradigm. *Cognition and Emotion, 19*(2), 217–243.

Fienberg, S. E., Stigler, S. M., & Tanur, J. M. (2007). The William Kruskal Legacy: 1919–2005. *Statistical Science, 22*(2), 255–261.

Fisher, R. A. (1921). On the probable error of a coefficient of correlation deduced from a small sample. *Metron, 1*, 3–32.

Fisher, R. A. (1922). On the interpretation of chi square from contingency tables, and the calculation of P. *Journal of the Royal Statistical Society, 85*, 87–94.

Fisher, R. A. (1925). *Statistical methods for research workers*. Edinburgh: Oliver & Boyd.

Fisher, R. A. (1925/1991). *Statistical methods, experimental design, and scientific inference*. Oxford: Oxford University Press. (This reference is for the 1991 reprint.).

Fisher, R. A. (1956). *Statistical methods and scientific inference*. New York: Hafner.

Flanagan, J. C. (1937). A proposed procedure for increasing the efficiency of objective tests. *Journal of Educational Psychology, 28*, 17–21.

Friedman, M. (1937). The use of ranks to avoid the assumption of normality implicit in the analysis of variance. *Journal of the American Statistical Association, 32*, 675–701.

Gallup, G. G. J., Burch, R. L., Zappieri, M. L., Parvez, R., Stockwell, M., & Davis, J. A. (2003). The human penis as a semen displacement device. *Evolution and Human Behavior, 24*, 277–289.

Games, P. A. (1983). Curvilinear transformations of the dependent variable. *Psychological Bulletin, 93*(2), 382–387.

Games, P. A. (1984). Data transformations, power, and skew: A rebuttal to Levine and Dunlap. *Psychological Bulletin, 95*(2), 345–347.

Games, P. A., & Lucas, P. A. (1966). Power of the analysis of variance of independent groups on non-normal and normally transformed data. *Educational and Psychological Measurement, 26*, 311–327.

Gelman, A., & Hill, J. (2007). *Data analysis using regression and multilevel/hierarchical models*. Cambridge: Cambridge University Press.

Girden, E. R. (1992). *ANOVA: Repeated measures*. Sage University Paper Series on Quantitative Applications in the Social Sciences, 07-084. Newbury Park, CA: Sage.

Glass, G. V. (1966). Testing homogeneity of variances. *American Educational Research Journal, 3*(3), 187–190.

Glass, G. V., Peckham, P. D., & Sanders, J. R. (1972). Consequences of failure to meet assumptions underlying the fixed effects analyses of variance and covariance. *Review of Educational Research, 42*(3), 237–288.

Graham, J. M., Guthrie, A. C., & Thompson, B. (2003). Consequences of not interpreting structure coefficients in published CFA research: A reminder. *Structural Equation Modeling, 10*(1), 142–153.

Grayson, D. (2004). Some myths and legends in quantitative psychology. *Understanding Statistics, 3*(1), 101–134.

Green, S. B. (1991). How many subjects does it take to do a regression analysis? *Multivariate Behavioral Research*, 26, 499–510.

Greenhouse, S. W., & Geisser, S. (1959). On methods in the analysis of profile data. *Psychometrika*, 24, 95–112.

Guadagnoli, E., & Velicer, W. F. (1988). Relation of sample size to the stability of component patterns. *Psychological Bulletin*, 103(2), 265–275.

Hakstian, A. R., Roed, J. C., & Lind, J. C. (1979). Two-sample T^2 procedure and the assumption of homogeneous covariance matrices. *Psychological Bulletin*, 86, 1255–1263.

Hardy, M. A. (1993). *Regression with dummy variables*. Sage University Paper Series on Quantitative Applications in the Social Sciences, 07-093. Newbury Park, CA: Sage.

Harman, B. H. (1976). *Modern factor analysis* (3rd ed., revised). Chicago: University of Chicago Press.

Harris, R. J. (1975). *A primer of multivariate statistics*. New York: Academic Press.

Hawton, K. (1989). Sexual dysfunctions. In K. Hawton, P. M. Salkovskis, J. Kirk, & D. M. Clark (Eds.), *Cognitive behaviour therapy for psychiatric problems: A practical guide*. (pp. 370–405). Oxford: Oxford University Press.

Hill, C., Abraham, C., & Wright, D. B. (2007). Can theory-based messages in combination with cognitive prompts promote exercise in classroom settings? *Social Science & Medicine*, 65, 1049–1058.

Hoaglin, D., & Welsch, R. (1978). The hat matrix in regression and ANOVA. *American Statistician*, 32, 17–22.

Hochberg, Y. (1988). A sharper Bonferroni procedure for multiple tests of significance. *Biometrika*, 75(4), 800–802.

Hoddle, G., Batty, D., & Ince, P. (1998). How not to take penalties in important soccer matches. *Journal of Cretinous Behaviour*, 1, 1–2.

Holm, S. (1979). A simple sequentially rejective multiple test procedure. *Scandinavian Journal of Statistics*, 6(2), 65–70.

Hommel, G. (1988). A stagewise rejective multiple test procedure based on a modified Bonferroni test. *Biometrika*, 75(2), 383–386.

Horn, J. L. (1965). A rationale and test for the number of factors in factor analysis. *Psychometrika*, 30, 179–185.

Hosmer, D. W., & Lemeshow, S. (1989). *Applied logistic regression*. New York: Wiley.

Howell, D. C. (1997). *Statistical methods for psychology* (4th ed.). Belmont, CA: Duxbury.

Howell, D. C. (2006). *Statistical methods for psychology* (6th ed.). Belmont, CA: Thomson.

Huberty, C. J., & Morris, J. D. (1989). Multivariate analysis versus multiple univariate analysis. *Psychological Bulletin*, 105(2), 302–308.

Hughes, J. P., Marice, H. P., & Gathright, J. B. (1976). Method of removing a hollow object from the rectum. *Diseases of the Colon & Rectum*, 19(1), 44–45.

Hume, D. (1739–40). *A treatise of human nature* (L. A. Selby-Bigge, Ed.). Oxford: Clarendon Press, 1965.

Hume, D. (1748). *An enquiry concerning human understanding*. Chicago: Open Court, 1927.

Hutcheson, G., & Sofroniou, N. (1999). *The multivariate social scientist*. London: Sage.

Huynh, H., & Feldt, L. S. (1976). Estimation of the Box correction for degrees of freedom from sample data in randomised block and split-plot designs. *Journal of Educational Statistics*, 1(1), 69–82.

Jolliffe, I. T. (1972). Discarding variables in a principal component analysis, I: Artificial data. *Applied Statistics*, 21, 160–173.

Jolliffe, I. T. (1986). *Principal component analysis*. New York: Springer.

Kahneman, D., & Krueger, A. B. (2006). Developments in the measurement of subjective well-being. *Journal of Economic Perspectives*, 20(1), 3–24.

Kaiser, H. F. (1960). The application of electronic computers to factor analysis. *Educational and Psychological Measurement*, 20, 141–151.

Kaiser, H. F. (1970). A second-generation little jiffy. *Psychometrika*, 35, 401–415.

Kaiser, H. F. (1974). An index of factorial simplicity. *Psychometrika*, 39, 31–36.

Kass, R. A., & Tinsley, H. E. A. (1979). Factor analysis. *Journal of Leisure Research*, 11, 120–138.

Kellett, S., Clarke, S., & McGill, P. (2008). Outcomes from psychological assessment regarding recommendations for cosmetic surgery. *Journal of Plastic, Reconstructive & Aesthetic Surgery*, 61, 512–517.

Keselman, H. J., & Keselman, J. C. (1988). Repeated measures multiple comparison procedures: Effects of violating multisample sphericity in unbalanced designs. *Journal of Educational Statistics*, 13(3), 215–226.

Kirk, R. E. (1996). Practical significance: A concept whose time has come. *Educational and Psychological Measurement*, 56(5), 746–759.

Kline, P. (1999). *The handbook of psychological testing* (2nd ed.). London: Routledge.

Klockars, A. J., & Sax, G. (1986). *Multiple comparisons*. Sage University Paper Series on Quantitative Applications in the Social Sciences, 07-061. Newbury Park, CA: Sage.

Koot, V. C. M., Peeters, P. H. M., Granath, F., Grobbee, D. E., & Nyren, O. (2003). Total and cause specific mortality among Swedish women with cosmetic breast implants: Prospective study. *British Medical Journal*, 326(7388), 527–528.

Kreft, I. G. G., & de Leeuw, J. (1998). *Introducing multilevel modeling*. London: Sage.

Kreft, I. G. G., de Leeuw, J., & Aiken, L. S. (1995). The effect of different forms of centering in hierarchical linear models. *Multivariate Behavioral Research*, 30, 1–21.

Kruskal, W. H., & Wallis, W. A. (1952). Use of ranks in one-criterion variance analysis. *Journal of the American Statistical Association*, 47, 583–621.

Lacourse, E., Claes, M., & Villeneuve, M. (2001). Heavy metal music and adolescent suicidal risk. *Journal of Youth and Adolescence*, *30*(3), 321–332.

Lehmann, E. L. (1993). The Fisher, Neyman-Pearson theories of testing hypotheses: One theory or two? *Journal of the American Statistical Association*, *88*, 1242–1249.

Lenth, R. V. (2001). Some practical guidelines for effective sample size determination. *American Statistician*, *55*(3), 187–193.

Levene, H. (1960). Robust tests for equality of variances. In I. Olkin, S. G. Ghurye, W. Hoeffding, W. G. Madow, & H. B. Mann (Eds.), *Contributions to probability and statistics: Essays in honor of Harold Hotelling* (pp. 278–292). Stanford, CA: Stanford University Press.

Levine, D. W., & Dunlap, W. P. (1982). Power of the F test with skewed data: Should one transform or not? *Psychological Bulletin*, *92*(1), 272–280.

Levine, D. W., & Dunlap, W. P. (1983). Data transformation, power, and skew: A rejoinder to Games. *Psychological Bulletin*, *93*(3), 596–599.

Lo, S. F., Wong, S. H., Leung, L. S., Law, I. C., & Yip, A. W. C. (2004). Traumatic rectal perforation by an eel. *Surgery*, *135*(1), 110–111.

Loftus, G. R., & Masson, M. E. J. (1994). Using confidence intervals in within-subject designs. *Psychonomic Bulletin and Review*, *1*(4), 476–490.

Lord, F. M. (1967). A paradox in the interpretation of group comparisons. *Psychological Bulletin*, *68*(5), 304–305.

Lord, F. M. (1969). Statistical adjustments when comparing preexisting groups. *Psychological Bulletin*, *72*(5), 336–337.

Lunney, G. H. (1970). Using analysis of variance with a dichotomous dependent variable: An empirical study. *Journal of Educational Measurement*, *7*(4), 263–269.

MacCallum, R. C., Widaman, K. F., Zhang, S., & Hong, S. (1999). Sample size in factor analysis. *Psychological Methods*, *4*(1), 84–99.

MacCallum, R. C., Zhang, S., Preacher, K. J., & Rucker, D. D. (2002). On the practice of dichotomization of quantitative variables. *Psychological Methods*, *7*(1), 19–40.

Mann, H. B., & Whitney, D. R. (1947). On a test of whether one of two random variables is stochastically larger than the other. *Annals of Mathematical Statistics*, *18*, 50–60.

Marzillier, S. L., & Davey, G. C. L. (2005). Anxiety and disgust: Evidence for a unidirectional relationship. *Cognition and Emotion*, *19*(5), 729–750.

Mather, K. (1951). R. A. Fisher's *Statistical Methods for Research Workers*: An appreciation. *Journal of the American Statistical Association*, *46*, 51–54.

Matthews, R. C., Domjan, M., Ramsey, M., & Crews, D. (2007). Learning effects on sperm competition and reproductive fitness. *Psychological Science*, *18*(9), 758–762.

Maxwell, S. E. (1980). Pairwise multiple comparisons in repeated measures designs. *Journal of Educational Statistics*, *5*(3), 269–287.

Maxwell, S. E., & Delaney, H. D. (1990). *Designing experiments and analyzing data*. Belmont, CA: Wadsworth.

McDonald, P. T., & Rosenthal, D. (1977). An unusual foreign body in the rectum – a baseball: Report of a case. *Diseases of the Colon & Rectum*, *20*(1), 56–57.

McGrath, R. E., & Meyer, G. J. (2006). When effect sizes disagree: The case of r and d. *Psychological Methods*, *11*(4), 386–401.

Menard, S. (1995). *Applied logistic regression analysis*. Sage University Paper Series on Quantitative Applications in the Social Sciences, 07-106. Thousand Oaks, CA: Sage.

Mendoza, J. L., Toothaker, L. E., & Crain, B. R. (1976). Necessary and sufficient conditions for F ratios in the L * J * K factorial design with two repeated factors. *Journal of the American Statistical Association*, *71*, 992–993.

Mendoza, J. L., Toothaker, L. E., & Nicewander, W. A. (1974). A Monte Carlo comparison of the univariate and multivariate methods for the groups by trials repeated measures design. *Multivariate Behavioural Research*, *9*, 165–177.

Miles, J. M. V., & Shevlin, M. (2001). *Applying regression and correlation: A guide for students and researchers*. London: Sage.

Miles, J. N. V., & Banyard, P. (2007). *Understanding and using statistics in psychology: A practical introduction*. London: Sage.

Mill, J. S. (1865). *A system of logic: ratiocinative and inductive*. London: Longmans, Green.

Miller, G., Tybur, J. M., & Jordan, B. D. (2007). Ovulatory cycle effects on tip earnings by lap dancers: Economic evidence for human estrus? *Evolution and Human Behavior*, *28*, 375–381.

Miller, G. A., & Chapman, J. P. (2001). Misunderstanding analysis of covariance. *Journal of Abnormal Psychology*, *110*(1), 40–48.

Mitzel, H. C., & Games, P. A. (1981). Circularity and multiple comparisons in repeated measures designs. *British Journal of Mathematical and Statistical Psychology*, *34*, 253–259.

Munzel, U., & Brunner, E. (2000). Nonparametric tests in the unbalanced multivariate one-way design. *Biometrical Journal*, *42*(7), 837–854.

Muris, P., Huijding, J., Mayer, B., & Hameetman, M. (2008). A space odyssey: Experimental manipulation of threat perception and anxiety-related interpretation bias in children. *Child Psychiatry and Human Development*, *39*(4), 469–480.

Myers, R. (1990). *Classical and modern regression with applications* (2nd ed.). Boston: Duxbury.

Nagelkerke, N. J. D. (1991). A note on a general definition of the coefficient of determination. *Biometrika*, *78*, 691–692.

Namboodiri, K. (1984). *Matrix algebra: An introduction*. Sage

University Paper Series on Quantitative Applications in the Social Sciences, 07-38. Beverly Hills, CA: Sage.

Nichols, L. A., & Nicki, R. (2004). Development of a psychometrically sound internet addiction scale: A preliminary step. *Psychology of Addictive Behaviors*, 18(4), 381–384.

Nunnally, J. C. (1978). *Psychometric theory*. New York: McGraw-Hill.

Nunnally, J. C., & Bernstein, I. H. (1994). *Psychometric theory* (3rd ed.). New York: McGraw-Hill.

O'Brien, M. G., & Kaiser, M. K. (1985). MANOVA method for analyzing repeated measures designs: An extensive primer. *Psychological Bulletin*, 97(2), 316–333.

Olson, C. L. (1974). Comparative robustness of six tests in multivariate analysis of variance. *Journal of the American Statistical Association*, 69, 894–908.

Olson, C. L. (1976). On choosing a test statistic in multivariate analysis of variance. *Psychological Bulletin*, 83, 579–586.

Olson, C. L. (1979). Practical considerations in choosing a MANOVA test statistic: A rejoinder to Stevens. *Psychological Bulletin*, 86, 1350–1352.

Ong, E. Y. L., Ang, R. P., Ho, J. C. M., Lim, J. C. Y., Goh, D. H., Lee, C. S., et al. (2011). Narcissism, extraversion and adolescents' self-presentation on Facebook. *Personality and Individual Differences*, 50(2), 180–185.

Pearson, E. S., & Hartley, H. O. (1954). *Biometrika tables for statisticians, Volume I*. New York: Cambridge University Press.

Pearson, K. (1894). Science and Monte Carlo. *Fortnightly Review*, 55, 183–193.

Pearson, K. (1900). On the criterion that a given system of deviations from the probable in the case of a correlated system of variables is such that it can be reasonably supposed to have arisen from random sampling. *Philosophical Magazine*, 50(5), 157–175.

Pedhazur, E., & Schmelkin, L. (1991). *Measurement, design and analysis:*

An integrated approach. Hillsdale, NJ: Erlbaum.

Pinheiro, J., Bates, D., DebRoy, S., Sarkar, S., & R Development Core Team. (2010). nlme: Linear and Nonlinear Mixed Effects Models. R package version (Version 3.1–97). Retrieved from http://CRAN.R-project.org/package=lme

Plackett, R. L. (1983). Karl Pearson and the chi-squared test. *International Statistical Review*, 51(1), 59–72.

Preacher, K. J., & MacCallum, R. C. (2003). Repairing Tom Swift's electric factor analysis machine. *Understanding Statistics*, 2(1), 13–43.

Ramsey, P. H. (1982). Empirical power of procedures for comparing two groups on *p* variables. *Journal of Educational Statistics*, 7, 139–156.

Raudenbush, S. W., & Bryk, A. S. (2002). *Hierarchical linear models* (2nd ed.). Thousand Oaks, CA: Sage.

Rockwell, R. C. (1975). Assessment of multicollinearity: The Haitovsky test of the determinant. *Sociological Methods and Research*, 3(4), 308–320.

Rosenthal, R. (1991). *Meta-analytic procedures for social research* (2nd ed.). Newbury Park, CA: Sage.

Rosnow, R. L., & Rosenthal, R. (2005). *Beginning behavioral research: A conceptual primer* (5th ed.). Upper Saddle River, NJ: Pearson/Prentice Hall.

Rosnow, R. L., Rosenthal, R., & Rubin, D. B. (2000). Contrasts and correlations in effect-size estimation. *Psychological Science*, 11, 446–453.

Rouanet, H., & Lépine, D. (1970). Comparison between treatments in a repeated-measurement design: ANOVA and multivariate methods. *British Journal of Mathematical and Statistical Psychology*, 23, 147–163.

Rulon, P. J. (1939). A simplified procedure for determining the reliability of a test by split-halves. *Harvard Educational Review*, 9, 99–103.

Sacco, W. P., Levine, B., Reed, D., & Thompson, K. (1991). Attitudes about condom use as

an AIDS-relevant behavior: Their factor structure and relation to condom use. *Psychological Assessment: A Journal of Consulting and Clinical Psychology*, 3(2), 265–272.

Sacco, W. P., Rickman, R. L., Thompson, K., Levine, B., & Reed, D. L. (1993). Gender differences in AIDS-relevant condom attitudes and condom use. *AIDS Education and Prevention*, 5(4), 311–326.

Sachdev, Y. V. (1967). An unusual foreign body in the rectum. *Diseases of the Colon & Rectum*, 10(3), 220–221.

Salsburg, D. (2002). *The lady tasting tea: How statistics revolutionized science in the twentieth century*. New York: Owl Books.

Savage, L. J. (1976). On re-reading R. A. Fisher. *Annals of Statistics*, 4, 441–500.

Scariano, S. M., & Davenport, J. M. (1987). The effects of violations of independence in the one-way ANOVA. *American Statistician*, 41(2), 123–129.

Schützwohl, A. (2008). The disengagement of attentive resources from task-irrelevant cues to sexual and emotional infidelity. *Personality and Individual Differences*, 44, 633–644.

Shackelford, T. K., LeBlanc, G. J., & Drass, E. (2000). Emotional reactions to infidelity. *Cognition & Emotion*, 14(5), 643–659.

Shee, J. C. (1964). Pargyline and the cheese reaction. *British Medical Journal*, 1(539), 1441.

Siegel, S., & Castellan, N. J. (1988). *Nonparametric statistics for the behavioral sciences* (2nd ed.). New York: McGraw-Hill.

Spearman, C. (1910). Correlation calculated with faulty data. *British Journal of Psychology*, 3, 271–295.

Stevens, J. P. (1979). Comment on Olson: Choosing a test statistic in multivariate analysis of variance. *Psychological Bulletin*, 86, 355–360.

Stevens, J. P. (1980). Power of the multivariate analysis of variance tests. *Psychological Bulletin*, 88, 728–737.

Stevens, J. P. (2002). *Applied multivariate statistics for the social sciences* (4th ed.). Hillsdale, NJ: Erlbaum.

Strahan, R. F. (1982). Assessing magnitude of effect from rank-order correlation coeffients. *Educational and Psychological Measurement, 42,* 763–765.

Stuart, E. W., Shimp, T. A., & Engle, R. W. (1987). Classical-conditioning of consumer attitudes – Four experiments in an advertising context. *Journal of Consumer Research, 14*(3), 334–349.

Studenmund, A. H., & Cassidy, H. J. (1987). *Using econometrics: a practical guide.* Boston: Little Brown.

Tabachnick, B. G., & Fidell, L. S. (2001). *Using multivariate statistics* (4th ed.). Boston: Allyn & Bacon.

Tabachnick, B. G., & Fidell, L. S. (2007). *Using multivariate statistics* (5th ed.). Boston: Allyn & Bacon.

Terrell, C. D. (1982). Significance tables for the biserial and the point biserial. *Educational and Psychological Measurement, 42,* 975–981.

Tinsley, H. E. A., & Tinsley, D. J. (1987). Uses of factor analysis in counseling psychology research. *Journal of Counseling Psychology, 34,* 414–424.

Toothaker, L. E. (1993). *Multiple comparison procedures.* Sage University Paper series on Quantitative Applications in the Social Sciences, 07-089. Newbury Park, CA: Sage.

Tufte, E. R. (2001). *The visual display of quantitative information* (2nd ed.). Cheshire, CT: Graphics Press.

Twisk, J. W. R. (2006). *Applied multilevel analysis: A practical guide.* Cambridge: Cambridge University Press.

Umpierre, S. A., Hill, J. A., & Anderson, D. J. (1985). Effect of Coke on sperm motility. *New England Journal of Medicine, 313*(21), 1351.

Wainer, H. (1984). How to display data badly. *American Statistician, 38*(2), 137–147.

Welch, B.L. (1951) On the comparison of several mean values: An alternative approach. *Biometrika, 38,* 330–336.

Wickham, H. (2009). *ggplot2: Elegant graphics for data analysis.* New York: Springer.

Widaman, K. F. (2007). Common factors versus components: Principals and principles, errors and misconception. In R. Cudeck & R. C. MacCallum (Eds.), *Factor analysis at 100: Historical developments and future directions.* Mahwah, NJ: Erlbaum.

Wilcox, R. R. (2003). Multiple comparisons based on a modified one-step M-estimator. *Journal of Applied Statistics, 30*(10), 1231–1241.

Wilcox, R. R. (2005). *Introduction to robust estimation and hypothesis testing* (2nd ed.). Burlington, MA: Elsevier.

Wilcoxon, F. (1945). Individual comparisons by ranking methods. *Biometrics, 1,* 80–83.

Wildt, A. R., & Ahtola, O. (1978). *Analysis of covariance.* Sage University Paper Series on Quantitative Applications in the Social Sciences, 07-012. Newbury Park, CA: Sage.

Wilkinson, L. (2005). *The grammar of graphics.* New York: Springer-Verlag.

Williams, J. M. G. (2001). *Suicide and attempted suicide.* London: Penguin.

Wright, D. B. (1998). Modeling clustered data in autobiographical memory research: The multilevel approach. *Applied Cognitive Psychology, 12,* 339–357.

Wright, D. B. (2003). Making friends with your data: Improving how statistics are conducted and reported. *British Journal of Educational Psychology, 73,* 123–136.

Wright, D. B., London, K., & Field, A. P. (2011). Using bootstrap estimation and the plug-in principle for clinical psychology data. *Journal of Experimental Psychopathology, 2*(2), 252–270.

Yang, X. W., Li, J. H., & Shoptaw, S. (2008). Imputation-based strategies for clinical trial longitudinal data with nonignorable missing values. *Statistics in Medicine, 27*(15), 2826–2849.

Yates, F. (1951). The influence of *Statistical methods for research workers* on the development of the science of statistics. *Journal of the American Statistical Association, 46,* 19–34.

Zabell, S. L. (1992). R. A. Fisher and fiducial argument. *Statistical Science, 7*(3), 369–387.

Zimmerman, D. W. (2004). A note on preliminary tests of equality of variances. *British Journal of Mathematical and Statistical Psychology, 57,* 173–181.

Zwick, W. R., & Velicer, W. F. (1986). Comparison of five rules for determining the number of components to retain. *Psychological Bulletin, 99*(3), 432–442.

Index

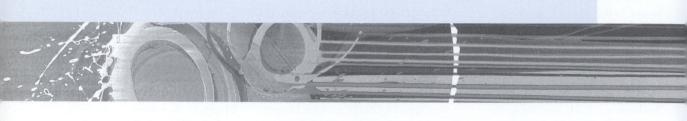

Functions in R

Packages in R

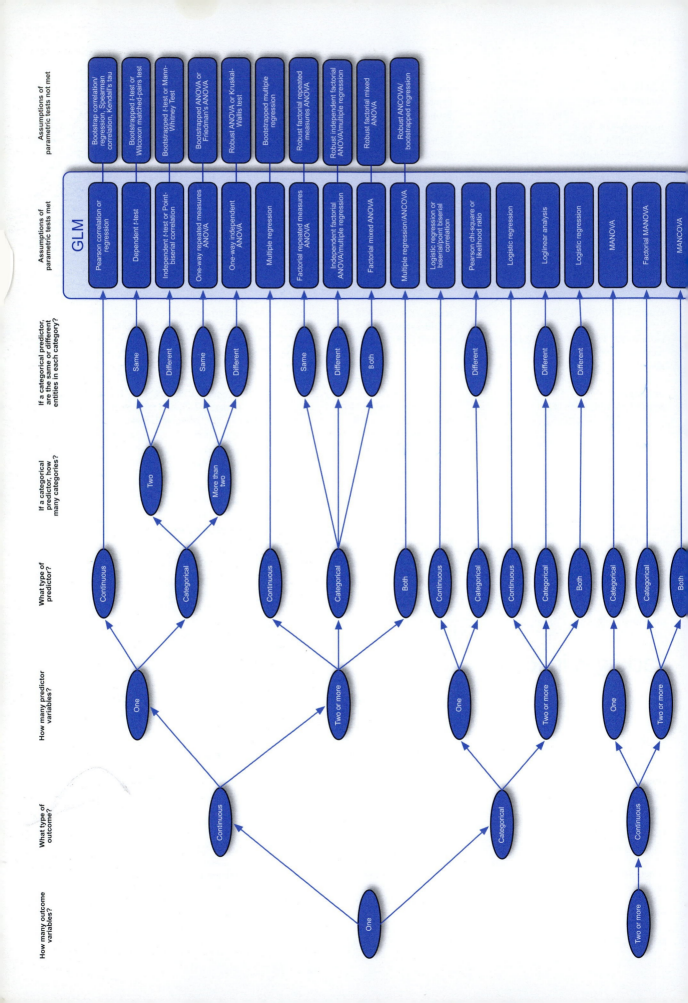